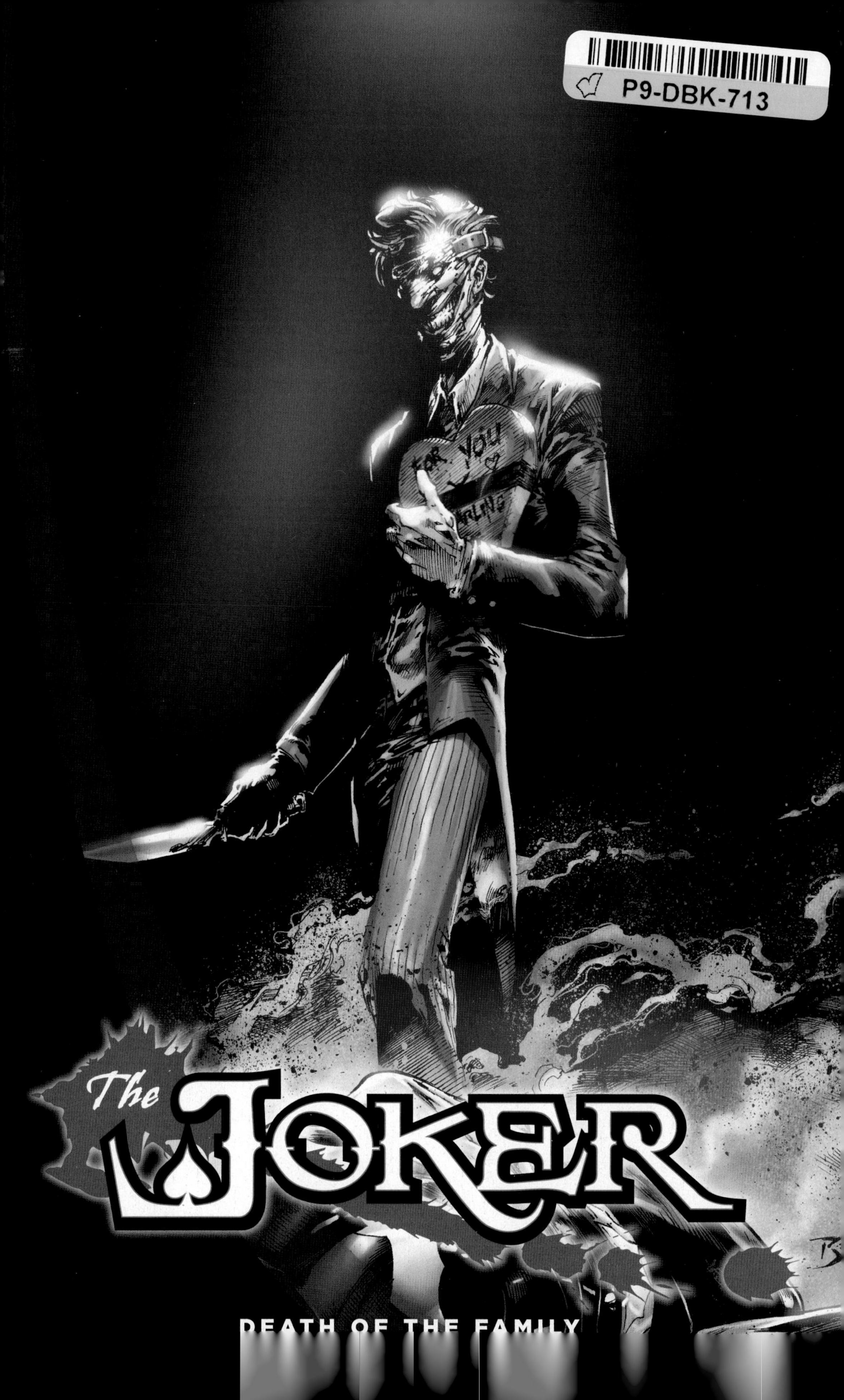
FOR YOU
The JOKER
DEATH OF THE FAMILY

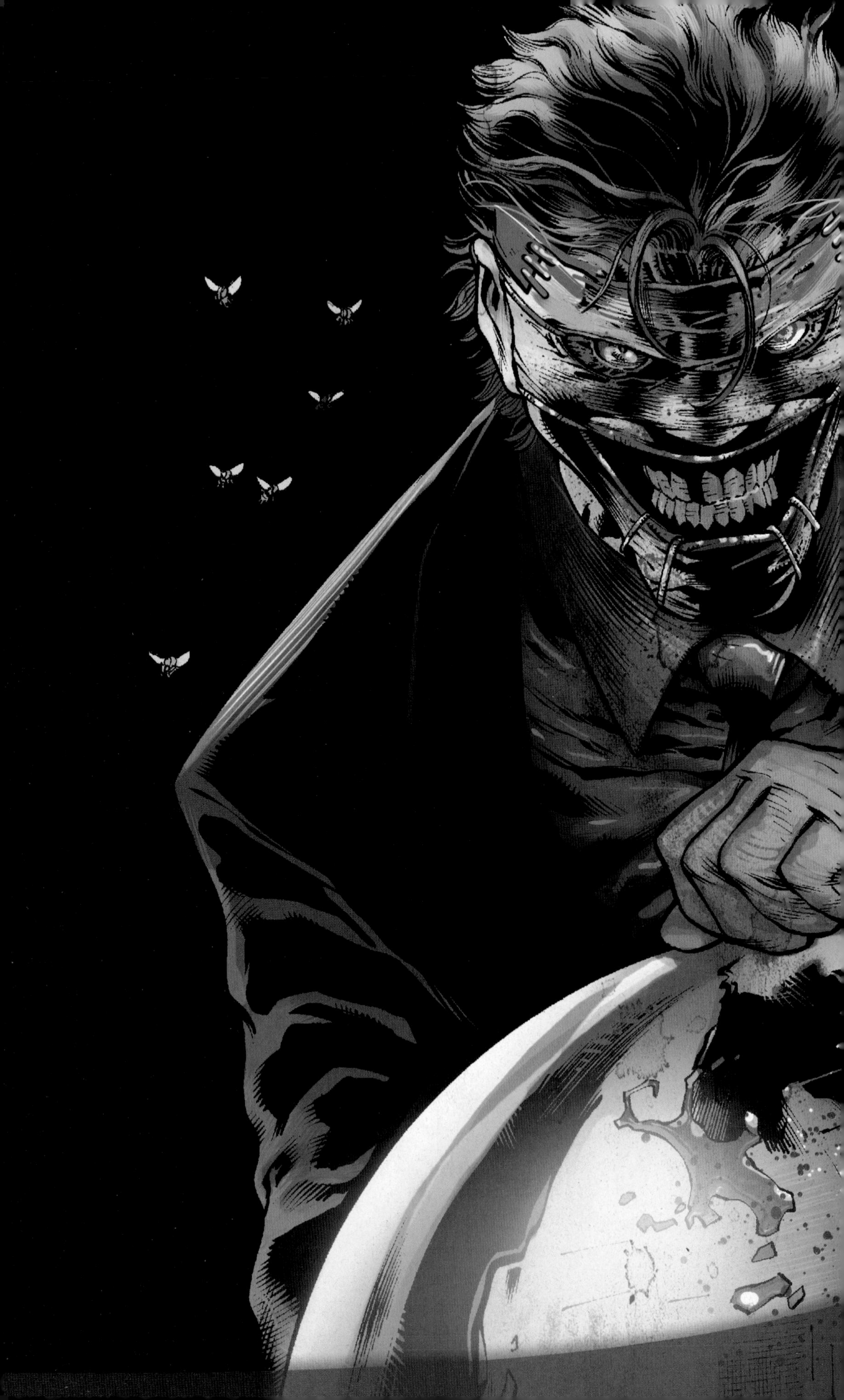

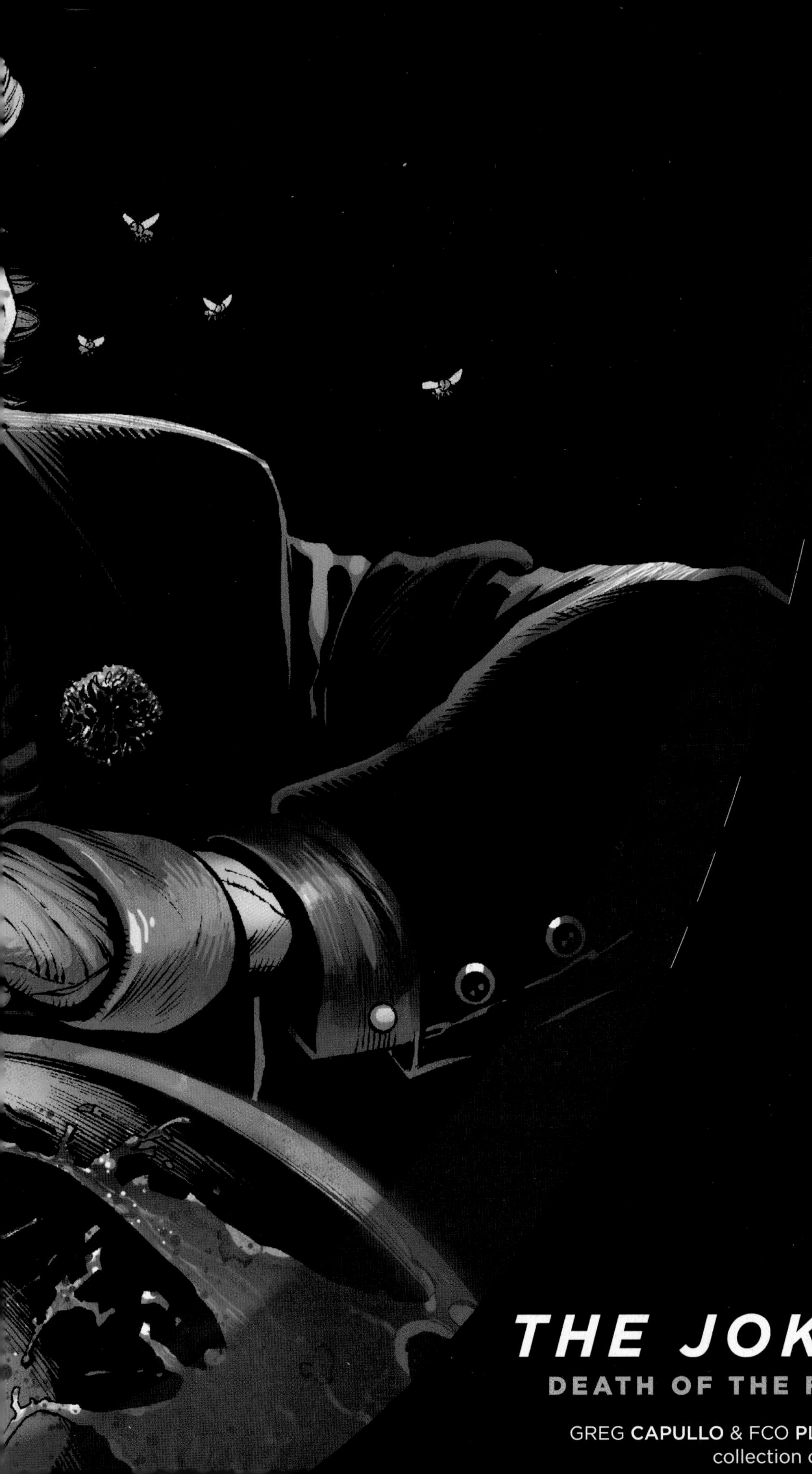

THE JOKER
DEATH OF THE FAMILY

GREG **CAPULLO** & FCO **PLASCENCIA**
collection cover artists

MIKE MARTS RACHEL GLUCKSTERN BRIAN SMITH BRIAN CUNNINGHAM EDDIE BERGANZA Editors – Original Series
KATIE KUBERT RICKEY PURDIN Associate Editors – Original Series DARREN SHAN Assistant Editor – Original Series
JEB WOODARD Group Editor – Collected Editions PETER HAMBOUSSI Editor – Collected Edition
ROBIN WILDMAN Assistant Editor – Collected Edition STEVE COOK Design Director – Books ROBBIE BIEDERMAN Publication Design

BOB HARRAS Senior VP – Editor-in-Chief, DC Comics

DIANE NELSON President DAN DiDIO Publisher JIM LEE Publisher GEOFF JOHNS President & Chief Creative Officer
AMIT DESAI Executive VP – Business & Marketing Strategy, Direct to Consumer & Global Franchise Management
SAM ADES Senior VP – Direct to Consumer BOBBIE CHASE VP – Talent Development
MARK CHIARELLO Senior VP – Art, Design & Collected Editions JOHN CUNNINGHAM Senior VP – Sales & Trade Marketing
ANNE DePIES Senior VP – Business Strategy, Finance & Administration DON FALLETTI VP – Manufacturing Operations
LAWRENCE GANEM VP – Editorial Administration & Talent Relations ALISON GILL Senior VP – Manufacturing & Operations
HANK KANALZ Senior VP – Editorial Strategy & Administration JAY KOGAN VP – Legal Affairs THOMAS LOFTUS VP – Business Affairs
JACK MAHAN VP – Business Affairs NICK J. NAPOLITANO VP – Manufacturing Administration EDDIE SCANNELL VP – Consumer Marketing
COURTNEY SIMMONS Senior VP – Publicity & Communications JIM (SKI) SOKOLOWSKI VP – Comic Book Specialty & Trade Marketing
NANCY SPEARS VP – Mass, Book, Digital Sales & Trade Marketing

THE JOKER: DEATH OF THE FAMILY

DC Comics, 2900 W. Alameda Avenue, Burbank, CA 91505
Printed by Transcontinental Interglobe, Beauceville, QC, Canada. 5/5/17. Fifth Printing.
ISBN: 978-1-4012-4646-4

Library of Congress Cataloging-in-Publication Data

The Joker : Death of the Family.
pages cm
"Originally published in single magazine form in Batman 13, 14, 17; Detective Comics 15-17; Catwoman 13-14; Suicide Squad 14-15; Batgirl 13-16;
Red Hood 13-16; Teen Titans 14-16; Nightwing 14-16; Batman and Robin 15-17."
ISBN 978-1-4012-4235-0
1. Joker (Fictitious character)—Comic books, strips, etc. 2. Graphic novels.
PN6728.B36J646 2013
741.5'973—dc23
2013020541

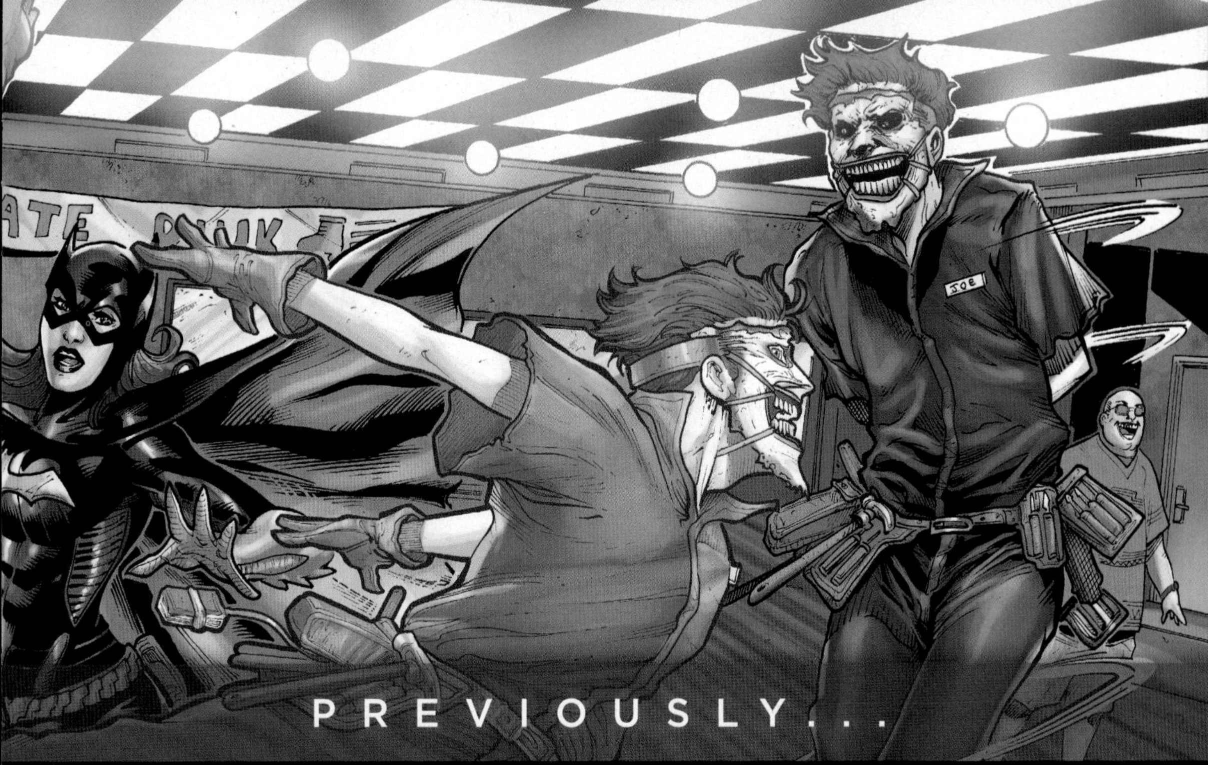
JOE

PREVIOUSLY...

A year ago, the Joker disappeared, seemingly forever. For his last terrifying stunt, he had the skin from his face removed, leaving it behind like a grisly calling card when he escaped Arkham Asylum. Afterwards, most believed him to be dead.

But they were wrong, and now he's back.

Wearing his decaying face like a mask, the Joker is in the midst of the most grisly murder spree Gotham has ever seen. He wants his "old friend" Batman to play along with him, but Batman has changed. The hero no longer works alone. He has an entire team of allies and friends.

But this family of Bats only weighs its leader down, making him weak and sentimental. To bring back the true Batman, the Joker will have to take them all out, one by one...

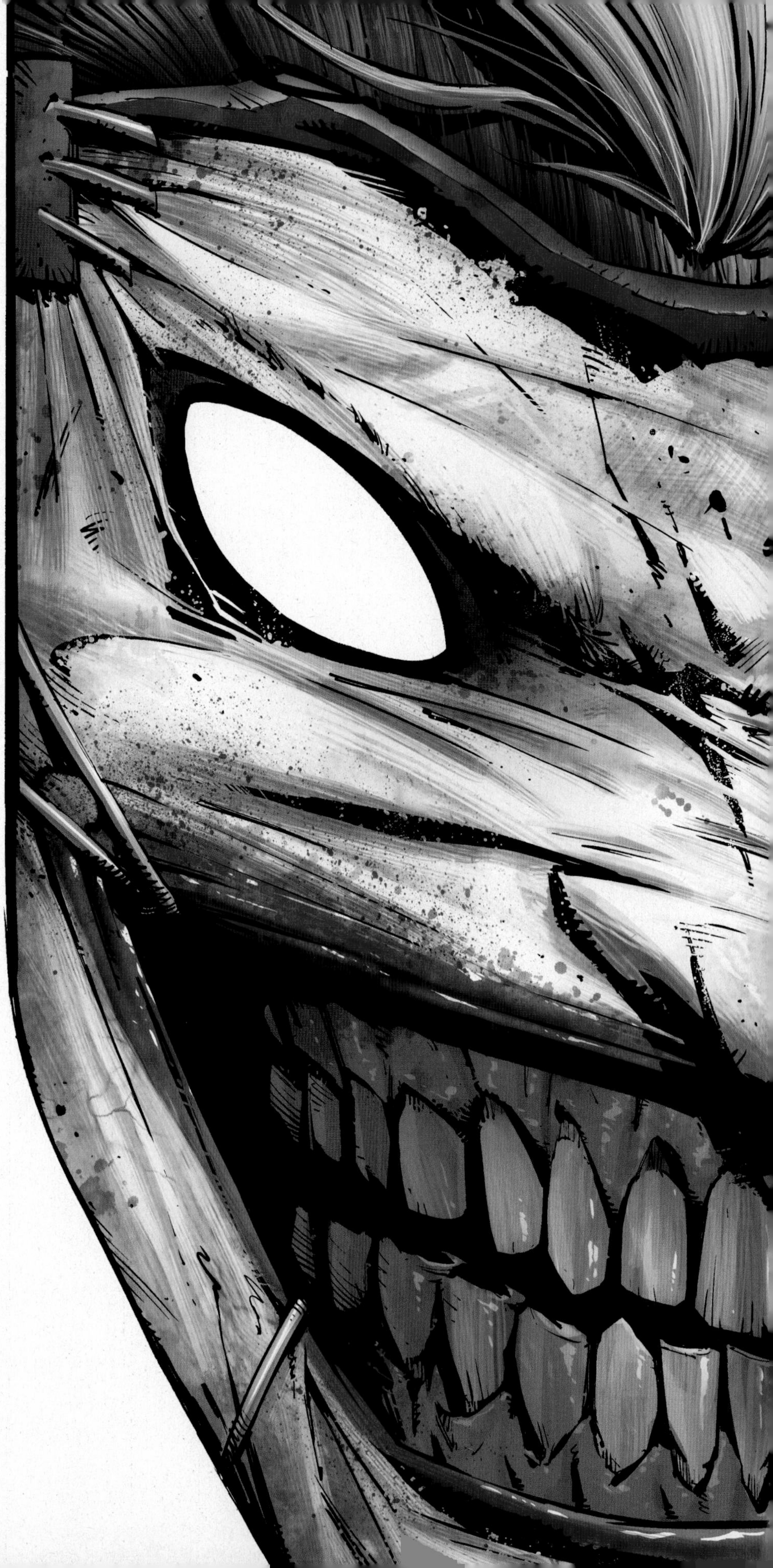

PART ONE
BATMAN

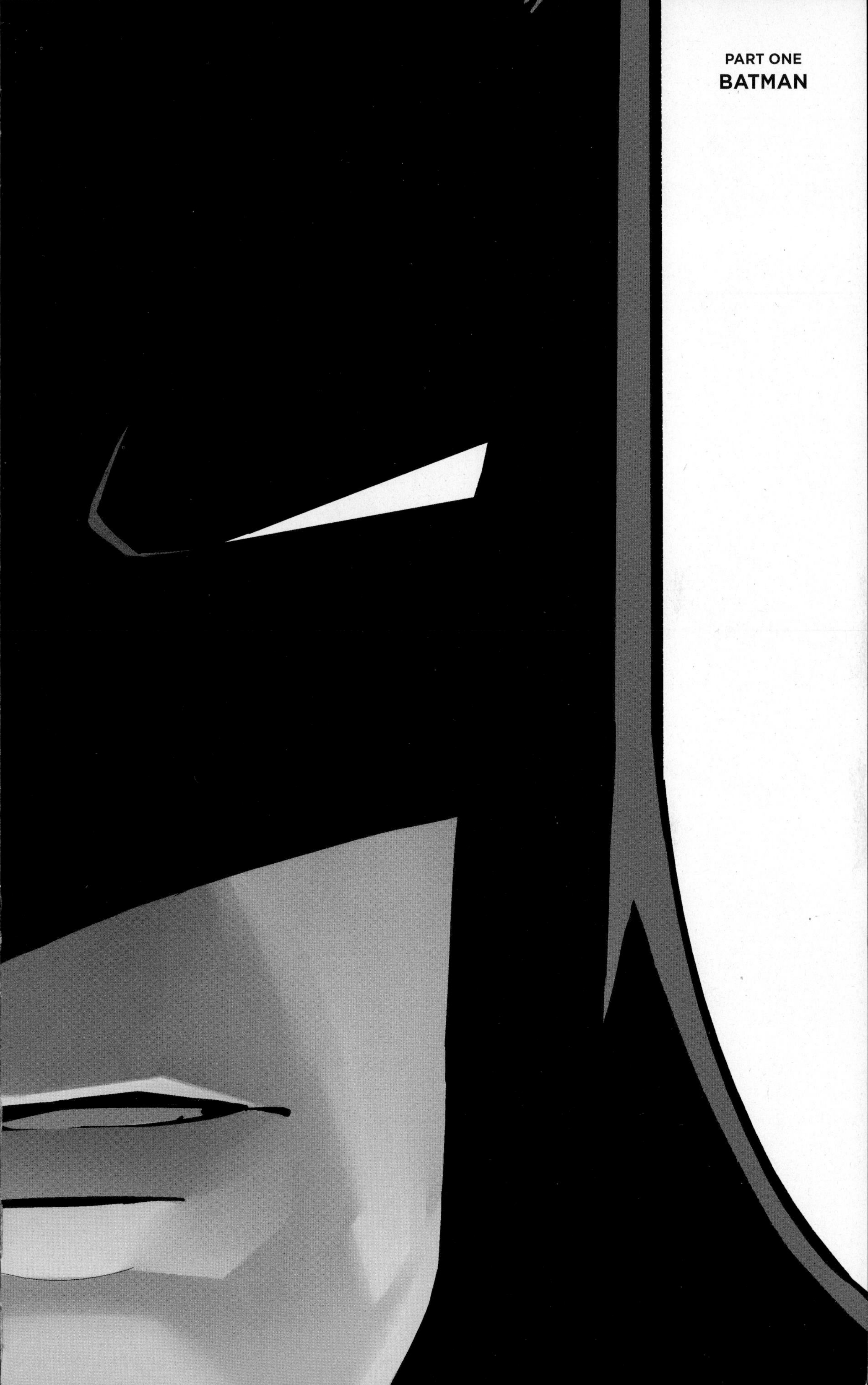

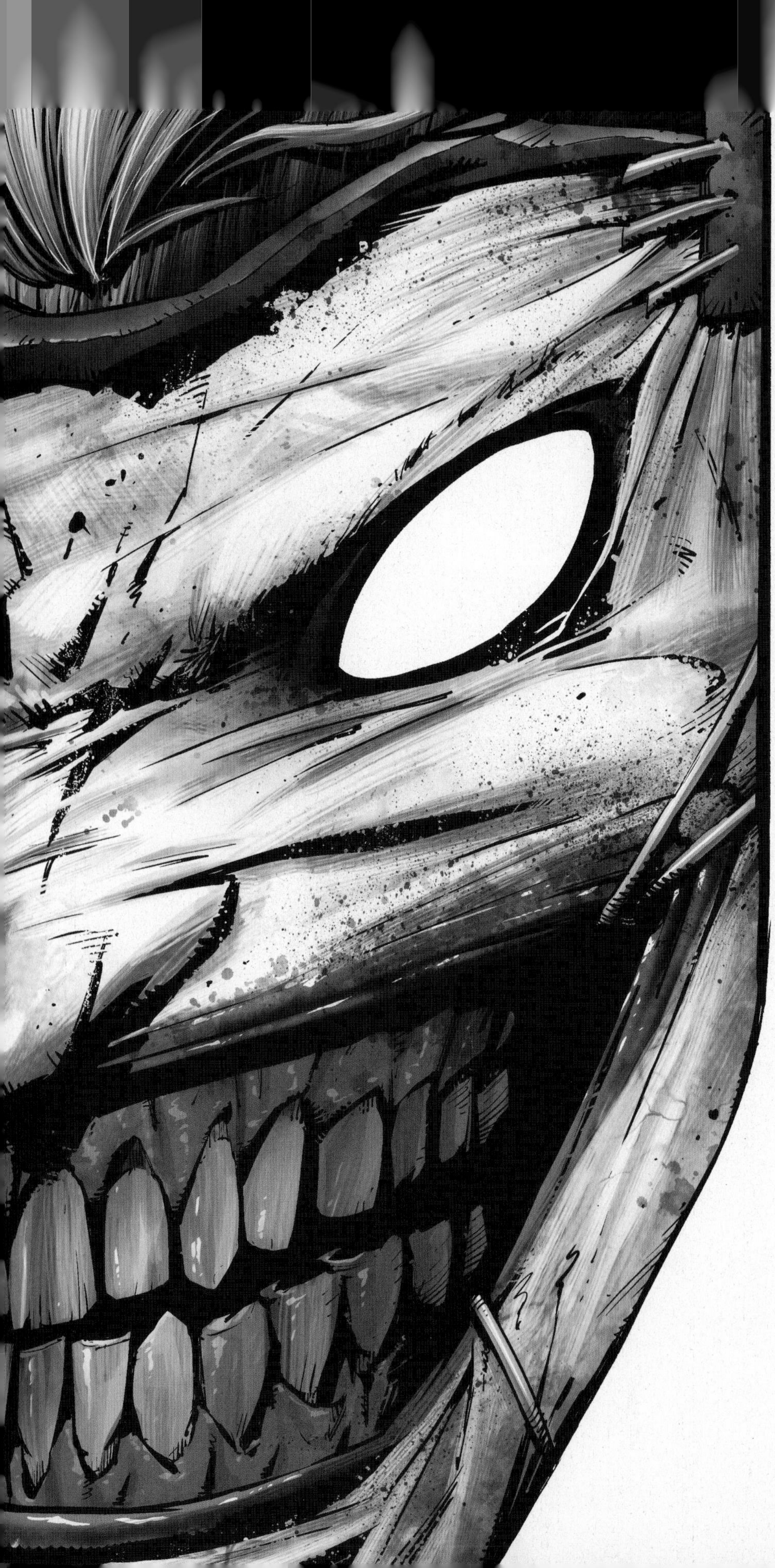

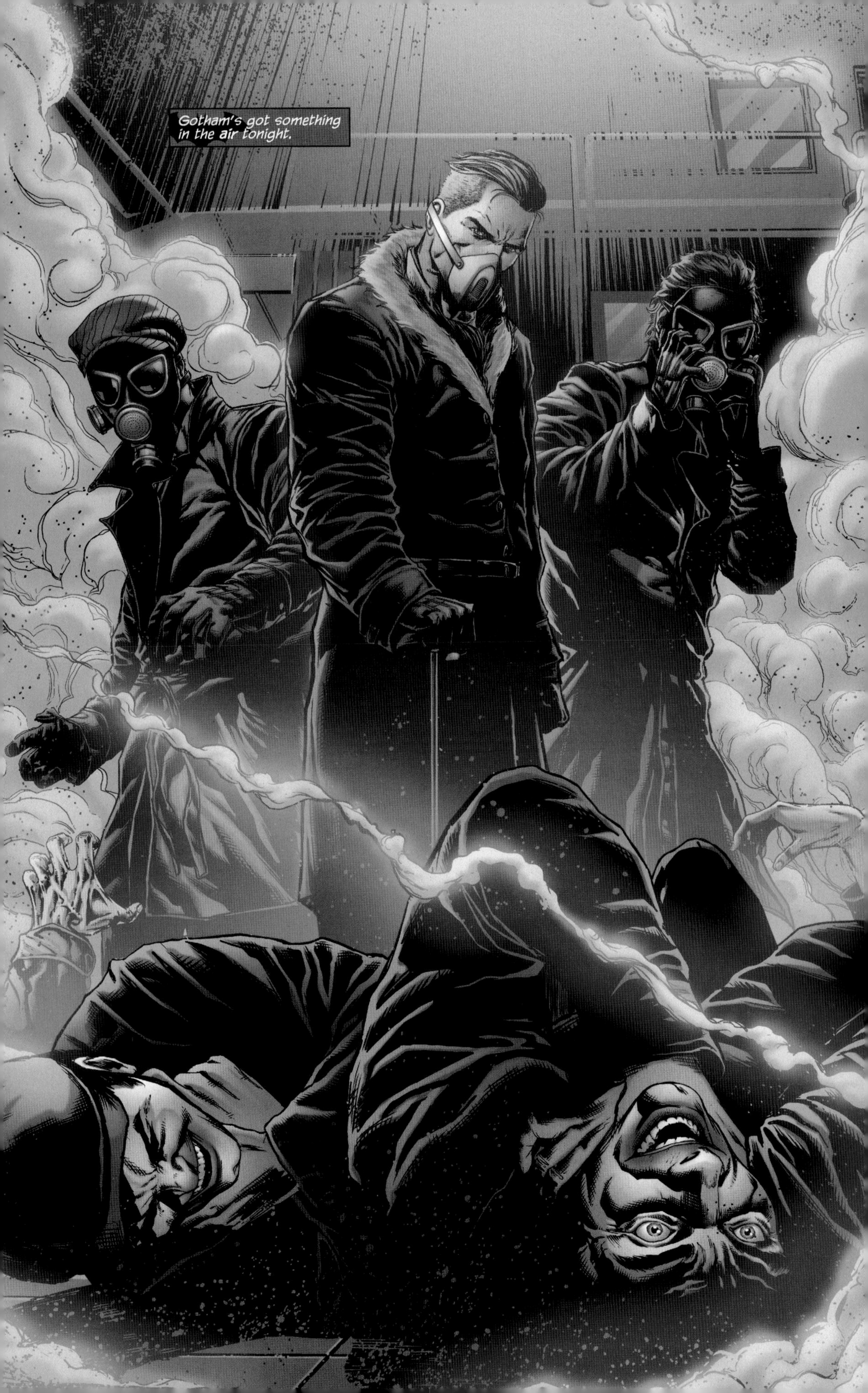
Gotham's got something in the air tonight.

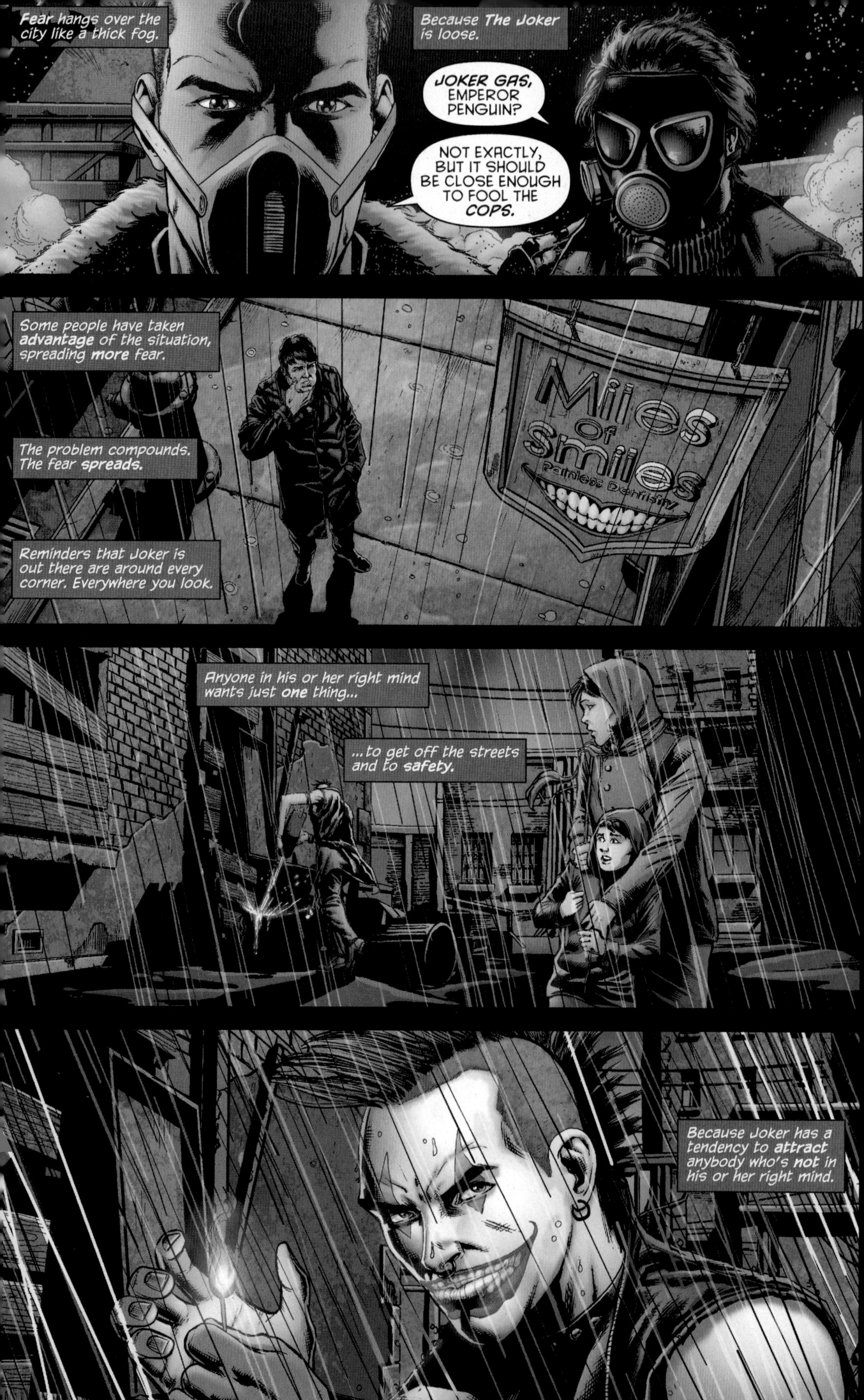
Fear hangs over the city like a thick fog.
Because The Joker is loose.
JOKER GAS, EMPEROR PENGUIN?
NOT EXACTLY, BUT IT SHOULD BE CLOSE ENOUGH TO FOOL THE COPS.
Some people have taken advantage of the situation, spreading more fear.
Miles Of Smiles Painless Dentistry
The problem compounds. The fear spreads.
Reminders that Joker is out there are around every corner. Everywhere you look.
Anyone in his or her right mind wants just one thing...
...to get off the streets and to safety.
Because Joker has a tendency to attract anybody who's not in his or her right mind.

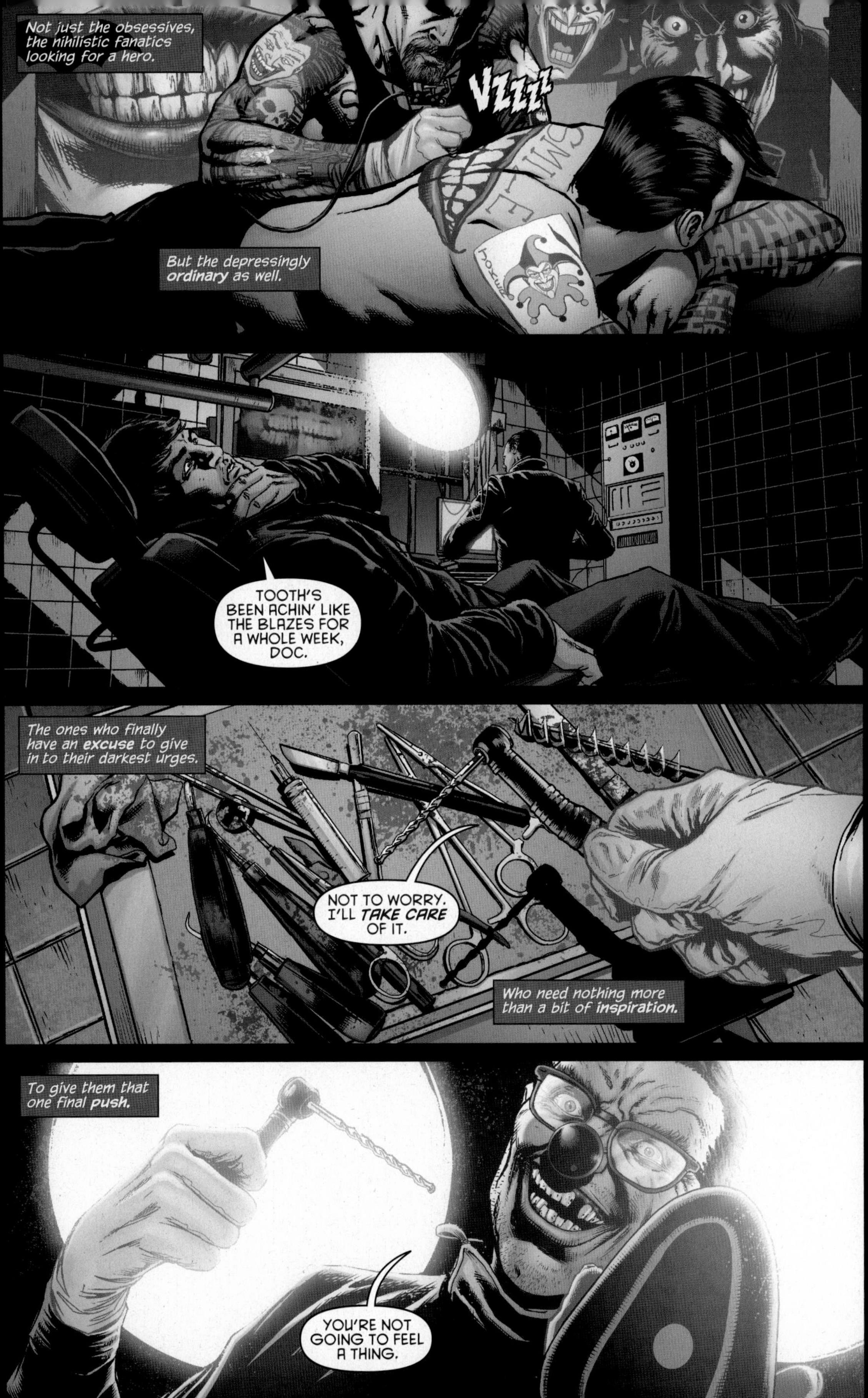
Not just the obsessives, the nihilistic fanatics looking for a hero.
VZZZZ
But the depressingly **ordinary** as well.
TOOTH'S BEEN ACHIN' LIKE THE BLAZES FOR A WHOLE WEEK, DOC.
The ones who finally have an **excuse** to give in to their darkest urges.
NOT TO WORRY. I'LL *TAKE CARE* OF IT.
Who need nothing more than a bit of **inspiration.**
To give them that one final **push.**
YOU'RE NOT GOING TO FEEL A THING.

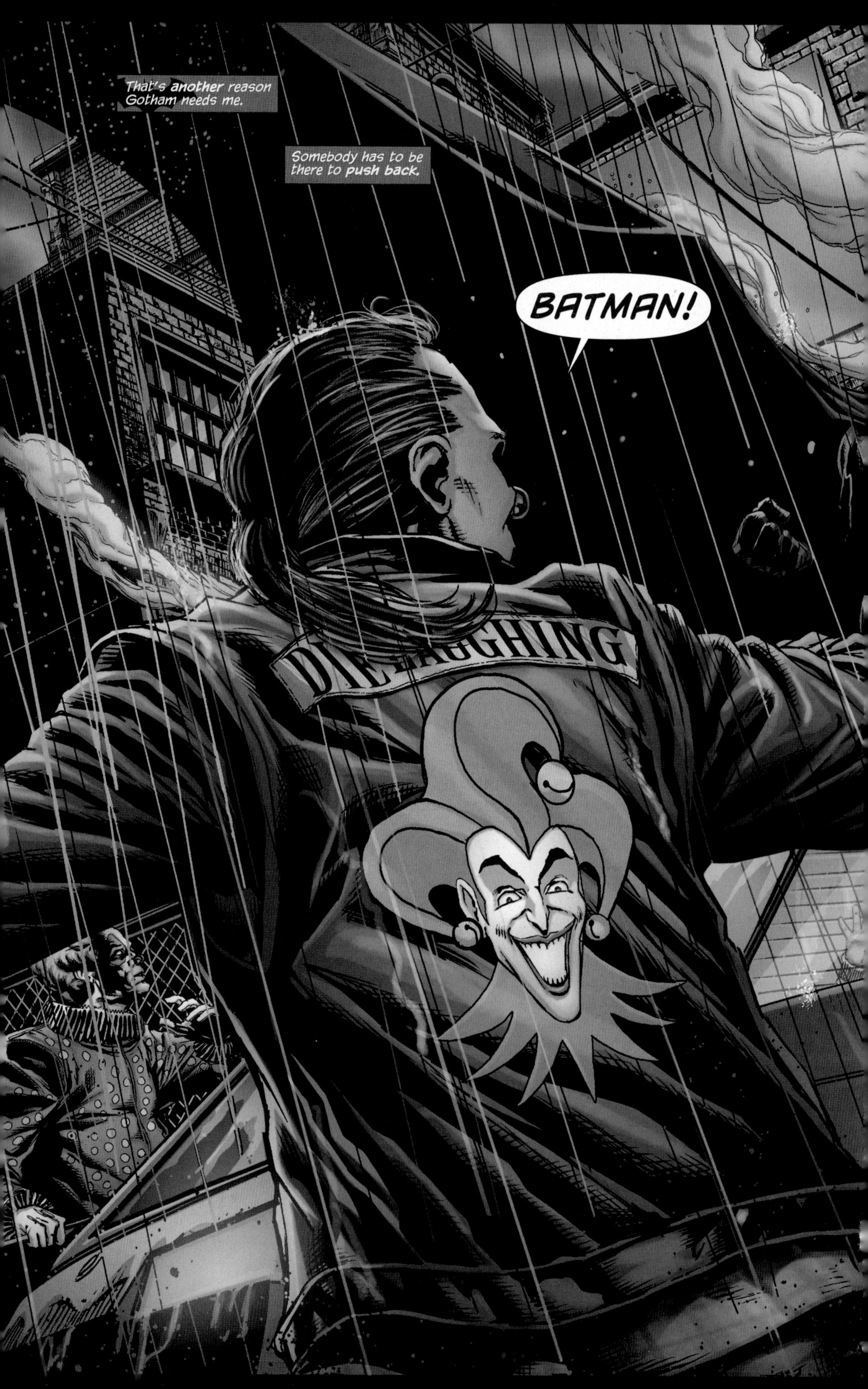
That's **another** reason Gotham needs me.
Somebody has to be there to **push back.**
BATMAN!
DIE LAUGHING

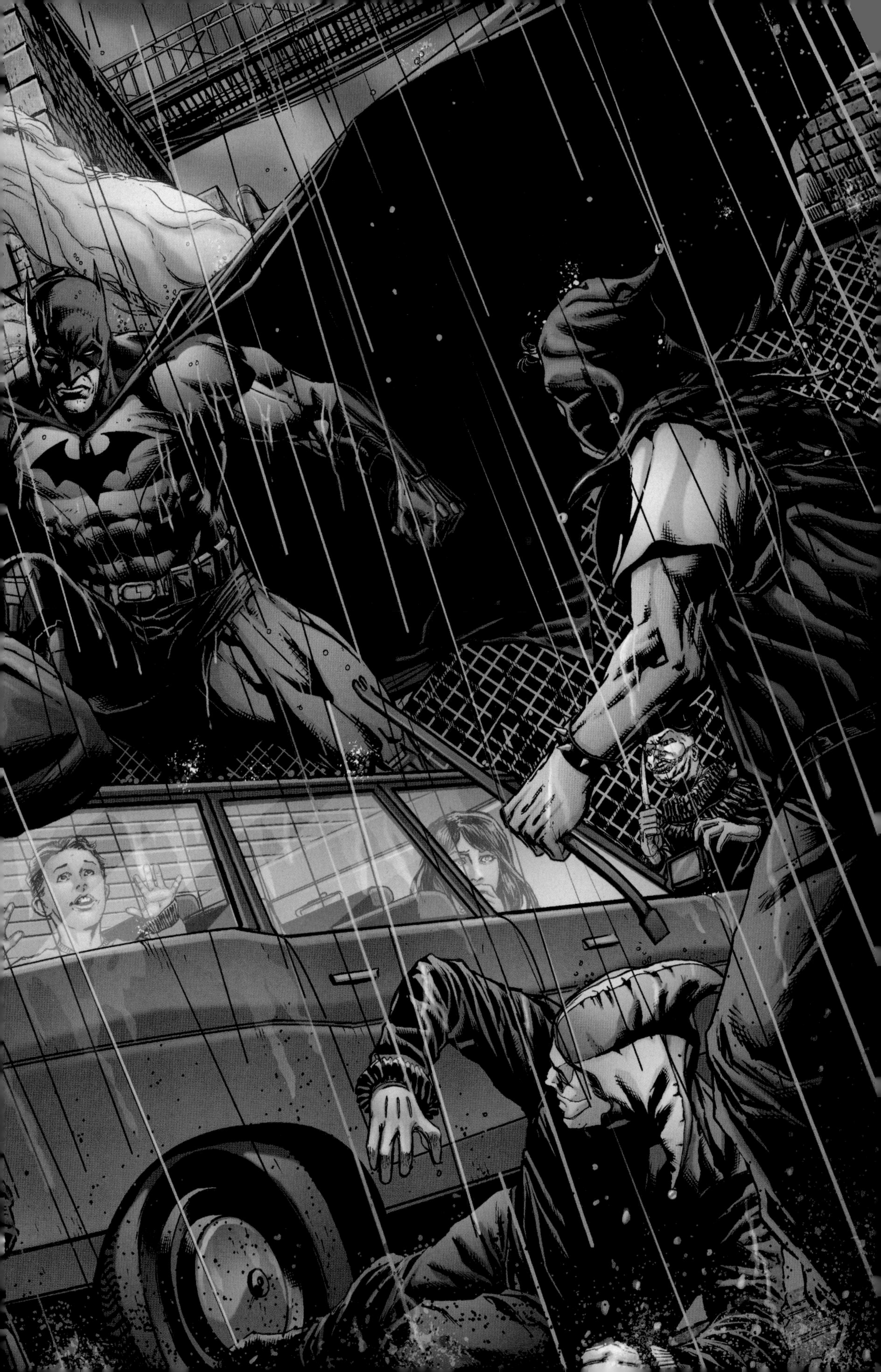

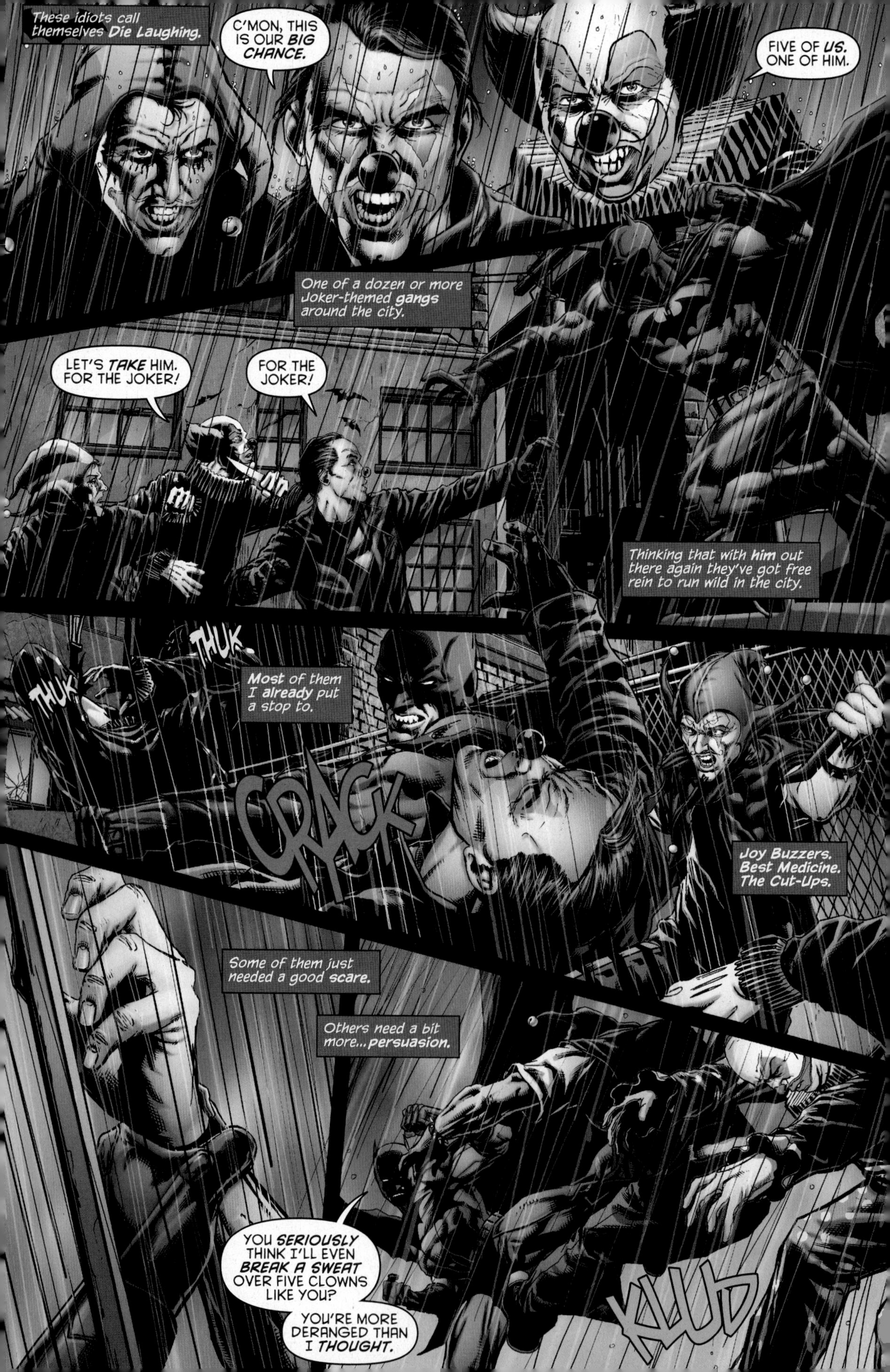
These idiots call themselves *Die Laughing.*
C'MON, THIS IS OUR *BIG CHANCE.*
FIVE OF *US.* ONE OF HIM.
One of a dozen or more Joker-themed **gangs** around the city.
LET'S *TAKE* HIM. FOR THE JOKER!
FOR THE JOKER!
Thinking that with **him** out there again they've got free rein to run wild in the city.
THUK
THUK
Most of them I *already* put a stop to.
CRACK
Joy Buzzers. Best Medicine. The Cut-Ups.
Some of them just needed a good **scare.**
Others need a bit more... **persuasion.**
YOU *SERIOUSLY* THINK I'LL EVEN *BREAK A SWEAT* OVER FIVE CLOWNS LIKE YOU?
YOU'RE MORE DERANGED THAN I *THOUGHT.*
KLUD

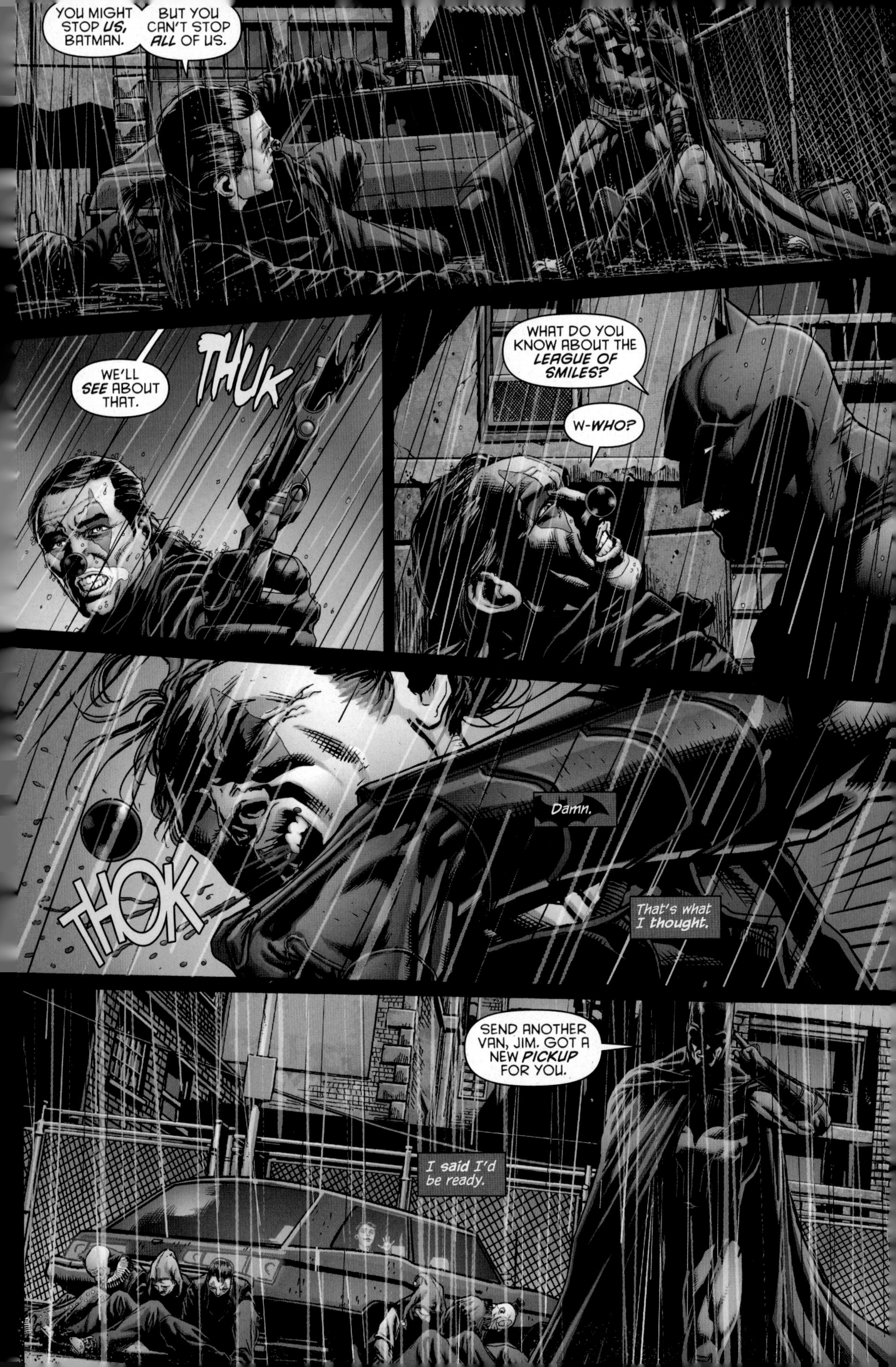

YOU MIGHT STOP *US,* BATMAN.
BUT YOU CAN'T STOP *ALL* OF US.
WE'LL *SEE* ABOUT THAT.
THUK
WHAT DO YOU KNOW ABOUT THE *LEAGUE OF SMILES?*
W-*WHO?*
THOK
Damn.
*That's what I **thought.***
SEND ANOTHER VAN, JIM. GOT A NEW *PICKUP* FOR YOU.
I said I'd be ready.

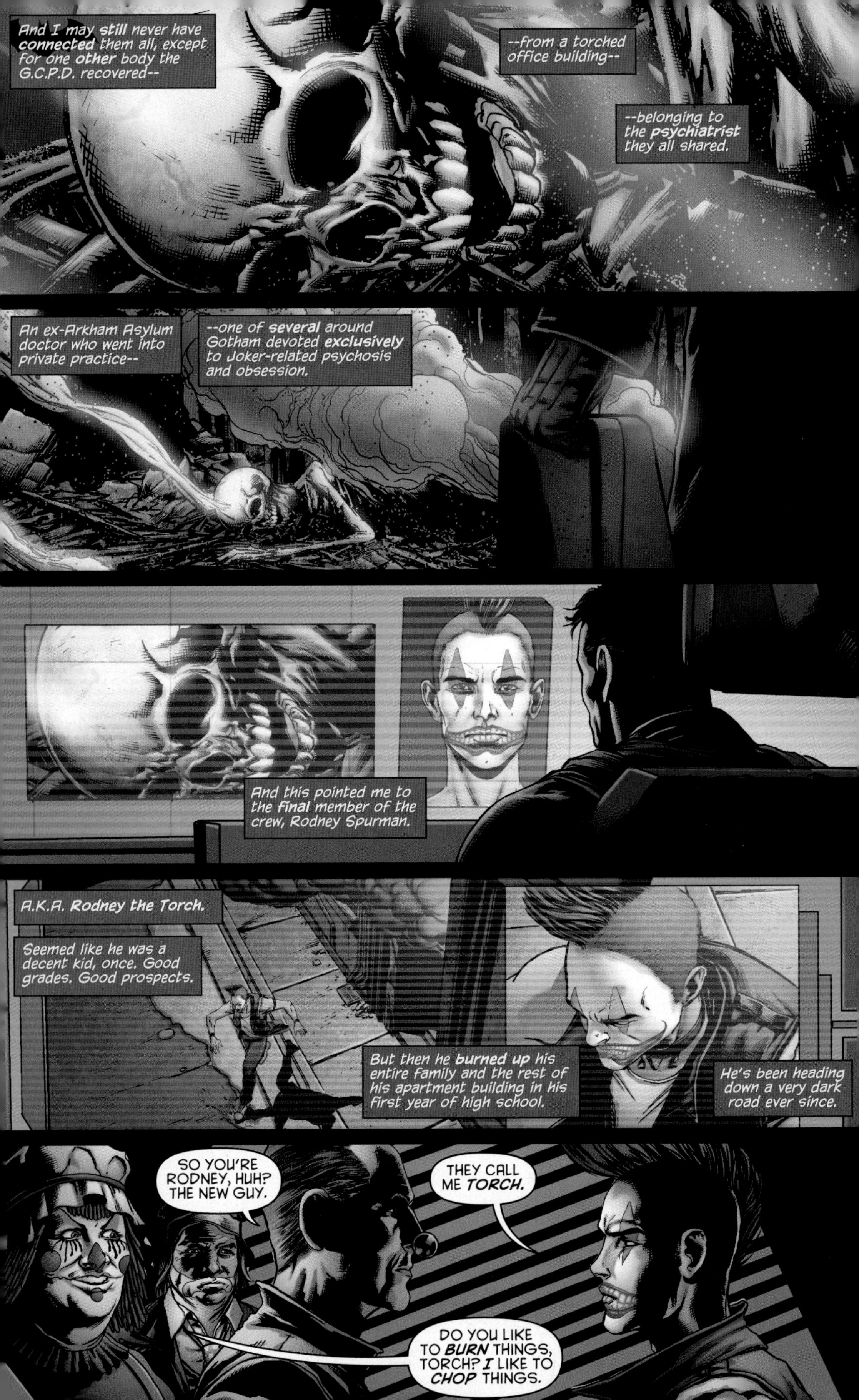
And I may still never have connected them all, except for one other body the G.C.P.D. recovered--
--from a torched office building--
--belonging to the psychiatrist they all shared.
An ex-Arkham Asylum doctor who went into private practice--
--one of several around Gotham devoted exclusively to Joker-related psychosis and obsession.
And this pointed me to the final member of the crew, Rodney Spurman.
A.K.A. Rodney the Torch.
Seemed like he was a decent kid, once. Good grades. Good prospects.
But then he burned up his entire family and the rest of his apartment building in his first year of high school.
He's been heading down a very dark road ever since.
SO YOU'RE RODNEY, HUH? THE NEW GUY.
THEY CALL ME TORCH.
DO YOU LIKE TO BURN THINGS, TORCH? I LIKE TO CHOP THINGS.

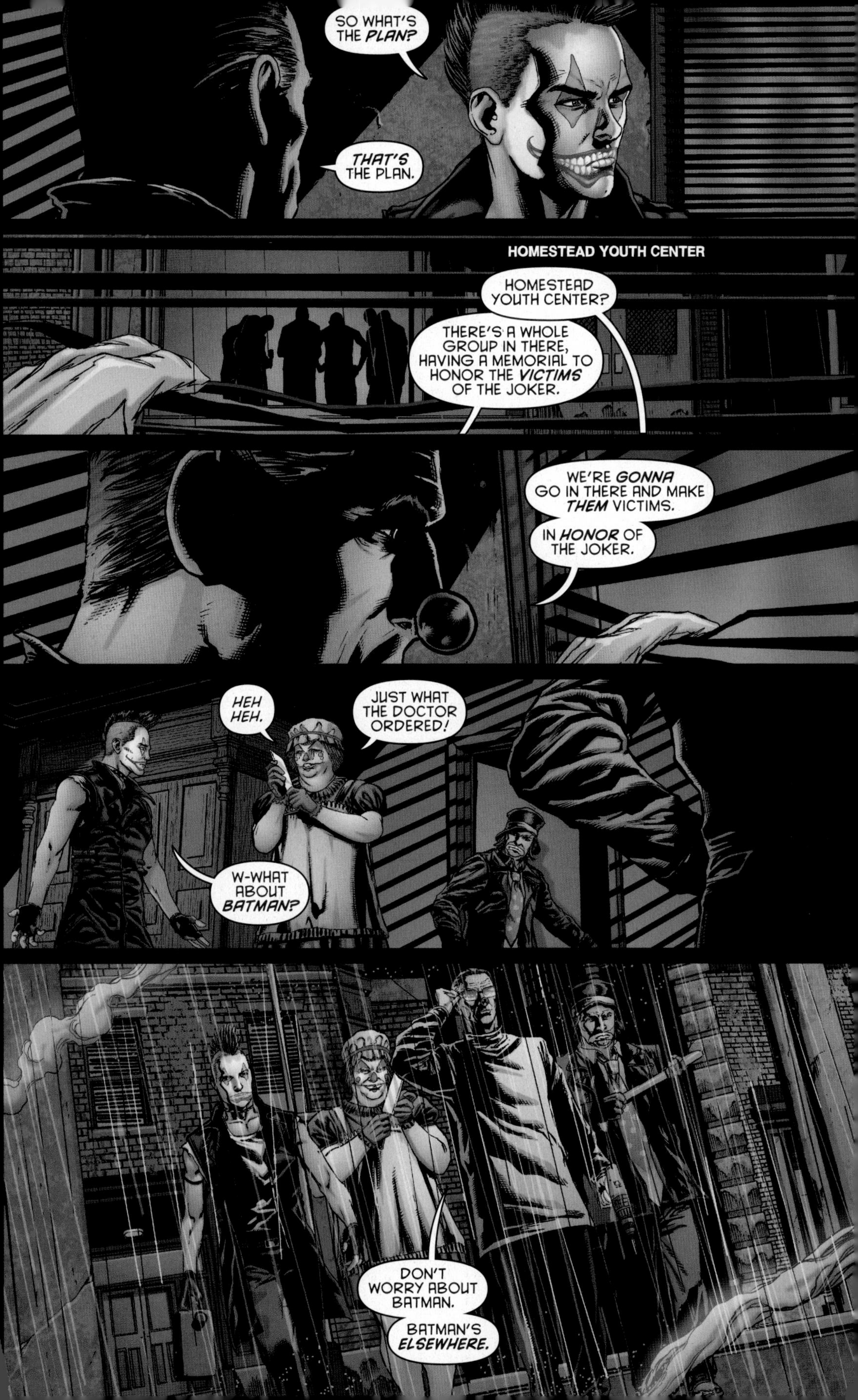
SO WHAT'S THE PLAN?
THAT'S THE PLAN.
HOMESTEAD YOUTH CENTER
HOMESTEAD YOUTH CENTER?
THERE'S A WHOLE GROUP IN THERE, HAVING A MEMORIAL TO HONOR THE VICTIMS OF THE JOKER.
WE'RE GONNA GO IN THERE AND MAKE THEM VICTIMS.
IN HONOR OF THE JOKER.
HEH HEH.
JUST WHAT THE DOCTOR ORDERED!
W-WHAT ABOUT BATMAN?
DON'T WORRY ABOUT BATMAN.
BATMAN'S ELSEWHERE.

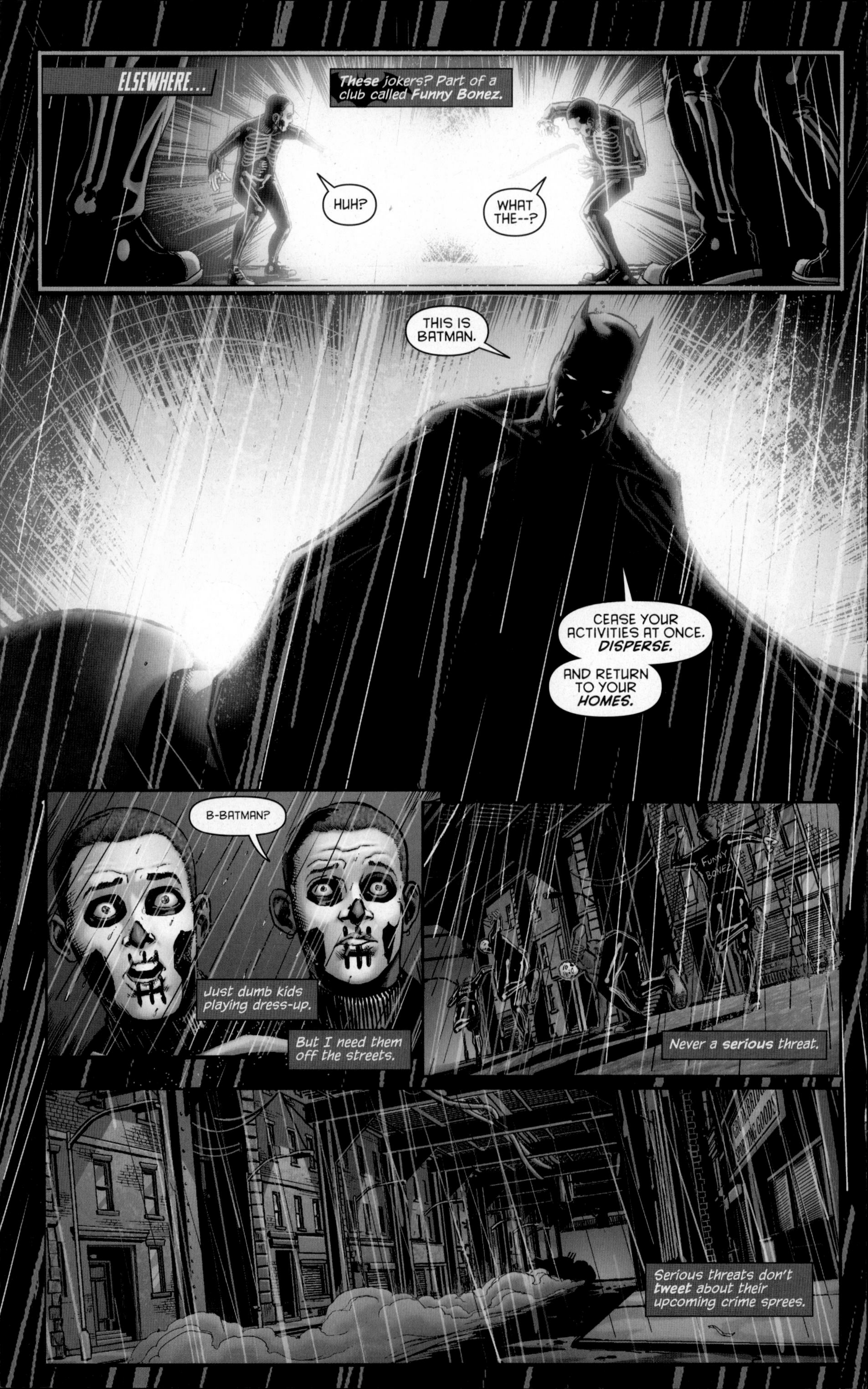
ELSEWHERE...
These jokers? Part of a club called Funny Bonez.
HUH?
WHAT THE--?
THIS IS BATMAN.
CEASE YOUR ACTIVITIES AT ONCE. DISPERSE.
AND RETURN TO YOUR HOMES.
B-BATMAN?
Just dumb kids playing dress-up.
But I need them off the streets.
FUNNY BONEZ
Never a serious threat.
Serious threats don't tweet about their upcoming crime sprees.

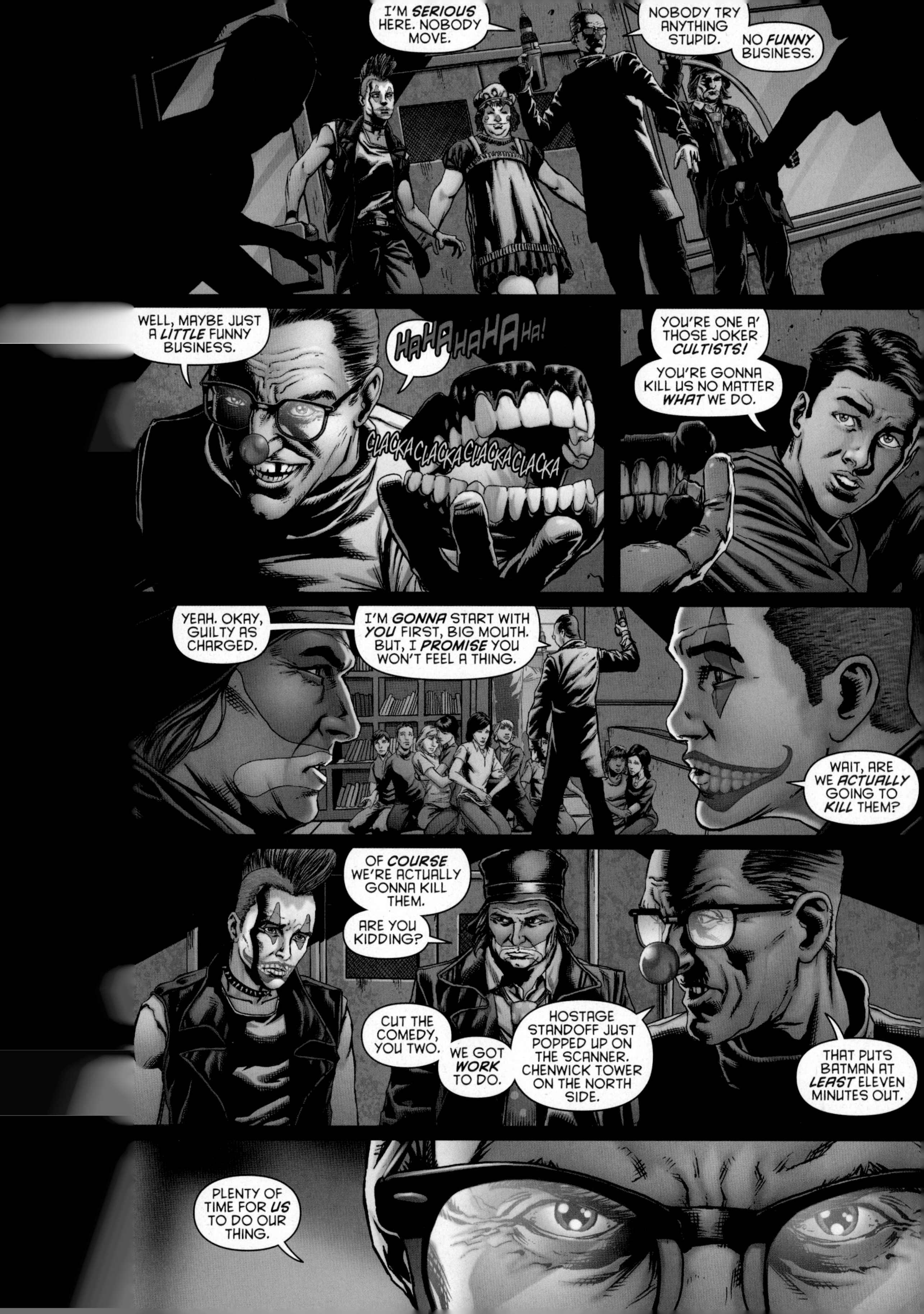
I'M SERIOUS HERE. NOBODY MOVE.
NOBODY TRY ANYTHING STUPID.
NO FUNNY BUSINESS.
WELL, MAYBE JUST A LITTLE FUNNY BUSINESS.
HAHAHAHAHAHA!
CLACKA CLACKA CLACKA CLACKA
YOU'RE ONE A' THOSE JOKER CULTISTS!
YOU'RE GONNA KILL US NO MATTER WHAT WE DO.
YEAH. OKAY, GUILTY AS CHARGED.
I'M GONNA START WITH YOU FIRST, BIG MOUTH. BUT, I PROMISE YOU WON'T FEEL A THING.
WAIT, ARE WE ACTUALLY GOING TO KILL THEM?
OF COURSE WE'RE ACTUALLY GONNA KILL THEM.
ARE YOU KIDDING?
CUT THE COMEDY, YOU TWO.
WE GOT WORK TO DO.
HOSTAGE STANDOFF JUST POPPED UP ON THE SCANNER. CHENWICK TOWER ON THE NORTH SIDE.
THAT PUTS BATMAN AT LEAST ELEVEN MINUTES OUT.
PLENTY OF TIME FOR US TO DO OUR THING.

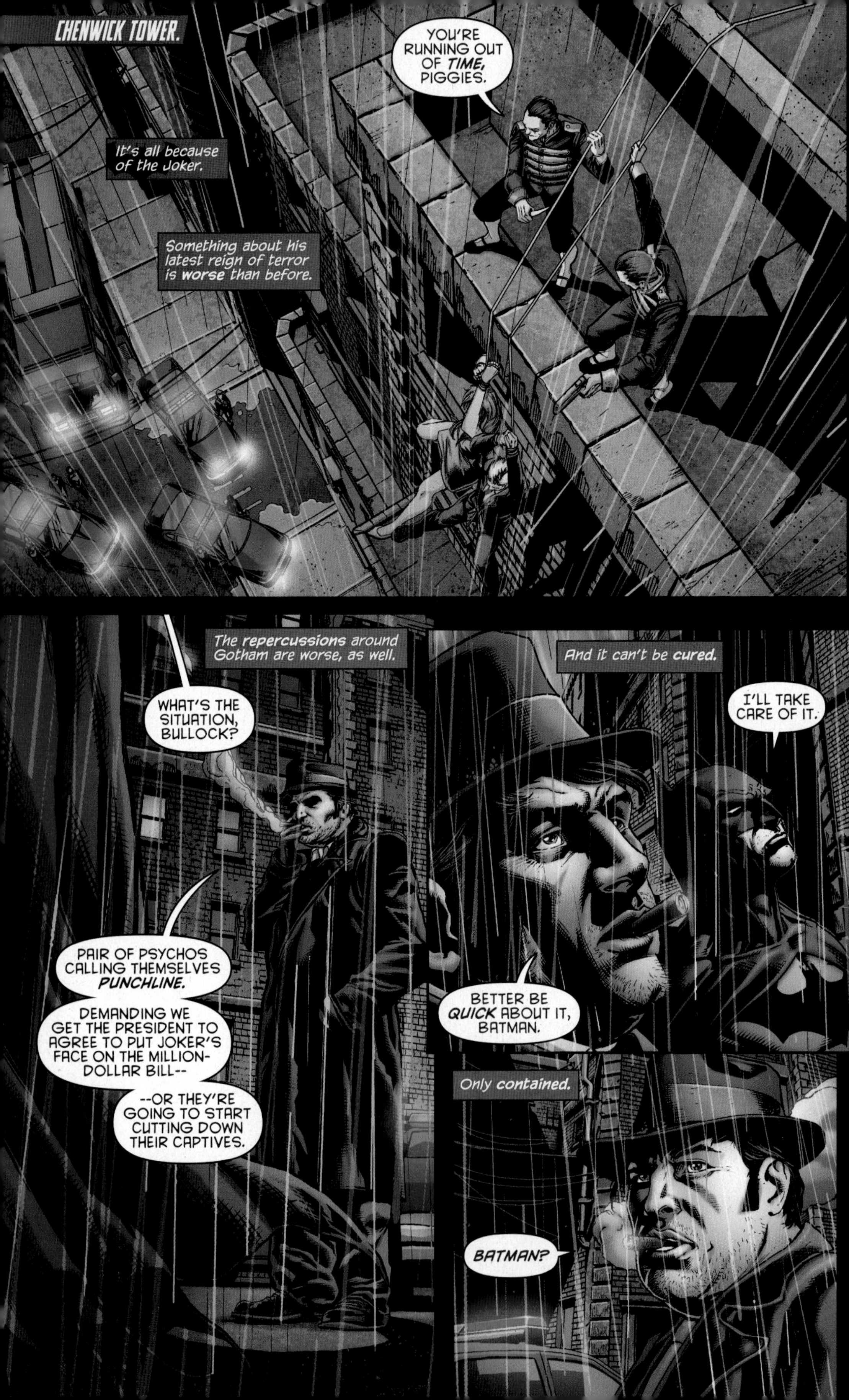
CHENWICK TOWER.
YOU'RE RUNNING OUT OF *TIME,* PIGGIES.
It's all because of the Joker.
Something about his latest reign of terror is **worse** than before.
The **repercussions** around Gotham are worse, as well.
WHAT'S THE SITUATION, BULLOCK?
PAIR OF PSYCHOS CALLING THEMSELVES *PUNCHLINE.*
DEMANDING WE GET THE PRESIDENT TO AGREE TO PUT JOKER'S FACE ON THE MILLION-DOLLAR BILL--
--OR THEY'RE GOING TO START CUTTING DOWN THEIR CAPTIVES.
And it can't be **cured.**
I'LL TAKE CARE OF IT.
BETTER BE *QUICK* ABOUT IT, BATMAN.
Only **contained.**
BATMAN?

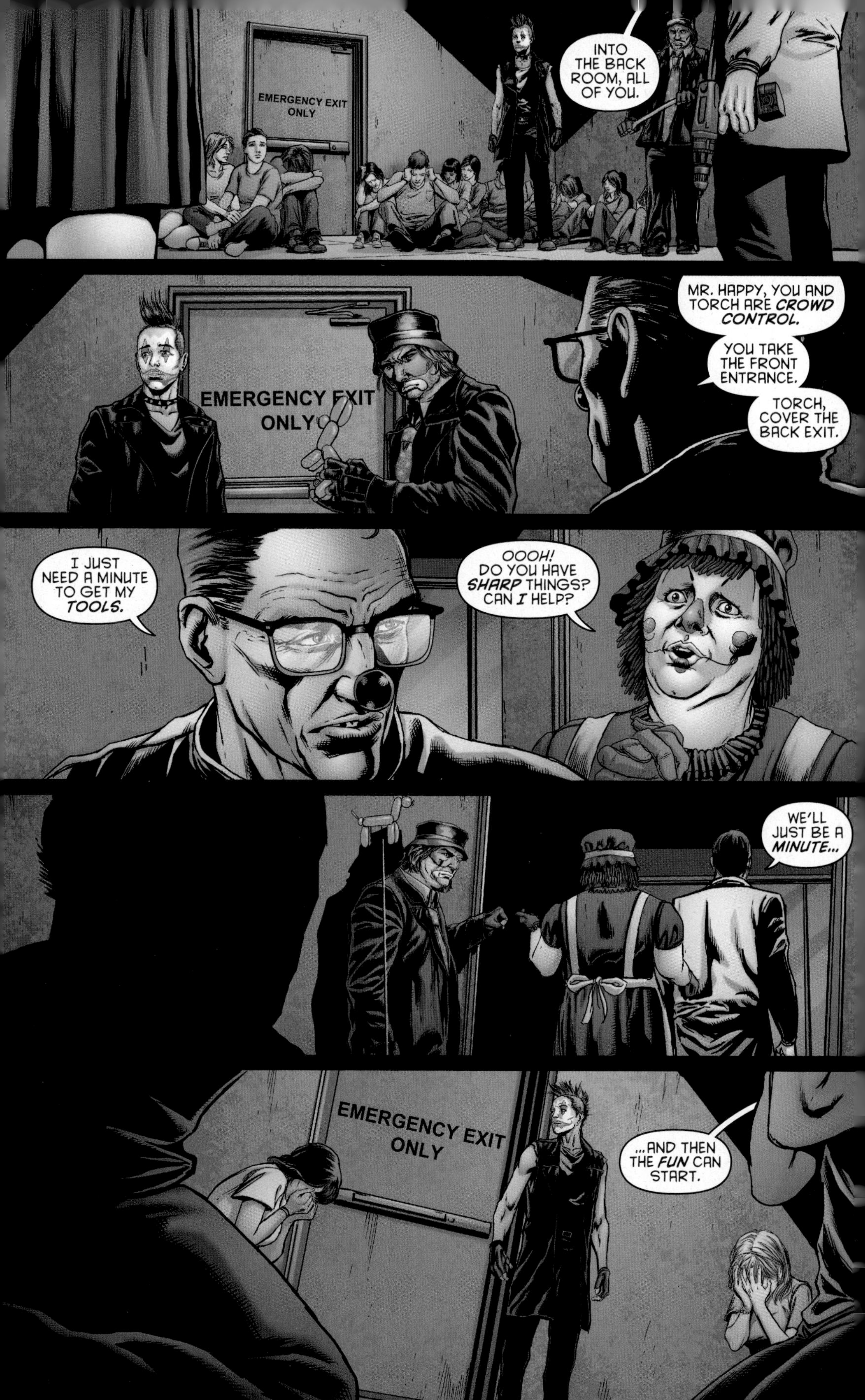

EMERGENCY EXIT ONLY
INTO THE BACK ROOM, ALL OF YOU.
EMERGENCY EXIT ONLY
MR. HAPPY, YOU AND TORCH ARE CROWD CONTROL.
YOU TAKE THE FRONT ENTRANCE.
TORCH, COVER THE BACK EXIT.
I JUST NEED A MINUTE TO GET MY TOOLS.
OOOH! DO YOU HAVE SHARP THINGS? CAN I HELP?
WE'LL JUST BE A MINUTE...
EMERGENCY EXIT ONLY
...AND THEN THE FUN CAN START.

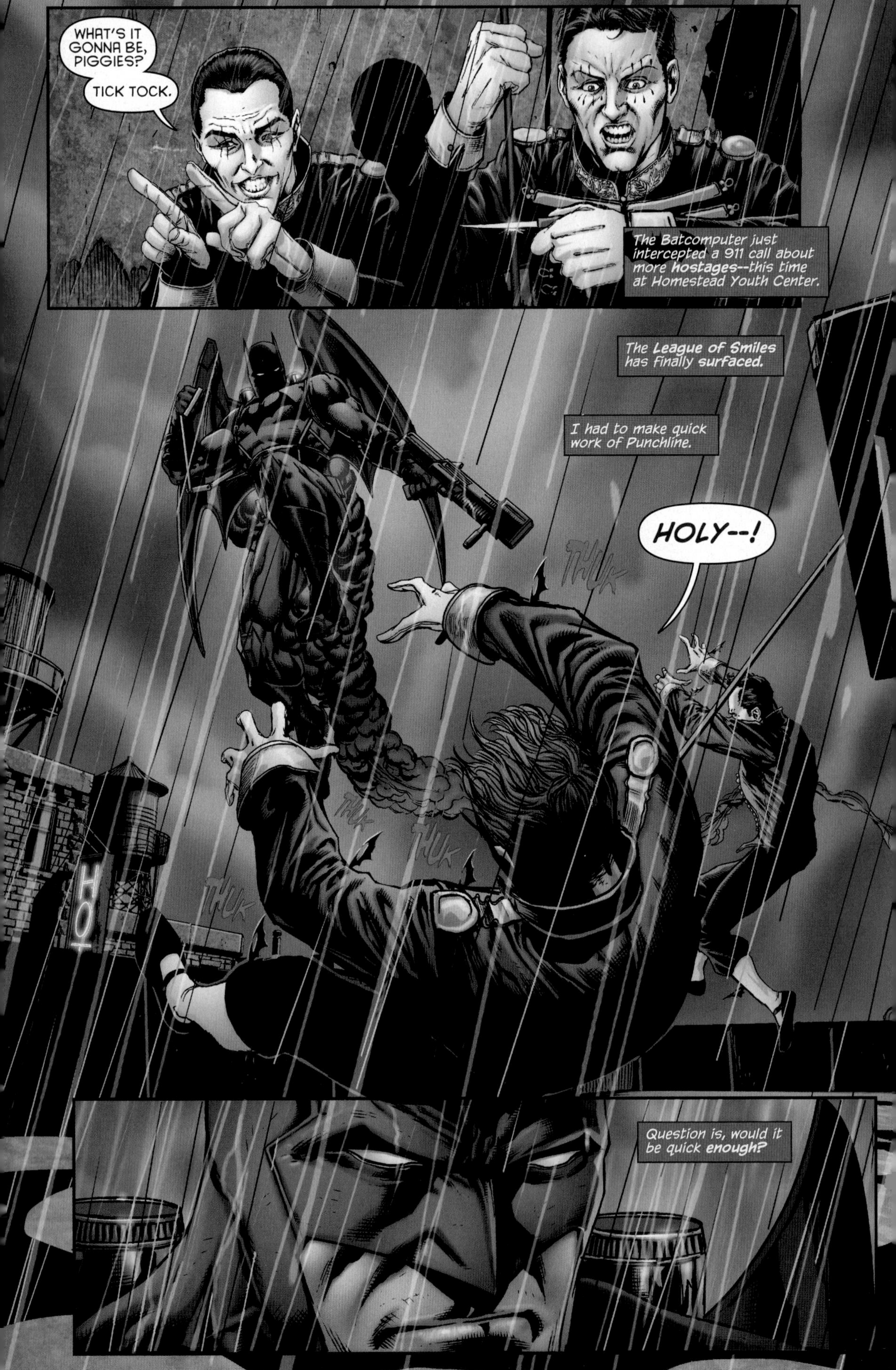
WHAT'S IT GONNA BE, PIGGIES?
TICK TOCK.
The Batcomputer just intercepted a 911 call about more **hostages**--this time at Homestead Youth Center.
The **League of Smiles** has finally **surfaced.**
I had to make quick work of Punchline.
HOLY--!
THUK
THUK
THUK
THUK
HO
Question is, would it be quick **enough?**

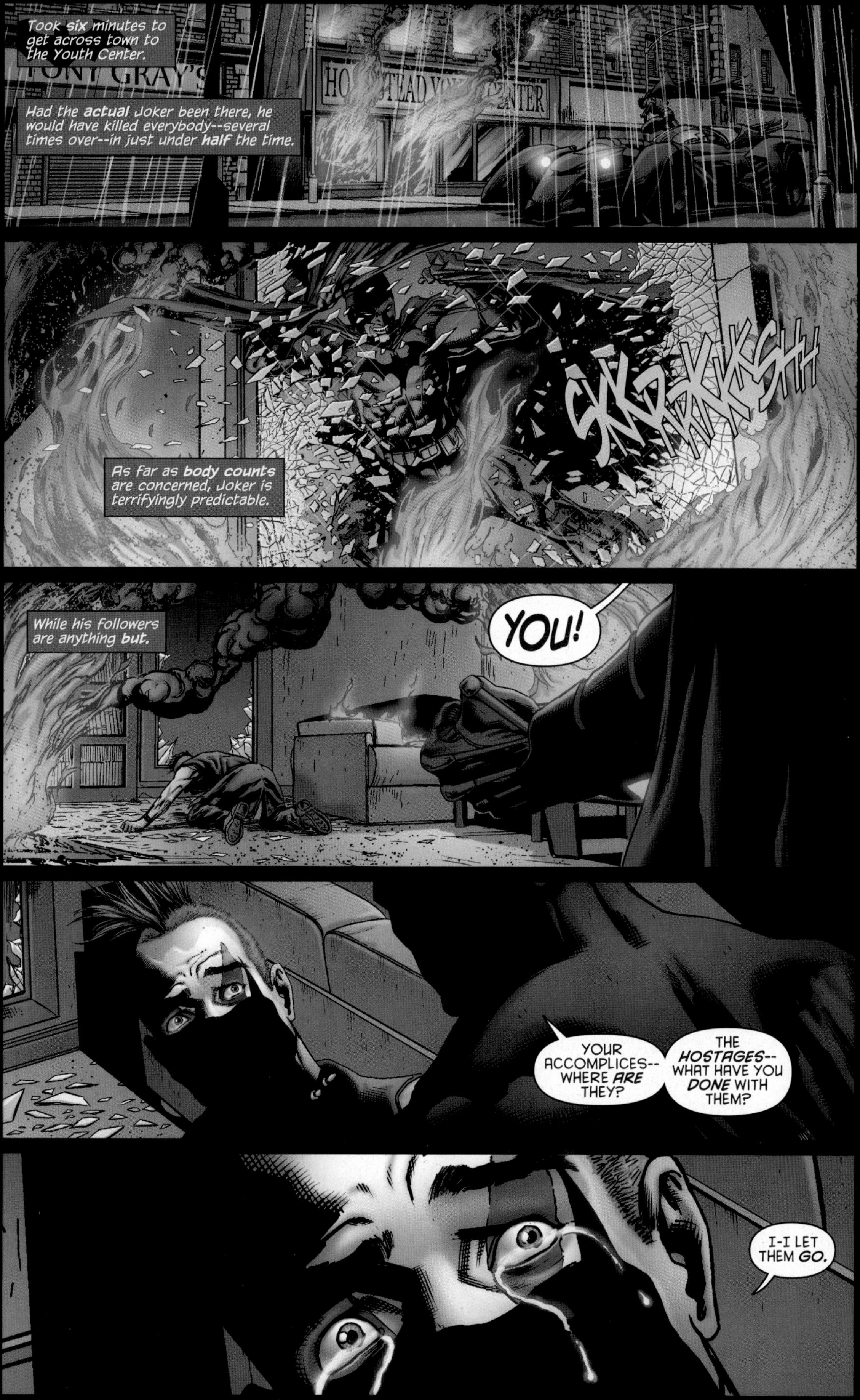
Took **six** minutes to get across town to the Youth Center.
TONY GRAY'S
HO STEAD YO CENTER
Had the **actual** Joker been there, he would have killed everybody--several times over--in just under **half** the time.
SKKRRKKKSHH
As far as **body counts** are concerned, Joker is terrifyingly predictable.
While his followers are anything **but.**
YOU!
YOUR ACCOMPLICES-- WHERE ***ARE*** THEY?
THE ***HOSTAGES***-- WHAT HAVE YOU ***DONE*** WITH THEM?
I-I LET THEM ***GO.***

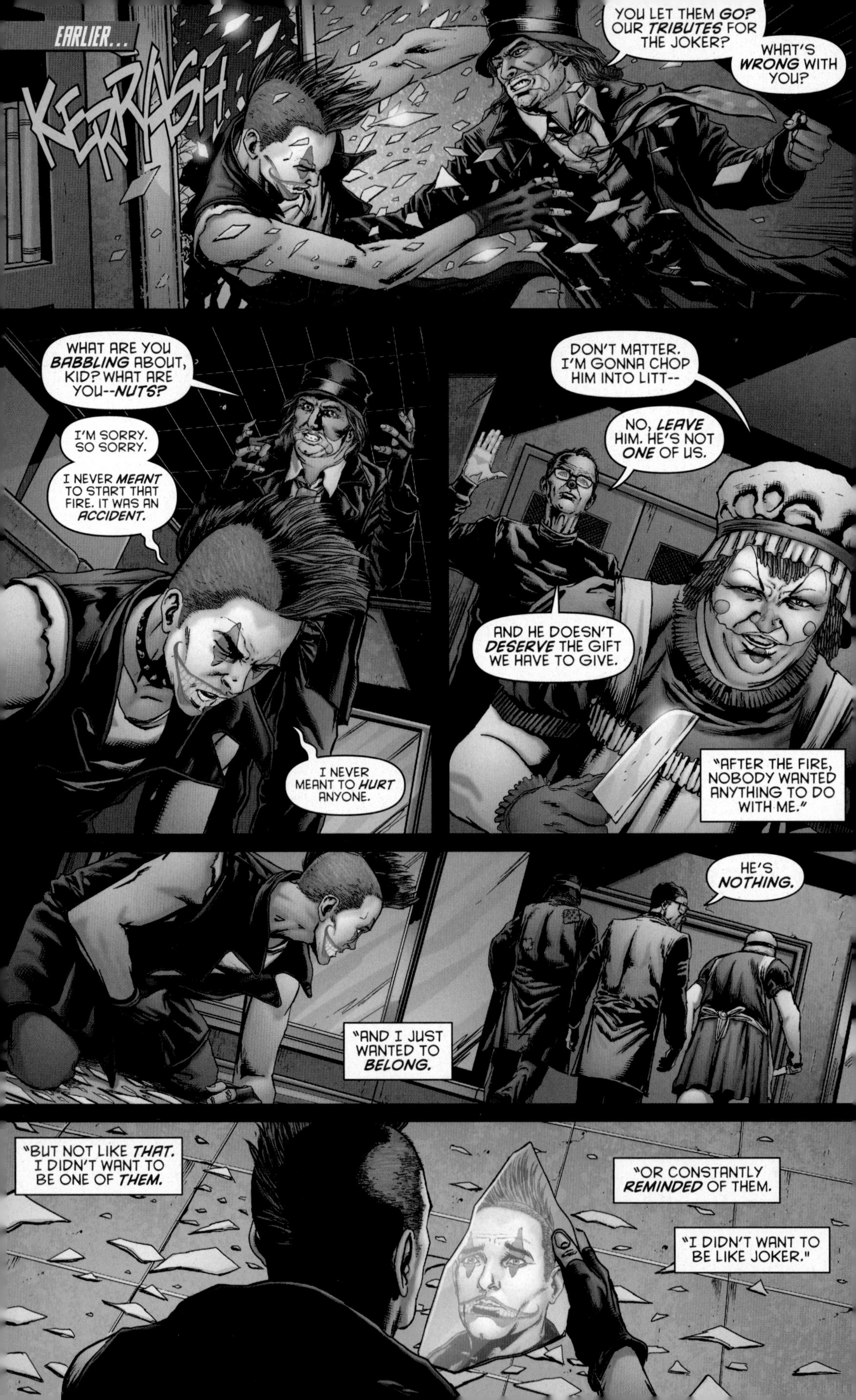
EARLIER...
KERRASH!
YOU LET THEM GO? OUR TRIBUTES FOR THE JOKER?
WHAT'S WRONG WITH YOU?
WHAT ARE YOU BABBLING ABOUT, KID? WHAT ARE YOU--NUTS?
I'M SORRY. SO SORRY.
I NEVER MEANT TO START THAT FIRE. IT WAS AN ACCIDENT.
I NEVER MEANT TO HURT ANYONE.
DON'T MATTER. I'M GONNA CHOP HIM INTO LITT--
NO, LEAVE HIM. HE'S NOT ONE OF US.
AND HE DOESN'T DESERVE THE GIFT WE HAVE TO GIVE.
"AFTER THE FIRE, NOBODY WANTED ANYTHING TO DO WITH ME."
"AND I JUST WANTED TO BELONG.
HE'S NOTHING.
"BUT NOT LIKE THAT. I DIDN'T WANT TO BE ONE OF THEM.
"OR CONSTANTLY REMINDED OF THEM.
"I DIDN'T WANT TO BE LIKE JOKER."

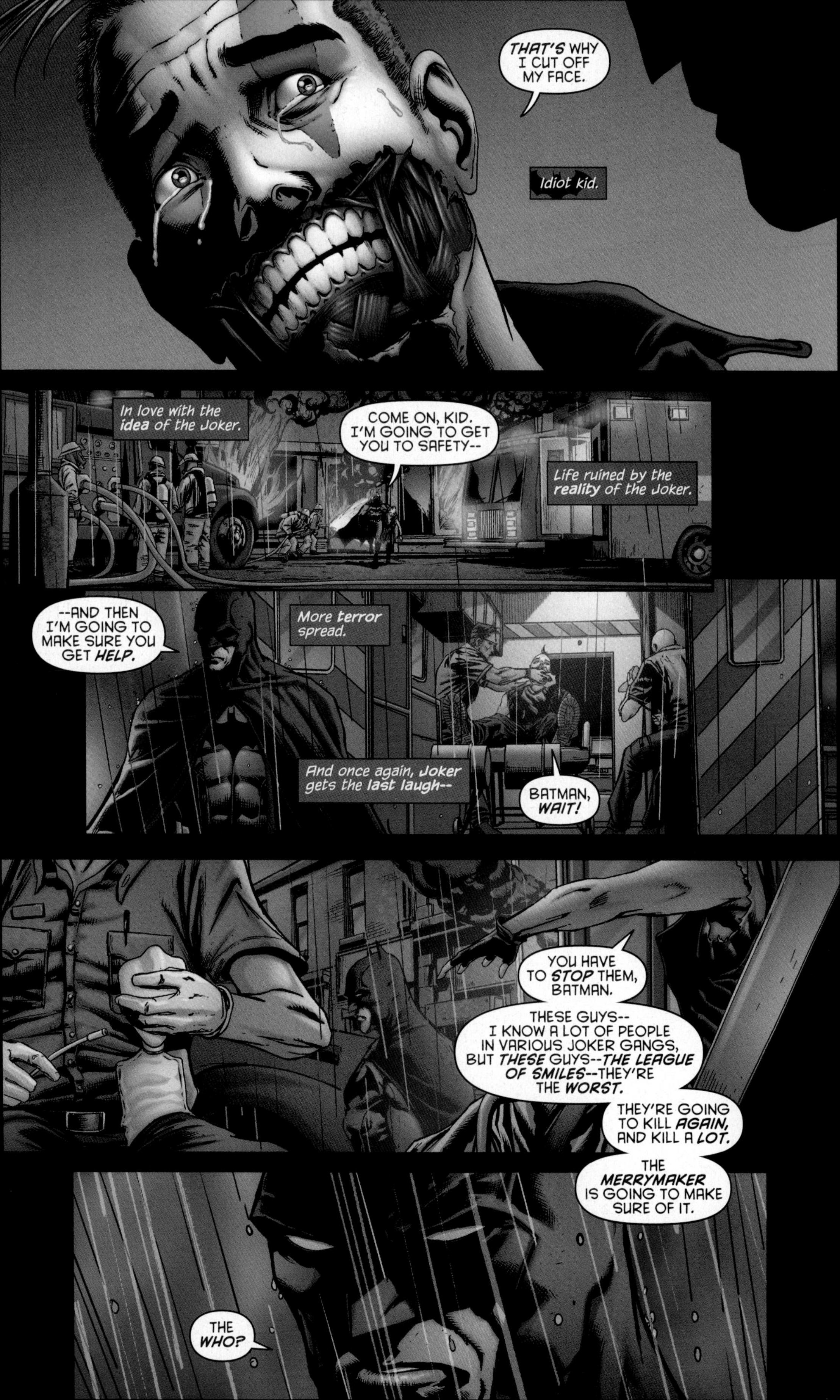
THAT'S WHY I CUT OFF MY FACE.
Idiot kid.
In love with the idea of the Joker.
COME ON, KID. I'M GOING TO GET YOU TO SAFETY--
Life ruined by the reality of the Joker.
--AND THEN I'M GOING TO MAKE SURE YOU GET HELP.
More terror spread.
And once again, Joker gets the last laugh--
BATMAN, WAIT!
YOU HAVE TO STOP THEM, BATMAN.
THESE GUYS-- I KNOW A LOT OF PEOPLE IN VARIOUS JOKER GANGS, BUT THESE GUYS--THE LEAGUE OF SMILES--THEY'RE THE WORST.
THEY'RE GOING TO KILL AGAIN, AND KILL A LOT.
THE MERRYMAKER IS GOING TO MAKE SURE OF IT.
THE WHO?

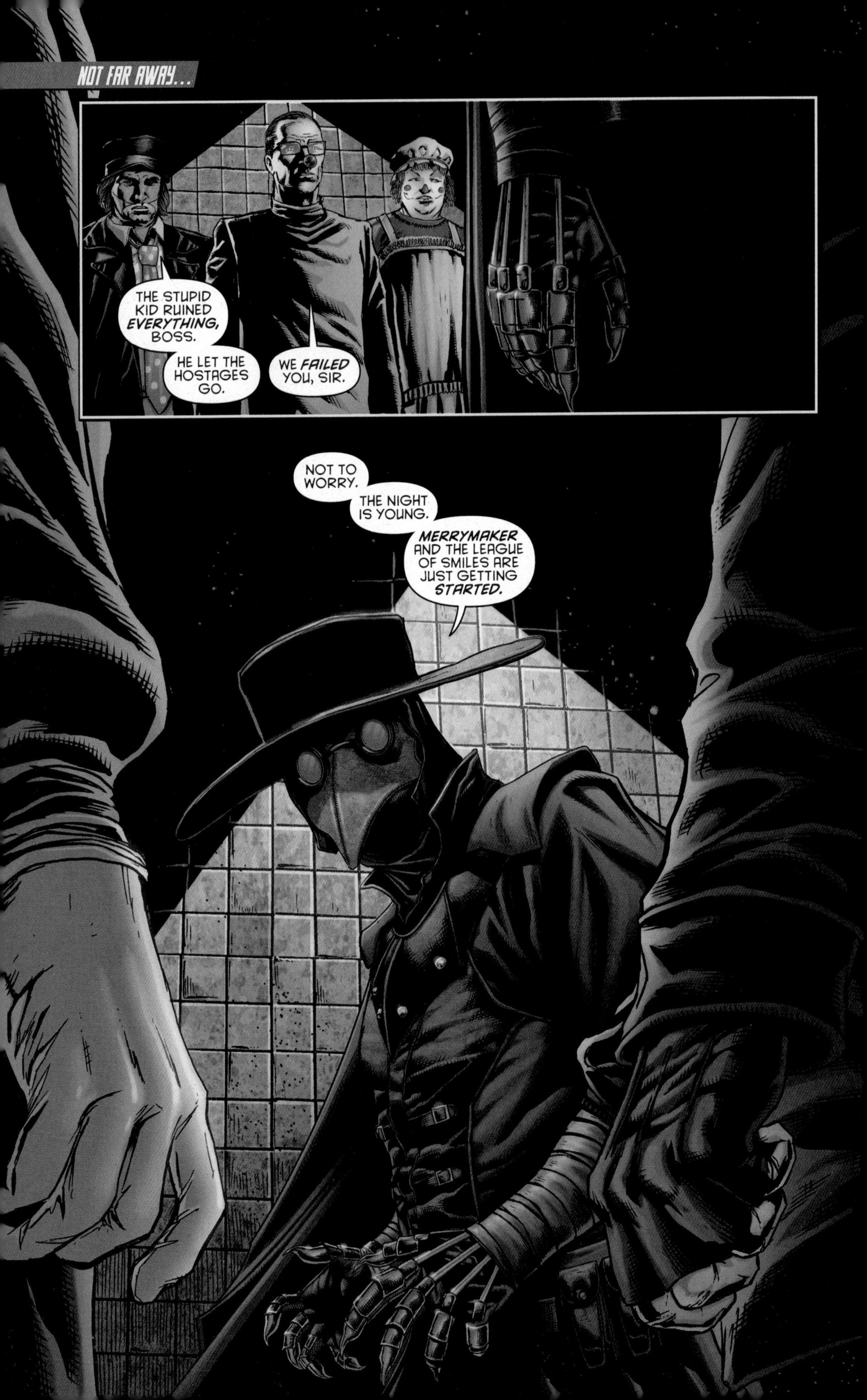
NOT FAR AWAY...
THE STUPID KID RUINED EVERYTHING, BOSS.
HE LET THE HOSTAGES GO.
WE FAILED YOU, SIR.
NOT TO WORRY.
THE NIGHT IS YOUNG.
MERRYMAKER AND THE LEAGUE OF SMILES ARE JUST GETTING STARTED.

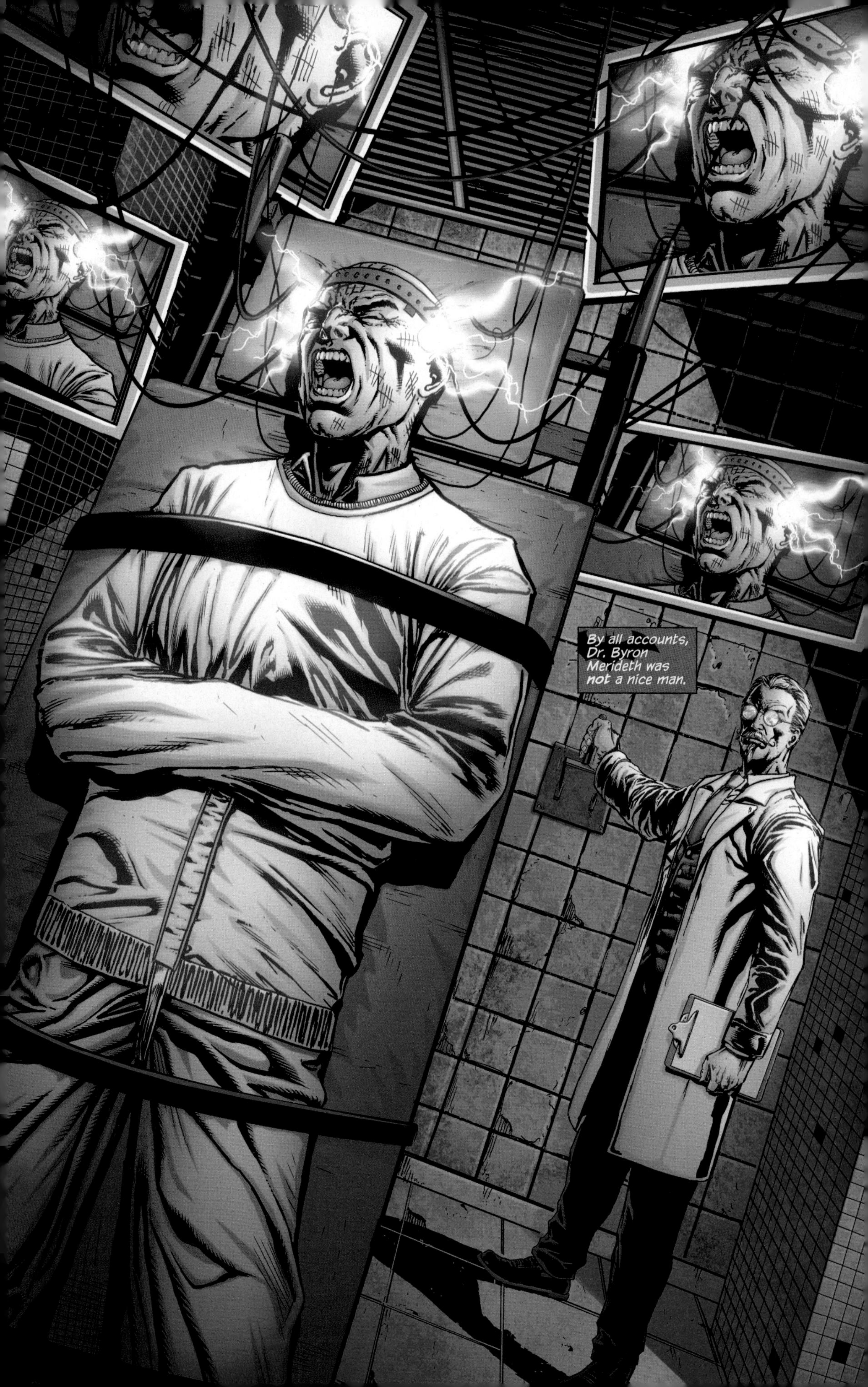
By all accounts, Dr. Byron Merideth was **not** a nice man.

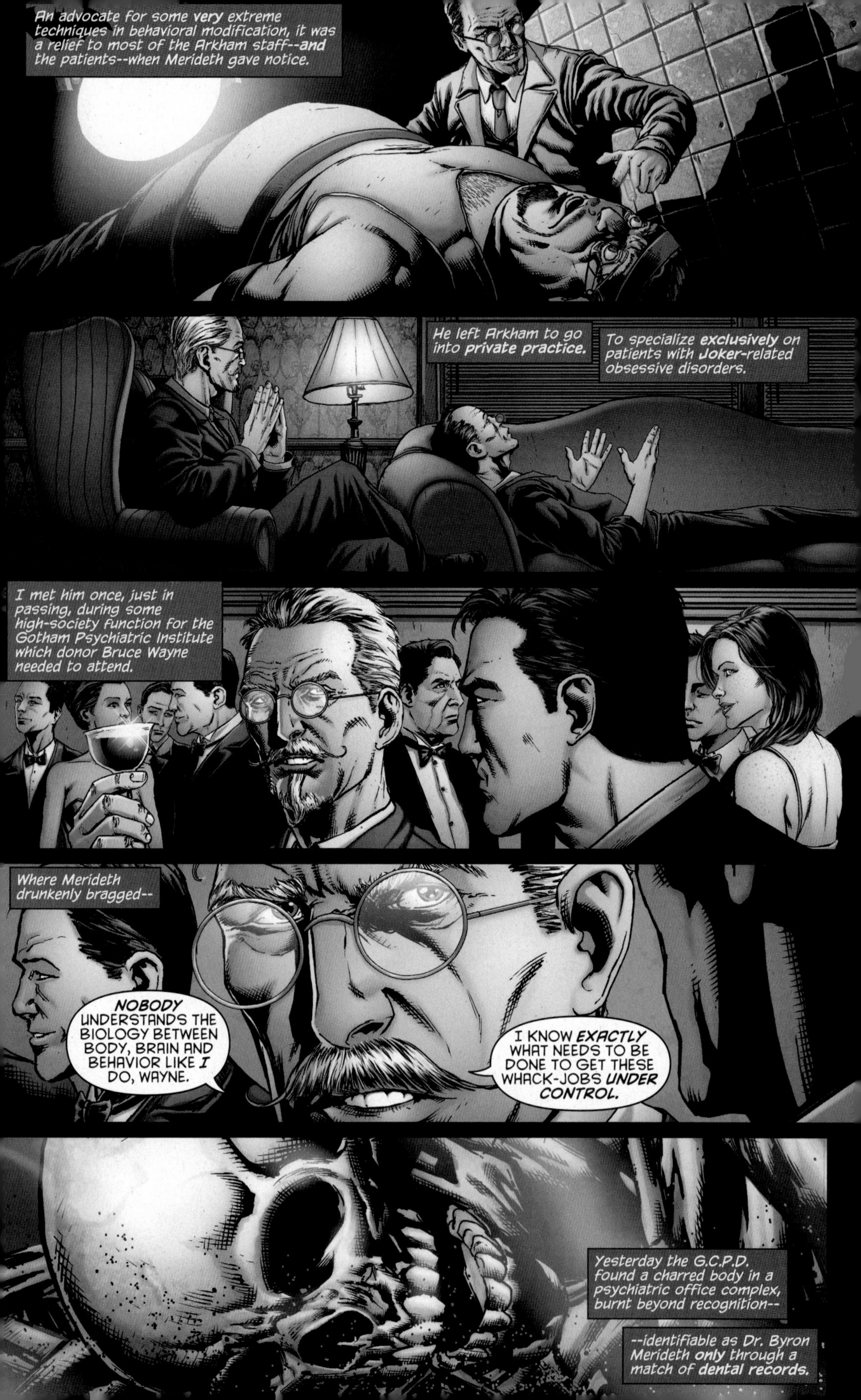
An advocate for some very extreme techniques in behavioral modification, it was a relief to most of the Arkham staff--and the patients--when Merideth gave notice.
He left Arkham to go into private practice.
To specialize exclusively on patients with Joker-related obsessive disorders.
I met him once, just in passing, during some high-society function for the Gotham Psychiatric Institute which donor Bruce Wayne needed to attend.
Where Merideth drunkenly bragged--
NOBODY UNDERSTANDS THE BIOLOGY BETWEEN BODY, BRAIN AND BEHAVIOR LIKE I DO, WAYNE.
I KNOW EXACTLY WHAT NEEDS TO BE DONE TO GET THESE WHACK-JOBS UNDER CONTROL.
Yesterday the G.C.P.D. found a charred body in a psychiatric office complex, burnt beyond recognition--
--identifiable as Dr. Byron Merideth only through a match of dental records.

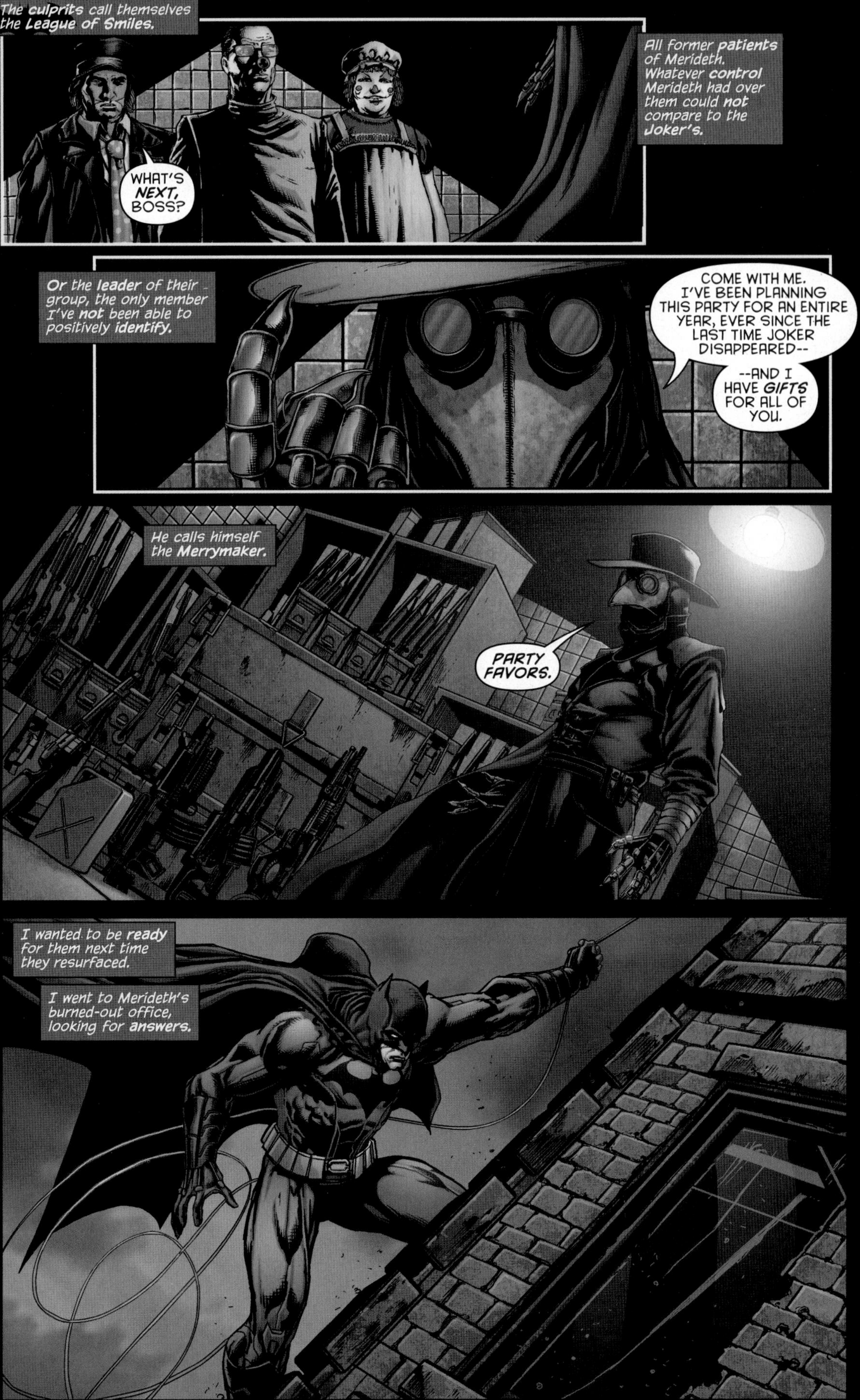
The culprits call themselves the League of Smiles.
All former patients of Merideth. Whatever control Merideth had over them could not compare to the Joker's.
WHAT'S NEXT, BOSS?
Or the leader of their group, the only member I've not been able to positively identify.
COME WITH ME. I'VE BEEN PLANNING THIS PARTY FOR AN ENTIRE YEAR, EVER SINCE THE LAST TIME JOKER DISAPPEARED--
--AND I HAVE GIFTS FOR ALL OF YOU.
He calls himself the Merrymaker.
PARTY FAVORS.
I wanted to be ready for them next time they resurfaced.
I went to Merideth's burned-out office, looking for answers.

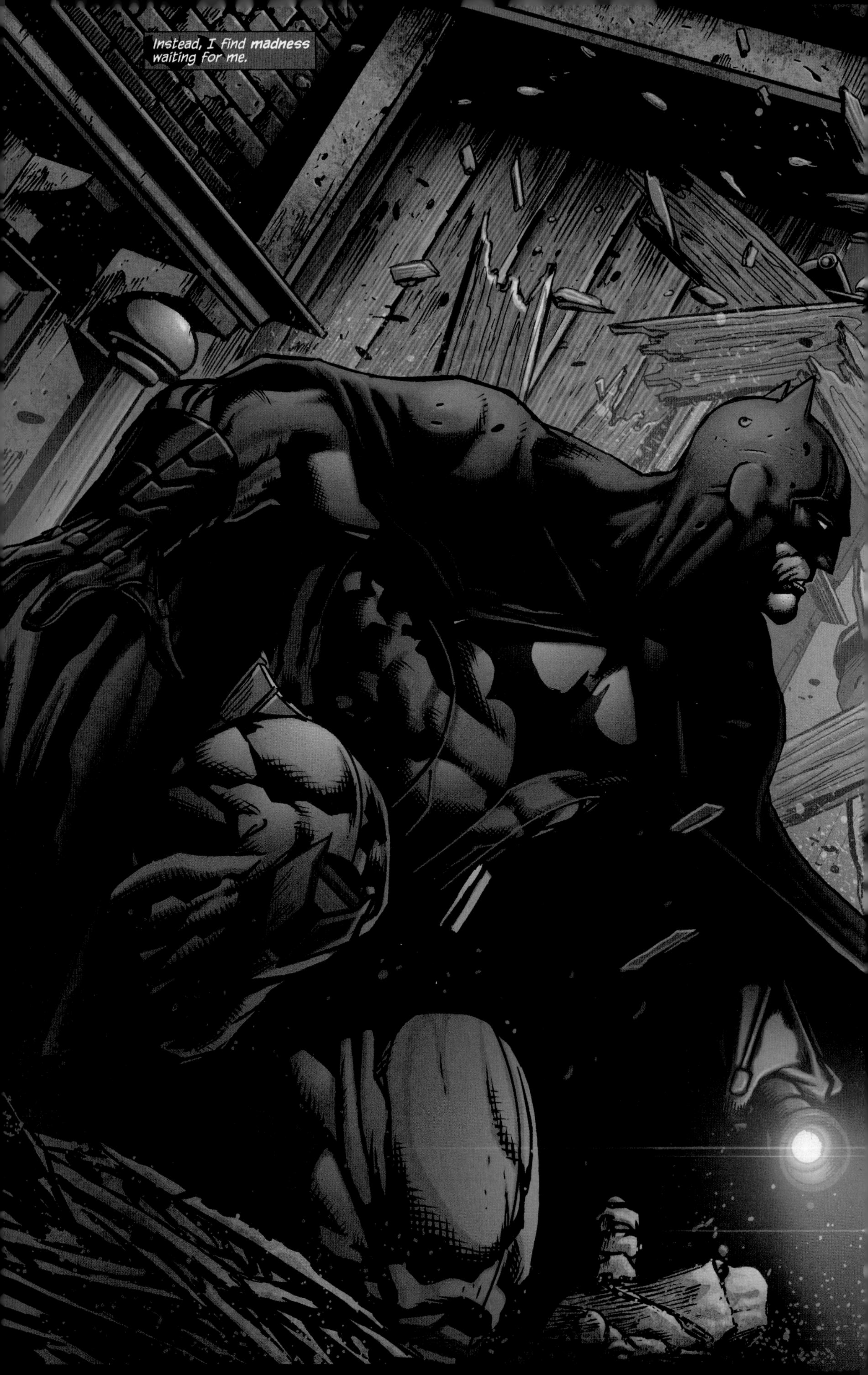
Instead, I find madness waiting for me.

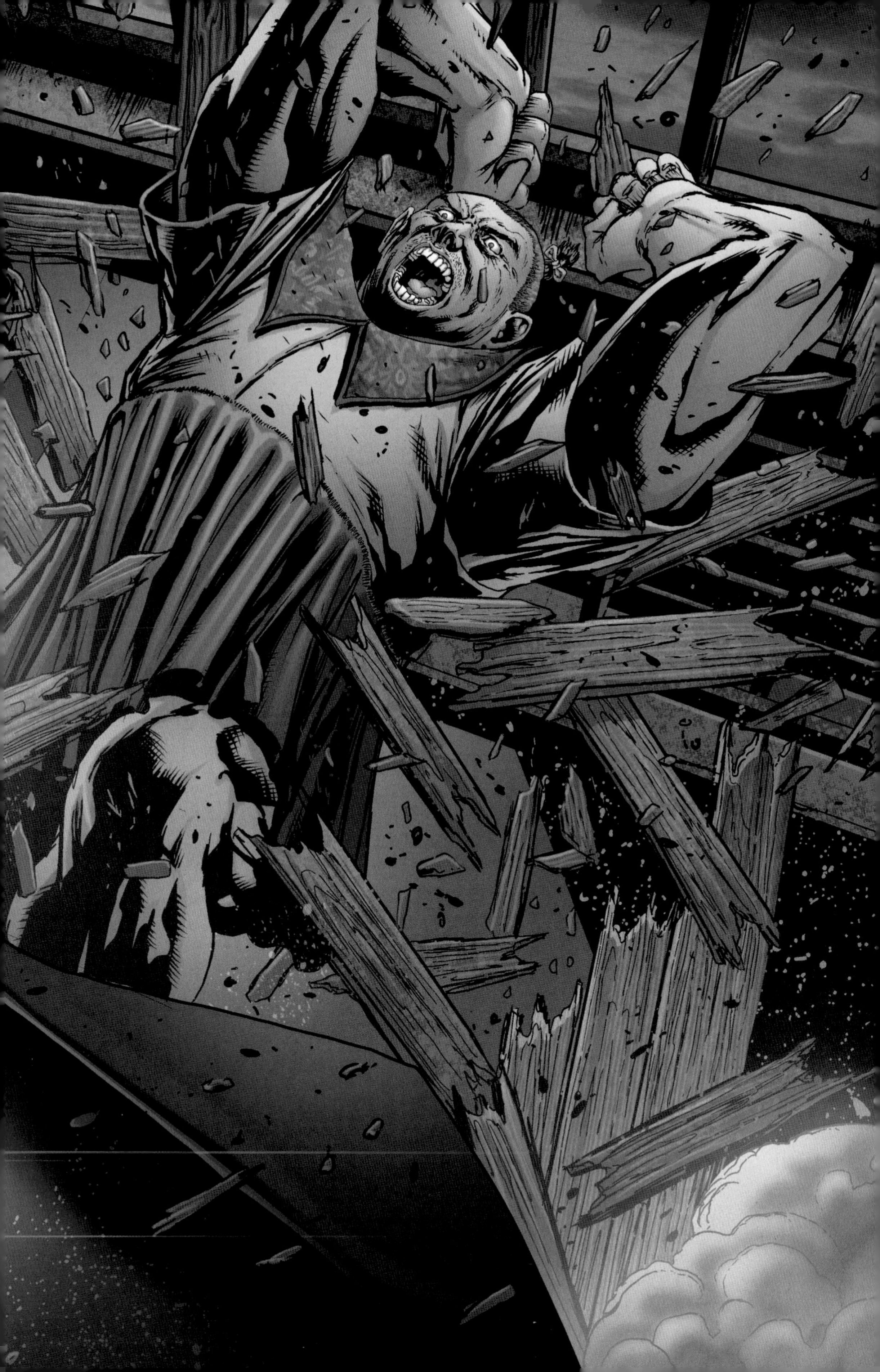

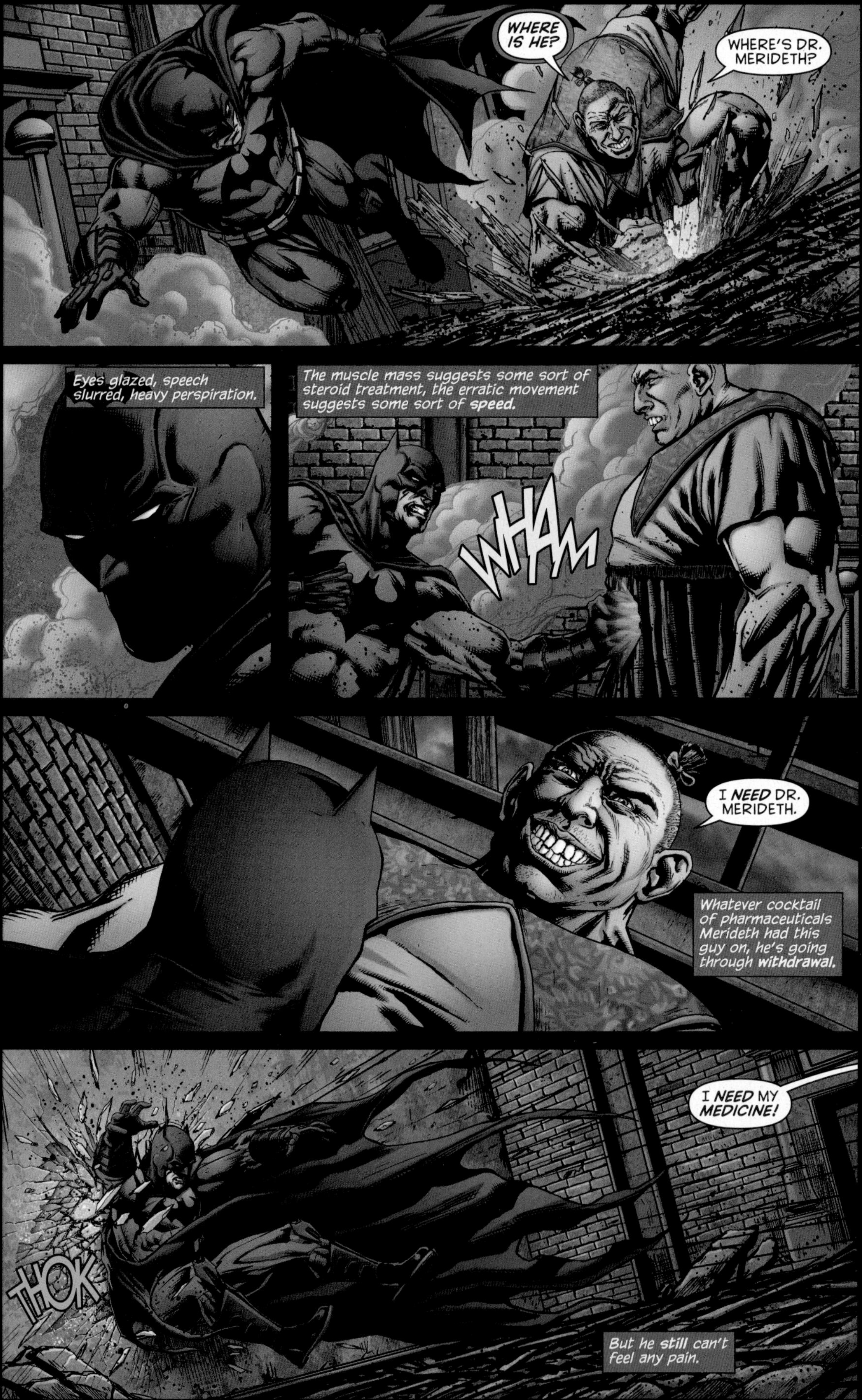
WHERE IS HE?
WHERE'S DR. MERIDETH?
Eyes glazed, speech slurred, heavy perspiration.
The muscle mass suggests some sort of steroid treatment, the erratic movement suggests some sort of speed.
WHAM
I NEED DR. MERIDETH.
Whatever cocktail of pharmaceuticals Merideth had this guy on, he's going through withdrawal.
I NEED MY MEDICINE!
THOK
But he still can't feel any pain.

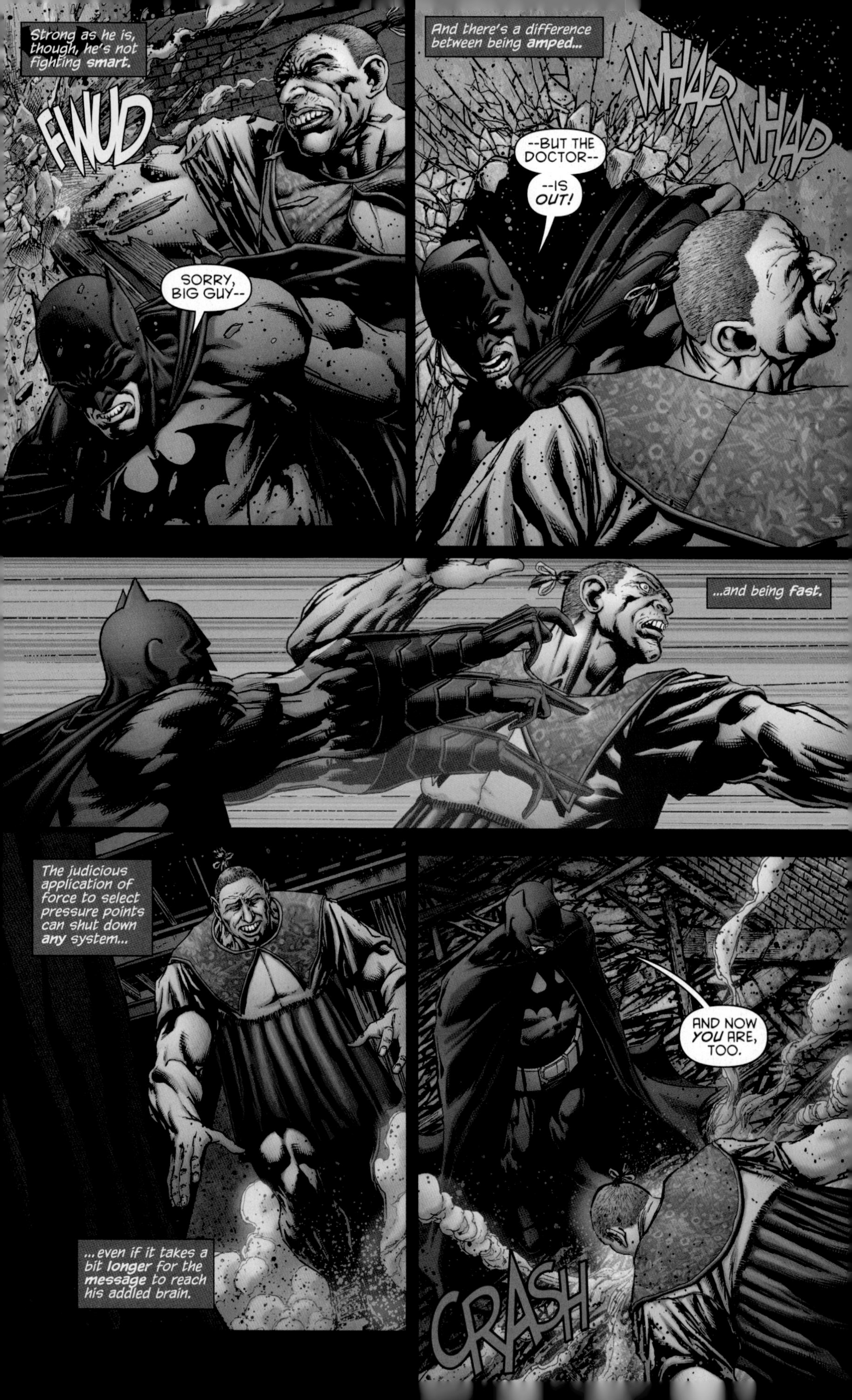
Strong as he is, though, he's not fighting smart.
FWUD
SORRY, BIG GUY--
And there's a difference between being amped...
WHAP WHAP
--BUT THE DOCTOR--
--IS OUT!
...and being fast.
The judicious application of force to select pressure points can shut down any system...
...even if it takes a bit longer for the message to reach his addled brain.
AND NOW YOU ARE, TOO.
CRASH

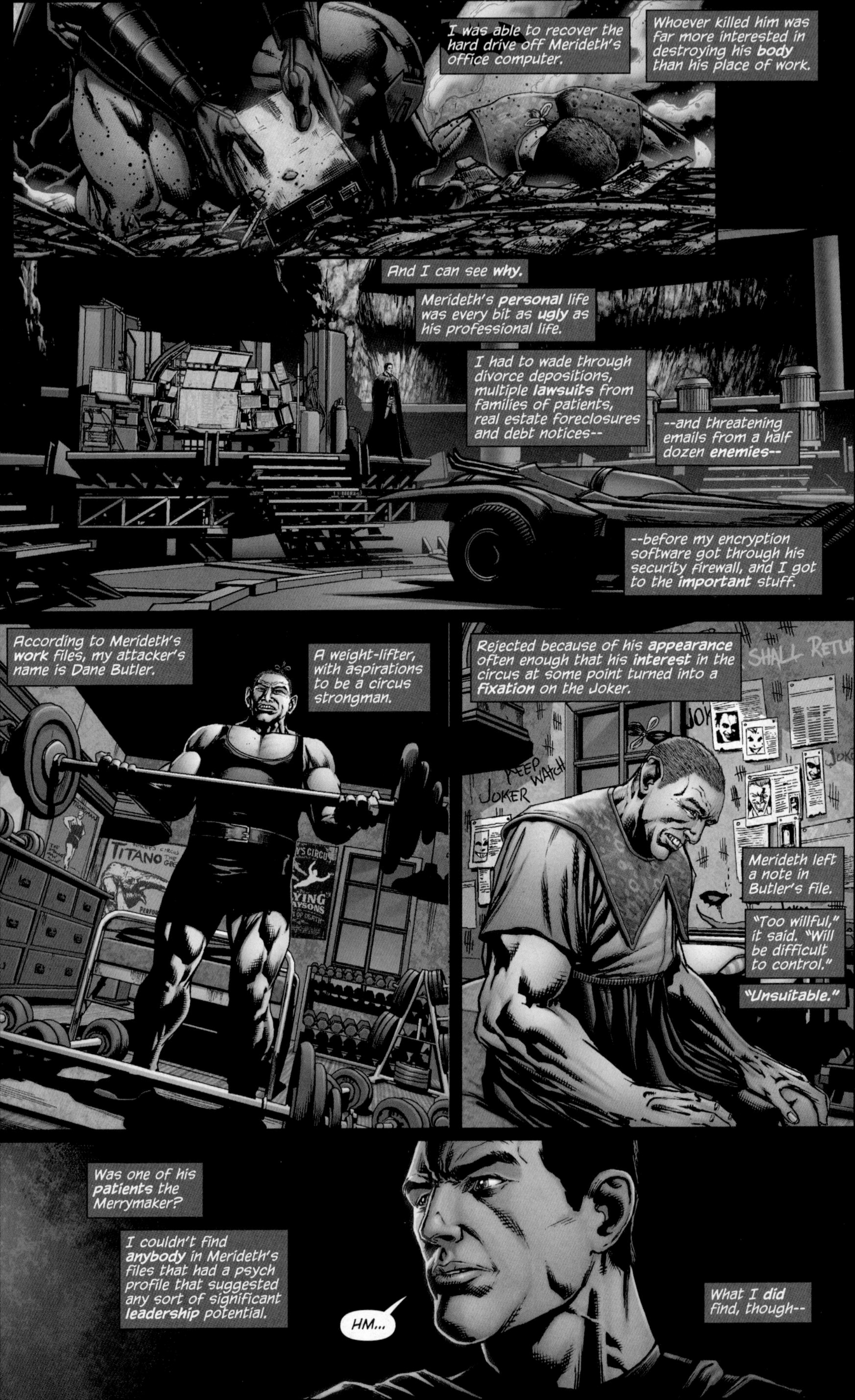

I was able to recover the hard drive off Merideth's office computer.
Whoever killed him was far more interested in destroying his **body** than his place of work.
And I can see **why.**
Merideth's **personal** life was every bit as **ugly** as his professional life.
I had to wade through divorce depositions, multiple **lawsuits** from families of patients, real estate foreclosures and debt notices--
--and threatening emails from a half dozen **enemies**--
--before my encryption software got through his security firewall, and I got to the **important** stuff.
According to Merideth's **work** files, my attacker's name is Dane Butler.
A weight-lifter, with aspirations to be a circus strongman.
TITANO
Rejected because of his **appearance** often enough that his **interest** in the circus at some point turned into a **fixation** on the Joker.
SHALL RETUR
KEEP WATCH
JOKER
Merideth left a note in Butler's file.
"Too willful," it said. "Will be difficult to control."
"Unsuitable."
Was one of his **patients** the Merrymaker?
I couldn't find **anybody** in Merideth's files that had a psych profile that suggested any sort of significant **leadership** potential.
HM...
What I **did** find, though--

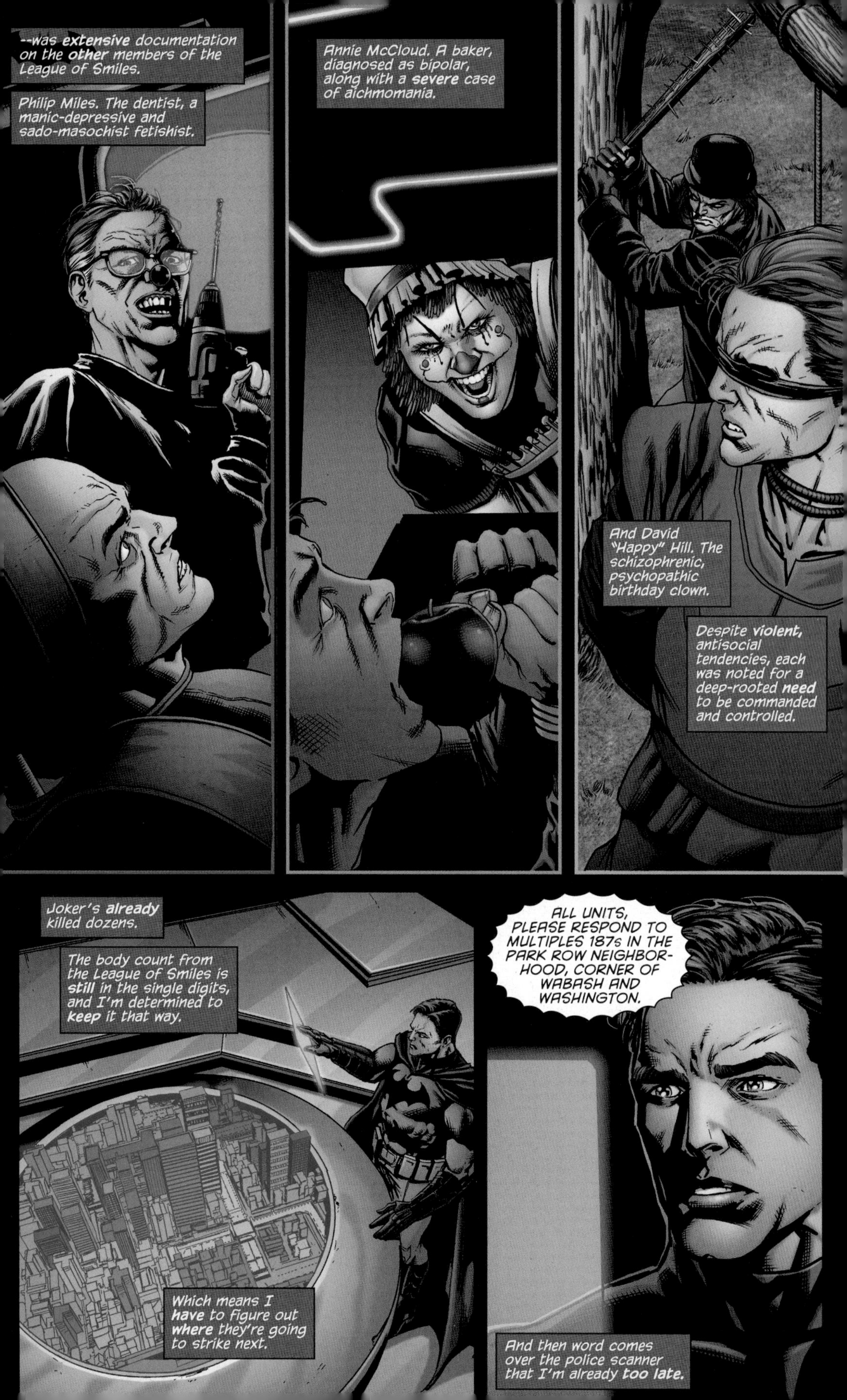
--was extensive documentation on the other members of the League of Smiles.
Philip Miles. The dentist, a manic-depressive and sado-masochist fetishist.
Annie McCloud. A baker, diagnosed as bipolar, along with a severe case of aichmomania.
And David "Happy" Hill. The schizophrenic, psychopathic birthday clown.
Despite violent, antisocial tendencies, each was noted for a deep-rooted need to be commanded and controlled.
Joker's already killed dozens.
The body count from the League of Smiles is still in the single digits, and I'm determined to keep it that way.
Which means I have to figure out where they're going to strike next.
ALL UNITS, PLEASE RESPOND TO MULTIPLES 187s IN THE PARK ROW NEIGHBOR-HOOD, CORNER OF WABASH AND WASHINGTON.
And then word comes over the police scanner that I'm already too late.

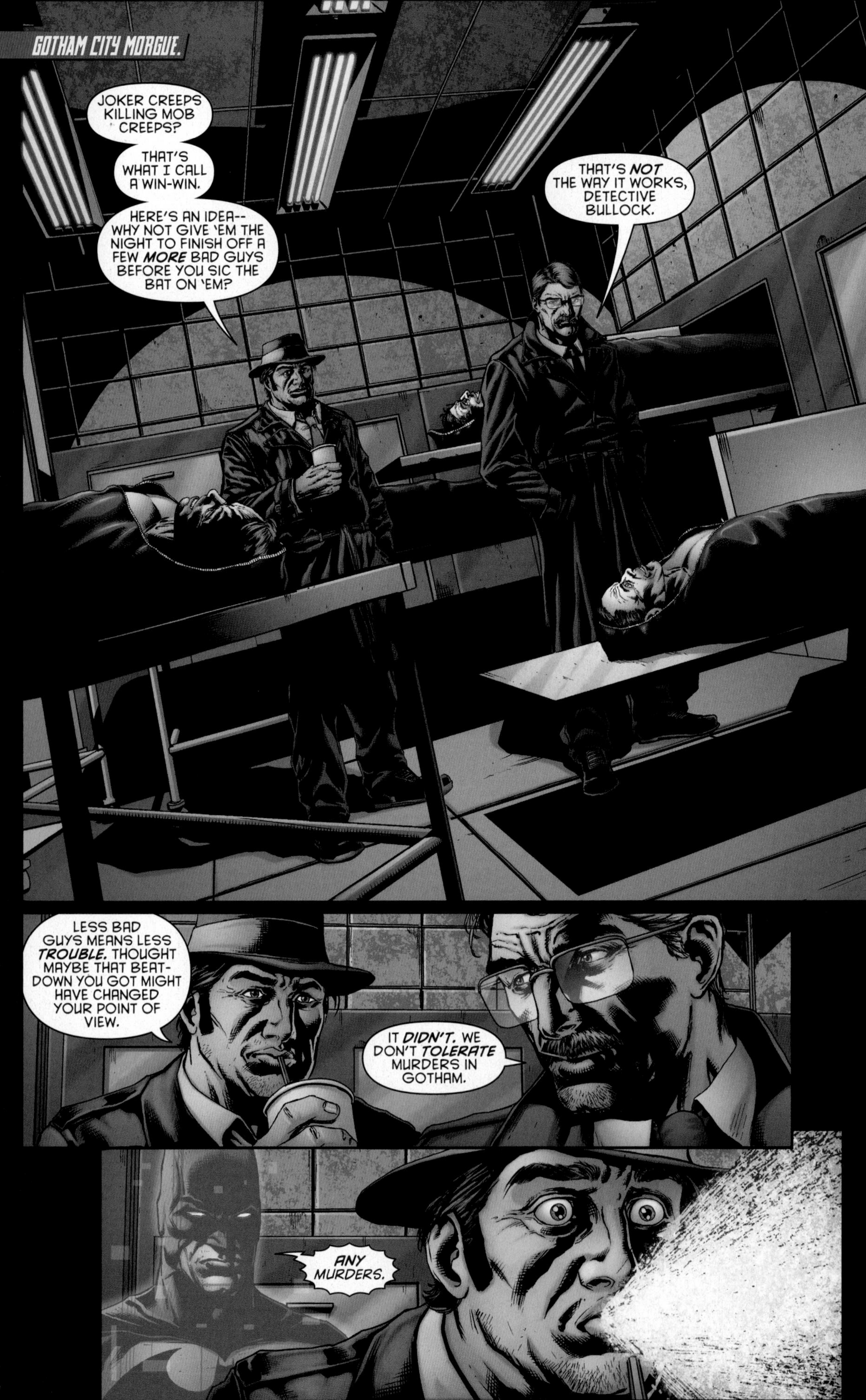
GOTHAM CITY MORGUE.
JOKER CREEPS KILLING MOB CREEPS?
THAT'S WHAT I CALL A WIN-WIN.
HERE'S AN IDEA-- WHY NOT GIVE 'EM THE NIGHT TO FINISH OFF A FEW MORE BAD GUYS BEFORE YOU SIC THE BAT ON 'EM?
THAT'S NOT THE WAY IT WORKS, DETECTIVE BULLOCK.
LESS BAD GUYS MEANS LESS TROUBLE. THOUGHT MAYBE THAT BEAT-DOWN YOU GOT MIGHT HAVE CHANGED YOUR POINT OF VIEW.
IT DIDN'T. WE DON'T TOLERATE MURDERS IN GOTHAM.
ANY MURDERS.

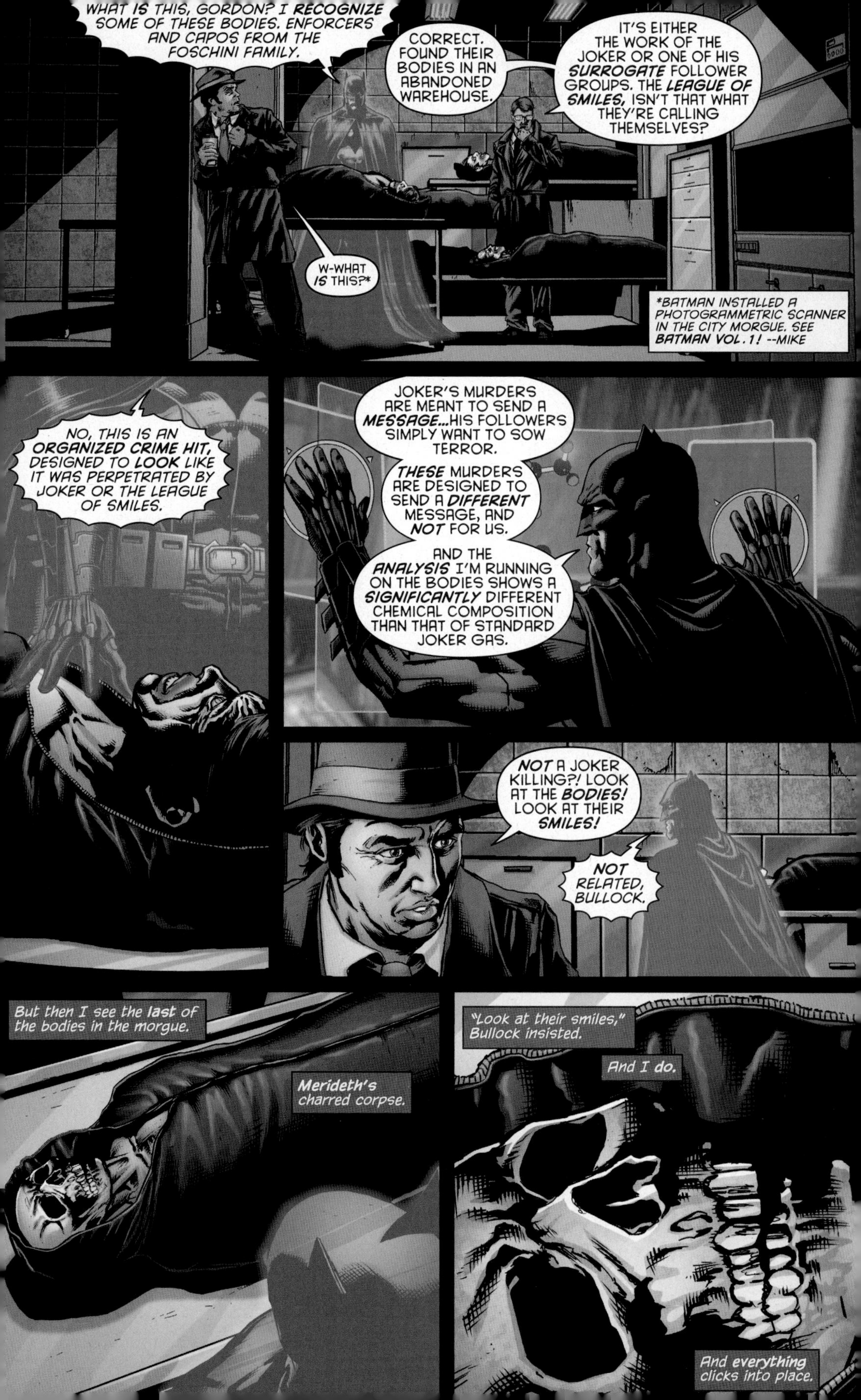
WHAT IS THIS, GORDON? I RECOGNIZE SOME OF THESE BODIES. ENFORCERS AND CAPOS FROM THE FOSCHINI FAMILY.
CORRECT. FOUND THEIR BODIES IN AN ABANDONED WAREHOUSE.
IT'S EITHER THE WORK OF THE JOKER OR ONE OF HIS SURROGATE FOLLOWER GROUPS. THE LEAGUE OF SMILES, ISN'T THAT WHAT THEY'RE CALLING THEMSELVES?
W-WHAT IS THIS?*
*BATMAN INSTALLED A PHOTOGRAMMETRIC SCANNER IN THE CITY MORGUE. SEE BATMAN VOL.1! --MIKE
NO, THIS IS AN ORGANIZED CRIME HIT, DESIGNED TO LOOK LIKE IT WAS PERPETRATED BY JOKER OR THE LEAGUE OF SMILES.
JOKER'S MURDERS ARE MEANT TO SEND A MESSAGE...HIS FOLLOWERS SIMPLY WANT TO SOW TERROR.
THESE MURDERS ARE DESIGNED TO SEND A DIFFERENT MESSAGE, AND NOT FOR US.
AND THE ANALYSIS I'M RUNNING ON THE BODIES SHOWS A SIGNIFICANTLY DIFFERENT CHEMICAL COMPOSITION THAN THAT OF STANDARD JOKER GAS.
NOT A JOKER KILLING?! LOOK AT THE BODIES! LOOK AT THEIR SMILES!
NOT RELATED, BULLOCK.
But then I see the last of the bodies in the morgue.
Merideth's charred corpse.
"Look at their smiles," Bullock insisted.
And I do.
And everything clicks into place.

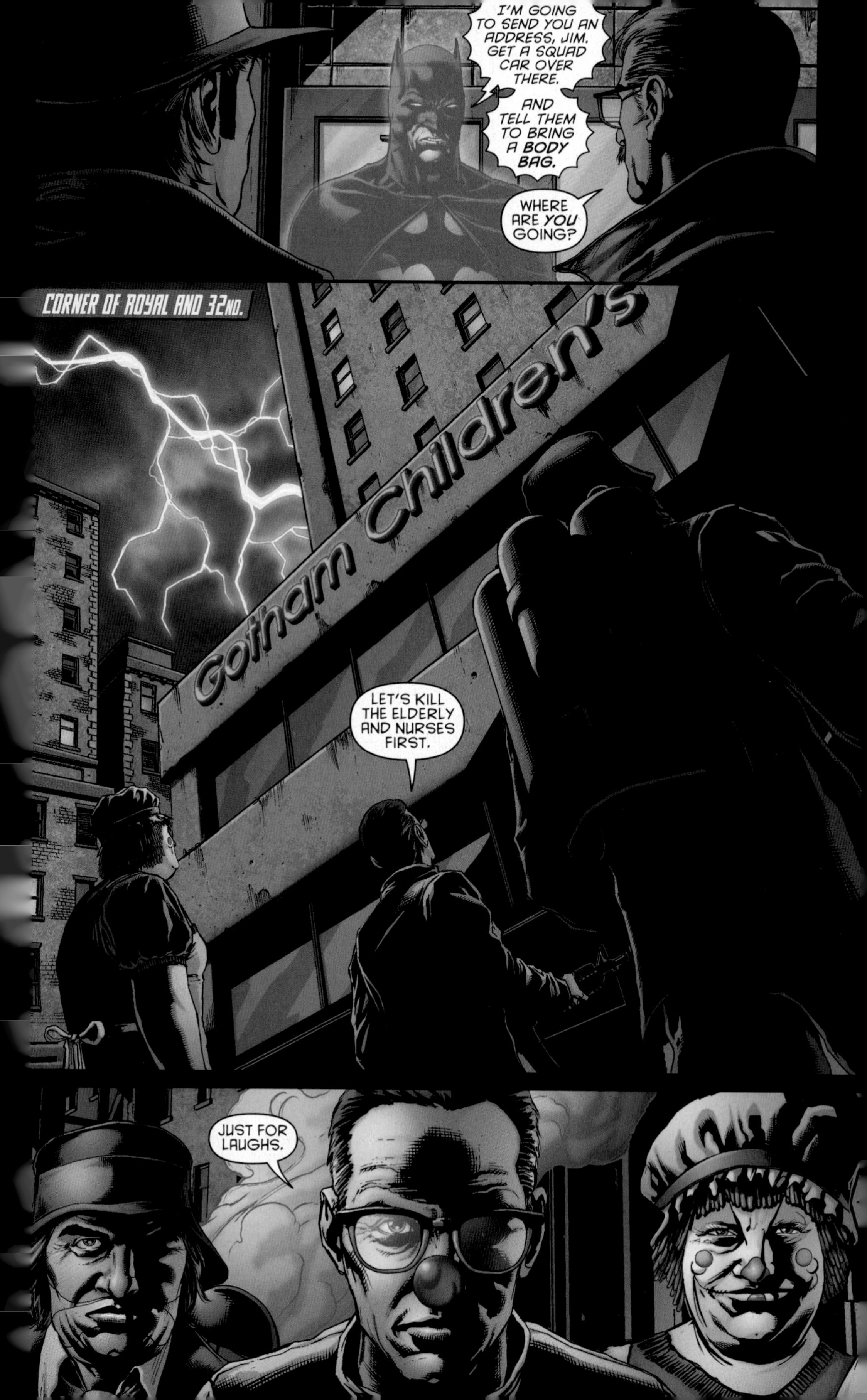
I'M GOING TO SEND YOU AN ADDRESS, JIM. GET A SQUAD CAR OVER THERE.
AND TELL THEM TO BRING A **BODY BAG.**
WHERE ARE *YOU* GOING?
CORNER OF ROYAL AND 32ND.
Gotham Children's
LET'S KILL THE ELDERLY AND NURSES FIRST.
JUST FOR LAUGHS.

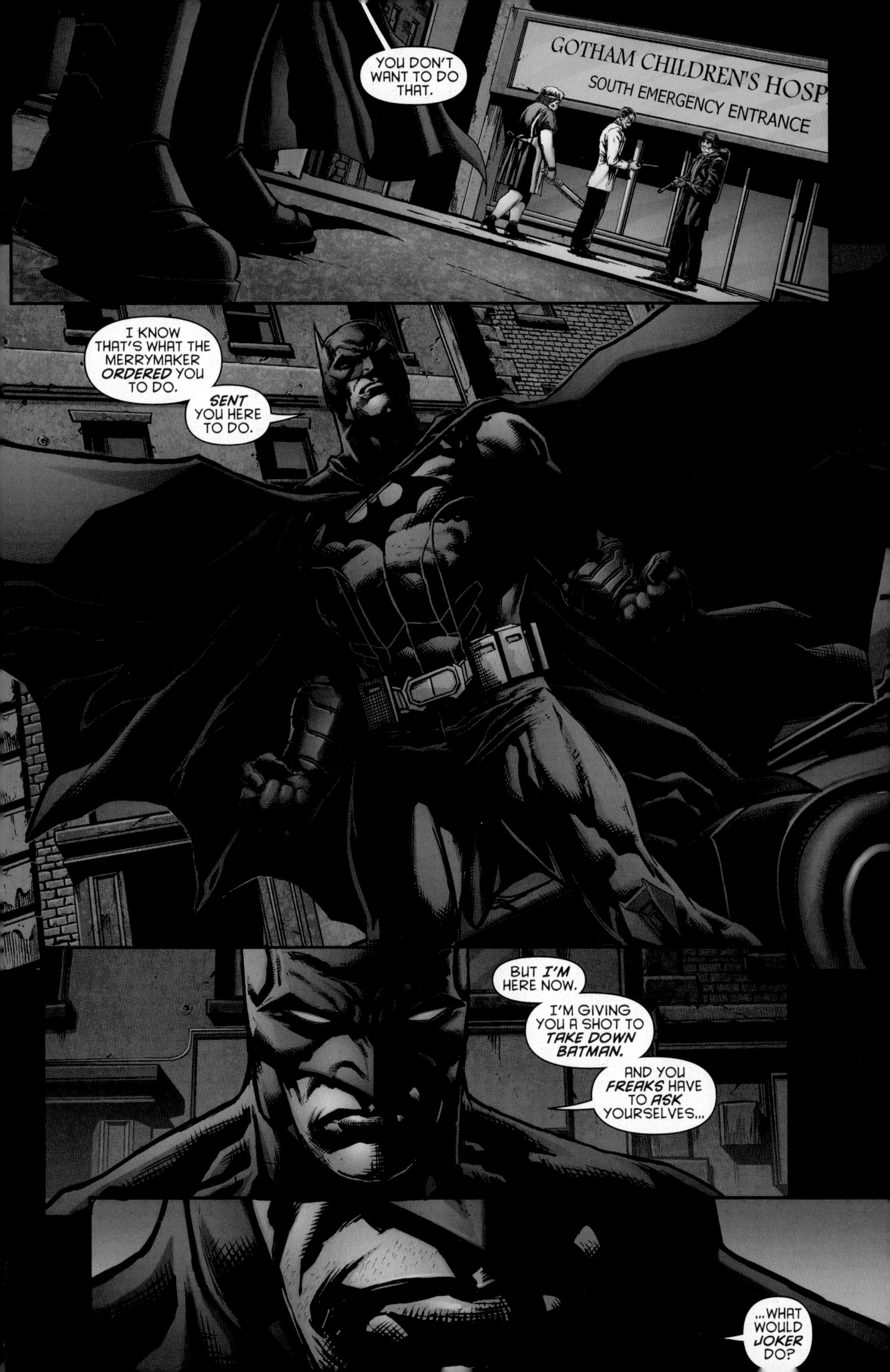
YOU DON'T WANT TO DO THAT.
GOTHAM CHILDREN'S HOSP
SOUTH EMERGENCY ENTRANCE
I KNOW THAT'S WHAT THE MERRYMAKER ORDERED YOU TO DO.
SENT YOU HERE TO DO.
BUT I'M HERE NOW.
I'M GIVING YOU A SHOT TO TAKE DOWN BATMAN.
AND YOU FREAKS HAVE TO ASK YOURSELVES...
...WHAT WOULD JOKER DO?

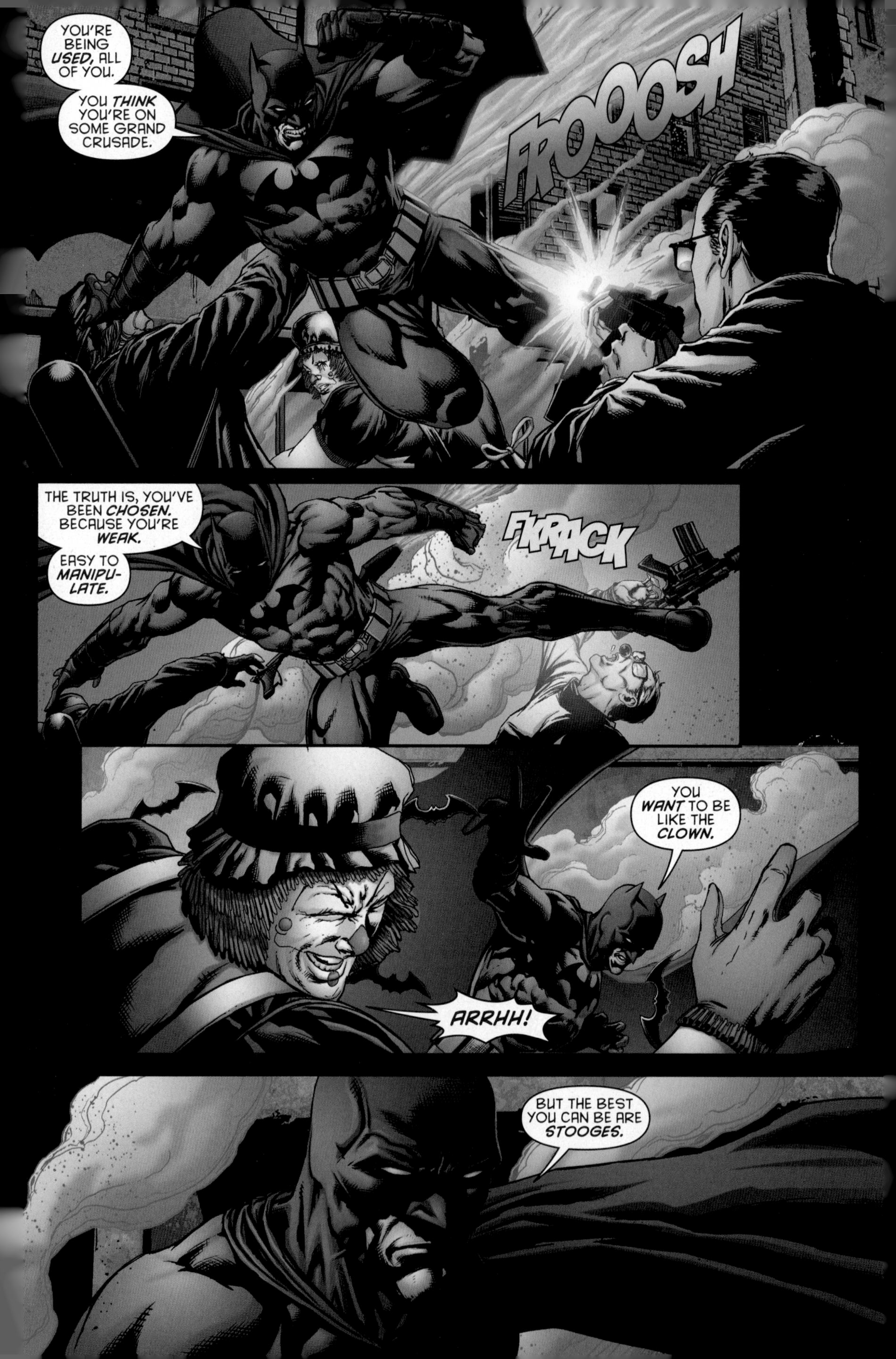
YOU'RE BEING USED, ALL OF YOU.
YOU THINK YOU'RE ON SOME GRAND CRUSADE.
FROOOSH
THE TRUTH IS, YOU'VE BEEN CHOSEN. BECAUSE YOU'RE WEAK.
EASY TO MANIPU-LATE.
FKRACK
YOU WANT TO BE LIKE THE CLOWN.
ARRHH!
BUT THE BEST YOU CAN BE ARE STOOGES.

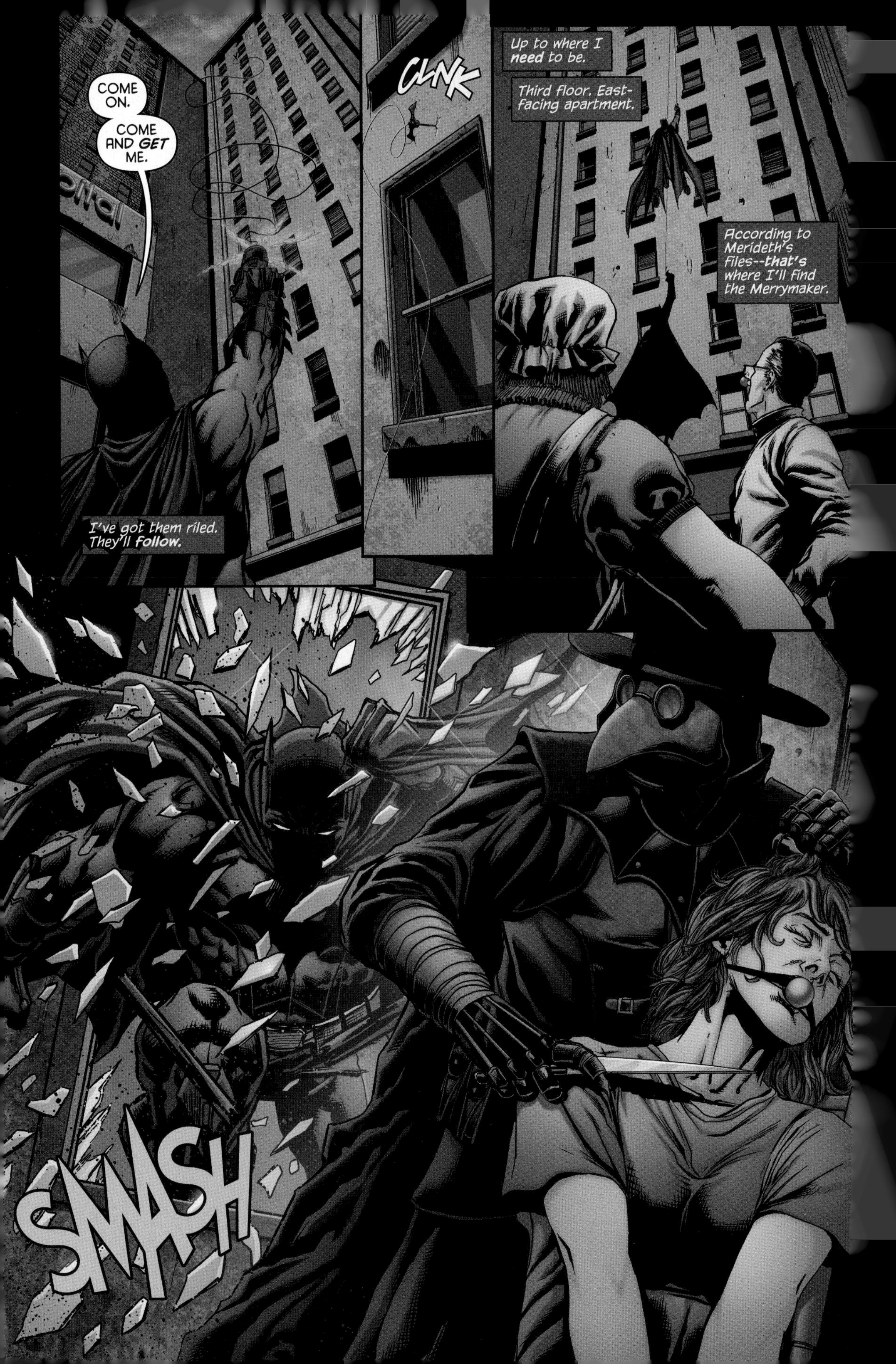

COME ON.
COME AND GET ME.
I've got them riled. They'll follow.
CLNK
Up to where I need to be.
Third floor. East-facing apartment.
According to Merideth's files--that's where I'll find the Merrymaker.
SMASH

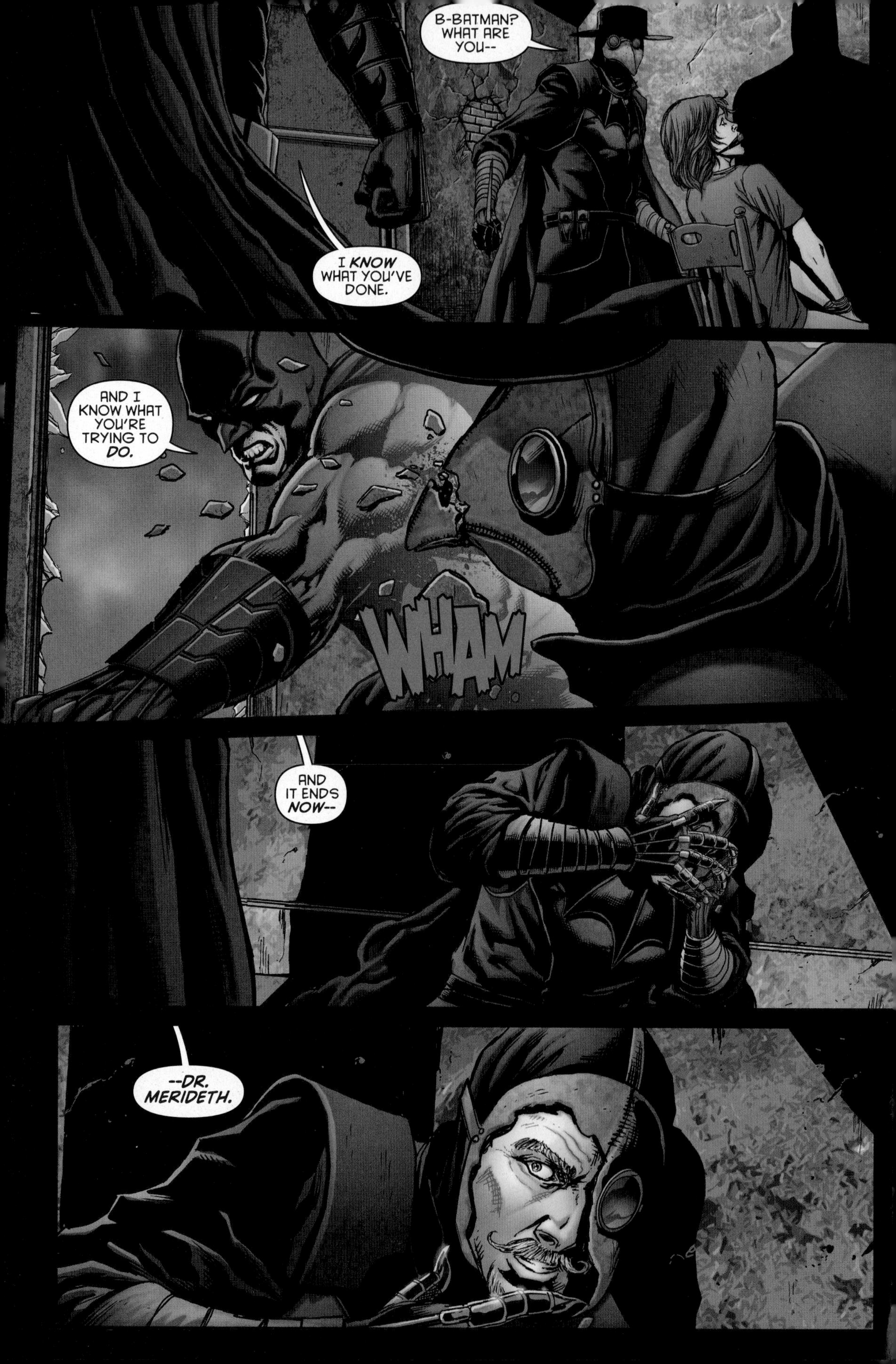
B-BATMAN? WHAT ARE YOU--
I KNOW WHAT YOU'VE DONE.
AND I KNOW WHAT YOU'RE TRYING TO DO.
WHAM
AND IT ENDS NOW--
--DR. MERIDETH.

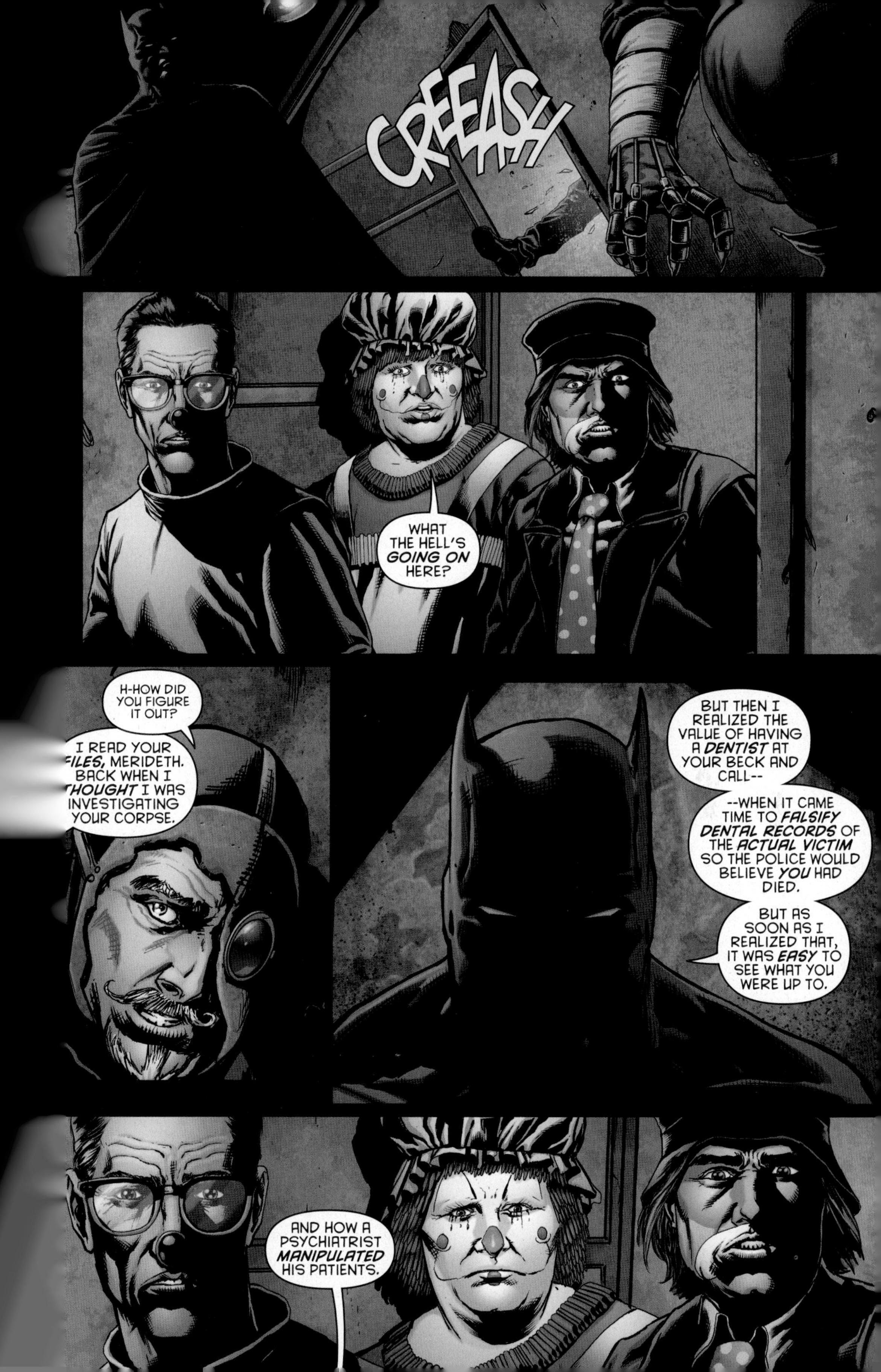
CREEASH
WHAT THE HELL'S GOING ON HERE?
H-HOW DID YOU FIGURE IT OUT?
I READ YOUR FILES, MERIDETH. BACK WHEN I THOUGHT I WAS INVESTIGATING YOUR CORPSE.
BUT THEN I REALIZED THE VALUE OF HAVING A DENTIST AT YOUR BECK AND CALL--
--WHEN IT CAME TIME TO FALSIFY DENTAL RECORDS OF THE ACTUAL VICTIM SO THE POLICE WOULD BELIEVE YOU HAD DIED.
BUT AS SOON AS I REALIZED THAT, IT WAS EASY TO SEE WHAT YOU WERE UP TO.
AND HOW A PSYCHIATRIST MANIPULATED HIS PATIENTS.

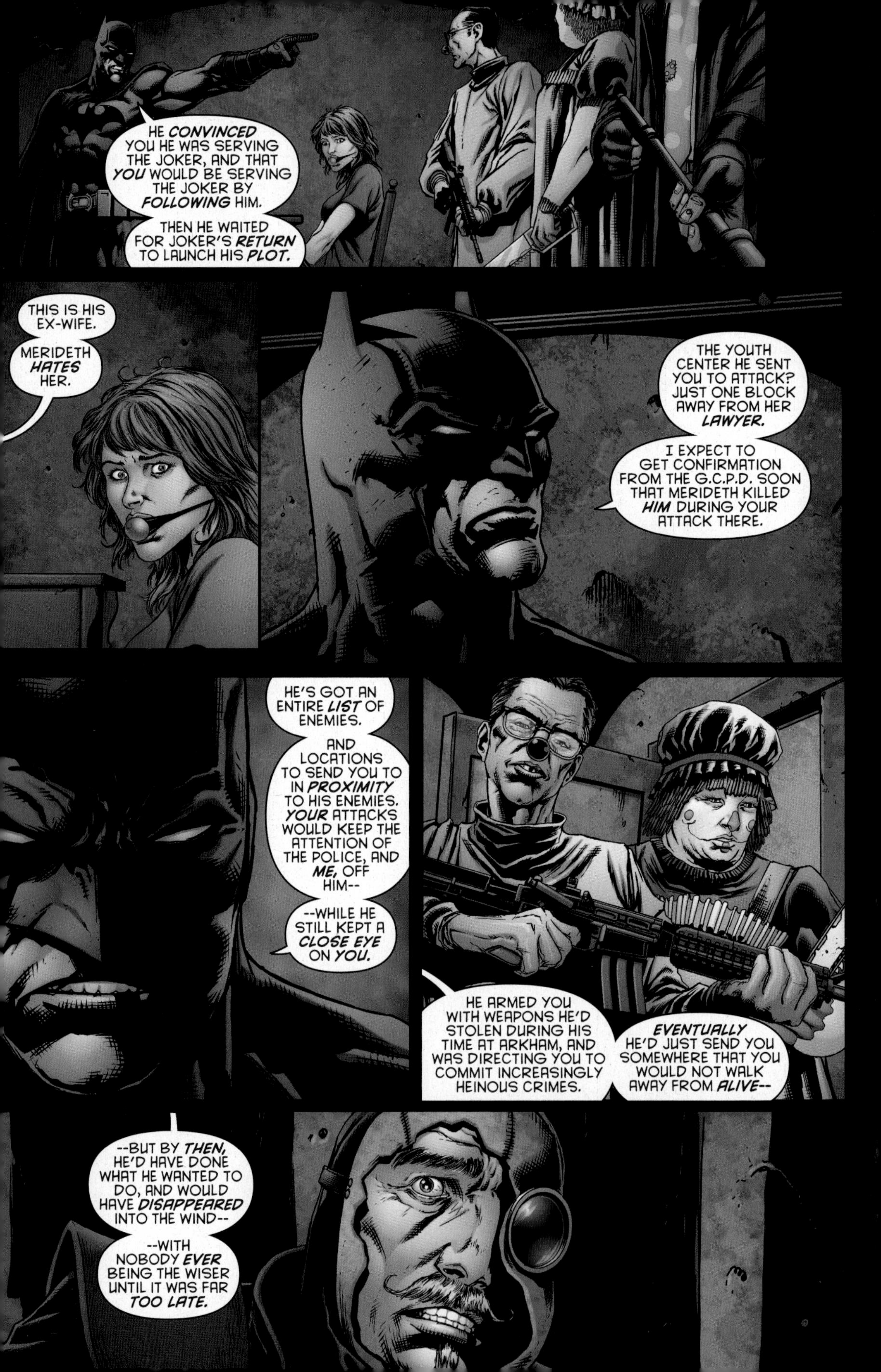
HE CONVINCED YOU HE WAS SERVING THE JOKER, AND THAT YOU WOULD BE SERVING THE JOKER BY FOLLOWING HIM.
THEN HE WAITED FOR JOKER'S RETURN TO LAUNCH HIS PLOT.
THIS IS HIS EX-WIFE.
MERIDETH HATES HER.
THE YOUTH CENTER HE SENT YOU TO ATTACK? JUST ONE BLOCK AWAY FROM HER LAWYER.
I EXPECT TO GET CONFIRMATION FROM THE G.C.P.D. SOON THAT MERIDETH KILLED HIM DURING YOUR ATTACK THERE.
HE'S GOT AN ENTIRE LIST OF ENEMIES.
AND LOCATIONS TO SEND YOU TO IN PROXIMITY TO HIS ENEMIES. YOUR ATTACKS WOULD KEEP THE ATTENTION OF THE POLICE, AND ME, OFF HIM--
--WHILE HE STILL KEPT A CLOSE EYE ON YOU.
HE ARMED YOU WITH WEAPONS HE'D STOLEN DURING HIS TIME AT ARKHAM, AND WAS DIRECTING YOU TO COMMIT INCREASINGLY HEINOUS CRIMES.
EVENTUALLY HE'D JUST SEND YOU SOMEWHERE THAT YOU WOULD NOT WALK AWAY FROM ALIVE--
--BUT BY THEN, HE'D HAVE DONE WHAT HE WANTED TO DO, AND WOULD HAVE DISAPPEARED INTO THE WIND--
--WITH NOBODY EVER BEING THE WISER UNTIL IT WAS FAR TOO LATE.

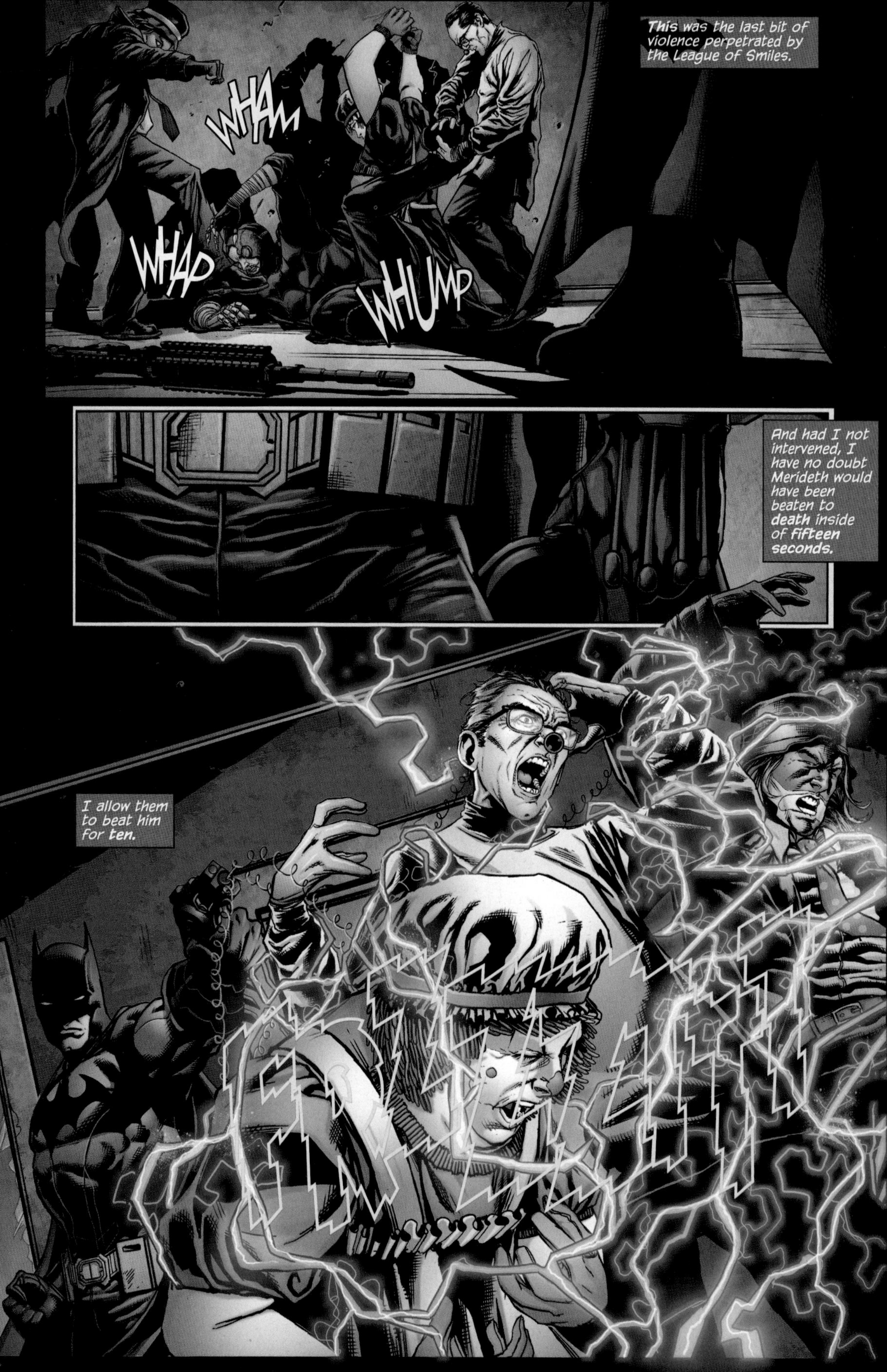
This was the last bit of violence perpetrated by the League of Smiles.
WHAM
WHAP
WHUMP
And had I not intervened, I have no doubt Merideth would have been beaten to death inside of fifteen seconds.
I allow them to beat him for ten.

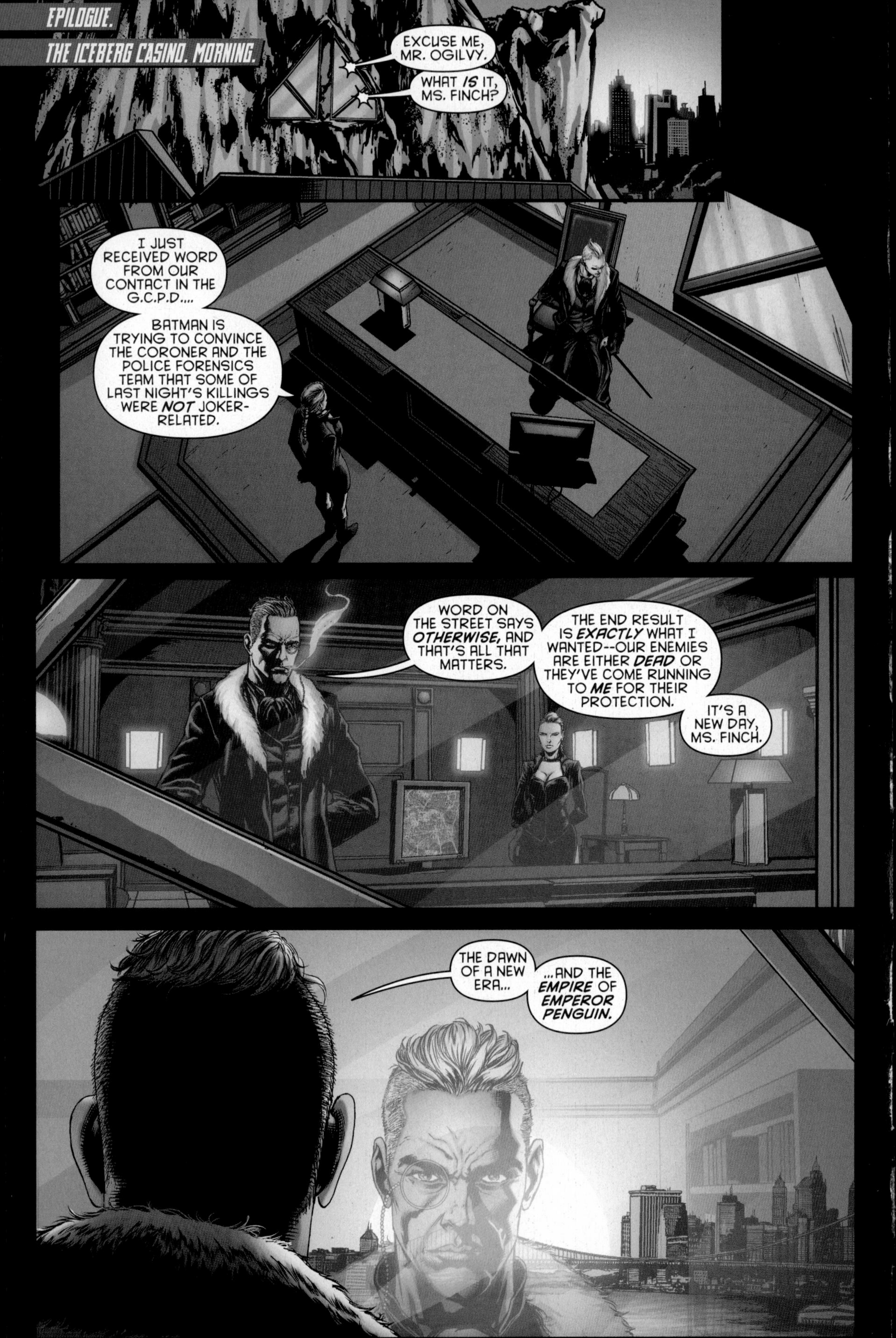

EPILOGUE.
THE ICEBERG CASINO. MORNING.
EXCUSE ME, MR. OGILVY.
WHAT IS IT, MS. FINCH?
I JUST RECEIVED WORD FROM OUR CONTACT IN THE G.C.P.D....
BATMAN IS TRYING TO CONVINCE THE CORONER AND THE POLICE FORENSICS TEAM THAT SOME OF LAST NIGHT'S KILLINGS WERE NOT JOKER-RELATED.
WORD ON THE STREET SAYS OTHERWISE, AND THAT'S ALL THAT MATTERS.
THE END RESULT IS EXACTLY WHAT I WANTED--OUR ENEMIES ARE EITHER DEAD OR THEY'VE COME RUNNING TO ME FOR THEIR PROTECTION.
IT'S A NEW DAY, MS. FINCH.
THE DAWN OF A NEW ERA...
...AND THE EMPIRE OF EMPEROR PENGUIN.

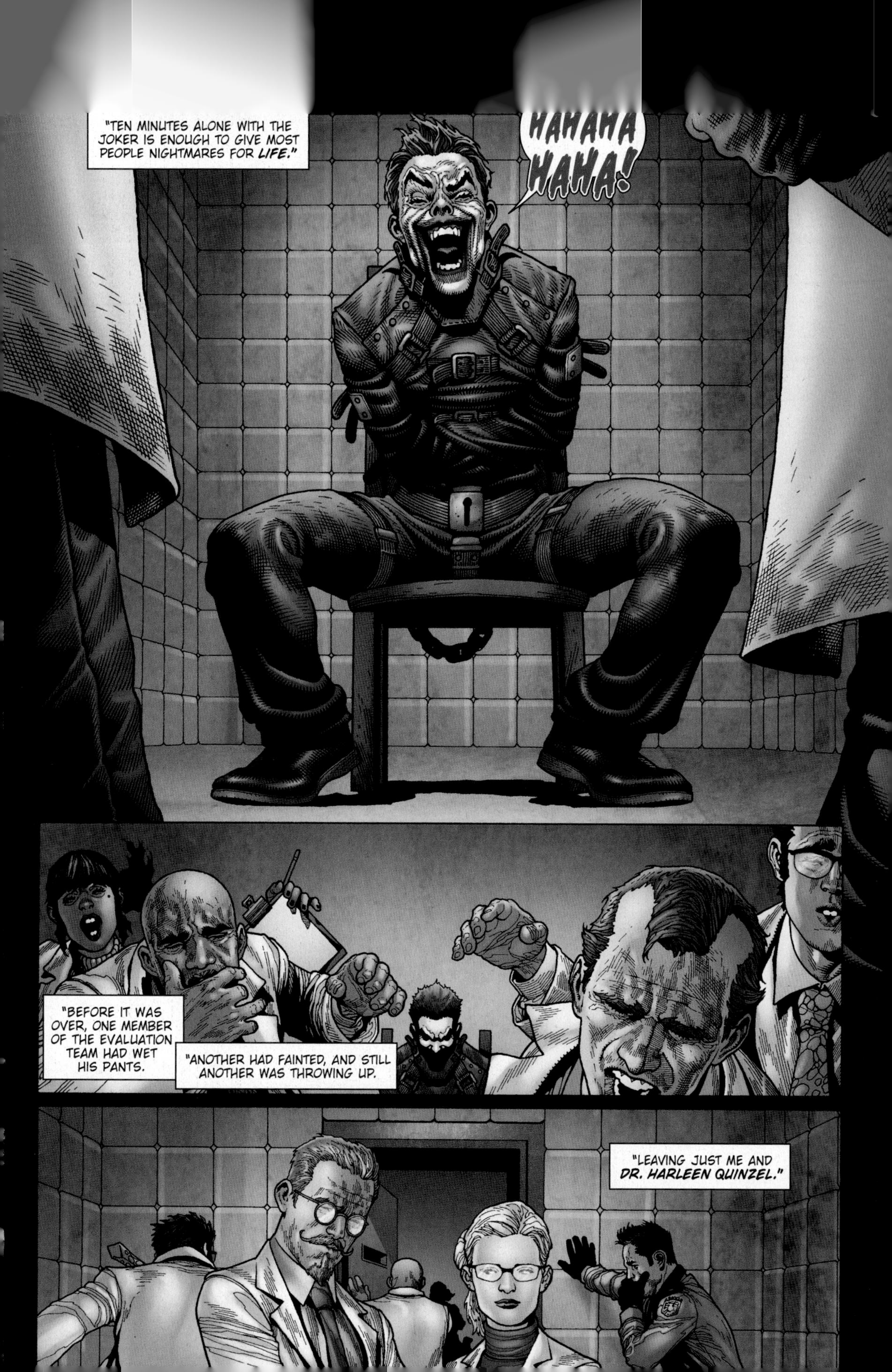

"TEN MINUTES ALONE WITH THE JOKER IS ENOUGH TO GIVE MOST PEOPLE NIGHTMARES FOR *LIFE.*"
HAHAHA HAHA!
"BEFORE IT WAS OVER, ONE MEMBER OF THE EVALUATION TEAM HAD WET HIS PANTS.
"ANOTHER HAD FAINTED, AND STILL ANOTHER WAS THROWING UP.
"LEAVING JUST ME AND *DR. HARLEEN QUINZEL.*"

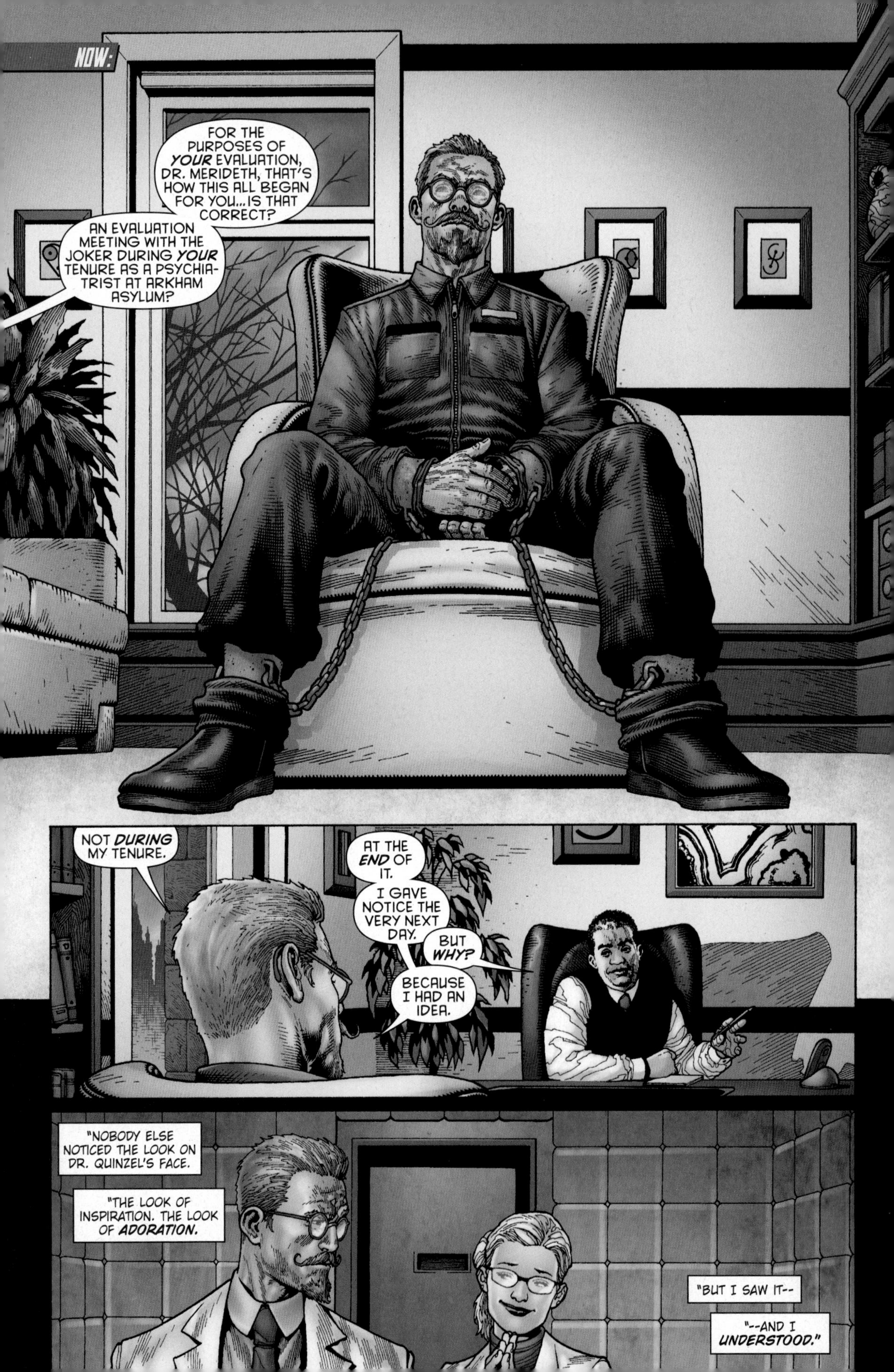
NOW:
FOR THE PURPOSES OF *YOUR* EVALUATION, DR. MERIDETH, THAT'S HOW THIS ALL BEGAN FOR YOU...IS THAT CORRECT?
AN EVALUATION MEETING WITH THE JOKER DURING *YOUR* TENURE AS A PSYCHIATRIST AT ARKHAM ASYLUM?
NOT *DURING* MY TENURE.
AT THE *END* OF IT.
I GAVE NOTICE THE VERY NEXT DAY.
BUT *WHY?*
BECAUSE I HAD AN IDEA.
"NOBODY ELSE NOTICED THE LOOK ON DR. QUINZEL'S FACE.
"THE LOOK OF INSPIRATION. THE LOOK OF *ADORATION.*
"BUT I SAW IT--
"--AND I *UNDERSTOOD.*"

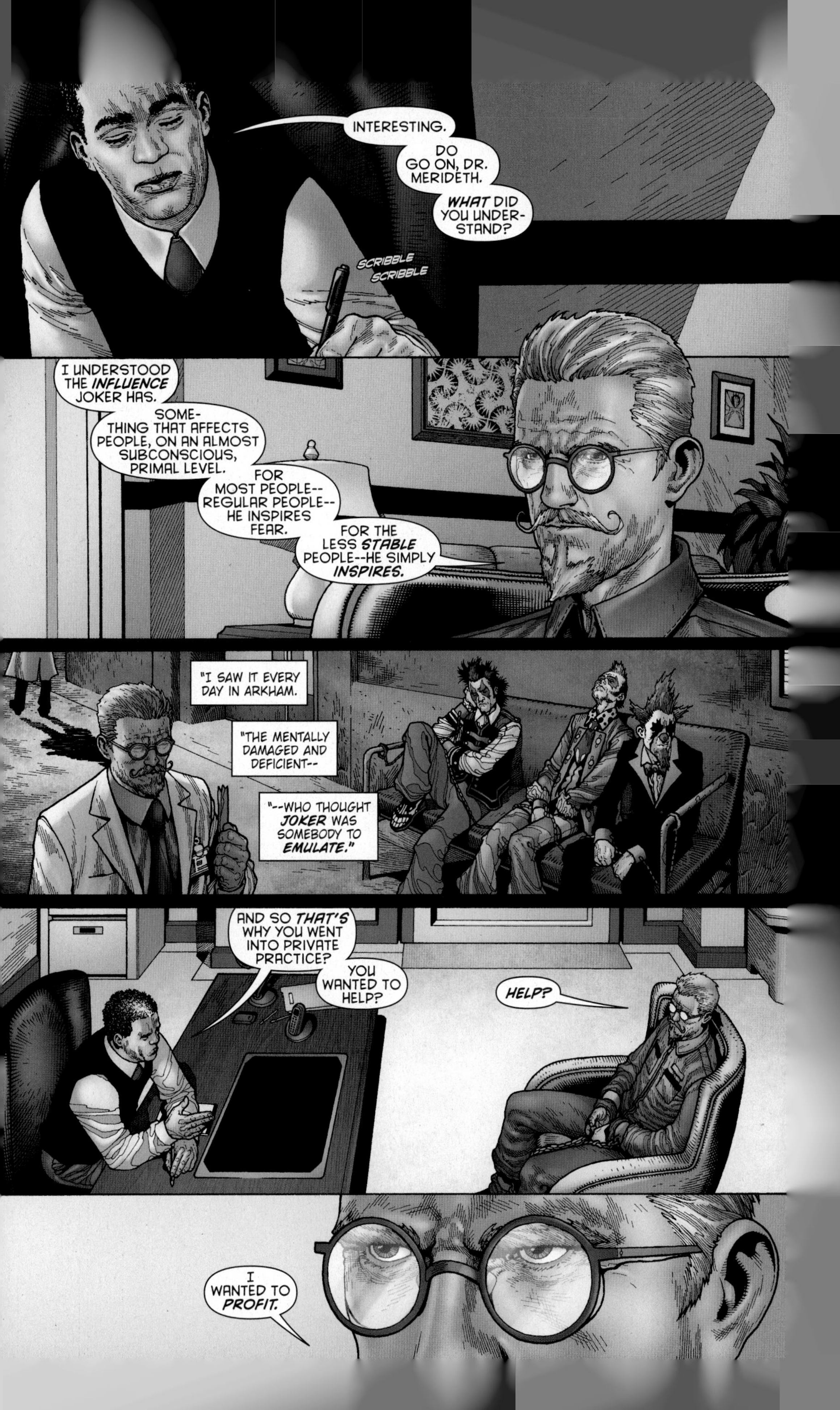
INTERESTING.
DO GO ON, DR. MERIDETH.
WHAT DID YOU UNDERSTAND?
SCRIBBLE SCRIBBLE
I UNDERSTOOD THE INFLUENCE JOKER HAS.
SOMETHING THAT AFFECTS PEOPLE, ON AN ALMOST SUBCONSCIOUS, PRIMAL LEVEL.
FOR MOST PEOPLE--REGULAR PEOPLE--HE INSPIRES FEAR.
FOR THE LESS STABLE PEOPLE--HE SIMPLY INSPIRES.
"I SAW IT EVERY DAY IN ARKHAM.
"THE MENTALLY DAMAGED AND DEFICIENT--
"--WHO THOUGHT JOKER WAS SOMEBODY TO EMULATE."
AND SO THAT'S WHY YOU WENT INTO PRIVATE PRACTICE?
YOU WANTED TO HELP?
HELP?
I WANTED TO PROFIT.

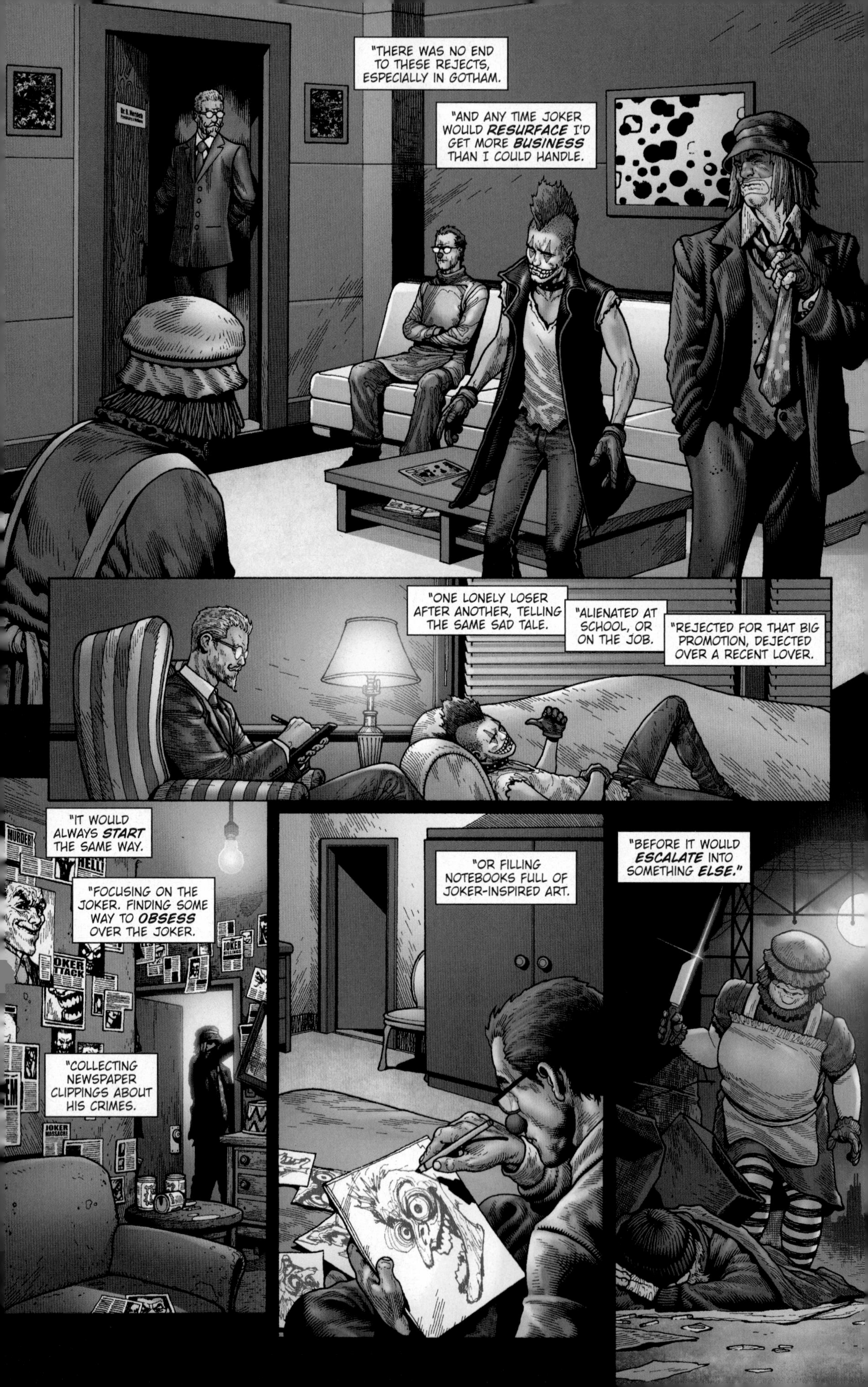
"THERE WAS NO END TO THESE REJECTS, ESPECIALLY IN GOTHAM.
"AND ANY TIME JOKER WOULD RESURFACE I'D GET MORE BUSINESS THAN I COULD HANDLE.
"ONE LONELY LOSER AFTER ANOTHER, TELLING THE SAME SAD TALE.
"ALIENATED AT SCHOOL, OR ON THE JOB.
"REJECTED FOR THAT BIG PROMOTION, DEJECTED OVER A RECENT LOVER.
"IT WOULD ALWAYS START THE SAME WAY.
"FOCUSING ON THE JOKER. FINDING SOME WAY TO OBSESS OVER THE JOKER.
"COLLECTING NEWSPAPER CLIPPINGS ABOUT HIS CRIMES.
"OR FILLING NOTEBOOKS FULL OF JOKER-INSPIRED ART.
"BEFORE IT WOULD ESCALATE INTO SOMETHING ELSE."

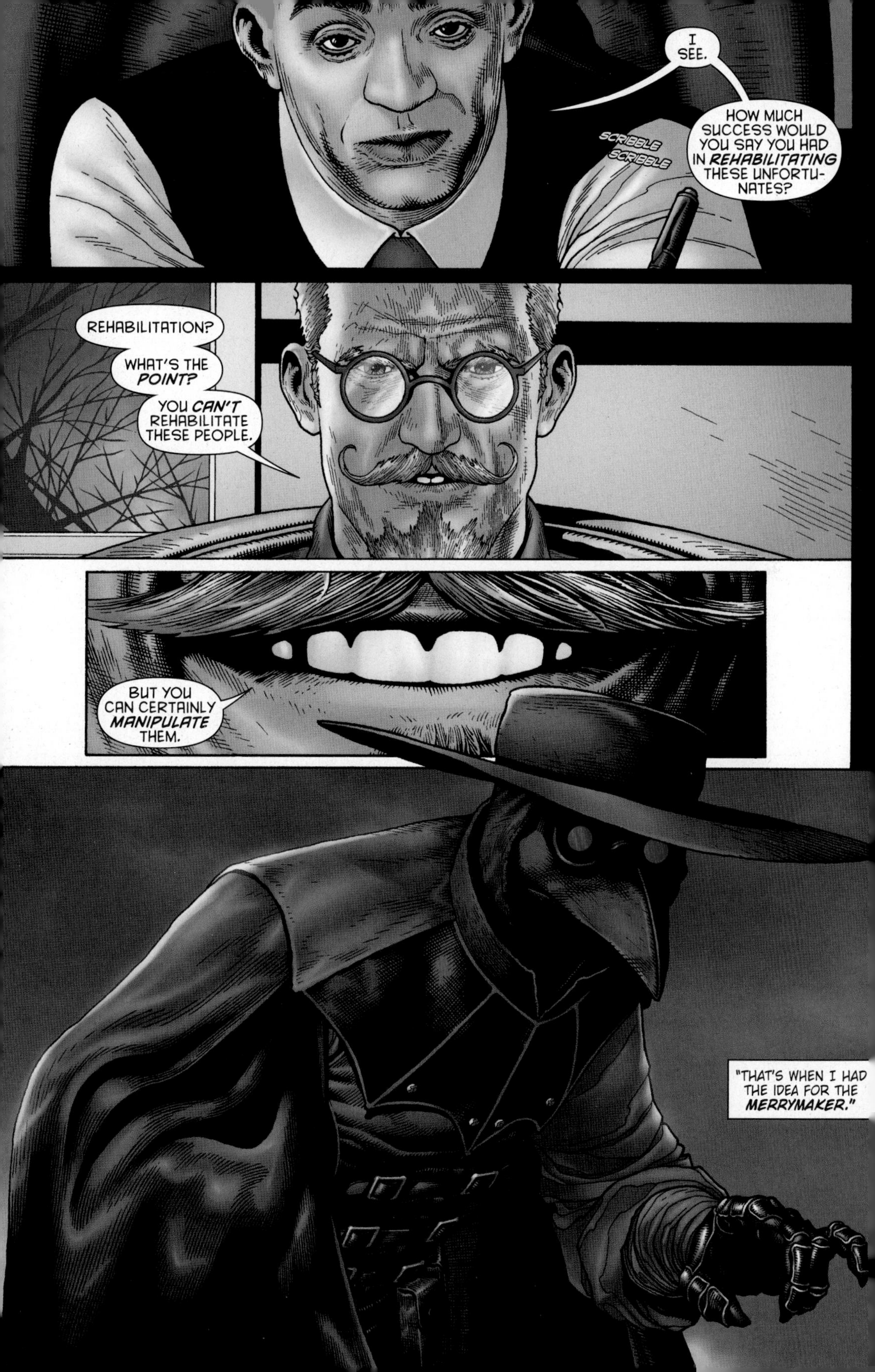
I SEE.
SCRIBBLE SCRIBBLE
HOW MUCH SUCCESS WOULD YOU SAY YOU HAD IN REHABILITATING THESE UNFORTU-NATES?
REHABILITATION?
WHAT'S THE POINT?
YOU CAN'T REHABILITATE THESE PEOPLE.
BUT YOU CAN CERTAINLY MANIPULATE THEM.
"THAT'S WHEN I HAD THE IDEA FOR THE MERRYMAKER."

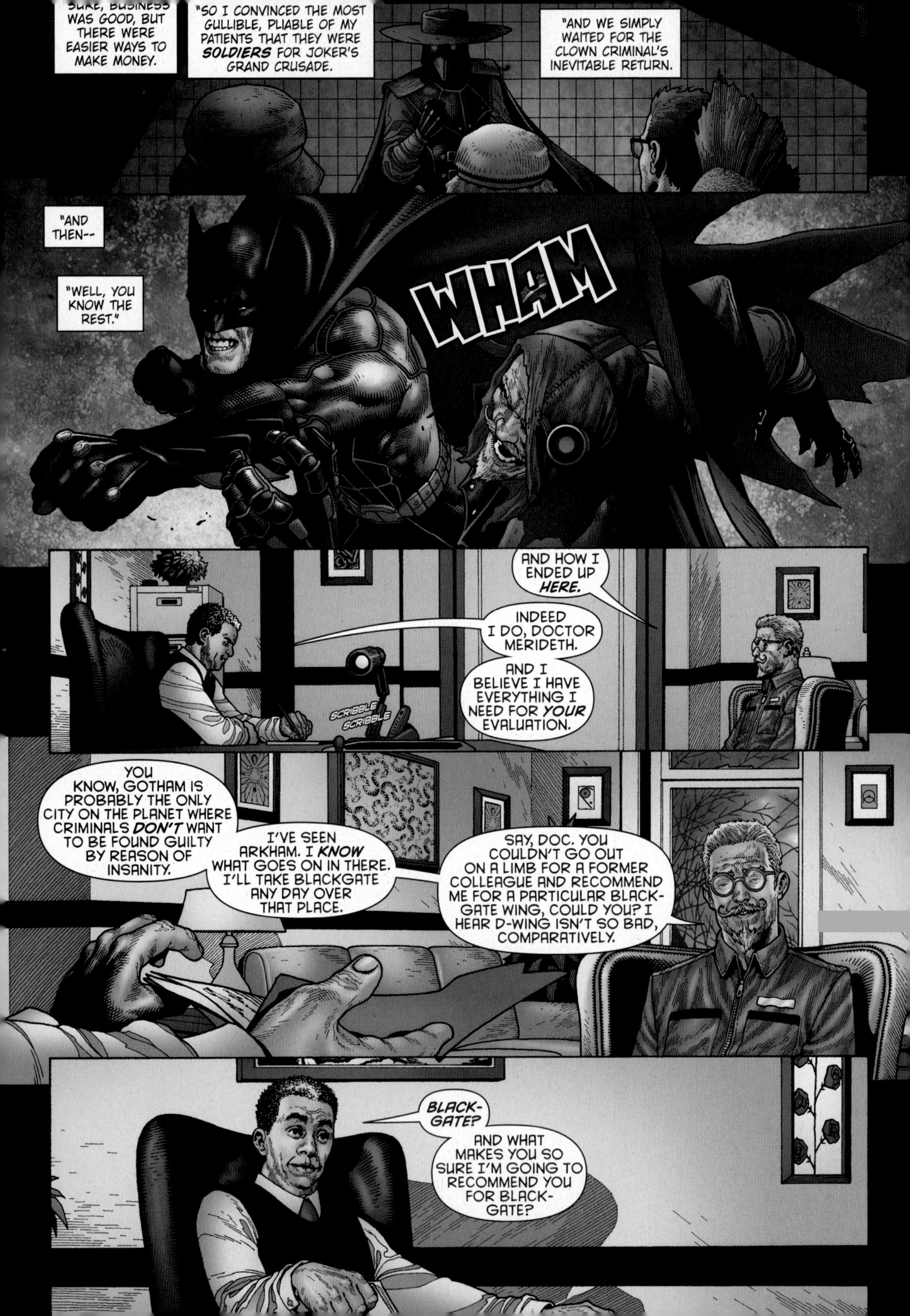
SURE, BUSINESS WAS GOOD, BUT THERE WERE EASIER WAYS TO MAKE MONEY.
"SO I CONVINCED THE MOST GULLIBLE, PLIABLE OF MY PATIENTS THAT THEY WERE SOLDIERS FOR JOKER'S GRAND CRUSADE.
"AND WE SIMPLY WAITED FOR THE CLOWN CRIMINAL'S INEVITABLE RETURN.
"AND THEN--
WHAM
"WELL, YOU KNOW THE REST."
AND HOW I ENDED UP HERE.
INDEED I DO, DOCTOR MERIDETH.
AND I BELIEVE I HAVE EVERYTHING I NEED FOR YOUR EVALUATION.
SCRIBBLE SCRIBBLE
YOU KNOW, GOTHAM IS PROBABLY THE ONLY CITY ON THE PLANET WHERE CRIMINALS DON'T WANT TO BE FOUND GUILTY BY REASON OF INSANITY.
I'VE SEEN ARKHAM. I KNOW WHAT GOES ON IN THERE. I'LL TAKE BLACKGATE ANY DAY OVER THAT PLACE.
SAY, DOC. YOU COULDN'T GO OUT ON A LIMB FOR A FORMER COLLEAGUE AND RECOMMEND ME FOR A PARTICULAR BLACKGATE WING, COULD YOU? I HEAR D-WING ISN'T SO BAD, COMPARATIVELY.
BLACKGATE?
AND WHAT MAKES YOU SO SURE I'M GOING TO RECOMMEND YOU FOR BLACKGATE?

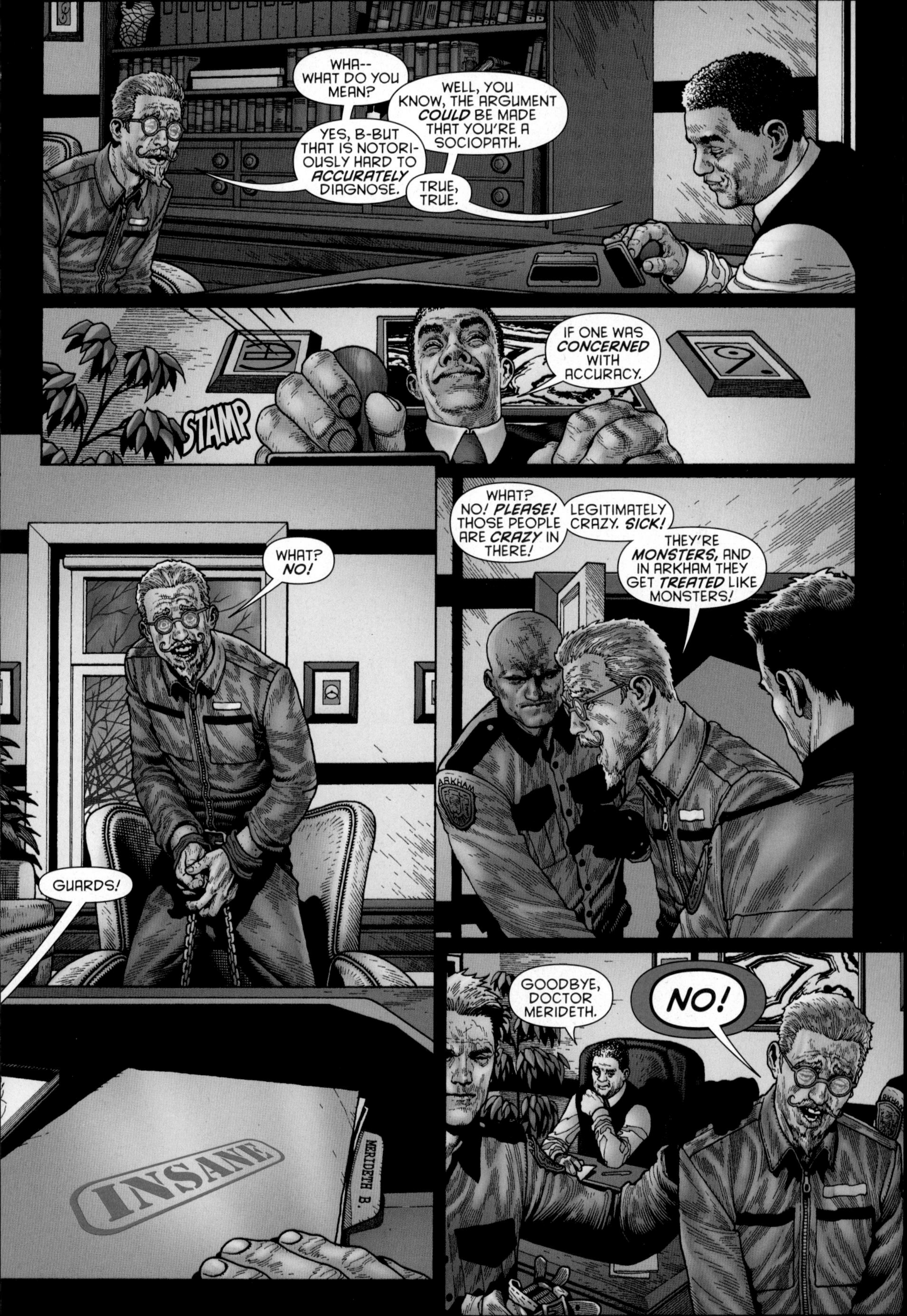

WHA-- WHAT DO YOU MEAN?
WELL, YOU KNOW, THE ARGUMENT COULD BE MADE THAT YOU'RE A SOCIOPATH.
YES, B-BUT THAT IS NOTORIOUSLY HARD TO ACCURATELY DIAGNOSE.
TRUE, TRUE.
IF ONE WAS CONCERNED WITH ACCURACY.
STAMP
WHAT? NO!
GUARDS!
INSANE
MERIDETH B.
WHAT? NO! PLEASE! THOSE PEOPLE ARE CRAZY IN THERE!
LEGITIMATELY CRAZY. SICK!
THEY'RE MONSTERS, AND IN ARKHAM THEY GET TREATED LIKE MONSTERS!
ARKHAM
GOODBYE, DOCTOR MERIDETH.
NO!

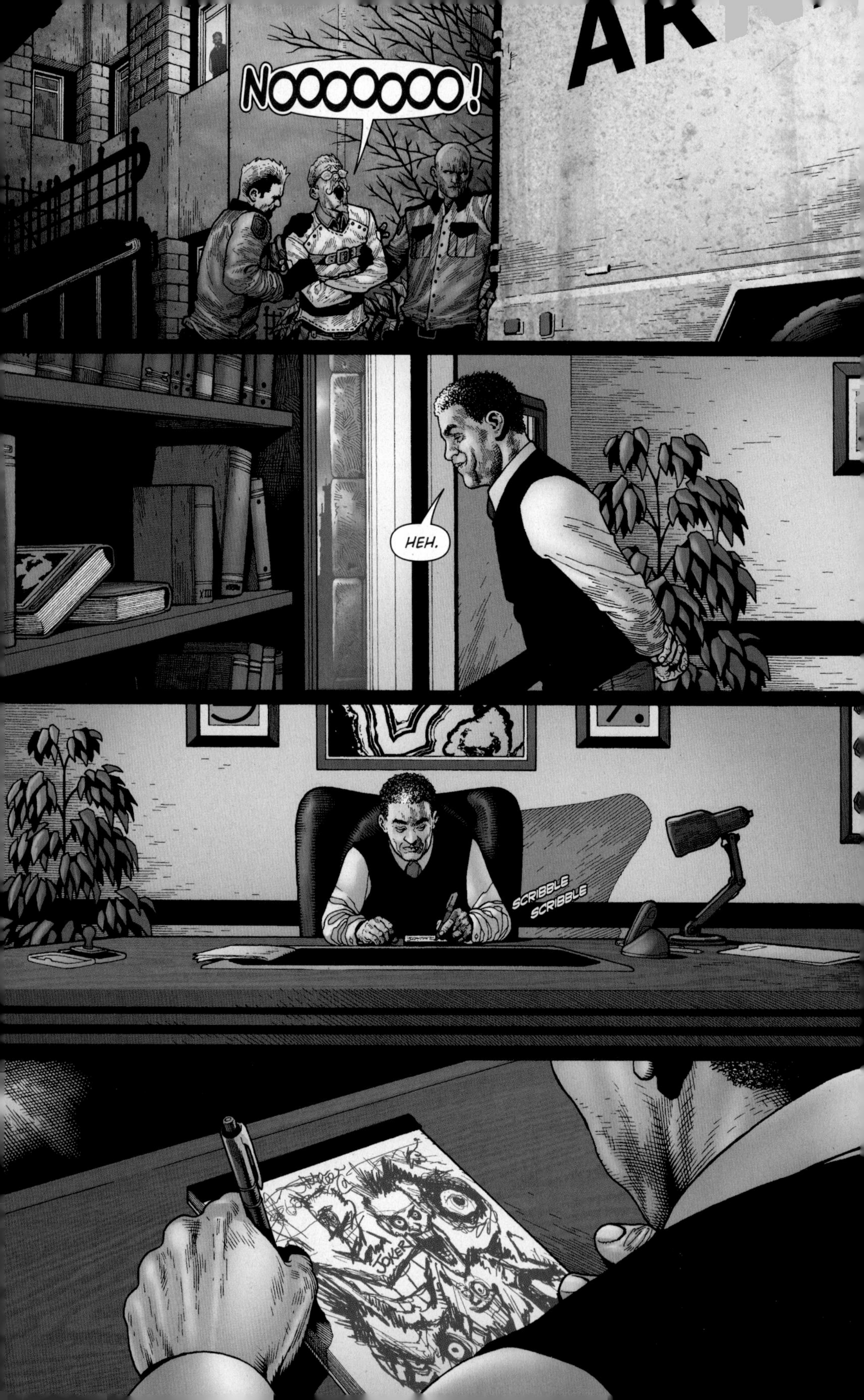
NOOOOOOO!
HEH.
SCRIBBLE
SCRIBBLE
JOKER

PART TWO
CATWOMAN

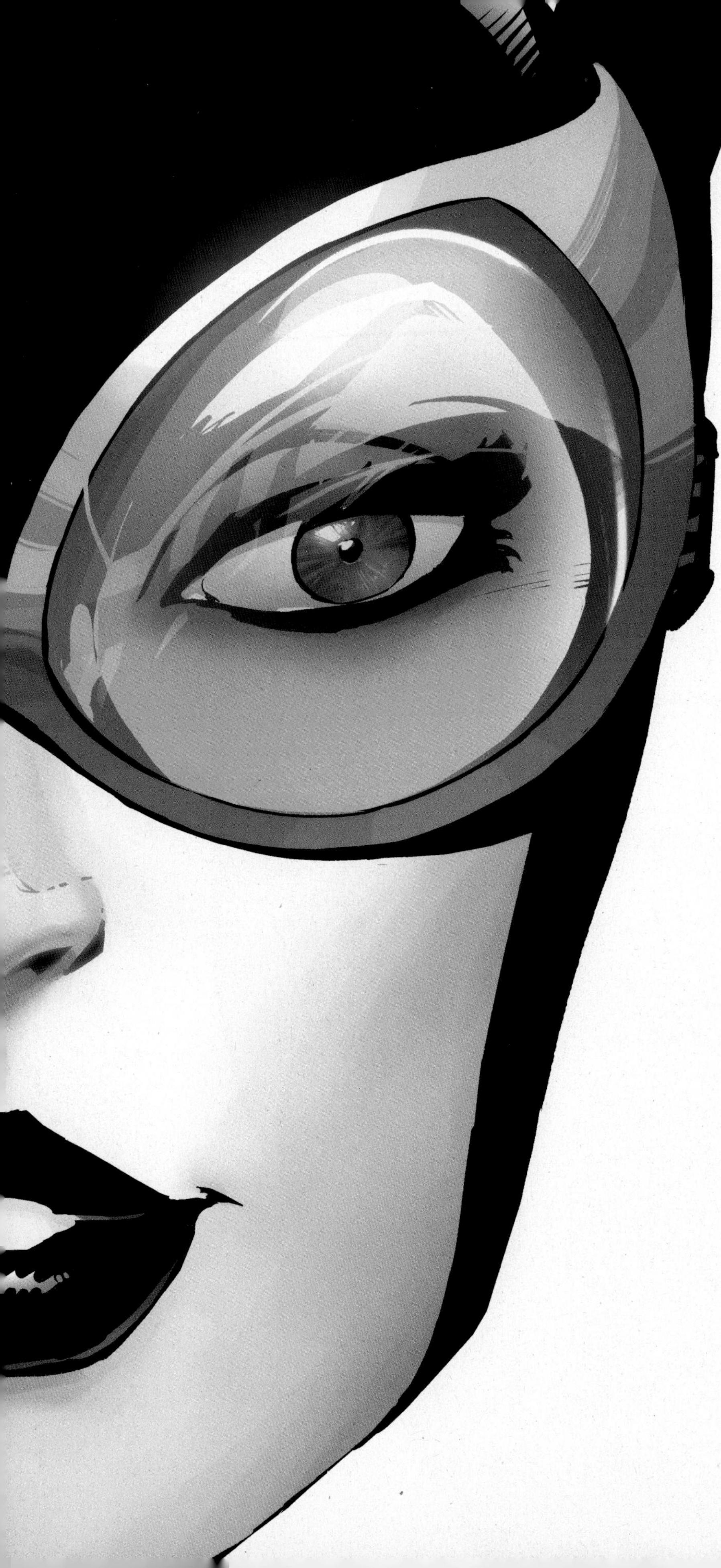

ANN NOCENTI writer **RAFA SANDOVAL** penciller **JORDI TARRAGONA** inker
SONIA OBACK colorist **CARLOS M. MANGUAL** letterer

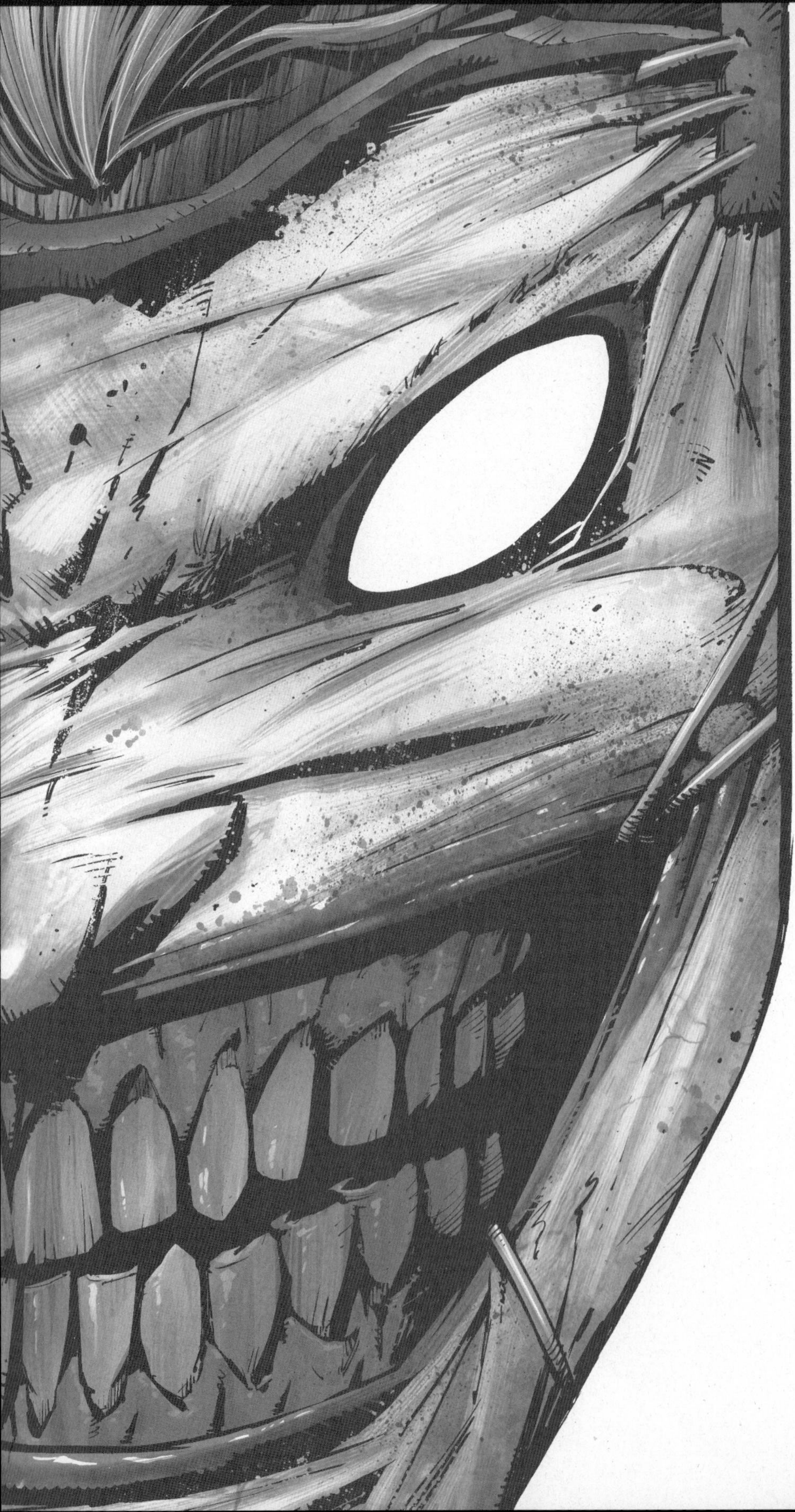

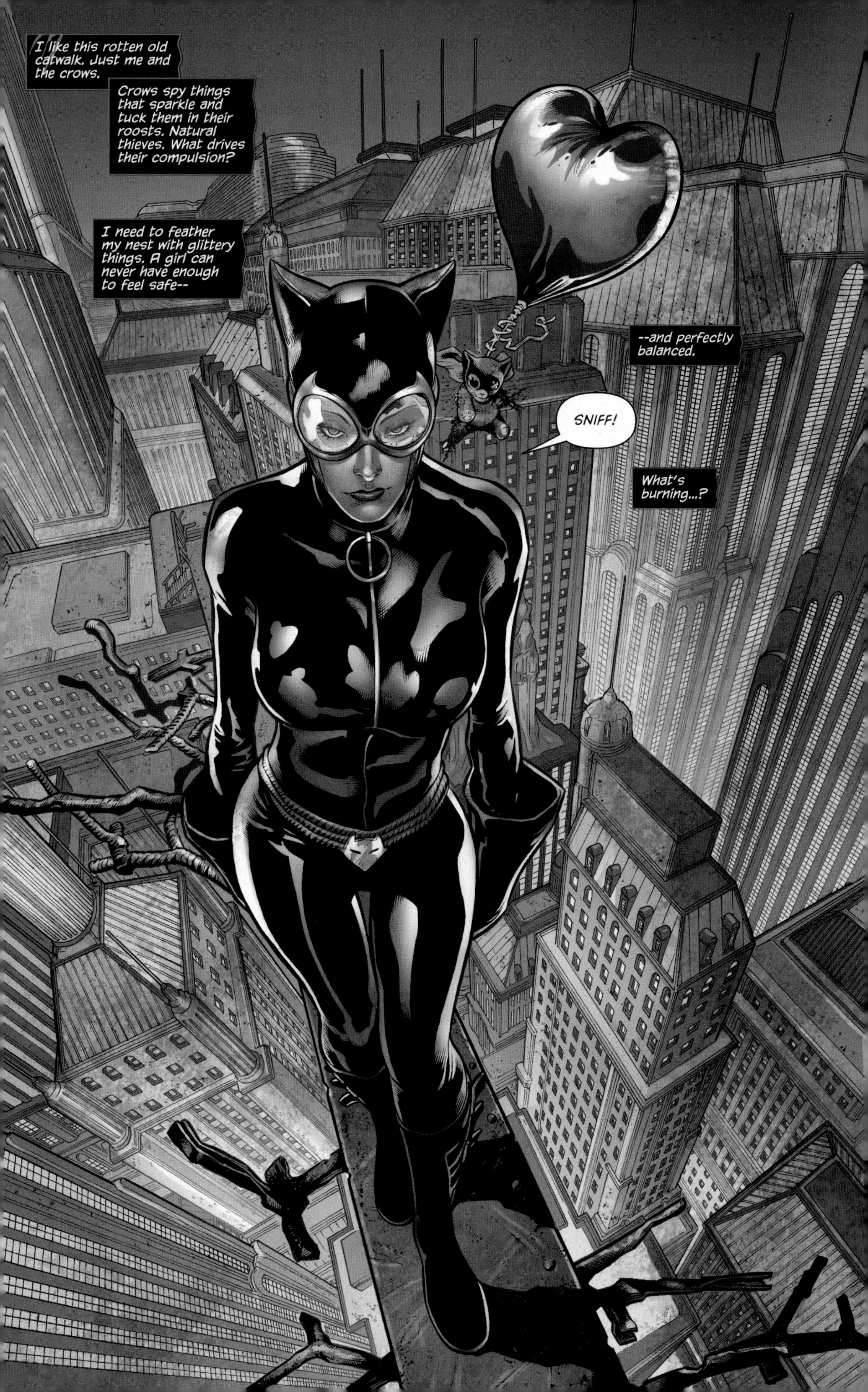
I like this rotten old catwalk. Just me and the crows.
Crows spy things that sparkle and tuck them in their roosts. Natural thieves. What drives their compulsion?
I need to feather my nest with glittery things. A girl can never have enough to feel safe--
--and perfectly balanced.
SNIFF!
What's burning...?

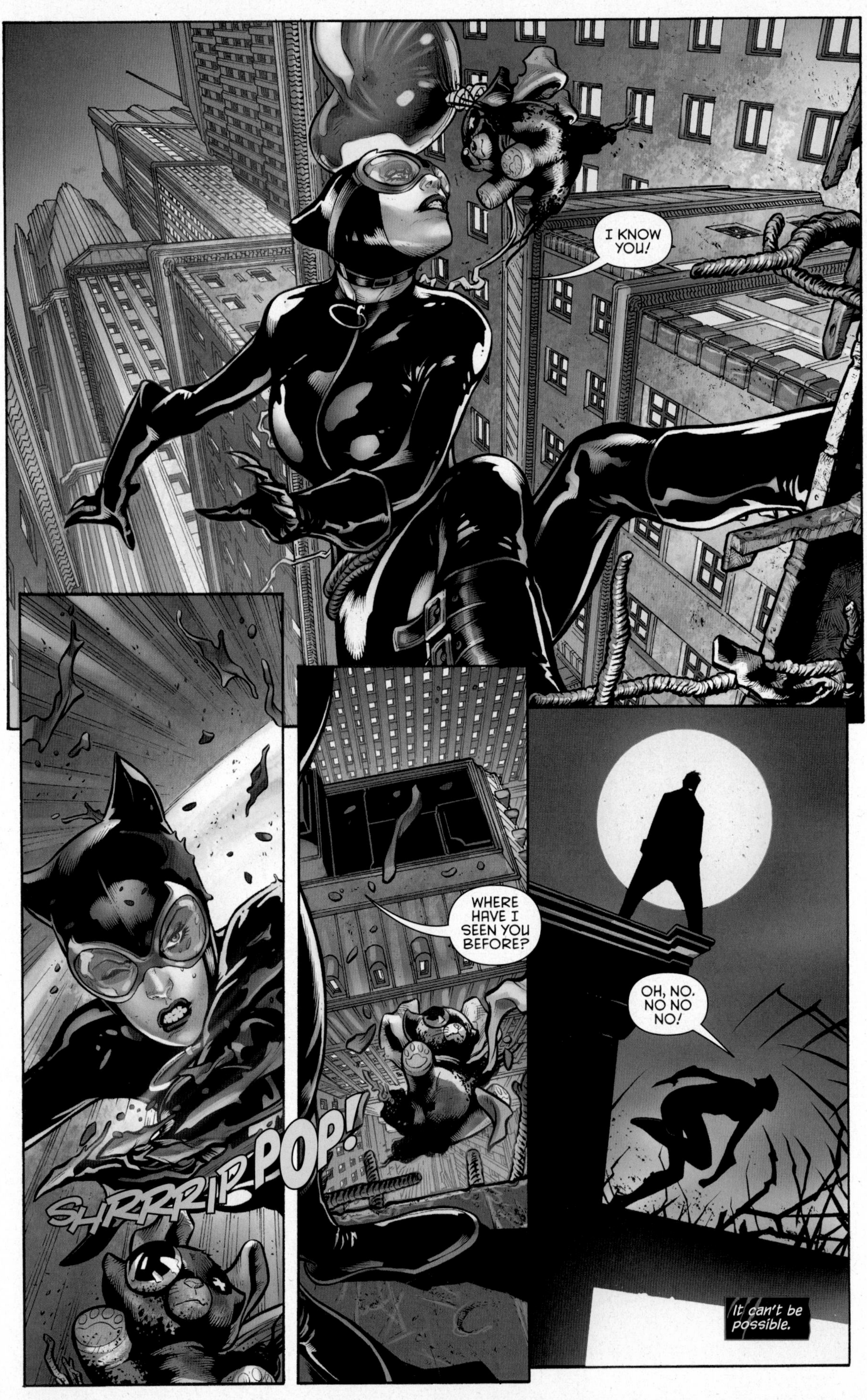
I KNOW YOU!
SHRRRIP
POP!
WHERE HAVE I SEEN YOU BEFORE?
OH, NO. NO NO NO!
It can't be possible.

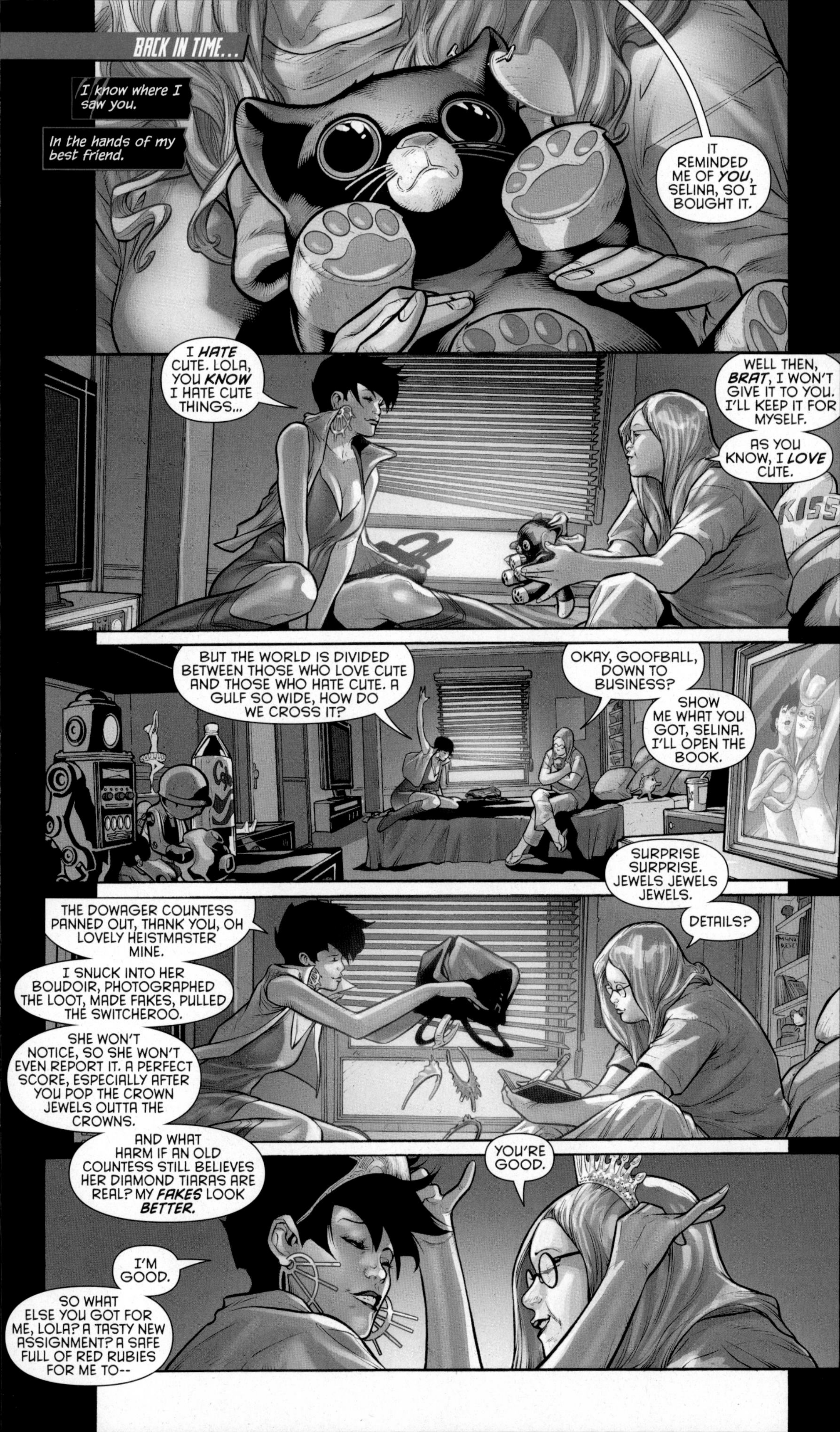
BACK IN TIME...
I know where I saw you.
In the hands of my best friend.
IT REMINDED ME OF YOU, SELINA, SO I BOUGHT IT.
I HATE CUTE. LOLA, YOU KNOW I HATE CUTE THINGS...
WELL THEN, BRAT, I WON'T GIVE IT TO YOU. I'LL KEEP IT FOR MYSELF.
AS YOU KNOW, I LOVE CUTE.
KISS
BUT THE WORLD IS DIVIDED BETWEEN THOSE WHO LOVE CUTE AND THOSE WHO HATE CUTE. A GULF SO WIDE, HOW DO WE CROSS IT?
OKAY, GOOFBALL, DOWN TO BUSINESS?
SHOW ME WHAT YOU GOT, SELINA. I'LL OPEN THE BOOK.
SURPRISE SURPRISE. JEWELS JEWELS JEWELS.
THE DOWAGER COUNTESS PANNED OUT, THANK YOU, OH LOVELY HEISTMASTER MINE.
DETAILS?
I SNUCK INTO HER BOUDOIR, PHOTOGRAPHED THE LOOT, MADE FAKES, PULLED THE SWITCHEROO.
SHE WON'T NOTICE, SO SHE WON'T EVEN REPORT IT. A PERFECT SCORE, ESPECIALLY AFTER YOU POP THE CROWN JEWELS OUTTA THE CROWNS.
AND WHAT HARM IF AN OLD COUNTESS STILL BELIEVES HER DIAMOND TIARAS ARE REAL? MY FAKES LOOK BETTER.
YOU'RE GOOD.
I'M GOOD.
SO WHAT ELSE YOU GOT FOR ME, LOLA? A TASTY NEW ASSIGNMENT? A SAFE FULL OF RED RUBIES FOR ME TO--

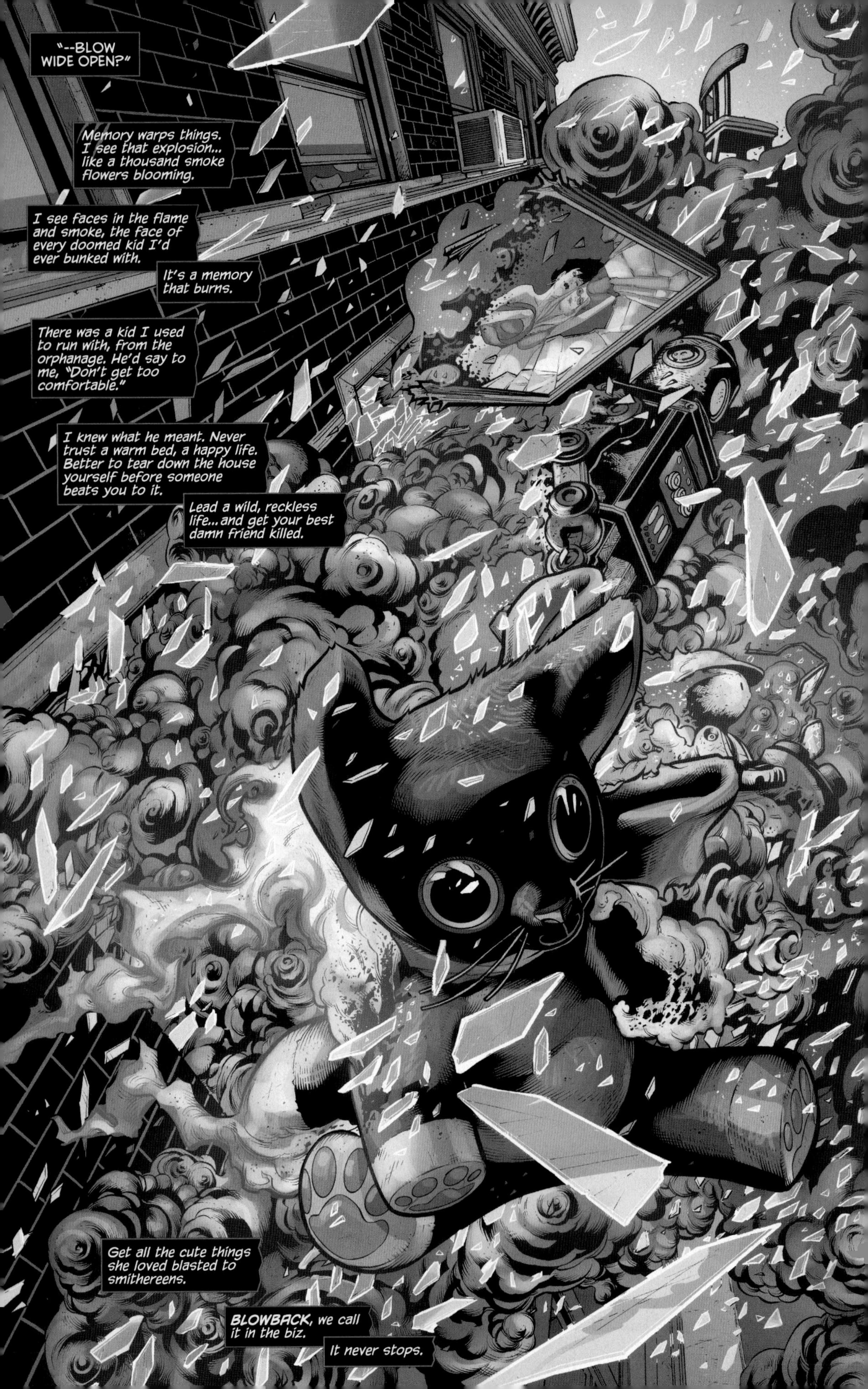
"--BLOW WIDE OPEN?"
Memory warps things. I see that explosion... like a thousand smoke flowers blooming.
I see faces in the flame and smoke, the face of every doomed kid I'd ever bunked with.
It's a memory that burns.
There was a kid I used to run with, from the orphanage. He'd say to me, "Don't get too comfortable."
I knew what he meant. Never trust a warm bed, a happy life. Better to tear down the house yourself before someone beats you to it.
Lead a wild, reckless life...and get your best damn friend killed.
Get all the cute things she loved blasted to smithereens.
BLOWBACK, we call it in the biz.
It never stops.

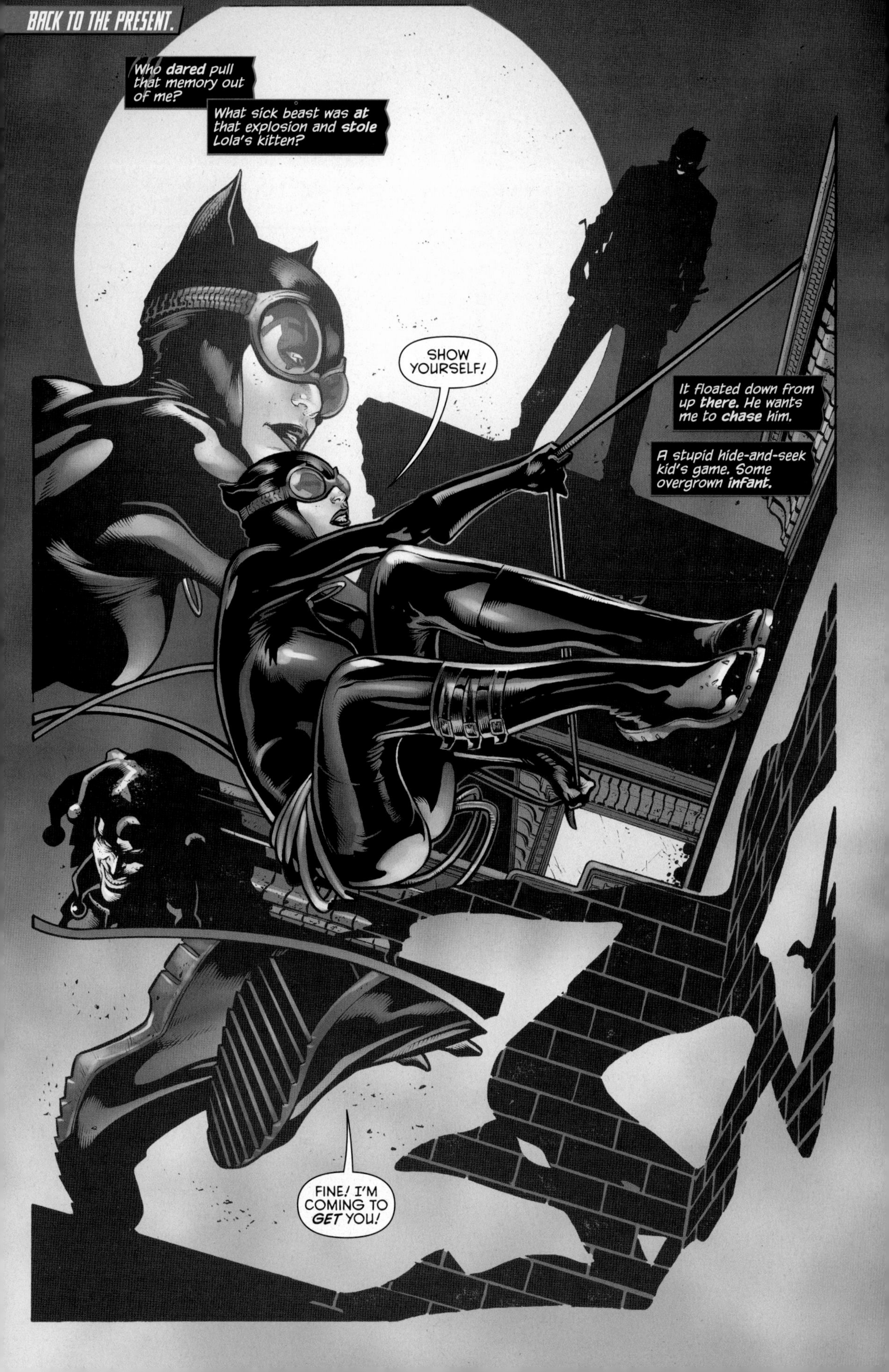
BACK TO THE PRESENT.
Who dared pull that memory out of me?
What sick beast was at that explosion and stole Lola's kitten?
SHOW YOURSELF!
It floated down from up there. He wants me to chase him.
A stupid hide-and-seek kid's game. Some overgrown infant.
FINE! I'M COMING TO GET YOU!

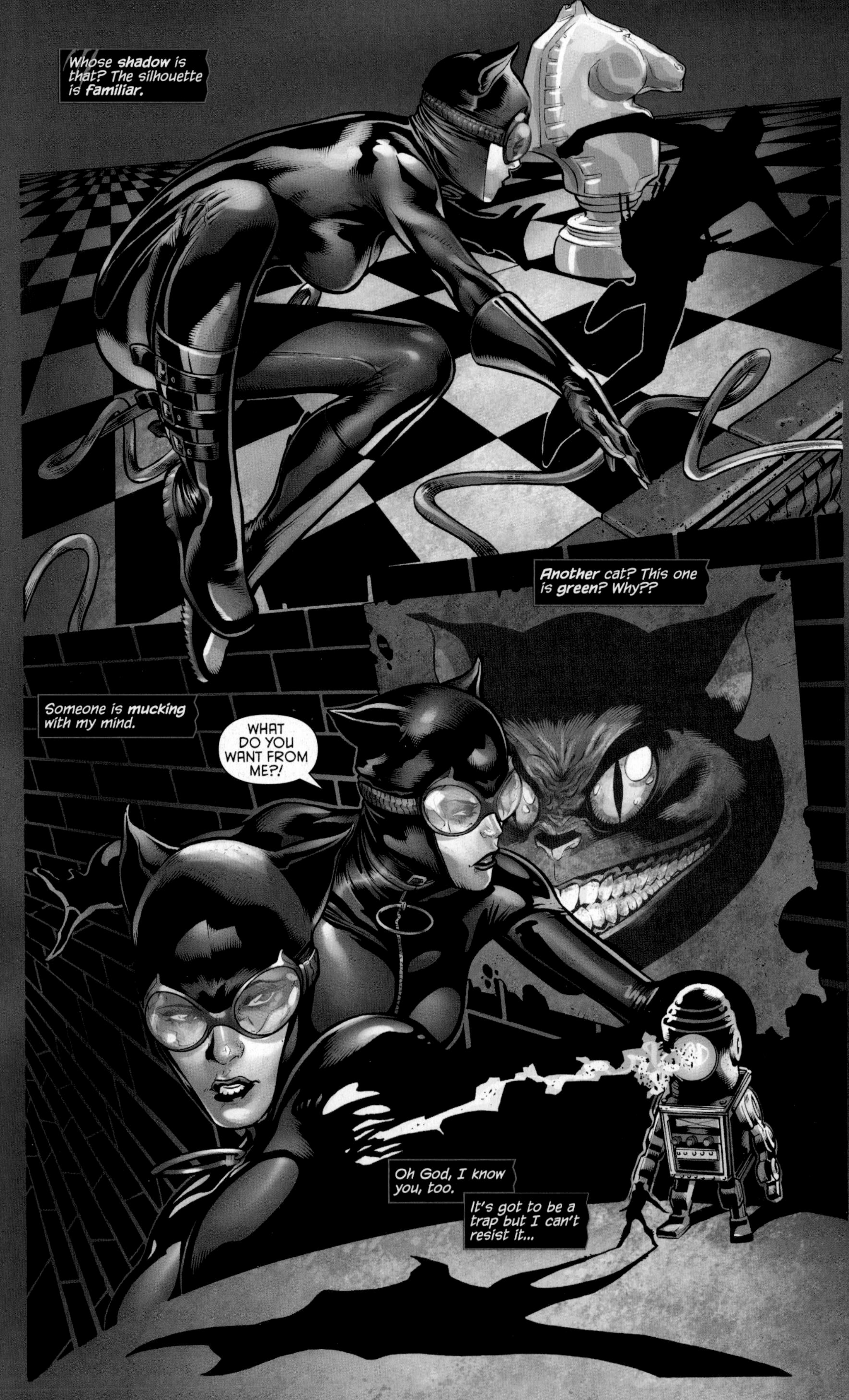
Whose shadow is that? The silhouette is familiar.
Another cat? This one is green? Why??
Someone is mucking with my mind.
WHAT DO YOU WANT FROM ME?!
Oh God, I know you, too.
It's got to be a trap but I can't resist it...

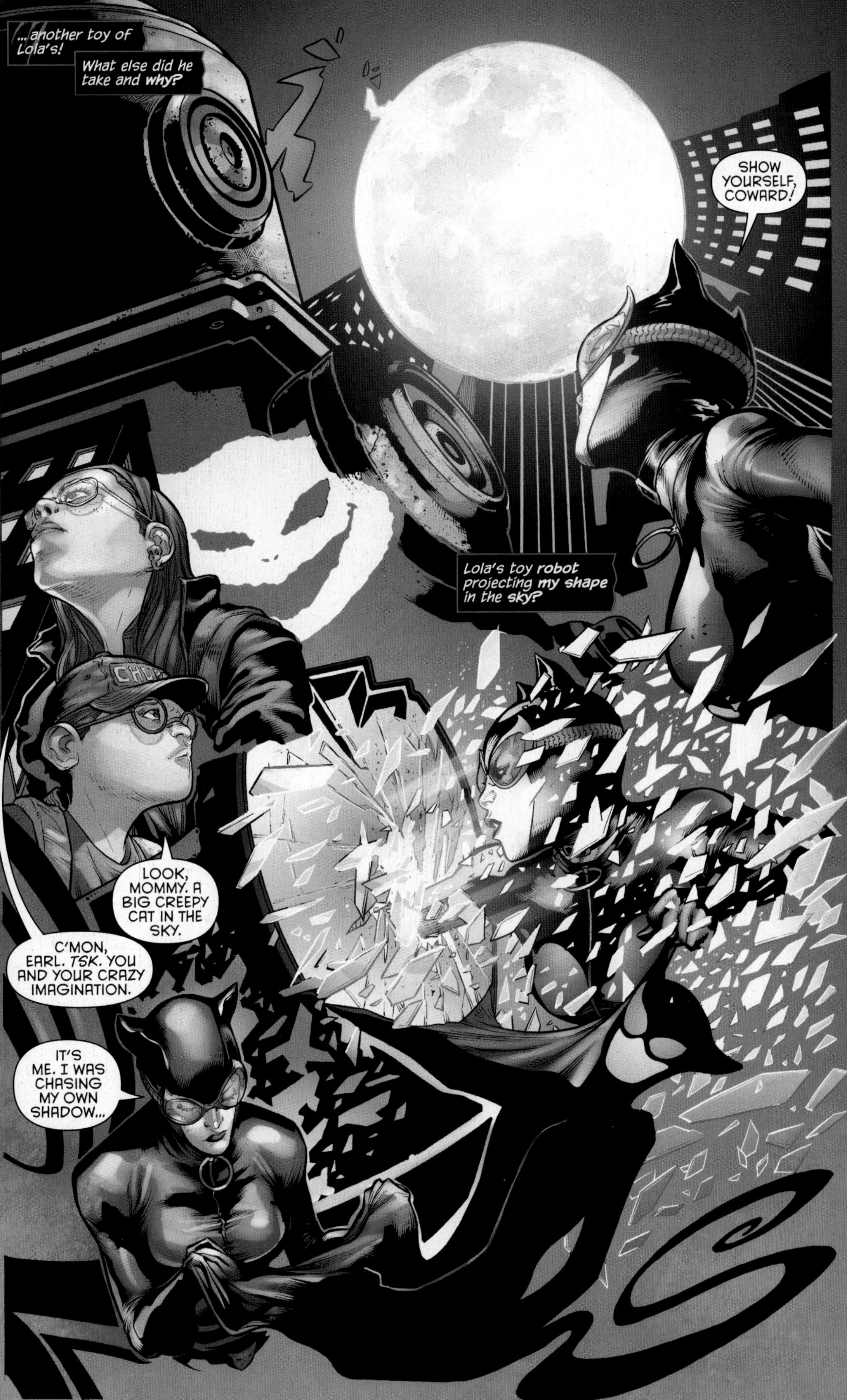
...another toy of Lola's!
What else did he take and why?
SHOW YOURSELF, COWARD!
Lola's toy robot projecting my shape in the sky?
LOOK, MOMMY. A BIG CREEPY CAT IN THE SKY.
C'MON, EARL. TSK. YOU AND YOUR CRAZY IMAGINATION.
IT'S ME. I WAS CHASING MY OWN SHADOW...

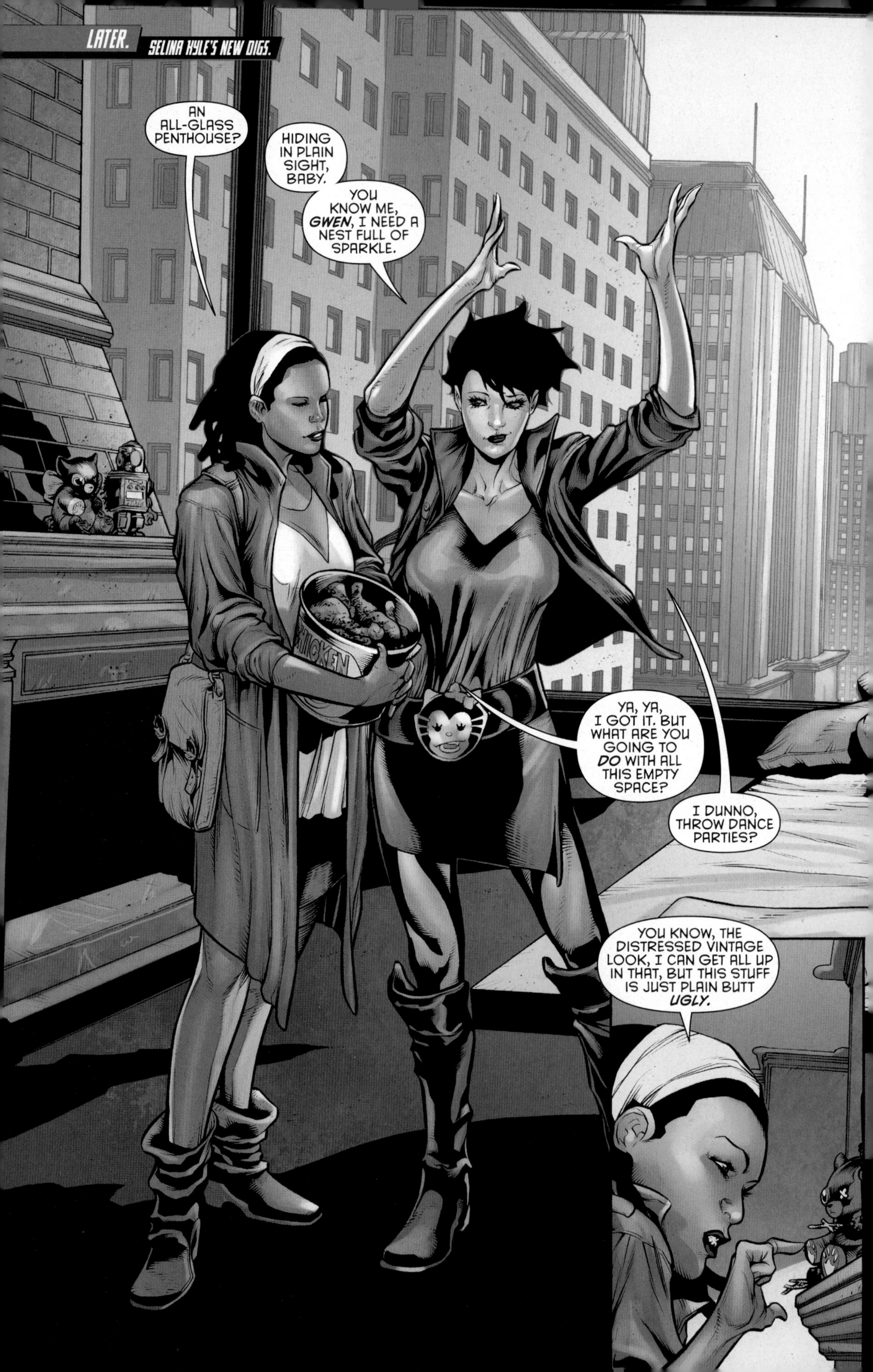
LATER.
SELINA KYLE'S NEW DIGS.
AN ALL-GLASS PENTHOUSE?
HIDING IN PLAIN SIGHT, BABY.
YOU KNOW ME, GWEN, I NEED A NEST FULL OF SPARKLE.
YA, YA, I GOT IT. BUT WHAT ARE YOU GOING TO DO WITH ALL THIS EMPTY SPACE?
I DUNNO, THROW DANCE PARTIES?
YOU KNOW, THE DISTRESSED VINTAGE LOOK, I CAN GET ALL UP IN THAT, BUT THIS STUFF IS JUST PLAIN BUTT UGLY.
CHICKEN

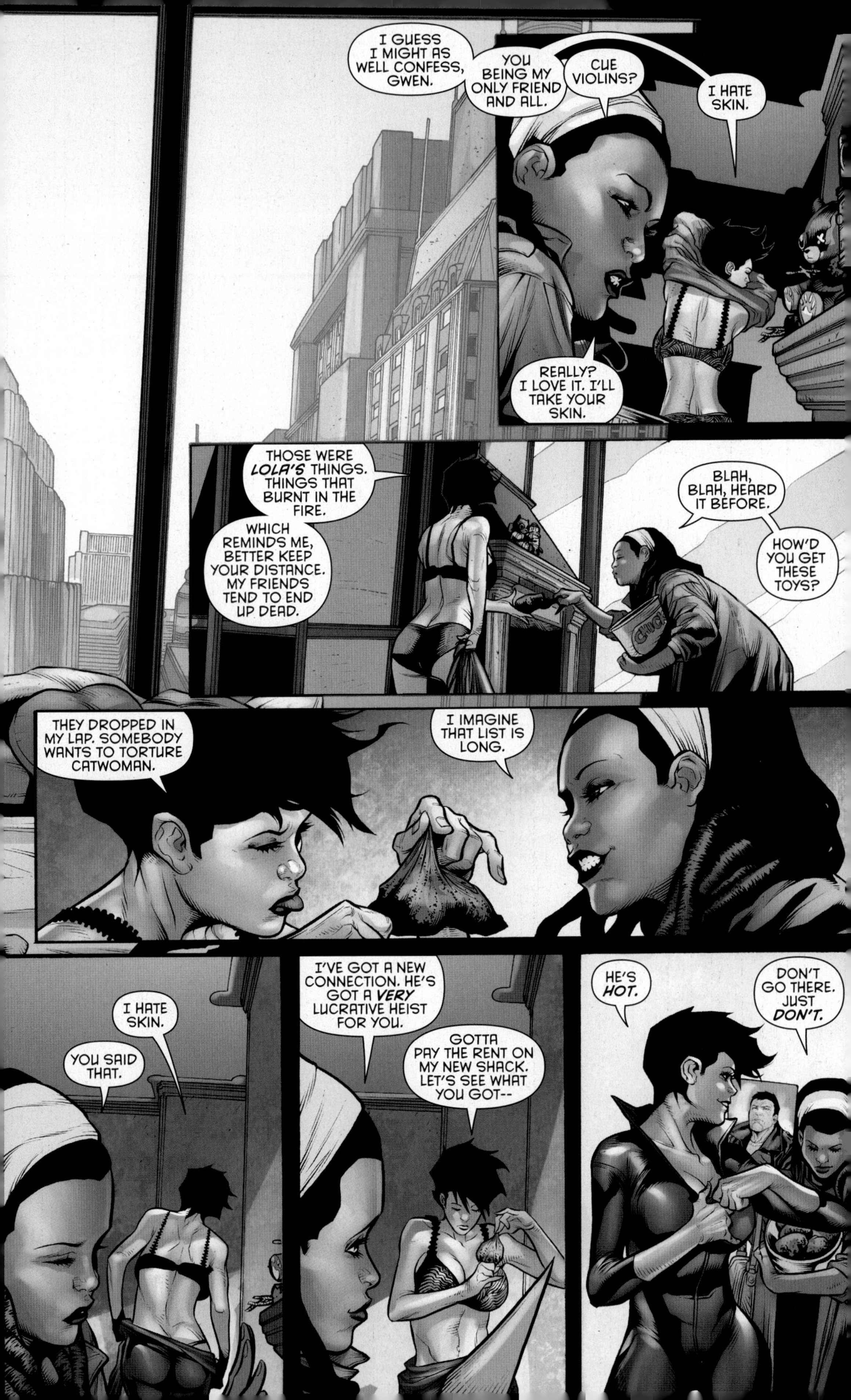
I GUESS I MIGHT AS WELL CONFESS, GWEN.
YOU BEING MY ONLY FRIEND AND ALL.
CUE VIOLINS?
I HATE SKIN.
REALLY? I LOVE IT. I'LL TAKE YOUR SKIN.
THOSE WERE LOLA'S THINGS. THINGS THAT BURNT IN THE FIRE.
WHICH REMINDS ME, BETTER KEEP YOUR DISTANCE. MY FRIENDS TEND TO END UP DEAD.
BLAH, BLAH, HEARD IT BEFORE.
HOW'D YOU GET THESE TOYS?
THEY DROPPED IN MY LAP. SOMEBODY WANTS TO TORTURE CATWOMAN.
I IMAGINE THAT LIST IS LONG.
I HATE SKIN.
YOU SAID THAT.
I'VE GOT A NEW CONNECTION. HE'S GOT A VERY LUCRATIVE HEIST FOR YOU.
GOTTA PAY THE RENT ON MY NEW SHACK. LET'S SEE WHAT YOU GOT--
HE'S HOT.
DON'T GO THERE. JUST DON'T.

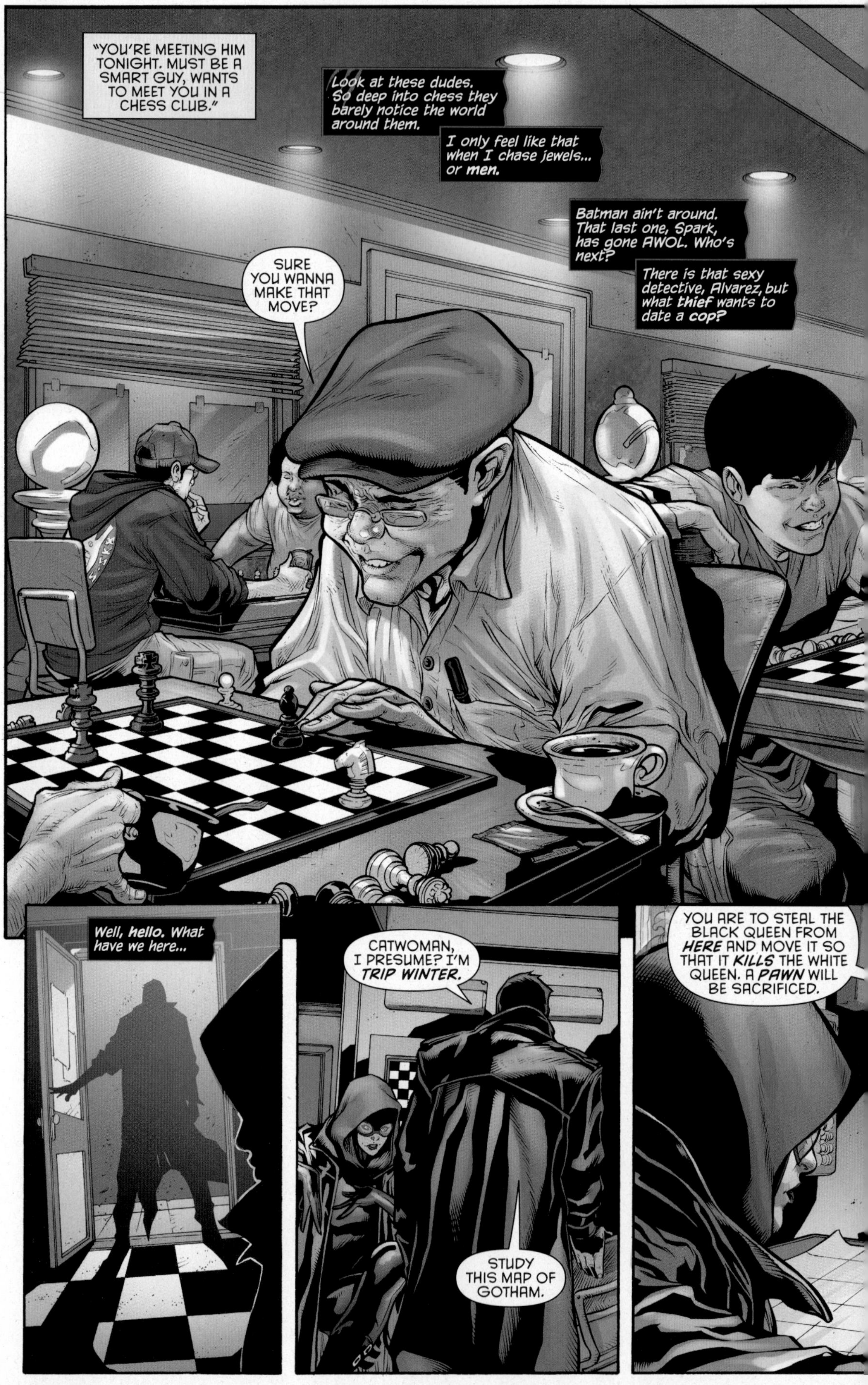
"YOU'RE MEETING HIM TONIGHT. MUST BE A SMART GUY, WANTS TO MEET YOU IN A CHESS CLUB."
Look at these dudes. So deep into chess they barely notice the world around them.
I only feel like that when I chase jewels... or **men**.
Batman ain't around. That last one, Spark, has gone AWOL. Who's next?
There is that sexy detective, Alvarez, but what **thief** wants to date a **cop?**
SURE YOU WANNA MAKE THAT MOVE?
Well, **hello**. What have we here...
CATWOMAN, I PRESUME? I'M ***TRIP WINTER***.
STUDY THIS MAP OF GOTHAM.
YOU ARE TO STEAL THE BLACK QUEEN FROM ***HERE*** AND MOVE IT SO THAT IT ***KILLS*** THE WHITE QUEEN. A ***PAWN*** WILL BE SACRIFICED.

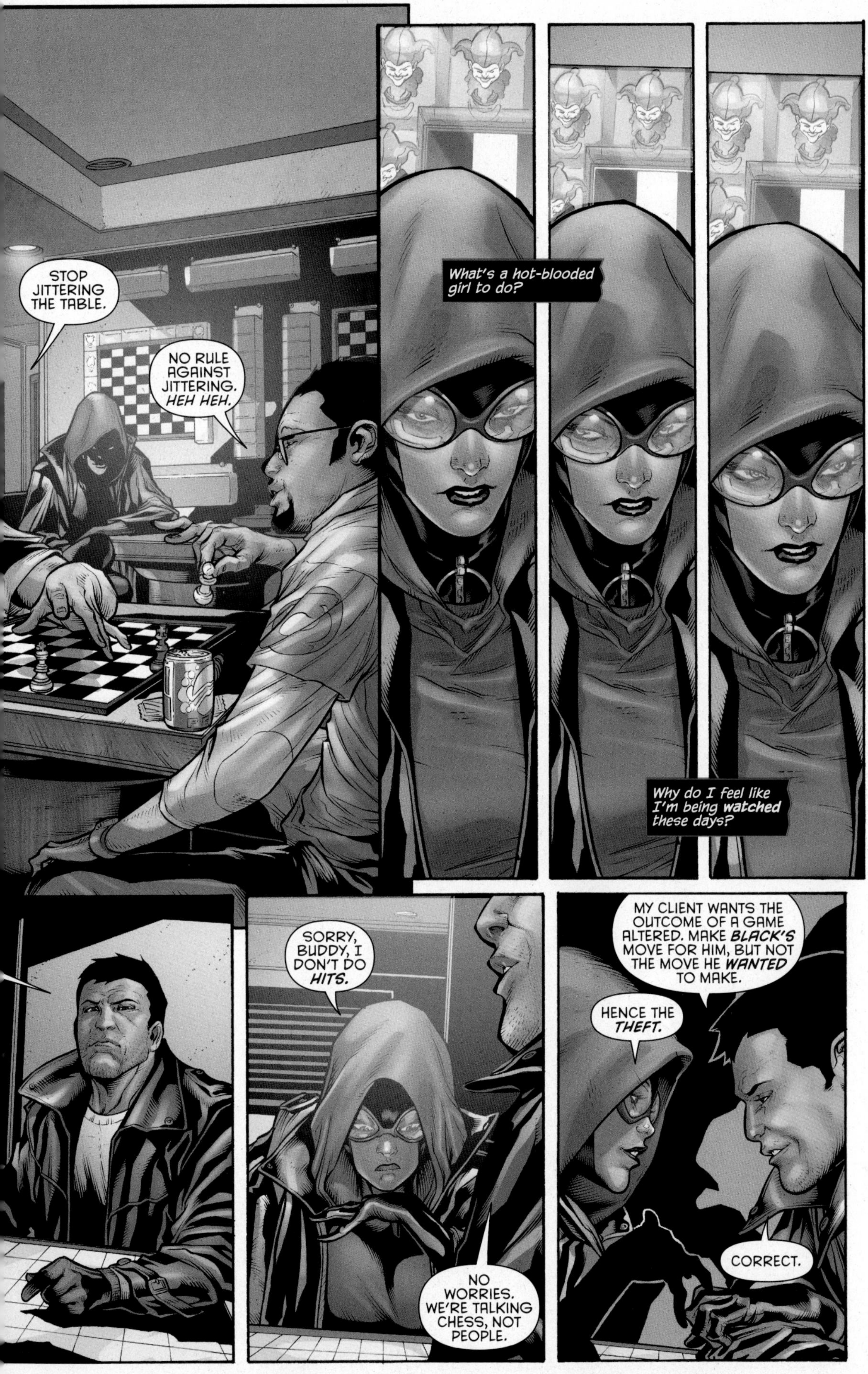

STOP JITTERING THE TABLE.
NO RULE AGAINST JITTERING. *HEH HEH.*
What's a hot-blooded girl to do?
*Why do I feel like I'm being **watched** these days?*
SORRY, BUDDY, I DON'T DO ***HITS.***
NO WORRIES. WE'RE TALKING CHESS, NOT PEOPLE.
MY CLIENT WANTS THE OUTCOME OF A GAME ALTERED. MAKE ***BLACK'S*** MOVE FOR HIM, BUT NOT THE MOVE HE ***WANTED*** TO MAKE.
HENCE THE ***THEFT.***
CORRECT.

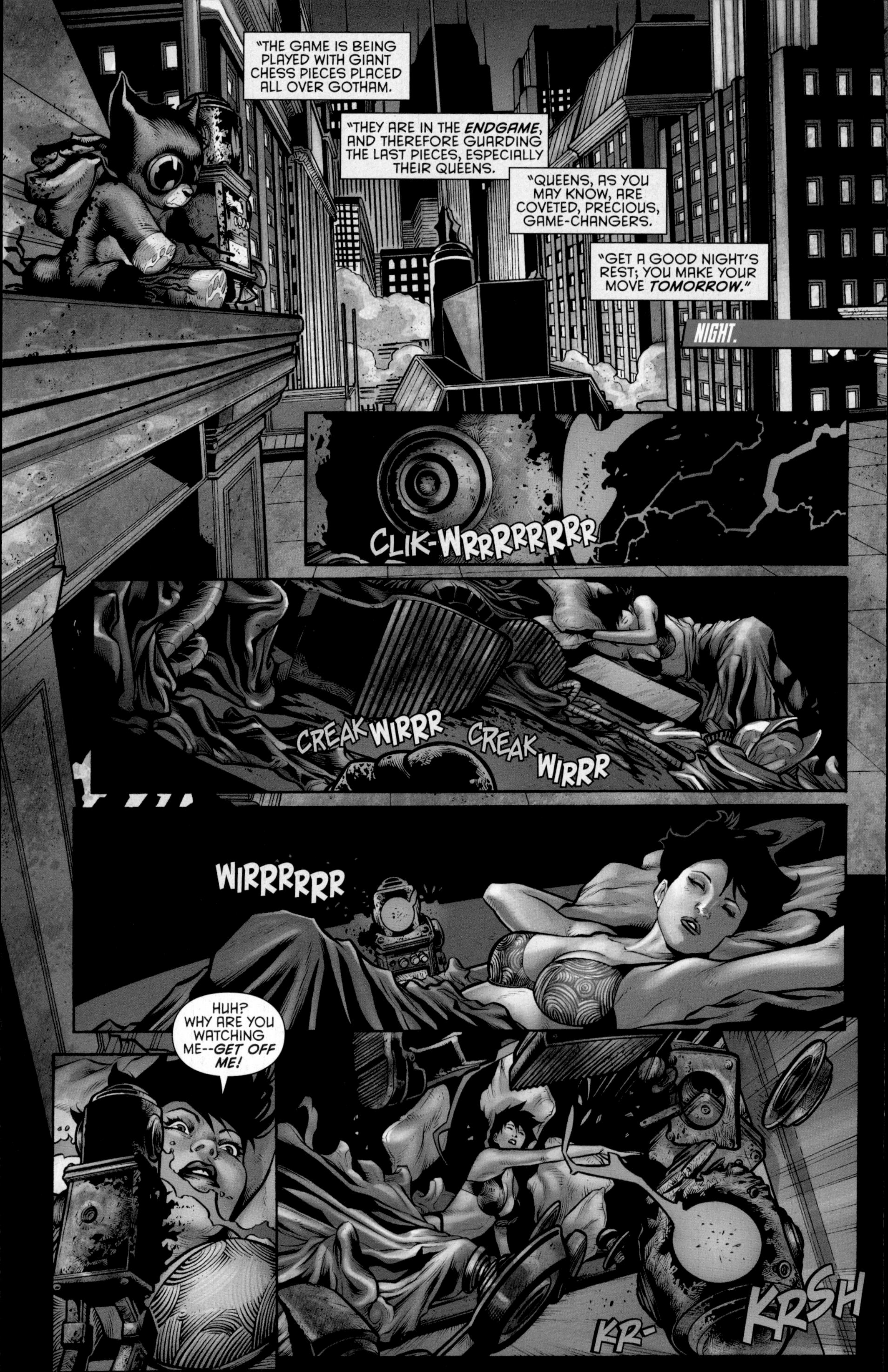
"THE GAME IS BEING PLAYED WITH GIANT CHESS PIECES PLACED ALL OVER GOTHAM.
"THEY ARE IN THE *ENDGAME*, AND THEREFORE GUARDING THE LAST PIECES, ESPECIALLY THEIR QUEENS.
"QUEENS, AS YOU MAY KNOW, ARE COVETED, PRECIOUS, GAME-CHANGERS.
"GET A GOOD NIGHT'S REST; YOU MAKE YOUR MOVE *TOMORROW*."
NIGHT.
CLIK-WRRRRRRRR
CREAK WIRRR CREAK WIRRR
WIRRRRRR
HUH? WHY ARE YOU WATCHING ME--*GET OFF ME!*
KR- KRSH

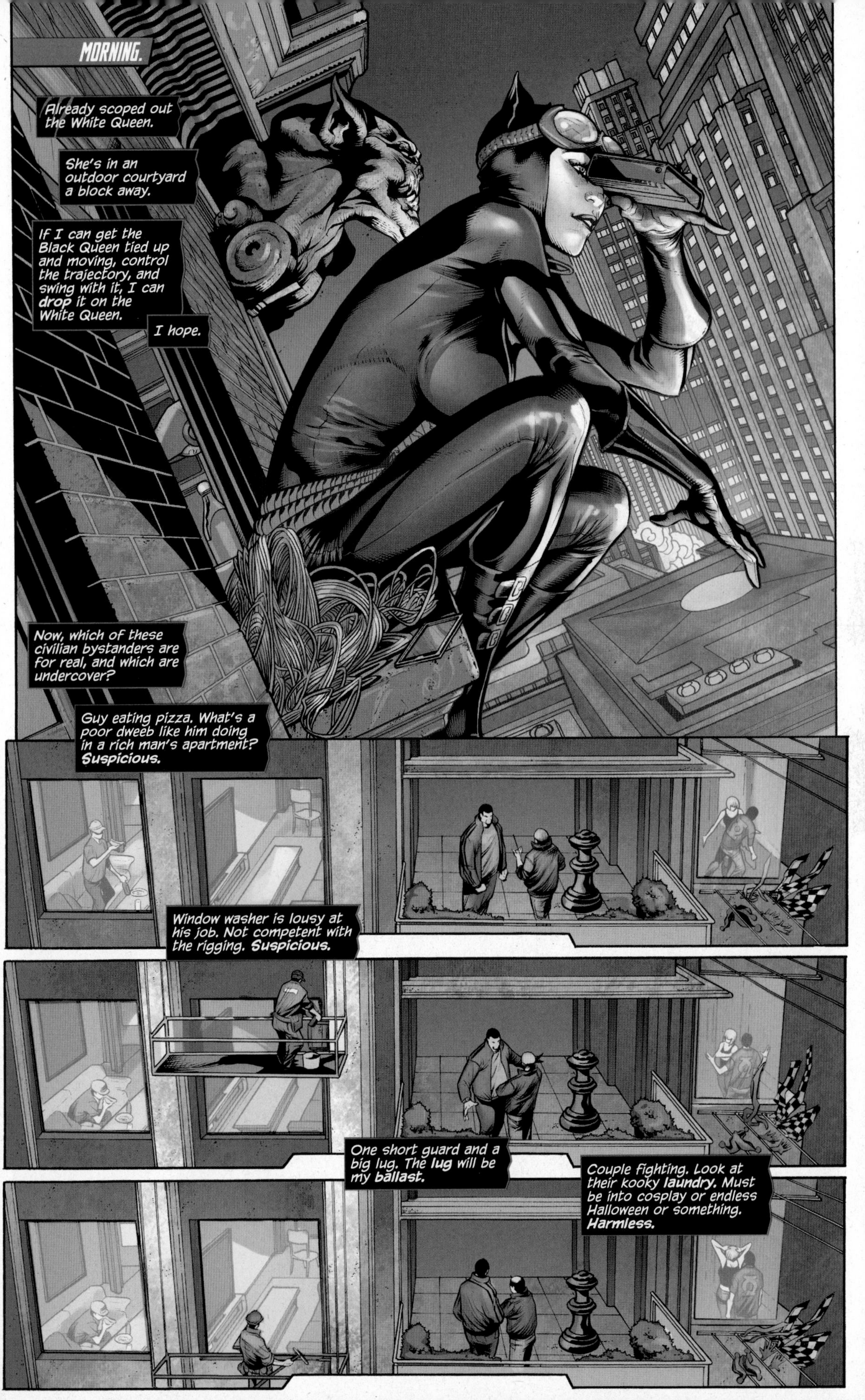
MORNING.
Already scoped out the White Queen.
She's in an outdoor courtyard a block away.
If I can get the Black Queen tied up and moving, control the trajectory, and swing with it, I can **drop** it on the White Queen.
I hope.
Now, which of these civilian bystanders are for real, and which are undercover?
Guy eating pizza. What's a poor dweeb like him doing in a rich man's apartment? **Suspicious.**
Window washer is lousy at his job. Not competent with the rigging. **Suspicious.**
One short guard and a big lug. The **lug** will be my **ballast.**
Couple fighting. Look at their kooky **laundry.** Must be into cosplay or endless Halloween or something. **Harmless.**

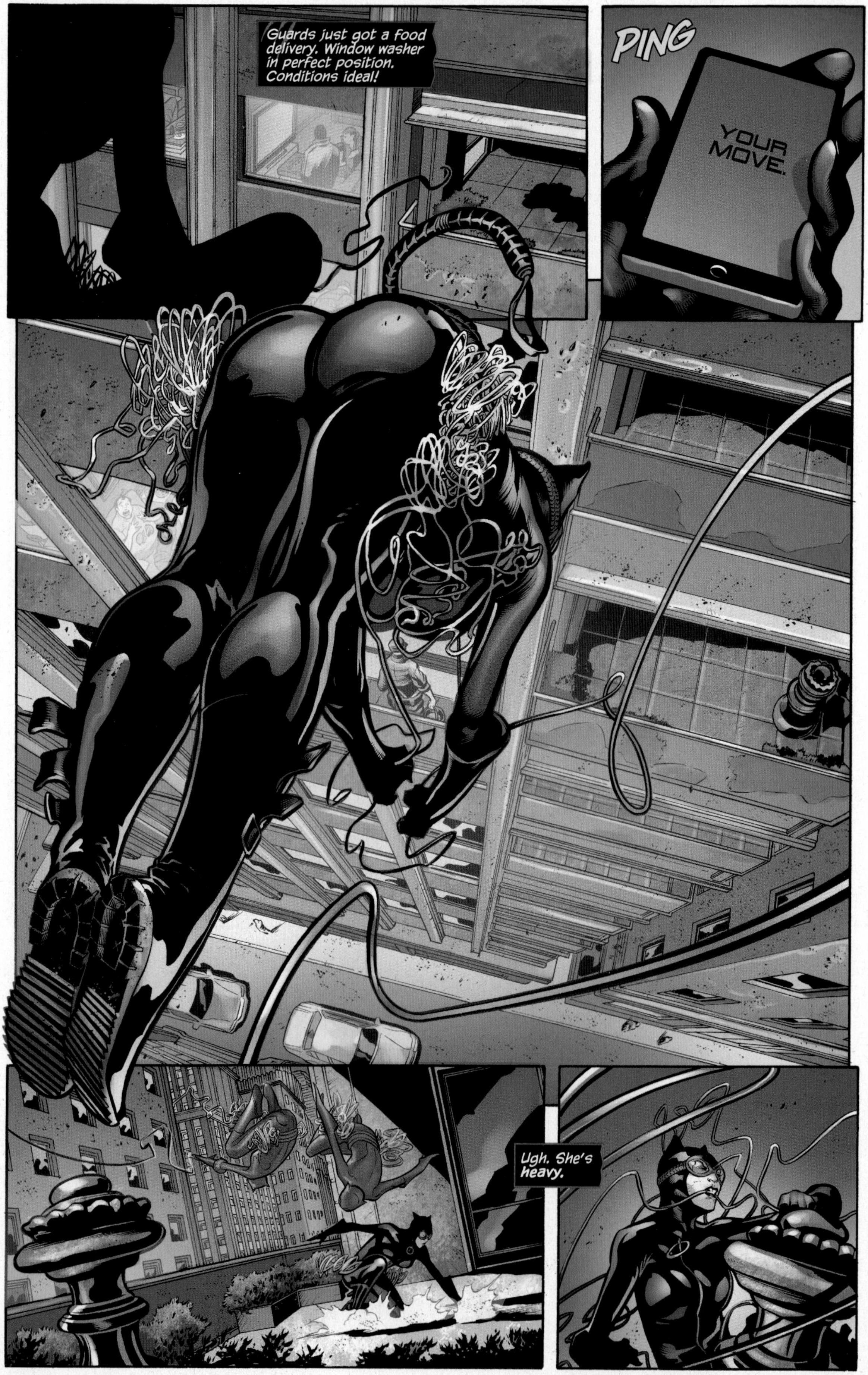
Guards just got a food delivery. Window washer in perfect position. Conditions ideal!
PING
YOUR MOVE.
Ugh. She's heavy.

They can't hear a thing over all that chewing and yakking.

IT'S ALWAYS LIKE, YOUR CHOLESTEROL, YOUR ARTERIES, YOUR BLOOD PRESSURE, BLAH BLAH NAG NAG.

DUDE, SHE DON'T WANT YOU TO DIE.

IF SHE COULD SEE ME NOW, EATING THIS GREASY SAUSAGE AN' EGG SANDWICH, PIZZA ON THE SIDE...

KILLER

--I MEAN, WHAT'S THE POINT OF LIVING AN EXTRA TEN YEARS IF YOU HAVE TO LIVE THEM WITHOUT THE COMPANIONSHIP OF SAUSAGE?

SHUT UP AN' GIMME A SLICE.

NA-HA. YOU ORDERED THE SALAD, DUDE. LIVE WITH IT.

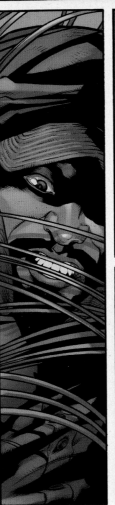

YOU HEAR SOMETHIN'?

YEAH, A THUNK.

UH-OH. WHERE'S THAT STUPID THING WE'RE GUARDING?

THUNK

K'RAK

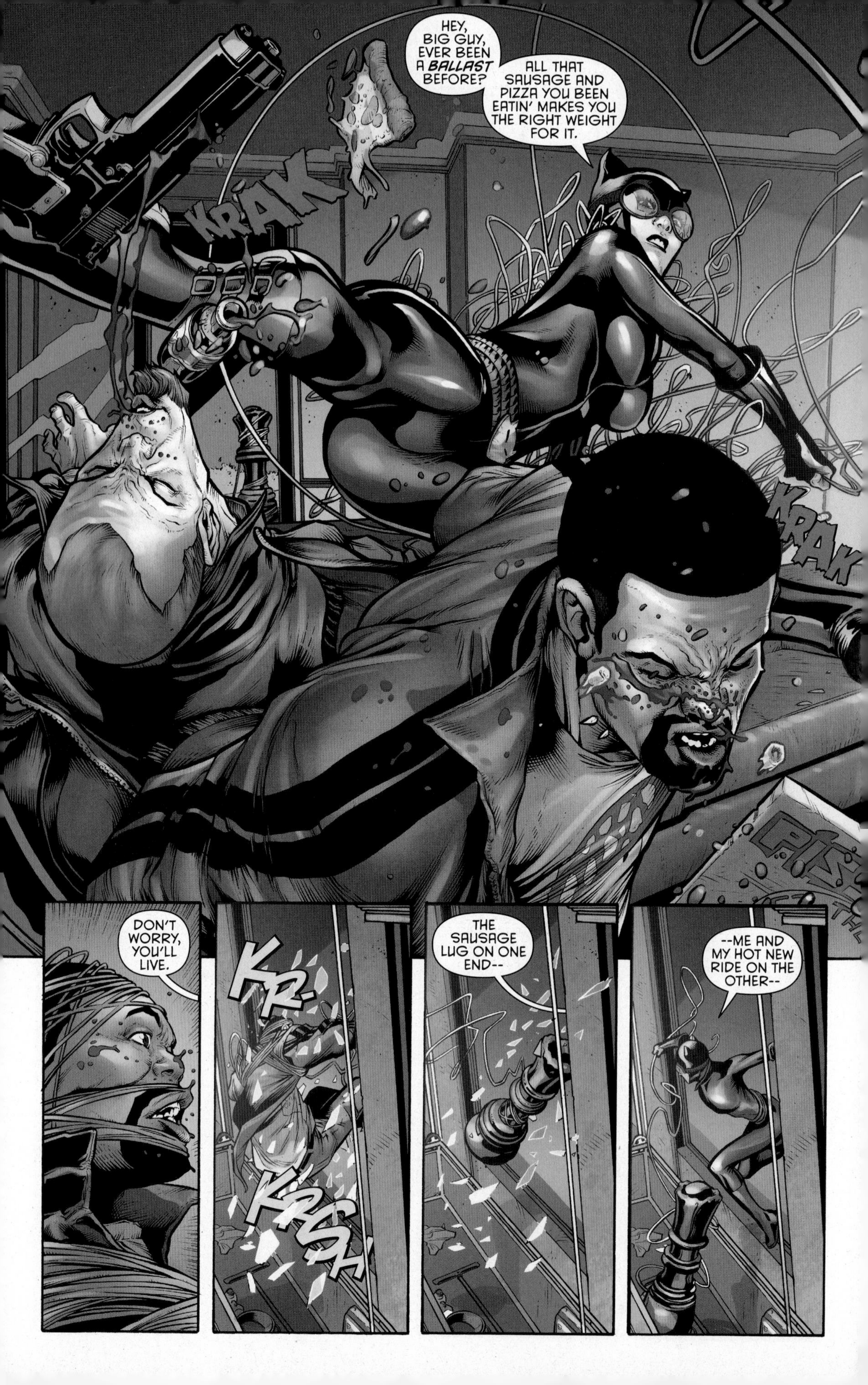
HEY, BIG GUY, EVER BEEN A BALLAST BEFORE?
ALL THAT SAUSAGE AND PIZZA YOU BEEN EATIN' MAKES YOU THE RIGHT WEIGHT FOR IT.
KRAK
KRAK
DON'T WORRY, YOU'LL LIVE.
KR-
KRSH
THE SAUSAGE LUG ON ONE END--
--ME AND MY HOT NEW RIDE ON THE OTHER--

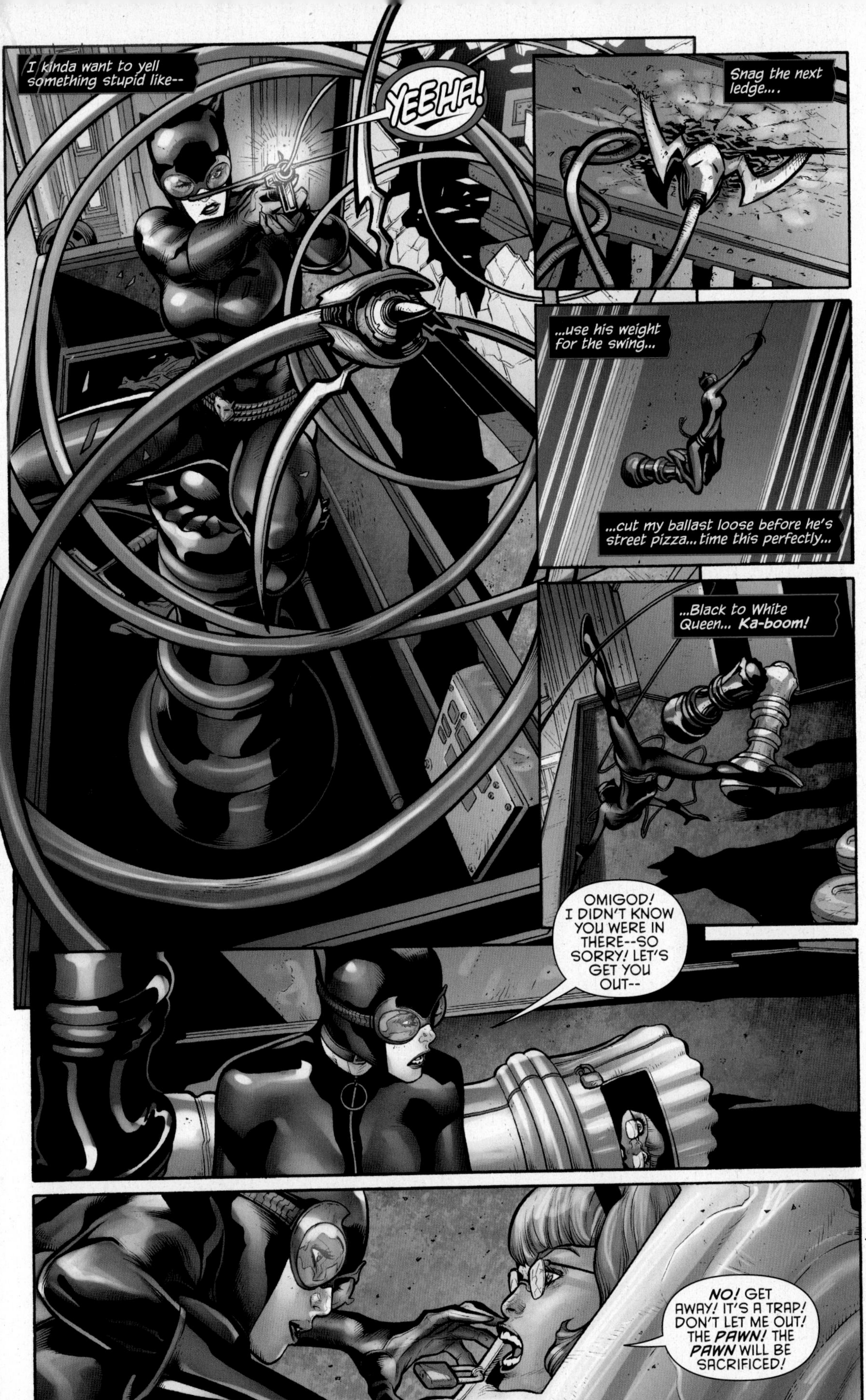
I kinda want to yell something stupid like--
YEEHA!
Snag the next ledge....
...use his weight for the swing...
...cut my ballast loose before he's street pizza...time this perfectly...
...Black to White Queen... Ka-boom!
OMIGOD! I DIDN'T KNOW YOU WERE IN THERE--SO SORRY! LET'S GET YOU OUT--
NO! GET AWAY! IT'S A TRAP! DON'T LET ME OUT! THE PAWN! THE PAWN WILL BE SACRIFICED!

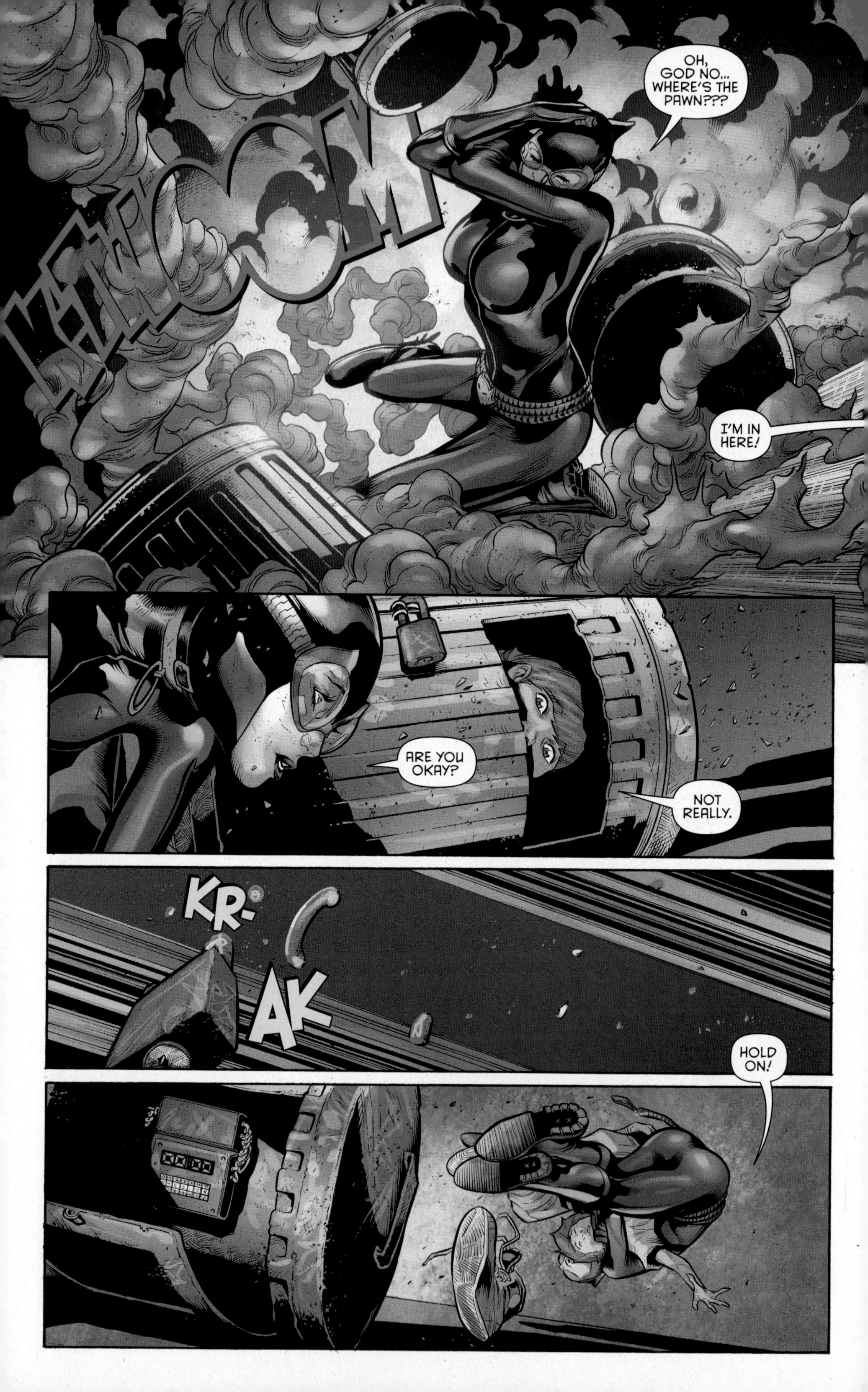
OH, GOD NO... WHERE'S THE PAWN???
I'M IN HERE!
ARE YOU OKAY?
NOT REALLY.
KR-
AK
HOLD ON!

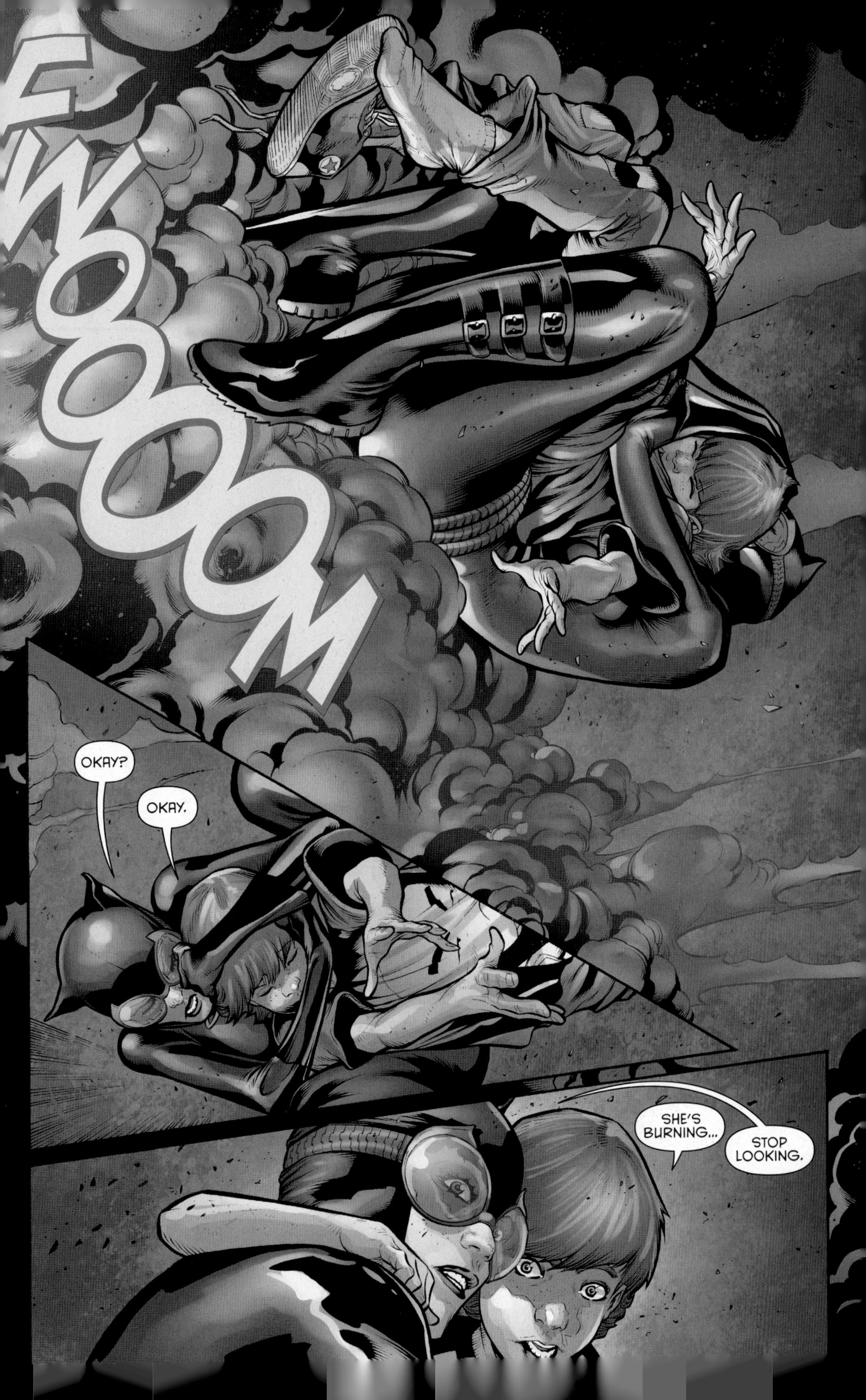

WOOOOOM
OKAY?
OKAY.
SHE'S BURNING...
STOP LOOKING.

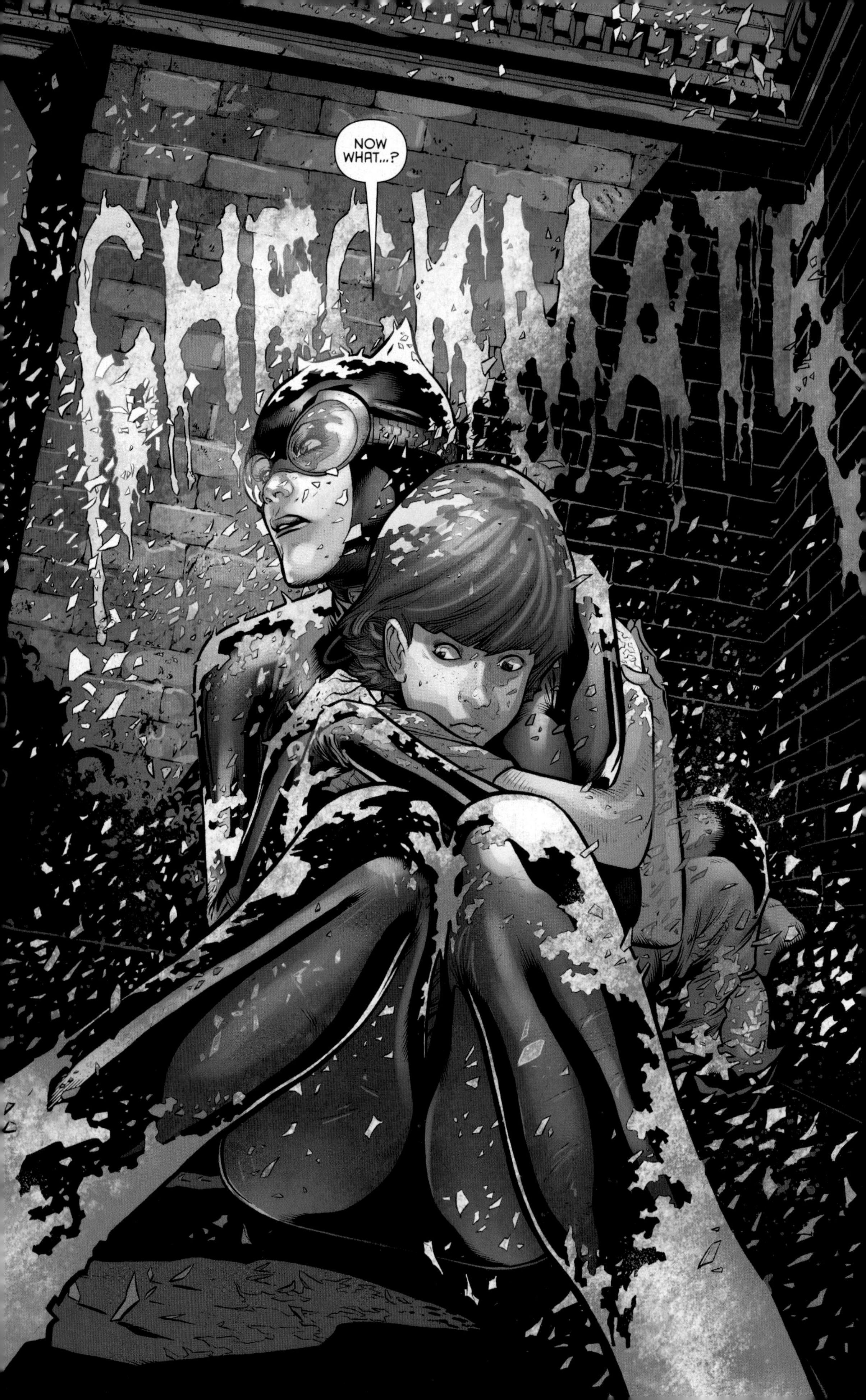
NOW WHAT...?

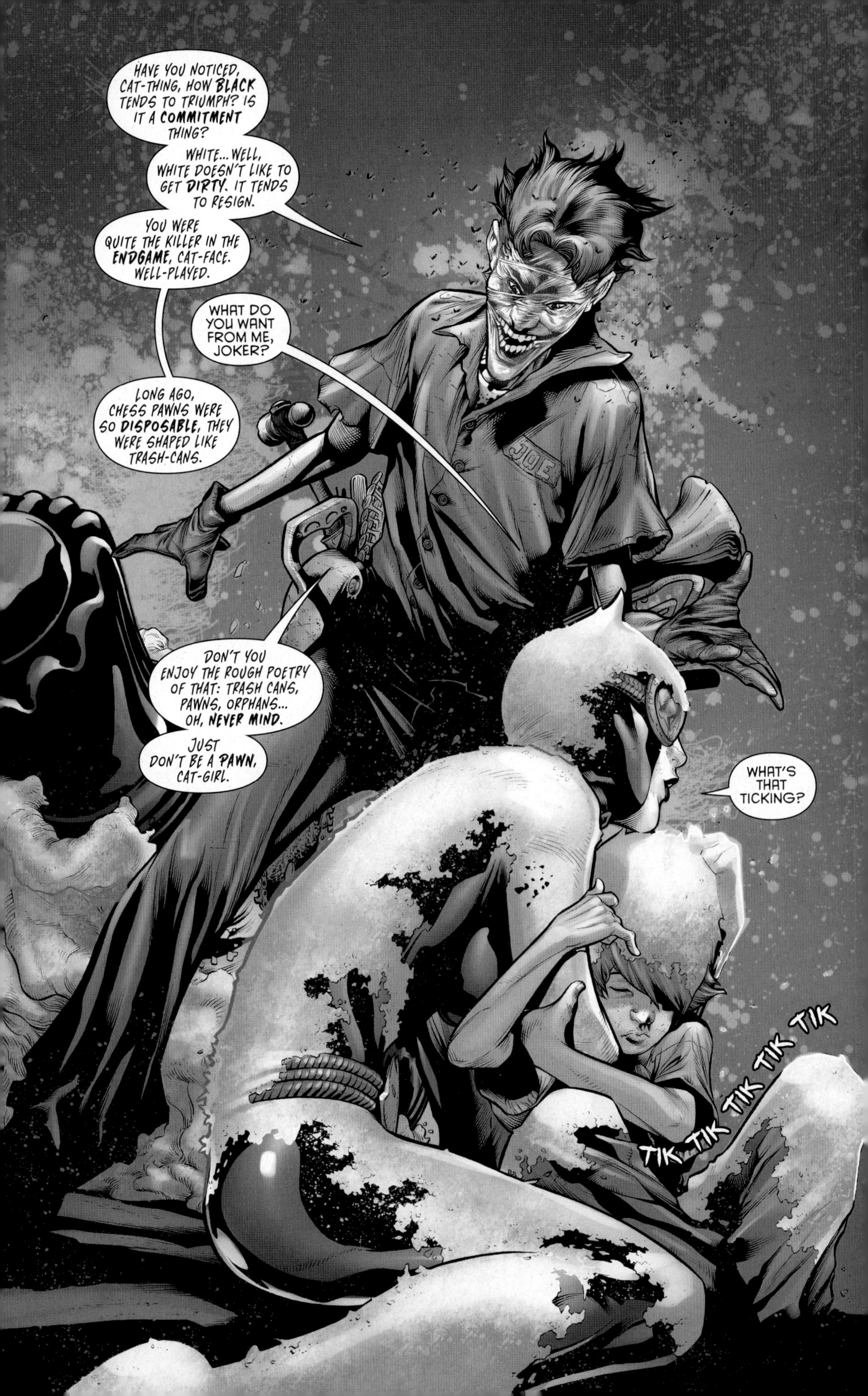
HAVE YOU NOTICED, CAT-THING, HOW BLACK TENDS TO TRIUMPH? IS IT A COMMITMENT THING?
WHITE... WELL, WHITE DOESN'T LIKE TO GET DIRTY. IT TENDS TO RESIGN.
YOU WERE QUITE THE KILLER IN THE ENDGAME, CAT-FACE. WELL-PLAYED.
WHAT DO YOU WANT FROM ME, JOKER?
LONG AGO, CHESS PAWNS WERE SO DISPOSABLE, THEY WERE SHAPED LIKE TRASH-CANS.
DON'T YOU ENJOY THE ROUGH POETRY OF THAT: TRASH CANS, PAWNS, ORPHANS... OH, NEVER MIND.
JUST DON'T BE A PAWN, CAT-GIRL.
WHAT'S THAT TICKING?
TIK TIK TIK TIK TIK TIK

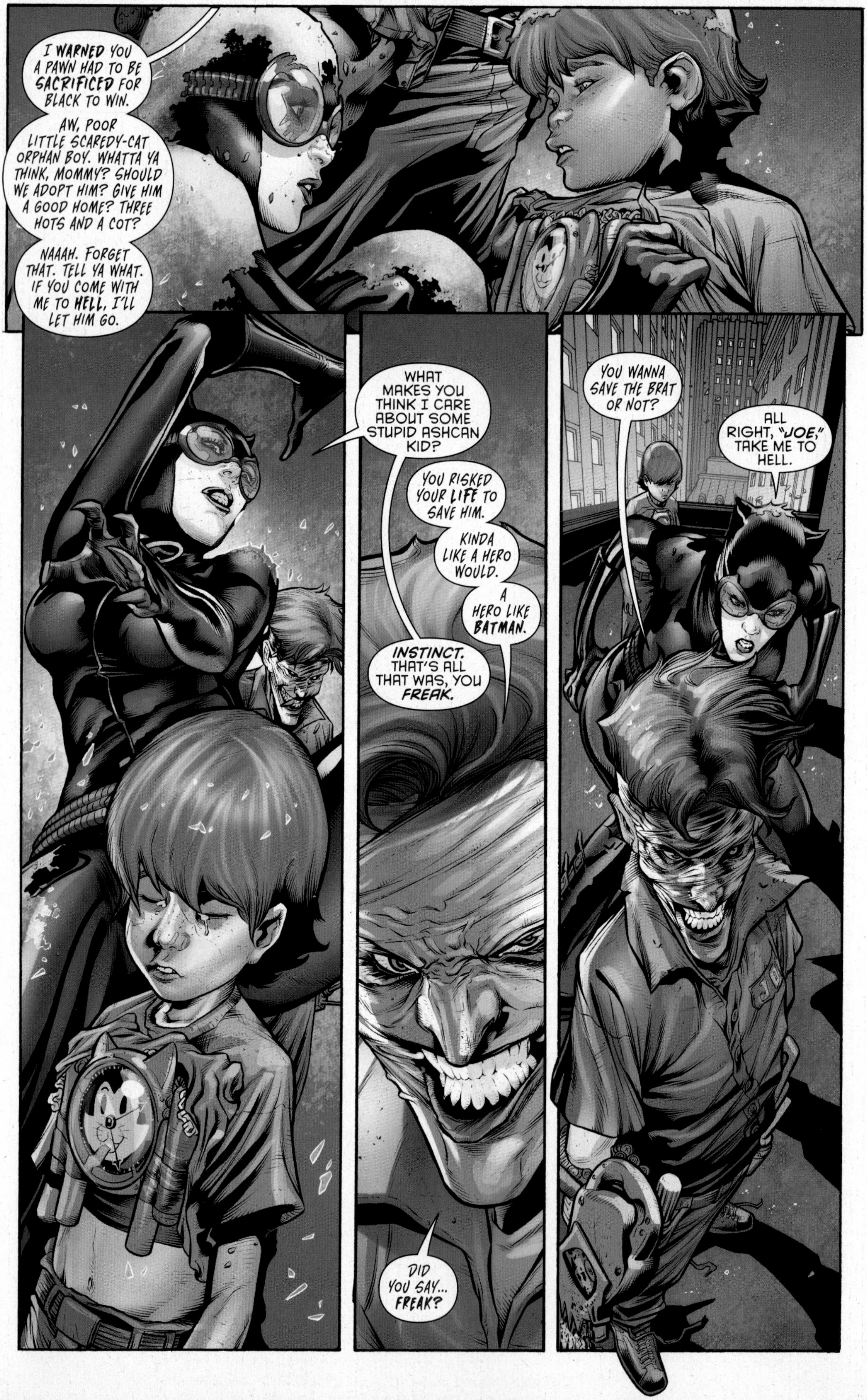
I WARNED YOU A PAWN HAD TO BE SACRIFICED FOR BLACK TO WIN.
AW, POOR LITTLE SCAREDY-CAT ORPHAN BOY. WHATTA YA THINK, MOMMY? SHOULD WE ADOPT HIM? GIVE HIM A GOOD HOME? THREE HOTS AND A COT?
NAAAH. FORGET THAT. TELL YA WHAT. IF YOU COME WITH ME TO HELL, I'LL LET HIM GO.
WHAT MAKES YOU THINK I CARE ABOUT SOME STUPID ASHCAN KID?
YOU RISKED YOUR LIFE TO SAVE HIM.
KINDA LIKE A HERO WOULD.
A HERO LIKE BATMAN.
INSTINCT. THAT'S ALL THAT WAS, YOU FREAK.
DID YOU SAY... FREAK?
YOU WANNA SAVE THE BRAT OR NOT?
ALL RIGHT, "JOE," TAKE ME TO HELL.

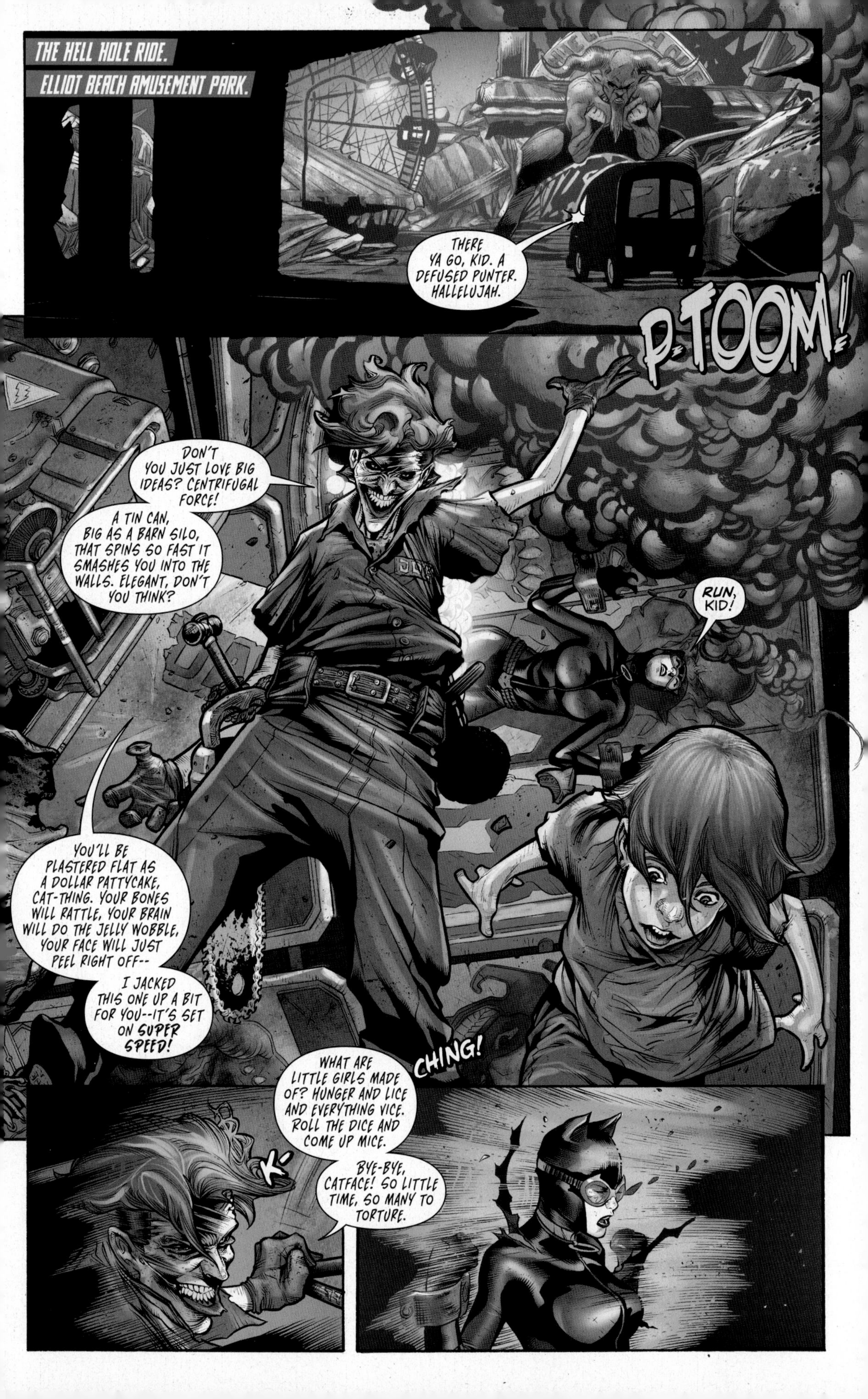
THE HELL HOLE RIDE.
ELLIOT BEACH AMUSEMENT PARK.
THERE YA GO, KID. A DEFUSED PUNTER. HALLELUJAH.
P-TOOM!
DON'T YOU JUST LOVE BIG IDEAS? CENTRIFUGAL FORCE!
A TIN CAN, BIG AS A BARN SILO, THAT SPINS SO FAST IT SMASHES YOU INTO THE WALLS. ELEGANT, DON'T YOU THINK?
RUN, KID!
YOU'LL BE PLASTERED FLAT AS A DOLLAR PATTYCAKE, CAT-THING. YOUR BONES WILL RATTLE, YOUR BRAIN WILL DO THE JELLY WOBBLE, YOUR FACE WILL JUST PEEL RIGHT OFF--
I JACKED THIS ONE UP A BIT FOR YOU--IT'S SET ON SUPER SPEED!
CHING!
WHAT ARE LITTLE GIRLS MADE OF? HUNGER AND LICE AND EVERYTHING VICE. ROLL THE DICE AND COME UP MICE.
K-
BYE-BYE, CATFACE! SO LITTLE TIME, SO MANY TO TORTURE.

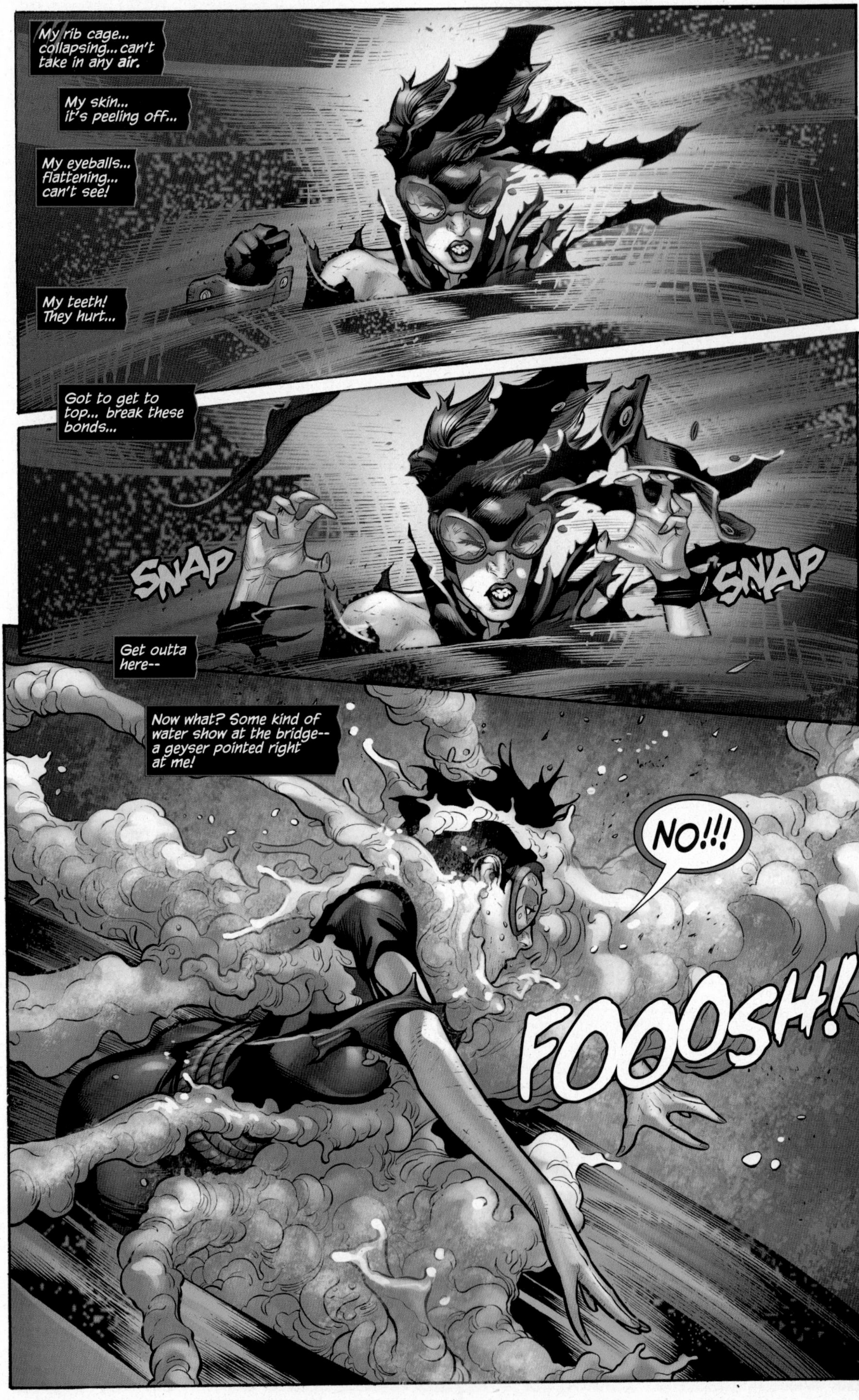
My rib cage... collapsing... can't take in any air.
My skin... it's peeling off...
My eyeballs... flattening... can't see!
My teeth! They hurt...
Got to get to top... break these bonds...
SNAP
SNAP
Get outta here--
Now what? Some kind of water show at the bridge-- a geyser pointed right at me!
NO!!!
FOOOSH!

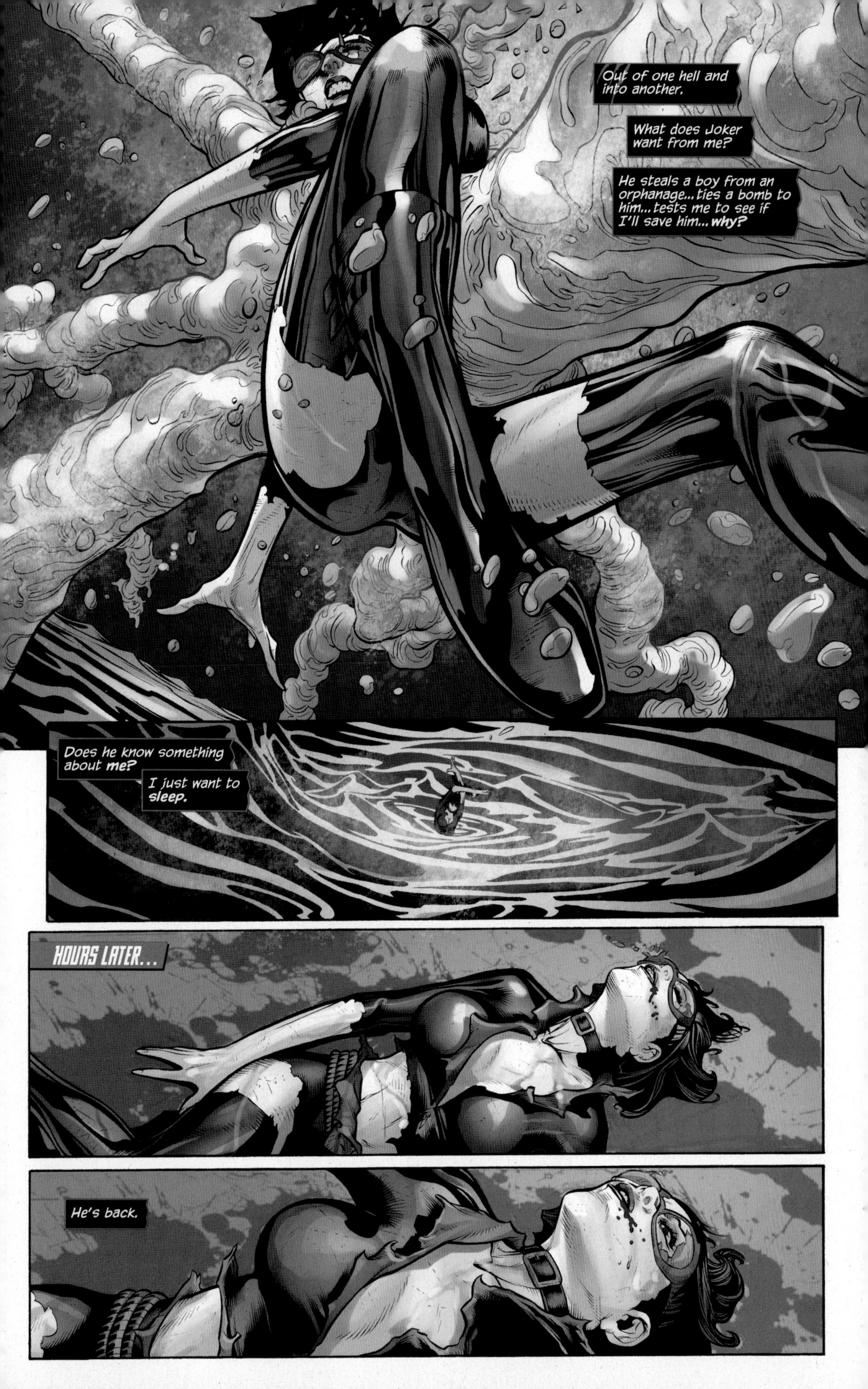
Out of one hell and into another.
What does Joker want from me?
He steals a boy from an orphanage...ties a bomb to him...tests me to see if I'll save him...why?
Does he know something about me?
I just want to sleep.
HOURS LATER...
He's back.

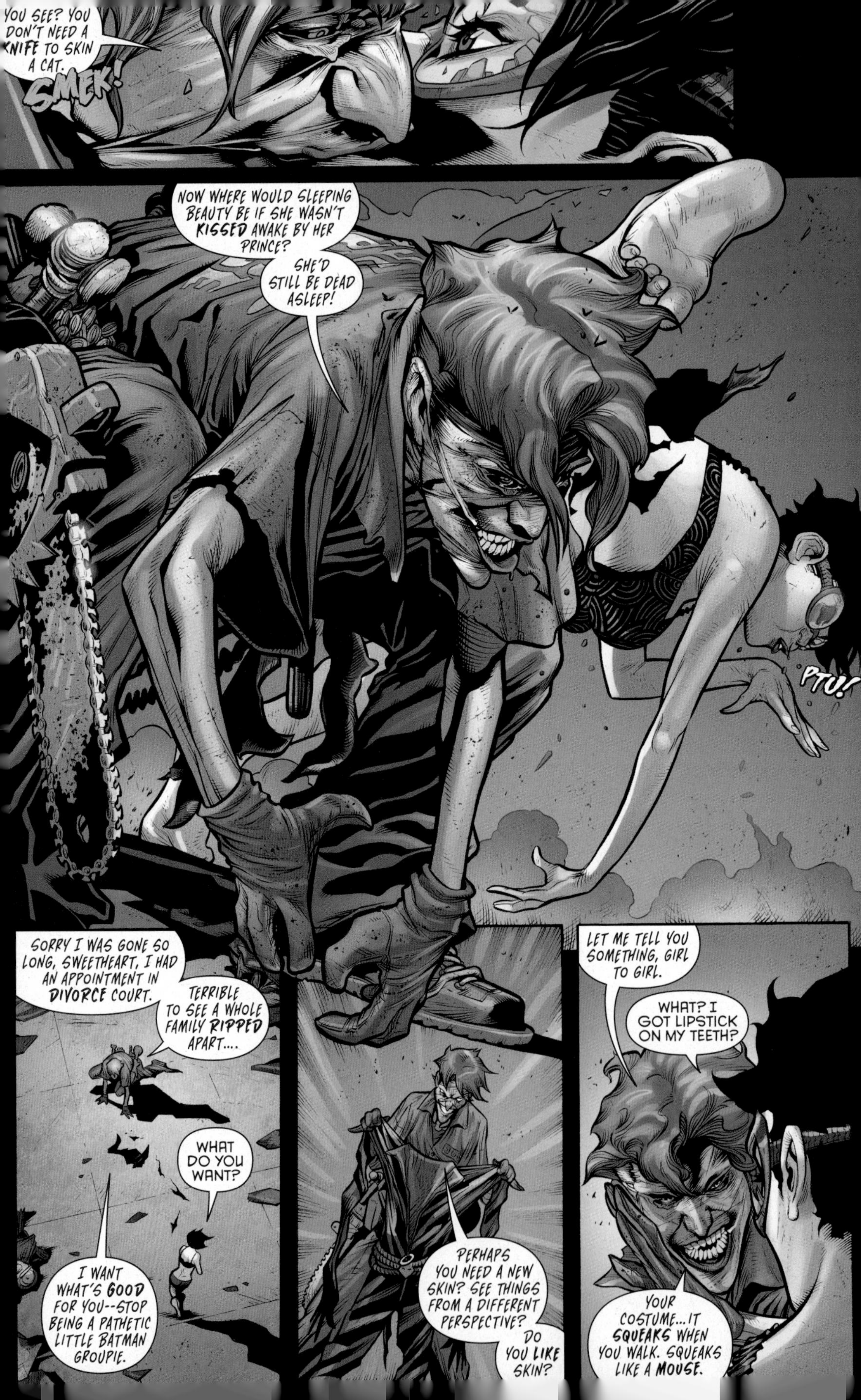
YOU SEE? YOU DON'T NEED A KNIFE TO SKIN A CAT.
SMEK!
NOW WHERE WOULD SLEEPING BEAUTY BE IF SHE WASN'T KISSED AWAKE BY HER PRINCE?
SHE'D STILL BE DEAD ASLEEP!
PTU!
SORRY I WAS GONE SO LONG, SWEETHEART, I HAD AN APPOINTMENT IN DIVORCE COURT.
TERRIBLE TO SEE A WHOLE FAMILY RIPPED APART....
WHAT DO YOU WANT?
I WANT WHAT'S GOOD FOR YOU--STOP BEING A PATHETIC LITTLE BATMAN GROUPIE.
PERHAPS YOU NEED A NEW SKIN? SEE THINGS FROM A DIFFERENT PERSPECTIVE?
DO YOU LIKE SKIN?
LET ME TELL YOU SOMETHING, GIRL TO GIRL.
WHAT? I GOT LIPSTICK ON MY TEETH?
YOUR COSTUME...IT SQUEAKS WHEN YOU WALK. SQUEAKS LIKE A MOUSE.

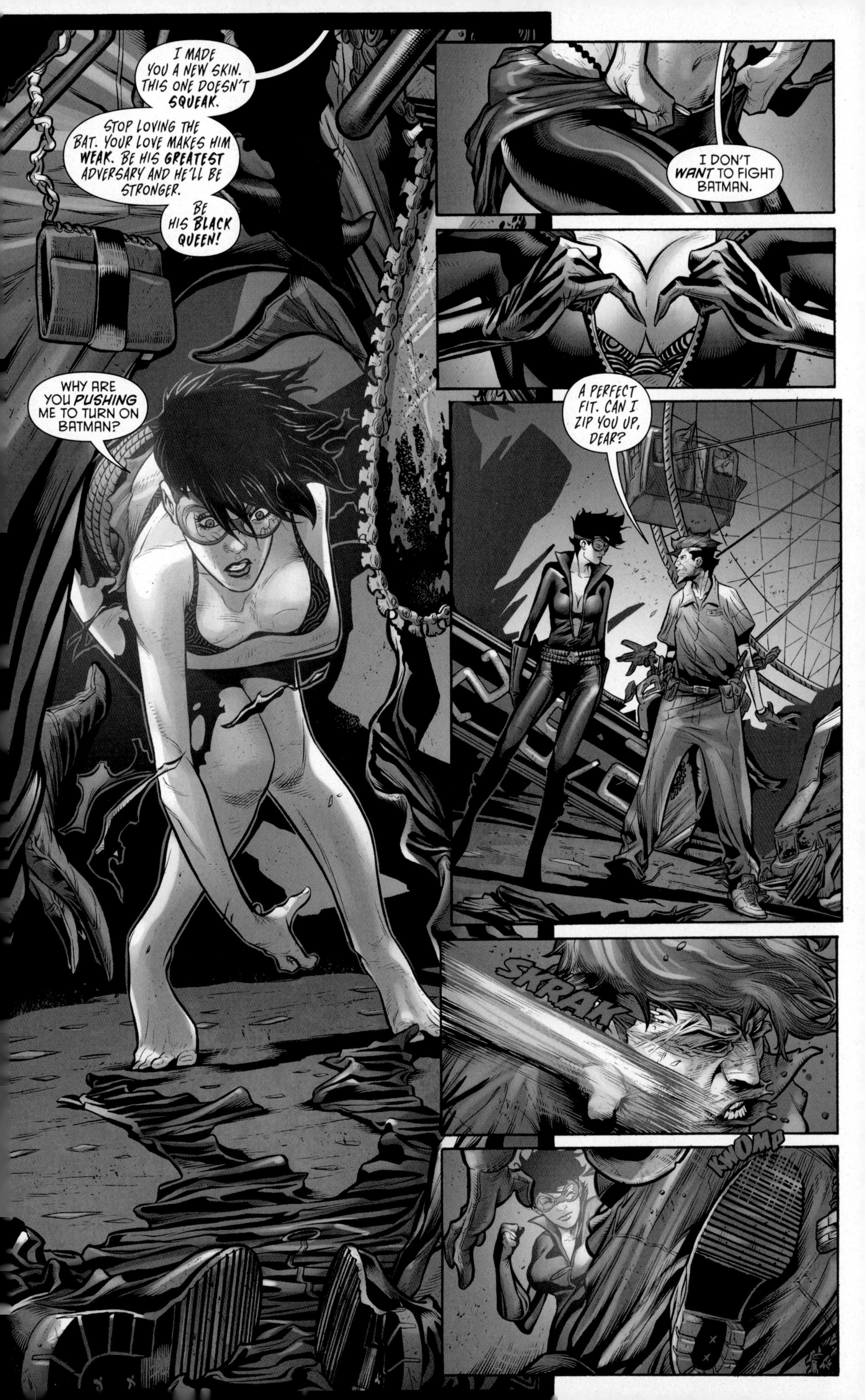
I MADE YOU A NEW SKIN. THIS ONE DOESN'T SQUEAK.
STOP LOVING THE BAT. YOUR LOVE MAKES HIM WEAK. BE HIS GREATEST ADVERSARY AND HE'LL BE STRONGER.
BE HIS BLACK QUEEN!
I DON'T WANT TO FIGHT BATMAN.
WHY ARE YOU PUSHING ME TO TURN ON BATMAN?
A PERFECT FIT. CAN I ZIP YOU UP, DEAR?
SKRAK
KWOMP

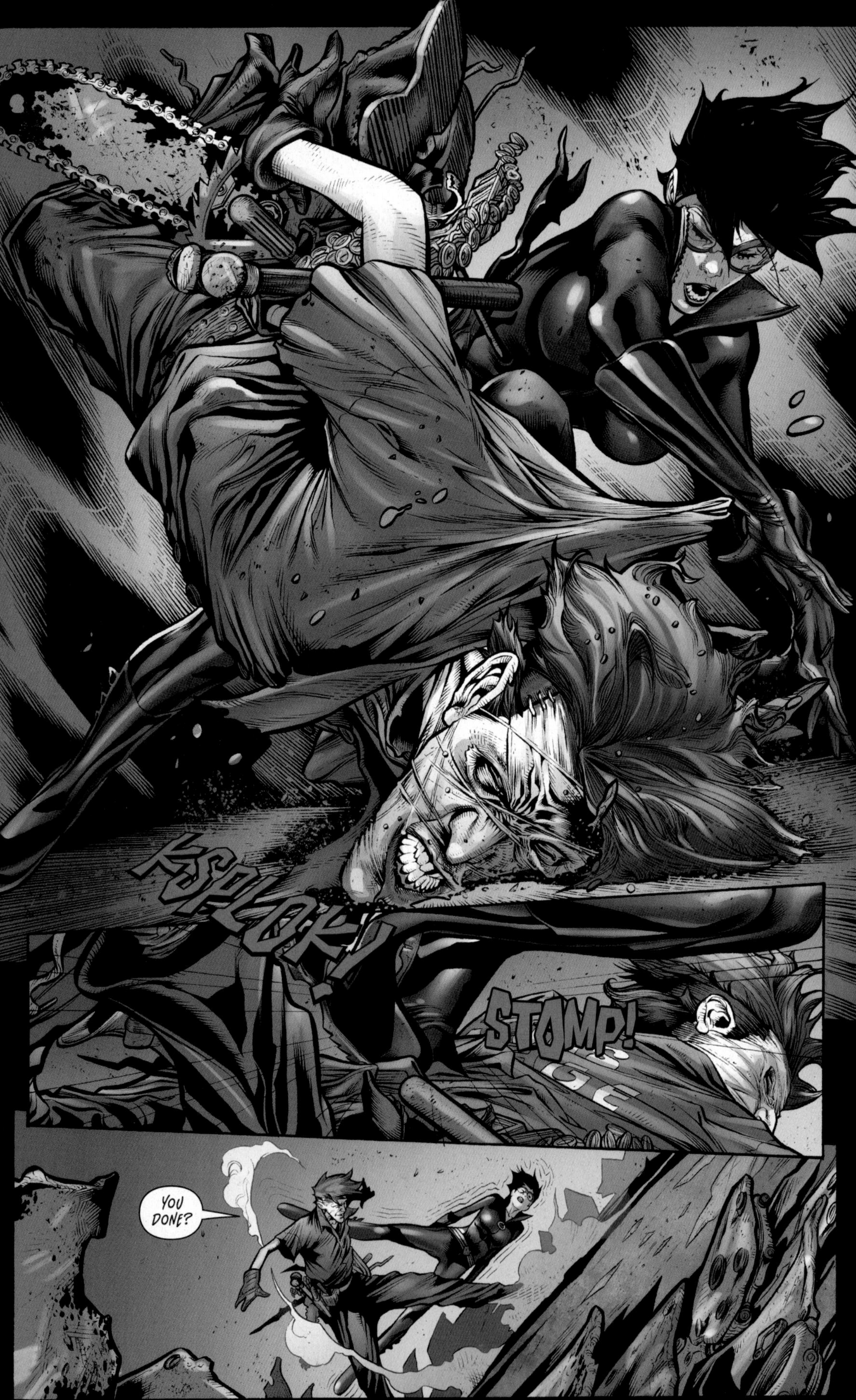
KSPLOK!
STOMP!
YOU DONE?

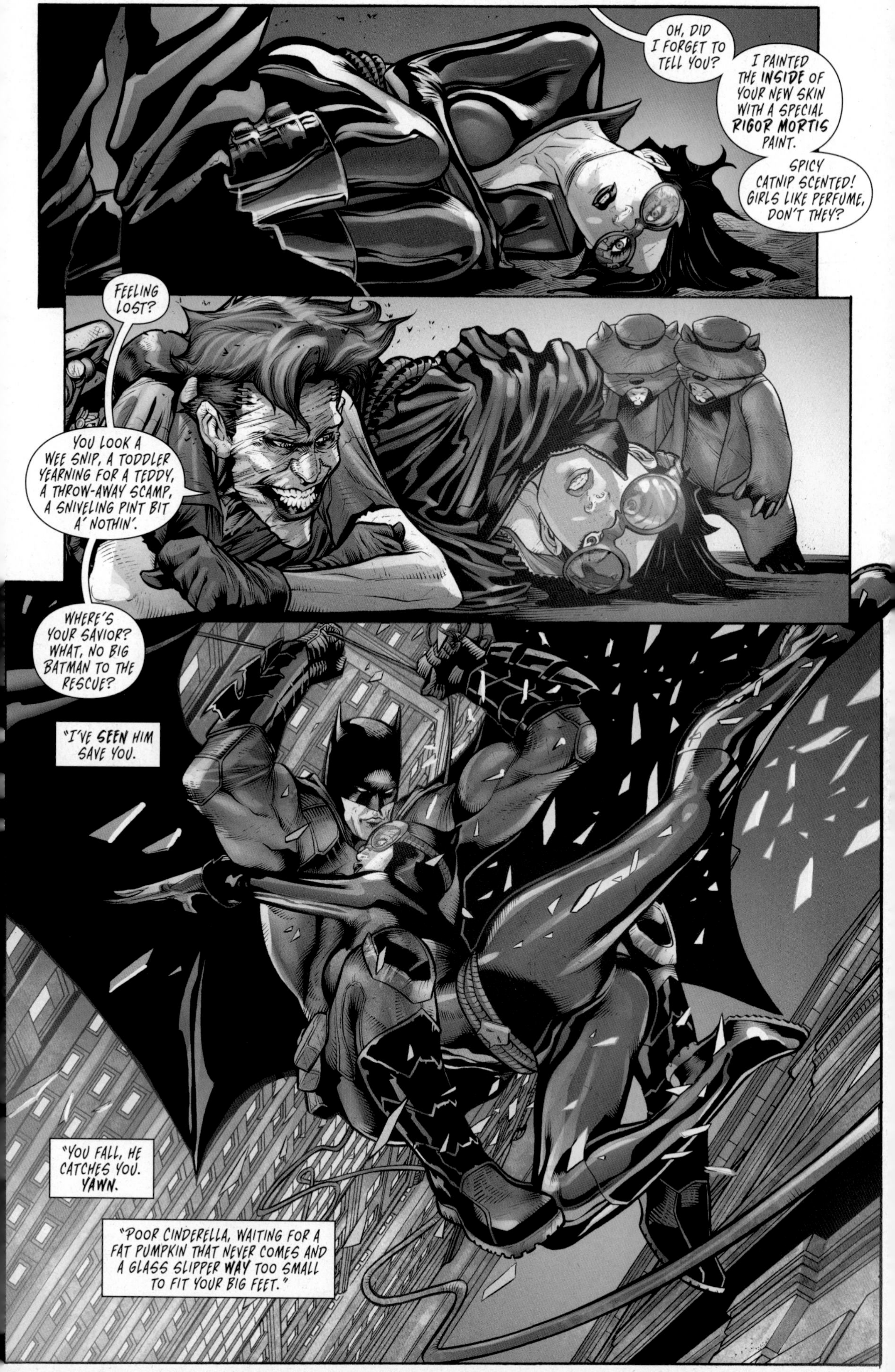
OH, DID I FORGET TO TELL YOU?
I PAINTED THE INSIDE OF YOUR NEW SKIN WITH A SPECIAL RIGOR MORTIS PAINT.
SPICY CATNIP SCENTED! GIRLS LIKE PERFUME, DON'T THEY?
FEELING LOST?
YOU LOOK A WEE SNIP, A TODDLER YEARNING FOR A TEDDY, A THROW-AWAY SCAMP, A SNIVELING PINT BIT A' NOTHIN'.
WHERE'S YOUR SAVIOR? WHAT, NO BIG BATMAN TO THE RESCUE?
"I'VE SEEN HIM SAVE YOU.
"YOU FALL, HE CATCHES YOU. YAWN.
"POOR CINDERELLA, WAITING FOR A FAT PUMPKIN THAT NEVER COMES AND A GLASS SLIPPER WAY TOO SMALL TO FIT YOUR BIG FEET."

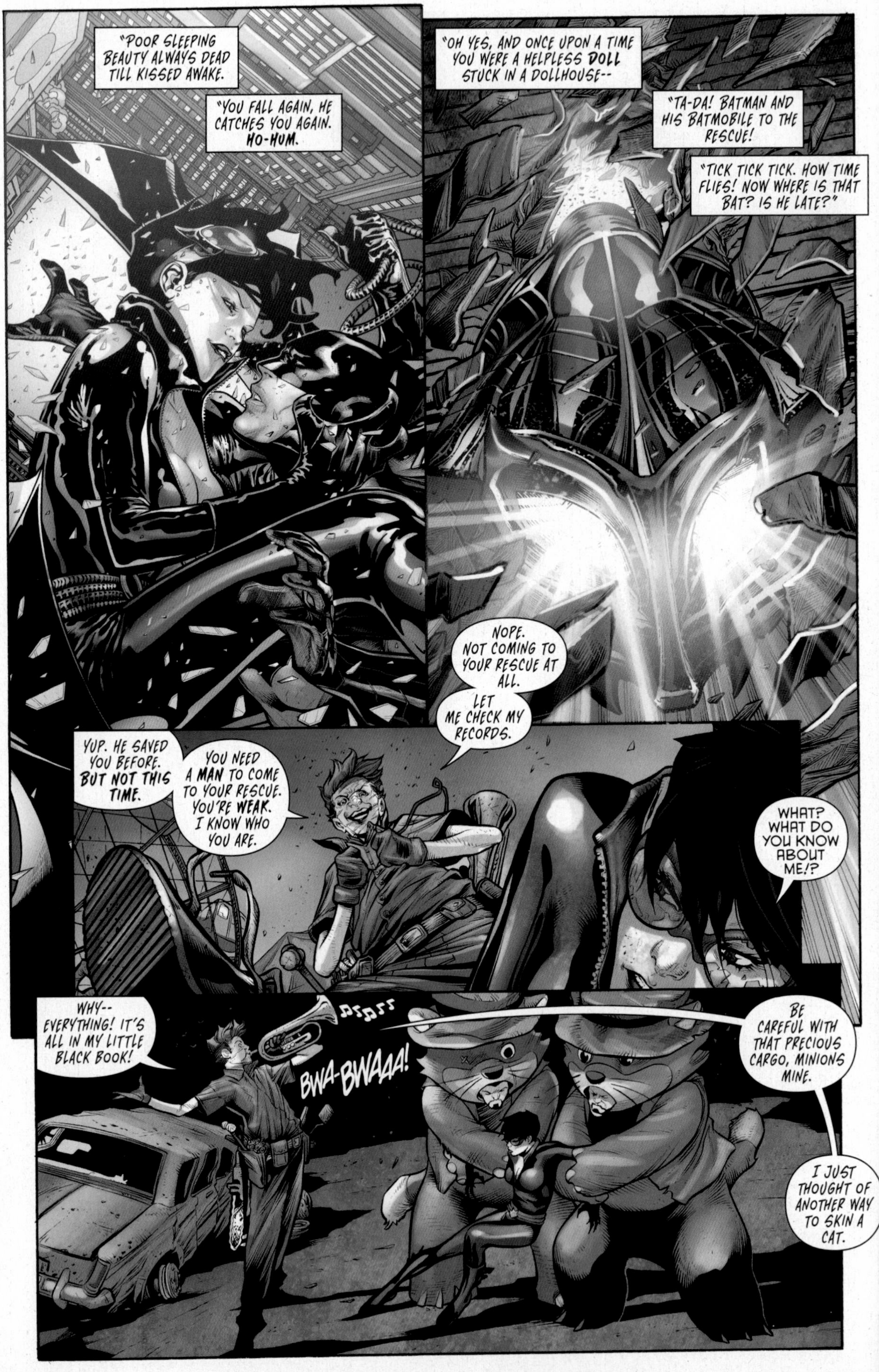
"POOR SLEEPING BEAUTY ALWAYS DEAD TILL KISSED AWAKE.
"YOU FALL AGAIN, HE CATCHES YOU AGAIN. **HO-HUM**.
"OH YES, AND ONCE UPON A TIME YOU WERE A HELPLESS **DOLL** STUCK IN A DOLLHOUSE--
"TA-DA! BATMAN AND HIS BATMOBILE TO THE RESCUE!
"TICK TICK TICK. HOW TIME FLIES! NOW WHERE IS THAT BAT? IS HE LATE?"
NOPE. NOT COMING TO YOUR RESCUE AT ALL.
LET ME CHECK MY RECORDS.
YUP. HE SAVED YOU BEFORE. **BUT NOT THIS TIME.**
YOU NEED A **MAN** TO COME TO YOUR RESCUE. YOU'RE **WEAK**. I KNOW WHO YOU ARE.
WHAT? WHAT DO YOU KNOW ABOUT ME!?
WHY-- EVERYTHING! IT'S ALL IN MY LITTLE BLACK BOOK!
BWA-BWAAA!
BE CAREFUL WITH THAT PRECIOUS CARGO, MINIONS MINE.
I JUST THOUGHT OF ANOTHER WAY TO SKIN A CAT.

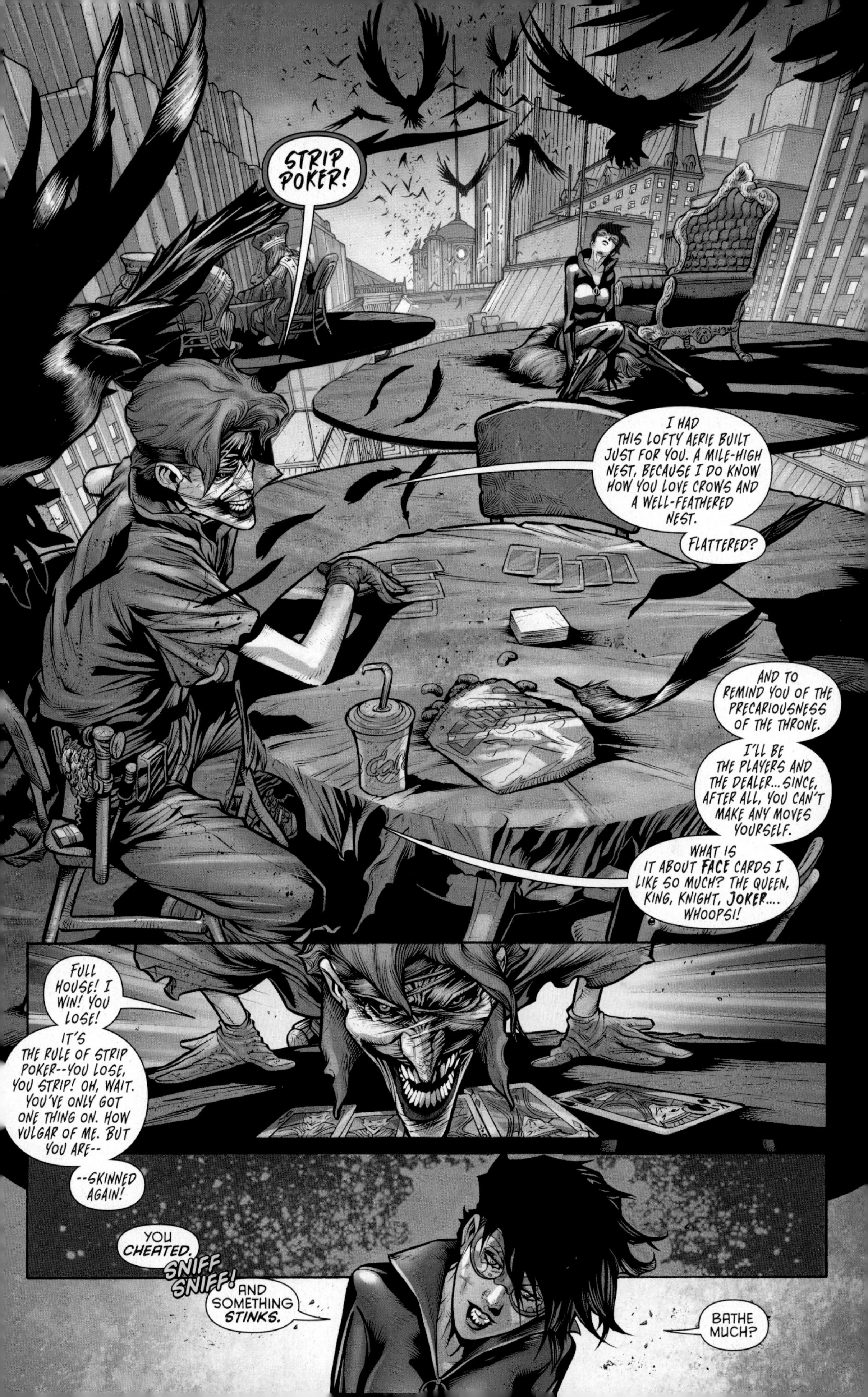
STRIP POKER!
I HAD THIS LOFTY AERIE BUILT JUST FOR YOU. A MILE-HIGH NEST, BECAUSE I DO KNOW HOW YOU LOVE CROWS AND A WELL-FEATHERED NEST.
FLATTERED?
AND TO REMIND YOU OF THE PRECARIOUSNESS OF THE THRONE.
I'LL BE THE PLAYERS AND THE DEALER... SINCE, AFTER ALL, YOU CAN'T MAKE ANY MOVES YOURSELF.
WHAT IS IT ABOUT FACE CARDS I LIKE SO MUCH? THE QUEEN, KING, KNIGHT, JOKER.... WHOOPS!!
FULL HOUSE! I WIN! YOU LOSE!
IT'S THE RULE OF STRIP POKER--YOU LOSE, YOU STRIP! OH, WAIT. YOU'VE ONLY GOT ONE THING ON. HOW VULGAR OF ME. BUT YOU ARE--
--SKINNED AGAIN!
YOU CHEATED.
SNIFF SNIFF!
AND SOMETHING STINKS.
BATHE MUCH?

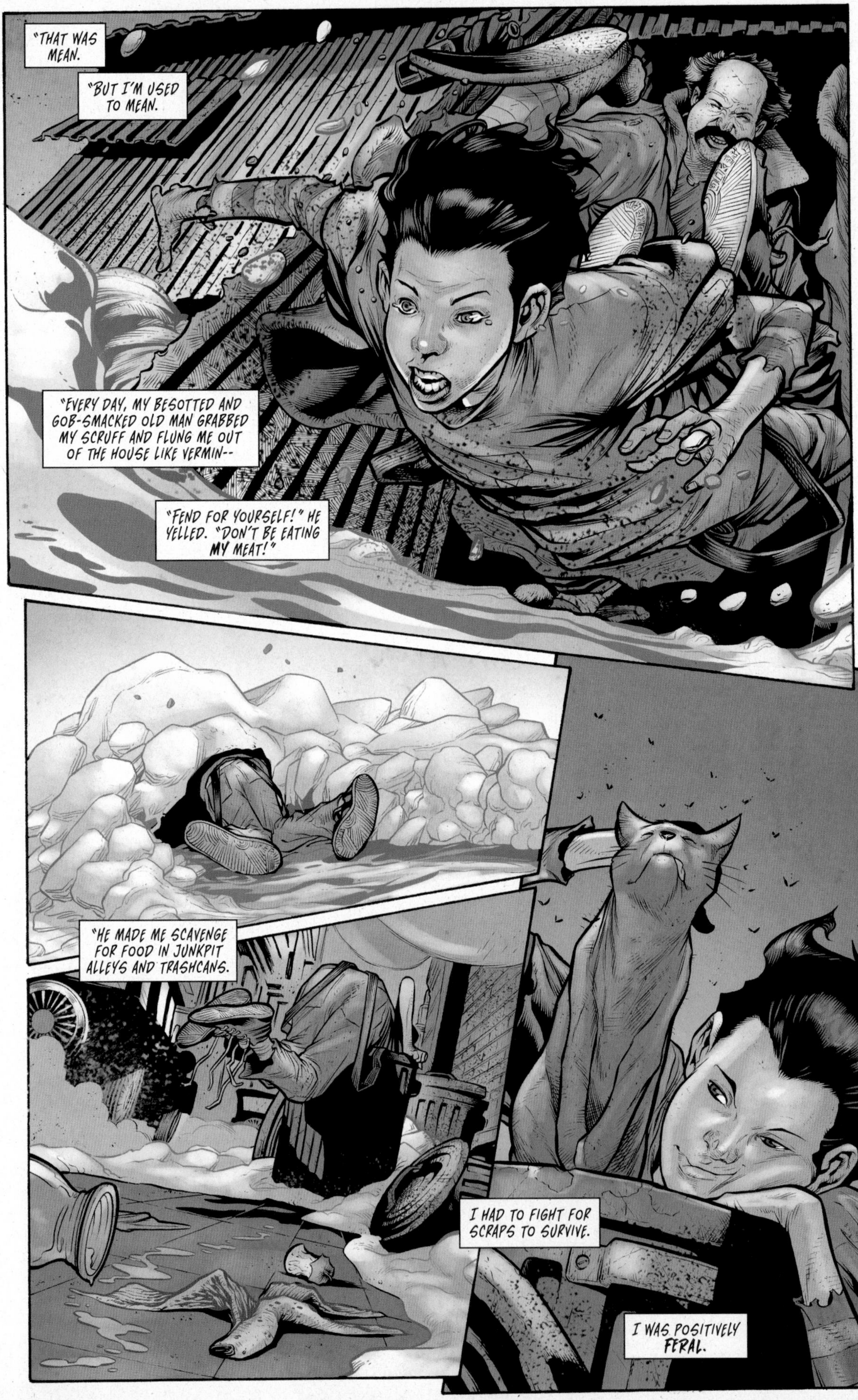
"THAT WAS MEAN.
"BUT I'M USED TO MEAN.
"EVERY DAY, MY BESOTTED AND GOB-SMACKED OLD MAN GRABBED MY SCRUFF AND FLUNG ME OUT OF THE HOUSE LIKE VERMIN--
"FEND FOR YOURSELF!" HE YELLED. "DON'T BE EATING MY MEAT!"
"HE MADE ME SCAVENGE FOR FOOD IN JUNKPIT ALLEYS AND TRASHCANS.
I HAD TO FIGHT FOR SCRAPS TO SURVIVE.
I WAS POSITIVELY FERAL.

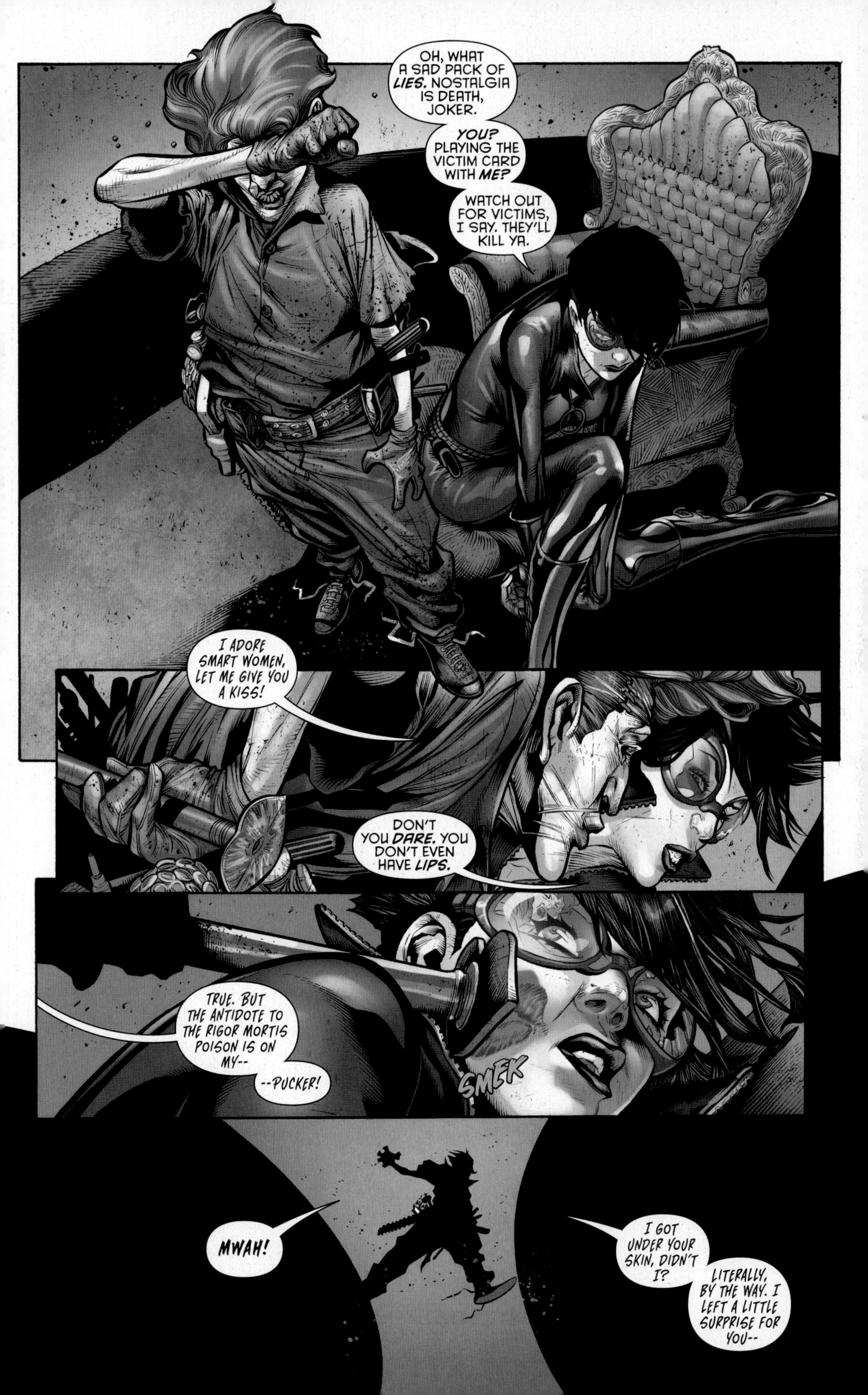
OH, WHAT A SAD PACK OF LIES. NOSTALGIA IS DEATH, JOKER.
YOU? PLAYING THE VICTIM CARD WITH ME?
WATCH OUT FOR VICTIMS, I SAY. THEY'LL KILL YA.
I ADORE SMART WOMEN, LET ME GIVE YOU A KISS!
DON'T YOU DARE. YOU DON'T EVEN HAVE LIPS.
TRUE. BUT THE ANTIDOTE TO THE RIGOR MORTIS POISON IS ON MY--
--PUCKER!
SMEK
MWAH!
I GOT UNDER YOUR SKIN, DIDN'T I?
LITERALLY, BY THE WAY. I LEFT A LITTLE SURPRISE FOR YOU--

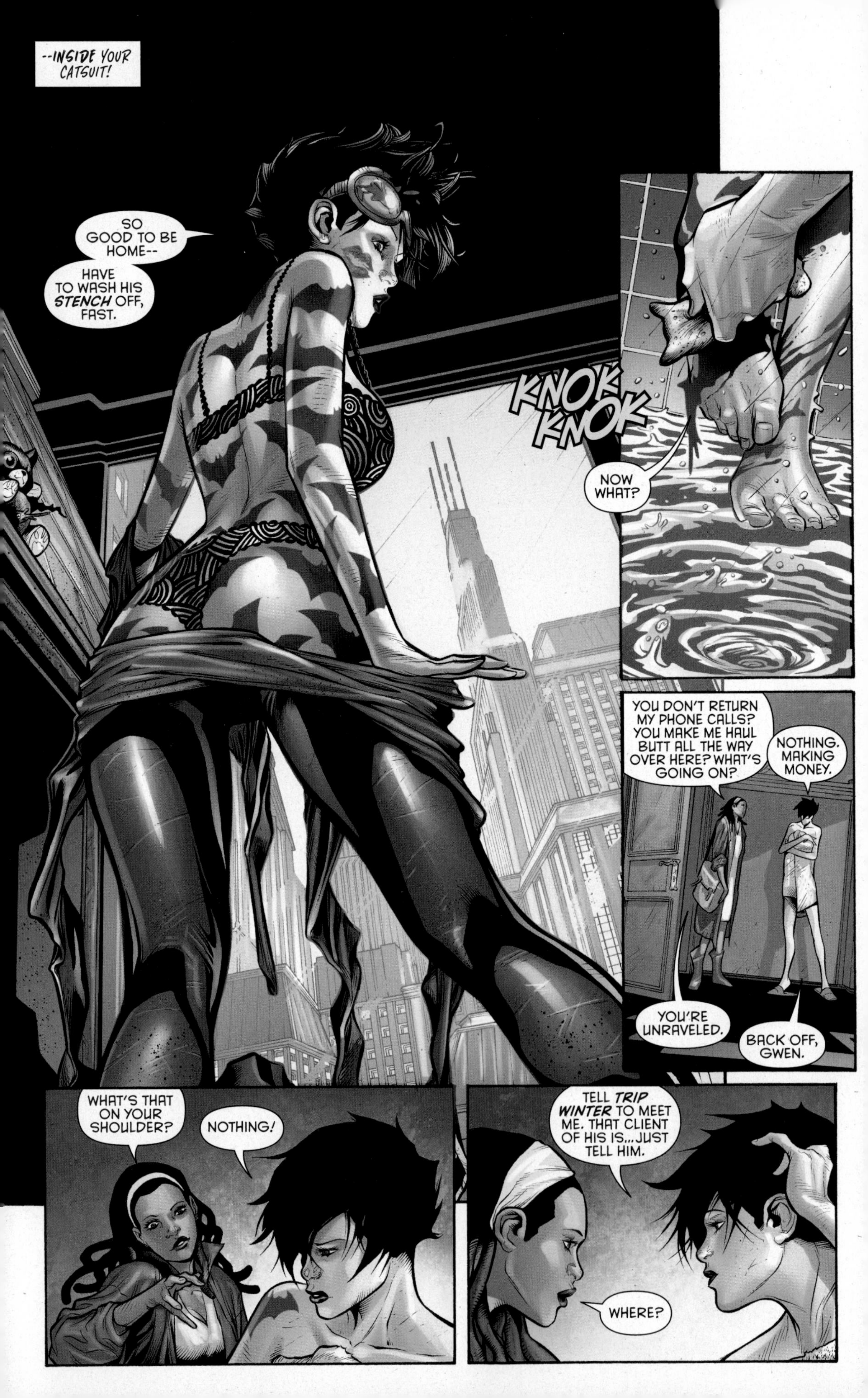
--INSIDE YOUR CATSUIT!
SO GOOD TO BE HOME--
HAVE TO WASH HIS STENCH OFF, FAST.
KNOK KNOK
NOW WHAT?
YOU DON'T RETURN MY PHONE CALLS? YOU MAKE ME HAUL BUTT ALL THE WAY OVER HERE? WHAT'S GOING ON?
NOTHING. MAKING MONEY.
YOU'RE UNRAVELED.
BACK OFF, GWEN.
WHAT'S THAT ON YOUR SHOULDER?
NOTHING!
TELL TRIP WINTER TO MEET ME. THAT CLIENT OF HIS IS...JUST TELL HIM.
WHERE?

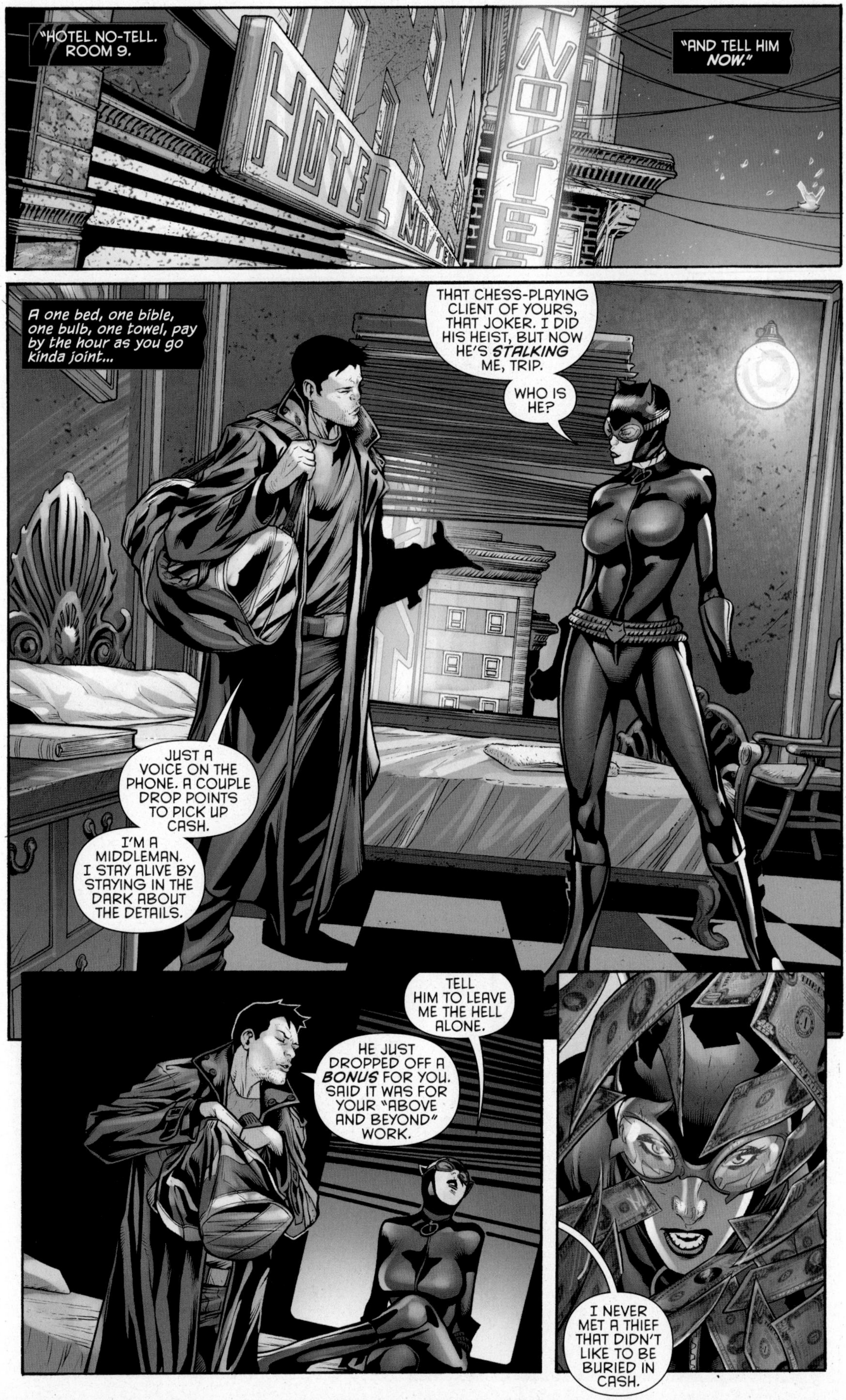
"HOTEL NO-TELL. ROOM 9.
"AND TELL HIM *NOW.*"
HOTEL NO/TELL
NO/TE
A one bed, one bible, one bulb, one towel, pay by the hour as you go kinda joint...
THAT CHESS-PLAYING CLIENT OF YOURS, THAT JOKER. I DID HIS HEIST, BUT NOW HE'S *STALKING* ME, TRIP.
WHO IS HE?
JUST A VOICE ON THE PHONE. A COUPLE DROP POINTS TO PICK UP CASH.
I'M A MIDDLEMAN. I STAY ALIVE BY STAYING IN THE DARK ABOUT THE DETAILS.
TELL HIM TO LEAVE ME THE HELL ALONE.
HE JUST DROPPED OFF A *BONUS* FOR YOU. SAID IT WAS FOR YOUR "ABOVE AND BEYOND" WORK.
I NEVER MET A THIEF THAT DIDN'T LIKE TO BE BURIED IN CASH.

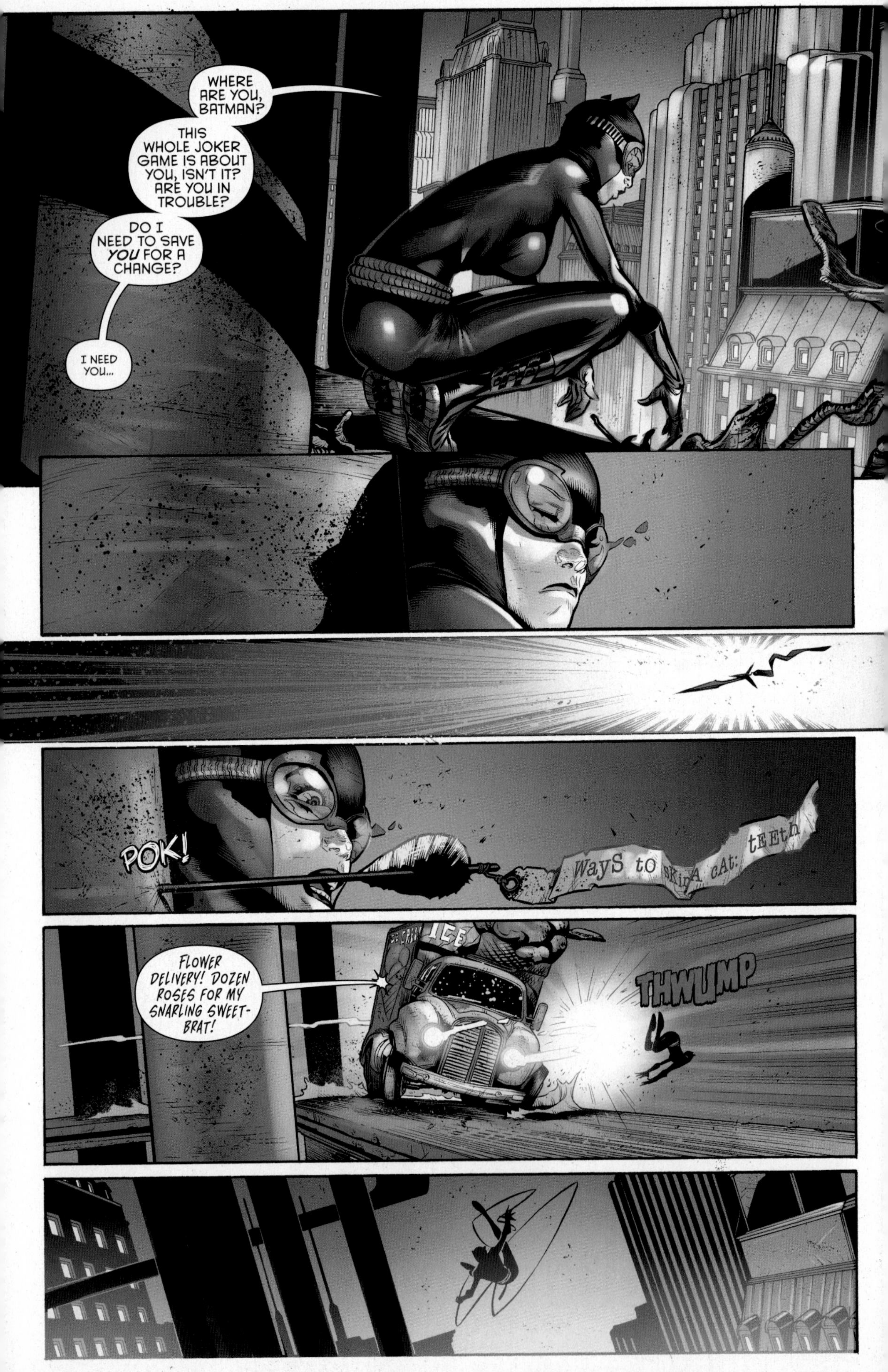
WHERE ARE YOU, BATMAN?
THIS WHOLE JOKER GAME IS ABOUT YOU, ISN'T IT? ARE YOU IN TROUBLE?
DO I NEED TO SAVE *YOU* FOR A CHANGE?
I NEED YOU...
POK!
WayS to sKin A cAt: tEEth
ICE
FLOWER DELIVERY! DOZEN ROSES FOR MY SNARLING SWEET-BRAT!
THWUMP

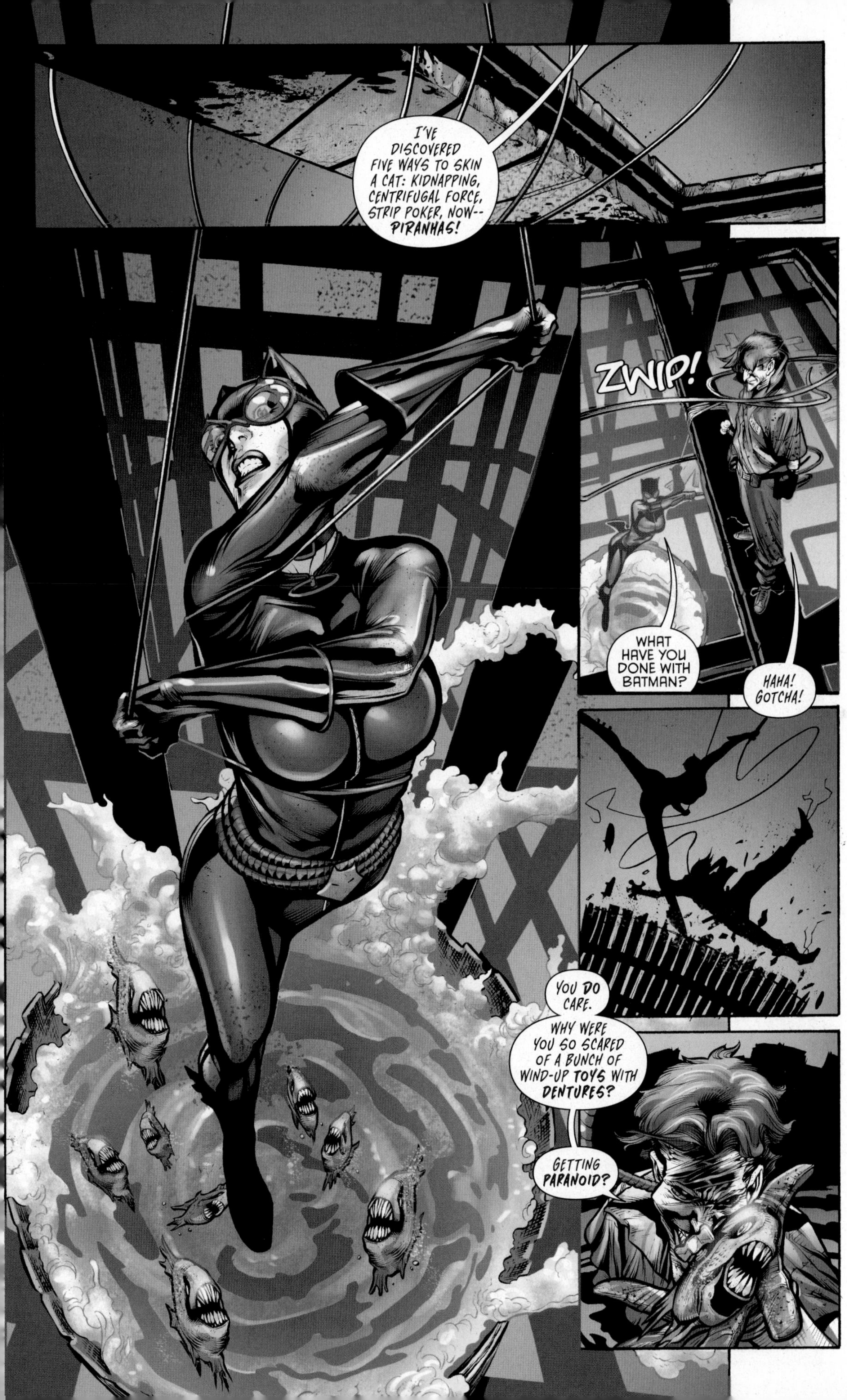
I'VE DISCOVERED FIVE WAYS TO SKIN A CAT: KIDNAPPING, CENTRIFUGAL FORCE, STRIP POKER, NOW-- PIRANHAS!
ZWIP!
WHAT HAVE YOU DONE WITH BATMAN?
HAHA! GOTCHA!
YOU DO CARE.
WHY WERE YOU SO SCARED OF A BUNCH OF WIND-UP TOYS WITH DENTURES?
GETTING PARANOID?

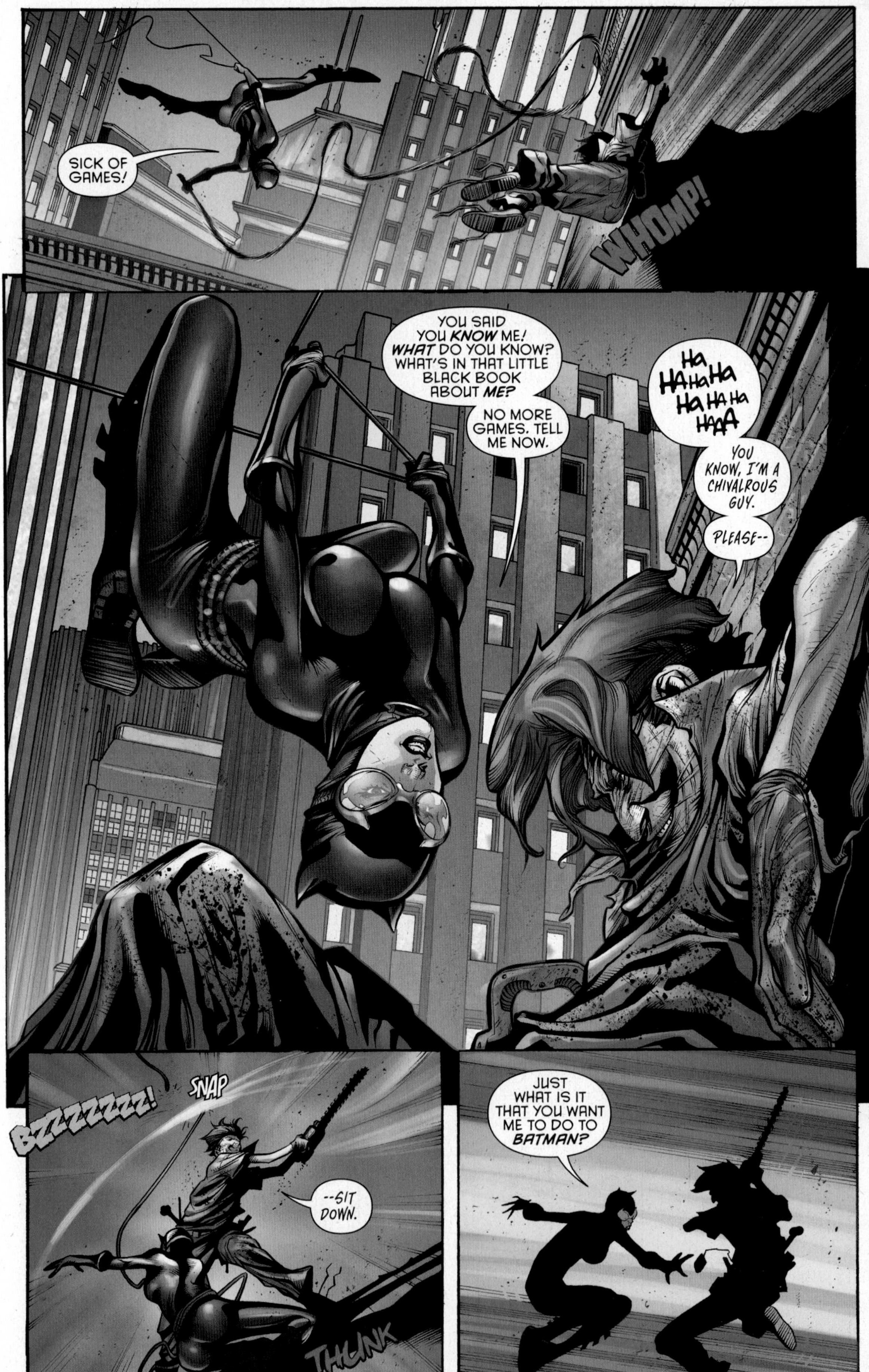
SICK OF GAMES!
WHOMP!
YOU SAID YOU KNOW ME! WHAT DO YOU KNOW? WHAT'S IN THAT LITTLE BLACK BOOK ABOUT ME?
NO MORE GAMES. TELL ME NOW.
HA HAHAHA HA HA HA HAAA
YOU KNOW, I'M A CHIVALROUS GUY.
PLEASE--
BZZZZZZZZ!
SNAP
--SIT DOWN.
THUNK
JUST WHAT IS IT THAT YOU WANT ME TO DO TO BATMAN?

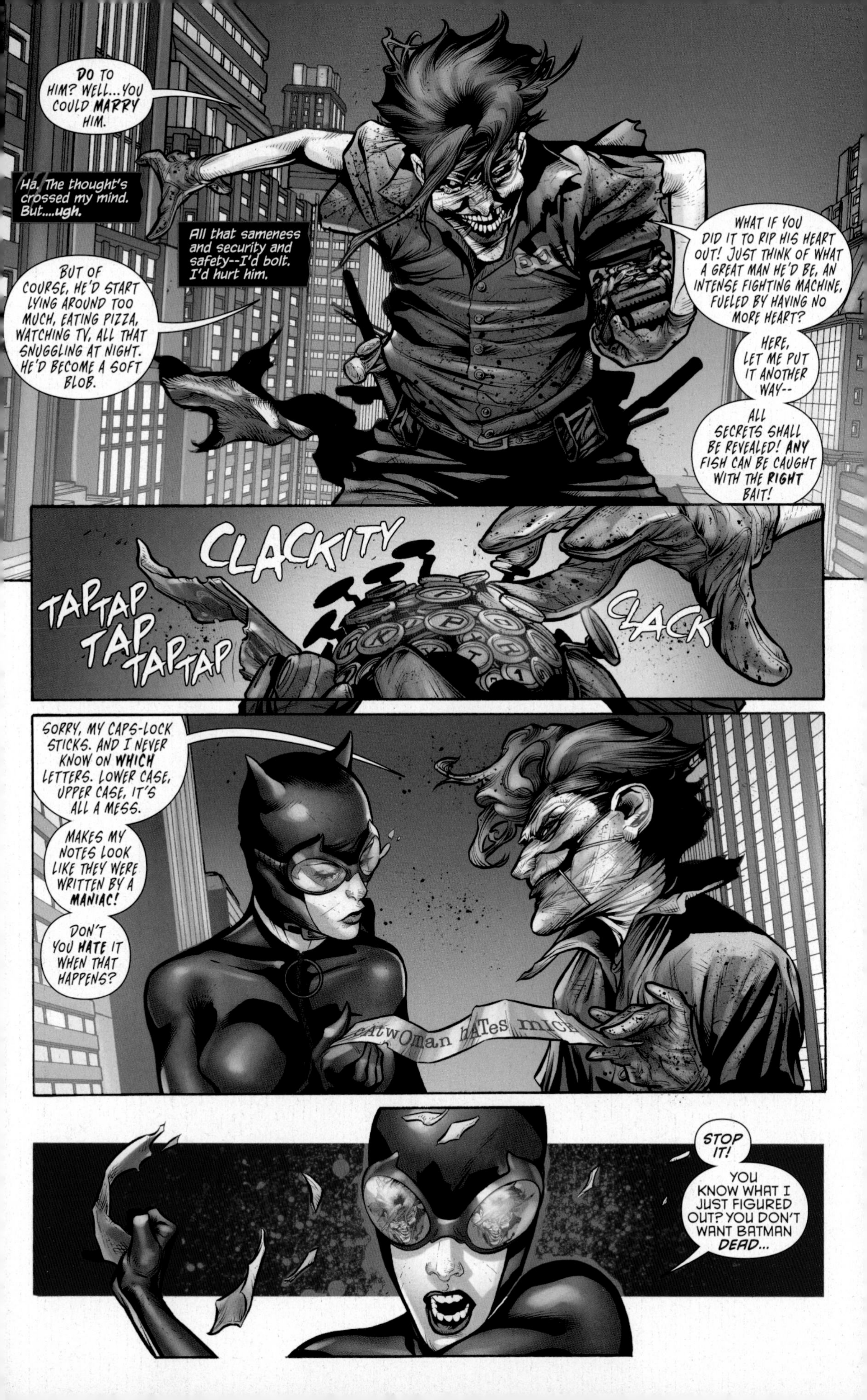
DO TO HIM? WELL...YOU COULD MARRY HIM.
Ha. The thought's crossed my mind. But....ugh.
All that sameness and security and safety--I'd bolt. I'd hurt him.
BUT OF COURSE, HE'D START LYING AROUND TOO MUCH, EATING PIZZA, WATCHING TV, ALL THAT SNUGGLING AT NIGHT. HE'D BECOME A SOFT BLOB.
WHAT IF YOU DID IT TO RIP HIS HEART OUT! JUST THINK OF WHAT A GREAT MAN HE'D BE, AN INTENSE FIGHTING MACHINE, FUELED BY HAVING NO MORE HEART?
HERE, LET ME PUT IT ANOTHER WAY--
ALL SECRETS SHALL BE REVEALED! ANY FISH CAN BE CAUGHT WITH THE RIGHT BAIT!
CLACKITY
TAP TAP TAP TAP TAP
CLACK
SORRY, MY CAPS-LOCK STICKS. AND I NEVER KNOW ON WHICH LETTERS. LOWER CASE, UPPER CASE, IT'S ALL A MESS.
MAKES MY NOTES LOOK LIKE THEY WERE WRITTEN BY A MANIAC!
DON'T YOU HATE IT WHEN THAT HAPPENS?
atwOman hATes mICE
STOP IT!
YOU KNOW WHAT I JUST FIGURED OUT? YOU DON'T WANT BATMAN DEAD...

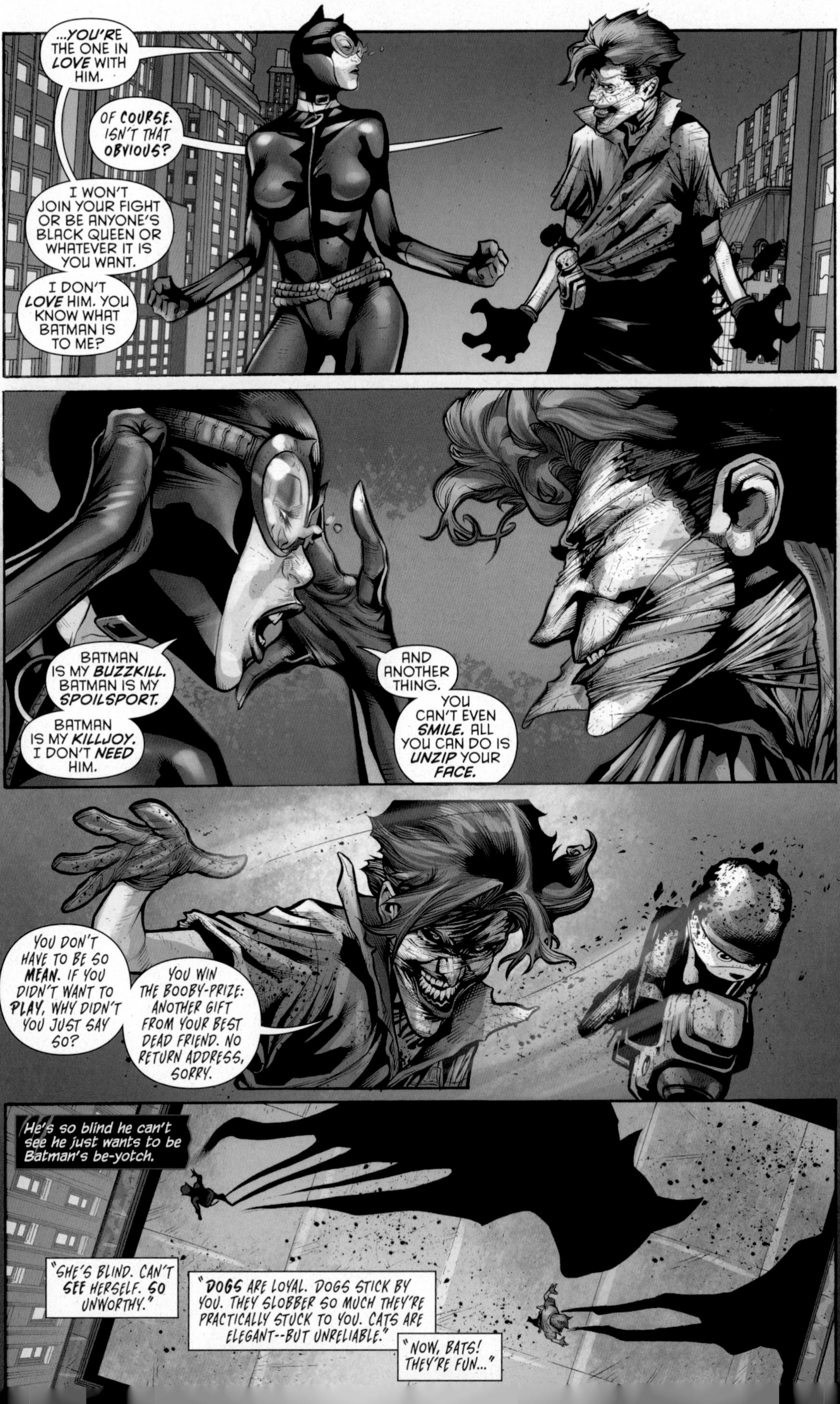
...YOU'RE THE ONE IN LOVE WITH HIM.
OF COURSE. ISN'T THAT OBVIOUS?
I WON'T JOIN YOUR FIGHT OR BE ANYONE'S BLACK QUEEN OR WHATEVER IT IS YOU WANT.
I DON'T LOVE HIM. YOU KNOW WHAT BATMAN IS TO ME?
BATMAN IS MY BUZZKILL. BATMAN IS MY SPOILSPORT.
BATMAN IS MY KILLJOY. I DON'T NEED HIM.
AND ANOTHER THING.
YOU CAN'T EVEN SMILE. ALL YOU CAN DO IS UNZIP YOUR FACE.
YOU DON'T HAVE TO BE SO MEAN. IF YOU DIDN'T WANT TO PLAY, WHY DIDN'T YOU JUST SAY SO?
YOU WIN THE BOOBY-PRIZE: ANOTHER GIFT FROM YOUR BEST DEAD FRIEND. NO RETURN ADDRESS, SORRY.
He's so blind he can't see he just wants to be Batman's be-yotch.
"SHE'S BLIND. CAN'T SEE HERSELF. SO UNWORTHY."
"DOGS ARE LOYAL. DOGS STICK BY YOU. THEY SLOBBER SO MUCH THEY'RE PRACTICALLY STUCK TO YOU. CATS ARE ELEGANT--BUT UNRELIABLE."
"NOW, BATS! THEY'RE FUN..."

PART THREE
HARLEY QUINN

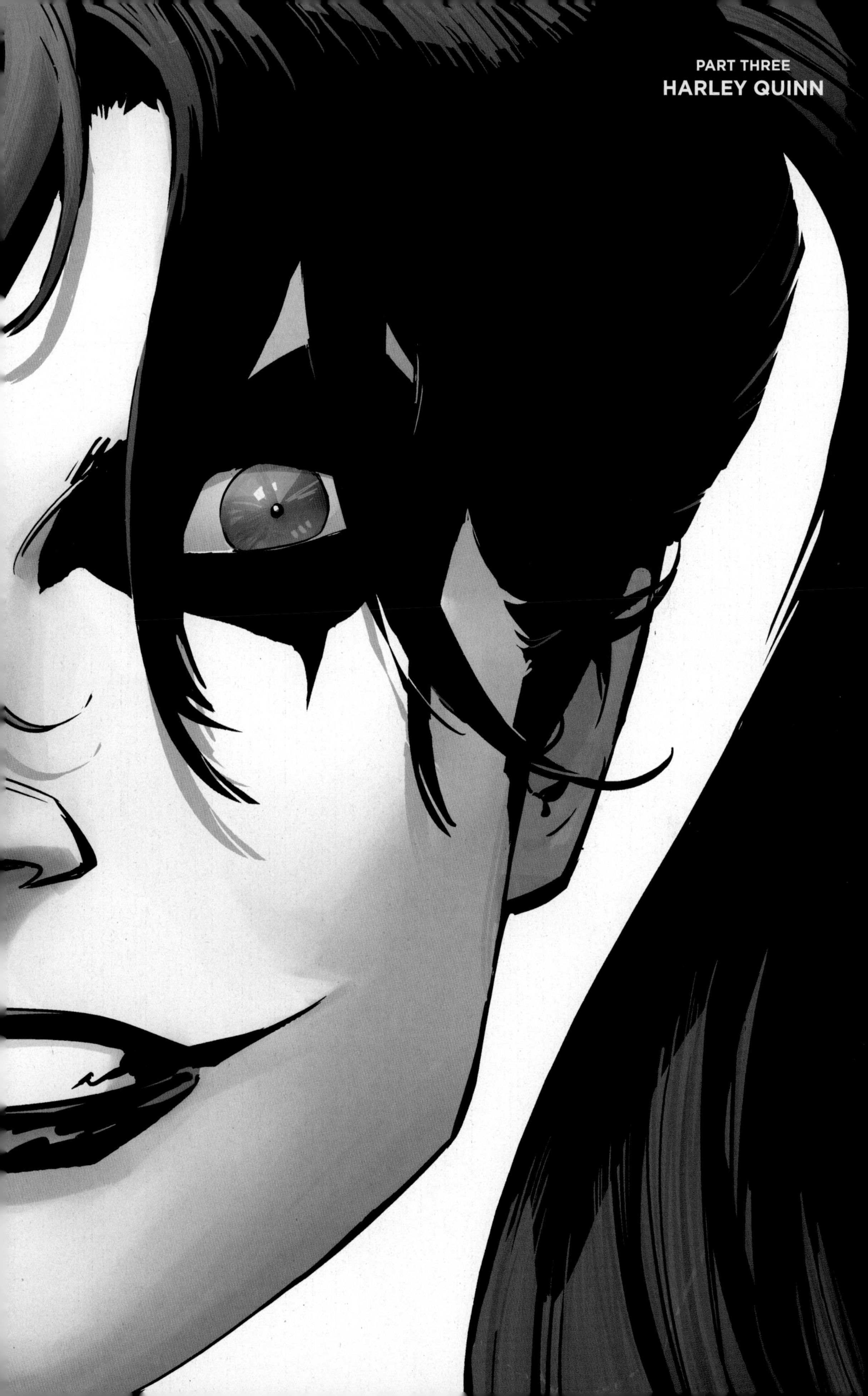

MATT YACKEY JOCK FCO PLASCENCIA colorists JARED K. FLETCHER SAL CIPRIANO RICHARD STARKINGS COMICRAFT'S JIMMY BETANCOURT letterers

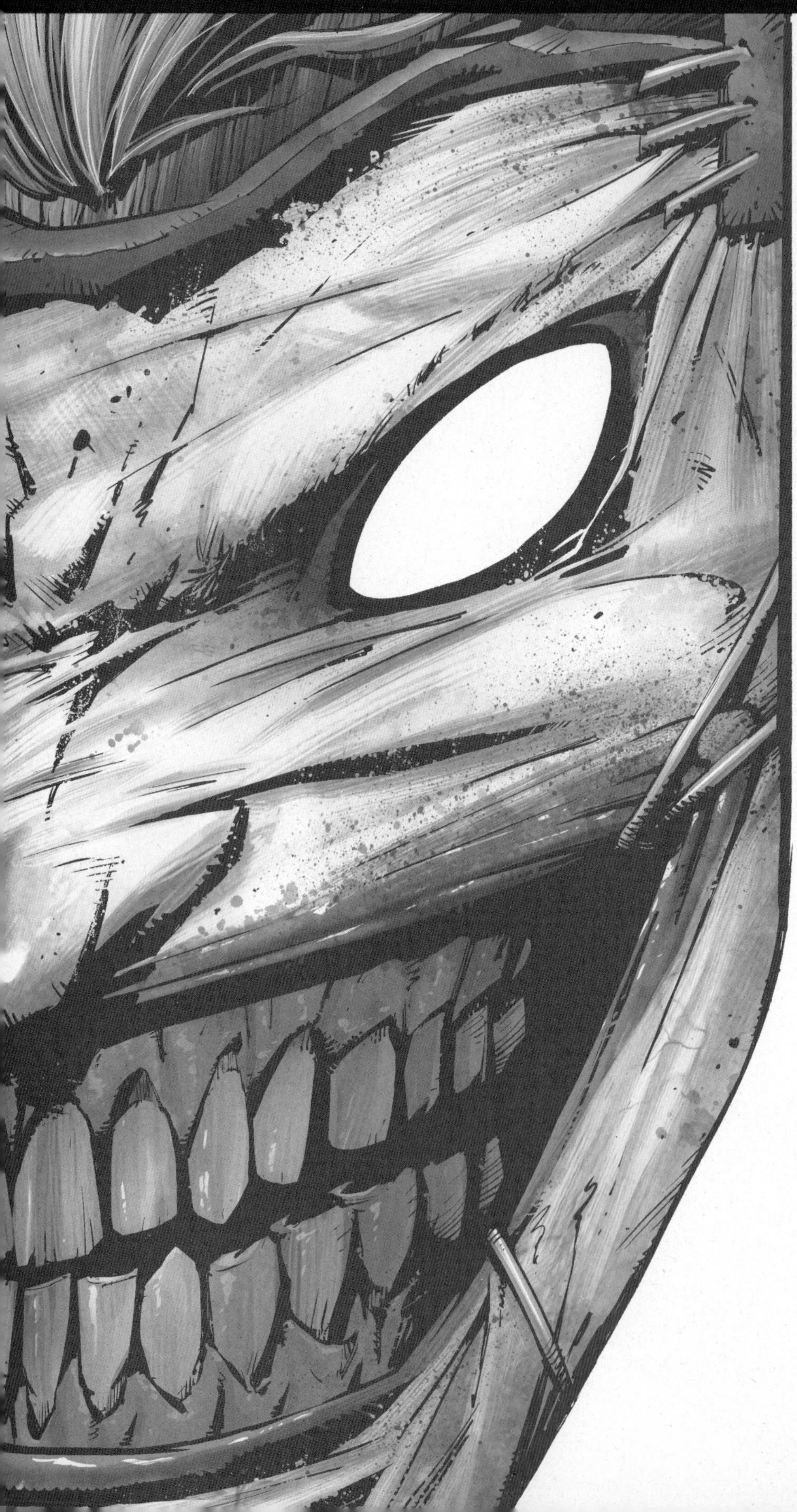

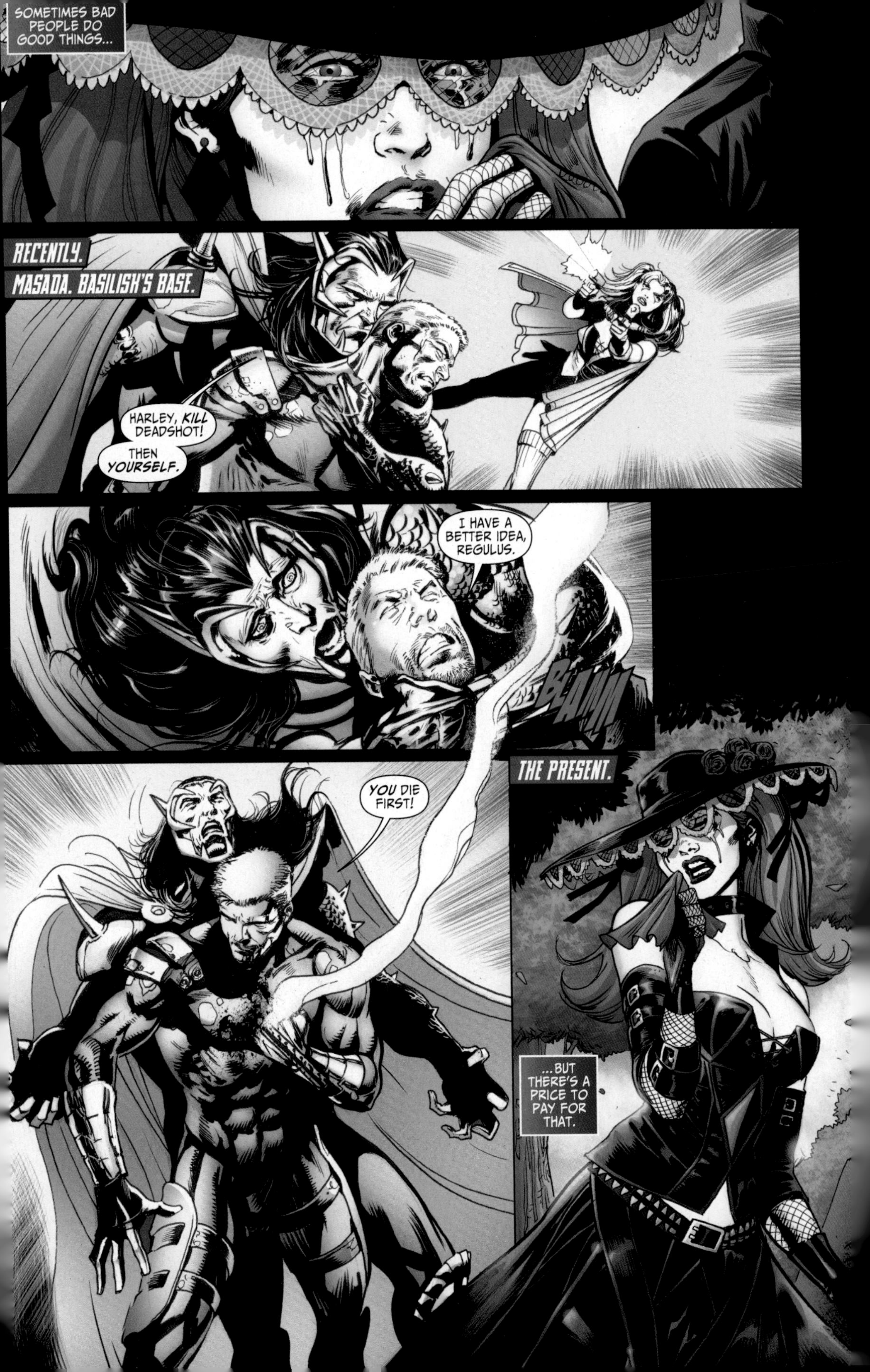

SOMETIMES BAD PEOPLE DO GOOD THINGS...
RECENTLY.
MASADA. BASILISK'S BASE.
HARLEY, KILL DEADSHOT!
THEN YOURSELF.
I HAVE A BETTER IDEA, REGULUS.
BLAM
YOU DIE FIRST!
THE PRESENT.
...BUT THERE'S A PRICE TO PAY FOR THAT.

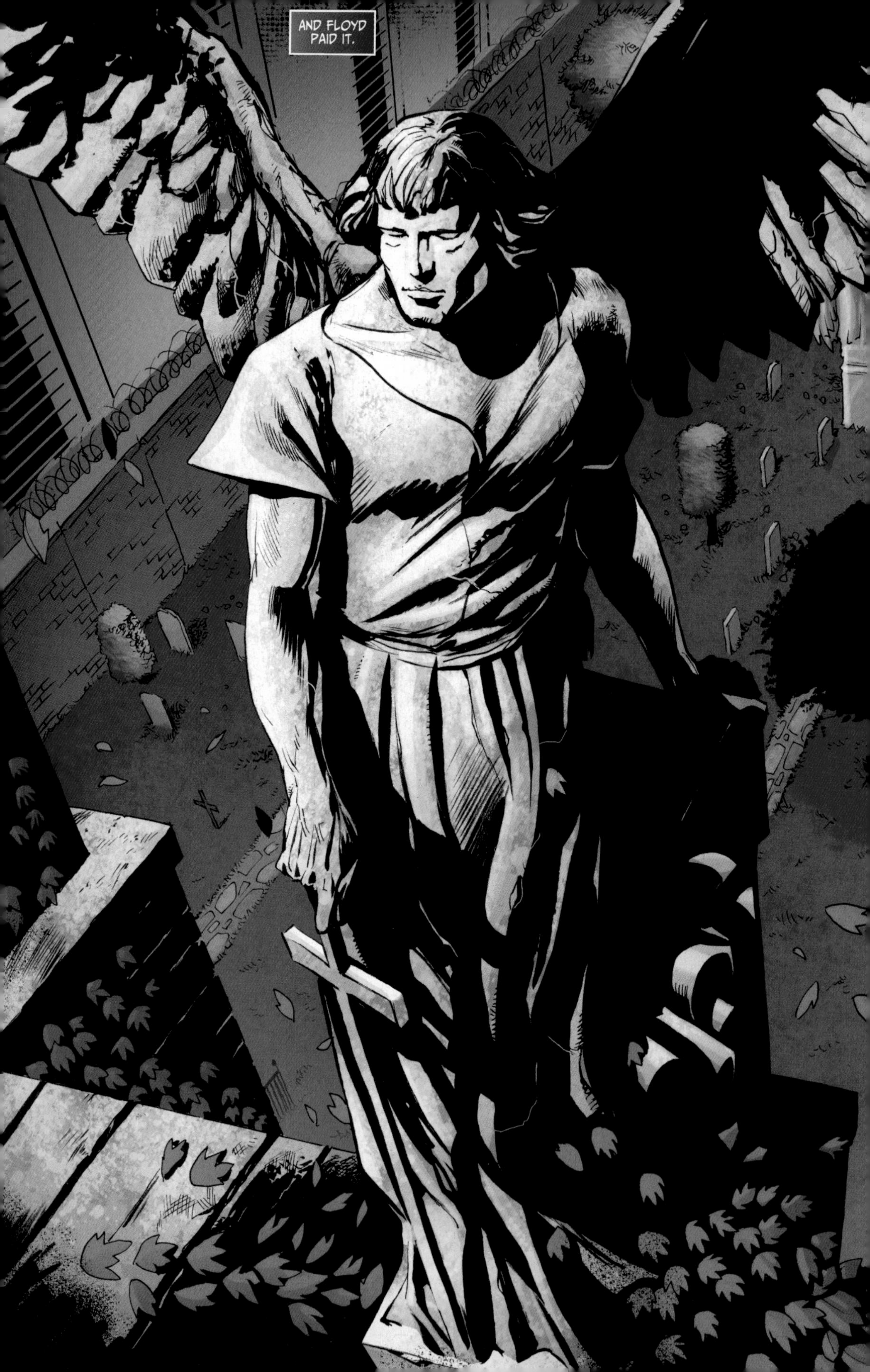
AND FLOYD PAID IT.

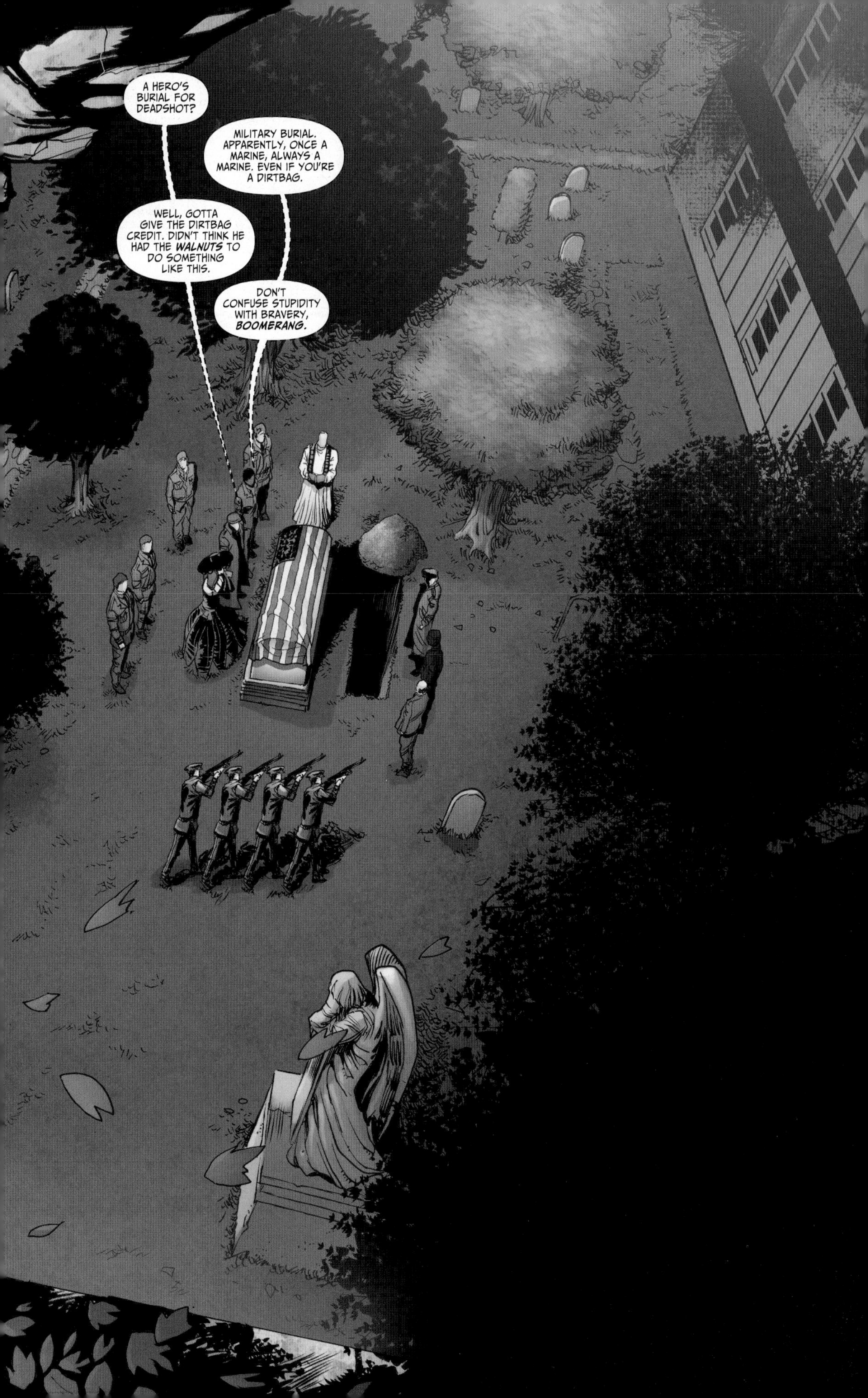
A HERO'S BURIAL FOR DEADSHOT?
MILITARY BURIAL. APPARENTLY, ONCE A MARINE, ALWAYS A MARINE. EVEN IF YOU'RE A DIRTBAG.
WELL, GOTTA GIVE THE DIRTBAG CREDIT. DIDN'T THINK HE HAD THE *WALNUTS* TO DO SOMETHING LIKE THIS.
DON'T CONFUSE STUPIDITY WITH BRAVERY, *BOOMERANG*.

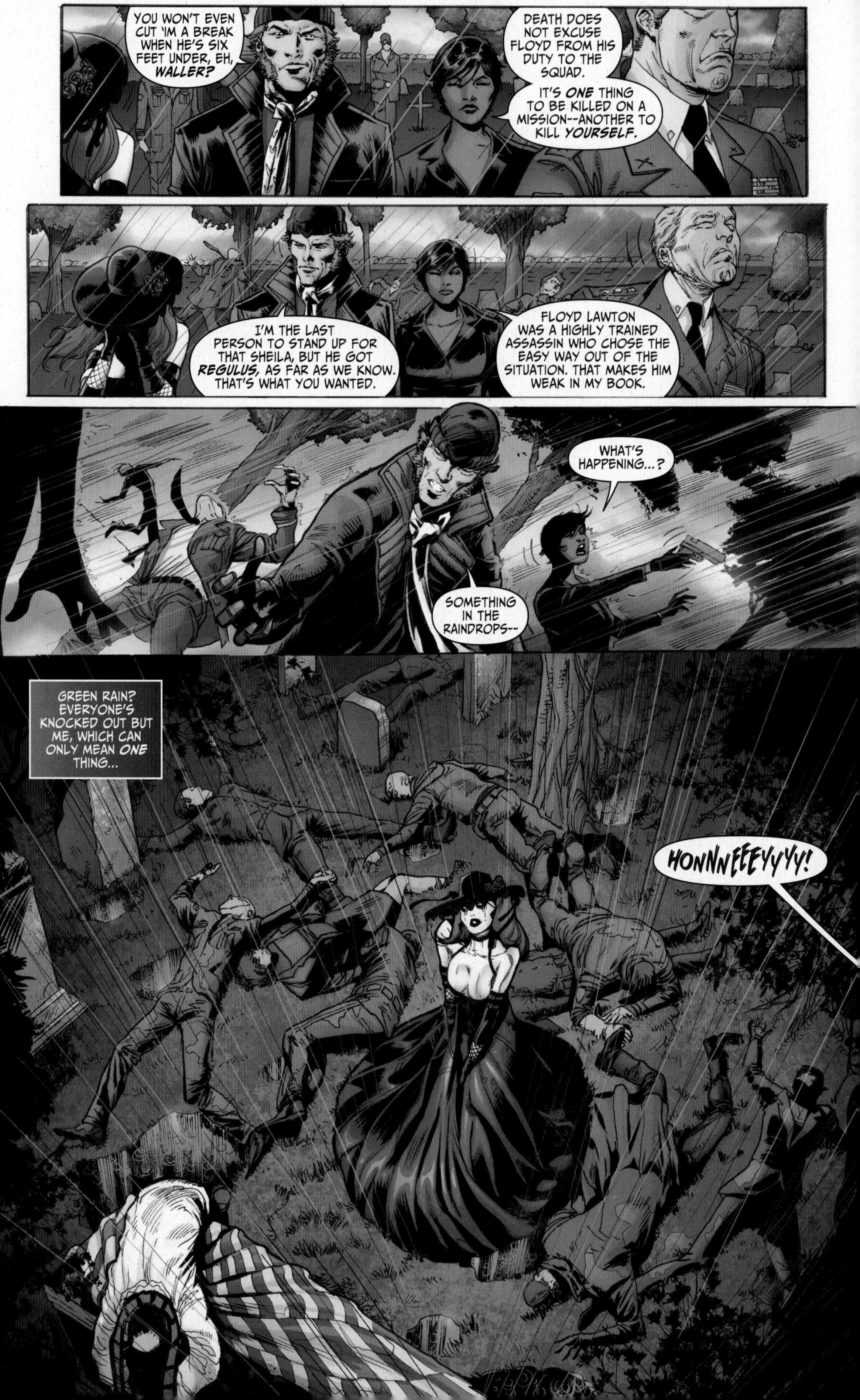

YOU WON'T EVEN CUT 'IM A BREAK WHEN HE'S SIX FEET UNDER, EH, WALLER?
DEATH DOES NOT EXCUSE FLOYD FROM HIS DUTY TO THE SQUAD.
IT'S ONE THING TO BE KILLED ON A MISSION--ANOTHER TO KILL YOURSELF.
I'M THE LAST PERSON TO STAND UP FOR THAT SHEILA, BUT HE GOT REGULUS, AS FAR AS WE KNOW. THAT'S WHAT YOU WANTED.
FLOYD LAWTON WAS A HIGHLY TRAINED ASSASSIN WHO CHOSE THE EASY WAY OUT OF THE SITUATION. THAT MAKES HIM WEAK IN MY BOOK.
WHAT'S HAPPENING...?
SOMETHING IN THE RAINDROPS--
GREEN RAIN? EVERYONE'S KNOCKED OUT BUT ME, WHICH CAN ONLY MEAN ONE THING...
HONNNEEEYYYY!

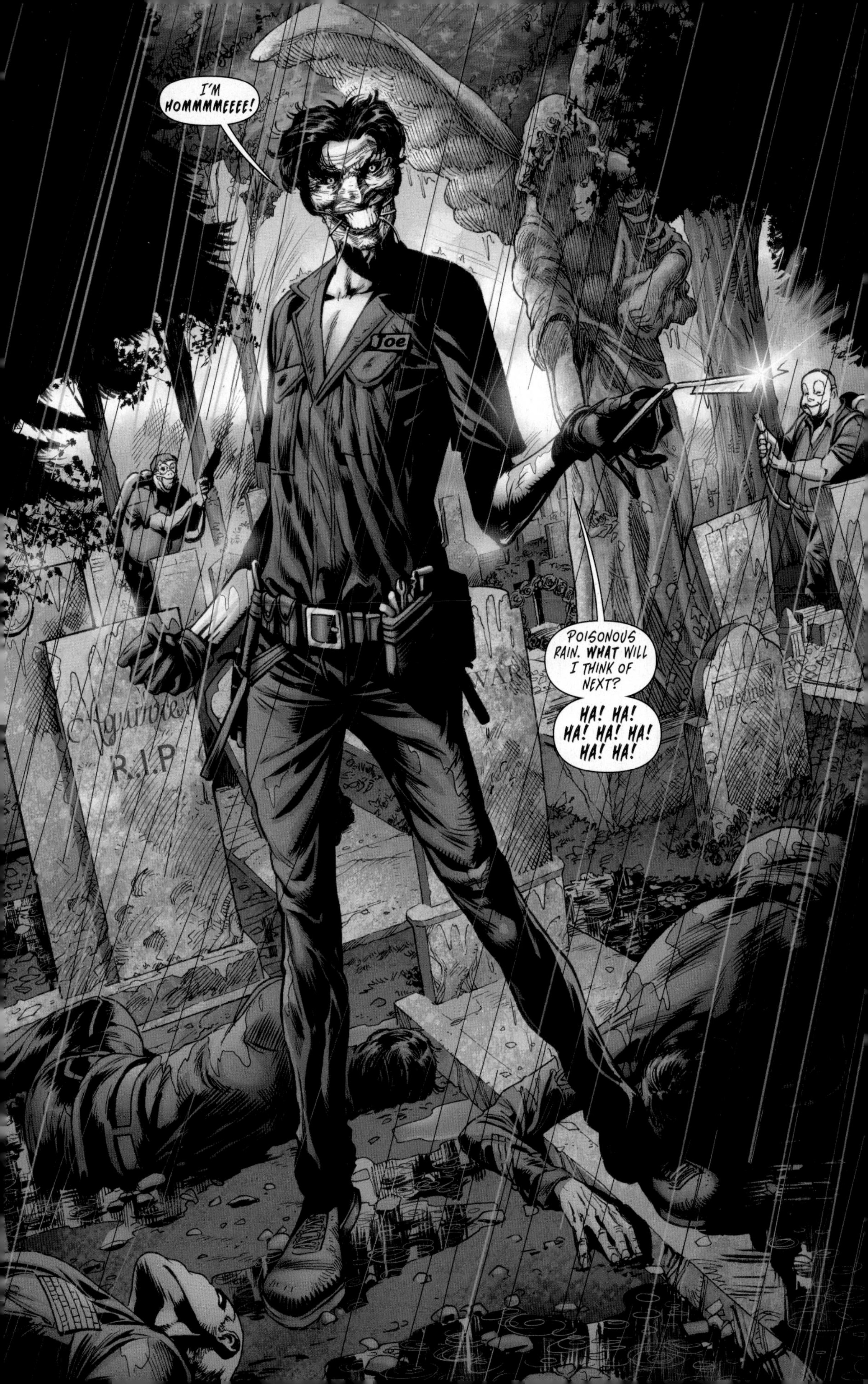
I'M HOMMMMEEEE!
POISONOUS RAIN. WHAT WILL I THINK OF NEXT?
HA! HA! HA! HA! HA! HA! HA!
Joe
R.I.P

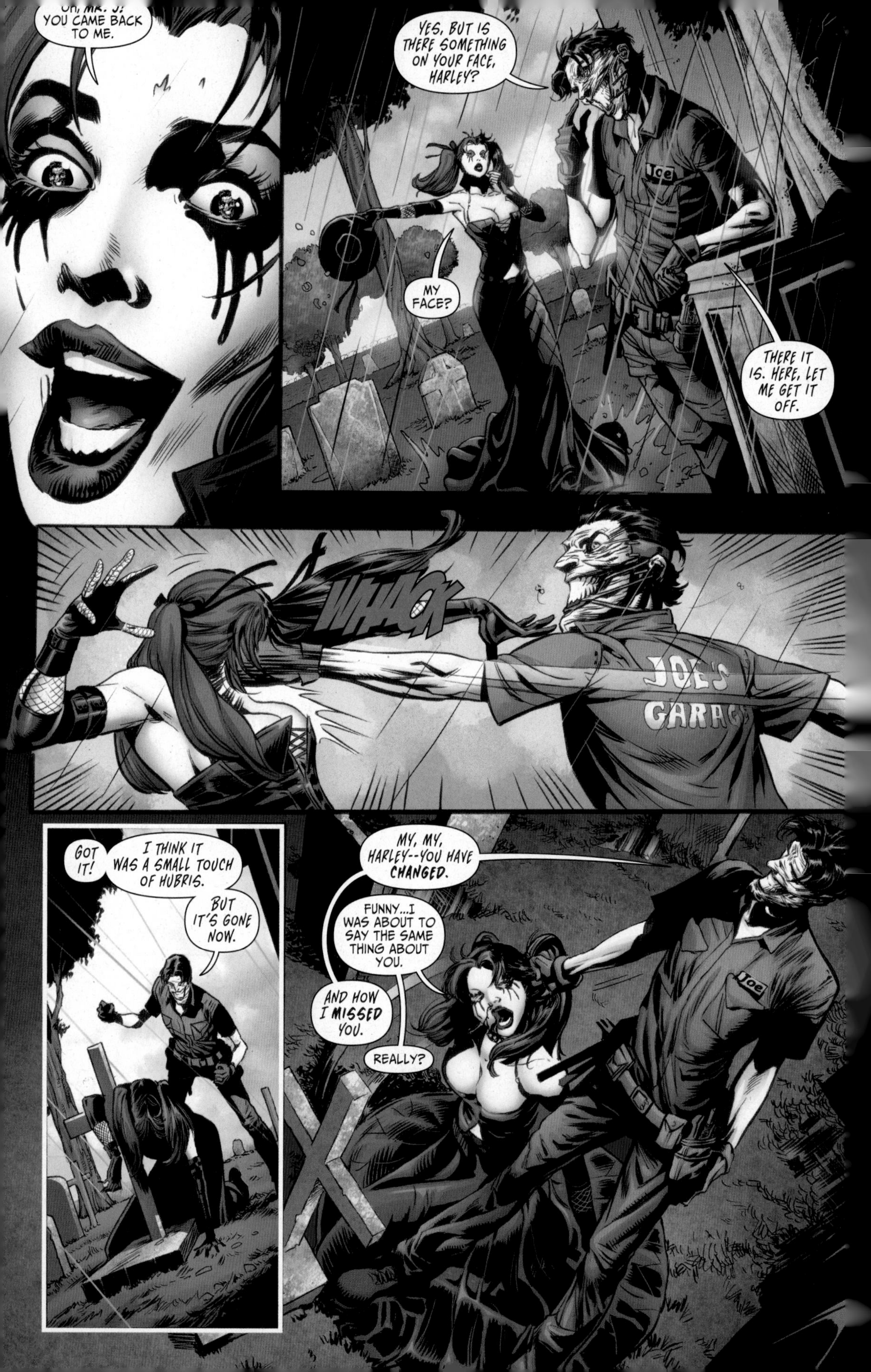
OH, MR. J. YOU CAME BACK TO ME.
YES, BUT IS THERE SOMETHING ON YOUR FACE, HARLEY?
MY FACE?
THERE IT IS. HERE, LET ME GET IT OFF.
WHACK
JOE'S GARAGE
GOT IT!
I THINK IT WAS A SMALL TOUCH OF HUBRIS.
BUT IT'S GONE NOW.
MY, MY, HARLEY--YOU HAVE CHANGED.
FUNNY...I WAS ABOUT TO SAY THE SAME THING ABOUT YOU.
AND HOW I MISSED YOU.
REALLY?

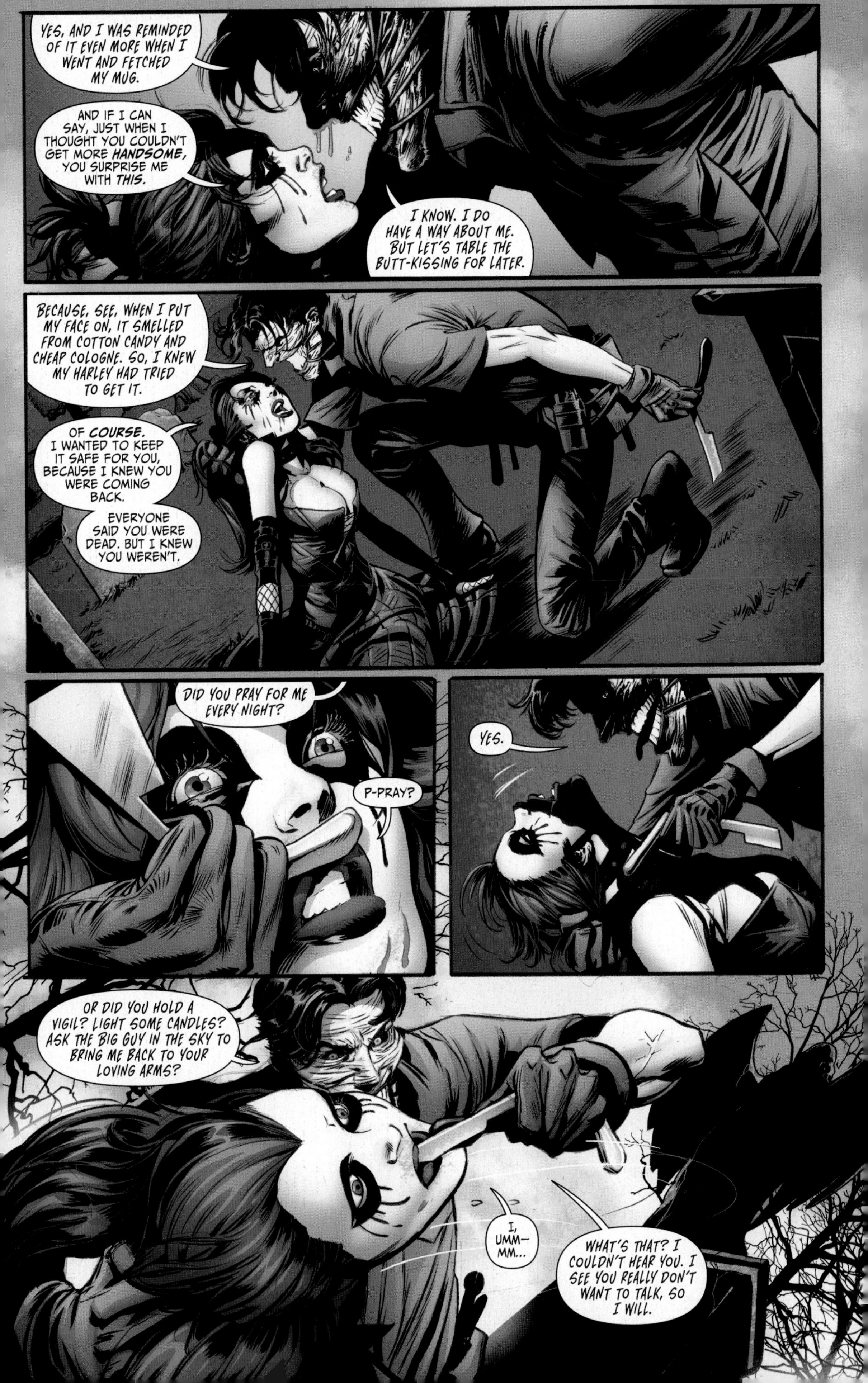
YES, AND I WAS REMINDED OF IT EVEN MORE WHEN I WENT AND FETCHED MY MUG.
AND IF I CAN SAY, JUST WHEN I THOUGHT YOU COULDN'T GET MORE HANDSOME, YOU SURPRISE ME WITH THIS.
I KNOW. I DO HAVE A WAY ABOUT ME. BUT LET'S TABLE THE BUTT-KISSING FOR LATER.
BECAUSE, SEE, WHEN I PUT MY FACE ON, IT SMELLED FROM COTTON CANDY AND CHEAP COLOGNE. SO, I KNEW MY HARLEY HAD TRIED TO GET IT.
OF COURSE. I WANTED TO KEEP IT SAFE FOR YOU, BECAUSE I KNEW YOU WERE COMING BACK.
EVERYONE SAID YOU WERE DEAD. BUT I KNEW YOU WEREN'T.
DID YOU PRAY FOR ME EVERY NIGHT?
P-PRAY?
YES.
OR DID YOU HOLD A VIGIL? LIGHT SOME CANDLES? ASK THE BIG GUY IN THE SKY TO BRING ME BACK TO YOUR LOVING ARMS?
I, UMM-MM...
WHAT'S THAT? I COULDN'T HEAR YOU. I SEE YOU REALLY DON'T WANT TO TALK, SO I WILL.

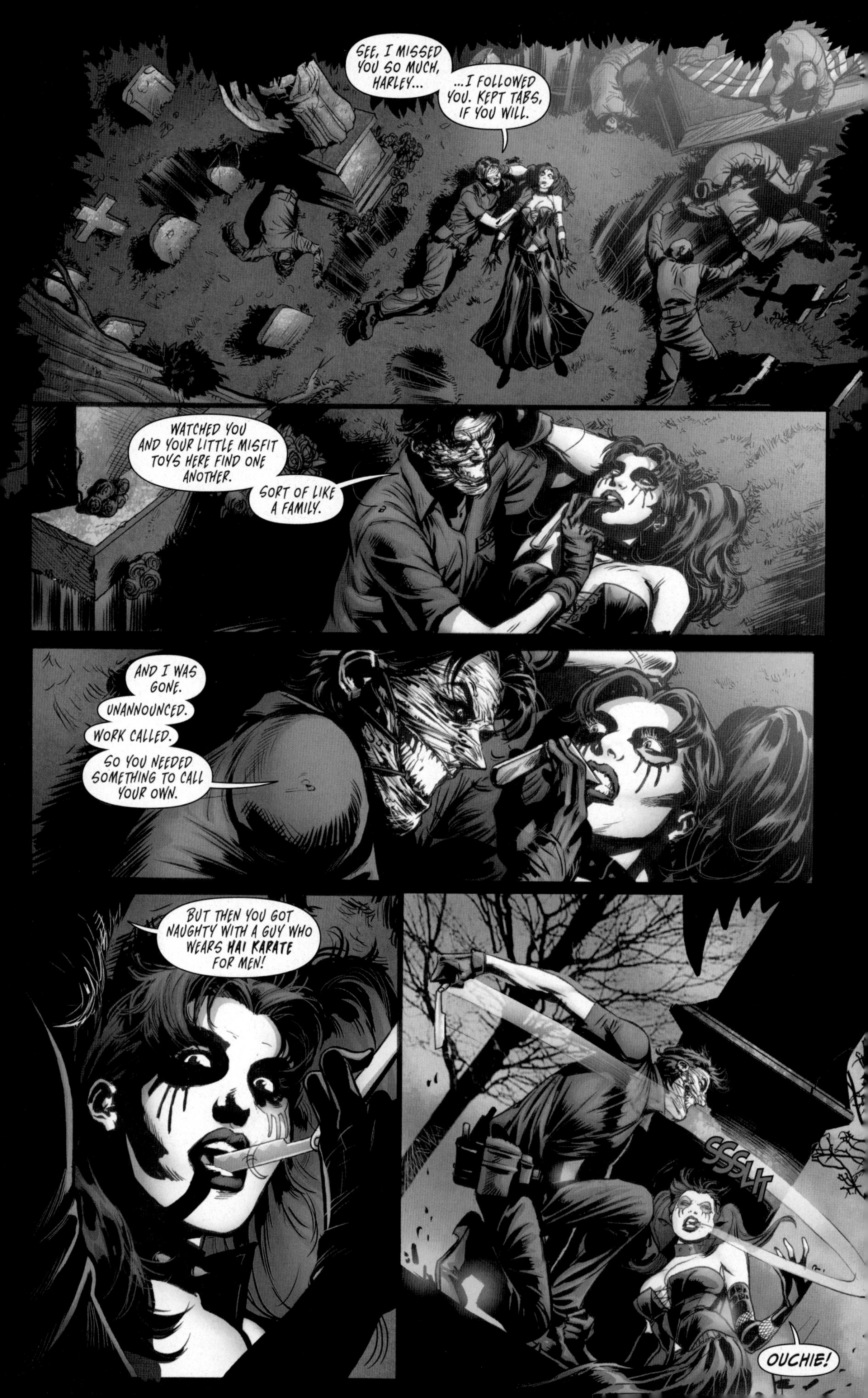
SEE, I MISSED YOU SO MUCH, HARLEY...
...I FOLLOWED YOU. KEPT TABS, IF YOU WILL.
WATCHED YOU AND YOUR LITTLE MISFIT TOYS HERE FIND ONE ANOTHER.
SORT OF LIKE A FAMILY.
AND I WAS GONE.
UNANNOUNCED.
WORK CALLED.
SO YOU NEEDED SOMETHING TO CALL YOUR OWN.
BUT THEN YOU GOT NAUGHTY WITH A GUY WHO WEARS HAI KARATE FOR MEN!
SSSLK
OUCHIE!

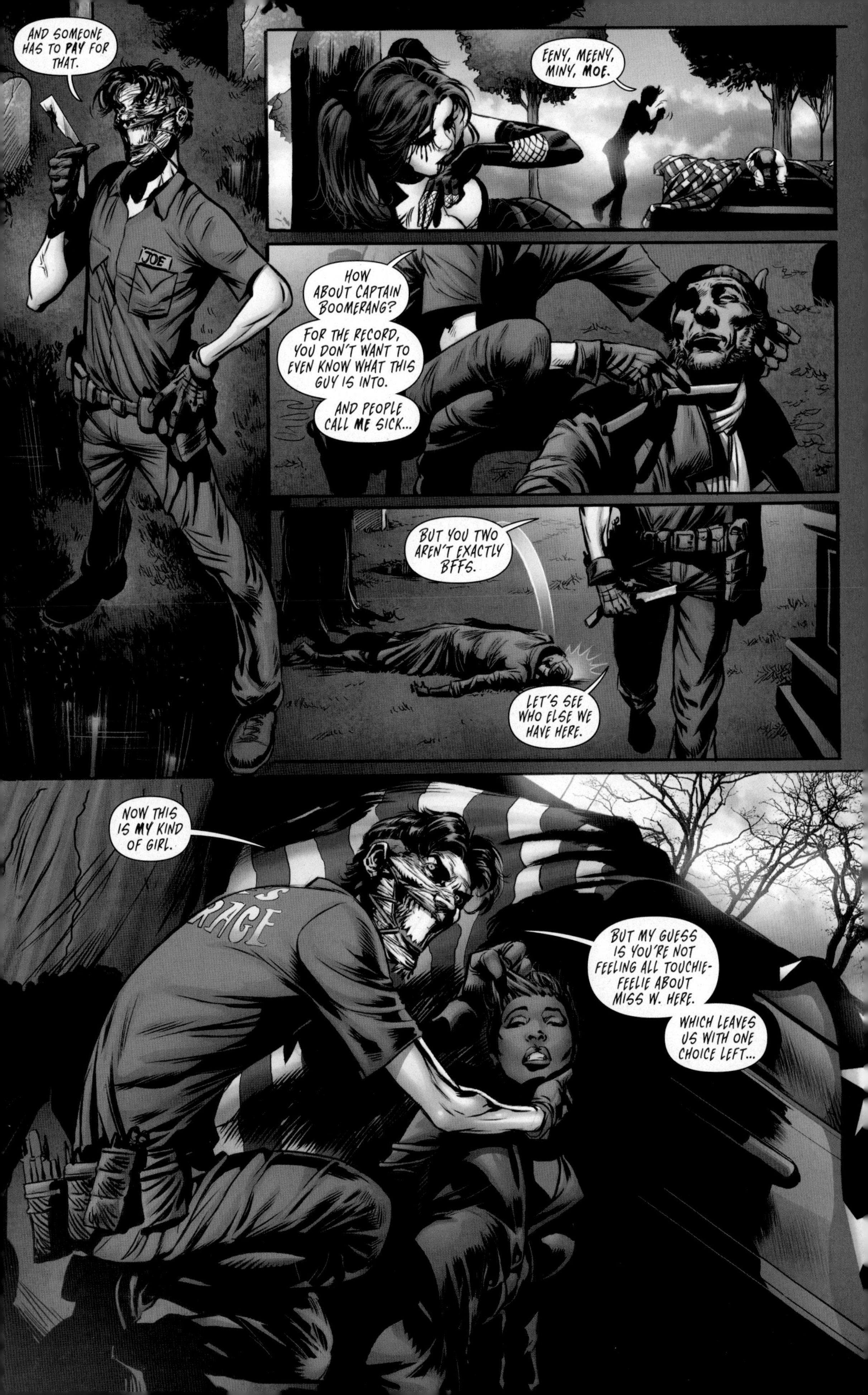
AND SOMEONE HAS TO PAY FOR THAT.
EENY, MEENY, MINY, MOE.
HOW ABOUT CAPTAIN BOOMERANG?
FOR THE RECORD, YOU DON'T WANT TO EVEN KNOW WHAT THIS GUY IS INTO.
AND PEOPLE CALL ME SICK...
BUT YOU TWO AREN'T EXACTLY BFFS.
LET'S SEE WHO ELSE WE HAVE HERE.
NOW THIS IS MY KIND OF GIRL.
BUT MY GUESS IS YOU'RE NOT FEELING ALL TOUCHIE-FEELIE ABOUT MISS W. HERE.
WHICH LEAVES US WITH ONE CHOICE LEFT...
JOE

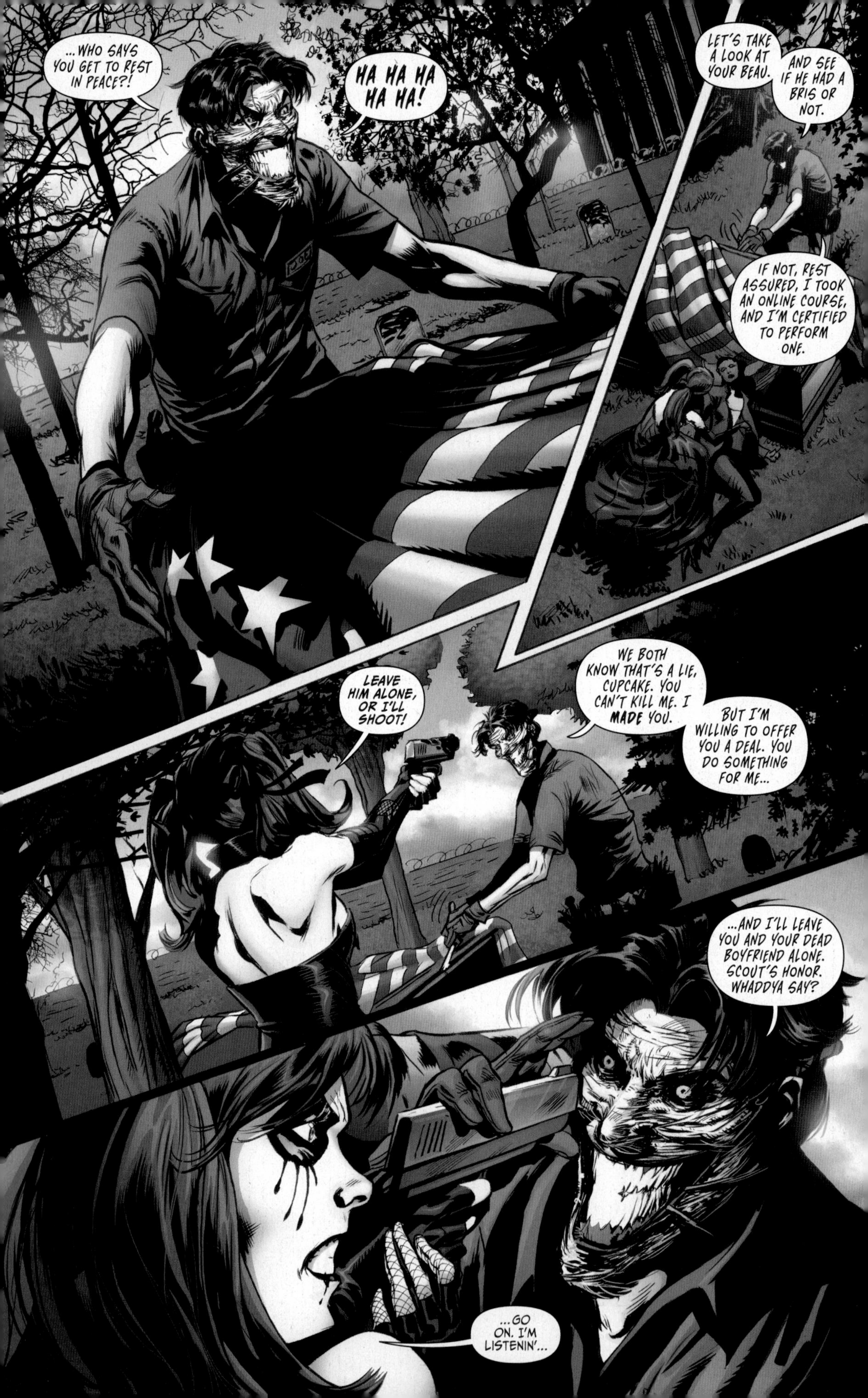
...WHO SAYS YOU GET TO REST IN PEACE?!
HA HA HA HA HA!
LET'S TAKE A LOOK AT YOUR BEAU.
AND SEE IF HE HAD A BRIS OR NOT.
IF NOT, REST ASSURED, I TOOK AN ONLINE COURSE, AND I'M CERTIFIED TO PERFORM ONE.
LEAVE HIM ALONE, OR I'LL SHOOT!
WE BOTH KNOW THAT'S A LIE, CUPCAKE. YOU CAN'T KILL ME. I MADE YOU.
BUT I'M WILLING TO OFFER YOU A DEAL. YOU DO SOMETHING FOR ME...
...AND I'LL LEAVE YOU AND YOUR DEAD BOYFRIEND ALONE. SCOUT'S HONOR. WHADDYA SAY?
...GO ON. I'M LISTENIN'...

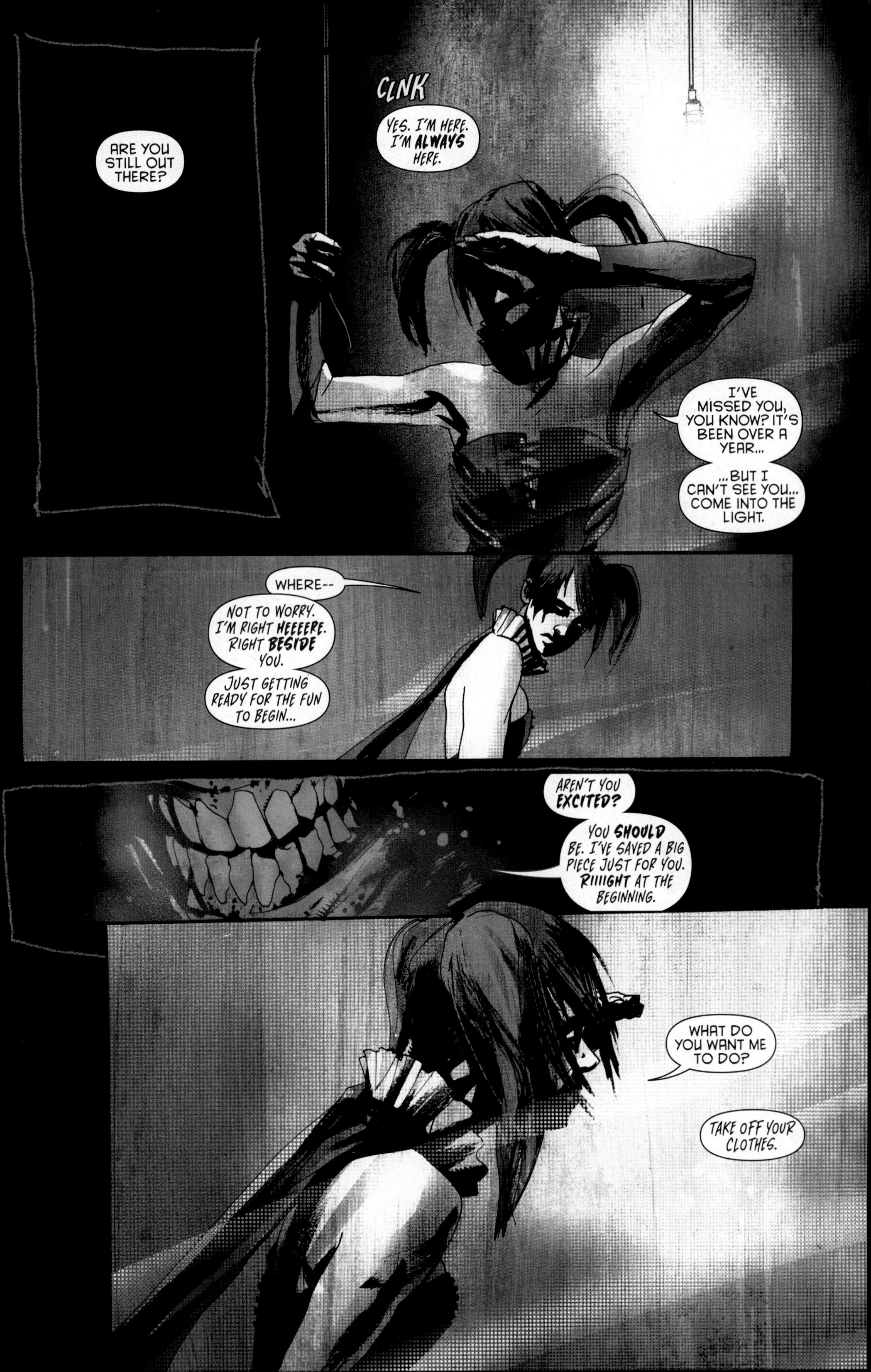
ARE YOU STILL OUT THERE?
CLNK
YES. I'M HERE. I'M ALWAYS HERE.
I'VE MISSED YOU, YOU KNOW? IT'S BEEN OVER A YEAR...
...BUT I CAN'T SEE YOU... COME INTO THE LIGHT.
WHERE--
NOT TO WORRY. I'M RIGHT HEEEERE. RIGHT BESIDE YOU.
JUST GETTING READY FOR THE FUN TO BEGIN...
AREN'T YOU EXCITED?
YOU SHOULD BE. I'VE SAVED A BIG PIECE JUST FOR YOU. RIIIIGHT AT THE BEGINNING.
WHAT DO YOU WANT ME TO DO?
TAKE OFF YOUR CLOTHES.

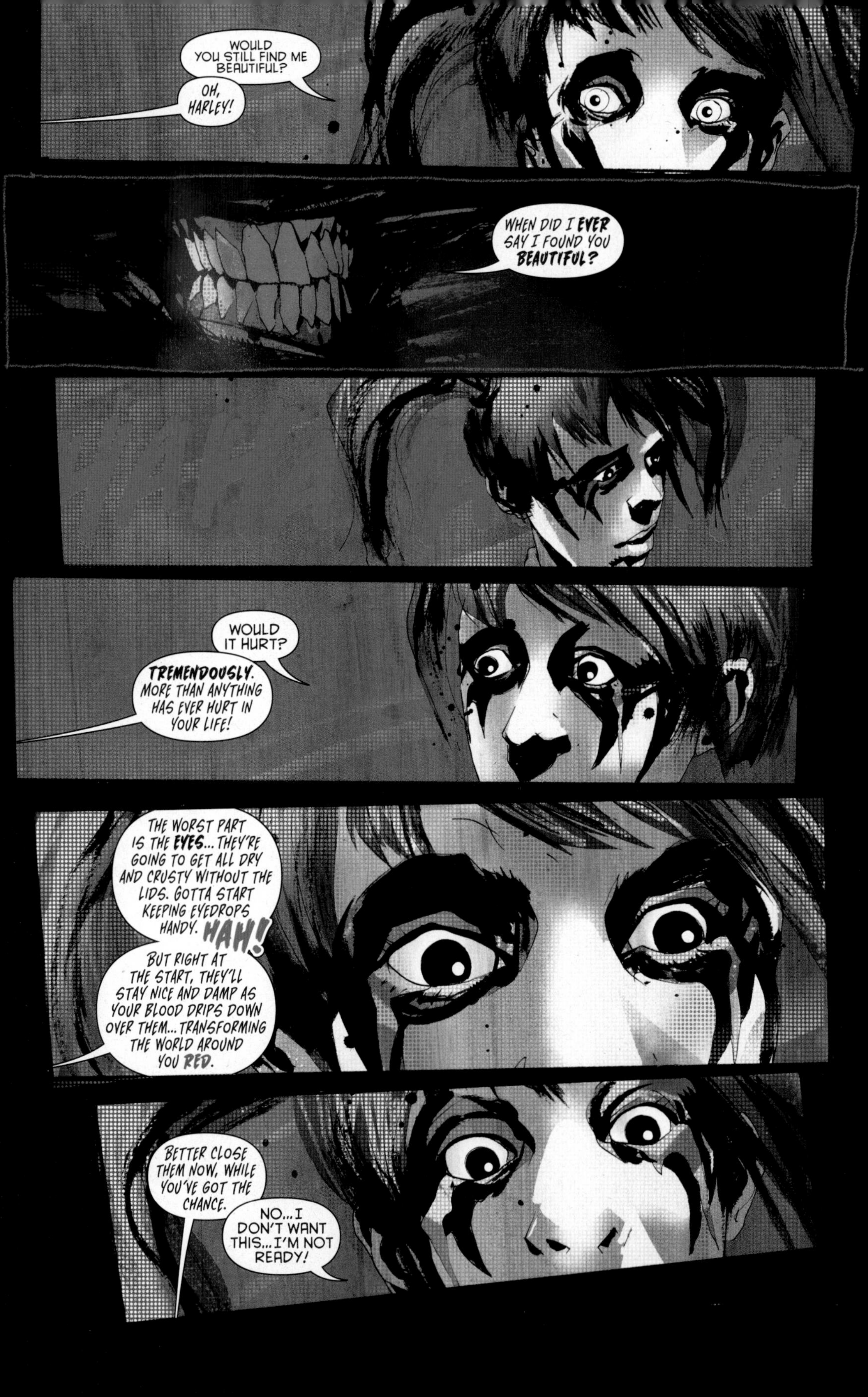
WOULD YOU STILL FIND ME BEAUTIFUL?
OH, HARLEY!
WHEN DID I EVER SAY I FOUND YOU BEAUTIFUL?
WOULD IT HURT?
TREMENDOUSLY. MORE THAN ANYTHING HAS EVER HURT IN YOUR LIFE!
THE WORST PART IS THE EYES... THEY'RE GOING TO GET ALL DRY AND CRUSTY WITHOUT THE LIDS. GOTTA START KEEPING EYEDROPS HANDY. HAH!
BUT RIGHT AT THE START, THEY'LL STAY NICE AND DAMP AS YOUR BLOOD DRIPS DOWN OVER THEM... TRANSFORMING THE WORLD AROUND YOU RED.
BETTER CLOSE THEM NOW, WHILE YOU'VE GOT THE CHANCE.
NO... I DON'T WANT THIS... I'M NOT READY!

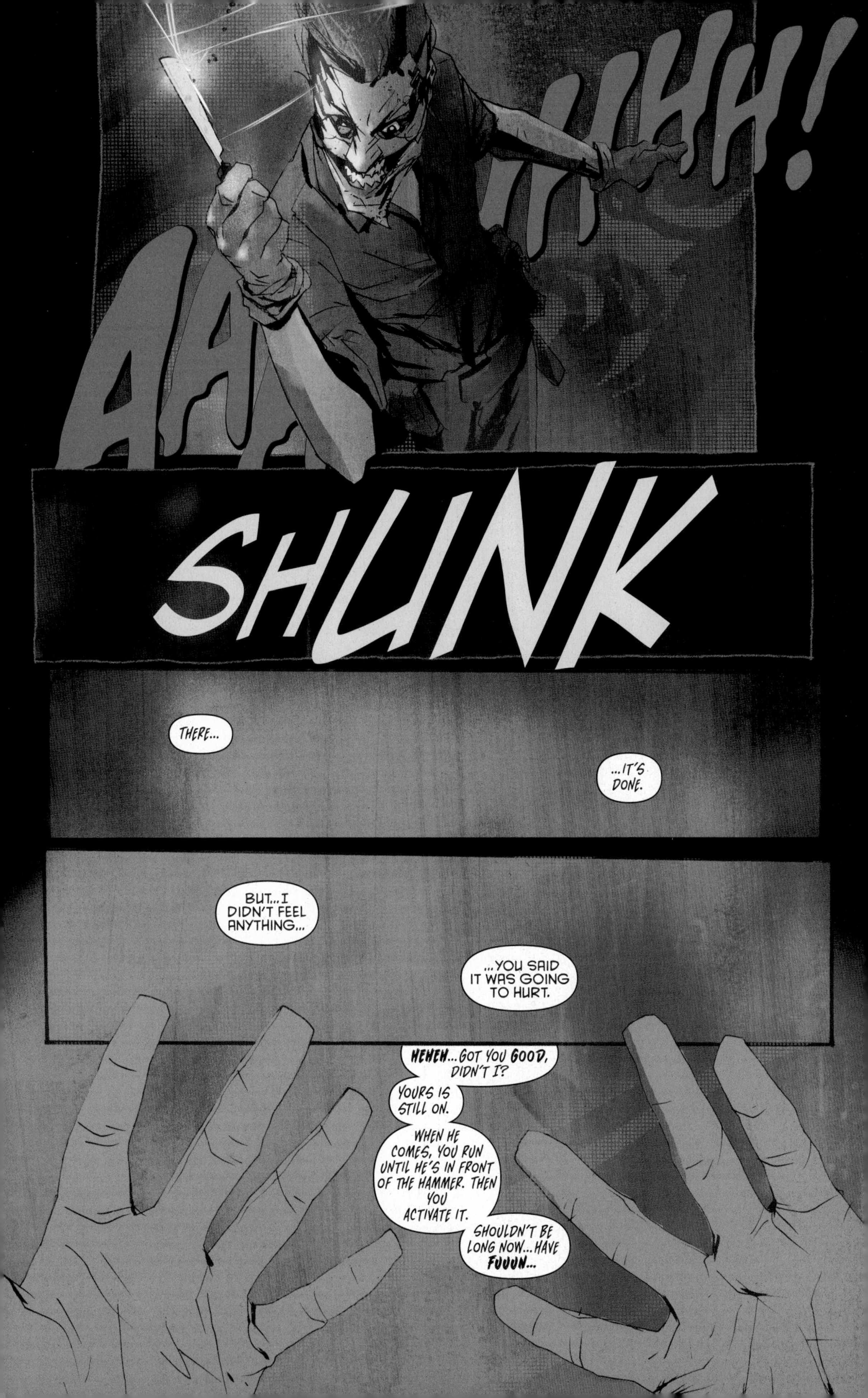
AAAHHH!
SHUNK
THERE...
...IT'S DONE.
BUT...I DIDN'T FEEL ANYTHING...
...YOU SAID IT WAS GOING TO HURT.
HEHEH...GOT YOU GOOD, DIDN'T I?
YOURS IS STILL ON.
WHEN HE COMES, YOU RUN UNTIL HE'S IN FRONT OF THE HAMMER. THEN YOU ACTIVATE IT.
SHOULDN'T BE LONG NOW...HAVE FUUUN...

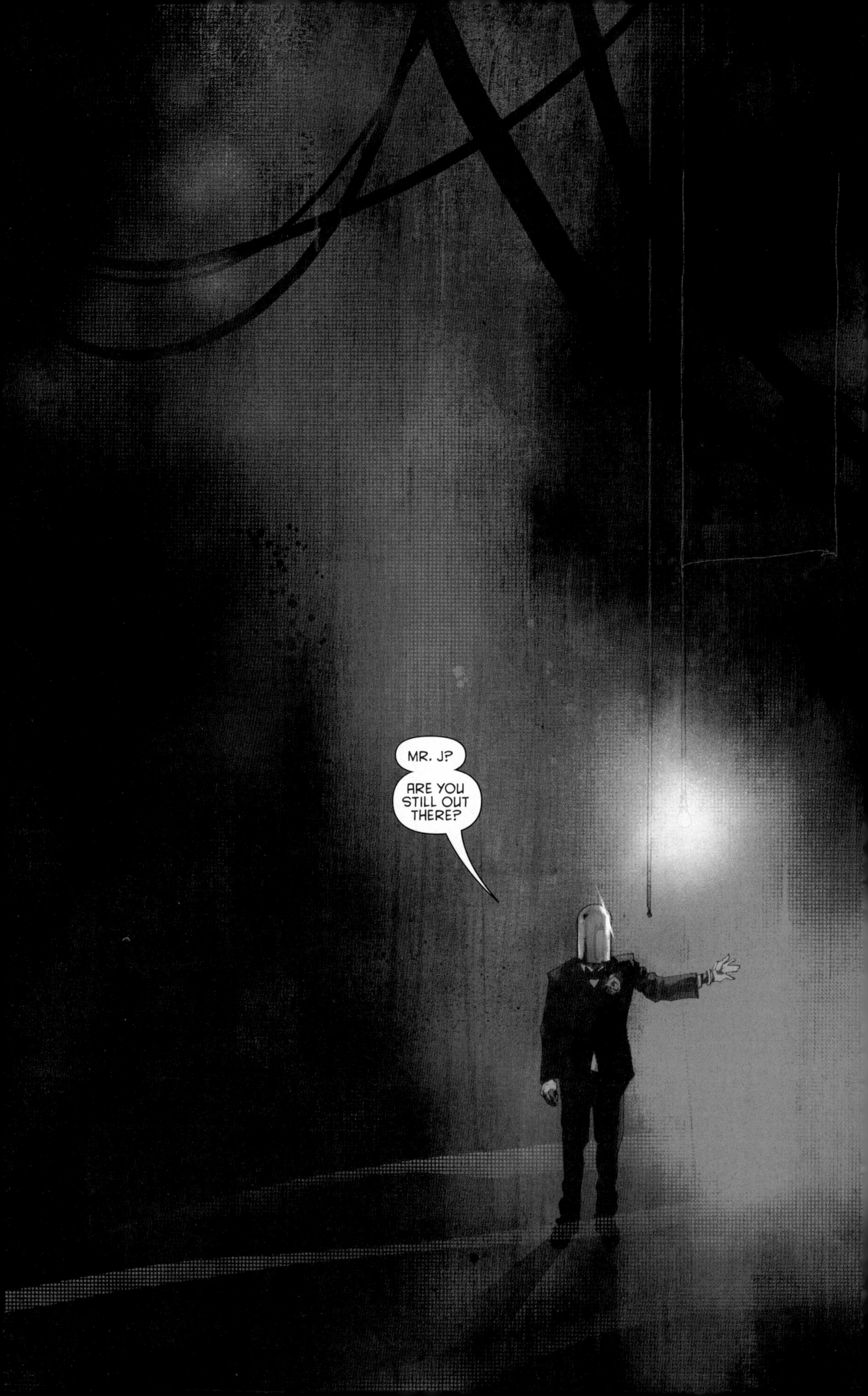
MR. J?
ARE YOU STILL OUT THERE?

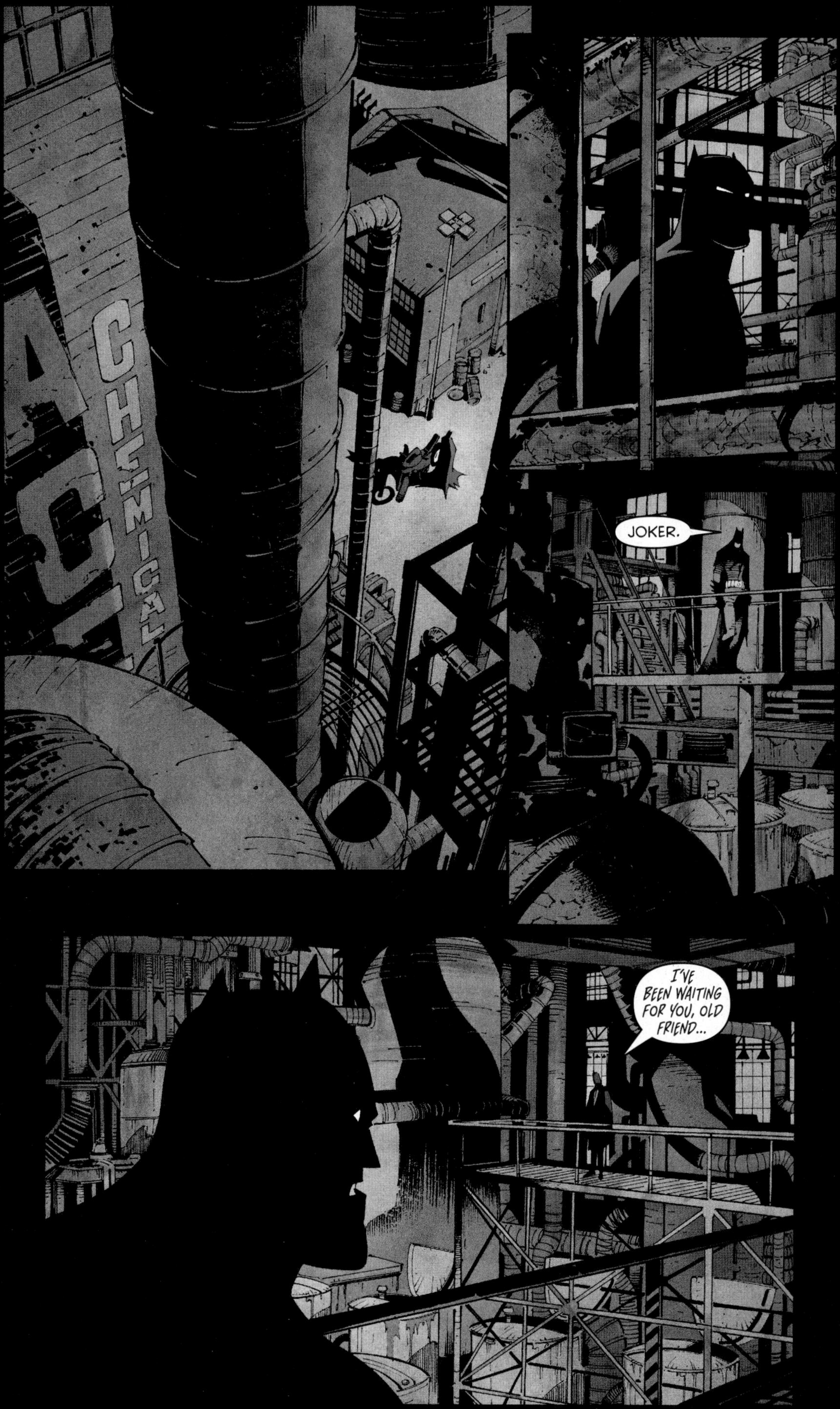
CHEMICAL
JOKER.
I'VE BEEN WAITING FOR YOU, OLD FRIEND...

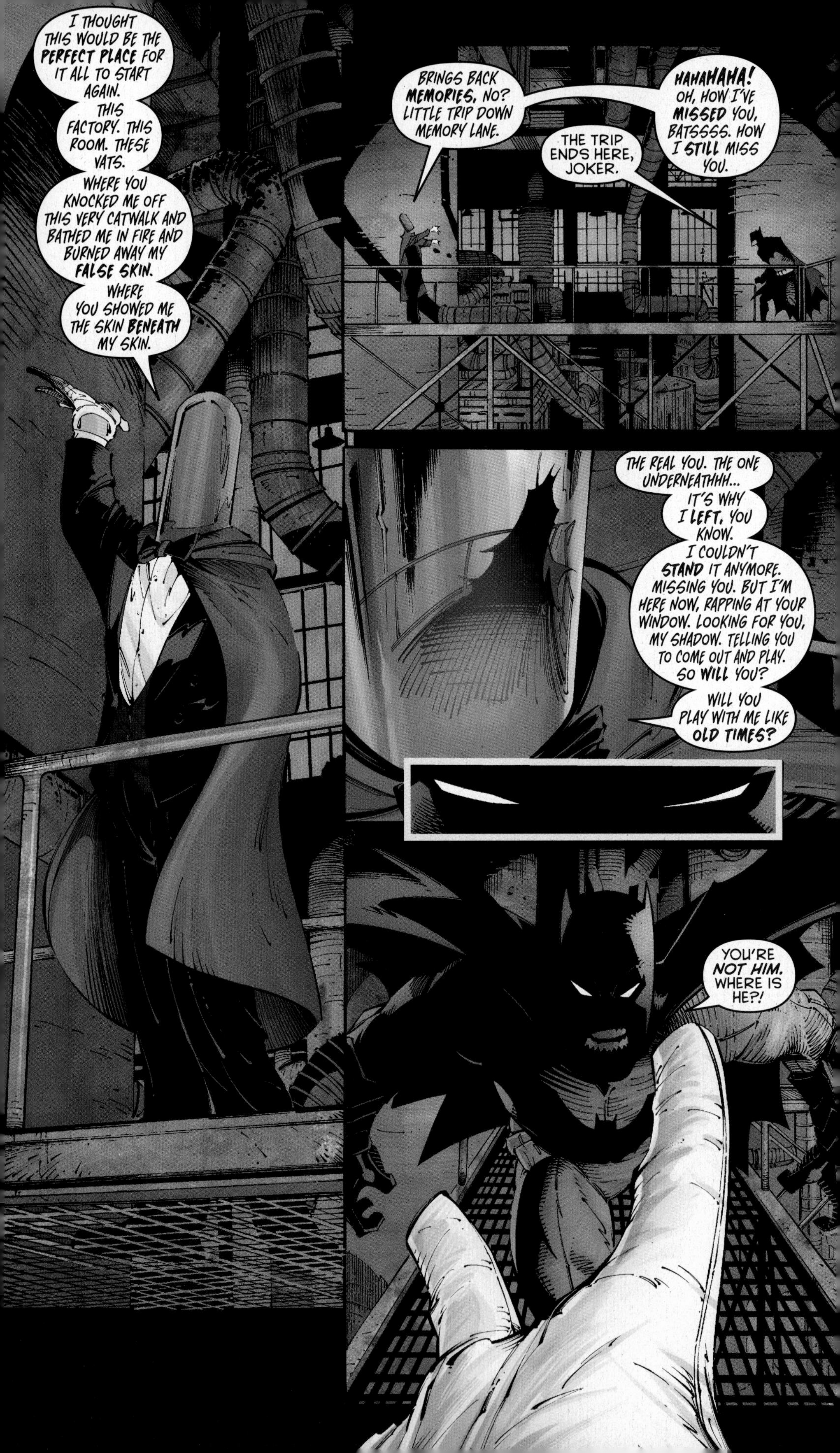
I THOUGHT THIS WOULD BE THE PERFECT PLACE FOR IT ALL TO START AGAIN.
THIS FACTORY. THIS ROOM. THESE VATS.
WHERE YOU KNOCKED ME OFF THIS VERY CATWALK AND BATHED ME IN FIRE AND BURNED AWAY MY FALSE SKIN.
WHERE YOU SHOWED ME THE SKIN BENEATH MY SKIN.
BRINGS BACK MEMORIES, NO? LITTLE TRIP DOWN MEMORY LANE.
THE TRIP ENDS HERE, JOKER.
HAHAHAHA! OH, HOW I'VE MISSED YOU, BATSSSS. HOW I STILL MISS YOU.
THE REAL YOU. THE ONE UNDERNEATHHH...
IT'S WHY I LEFT, YOU KNOW.
I COULDN'T STAND IT ANYMORE. MISSING YOU. BUT I'M HERE NOW, RAPPING AT YOUR WINDOW. LOOKING FOR YOU, MY SHADOW. TELLING YOU TO COME OUT AND PLAY. SO WILL YOU?
WILL YOU PLAY WITH ME LIKE OLD TIMES?
YOU'RE NOT HIM. WHERE IS HE?!

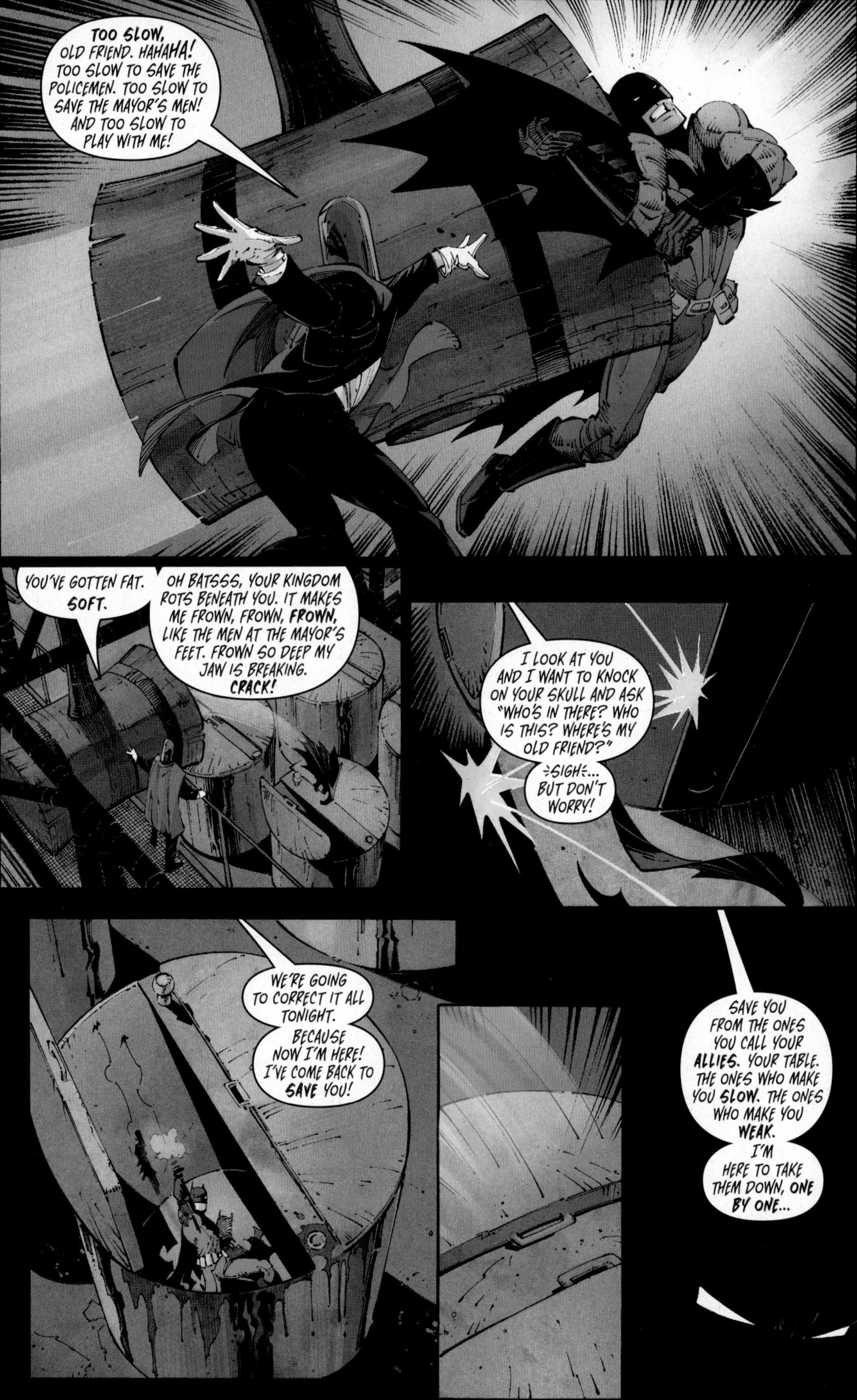
TOO SLOW, OLD FRIEND. HAHAHA! TOO SLOW TO SAVE THE POLICEMEN. TOO SLOW TO SAVE THE MAYOR'S MEN! AND TOO SLOW TO PLAY WITH ME!
YOU'VE GOTTEN FAT. SOFT.
OH BATSSS, YOUR KINGDOM ROTS BENEATH YOU. IT MAKES ME FROWN, FROWN, FROWN, LIKE THE MEN AT THE MAYOR'S FEET. FROWN SO DEEP MY JAW IS BREAKING. CRACK!
I LOOK AT YOU AND I WANT TO KNOCK ON YOUR SKULL AND ASK "WHO'S IN THERE? WHO IS THIS? WHERE'S MY OLD FRIEND?"
SIGH... BUT DON'T WORRY!
WE'RE GOING TO CORRECT IT ALL TONIGHT.
BECAUSE NOW I'M HERE! I'VE COME BACK TO SAVE YOU!
SAVE YOU FROM THE ONES YOU CALL YOUR ALLIES. YOUR TABLE. THE ONES WHO MAKE YOU SLOW. THE ONES WHO MAKE YOU WEAK.
I'M HERE TO TAKE THEM DOWN, ONE BY ONE...

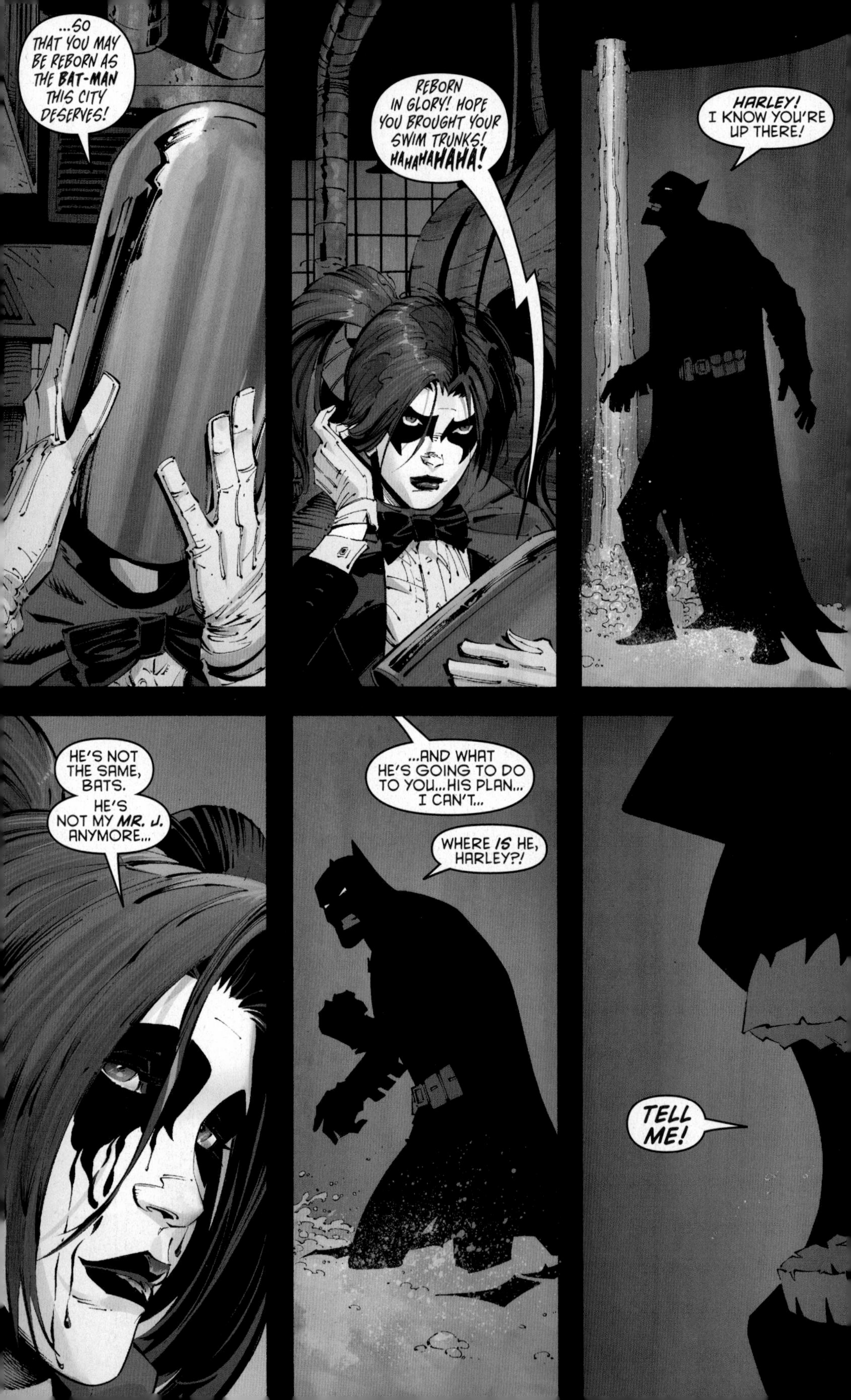
...SO THAT YOU MAY BE REBORN AS THE BAT-MAN THIS CITY DESERVES!
REBORN IN GLORY! HOPE YOU BROUGHT YOUR SWIM TRUNKS! HAHAHAHAHA!
HARLEY! I KNOW YOU'RE UP THERE!
HE'S NOT THE SAME, BATS.
HE'S NOT MY MR. J. ANYMORE...
...AND WHAT HE'S GOING TO DO TO YOU...HIS PLAN... I CAN'T...
WHERE IS HE, HARLEY?!
TELL ME!

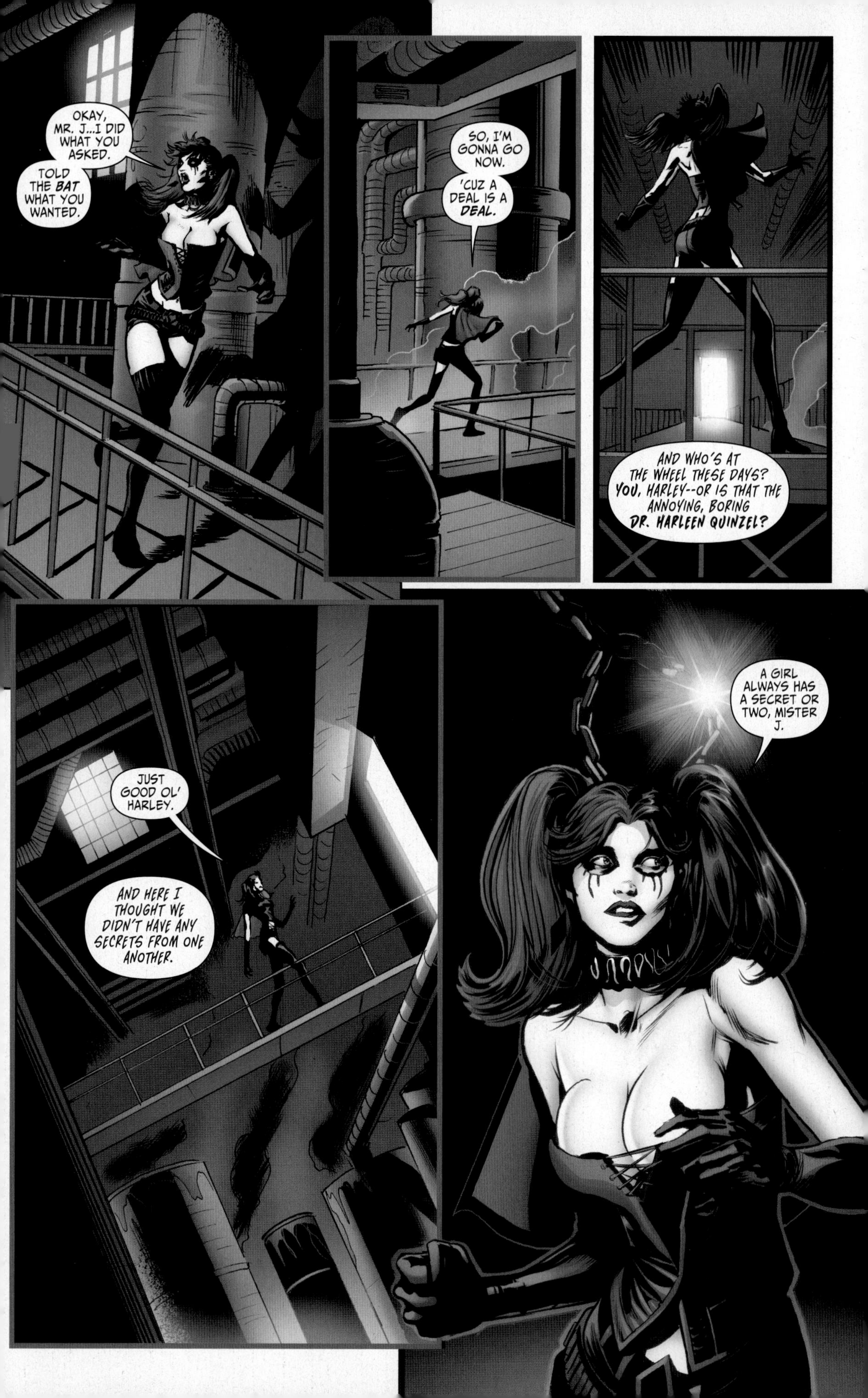
OKAY, MR. J...I DID WHAT YOU ASKED.
TOLD THE BAT WHAT YOU WANTED.
SO, I'M GONNA GO NOW.
'CUZ A DEAL IS A DEAL.
AND WHO'S AT THE WHEEL THESE DAYS? YOU, HARLEY--OR IS THAT THE ANNOYING, BORING DR. HARLEEN QUINZEL?
JUST GOOD OL' HARLEY.
AND HERE I THOUGHT WE DIDN'T HAVE ANY SECRETS FROM ONE ANOTHER.
A GIRL ALWAYS HAS A SECRET OR TWO, MISTER J.

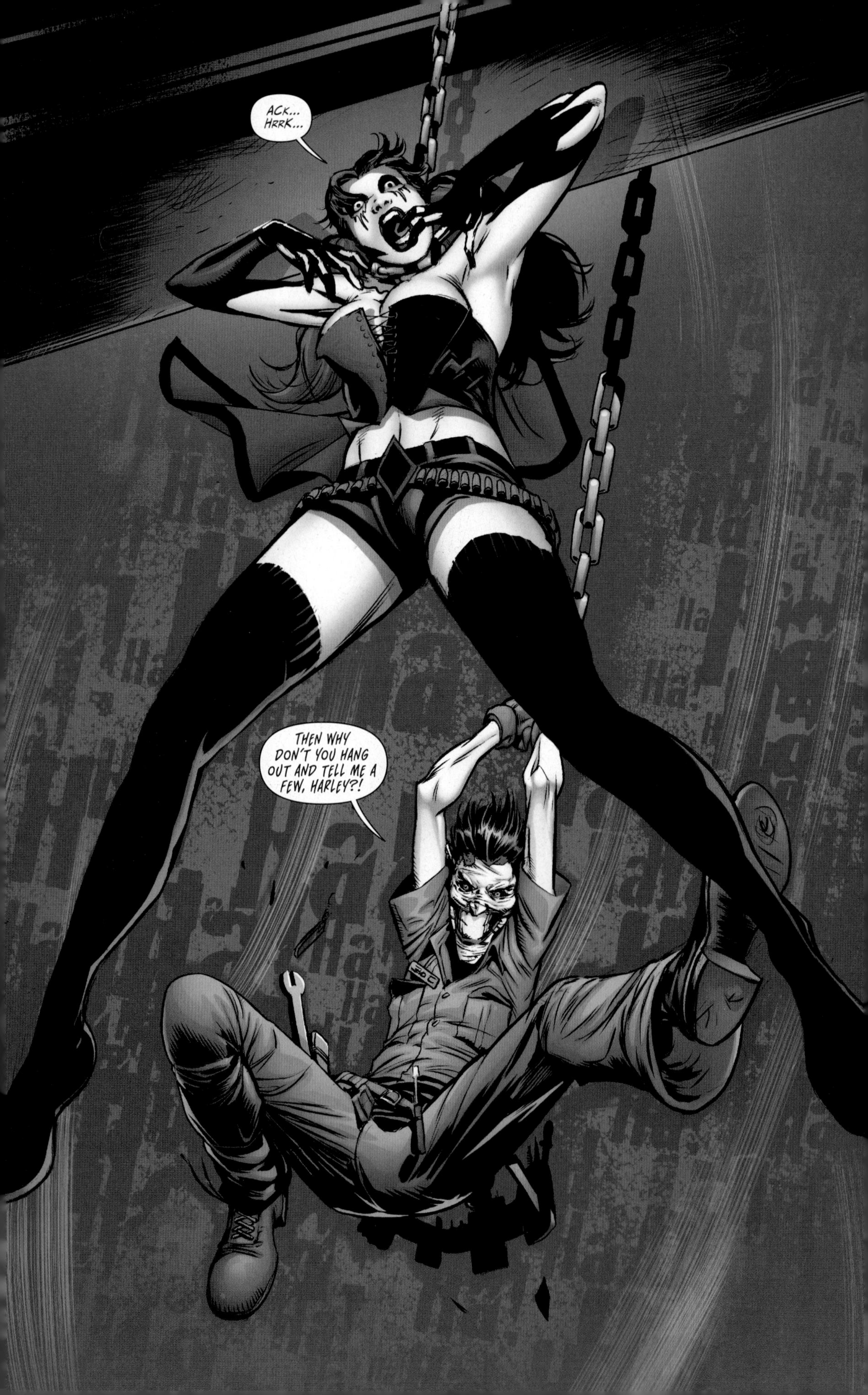
ACK... HRRK...
THEN WHY DON'T YOU HANG OUT AND TELL ME A FEW, HARLEY?!

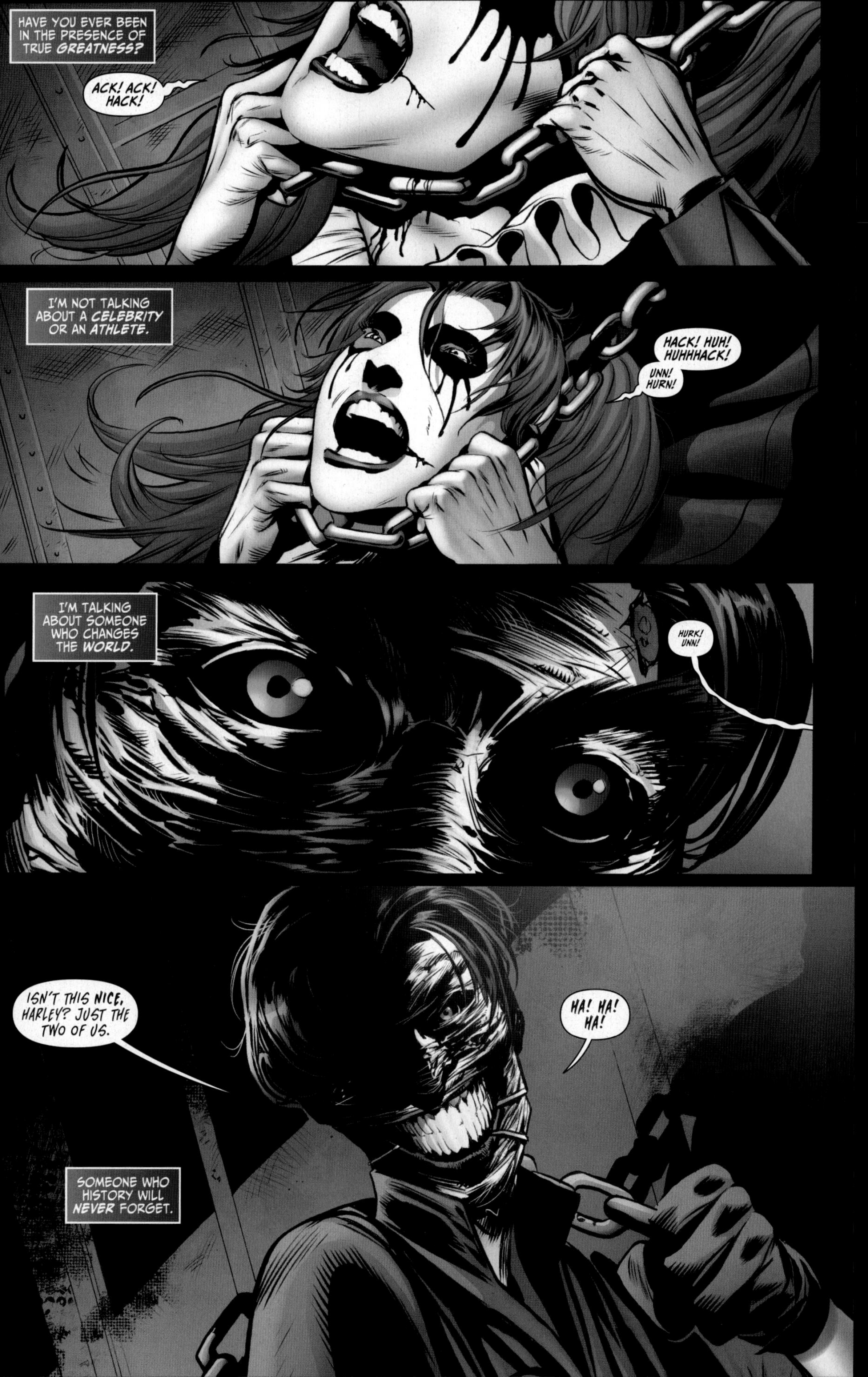
HAVE YOU EVER BEEN IN THE PRESENCE OF TRUE GREATNESS?
ACK! ACK! HACK!
I'M NOT TALKING ABOUT A CELEBRITY OR AN ATHLETE.
HACK! HUH! HUHHHACK!
UNN! HURN!
I'M TALKING ABOUT SOMEONE WHO CHANGES THE WORLD.
HURK! UNN!
ISN'T THIS NICE, HARLEY? JUST THE TWO OF US.
HA! HA! HA!
SOMEONE WHO HISTORY WILL NEVER FORGET.

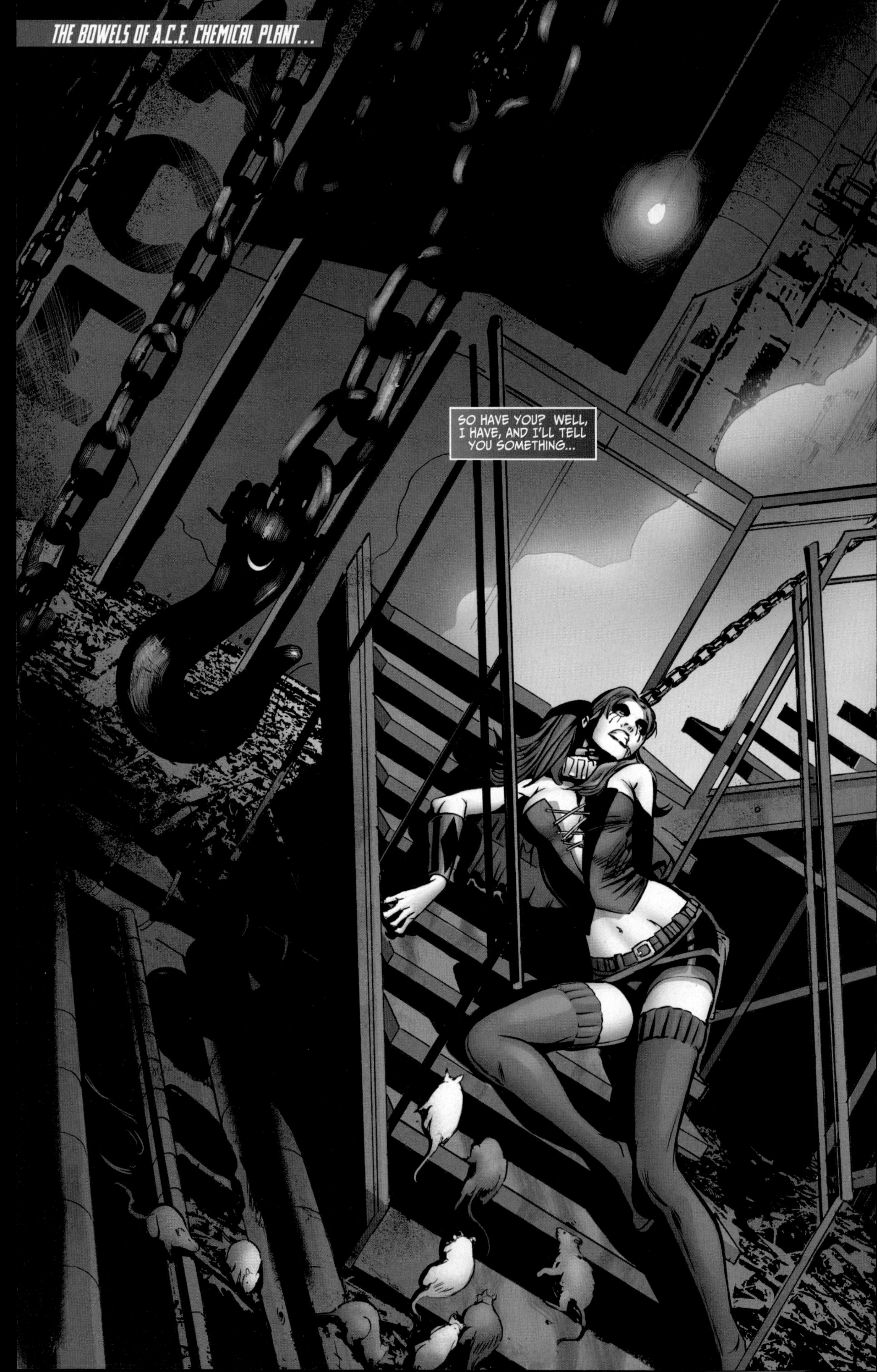
THE BOWELS OF A.C.E. CHEMICAL PLANT...
SO HAVE YOU? WELL, I HAVE, AND I'LL TELL YOU SOMETHING...

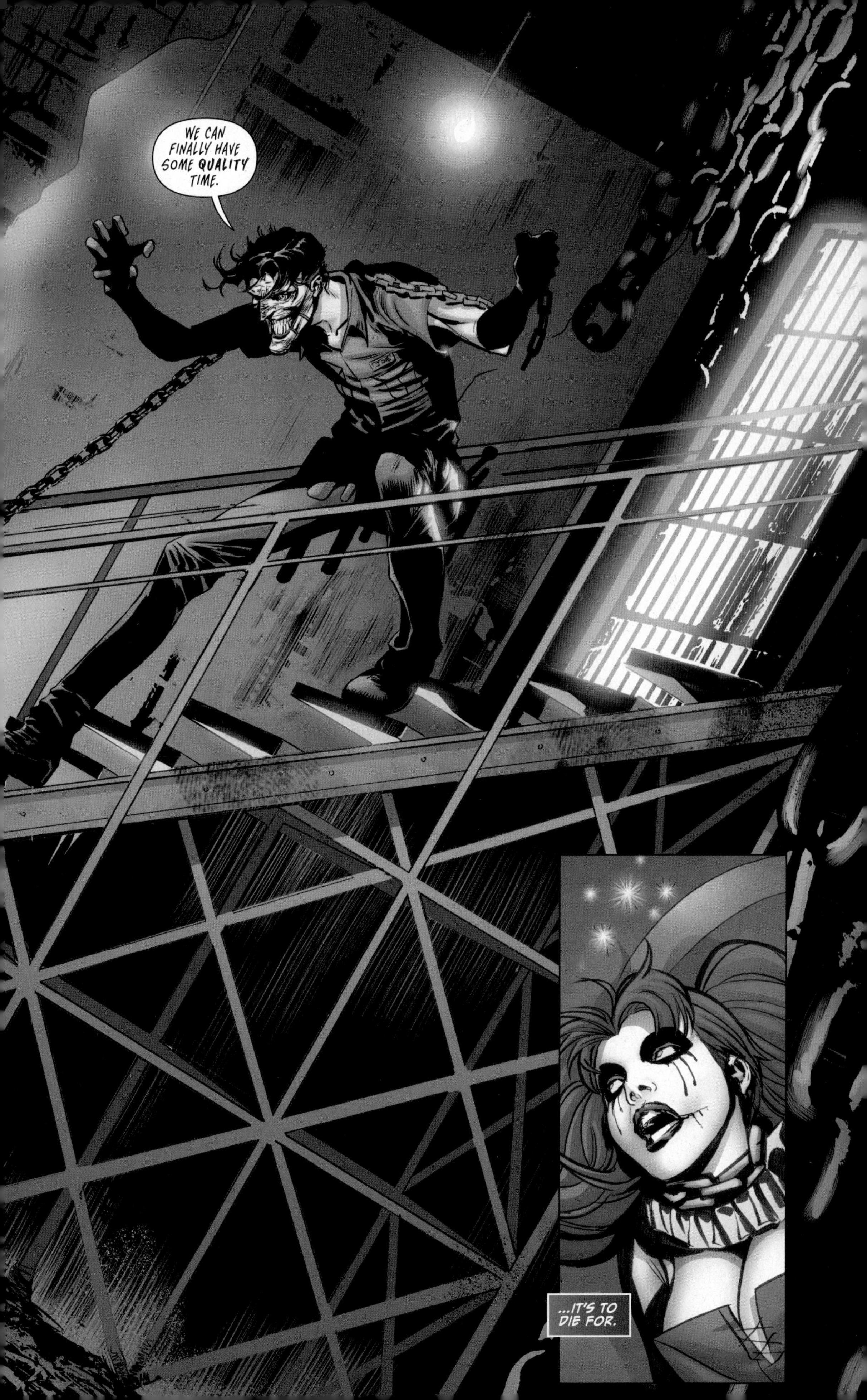
WE CAN FINALLY HAVE SOME QUALITY TIME.
...IT'S TO DIE FOR.

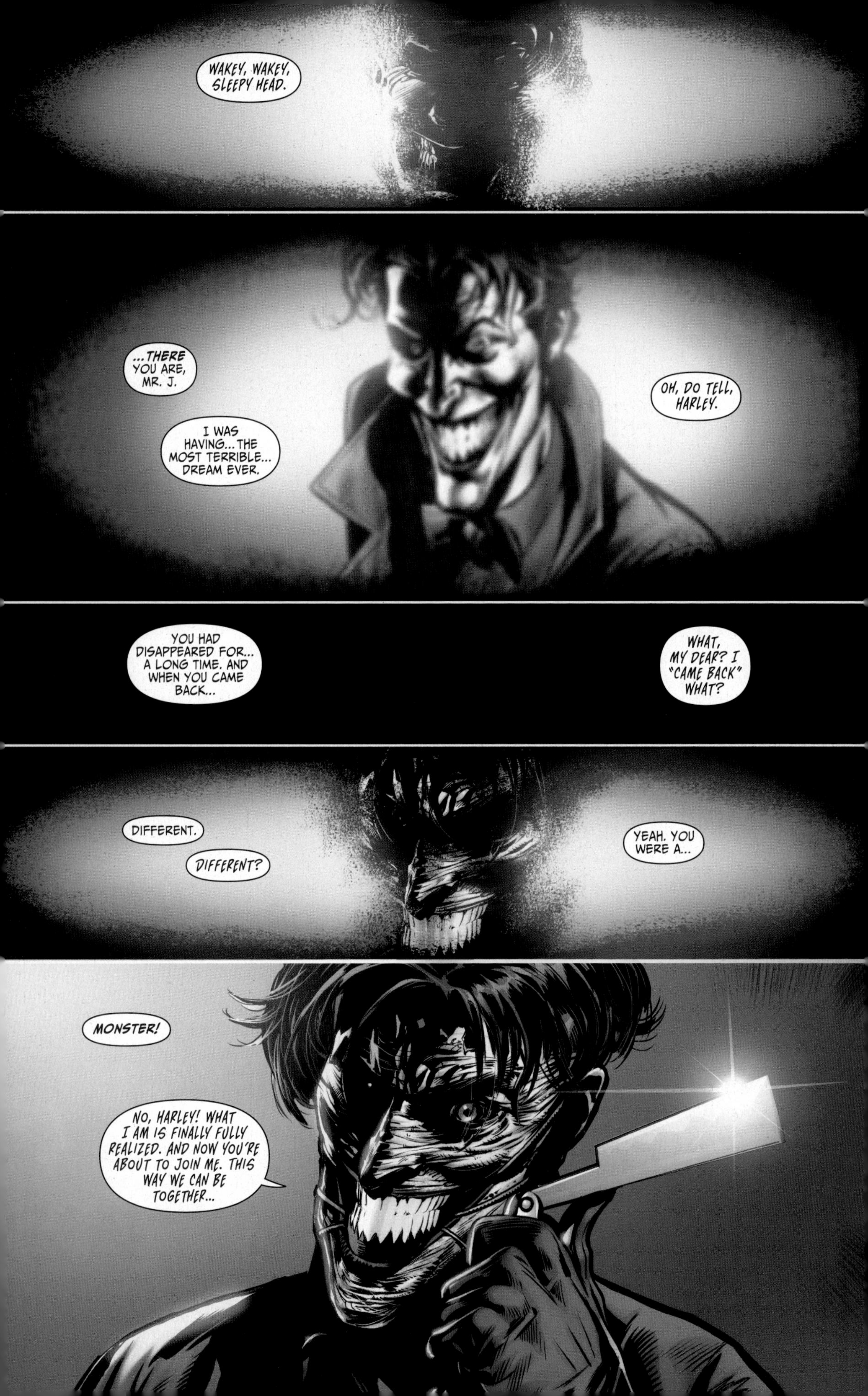
WAKEY, WAKEY, SLEEPY HEAD.
...THERE YOU ARE, MR. J.
I WAS HAVING... THE MOST TERRIBLE... DREAM EVER.
OH, DO TELL, HARLEY.
YOU HAD DISAPPEARED FOR... A LONG TIME. AND WHEN YOU CAME BACK...
WHAT, MY DEAR? I "CAME BACK" WHAT?
DIFFERENT.
DIFFERENT?
YEAH. YOU WERE A...
MONSTER!
NO, HARLEY! WHAT I AM IS FINALLY FULLY REALIZED. AND NOW YOU'RE ABOUT TO JOIN ME. THIS WAY WE CAN BE TOGETHER...

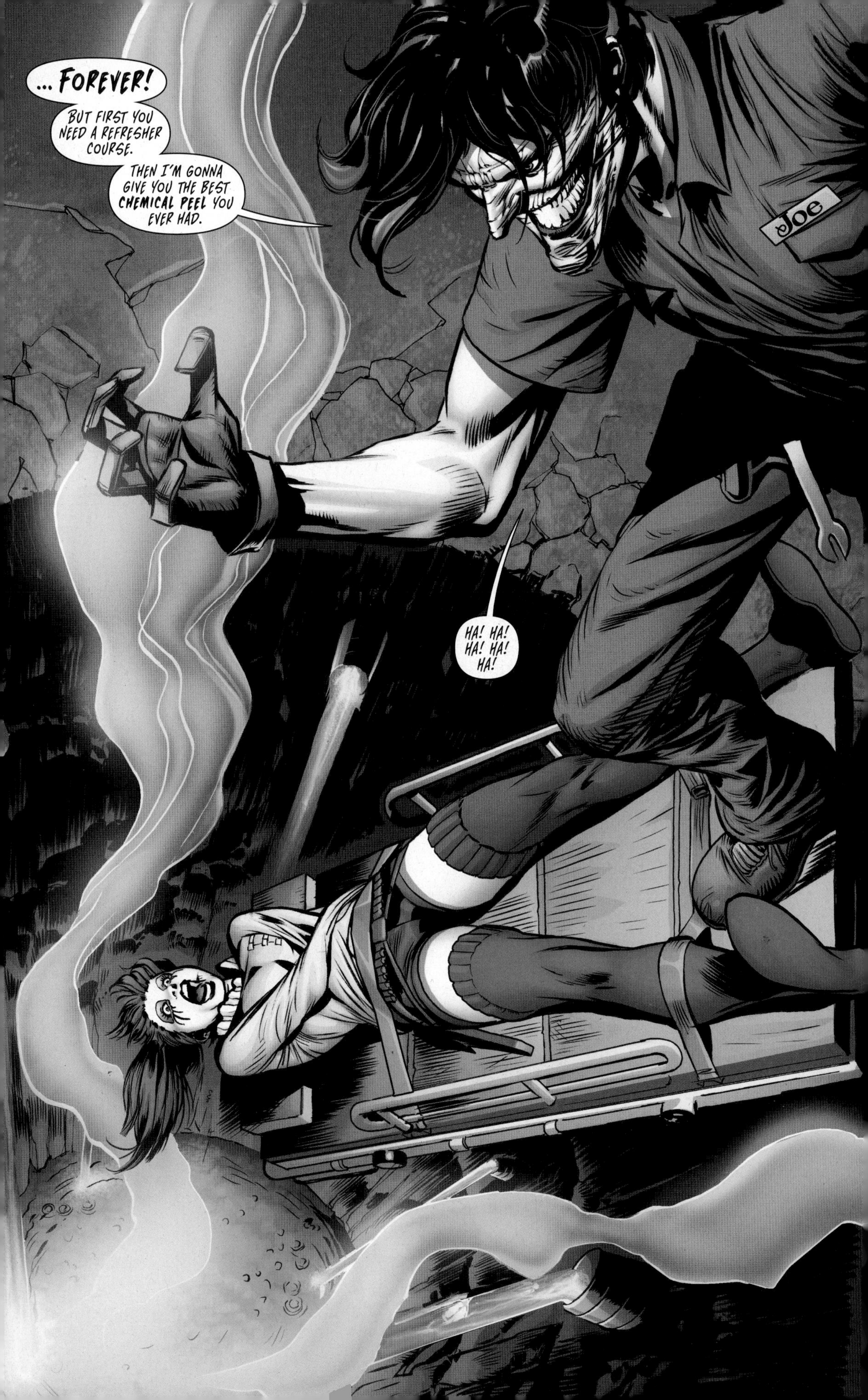
... FOREVER!
BUT FIRST YOU NEED A REFRESHER COURSE.
THEN I'M GONNA GIVE YOU THE BEST CHEMICAL PEEL YOU EVER HAD.
Joe
HA! HA! HA! HA! HA!

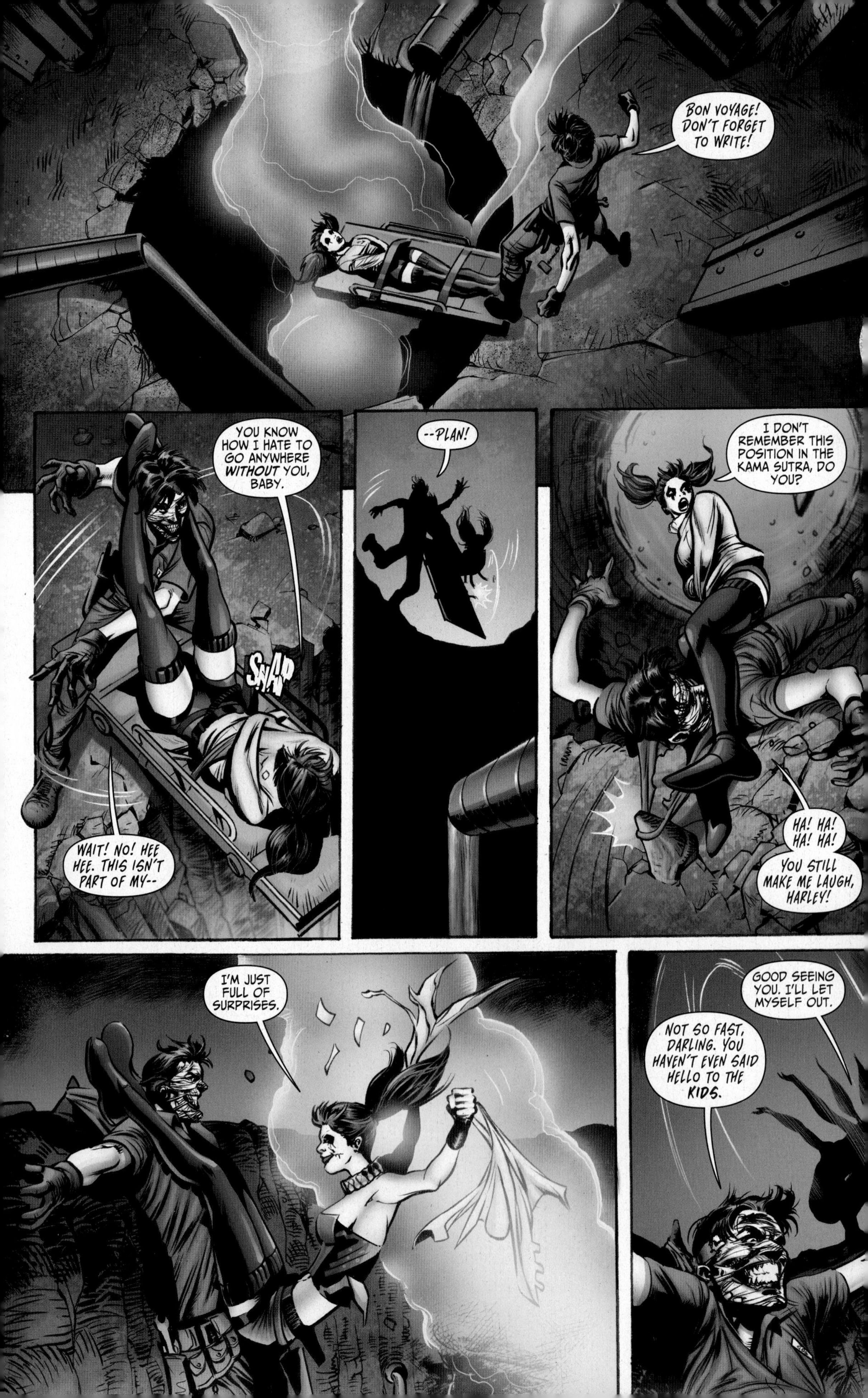

BON VOYAGE! DON'T FORGET TO WRITE!
YOU KNOW HOW I HATE TO GO ANYWHERE WITHOUT YOU, BABY.
SNAP
WAIT! NO! HEE HEE. THIS ISN'T PART OF MY--
--PLAN!
I DON'T REMEMBER THIS POSITION IN THE KAMA SUTRA, DO YOU?
HA! HA! HA! HA!
YOU STILL MAKE ME LAUGH, HARLEY!
I'M JUST FULL OF SURPRISES.
GOOD SEEING YOU. I'LL LET MYSELF OUT.
NOT SO FAST, DARLING. YOU HAVEN'T EVEN SAID HELLO TO THE KIDS.

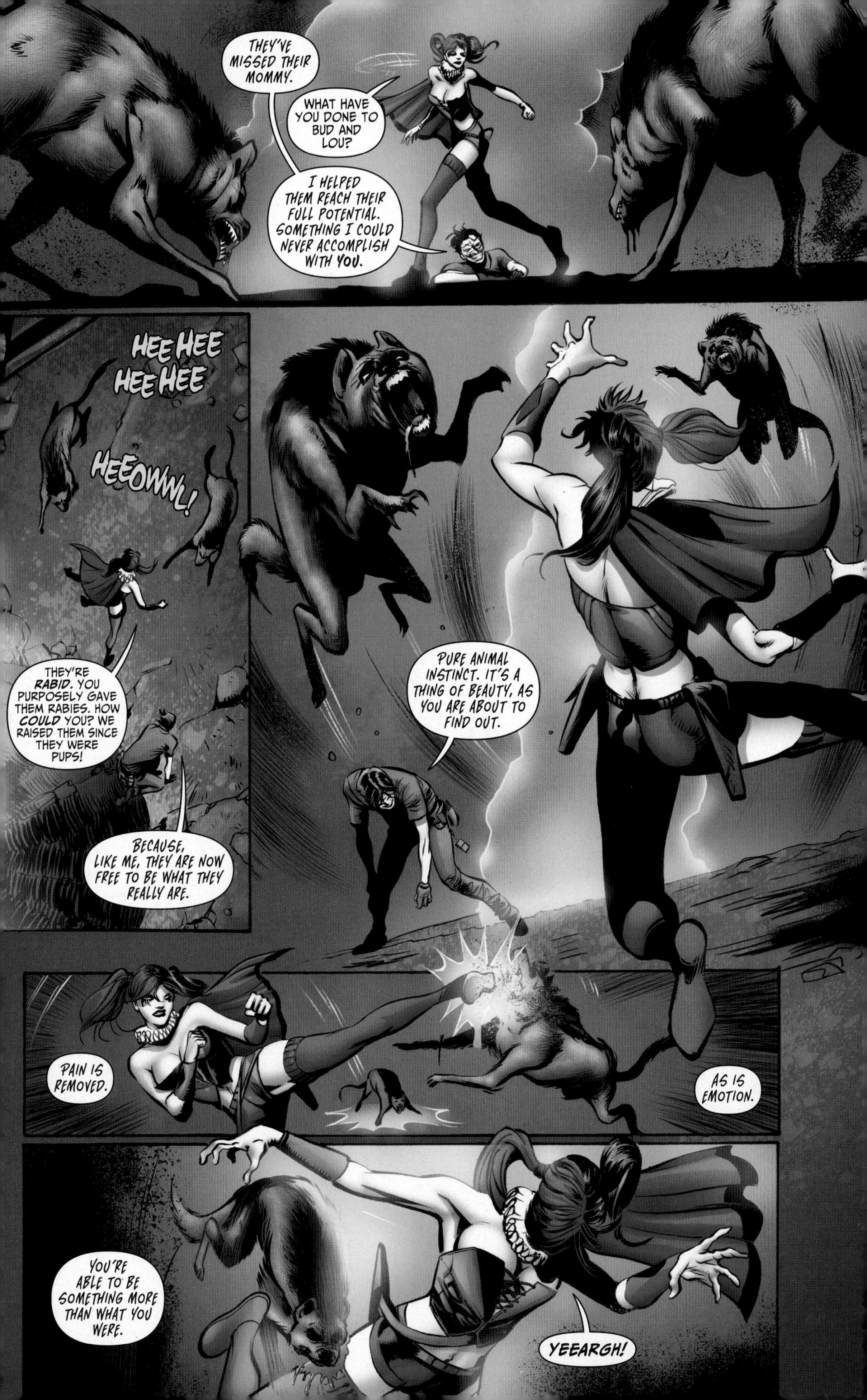

THEY'VE MISSED THEIR MOMMY.
WHAT HAVE YOU DONE TO BUD AND LOU?
I HELPED THEM REACH THEIR FULL POTENTIAL. SOMETHING I COULD NEVER ACCOMPLISH WITH YOU.
HEE HEE HEE HEE
HEEOWWL!
THEY'RE RABID. YOU PURPOSELY GAVE THEM RABIES. HOW COULD YOU? WE RAISED THEM SINCE THEY WERE PUPS!
BECAUSE, LIKE ME, THEY ARE NOW FREE TO BE WHAT THEY REALLY ARE.
PURE ANIMAL INSTINCT. IT'S A THING OF BEAUTY, AS YOU ARE ABOUT TO FIND OUT.
PAIN IS REMOVED.
AS IS EMOTION.
YOU'RE ABLE TO BE SOMETHING MORE THAN WHAT YOU WERE.
YEEARGH!

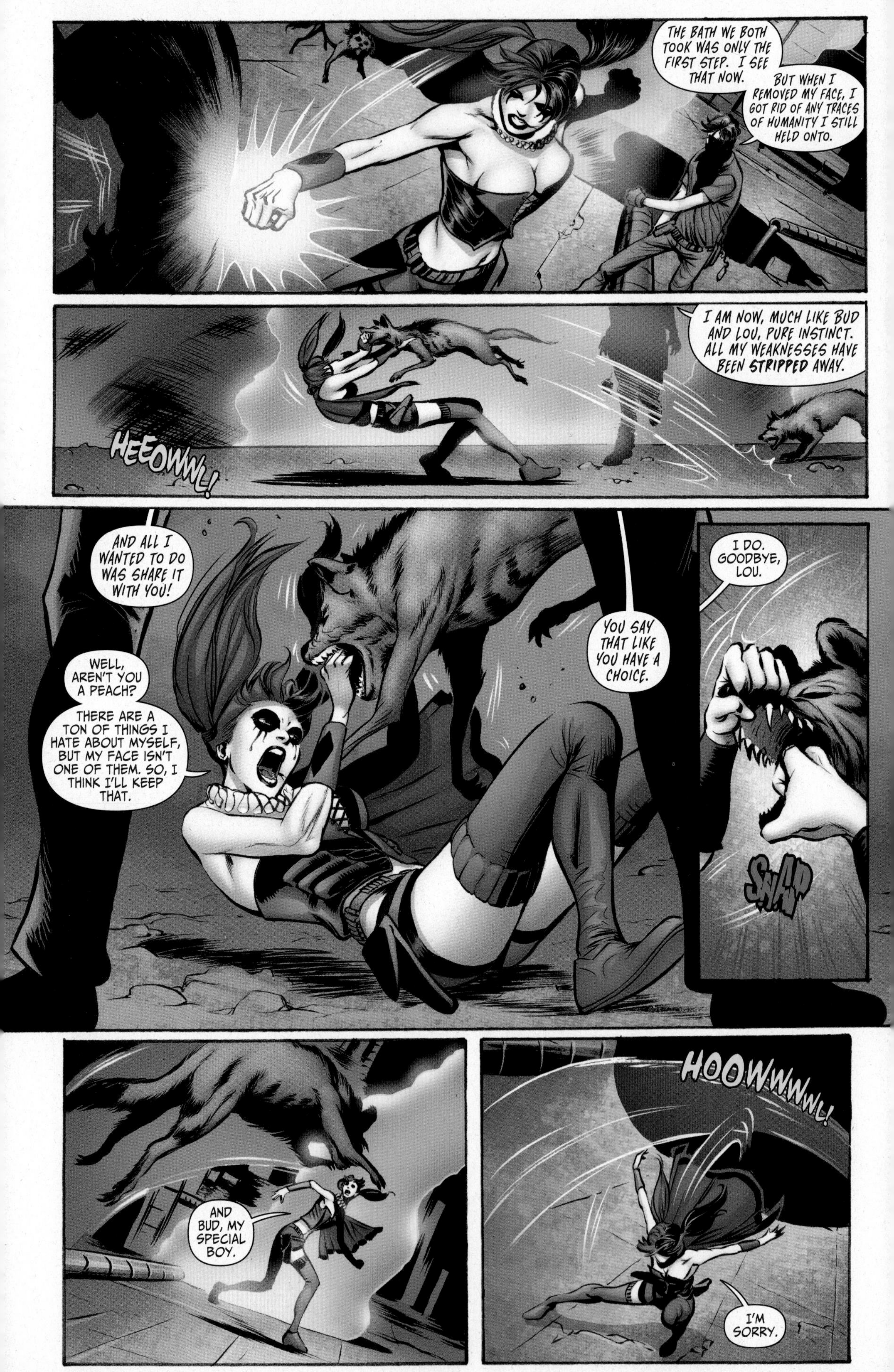
THE BATH WE BOTH TOOK WAS ONLY THE FIRST STEP. I SEE THAT NOW.
BUT WHEN I REMOVED MY FACE, I GOT RID OF ANY TRACES OF HUMANITY I STILL HELD ONTO.
I AM NOW, MUCH LIKE BUD AND LOU, PURE INSTINCT. ALL MY WEAKNESSES HAVE BEEN STRIPPED AWAY.
HEEOWWL!
AND ALL I WANTED TO DO WAS SHARE IT WITH YOU!
WELL, AREN'T YOU A PEACH?
THERE ARE A TON OF THINGS I HATE ABOUT MYSELF, BUT MY FACE ISN'T ONE OF THEM. SO, I THINK I'LL KEEP THAT.
YOU SAY THAT LIKE YOU HAVE A CHOICE.
I DO. GOODBYE, LOU.
SNAP
AND BUD, MY SPECIAL BOY.
HOOWWWWL!
I'M SORRY.

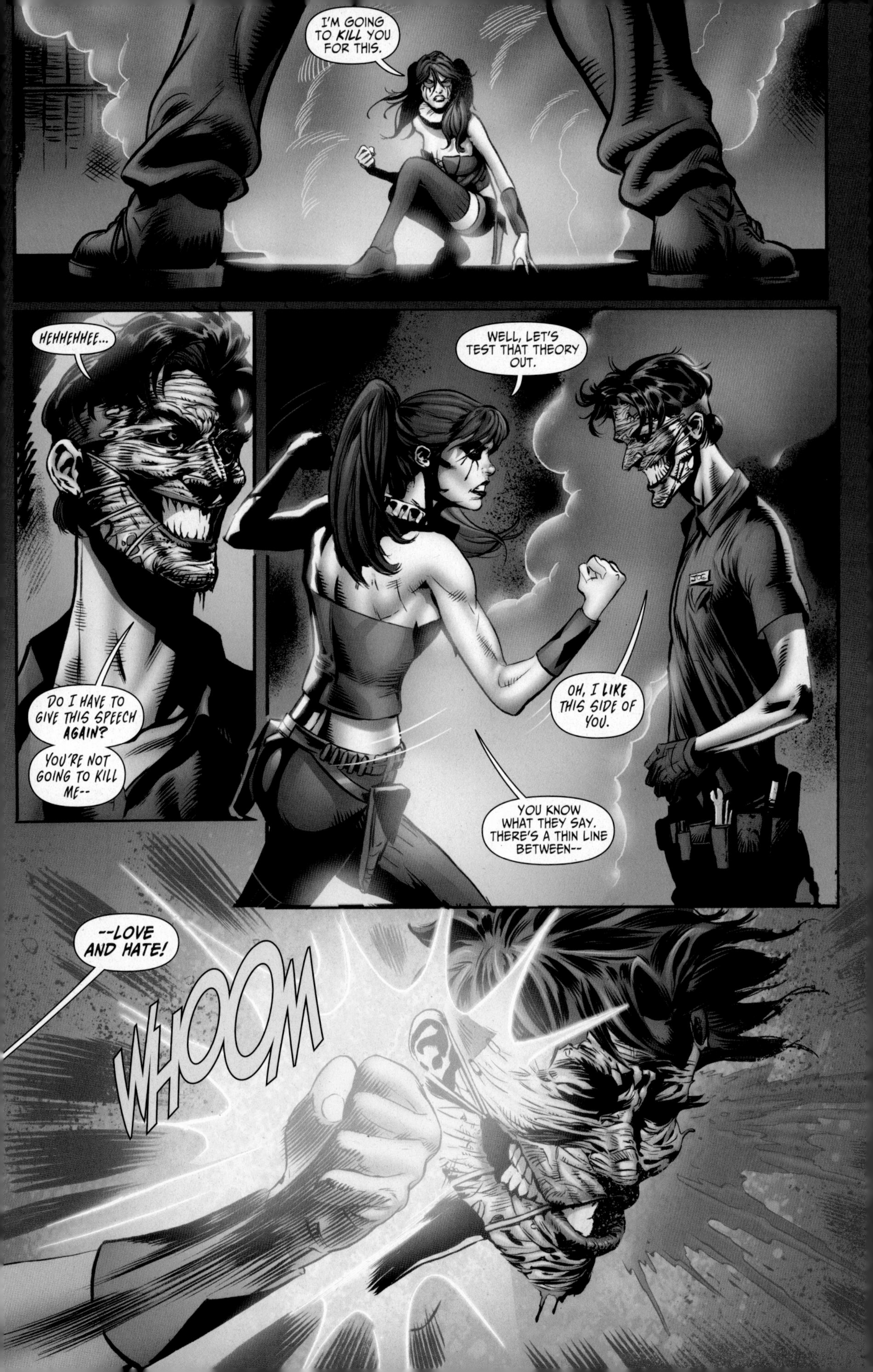
I'M GOING TO KILL YOU FOR THIS.
HEHHEHHEE...
DO I HAVE TO GIVE THIS SPEECH AGAIN?
YOU'RE NOT GOING TO KILL ME--
WELL, LET'S TEST THAT THEORY OUT.
OH, I LIKE THIS SIDE OF YOU.
YOU KNOW WHAT THEY SAY. THERE'S A THIN LINE BETWEEN--
--LOVE AND HATE!
WHOOM

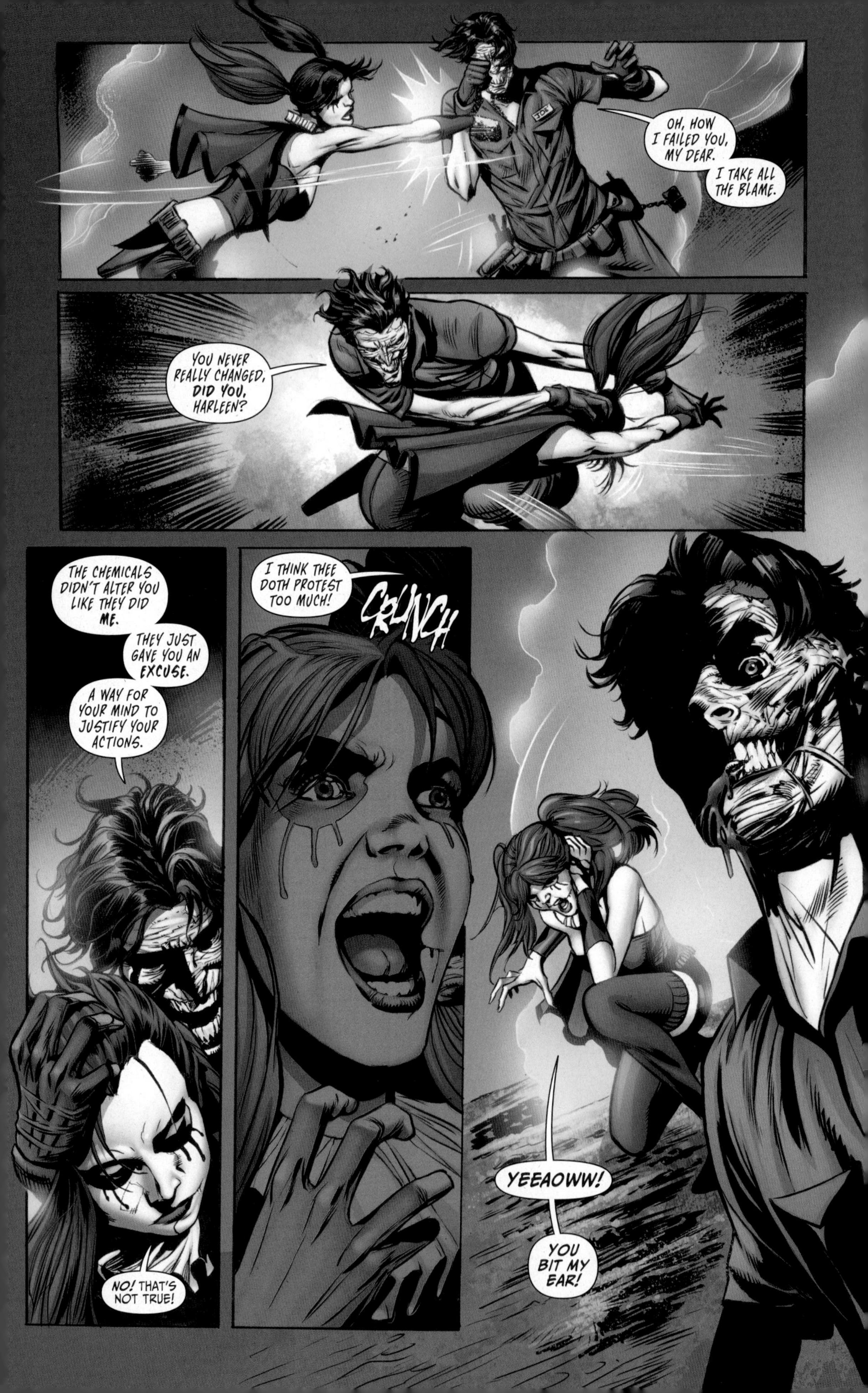
OH, HOW I FAILED YOU, MY DEAR.
I TAKE ALL THE BLAME.
YOU NEVER REALLY CHANGED, DID YOU, HARLEEN?
THE CHEMICALS DIDN'T ALTER YOU LIKE THEY DID ME.
THEY JUST GAVE YOU AN EXCUSE.
A WAY FOR YOUR MIND TO JUSTIFY YOUR ACTIONS.
NO! THAT'S NOT TRUE!
I THINK THEE DOTH PROTEST TOO MUCH!
CRUNCH
YEEAOWW!
YOU BIT MY EAR!

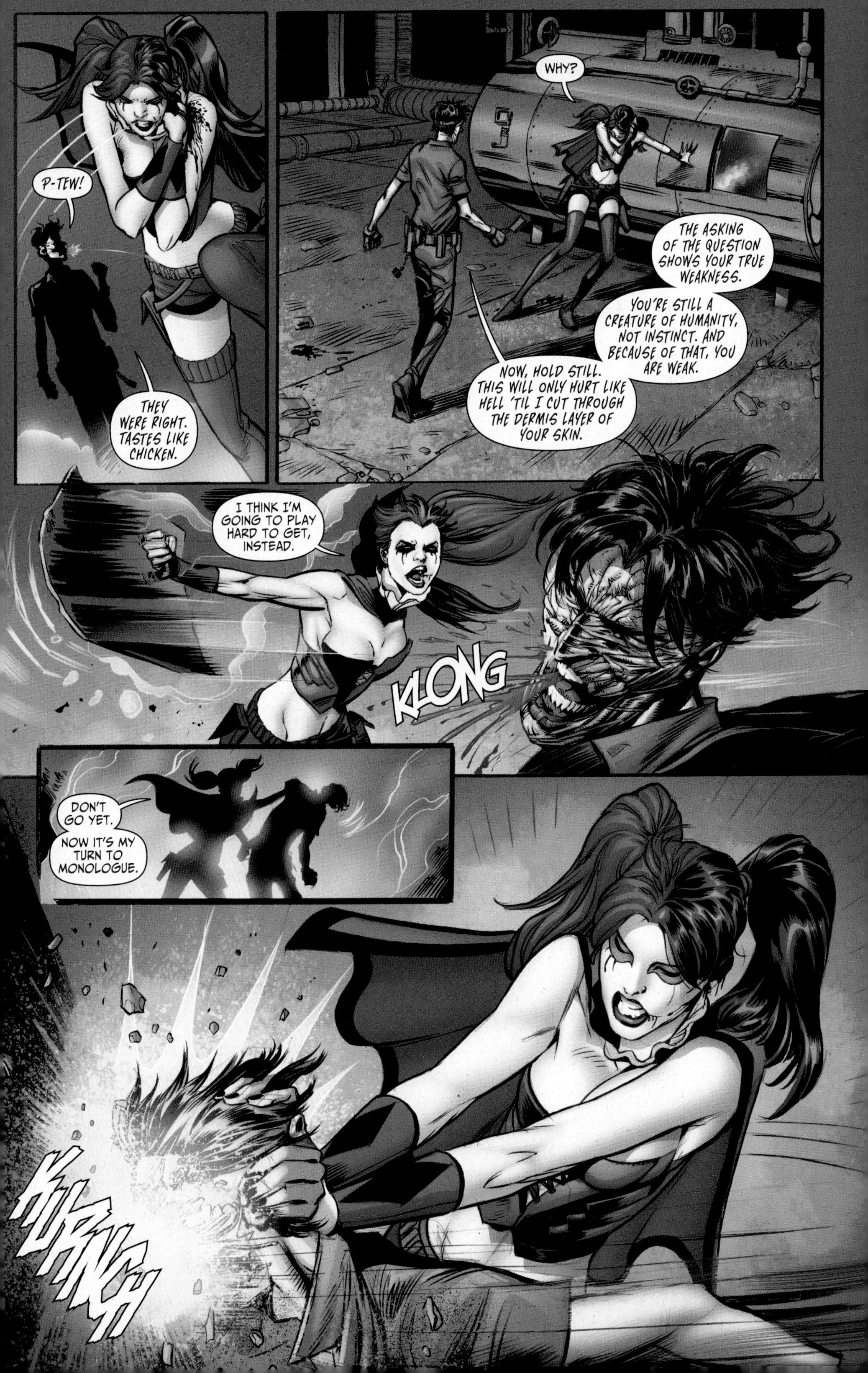
P-TEW!
THEY WERE RIGHT. TASTES LIKE CHICKEN.
WHY?
THE ASKING OF THE QUESTION SHOWS YOUR TRUE WEAKNESS.
YOU'RE STILL A CREATURE OF HUMANITY, NOT INSTINCT. AND BECAUSE OF THAT, YOU ARE WEAK.
NOW, HOLD STILL. THIS WILL ONLY HURT LIKE HELL 'TIL I CUT THROUGH THE DERMIS LAYER OF YOUR SKIN.
I THINK I'M GOING TO PLAY HARD TO GET, INSTEAD.
KLONG
DON'T GO YET.
NOW IT'S MY TURN TO MONOLOGUE.
KURNCH

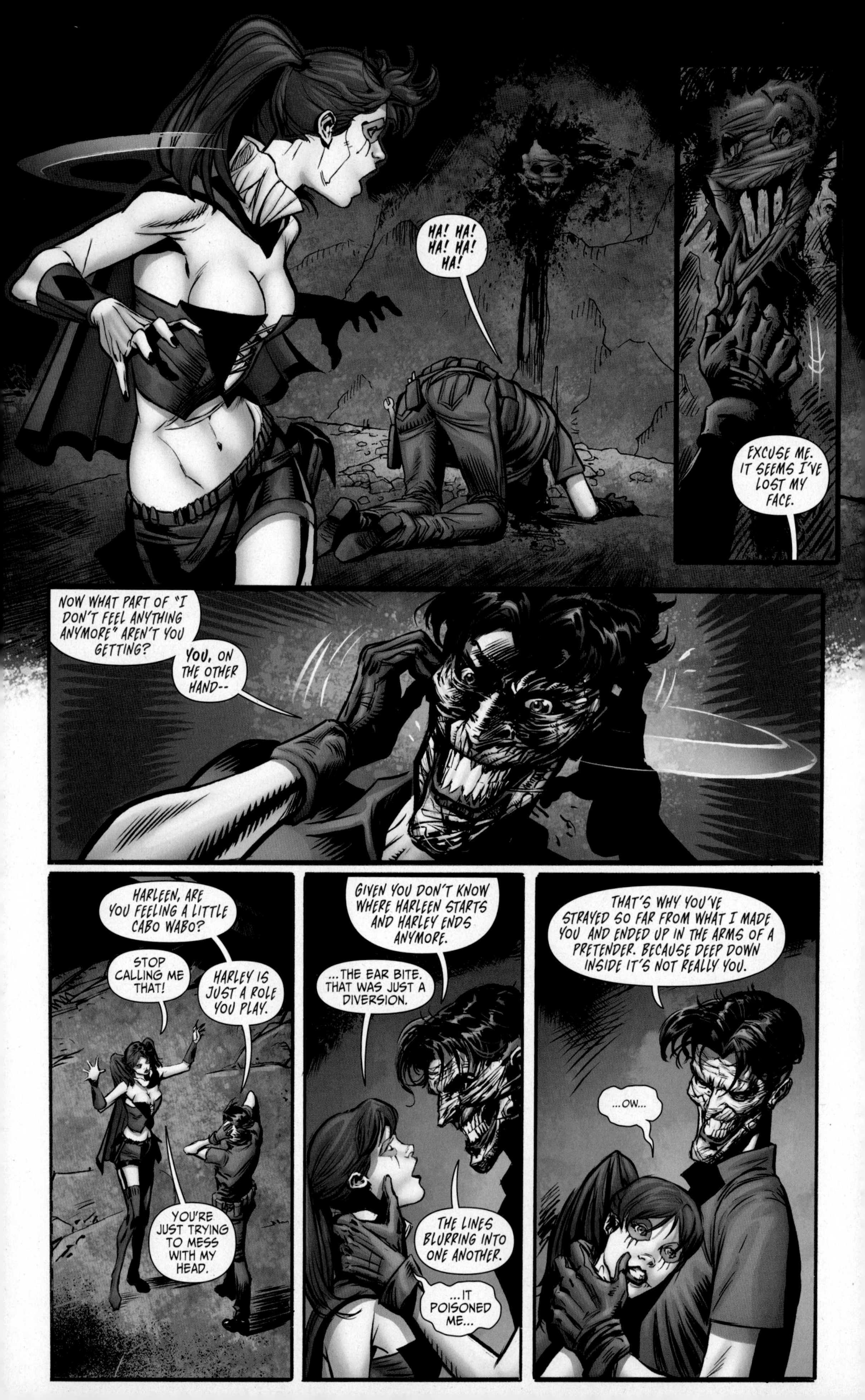
HA! HA! HA! HA! HA!
EXCUSE ME. IT SEEMS I'VE LOST MY FACE.
NOW WHAT PART OF "I DON'T FEEL ANYTHING ANYMORE" AREN'T YOU GETTING?
YOU, ON THE OTHER HAND--
HARLEEN, ARE YOU FEELING A LITTLE CABO WABO?
STOP CALLING ME THAT!
HARLEY IS JUST A ROLE YOU PLAY.
YOU'RE JUST TRYING TO MESS WITH MY HEAD.
GIVEN YOU DON'T KNOW WHERE HARLEEN STARTS AND HARLEY ENDS ANYMORE.
...THE EAR BITE. THAT WAS JUST A DIVERSION.
THE LINES BLURRING INTO ONE ANOTHER.
...IT POISONED ME...
THAT'S WHY YOU'VE STRAYED SO FAR FROM WHAT I MADE YOU AND ENDED UP IN THE ARMS OF A PRETENDER. BECAUSE DEEP DOWN INSIDE IT'S NOT REALLY YOU.
...OW...

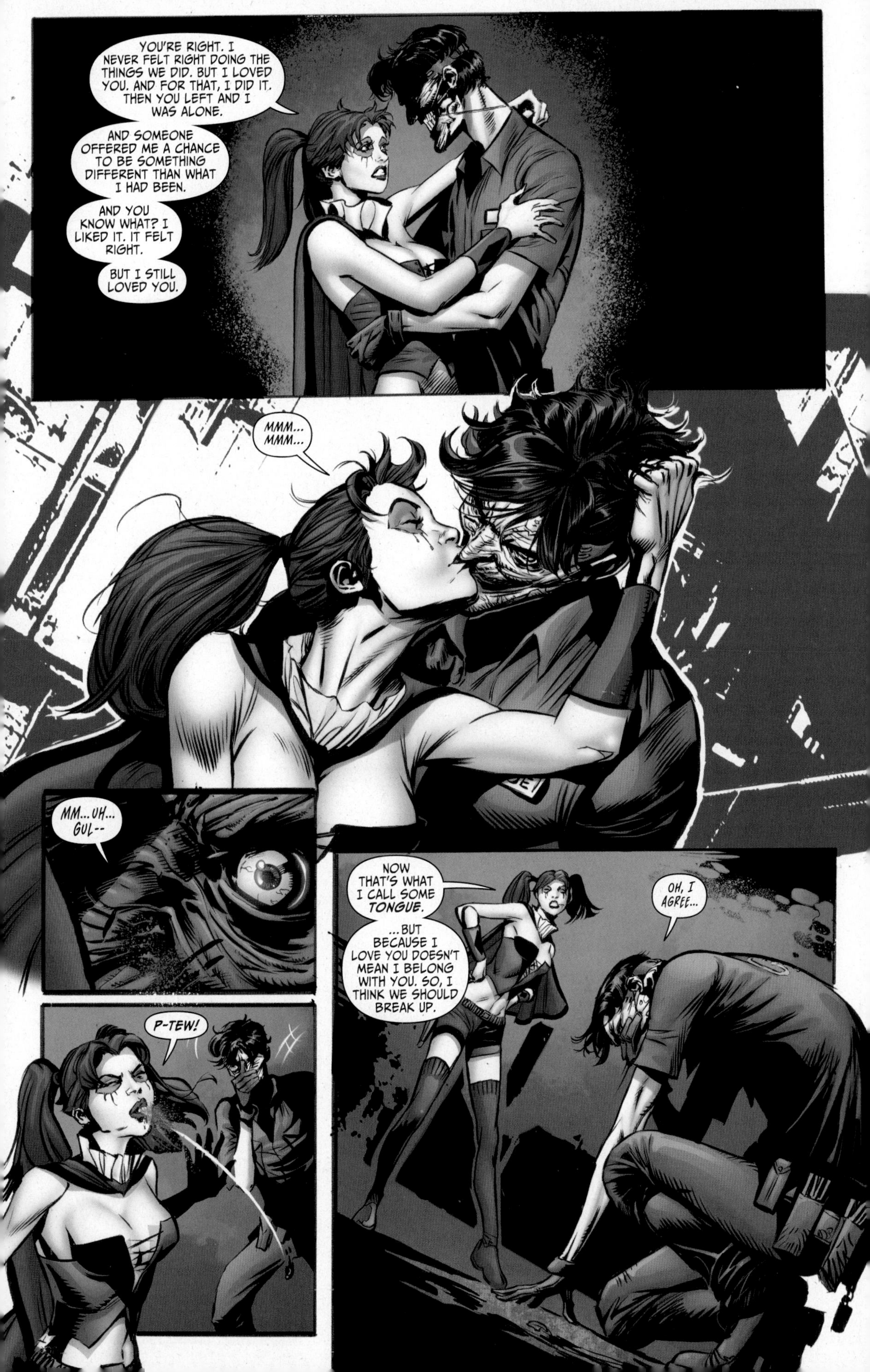
YOU'RE RIGHT. I NEVER FELT RIGHT DOING THE THINGS WE DID. BUT I LOVED YOU. AND FOR THAT, I DID IT. THEN YOU LEFT AND I WAS ALONE.
AND SOMEONE OFFERED ME A CHANCE TO BE SOMETHING DIFFERENT THAN WHAT I HAD BEEN.
AND YOU KNOW WHAT? I LIKED IT. IT FELT RIGHT.
BUT I STILL LOVED YOU.
MMM... MMM...
MM...UH... GUL--
P-TEW!
NOW THAT'S WHAT I CALL SOME *TONGUE*.
...BUT BECAUSE I LOVE YOU DOESN'T MEAN I BELONG WITH YOU. SO, I THINK WE SHOULD BREAK UP.
OH, I AGREE...

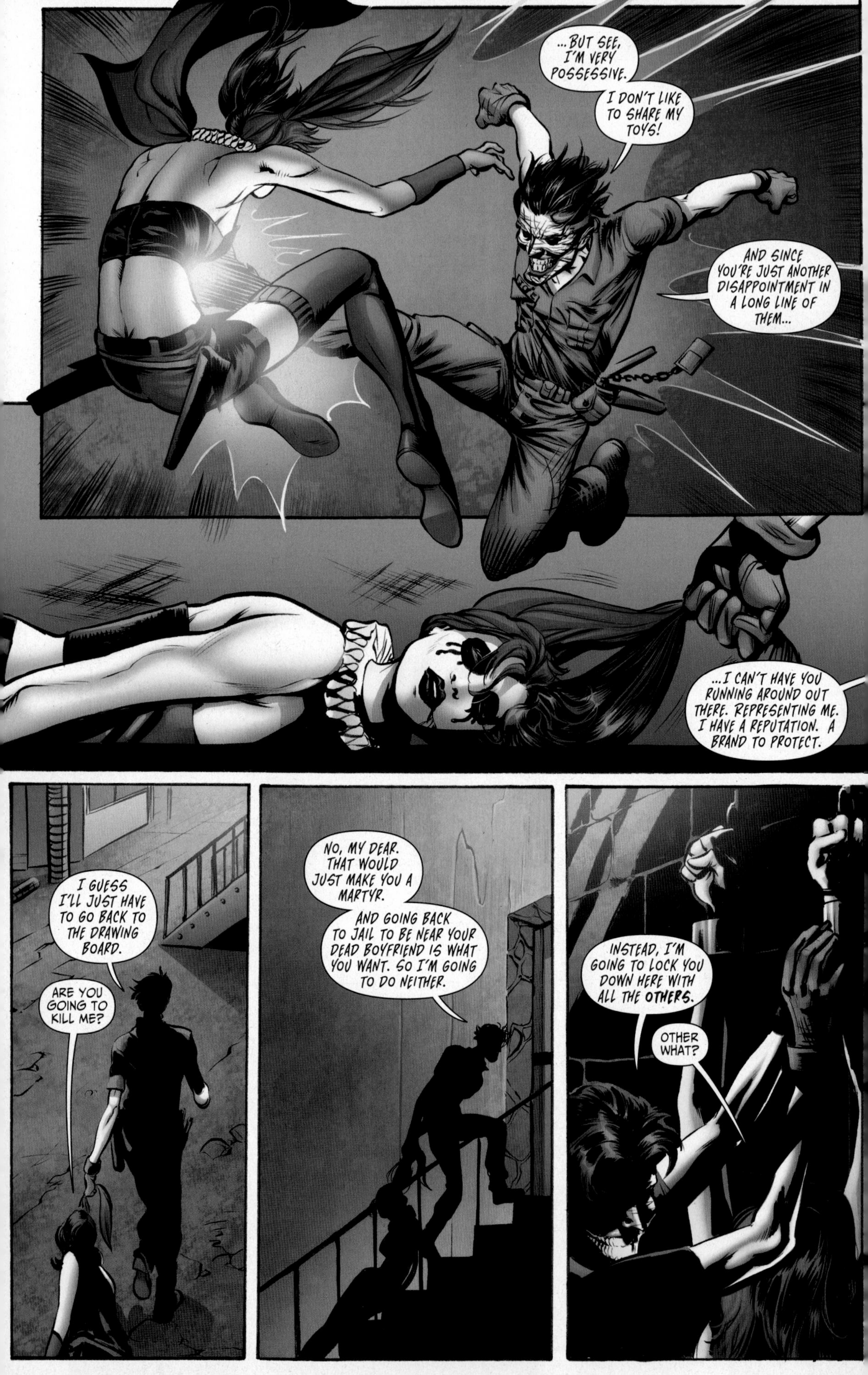
...BUT SEE, I'M VERY POSSESSIVE.
I DON'T LIKE TO SHARE MY TOYS!
AND SINCE YOU'RE JUST ANOTHER DISAPPOINTMENT IN A LONG LINE OF THEM...
...I CAN'T HAVE YOU RUNNING AROUND OUT THERE. REPRESENTING ME. I HAVE A REPUTATION. A BRAND TO PROTECT.
I GUESS I'LL JUST HAVE TO GO BACK TO THE DRAWING BOARD.
ARE YOU GOING TO KILL ME?
NO, MY DEAR. THAT WOULD JUST MAKE YOU A MARTYR.
AND GOING BACK TO JAIL TO BE NEAR YOUR DEAD BOYFRIEND IS WHAT YOU WANT. SO I'M GOING TO DO NEITHER.
INSTEAD, I'M GOING TO LOCK YOU DOWN HERE WITH ALL THE OTHERS.
OTHER WHAT?

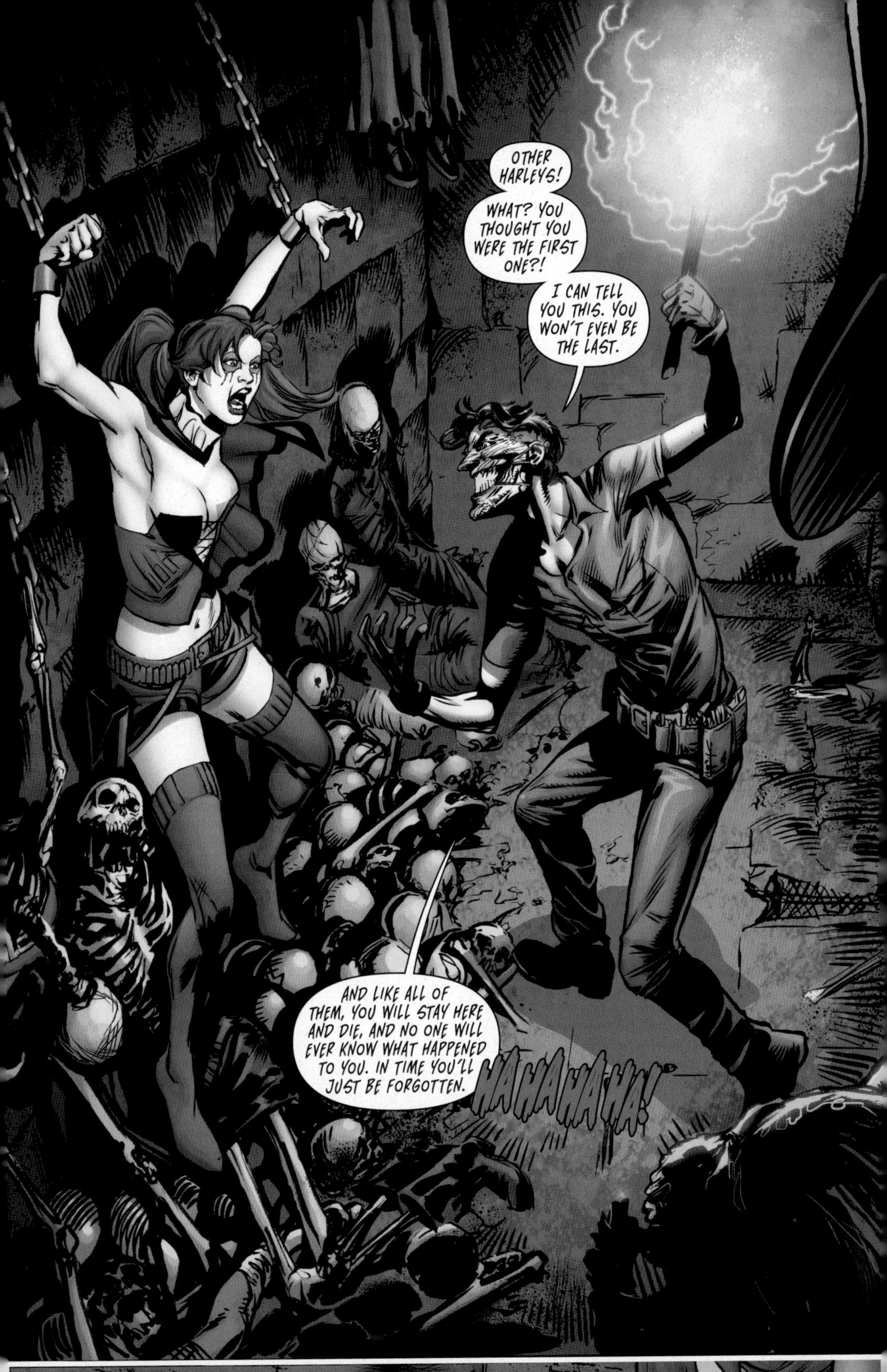
OTHER HARLEYS!
WHAT? YOU THOUGHT YOU WERE THE FIRST ONE?!
I CAN TELL YOU THIS. YOU WON'T EVEN BE THE LAST.
AND LIKE ALL OF THEM, YOU WILL STAY HERE AND DIE, AND NO ONE WILL EVER KNOW WHAT HAPPENED TO YOU. IN TIME YOU'LL JUST BE FORGOTTEN.
HA HA HA HA HA!

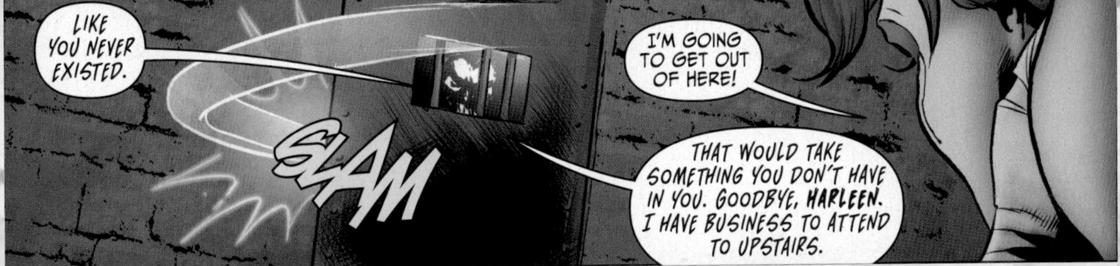
LIKE YOU NEVER EXISTED.
I'M GOING TO GET OUT OF HERE!
SLAM
THAT WOULD TAKE SOMETHING YOU DON'T HAVE IN YOU. GOODBYE, **HARLEEN**. I HAVE BUSINESS TO ATTEND TO UPSTAIRS.

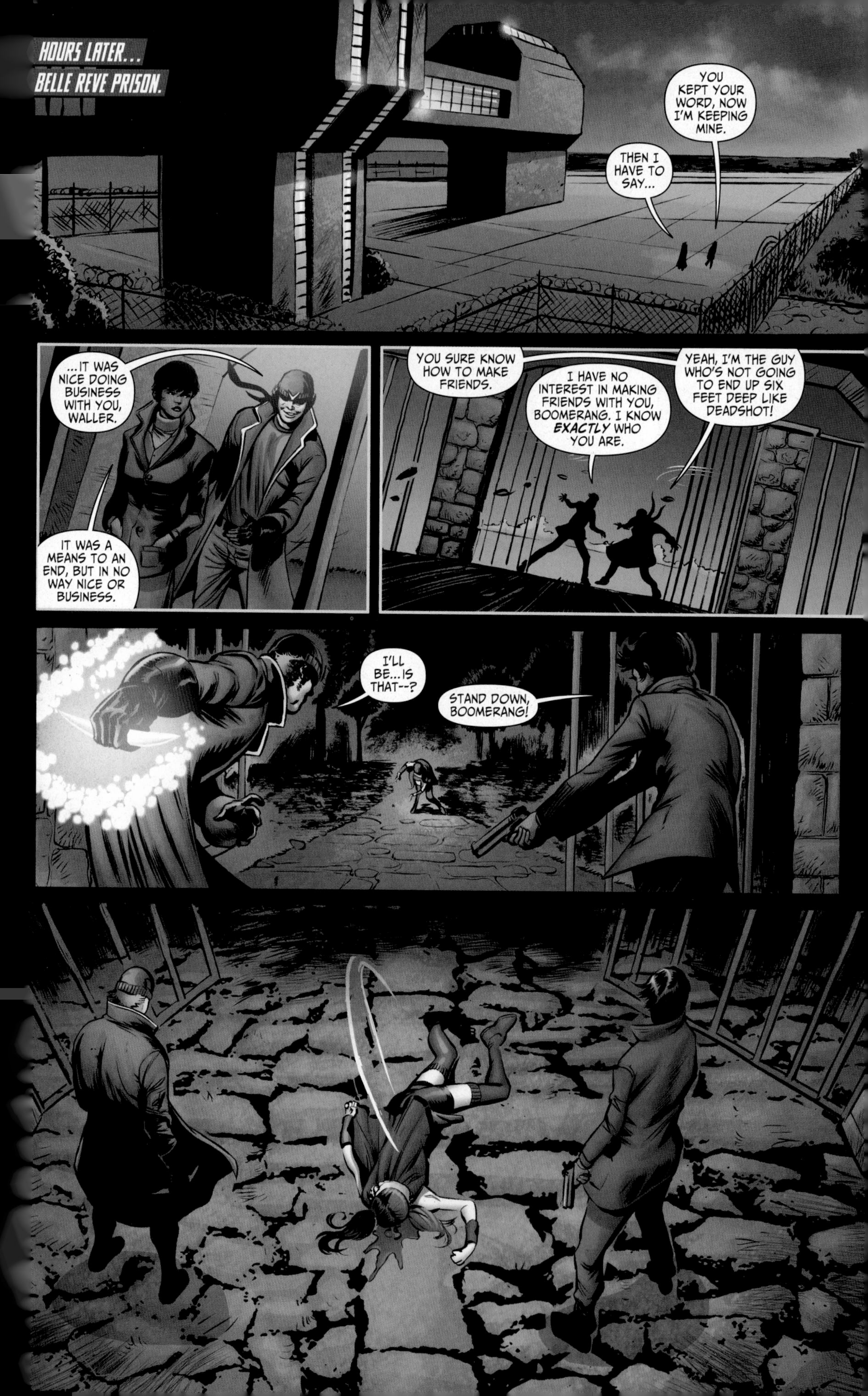
HOURS LATER...
BELLE REVE PRISON.
THEN I HAVE TO SAY...
YOU KEPT YOUR WORD, NOW I'M KEEPING MINE.
...IT WAS NICE DOING BUSINESS WITH YOU, WALLER.
IT WAS A MEANS TO AN END, BUT IN NO WAY NICE OR BUSINESS.
YOU SURE KNOW HOW TO MAKE FRIENDS.
I HAVE NO INTEREST IN MAKING FRIENDS WITH YOU, BOOMERANG. I KNOW EXACTLY WHO YOU ARE.
YEAH, I'M THE GUY WHO'S NOT GOING TO END UP SIX FEET DEEP LIKE DEADSHOT!
I'LL BE...IS THAT--?
STAND DOWN, BOOMERANG!

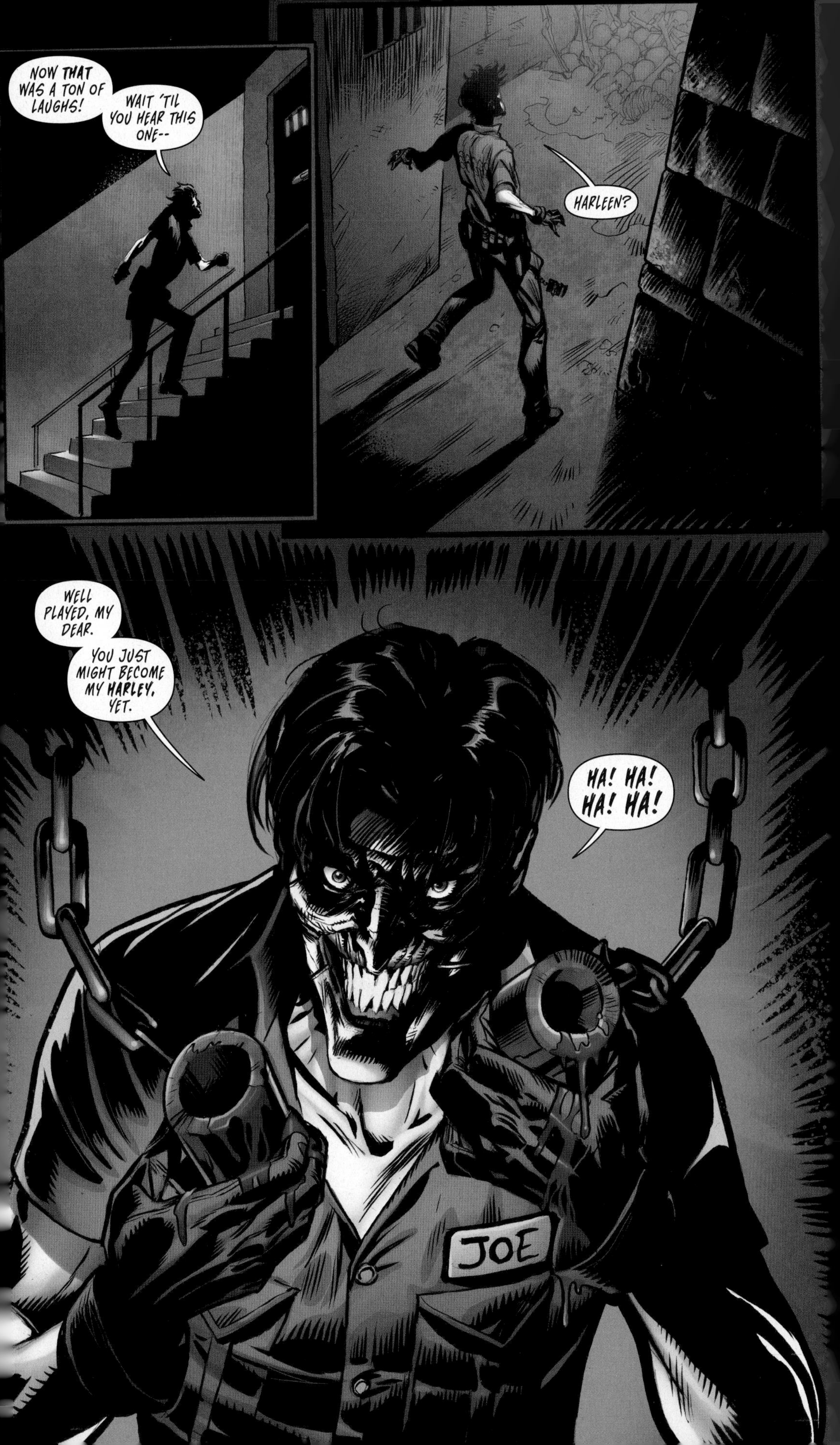
NOW THAT WAS A TON OF LAUGHS!
WAIT 'TIL YOU HEAR THIS ONE--
HARLEEN?
WELL PLAYED, MY DEAR.
YOU JUST MIGHT BECOME MY HARLEY, YET.
HA! HA! HA! HA!
JOE

PART FOUR
BATGIRL

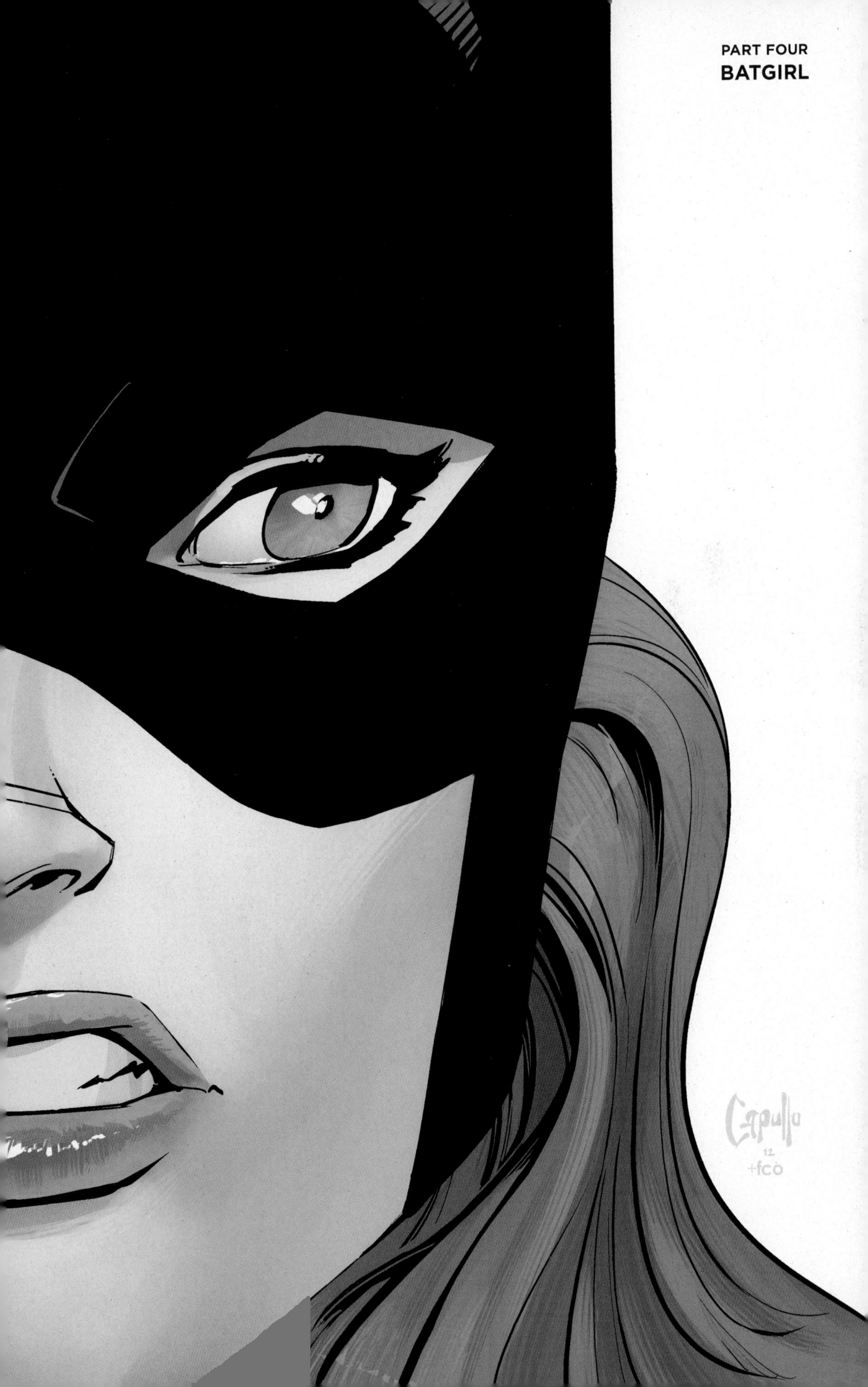

ULISES ARREOLA KYLE RITTER colorists DAVE SHARPE letterer

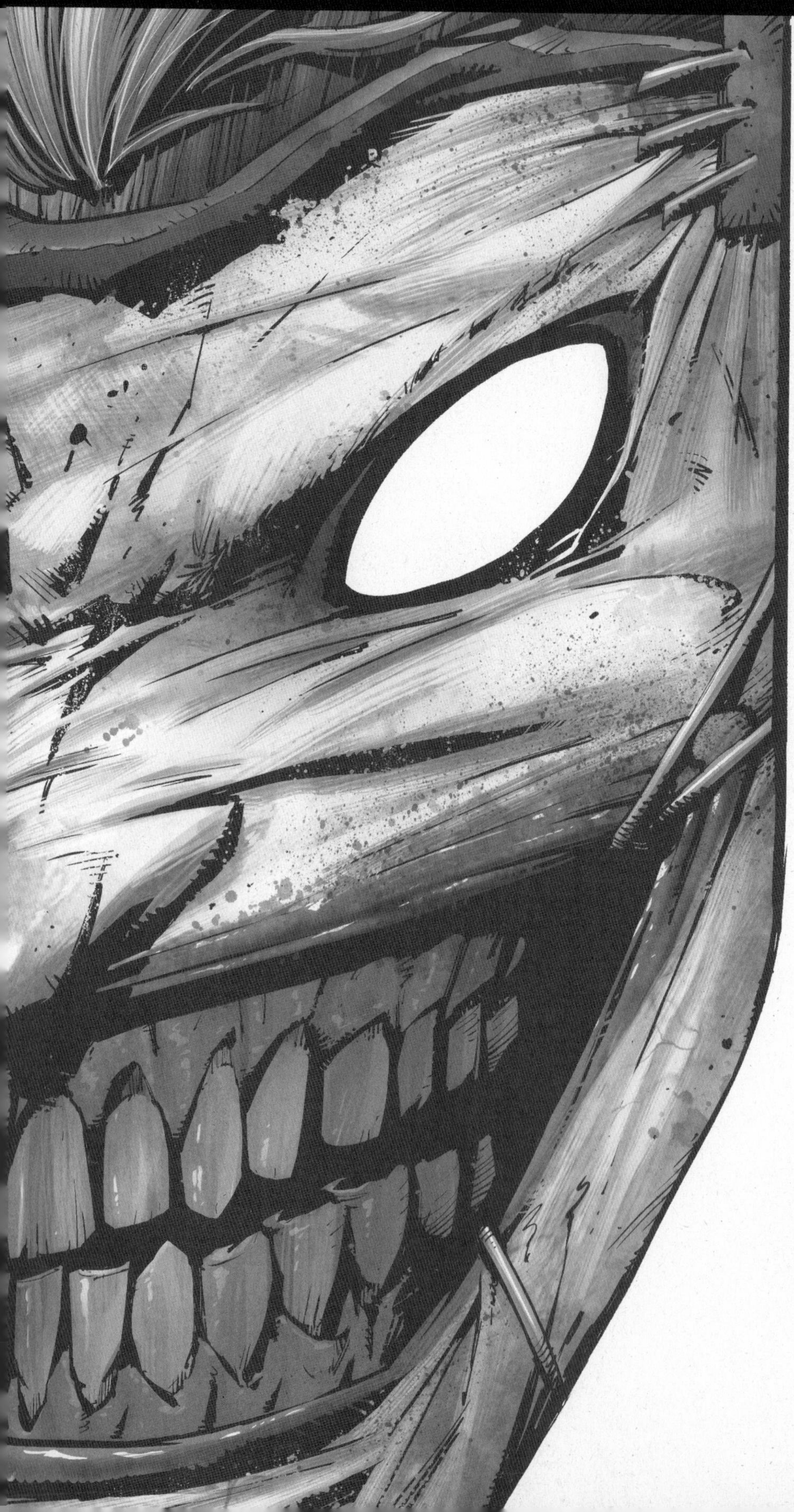

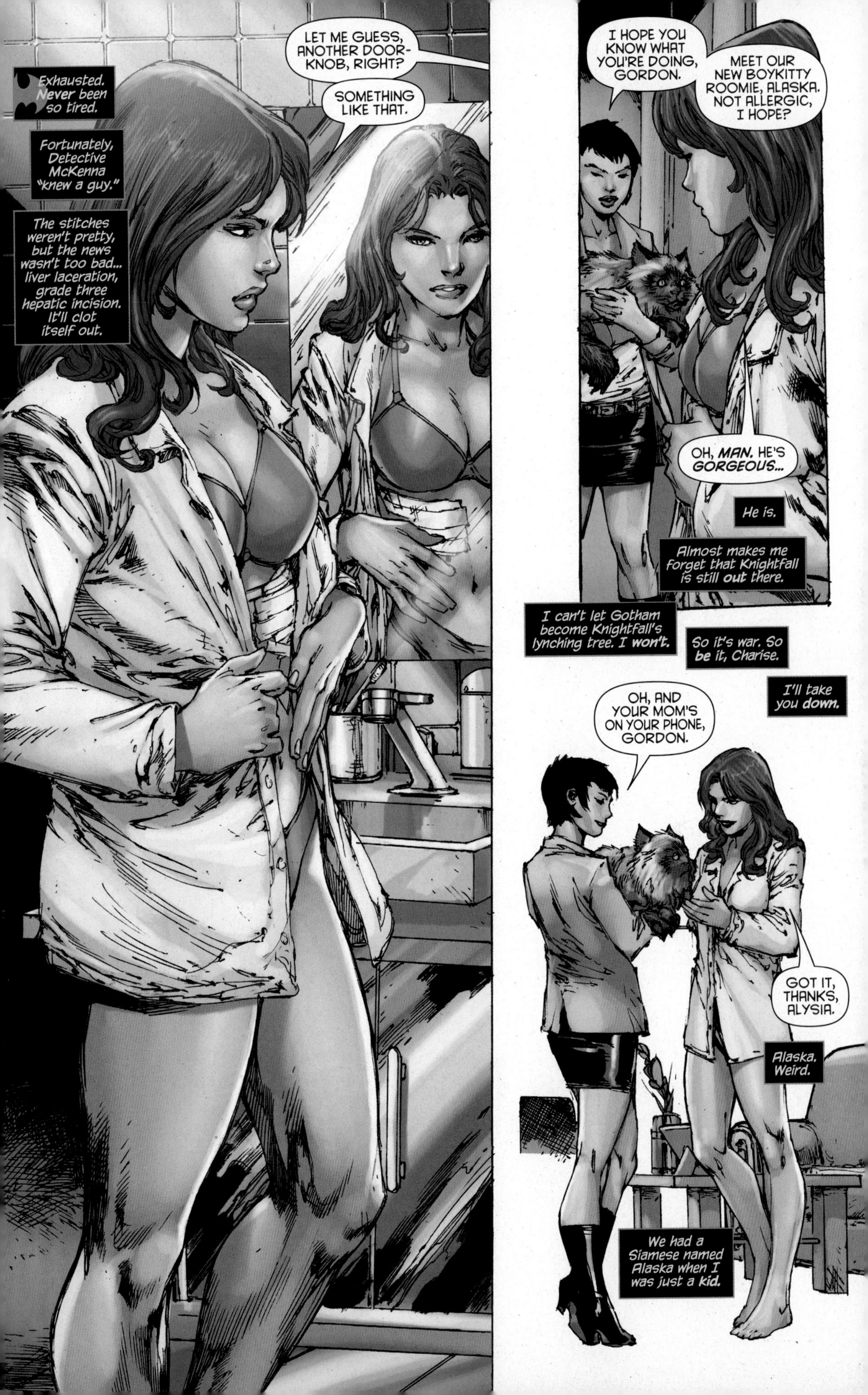

Exhausted. Never been so tired.
Fortunately, Detective McKenna "knew a guy."
The stitches weren't pretty, but the news wasn't too bad... liver laceration, grade three hepatic incision. It'll clot itself out.
LET ME GUESS, ANOTHER DOOR-KNOB, RIGHT?
SOMETHING LIKE THAT.
I HOPE YOU KNOW WHAT YOU'RE DOING, GORDON.
MEET OUR NEW BOYKITTY ROOMIE, ALASKA. NOT ALLERGIC, I HOPE?
OH, MAN. HE'S GORGEOUS...
He is.
Almost makes me forget that Knightfall is still out there.
I can't let Gotham become Knightfall's lynching tree. I won't.
So it's war. So be it, Charise.
I'll take you down.
OH, AND YOUR MOM'S ON YOUR PHONE, GORDON.
GOT IT, THANKS, ALYSIA.
Alaska. Weird.
We had a Siamese named Alaska when I was just a kid.

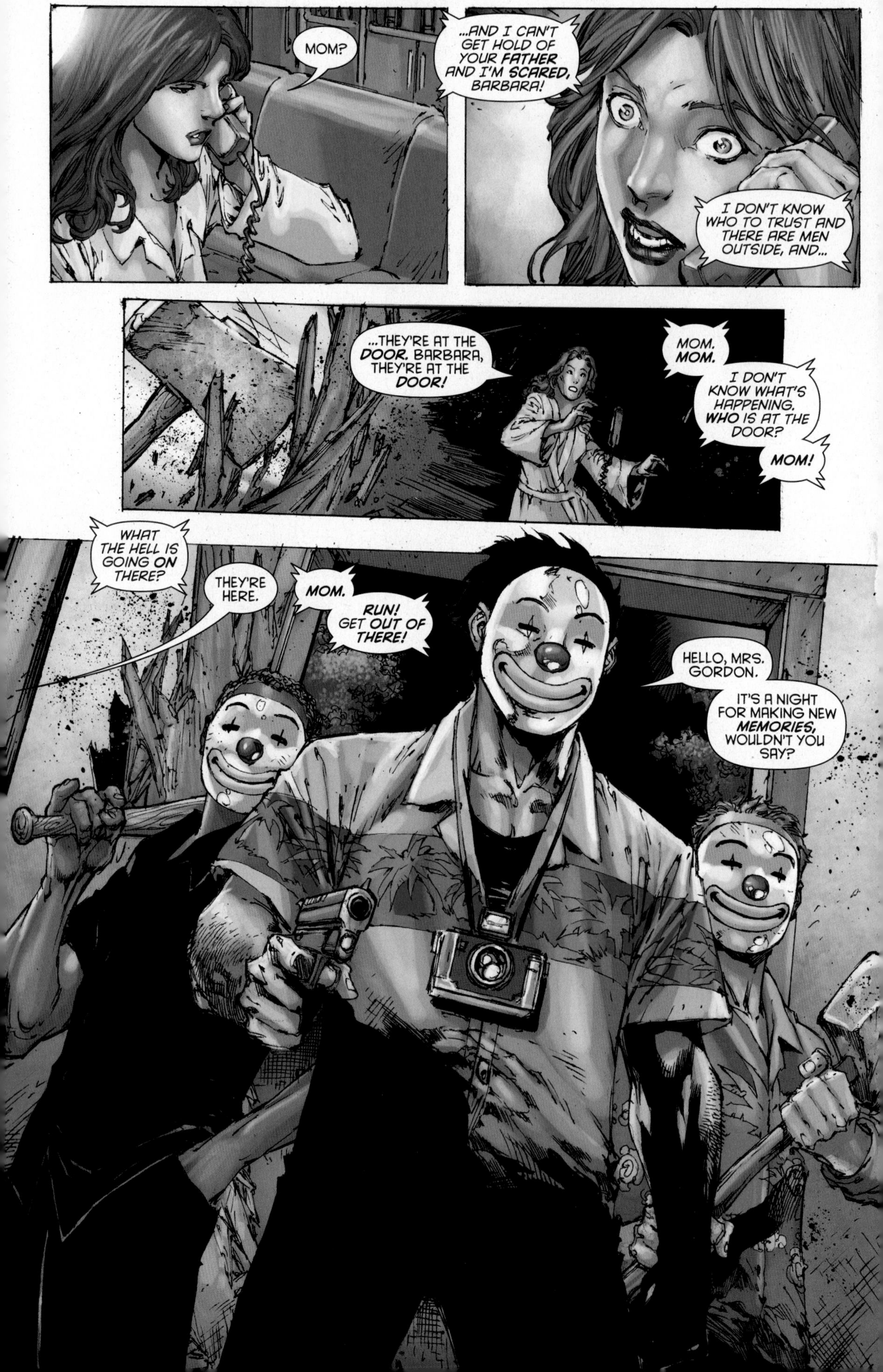
MOM?
...AND I CAN'T GET HOLD OF YOUR FATHER AND I'M SCARED, BARBARA!
I DON'T KNOW WHO TO TRUST AND THERE ARE MEN OUTSIDE, AND...
...THEY'RE AT THE DOOR. BARBARA, THEY'RE AT THE DOOR!
MOM. MOM.
I DON'T KNOW WHAT'S HAPPENING. WHO IS AT THE DOOR?
MOM!
WHAT THE HELL IS GOING ON THERE?
THEY'RE HERE.
MOM.
RUN! GET OUT OF THERE!
HELLO, MRS. GORDON.
IT'S A NIGHT FOR MAKING NEW MEMORIES, WOULDN'T YOU SAY?

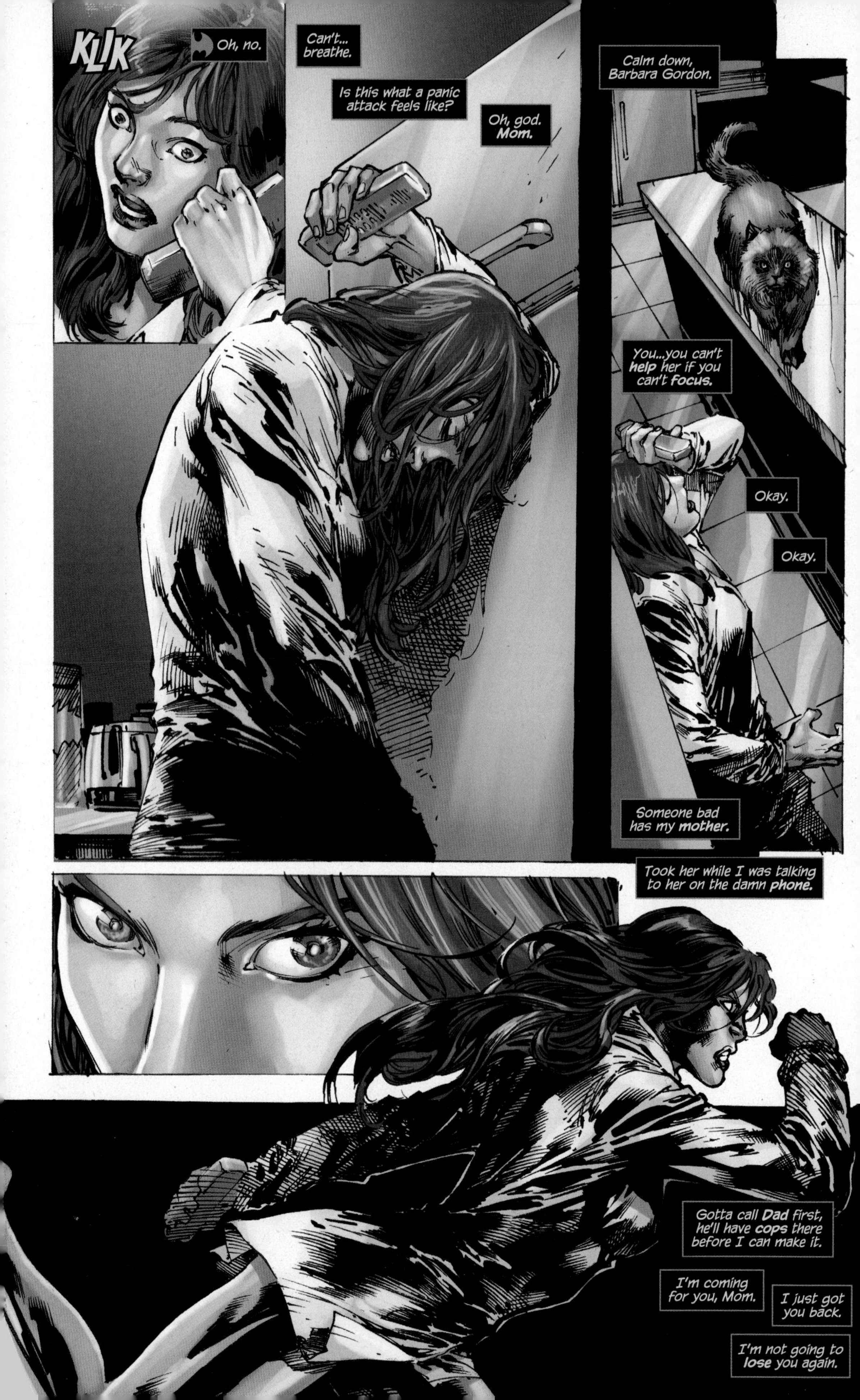
KLIK
Oh, no.
Can't... breathe.
Is this what a panic attack feels like?
Oh, god. **Mom.**
Calm down, Barbara Gordon.
You...you can't **help** her if you can't **focus.**
Okay.
Okay.
Someone bad has my **mother.**
Took her while I was talking to her on the damn **phone.**
Gotta call **Dad** first, he'll have **cops** there before I can make it.
I'm coming for you, Mom.
I just got you back.
I'm not going to **lose** you again.

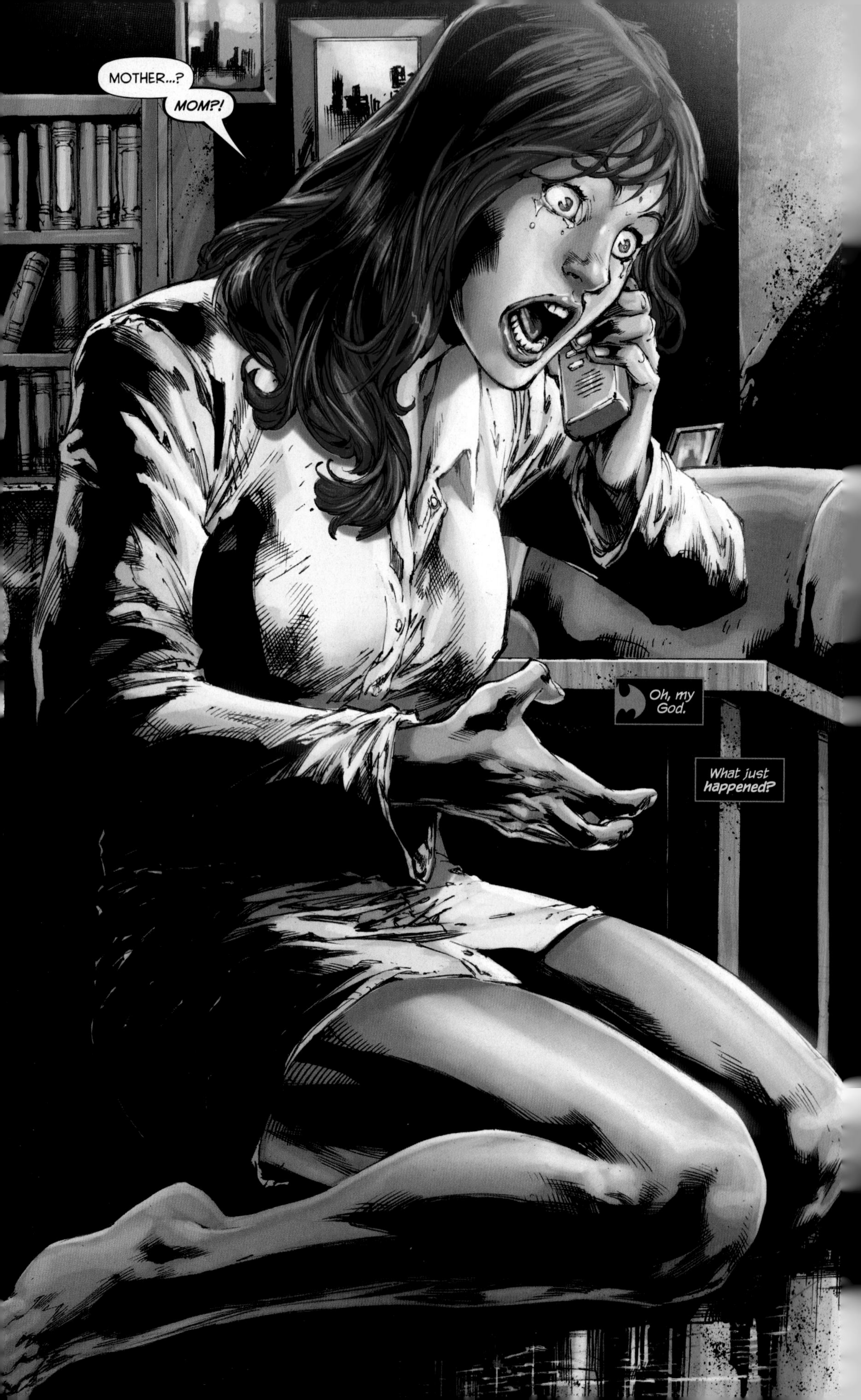
MOTHER...?
MOM?!
Oh, my God.
What just happened?

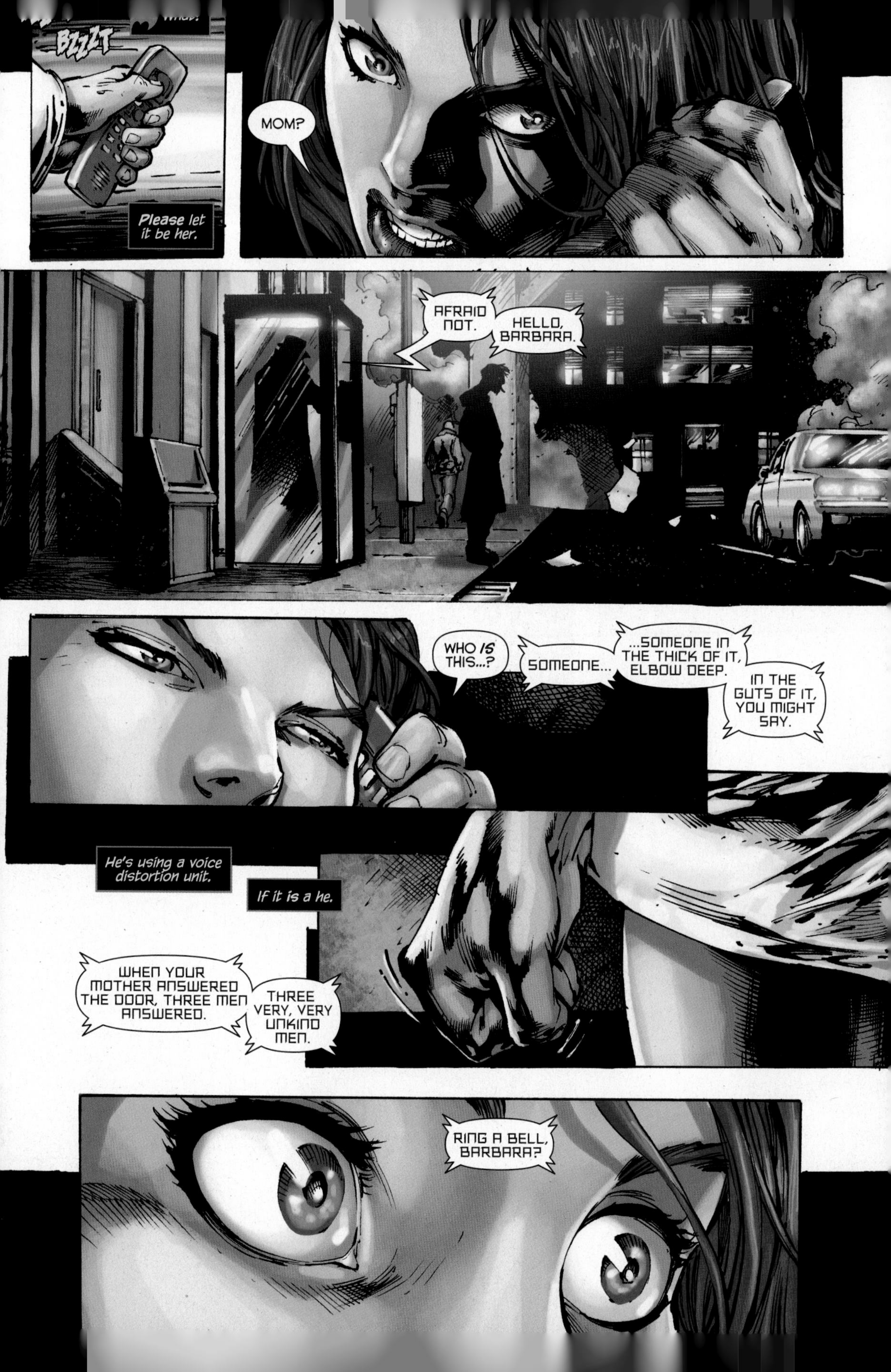
BZZZT
Please let it be her.
MOM?
AFRAID NOT.
HELLO, BARBARA.
WHO *IS* THIS...?
SOMEONE...
...SOMEONE IN THE THICK OF IT, ELBOW DEEP.
IN THE GUTS OF IT, YOU MIGHT SAY.
He's using a voice distortion unit.
If it *is* a he.
WHEN YOUR MOTHER ANSWERED THE DOOR, THREE MEN ANSWERED.
THREE VERY, VERY UNKIND MEN.
RING A BELL, BARBARA?

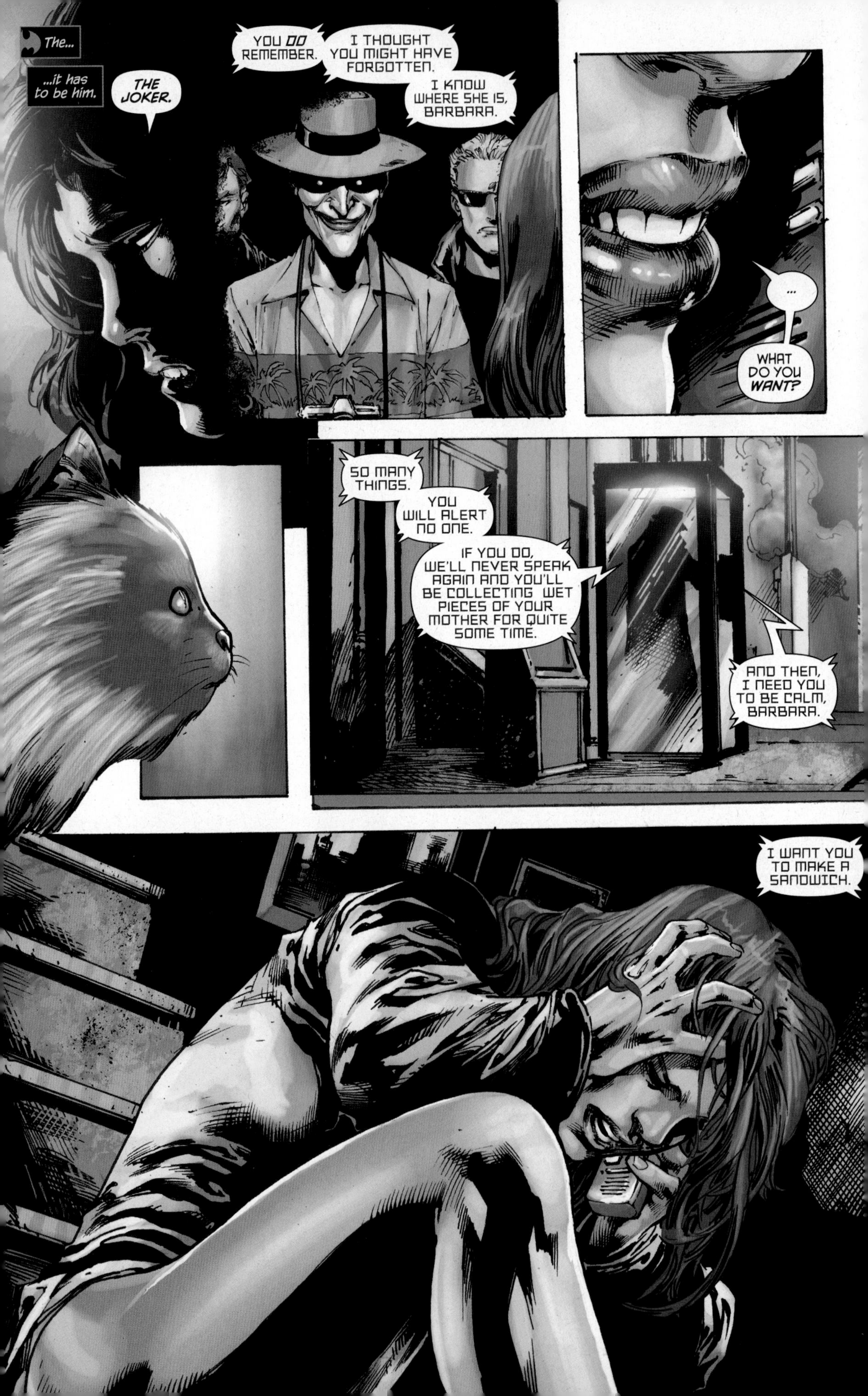
The...
...it has to be him.
THE JOKER.
YOU DO REMEMBER.
I THOUGHT YOU MIGHT HAVE FORGOTTEN.
I KNOW WHERE SHE IS, BARBARA.
...
WHAT DO YOU WANT?
SO MANY THINGS.
YOU WILL ALERT NO ONE.
IF YOU DO, WE'LL NEVER SPEAK AGAIN AND YOU'LL BE COLLECTING WET PIECES OF YOUR MOTHER FOR QUITE SOME TIME.
AND THEN, I NEED YOU TO BE CALM, BARBARA.
I WANT YOU TO MAKE A SANDWICH.

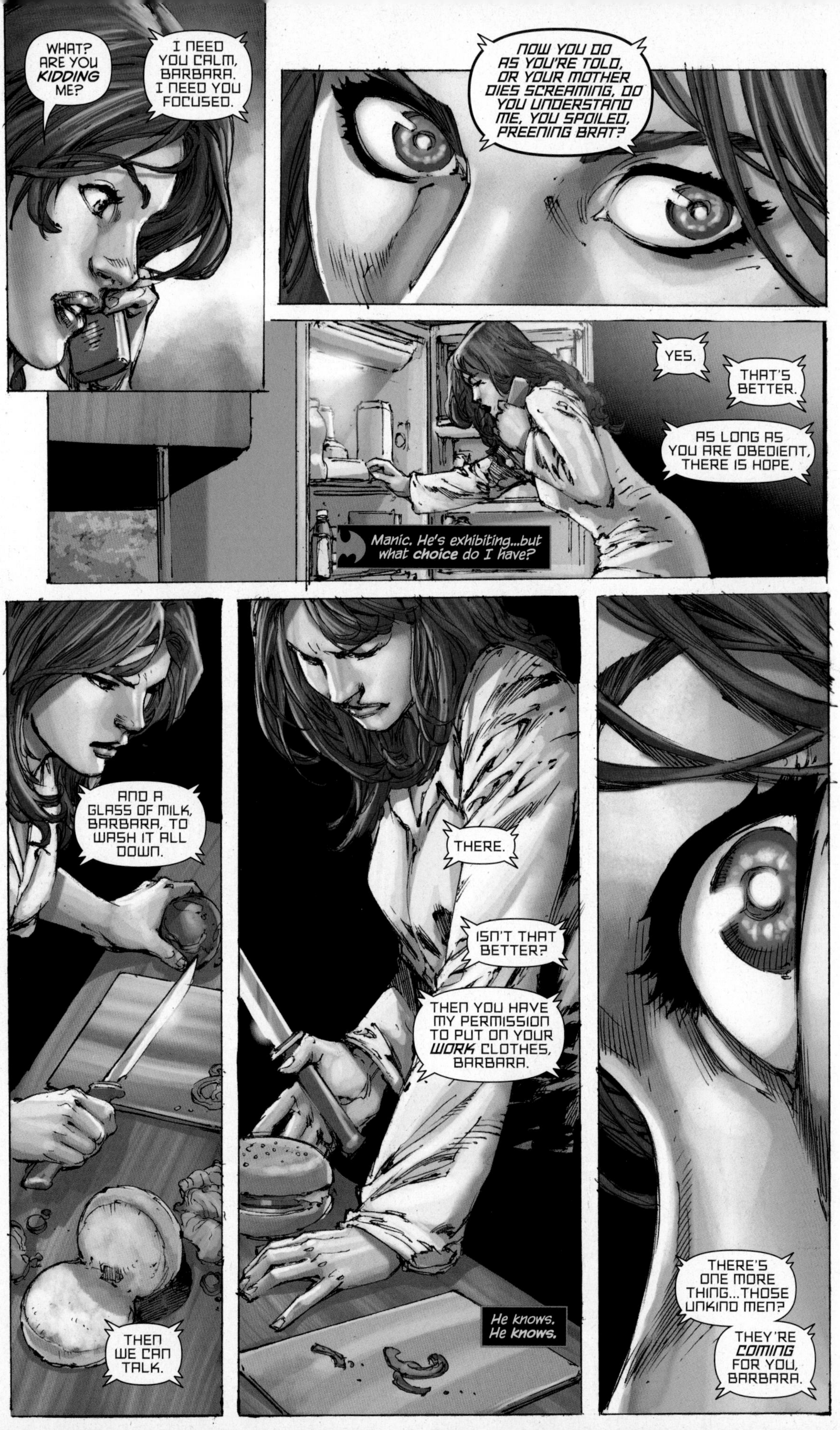
WHAT? ARE YOU *KIDDING* ME?
I NEED YOU CALM, BARBARA. I NEED YOU FOCUSED.
NOW YOU DO AS YOU'RE TOLD, OR YOUR MOTHER DIES SCREAMING, DO YOU UNDERSTAND ME, YOU SPOILED, PREENING BRAT?
YES.
THAT'S BETTER.
AS LONG AS YOU ARE OBEDIENT, THERE IS HOPE.
Manic. He's exhibiting...but what *choice* do I have?
AND A GLASS OF MILK, BARBARA, TO WASH IT ALL DOWN.
THEN WE CAN TALK.
THERE.
ISN'T THAT BETTER?
THEN YOU HAVE MY PERMISSION TO PUT ON YOUR *WORK* CLOTHES, BARBARA.
He knows. He *knows*.
THERE'S ONE MORE THING...THOSE UNKIND MEN?
THEY'RE *COMING* FOR YOU, BARBARA.

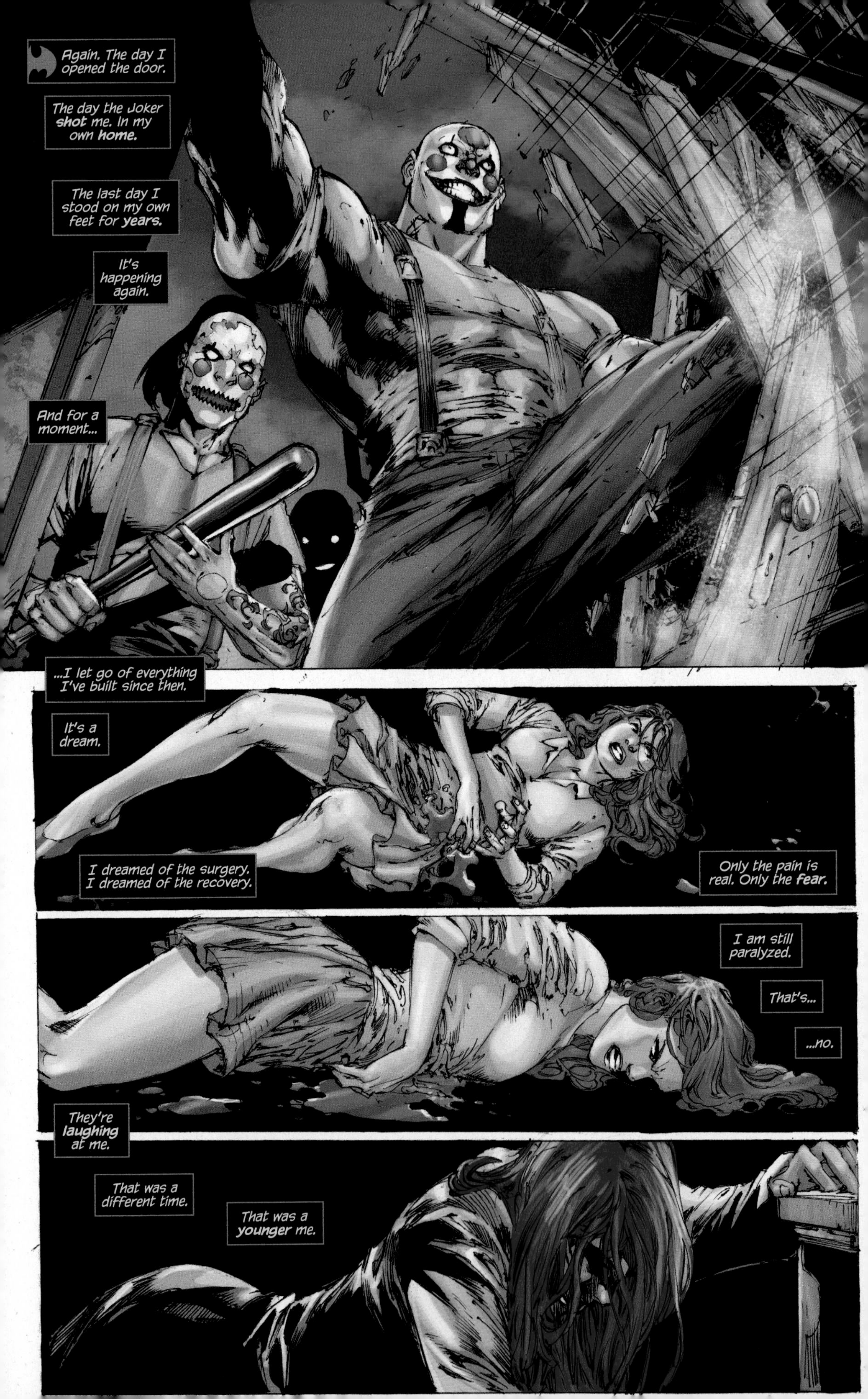
Again. The day I opened the door.
The day the Joker **shot** me. In my own **home.**
The last day I stood on my own feet for **years.**
It's happening again.
And for a moment...
...I let go of everything I've built since then.
It's a dream.
I dreamed of the surgery. I dreamed of the recovery.
Only the pain is real. Only the **fear.**
I am still paralyzed.
That's...
...no.
They're **laughing** at me.
That was a different time.
That was a **younger** me.

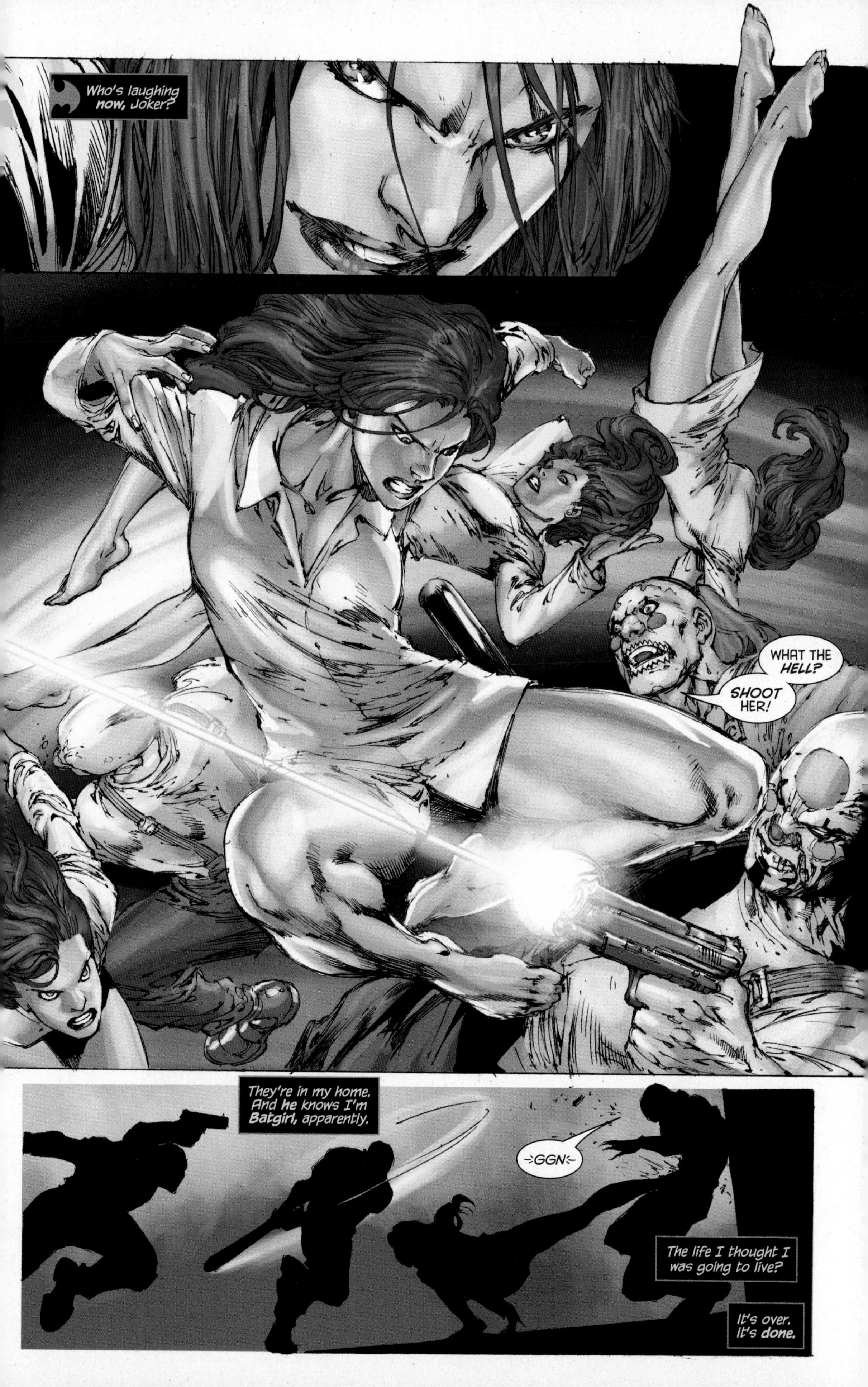
Who's laughing now, Joker?
WHAT THE HELL?
SHOOT HER!
They're in my home. And he knows I'm Batgirl, apparently.
GGN
The life I thought I was going to live?
It's over. It's done.

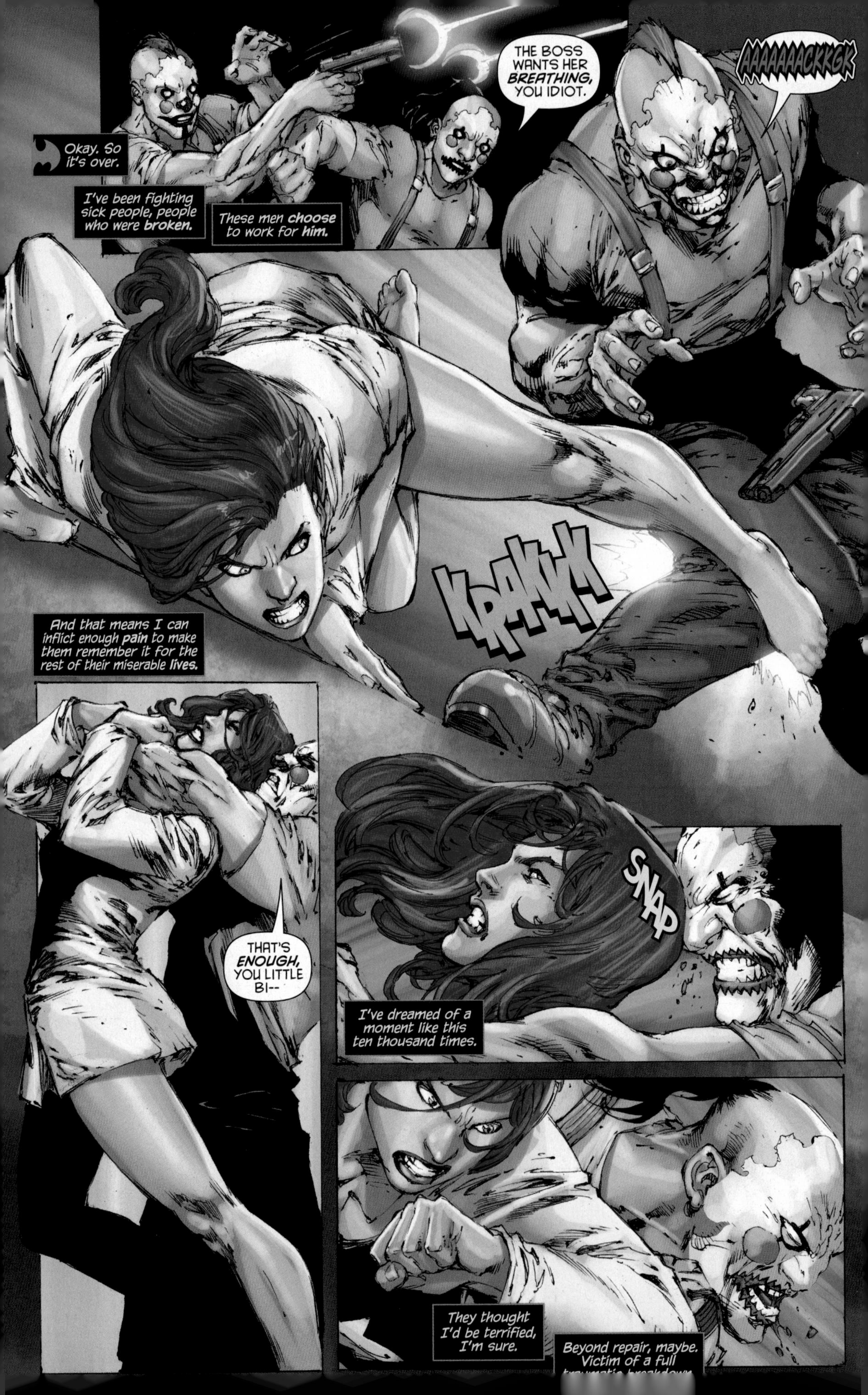

Okay. So it's over.
I've been fighting sick people, people who were broken.
These men choose to work for him.
THE BOSS WANTS HER BREATHING, YOU IDIOT.
AAAAAAACKKGK
And that means I can inflict enough pain to make them remember it for the rest of their miserable lives.
KRAKKK
THAT'S ENOUGH, YOU LITTLE BI--
SNAP
I've dreamed of a moment like this ten thousand times.
They thought I'd be terrified, I'm sure.
Beyond repair, maybe. Victim of a full

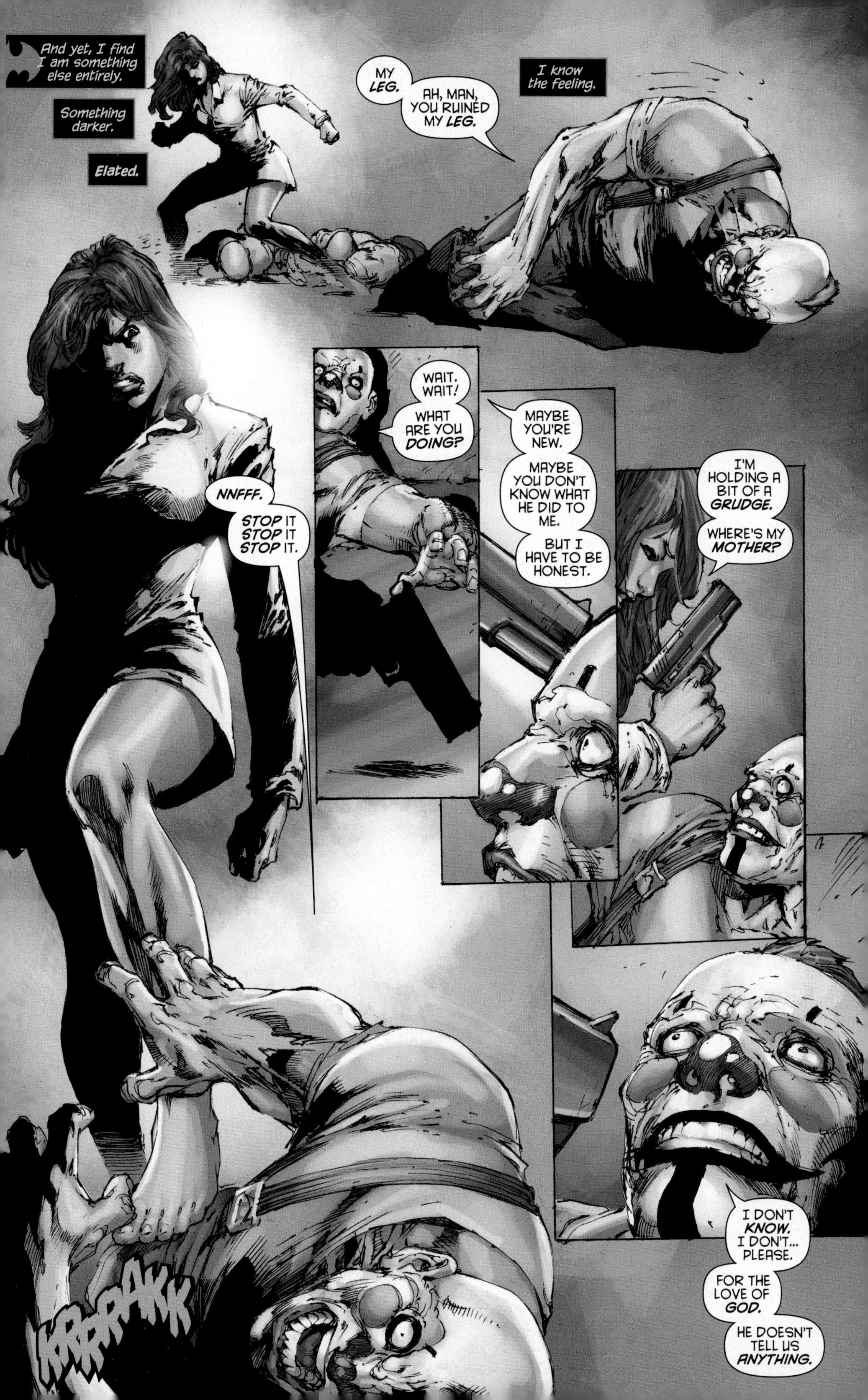
And yet, I find I am something else entirely.
Something darker.
Elated.
MY LEG.
AH, MAN, YOU RUINED MY LEG.
I know the feeling.
NNFFF.
STOP IT STOP IT STOP IT.
WAIT. WAIT!
WHAT ARE YOU DOING?
MAYBE YOU'RE NEW.
MAYBE YOU DON'T KNOW WHAT HE DID TO ME.
BUT I HAVE TO BE HONEST.
I'M HOLDING A BIT OF A GRUDGE.
WHERE'S MY MOTHER?
KRRAKK
I DON'T KNOW. I DON'T... PLEASE.
FOR THE LOVE OF GOD.
HE DOESN'T TELL US ANYTHING.

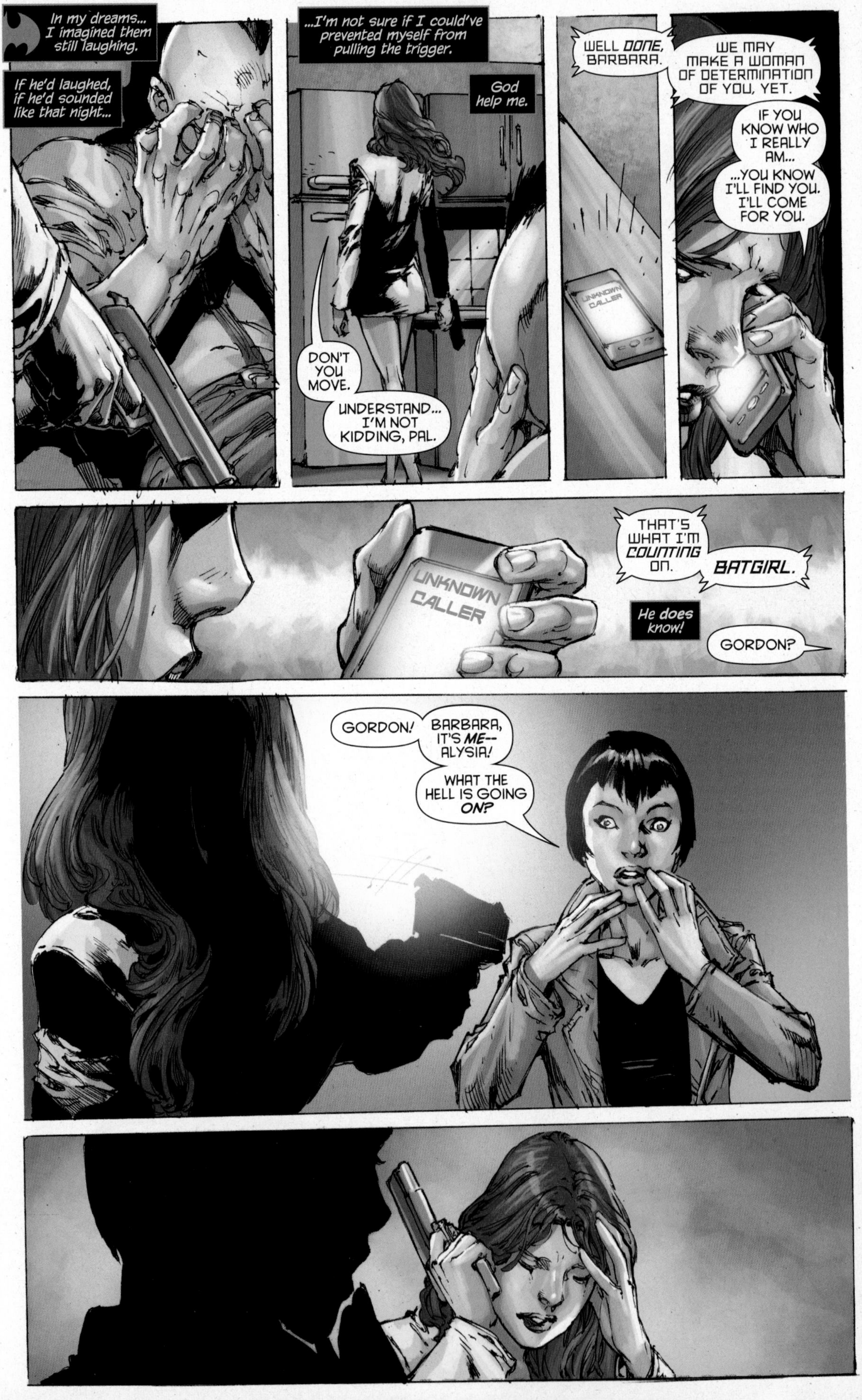
In my dreams... I imagined them still laughing.
If he'd laughed, if he'd sounded like that night...
...I'm not sure if I could've prevented myself from pulling the trigger.
God help me.
DON'T YOU MOVE.
UNDERSTAND... I'M NOT KIDDING, PAL.
WELL DONE, BARBARA.
WE MAY MAKE A WOMAN OF DETERMINATION OF YOU, YET.
IF YOU KNOW WHO I REALLY AM...
...YOU KNOW I'LL FIND YOU. I'LL COME FOR YOU.
UNKNOWN CALLER
UNKNOWN CALLER
THAT'S WHAT I'M COUNTING ON.
BATGIRL.
He does know!
GORDON?
GORDON!
BARBARA, IT'S ME-- ALYSIA!
WHAT THE HELL IS GOING ON?

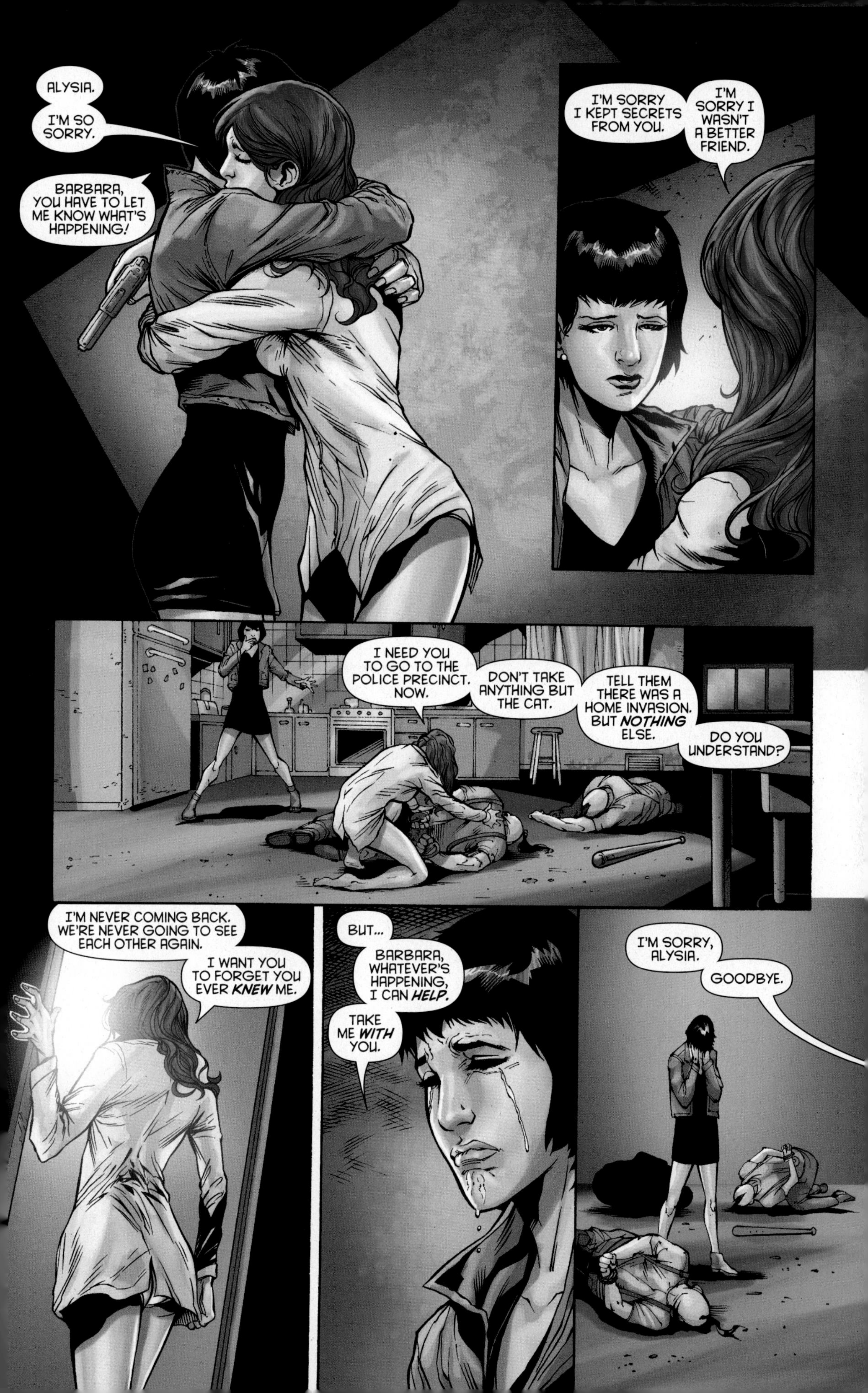
ALYSIA.
I'M SO SORRY.
BARBARA, YOU HAVE TO LET ME KNOW WHAT'S HAPPENING!
I'M SORRY I KEPT SECRETS FROM YOU.
I'M SORRY I WASN'T A BETTER FRIEND.
I NEED YOU TO GO TO THE POLICE PRECINCT. NOW.
DON'T TAKE ANYTHING BUT THE CAT.
TELL THEM THERE WAS A HOME INVASION. BUT NOTHING ELSE.
DO YOU UNDERSTAND?
I'M NEVER COMING BACK. WE'RE NEVER GOING TO SEE EACH OTHER AGAIN.
I WANT YOU TO FORGET YOU EVER KNEW ME.
BUT...
BARBARA, WHATEVER'S HAPPENING, I CAN HELP.
TAKE ME WITH YOU.
I'M SORRY, ALYSIA.
GOODBYE.

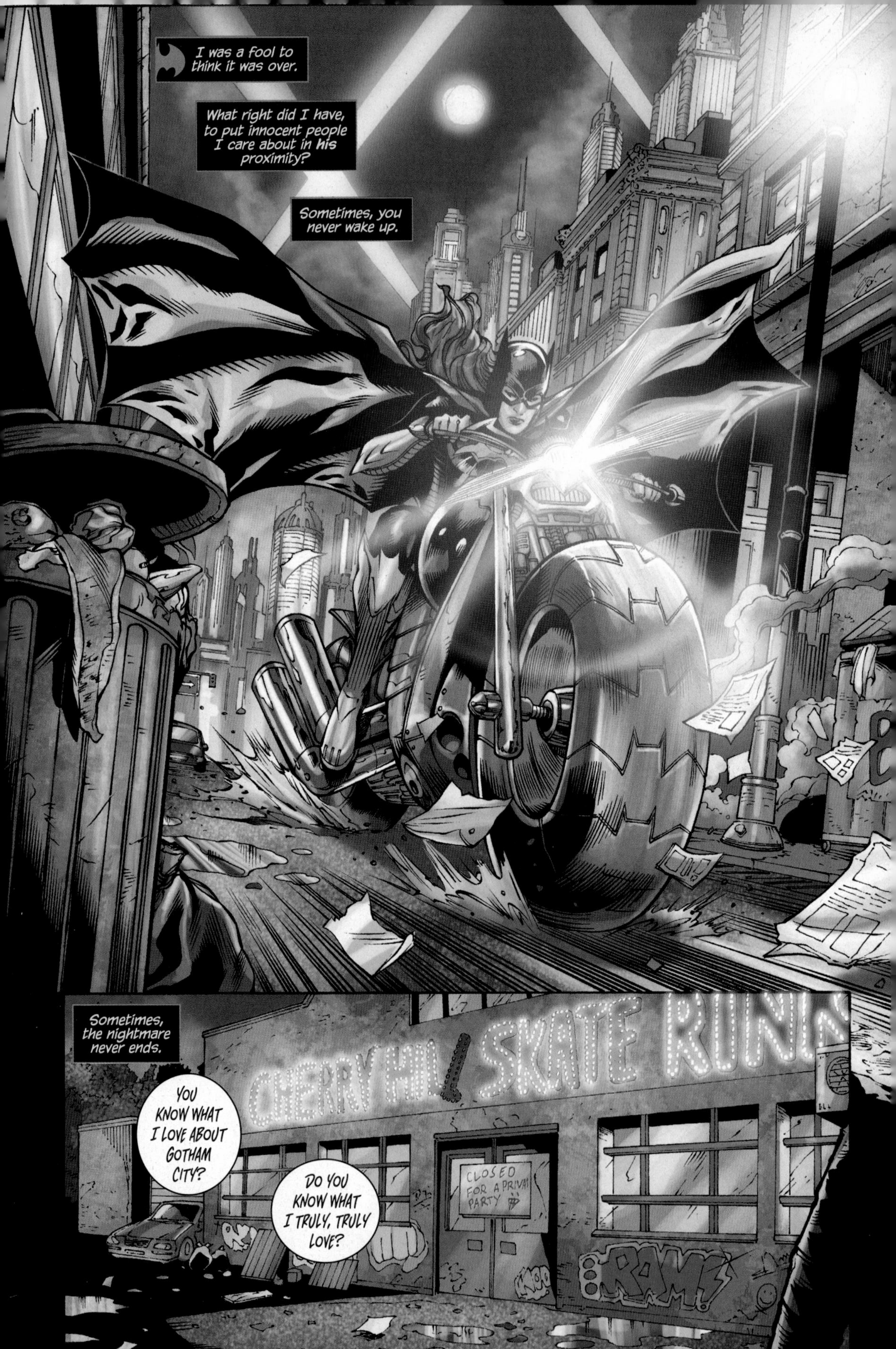

I was a fool to think it was over.
What right did I have, to put innocent people I care about in **his** proximity?
Sometimes, you never wake up.
Sometimes, the nightmare never ends.
SKATE
YOU KNOW WHAT I LOVE ABOUT GOTHAM CITY?
DO YOU KNOW WHAT I TRULY, TRULY LOVE?
CLOSED FOR A PRIVA PARTY
RAM!

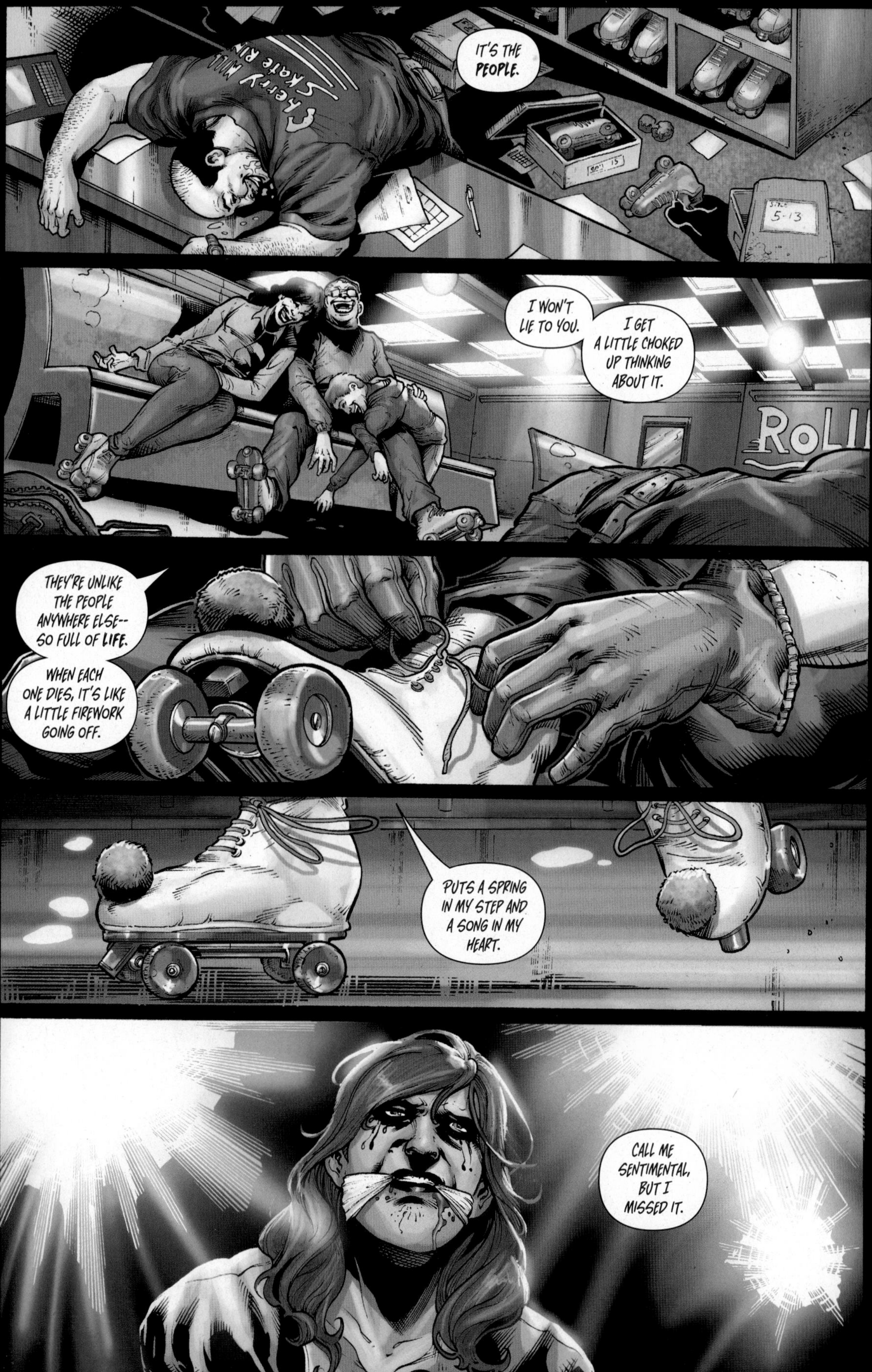
Cherry Hill Skate Rink
IT'S THE PEOPLE.
I WON'T LIE TO YOU.
I GET A LITTLE CHOKED UP THINKING ABOUT IT.
THEY'RE UNLIKE THE PEOPLE ANYWHERE ELSE-- SO FULL OF LIFE.
WHEN EACH ONE DIES, IT'S LIKE A LITTLE FIREWORK GOING OFF.
PUTS A SPRING IN MY STEP AND A SONG IN MY HEART.
CALL ME SENTIMENTAL, BUT I MISSED IT.

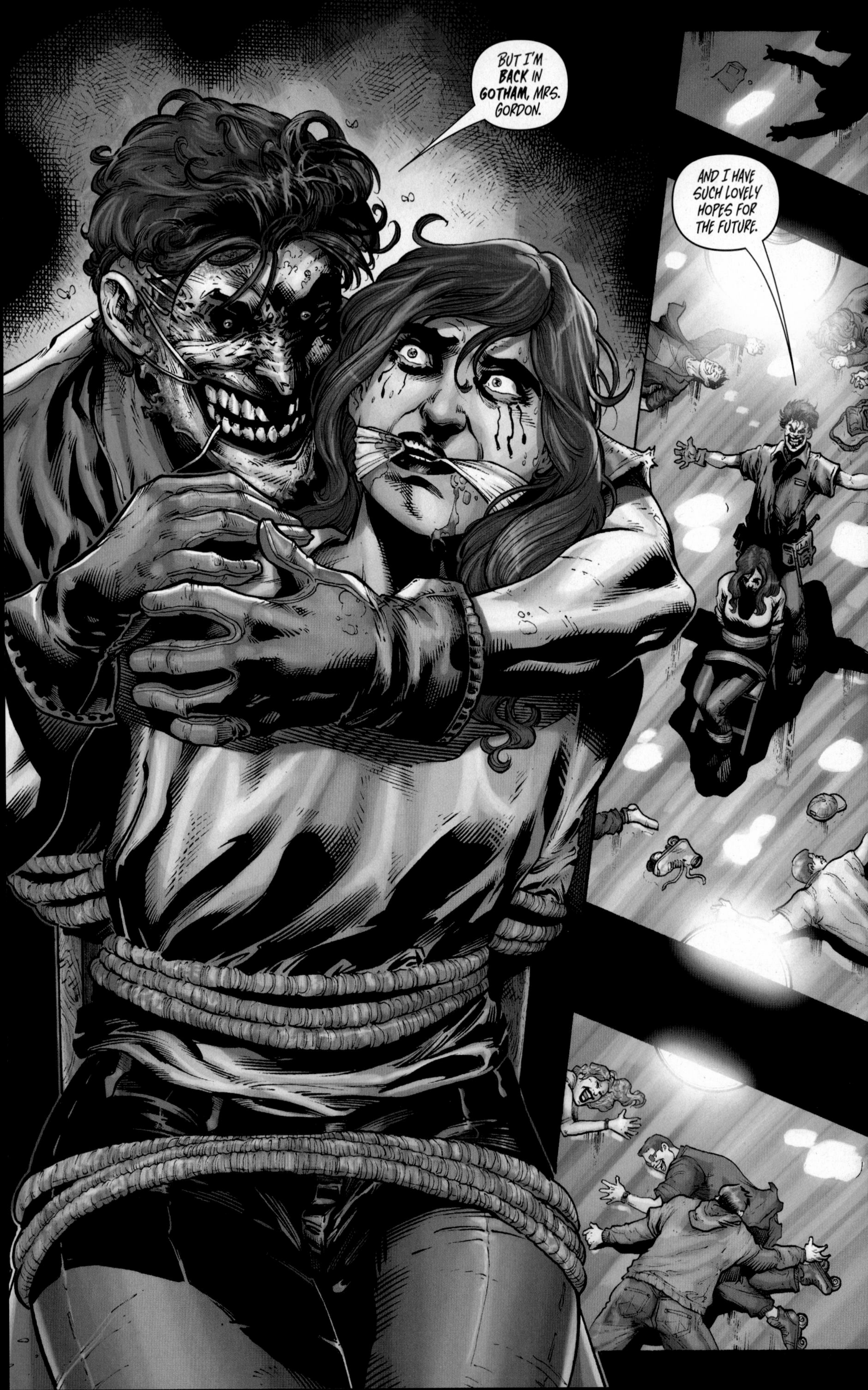
BUT I'M BACK IN GOTHAM, MRS. GORDON.
AND I HAVE SUCH LOVELY HOPES FOR THE FUTURE.

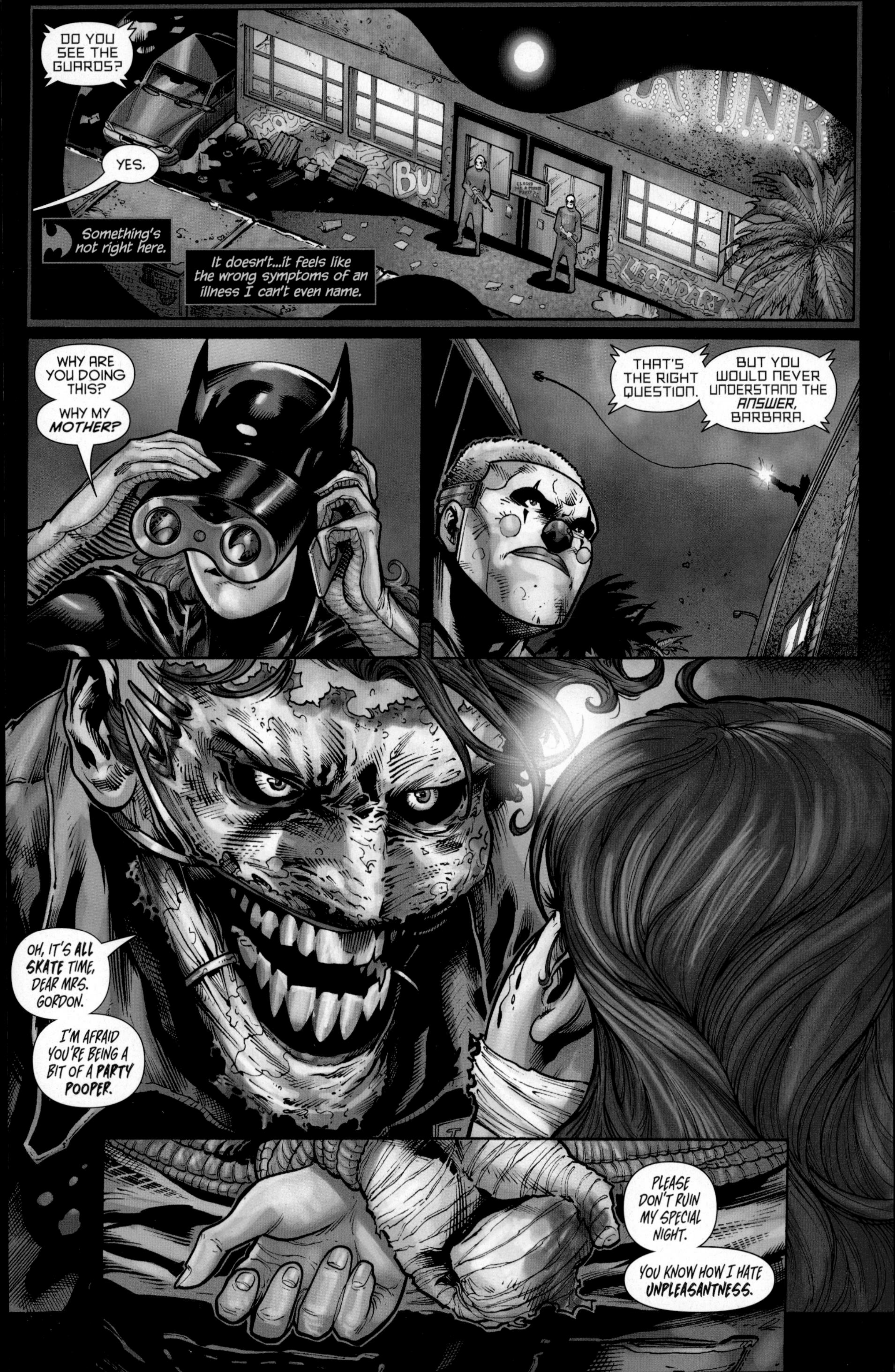

DO YOU SEE THE GUARDS?
YES.
Something's not right here.
It doesn't...it feels like the wrong symptoms of an illness I can't even name.
WHY ARE YOU DOING THIS?
WHY MY MOTHER?
THAT'S THE RIGHT QUESTION.
BUT YOU WOULD NEVER UNDERSTAND THE ANSWER, BARBARA.
OH, IT'S ALL SKATE TIME, DEAR MRS. GORDON.
I'M AFRAID YOU'RE BEING A BIT OF A PARTY POOPER.
PLEASE DON'T RUIN MY SPECIAL NIGHT.
YOU KNOW HOW I HATE UNPLEASANTNESS.

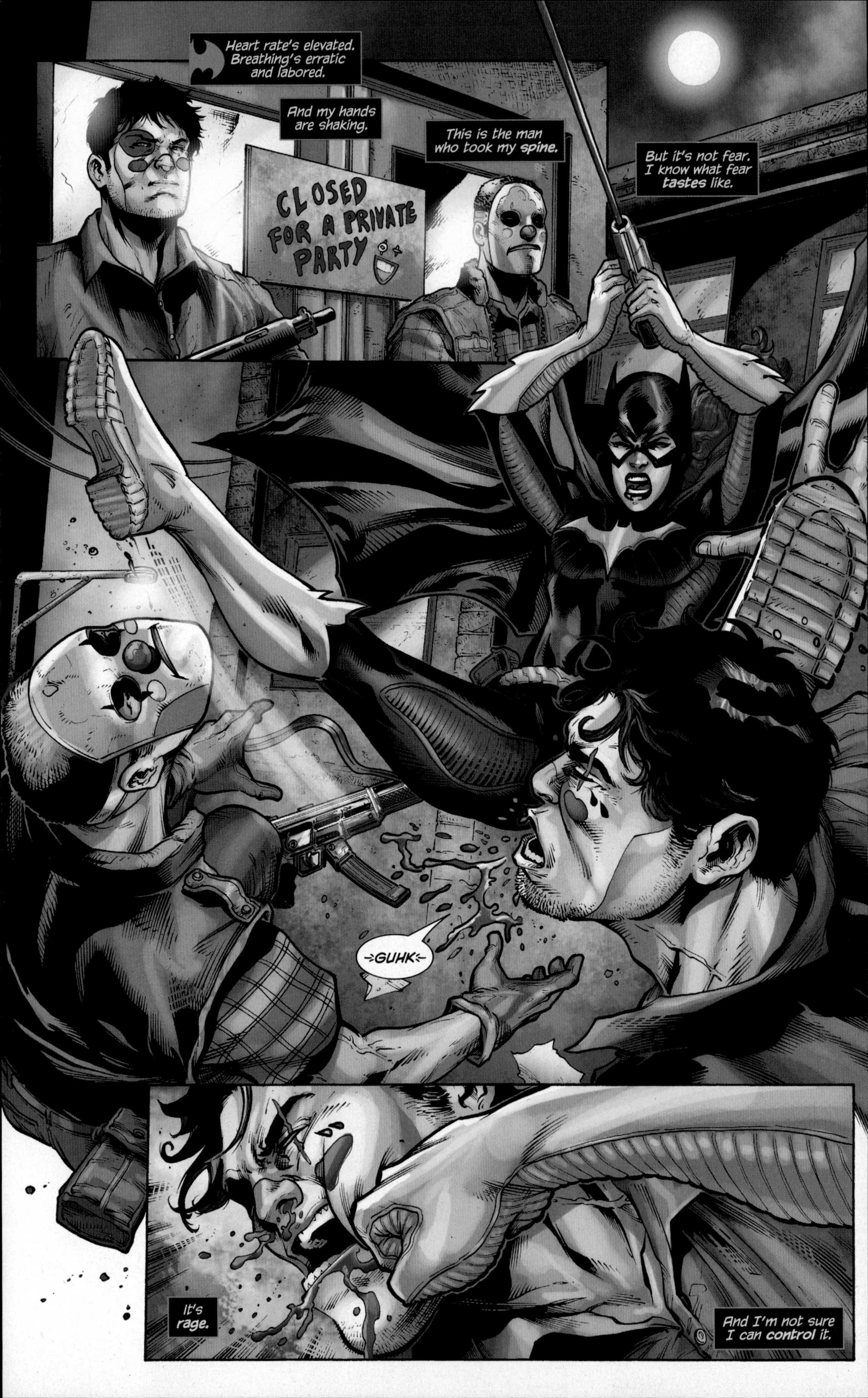

Heart rate's elevated. Breathing's erratic and labored.
And my hands are shaking.
CLOSED FOR A PRIVATE PARTY
This is the man who took my spine.
But it's not fear. I know what fear tastes like.
GUHK
It's rage.
And I'm not sure I can control it.

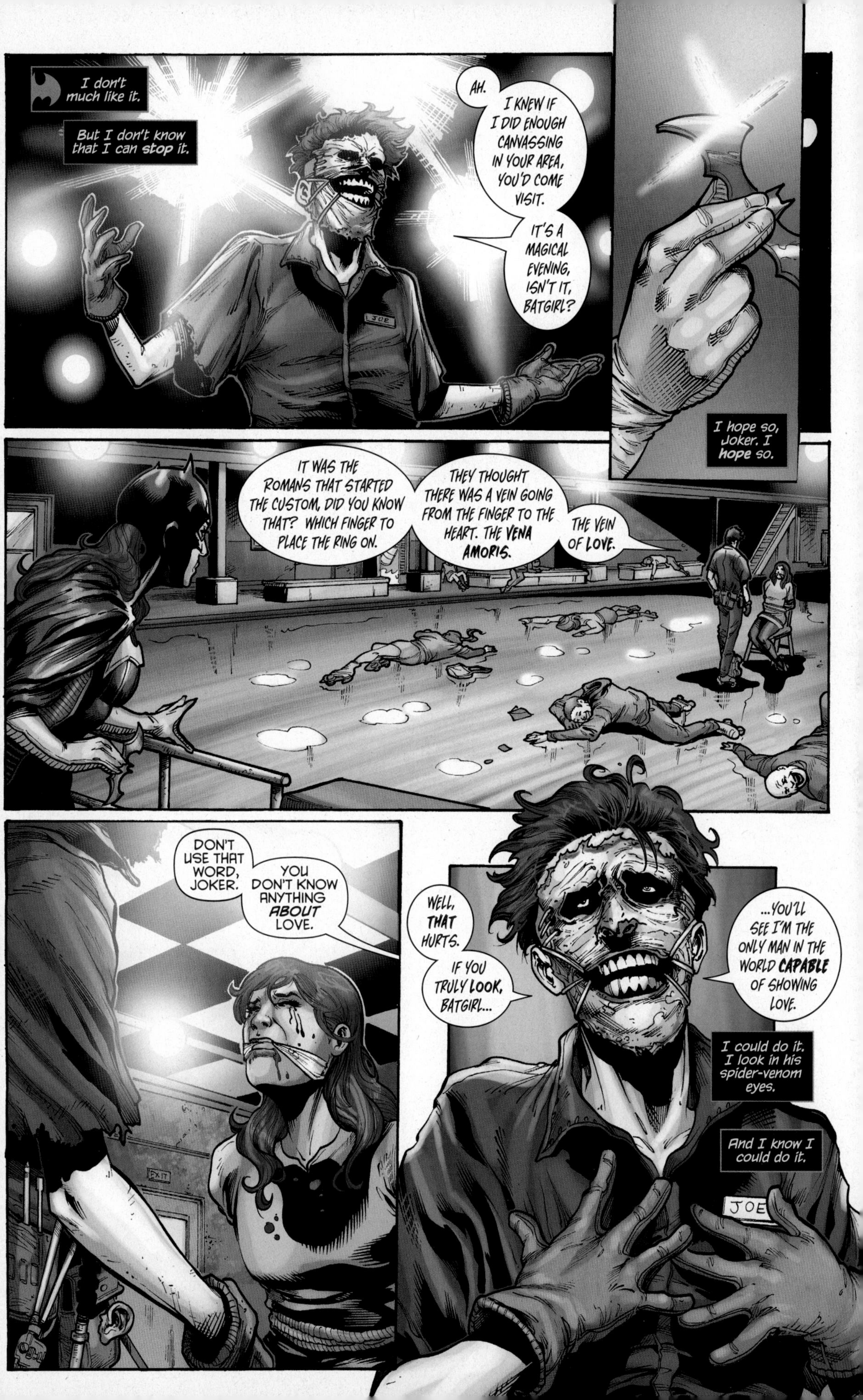
I don't much like it.
But I don't know that I can stop it.
AH.
I KNEW IF I DID ENOUGH CANVASSING IN YOUR AREA, YOU'D COME VISIT.
IT'S A MAGICAL EVENING, ISN'T IT, BATGIRL?
JOE
I hope so, Joker. I hope so.
IT WAS THE ROMANS THAT STARTED THE CUSTOM, DID YOU KNOW THAT? WHICH FINGER TO PLACE THE RING ON.
THEY THOUGHT THERE WAS A VEIN GOING FROM THE FINGER TO THE HEART. THE VENA AMORIS.
THE VEIN OF LOVE.
DON'T USE THAT WORD, JOKER.
YOU DON'T KNOW ANYTHING ABOUT LOVE.
WELL, THAT HURTS.
IF YOU TRULY LOOK, BATGIRL...
...YOU'LL SEE I'M THE ONLY MAN IN THE WORLD CAPABLE OF SHOWING LOVE.
I could do it. I look in his spider-venom eyes.
And I know I could do it.
EXIT
JOE

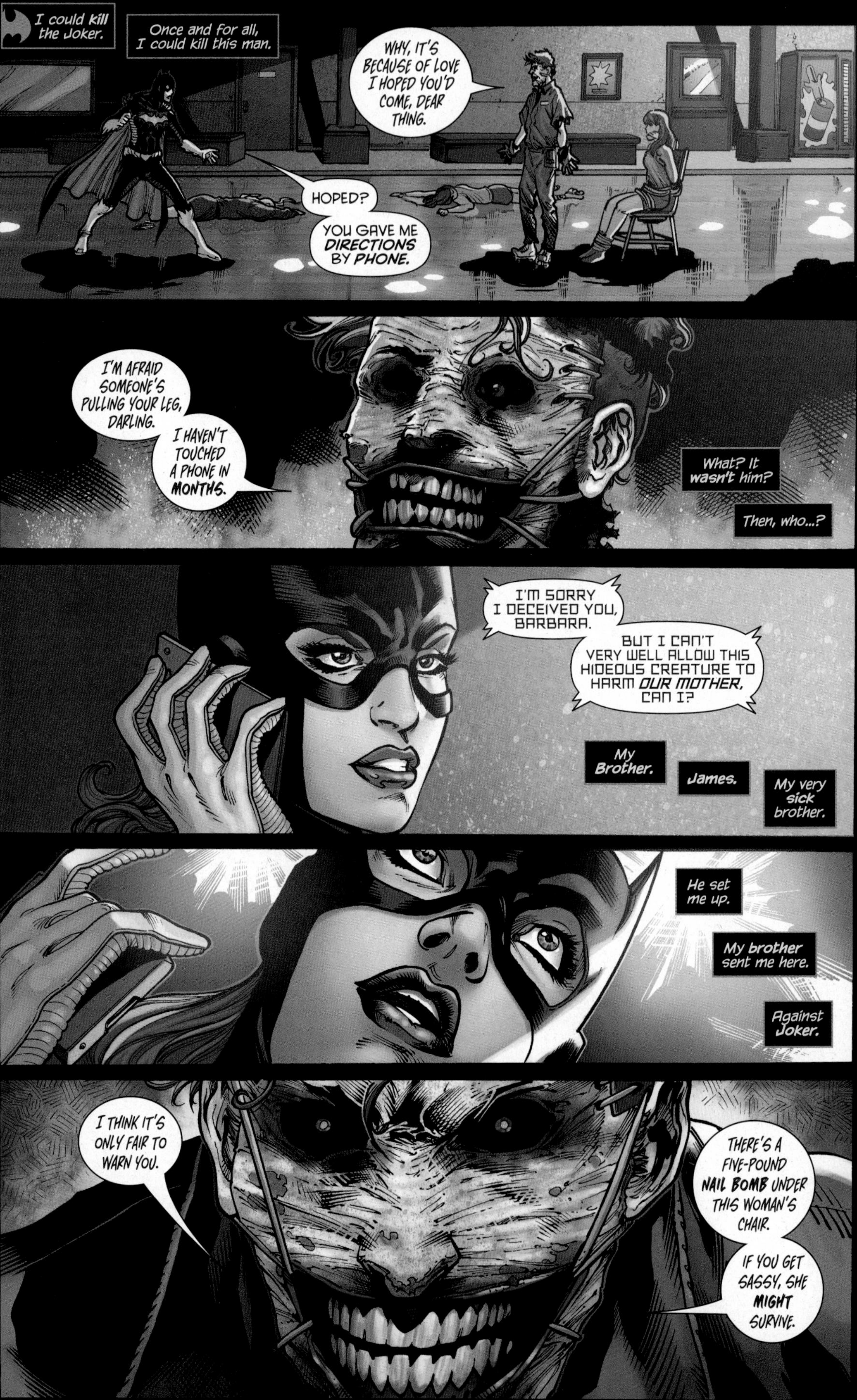
I could kill the Joker.
Once and for all, I could kill this man.
WHY, IT'S BECAUSE OF LOVE I HOPED YOU'D COME, DEAR THING.
HOPED?
YOU GAVE ME DIRECTIONS BY PHONE.
I'M AFRAID SOMEONE'S PULLING YOUR LEG, DARLING.
I HAVEN'T TOUCHED A PHONE IN MONTHS.
What? It wasn't him?
Then, who...?
I'M SORRY I DECEIVED YOU, BARBARA.
BUT I CAN'T VERY WELL ALLOW THIS HIDEOUS CREATURE TO HARM OUR MOTHER, CAN I?
My Brother.
James.
My very sick brother.
He set me up.
My brother sent me here.
Against Joker.
I THINK IT'S ONLY FAIR TO WARN YOU.
THERE'S A FIVE-POUND NAIL BOMB UNDER THIS WOMAN'S CHAIR.
IF YOU GET SASSY, SHE MIGHT SURVIVE.

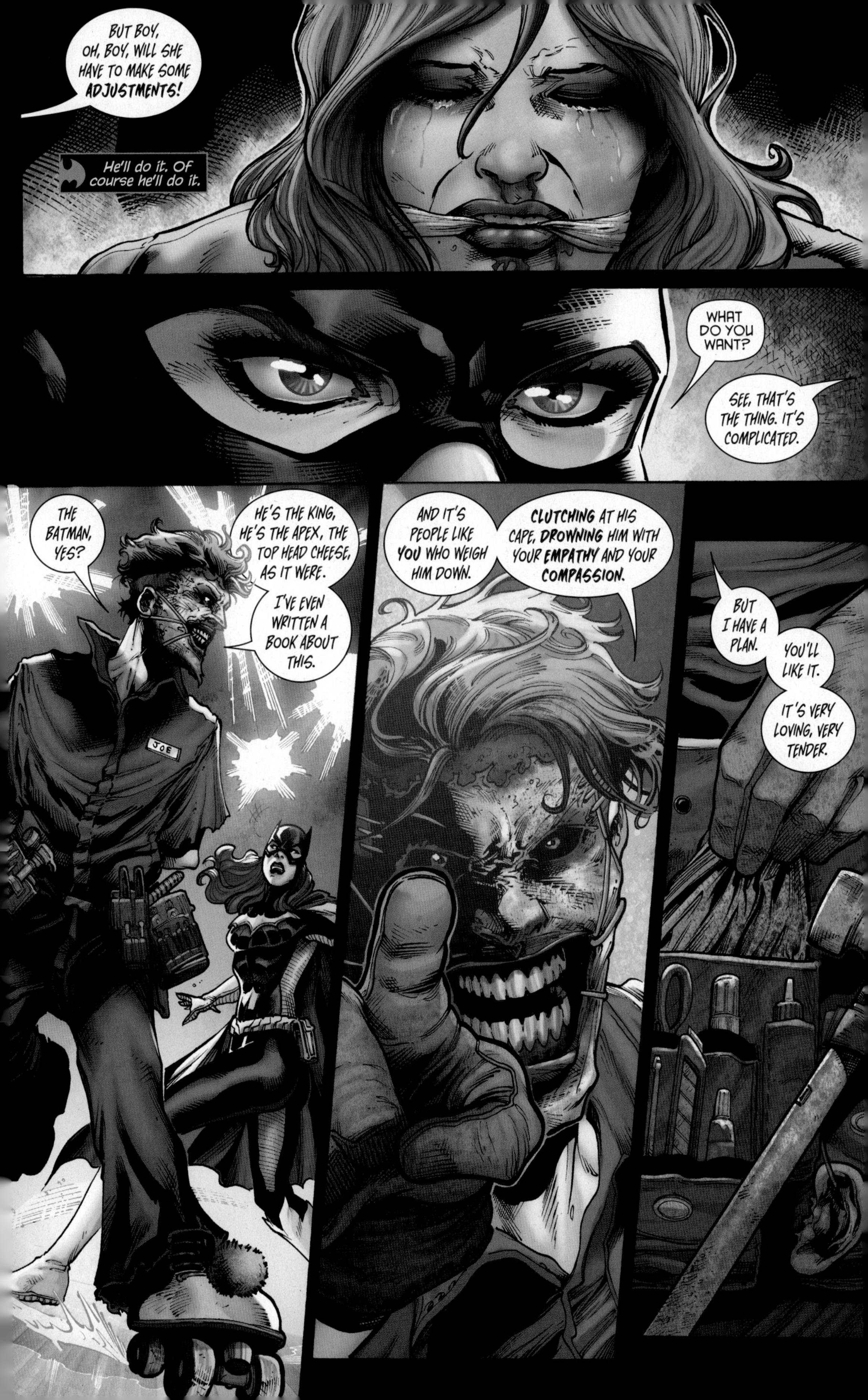
BUT BOY, OH, BOY, WILL SHE HAVE TO MAKE SOME ADJUSTMENTS!
He'll do it. Of course he'll do it.
WHAT DO YOU WANT?
SEE, THAT'S THE THING. IT'S COMPLICATED.
THE BATMAN, YES?
HE'S THE KING, HE'S THE APEX, THE TOP HEAD CHEESE, AS IT WERE.
I'VE EVEN WRITTEN A BOOK ABOUT THIS.
JOE
AND IT'S PEOPLE LIKE YOU WHO WEIGH HIM DOWN.
CLUTCHING AT HIS CAPE, DROWNING HIM WITH YOUR EMPATHY AND YOUR COMPASSION.
BUT I HAVE A PLAN.
YOU'LL LIKE IT.
IT'S VERY LOVING, VERY TENDER.

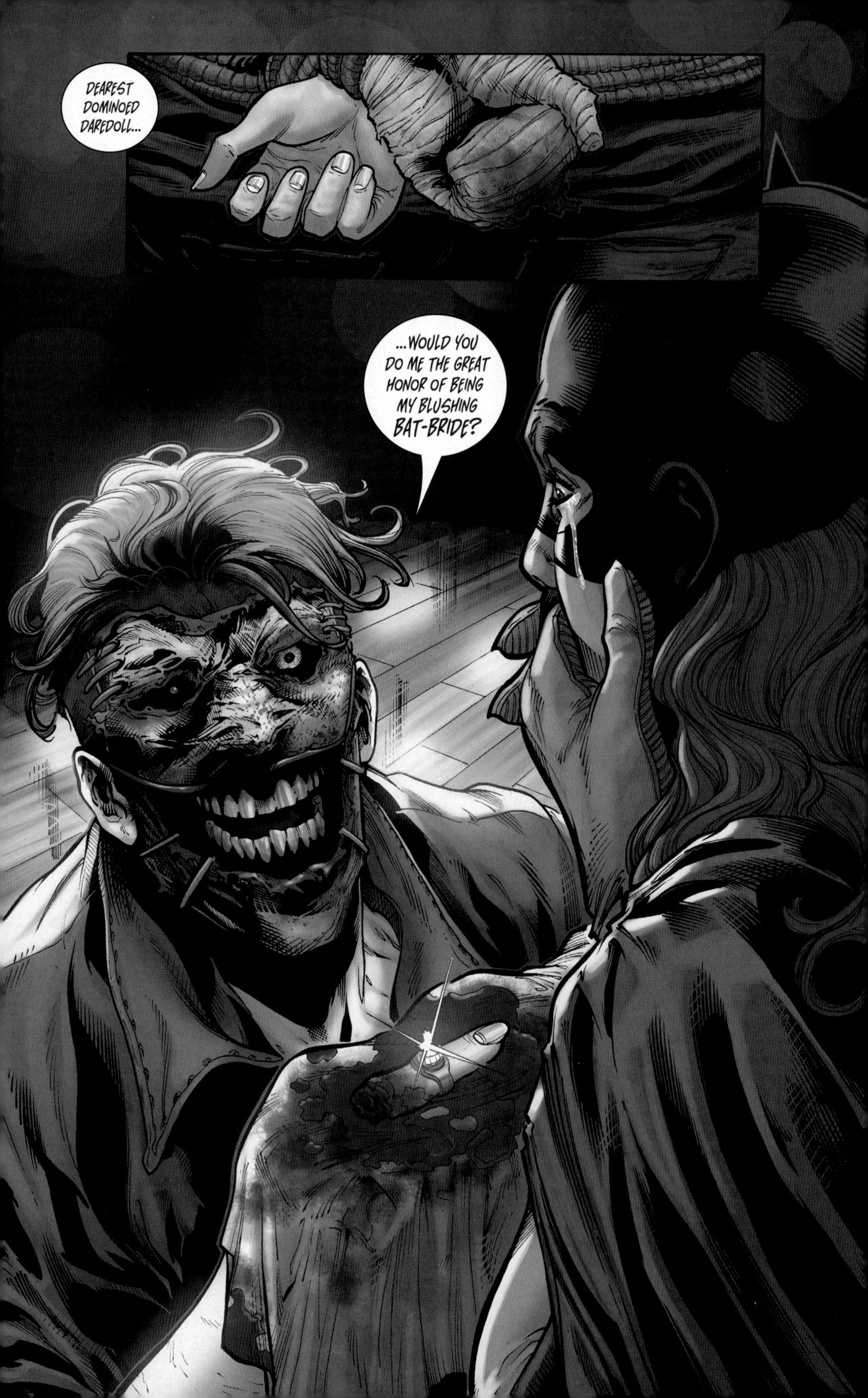
DEAREST DOMINOED DAREDOLL...
...WOULD YOU DO ME THE GREAT HONOR OF BEING MY BLUSHING BAT-BRIDE?

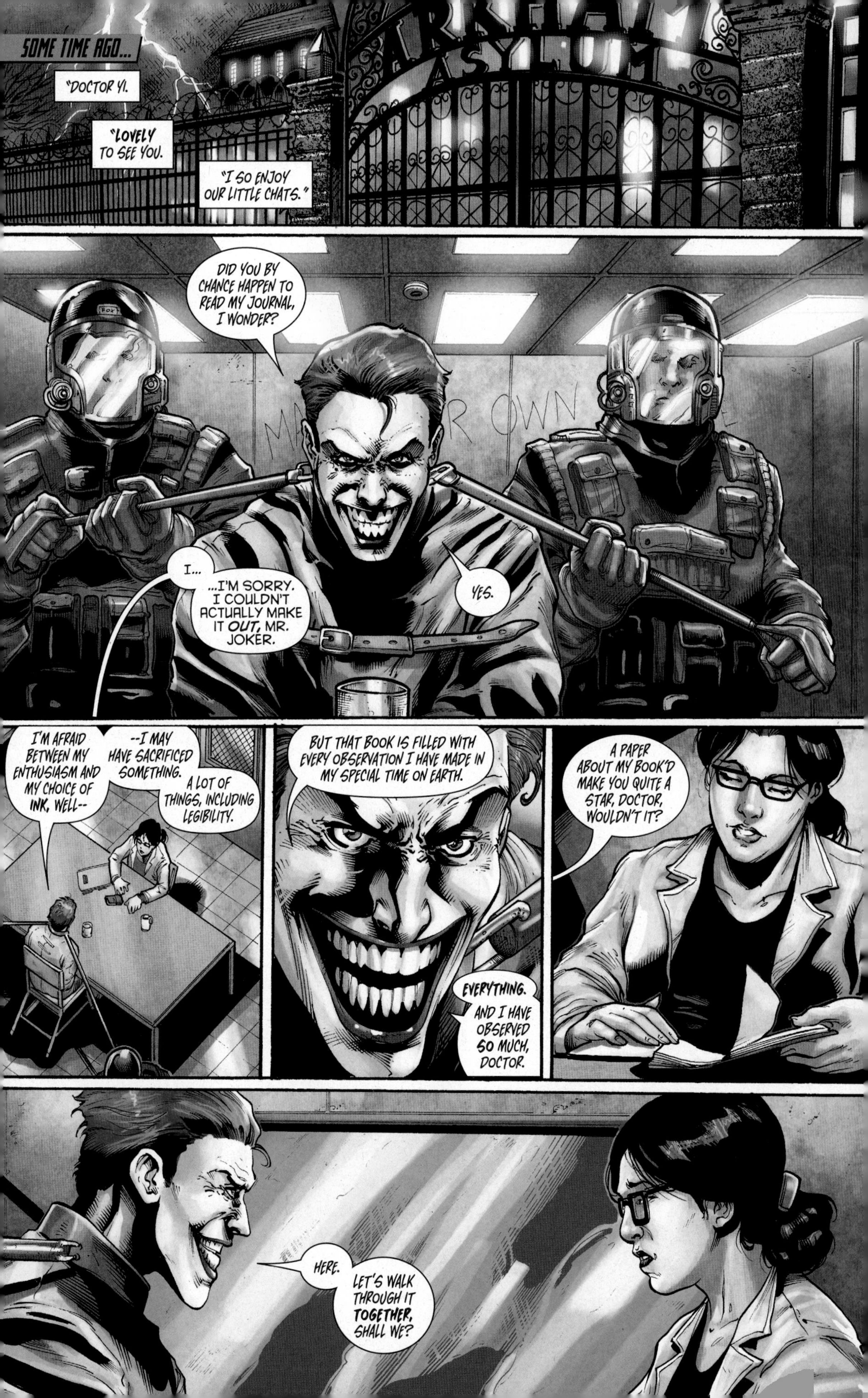
SOME TIME AGO...
"DOCTOR YI.
"LOVELY TO SEE YOU.
"I SO ENJOY OUR LITTLE CHATS."
DID YOU BY CHANCE HAPPEN TO READ MY JOURNAL, I WONDER?
I...
...I'M SORRY. I COULDN'T ACTUALLY MAKE IT OUT, MR. JOKER.
YES.
I'M AFRAID BETWEEN MY ENTHUSIASM AND MY CHOICE OF INK, WELL--
--I MAY HAVE SACRIFICED SOMETHING.
A LOT OF THINGS, INCLUDING LEGIBILITY.
BUT THAT BOOK IS FILLED WITH EVERY OBSERVATION I HAVE MADE IN MY SPECIAL TIME ON EARTH.
EVERYTHING.
AND I HAVE OBSERVED SO MUCH, DOCTOR.
A PAPER ABOUT MY BOOK'D MAKE YOU QUITE A STAR, DOCTOR, WOULDN'T IT?
HERE.
LET'S WALK THROUGH IT TOGETHER, SHALL WE?

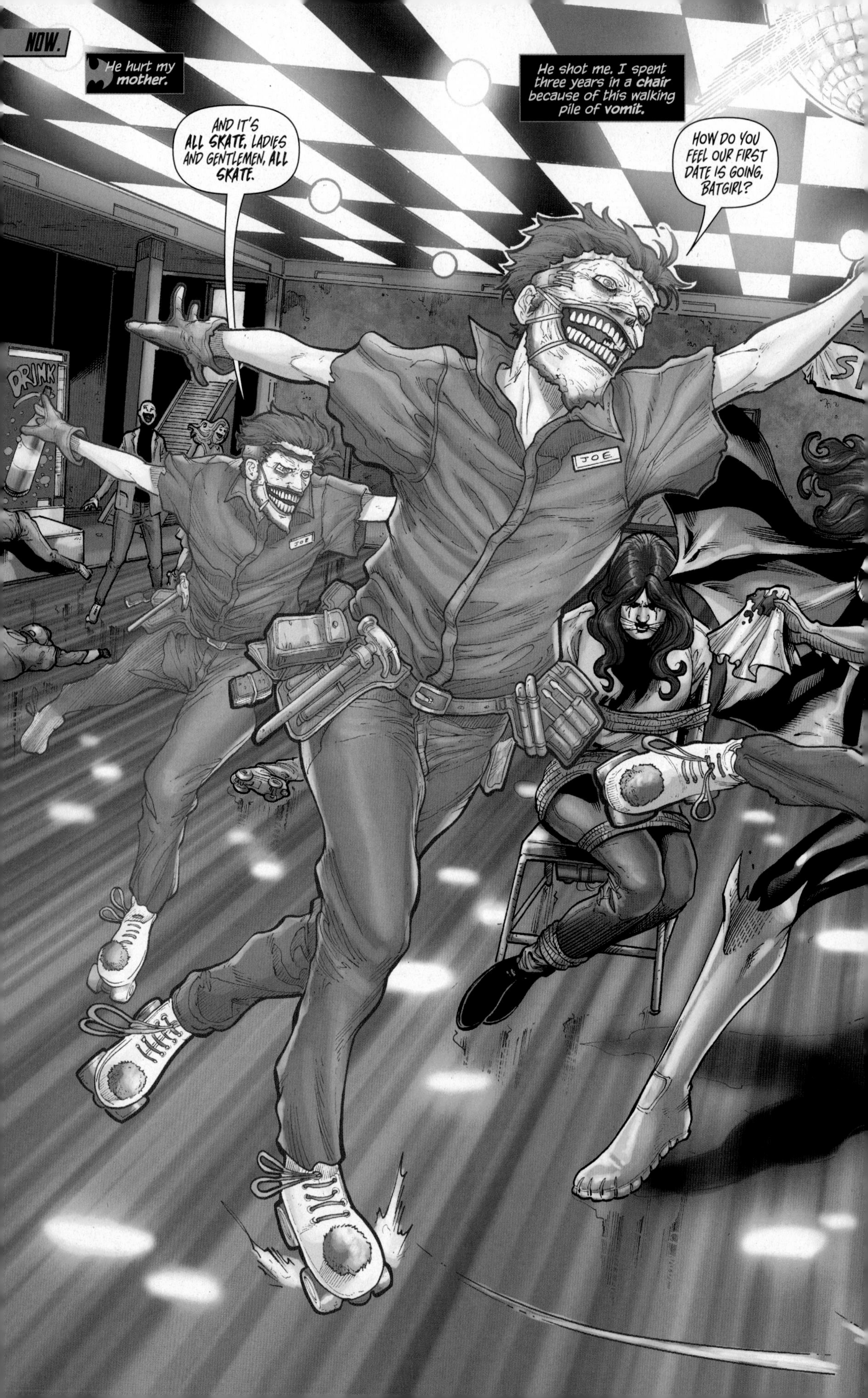
NOW.
He hurt my mother.
He shot me. I spent three years in a chair because of this walking pile of vomit.
AND IT'S ALL SKATE, LADIES AND GENTLEMEN, ALL SKATE.
HOW DO YOU FEEL OUR FIRST DATE IS GOING, BATGIRL?
DRINK
JOE
JOE

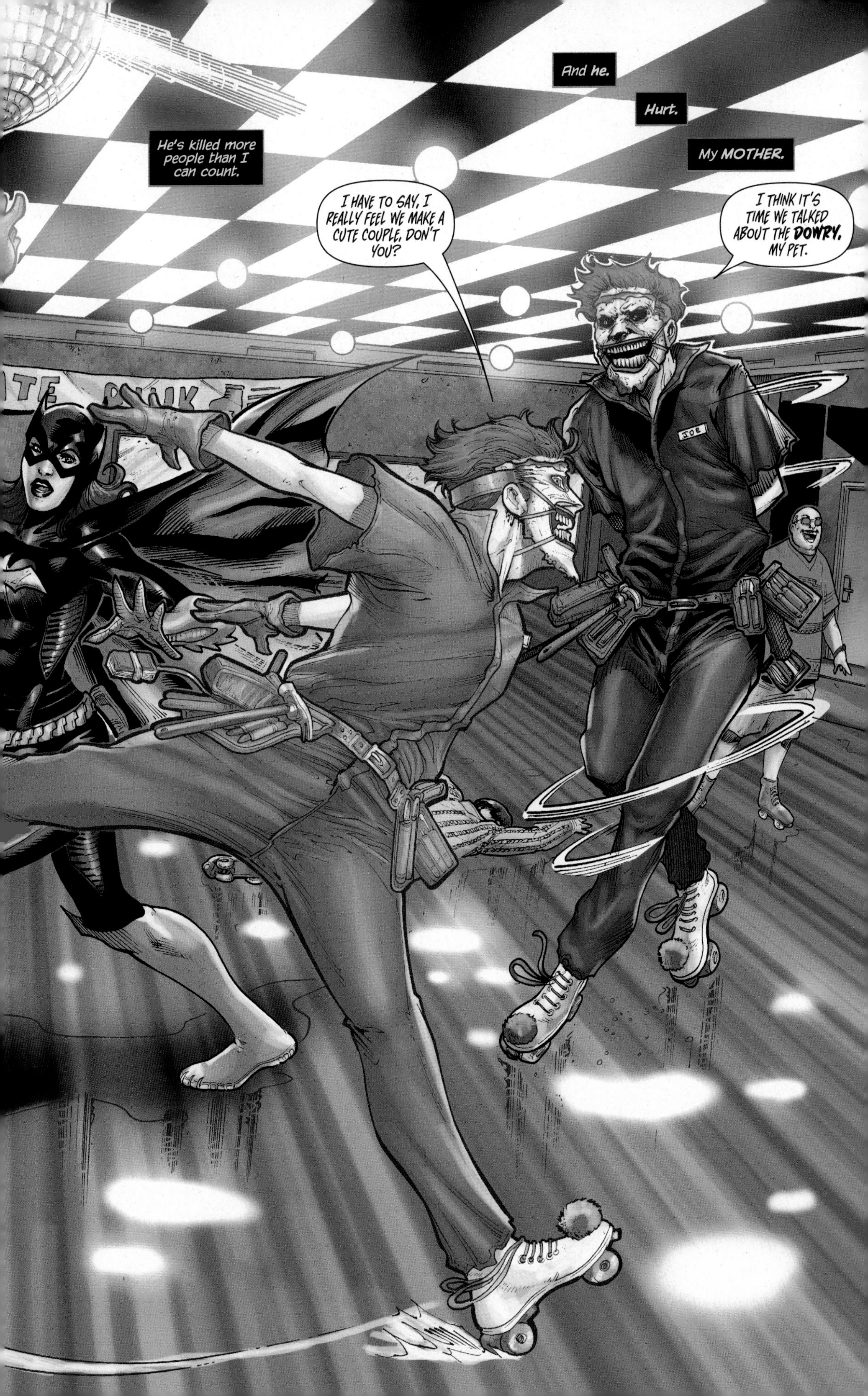
He's killed more people than I can count.
And he.
Hurt.
My MOTHER.
I HAVE TO SAY, I REALLY FEEL WE MAKE A CUTE COUPLE, DON'T YOU?
I THINK IT'S TIME WE TALKED ABOUT THE DOWRY, MY PET.
JOE

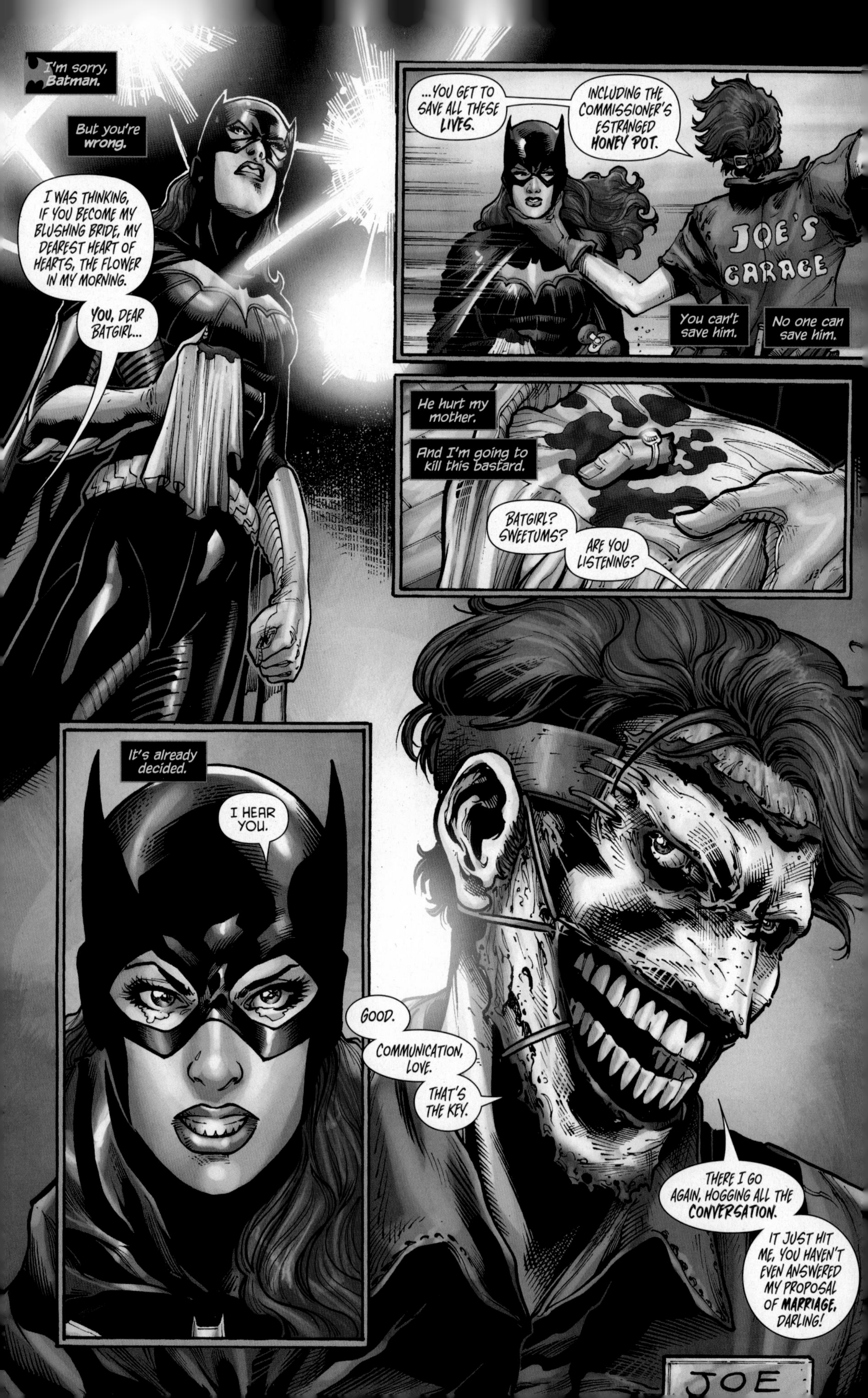

I'm sorry, Batman.
But you're wrong.
I WAS THINKING, IF YOU BECOME MY BLUSHING BRIDE, MY DEAREST HEART OF HEARTS, THE FLOWER IN MY MORNING.
YOU, DEAR BATGIRL...
...YOU GET TO SAVE ALL THESE LIVES.
INCLUDING THE COMMISSIONER'S ESTRANGED HONEY POT.
JOE'S GARAGE
You can't save him.
No one can save him.
He hurt my mother.
And I'm going to kill this bastard.
BATGIRL? SWEETUMS?
ARE YOU LISTENING?
It's already decided.
I HEAR YOU.
GOOD.
COMMUNICATION, LOVE.
THAT'S THE KEY.
THERE I GO AGAIN, HOGGING ALL THE CONVERSATION.
IT JUST HIT ME, YOU HAVEN'T EVEN ANSWERED MY PROPOSAL OF MARRIAGE, DARLING!
JOE

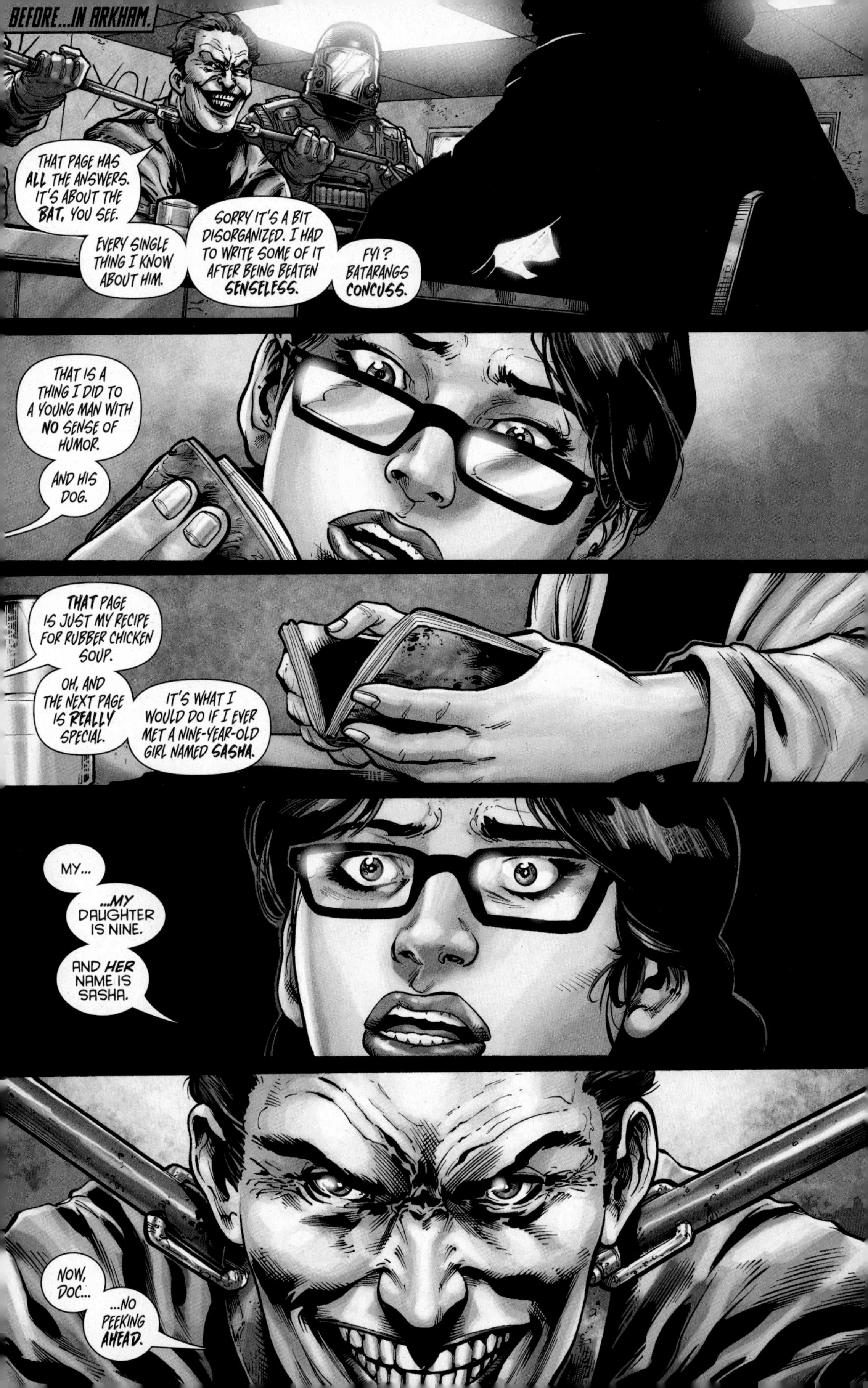
BEFORE...IN ARKHAM.
THAT PAGE HAS ALL THE ANSWERS. IT'S ABOUT THE BAT, YOU SEE.
EVERY SINGLE THING I KNOW ABOUT HIM.
SORRY IT'S A BIT DISORGANIZED. I HAD TO WRITE SOME OF IT AFTER BEING BEATEN SENSELESS.
FYI? BATARANGS CONCUSS.
THAT IS A THING I DID TO A YOUNG MAN WITH NO SENSE OF HUMOR.
AND HIS DOG.
THAT PAGE IS JUST MY RECIPE FOR RUBBER CHICKEN SOUP.
OH, AND THE NEXT PAGE IS REALLY SPECIAL.
IT'S WHAT I WOULD DO IF I EVER MET A NINE-YEAR-OLD GIRL NAMED SASHA.
MY...
...MY DAUGHTER IS NINE.
AND HER NAME IS SASHA.
NOW, DOC...
...NO PEEKING AHEAD.

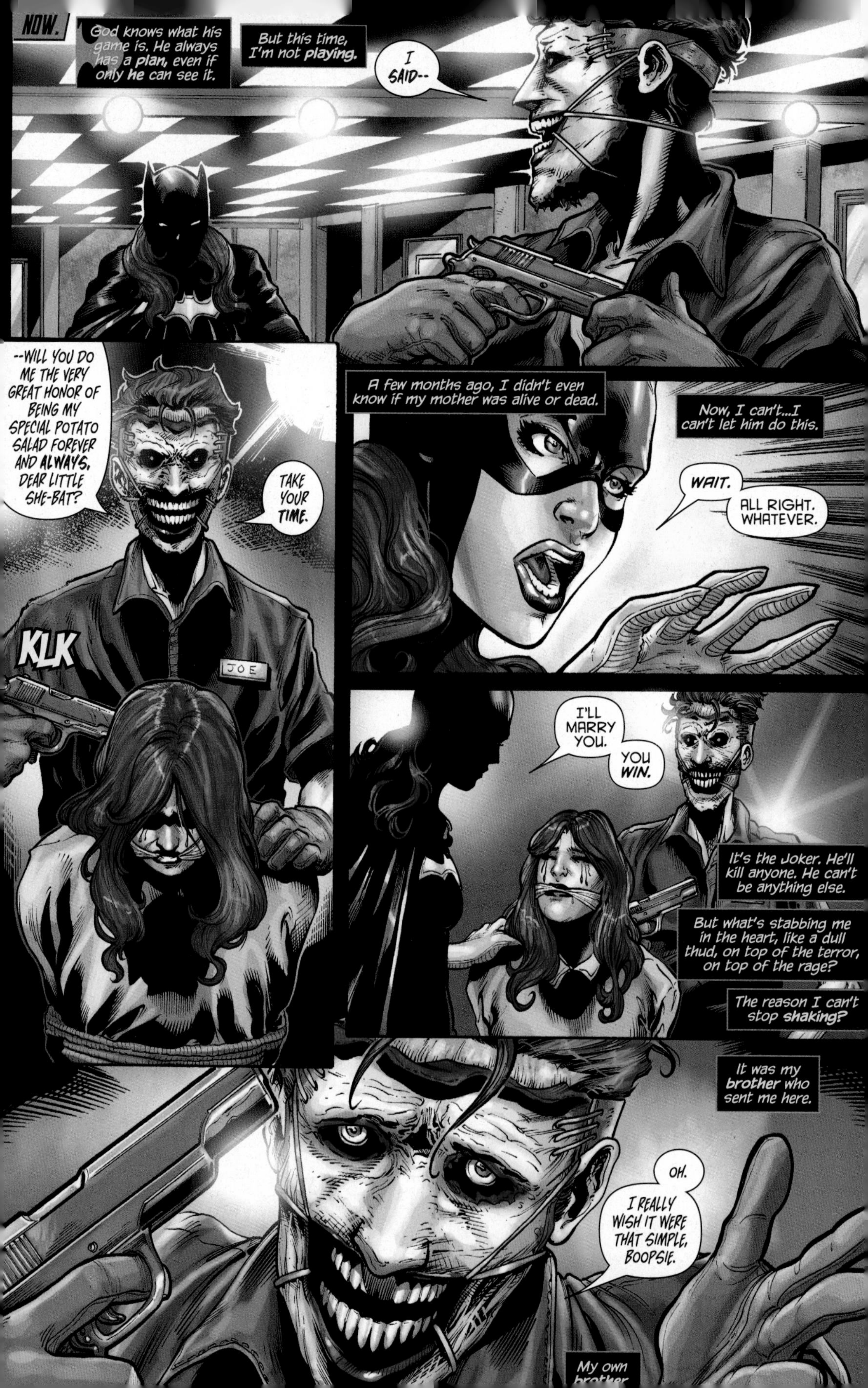
NOW.
God knows what his game is. He always has a plan, even if only he can see it.
But this time, I'm not playing.
I SAID--
--WILL YOU DO ME THE VERY GREAT HONOR OF BEING MY SPECIAL POTATO SALAD FOREVER AND ALWAYS, DEAR LITTLE SHE-BAT?
TAKE YOUR TIME.
KLK
JOE
A few months ago, I didn't even know if my mother was alive or dead.
Now, I can't...I can't let him do this.
WAIT.
ALL RIGHT. WHATEVER.
I'LL MARRY YOU.
YOU WIN.
It's the Joker. He'll kill anyone. He can't be anything else.
But what's stabbing me in the heart, like a dull thud, on top of the terror, on top of the rage?
The reason I can't stop shaking?
It was my brother who sent me here.
OH.
I REALLY WISH IT WERE THAT SIMPLE, BOOPSIE.
My own

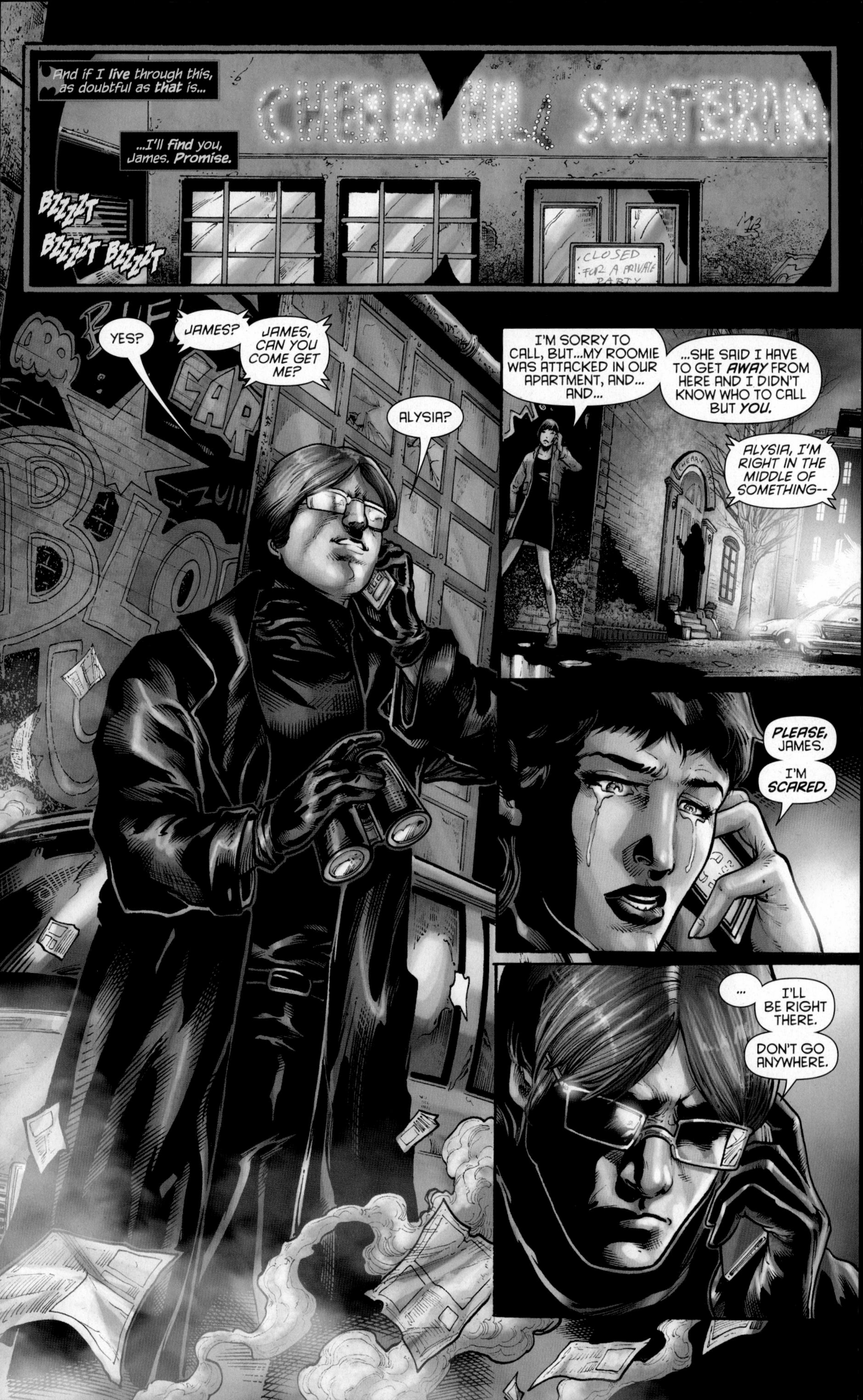
And if I live through this, as doubtful as that is...
...I'll find you, James. Promise.
CHERRY HILL SKATERIN
BZZZZT
BZZZZT BZZZZT
CLOSED FOR A PRIVATE PARTY
YES?
JAMES?
JAMES, CAN YOU COME GET ME?
ALYSIA?
I'M SORRY TO CALL, BUT...MY ROOMIE WAS ATTACKED IN OUR APARTMENT, AND... AND...
...SHE SAID I HAVE TO GET AWAY FROM HERE AND I DIDN'T KNOW WHO TO CALL BUT YOU.
ALYSIA, I'M RIGHT IN THE MIDDLE OF SOMETHING--
PLEASE, JAMES.
I'M SCARED.
...
I'LL BE RIGHT THERE.
DON'T GO ANYWHERE.

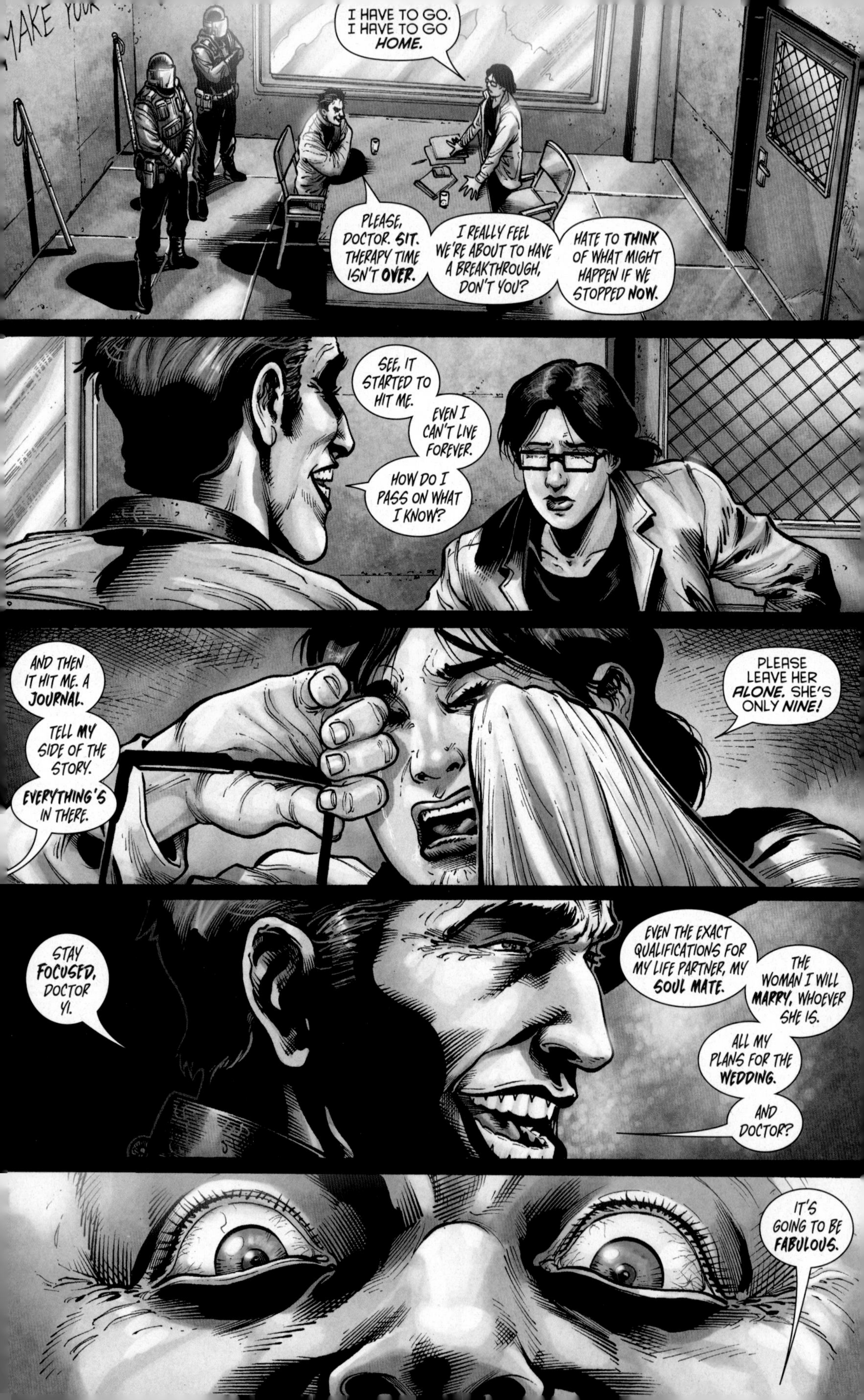
I HAVE TO GO. I HAVE TO GO HOME.
PLEASE, DOCTOR. SIT. THERAPY TIME ISN'T OVER.
I REALLY FEEL WE'RE ABOUT TO HAVE A BREAKTHROUGH, DON'T YOU?
HATE TO THINK OF WHAT MIGHT HAPPEN IF WE STOPPED NOW.
SEE, IT STARTED TO HIT ME.
EVEN I CAN'T LIVE FOREVER.
HOW DO I PASS ON WHAT I KNOW?
AND THEN IT HIT ME. A JOURNAL.
TELL MY SIDE OF THE STORY.
EVERYTHING'S IN THERE.
PLEASE LEAVE HER ALONE. SHE'S ONLY NINE!
STAY FOCUSED, DOCTOR YI.
EVEN THE EXACT QUALIFICATIONS FOR MY LIFE PARTNER, MY SOUL MATE.
THE WOMAN I WILL MARRY, WHOEVER SHE IS.
ALL MY PLANS FOR THE WEDDING.
AND DOCTOR?
IT'S GOING TO BE FABULOUS.

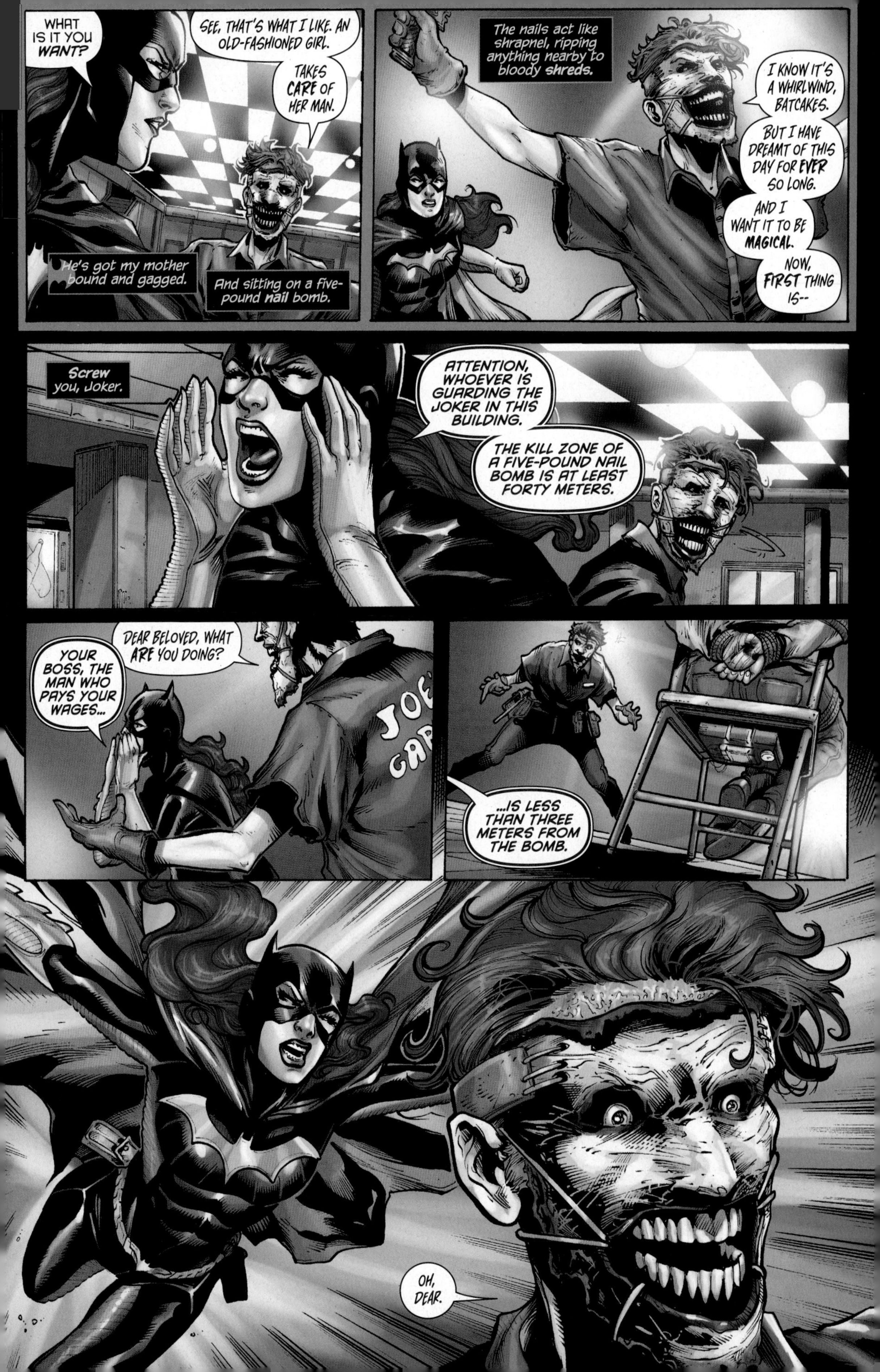

WHAT IS IT YOU WANT?
SEE, THAT'S WHAT I LIKE. AN OLD-FASHIONED GIRL.
TAKES CARE OF HER MAN.
He's got my mother bound and gagged.
And sitting on a five-pound nail bomb.
The nails act like shrapnel, ripping anything nearby to bloody shreds.
I KNOW IT'S A WHIRLWIND, BATCAKES.
BUT I HAVE DREAMT OF THIS DAY FOR EVER SO LONG.
AND I WANT IT TO BE MAGICAL.
NOW, FIRST THING IS--
Screw you, Joker.
ATTENTION, WHOEVER IS GUARDING THE JOKER IN THIS BUILDING.
THE KILL ZONE OF A FIVE-POUND NAIL BOMB IS AT LEAST FORTY METERS.
YOUR BOSS, THE MAN WHO PAYS YOUR WAGES...
DEAR BELOVED, WHAT ARE YOU DOING?
...IS LESS THAN THREE METERS FROM THE BOMB.
OH, DEAR.

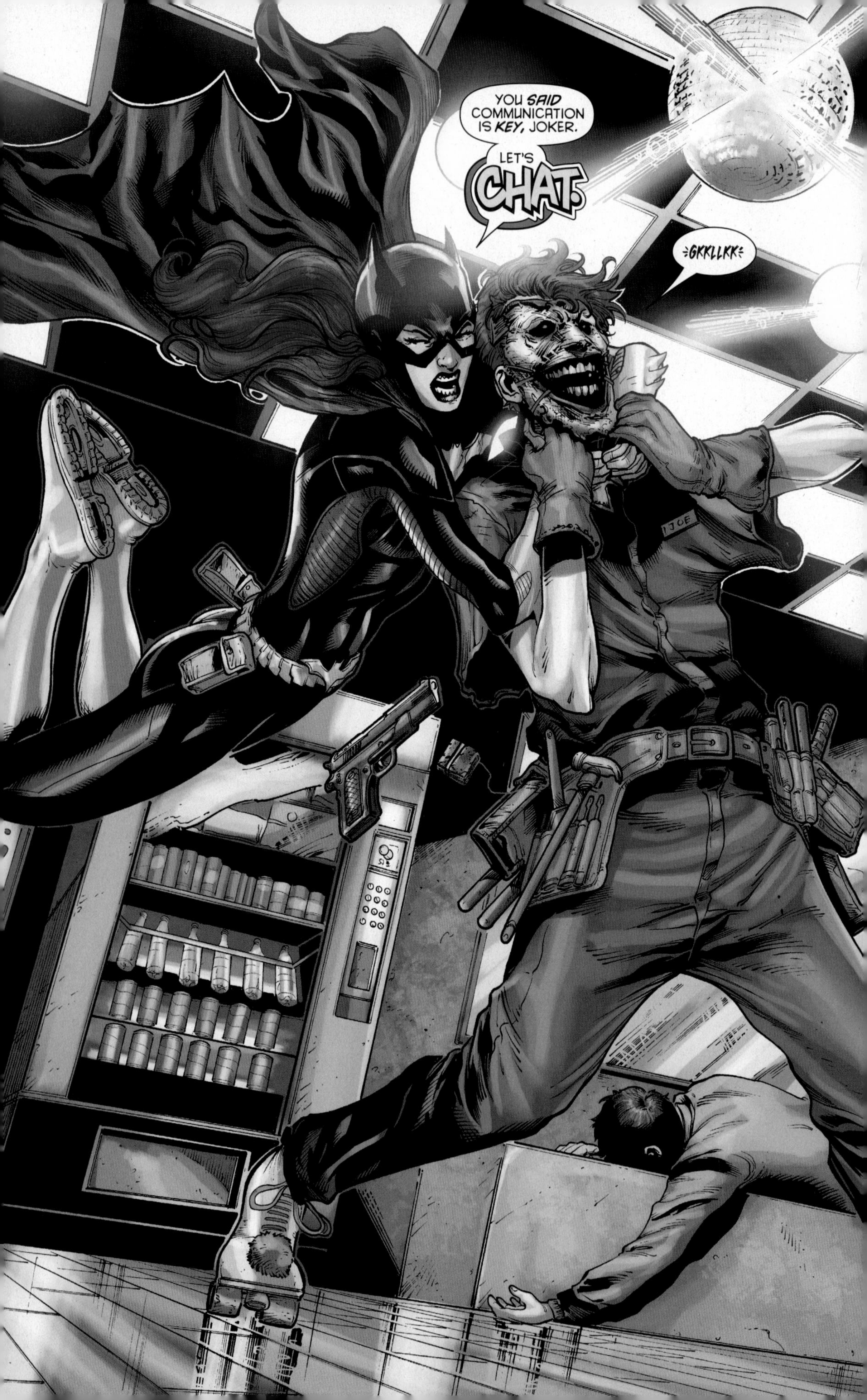
YOU SAID COMMUNICATION IS KEY, JOKER.
LET'S CHAT.
GKKLLKK

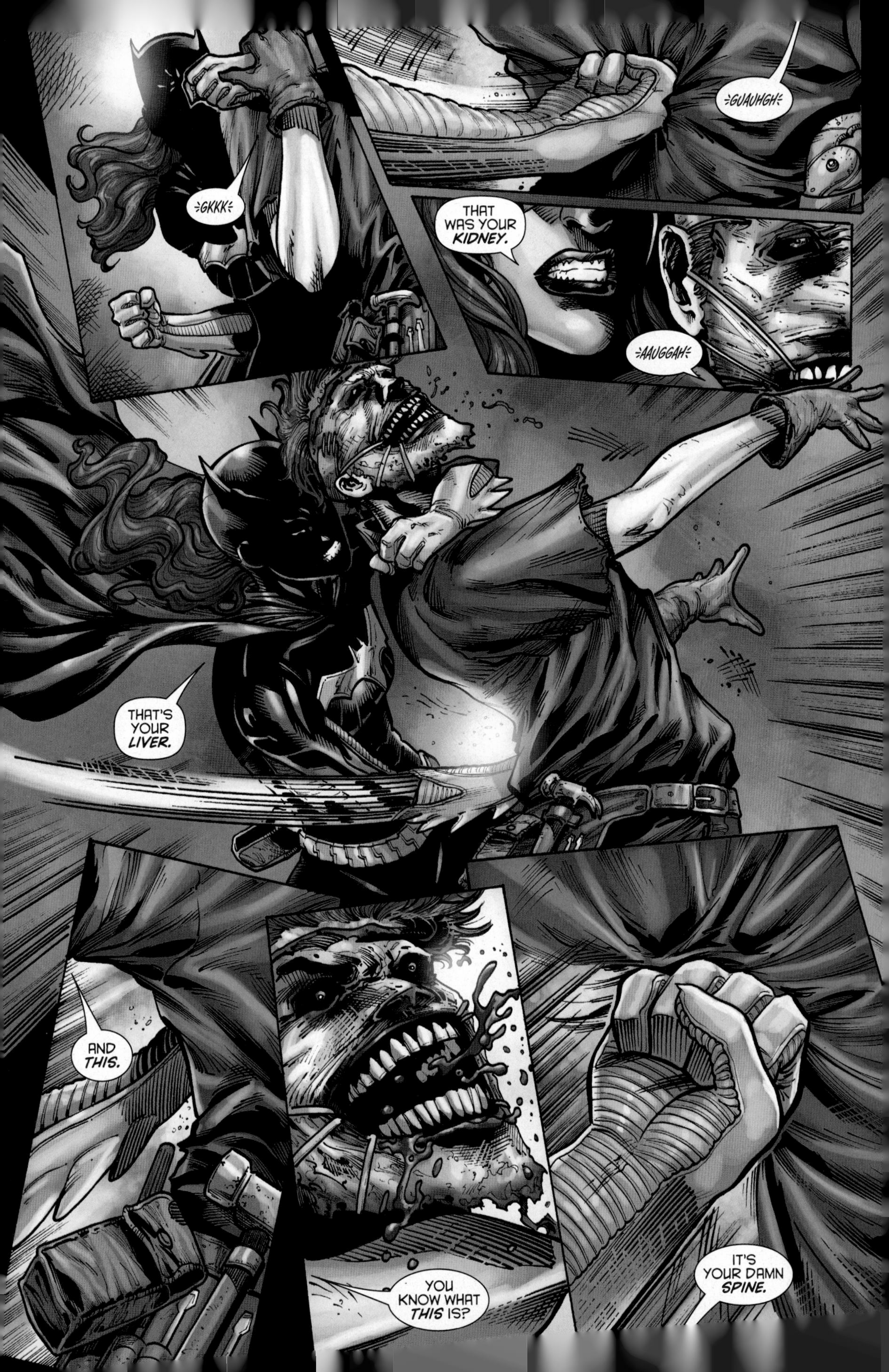

GKKK
GUAUHGH
THAT WAS YOUR KIDNEY.
AAUGGAH
THAT'S YOUR LIVER.
AND THIS.
YOU KNOW WHAT THIS IS?
IT'S YOUR DAMN SPINE.

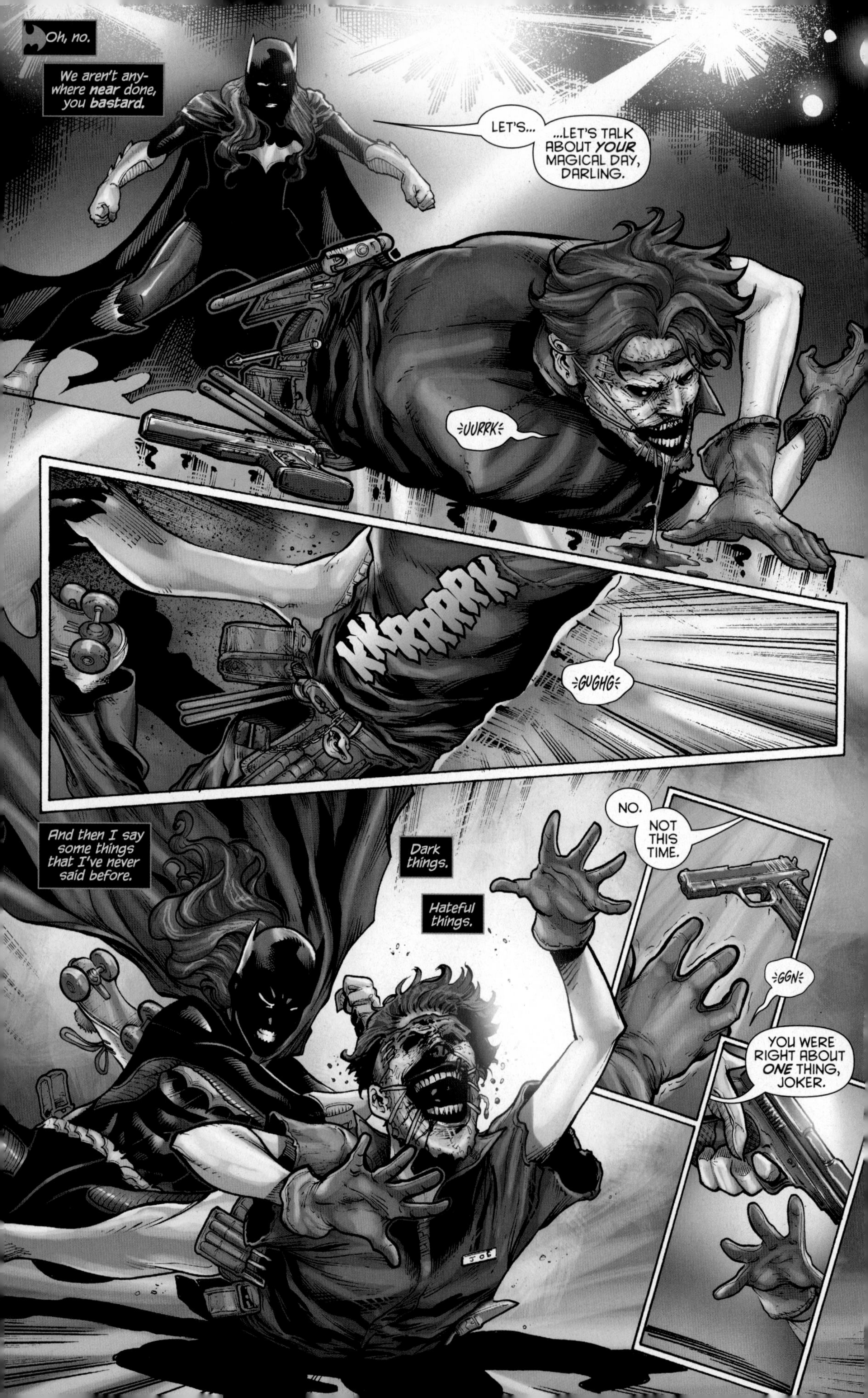
Oh, no.
We aren't anywhere near done, you bastard.
LET'S...
...LET'S TALK ABOUT YOUR MAGICAL DAY, DARLING.
UURRK
KKRRRRK
GUGHG
And then I say some things that I've never said before.
Dark things.
Hateful things.
NO.
NOT THIS TIME.
GGN
YOU WERE RIGHT ABOUT ONE THING, JOKER.

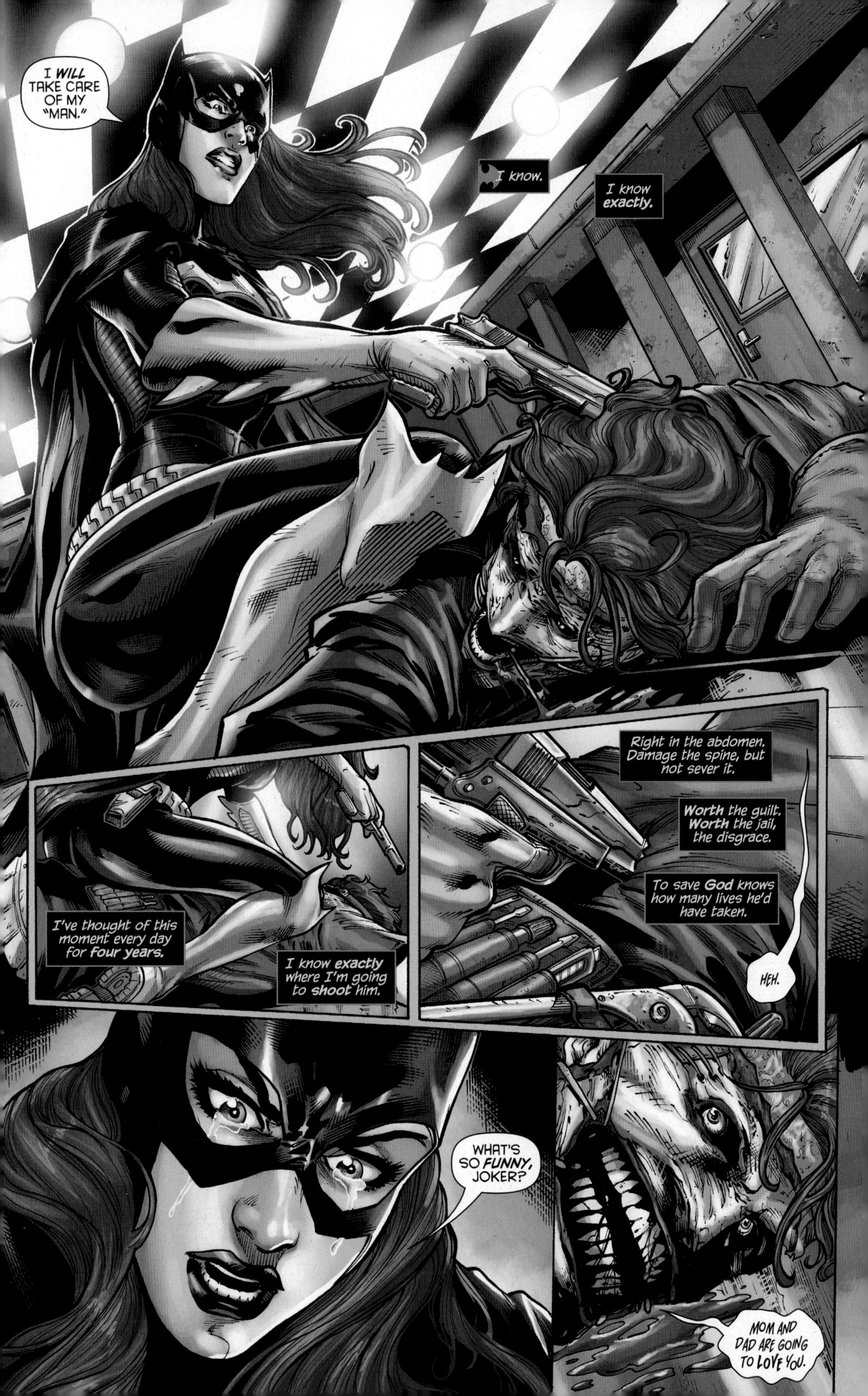

I WILL TAKE CARE OF MY "MAN."
I know.
I know exactly.
I've thought of this moment every day for four years.
I know exactly where I'm going to shoot him.
Right in the abdomen. Damage the spine, but not sever it.
Worth the guilt. Worth the jail, the disgrace.
To save God knows how many lives he'd have taken.
HEH.
WHAT'S SO FUNNY, JOKER?
MOM AND DAD ARE GOING TO LOVE YOU.

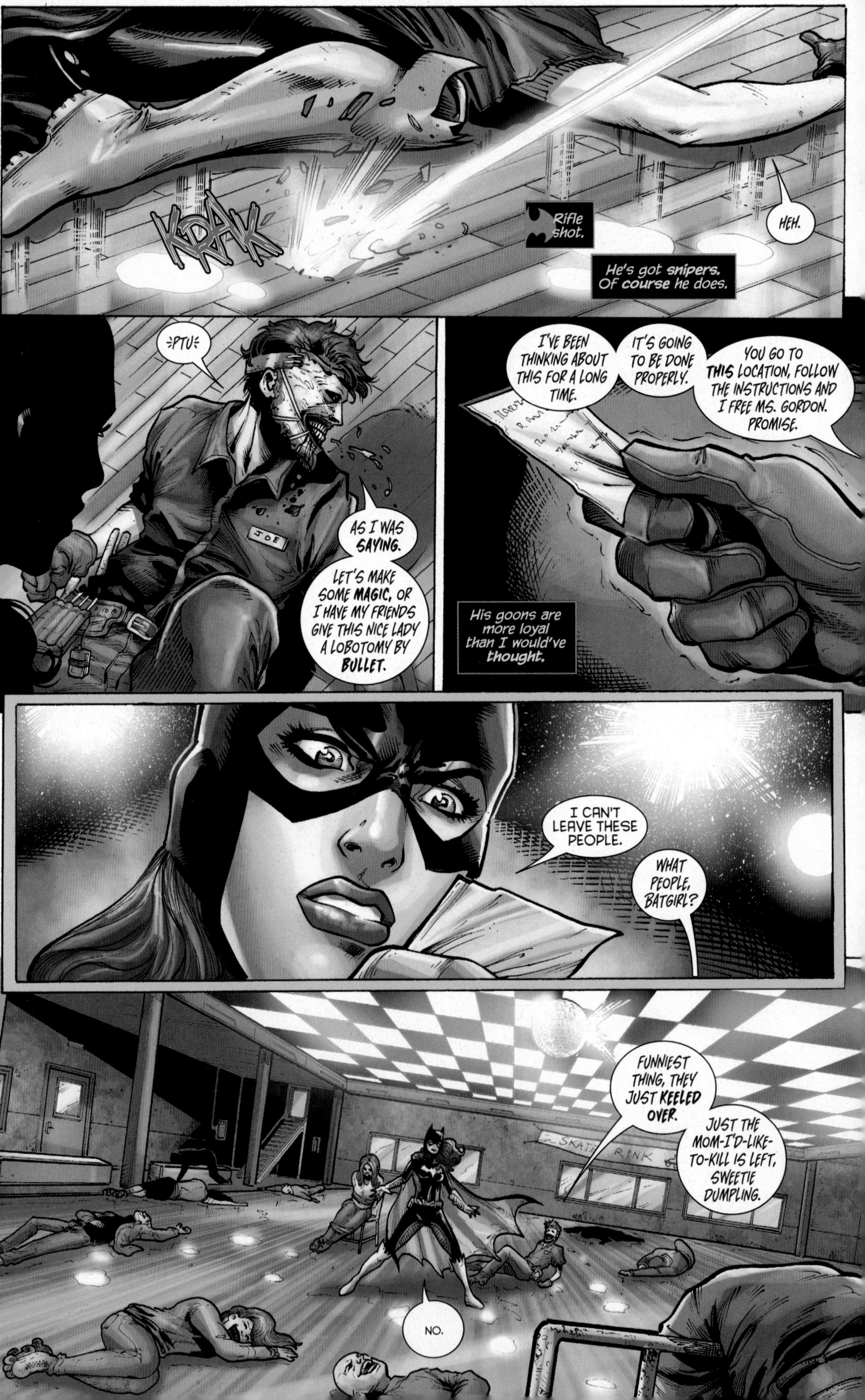
KRAK
Rifle shot.
HEH.
He's got snipers. Of course he does.
PTU
AS I WAS SAYING.
LET'S MAKE SOME MAGIC, OR I HAVE MY FRIENDS GIVE THIS NICE LADY A LOBOTOMY BY BULLET.
I'VE BEEN THINKING ABOUT THIS FOR A LONG TIME.
IT'S GOING TO BE DONE PROPERLY.
YOU GO TO THIS LOCATION, FOLLOW THE INSTRUCTIONS AND I FREE MS. GORDON. PROMISE.
His goons are more loyal than I would've thought.
I CAN'T LEAVE THESE PEOPLE.
WHAT PEOPLE, BATGIRL?
FUNNIEST THING, THEY JUST KEELED OVER.
JUST THE MOM-I'D-LIKE-TO-KILL IS LEFT, SWEETIE DUMPLING.
NO.

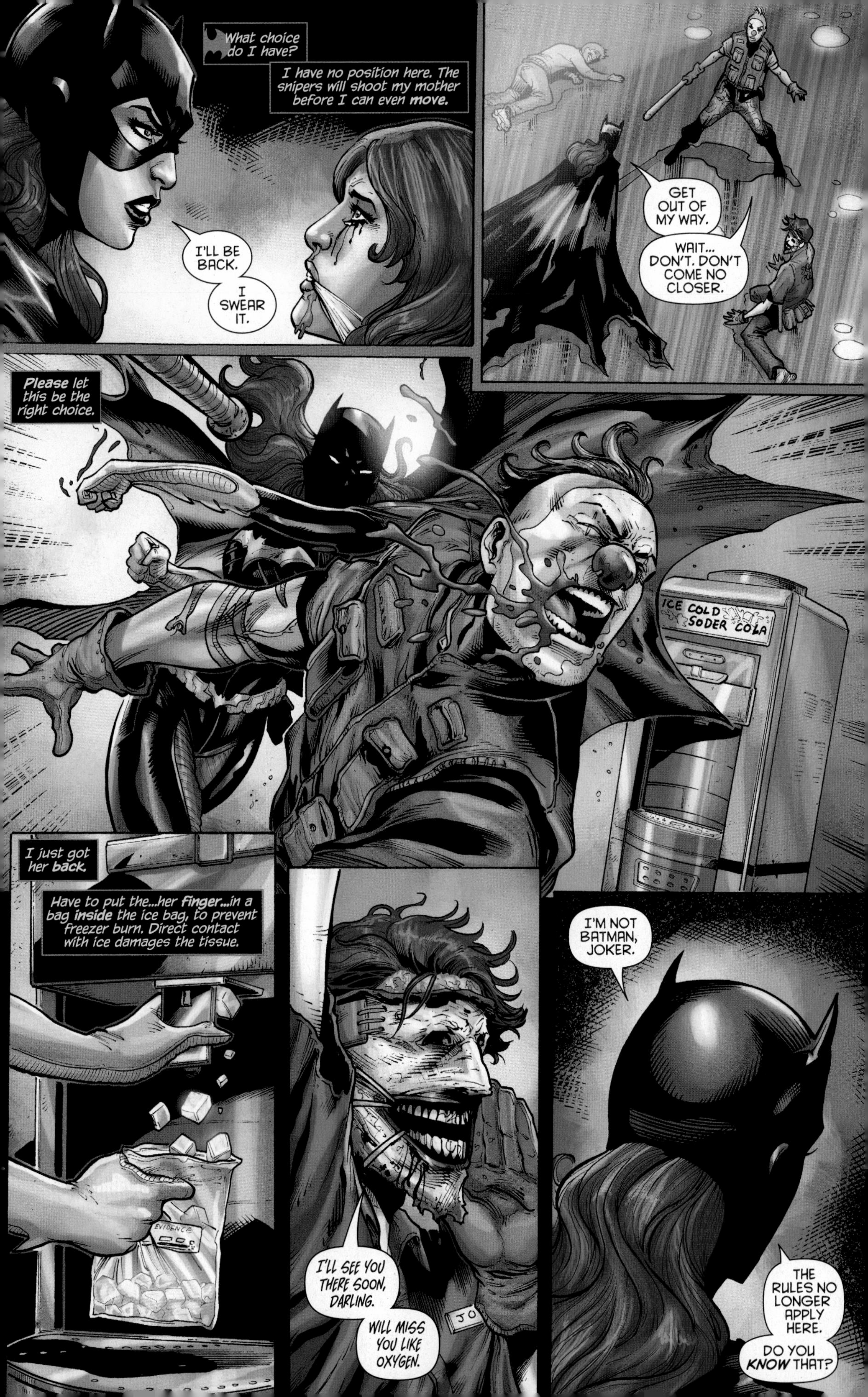

What choice do I have?
I have no position here. The snipers will shoot my mother before I can even **move.**
I'LL BE BACK.
I SWEAR IT.
GET OUT OF MY WAY.
WAIT... DON'T. DON'T COME NO CLOSER.
Please let this be the right choice.
ICE COLD SODER COLA
I just got her **back.**
Have to put the...her **finger**...in a bag **inside** the ice bag, to prevent freezer burn. Direct contact with ice damages the tissue.
EVIDENCE
I'LL SEE YOU THERE SOON, DARLING.
WILL MISS YOU LIKE OXYGEN.
I'M NOT BATMAN, JOKER.
THE RULES NO LONGER APPLY HERE.
DO YOU ***KNOW*** THAT?

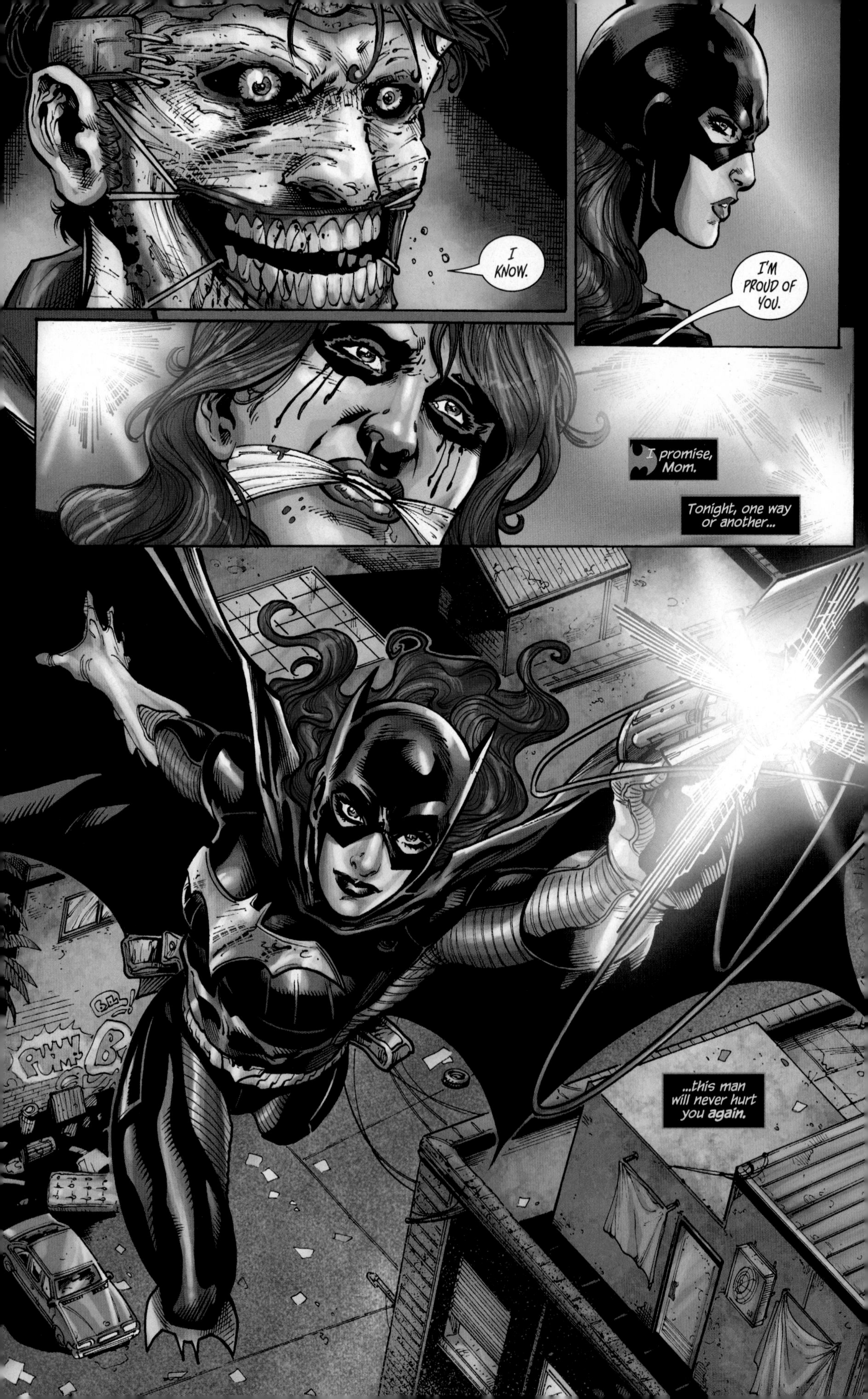
I KNOW.
I'M PROUD OF YOU.
I promise, Mom.
Tonight, one way or another...
...this man will never hurt you again.

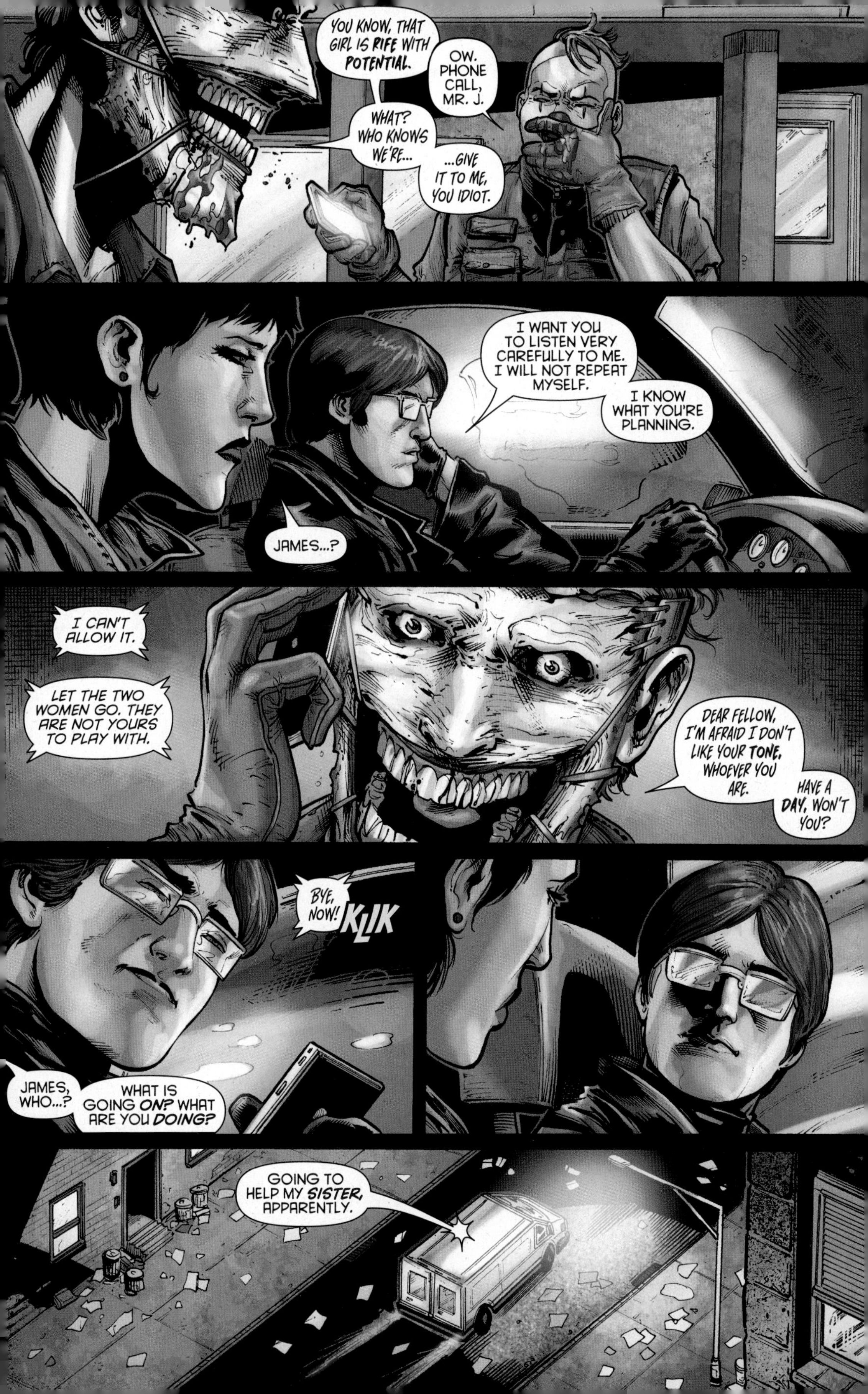

YOU KNOW, THAT GIRL IS RIFE WITH POTENTIAL.
OW. PHONE CALL, MR. J.
WHAT? WHO KNOWS WE'RE...
...GIVE IT TO ME, YOU IDIOT.
I WANT YOU TO LISTEN VERY CAREFULLY TO ME. I WILL NOT REPEAT MYSELF.
I KNOW WHAT YOU'RE PLANNING.
JAMES...?
I CAN'T ALLOW IT.
LET THE TWO WOMEN GO. THEY ARE NOT YOURS TO PLAY WITH.
DEAR FELLOW, I'M AFRAID I DON'T LIKE YOUR TONE, WHOEVER YOU ARE.
HAVE A DAY, WON'T YOU?
BYE, NOW!
KLIK
JAMES, WHO...?
WHAT IS GOING ON? WHAT ARE YOU DOING?
GOING TO HELP MY SISTER, APPARENTLY.

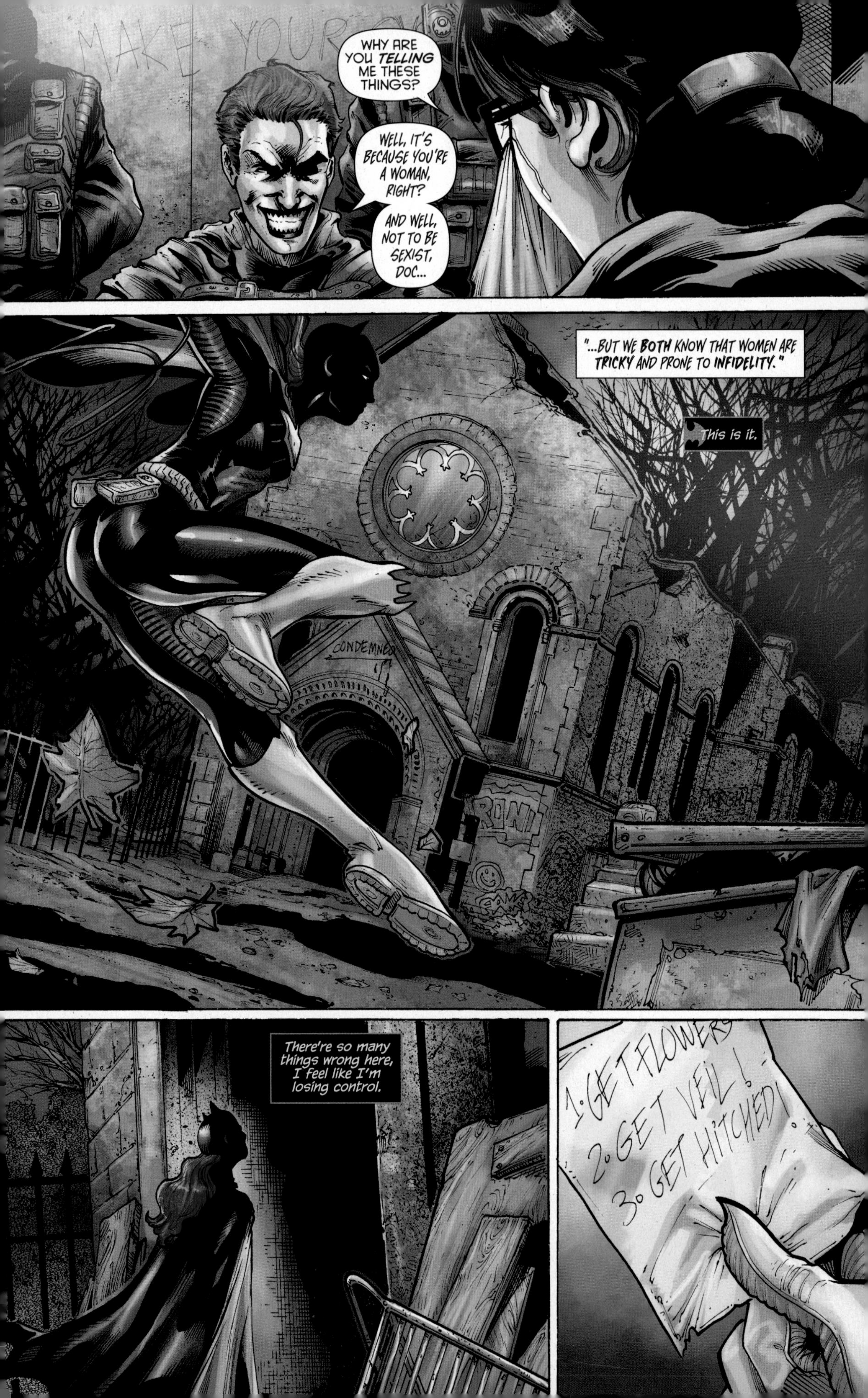

MAKE YOUR
WHY ARE YOU TELLING ME THESE THINGS?
WELL, IT'S BECAUSE YOU'RE A WOMAN, RIGHT?
AND WELL, NOT TO BE SEXIST, DOC...
"...BUT WE BOTH KNOW THAT WOMEN ARE TRICKY AND PRONE TO INFIDELITY."
This is it.
CONDEMNED
There're so many things wrong here, I feel like I'm losing control.
1. GET FLOWERS
2. GET VEIL!
3. GET HITCHED!

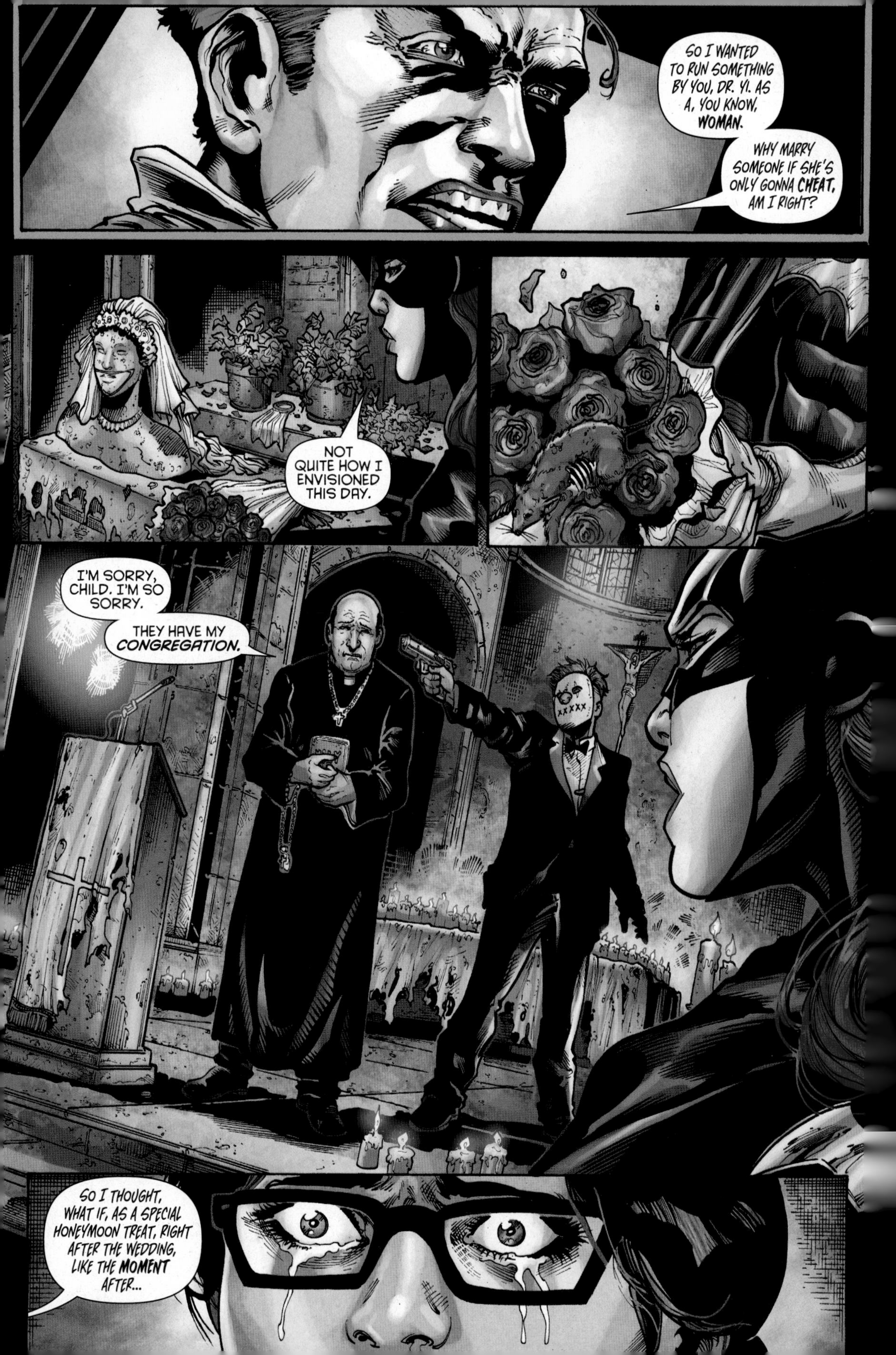
SO I WANTED TO RUN SOMETHING BY YOU, DR. YI. AS A, YOU KNOW, **WOMAN.**
WHY MARRY SOMEONE IF SHE'S ONLY GONNA **CHEAT,** AM I RIGHT?
NOT QUITE HOW I ENVISIONED THIS DAY.
I'M SORRY, CHILD. I'M SO SORRY.
THEY HAVE MY ***CONGREGATION.***
SO I THOUGHT, WHAT IF, AS A SPECIAL HONEYMOON TREAT, RIGHT AFTER THE WEDDING, LIKE THE **MOMENT** AFTER...

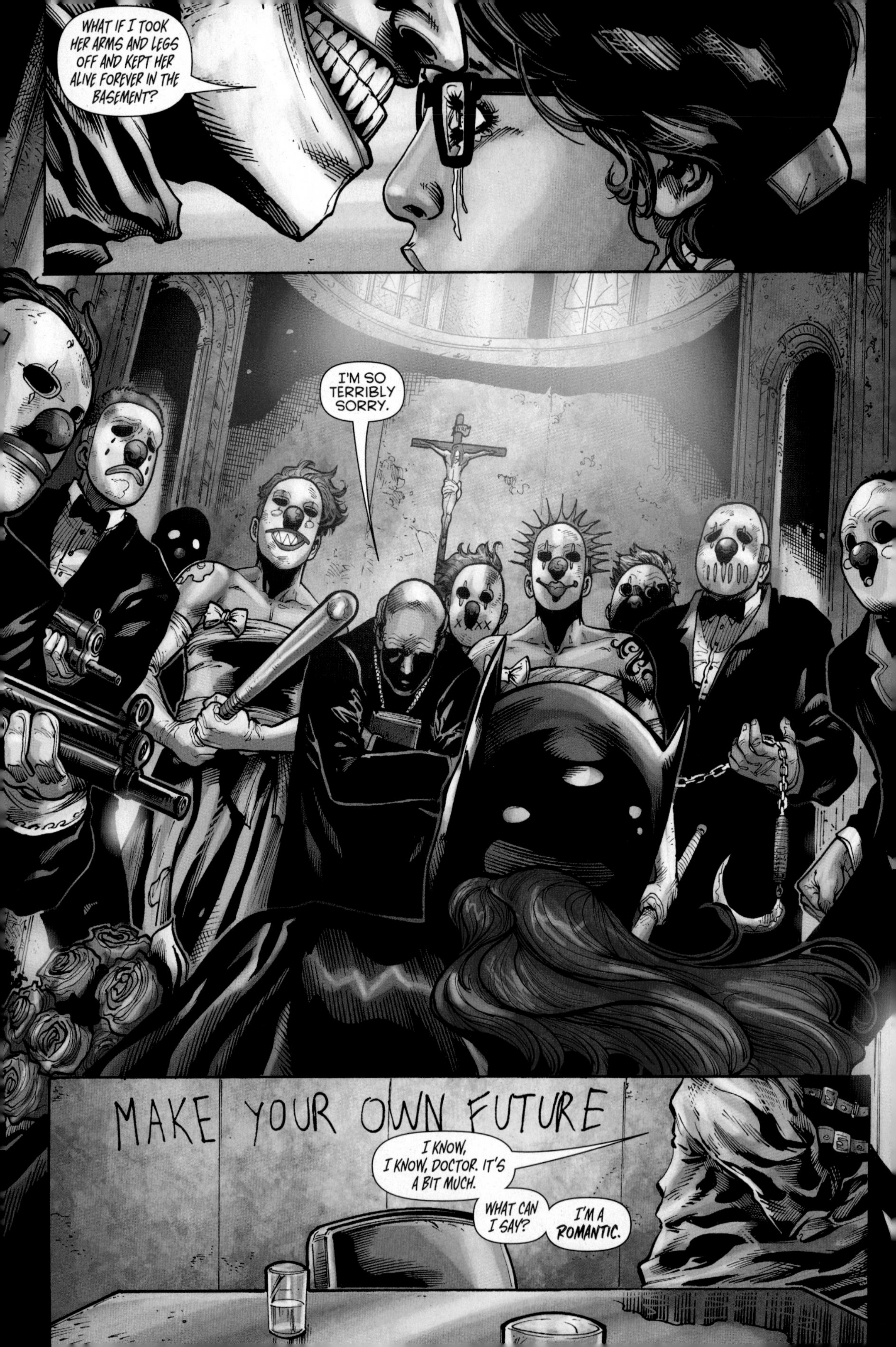
WHAT IF I TOOK HER ARMS AND LEGS OFF AND KEPT HER ALIVE FOREVER IN THE BASEMENT?
I'M SO TERRIBLY SORRY.
MAKE YOUR OWN FUTURE
I KNOW, I KNOW, DOCTOR. IT'S A BIT MUCH.
WHAT CAN I SAY?
I'M A ROMANTIC.

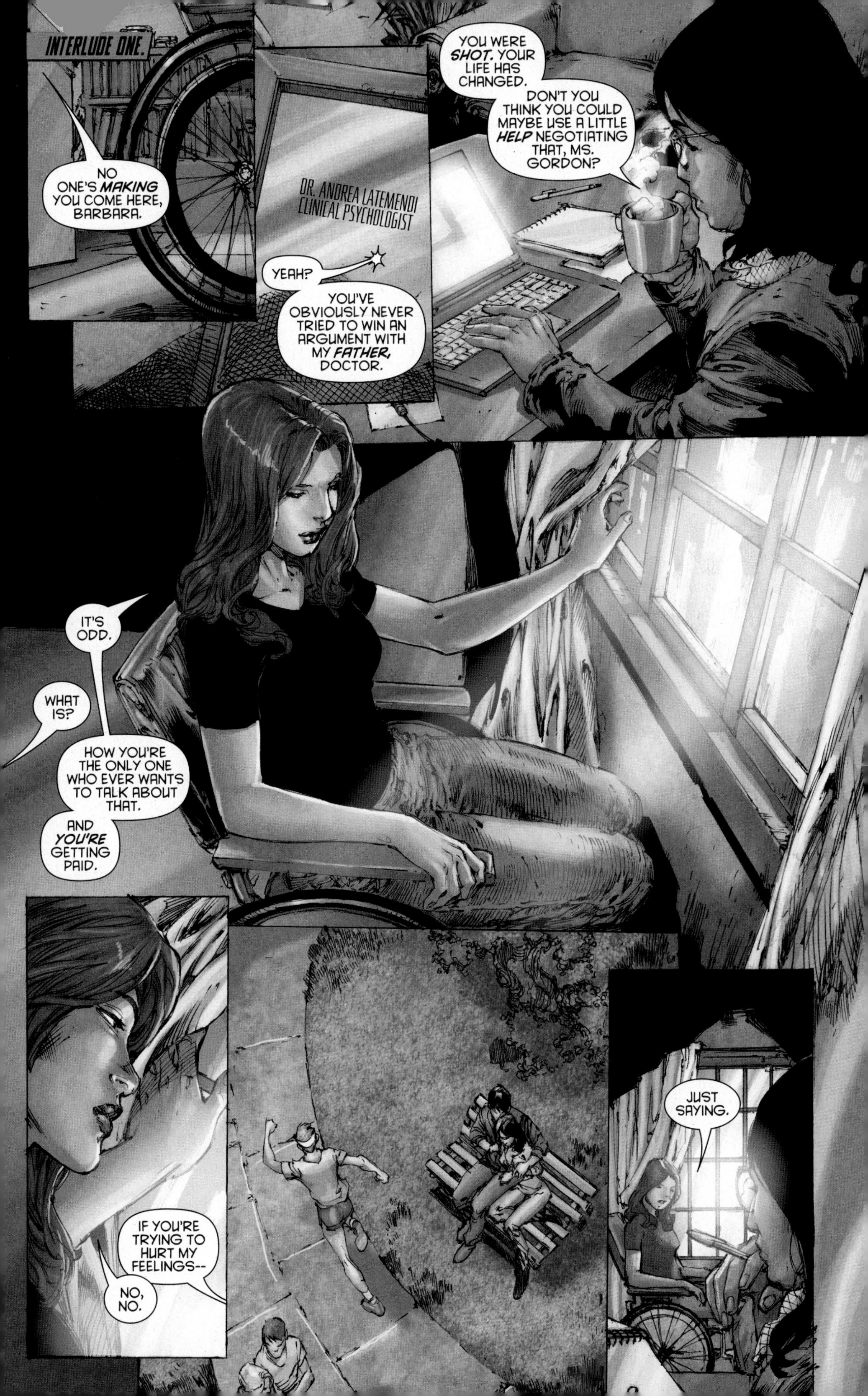
INTERLUDE ONE.
NO ONE'S MAKING YOU COME HERE, BARBARA.
DR. ANDREA LATEMENDI CLINICAL PSYCHOLOGIST
YEAH?
YOU'VE OBVIOUSLY NEVER TRIED TO WIN AN ARGUMENT WITH MY FATHER, DOCTOR.
YOU WERE SHOT. YOUR LIFE HAS CHANGED.
DON'T YOU THINK YOU COULD MAYBE USE A LITTLE HELP NEGOTIATING THAT, MS. GORDON?
IT'S ODD.
WHAT IS?
HOW YOU'RE THE ONLY ONE WHO EVER WANTS TO TALK ABOUT THAT.
AND YOU'RE GETTING PAID.
IF YOU'RE TRYING TO HURT MY FEELINGS--
NO, NO.
JUST SAYING.

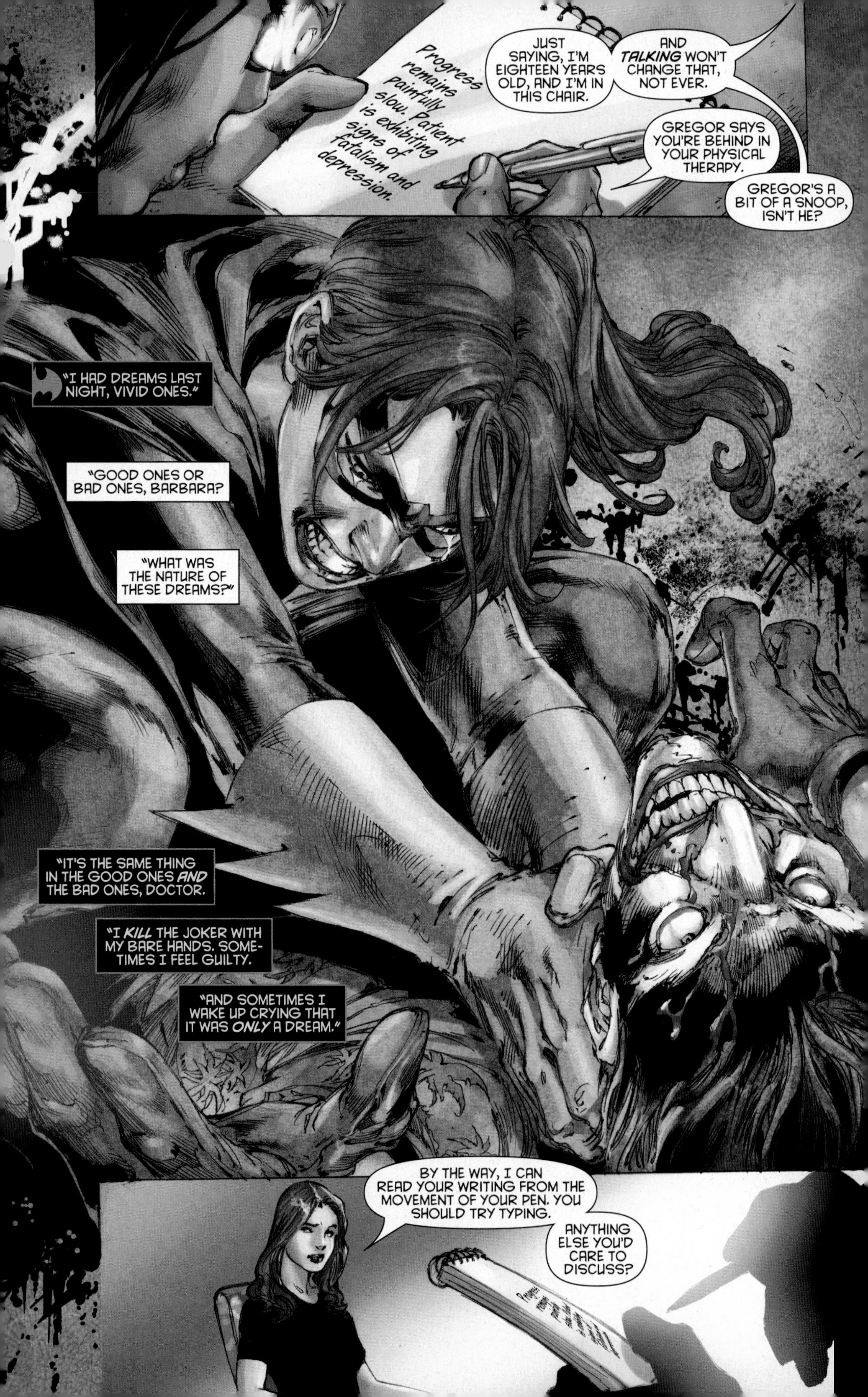
Progress remains painfully slow. Patient is exhibiting signs of fatalism and depression.
JUST SAYING, I'M EIGHTEEN YEARS OLD, AND I'M IN THIS CHAIR.
AND TALKING WON'T CHANGE THAT, NOT EVER.
GREGOR SAYS YOU'RE BEHIND IN YOUR PHYSICAL THERAPY.
GREGOR'S A BIT OF A SNOOP, ISN'T HE?
"I HAD DREAMS LAST NIGHT, VIVID ONES."
"GOOD ONES OR BAD ONES, BARBARA?
"WHAT WAS THE NATURE OF THESE DREAMS?"
"IT'S THE SAME THING IN THE GOOD ONES AND THE BAD ONES, DOCTOR.
"I KILL THE JOKER WITH MY BARE HANDS. SOMETIMES I FEEL GUILTY.
"AND SOMETIMES I WAKE UP CRYING THAT IT WAS ONLY A DREAM."
BY THE WAY, I CAN READ YOUR WRITING FROM THE MOVEMENT OF YOUR PEN. YOU SHOULD TRY TYPING.
ANYTHING ELSE YOU'D CARE TO DISCUSS?

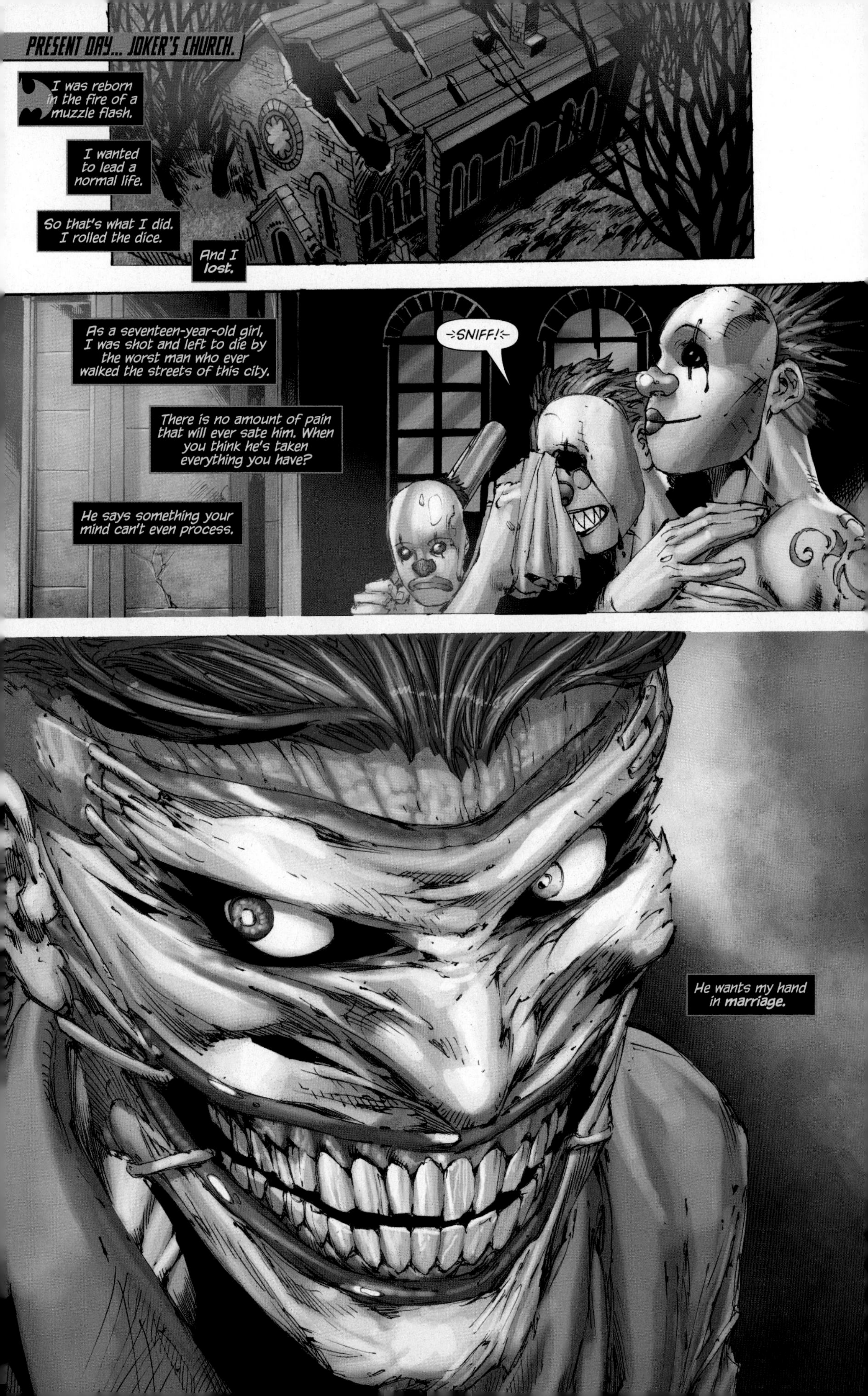
PRESENT DAY... JOKER'S CHURCH.
I was reborn in the fire of a muzzle flash.
I wanted to lead a normal life.
So that's what I did. I rolled the dice.
And I lost.
As a seventeen-year-old girl, I was shot and left to die by the worst man who ever walked the streets of this city.
-SNIFF!-
There is no amount of pain that will ever sate him. When you think he's taken everything you have?
He says something your mind can't even process.
He wants my hand in marriage.

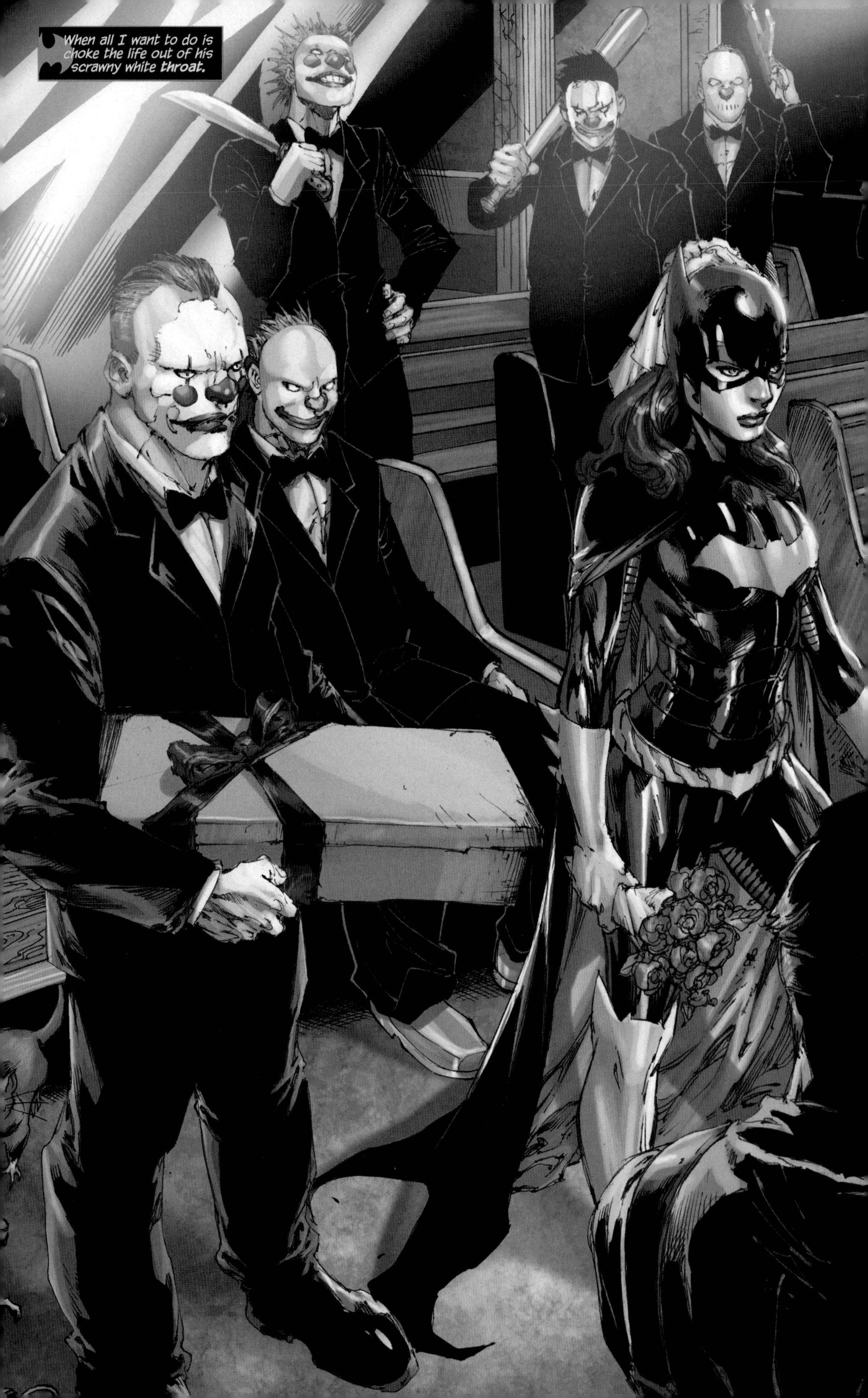
When all I want to do is choke the life out of his scrawny white **throat.**

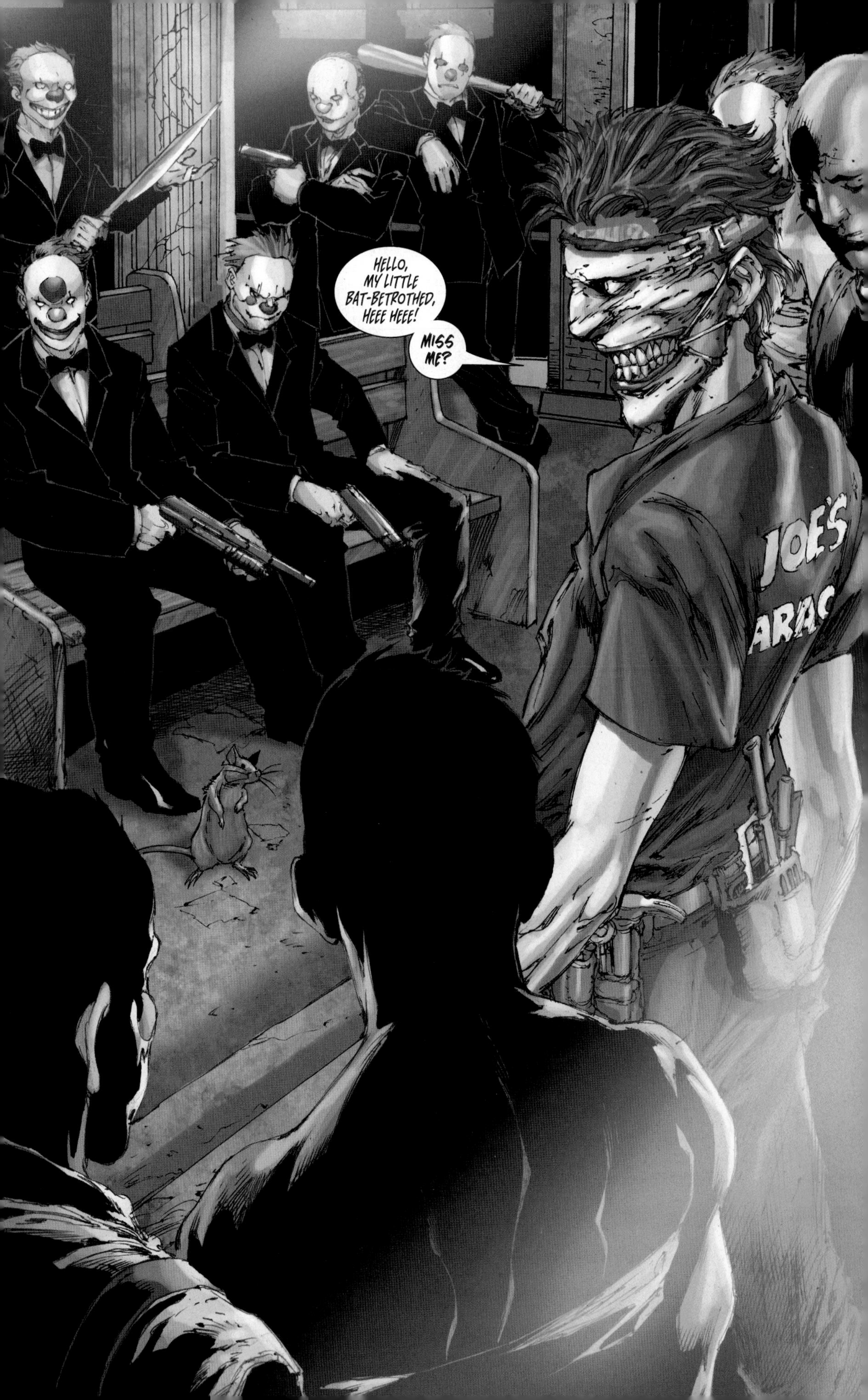
HELLO, MY LITTLE BAT-BETROTHED, HEEE HEEE!
MISS ME?
JOE'S

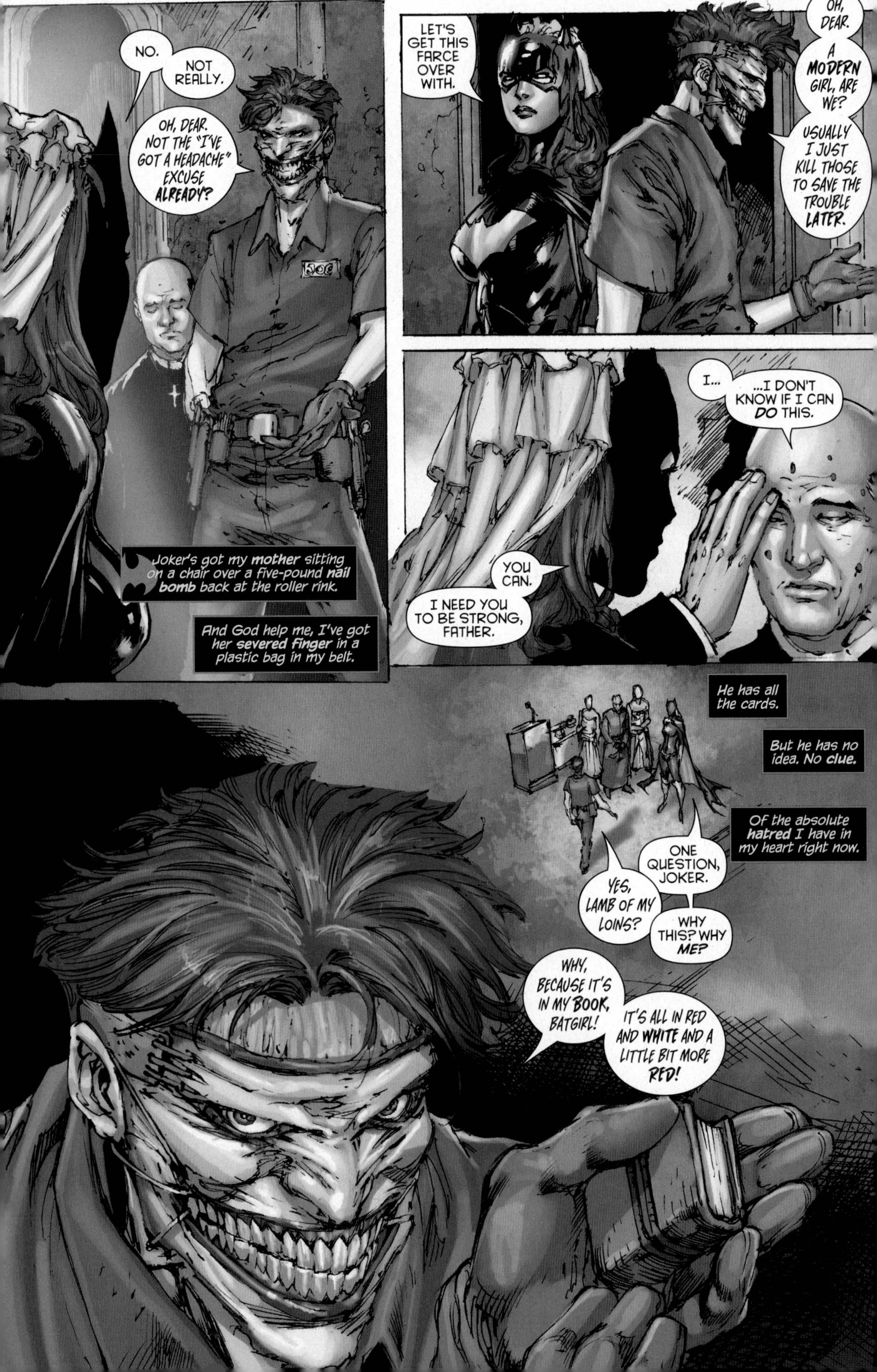
NO.
NOT REALLY.
OH, DEAR. NOT THE "I'VE GOT A HEADACHE" EXCUSE ALREADY?
Joker's got my mother sitting on a chair over a five-pound nail bomb back at the roller rink.
And God help me, I've got her severed finger in a plastic bag in my belt.
LET'S GET THIS FARCE OVER WITH.
OH, DEAR.
A MODERN GIRL, ARE WE?
USUALLY I JUST KILL THOSE TO SAVE THE TROUBLE LATER.
I...
...I DON'T KNOW IF I CAN DO THIS.
YOU CAN.
I NEED YOU TO BE STRONG, FATHER.
He has all the cards.
But he has no idea. No clue.
Of the absolute hatred I have in my heart right now.
ONE QUESTION, JOKER.
YES, LAMB OF MY LOINS?
WHY THIS? WHY ME?
WHY, BECAUSE IT'S IN MY BOOK, BATGIRL!
IT'S ALL IN RED AND WHITE AND A LITTLE BIT MORE RED!

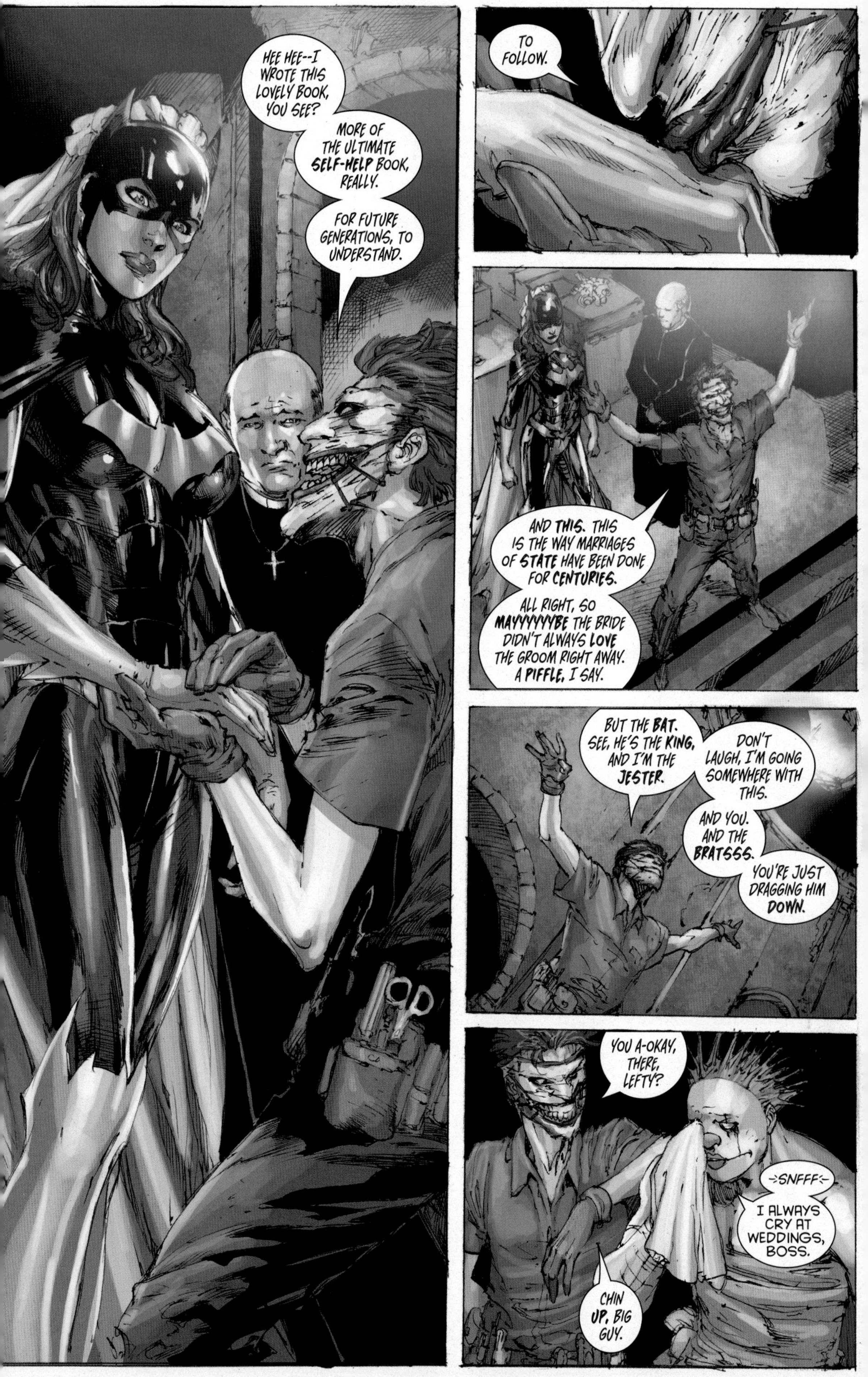
HEE HEE--I WROTE THIS LOVELY BOOK, YOU SEE?
MORE OF THE ULTIMATE SELF-HELP BOOK, REALLY.
FOR FUTURE GENERATIONS, TO UNDERSTAND.
TO FOLLOW.
AND THIS. THIS IS THE WAY MARRIAGES OF STATE HAVE BEEN DONE FOR CENTURIES.
ALL RIGHT, SO MAYYYYYYBE THE BRIDE DIDN'T ALWAYS LOVE THE GROOM RIGHT AWAY. A PIFFLE, I SAY.
BUT THE BAT. SEE, HE'S THE KING, AND I'M THE JESTER.
DON'T LAUGH, I'M GOING SOMEWHERE WITH THIS.
AND YOU. AND THE BRATSSS.
YOU'RE JUST DRAGGING HIM DOWN.
YOU A-OKAY, THERE, LEFTY?
SNFFF
I ALWAYS CRY AT WEDDINGS, BOSS.
CHIN UP, BIG GUY.

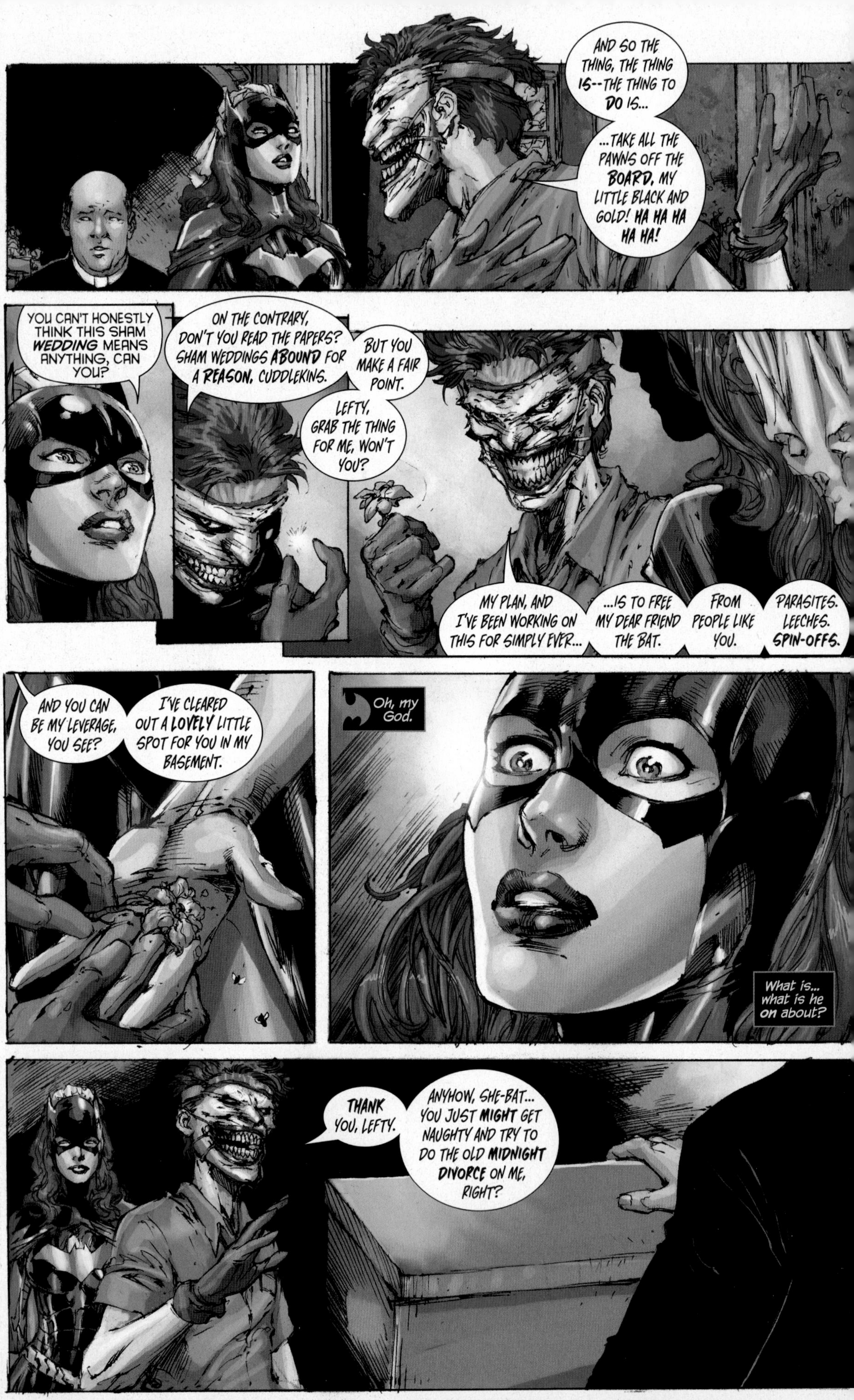
AND SO THE THING, THE THING IS--THE THING TO DO IS...
...TAKE ALL THE PAWNS OFF THE BOARD, MY LITTLE BLACK AND GOLD! HA HA HA HA HA!
YOU CAN'T HONESTLY THINK THIS SHAM WEDDING MEANS ANYTHING, CAN YOU?
ON THE CONTRARY, DON'T YOU READ THE PAPERS? SHAM WEDDINGS ABOUND FOR A REASON, CUDDLEKINS.
BUT YOU MAKE A FAIR POINT.
LEFTY, GRAB THE THING FOR ME, WON'T YOU?
MY PLAN, AND I'VE BEEN WORKING ON THIS FOR SIMPLY EVER...
...IS TO FREE MY DEAR FRIEND THE BAT.
FROM PEOPLE LIKE YOU.
PARASITES. LEECHES. SPIN-OFFS.
AND YOU CAN BE MY LEVERAGE, YOU SEE?
I'VE CLEARED OUT A LOVELY LITTLE SPOT FOR YOU IN MY BASEMENT.
Oh, my God.
What is... what is he on about?
THANK YOU, LEFTY.
ANYHOW, SHE-BAT... YOU JUST MIGHT GET NAUGHTY AND TRY TO DO THE OLD MIDNIGHT DIVORCE ON ME, RIGHT?

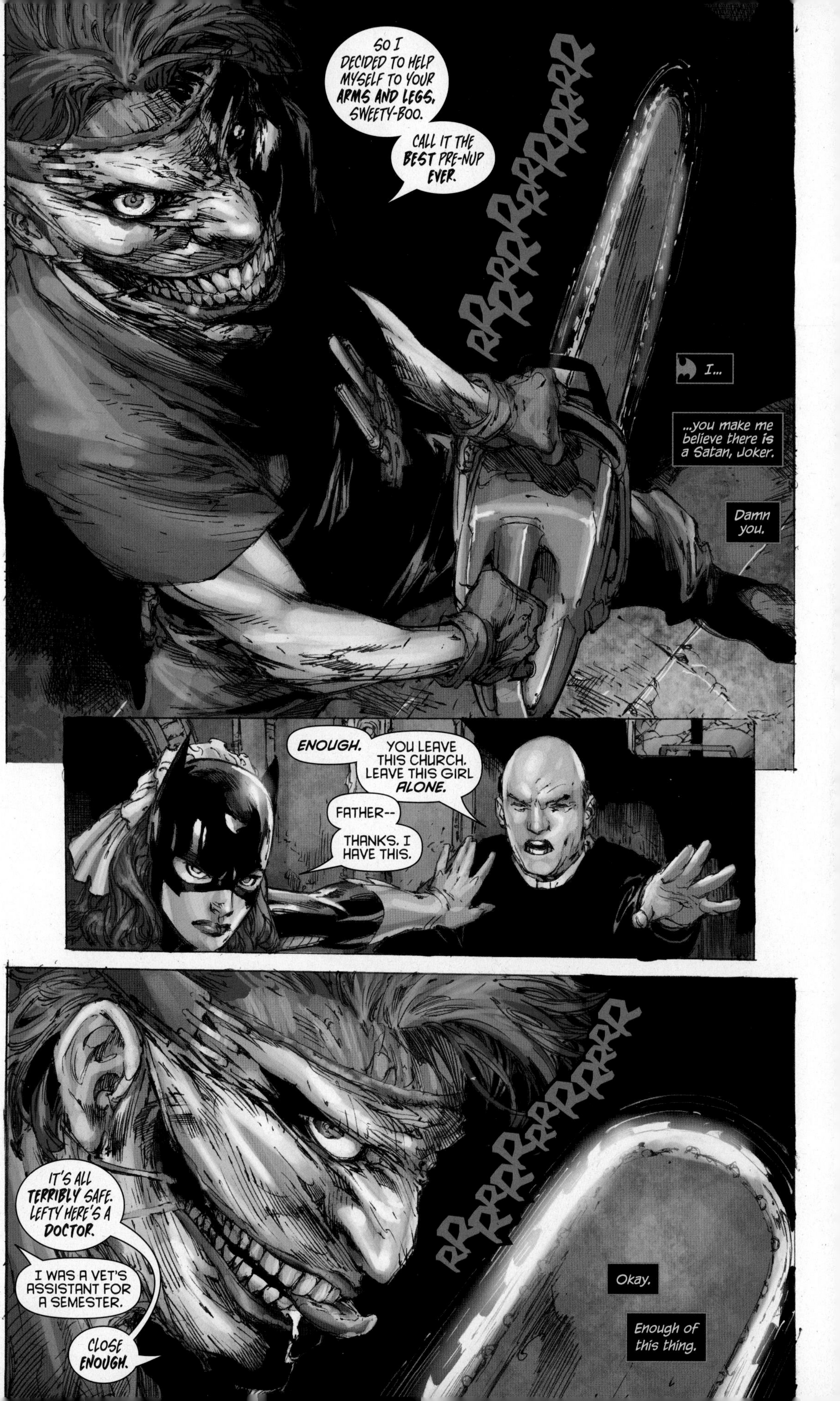
SO I DECIDED TO HELP MYSELF TO YOUR ARMS AND LEGS, SWEETY-BOO.
CALL IT THE BEST PRE-NUP EVER.
RRRRRRRRRRRRRR
I...
...you make me believe there is a Satan, Joker.
Damn you.
ENOUGH.
YOU LEAVE THIS CHURCH. LEAVE THIS GIRL ALONE.
FATHER--
THANKS. I HAVE THIS.
RRRRRRRRRRRRRRR
IT'S ALL TERRIBLY SAFE. LEFTY HERE'S A DOCTOR.
I WAS A VET'S ASSISTANT FOR A SEMESTER.
CLOSE ENOUGH.
Okay.
Enough of this thing.

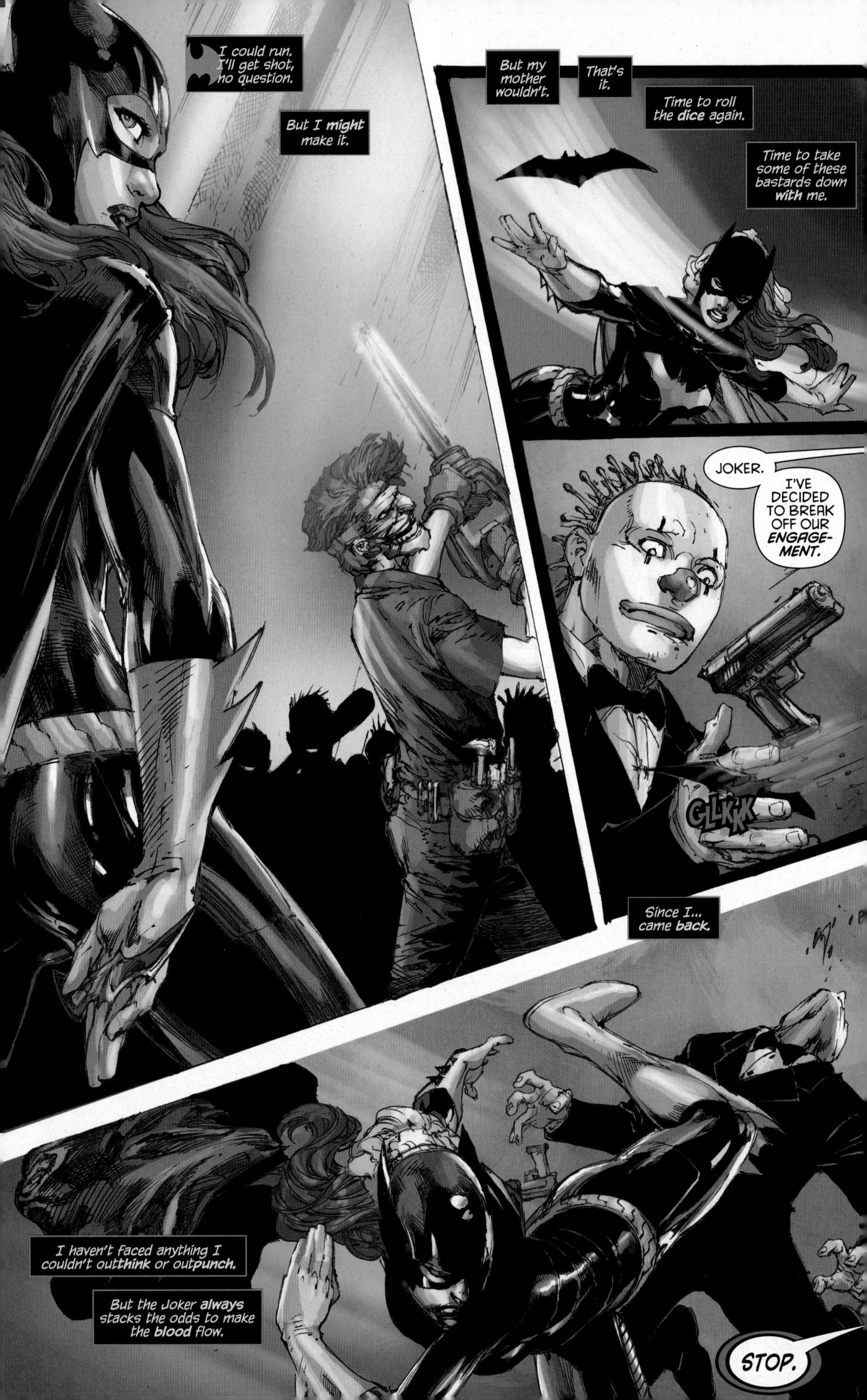
I could run. I'll get shot, no question.
But I might make it.
But my mother wouldn't.
That's it.
Time to roll the dice again.
Time to take some of these bastards down with me.
JOKER.
I'VE DECIDED TO BREAK OFF OUR ENGAGE-MENT.
GLLKKK
Since I... came back.
I haven't faced anything I couldn't outthink or outpunch.
But the Joker always stacks the odds to make the blood flow.
STOP.

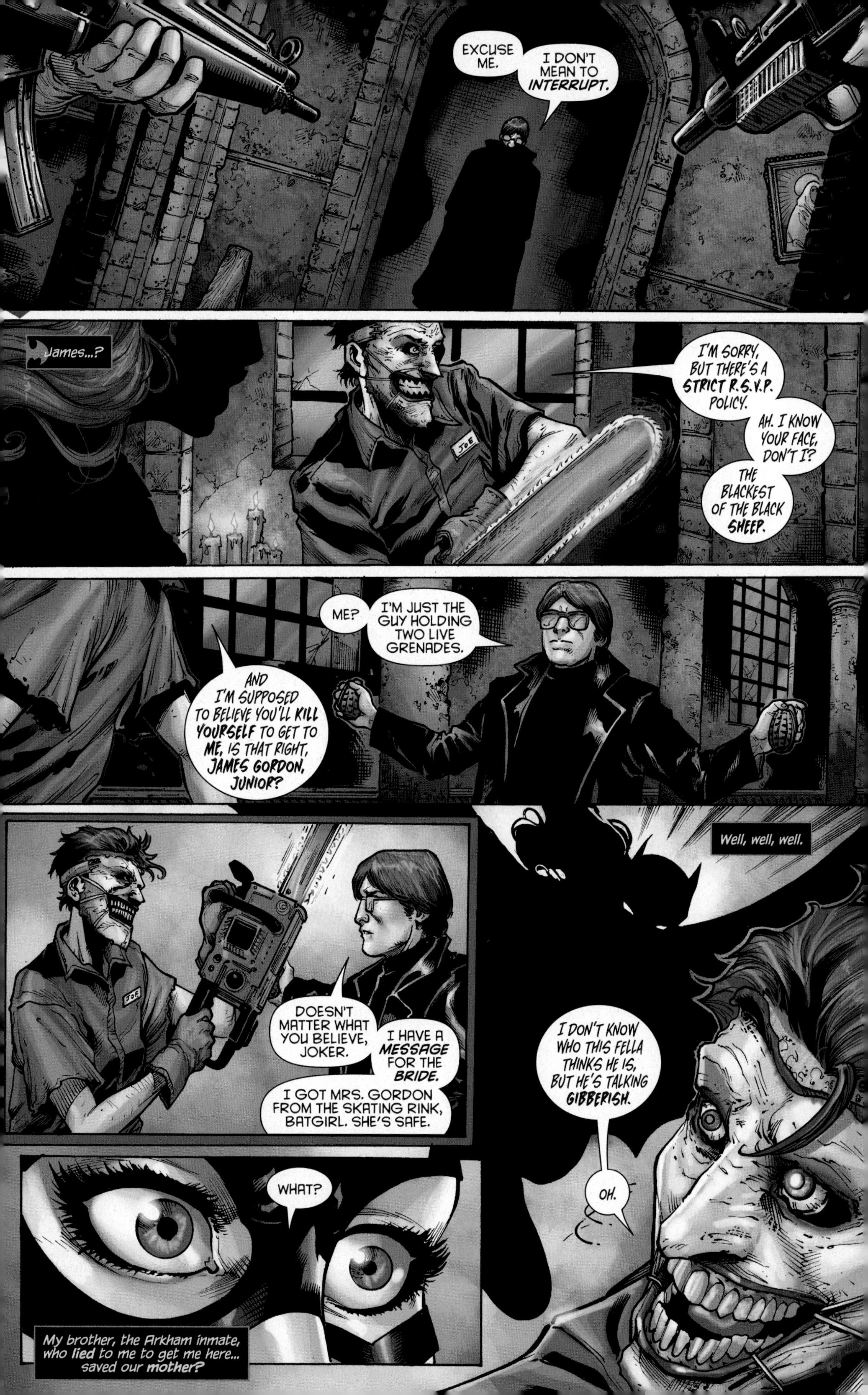
EXCUSE ME.
I DON'T MEAN TO INTERRUPT.
James...?
I'M SORRY, BUT THERE'S A STRICT R.S.V.P. POLICY.
AH. I KNOW YOUR FACE, DON'T I?
THE BLACKEST OF THE BLACK SHEEP.
ME?
I'M JUST THE GUY HOLDING TWO LIVE GRENADES.
AND I'M SUPPOSED TO BELIEVE YOU'LL KILL YOURSELF TO GET TO ME, IS THAT RIGHT, JAMES GORDON, JUNIOR?
DOESN'T MATTER WHAT YOU BELIEVE, JOKER.
I HAVE A MESSAGE FOR THE BRIDE.
I GOT MRS. GORDON FROM THE SKATING RINK, BATGIRL. SHE'S SAFE.
Well, well, well.
I DON'T KNOW WHO THIS FELLA THINKS HE IS, BUT HE'S TALKING GIBBERISH.
WHAT?
OH.
My brother, the Arkham inmate, who lied to me to get me here... saved our mother?

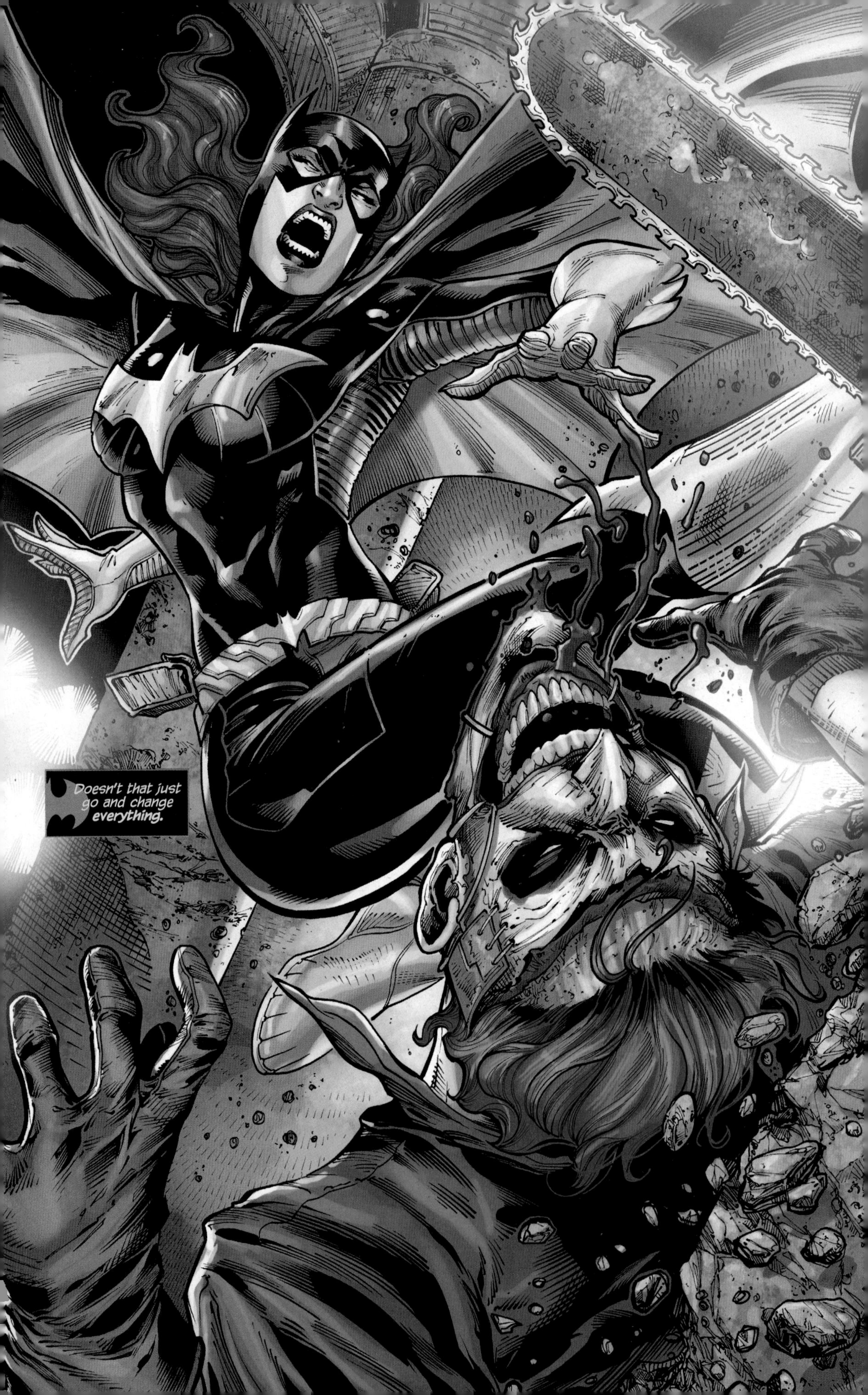
Doesn't that just go and change everything.

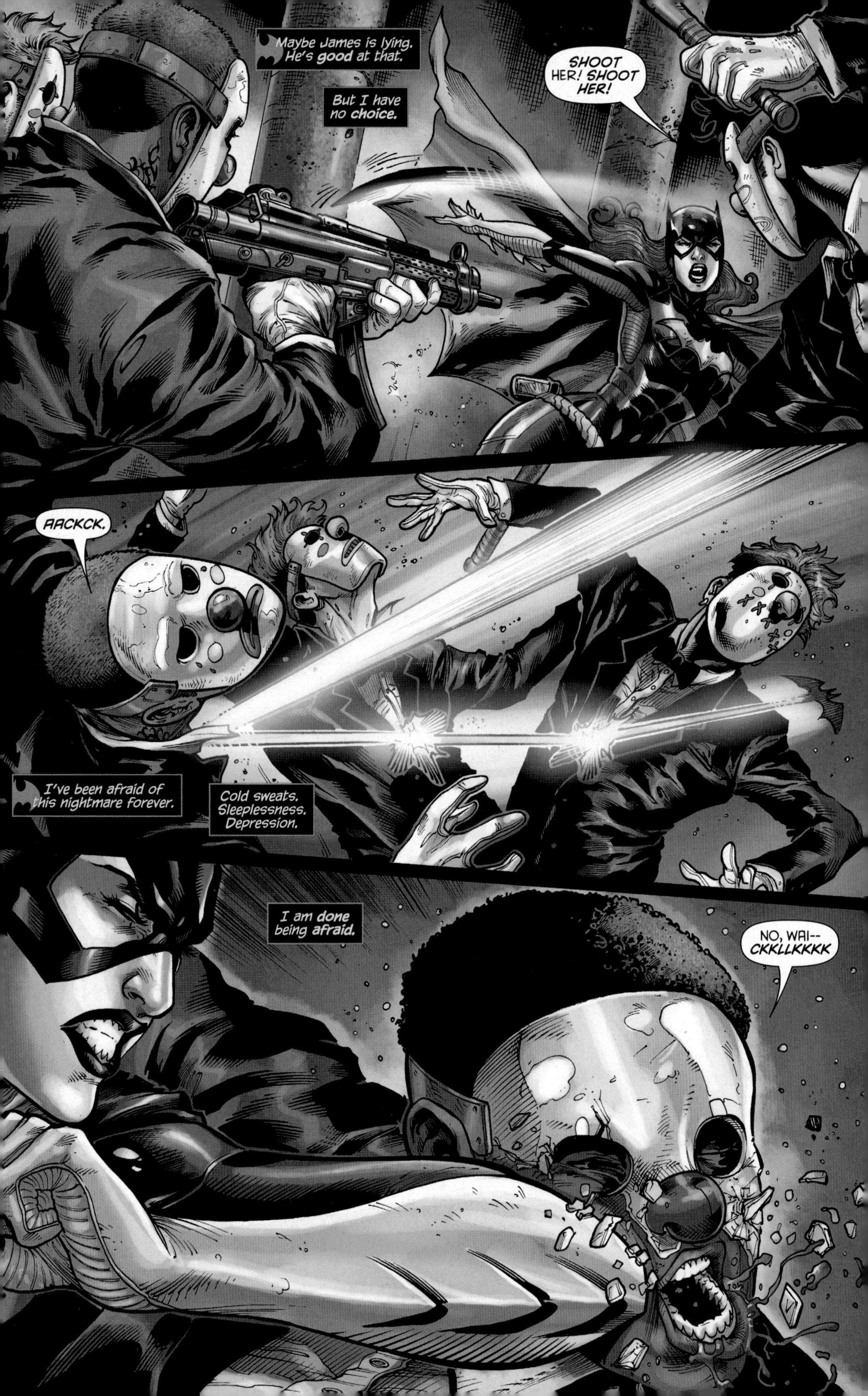
Maybe James is lying. He's good at that.
But I have no choice.
SHOOT HER! SHOOT HER!
AACKCK.
I've been afraid of this nightmare forever.
Cold sweats. Sleeplessness. Depression.
I am done being afraid.
NO, WAI-- CKKLLKKKK

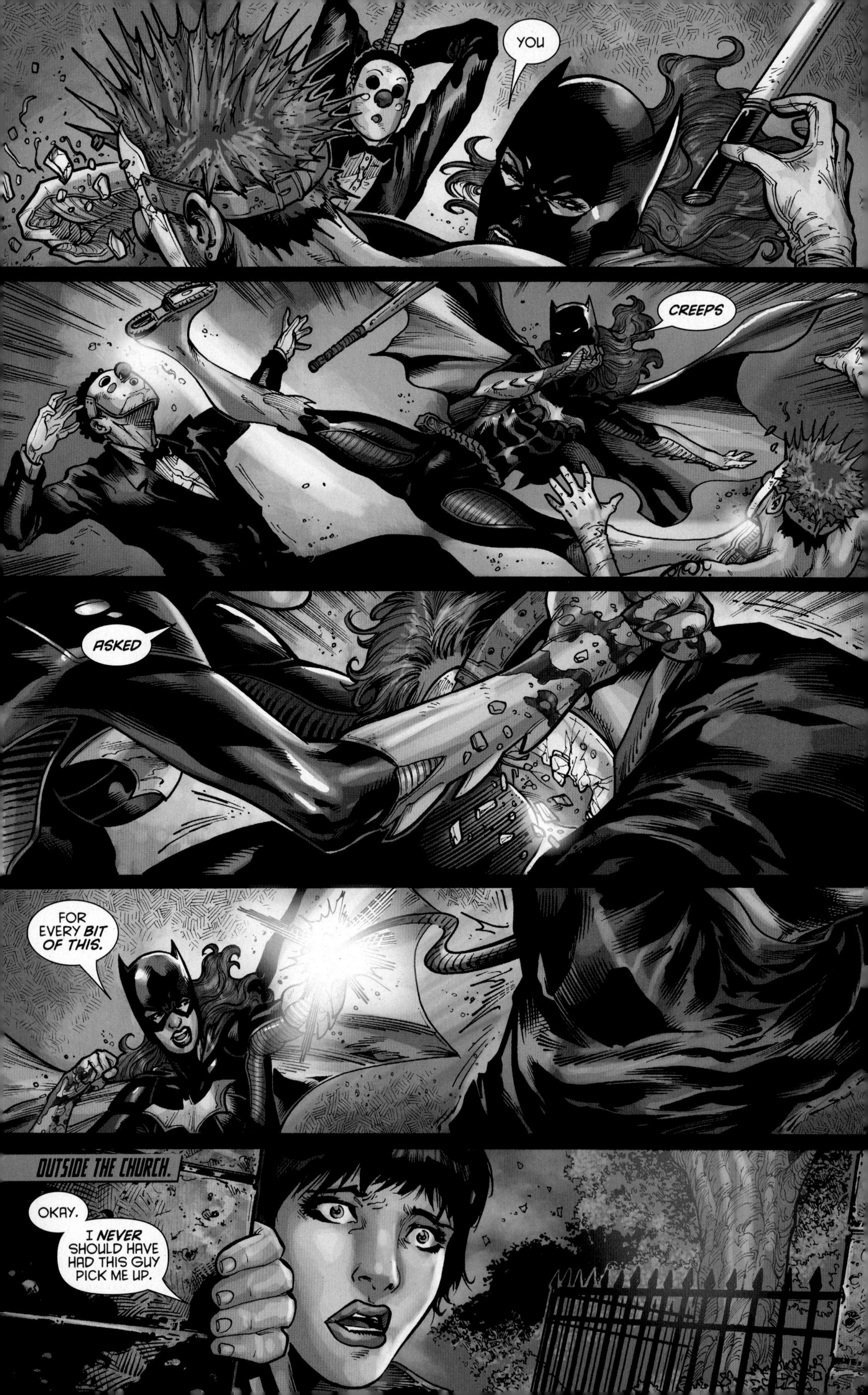
YOU
CREEPS
ASKED
FOR EVERY BIT OF THIS.
OUTSIDE THE CHURCH.
OKAY.
I NEVER SHOULD HAVE HAD THIS GUY PICK ME UP.

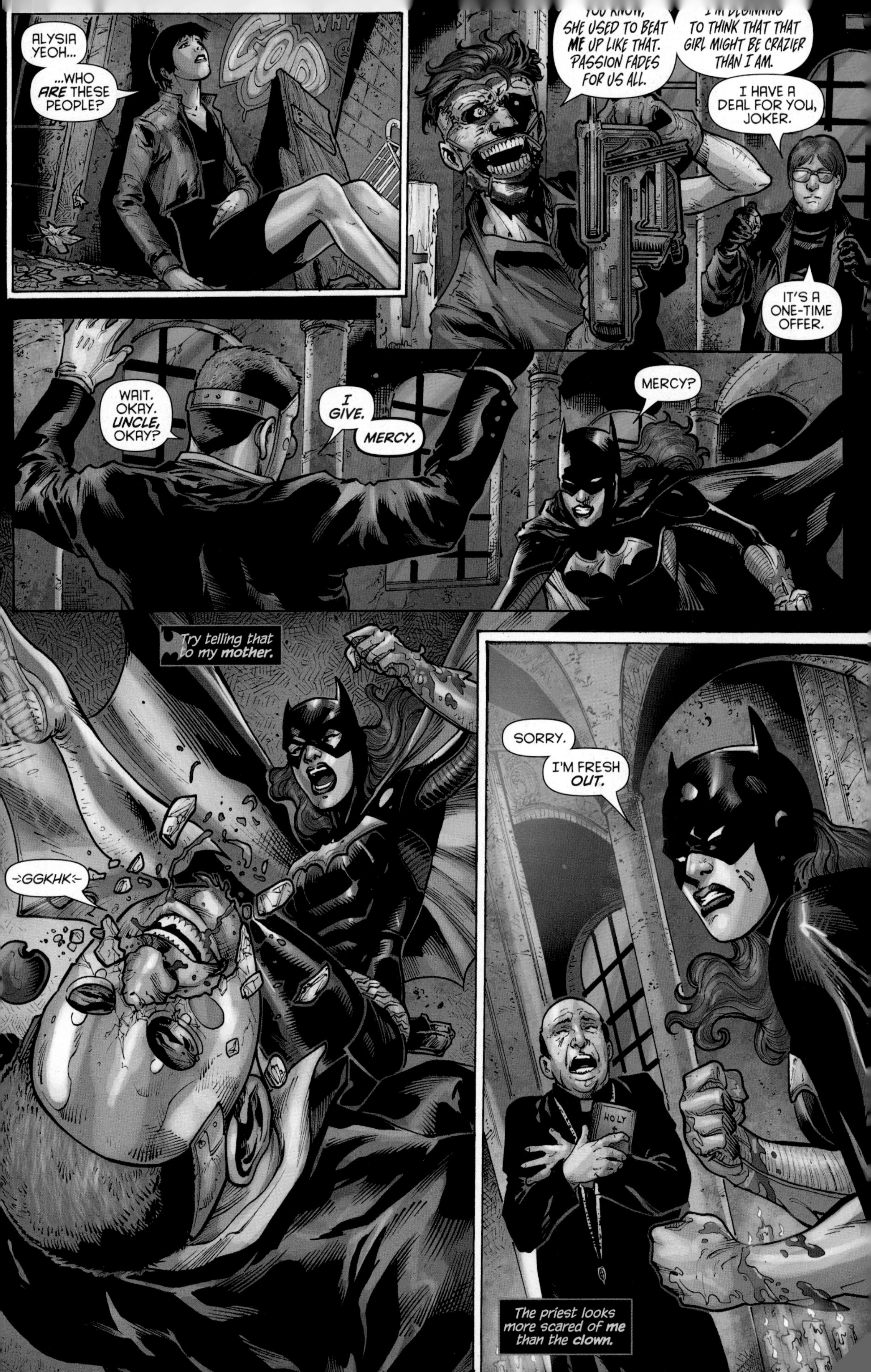
ALYSIA YEOH...
...WHO ARE THESE PEOPLE?
SHE USED TO BEAT ME UP LIKE THAT. PASSION FADES FOR US ALL.
TO THINK THAT THAT GIRL MIGHT BE CRAZIER THAN I AM.
I HAVE A DEAL FOR YOU, JOKER.
IT'S A ONE-TIME OFFER.
WAIT. OKAY. UNCLE, OKAY?
I GIVE.
MERCY.
MERCY?
Try telling that to my mother.
GGKHK
SORRY.
I'M FRESH OUT.
The priest looks more scared of me than the clown.
HOLY

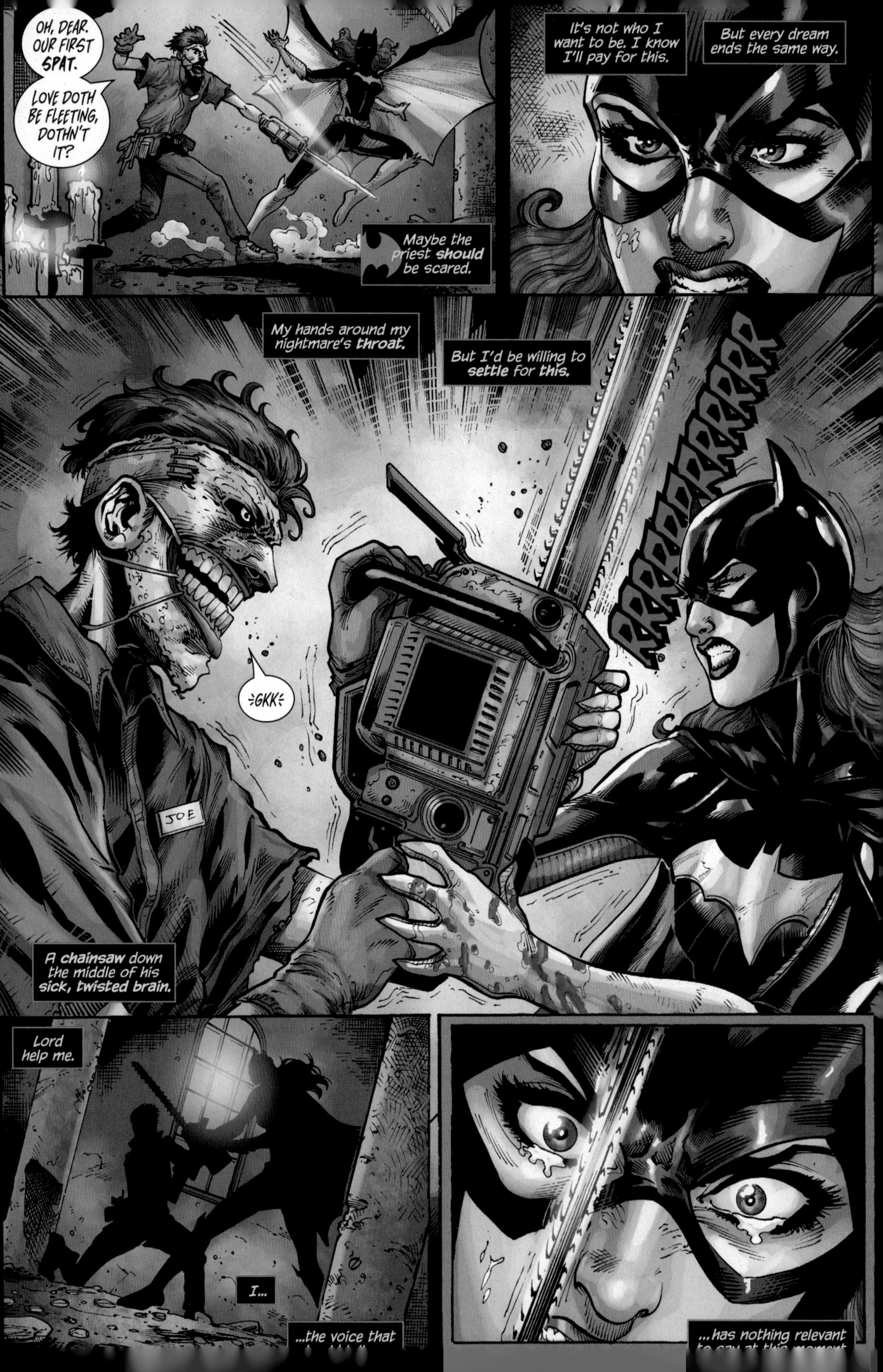
OH, DEAR. OUR FIRST SPAT.
LOVE DOTH BE FLEETING, DOTHN'T IT?
Maybe the priest should be scared.
It's not who I want to be. I know I'll pay for this.
But every dream ends the same way.
My hands around my nightmare's throat.
But I'd be willing to settle for this.
RRRRRRRRRRRR
GKK
JOE
A chainsaw down the middle of his sick, twisted brain.
Lord help me.
I...
...the voice that
...has nothing relevant

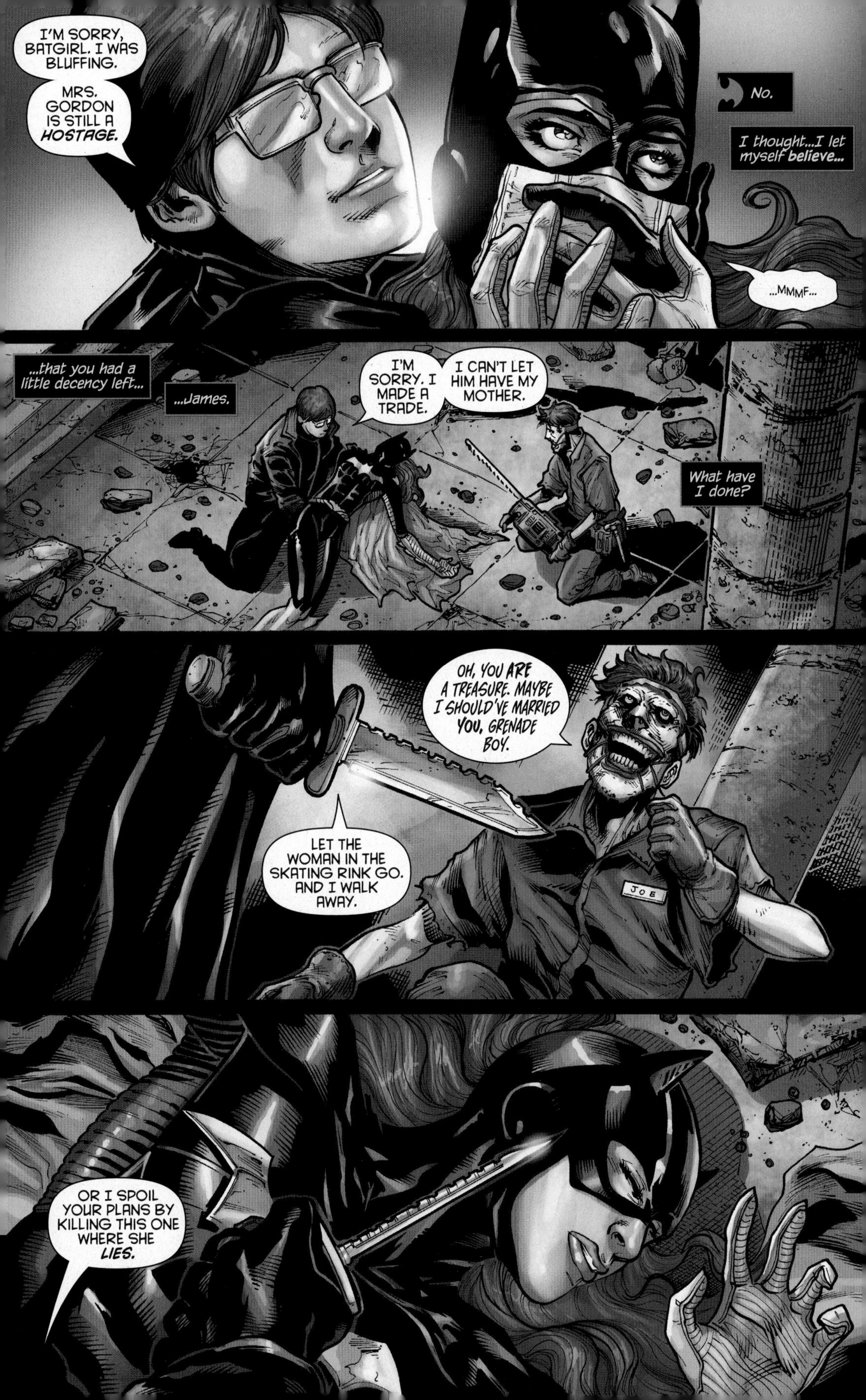
I'M SORRY, BATGIRL. I WAS BLUFFING.
MRS. GORDON IS STILL A HOSTAGE.
No.
I thought...I let myself believe...
...MMMF...
...that you had a little decency left...
...James.
I'M SORRY. I MADE A TRADE.
I CAN'T LET HIM HAVE MY MOTHER.
What have I done?
OH, YOU ARE A TREASURE. MAYBE I SHOULD'VE MARRIED YOU, GRENADE BOY.
LET THE WOMAN IN THE SKATING RINK GO. AND I WALK AWAY.
JOE
OR I SPOIL YOUR PLANS BY KILLING THIS ONE WHERE SHE LIES.

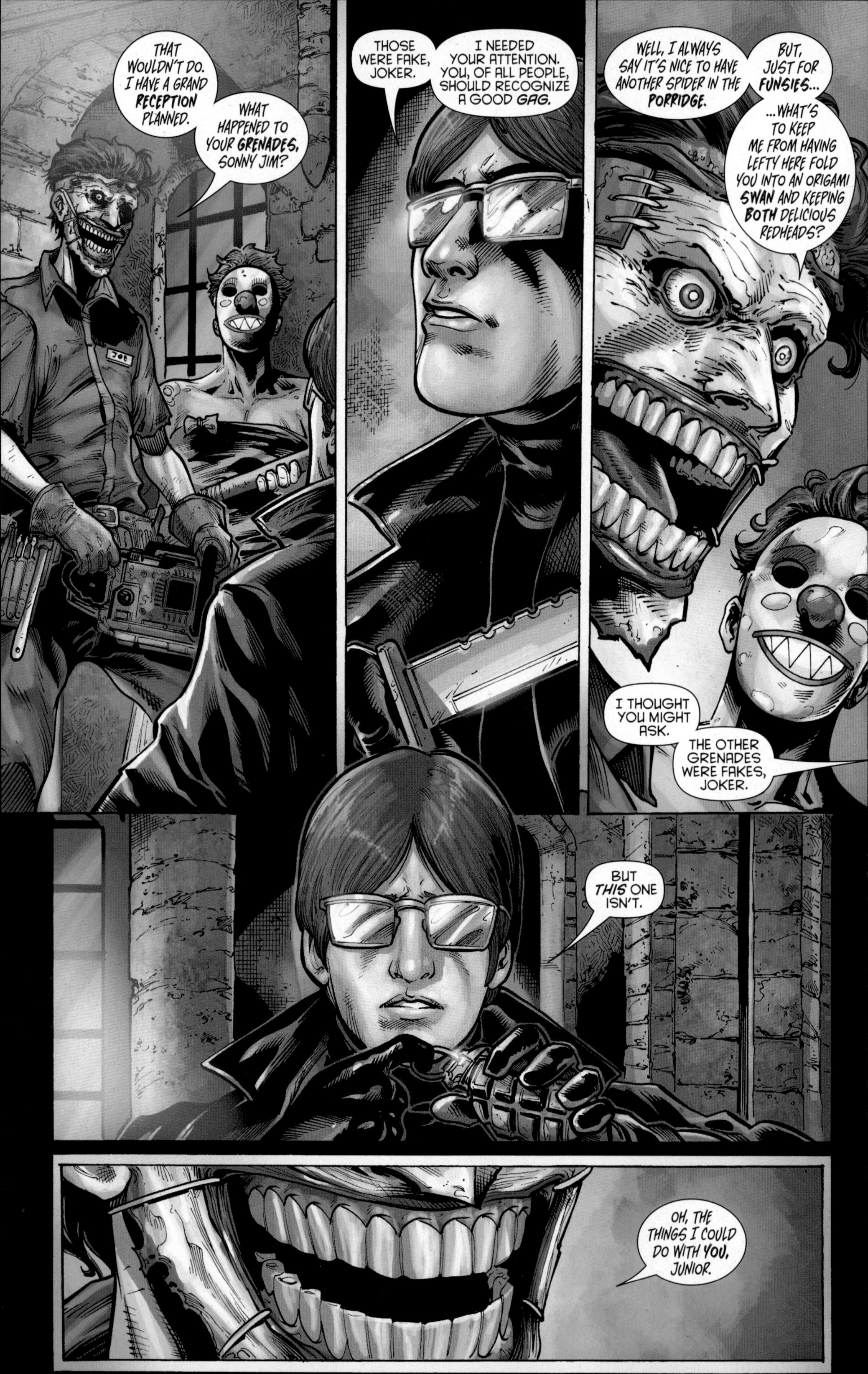
THAT WOULDN'T DO. I HAVE A GRAND RECEPTION PLANNED.
WHAT HAPPENED TO YOUR GRENADES, SONNY JIM?
THOSE WERE FAKE, JOKER.
I NEEDED YOUR ATTENTION. YOU, OF ALL PEOPLE, SHOULD RECOGNIZE A GOOD GAG.
WELL, I ALWAYS SAY IT'S NICE TO HAVE ANOTHER SPIDER IN THE PORRIDGE.
BUT, JUST FOR FUNSIES...
...WHAT'S TO KEEP ME FROM HAVING LEFTY HERE FOLD YOU INTO AN ORIGAMI SWAN AND KEEPING BOTH DELICIOUS REDHEADS?
I THOUGHT YOU MIGHT ASK.
THE OTHER GRENADES WERE FAKES, JOKER.
BUT THIS ONE ISN'T.
OH, THE THINGS I COULD DO WITH YOU, JUNIOR.

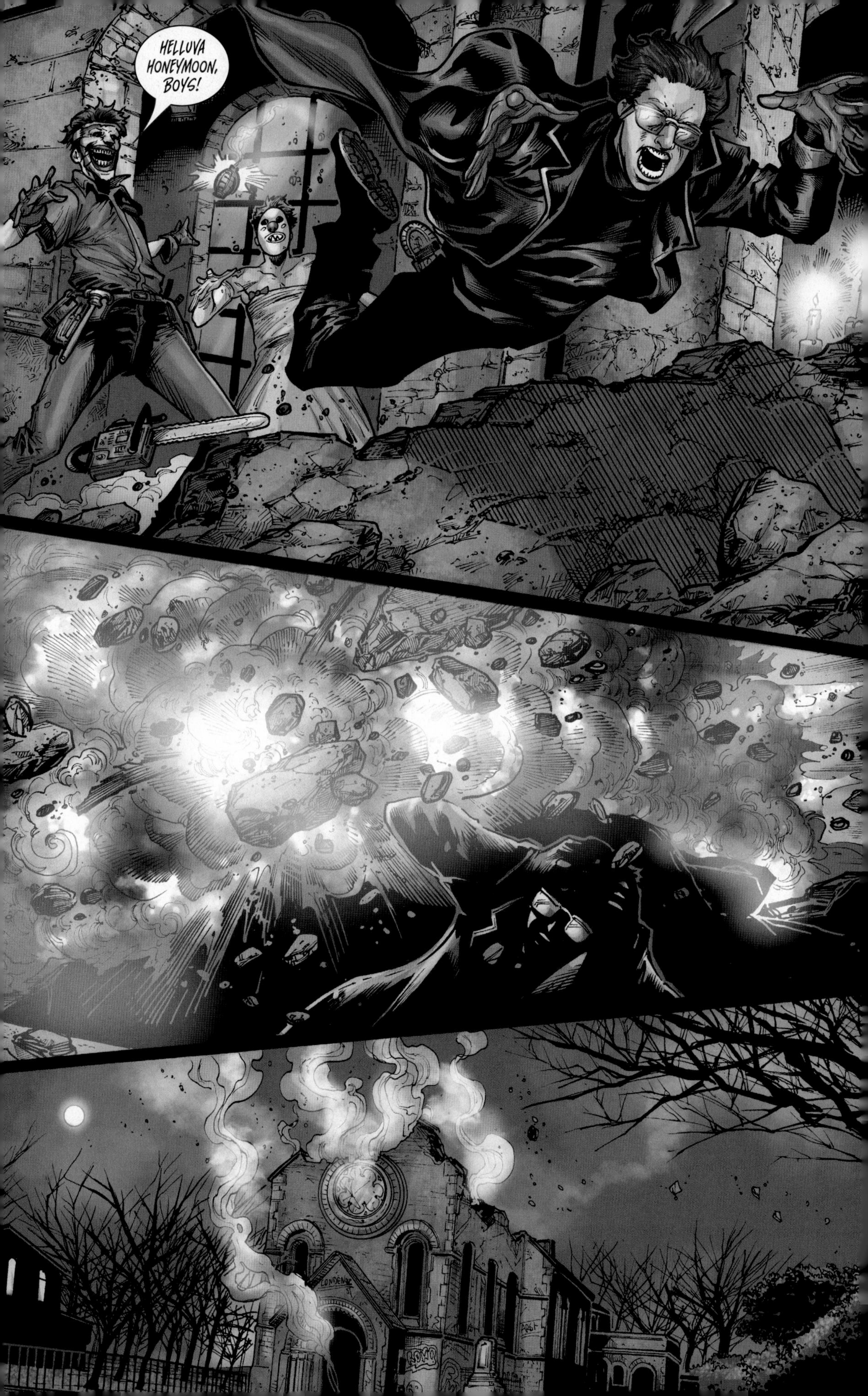
HELLUVA HONEYMOON, BOYS!

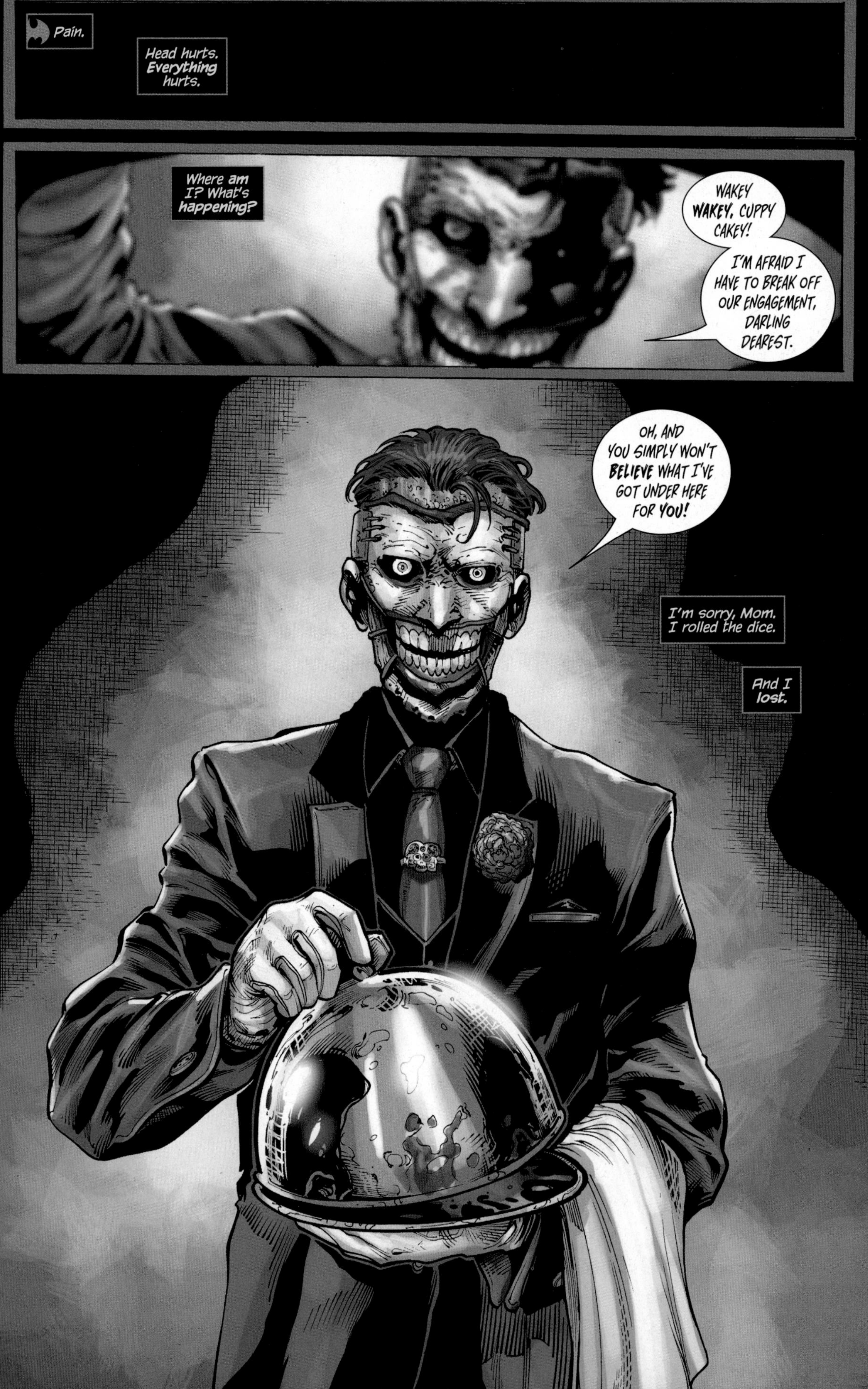
Pain.
Head hurts. Everything hurts.
Where am I? What's happening?
WAKEY WAKEY, CUPPY CAKEY!
I'M AFRAID I HAVE TO BREAK OFF OUR ENGAGEMENT, DARLING DEAREST.
OH, AND YOU SIMPLY WON'T BELIEVE WHAT I'VE GOT UNDER HERE FOR YOU!
I'm sorry, Mom. I rolled the dice.
And I lost.

PART FIVE

RED HOOD AND RED ROBIN

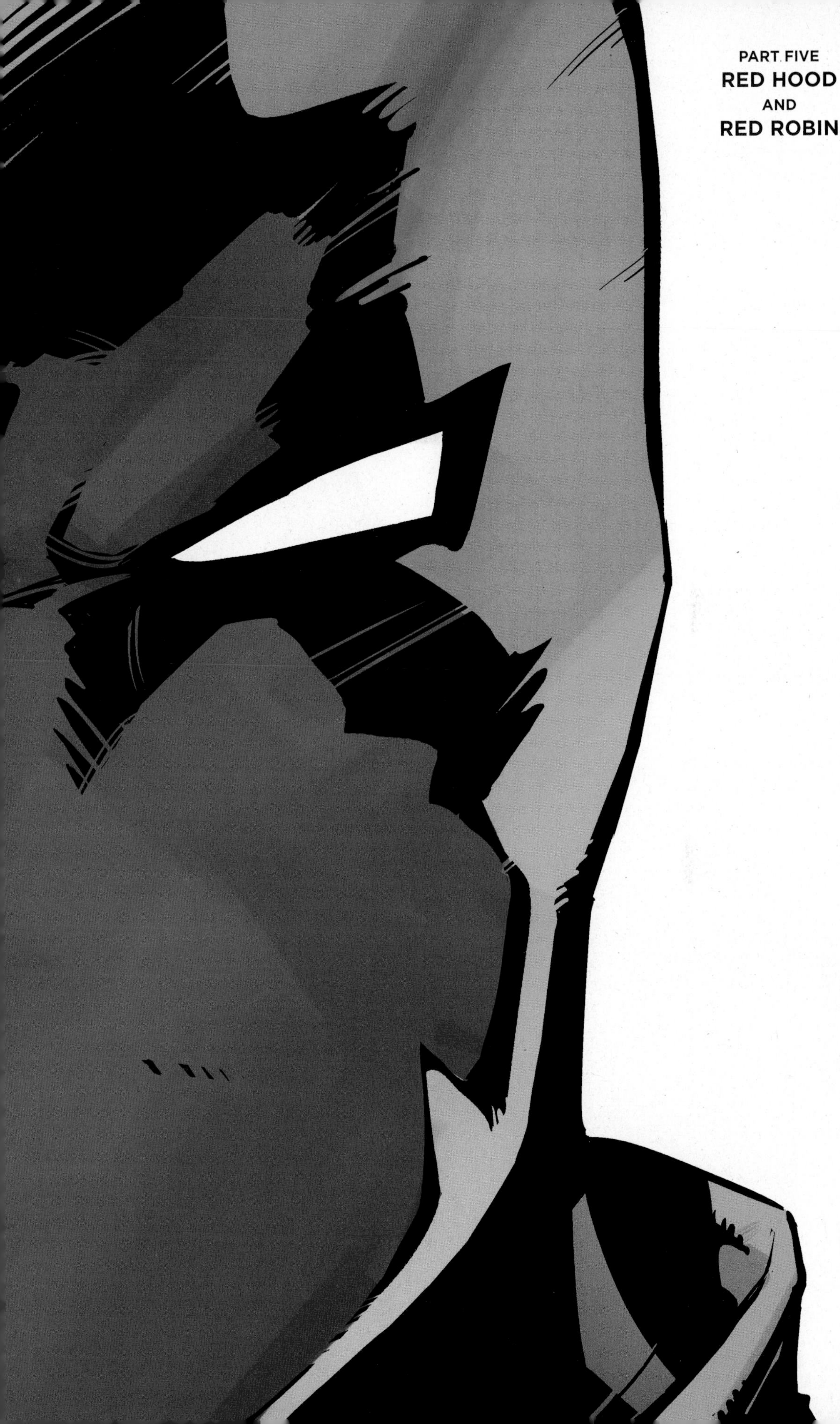

SCOTT LOBDELL FABIAN NICIEZA writers TIMOTHY GREEN II BRETT BOOTH NORM RAPMUND WAYNE FAUCHER PASCAL ALIXE ALE GARZA artists
ANDREW DALHOUSE BLOND colorists TRAVIS LANHAM DAVE SHARPE TAYLOR ESPOSITO letterers

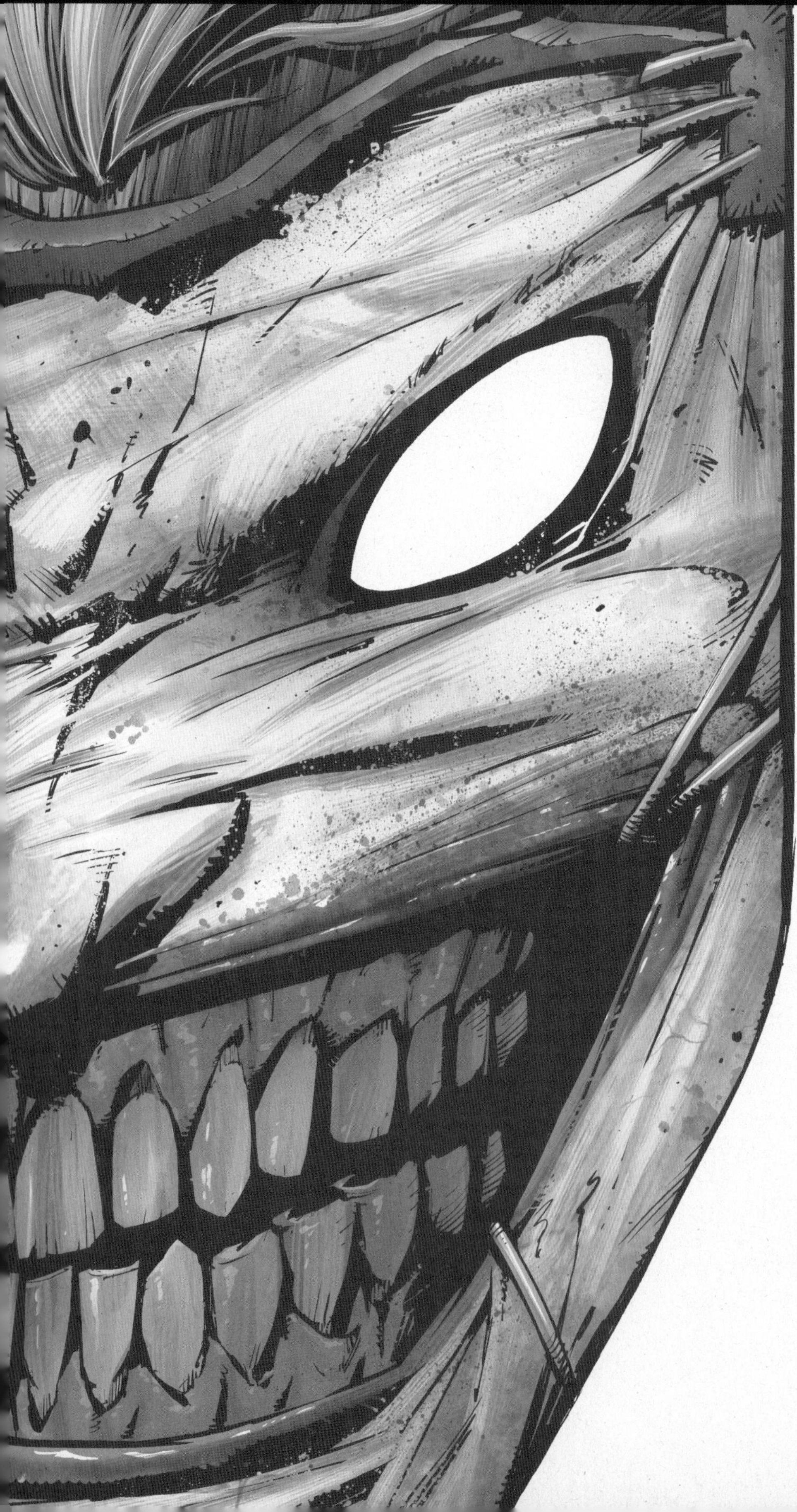

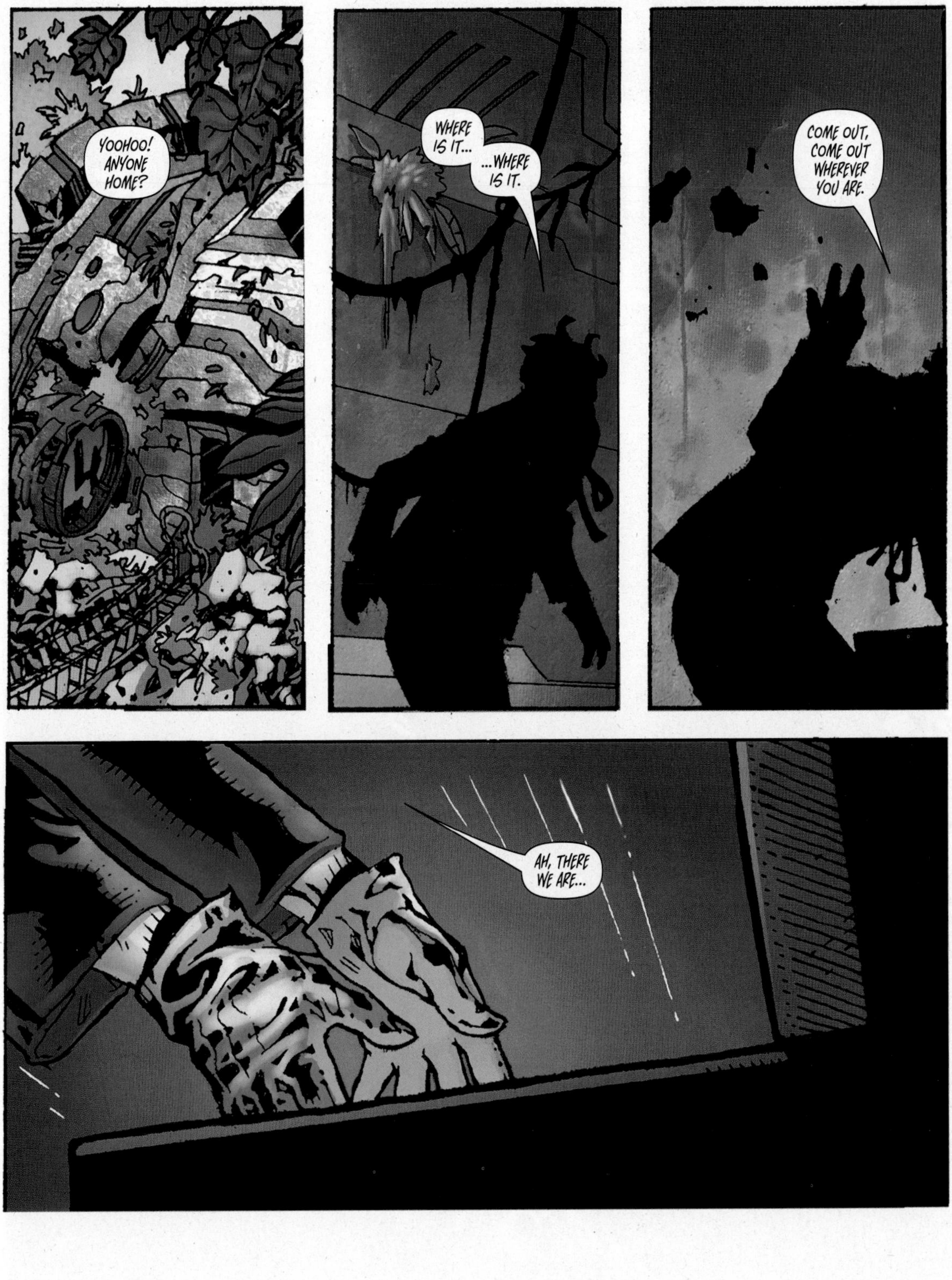
YOOHOO! ANYONE HOME?
WHERE IS IT...
...WHERE IS IT.
COME OUT, COME OUT WHEREVER YOU ARE.
AH, THERE WE ARE...

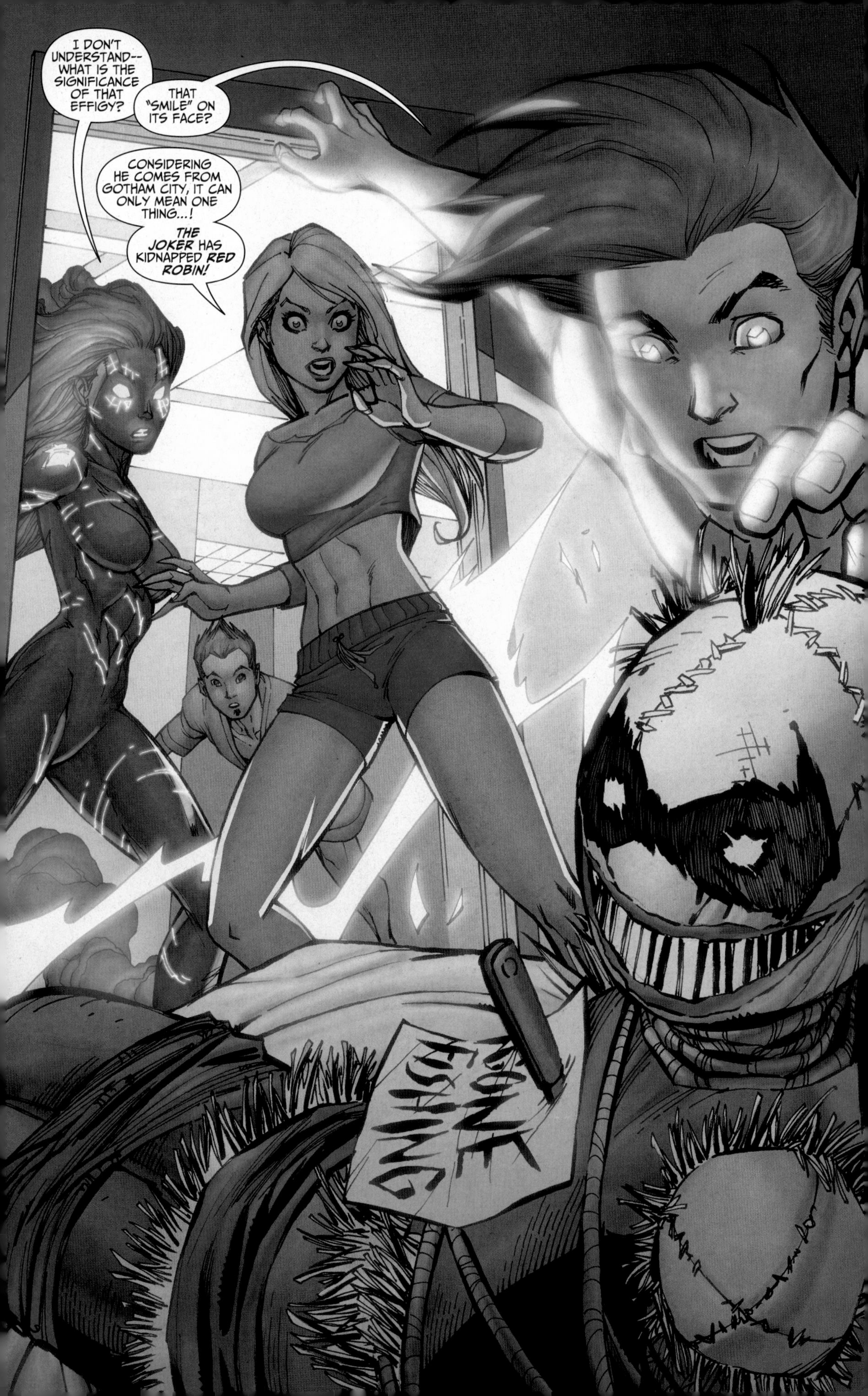
I DON'T UNDERSTAND-- WHAT IS THE SIGNIFICANCE OF THAT EFFIGY?
THAT "SMILE" ON ITS FACE?
CONSIDERING HE COMES FROM GOTHAM CITY, IT CAN ONLY MEAN ONE THING...!
THE JOKER HAS KIDNAPPED RED ROBIN!
GONE FISHING

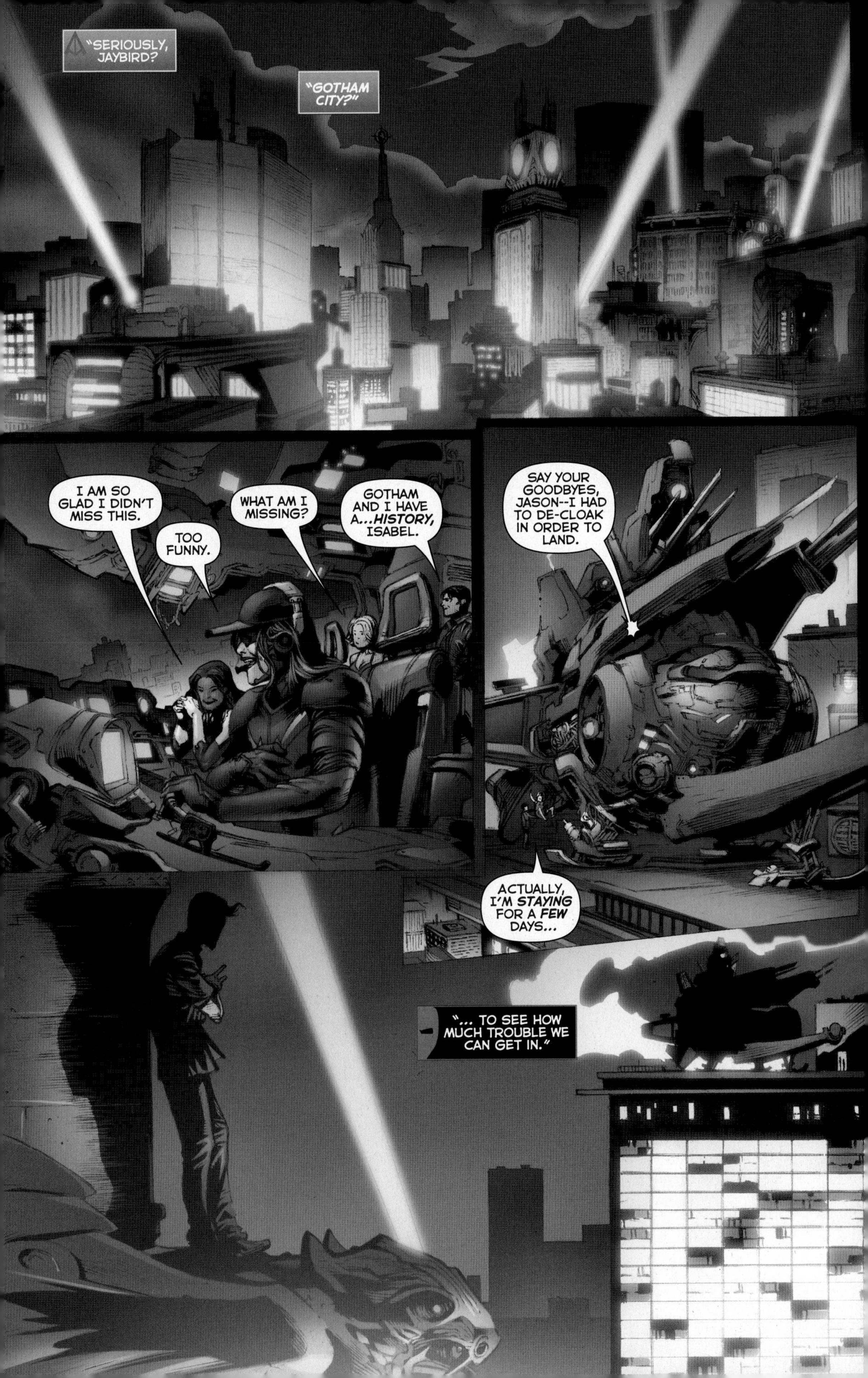
"SERIOUSLY, JAYBIRD?
"GOTHAM CITY?"
I AM SO GLAD I DIDN'T MISS THIS.
TOO FUNNY.
WHAT AM I MISSING?
GOTHAM AND I HAVE A...HISTORY, ISABEL.
SAY YOUR GOODBYES, JASON--I HAD TO DE-CLOAK IN ORDER TO LAND.
ACTUALLY, I'M STAYING FOR A FEW DAYS...
"... TO SEE HOW MUCH TROUBLE WE CAN GET IN."

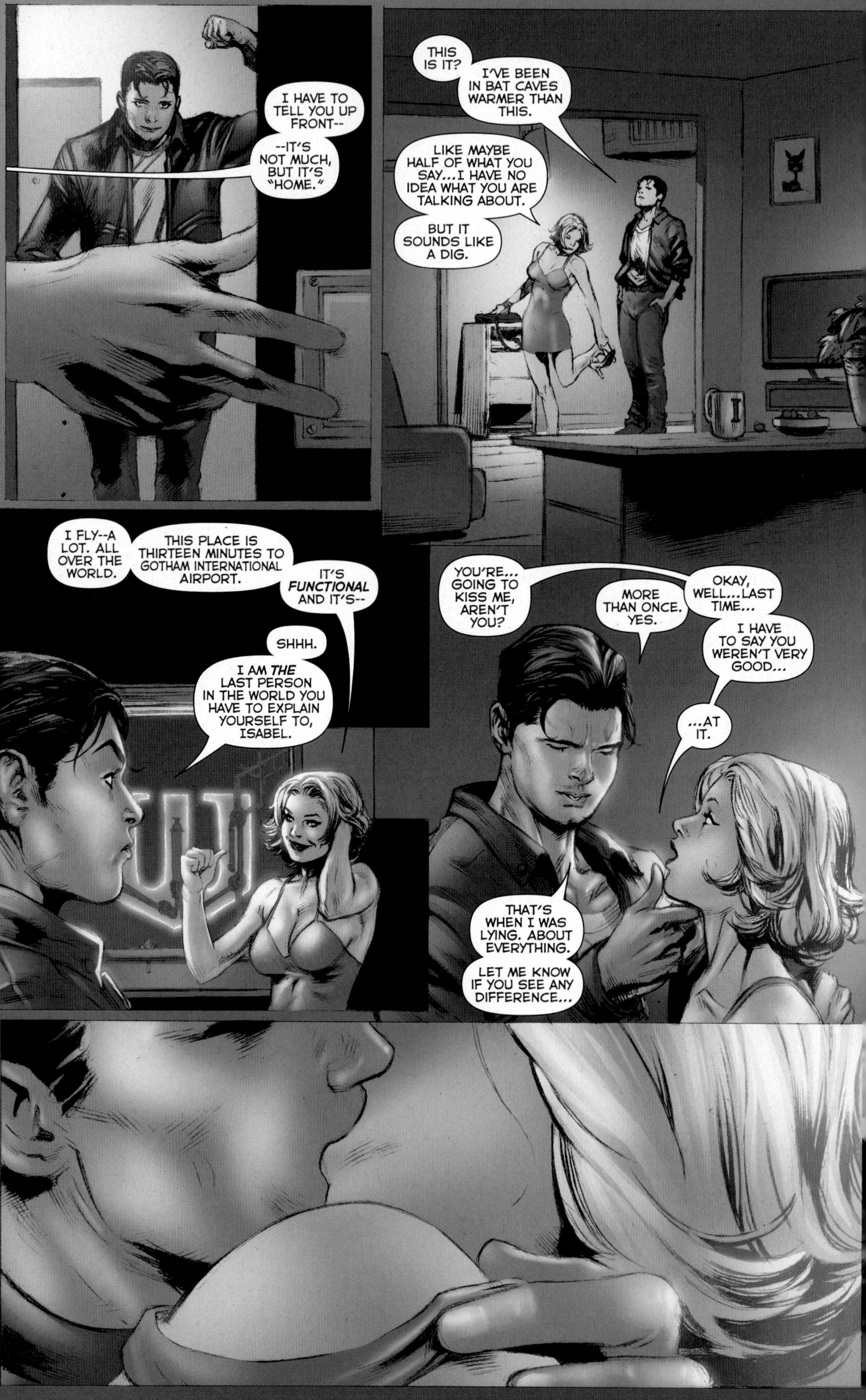
I HAVE TO TELL YOU UP FRONT--
--IT'S NOT MUCH, BUT IT'S "HOME."
THIS IS IT?
I'VE BEEN IN BAT CAVES WARMER THAN THIS.
LIKE MAYBE HALF OF WHAT YOU SAY...I HAVE NO IDEA WHAT YOU ARE TALKING ABOUT.
BUT IT SOUNDS LIKE A DIG.
I FLY--A LOT. ALL OVER THE WORLD.
THIS PLACE IS THIRTEEN MINUTES TO GOTHAM INTERNATIONAL AIRPORT.
IT'S *FUNCTIONAL* AND IT'S--
SHHH.
I AM *THE* LAST PERSON IN THE WORLD YOU HAVE TO EXPLAIN YOURSELF TO, ISABEL.
YOU'RE... GOING TO KISS ME, AREN'T YOU?
MORE THAN ONCE. YES.
OKAY, WELL...LAST TIME...
I HAVE TO SAY YOU WEREN'T VERY GOOD...
...AT IT.
THAT'S WHEN I WAS LYING. ABOUT EVERYTHING.
LET ME KNOW IF YOU SEE ANY DIFFERENCE...

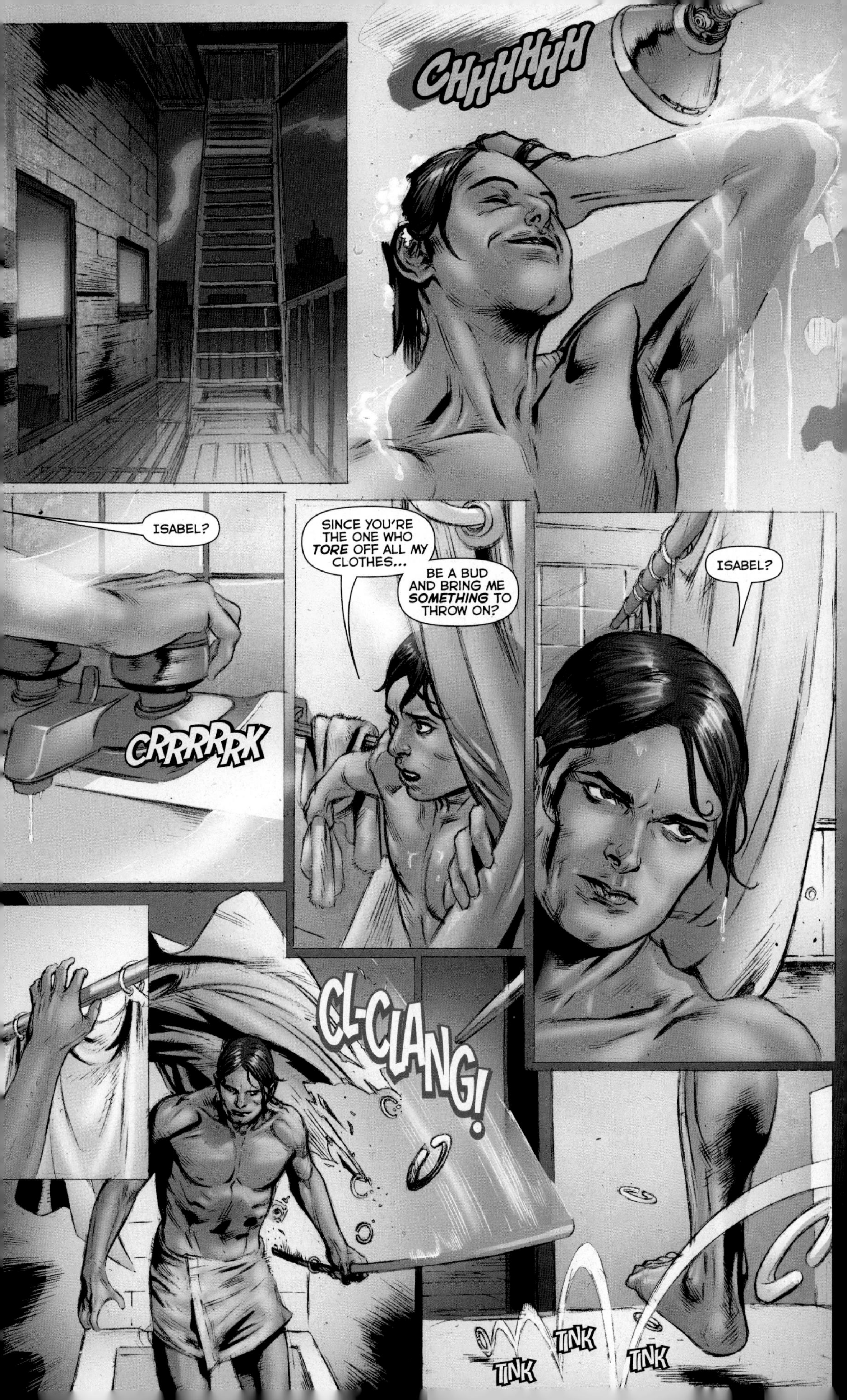
CHHHHHH
ISABEL?
CRRRRRK
SINCE YOU'RE THE ONE WHO TORE OFF ALL MY CLOTHES...
BE A BUD AND BRING ME SOMETHING TO THROW ON?
ISABEL?
CL-CLANG!
TINK
TINK
TINK
TINK

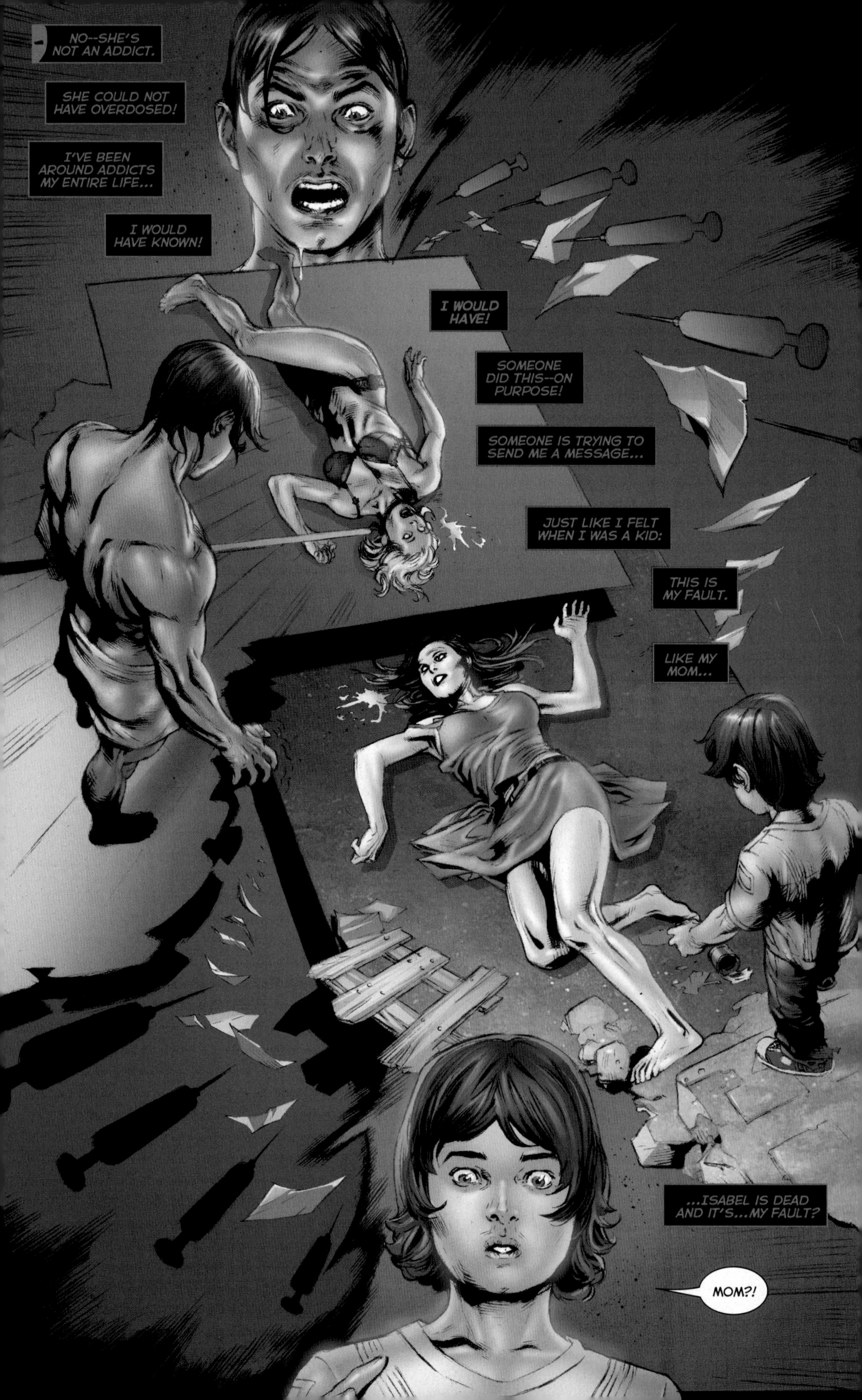
NO--SHE'S NOT AN ADDICT.
SHE COULD NOT HAVE OVERDOSED!
I'VE BEEN AROUND ADDICTS MY ENTIRE LIFE...
I WOULD HAVE KNOWN!
I WOULD HAVE!
SOMEONE DID THIS--ON PURPOSE!
SOMEONE IS TRYING TO SEND ME A MESSAGE...
JUST LIKE I FELT WHEN I WAS A KID:
THIS IS MY FAULT.
LIKE MY MOM...
...ISABEL IS DEAD AND IT'S...MY FAULT?
MOM?!

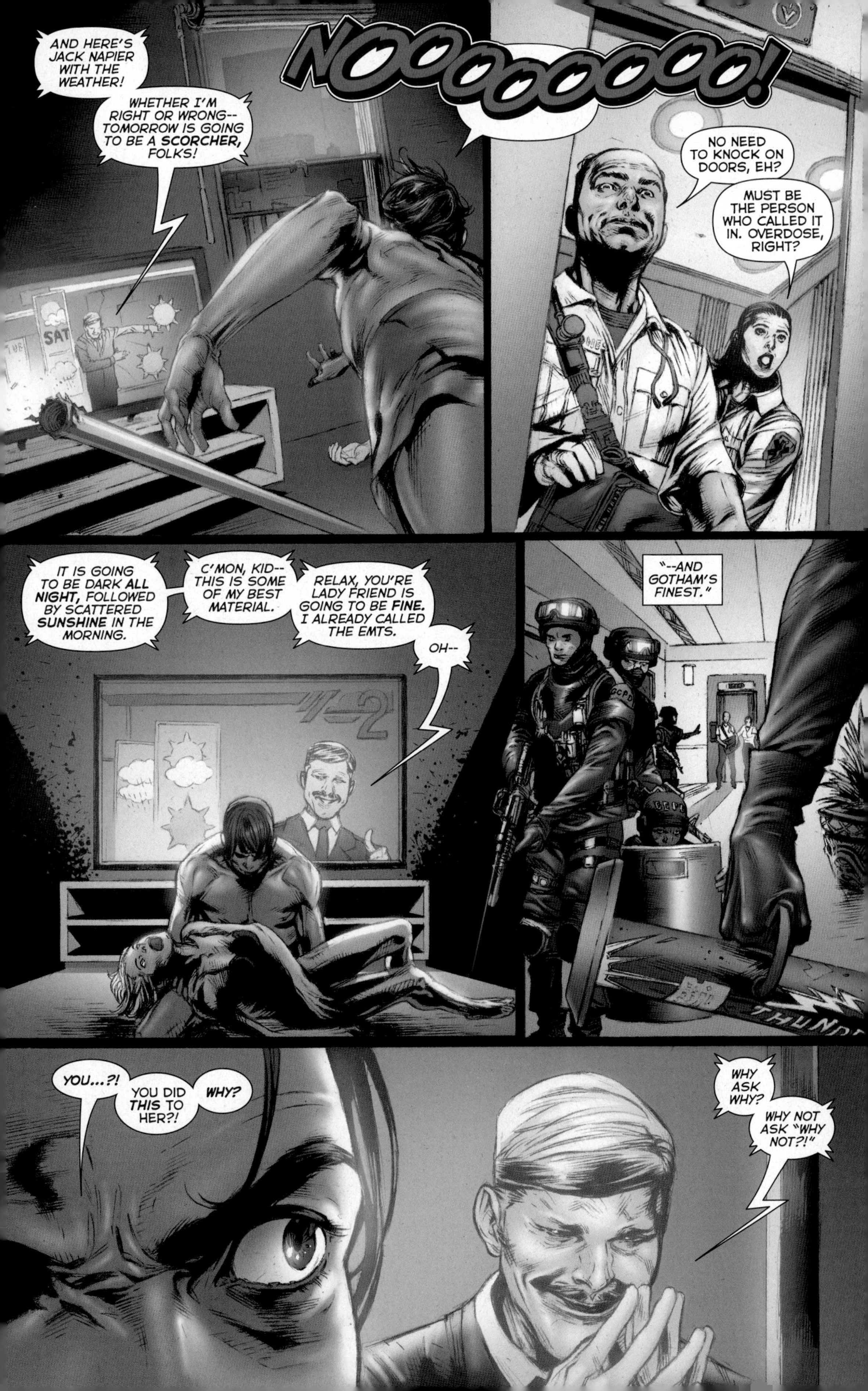
AND HERE'S JACK NAPIER WITH THE WEATHER!
WHETHER I'M RIGHT OR WRONG-- TOMORROW IS GOING TO BE A SCORCHER, FOLKS!
NOOOOOOOOOO!
SAT
NO NEED TO KNOCK ON DOORS, EH?
MUST BE THE PERSON WHO CALLED IT IN. OVERDOSE, RIGHT?
IT IS GOING TO BE DARK ALL NIGHT, FOLLOWED BY SCATTERED SUNSHINE IN THE MORNING.
C'MON, KID-- THIS IS SOME OF MY BEST MATERIAL.
RELAX, YOU'RE LADY FRIEND IS GOING TO BE FINE. I ALREADY CALLED THE EMTS.
OH--
"--AND GOTHAM'S FINEST."
GCPD
YOU...?!
YOU DID THIS TO HER?!
WHY?
WHY ASK WHY?
WHY NOT ASK "WHY NOT?!"

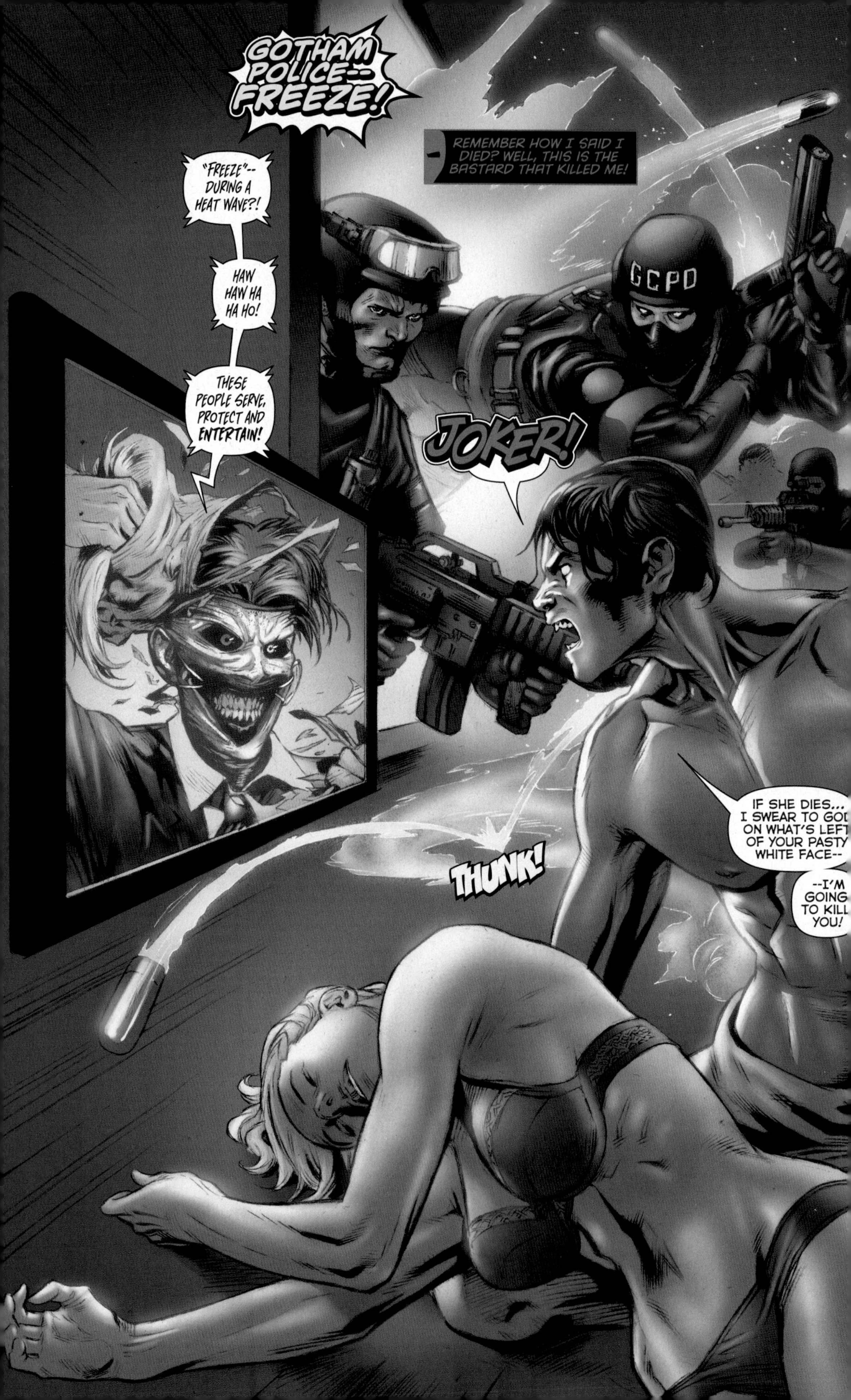
GOTHAM POLICE-- FREEZE!
REMEMBER HOW I SAID I DIED? WELL, THIS IS THE BASTARD THAT KILLED ME!
"FREEZE"-- DURING A HEAT WAVE?!
HAW HAW HA HA HO!
THESE PEOPLE SERVE, PROTECT AND ENTERTAIN!
JOKER!
THUNK!
IF SHE DIES... I SWEAR TO GOD ON WHAT'S LEFT OF YOUR PASTY WHITE FACE--
--I'M GOING TO KILL YOU!

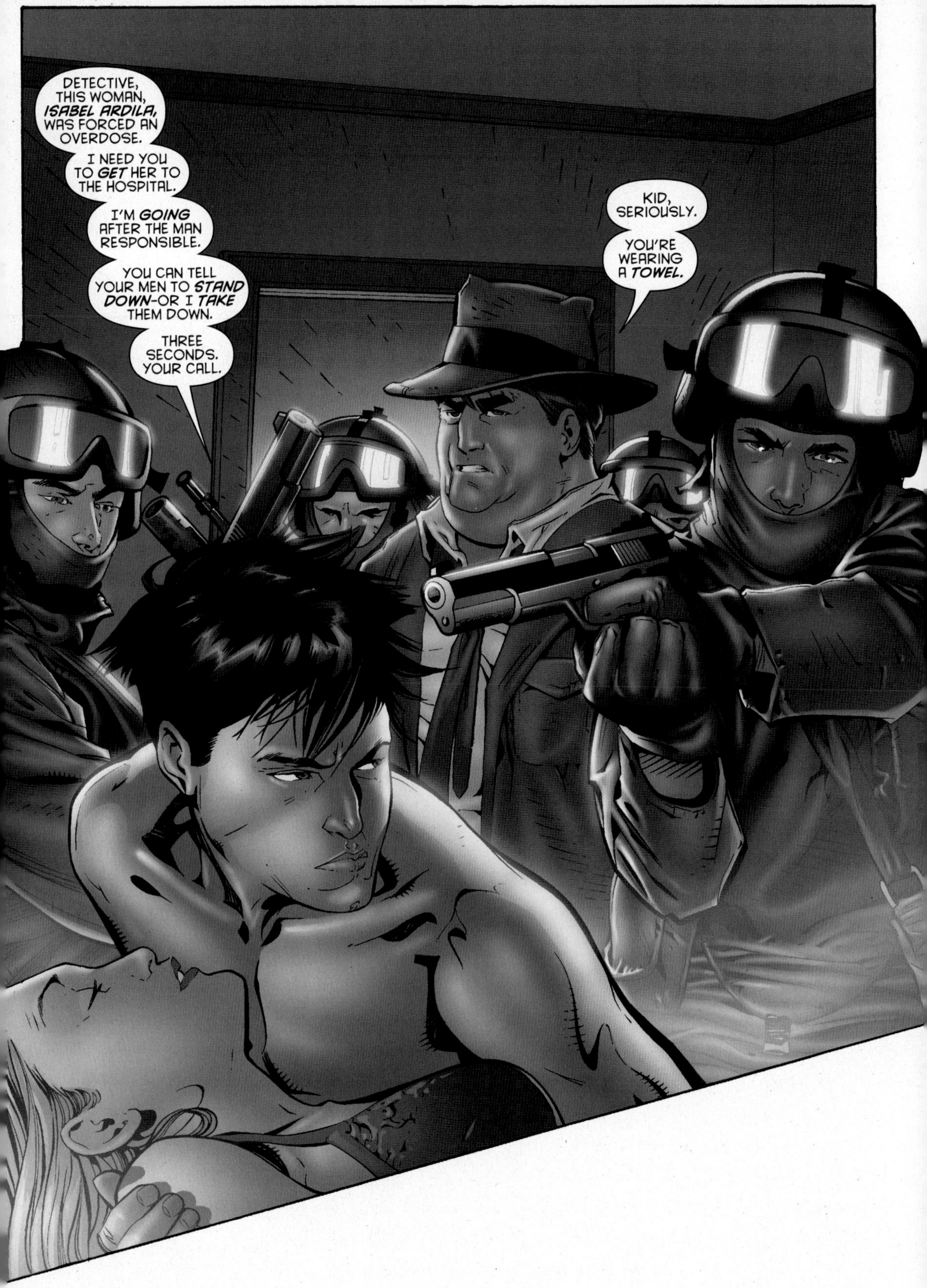
DETECTIVE, THIS WOMAN, ISABEL ARDILA, WAS FORCED AN OVERDOSE.
I NEED YOU TO GET HER TO THE HOSPITAL.
I'M GOING AFTER THE MAN RESPONSIBLE.
YOU CAN TELL YOUR MEN TO STAND DOWN--OR I TAKE THEM DOWN.
THREE SECONDS. YOUR CALL.
KID, SERIOUSLY.
YOU'RE WEARING A TOWEL.

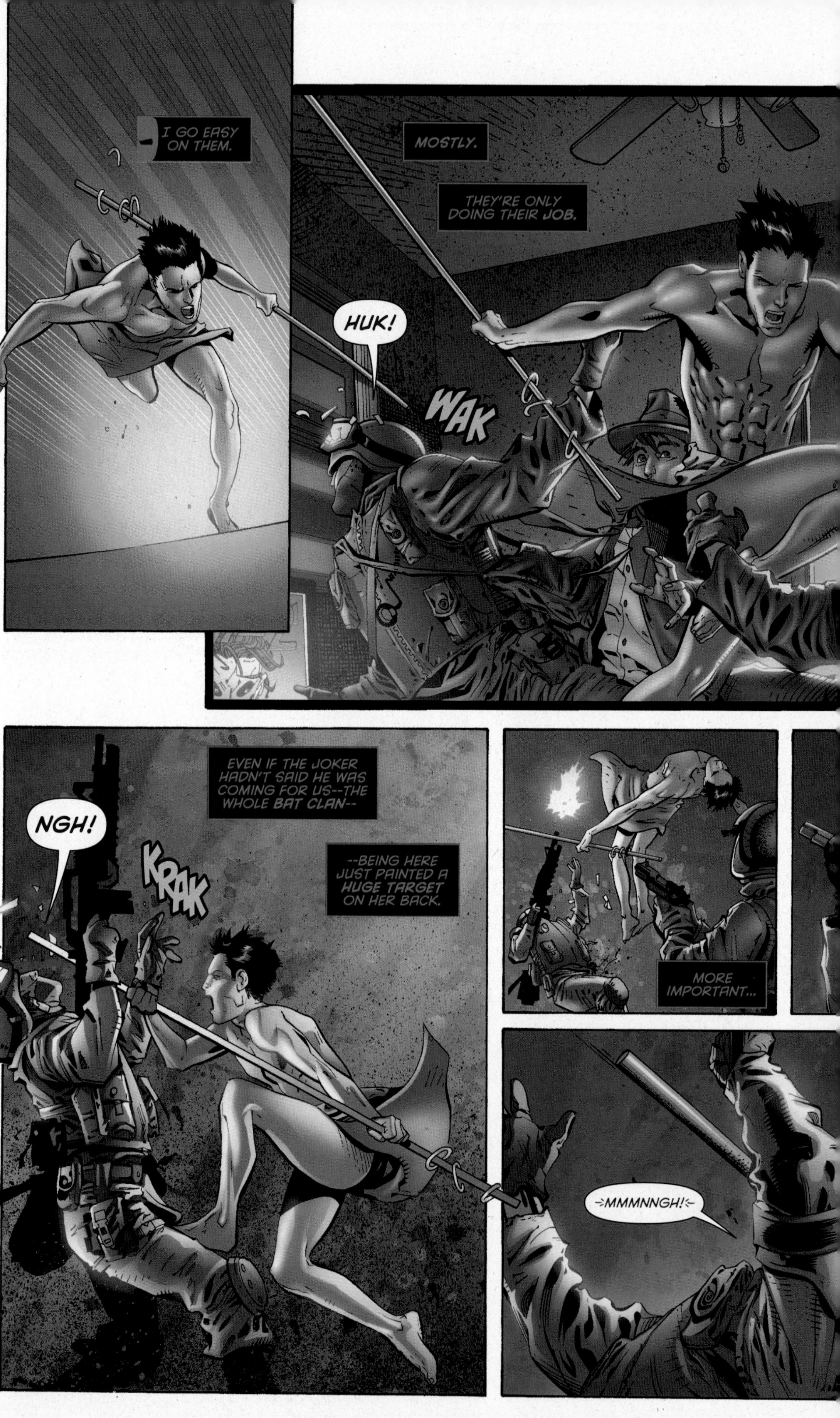

I GO EASY ON THEM.
MOSTLY.
THEY'RE ONLY DOING THEIR JOB.
HUK!
WAK
EVEN IF THE JOKER HADN'T SAID HE WAS COMING FOR US--THE WHOLE BAT CLAN--
NGH!
KRAK
--BEING HERE JUST PAINTED A HUGE TARGET ON HER BACK.
MORE IMPORTANT...
MMMNNGH!

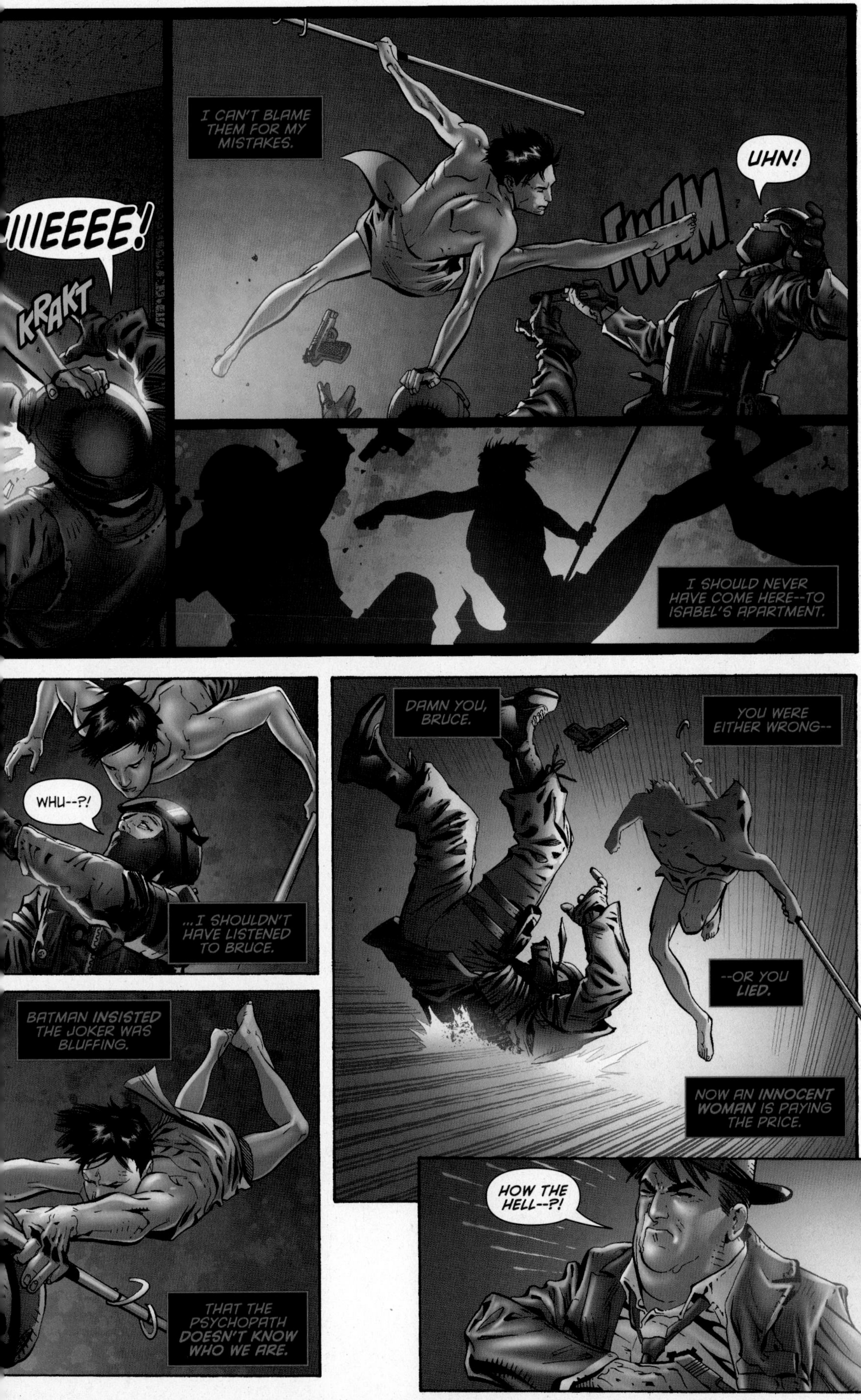
IIIIEEEEE!
KRAKT
I CAN'T BLAME THEM FOR MY MISTAKES.
UHN!
FWAM
I SHOULD NEVER HAVE COME HERE--TO ISABEL'S APARTMENT.
WHU--?!
...I SHOULDN'T HAVE LISTENED TO BRUCE.
BATMAN INSISTED THE JOKER WAS BLUFFING.
THAT THE PSYCHOPATH DOESN'T KNOW WHO WE ARE.
DAMN YOU, BRUCE.
YOU WERE EITHER WRONG--
--OR YOU LIED.
NOW AN INNOCENT WOMAN IS PAYING THE PRICE.
HOW THE HELL--?!

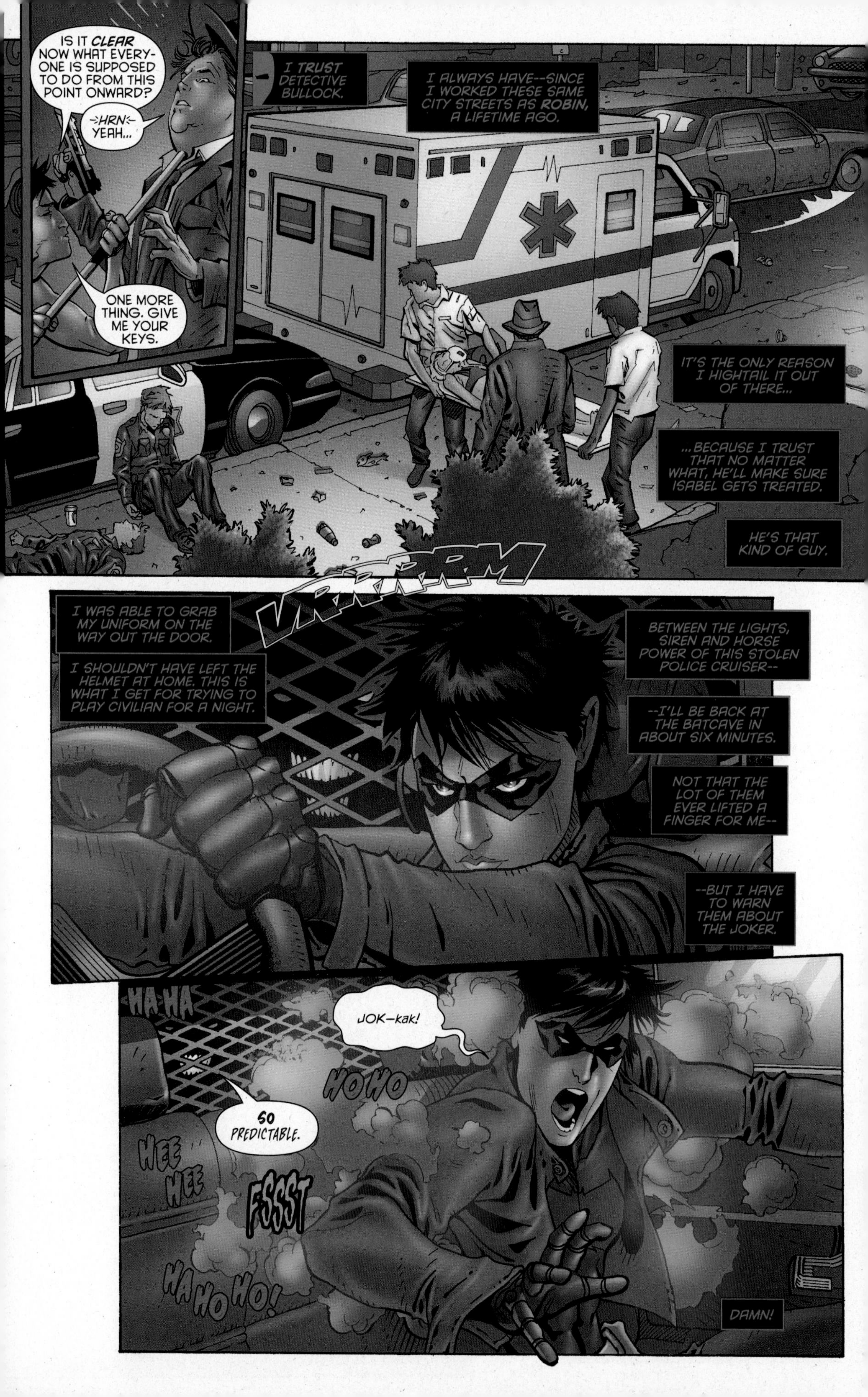
IS IT CLEAR NOW WHAT EVERY-ONE IS SUPPOSED TO DO FROM THIS POINT ONWARD?
-HRN- YEAH...
ONE MORE THING. GIVE ME YOUR KEYS.
I TRUST DETECTIVE BULLOCK.
I ALWAYS HAVE--SINCE I WORKED THESE SAME CITY STREETS AS ROBIN, A LIFETIME AGO.
IT'S THE ONLY REASON I HIGHTAIL IT OUT OF THERE...
...BECAUSE I TRUST THAT NO MATTER WHAT, HE'LL MAKE SURE ISABEL GETS TREATED.
HE'S THAT KIND OF GUY.
VRRRROOM
I WAS ABLE TO GRAB MY UNIFORM ON THE WAY OUT THE DOOR.
I SHOULDN'T HAVE LEFT THE HELMET AT HOME. THIS IS WHAT I GET FOR TRYING TO PLAY CIVILIAN FOR A NIGHT.
BETWEEN THE LIGHTS, SIREN AND HORSE POWER OF THIS STOLEN POLICE CRUISER--
--I'LL BE BACK AT THE BATCAVE IN ABOUT SIX MINUTES.
NOT THAT THE LOT OF THEM EVER LIFTED A FINGER FOR ME--
--BUT I HAVE TO WARN THEM ABOUT THE JOKER.
HA HA
JOK-kak!
HO HO
SO PREDICTABLE.
HEE HEE
FSSST
HA HO HO!
DAMN!

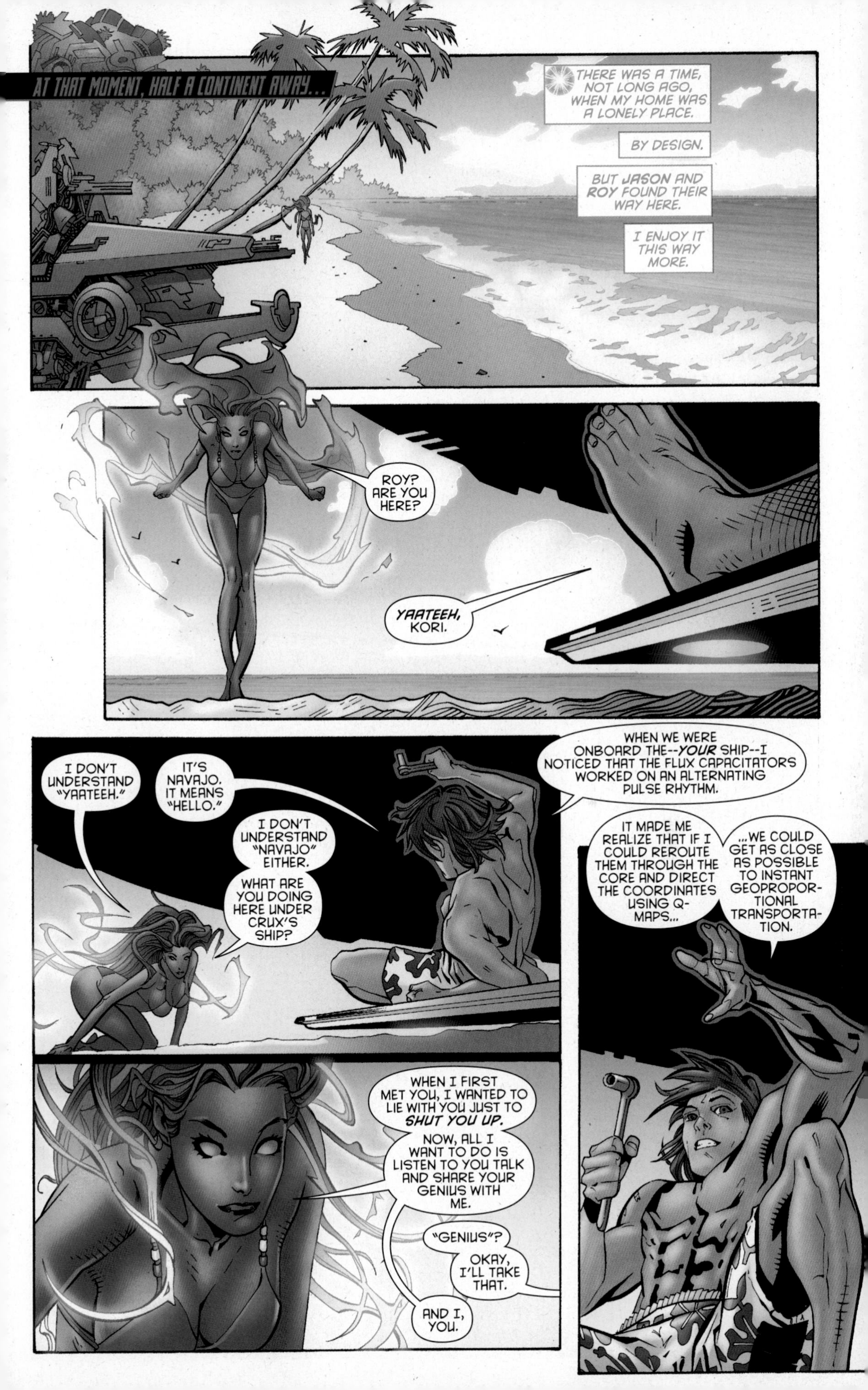
AT THAT MOMENT, HALF A CONTINENT AWAY...
THERE WAS A TIME, NOT LONG AGO, WHEN MY HOME WAS A LONELY PLACE.
BY DESIGN.
BUT JASON AND ROY FOUND THEIR WAY HERE.
I ENJOY IT THIS WAY MORE.
ROY? ARE YOU HERE?
YAATEEH, KORI.
I DON'T UNDERSTAND "YAATEEH."
IT'S NAVAJO. IT MEANS "HELLO."
I DON'T UNDERSTAND "NAVAJO" EITHER.
WHAT ARE YOU DOING HERE UNDER CRUX'S SHIP?
WHEN WE WERE ONBOARD THE--YOUR SHIP--I NOTICED THAT THE FLUX CAPACITATORS WORKED ON AN ALTERNATING PULSE RHYTHM.
IT MADE ME REALIZE THAT IF I COULD REROUTE THEM THROUGH THE CORE AND DIRECT THE COORDINATES USING Q-MAPS...
...WE COULD GET AS CLOSE AS POSSIBLE TO INSTANT GEOPROPORTIONAL TRANSPORTATION.
WHEN I FIRST MET YOU, I WANTED TO LIE WITH YOU JUST TO SHUT YOU UP.
NOW, ALL I WANT TO DO IS LISTEN TO YOU TALK AND SHARE YOUR GENIUS WITH ME.
"GENIUS"?
OKAY, I'LL TAKE THAT.
AND I, YOU.

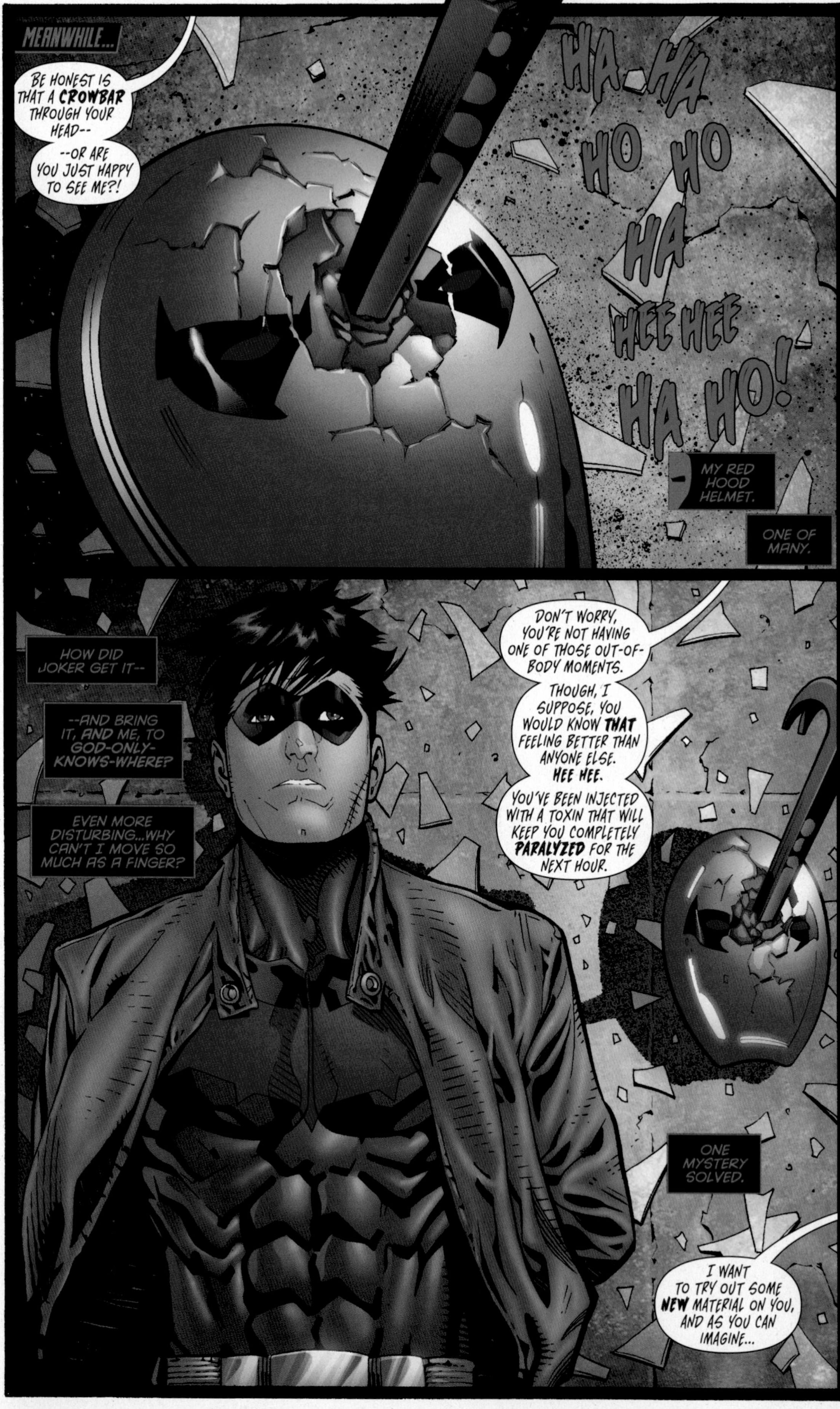
MEANWHILE...
BE HONEST IS THAT A CROWBAR THROUGH YOUR HEAD--
--OR ARE YOU JUST HAPPY TO SEE ME?!
HA HA HO HO HA HEE HEE HA HO!
MY RED HOOD HELMET.
ONE OF MANY.
HOW DID JOKER GET IT--
--AND BRING IT, AND ME, TO GOD-ONLY-KNOWS-WHERE?
EVEN MORE DISTURBING...WHY CAN'T I MOVE SO MUCH AS A FINGER?
DON'T WORRY, YOU'RE NOT HAVING ONE OF THOSE OUT-OF-BODY MOMENTS.
THOUGH, I SUPPOSE, YOU WOULD KNOW THAT FEELING BETTER THAN ANYONE ELSE. HEE HEE.
YOU'VE BEEN INJECTED WITH A TOXIN THAT WILL KEEP YOU COMPLETELY PARALYZED FOR THE NEXT HOUR.
ONE MYSTERY SOLVED.
I WANT TO TRY OUT SOME NEW MATERIAL ON YOU, AND AS YOU CAN IMAGINE...

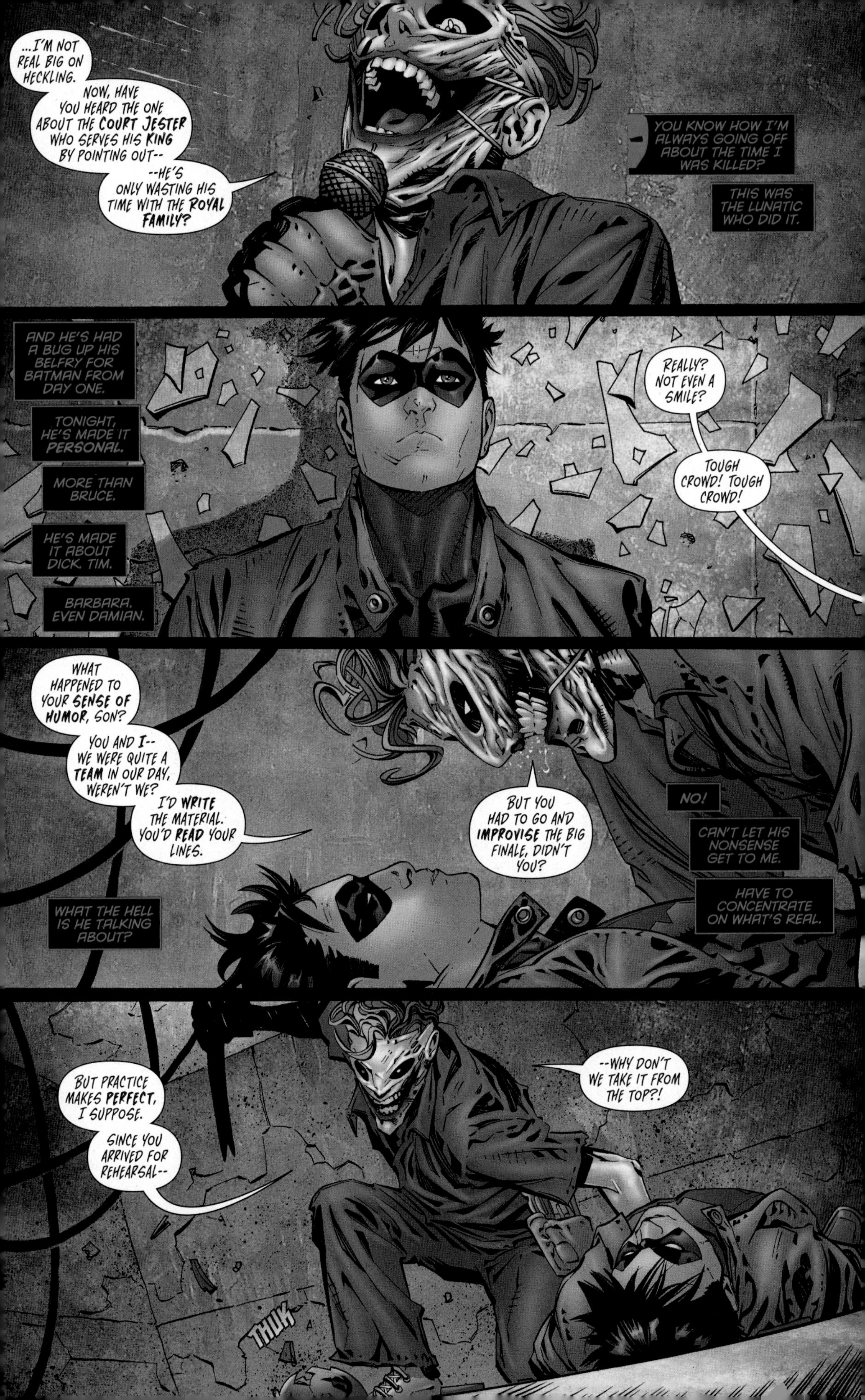
...I'M NOT REAL BIG ON HECKLING.
NOW, HAVE YOU HEARD THE ONE ABOUT THE COURT JESTER WHO SERVES HIS KING BY POINTING OUT--
--HE'S ONLY WASTING HIS TIME WITH THE ROYAL FAMILY?
YOU KNOW HOW I'M ALWAYS GOING OFF ABOUT THE TIME I WAS KILLED?
THIS WAS THE LUNATIC WHO DID IT.
AND HE'S HAD A BUG UP HIS BELFRY FOR BATMAN FROM DAY ONE.
TONIGHT, HE'S MADE IT PERSONAL.
MORE THAN BRUCE.
HE'S MADE IT ABOUT DICK. TIM.
BARBARA. EVEN DAMIAN.
REALLY? NOT EVEN A SMILE?
TOUGH CROWD! TOUGH CROWD!
WHAT HAPPENED TO YOUR SENSE OF HUMOR, SON?
YOU AND I--WE WERE QUITE A TEAM IN OUR DAY, WEREN'T WE?
I'D WRITE THE MATERIAL. YOU'D READ YOUR LINES.
BUT YOU HAD TO GO AND IMPROVISE THE BIG FINALE, DIDN'T YOU?
NO!
CAN'T LET HIS NONSENSE GET TO ME.
HAVE TO CONCENTRATE ON WHAT'S REAL.
WHAT THE HELL IS HE TALKING ABOUT?
BUT PRACTICE MAKES PERFECT, I SUPPOSE.
SINCE YOU ARRIVED FOR REHEARSAL--
--WHY DON'T WE TAKE IT FROM THE TOP?!
THUK

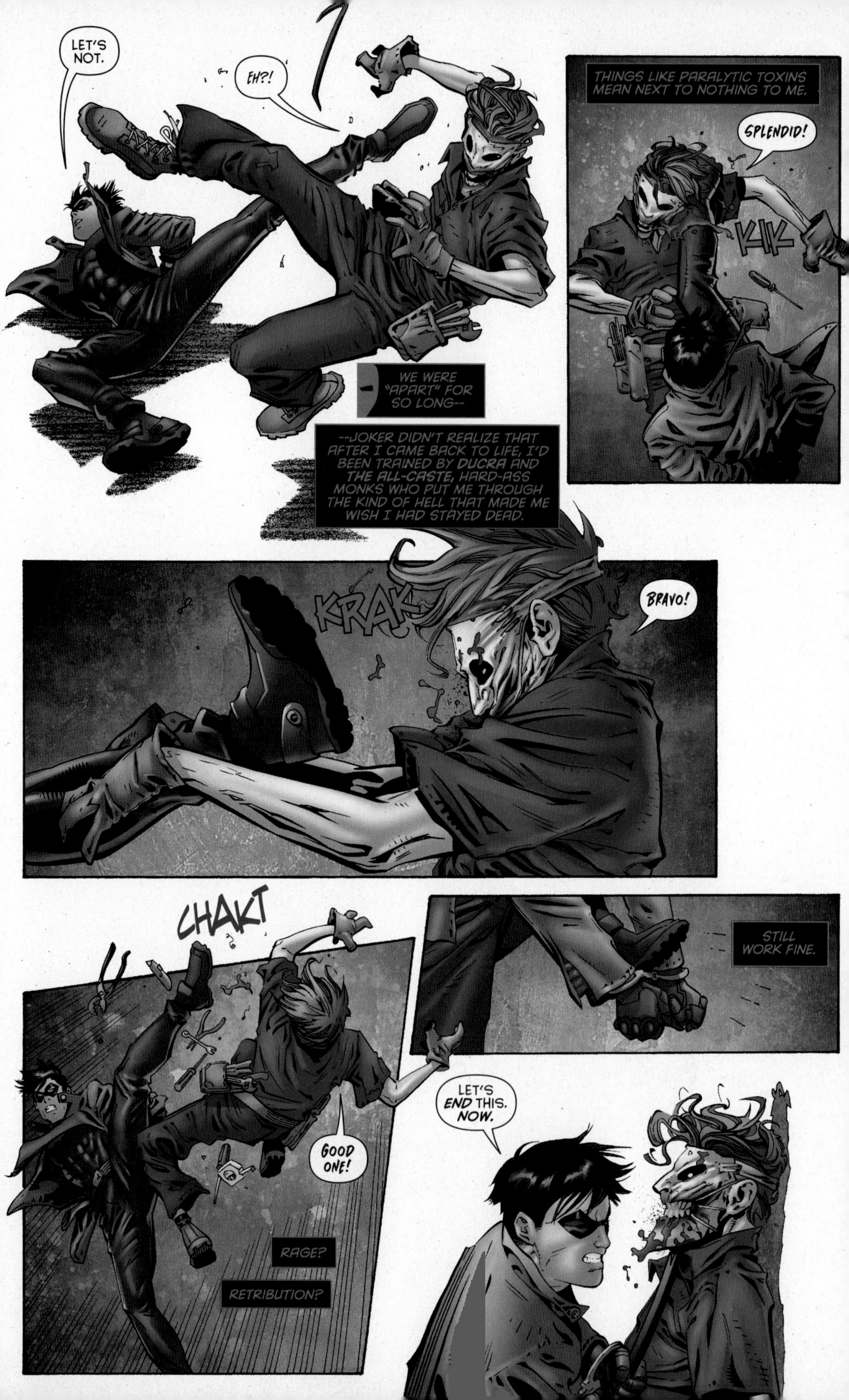
LET'S NOT.
EH?!
THINGS LIKE PARALYTIC TOXINS MEAN NEXT TO NOTHING TO ME.
SPLENDID!
KLIK
WE WERE "APART" FOR SO LONG--
--JOKER DIDN'T REALIZE THAT AFTER I CAME BACK TO LIFE, I'D BEEN TRAINED BY DUCRA AND THE ALL-CASTE, HARD-ASS MONKS WHO PUT ME THROUGH THE KIND OF HELL THAT MADE ME WISH I HAD STAYED DEAD.
KRAK
BRAVO!
CHAKT
GOOD ONE!
RAGE?
RETRIBUTION?
STILL WORK FINE.
LET'S END THIS. NOW.

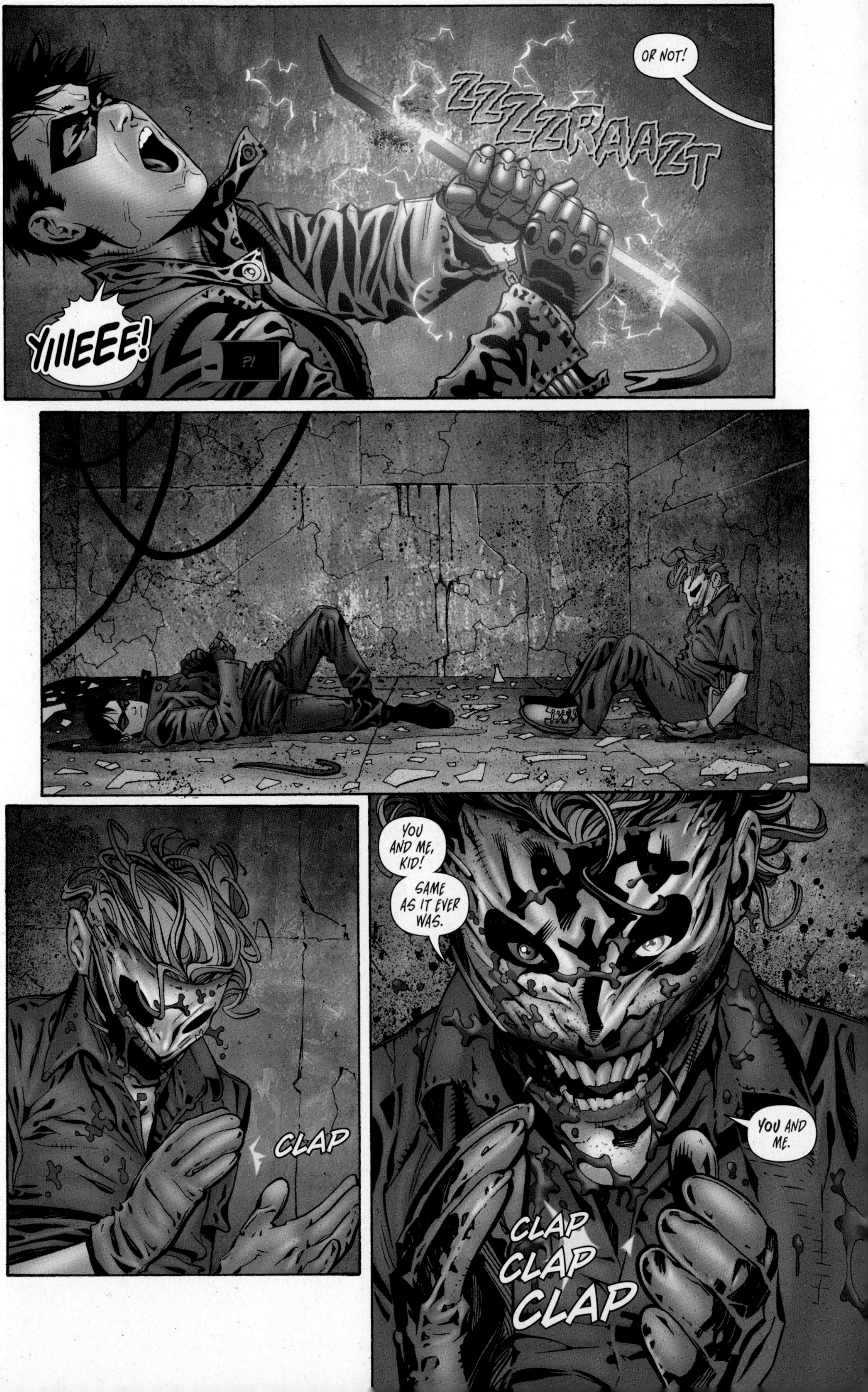
OR NOT!
ZZZZRAAZT
YIIIEEE!
?!
YOU AND ME, KID!
SAME AS IT EVER WAS.
CLAP
YOU AND ME.
CLAP
CLAP
CLAP

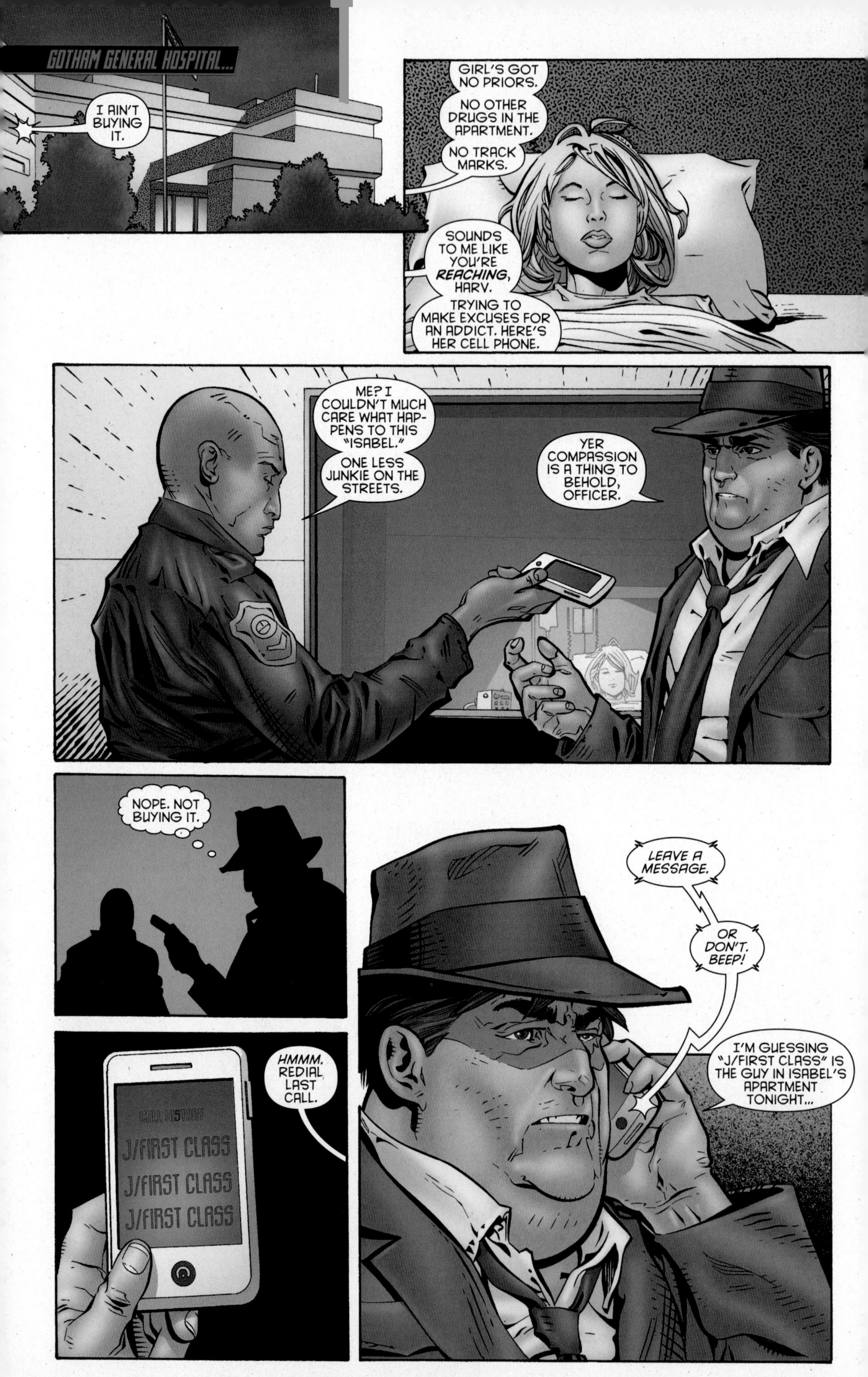
GOTHAM GENERAL HOSPITAL...
I AIN'T BUYING IT.
GIRL'S GOT NO PRIORS.
NO OTHER DRUGS IN THE APARTMENT.
NO TRACK MARKS.
SOUNDS TO ME LIKE YOU'RE *REACHING*, HARV.
TRYING TO MAKE EXCUSES FOR AN ADDICT. HERE'S HER CELL PHONE.
ME? I COULDN'T MUCH CARE WHAT HAPPENS TO THIS "ISABEL."
ONE LESS JUNKIE ON THE STREETS.
YER COMPASSION IS A THING TO BEHOLD, OFFICER.
NOPE. NOT BUYING IT.
CALL HISTORY
J/FIRST CLASS
J/FIRST CLASS
J/FIRST CLASS
HMMM. REDIAL LAST CALL.
LEAVE A MESSAGE.
OR DON'T. BEEP!
I'M GUESSING "J/FIRST CLASS" IS THE GUY IN ISABEL'S APARTMENT TONIGHT...

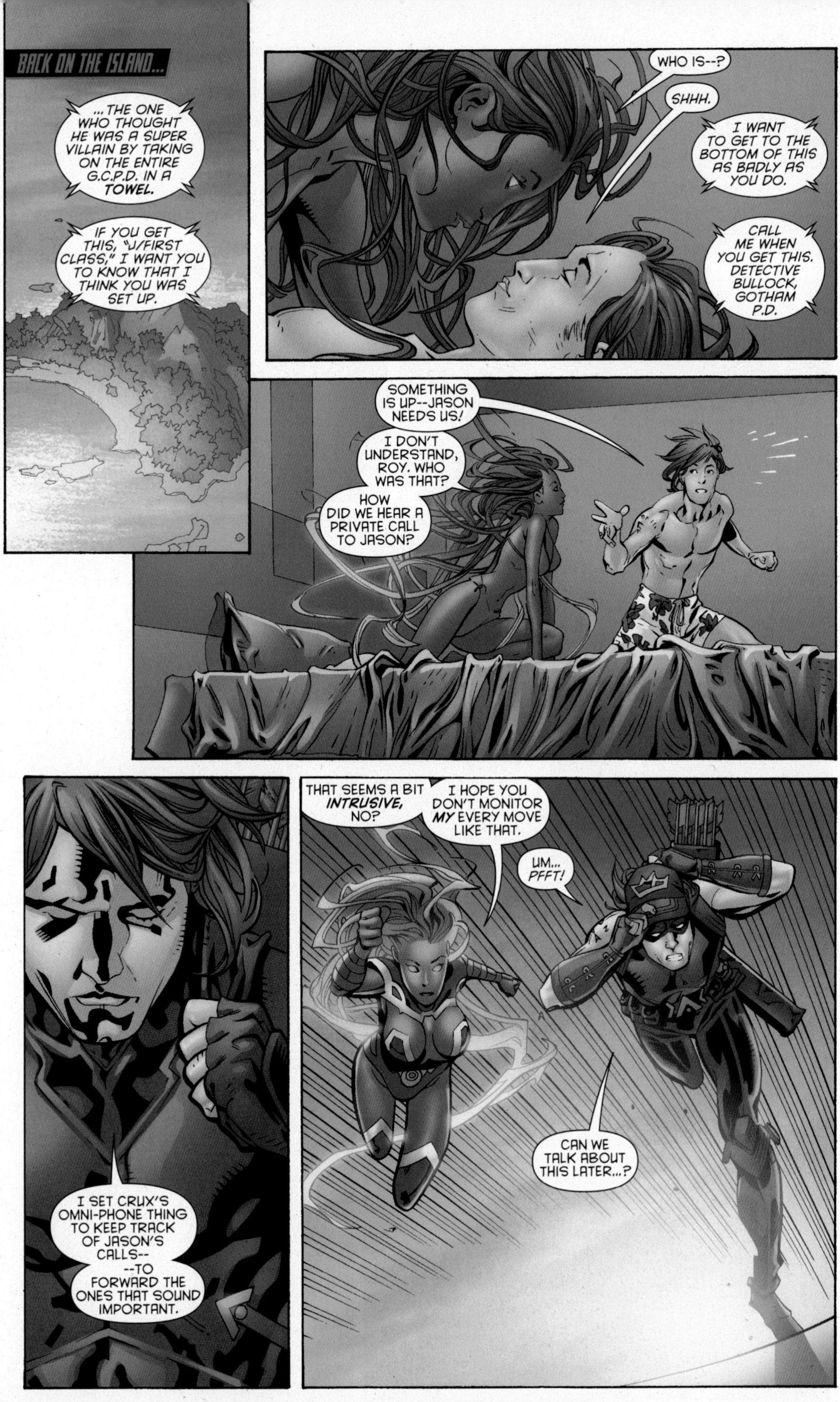
BACK ON THE ISLAND...
...THE ONE WHO THOUGHT HE WAS A SUPER VILLAIN BY TAKING ON THE ENTIRE G.C.P.D. IN A TOWEL.
IF YOU GET THIS, "J/FIRST CLASS," I WANT YOU TO KNOW THAT I THINK YOU WAS SET UP.
WHO IS--?
SHHH.
I WANT TO GET TO THE BOTTOM OF THIS AS BADLY AS YOU DO.
CALL ME WHEN YOU GET THIS. DETECTIVE BULLOCK, GOTHAM P.D.
SOMETHING IS UP--JASON NEEDS US!
I DON'T UNDERSTAND, ROY. WHO WAS THAT?
HOW DID WE HEAR A PRIVATE CALL TO JASON?
I SET CRUX'S OMNI-PHONE THING TO KEEP TRACK OF JASON'S CALLS--
--TO FORWARD THE ONES THAT SOUND IMPORTANT.
THAT SEEMS A BIT INTRUSIVE, NO?
I HOPE YOU DON'T MONITOR MY EVERY MOVE LIKE THAT.
UM... PFFT!
CAN WE TALK ABOUT THIS LATER...?

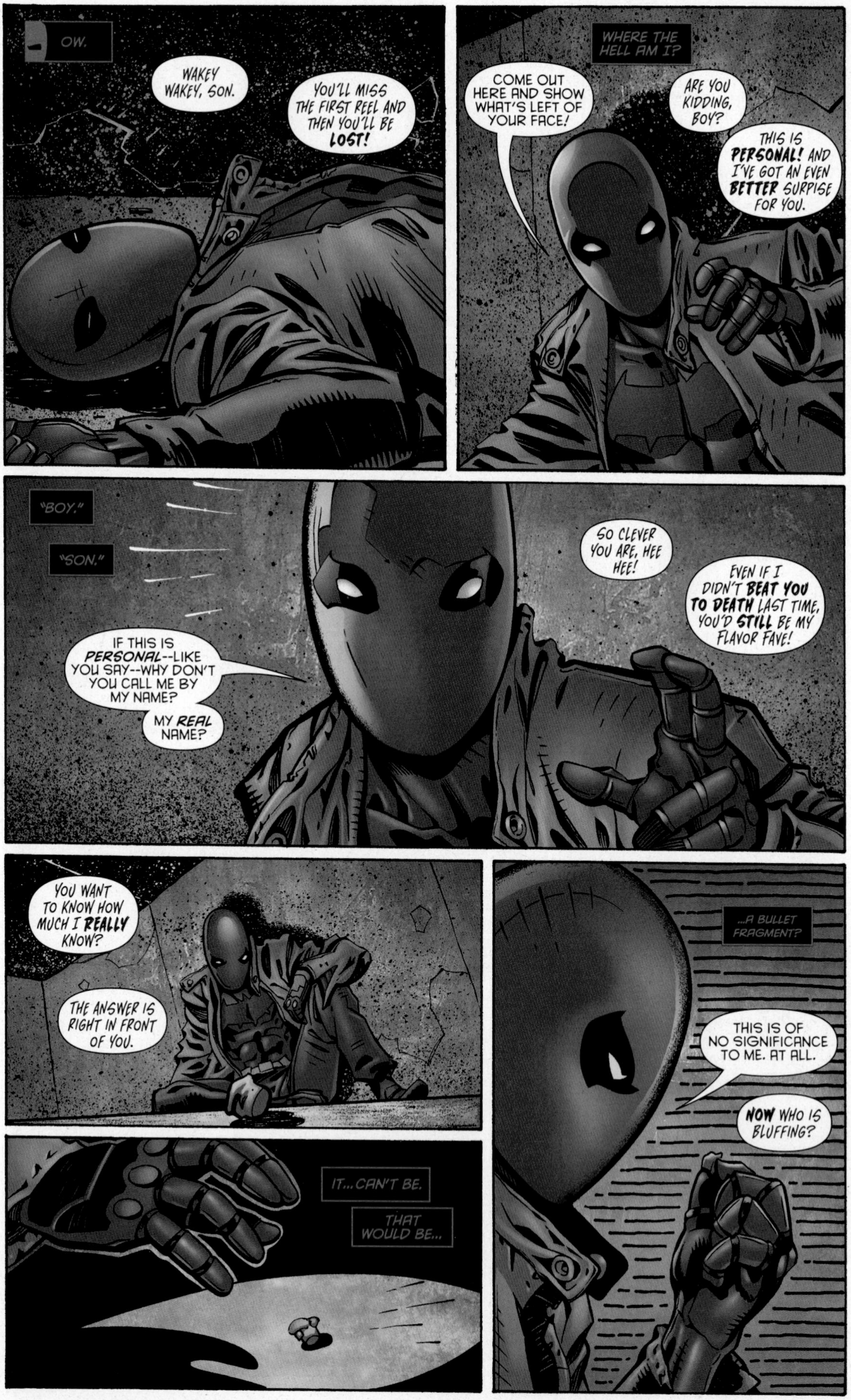
OW.
WAKEY WAKEY, SON.
YOU'LL MISS THE FIRST REEL AND THEN YOU'LL BE LOST!
WHERE THE HELL AM I?
COME OUT HERE AND SHOW WHAT'S LEFT OF YOUR FACE!
ARE YOU KIDDING, BOY?
THIS IS PERSONAL! AND I'VE GOT AN EVEN BETTER SURPISE FOR YOU.
"BOY."
"SON."
SO CLEVER YOU ARE, HEE HEE!
EVEN IF I DIDN'T BEAT YOU TO DEATH LAST TIME, YOU'D STILL BE MY FLAVOR FAVE!
IF THIS IS PERSONAL--LIKE YOU SAY--WHY DON'T YOU CALL ME BY MY NAME?
MY REAL NAME?
YOU WANT TO KNOW HOW MUCH I REALLY KNOW?
THE ANSWER IS RIGHT IN FRONT OF YOU.
IT...CAN'T BE.
THAT WOULD BE...
...A BULLET FRAGMENT?
THIS IS OF NO SIGNIFICANCE TO ME. AT ALL.
NOW WHO IS BLUFFING?

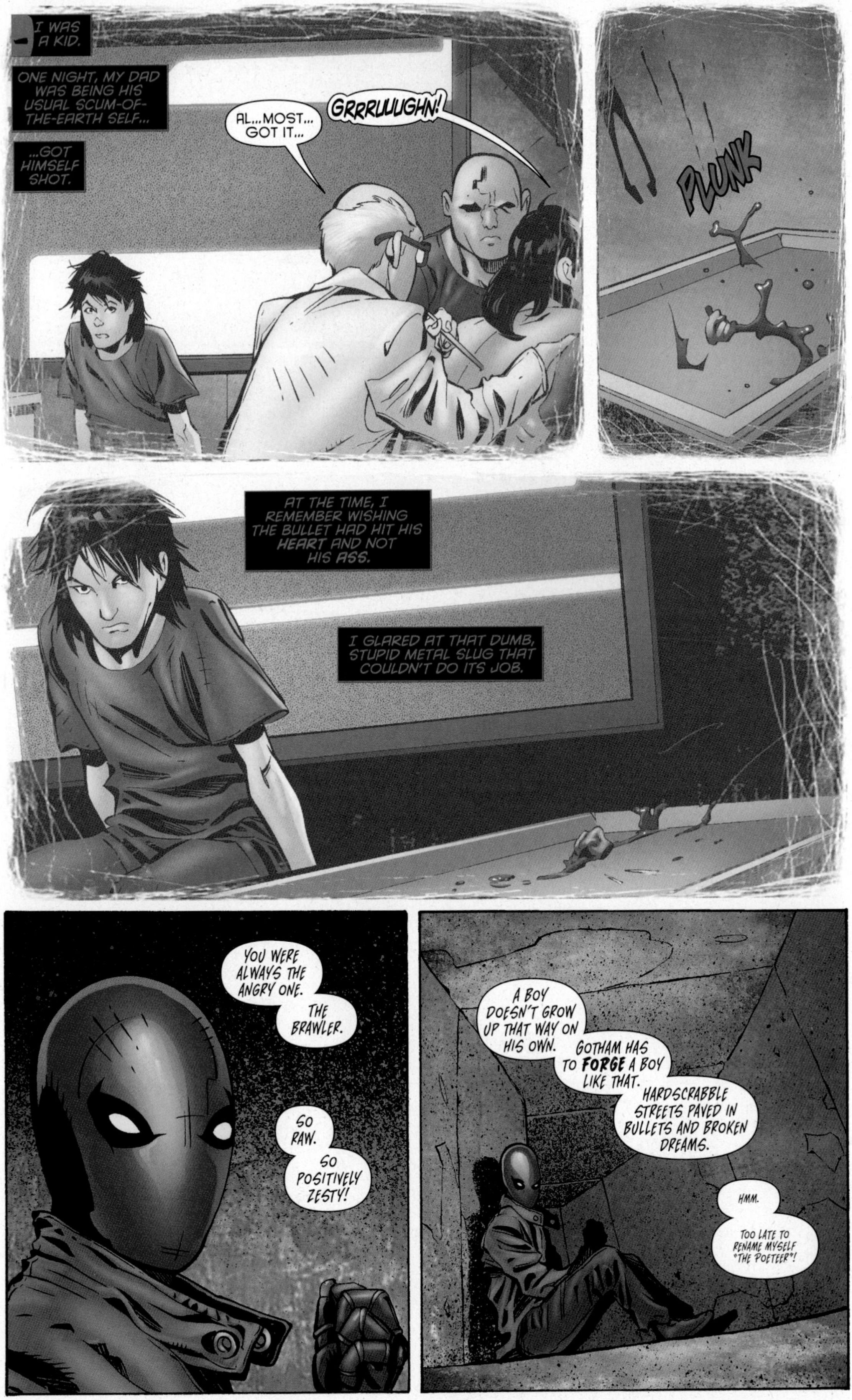
I WAS A KID.
ONE NIGHT, MY DAD WAS BEING HIS USUAL SCUM-OF-THE-EARTH SELF...
...GOT HIMSELF SHOT.
AL...MOST... GOT IT...
GRRRUUUGHN!
PLUNK
AT THE TIME, I REMEMBER WISHING THE BULLET HAD HIT HIS HEART AND NOT HIS ASS.
I GLARED AT THAT DUMB, STUPID METAL SLUG THAT COULDN'T DO ITS JOB.
YOU WERE ALWAYS THE ANGRY ONE.
THE BRAWLER.
SO RAW.
SO POSITIVELY ZESTY!
A BOY DOESN'T GROW UP THAT WAY ON HIS OWN.
GOTHAM HAS TO FORGE A BOY LIKE THAT.
HARDSCRABBLE STREETS PAVED IN BULLETS AND BROKEN DREAMS.
HMM.
TOO LATE TO RENAME MYSELF "THE POETEER"?

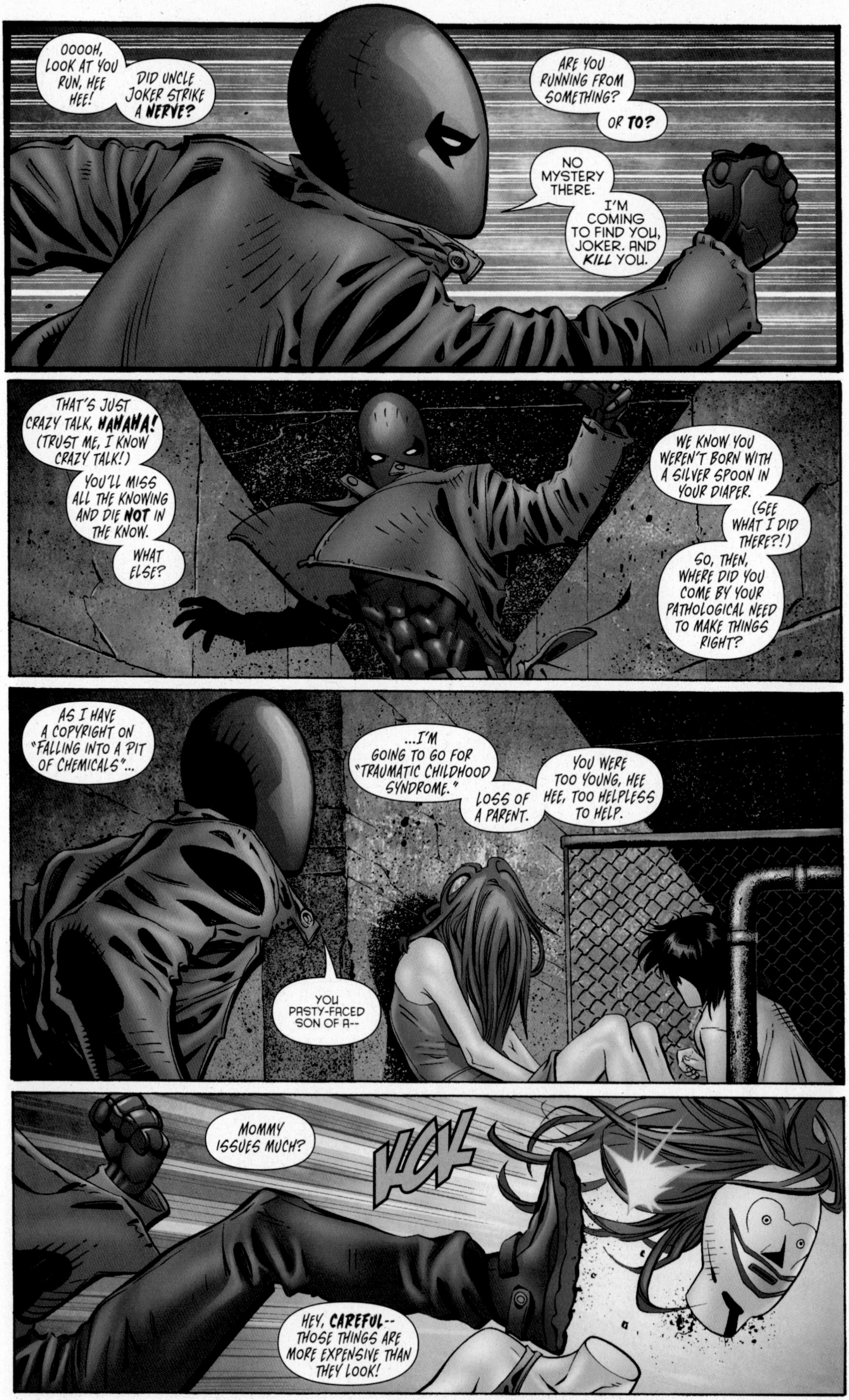

OOOOH, LOOK AT YOU RUN, HEE HEE!
DID UNCLE JOKER STRIKE A NERVE?
ARE YOU RUNNING FROM SOMETHING?
OR TO?
NO MYSTERY THERE.
I'M COMING TO FIND YOU, JOKER. AND KILL YOU.
THAT'S JUST CRAZY TALK, HAHAHA! (TRUST ME, I KNOW CRAZY TALK!)
YOU'LL MISS ALL THE KNOWING AND DIE NOT IN THE KNOW.
WHAT ELSE?
WE KNOW YOU WEREN'T BORN WITH A SILVER SPOON IN YOUR DIAPER.
(SEE WHAT I DID THERE?!)
SO, THEN, WHERE DID YOU COME BY YOUR PATHOLOGICAL NEED TO MAKE THINGS RIGHT?
AS I HAVE A COPYRIGHT ON "FALLING INTO A PIT OF CHEMICALS"...
...I'M GOING TO GO FOR "TRAUMATIC CHILDHOOD SYNDROME."
LOSS OF A PARENT.
YOU WERE TOO YOUNG, HEE HEE, TOO HELPLESS TO HELP.
YOU PASTY-FACED SON OF A--
MOMMY ISSUES MUCH?
HEY, CAREFUL-- THOSE THINGS ARE MORE EXPENSIVE THAN THEY LOOK!

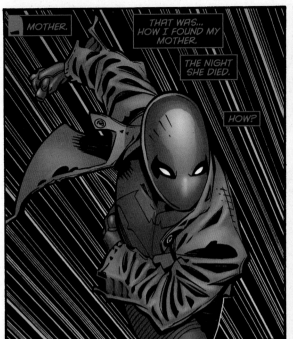

MOTHER.

THAT WAS... HOW I FOUND MY MOTHER.

THE NIGHT SHE DIED.

HOW?

HOW COULD JOKER--

CHUK-T

BUT IT DIDN'T TAKE.

YOU STRAYED OFF THE BEATEN NARROW.

DARE I SAY STUMBLED?

SLAMM

WHERE DID IT GO?

ALL THAT COMPASSION?

DID YOU LEAVE IT IN THE GRAVE?

OR DID YOU JUST LOCK IT UP IN A BOX SOMEWHERE: ONLY OPEN IN CASE OF EMERGENCY?

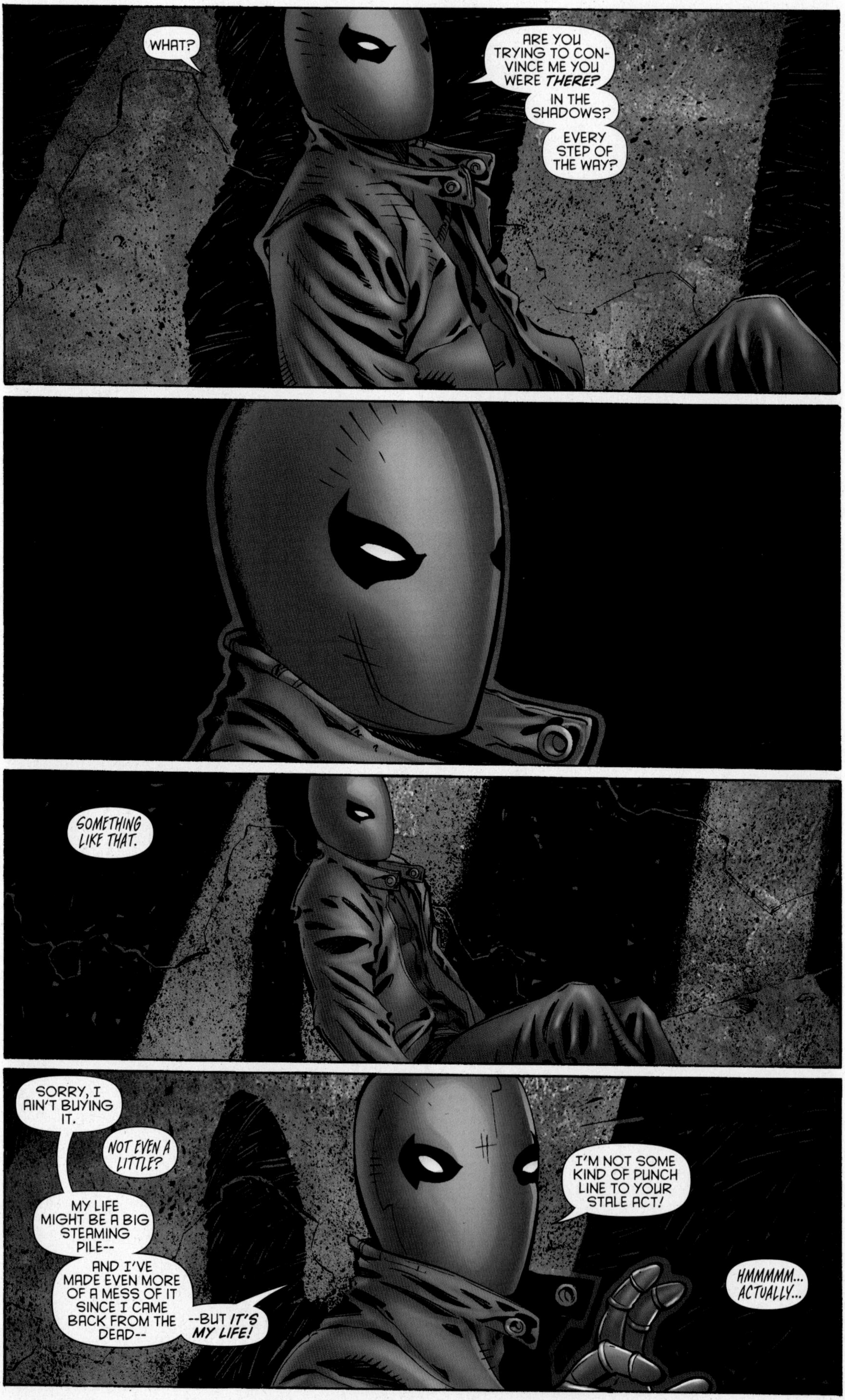
WHAT?
ARE YOU TRYING TO CONVINCE ME YOU WERE THERE?
IN THE SHADOWS?
EVERY STEP OF THE WAY?
SOMETHING LIKE THAT.
SORRY, I AIN'T BUYING IT.
NOT EVEN A LITTLE?
MY LIFE MIGHT BE A BIG STEAMING PILE--
AND I'VE MADE EVEN MORE OF A MESS OF IT SINCE I CAME BACK FROM THE DEAD--
--BUT IT'S MY LIFE!
I'M NOT SOME KIND OF PUNCH LINE TO YOUR STALE ACT!
HMMMMM... ACTUALLY...

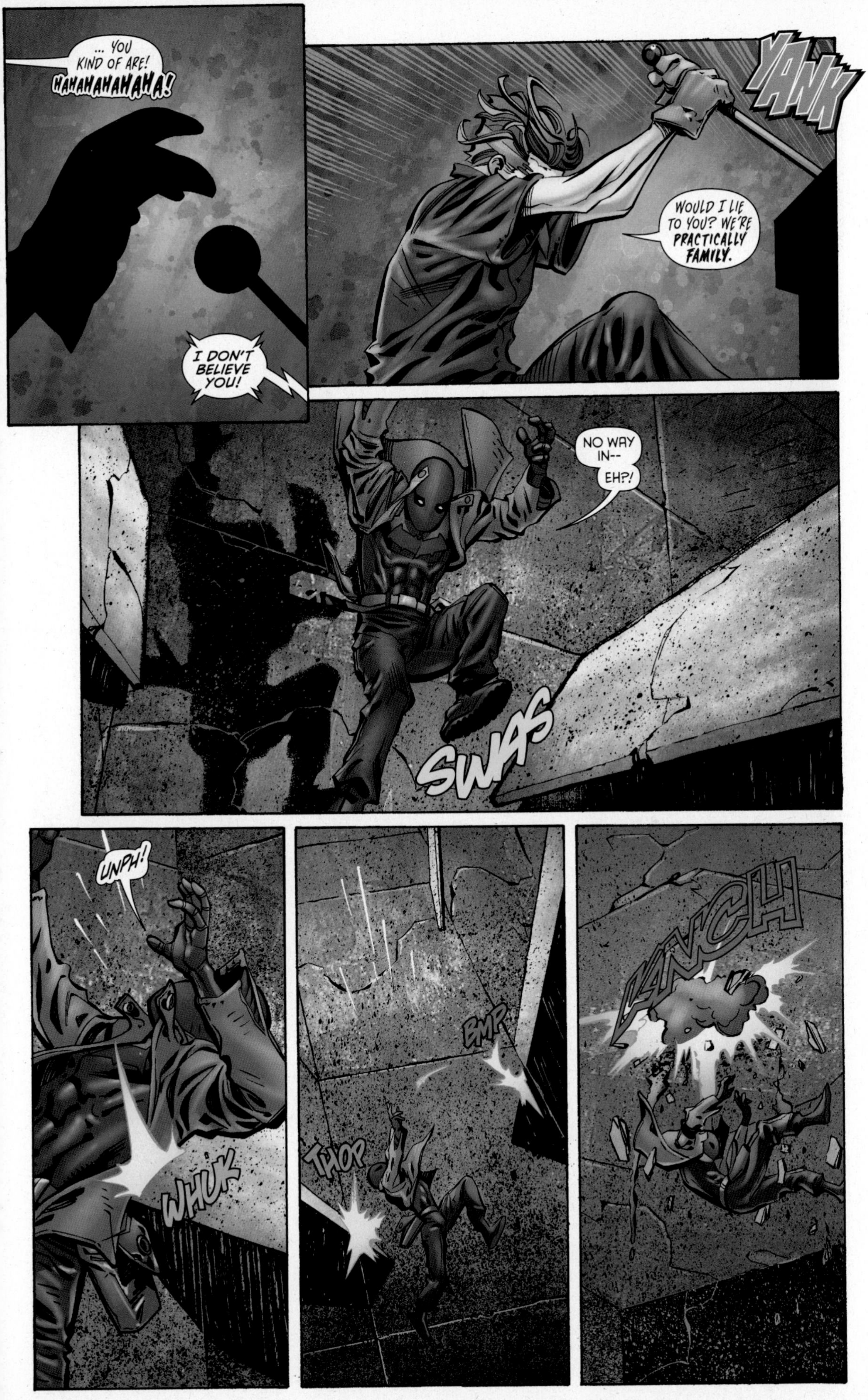

... YOU KIND OF ARE! HAHAHAHAHAHA!
I DON'T BELIEVE YOU!
YANK
WOULD I LIE TO YOU? WE'RE PRACTICALLY FAMILY.
NO WAY IN-- EH?!
SWAS
UNPH!
WHUK
BMP
THOP

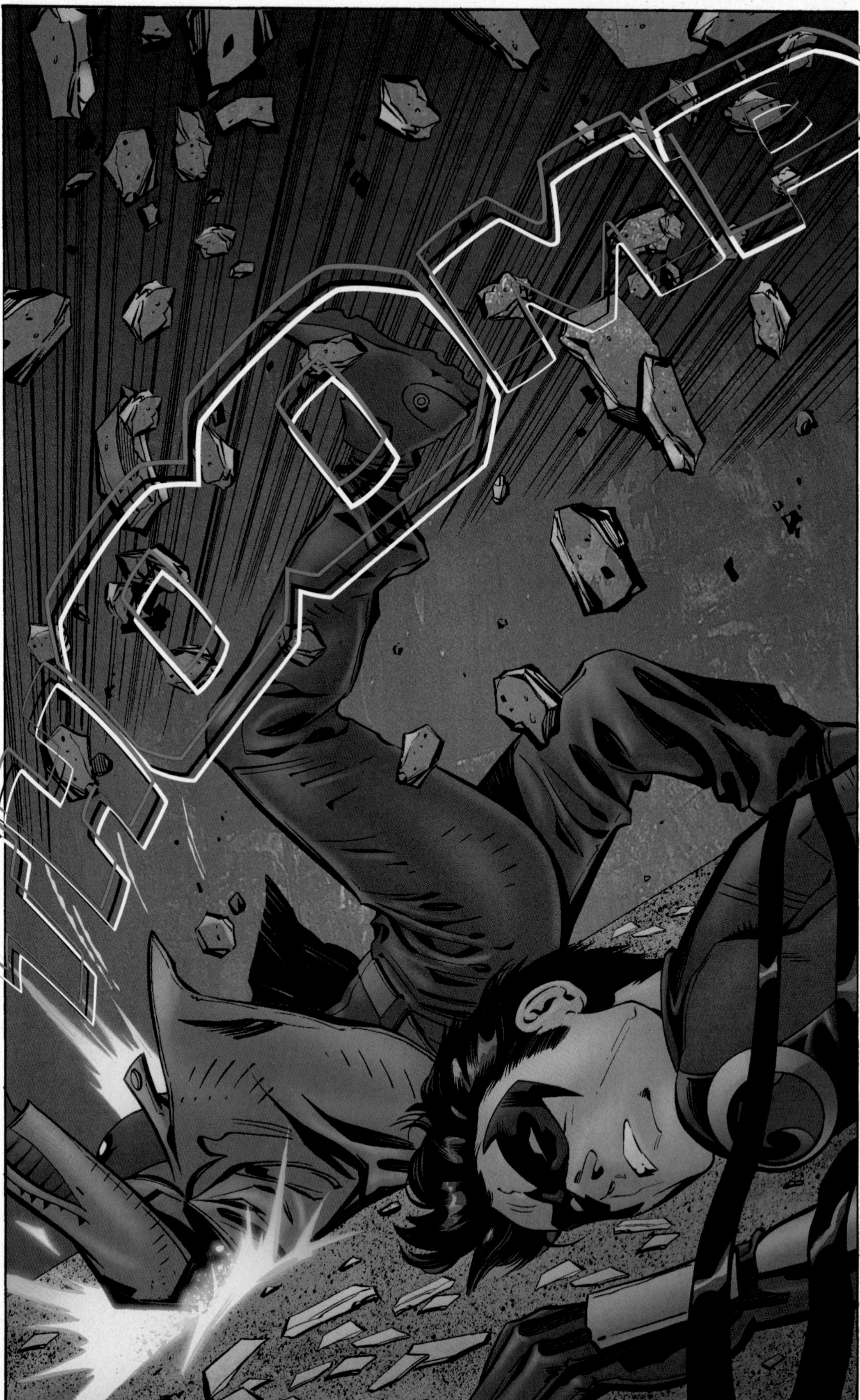
THOOMP

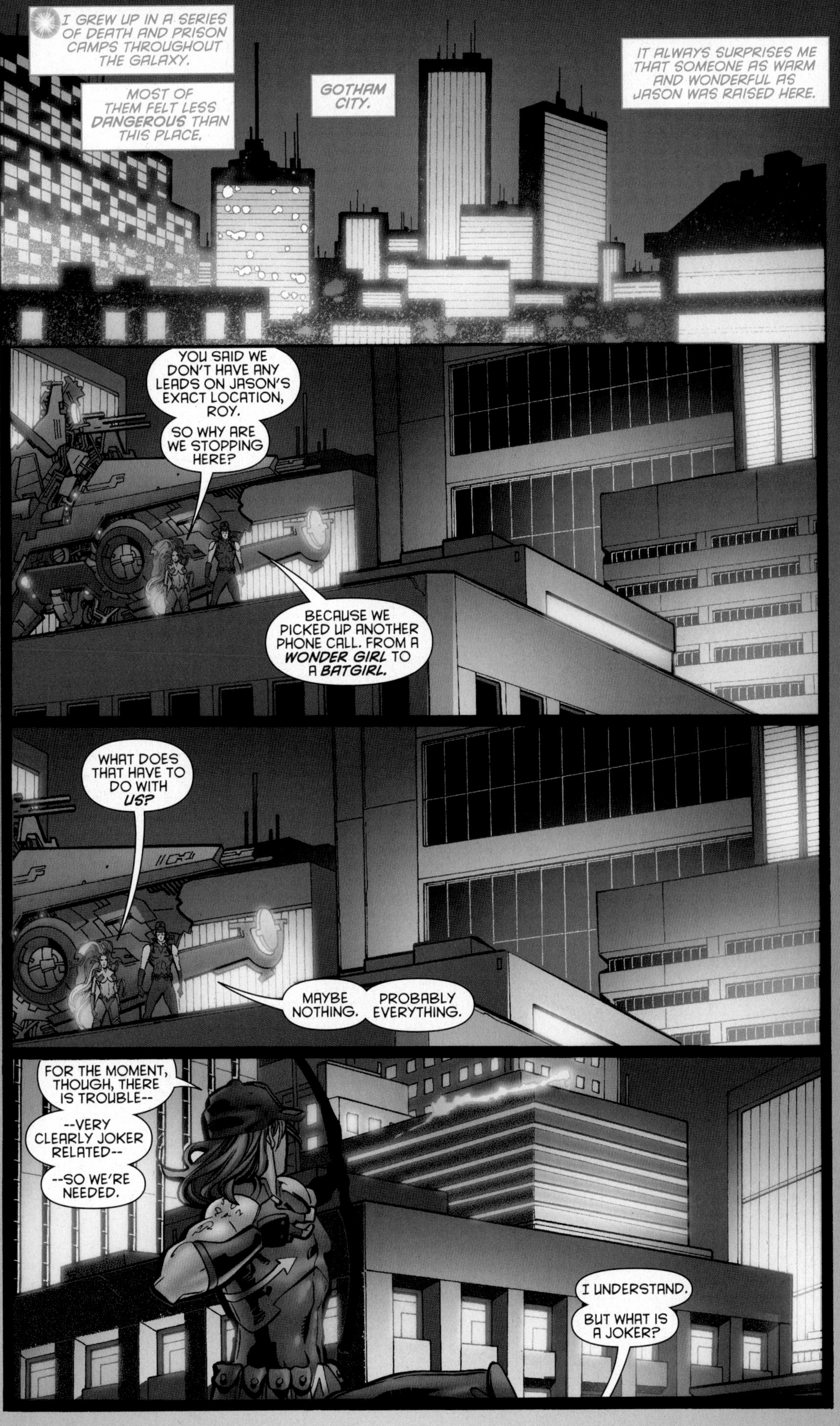
I GREW UP IN A SERIES OF DEATH AND PRISON CAMPS THROUGHOUT THE GALAXY.
MOST OF THEM FELT LESS DANGEROUS THAN THIS PLACE.
GOTHAM CITY.
IT ALWAYS SURPRISES ME THAT SOMEONE AS WARM AND WONDERFUL AS JASON WAS RAISED HERE.
YOU SAID WE DON'T HAVE ANY LEADS ON JASON'S EXACT LOCATION, ROY.
SO WHY ARE WE STOPPING HERE?
BECAUSE WE PICKED UP ANOTHER PHONE CALL. FROM A WONDER GIRL TO A BATGIRL.
WHAT DOES THAT HAVE TO DO WITH US?
MAYBE NOTHING.
PROBABLY EVERYTHING.
FOR THE MOMENT, THOUGH, THERE IS TROUBLE--
--VERY CLEARLY JOKER RELATED--
--SO WE'RE NEEDED.
I UNDERSTAND.
BUT WHAT IS A JOKER?

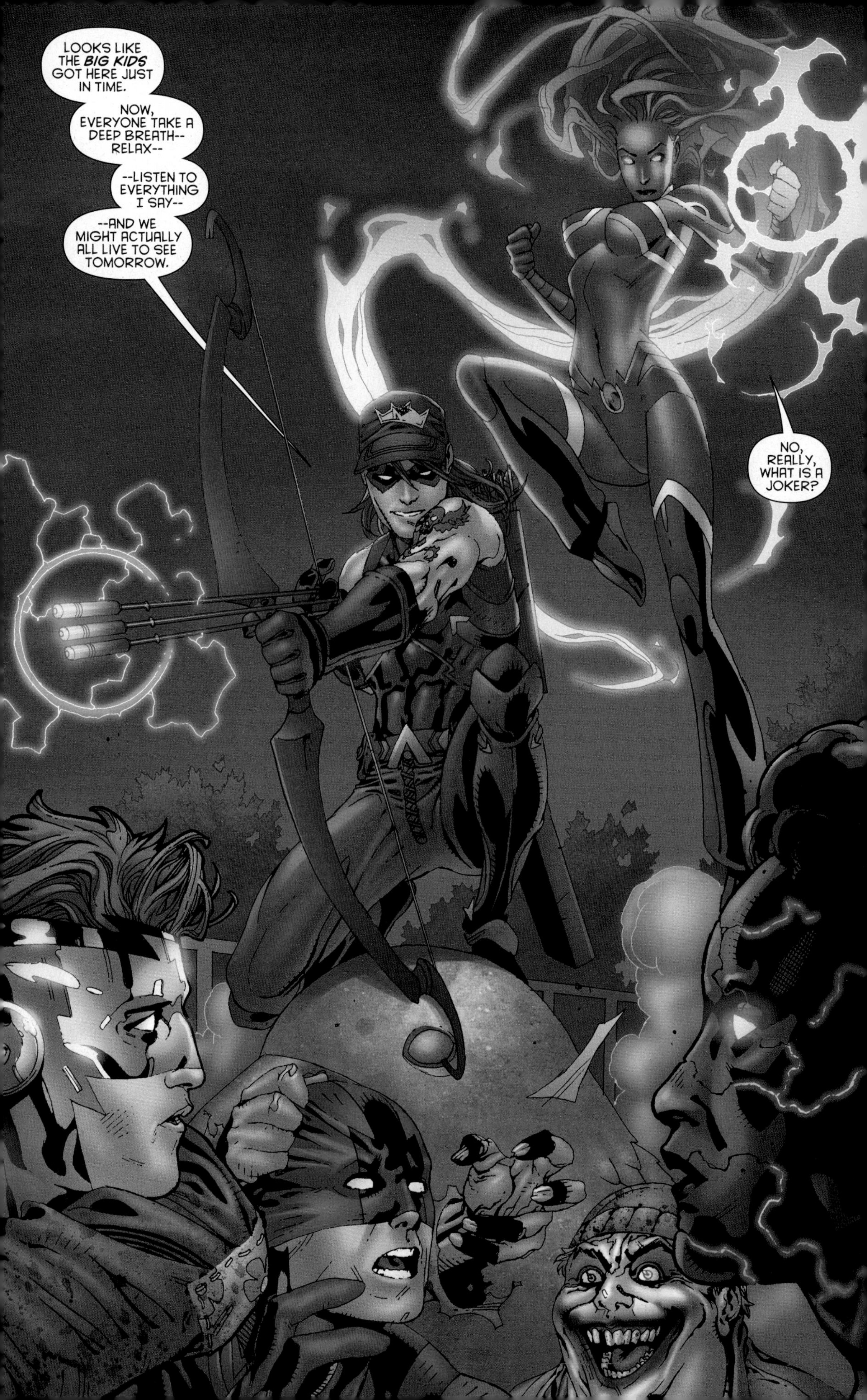
LOOKS LIKE THE *BIG KIDS* GOT HERE JUST IN TIME.
NOW, EVERYONE TAKE A DEEP BREATH-- RELAX--
--LISTEN TO EVERYTHING I SAY--
--AND WE MIGHT ACTUALLY ALL LIVE TO SEE TOMORROW.
NO, REALLY, WHAT IS A JOKER?

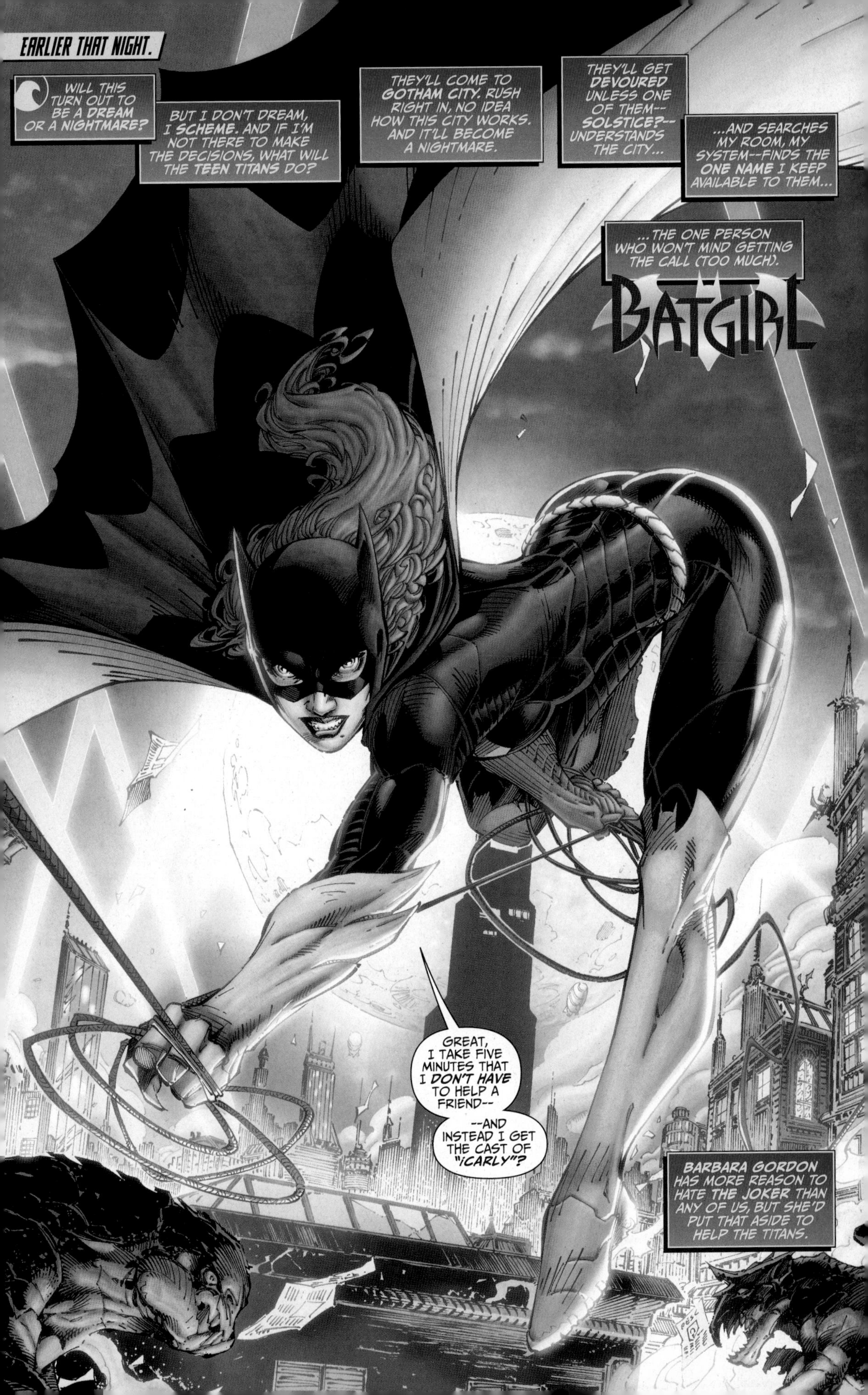
EARLIER THAT NIGHT.
WILL THIS TURN OUT TO BE A DREAM OR A NIGHTMARE?
BUT I DON'T DREAM, I SCHEME. AND IF I'M NOT THERE TO MAKE THE DECISIONS, WHAT WILL THE TEEN TITANS DO?
THEY'LL COME TO GOTHAM CITY. RUSH RIGHT IN, NO IDEA HOW THIS CITY WORKS. AND IT'LL BECOME A NIGHTMARE.
THEY'LL GET DEVOURED UNLESS ONE OF THEM--SOLSTICE?--UNDERSTANDS THE CITY...
...AND SEARCHES MY ROOM, MY SYSTEM--FINDS THE ONE NAME I KEEP AVAILABLE TO THEM...
...THE ONE PERSON WHO WON'T MIND GETTING THE CALL (TOO MUCH).
BATGIRL
GREAT, I TAKE FIVE MINUTES THAT I DON'T HAVE TO HELP A FRIEND--
--AND INSTEAD I GET THE CAST OF "iCARLY"?
BARBARA GORDON HAS MORE REASON TO HATE THE JOKER THAN ANY OF US, BUT SHE'D PUT THAT ASIDE TO HELP THE TITANS.

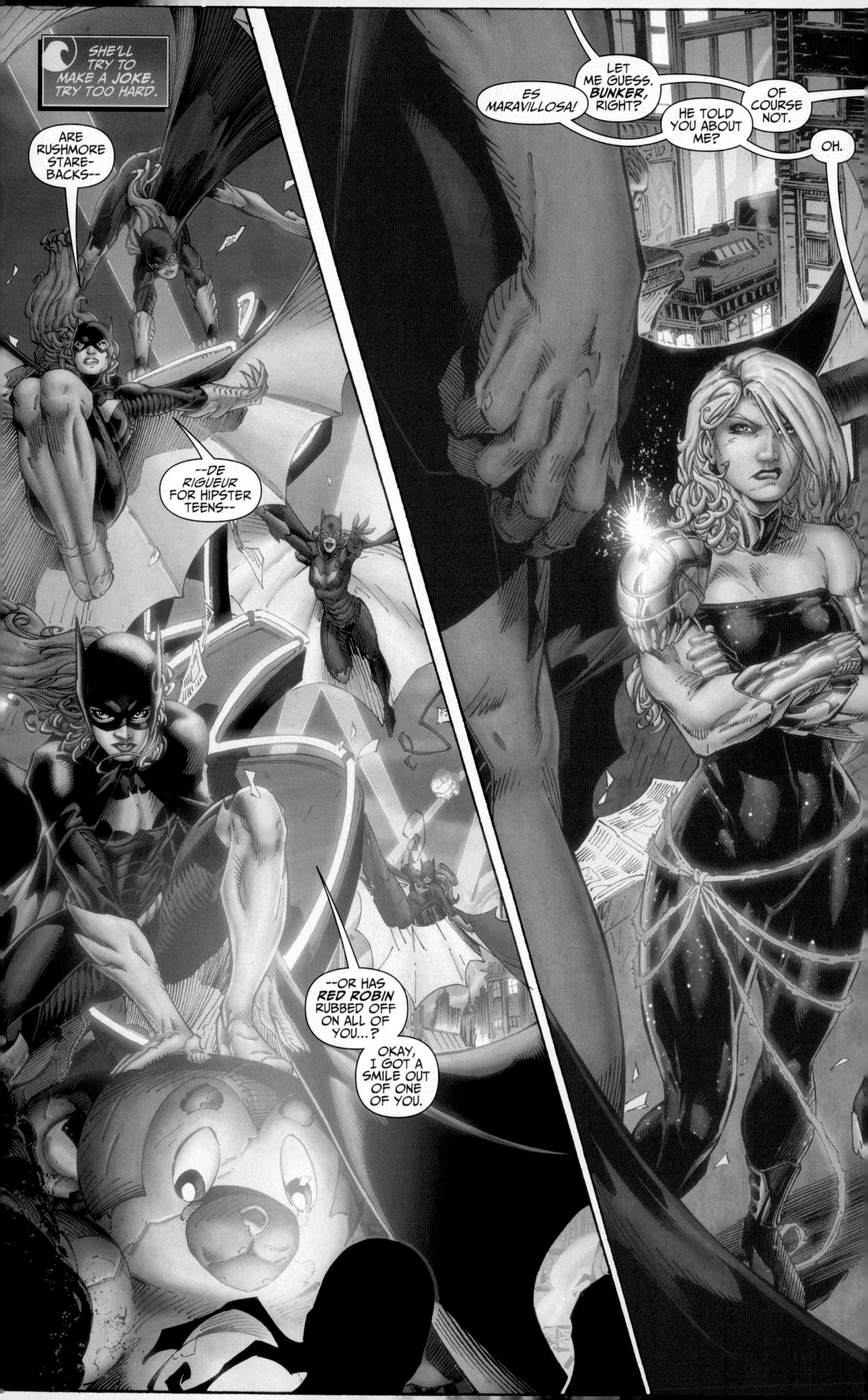

SHE'LL TRY TO MAKE A JOKE. TRY TOO HARD.
ARE RUSHMORE STARE-BACKS--
--DE RIGUEUR FOR HIPSTER TEENS--
--OR HAS RED ROBIN RUBBED OFF ON ALL OF YOU...?
OKAY, I GOT A SMILE OUT OF ONE OF YOU.
ES MARAVILLOSA!
LET ME GUESS. BUNKER, RIGHT?
HE TOLD YOU ABOUT ME?
OF COURSE NOT.
OH.

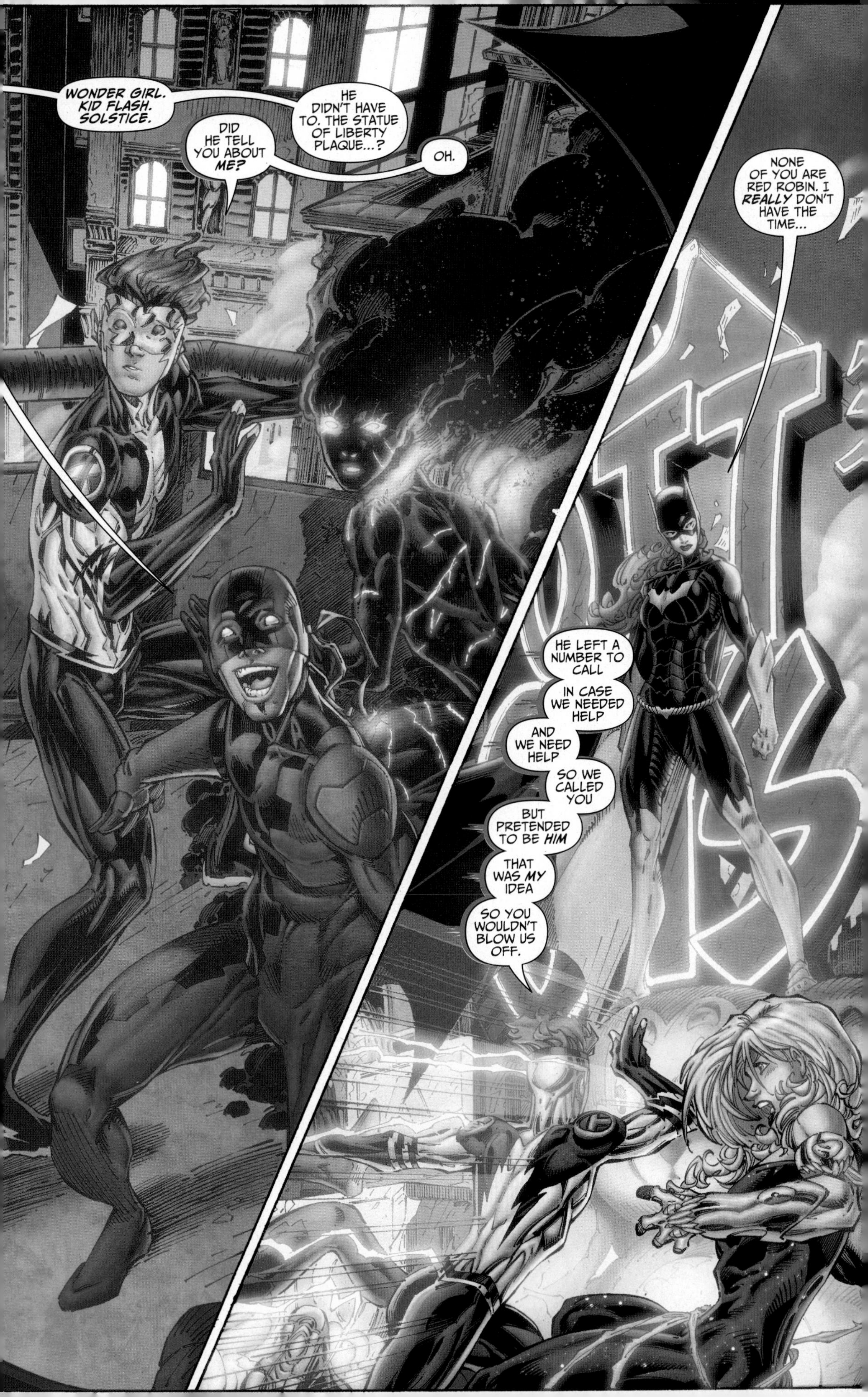
WONDER GIRL. KID FLASH. SOLSTICE.
HE DIDN'T HAVE TO. THE STATUE OF LIBERTY PLAQUE...?
DID HE TELL YOU ABOUT ME?
OH.
NONE OF YOU ARE RED ROBIN. I REALLY DON'T HAVE THE TIME...
HE LEFT A NUMBER TO CALL
IN CASE WE NEEDED HELP
AND WE NEED HELP
SO WE CALLED YOU
BUT PRETENDED TO BE HIM
THAT WAS MY IDEA
SO YOU WOULDN'T BLOW US OFF.

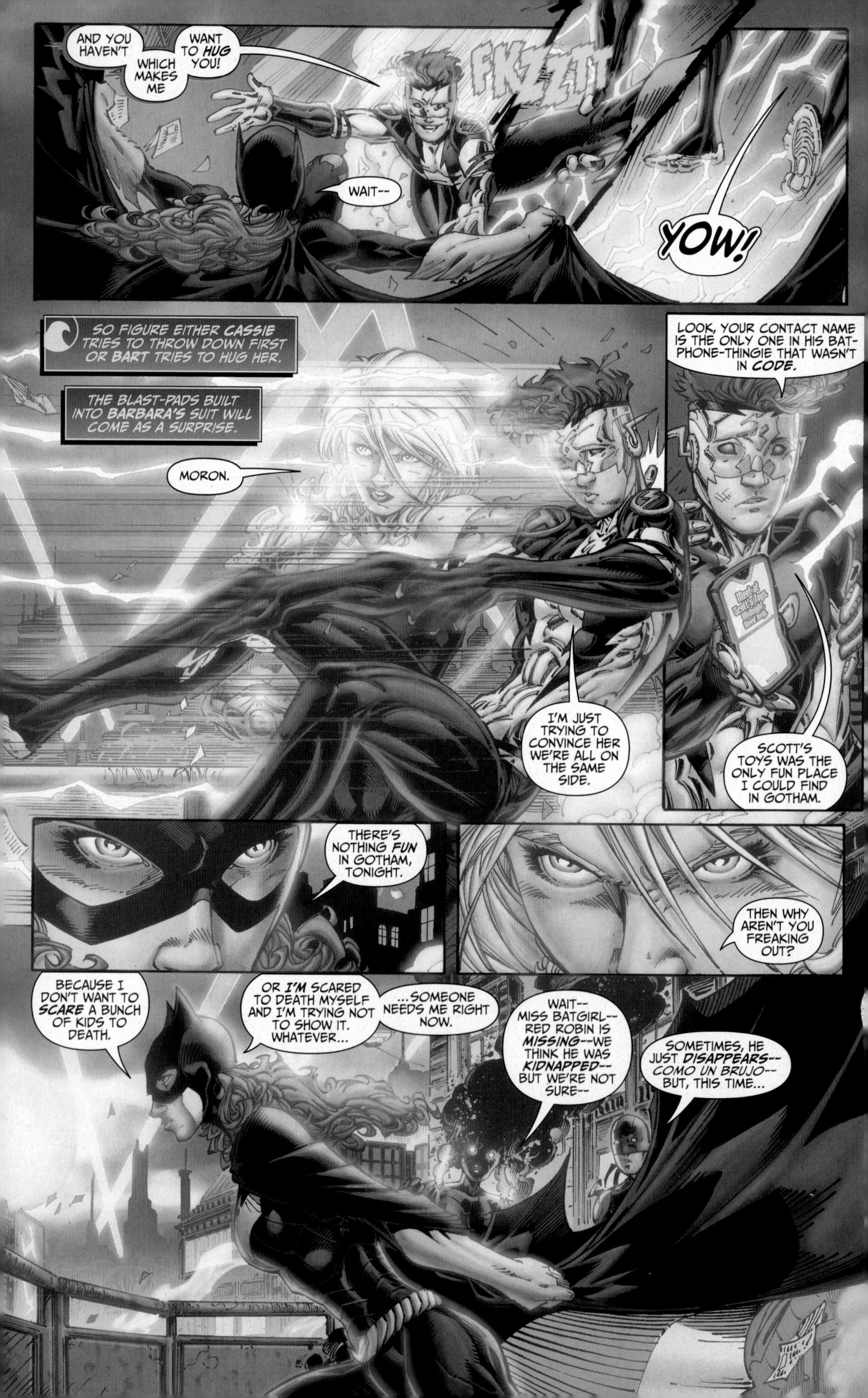
AND YOU HAVEN'T
WHICH MAKES ME
WANT TO HUG YOU!
FKZZTT
WAIT--
YOW!
SO FIGURE EITHER CASSIE TRIES TO THROW DOWN FIRST OR BART TRIES TO HUG HER.
THE BLAST-PADS BUILT INTO BARBARA'S SUIT WILL COME AS A SURPRISE.
MORON.
I'M JUST TRYING TO CONVINCE HER WE'RE ALL ON THE SAME SIDE.
LOOK, YOUR CONTACT NAME IS THE ONLY ONE IN HIS BAT-PHONE-THINGIE THAT WASN'T IN CODE.
SCOTT'S TOYS WAS THE ONLY FUN PLACE I COULD FIND IN GOTHAM.
THERE'S NOTHING FUN IN GOTHAM, TONIGHT.
THEN WHY AREN'T YOU FREAKING OUT?
BECAUSE I DON'T WANT TO SCARE A BUNCH OF KIDS TO DEATH.
OR I'M SCARED TO DEATH MYSELF AND I'M TRYING NOT TO SHOW IT. WHATEVER...
...SOMEONE NEEDS ME RIGHT NOW.
WAIT-- MISS BATGIRL-- RED ROBIN IS MISSING--WE THINK HE WAS KIDNAPPED-- BUT WE'RE NOT SURE--
SOMETIMES, HE JUST DISAPPEARS-- COMO UN BRUJO-- BUT, THIS TIME...

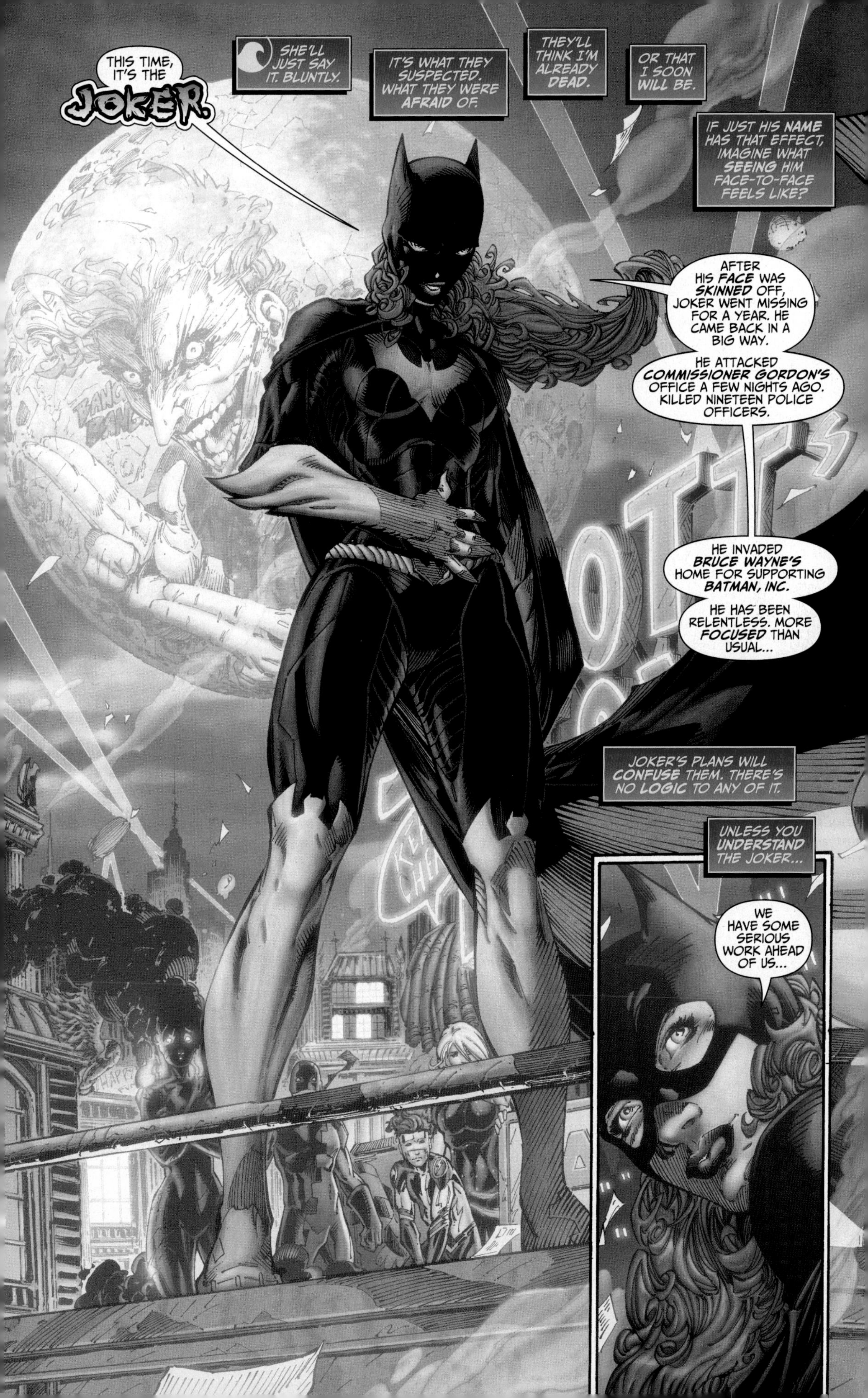
THIS TIME, IT'S THE JOKER.
SHE'LL JUST SAY IT. BLUNTLY.
IT'S WHAT THEY SUSPECTED. WHAT THEY WERE AFRAID OF.
THEY'LL THINK I'M ALREADY DEAD.
OR THAT I SOON WILL BE.
IF JUST HIS NAME HAS THAT EFFECT, IMAGINE WHAT SEEING HIM FACE-TO-FACE FEELS LIKE?
AFTER HIS FACE WAS SKINNED OFF, JOKER WENT MISSING FOR A YEAR. HE CAME BACK IN A BIG WAY.
HE ATTACKED COMMISSIONER GORDON'S OFFICE A FEW NIGHTS AGO. KILLED NINETEEN POLICE OFFICERS.
HE INVADED BRUCE WAYNE'S HOME FOR SUPPORTING BATMAN, INC.
HE HAS BEEN RELENTLESS. MORE FOCUSED THAN USUAL...
JOKER'S PLANS WILL CONFUSE THEM. THERE'S NO LOGIC TO ANY OF IT.
UNLESS YOU UNDERSTAND THE JOKER...
WE HAVE SOME SERIOUS WORK AHEAD OF US...

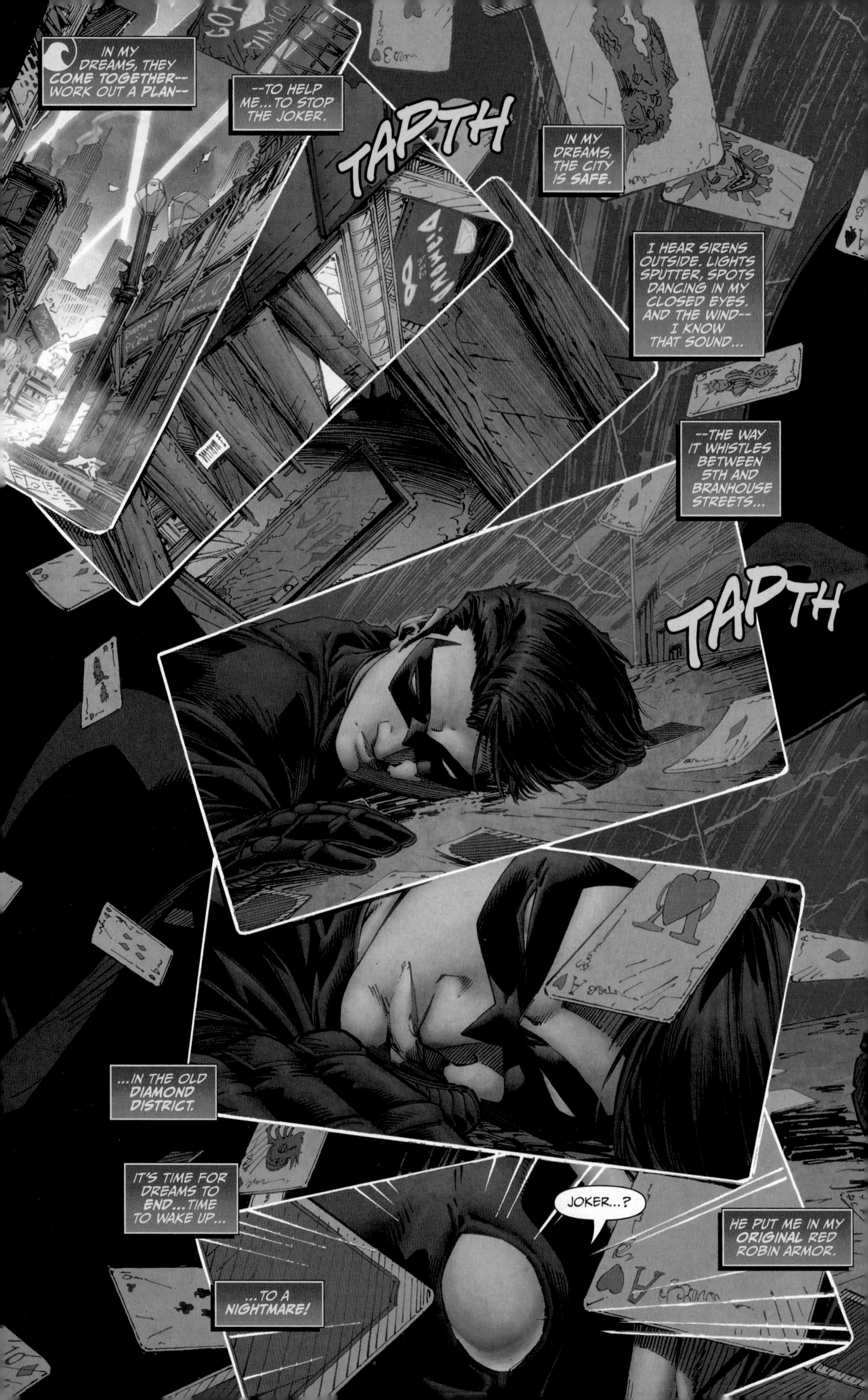
IN MY DREAMS, THEY COME TOGETHER-- WORK OUT A PLAN--
--TO HELP ME...TO STOP THE JOKER.
TAPTH
IN MY DREAMS, THE CITY IS SAFE.
I HEAR SIRENS OUTSIDE. LIGHTS SPUTTER, SPOTS DANCING IN MY CLOSED EYES. AND THE WIND-- I KNOW THAT SOUND...
--THE WAY IT WHISTLES BETWEEN 5TH AND BRANHOUSE STREETS...
TAPTH
...IN THE OLD DIAMOND DISTRICT.
IT'S TIME FOR DREAMS TO END...TIME TO WAKE UP...
...TO A NIGHTMARE!
JOKER...?
HE PUT ME IN MY ORIGINAL RED ROBIN ARMOR.

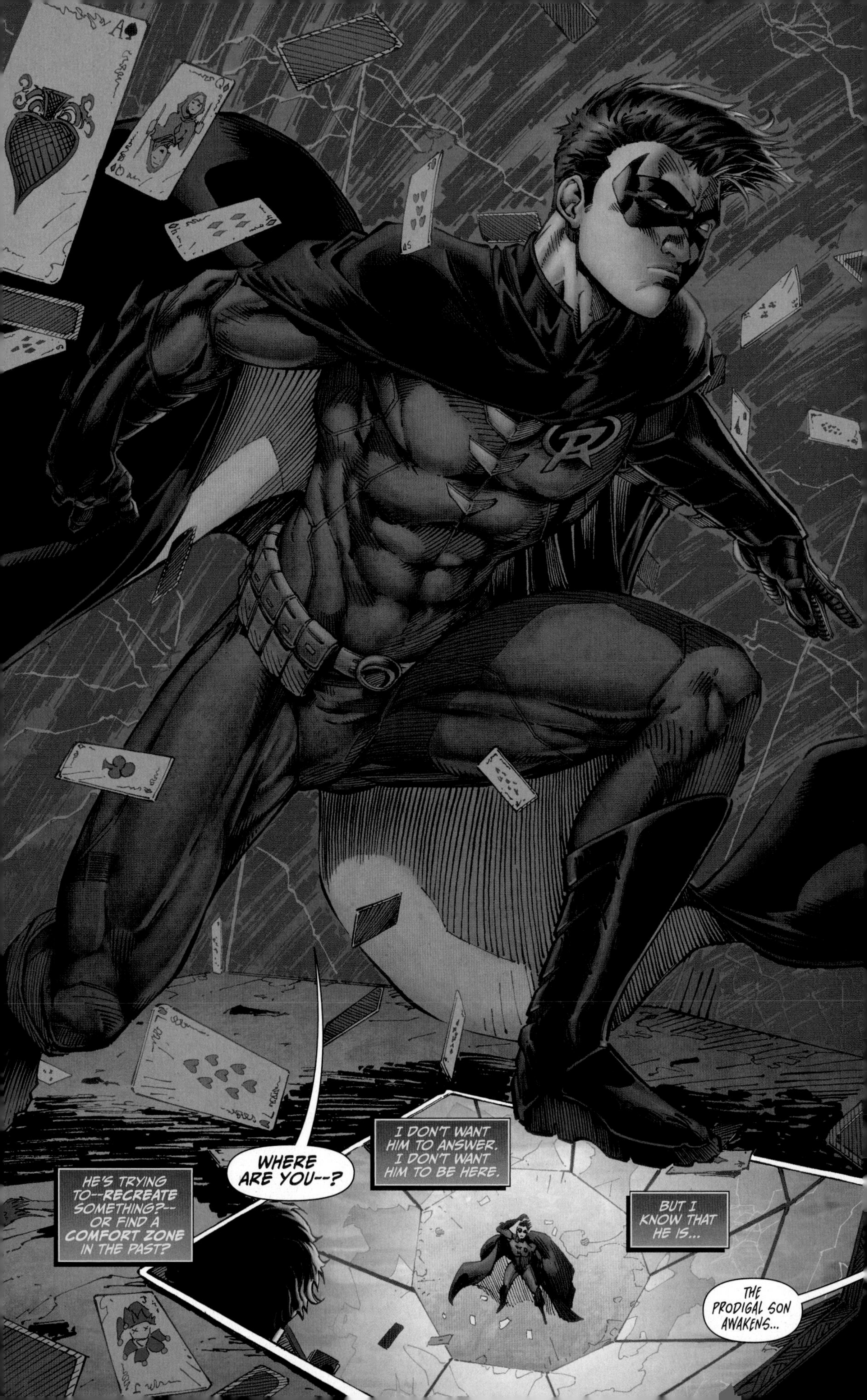
HE'S TRYING TO--RECREATE SOMETHING?-- OR FIND A COMFORT ZONE IN THE PAST?
WHERE ARE YOU--?
I DON'T WANT HIM TO ANSWER. I DON'T WANT HIM TO BE HERE.
BUT I KNOW THAT HE IS...
THE PRODIGAL SON AWAKENS...

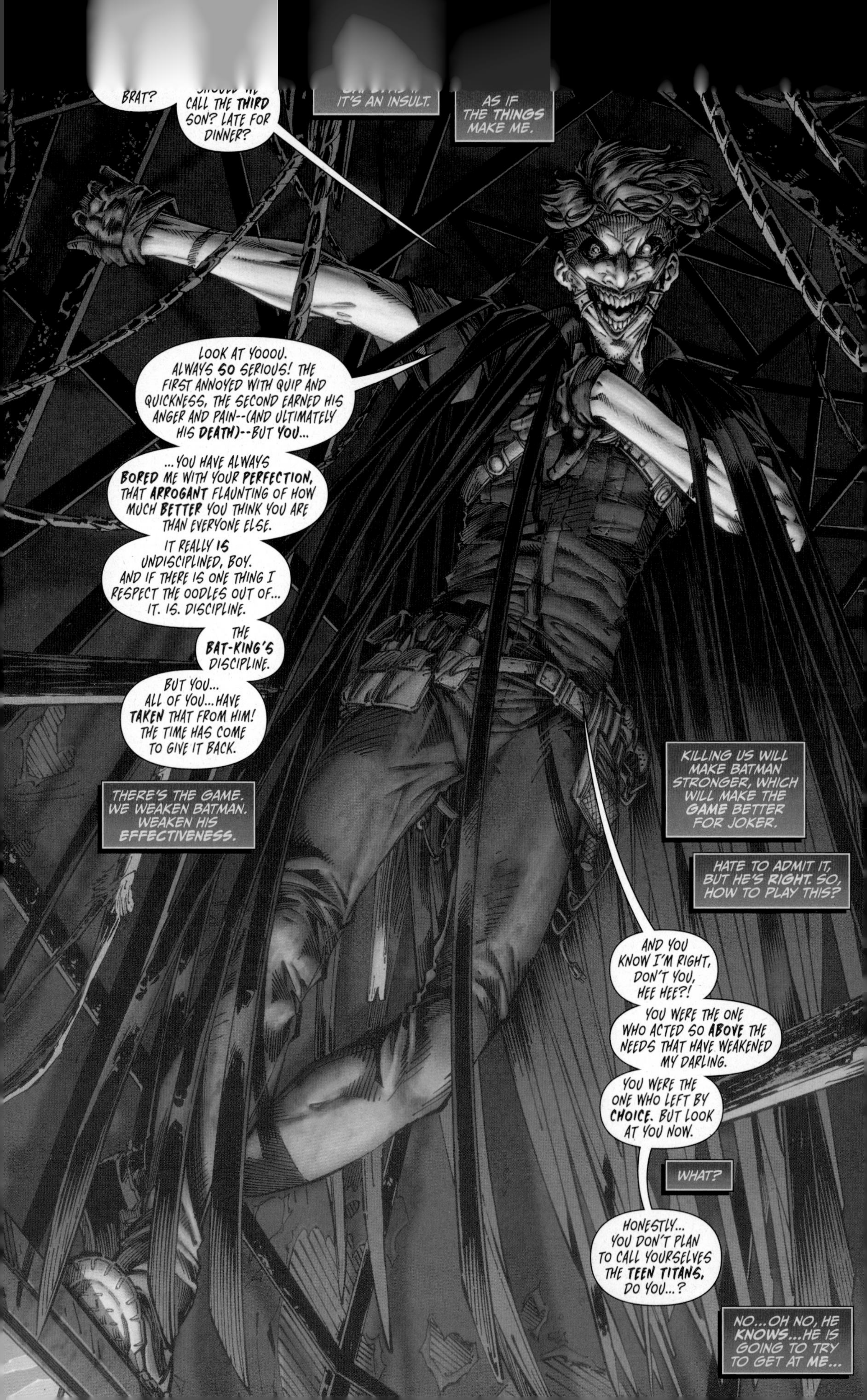
BRAT?
CALL THE THIRD SON? LATE FOR DINNER?
IT'S AN INSULT.
AS IF THE THINGS MAKE ME.
LOOK AT YOOOU. ALWAYS SO SERIOUS! THE FIRST ANNOYED WITH QUIP AND QUICKNESS, THE SECOND EARNED HIS ANGER AND PAIN--(AND ULTIMATELY HIS DEATH)--BUT YOU...
...YOU HAVE ALWAYS BORED ME WITH YOUR PERFECTION, THAT ARROGANT FLAUNTING OF HOW MUCH BETTER YOU THINK YOU ARE THAN EVERYONE ELSE.
IT REALLY IS UNDISCIPLINED, BOY. AND IF THERE IS ONE THING I RESPECT THE OODLES OUT OF... IT. IS. DISCIPLINE.
THE BAT-KING'S DISCIPLINE.
BUT YOU... ALL OF YOU...HAVE TAKEN THAT FROM HIM! THE TIME HAS COME TO GIVE IT BACK.
THERE'S THE GAME. WE WEAKEN BATMAN. WEAKEN HIS EFFECTIVENESS.
KILLING US WILL MAKE BATMAN STRONGER, WHICH WILL MAKE THE GAME BETTER FOR JOKER.
HATE TO ADMIT IT, BUT HE'S RIGHT. SO, HOW TO PLAY THIS?
AND YOU KNOW I'M RIGHT, DON'T YOU, HEE HEE?!
YOU WERE THE ONE WHO ACTED SO ABOVE THE NEEDS THAT HAVE WEAKENED MY DARLING.
YOU WERE THE ONE WHO LEFT BY CHOICE. BUT LOOK AT YOU NOW.
WHAT?
HONESTLY... YOU DON'T PLAN TO CALL YOURSELVES THE TEEN TITANS, DO YOU...?
NO...OH NO, HE KNOWS...HE IS GOING TO TRY TO GET AT ME...

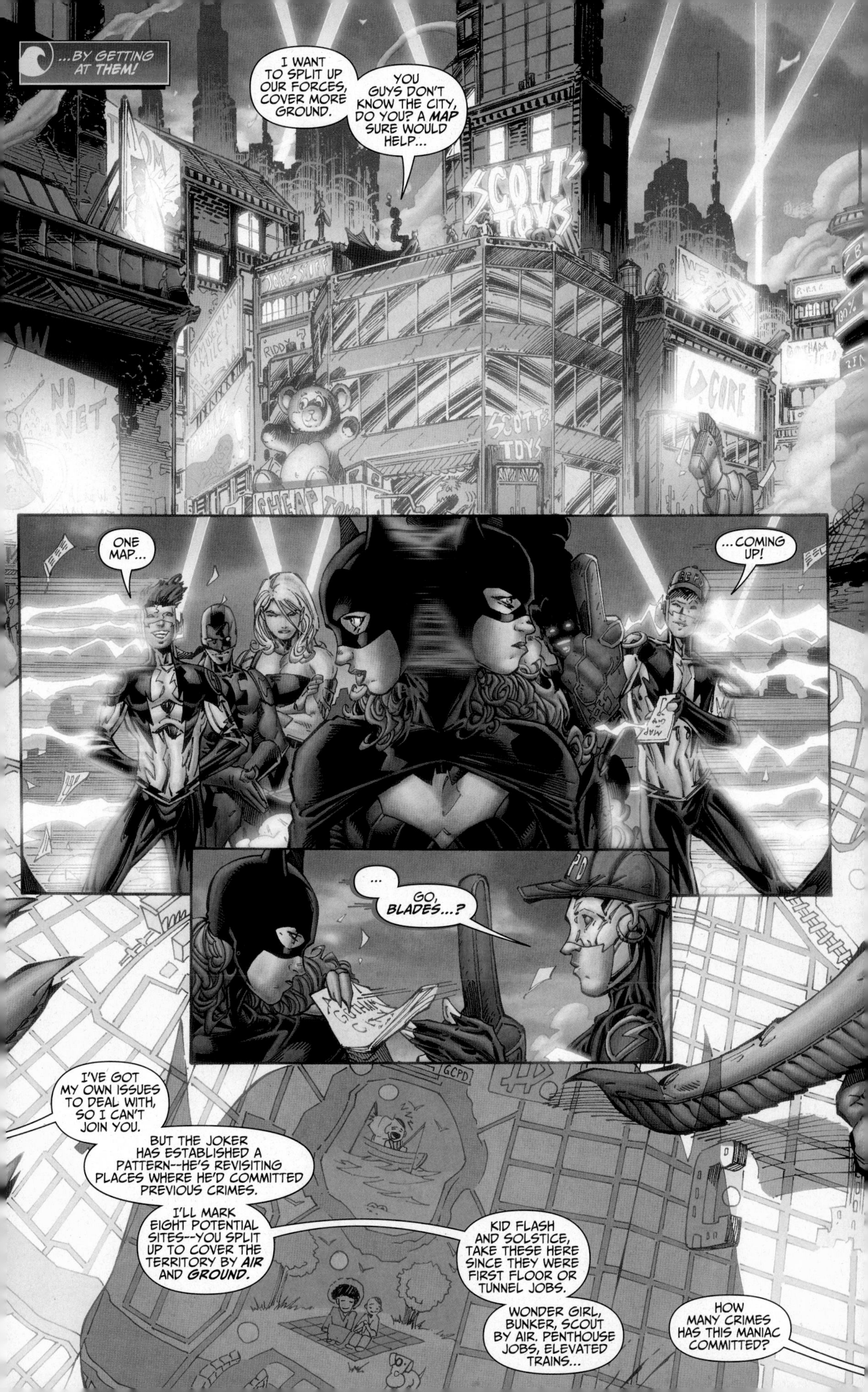
...BY GETTING AT THEM!
I WANT TO SPLIT UP OUR FORCES, COVER MORE GROUND.
YOU GUYS DON'T KNOW THE CITY, DO YOU? A MAP SURE WOULD HELP...
SCOTT'S TOYS
ONE MAP...
...COMING UP!
... GO, BLADES...?
I'VE GOT MY OWN ISSUES TO DEAL WITH, SO I CAN'T JOIN YOU.
BUT THE JOKER HAS ESTABLISHED A PATTERN--HE'S REVISITING PLACES WHERE HE'D COMMITTED PREVIOUS CRIMES.
I'LL MARK EIGHT POTENTIAL SITES--YOU SPLIT UP TO COVER THE TERRITORY BY AIR AND GROUND.
KID FLASH AND SOLSTICE, TAKE THESE HERE SINCE THEY WERE FIRST FLOOR OR TUNNEL JOBS.
WONDER GIRL, BUNKER, SCOUT BY AIR. PENTHOUSE JOBS, ELEVATED TRAINS...
HOW MANY CRIMES HAS THIS MANIAC COMMITTED?

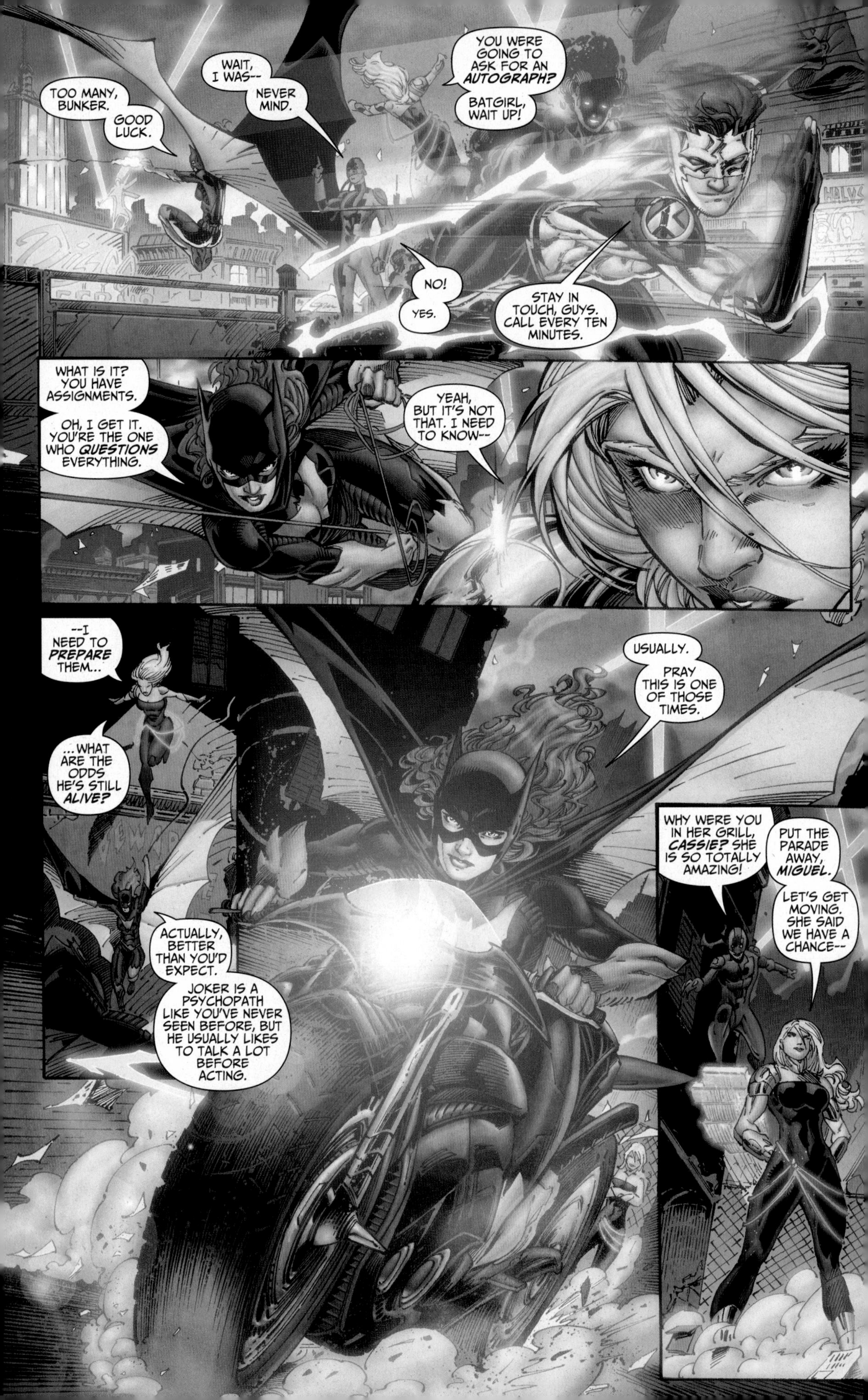
TOO MANY, BUNKER.
GOOD LUCK.
WAIT, I WAS--
NEVER MIND.
YOU WERE GOING TO ASK FOR AN AUTOGRAPH?
BATGIRL, WAIT UP!
NO!
YES.
STAY IN TOUCH, GUYS. CALL EVERY TEN MINUTES.
WHAT IS IT? YOU HAVE ASSIGNMENTS.
OH, I GET IT. YOU'RE THE ONE WHO QUESTIONS EVERYTHING.
YEAH, BUT IT'S NOT THAT. I NEED TO KNOW--
--I NEED TO PREPARE THEM...
...WHAT ARE THE ODDS HE'S STILL ALIVE?
ACTUALLY, BETTER THAN YOU'D EXPECT.
JOKER IS A PSYCHOPATH LIKE YOU'VE NEVER SEEN BEFORE, BUT HE USUALLY LIKES TO TALK A LOT BEFORE ACTING.
USUALLY.
PRAY THIS IS ONE OF THOSE TIMES.
WHY WERE YOU IN HER GRILL, CASSIE? SHE IS SO TOTALLY AMAZING!
PUT THE PARADE AWAY, MIGUEL.
LET'S GET MOVING. SHE SAID WE HAVE A CHANCE--

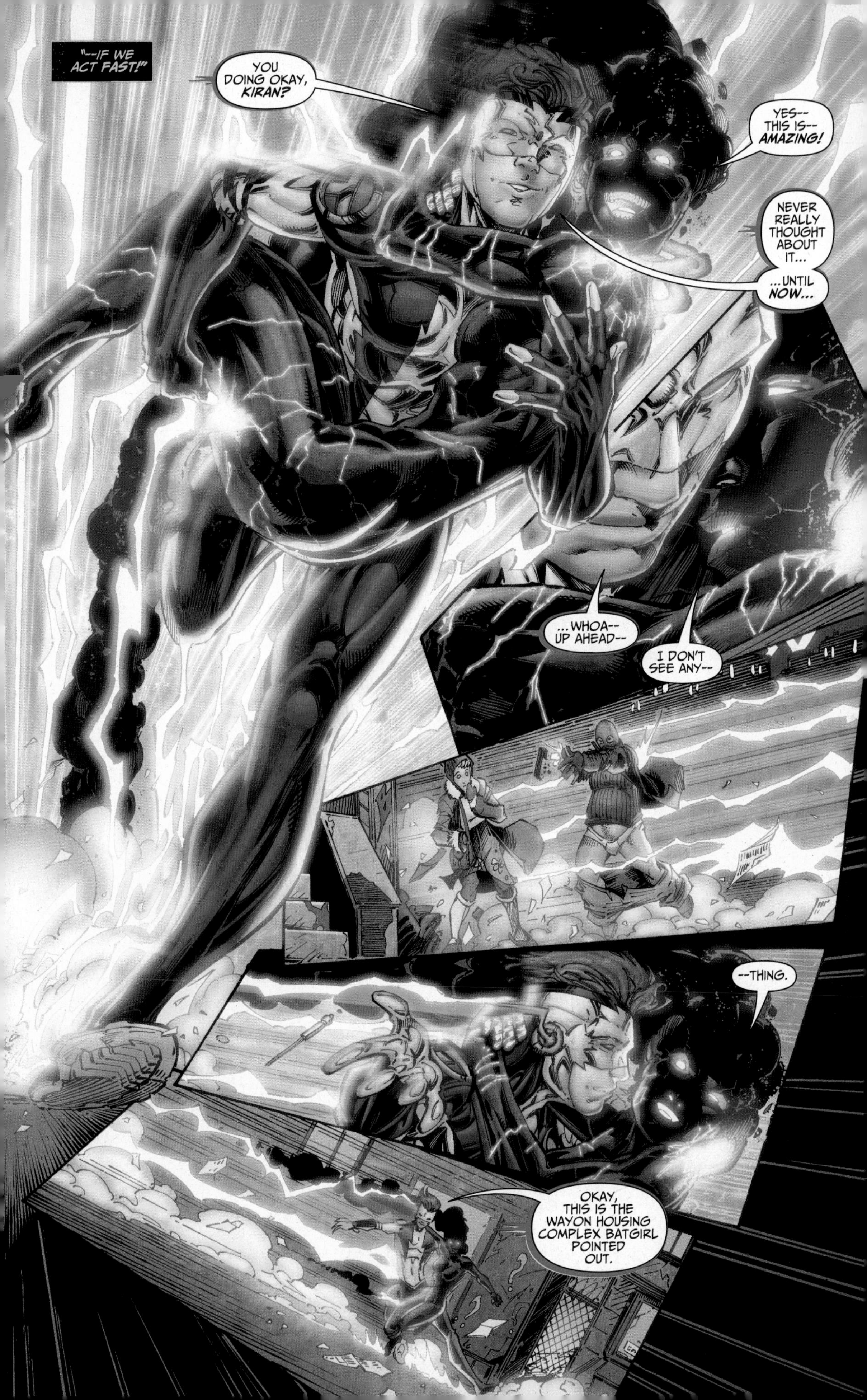
"--IF WE ACT FAST!"
YOU DOING OKAY, KIRAN?
YES-- THIS IS-- AMAZING!
NEVER REALLY THOUGHT ABOUT IT...
...UNTIL NOW...
...WHOA-- UP AHEAD--
I DON'T SEE ANY--
--THING.
OKAY, THIS IS THE WAYON HOUSING COMPLEX BATGIRL POINTED OUT.

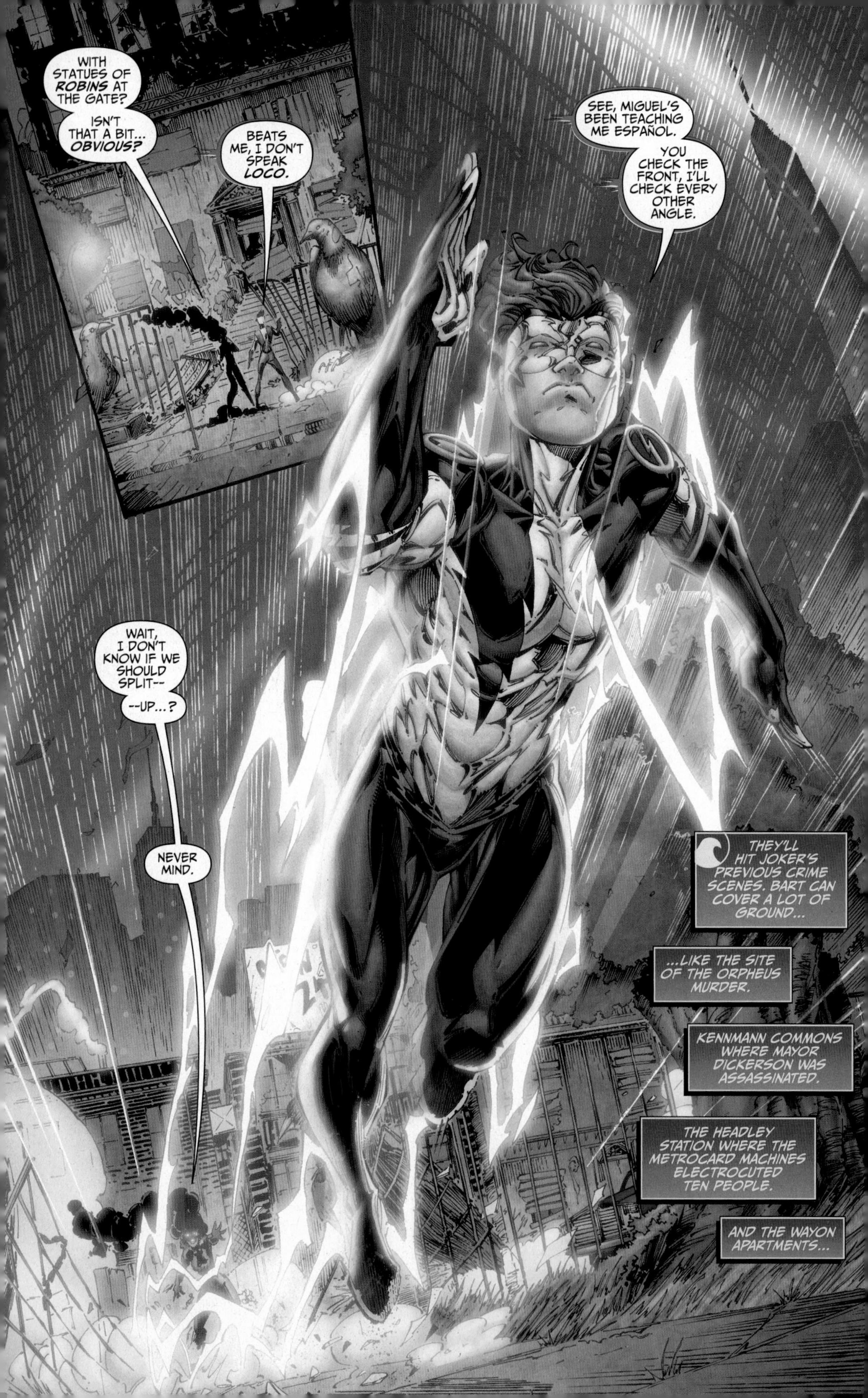

WITH STATUES OF ROBINS AT THE GATE?
ISN'T THAT A BIT... OBVIOUS?
BEATS ME, I DON'T SPEAK LOCO.
SEE, MIGUEL'S BEEN TEACHING ME ESPAÑOL.
YOU CHECK THE FRONT, I'LL CHECK EVERY OTHER ANGLE.
WAIT, I DON'T KNOW IF WE SHOULD SPLIT--
--UP...?
NEVER MIND.
THEY'LL HIT JOKER'S PREVIOUS CRIME SCENES. BART CAN COVER A LOT OF GROUND...
...LIKE THE SITE OF THE ORPHEUS MURDER.
KENMANN COMMONS WHERE MAYOR DICKERSON WAS ASSASSINATED.
THE HEADLEY STATION WHERE THE METROCARD MACHINES ELECTROCUTED TEN PEOPLE.
AND THE WAYON APARTMENTS...

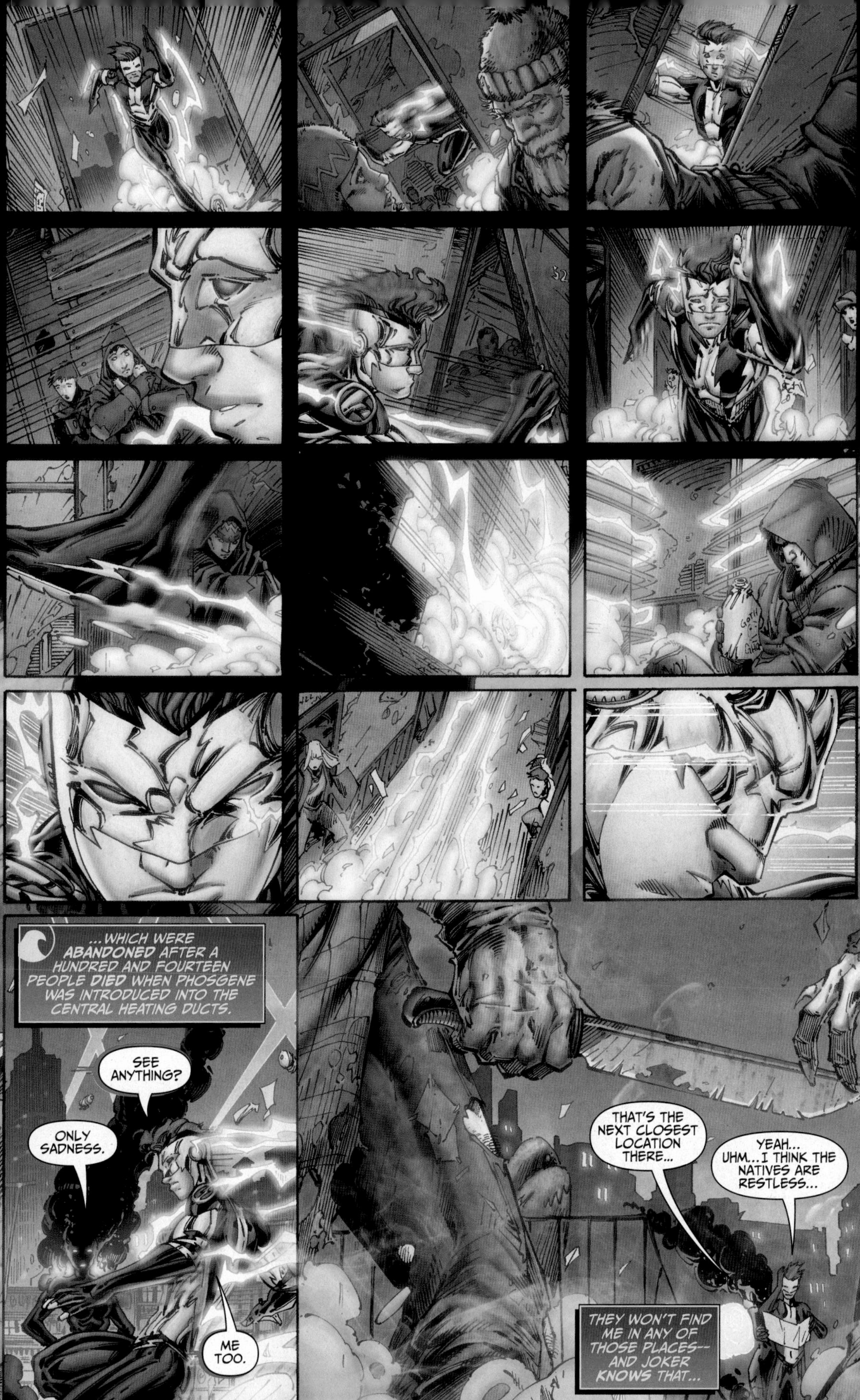
...WHICH WERE ABANDONED AFTER A HUNDRED AND FOURTEEN PEOPLE DIED WHEN PHOSGENE WAS INTRODUCED INTO THE CENTRAL HEATING DUCTS.
SEE ANYTHING?
ONLY SADNESS.
ME TOO.
THAT'S THE NEXT CLOSEST LOCATION THERE...
YEAH... UHM...I THINK THE NATIVES ARE RESTLESS...
THEY WON'T FIND ME IN ANY OF THOSE PLACES-- AND JOKER KNOWS THAT...

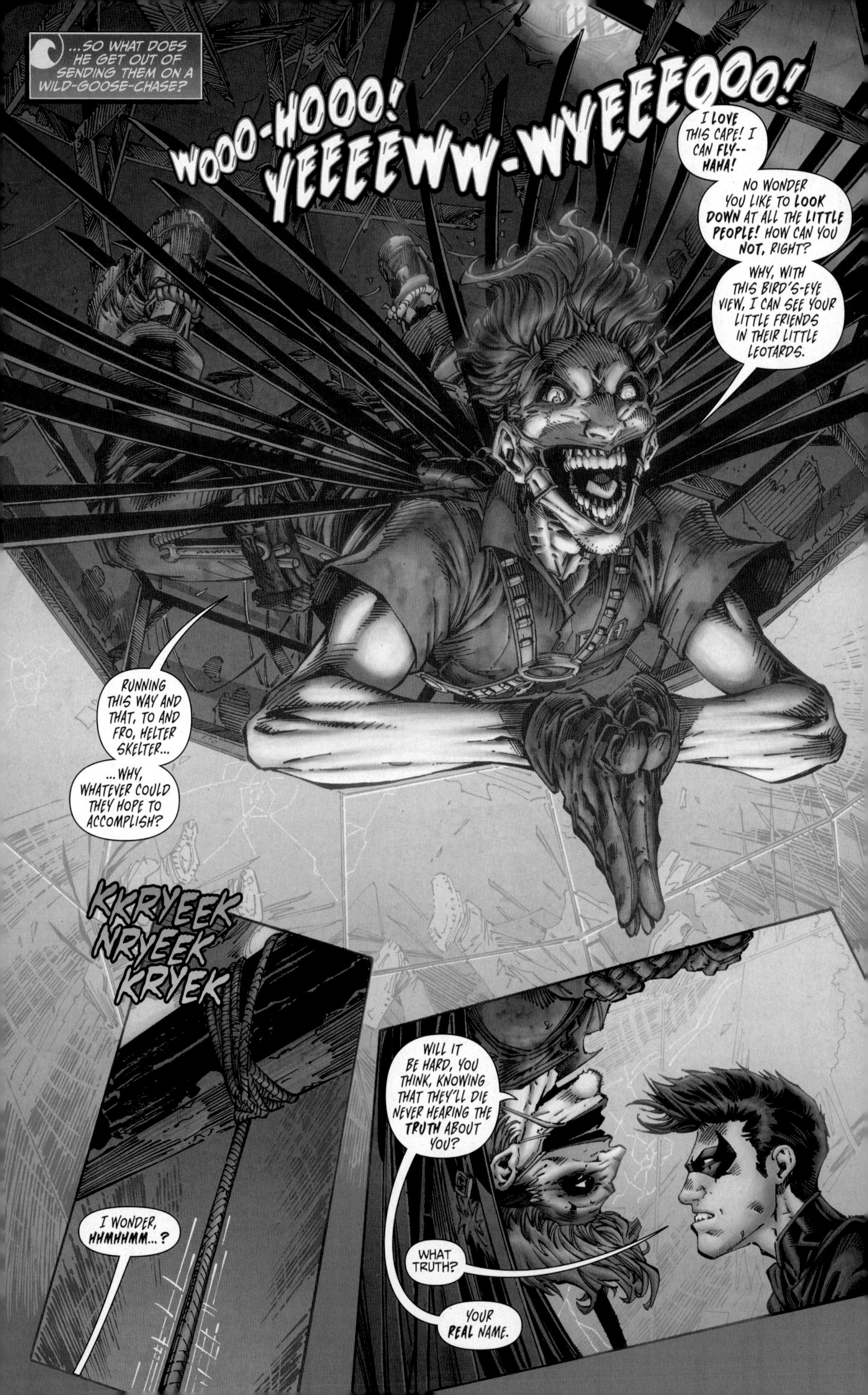
...SO WHAT DOES HE GET OUT OF SENDING THEM ON A WILD-GOOSE-CHASE?
WOOO-HOOO! YEEEEWW-WYEEEOOO!
I LOVE THIS CAPE! I CAN FLY-- HAHA!
NO WONDER YOU LIKE TO LOOK DOWN AT ALL THE LITTLE PEOPLE! HOW CAN YOU NOT, RIGHT?
WHY, WITH THIS BIRD'S-EYE VIEW, I CAN SEE YOUR LITTLE FRIENDS IN THEIR LITTLE LEOTARDS.
RUNNING THIS WAY AND THAT, TO AND FRO, HELTER SKELTER...
...WHY, WHATEVER COULD THEY HOPE TO ACCOMPLISH?
KKRYEEK NRYEEK KRYEK
I WONDER, HMHMHMM...?
WILL IT BE HARD, YOU THINK, KNOWING THAT THEY'LL DIE NEVER HEARING THE TRUTH ABOUT YOU?
WHAT TRUTH?
YOUR REAL NAME.

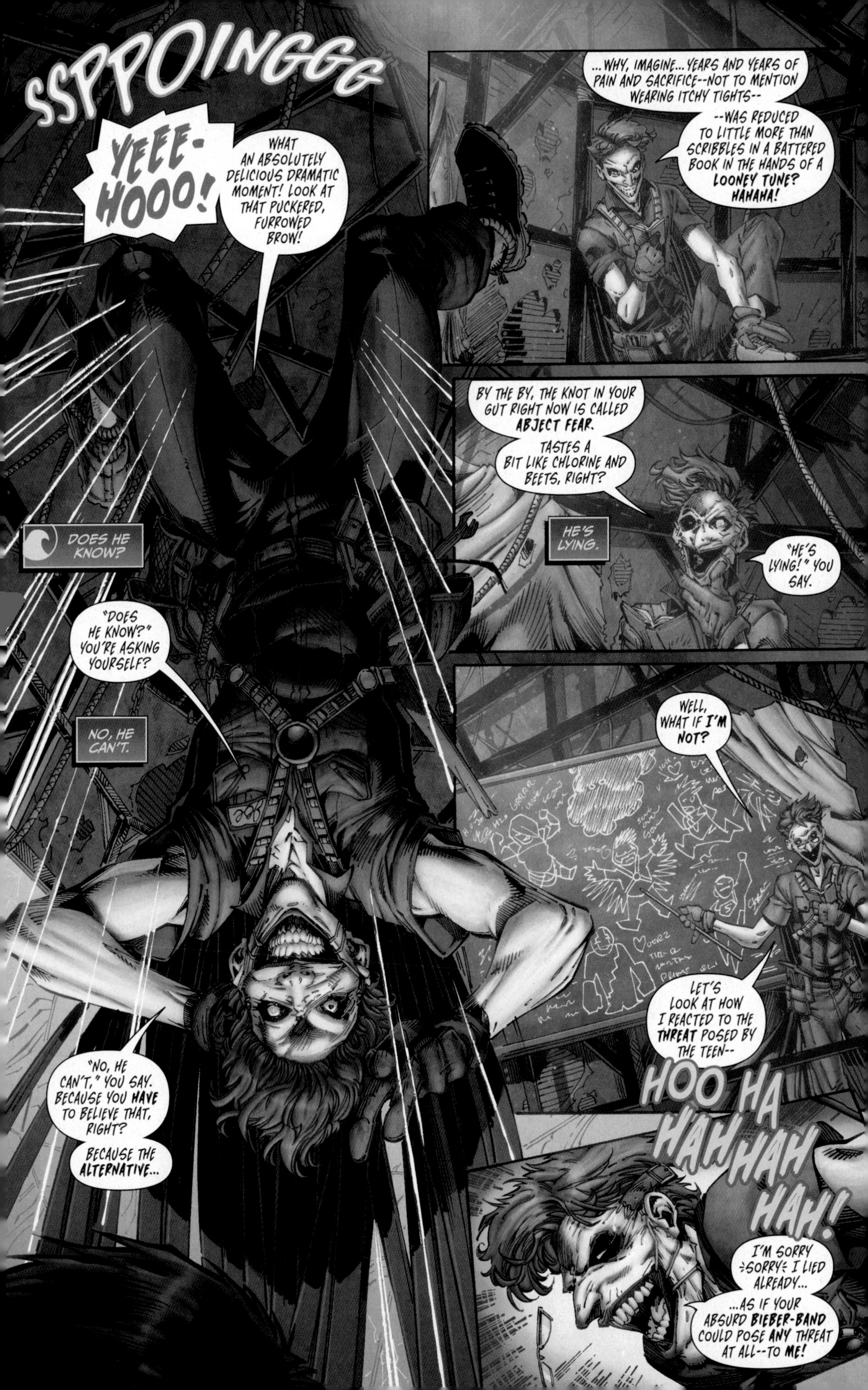
SSPPOINGGG
YEEE-HOOO!
WHAT AN ABSOLUTELY DELICIOUS DRAMATIC MOMENT! LOOK AT THAT PUCKERED, FURROWED BROW!
DOES HE KNOW?
"DOES HE KNOW?" YOU'RE ASKING YOURSELF?
NO, HE CAN'T.
"NO, HE CAN'T," YOU SAY. BECAUSE YOU HAVE TO BELIEVE THAT, RIGHT?
BECAUSE THE ALTERNATIVE...
...WHY, IMAGINE... YEARS AND YEARS OF PAIN AND SACRIFICE--NOT TO MENTION WEARING ITCHY TIGHTS--
--WAS REDUCED TO LITTLE MORE THAN SCRIBBLES IN A BATTERED BOOK IN THE HANDS OF A LOONEY TUNE? HAHAHA!
BY THE BY, THE KNOT IN YOUR GUT RIGHT NOW IS CALLED ABJECT FEAR.
TASTES A BIT LIKE CHLORINE AND BEETS, RIGHT?
HE'S LYING.
"HE'S LYING!" YOU SAY.
WELL, WHAT IF I'M NOT?
LET'S LOOK AT HOW I REACTED TO THE THREAT POSED BY THE TEEN--
HOO HA HAH HAH HAH!
I'M SORRY SORRY I LIED ALREADY...
...AS IF YOUR ABSURD BIEBER-BAND COULD POSE ANY THREAT AT ALL--TO ME!

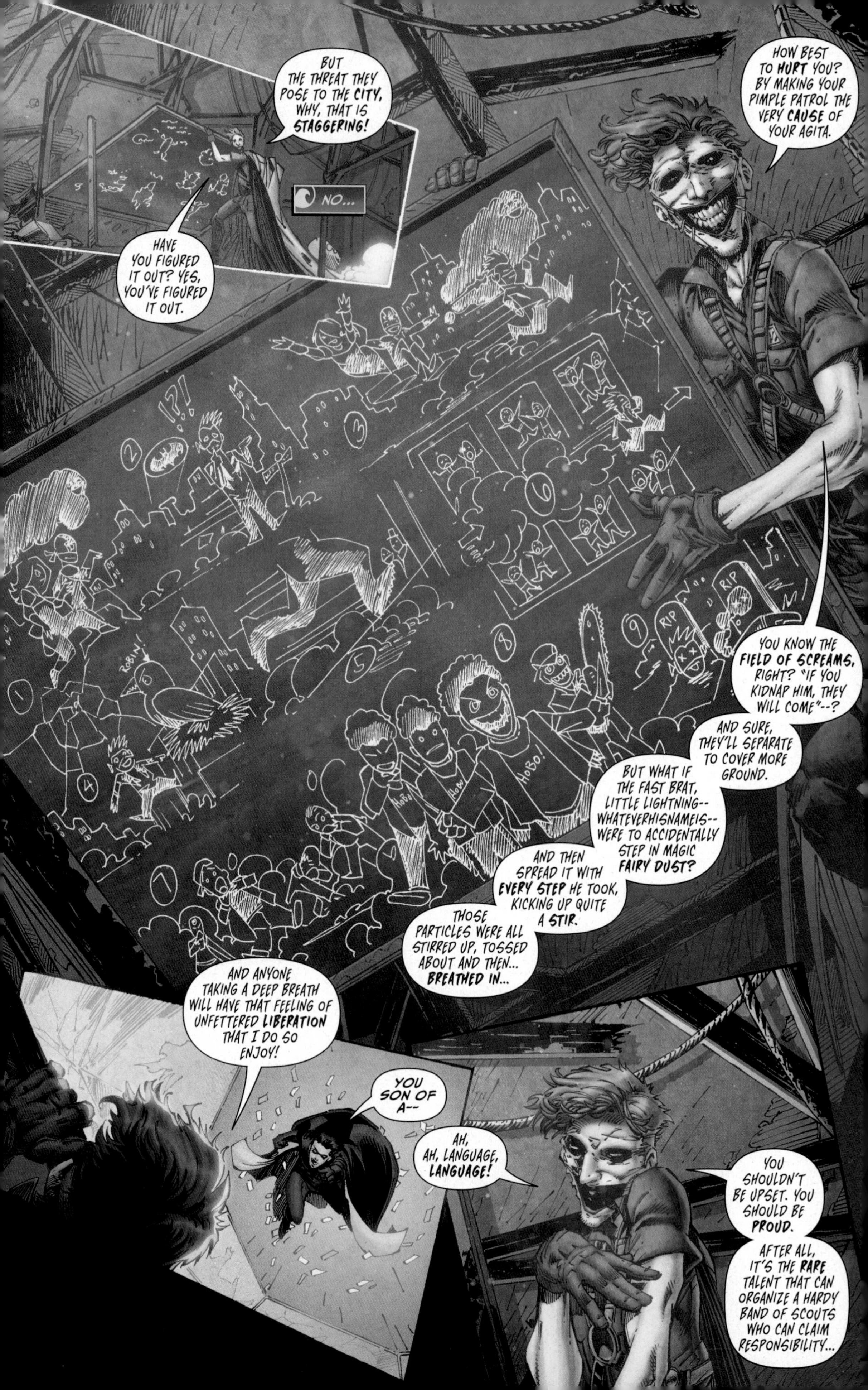
BUT THE THREAT THEY POSE TO THE CITY, WHY, THAT IS STAGGERING!
NO...
HAVE YOU FIGURED IT OUT? YES, YOU'VE FIGURED IT OUT.
HOW BEST TO HURT YOU? BY MAKING YOUR PIMPLE PATROL THE VERY CAUSE OF YOUR AGITA.
YOU KNOW THE FIELD OF SCREAMS, RIGHT? "IF YOU KIDNAP HIM, THEY WILL COME"--?
AND SURE, THEY'LL SEPARATE TO COVER MORE GROUND.
BUT WHAT IF THE FAST BRAT, LITTLE LIGHTNING--WHATEVERHISNAMEIS--WERE TO ACCIDENTALLY STEP IN MAGIC FAIRY DUST?
AND THEN SPREAD IT WITH EVERY STEP HE TOOK, KICKING UP QUITE A STIR.
THOSE PARTICLES WERE ALL STIRRED UP, TOSSED ABOUT AND THEN... BREATHED IN...
AND ANYONE TAKING A DEEP BREATH WILL HAVE THAT FEELING OF UNFETTERED LIBERATION THAT I DO SO ENJOY!
YOU SON OF A--
AH, AH, LANGUAGE, LANGUAGE!
YOU SHOULDN'T BE UPSET. YOU SHOULD BE PROUD.
AFTER ALL, IT'S THE RARE TALENT THAT CAN ORGANIZE A HARDY BAND OF SCOUTS WHO CAN CLAIM RESPONSIBILITY...

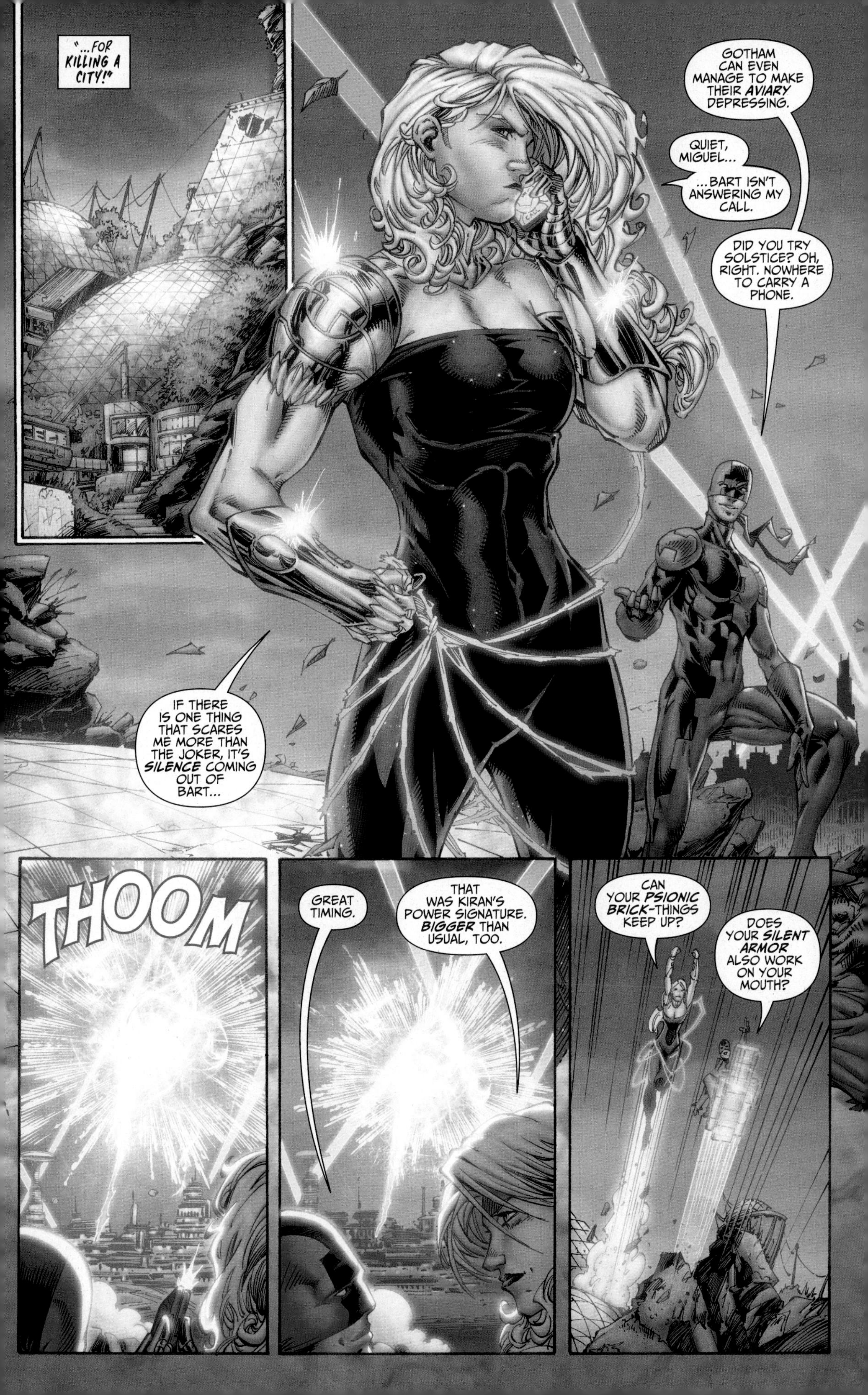
"...FOR KILLING A CITY!"
GOTHAM CAN EVEN MANAGE TO MAKE THEIR AVIARY DEPRESSING.
QUIET, MIGUEL...
...BART ISN'T ANSWERING MY CALL.
DID YOU TRY SOLSTICE? OH, RIGHT. NOWHERE TO CARRY A PHONE.
IF THERE IS ONE THING THAT SCARES ME MORE THAN THE JOKER, IT'S SILENCE COMING OUT OF BART...
THOOM
GREAT TIMING.
THAT WAS KIRAN'S POWER SIGNATURE. BIGGER THAN USUAL, TOO.
CAN YOUR PSIONIC BRICK-THINGS KEEP UP?
DOES YOUR SILENT ARMOR ALSO WORK ON YOUR MOUTH?

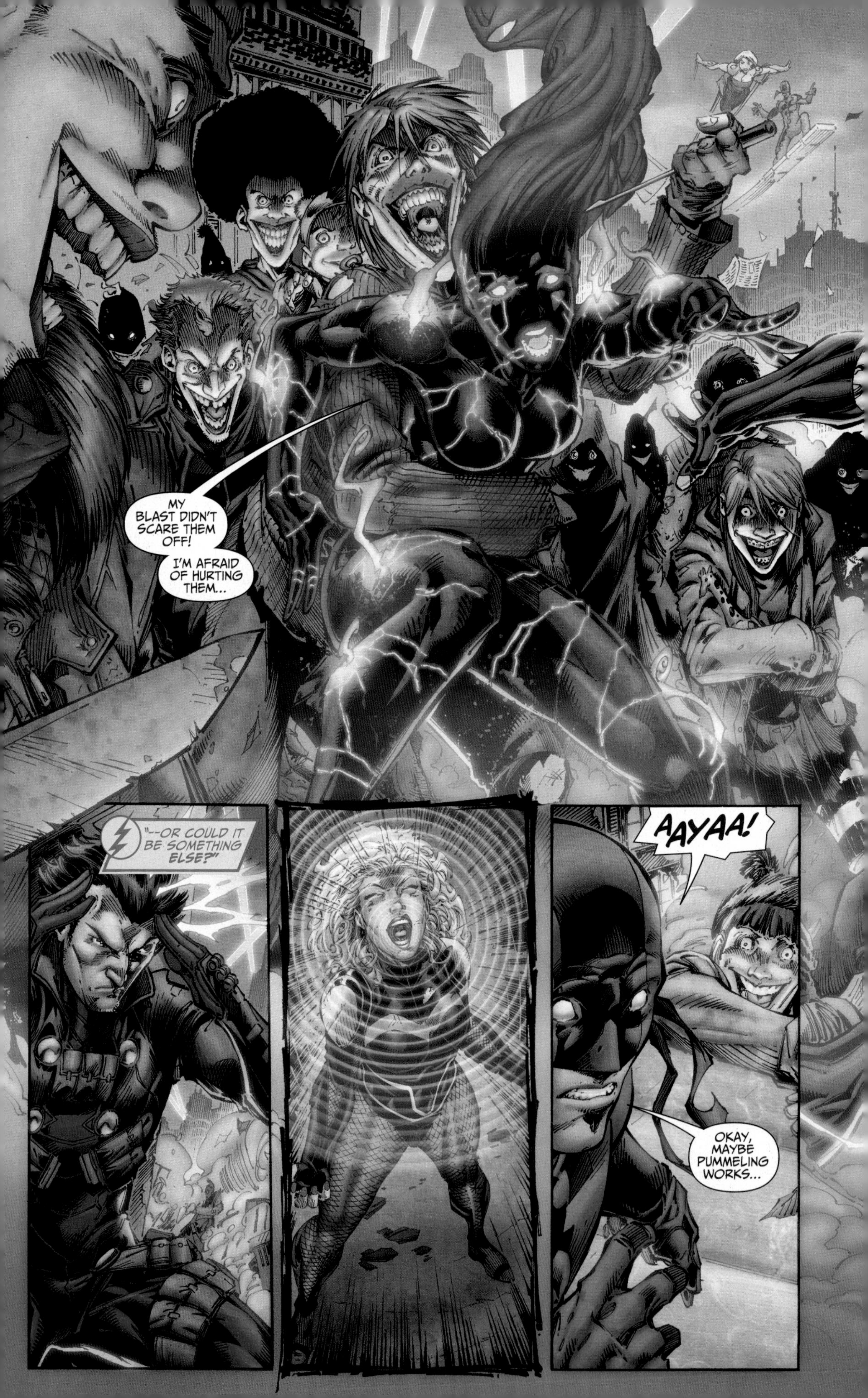
MY BLAST DIDN'T SCARE THEM OFF!
I'M AFRAID OF HURTING THEM...
"--OR COULD IT BE SOMETHING ELSE?"
AAYAA!
OKAY, MAYBE PUMMELING WORKS...

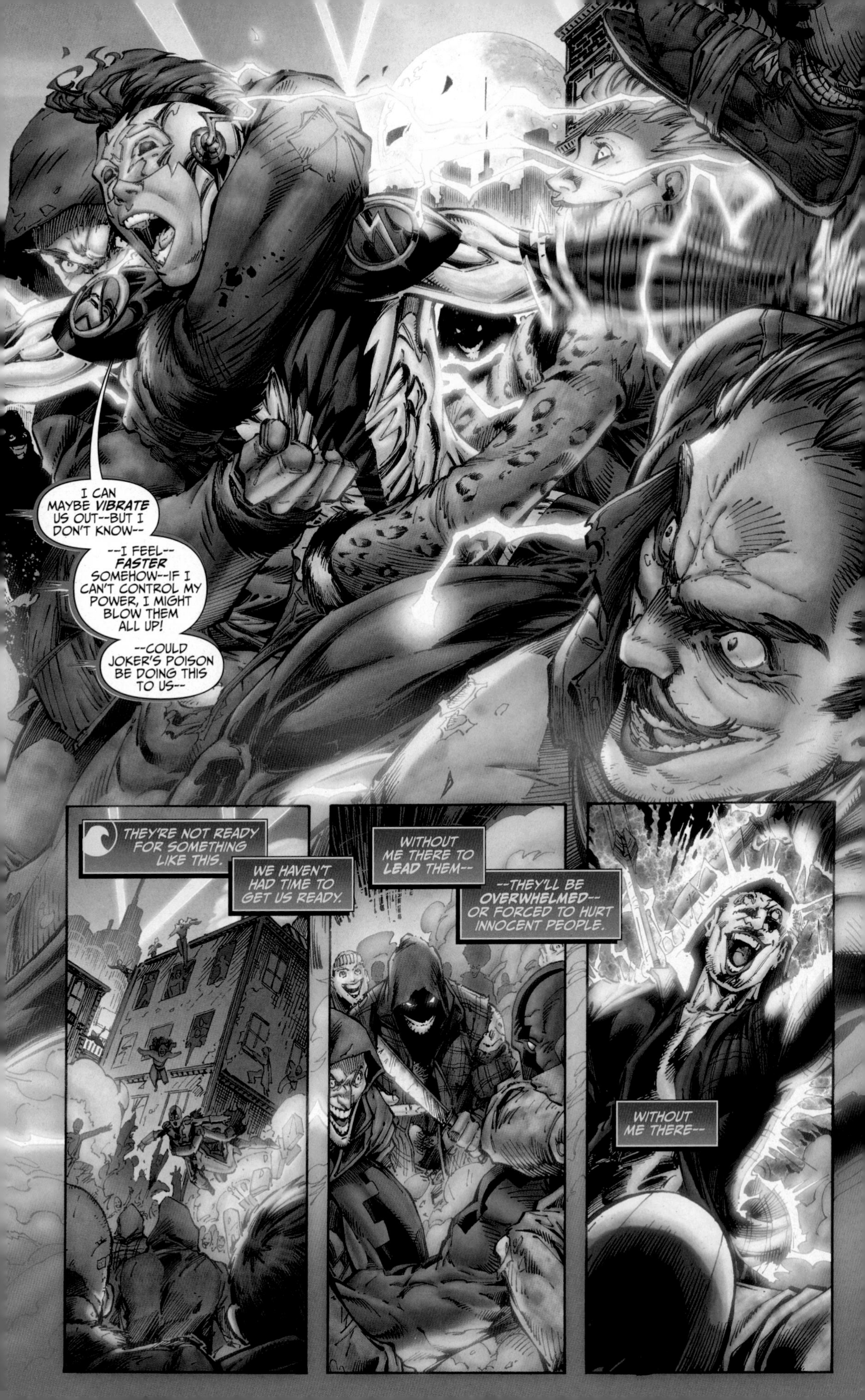
I CAN MAYBE VIBRATE US OUT--BUT I DON'T KNOW--
--I FEEL-- FASTER SOMEHOW--IF I CAN'T CONTROL MY POWER, I MIGHT BLOW THEM ALL UP!
--COULD JOKER'S POISON BE DOING THIS TO US--
THEY'RE NOT READY FOR SOMETHING LIKE THIS.
WE HAVEN'T HAD TIME TO GET US READY.
WITHOUT ME THERE TO LEAD THEM--
--THEY'LL BE OVERWHELMED-- OR FORCED TO HURT INNOCENT PEOPLE.
WITHOUT ME THERE--

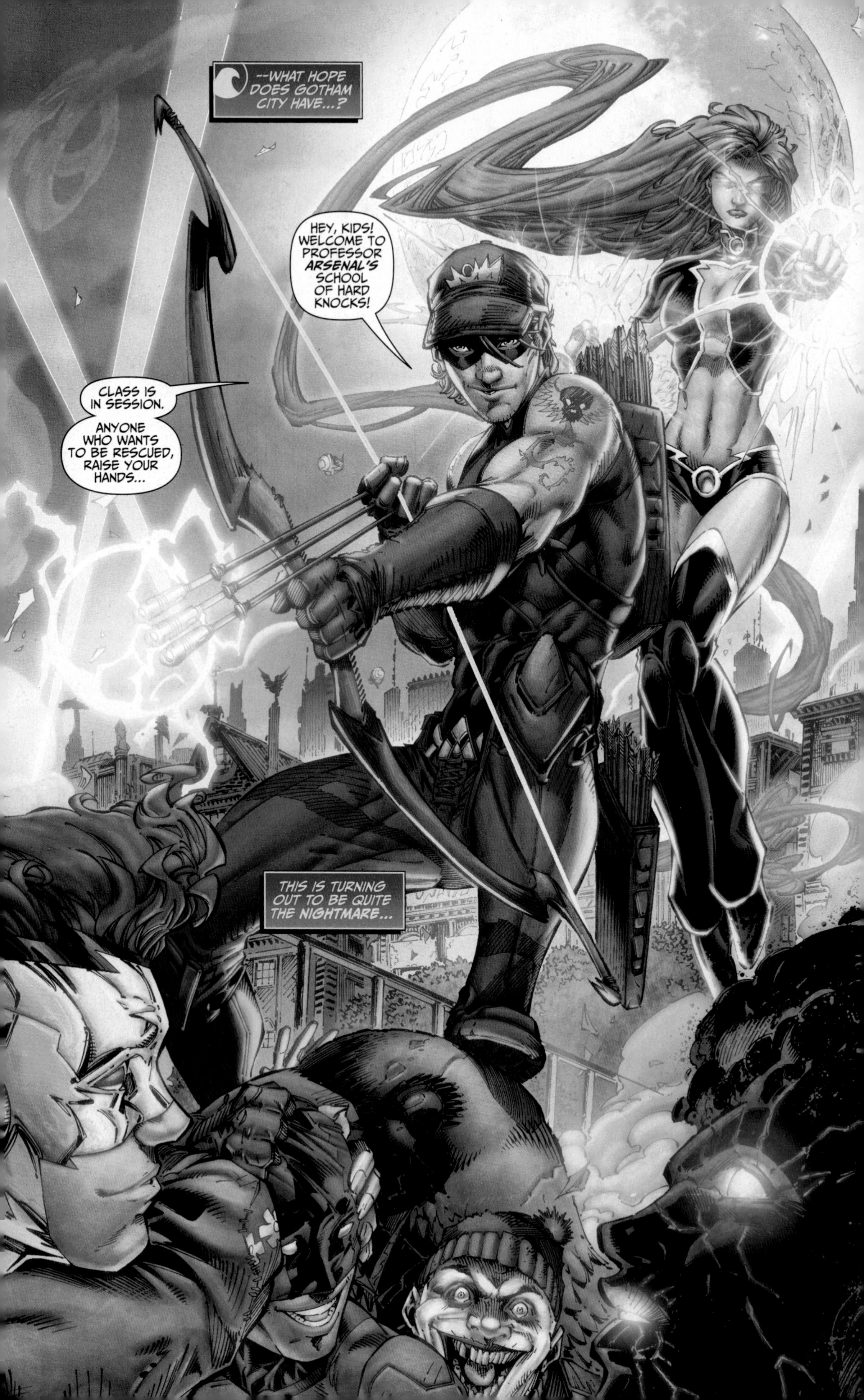
--WHAT HOPE DOES GOTHAM CITY HAVE...?
HEY, KIDS! WELCOME TO PROFESSOR ARSENAL'S SCHOOL OF HARD KNOCKS!
CLASS IS IN SESSION.
ANYONE WHO WANTS TO BE RESCUED, RAISE YOUR HANDS...
THIS IS TURNING OUT TO BE QUITE THE NIGHTMARE...

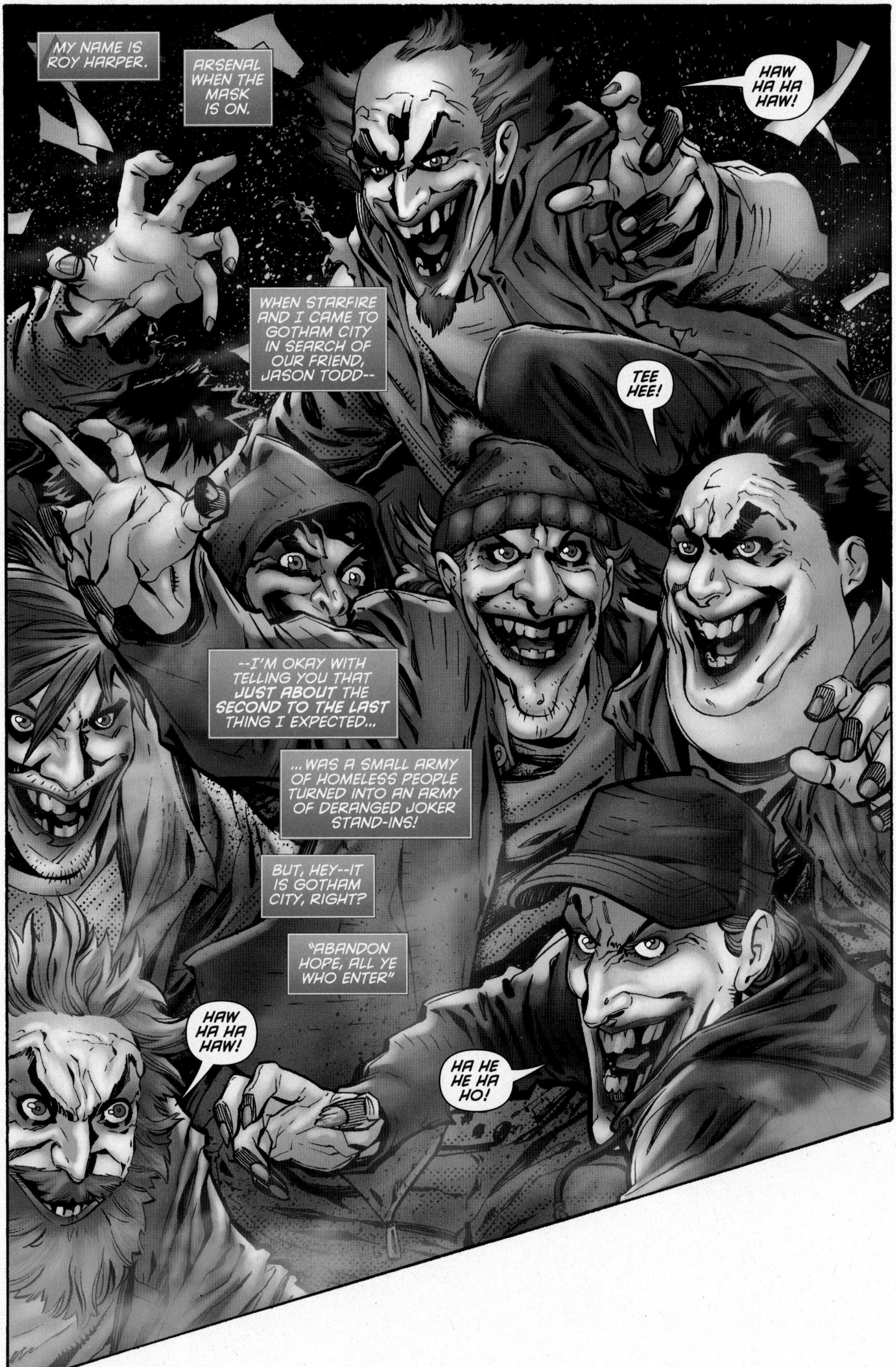

MY NAME IS ROY HARPER.
ARSENAL WHEN THE MASK IS ON.
HAW HA HA HAW!
WHEN STARFIRE AND I CAME TO GOTHAM CITY IN SEARCH OF OUR FRIEND, JASON TODD--
TEE HEE!
--I'M OKAY WITH TELLING YOU THAT JUST ABOUT THE SECOND TO THE LAST THING I EXPECTED...
...WAS A SMALL ARMY OF HOMELESS PEOPLE TURNED INTO AN ARMY OF DERANGED JOKER STAND-INS!
BUT, HEY--IT IS GOTHAM CITY, RIGHT?
"ABANDON HOPE, ALL YE WHO ENTER"
HAW HA HA HAW!
HA HE HE HA HO!

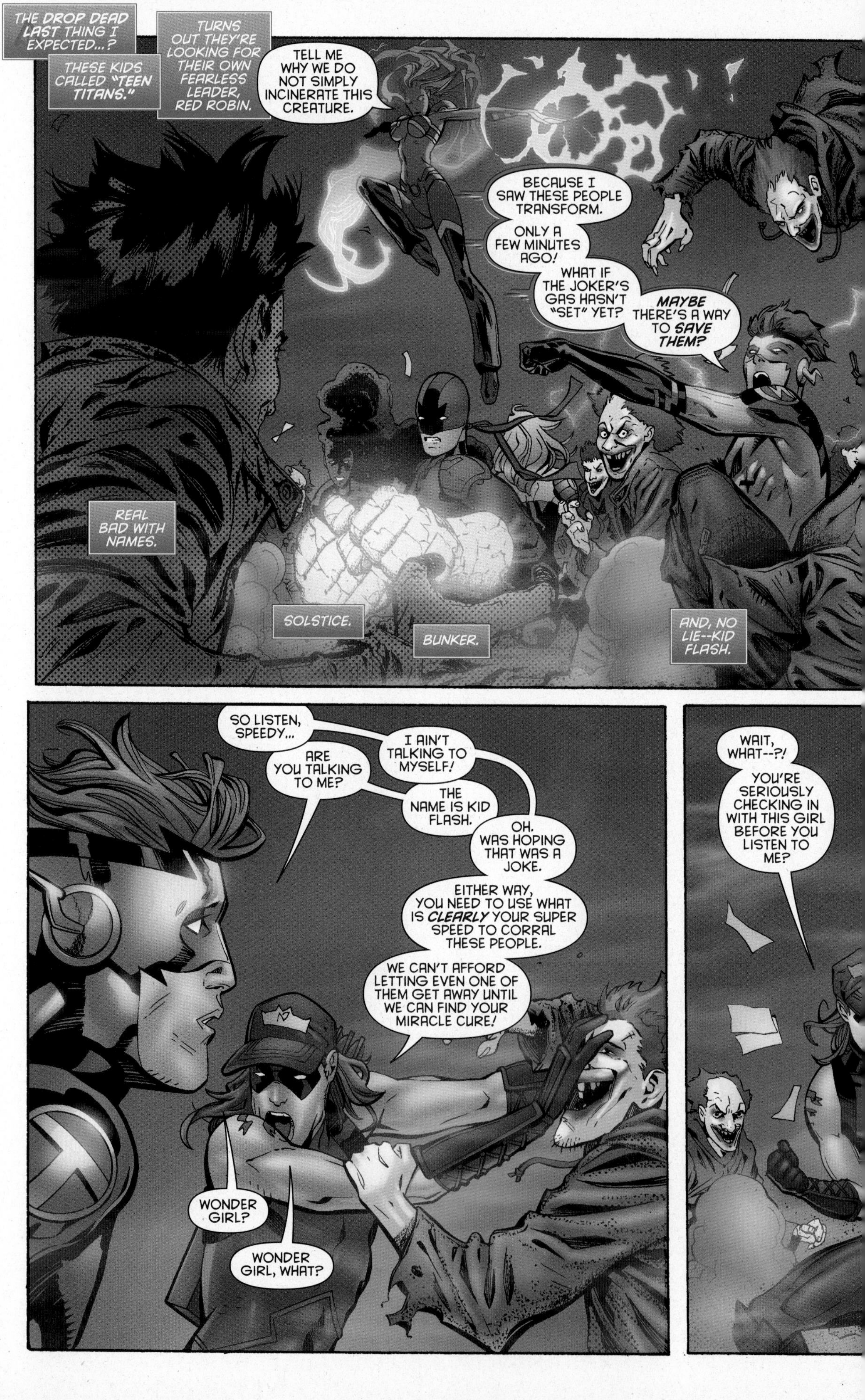
THE DROP DEAD LAST THING I EXPECTED...?
THESE KIDS CALLED "TEEN TITANS."
TURNS OUT THEY'RE LOOKING FOR THEIR OWN FEARLESS LEADER, RED ROBIN.
TELL ME WHY WE DO NOT SIMPLY INCINERATE THIS CREATURE.
BECAUSE I SAW THESE PEOPLE TRANSFORM.
ONLY A FEW MINUTES AGO!
WHAT IF THE JOKER'S GAS HASN'T "SET" YET?
MAYBE THERE'S A WAY TO SAVE THEM?
REAL BAD WITH NAMES.
SOLSTICE.
BUNKER.
AND, NO LIE--KID FLASH.
SO LISTEN, SPEEDY...
ARE YOU TALKING TO ME?
I AIN'T TALKING TO MYSELF!
THE NAME IS KID FLASH.
OH. WAS HOPING THAT WAS A JOKE.
EITHER WAY, YOU NEED TO USE WHAT IS CLEARLY YOUR SUPER SPEED TO CORRAL THESE PEOPLE.
WE CAN'T AFFORD LETTING EVEN ONE OF THEM GET AWAY UNTIL WE CAN FIND YOUR MIRACLE CURE!
WONDER GIRL?
WONDER GIRL, WHAT?
WAIT, WHAT--?!
YOU'RE SERIOUSLY CHECKING IN WITH THIS GIRL BEFORE YOU LISTEN TO ME?

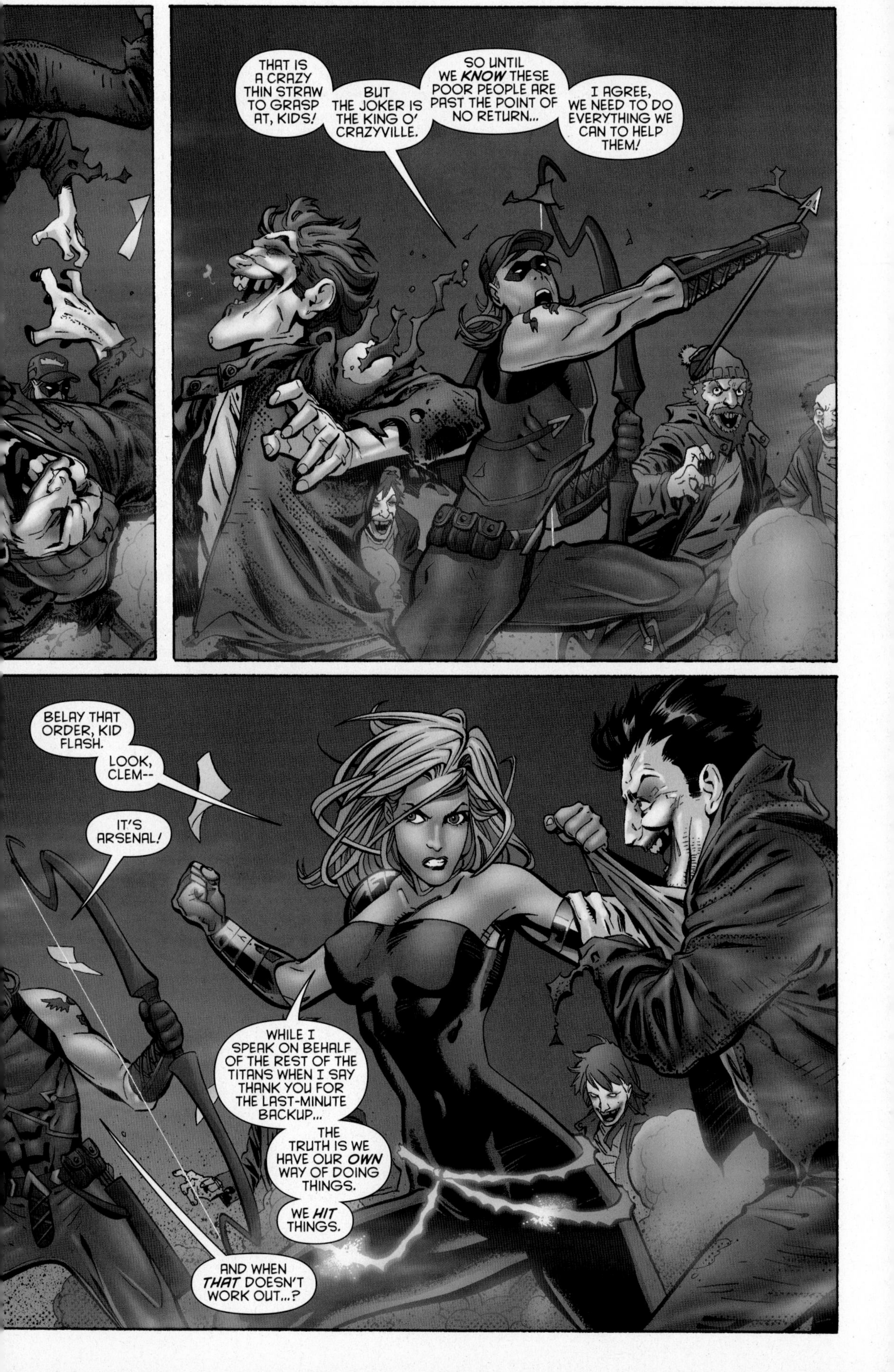
THAT IS A CRAZY THIN STRAW TO GRASP AT, KIDS!
BUT THE JOKER IS THE KING O' CRAZYVILLE.
SO UNTIL WE KNOW THESE POOR PEOPLE ARE PAST THE POINT OF NO RETURN...
I AGREE, WE NEED TO DO EVERYTHING WE CAN TO HELP THEM!
BELAY THAT ORDER, KID FLASH.
LOOK, CLEM--
IT'S ARSENAL!
WHILE I SPEAK ON BEHALF OF THE REST OF THE TITANS WHEN I SAY THANK YOU FOR THE LAST-MINUTE BACKUP...
THE TRUTH IS WE HAVE OUR OWN WAY OF DOING THINGS.
WE HIT THINGS.
AND WHEN THAT DOESN'T WORK OUT...?

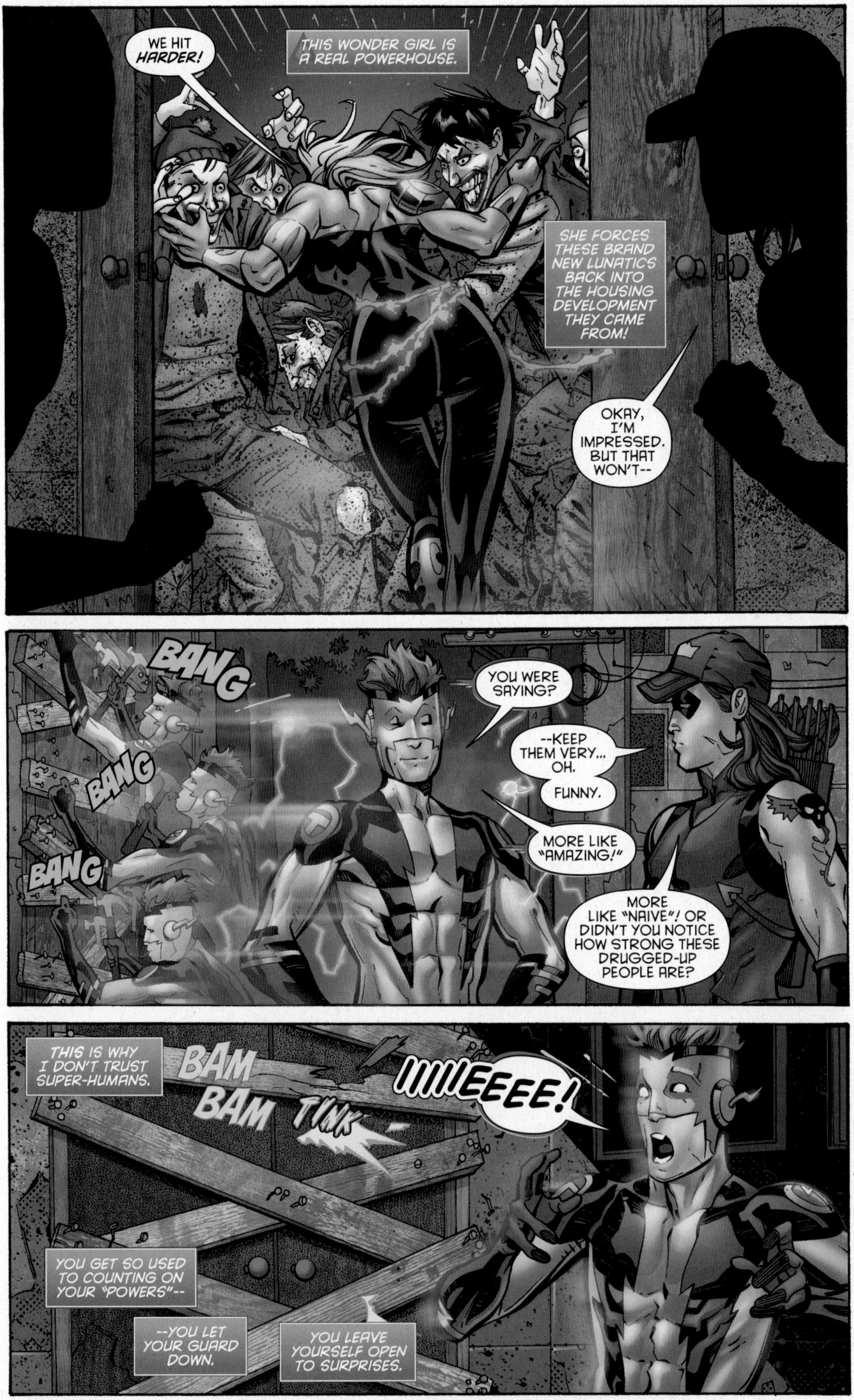
THIS WONDER GIRL IS A REAL POWERHOUSE.
WE HIT HARDER!
SHE FORCES THESE BRAND NEW LUNATICS BACK INTO THE HOUSING DEVELOPMENT THEY CAME FROM!
OKAY, I'M IMPRESSED. BUT THAT WON'T--
BANG
BANG
BANG
YOU WERE SAYING?
--KEEP THEM VERY... OH.
FUNNY.
MORE LIKE "AMAZING!"
MORE LIKE "NAIVE"! OR DIDN'T YOU NOTICE HOW STRONG THESE DRUGGED-UP PEOPLE ARE?
THIS IS WHY I DON'T TRUST SUPER-HUMANS.
BAM
BAM
TINK
IIIIIEEEEE!
YOU GET SO USED TO COUNTING ON YOUR "POWERS"--
--YOU LET YOUR GUARD DOWN.
YOU LEAVE YOURSELF OPEN TO SURPRISES.

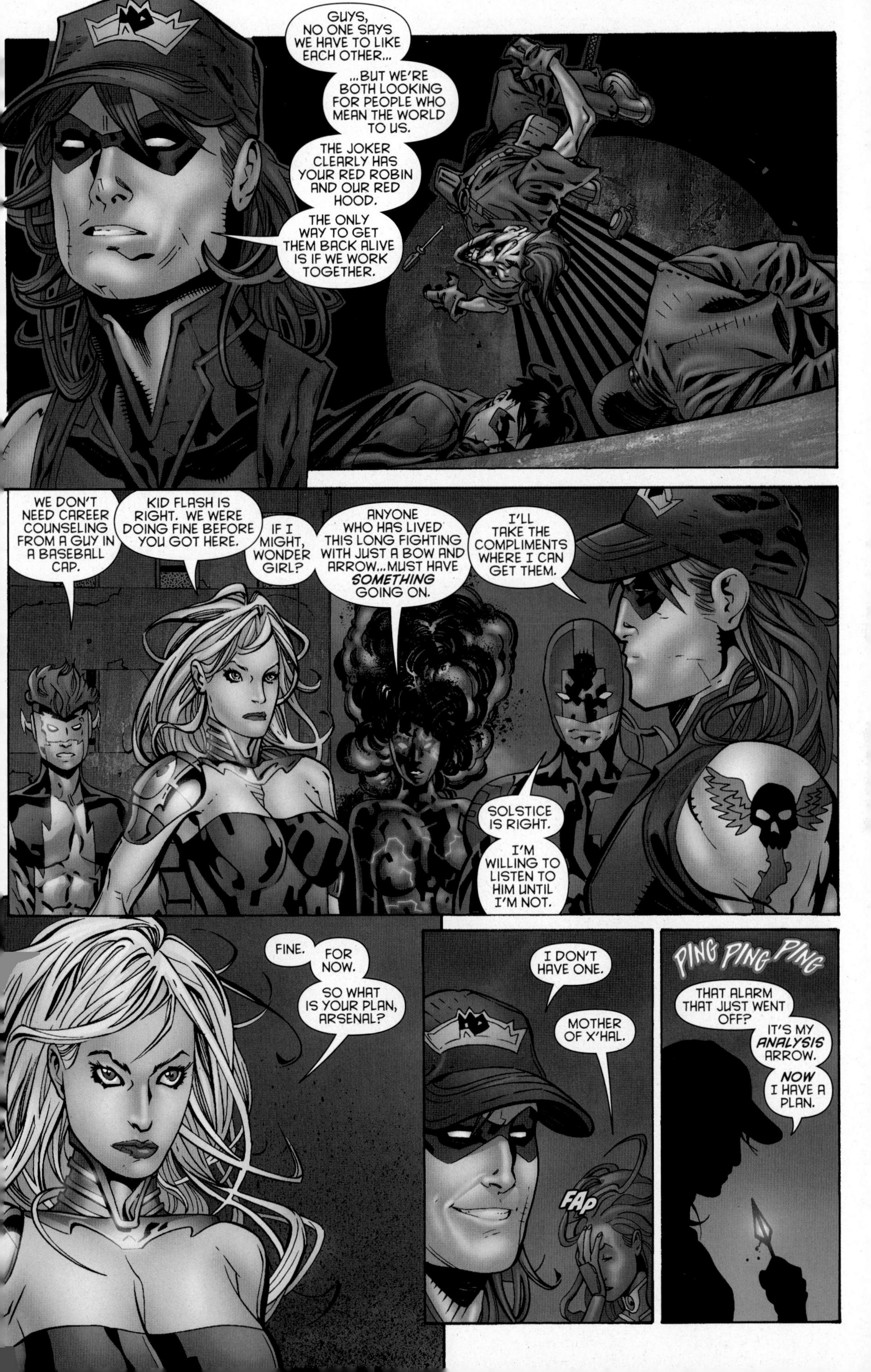
GUYS, NO ONE SAYS WE HAVE TO LIKE EACH OTHER...
...BUT WE'RE BOTH LOOKING FOR PEOPLE WHO MEAN THE WORLD TO US.
THE JOKER CLEARLY HAS YOUR RED ROBIN AND OUR RED HOOD.
THE ONLY WAY TO GET THEM BACK ALIVE IS IF WE WORK TOGETHER.
WE DON'T NEED CAREER COUNSELING FROM A GUY IN A BASEBALL CAP.
KID FLASH IS RIGHT. WE WERE DOING FINE BEFORE YOU GOT HERE.
IF I MIGHT, WONDER GIRL?
ANYONE WHO HAS LIVED THIS LONG FIGHTING WITH JUST A BOW AND ARROW...MUST HAVE SOMETHING GOING ON.
I'LL TAKE THE COMPLIMENTS WHERE I CAN GET THEM.
SOLSTICE IS RIGHT.
I'M WILLING TO LISTEN TO HIM UNTIL I'M NOT.
FINE.
FOR NOW.
SO WHAT IS YOUR PLAN, ARSENAL?
I DON'T HAVE ONE.
MOTHER OF X'HAL.
FAP
PING PING PING
THAT ALARM THAT JUST WENT OFF?
IT'S MY ANALYSIS ARROW.
NOW I HAVE A PLAN.

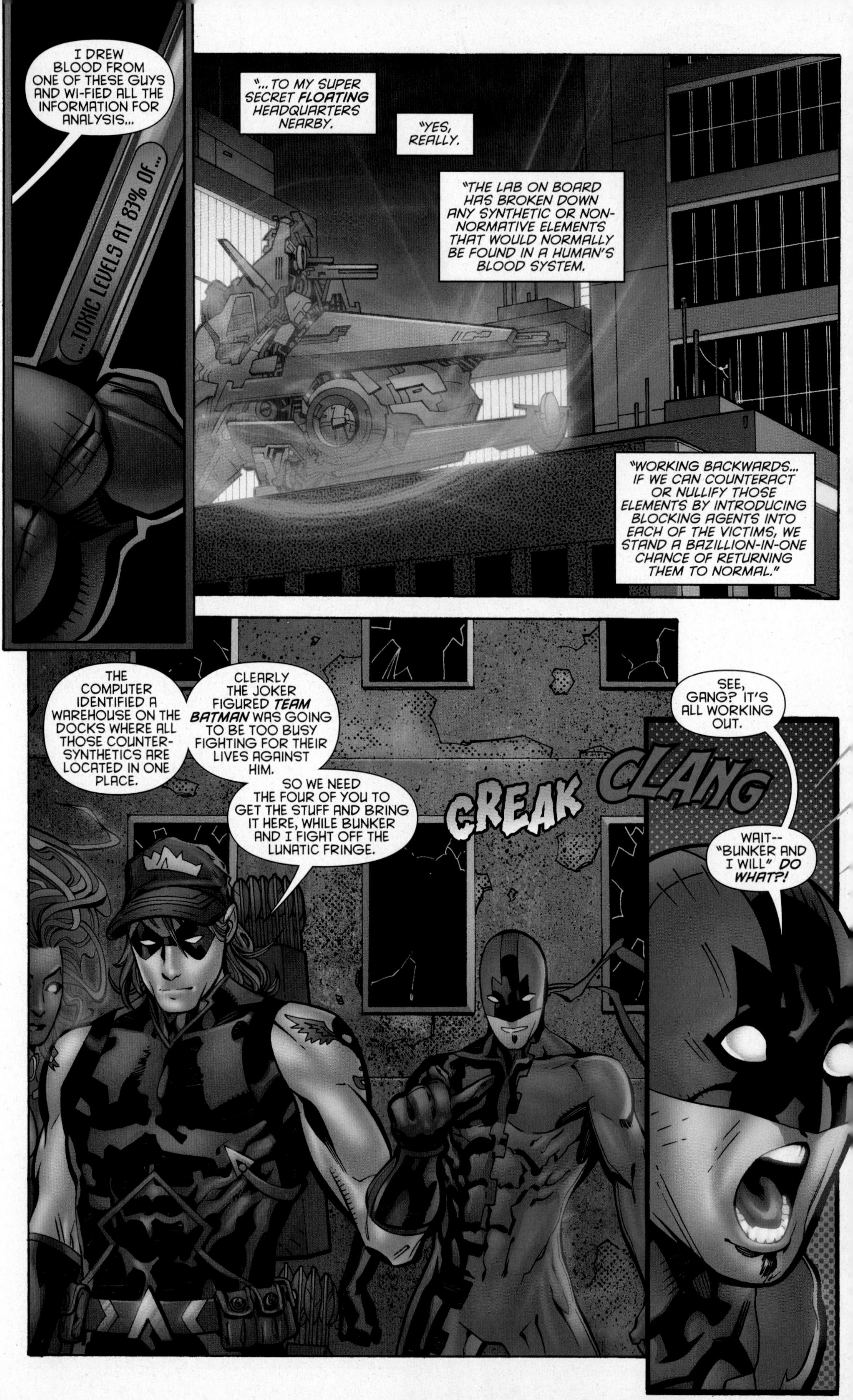
I DREW BLOOD FROM ONE OF THESE GUYS AND WI-FIED ALL THE INFORMATION FOR ANALYSIS...
...TOXIC LEVELS AT 83% OF...
"...TO MY SUPER SECRET FLOATING HEADQUARTERS NEARBY.
"YES, REALLY.
"THE LAB ON BOARD HAS BROKEN DOWN ANY SYNTHETIC OR NON-NORMATIVE ELEMENTS THAT WOULD NORMALLY BE FOUND IN A HUMAN'S BLOOD SYSTEM.
"WORKING BACKWARDS... IF WE CAN COUNTERACT OR NULLIFY THOSE ELEMENTS BY INTRODUCING BLOCKING AGENTS INTO EACH OF THE VICTIMS, WE STAND A BAZILLION-IN-ONE CHANCE OF RETURNING THEM TO NORMAL."
THE COMPUTER IDENTIFIED A WAREHOUSE ON THE DOCKS WHERE ALL THOSE COUNTER-SYNTHETICS ARE LOCATED IN ONE PLACE.
CLEARLY THE JOKER FIGURED TEAM BATMAN WAS GOING TO BE TOO BUSY FIGHTING FOR THEIR LIVES AGAINST HIM.
SO WE NEED THE FOUR OF YOU TO GET THE STUFF AND BRING IT HERE, WHILE BUNKER AND I FIGHT OFF THE LUNATIC FRINGE.
CREAK
CLANG
SEE, GANG? IT'S ALL WORKING OUT.
WAIT-- "BUNKER AND I WILL" DO WHAT?!

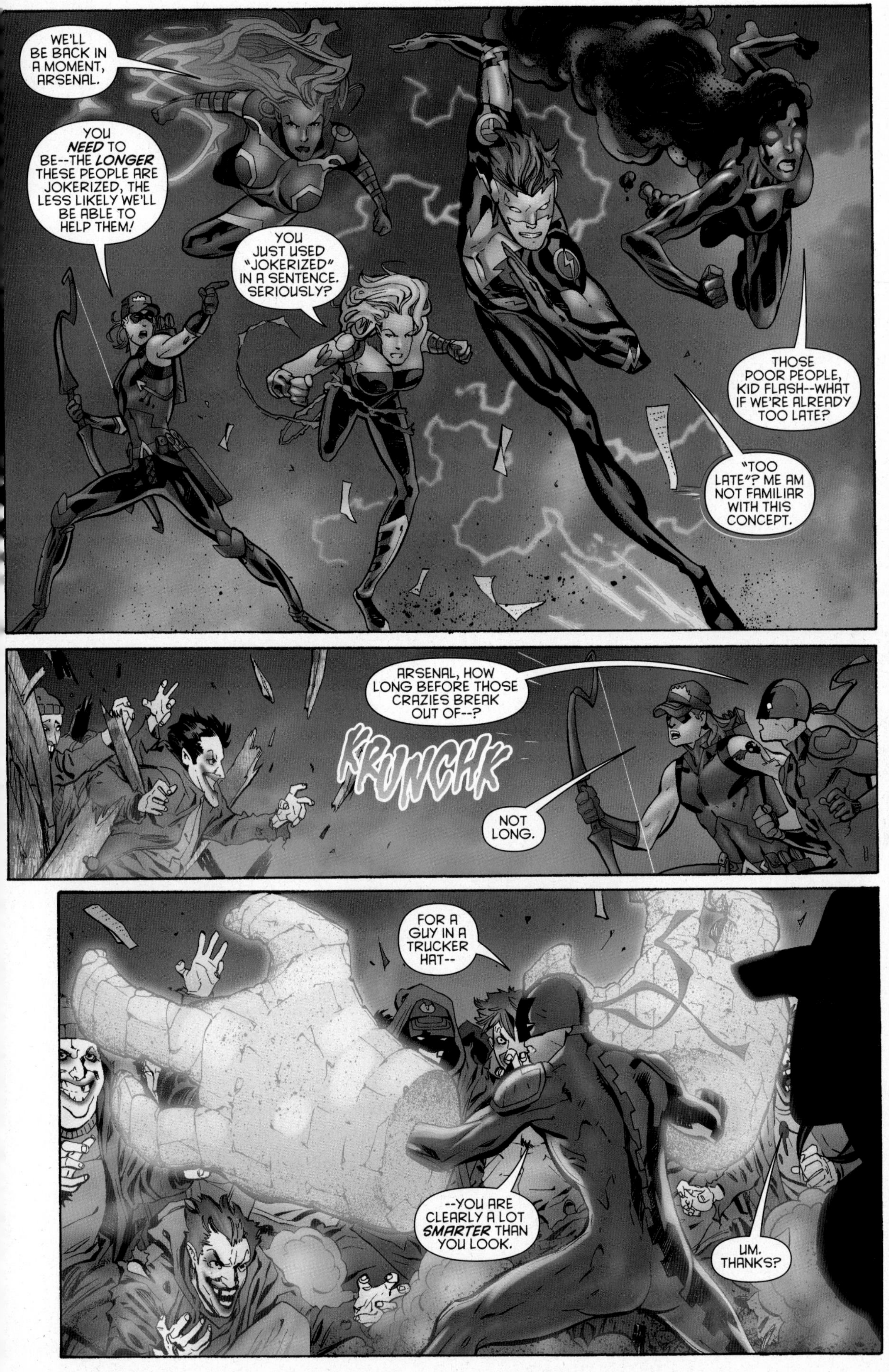
WE'LL BE BACK IN A MOMENT, ARSENAL.
YOU NEED TO BE--THE LONGER THESE PEOPLE ARE JOKERIZED, THE LESS LIKELY WE'LL BE ABLE TO HELP THEM!
YOU JUST USED "JOKERIZED" IN A SENTENCE. SERIOUSLY?
THOSE POOR PEOPLE, KID FLASH--WHAT IF WE'RE ALREADY TOO LATE?
"TOO LATE"? ME AM NOT FAMILIAR WITH THIS CONCEPT.
ARSENAL, HOW LONG BEFORE THOSE CRAZIES BREAK OUT OF--?
KRUNCHK
NOT LONG.
FOR A GUY IN A TRUCKER HAT--
--YOU ARE CLEARLY A LOT SMARTER THAN YOU LOOK.
UM. THANKS?

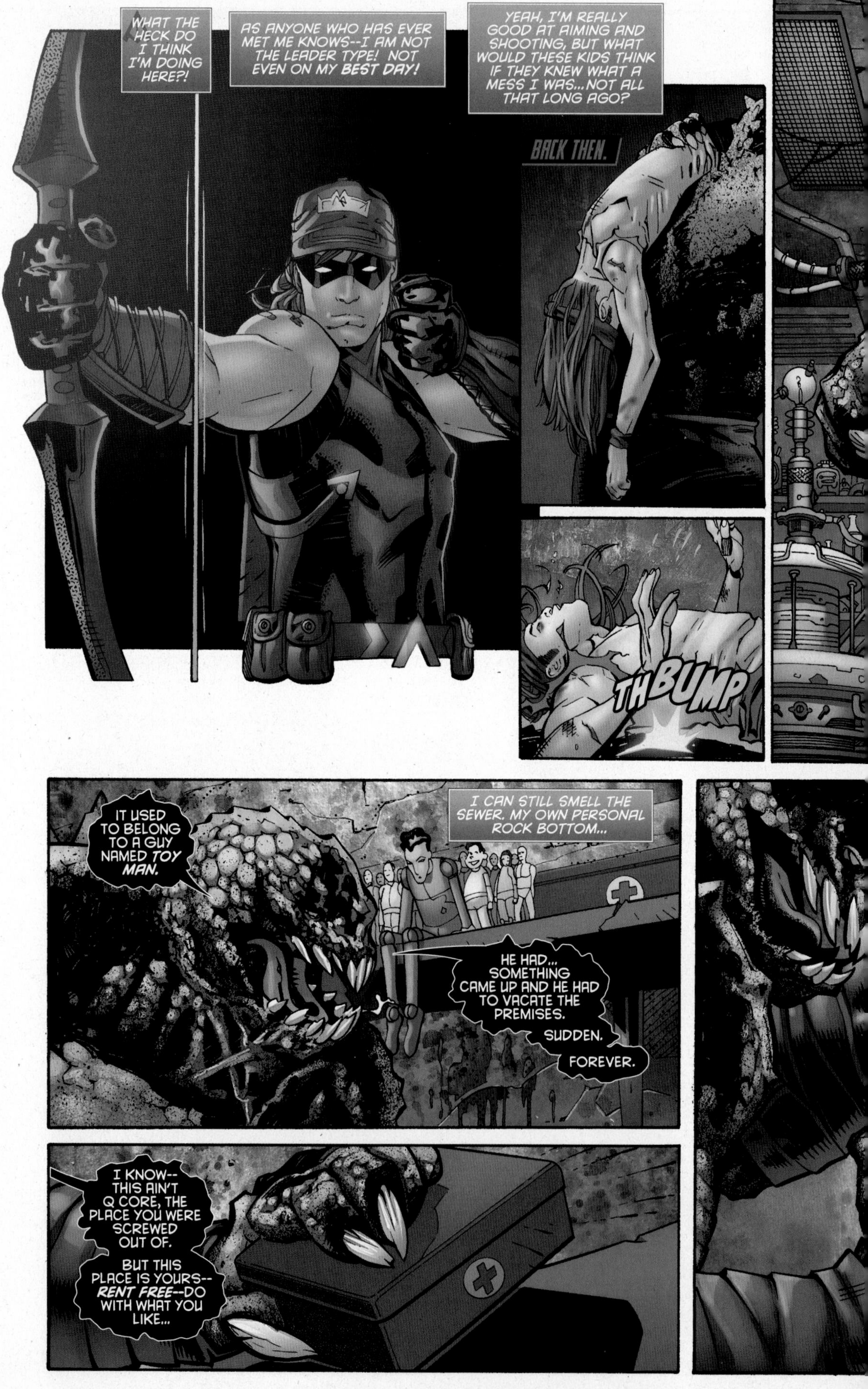

WHAT THE HECK DO I THINK I'M DOING HERE?!
AS ANYONE WHO HAS EVER MET ME KNOWS--I AM NOT THE LEADER TYPE! NOT EVEN ON MY BEST DAY!
YEAH, I'M REALLY GOOD AT AIMING AND SHOOTING, BUT WHAT WOULD THESE KIDS THINK IF THEY KNEW WHAT A MESS I WAS...NOT ALL THAT LONG AGO?
BACK THEN.
THBUMP
I CAN STILL SMELL THE SEWER. MY OWN PERSONAL ROCK BOTTOM...
IT USED TO BELONG TO A GUY NAMED TOY MAN.
HE HAD... SOMETHING CAME UP AND HE HAD TO VACATE THE PREMISES.
SUDDEN.
FOREVER.
I KNOW--THIS AIN'T Q CORE, THE PLACE YOU WERE SCREWED OUT OF.
BUT THIS PLACE IS YOURS--RENT FREE--DO WITH WHAT YOU LIKE...

HOLY SPIT--WHAT THE *HELL* IS THIS *PLACE?!*

...SO LONG AS YOU STAY IN THE PROGRAM.

"THE PROG--" YOU MEAN, A.A.?

SERIOUSLY? KILLER CROC IS BADGERING ME INTO GOING TO A.A.?

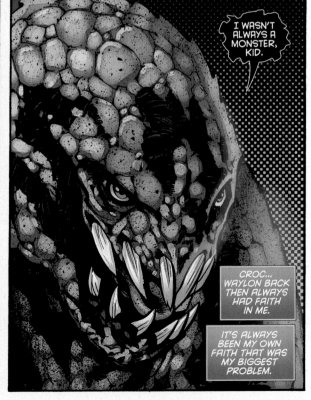

I WASN'T ALWAYS A MONSTER, KID.

CROC... WAYLON BACK THEN ALWAYS HAD FAITH IN ME.

IT'S ALWAYS BEEN MY OWN FAITH THAT WAS MY BIGGEST PROBLEM.

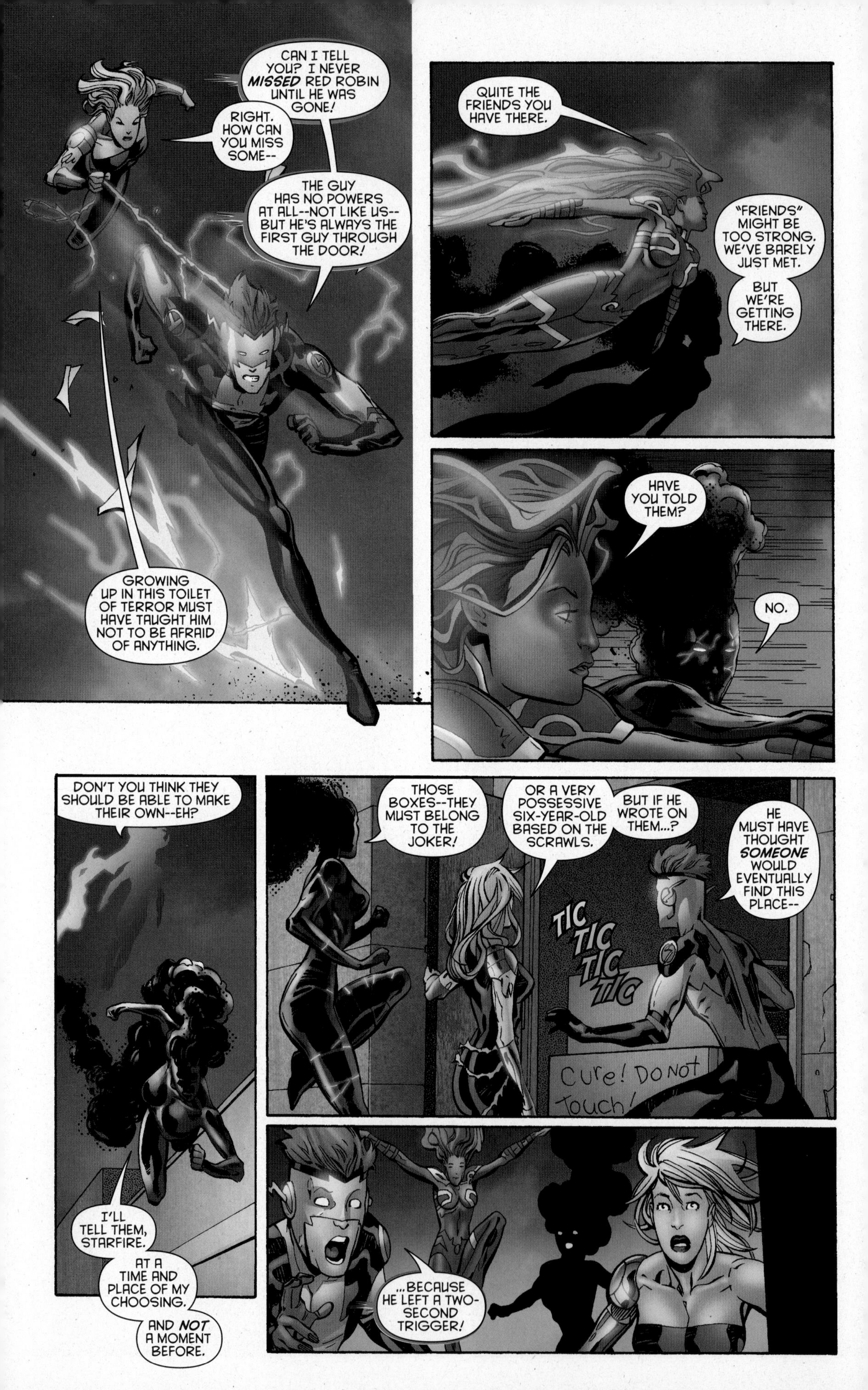

CAN I TELL YOU? I NEVER MISSED RED ROBIN UNTIL HE WAS GONE!
RIGHT. HOW CAN YOU MISS SOME--
THE GUY HAS NO POWERS AT ALL--NOT LIKE US--BUT HE'S ALWAYS THE FIRST GUY THROUGH THE DOOR!
GROWING UP IN THIS TOILET OF TERROR MUST HAVE TAUGHT HIM NOT TO BE AFRAID OF ANYTHING.
QUITE THE FRIENDS YOU HAVE THERE.
"FRIENDS" MIGHT BE TOO STRONG. WE'VE BARELY JUST MET.
BUT WE'RE GETTING THERE.
HAVE YOU TOLD THEM?
NO.
DON'T YOU THINK THEY SHOULD BE ABLE TO MAKE THEIR OWN--EH?
I'LL TELL THEM, STARFIRE.
AT A TIME AND PLACE OF MY CHOOSING.
AND NOT A MOMENT BEFORE.
THOSE BOXES--THEY MUST BELONG TO THE JOKER!
OR A VERY POSSESSIVE SIX-YEAR-OLD BASED ON THE SCRAWLS.
BUT IF HE WROTE ON THEM...?
HE MUST HAVE THOUGHT SOMEONE WOULD EVENTUALLY FIND THIS PLACE--
TIC TIC TIC TIC
Cure! Do not Touch!
...BECAUSE HE LEFT A TWO-SECOND TRIGGER!

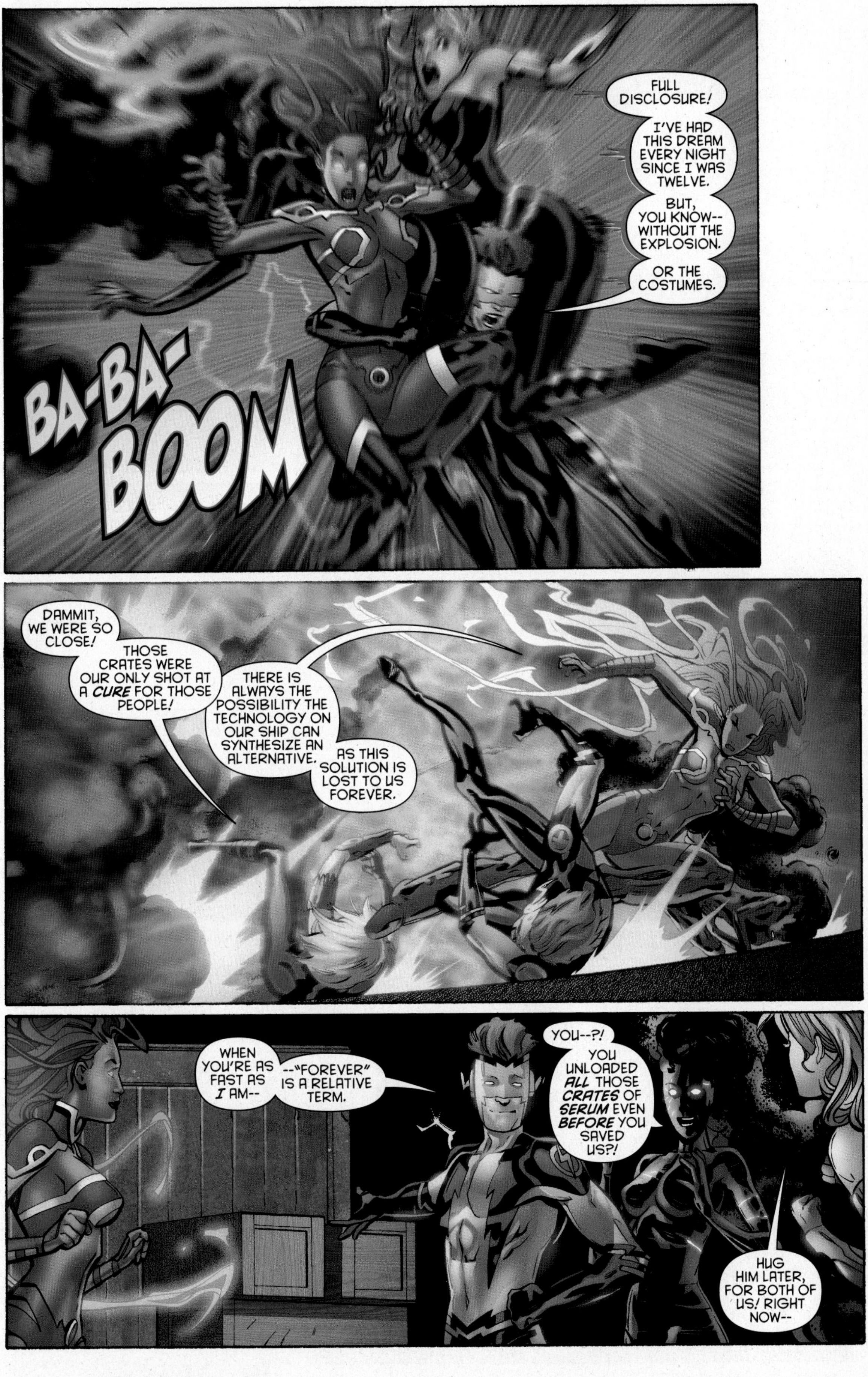
FULL DISCLOSURE!
I'VE HAD THIS DREAM EVERY NIGHT SINCE I WAS TWELVE.
BUT, YOU KNOW-- WITHOUT THE EXPLOSION.
OR THE COSTUMES.
BA-BA-BOOM
DAMMIT, WE WERE SO CLOSE!
THOSE CRATES WERE OUR ONLY SHOT AT A CURE FOR THOSE PEOPLE!
THERE IS ALWAYS THE POSSIBILITY THE TECHNOLOGY ON OUR SHIP CAN SYNTHESIZE AN ALTERNATIVE.
AS THIS SOLUTION IS LOST TO US FOREVER.
WHEN YOU'RE AS FAST AS I AM--
--"FOREVER" IS A RELATIVE TERM.
YOU--?!
YOU UNLOADED ALL THOSE CRATES OF SERUM EVEN BEFORE YOU SAVED US?!
HUG HIM LATER, FOR BOTH OF US! RIGHT NOW--

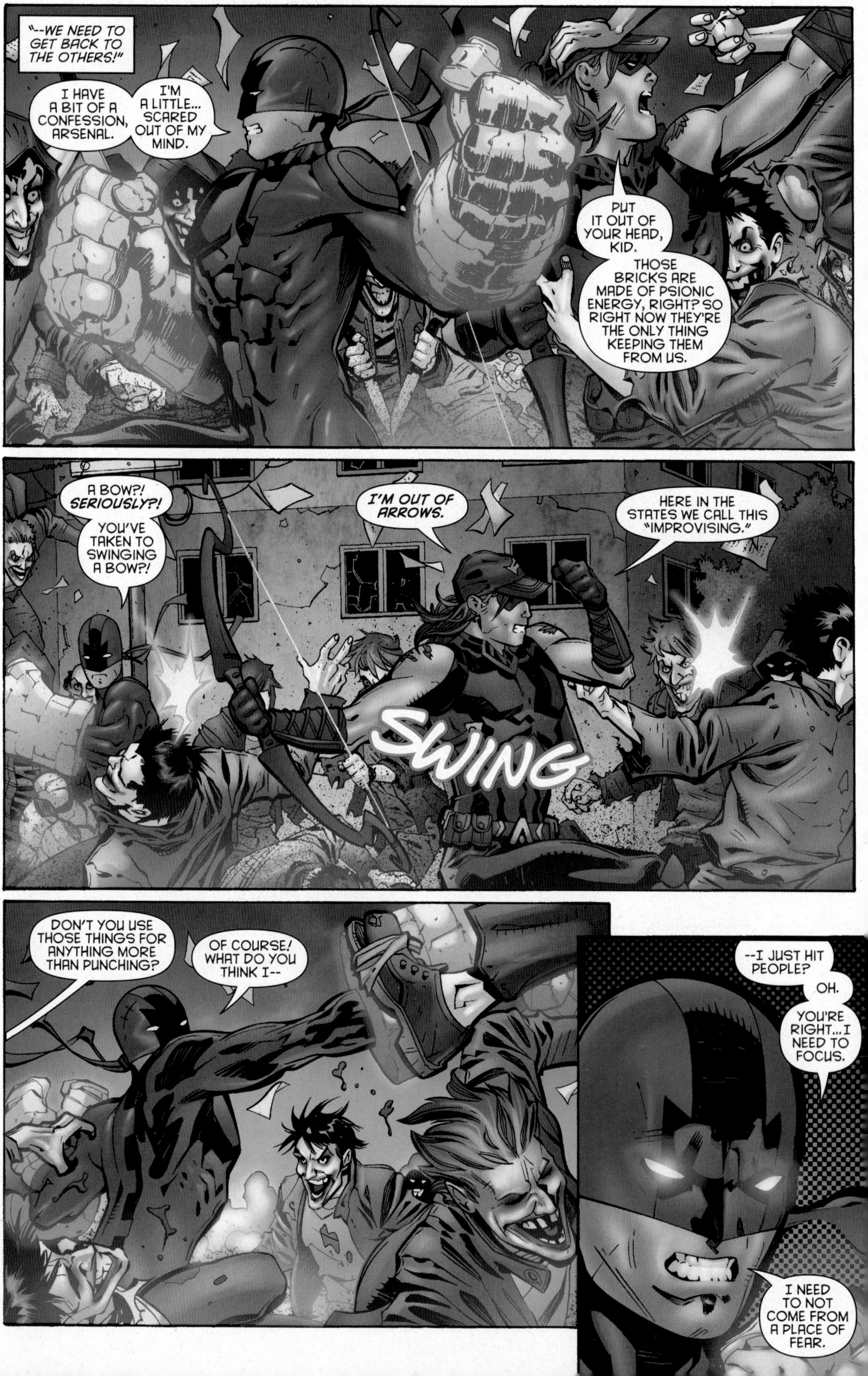
"--WE NEED TO GET BACK TO THE OTHERS!"
I HAVE A BIT OF A CONFESSION, ARSENAL.
I'M A LITTLE... SCARED OUT OF MY MIND.
PUT IT OUT OF YOUR HEAD, KID.
THOSE BRICKS ARE MADE OF PSIONIC ENERGY, RIGHT? SO RIGHT NOW THEY'RE THE ONLY THING KEEPING THEM FROM US.
A BOW?! SERIOUSLY?!
YOU'VE TAKEN TO SWINGING A BOW?!
I'M OUT OF ARROWS.
HERE IN THE STATES WE CALL THIS "IMPROVISING."
SWING
DON'T YOU USE THOSE THINGS FOR ANYTHING MORE THAN PUNCHING?
OF COURSE! WHAT DO YOU THINK I--
--I JUST HIT PEOPLE?
OH.
YOU'RE RIGHT...I NEED TO FOCUS.
I NEED TO NOT COME FROM A PLACE OF FEAR.

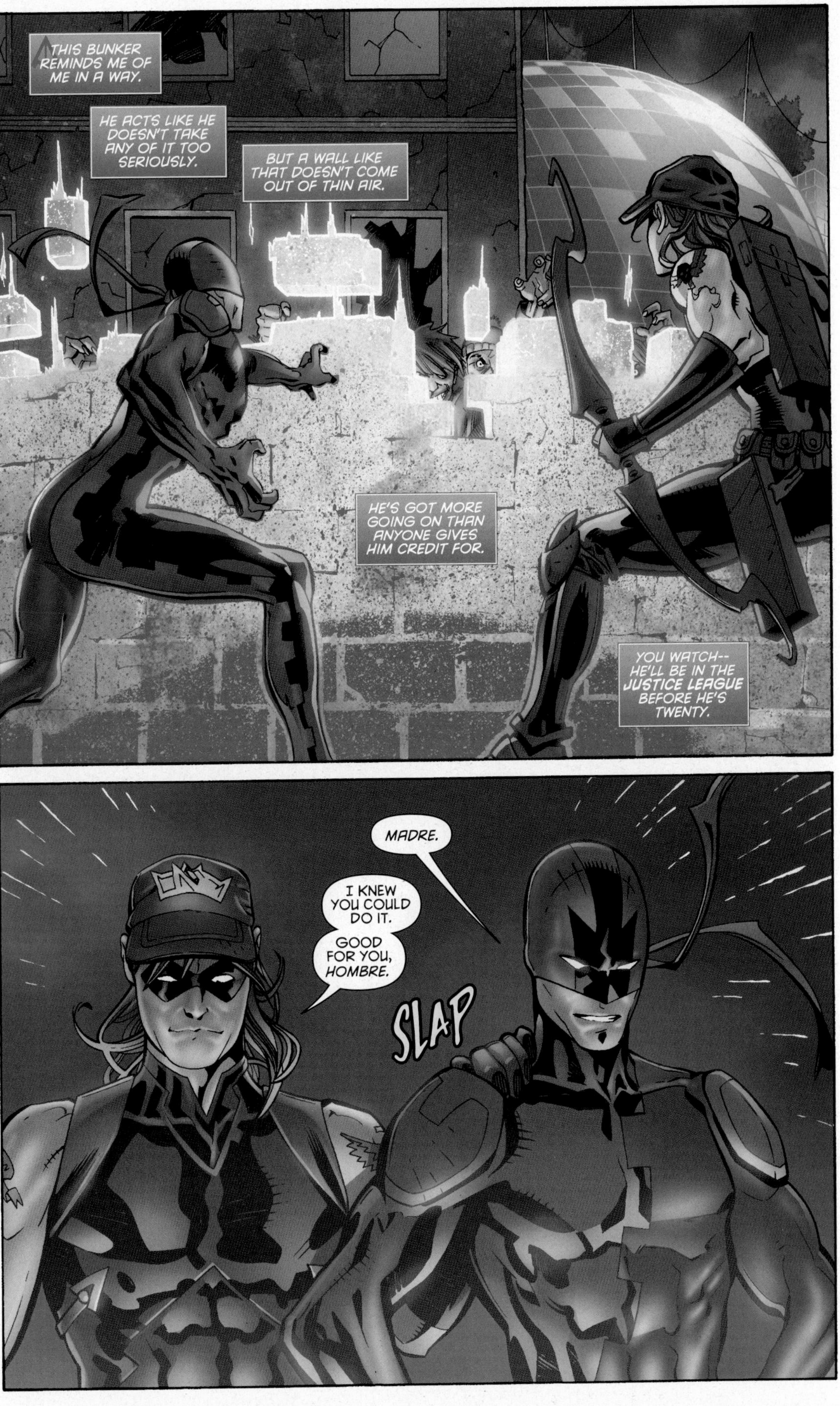
THIS BUNKER REMINDS ME OF ME IN A WAY.
HE ACTS LIKE HE DOESN'T TAKE ANY OF IT TOO SERIOUSLY.
BUT A WALL LIKE THAT DOESN'T COME OUT OF THIN AIR.
HE'S GOT MORE GOING ON THAN ANYONE GIVES HIM CREDIT FOR.
YOU WATCH-- HE'LL BE IN THE JUSTICE LEAGUE BEFORE HE'S TWENTY.
MADRE.
I KNEW YOU COULD DO IT.
GOOD FOR YOU, HOMBRE.
SLAP

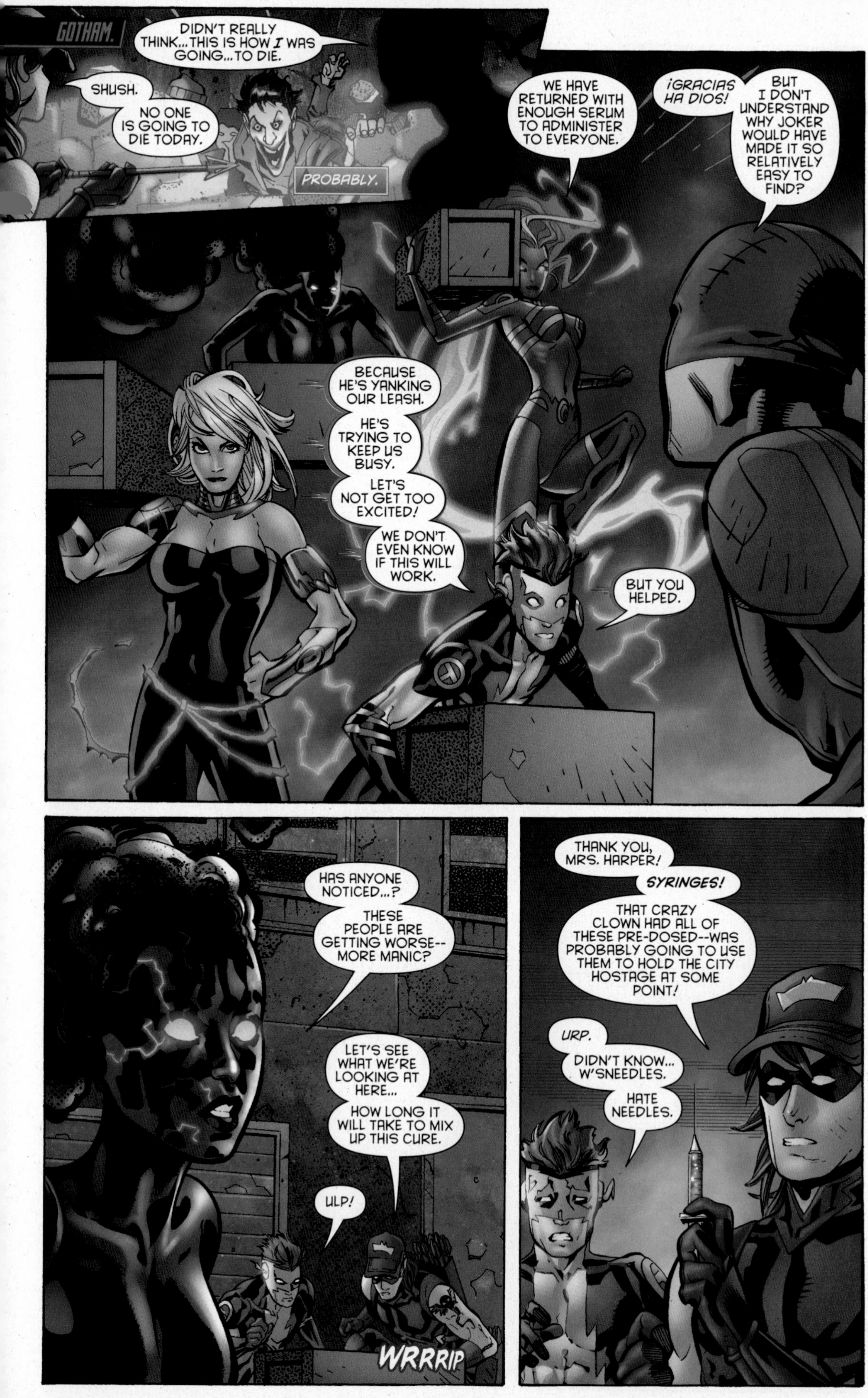
GOTHAM.
DIDN'T REALLY THINK...THIS IS HOW I WAS GOING...TO DIE.
SHUSH.
NO ONE IS GOING TO DIE TODAY.
PROBABLY.
WE HAVE RETURNED WITH ENOUGH SERUM TO ADMINISTER TO EVERYONE.
¡GRACIAS HA DIOS!
BUT I DON'T UNDERSTAND WHY JOKER WOULD HAVE MADE IT SO RELATIVELY EASY TO FIND?
BECAUSE HE'S YANKING OUR LEASH.
HE'S TRYING TO KEEP US BUSY.
LET'S NOT GET TOO EXCITED!
WE DON'T EVEN KNOW IF THIS WILL WORK.
BUT YOU HELPED.
HAS ANYONE NOTICED...?
THESE PEOPLE ARE GETTING WORSE--MORE MANIC?
LET'S SEE WHAT WE'RE LOOKING AT HERE...
HOW LONG IT WILL TAKE TO MIX UP THIS CURE.
ULP!
WRRRIP
THANK YOU, MRS. HARPER!
SYRINGES!
THAT CRAZY CLOWN HAD ALL OF THESE PRE-DOSED--WAS PROBABLY GOING TO USE THEM TO HOLD THE CITY HOSTAGE AT SOME POINT!
URP.
DIDN'T KNOW... W'SNEEDLES.
HATE NEEDLES.

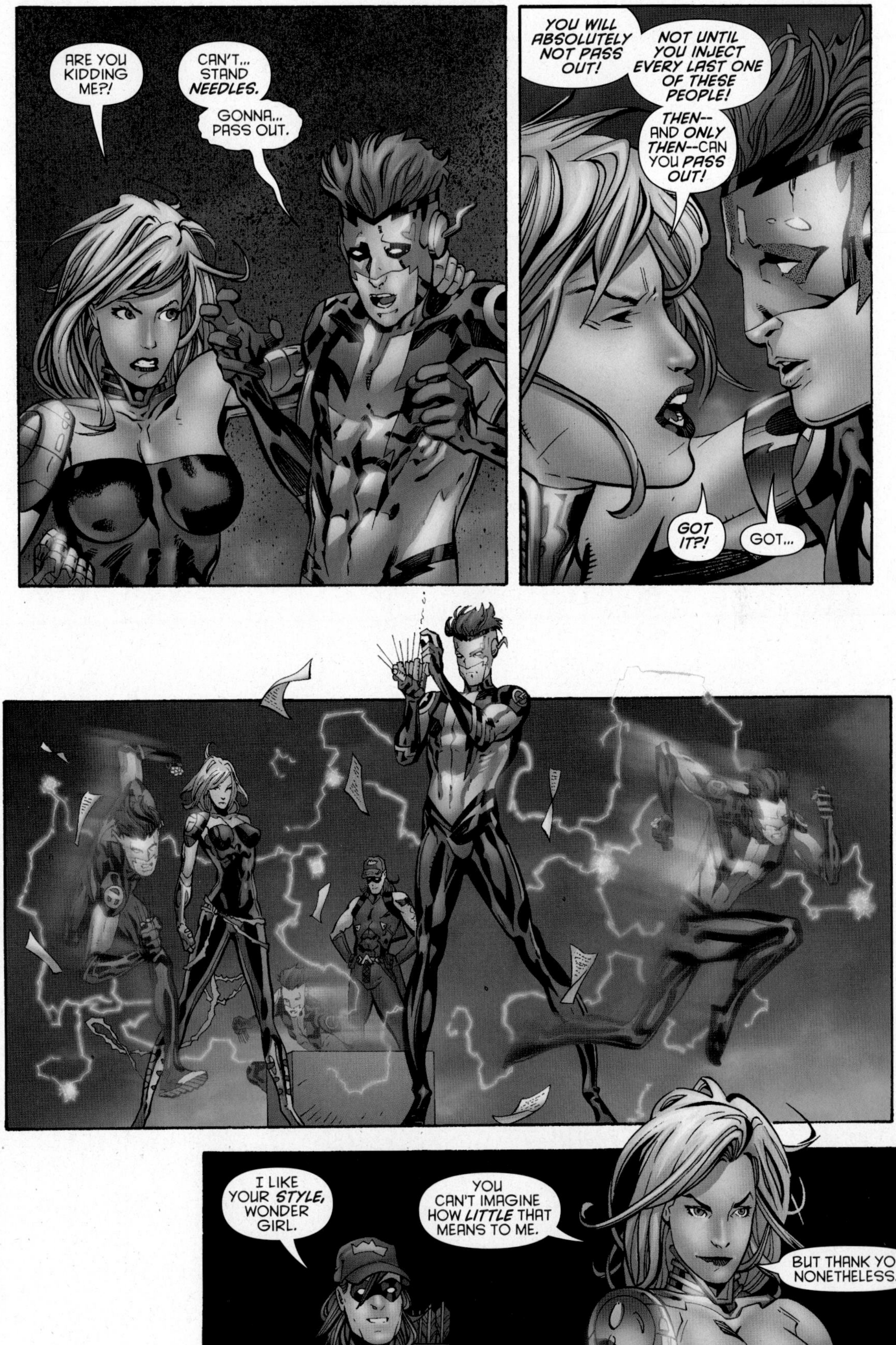
ARE YOU KIDDING ME?!
CAN'T... STAND NEEDLES.
GONNA... PASS OUT.
YOU WILL ABSOLUTELY NOT PASS OUT!
NOT UNTIL YOU INJECT EVERY LAST ONE OF THESE PEOPLE!
THEN-- AND ONLY THEN--CAN YOU PASS OUT!
GOT IT?!
GOT...
I LIKE YOUR STYLE, WONDER GIRL.
YOU CAN'T IMAGINE HOW LITTLE THAT MEANS TO ME.
BUT THANK YOU NONETHELESS.

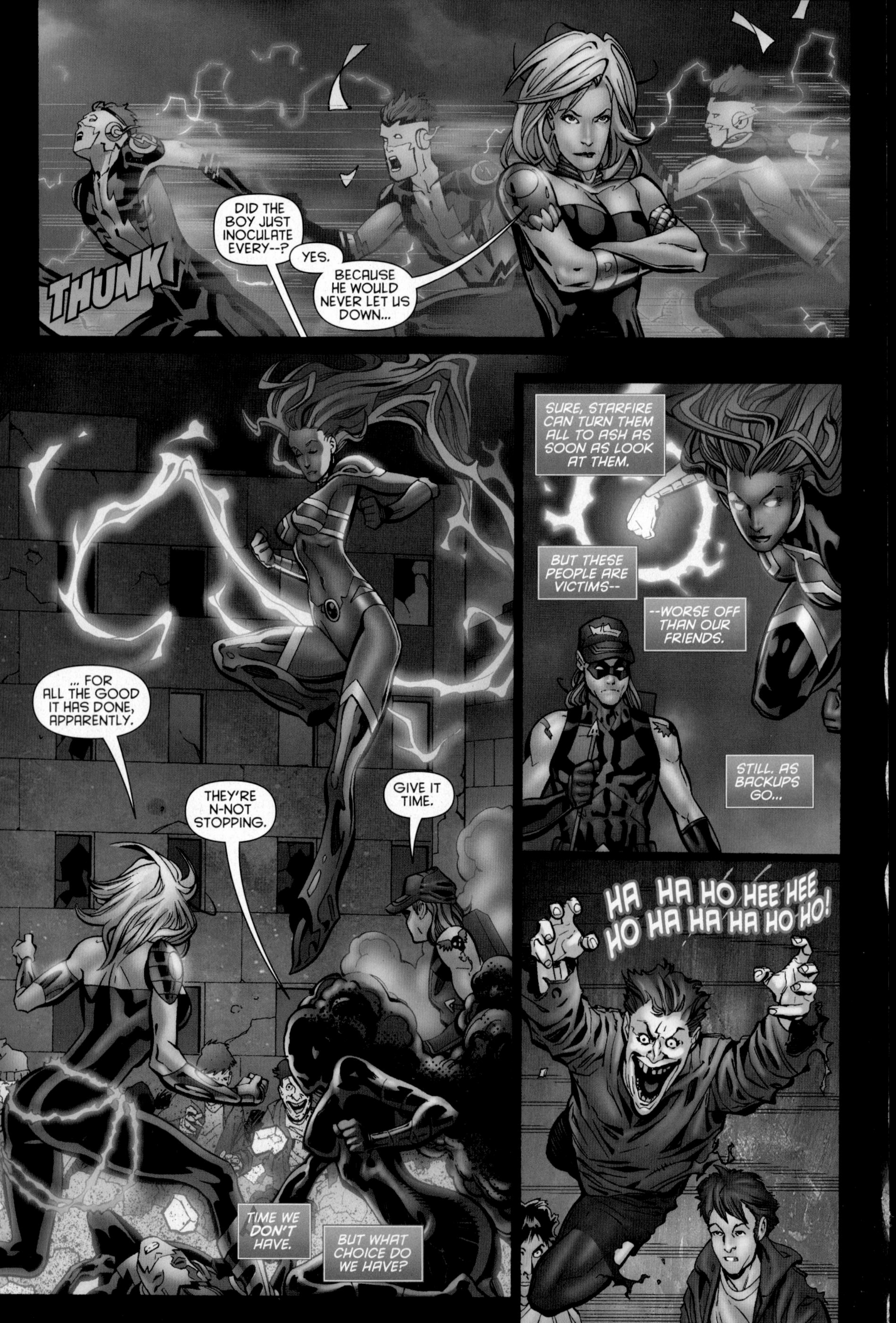
THUNK
DID THE BOY JUST INOCULATE EVERY--?
YES.
BECAUSE HE WOULD NEVER LET US DOWN...
... FOR ALL THE GOOD IT HAS DONE, APPARENTLY.
THEY'RE N-NOT STOPPING.
GIVE IT TIME.
TIME WE DON'T HAVE.
BUT WHAT CHOICE DO WE HAVE?
SURE, STARFIRE CAN TURN THEM ALL TO ASH AS SOON AS LOOK AT THEM.
BUT THESE PEOPLE ARE VICTIMS--
--WORSE OFF THAN OUR FRIENDS.
STILL. AS BACKUPS GO...
HA HA HO HEE HEE HO HA HA HA HO HO!

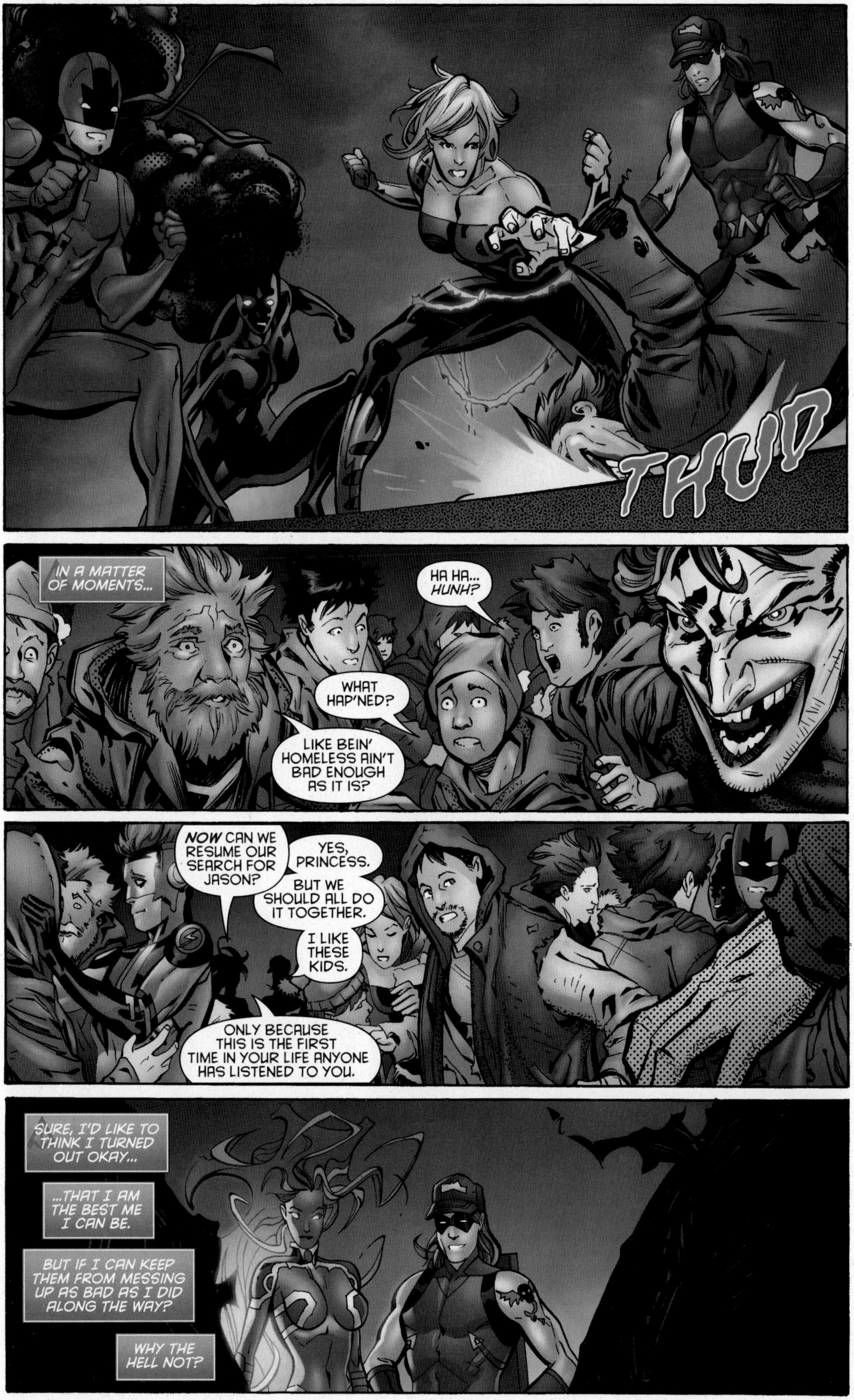
THUD
IN A MATTER OF MOMENTS...
HA HA... HUNH?
WHAT HAP'NED?
LIKE BEIN' HOMELESS AIN'T BAD ENOUGH AS IT IS?
NOW CAN WE RESUME OUR SEARCH FOR JASON?
YES, PRINCESS.
BUT WE SHOULD ALL DO IT TOGETHER.
I LIKE THESE KIDS.
ONLY BECAUSE THIS IS THE FIRST TIME IN YOUR LIFE ANYONE HAS LISTENED TO YOU.
SURE, I'D LIKE TO THINK I TURNED OUT OKAY...
...THAT I AM THE BEST ME I CAN BE.
BUT IF I CAN KEEP THEM FROM MESSING UP AS BAD AS I DID ALONG THE WAY?
WHY THE HELL NOT?

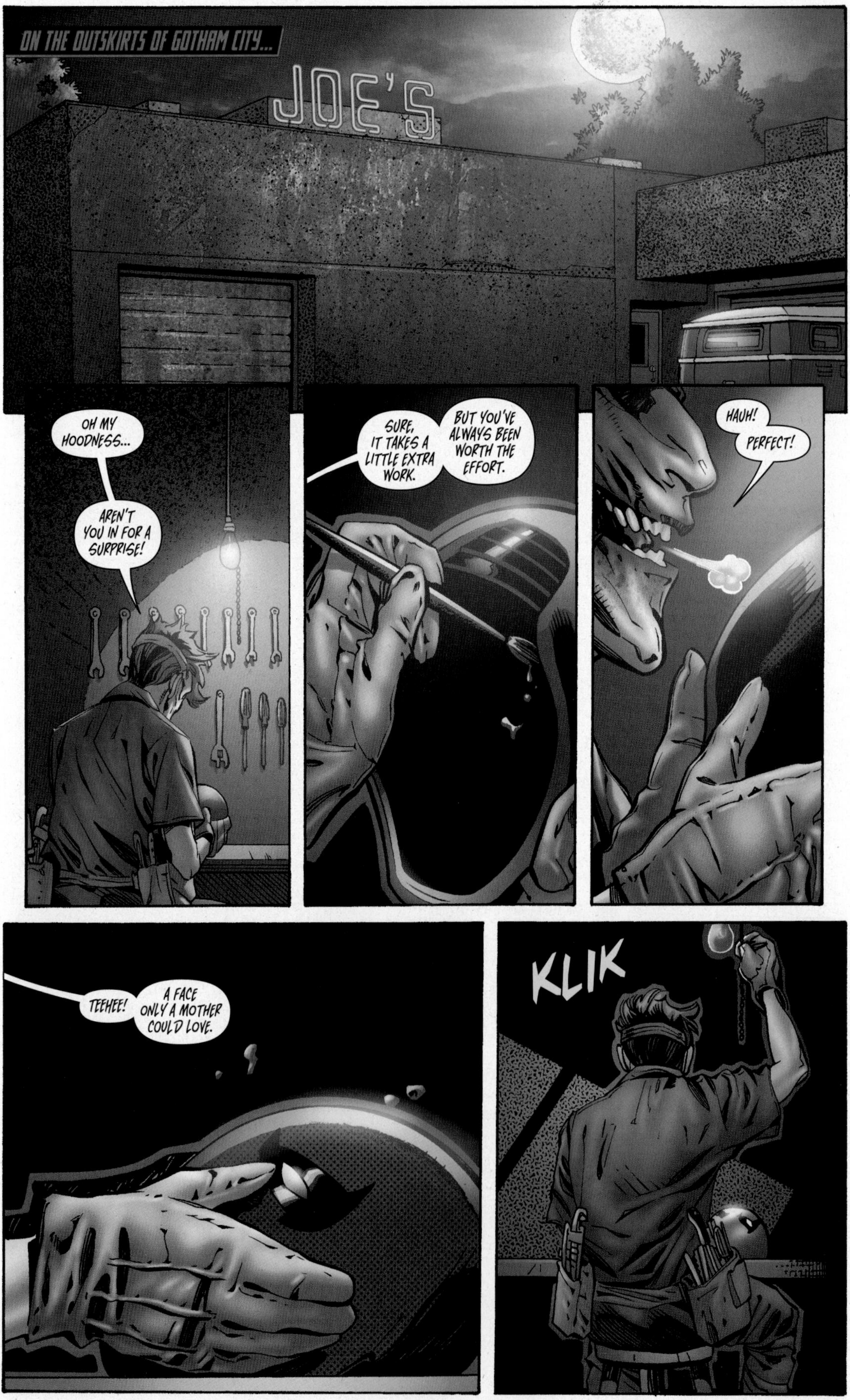
ON THE OUTSKIRTS OF GOTHAM CITY...
JOE'S
OH MY HOODNESS...
AREN'T YOU IN FOR A SURPRISE!
SURE, IT TAKES A LITTLE EXTRA WORK.
BUT YOU'VE ALWAYS BEEN WORTH THE EFFORT.
HAUH!
PERFECT!
TEEHEE!
A FACE ONLY A MOTHER COULD LOVE.
KLIK

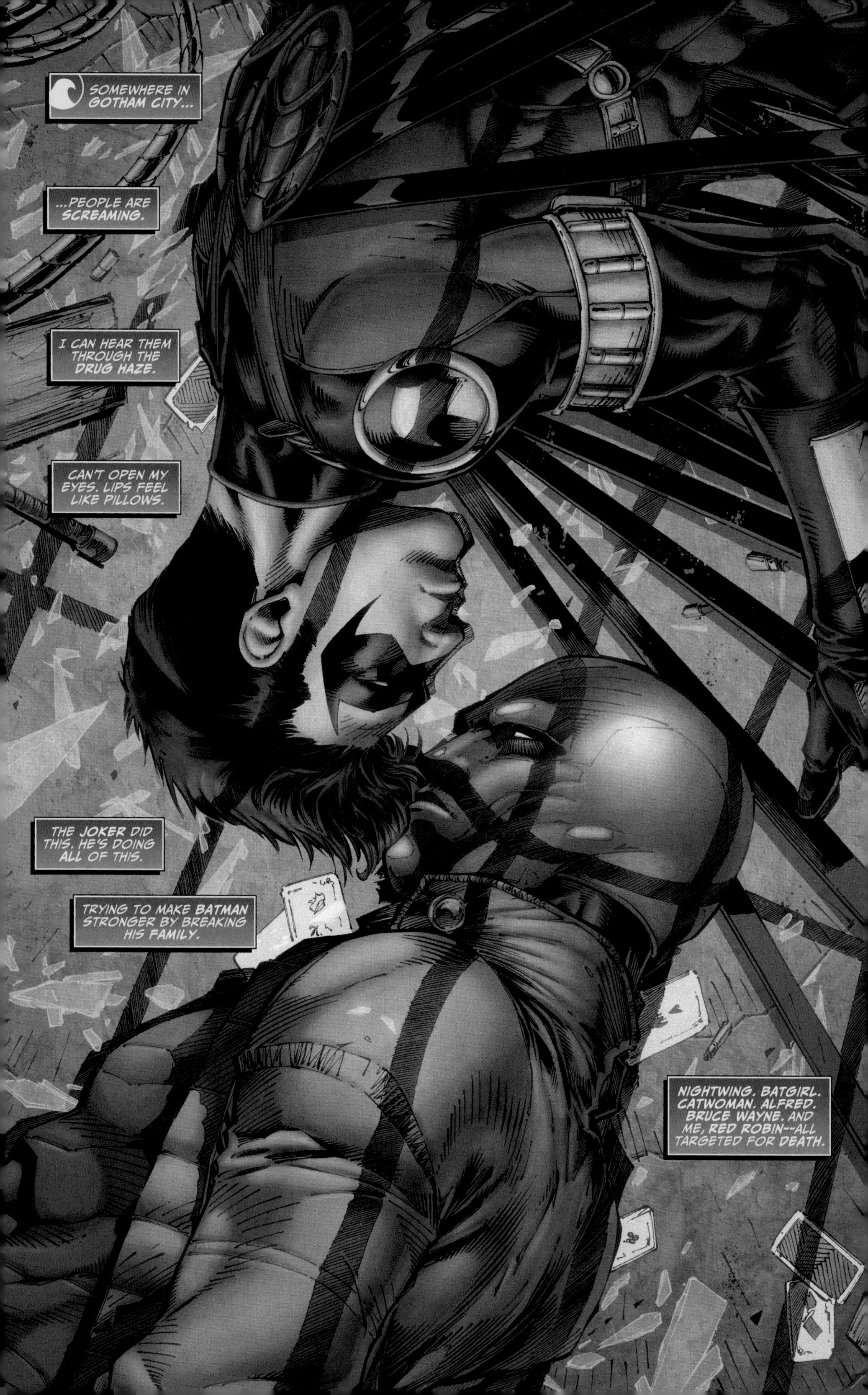
SOMEWHERE IN GOTHAM CITY...
...PEOPLE ARE SCREAMING.
I CAN HEAR THEM THROUGH THE DRUG HAZE.
CAN'T OPEN MY EYES. LIPS FEEL LIKE PILLOWS.
THE JOKER DID THIS. HE'S DOING ALL OF THIS.
TRYING TO MAKE BATMAN STRONGER BY BREAKING HIS FAMILY.
NIGHTWING. BATGIRL. CATWOMAN. ALFRED. BRUCE WAYNE. AND ME, RED ROBIN--ALL TARGETED FOR DEATH.

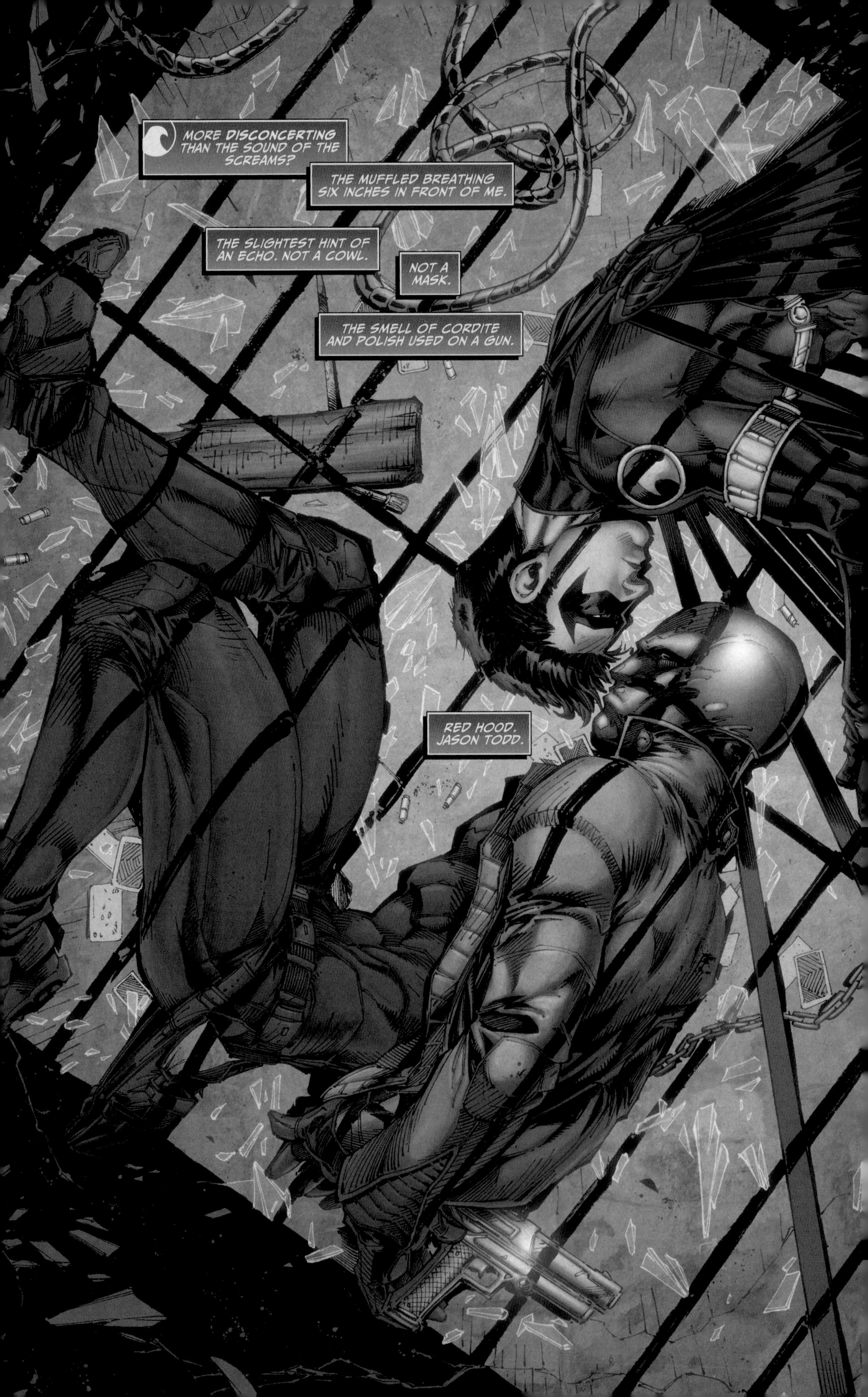
MORE DISCONCERTING THAN THE SOUND OF THE SCREAMS?
THE MUFFLED BREATHING SIX INCHES IN FRONT OF ME.
THE SLIGHTEST HINT OF AN ECHO. NOT A COWL.
NOT A MASK.
THE SMELL OF CORDITE AND POLISH USED ON A GUN.
RED HOOD, JASON TODD.

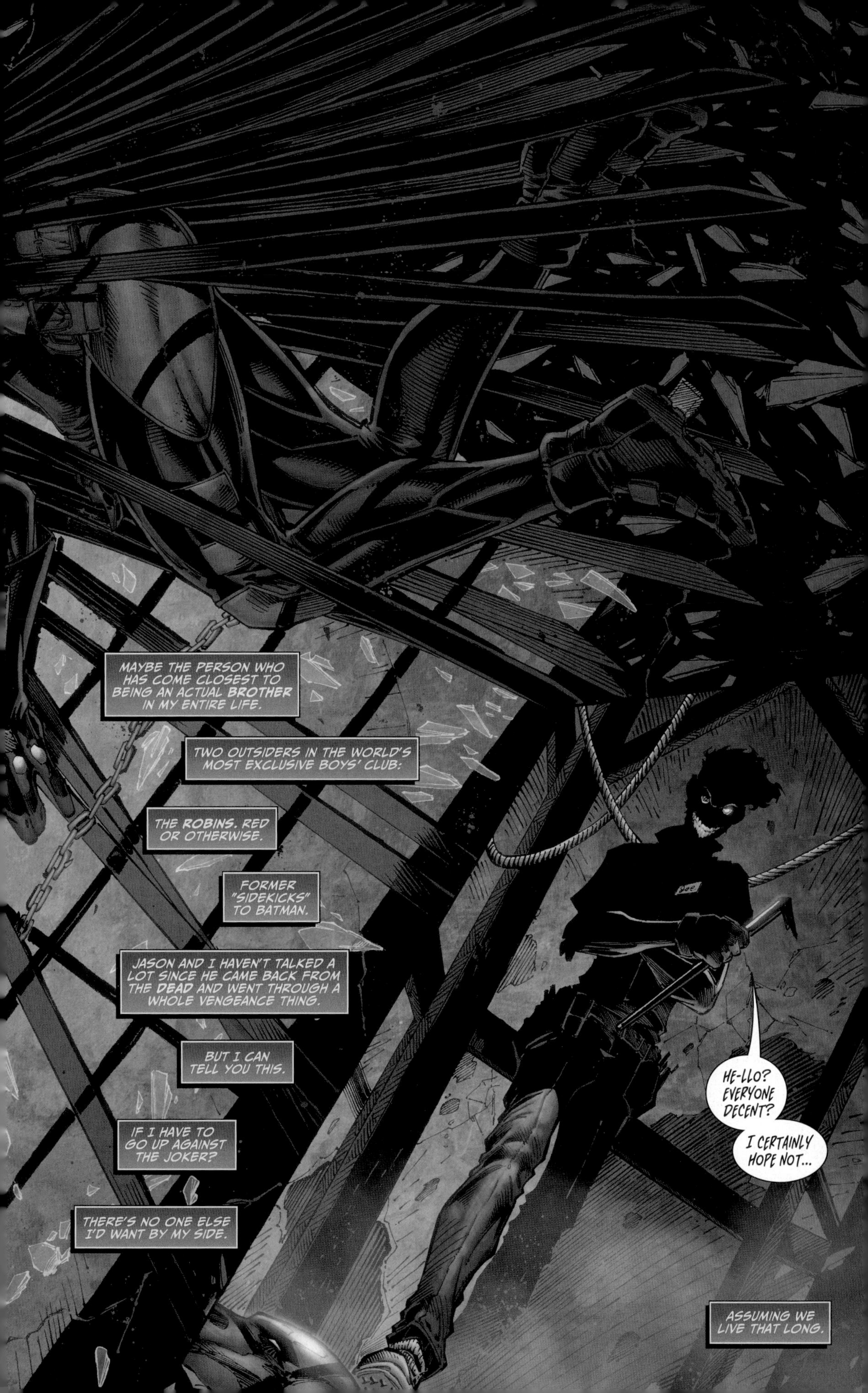
MAYBE THE PERSON WHO HAS COME CLOSEST TO BEING AN ACTUAL BROTHER IN MY ENTIRE LIFE.
TWO OUTSIDERS IN THE WORLD'S MOST EXCLUSIVE BOYS' CLUB:
THE ROBINS. RED OR OTHERWISE.
FORMER "SIDEKICKS" TO BATMAN.
JASON AND I HAVEN'T TALKED A LOT SINCE HE CAME BACK FROM THE DEAD AND WENT THROUGH A WHOLE VENGEANCE THING.
BUT I CAN TELL YOU THIS.
IF I HAVE TO GO UP AGAINST THE JOKER?
THERE'S NO ONE ELSE I'D WANT BY MY SIDE.
HE-LLO? EVERYONE DECENT?
I CERTAINLY HOPE NOT...
ASSUMING WE LIVE THAT LONG.

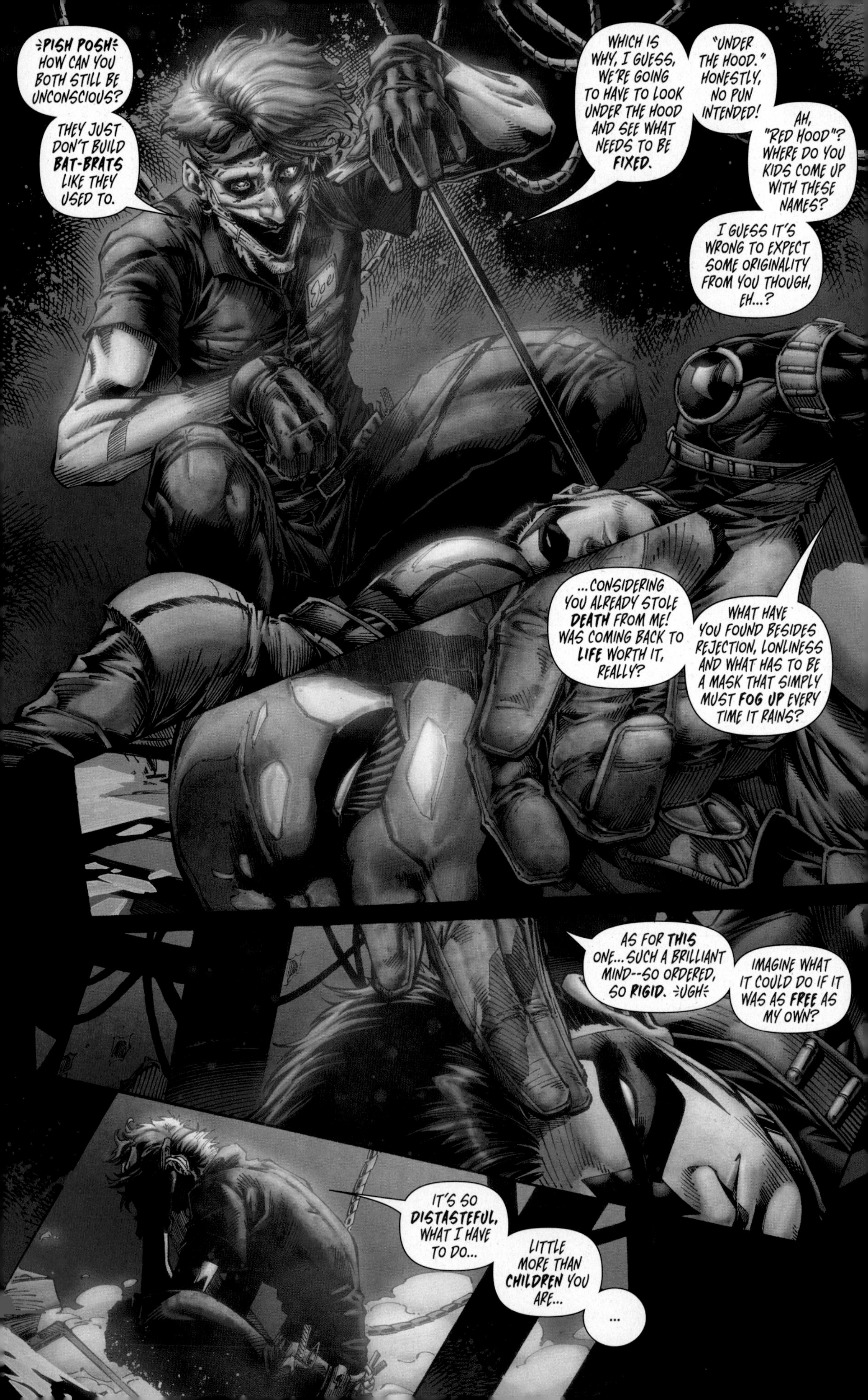
PISH POSH HOW CAN YOU BOTH STILL BE UNCONSCIOUS?
THEY JUST DON'T BUILD BAT-BRATS LIKE THEY USED TO.
WHICH IS WHY, I GUESS, WE'RE GOING TO HAVE TO LOOK UNDER THE HOOD AND SEE WHAT NEEDS TO BE FIXED.
"UNDER THE HOOD." HONESTLY, NO PUN INTENDED!
AH, "RED HOOD"? WHERE DO YOU KIDS COME UP WITH THESE NAMES?
I GUESS IT'S WRONG TO EXPECT SOME ORIGINALITY FROM YOU THOUGH, EH...?
...CONSIDERING YOU ALREADY STOLE DEATH FROM ME! WAS COMING BACK TO LIFE WORTH IT, REALLY?
WHAT HAVE YOU FOUND BESIDES REJECTION, LONLINESS AND WHAT HAS TO BE A MASK THAT SIMPLY MUST FOG UP EVERY TIME IT RAINS?
AS FOR THIS ONE... SUCH A BRILLIANT MIND--SO ORDERED, SO RIGID. UGH
IMAGINE WHAT IT COULD DO IF IT WAS AS FREE AS MY OWN?
IT'S SO DISTASTEFUL, WHAT I HAVE TO DO...
LITTLE MORE THAN CHILDREN YOU ARE...
...

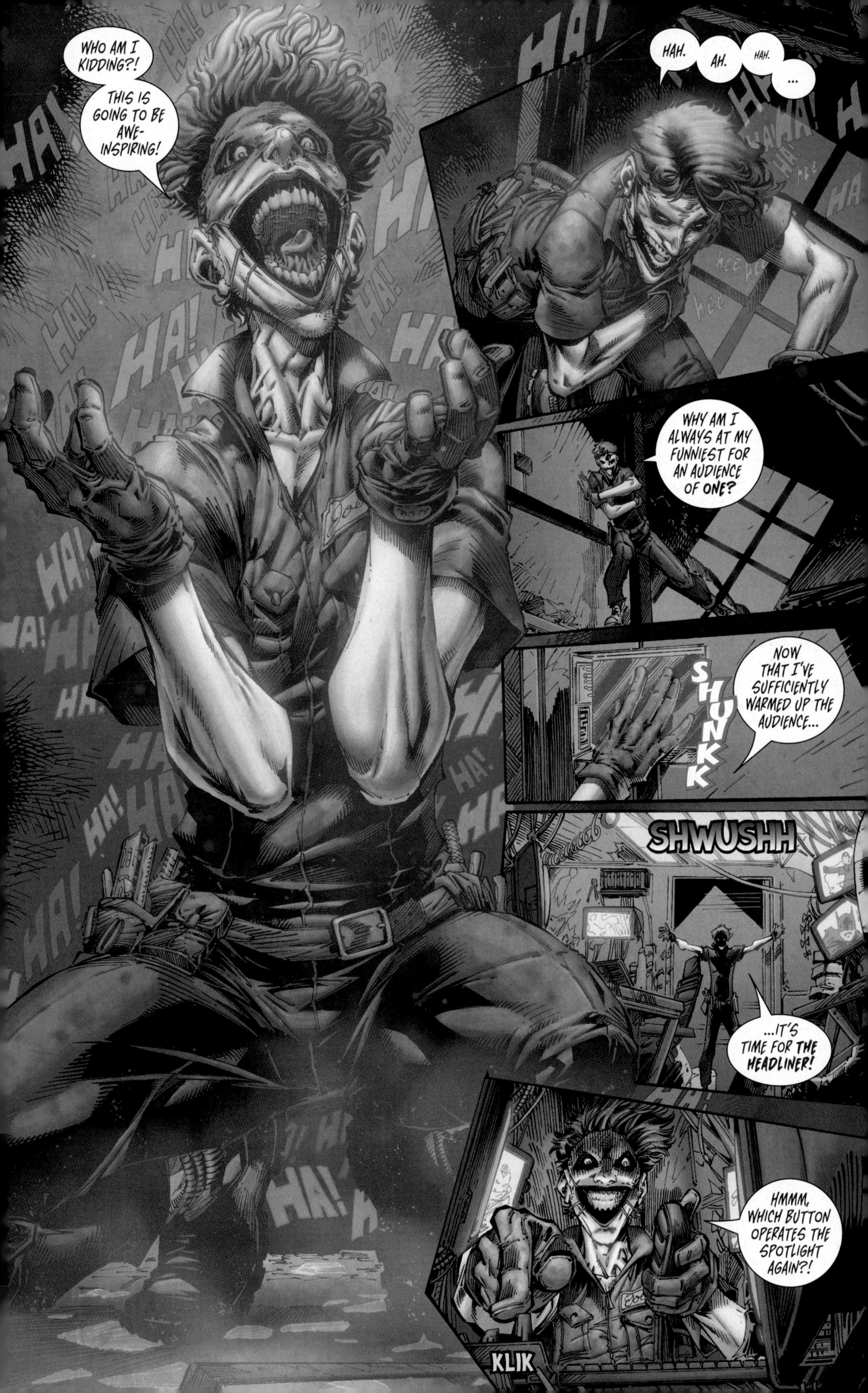
WHO AM I KIDDING?!
THIS IS GOING TO BE AWE-INSPIRING!
HA! HA! HA! HA! HA! HA! HA!
HAH.
AH.
HAH.
...
hee hee hee
WHY AM I ALWAYS AT MY FUNNIEST FOR AN AUDIENCE OF ONE?
SHUNKK
NOW THAT I'VE SUFFICIENTLY WARMED UP THE AUDIENCE...
SHWUSHH
...IT'S TIME FOR THE HEADLINER!
HMMM, WHICH BUTTON OPERATES THE SPOTLIGHT AGAIN?!
KLIK

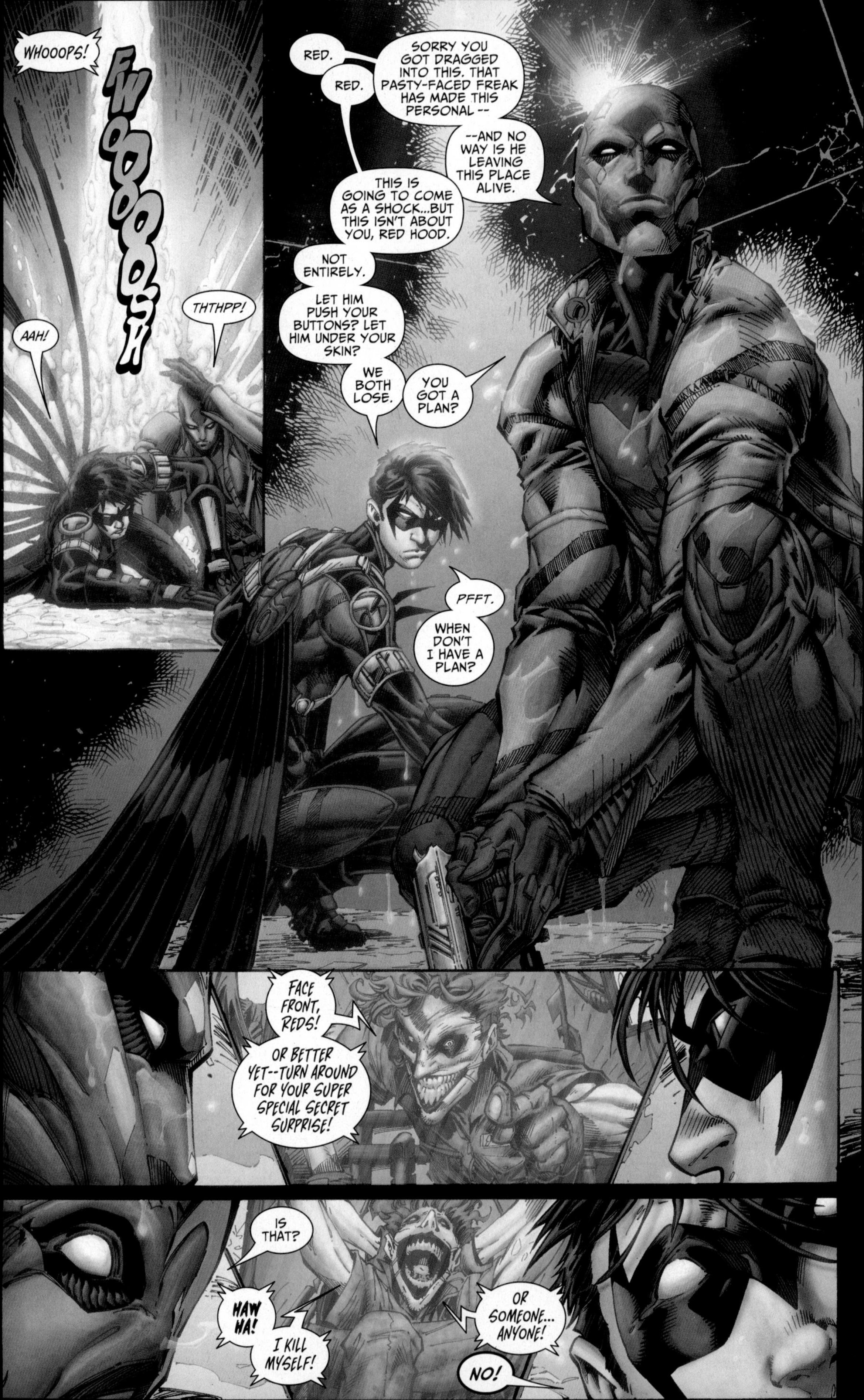
WHOOOPS!
FWOOOOOOSH
THTHPP!
AAH!
RED.
RED.
SORRY YOU GOT DRAGGED INTO THIS. THAT PASTY-FACED FREAK HAS MADE THIS PERSONAL --
--AND NO WAY IS HE LEAVING THIS PLACE ALIVE.
THIS IS GOING TO COME AS A SHOCK...BUT THIS ISN'T ABOUT YOU, RED HOOD.
NOT ENTIRELY.
LET HIM PUSH YOUR BUTTONS? LET HIM UNDER YOUR SKIN?
WE BOTH LOSE.
YOU GOT A PLAN?
PFFT.
WHEN DON'T I HAVE A PLAN?
FACE FRONT, REDS!
OR BETTER YET--TURN AROUND FOR YOUR SUPER SPECIAL SECRET SURPRISE!
IS THAT?
HAW HA!
I KILL MYSELF!
OR SOMEONE... ANYONE!
NO!

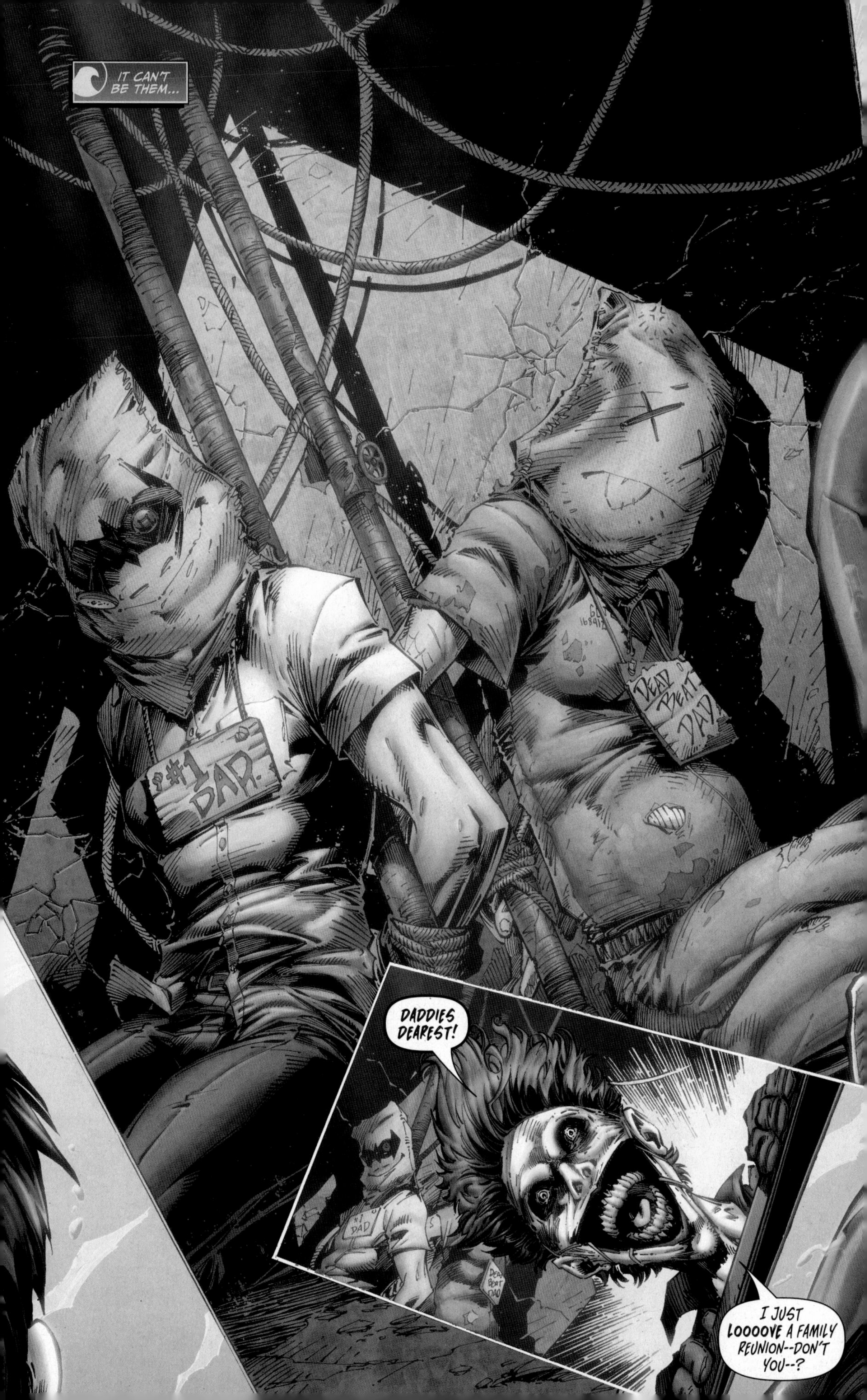
IT CAN'T BE THEM...
#1 DAD
DEAD BEAT DAD
DADDIES DEAREST!
I JUST LOOOOVE A FAMILY REUNION--DON'T YOU--?

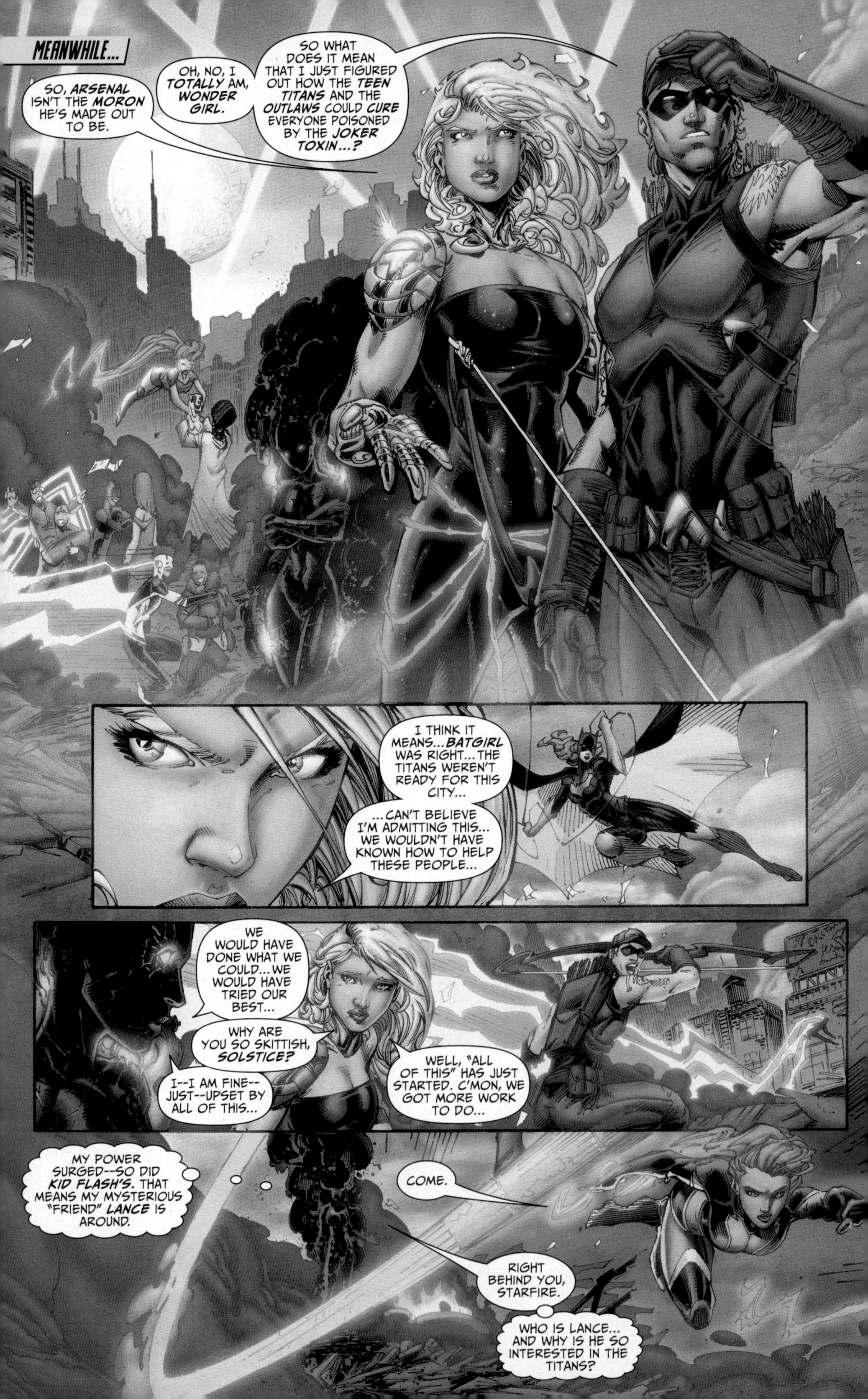
MEANWHILE...
SO, ARSENAL ISN'T THE MORON HE'S MADE OUT TO BE.
OH, NO, I TOTALLY AM, WONDER GIRL.
SO WHAT DOES IT MEAN THAT I JUST FIGURED OUT HOW THE TEEN TITANS AND THE OUTLAWS COULD CURE EVERYONE POISONED BY THE JOKER TOXIN...?
I THINK IT MEANS...BATGIRL WAS RIGHT...THE TITANS WEREN'T READY FOR THIS CITY...
...CAN'T BELIEVE I'M ADMITTING THIS... WE WOULDN'T HAVE KNOWN HOW TO HELP THESE PEOPLE...
WE WOULD HAVE DONE WHAT WE COULD...WE WOULD HAVE TRIED OUR BEST...
WHY ARE YOU SO SKITTISH, SOLSTICE?
I--I AM FINE-- JUST--UPSET BY ALL OF THIS...
WELL, "ALL OF THIS" HAS JUST STARTED. C'MON, WE GOT MORE WORK TO DO...
MY POWER SURGED--SO DID KID FLASH'S. THAT MEANS MY MYSTERIOUS "FRIEND" LANCE IS AROUND.
COME.
RIGHT BEHIND YOU, STARFIRE.
WHO IS LANCE... AND WHY IS HE SO INTERESTED IN THE TITANS?

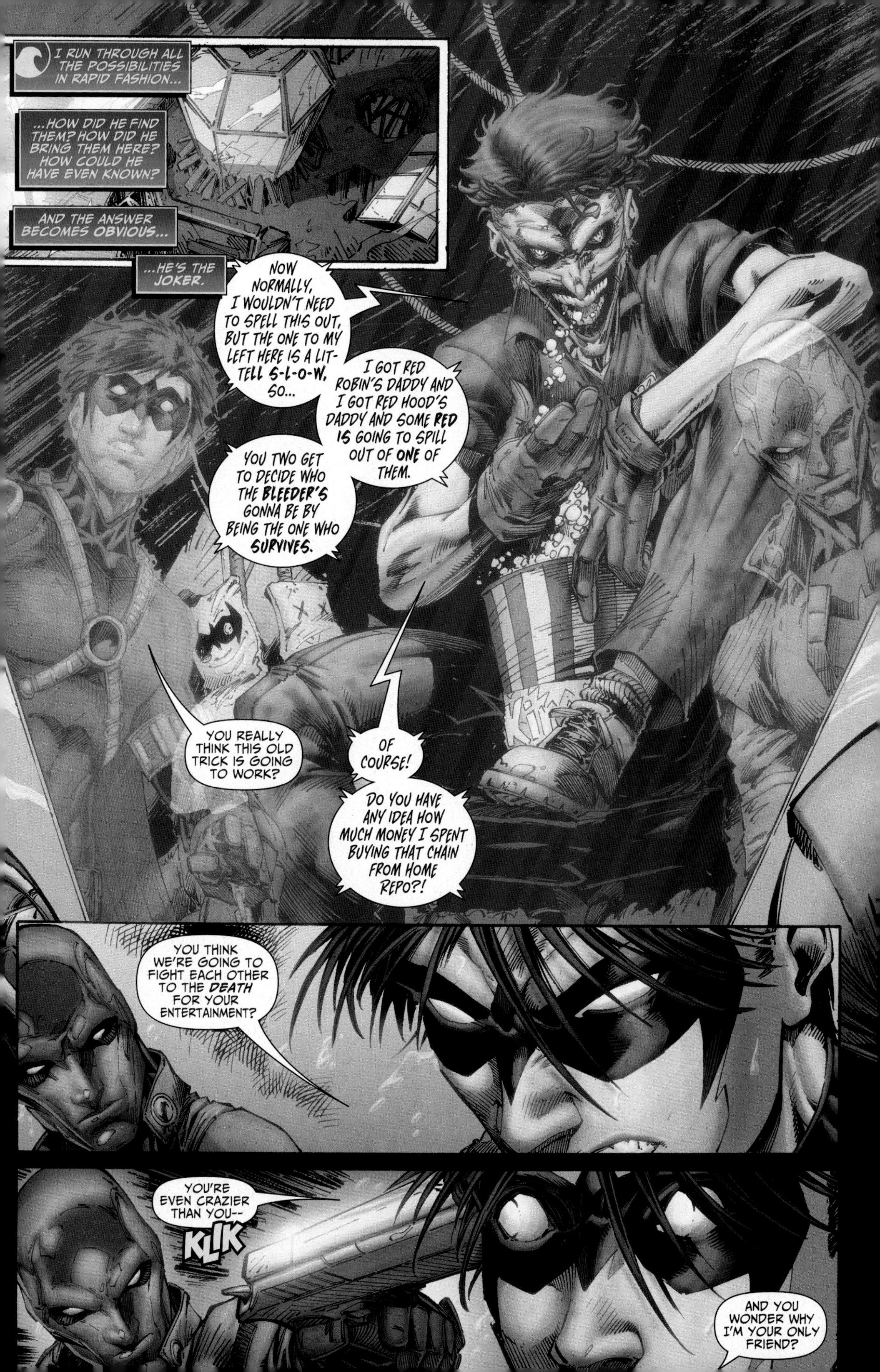
I RUN THROUGH ALL THE POSSIBILITIES IN RAPID FASHION...
...HOW DID HE FIND THEM? HOW DID HE BRING THEM HERE? HOW COULD HE HAVE EVEN KNOWN?
AND THE ANSWER BECOMES OBVIOUS...
...HE'S THE JOKER.
NOW NORMALLY, I WOULDN'T NEED TO SPELL THIS OUT, BUT THE ONE TO MY LEFT HERE IS A LIT-TELL S-L-O-W, SO...
I GOT RED ROBIN'S DADDY AND I GOT RED HOOD'S DADDY AND SOME RED IS GOING TO SPILL OUT OF ONE OF THEM.
YOU TWO GET TO DECIDE WHO THE BLEEDER'S GONNA BE BY BEING THE ONE WHO SURVIVES.
YOU REALLY THINK THIS OLD TRICK IS GOING TO WORK?
OF COURSE!
DO YOU HAVE ANY IDEA HOW MUCH MONEY I SPENT BUYING THAT CHAIN FROM HOME REPO?!
YOU THINK WE'RE GOING TO FIGHT EACH OTHER TO THE DEATH FOR YOUR ENTERTAINMENT?
YOU'RE EVEN CRAZIER THAN YOU--
KLIK
AND YOU WONDER WHY I'M YOUR ONLY FRIEND?

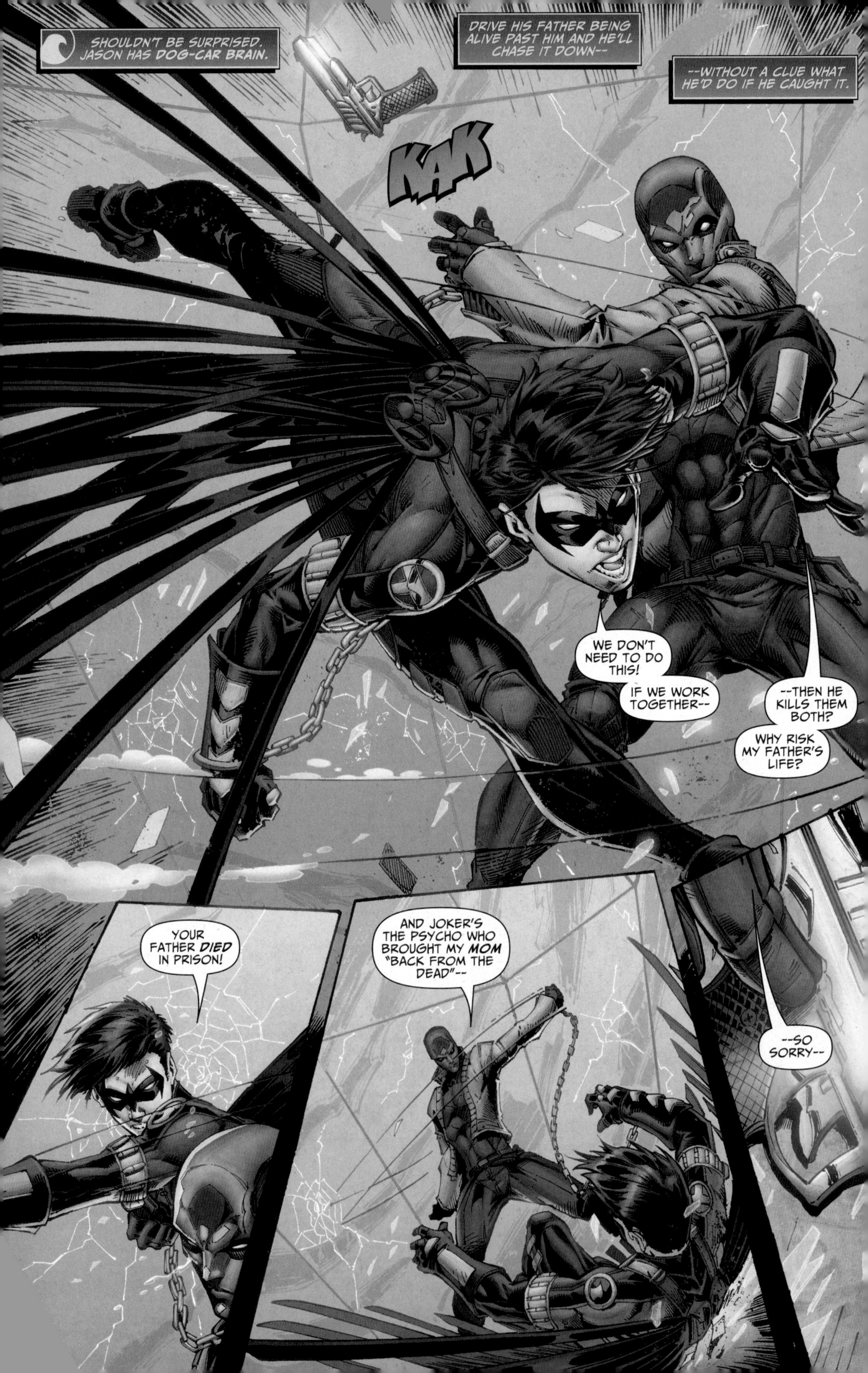

SHOULDN'T BE SURPRISED. JASON HAS DOG-CAR BRAIN.
DRIVE HIS FATHER BEING ALIVE PAST HIM AND HE'LL CHASE IT DOWN--
--WITHOUT A CLUE WHAT HE'D DO IF HE CAUGHT IT.
KAK
WE DON'T NEED TO DO THIS!
IF WE WORK TOGETHER--
--THEN HE KILLS THEM BOTH?
WHY RISK MY FATHER'S LIFE?
YOUR FATHER DIED IN PRISON!
AND JOKER'S THE PSYCHO WHO BROUGHT MY MOM "BACK FROM THE DEAD"--
--SO SORRY--

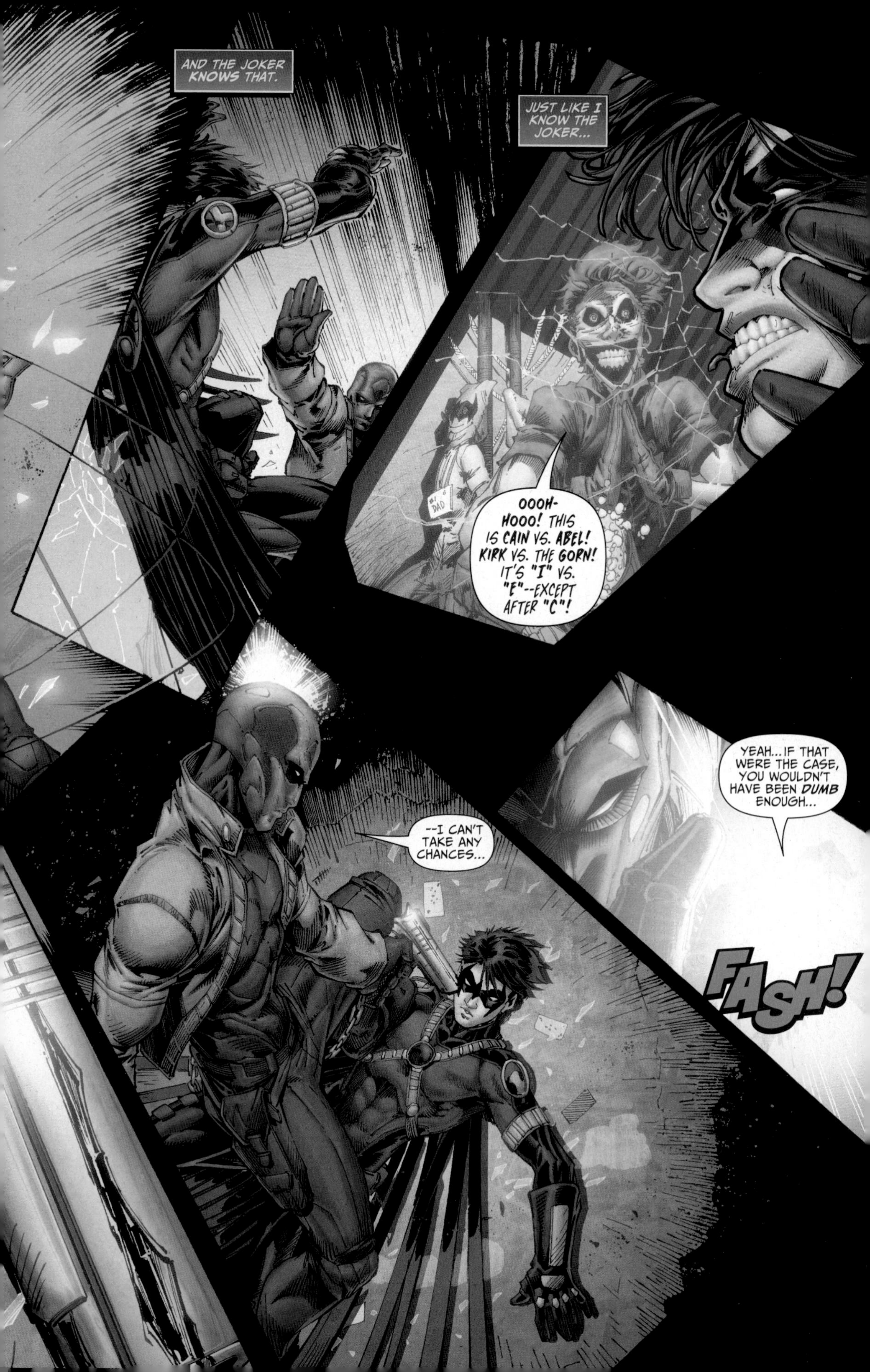
AND THE JOKER KNOWS THAT.
JUST LIKE I KNOW THE JOKER...
OOOH-HOOO! THIS IS CAIN VS. ABEL! KIRK VS. THE GORN! IT'S "I" VS. "E"--EXCEPT AFTER "C"!
--I CAN'T TAKE ANY CHANCES...
YEAH...IF THAT WERE THE CASE, YOU WOULDN'T HAVE BEEN DUMB ENOUGH...
FASH!

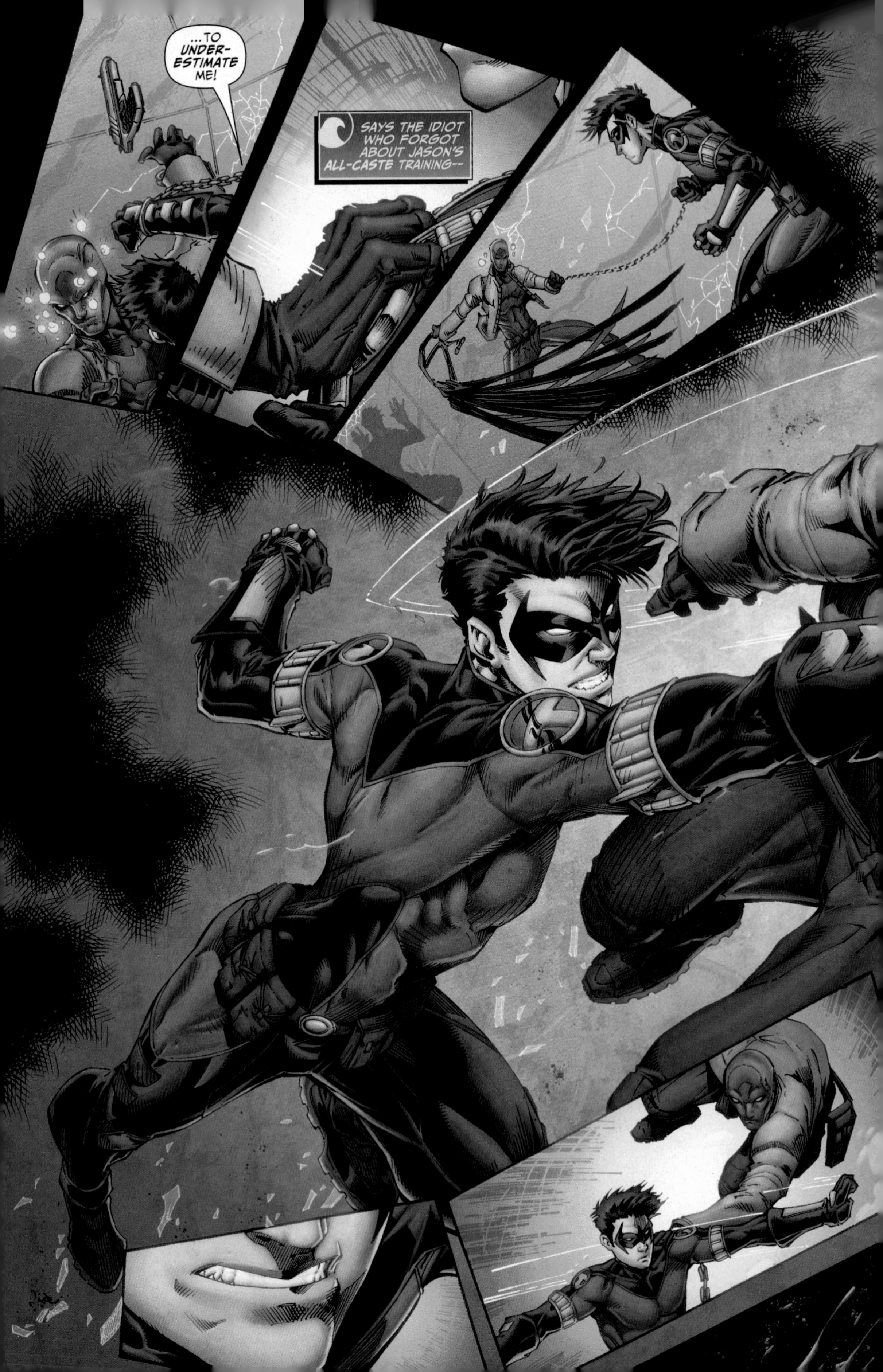
...TO UNDER-ESTIMATE ME!
SAYS THE IDIOT WHO FORGOT ABOUT JASON'S ALL-CASTE TRAINING--

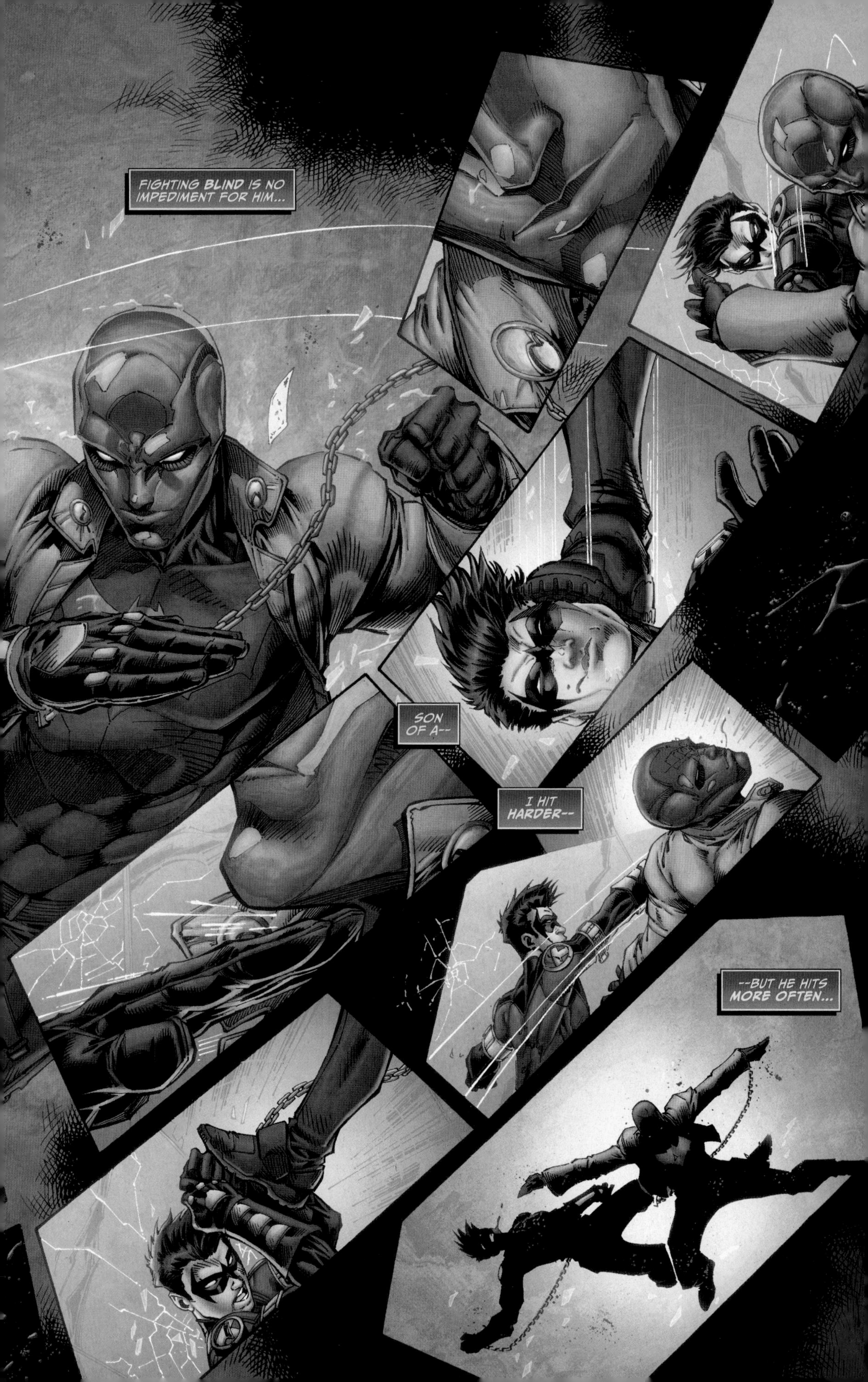
FIGHTING BLIND IS NO IMPEDIMENT FOR HIM...
SON OF A--
I HIT HARDER--
--BUT HE HITS MORE OFTEN...

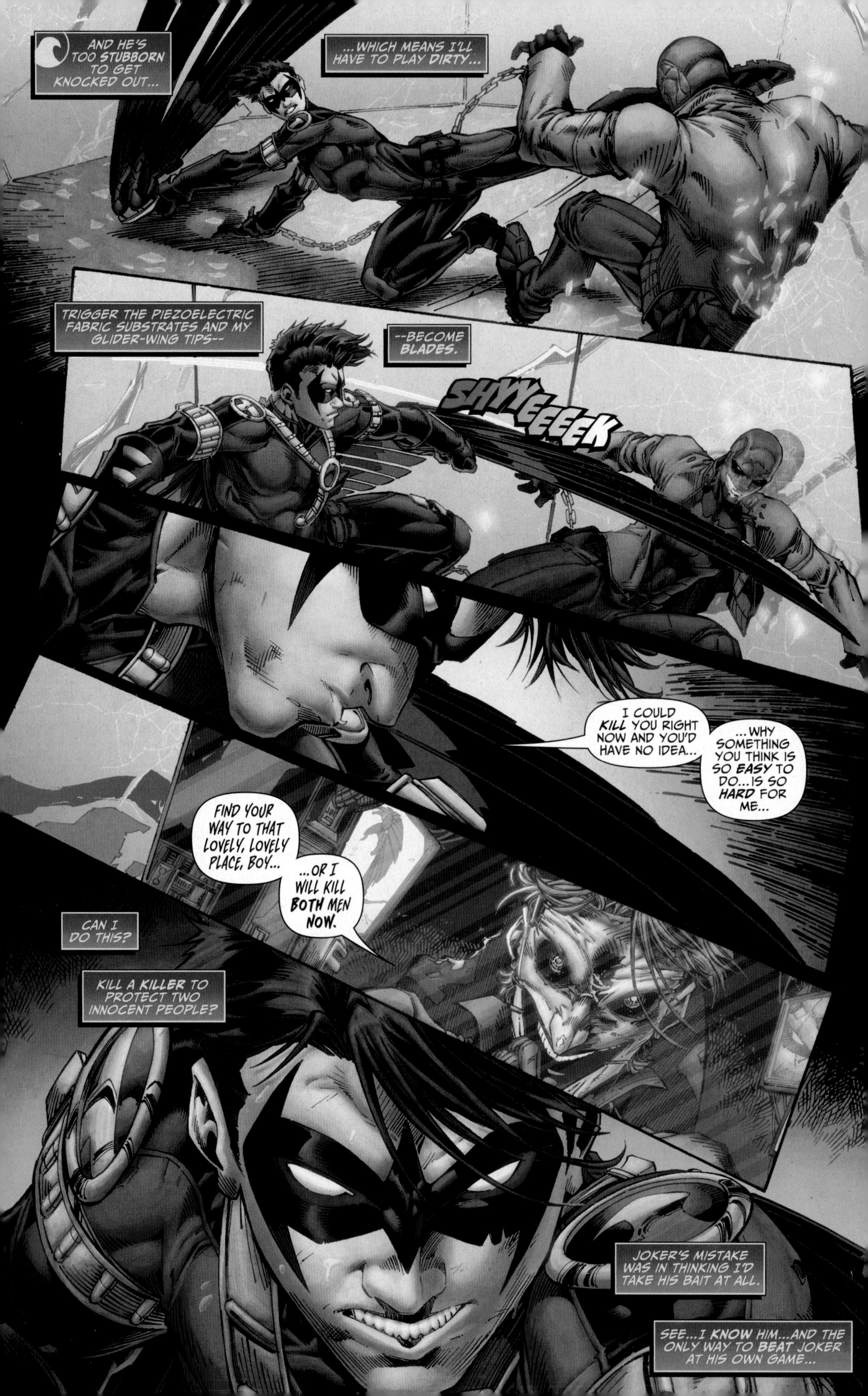
AND HE'S TOO STUBBORN TO GET KNOCKED OUT...
...WHICH MEANS I'LL HAVE TO PLAY DIRTY...
TRIGGER THE PIEZOELECTRIC FABRIC SUBSTRATES AND MY GLIDER-WING TIPS--
--BECOME BLADES.
SHYYEEEEK
I COULD KILL YOU RIGHT NOW AND YOU'D HAVE NO IDEA...
...WHY SOMETHING YOU THINK IS SO EASY TO DO...IS SO HARD FOR ME...
FIND YOUR WAY TO THAT LOVELY, LOVELY PLACE, BOY...
...OR I WILL KILL BOTH MEN NOW.
CAN I DO THIS?
KILL A KILLER TO PROTECT TWO INNOCENT PEOPLE?
JOKER'S MISTAKE WAS IN THINKING I'D TAKE HIS BAIT AT ALL.
SEE...I KNOW HIM...AND THE ONLY WAY TO BEAT JOKER AT HIS OWN GAME...

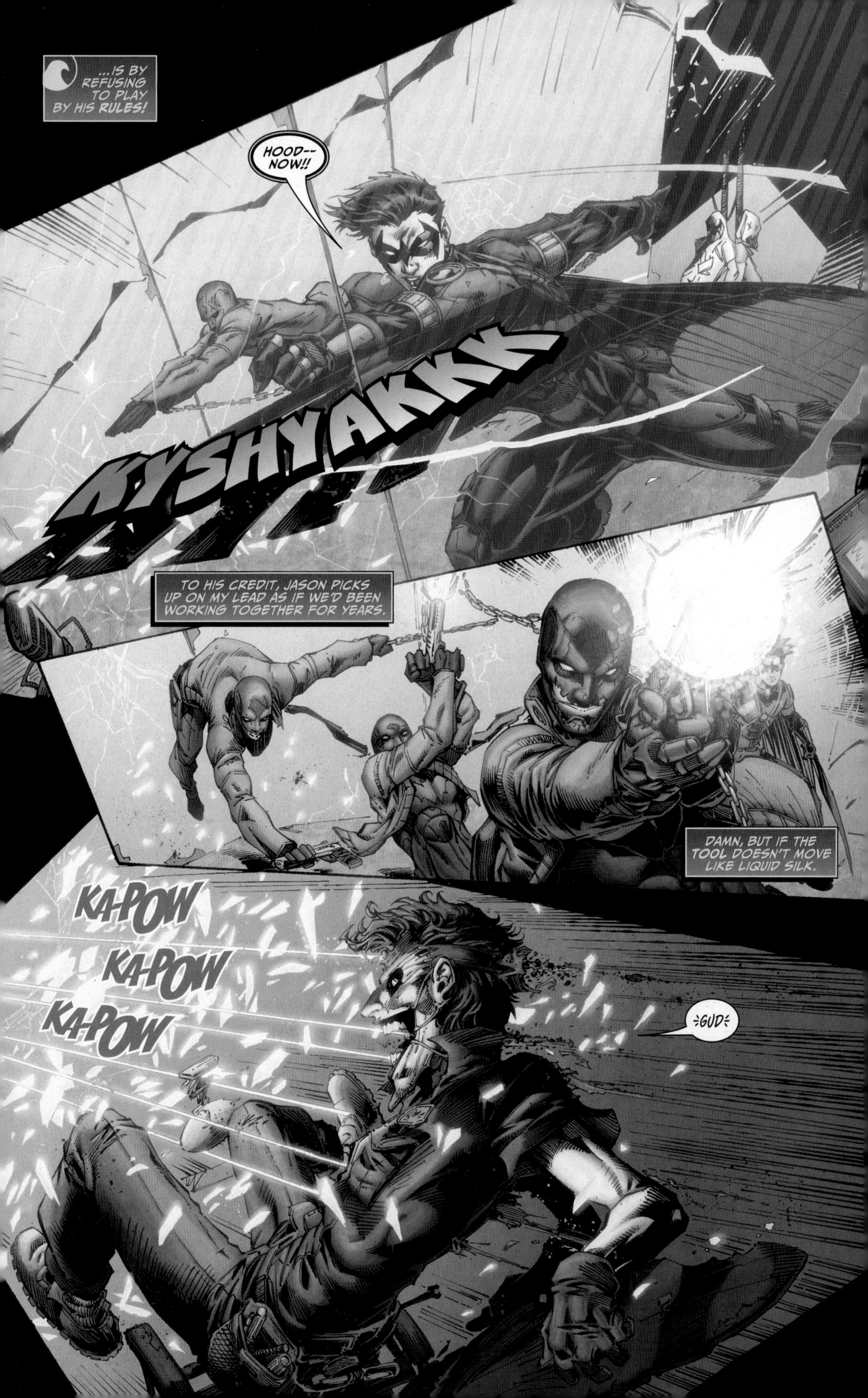
...IS BY REFUSING TO PLAY BY HIS RULES!
HOOD-- NOW!!
KYSHYAKKK
TO HIS CREDIT, JASON PICKS UP ON MY LEAD AS IF WE'D BEEN WORKING TOGETHER FOR YEARS.
DAMN, BUT IF THE TOOL DOESN'T MOVE LIKE LIQUID SILK.
KA-POW
KA-POW
KA-POW
GUD

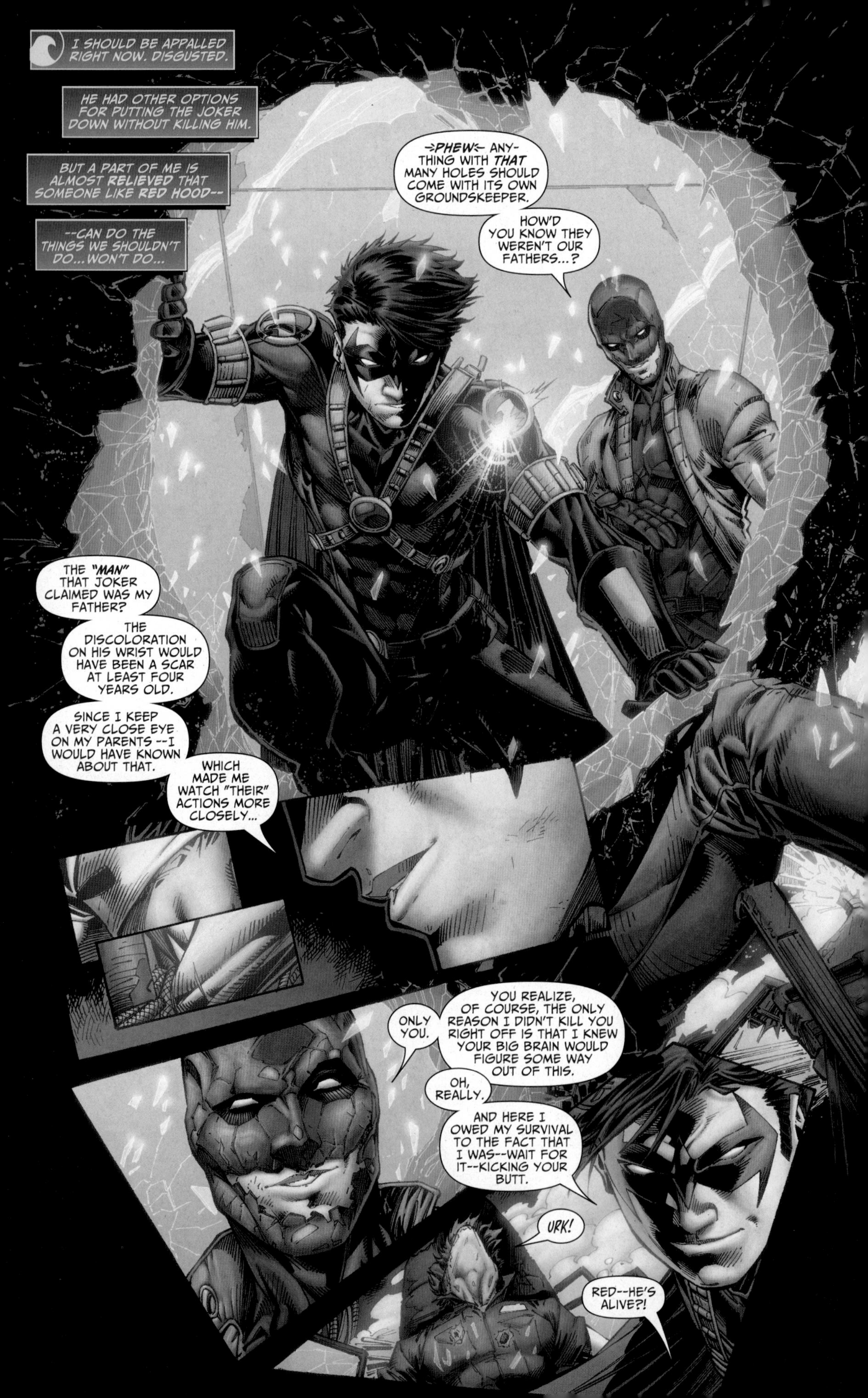
I SHOULD BE APPALLED RIGHT NOW. DISGUSTED.
HE HAD OTHER OPTIONS FOR PUTTING THE JOKER DOWN WITHOUT KILLING HIM.
BUT A PART OF ME IS ALMOST RELIEVED THAT SOMEONE LIKE RED HOOD--
--CAN DO THE THINGS WE SHOULDN'T DO...WON'T DO...
-PHEW- ANY-THING WITH THAT MANY HOLES SHOULD COME WITH ITS OWN GROUNDSKEEPER.
HOW'D YOU KNOW THEY WEREN'T OUR FATHERS...?
THE "MAN" THAT JOKER CLAIMED WAS MY FATHER?
THE DISCOLORATION ON HIS WRIST WOULD HAVE BEEN A SCAR AT LEAST FOUR YEARS OLD.
SINCE I KEEP A VERY CLOSE EYE ON MY PARENTS --I WOULD HAVE KNOWN ABOUT THAT.
WHICH MADE ME WATCH "THEIR" ACTIONS MORE CLOSELY...
ONLY YOU.
YOU REALIZE, OF COURSE, THE ONLY REASON I DIDN'T KILL YOU RIGHT OFF IS THAT I KNEW YOUR BIG BRAIN WOULD FIGURE SOME WAY OUT OF THIS.
OH, REALLY.
AND HERE I OWED MY SURVIVAL TO THE FACT THAT I WAS--WAIT FOR IT--KICKING YOUR BUTT.
URK!
RED--HE'S ALIVE?!

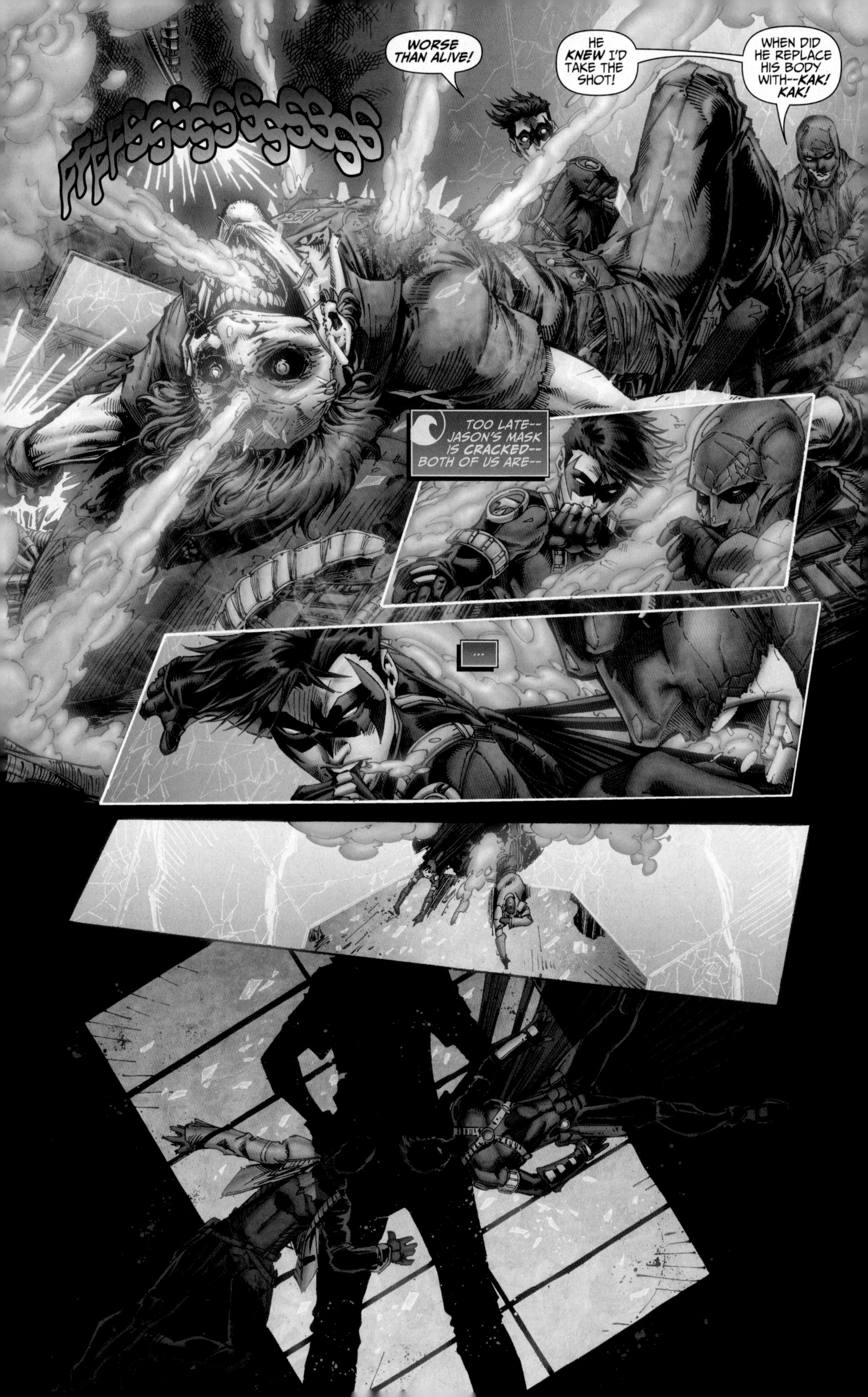
FFFSSSSSSSSSSS
WORSE THAN ALIVE!
HE KNEW I'D TAKE THE SHOT!
WHEN DID HE REPLACE HIS BODY WITH--KAK! KAK!
TOO LATE-- JASON'S MASK IS CRACKED-- BOTH OF US ARE--
...

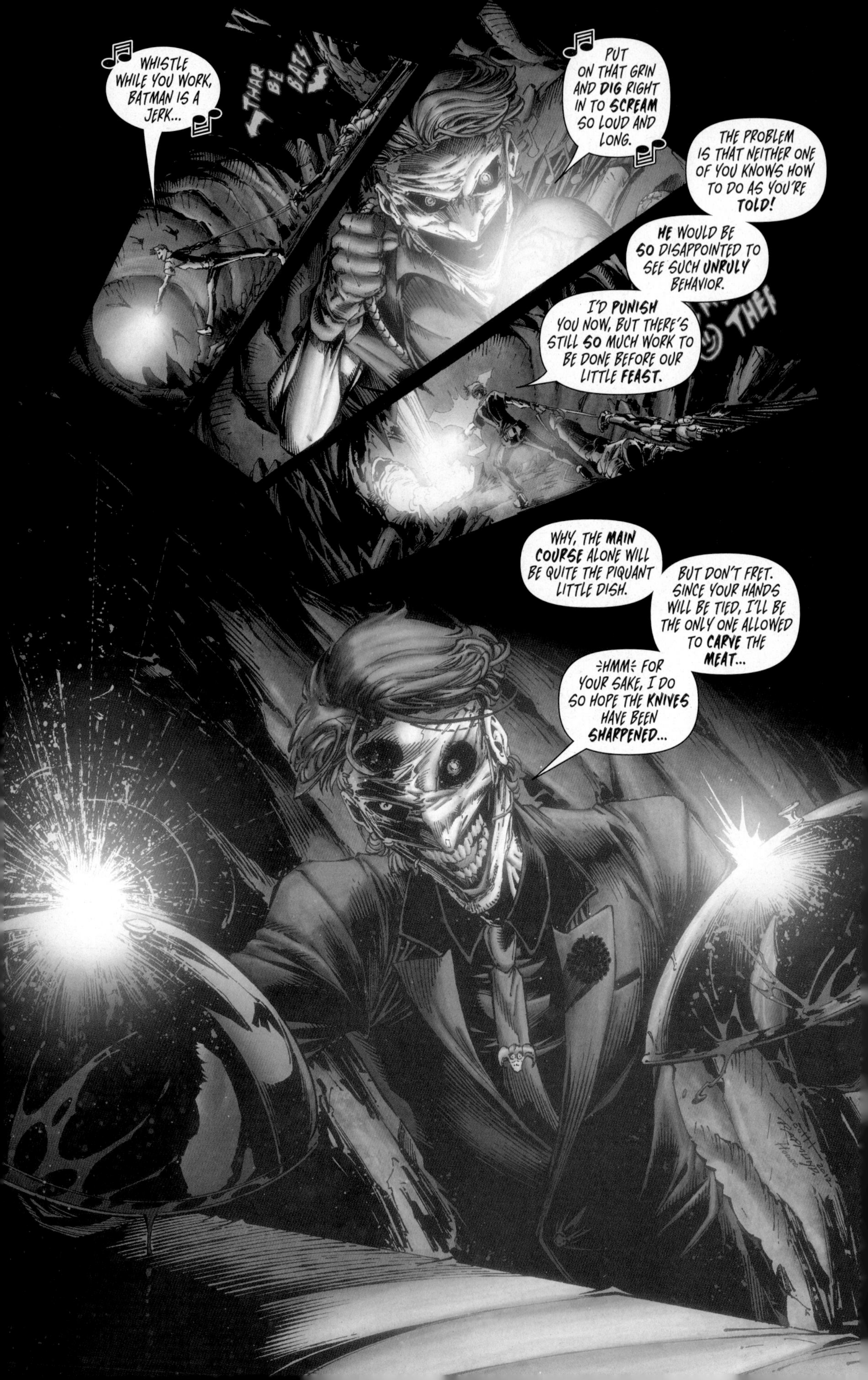
WHISTLE WHILE YOU WORK, BATMAN IS A JERK...
THAR BE BATS
PUT ON THAT GRIN AND DIG RIGHT IN TO SCREAM SO LOUD AND LONG.
THE PROBLEM IS THAT NEITHER ONE OF YOU KNOWS HOW TO DO AS YOU'RE TOLD!
HE WOULD BE SO DISAPPOINTED TO SEE SUCH UNRULY BEHAVIOR.
I'D PUNISH YOU NOW, BUT THERE'S STILL SO MUCH WORK TO BE DONE BEFORE OUR LITTLE FEAST.
WHY, THE MAIN COURSE ALONE WILL BE QUITE THE PIQUANT LITTLE DISH.
BUT DON'T FRET. SINCE YOUR HANDS WILL BE TIED, I'LL BE THE ONLY ONE ALLOWED TO CARVE THE MEAT...
HMM FOR YOUR SAKE, I DO SO HOPE THE KNIVES HAVE BEEN SHARPENED...

PART SIX
NIGHTWING

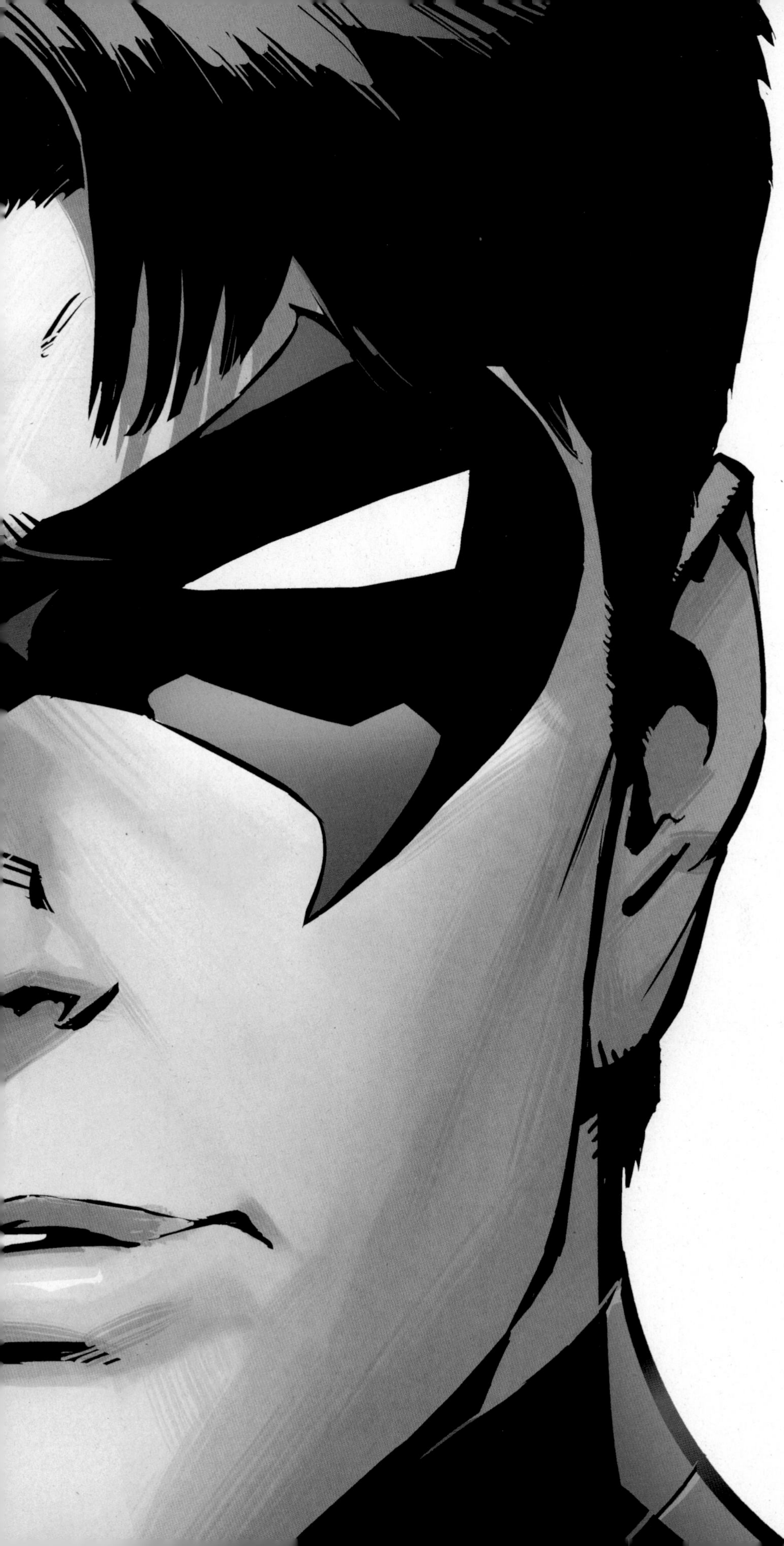

KYLE HIGGINS TOM DEFALCO writers EDDY BARROWS ANDRES GUINALDO pencillers EBER FERREIRA MARK IRWIN inkers
ROD REIS PETE PANTAZIS colorists CARLOS M. MANGUAL DAVE SHARPE letterers NIGHTWING created by MARV WOLFMAN and GEORGE PÉREZ

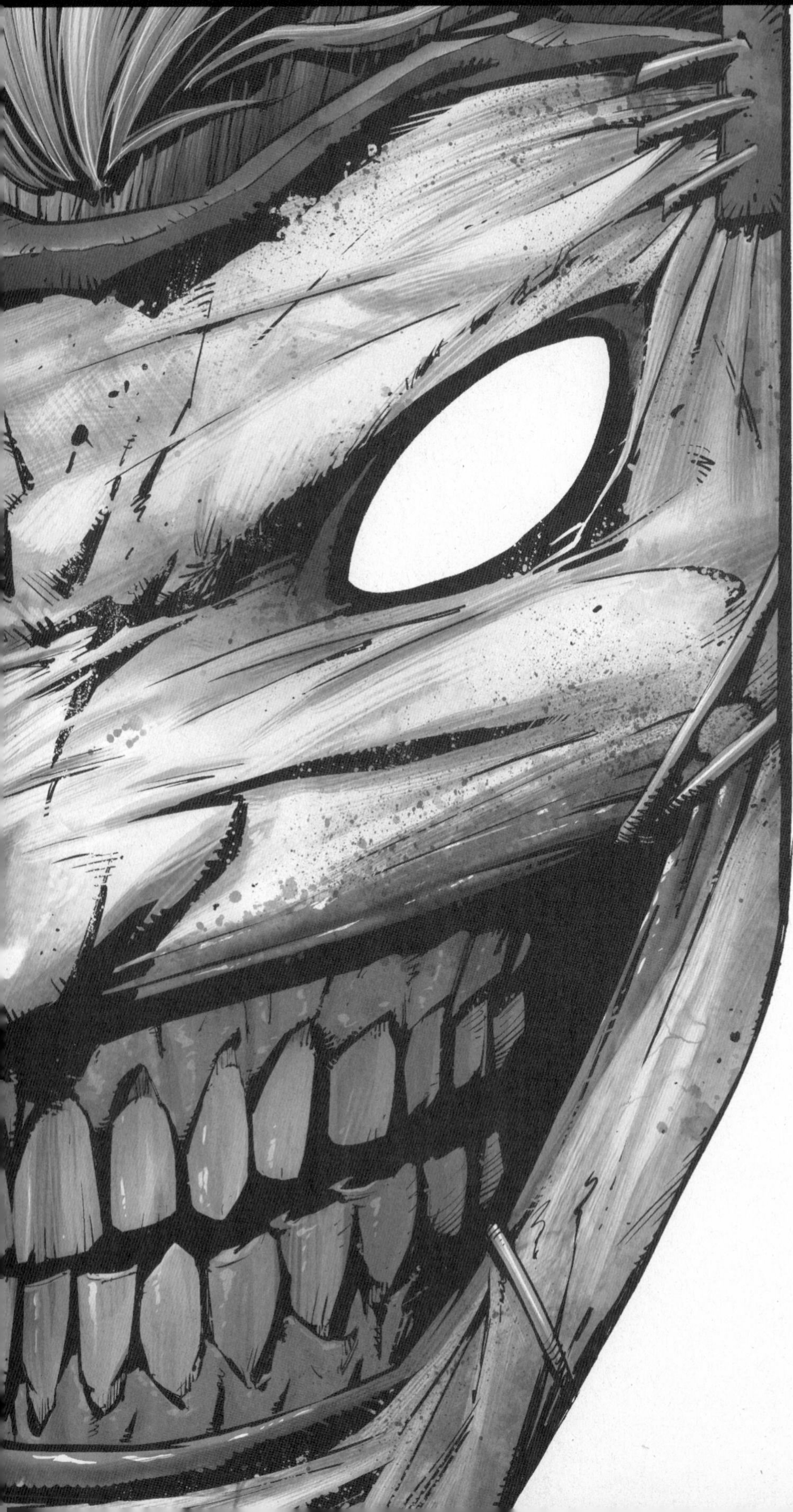

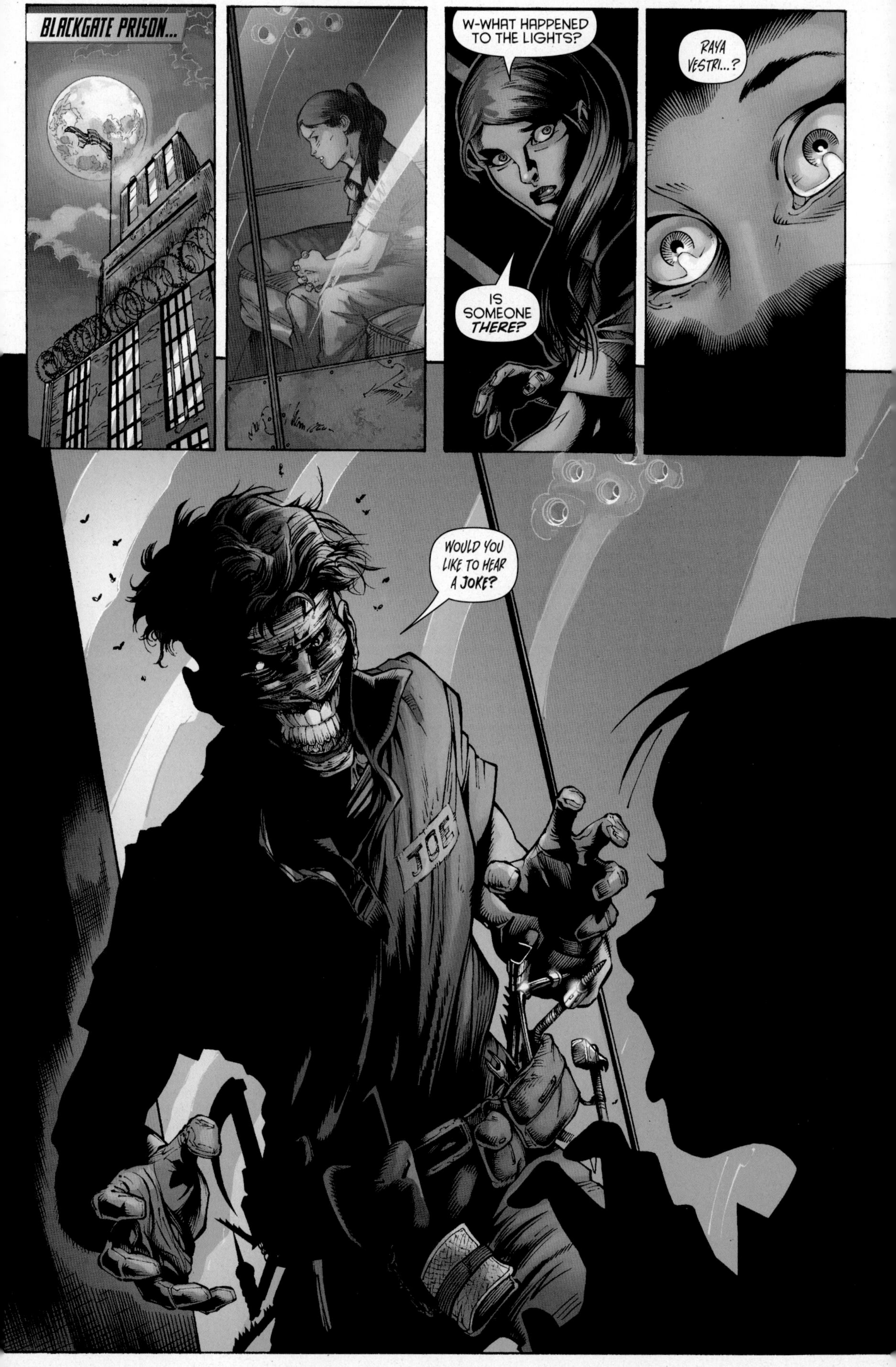
BLACKGATE PRISON...
W-WHAT HAPPENED TO THE LIGHTS?
IS SOMEONE THERE?
RAYA VESTRI...?
WOULD YOU LIKE TO HEAR A JOKE?
JOE

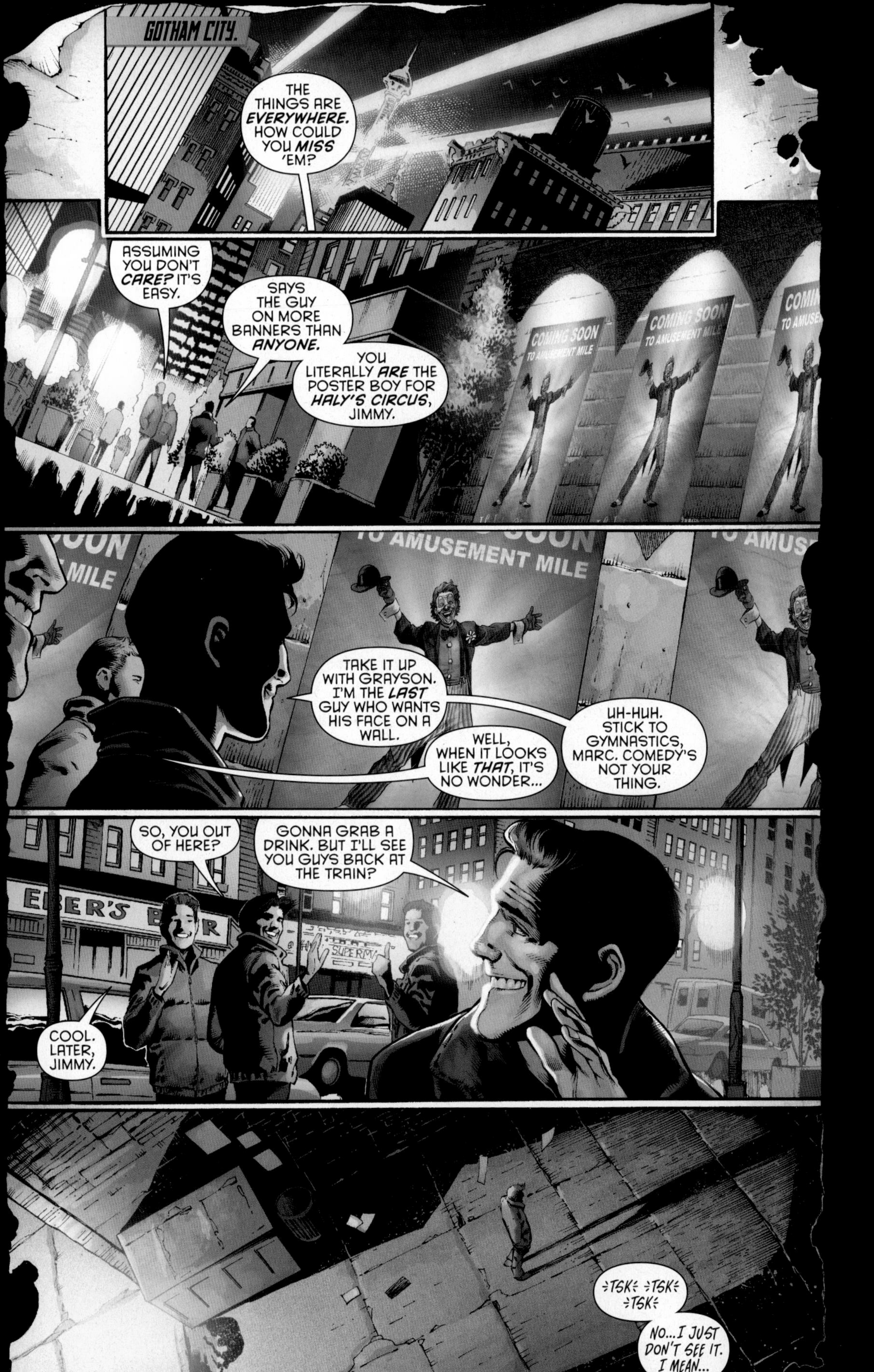
GOTHAM CITY.
THE THINGS ARE EVERYWHERE. HOW COULD YOU MISS 'EM?
ASSUMING YOU DON'T CARE? IT'S EASY.
SAYS THE GUY ON MORE BANNERS THAN ANYONE.
YOU LITERALLY ARE THE POSTER BOY FOR HALY'S CIRCUS, JIMMY.
COMING SOON TO AMUSEMENT MILE
TAKE IT UP WITH GRAYSON. I'M THE LAST GUY WHO WANTS HIS FACE ON A WALL.
WELL, WHEN IT LOOKS LIKE THAT, IT'S NO WONDER...
UH-HUH. STICK TO GYMNASTICS, MARC. COMEDY'S NOT YOUR THING.
SO, YOU OUT OF HERE?
GONNA GRAB A DRINK. BUT I'LL SEE YOU GUYS BACK AT THE TRAIN?
COOL. LATER, JIMMY.
TSK TSK TSK
NO...I JUST DON'T SEE IT. I MEAN...

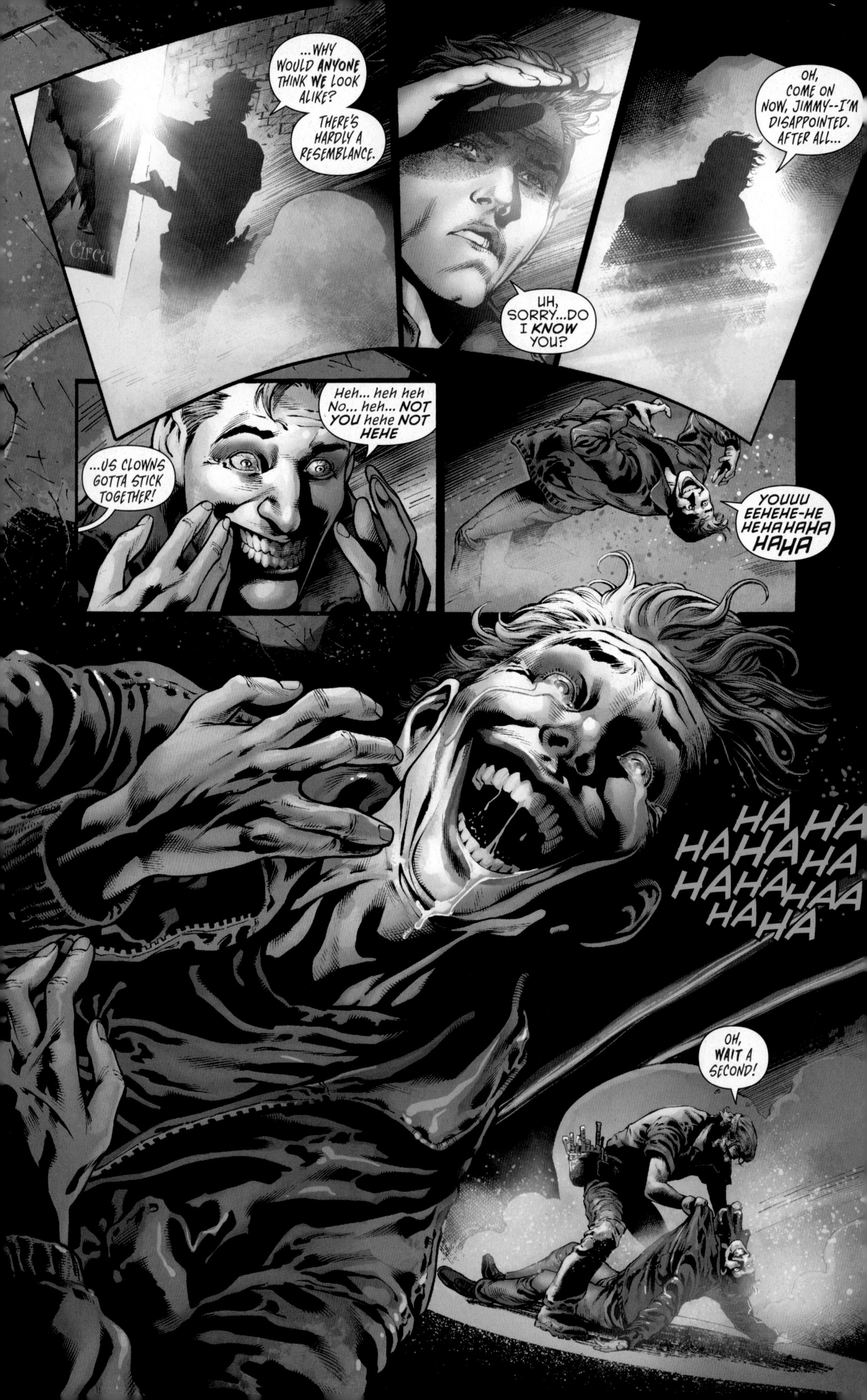
...WHY WOULD ANYONE THINK WE LOOK ALIKE?
THERE'S HARDLY A RESEMBLANCE.
UH, SORRY...DO I KNOW YOU?
OH, COME ON NOW, JIMMY--I'M DISAPPOINTED. AFTER ALL...
...US CLOWNS GOTTA STICK TOGETHER!
Heh... heh heh No... heh... NOT YOU hehe NOT HEHE
YOUUU EEHEHE-HE HEHAHAHA HAHA
HA HA HAHAHA HAHAHAA HAHA
OH, WAIT A SECOND!

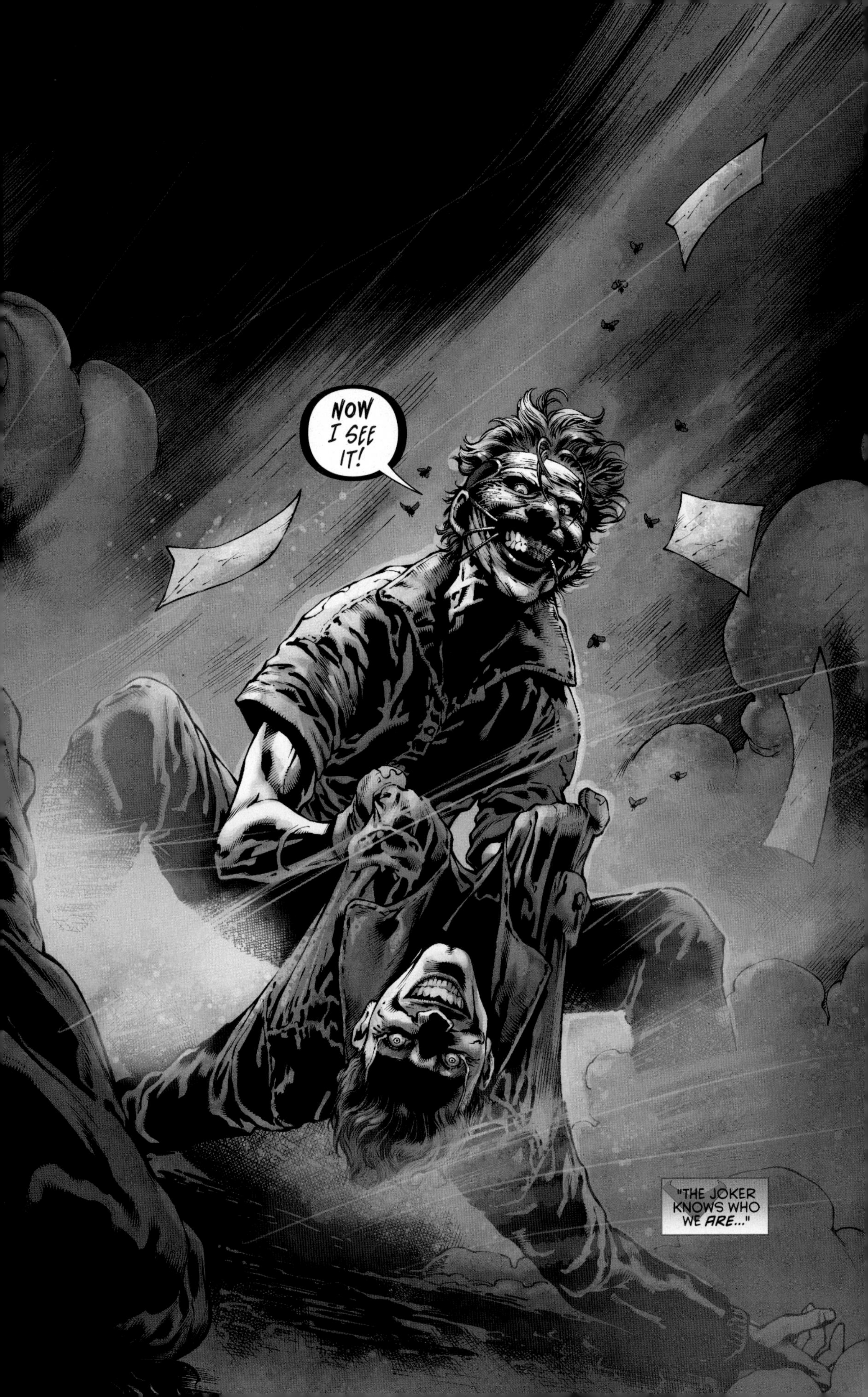
NOW I SEE IT!
"THE JOKER KNOWS WHO WE ARE..."

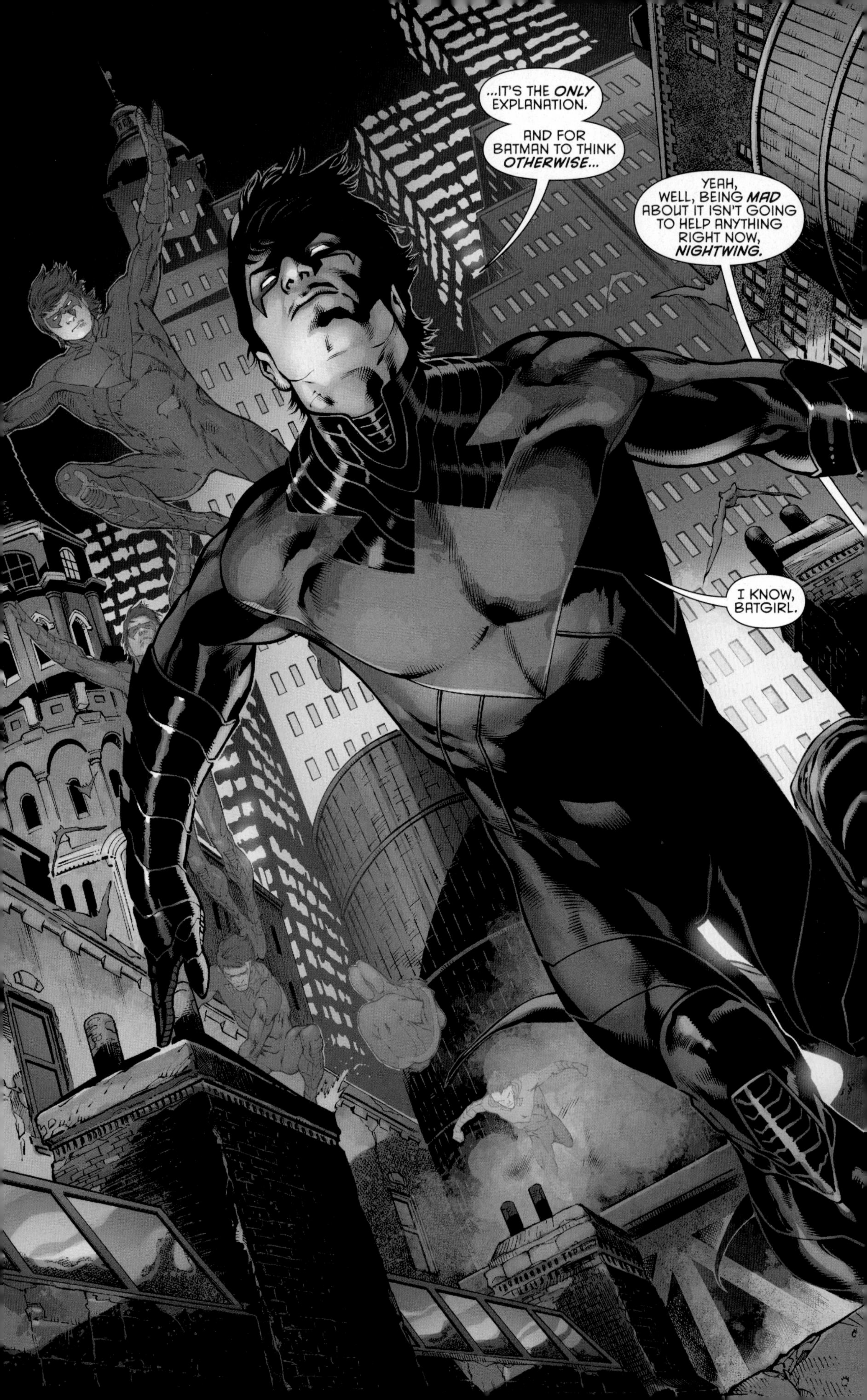
...IT'S THE ONLY EXPLANATION.
AND FOR BATMAN TO THINK OTHERWISE...
YEAH, WELL, BEING MAD ABOUT IT ISN'T GOING TO HELP ANYTHING RIGHT NOW, NIGHTWING.
I KNOW, BATGIRL.

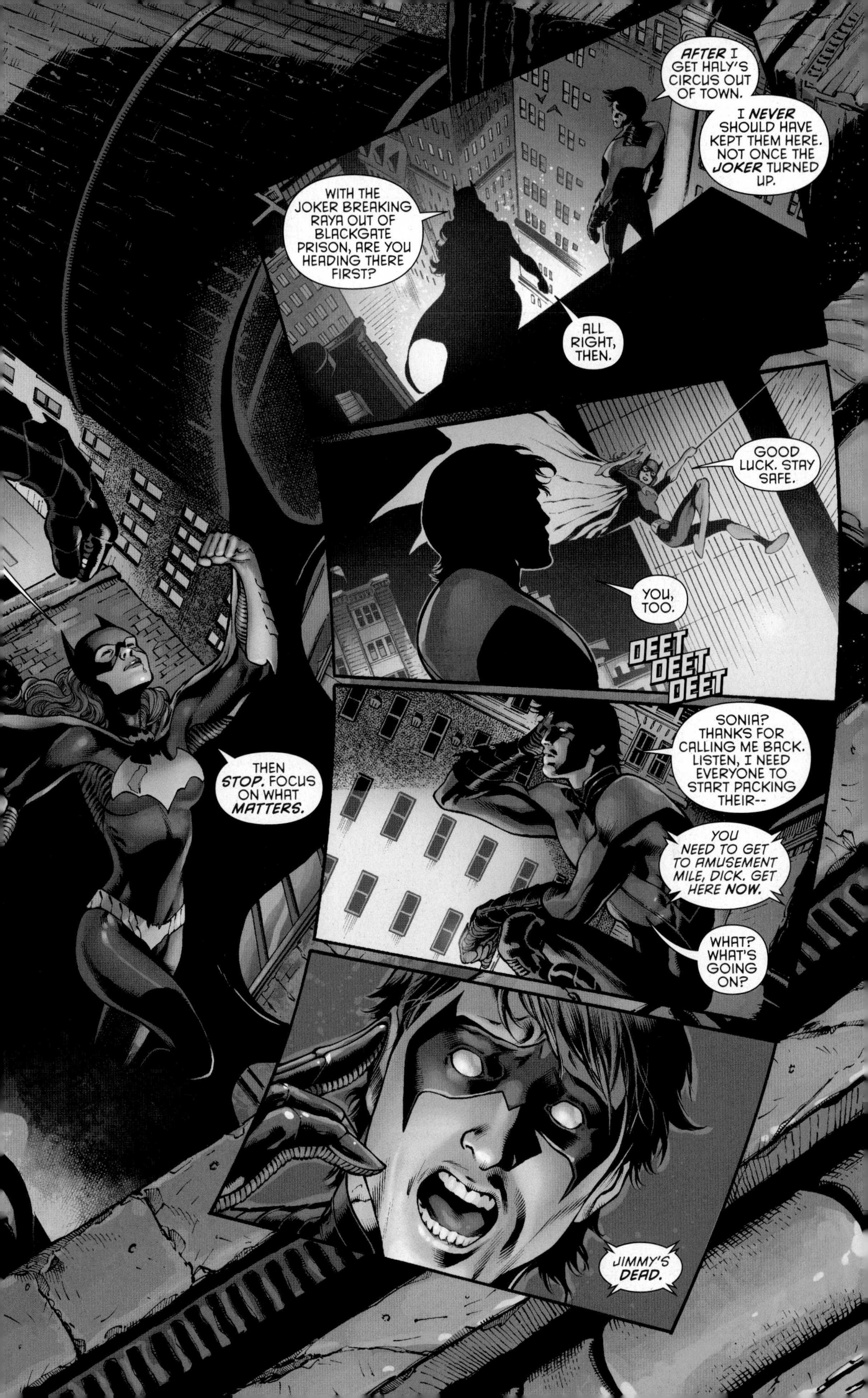
WITH THE JOKER BREAKING RAYA OUT OF BLACKGATE PRISON, ARE YOU HEADING THERE FIRST?
AFTER I GET HALY'S CIRCUS OUT OF TOWN.
I NEVER SHOULD HAVE KEPT THEM HERE. NOT ONCE THE JOKER TURNED UP.
ALL RIGHT, THEN.
GOOD LUCK. STAY SAFE.
YOU, TOO.
DEET DEET DEET
SONIA? THANKS FOR CALLING ME BACK. LISTEN, I NEED EVERYONE TO START PACKING THEIR--
YOU NEED TO GET TO AMUSEMENT MILE, DICK. GET HERE NOW.
WHAT? WHAT'S GOING ON?
JIMMY'S DEAD.
THEN STOP. FOCUS ON WHAT MATTERS.

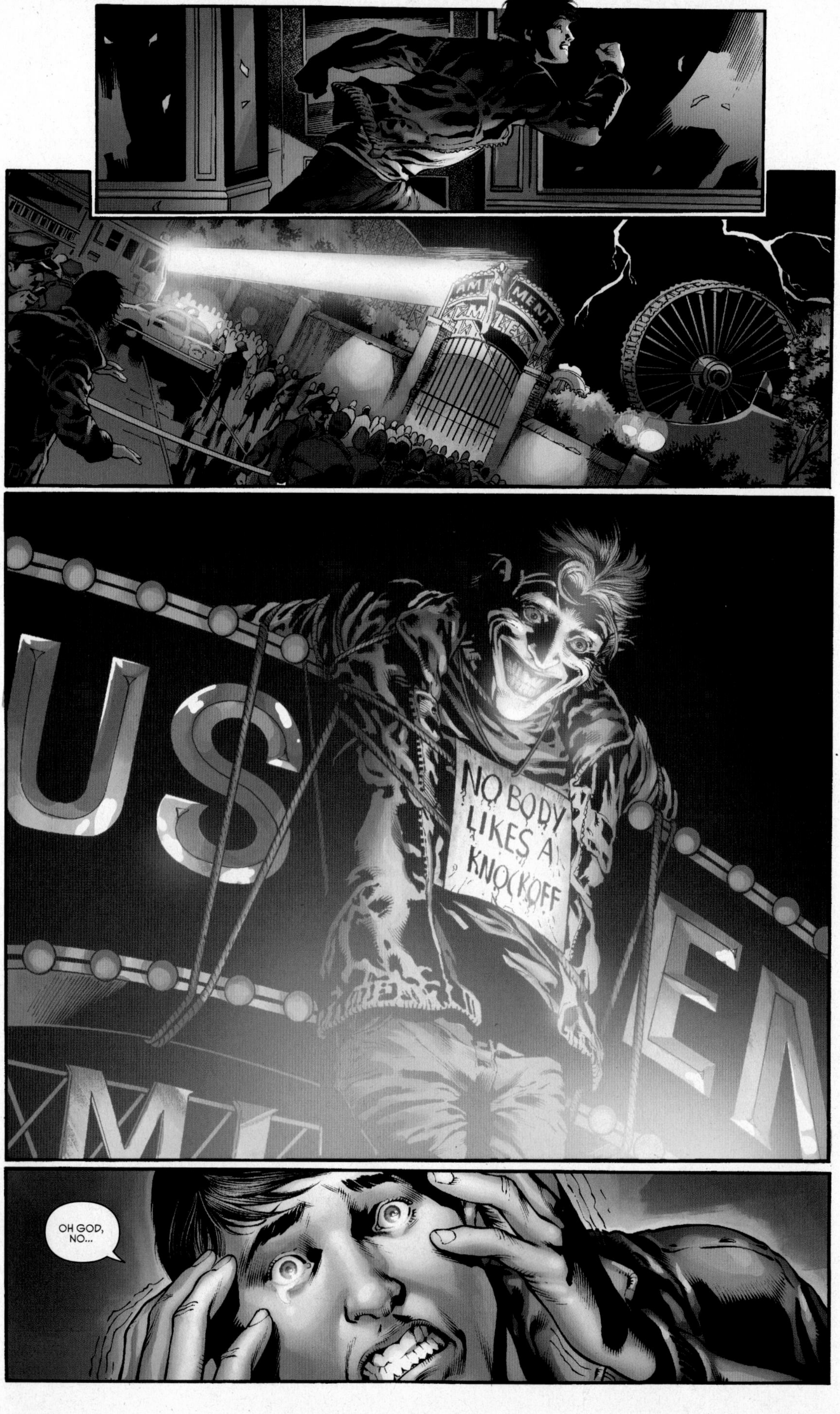
AMUSEMENT
NO BODY LIKES A KNOCKOFF
OH GOD, NO...

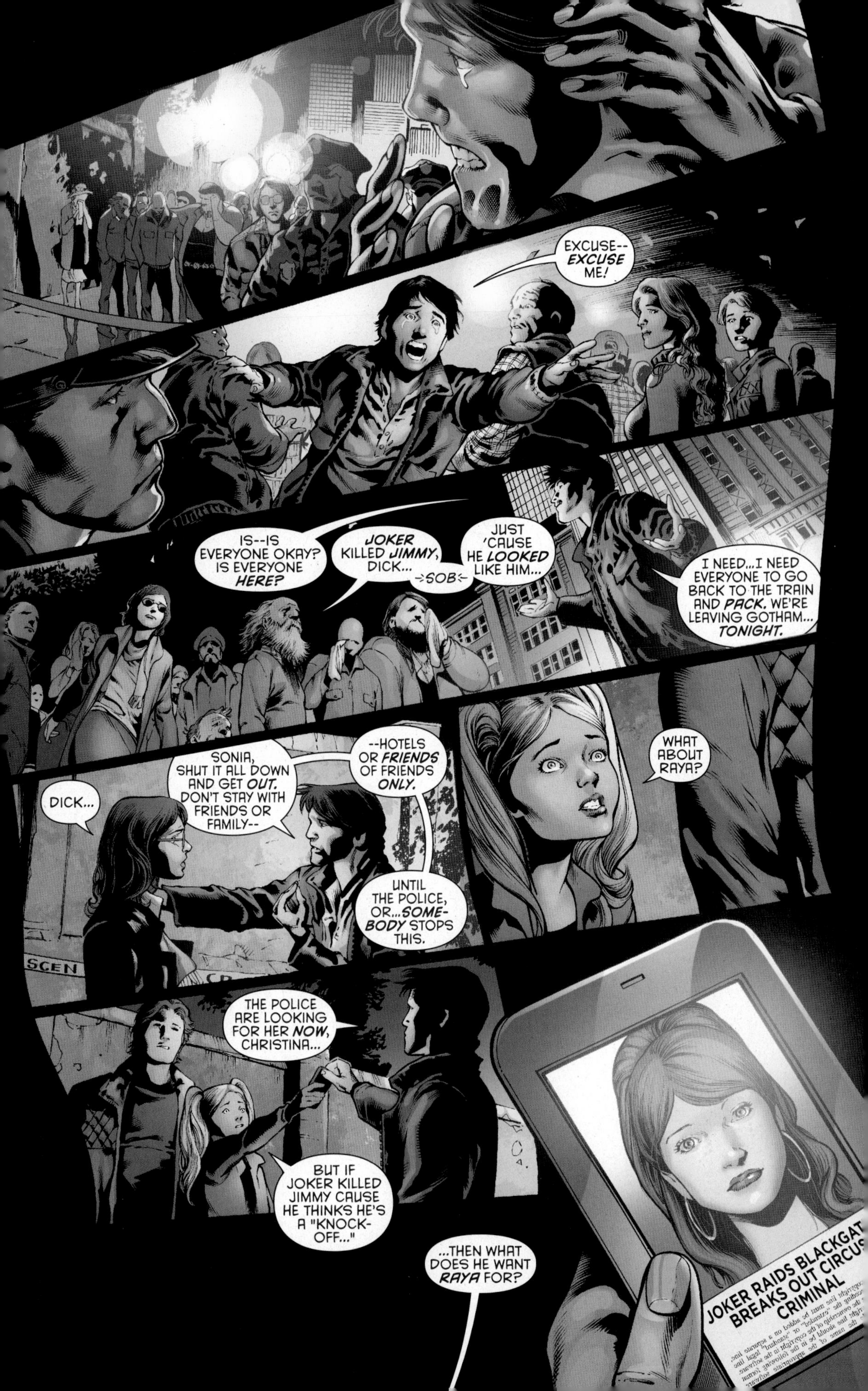

EXCUSE-- EXCUSE ME!
IS--IS EVERYONE OKAY? IS EVERYONE HERE?
JOKER KILLED JIMMY, DICK...
SOB
JUST 'CAUSE HE LOOKED LIKE HIM...
I NEED...I NEED EVERYONE TO GO BACK TO THE TRAIN AND PACK. WE'RE LEAVING GOTHAM... TONIGHT.
WHAT ABOUT RAYA?
DICK...
SONIA, SHUT IT ALL DOWN AND GET OUT. DON'T STAY WITH FRIENDS OR FAMILY--
--HOTELS OR FRIENDS OF FRIENDS ONLY.
UNTIL THE POLICE, OR...SOMEBODY STOPS THIS.
THE POLICE ARE LOOKING FOR HER NOW, CHRISTINA...
BUT IF JOKER KILLED JIMMY CAUSE HE THINKS HE'S A "KNOCK-OFF..."
...THEN WHAT DOES HE WANT RAYA FOR?
JOKER RAIDS BLACKGAT
BREAKS OUT CIRCUS
CRIMINAL

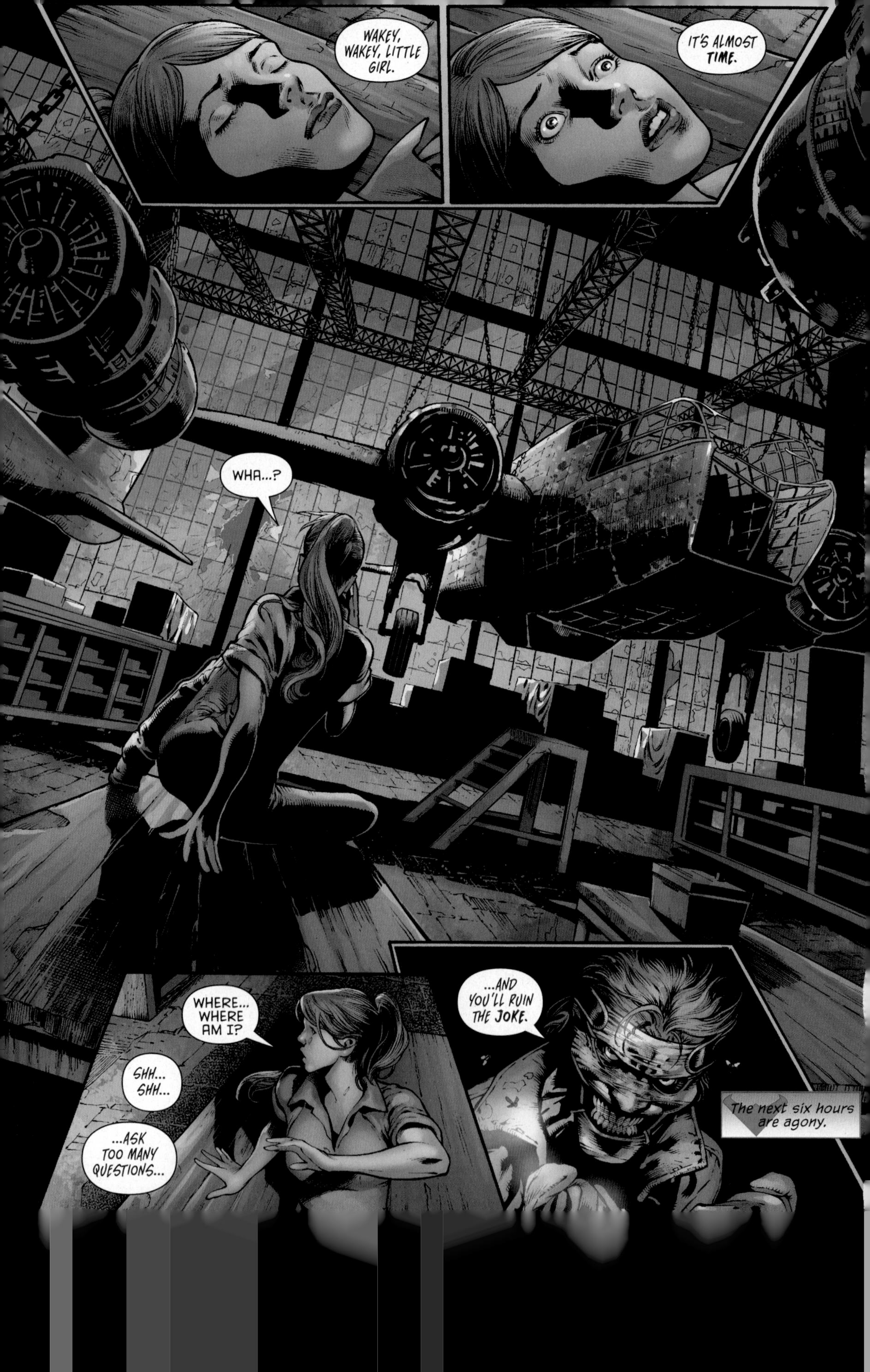
WAKEY, WAKEY, LITTLE GIRL.
IT'S ALMOST TIME.
WHA...?
WHERE... WHERE AM I?
SHH... SHH...
...ASK TOO MANY QUESTIONS...
...AND YOU'LL RUIN THE JOKE.
The next six hours are agony.

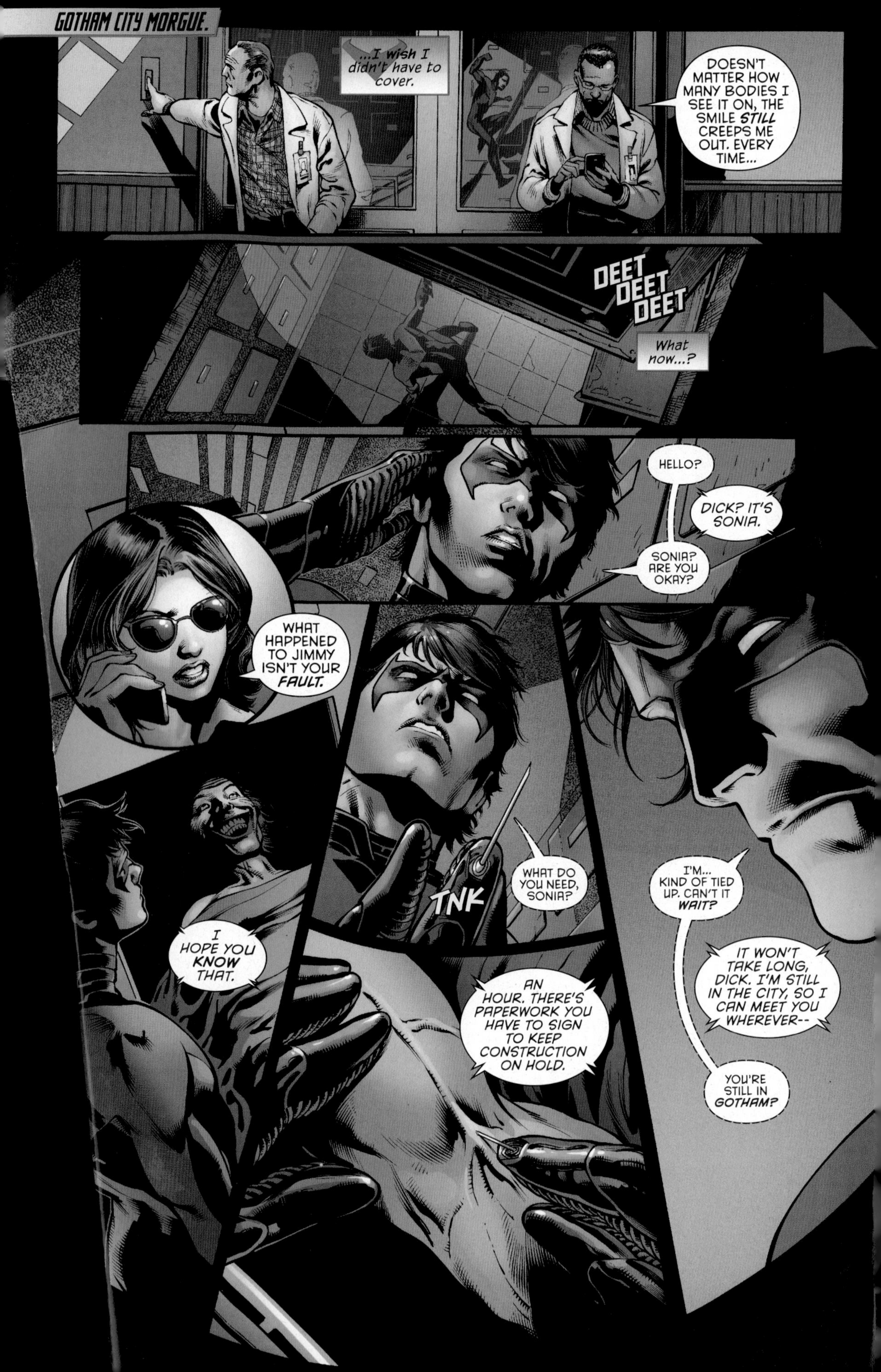
GOTHAM CITY MORGUE.
...I wish I didn't have to cover.
DOESN'T MATTER HOW MANY BODIES I SEE IT ON, THE SMILE STILL CREEPS ME OUT. EVERY TIME...
DEET DEET DEET
What now...?
HELLO?
DICK? IT'S SONIA.
SONIA? ARE YOU OKAY?
WHAT HAPPENED TO JIMMY ISN'T YOUR FAULT.
I HOPE YOU KNOW THAT.
TNK
WHAT DO YOU NEED, SONIA?
I'M... KIND OF TIED UP. CAN'T IT WAIT?
IT WON'T TAKE LONG, DICK. I'M STILL IN THE CITY, SO I CAN MEET YOU WHEREVER--
YOU'RE STILL IN GOTHAM?
AN HOUR. THERE'S PAPERWORK YOU HAVE TO SIGN TO KEEP CONSTRUCTION ON HOLD.

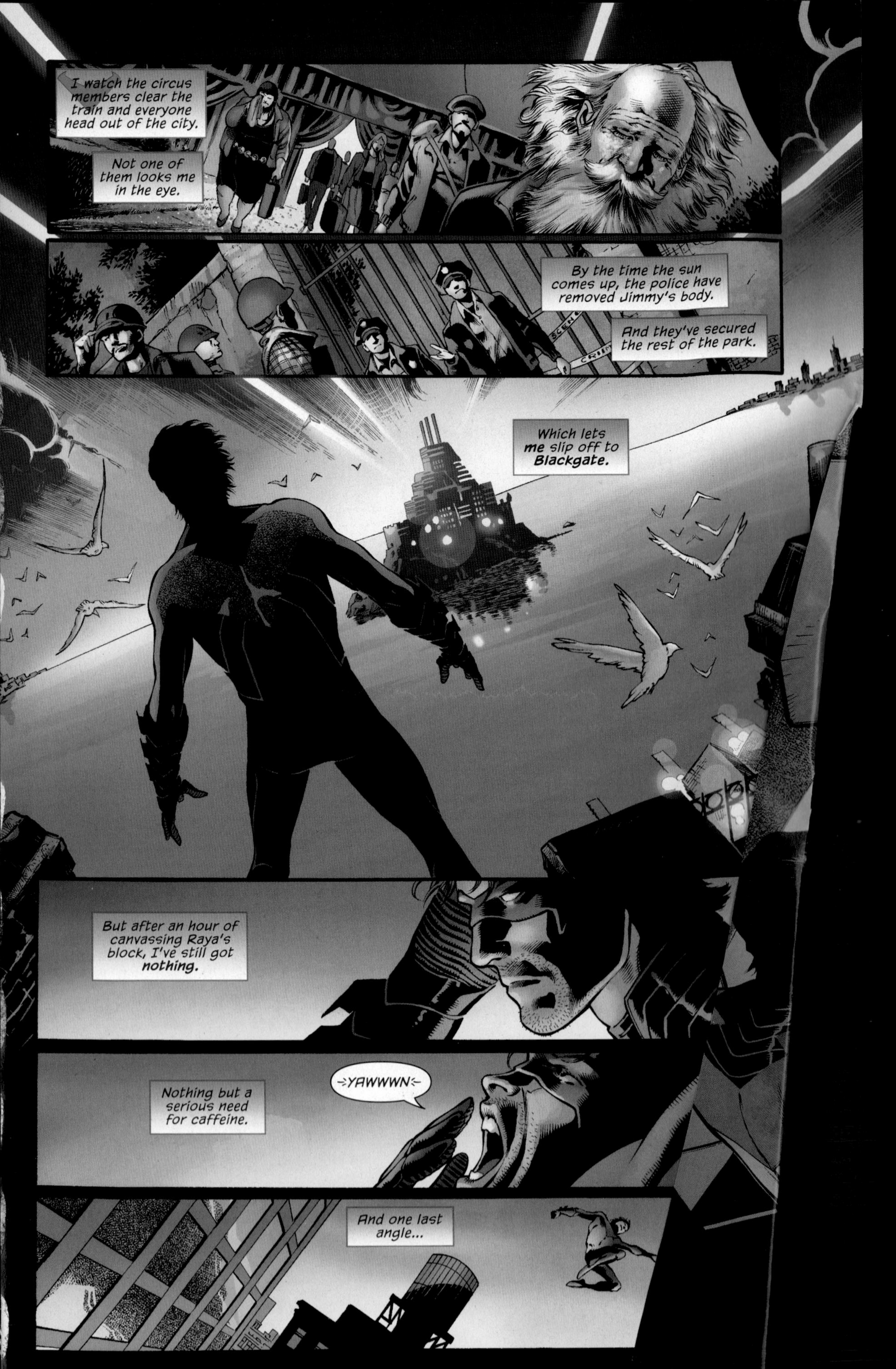

I watch the circus members clear the train and everyone head out of the city.
Not one of them looks me in the eye.
By the time the sun comes up, the police have removed Jimmy's body.
And they've secured the rest of the park.
Which lets **me** slip off to **Blackgate.**
But after an hour of canvassing Raya's block, I've still got **nothing.**
Nothing but a serious need for caffeine.
YAWWWN
And one last angle...

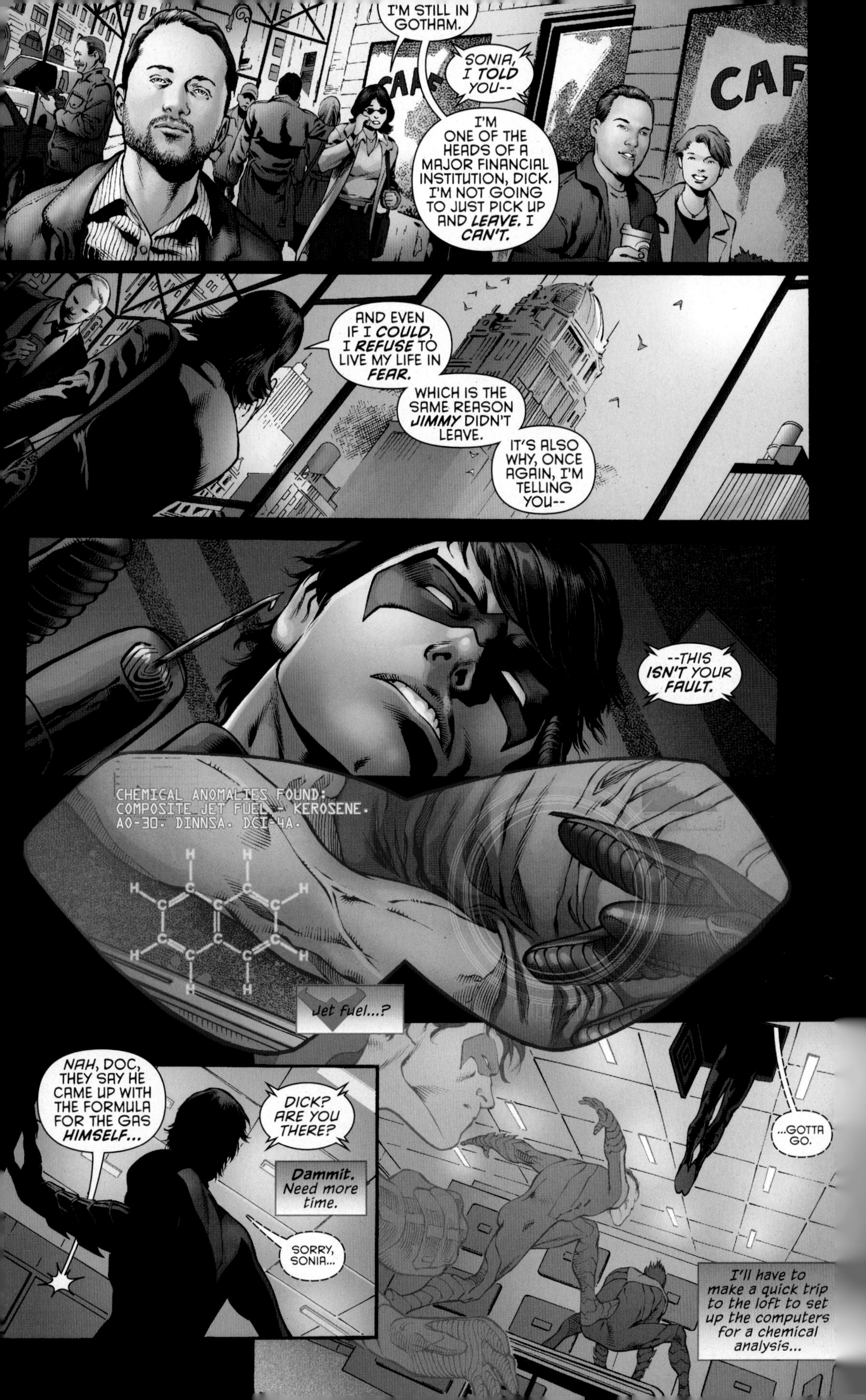
I'M STILL IN GOTHAM.
SONIA, I TOLD YOU--
I'M ONE OF THE HEADS OF A MAJOR FINANCIAL INSTITUTION, DICK. I'M NOT GOING TO JUST PICK UP AND LEAVE. I CAN'T.
CAF
AND EVEN IF I COULD, I REFUSE TO LIVE MY LIFE IN FEAR.
WHICH IS THE SAME REASON JIMMY DIDN'T LEAVE.
IT'S ALSO WHY, ONCE AGAIN, I'M TELLING YOU--
--THIS ISN'T YOUR FAULT.
CHEMICAL ANOMALIES FOUND:
COMPOSITE JET FUEL - KEROSENE.
AO-30. DINNSA. DCI-4A.
Jet fuel...?
NAH, DOC, THEY SAY HE CAME UP WITH THE FORMULA FOR THE GAS HIMSELF...
DICK? ARE YOU THERE?
Dammit. Need more time.
SORRY, SONIA...
...GOTTA GO.
I'll have to make a quick trip to the loft to set up the computers for a chemical analysis...

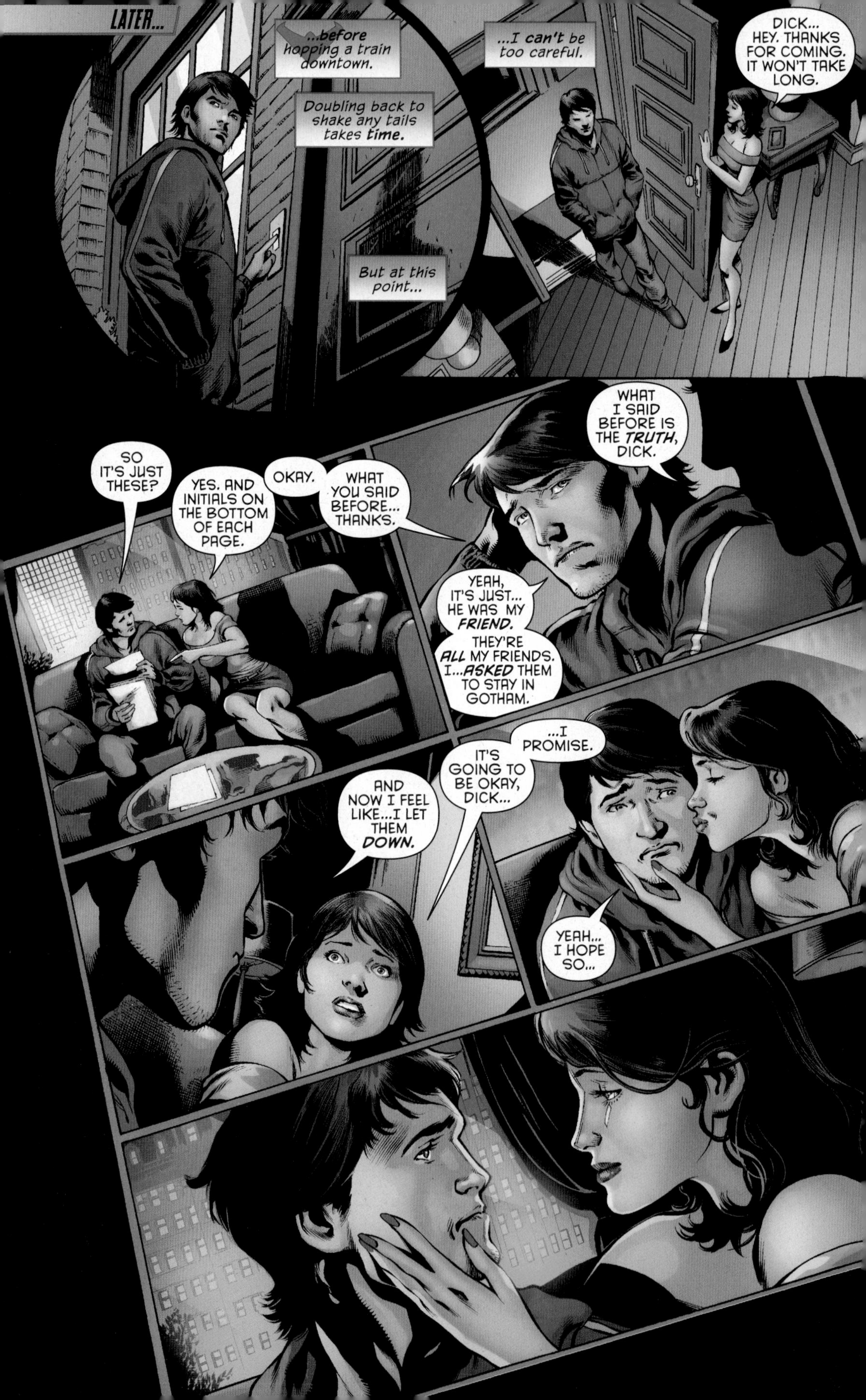
LATER...
...before hopping a train downtown.
Doubling back to shake any tails takes time.
But at this point...
...I can't be too careful.
DICK... HEY. THANKS FOR COMING. IT WON'T TAKE LONG.
SO IT'S JUST THESE?
YES. AND INITIALS ON THE BOTTOM OF EACH PAGE.
OKAY.
WHAT YOU SAID BEFORE... THANKS.
WHAT I SAID BEFORE IS THE TRUTH, DICK.
YEAH, IT'S JUST... HE WAS MY FRIEND.
THEY'RE ALL MY FRIENDS. I...ASKED THEM TO STAY IN GOTHAM.
AND NOW I FEEL LIKE...I LET THEM DOWN.
IT'S GOING TO BE OKAY, DICK...
...I PROMISE.
YEAH... I HOPE SO...

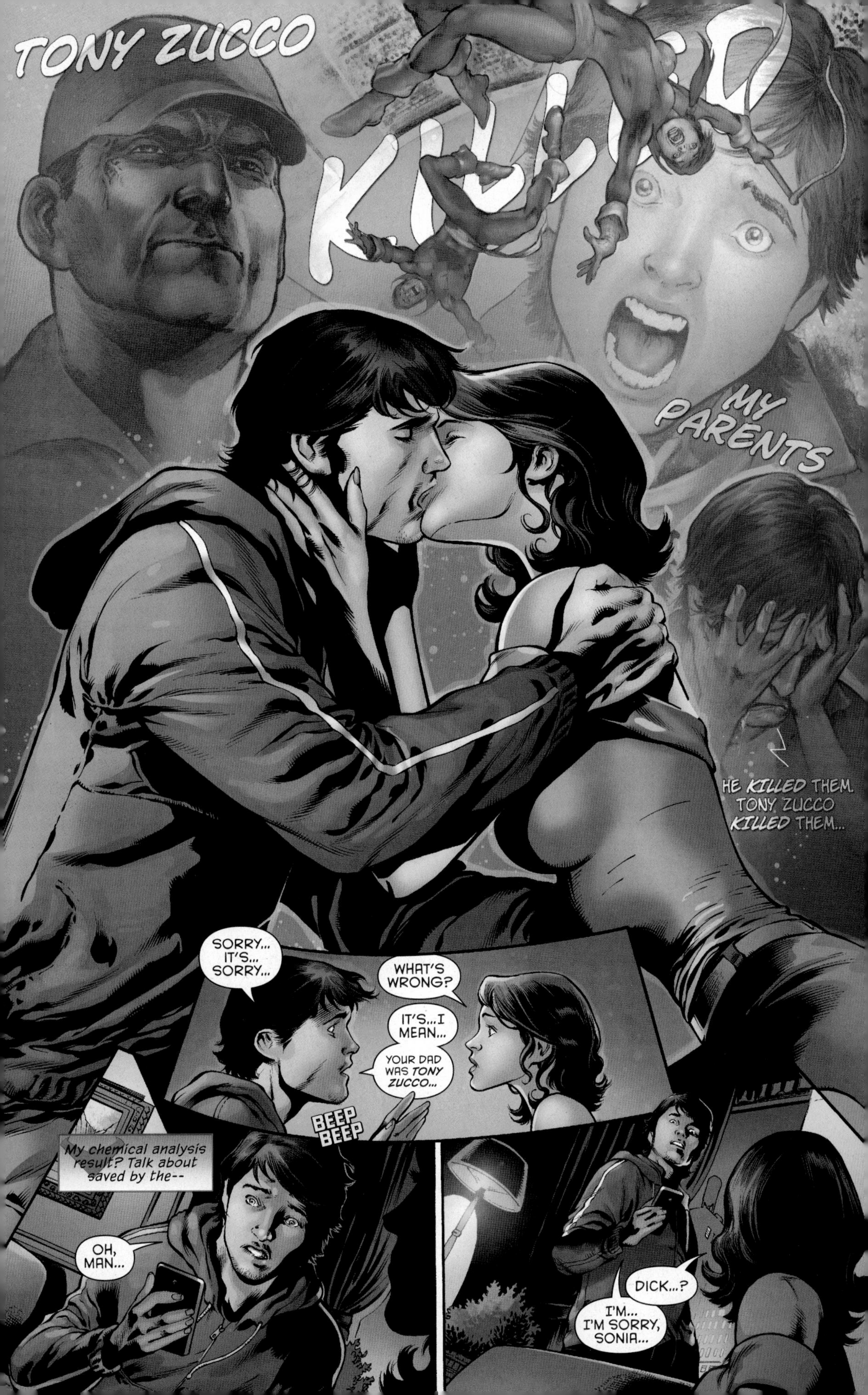
TONY ZUCCO
KILLED
MY PARENTS
HE KILLED THEM. TONY ZUCCO KILLED THEM...
SORRY... IT'S... SORRY...
WHAT'S WRONG?
IT'S...I MEAN...
YOUR DAD WAS TONY ZUCCO...
BEEP BEEP
My chemical analysis result? Talk about saved by the--
OH, MAN...
DICK...?
I'M... I'M SORRY, SONIA...

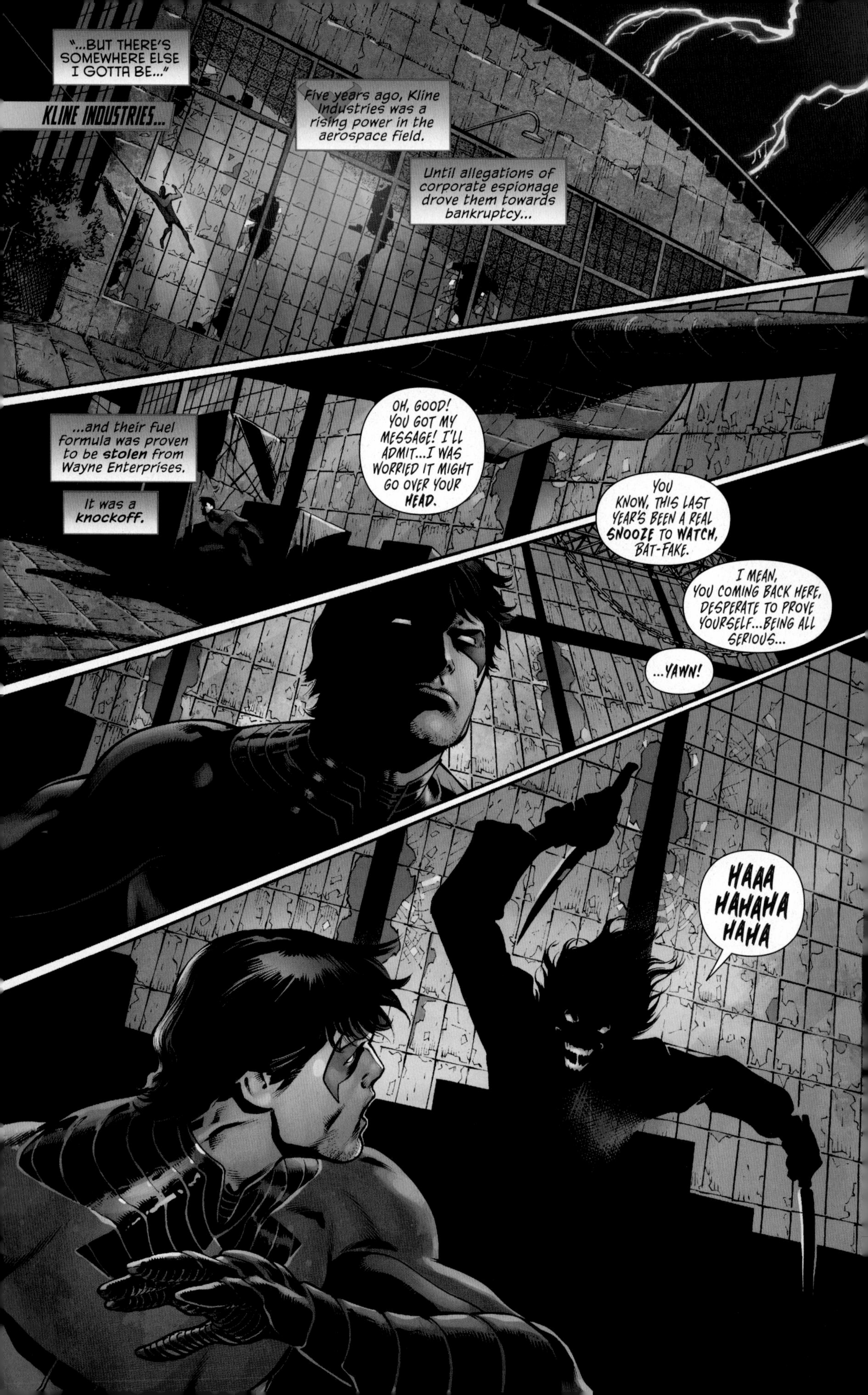
"...BUT THERE'S SOMEWHERE ELSE I GOTTA BE..."
KLINE INDUSTRIES...
Five years ago, Kline Industries was a rising power in the aerospace field.
Until allegations of corporate espionage drove them towards bankruptcy...
...and their fuel formula was proven to be stolen from Wayne Enterprises.
It was a knockoff.
OH, GOOD! YOU GOT MY MESSAGE! I'LL ADMIT...I WAS WORRIED IT MIGHT GO OVER YOUR HEAD.
YOU KNOW, THIS LAST YEAR'S BEEN A REAL SNOOZE TO WATCH, BAT-FAKE.
I MEAN, YOU COMING BACK HERE, DESPERATE TO PROVE YOURSELF...BEING ALL SERIOUS...
...YAWN!
HAAA HAHAHA HAHA

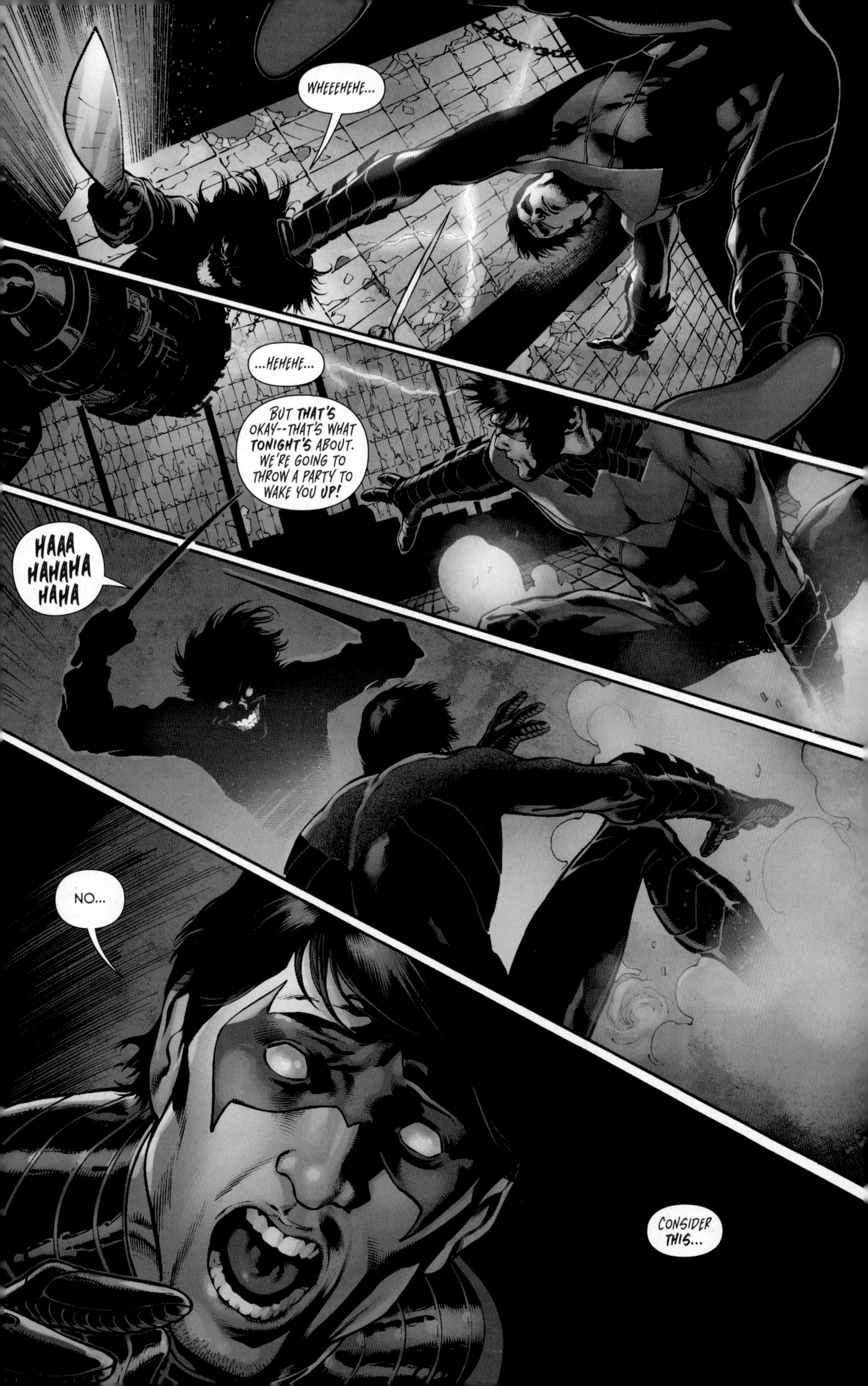

WHEEEHEHE...
...HEHEHE...
BUT THAT'S OKAY--THAT'S WHAT TONIGHT'S ABOUT. WE'RE GOING TO THROW A PARTY TO WAKE YOU UP!
HAAA HAHAHA HAHA
NO...
CONSIDER THIS...

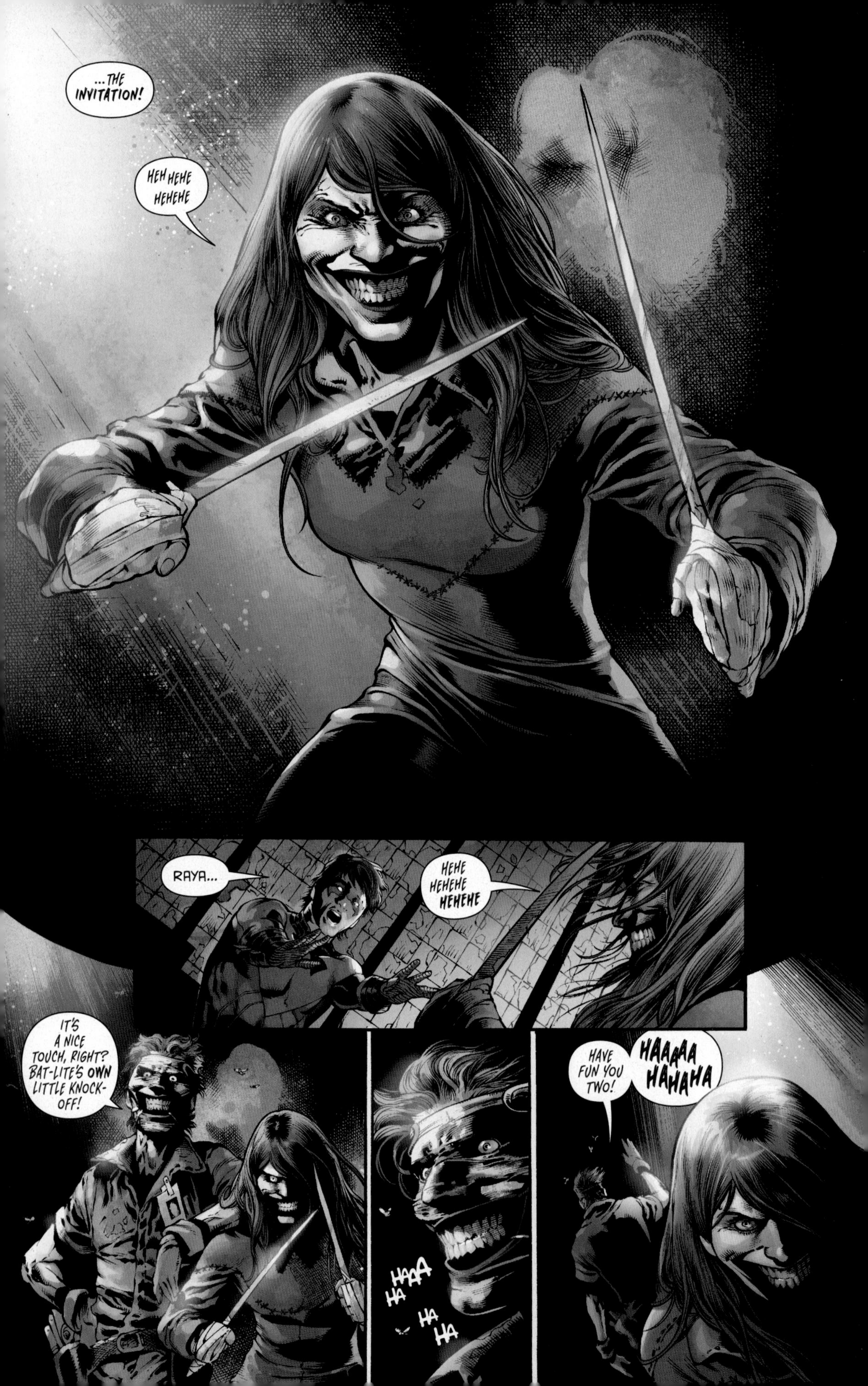
...THE INVITATION!
HEH HEHE HEHEHE
RAYA...
HEHE HEHEHE HEHEHE
IT'S A NICE TOUCH, RIGHT? BAT-LITE'S OWN LITTLE KNOCK-OFF!
HAAA HA
HA
HA
HAVE FUN YOU TWO!
HAAAAA HAHAHA

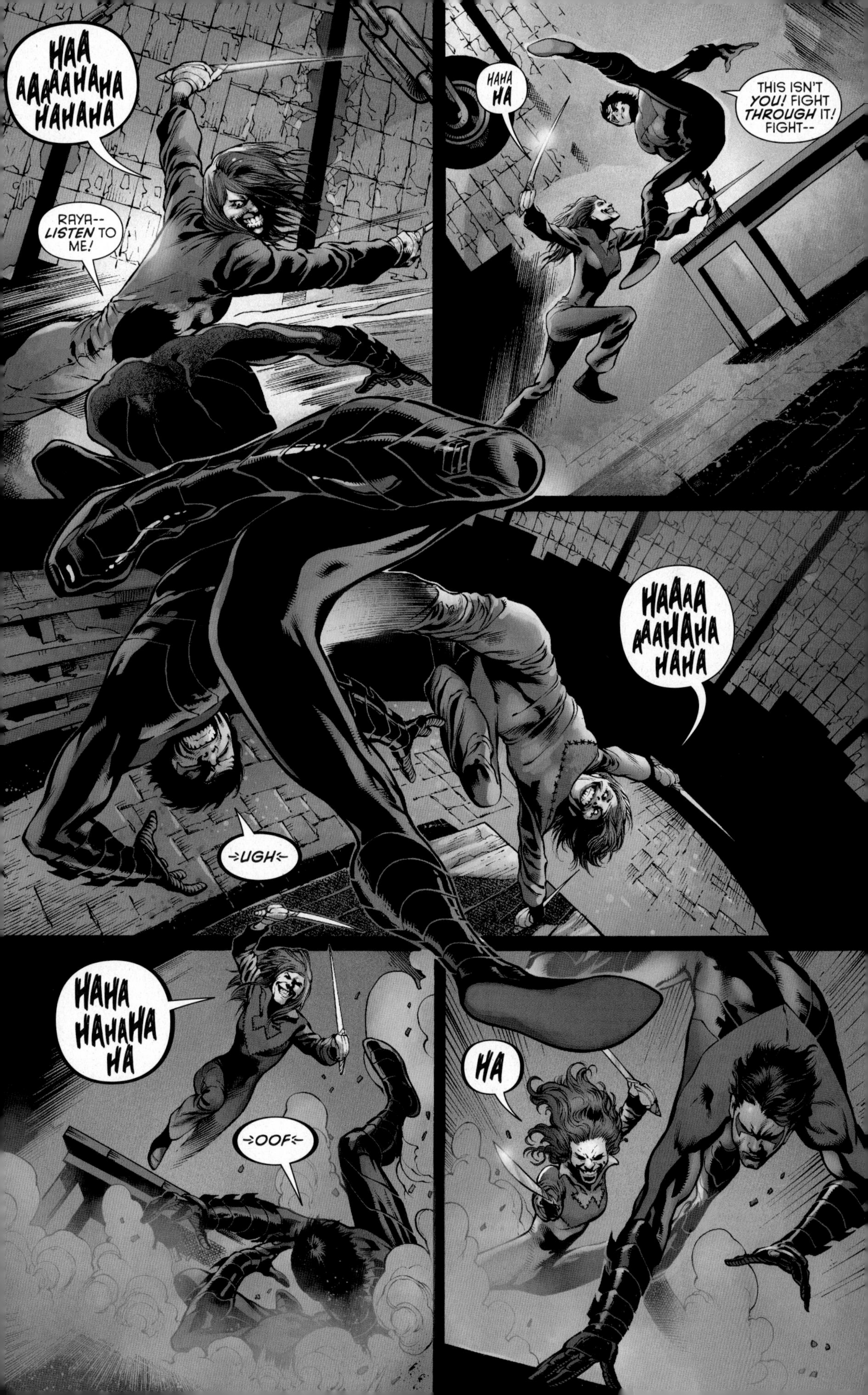
HAA AAAAAHAHA HAHAHA
RAYA-- LISTEN TO ME!
HAHA HA
THIS ISN'T YOU! FIGHT THROUGH IT! FIGHT--
HAAAA AAAHAHA HAHA
UGH
HAHA HAHAHA HA
OOF
HA

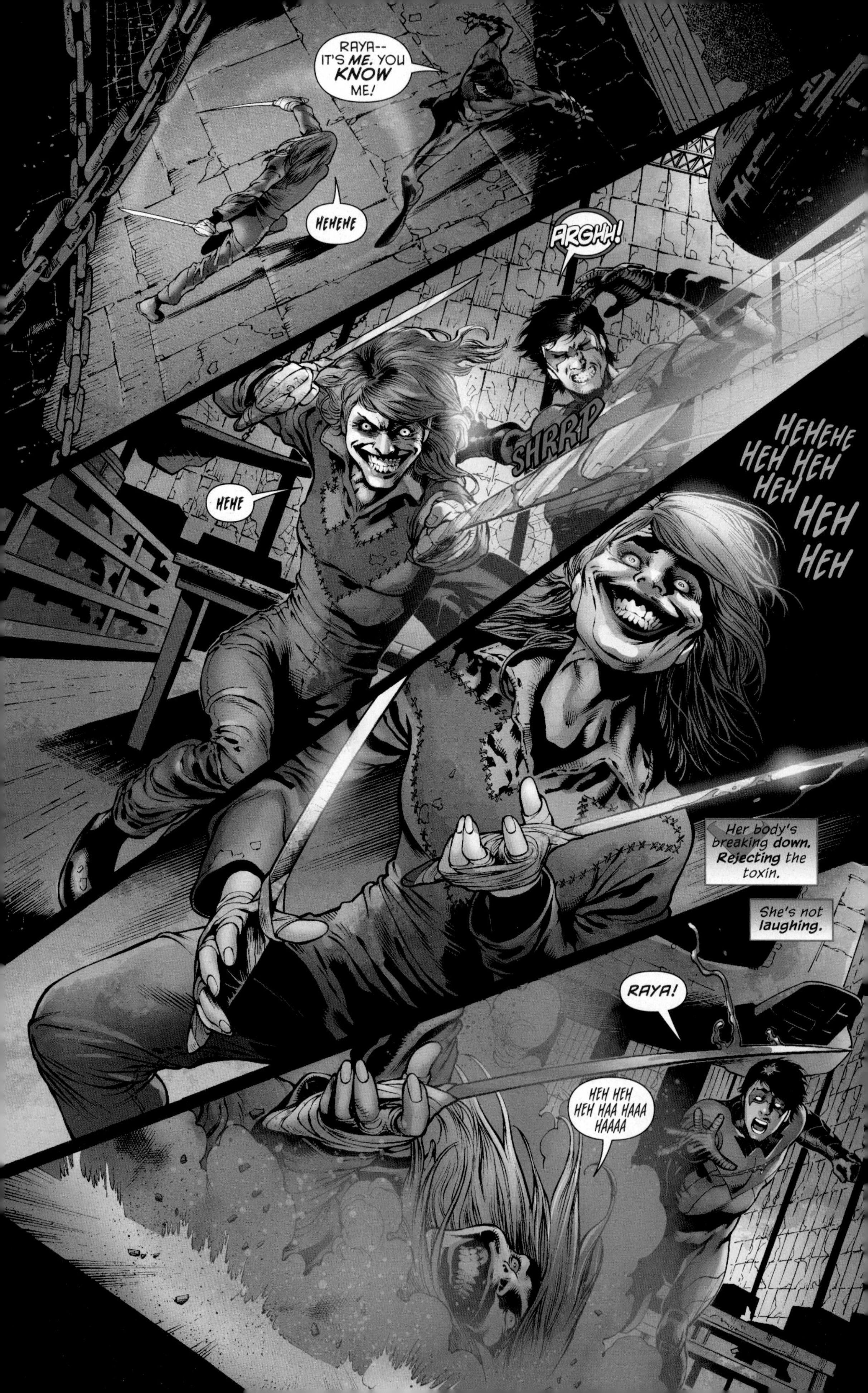
RAYA-- IT'S ME. YOU KNOW ME!
HEHEHE
ARGHH!
SHRRP
HEHE
HEHEHE HEH HEH HEH HEH HEH
Her body's breaking down. Rejecting the toxin.
She's not laughing.
RAYA!
HEH HEH HEH HAA HAAA HAAAA

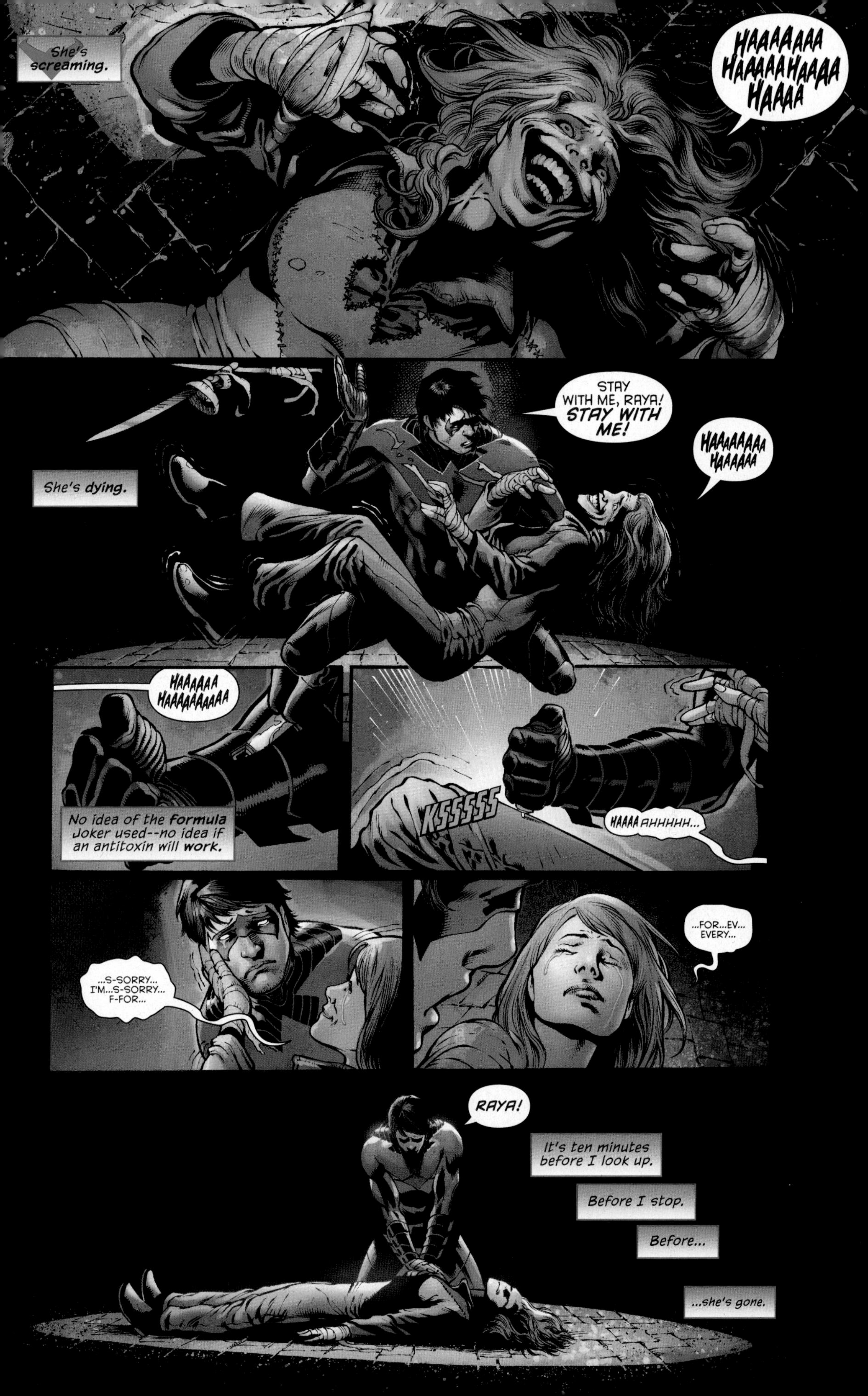
She's screaming.
HAAAAAAA HAAAAAHAAAA HAAAA
STAY WITH ME, RAYA! STAY WITH ME!
HAAAAAAAA HAAAAAA
She's dying.
HAAAAAA HAAAAAAAAAA
No idea of the formula Joker used--no idea if an antitoxin will work.
KSSSSS
HAAAA AHHHHHH...
...S-SORRY... I'M...S-SORRY... F-FOR...
...FOR...EV... EVERY...
RAYA!
It's ten minutes before I look up.
Before I stop.
Before...
...she's gone.

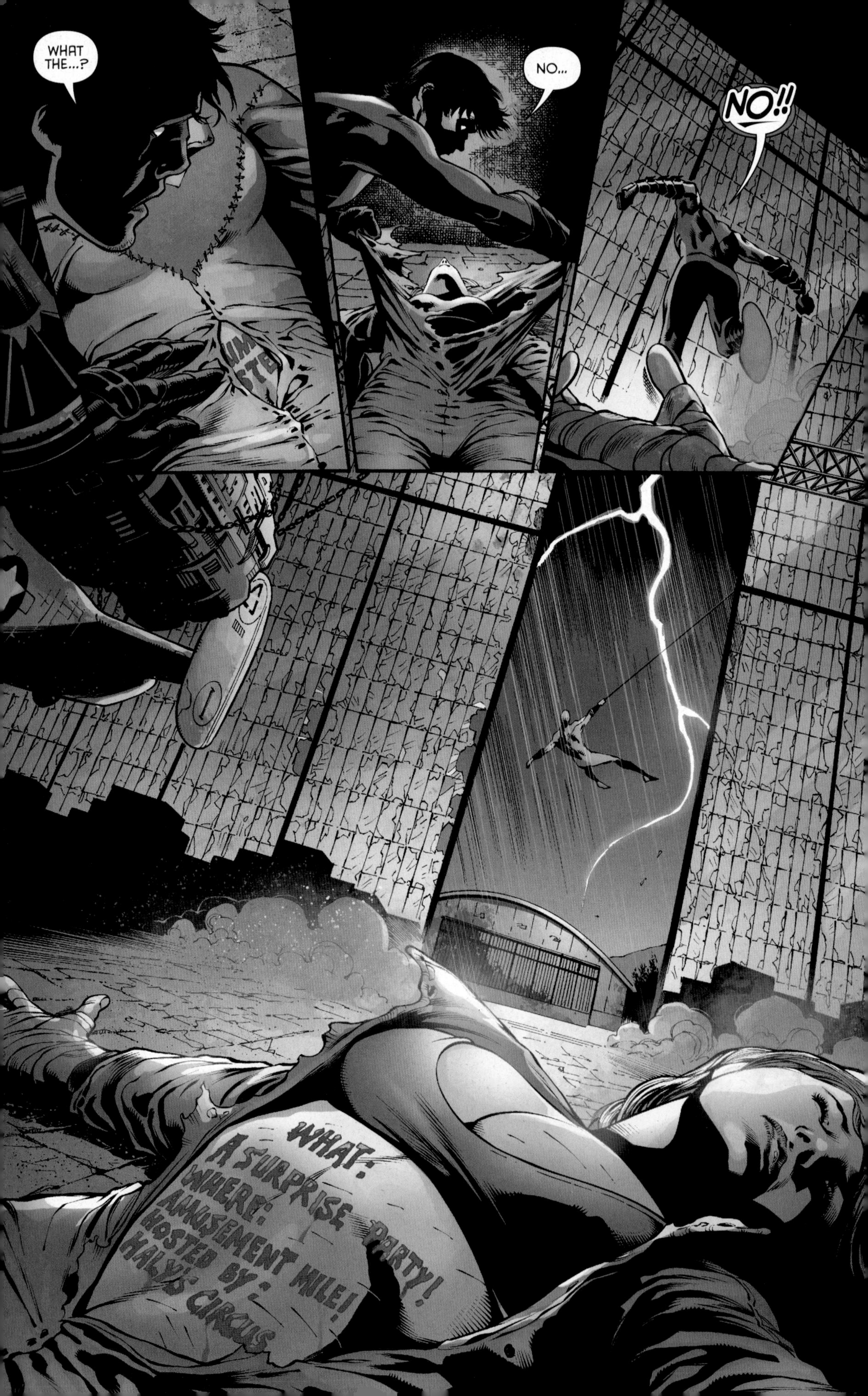
WHAT THE...?
NO...
NO!!
WHAT:
A SURPRISE PARTY!
WHERE:
AMUSEMENT MILE!
HOSTED BY:
HALY'S CIRCUS

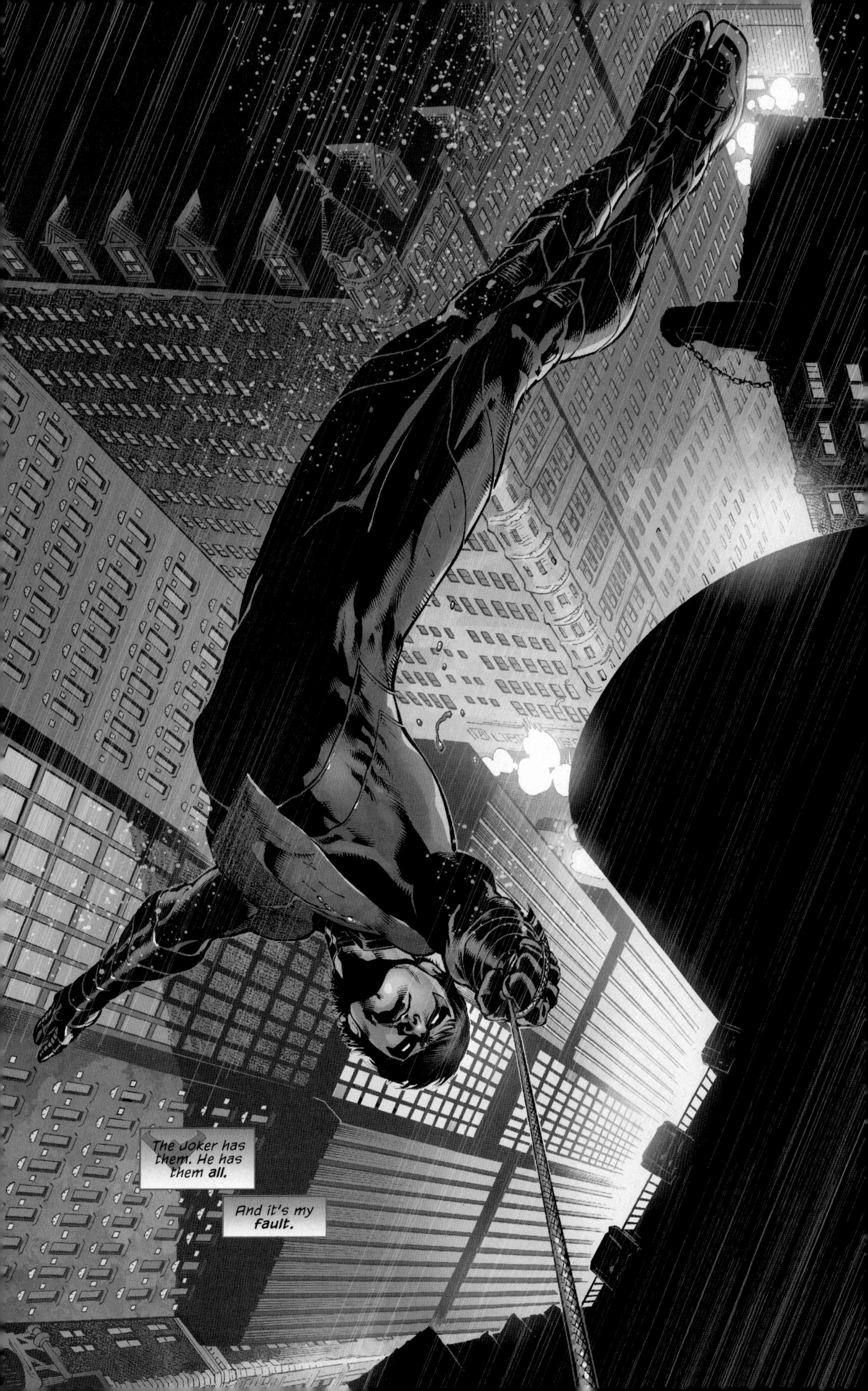

The Joker has them. He has them all.
And it's my fault.

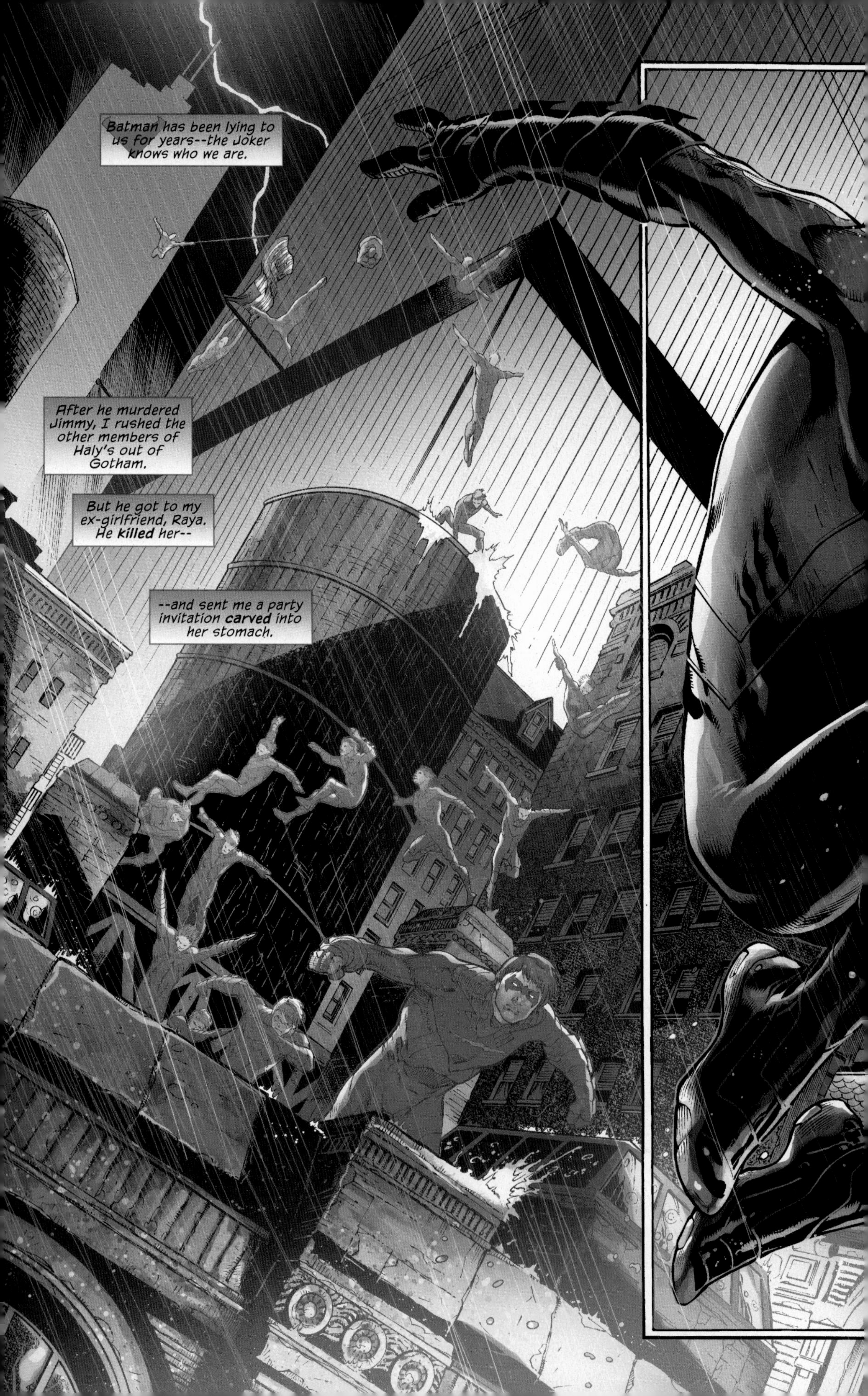
Batman has been lying to us for years--the Joker knows who we are.
After he murdered Jimmy, I rushed the other members of Haly's out of Gotham.
But he got to my ex-girlfriend, Raya. He **killed** her--
--and sent me a party invitation **carved** into her stomach.

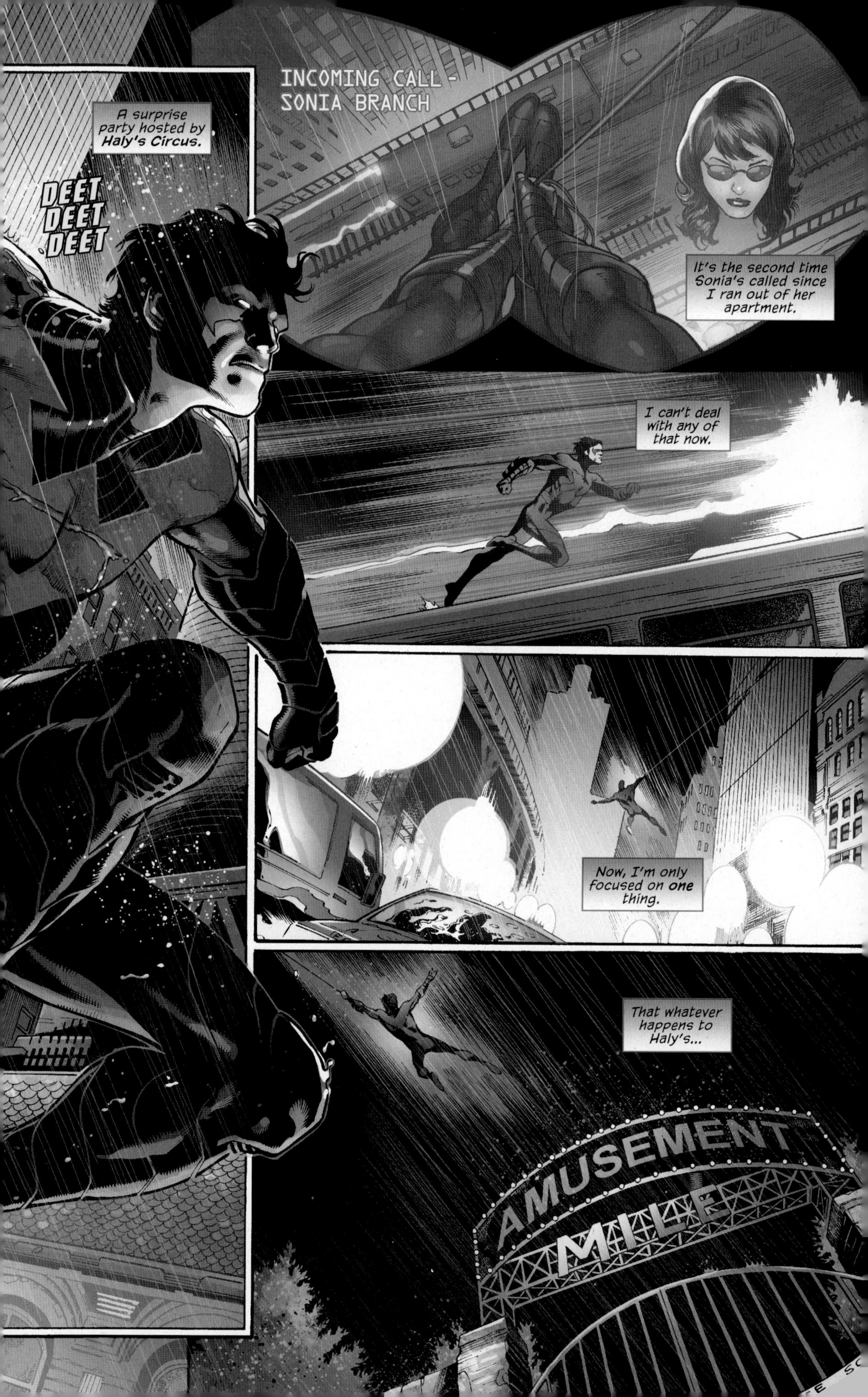
A surprise party hosted by Haly's Circus.
DEET DEET DEET
INCOMING CALL - SONIA BRANCH
It's the second time Sonia's called since I ran out of her apartment.
I can't deal with any of that now.
Now, I'm only focused on one thing.
That whatever happens to Haly's...
AMUSEMENT MILE

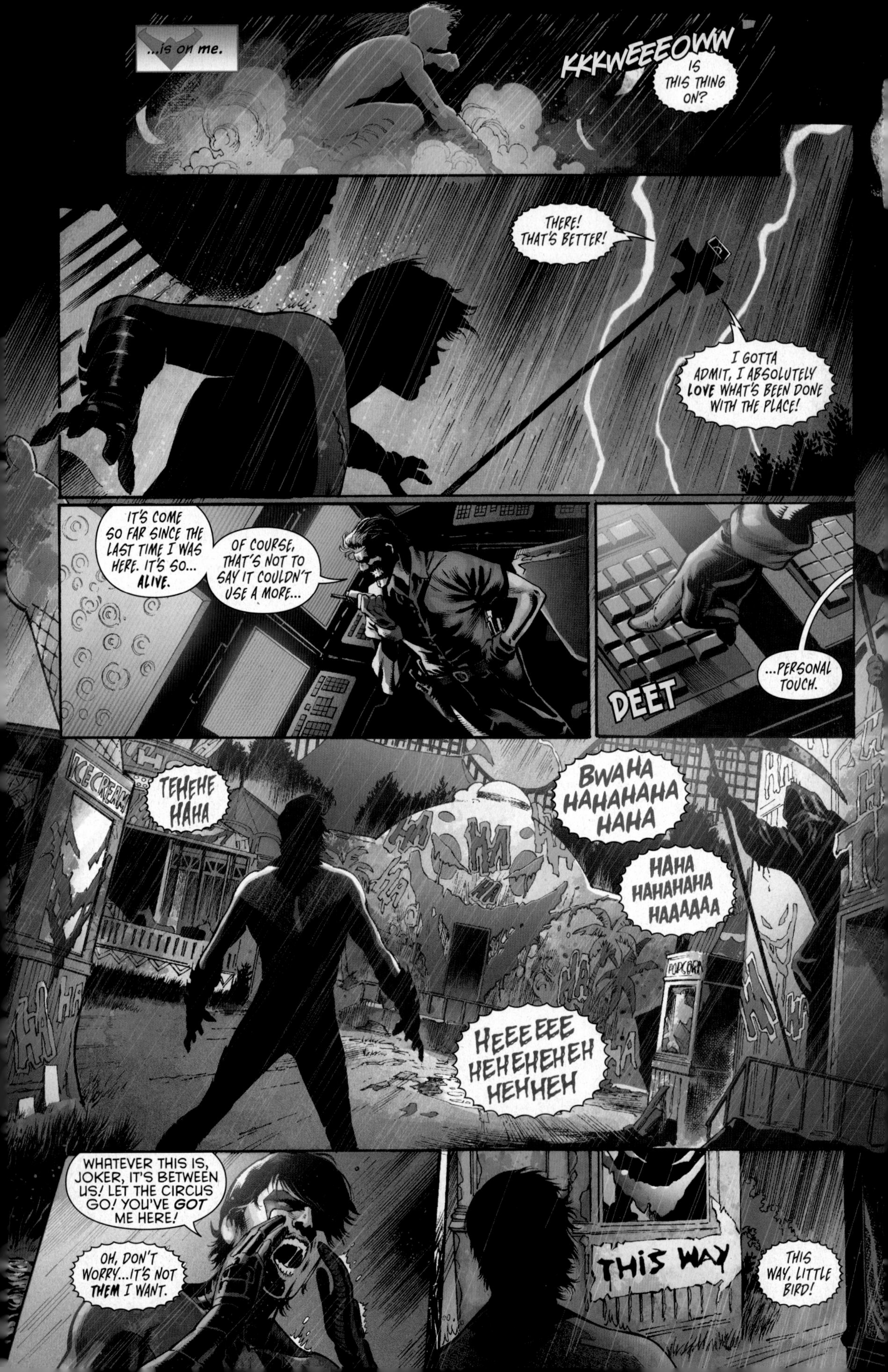
...is on me.
KKKWEEEOWN
IS THIS THING ON?
THERE! THAT'S BETTER!
I GOTTA ADMIT, I ABSOLUTELY LOVE WHAT'S BEEN DONE WITH THE PLACE!
IT'S COME SO FAR SINCE THE LAST TIME I WAS HERE. IT'S SO... ALIVE.
OF COURSE, THAT'S NOT TO SAY IT COULDN'T USE A MORE...
DEET
...PERSONAL TOUCH.
ICE CREAM
TEHEHE HAHA
BWAHA HAHAHAHA HAHA
HAHA HAHAHAHA HAAAAAA
POPCORN
HEEEEEE HEHEHEHEH HEHHEH
WHATEVER THIS IS, JOKER, IT'S BETWEEN US! LET THE CIRCUS GO! YOU'VE GOT ME HERE!
OH, DON'T WORRY...IT'S NOT THEM I WANT.
THIS WAY
THIS WAY, LITTLE BIRD!

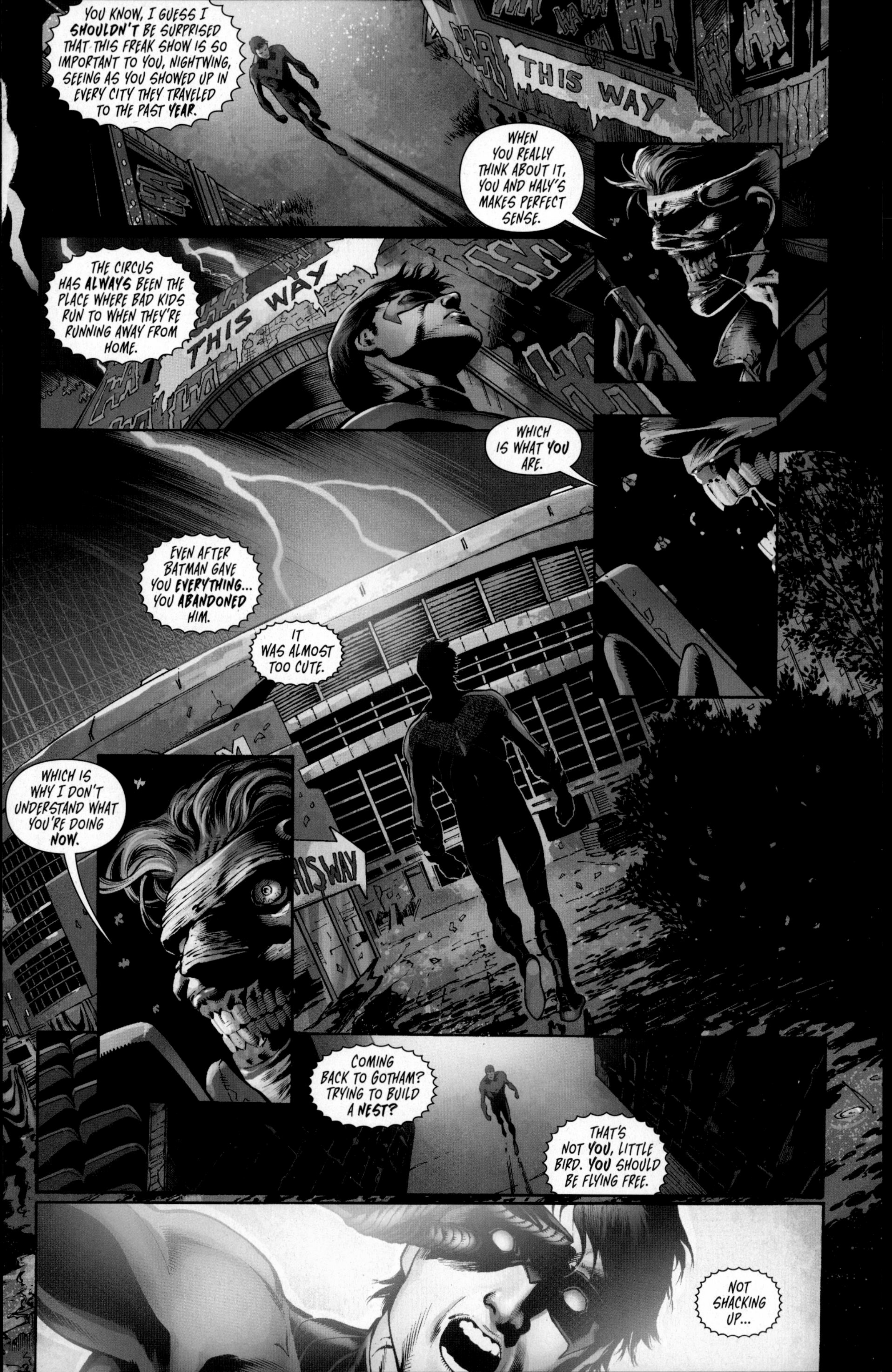
YOU KNOW, I GUESS I SHOULDN'T BE SURPRISED THAT THIS FREAK SHOW IS SO IMPORTANT TO YOU, NIGHTWING, SEEING AS YOU SHOWED UP IN EVERY CITY THEY TRAVELED TO THE PAST YEAR.
THIS WAY
WHEN YOU REALLY THINK ABOUT IT, YOU AND HALY'S MAKES PERFECT SENSE.
THE CIRCUS HAS ALWAYS BEEN THE PLACE WHERE BAD KIDS RUN TO WHEN THEY'RE RUNNING AWAY FROM HOME.
THIS WAY
WHICH IS WHAT YOU ARE.
EVEN AFTER BATMAN GAVE YOU EVERYTHING... YOU ABANDONED HIM.
IT WAS ALMOST TOO CUTE.
WHICH IS WHY I DON'T UNDERSTAND WHAT YOU'RE DOING NOW.
COMING BACK TO GOTHAM? TRYING TO BUILD A NEST?
THAT'S NOT YOU, LITTLE BIRD. YOU SHOULD BE FLYING FREE.
NOT SHACKING UP...

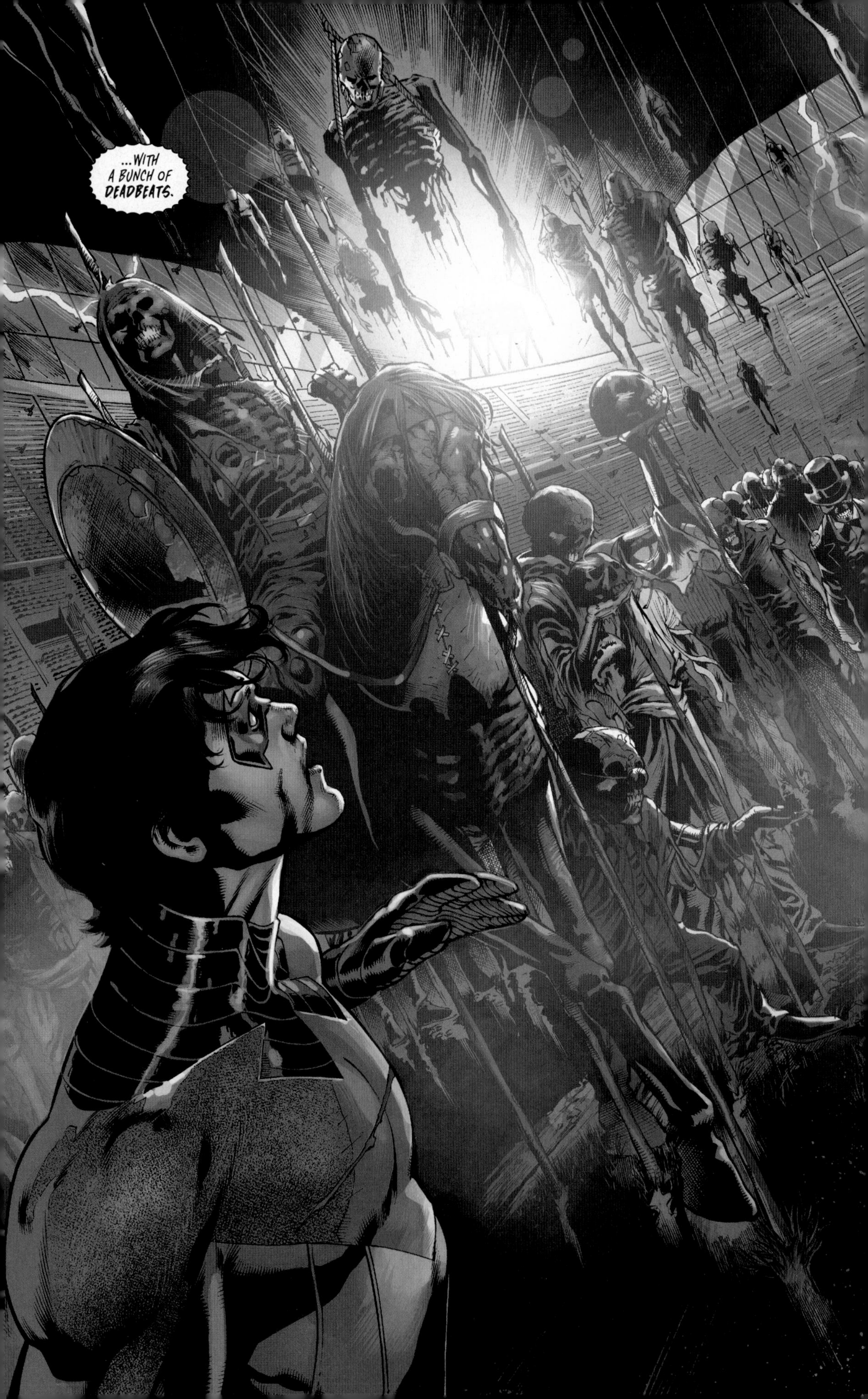
...WITH A BUNCH OF DEADBEATS.

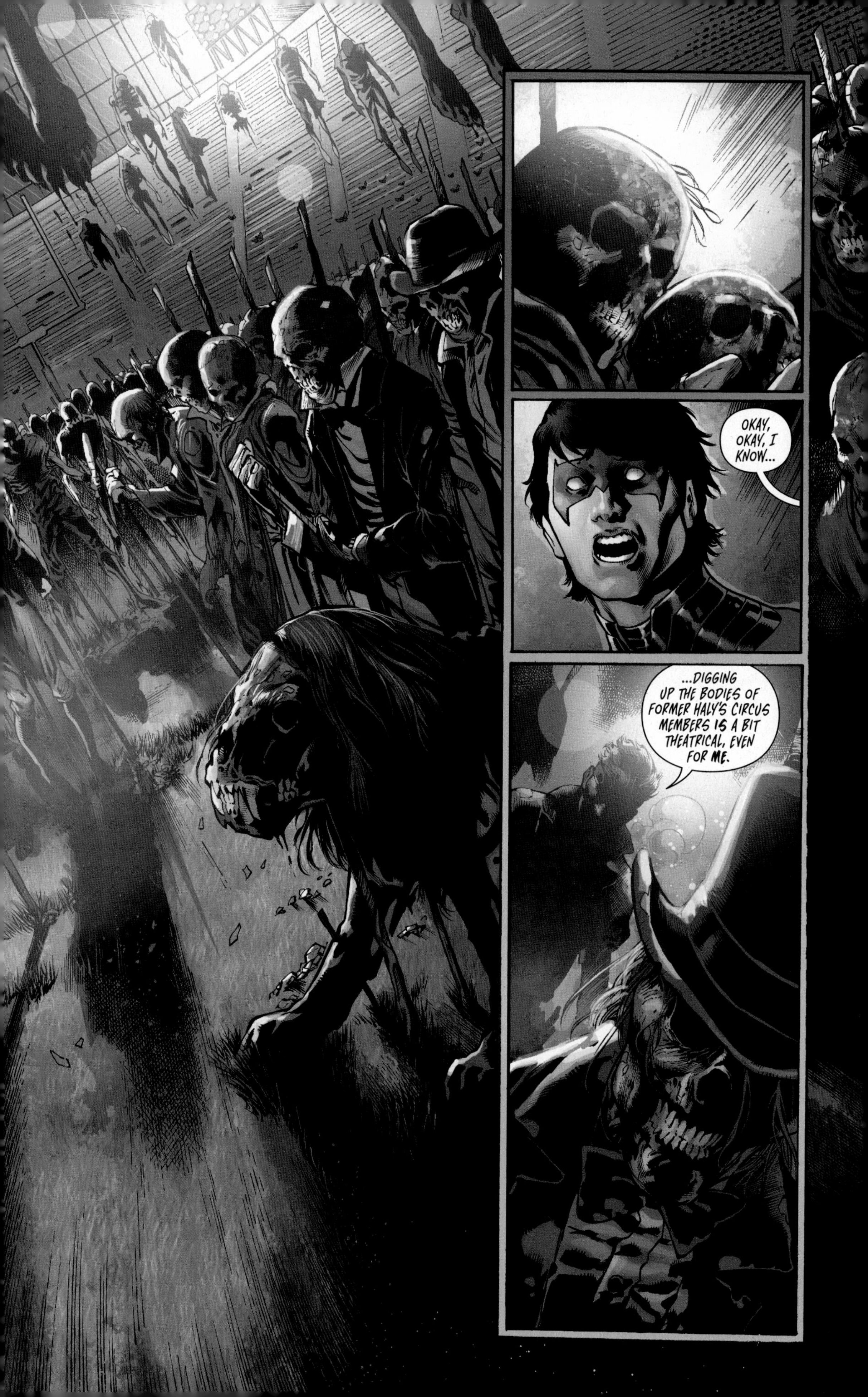
OKAY, OKAY, I KNOW...
...DIGGING UP THE BODIES OF FORMER HALY'S CIRCUS MEMBERS IS A BIT THEATRICAL, EVEN FOR ME.

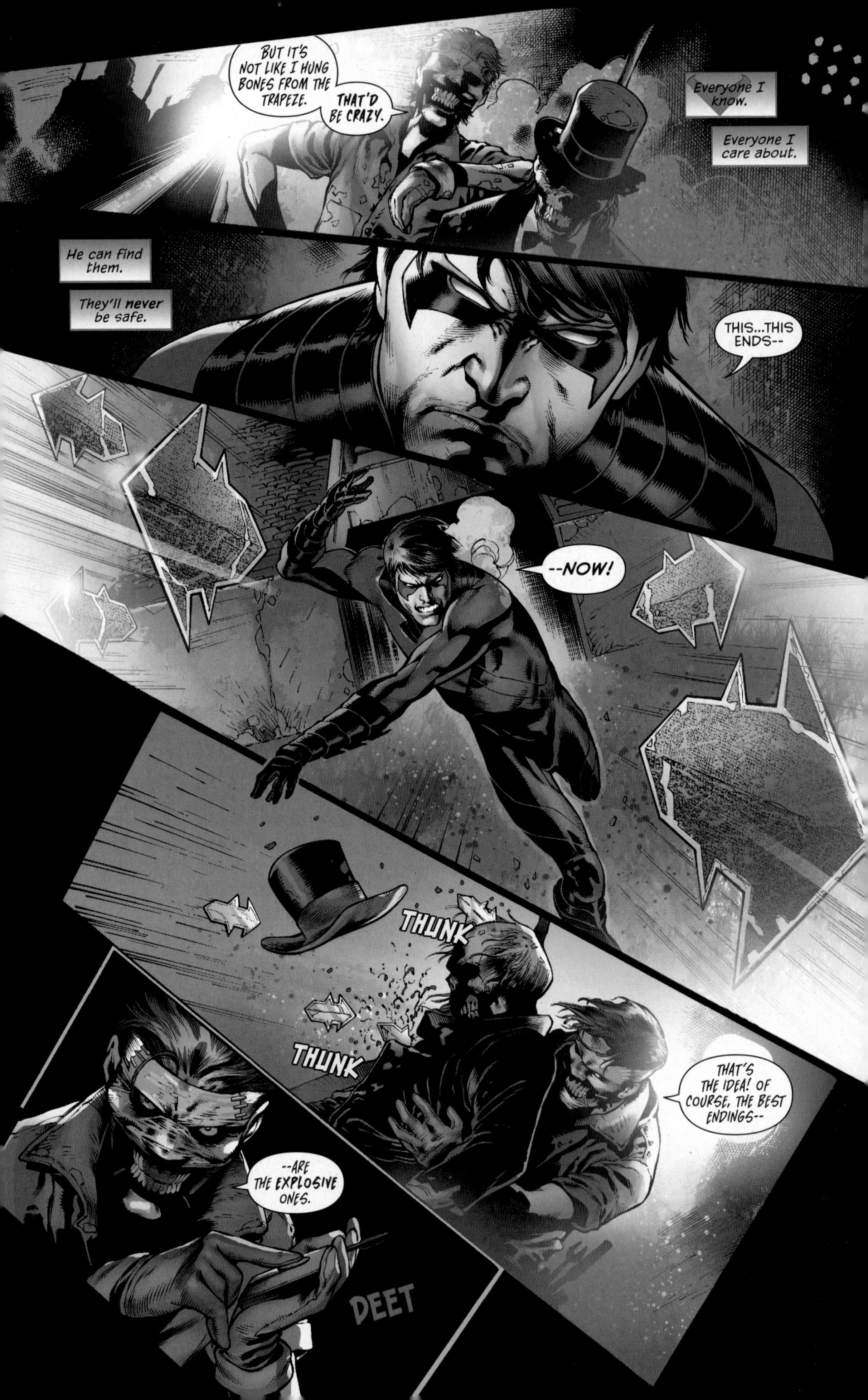

BUT IT'S NOT LIKE I HUNG BONES FROM THE TRAPEZE.
THAT'D BE CRAZY.
Everyone I know.
Everyone I care about.
He can find them.
They'll never be safe.
THIS...THIS ENDS--
--NOW!
THUNK
THUNK
THAT'S THE IDEA! OF COURSE, THE BEST ENDINGS--
--ARE THE EXPLOSIVE ONES.
DEET

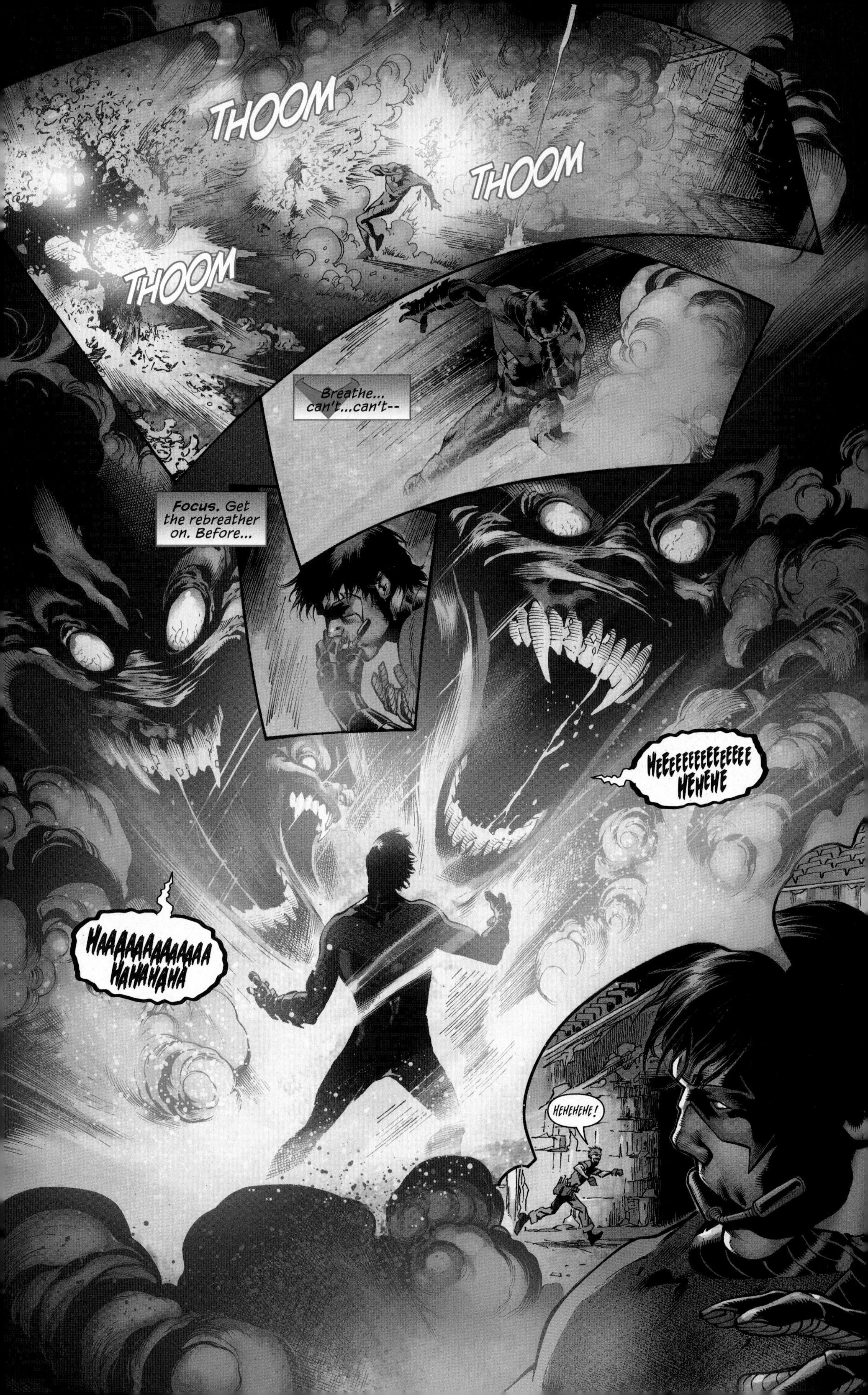
THOOM
THOOM
THOOM
Breathe... can't...can't--
Focus. Get the rebreather on. Before...
HEEEEEEEEEEEEEE HEHEHE
HAAAAAAAAAAAAA HAHAHAHA
HEHEHEHE!

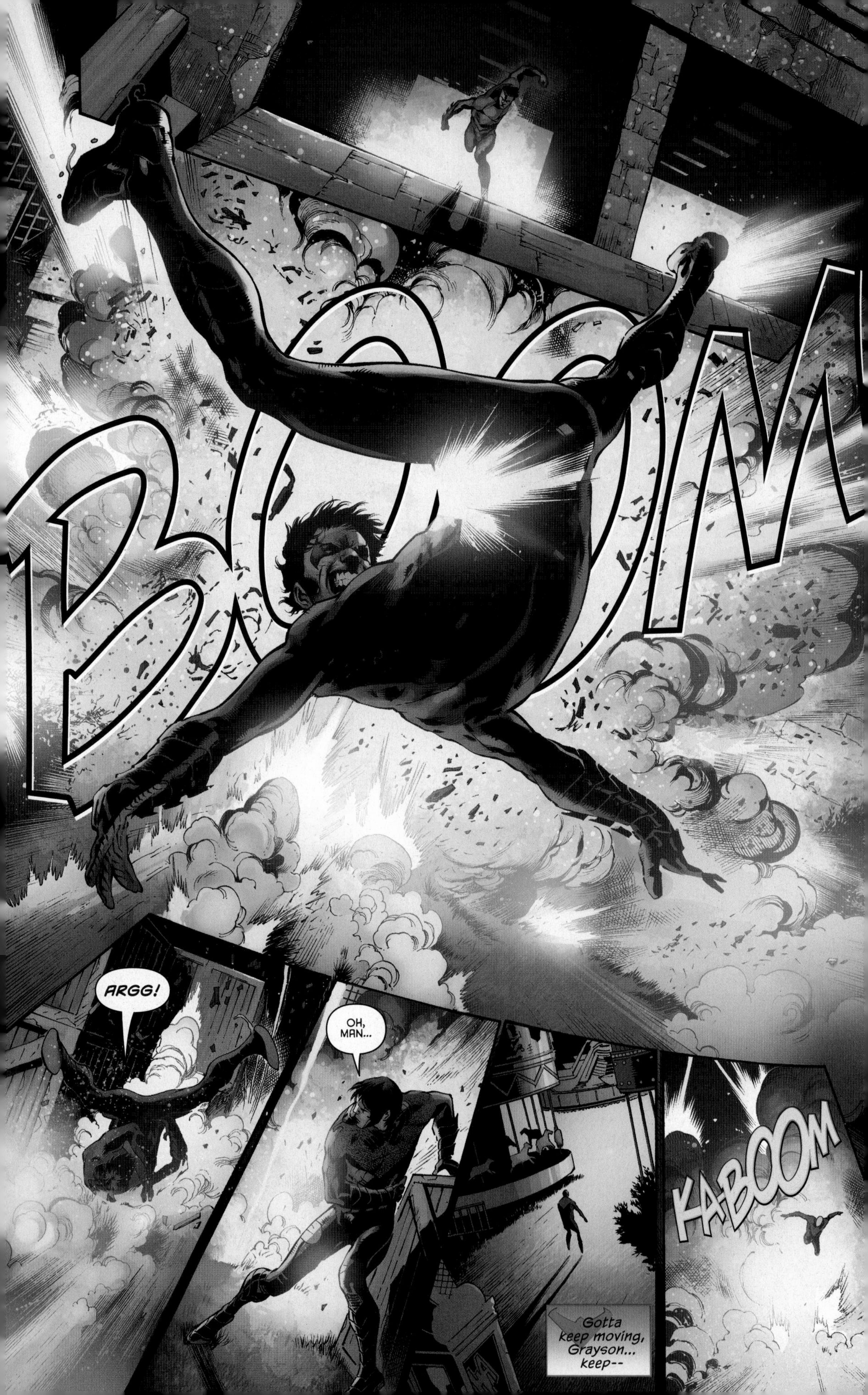
BOOM
ARGG!
OH, MAN...
KA-BOOM
Gotta keep moving, Grayson... keep--

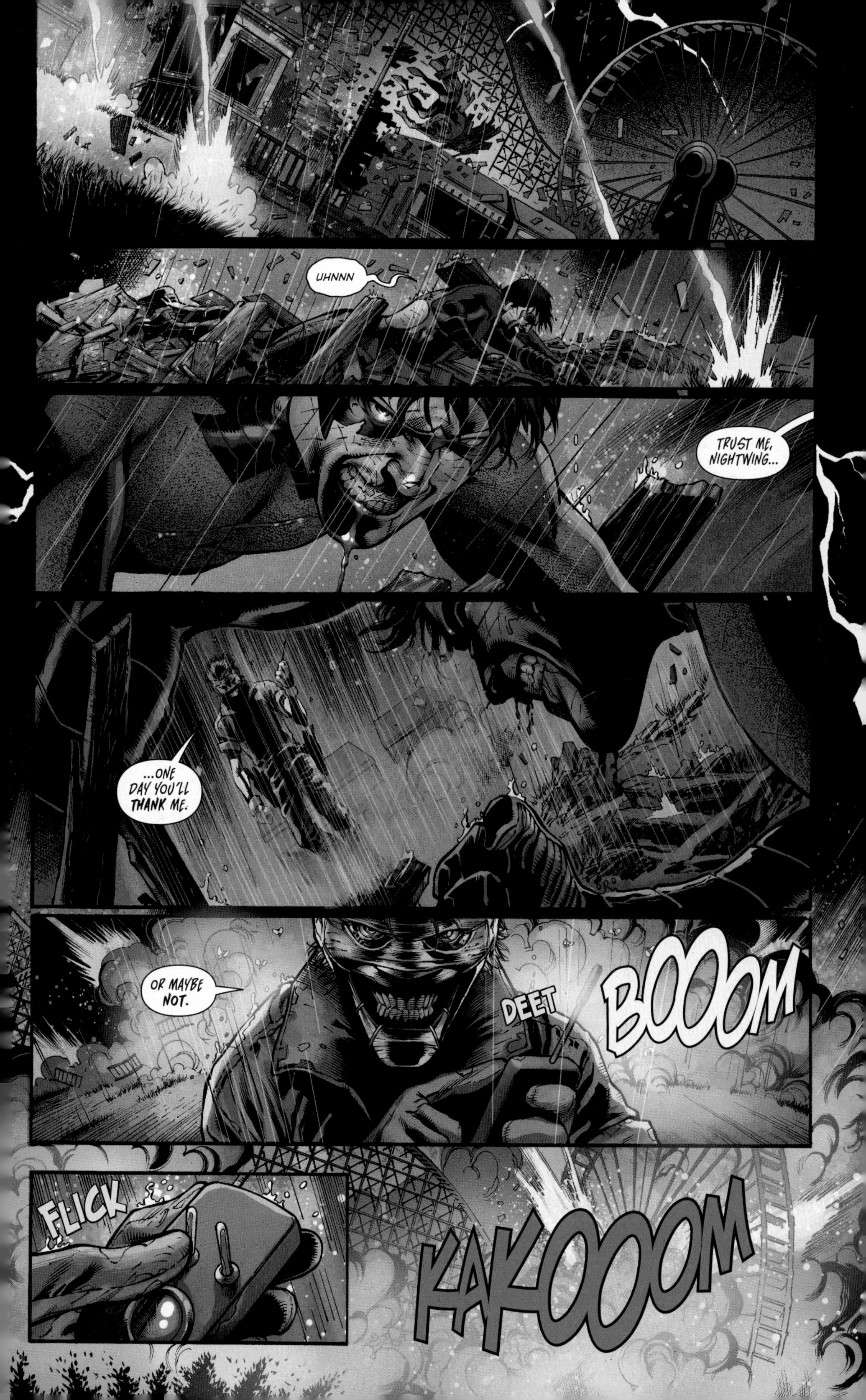
UHNNN
TRUST ME, NIGHTWING...
...ONE DAY YOU'LL THANK ME.
OR MAYBE NOT.
DEET
BOOOM
FLICK
KAKOOOM

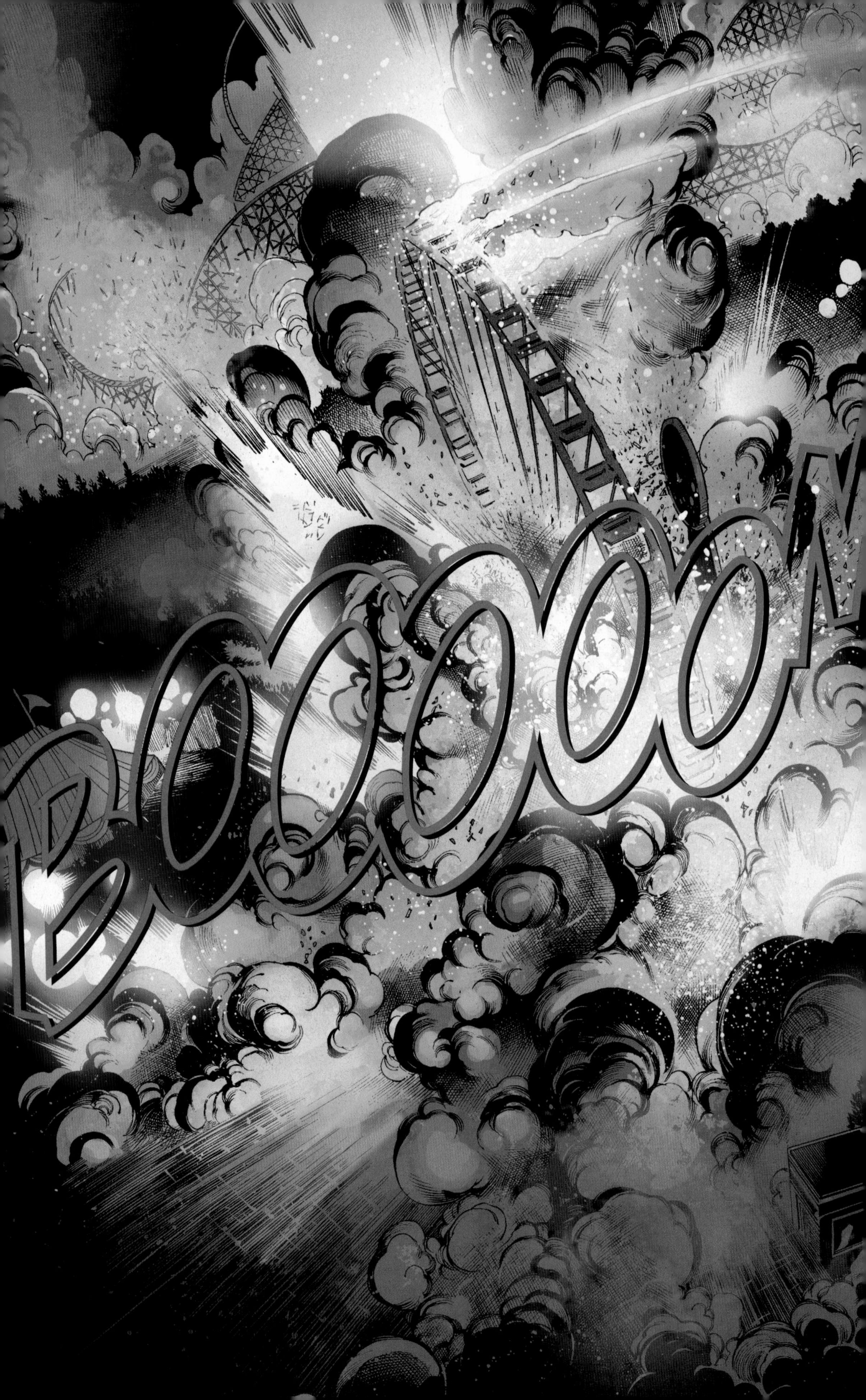
BOOOOOOM

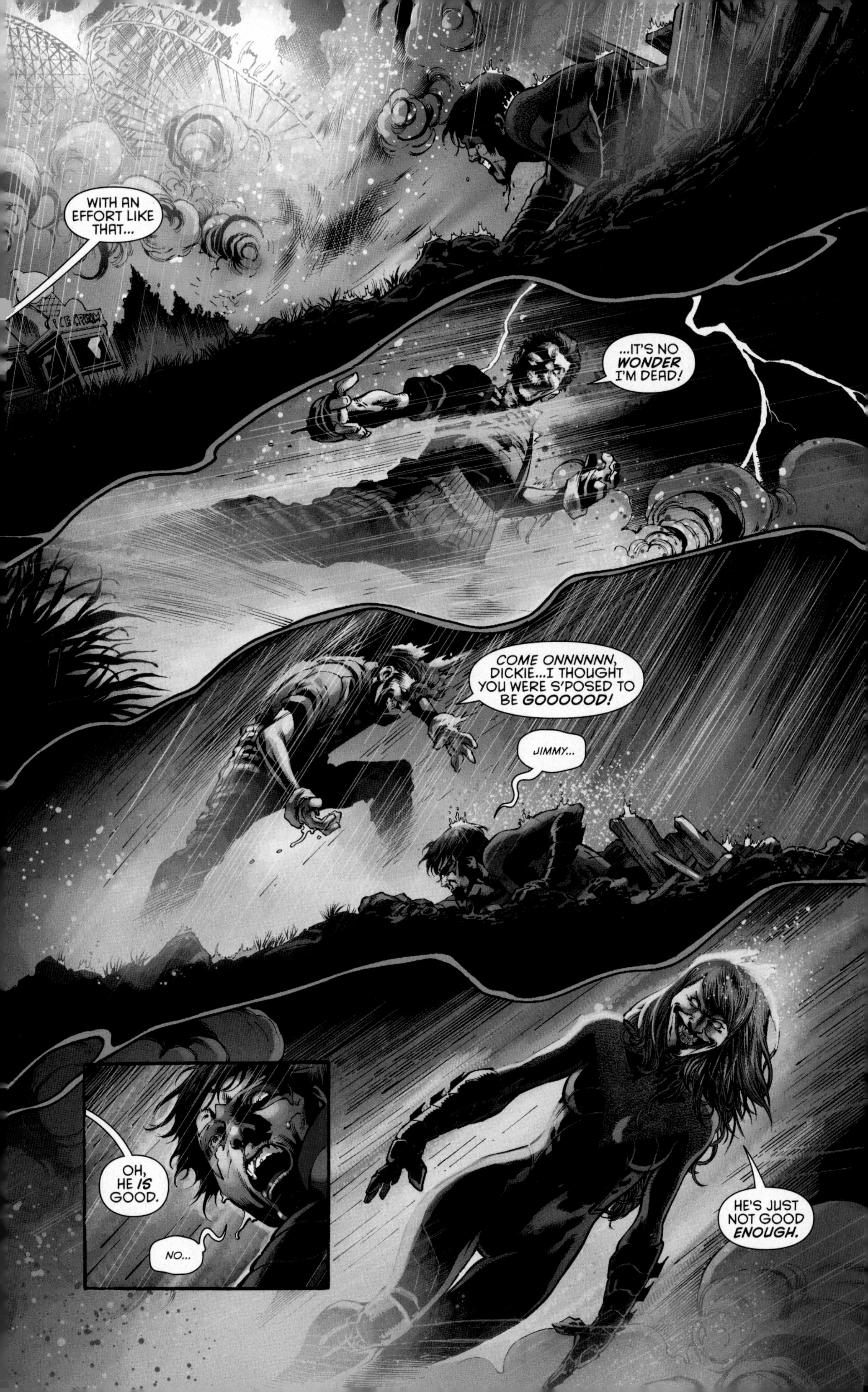
WITH AN EFFORT LIKE THAT...
...IT'S NO *WONDER* I'M DEAD!
*COME ONNNNNN, DICKIE...I THOUGHT YOU WERE S'POSED TO BE **GOOOOOD!***
JIMMY...
OH, HE ***IS*** GOOD.
NO...
HE'S JUST NOT GOOD ***ENOUGH.***

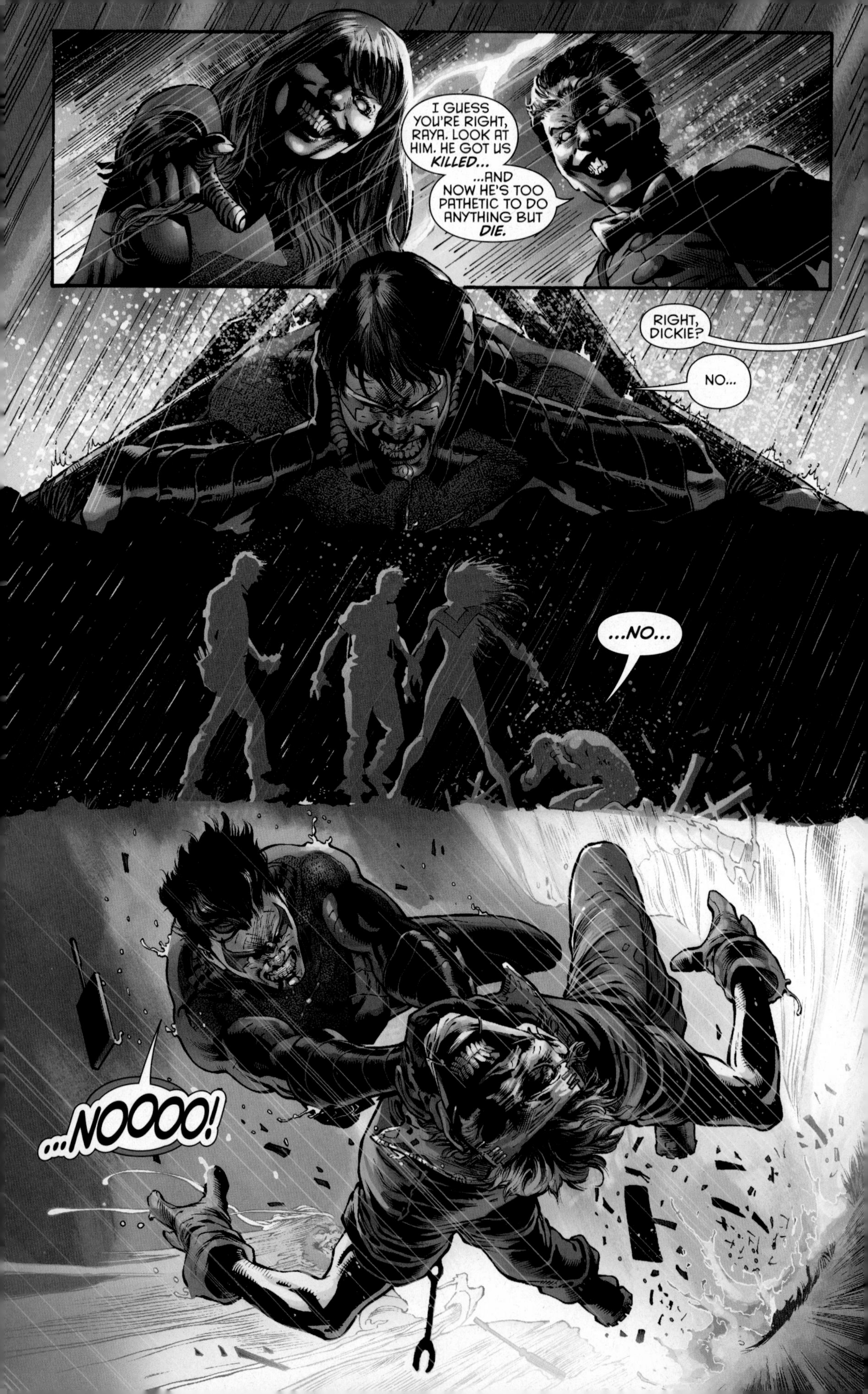
I GUESS YOU'RE RIGHT, RAYA. LOOK AT HIM. HE GOT US *KILLED...*
...AND NOW HE'S TOO PATHETIC TO DO ANYTHING BUT *DIE.*
RIGHT, DICKIE?
NO...
...NO...
...NOOOO!

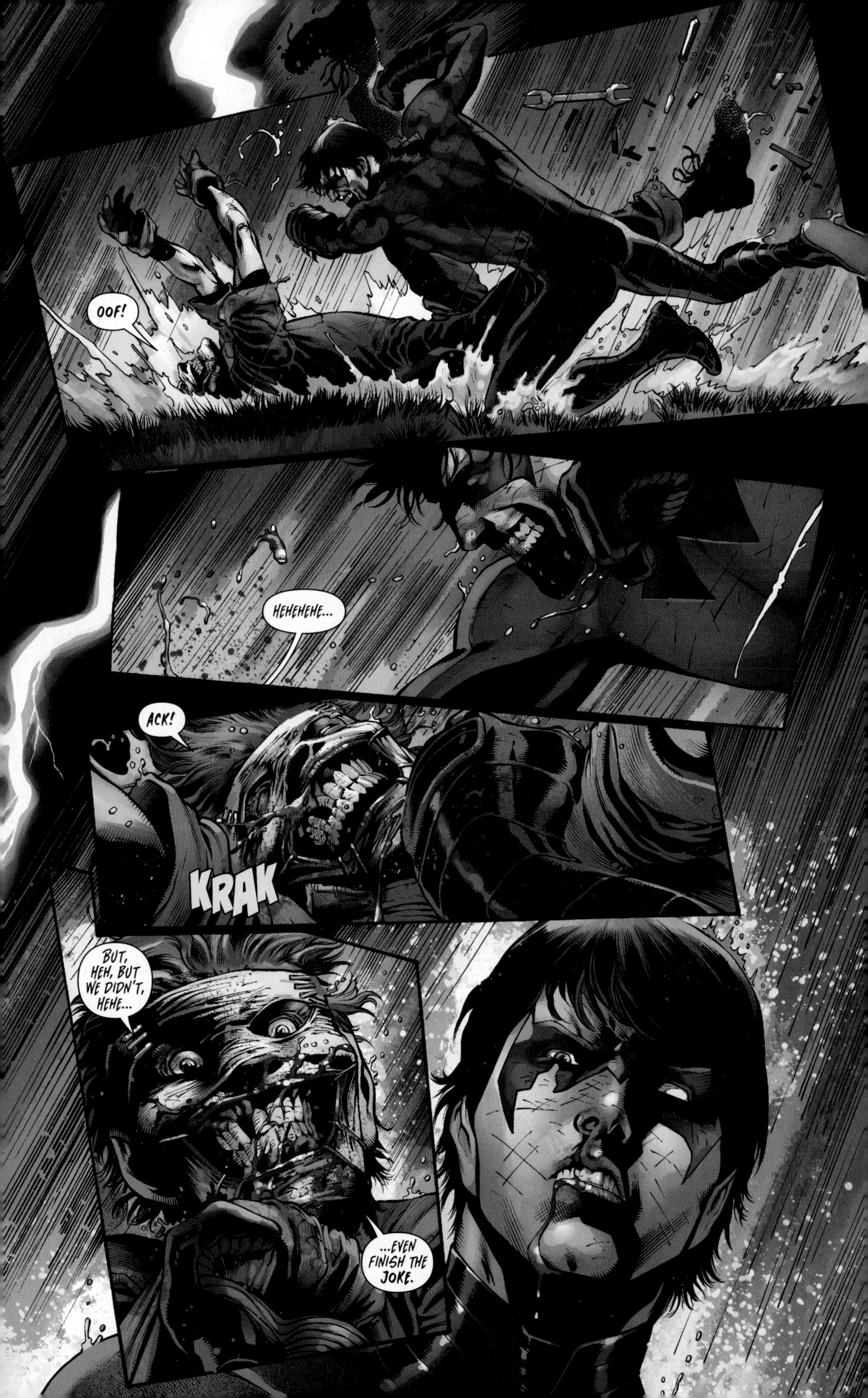
OOF!
HEHEHEHE...
ACK!
KRAK
BUT, HEH, BUT WE DIDN'T, HEHE...
...EVEN FINISH THE JOKE.

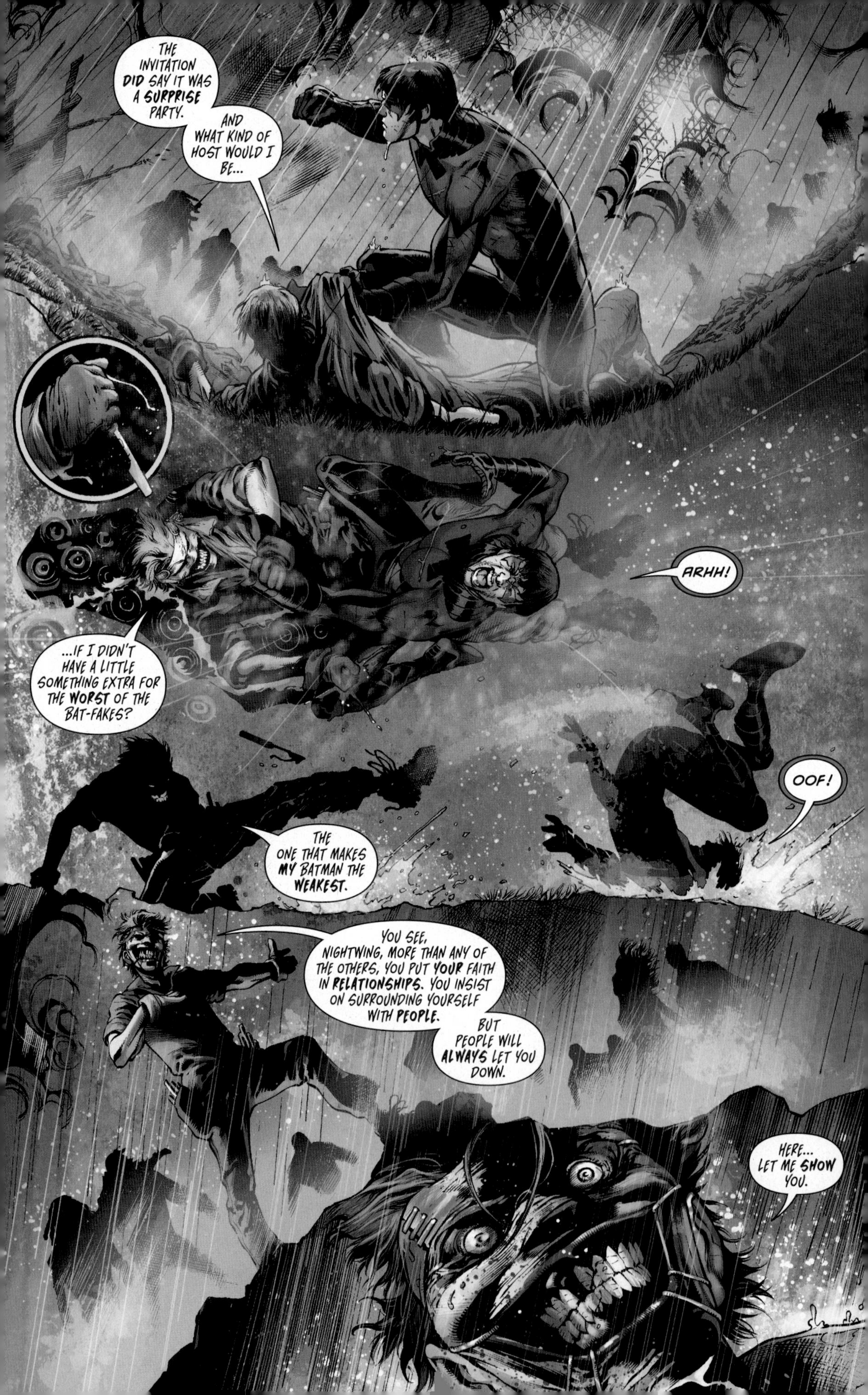
THE INVITATION DID SAY IT WAS A SURPRISE PARTY.
AND WHAT KIND OF HOST WOULD I BE...
ARHH!
...IF I DIDN'T HAVE A LITTLE SOMETHING EXTRA FOR THE WORST OF THE BAT-FAKES?
OOF!
THE ONE THAT MAKES MY BATMAN THE WEAKEST.
YOU SEE, NIGHTWING, MORE THAN ANY OF THE OTHERS, YOU PUT YOUR FAITH IN RELATIONSHIPS. YOU INSIST ON SURROUNDING YOURSELF WITH PEOPLE.
BUT PEOPLE WILL ALWAYS LET YOU DOWN.
HERE... LET ME SHOW YOU.

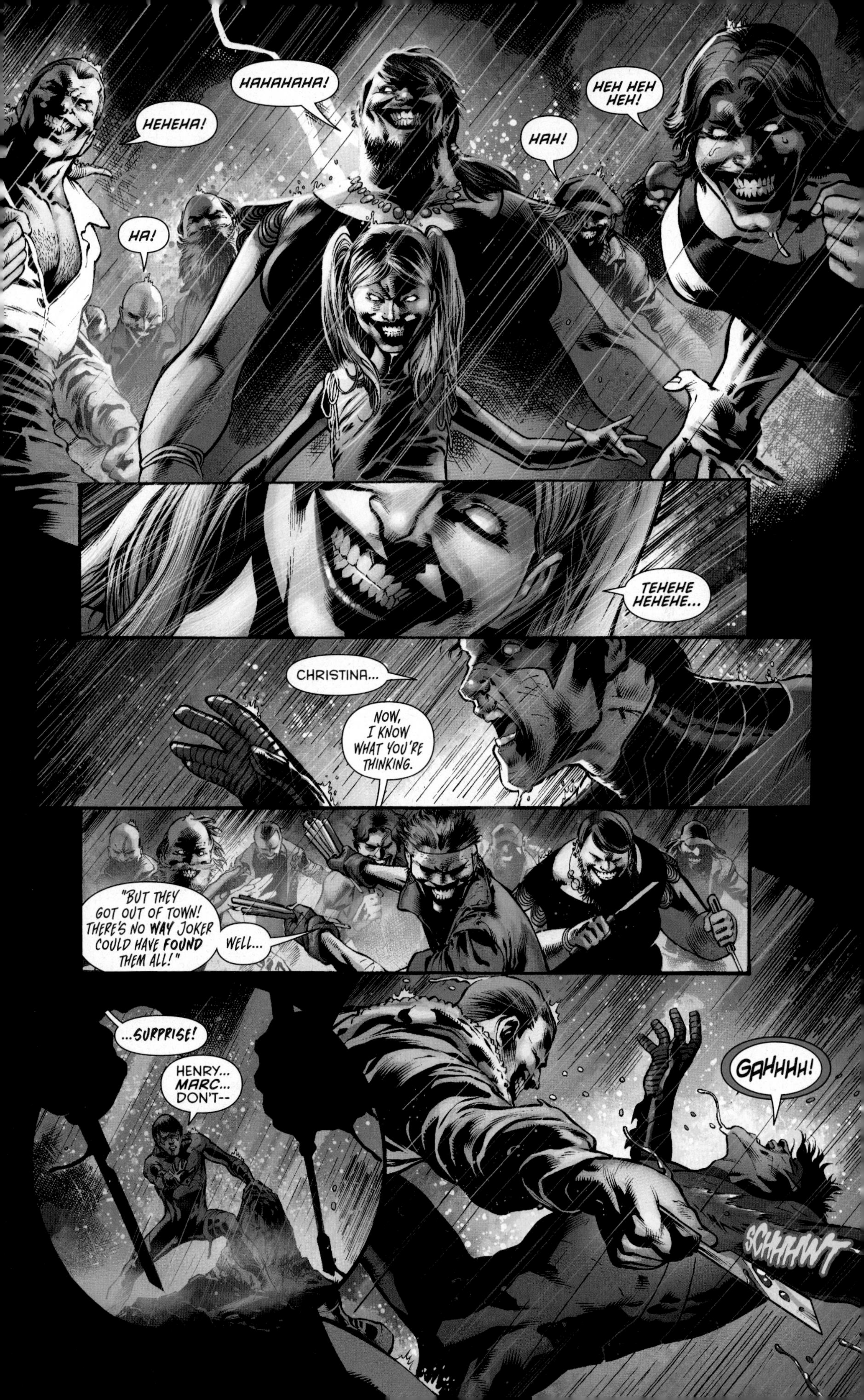
HEHEHA!
HAHAHAHA!
HA!
HAH!
HEH HEH HEH!
TEHEHE HEHEHE...
CHRISTINA...
NOW, I KNOW WHAT YOU'RE THINKING.
"BUT THEY GOT OUT OF TOWN! THERE'S NO WAY JOKER COULD HAVE FOUND THEM ALL!"
WELL...
...SURPRISE!
HENRY... MARC... DON'T--
GAHHHH!
SCHHHWT

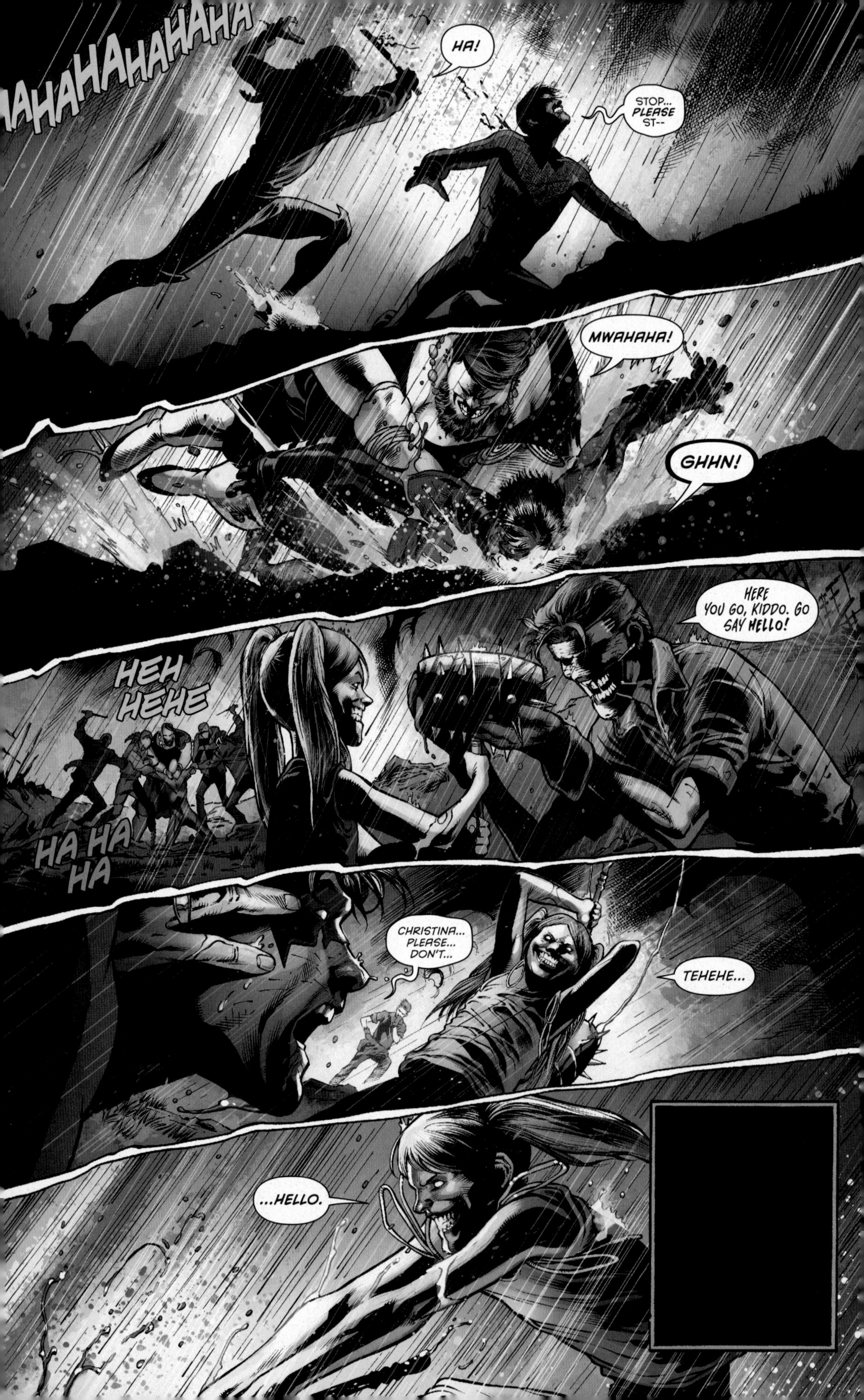
AHAHAHAHAHAHAHA
HA!
STOP... PLEASE ST--
MWAHAHA!
GHHN!
HEH HEHE
HERE YOU GO, KIDDO. GO SAY HELLO!
HA HA HA
CHRISTINA... PLEASE... DON'T...
TEHEHE...
...HELLO.

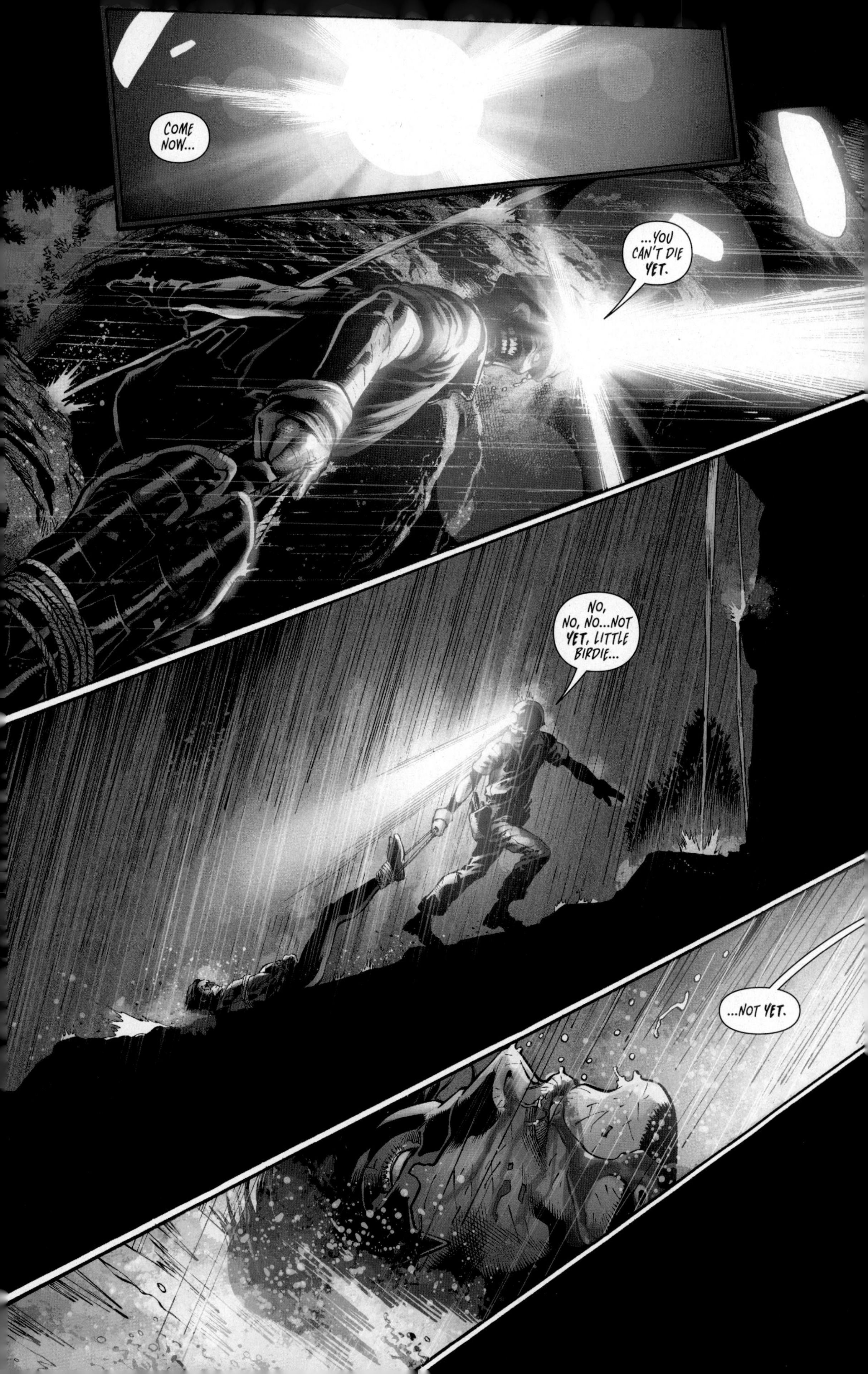
COME NOW...
...YOU CAN'T DIE YET.
NO, NO, NO...NOT YET, LITTLE BIRDIE...
...NOT YET.

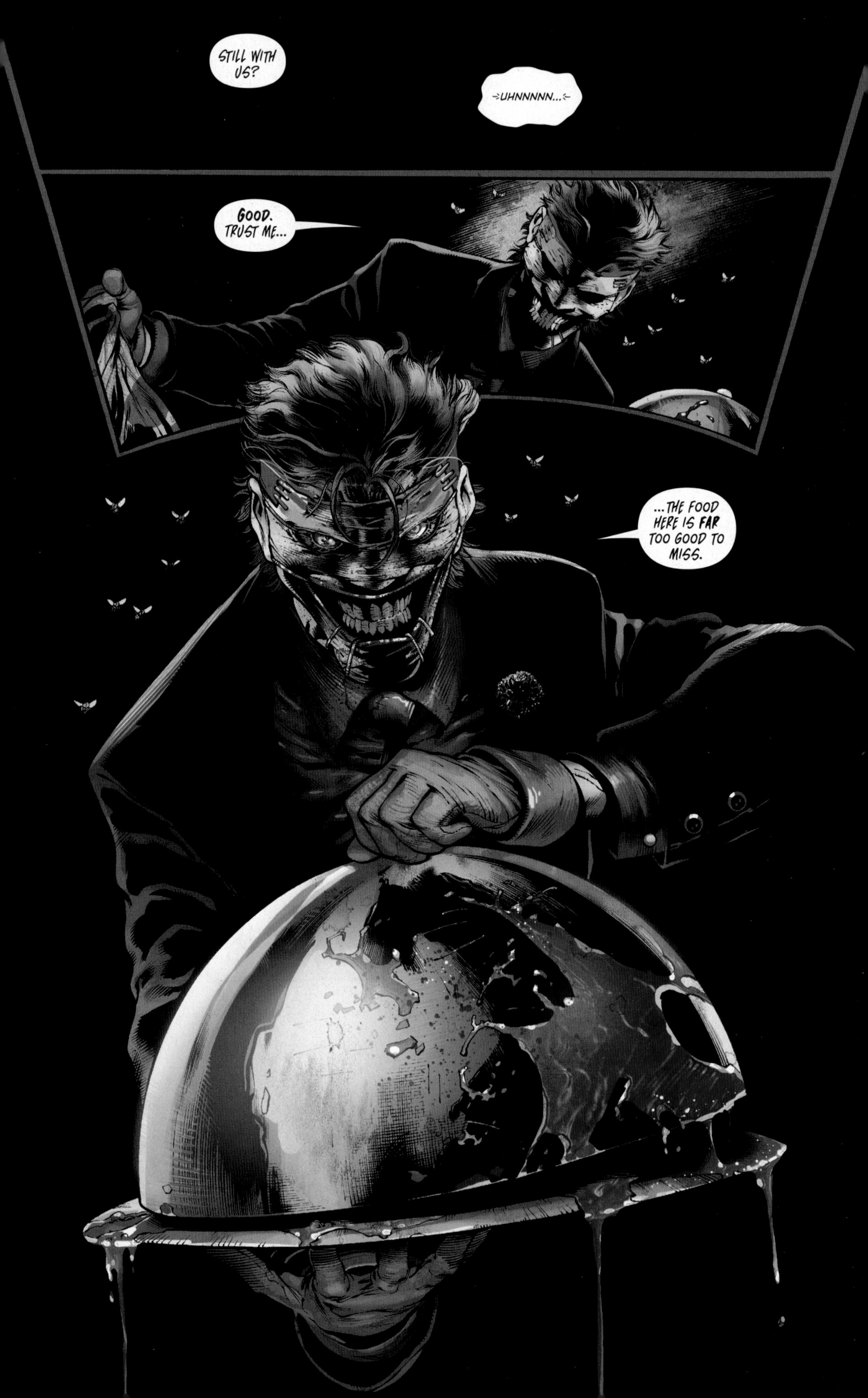
STILL WITH US?
UHNNNNN...
GOOD. TRUST ME...
...THE FOOD HERE IS FAR TOO GOOD TO MISS.

PART SEVEN

ROBIN

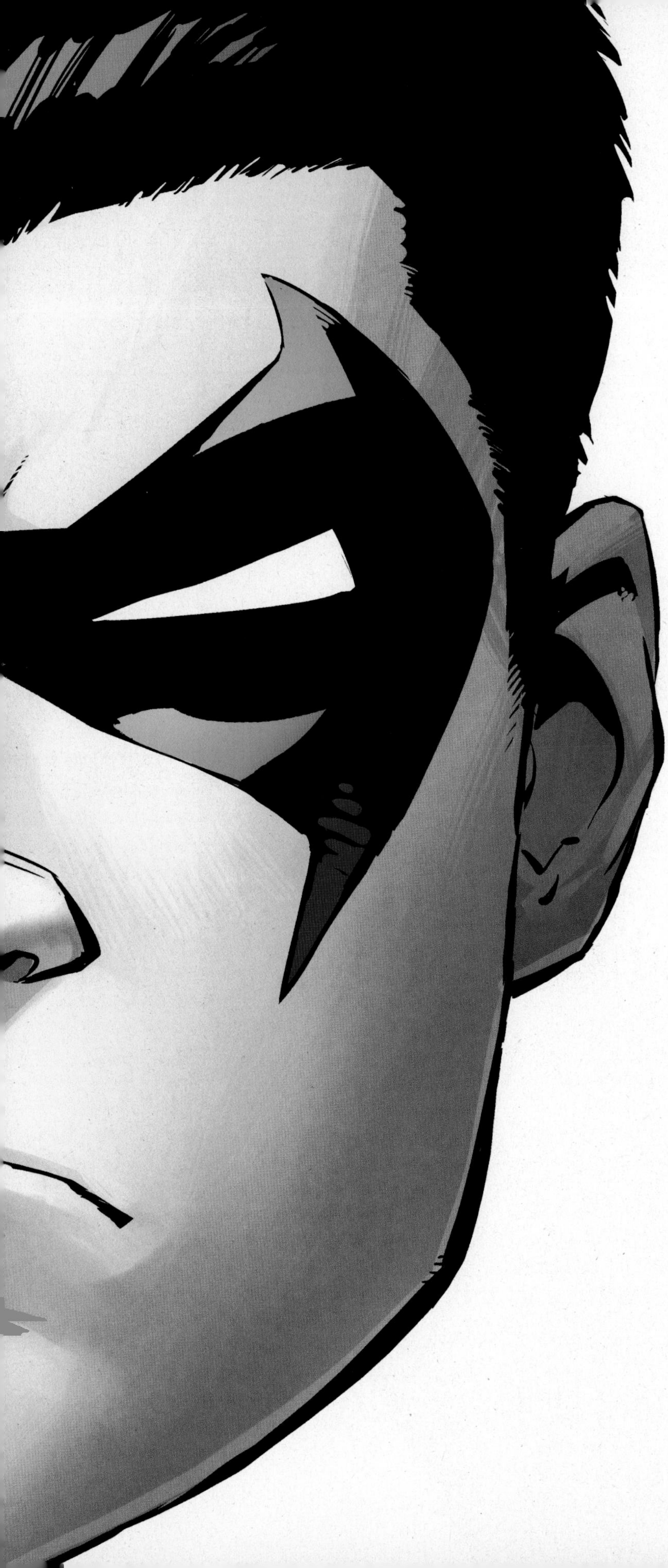

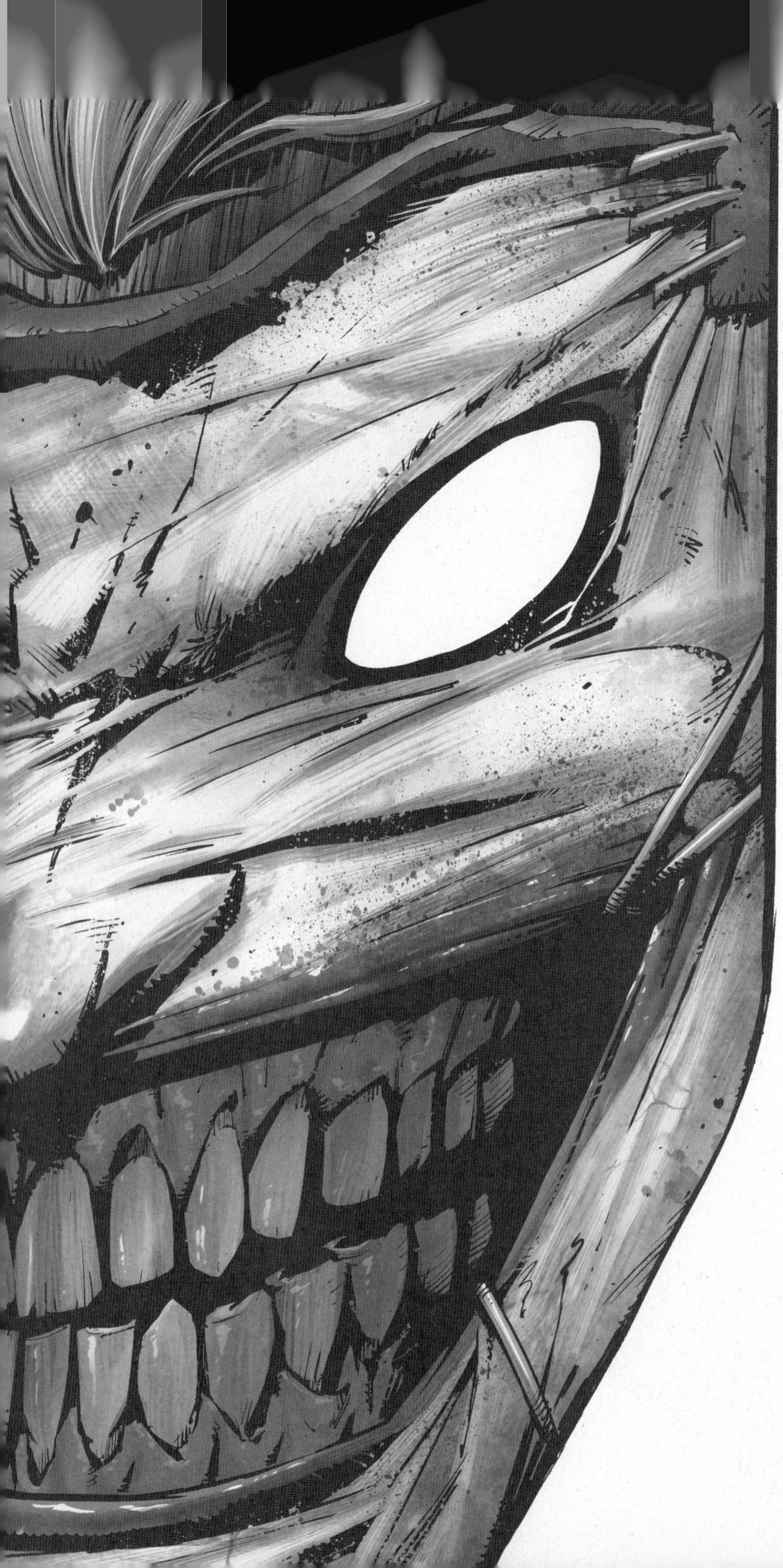

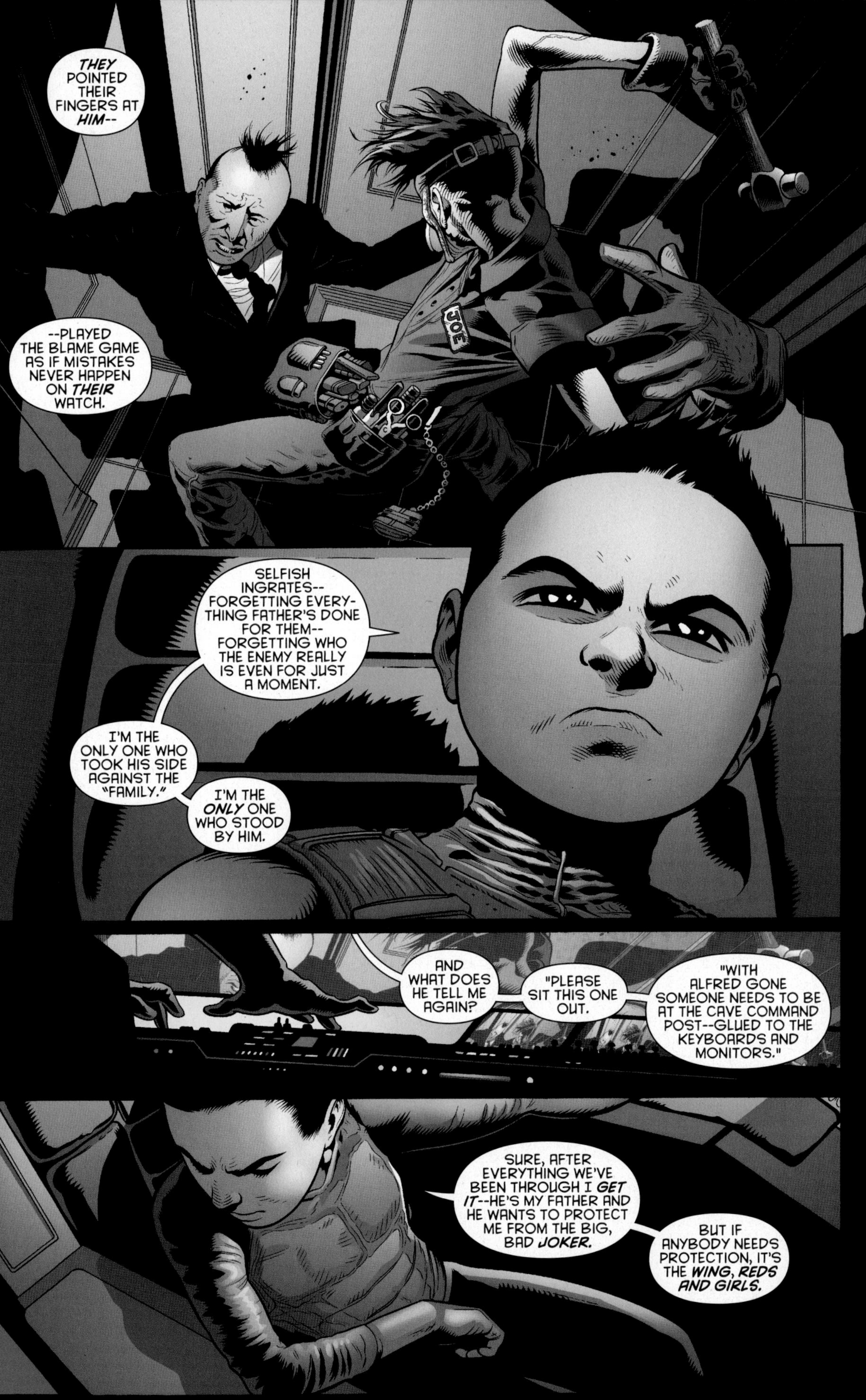

THEY POINTED THEIR FINGERS AT HIM--
--PLAYED THE BLAME GAME AS IF MISTAKES NEVER HAPPEN ON THEIR WATCH.
JOE
SELFISH INGRATES--FORGETTING EVERYTHING FATHER'S DONE FOR THEM--FORGETTING WHO THE ENEMY REALLY IS EVEN FOR JUST A MOMENT.
I'M THE ONLY ONE WHO TOOK HIS SIDE AGAINST THE "FAMILY."
I'M THE ONLY ONE WHO STOOD BY HIM.
AND WHAT DOES HE TELL ME AGAIN?
"PLEASE SIT THIS ONE OUT.
"WITH ALFRED GONE SOMEONE NEEDS TO BE AT THE CAVE COMMAND POST--GLUED TO THE KEYBOARDS AND MONITORS."
SURE, AFTER EVERYTHING WE'VE BEEN THROUGH I GET IT--HE'S MY FATHER AND HE WANTS TO PROTECT ME FROM THE BIG, BAD JOKER.
BUT IF ANYBODY NEEDS PROTECTION, IT'S THE WING, REDS AND GIRLS.

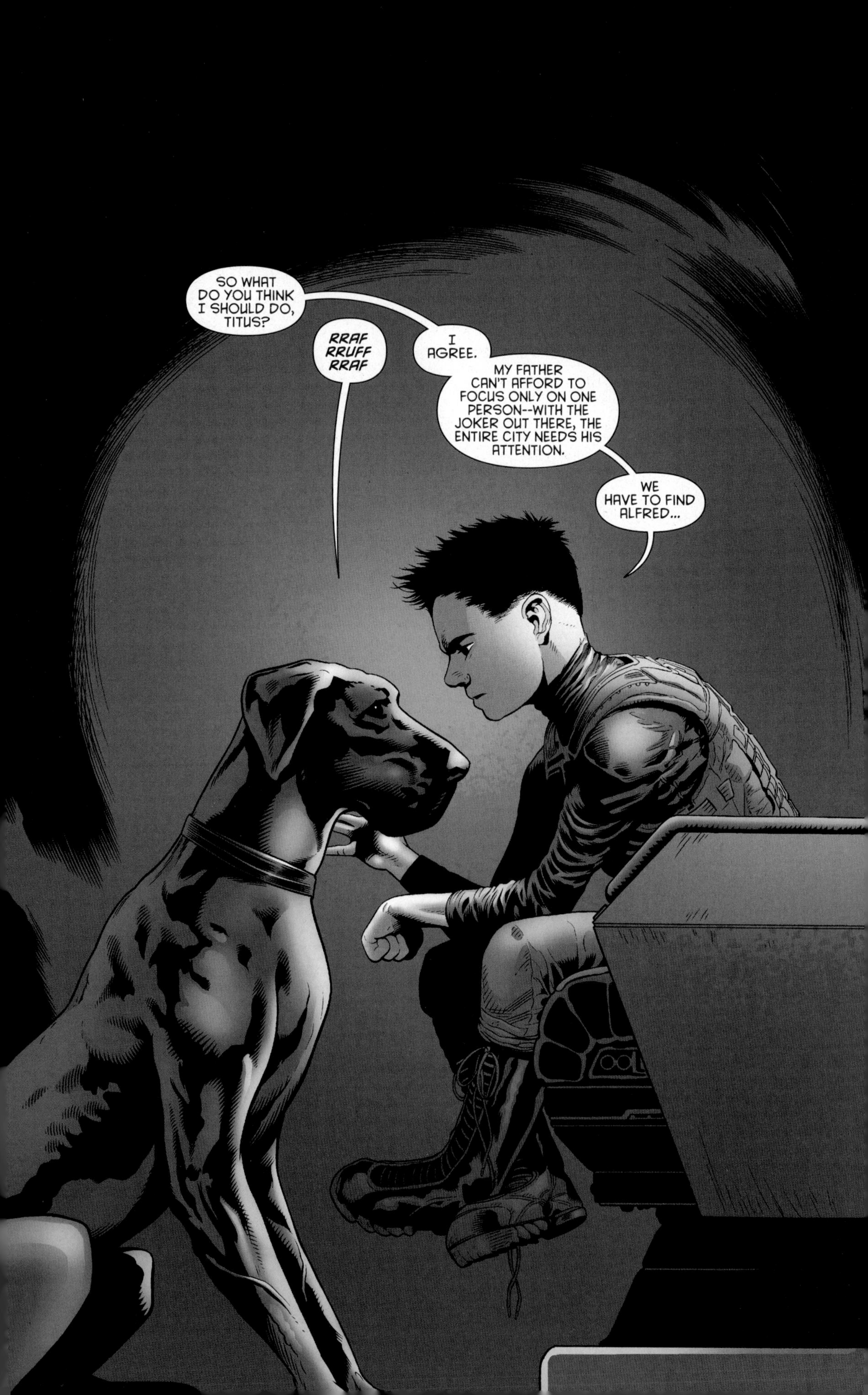
SO WHAT DO YOU THINK I SHOULD DO, TITUS?
RRAF RRUFF RRAF
I AGREE.
MY FATHER CAN'T AFFORD TO FOCUS ONLY ON ONE PERSON--WITH THE JOKER OUT THERE, THE ENTIRE CITY NEEDS HIS ATTENTION.
WE HAVE TO FIND ALFRED...

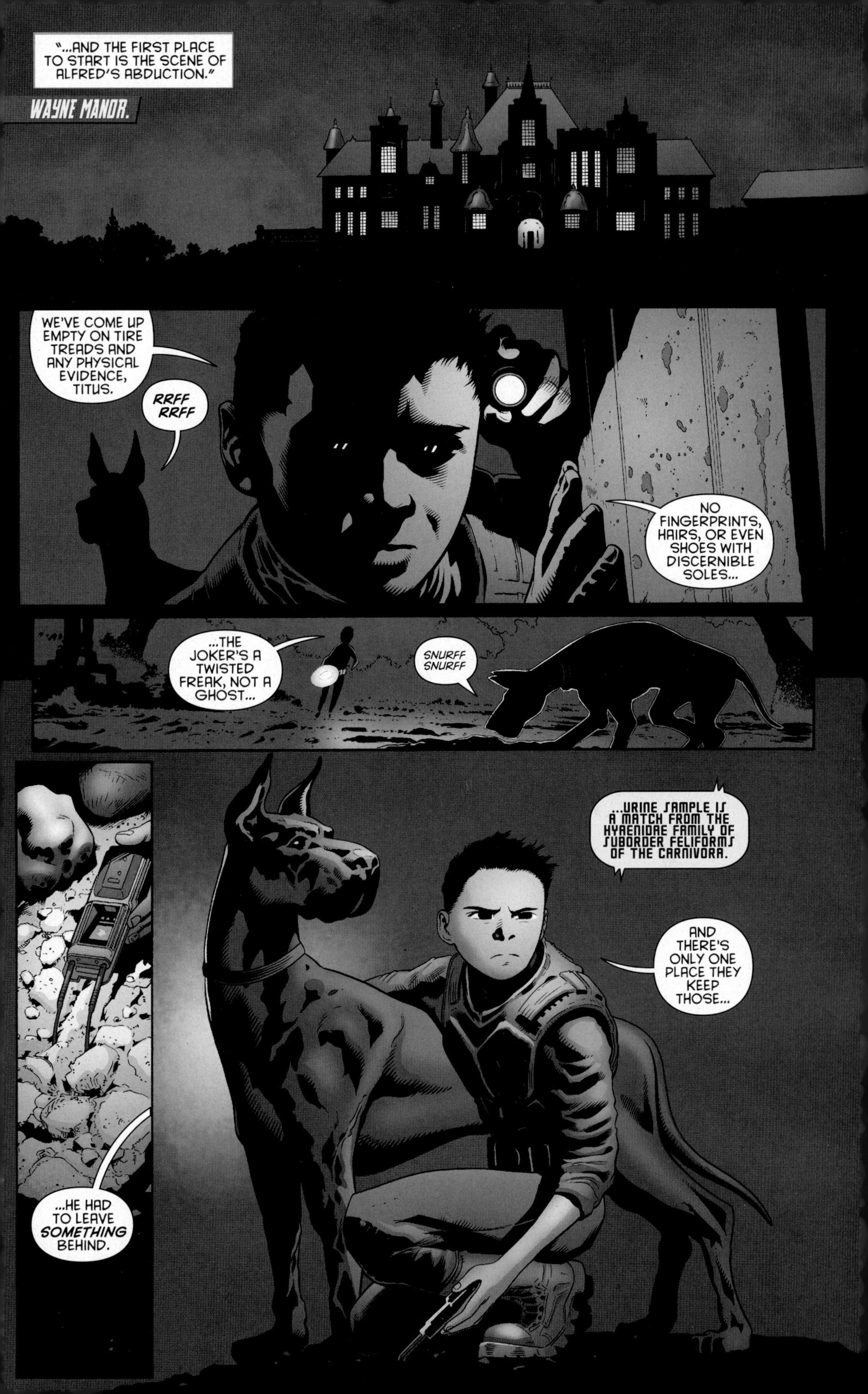
"...AND THE FIRST PLACE TO START IS THE SCENE OF ALFRED'S ABDUCTION."
WAYNE MANOR.
WE'VE COME UP EMPTY ON TIRE TREADS AND ANY PHYSICAL EVIDENCE, TITUS.
RRFF RRFF
NO FINGERPRINTS, HAIRS, OR EVEN SHOES WITH DISCERNIBLE SOLES...
...THE JOKER'S A TWISTED FREAK, NOT A GHOST...
SNURFF SNURFF
...HE HAD TO LEAVE SOMETHING BEHIND.
...URINE SAMPLE IS A MATCH FROM THE HYAENIDAE FAMILY OF SUBORDER FELIFORMS OF THE CARNIVORA.
AND THERE'S ONLY ONE PLACE THEY KEEP THOSE...

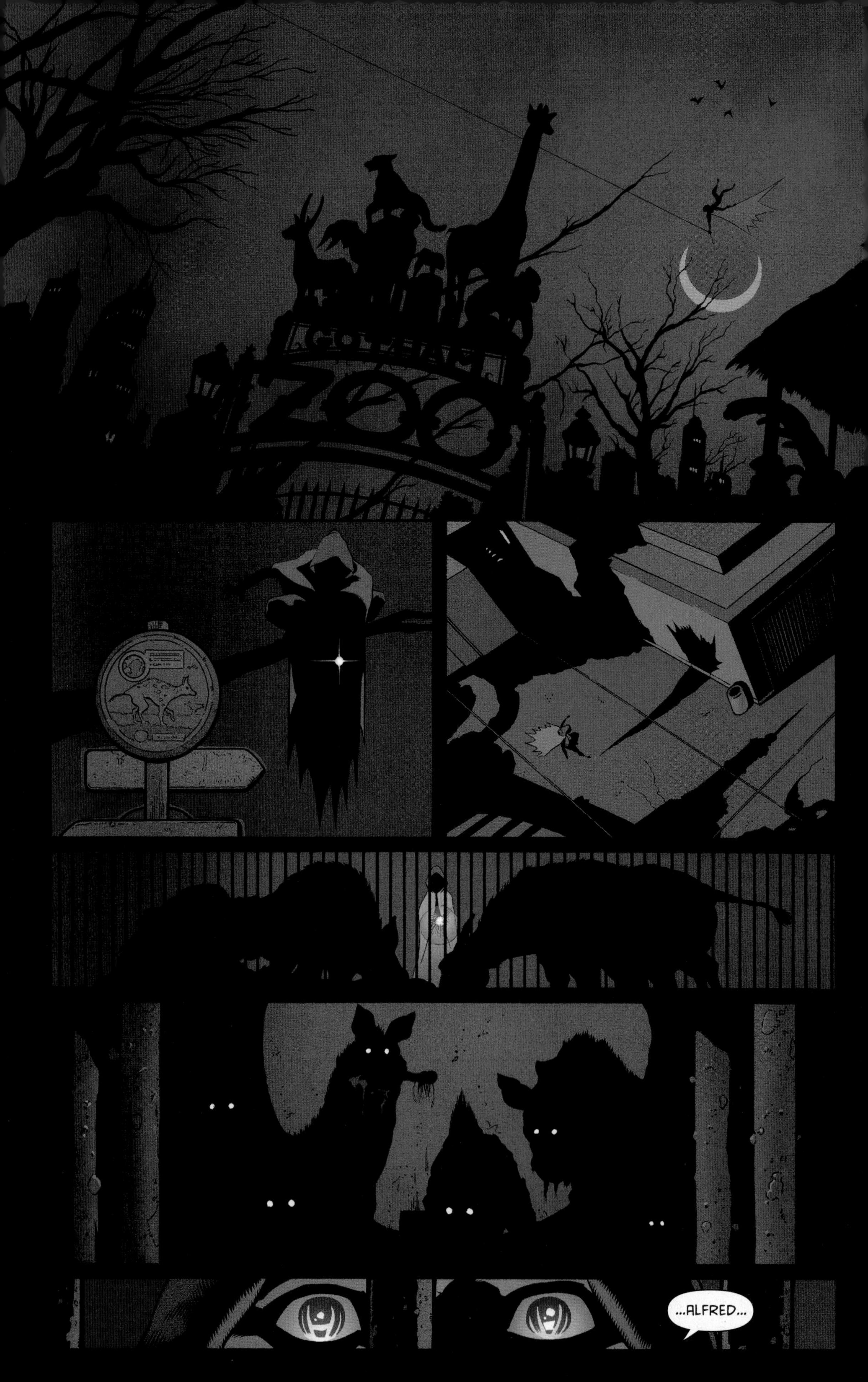
GOTHAM
ZOO
...ALFRED...

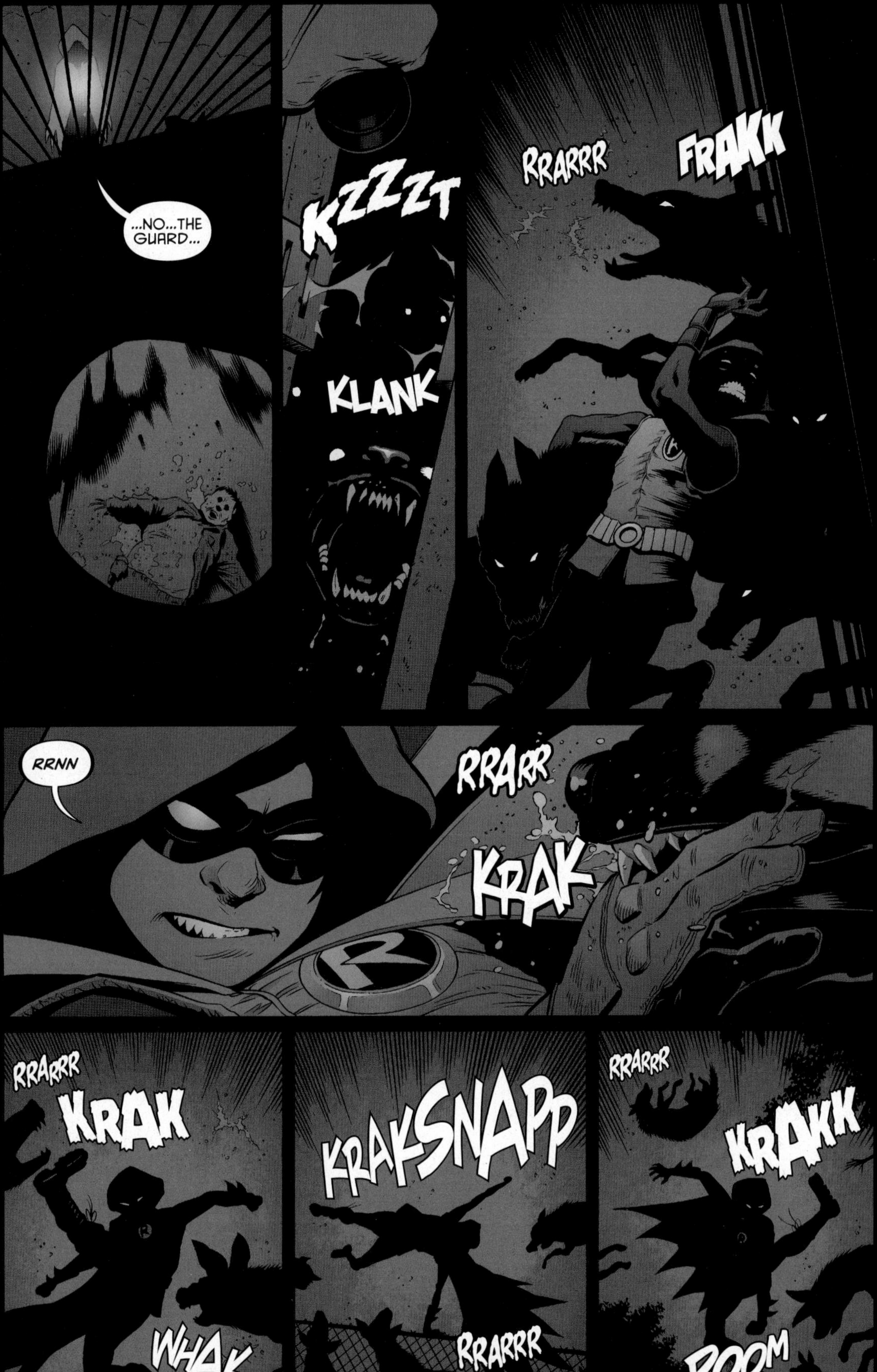
...NO...THE GUARD...
KZZZZT
KLANK
RRARRR
FRAKK
RRNN
RRARR
KRAK
RRARRR
KRAK
WHAK
KRAKSNAPP
RRARRR
RRARRR
KRAKK
POOM

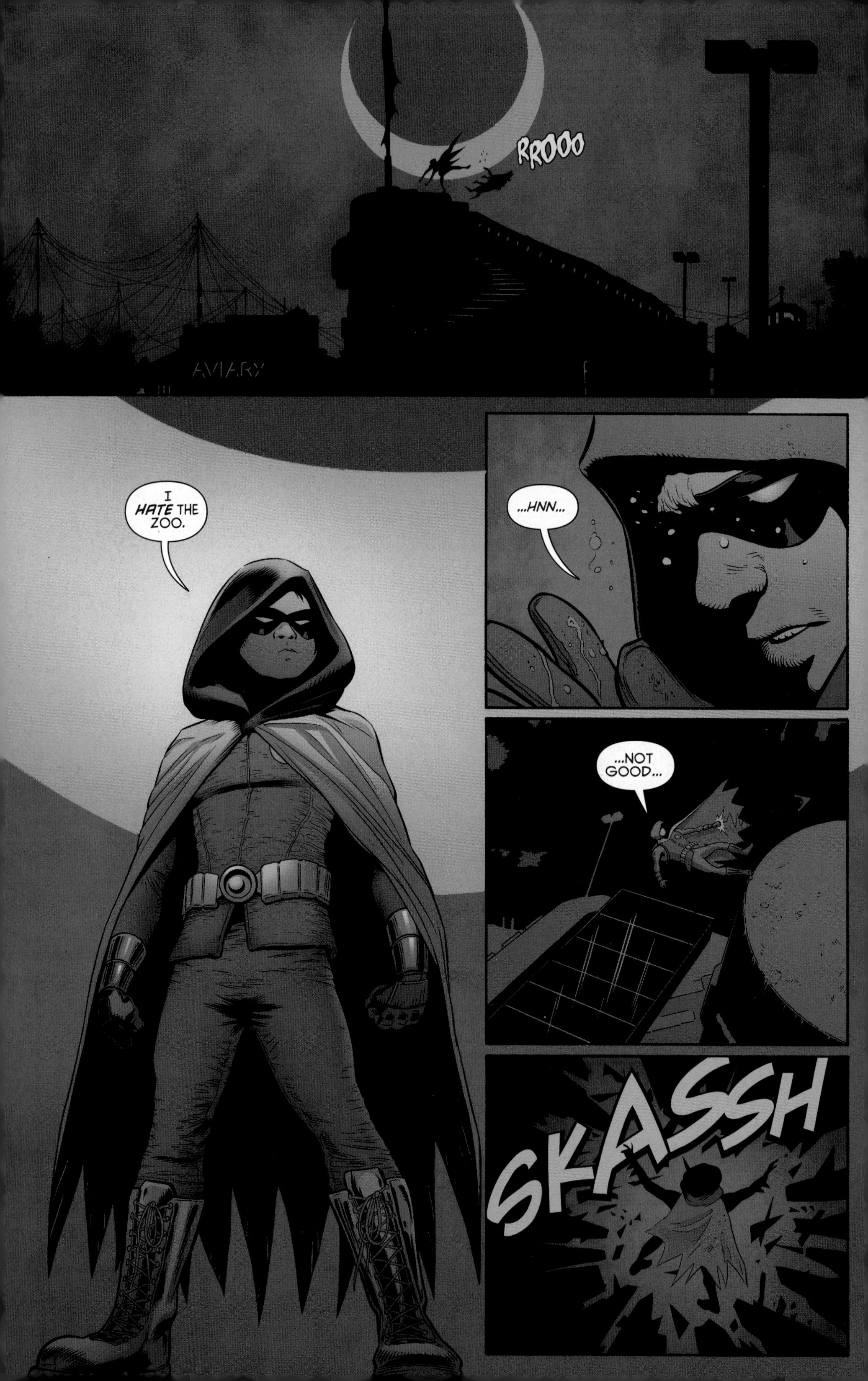
RROOO
AVIARY
I HATE THE ZOO.
...HNN...
...NOT GOOD...
SKASSH

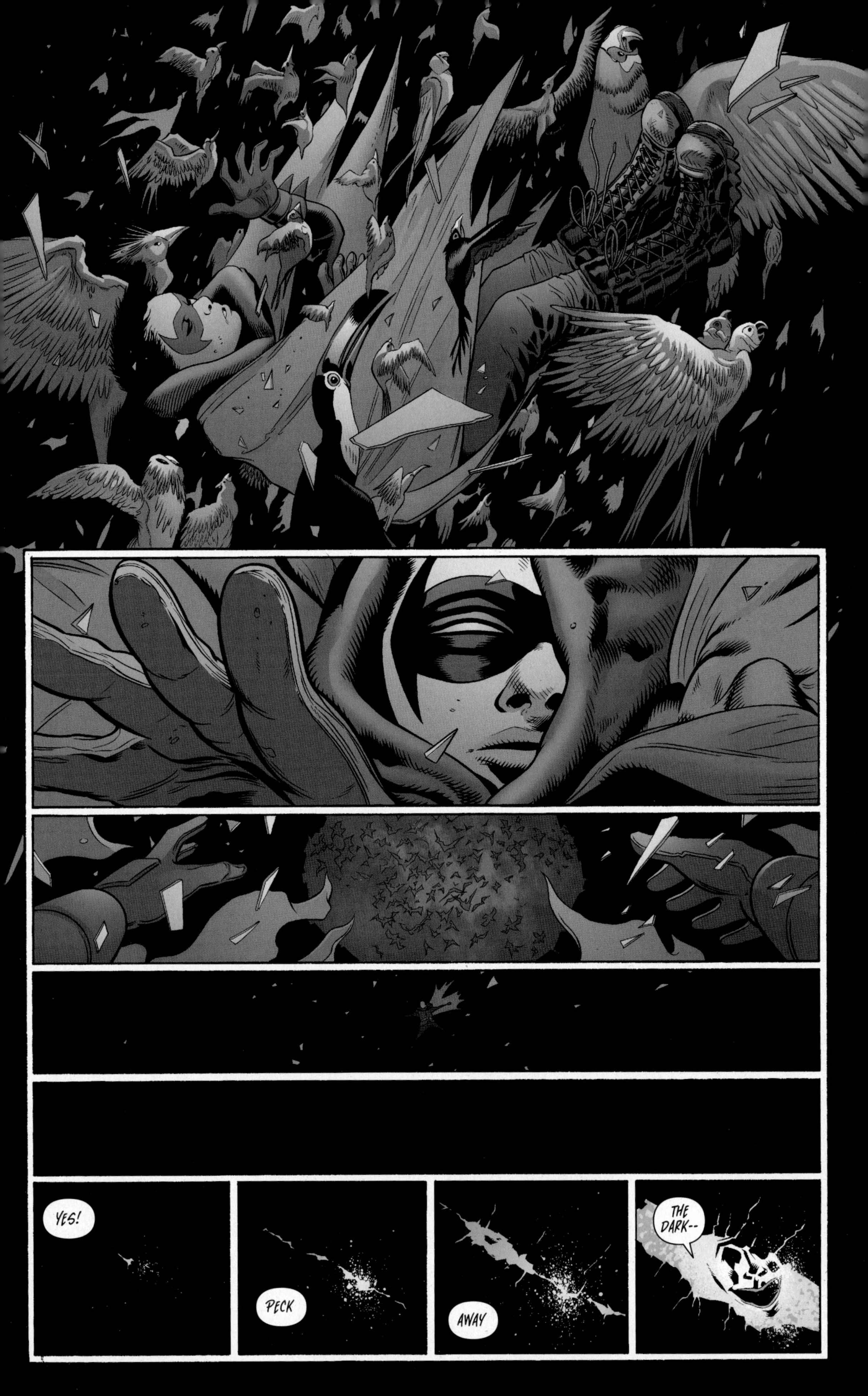
YES!
PECK
AWAY
THE DARK--

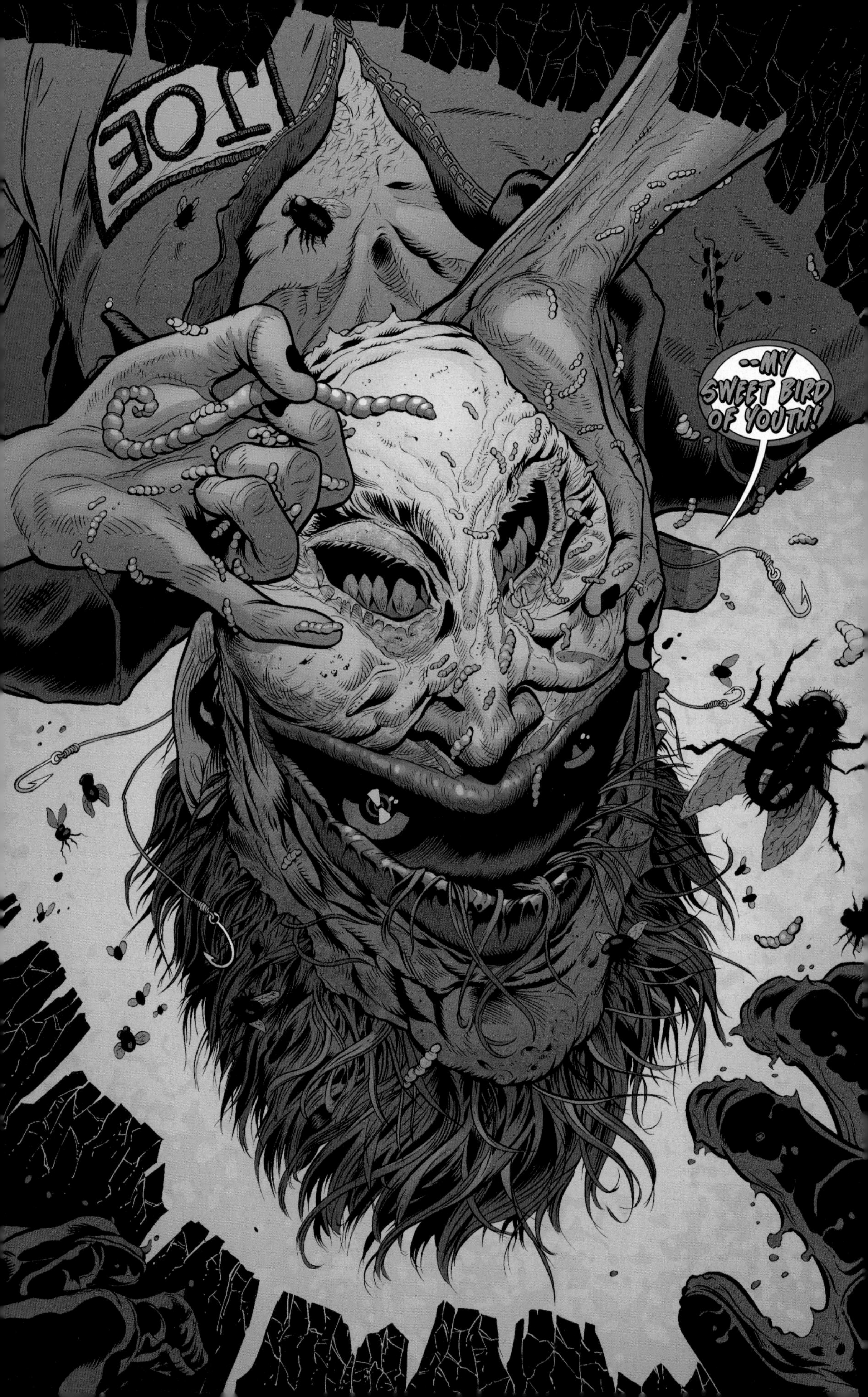
--MY SWEET BIRD OF YOUTH!

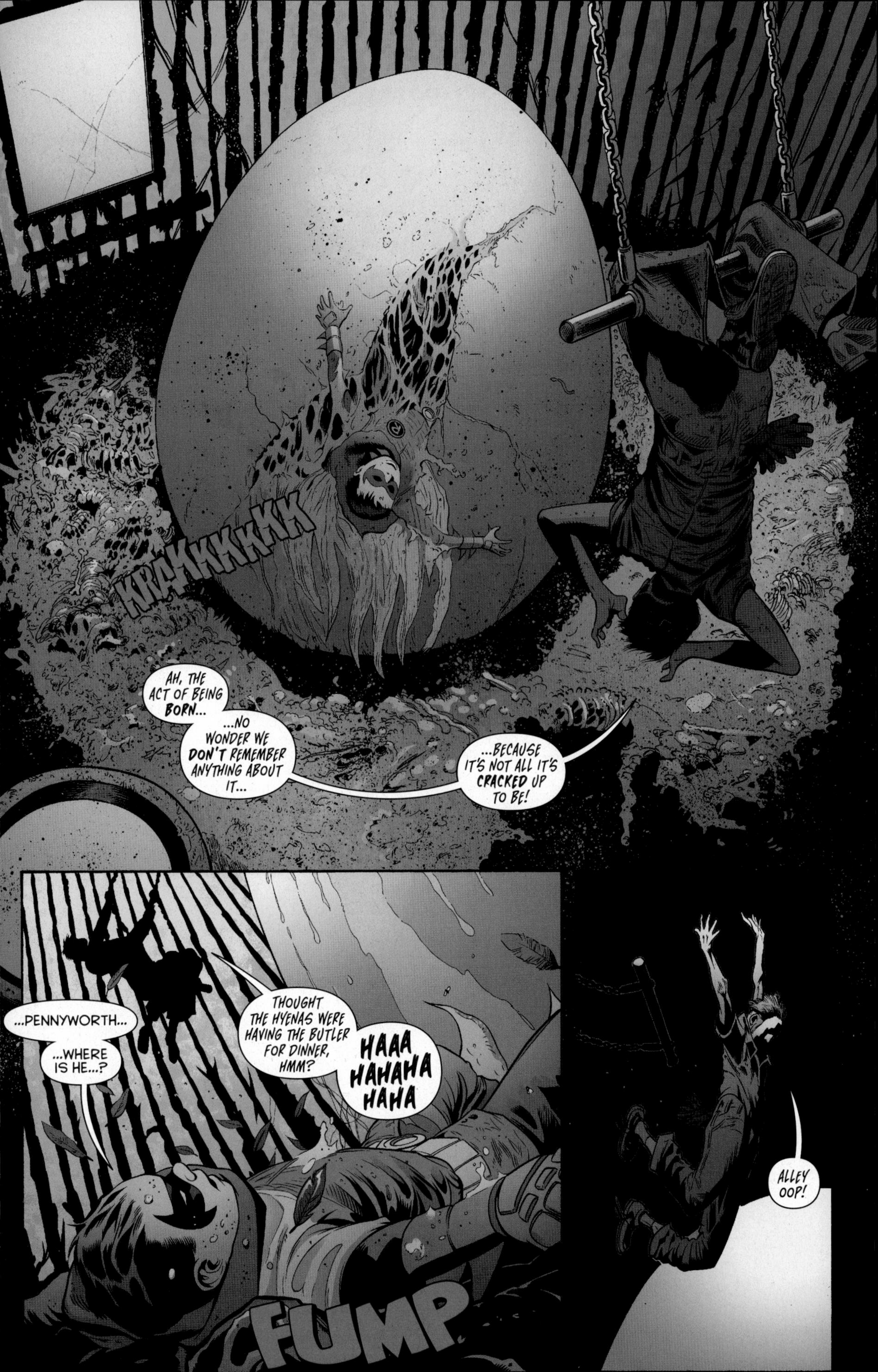
KRAKKKKKKK
AH, THE ACT OF BEING BORN...
...NO WONDER WE DON'T REMEMBER ANYTHING ABOUT IT...
...BECAUSE IT'S NOT ALL IT'S CRACKED UP TO BE!
...PENNYWORTH...
...WHERE IS HE...?
THOUGHT THE HYENAS WERE HAVING THE BUTLER FOR DINNER, HMM?
HAAA HAHAHA HAHA
ALLEY OOP!
FUMP

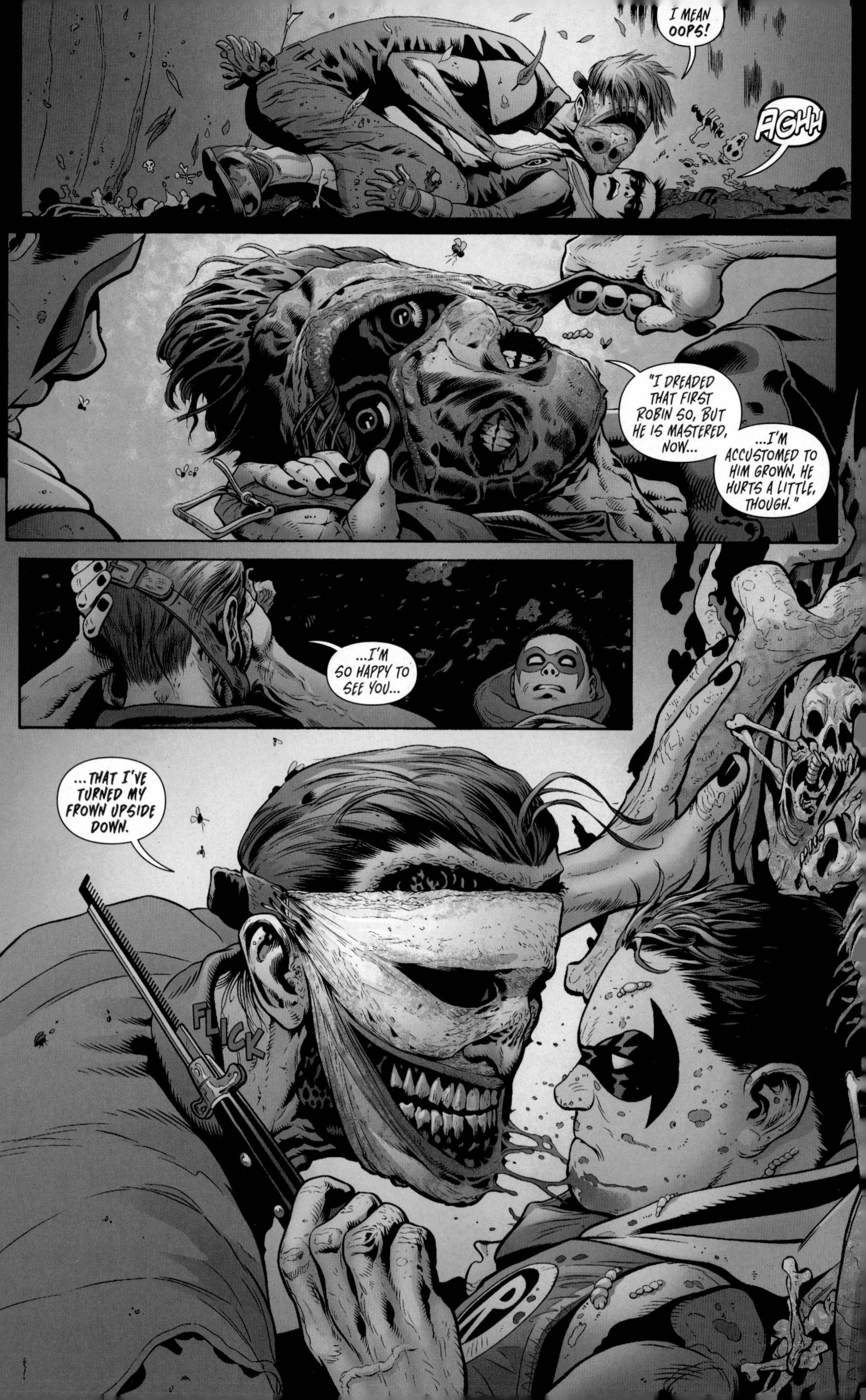
I MEAN OOPS!
AGHH
"I DREADED THAT FIRST ROBIN SO, BUT HE IS MASTERED, NOW...
...I'M ACCUSTOMED TO HIM GROWN, HE HURTS A LITTLE, THOUGH."
...I'M SO HAPPY TO SEE YOU...
...THAT I'VE TURNED MY FROWN UPSIDE DOWN.
FLICK

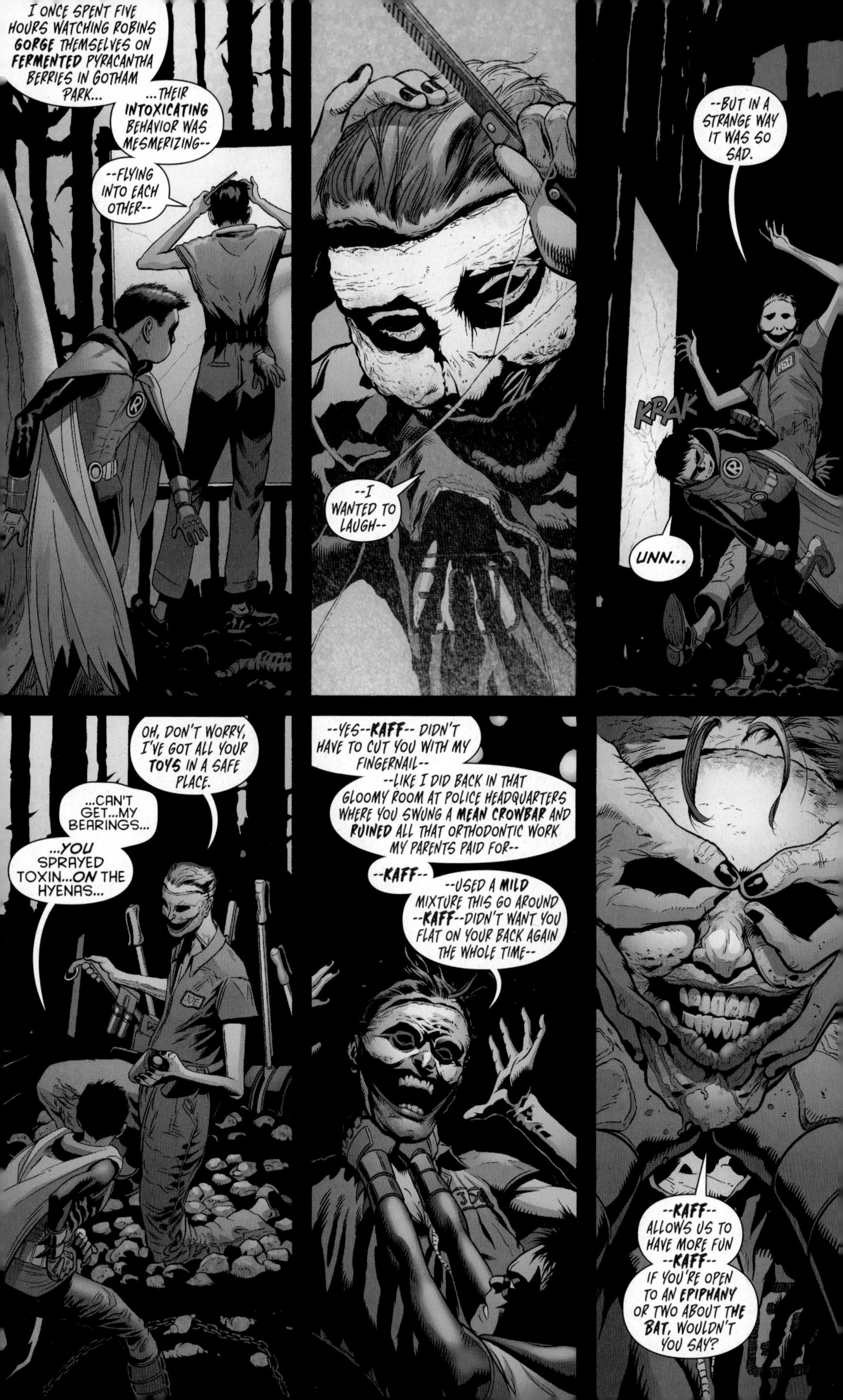
I ONCE SPENT FIVE HOURS WATCHING ROBINS GORGE THEMSELVES ON FERMENTED PYRACANTHA BERRIES IN GOTHAM PARK...
...THEIR INTOXICATING BEHAVIOR WAS MESMERIZING--
--FLYING INTO EACH OTHER--
--I WANTED TO LAUGH--
--BUT IN A STRANGE WAY IT WAS SO SAD.
KRAK
UNN...
OH, DON'T WORRY, I'VE GOT ALL YOUR TOYS IN A SAFE PLACE.
...CAN'T GET...MY BEARINGS...
...YOU SPRAYED TOXIN...ON THE HYENAS...
--YES--KAFF-- DIDN'T HAVE TO CUT YOU WITH MY FINGERNAIL--
--LIKE I DID BACK IN THAT GLOOMY ROOM AT POLICE HEADQUARTERS WHERE YOU SWUNG A MEAN CROWBAR AND RUINED ALL THAT ORTHODONTIC WORK MY PARENTS PAID FOR--
--KAFF--
--USED A MILD MIXTURE THIS GO AROUND --KAFF--DIDN'T WANT YOU FLAT ON YOUR BACK AGAIN THE WHOLE TIME--
--KAFF-- ALLOWS US TO HAVE MORE FUN --KAFF-- IF YOU'RE OPEN TO AN EPIPHANY OR TWO ABOUT THE BAT, WOULDN'T YOU SAY?

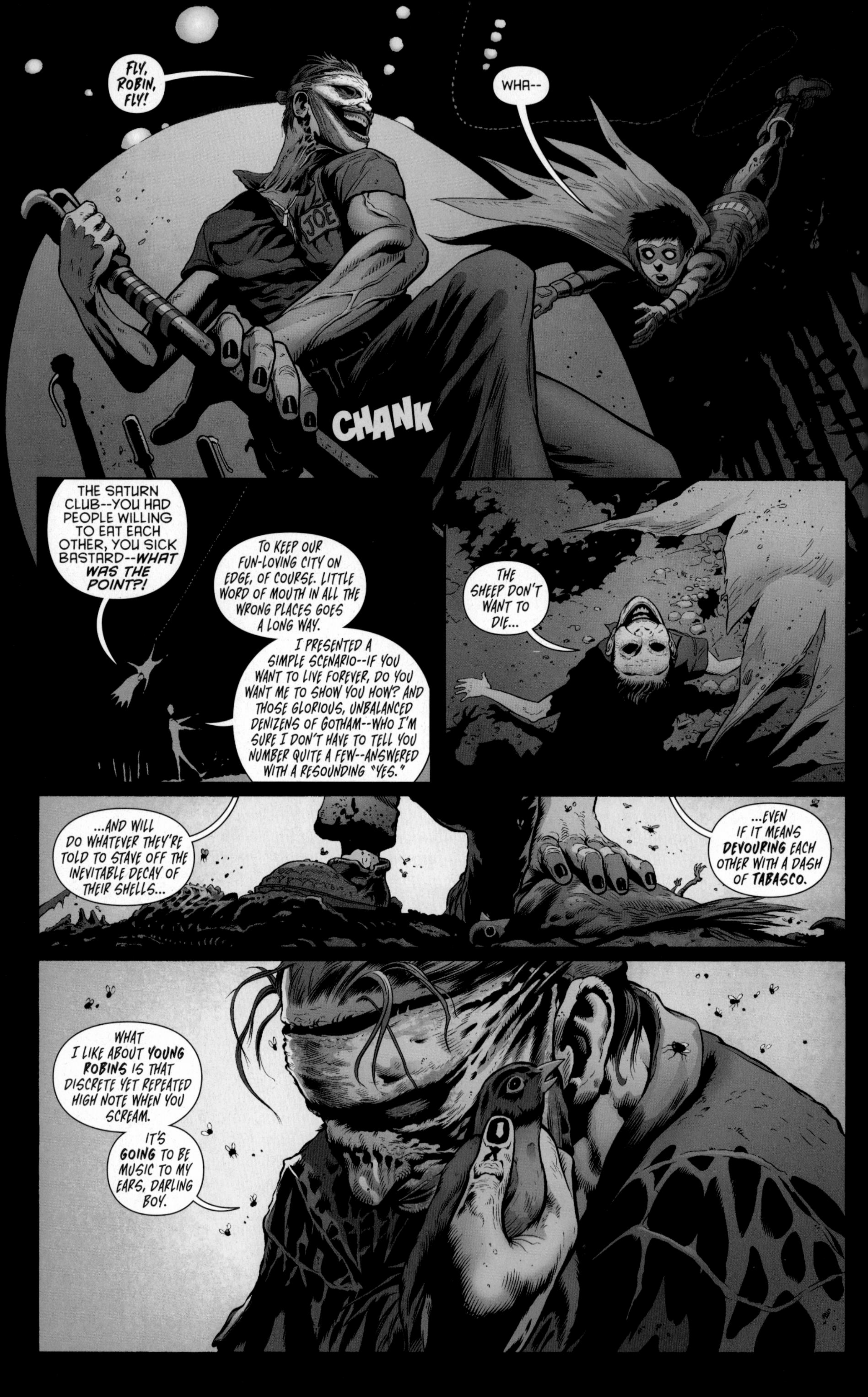
FLY, ROBIN, FLY!
WHA--
JOE
CHANK
THE SATURN CLUB--YOU HAD PEOPLE WILLING TO EAT EACH OTHER, YOU SICK BASTARD--WHAT WAS THE POINT?!
TO KEEP OUR FUN-LOVING CITY ON EDGE, OF COURSE. LITTLE WORD OF MOUTH IN ALL THE WRONG PLACES GOES A LONG WAY.
I PRESENTED A SIMPLE SCENARIO--IF YOU WANT TO LIVE FOREVER, DO YOU WANT ME TO SHOW YOU HOW? AND THOSE GLORIOUS, UNBALANCED DENIZENS OF GOTHAM--WHO I'M SURE I DON'T HAVE TO TELL YOU NUMBER QUITE A FEW--ANSWERED WITH A RESOUNDING "YES."
THE SHEEP DON'T WANT TO DIE...
...AND WILL DO WHATEVER THEY'RE TOLD TO STAVE OFF THE INEVITABLE DECAY OF THEIR SHELLS...
...EVEN IF IT MEANS DEVOURING EACH OTHER WITH A DASH OF TABASCO.
WHAT I LIKE ABOUT YOUNG ROBINS IS THAT DISCRETE YET REPEATED HIGH NOTE WHEN YOU SCREAM.
IT'S GOING TO BE MUSIC TO MY EARS, DARLING BOY.

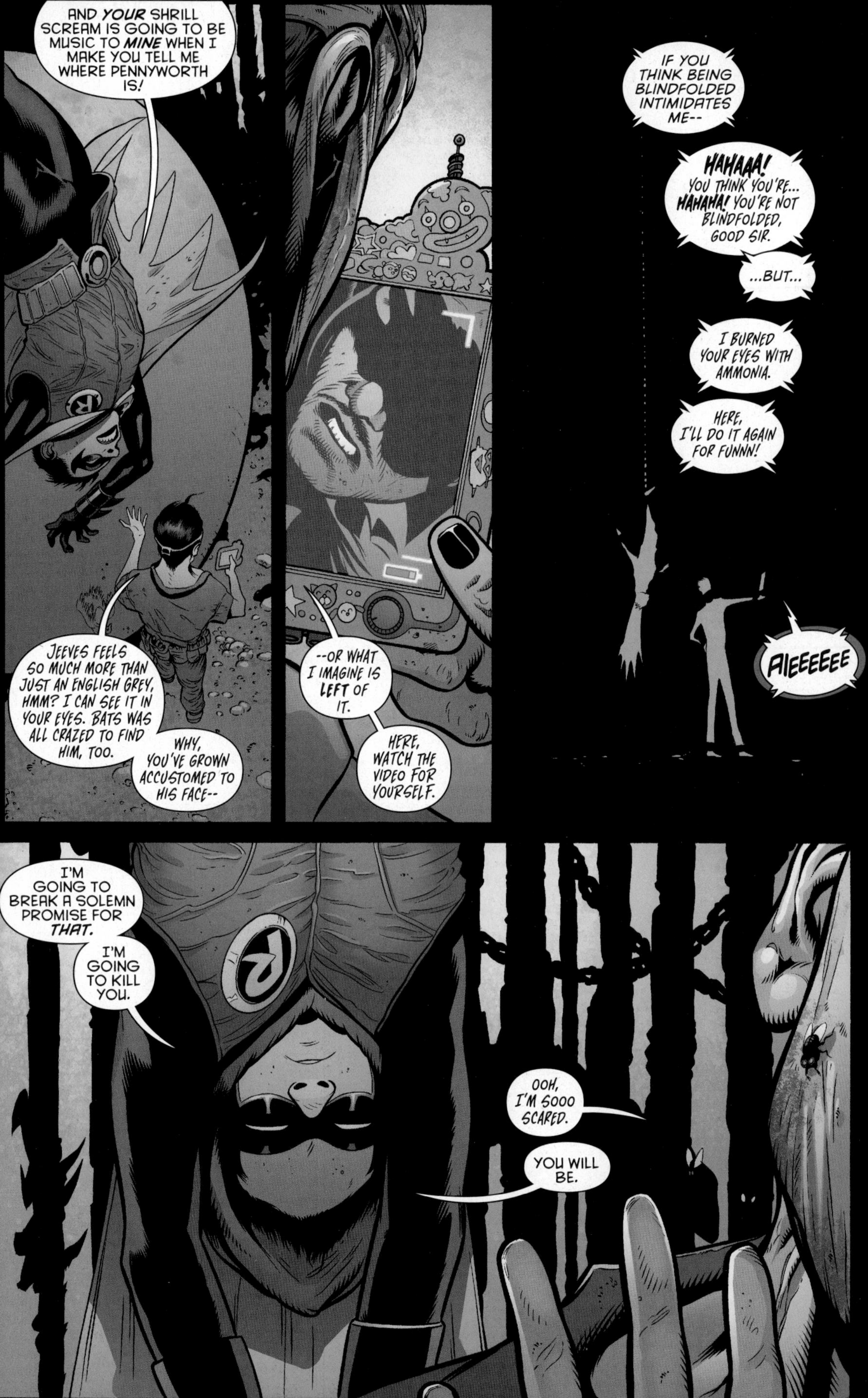
AND YOUR SHRILL SCREAM IS GOING TO BE MUSIC TO MINE WHEN I MAKE YOU TELL ME WHERE PENNYWORTH IS!
JEEVES FEELS SO MUCH MORE THAN JUST AN ENGLISH GREY, HMM? I CAN SEE IT IN YOUR EYES. BATS WAS ALL CRAZED TO FIND HIM, TOO.
WHY, YOU'VE GROWN ACCUSTOMED TO HIS FACE--
--OR WHAT I IMAGINE IS LEFT OF IT.
HERE, WATCH THE VIDEO FOR YOURSELF.
IF YOU THINK BEING BLINDFOLDED INTIMIDATES ME--
HAHAAA! YOU THINK YOU'RE... HAHAHA! YOU'RE NOT BLINDFOLDED, GOOD SIR.
...BUT...
I BURNED YOUR EYES WITH AMMONIA.
HERE, I'LL DO IT AGAIN FOR FUNNN!
AIEEEEEE
I'M GOING TO BREAK A SOLEMN PROMISE FOR THAT.
I'M GOING TO KILL YOU.
OOH, I'M SOOO SCARED.
YOU WILL BE.

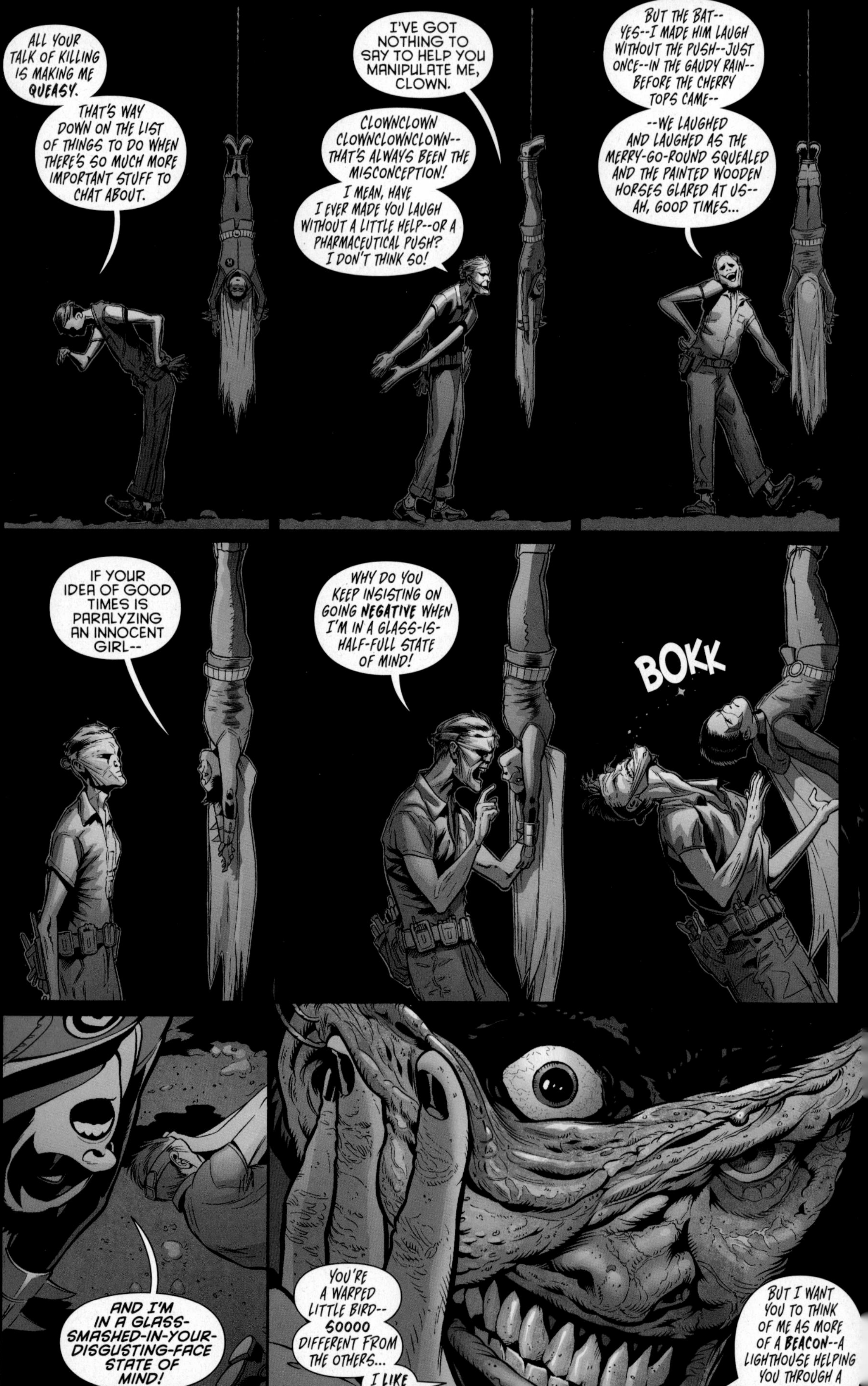
ALL YOUR TALK OF KILLING IS MAKING ME QUEASY.
THAT'S WAY DOWN ON THE LIST OF THINGS TO DO WHEN THERE'S SO MUCH MORE IMPORTANT STUFF TO CHAT ABOUT.
I'VE GOT NOTHING TO SAY TO HELP YOU MANIPULATE ME, CLOWN.
CLOWNCLOWN CLOWNCLOWNCLOWN-- THAT'S ALWAYS BEEN THE MISCONCEPTION!
I MEAN, HAVE I EVER MADE YOU LAUGH WITHOUT A LITTLE HELP--OR A PHARMACEUTICAL PUSH? I DON'T THINK SO!
BUT THE BAT-- YES--I MADE HIM LAUGH WITHOUT THE PUSH--JUST ONCE--IN THE GAUDY RAIN-- BEFORE THE CHERRY TOPS CAME--
--WE LAUGHED AND LAUGHED AS THE MERRY-GO-ROUND SQUEALED AND THE PAINTED WOODEN HORSES GLARED AT US-- AH, GOOD TIMES...
IF YOUR IDEA OF GOOD TIMES IS PARALYZING AN INNOCENT GIRL--
WHY DO YOU KEEP INSISTING ON GOING NEGATIVE WHEN I'M IN A GLASS-IS-HALF-FULL STATE OF MIND!
BOKK
AND I'M IN A GLASS-SMASHED-IN-YOUR-DISGUSTING-FACE STATE OF MIND!
YOU'RE A WARPED LITTLE BIRD-- SOOOO DIFFERENT FROM THE OTHERS...
I LIKE THAT.
BUT I WANT YOU TO THINK OF ME AS MORE OF A BEACON--A LIGHTHOUSE HELPING YOU THROUGH A STORM OF THE SOUL.

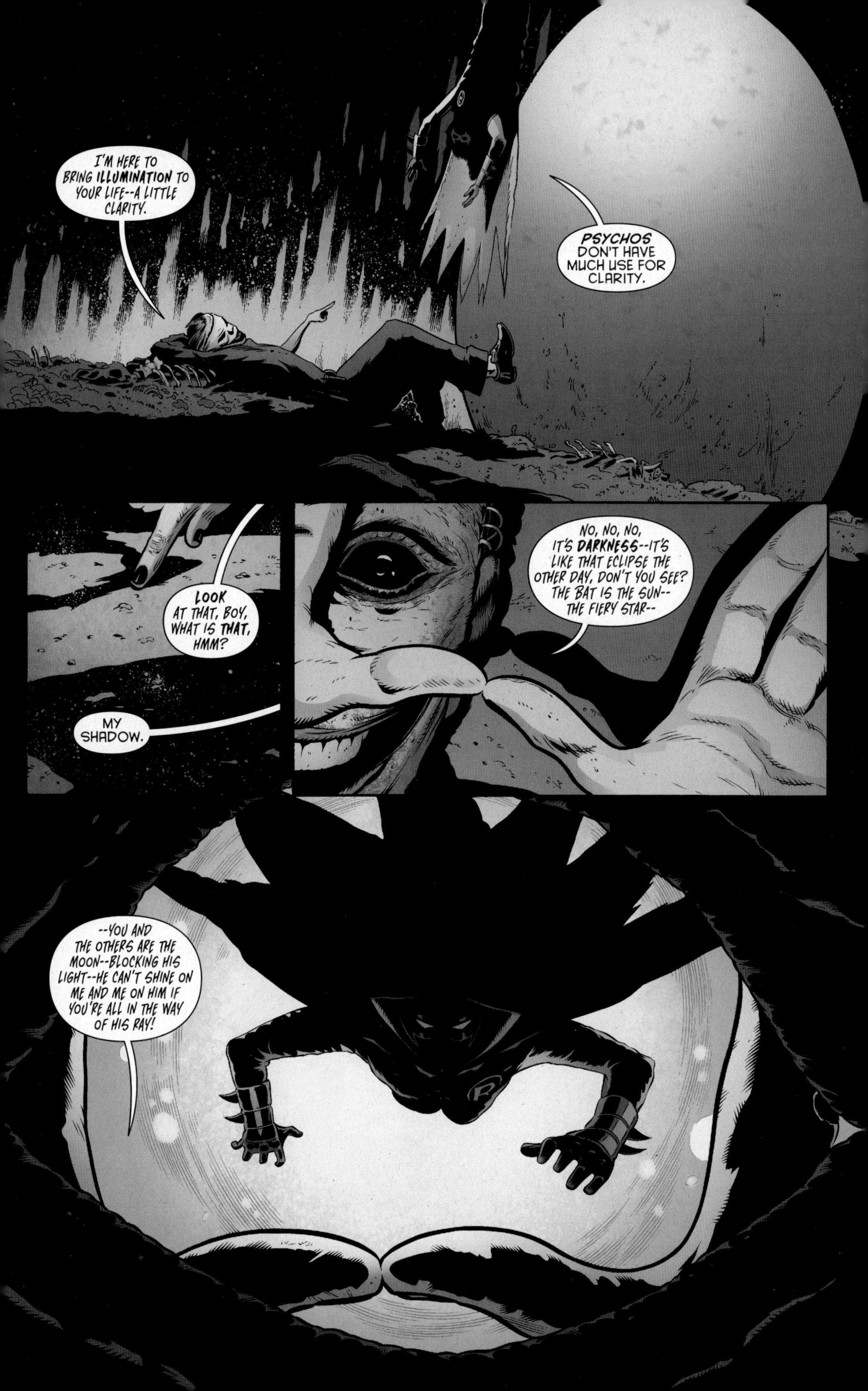
I'M HERE TO BRING ILLUMINATION TO YOUR LIFE--A LITTLE CLARITY.
PSYCHOS DON'T HAVE MUCH USE FOR CLARITY.
LOOK AT THAT, BOY, WHAT IS THAT, HMM?
MY SHADOW.
NO, NO, NO, IT'S DARKNESS--IT'S LIKE THAT ECLIPSE THE OTHER DAY, DON'T YOU SEE? THE BAT IS THE SUN--THE FIERY STAR--
--YOU AND THE OTHERS ARE THE MOON--BLOCKING HIS LIGHT--HE CAN'T SHINE ON ME AND ME ON HIM IF YOU'RE ALL IN THE WAY OF HIS RAY!

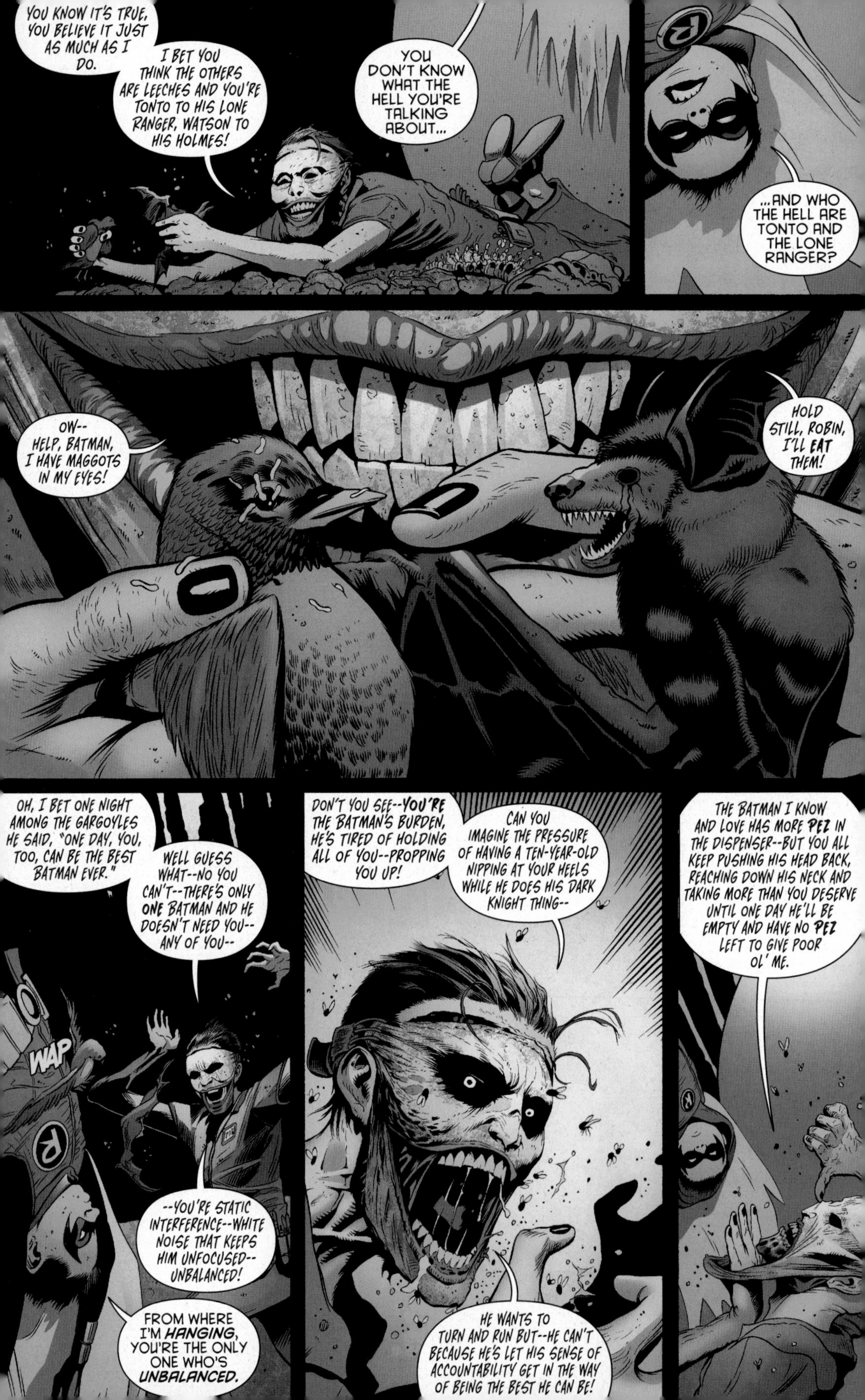
YOU KNOW IT'S TRUE, YOU BELIEVE IT JUST AS MUCH AS I DO.
I BET YOU THINK THE OTHERS ARE LEECHES AND YOU'RE TONTO TO HIS LONE RANGER, WATSON TO HIS HOLMES!
YOU DON'T KNOW WHAT THE HELL YOU'RE TALKING ABOUT...
...AND WHO THE HELL ARE TONTO AND THE LONE RANGER?
OW-- HELP, BATMAN, I HAVE MAGGOTS IN MY EYES!
HOLD STILL, ROBIN, I'LL EAT THEM!
OH, I BET ONE NIGHT AMONG THE GARGOYLES HE SAID, "ONE DAY, YOU, TOO, CAN BE THE BEST BATMAN EVER."
WELL GUESS WHAT--NO YOU CAN'T--THERE'S ONLY ONE BATMAN AND HE DOESN'T NEED YOU--ANY OF YOU--
WAP
--YOU'RE STATIC INTERFERENCE--WHITE NOISE THAT KEEPS HIM UNFOCUSED--UNBALANCED!
FROM WHERE I'M HANGING, YOU'RE THE ONLY ONE WHO'S UNBALANCED.
DON'T YOU SEE--YOU'RE THE BATMAN'S BURDEN, HE'S TIRED OF HOLDING ALL OF YOU--PROPPING YOU UP!
CAN YOU IMAGINE THE PRESSURE OF HAVING A TEN-YEAR-OLD NIPPING AT YOUR HEELS WHILE HE DOES HIS DARK KNIGHT THING--
HE WANTS TO TURN AND RUN BUT--HE CAN'T BECAUSE HE'S LET HIS SENSE OF ACCOUNTABILITY GET IN THE WAY OF BEING THE BEST HE CAN BE!
THE BATMAN I KNOW AND LOVE HAS MORE PEZ IN THE DISPENSER--BUT YOU ALL KEEP PUSHING HIS HEAD BACK, REACHING DOWN HIS NECK AND TAKING MORE THAN YOU DESERVE UNTIL ONE DAY HE'LL BE EMPTY AND HAVE NO PEZ LEFT TO GIVE POOR OL' ME.

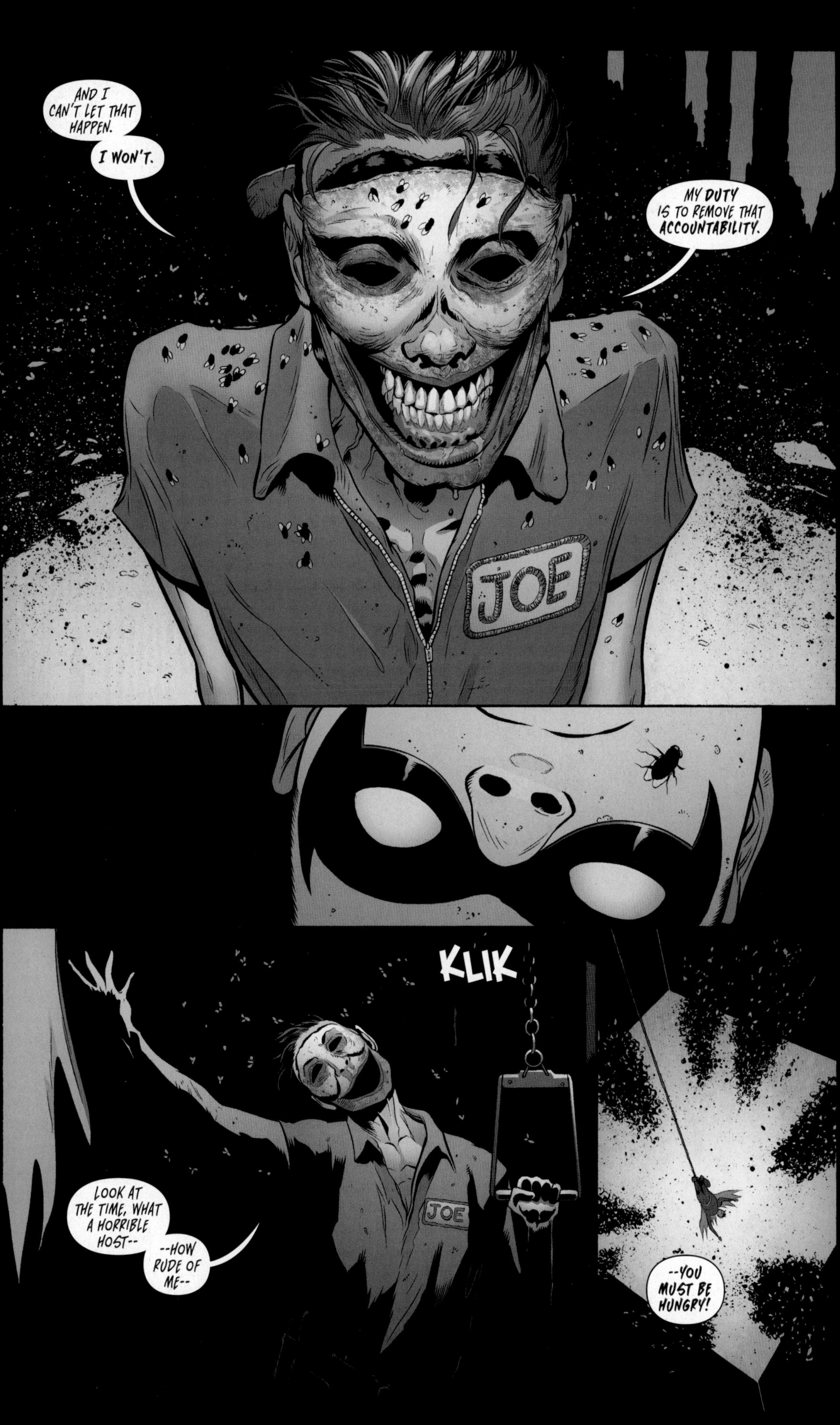
AND I CAN'T LET THAT HAPPEN.
I WON'T.
MY DUTY IS TO REMOVE THAT ACCOUNTABILITY.
KLIK
LOOK AT THE TIME, WHAT A HORRIBLE HOST--
--HOW RUDE OF ME--
--YOU MUST BE HUNGRY!

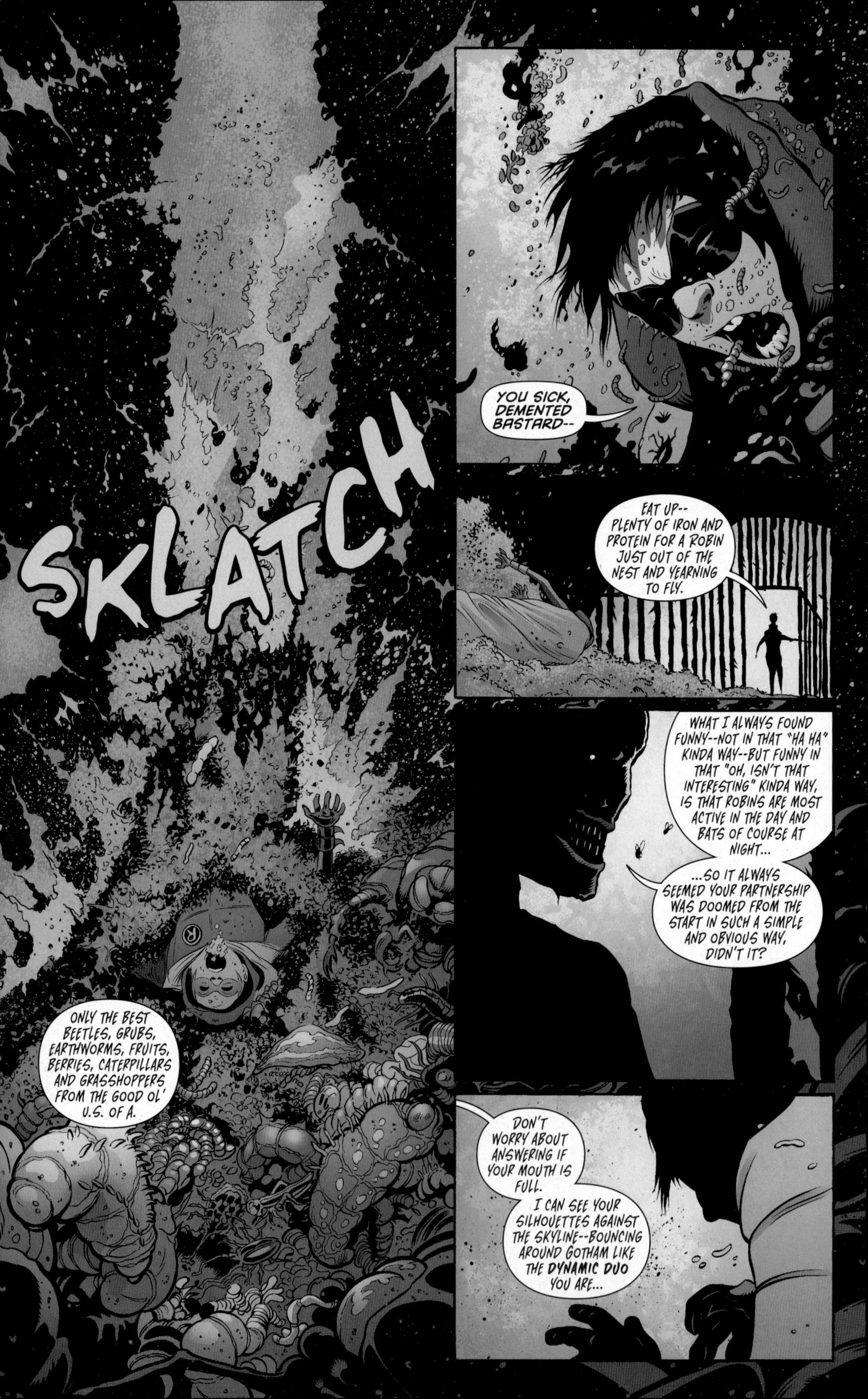
SKLATCH
ONLY THE BEST BEETLES, GRUBS, EARTHWORMS, FRUITS, BERRIES, CATERPILLARS AND GRASSHOPPERS FROM THE GOOD OL' U.S. OF A.
YOU SICK, DEMENTED BASTARD--
EAT UP-- PLENTY OF IRON AND PROTEIN FOR A ROBIN JUST OUT OF THE NEST AND YEARNING TO FLY.
WHAT I ALWAYS FOUND FUNNY--NOT IN THAT "HA HA" KINDA WAY--BUT FUNNY IN THAT "OH, ISN'T THAT INTERESTING" KINDA WAY, IS THAT ROBINS ARE MOST ACTIVE IN THE DAY AND BATS OF COURSE AT NIGHT...
...SO IT ALWAYS SEEMED YOUR PARTNERSHIP WAS DOOMED FROM THE START IN SUCH A SIMPLE AND OBVIOUS WAY, DIDN'T IT?
DON'T WORRY ABOUT ANSWERING IF YOUR MOUTH IS FULL.
I CAN SEE YOUR SILHOUETTES AGAINST THE SKYLINE--BOUNCING AROUND GOTHAM LIKE THE DYNAMIC DUO YOU ARE...

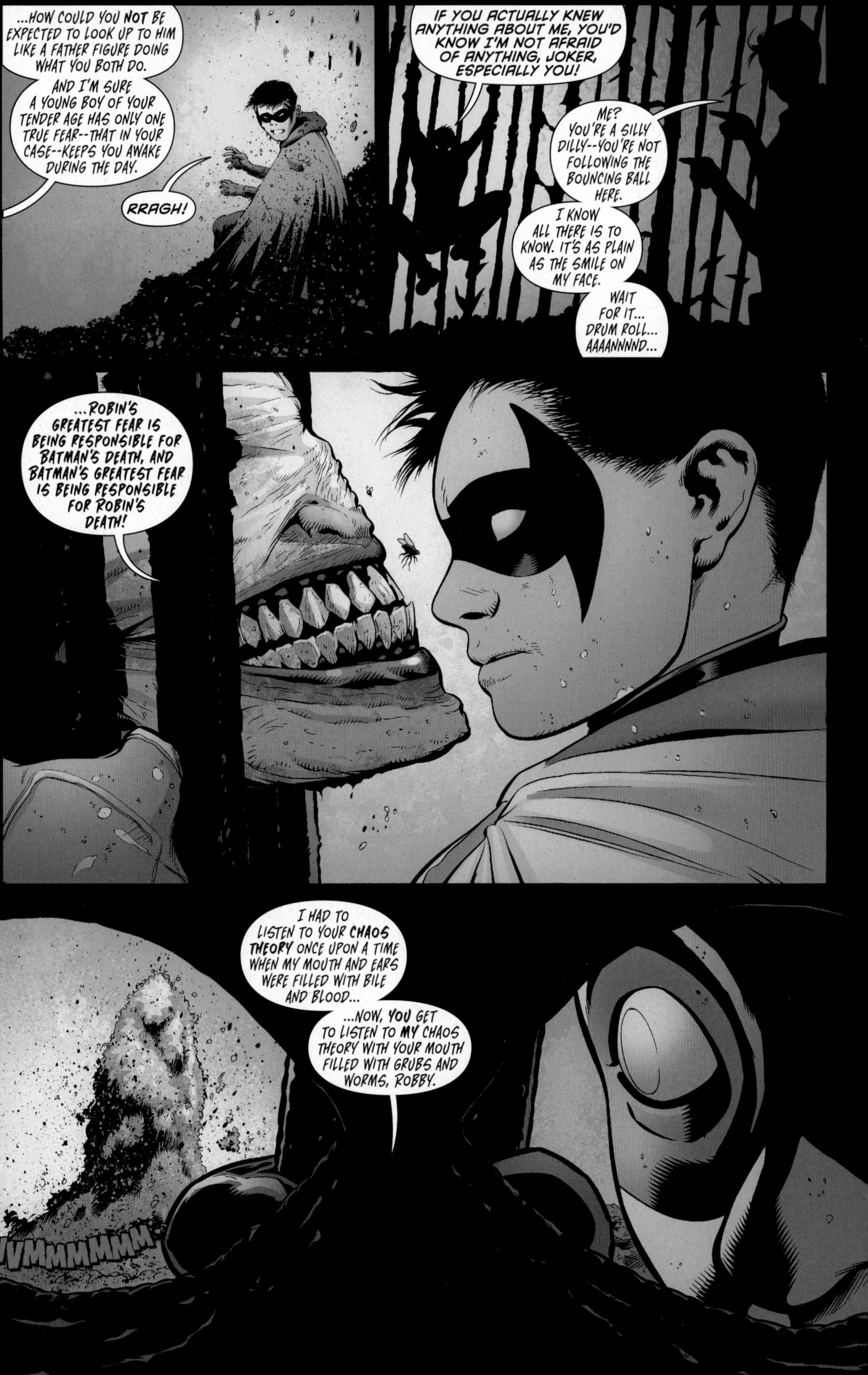
...HOW COULD YOU NOT BE EXPECTED TO LOOK UP TO HIM LIKE A FATHER FIGURE DOING WHAT YOU BOTH DO.
AND I'M SURE A YOUNG BOY OF YOUR TENDER AGE HAS ONLY ONE TRUE FEAR--THAT IN YOUR CASE--KEEPS YOU AWAKE DURING THE DAY.
RRAGH!
IF YOU ACTUALLY KNEW ANYTHING ABOUT ME, YOU'D KNOW I'M NOT AFRAID OF ANYTHING, JOKER, ESPECIALLY YOU!
ME? YOU'RE A SILLY DILLY--YOU'RE NOT FOLLOWING THE BOUNCING BALL HERE.
I KNOW ALL THERE IS TO KNOW. IT'S AS PLAIN AS THE SMILE ON MY FACE.
WAIT FOR IT... DRUM ROLL... AAAANNNND...
...ROBIN'S GREATEST FEAR IS BEING RESPONSIBLE FOR BATMAN'S DEATH, AND BATMAN'S GREATEST FEAR IS BEING RESPONSIBLE FOR ROBIN'S DEATH!
I HAD TO LISTEN TO YOUR CHAOS THEORY ONCE UPON A TIME WHEN MY MOUTH AND EARS WERE FILLED WITH BILE AND BLOOD...
...NOW, YOU GET TO LISTEN TO MY CHAOS THEORY WITH YOUR MOUTH FILLED WITH GRUBS AND WORMS, ROBBY.
VVMMMMMMM

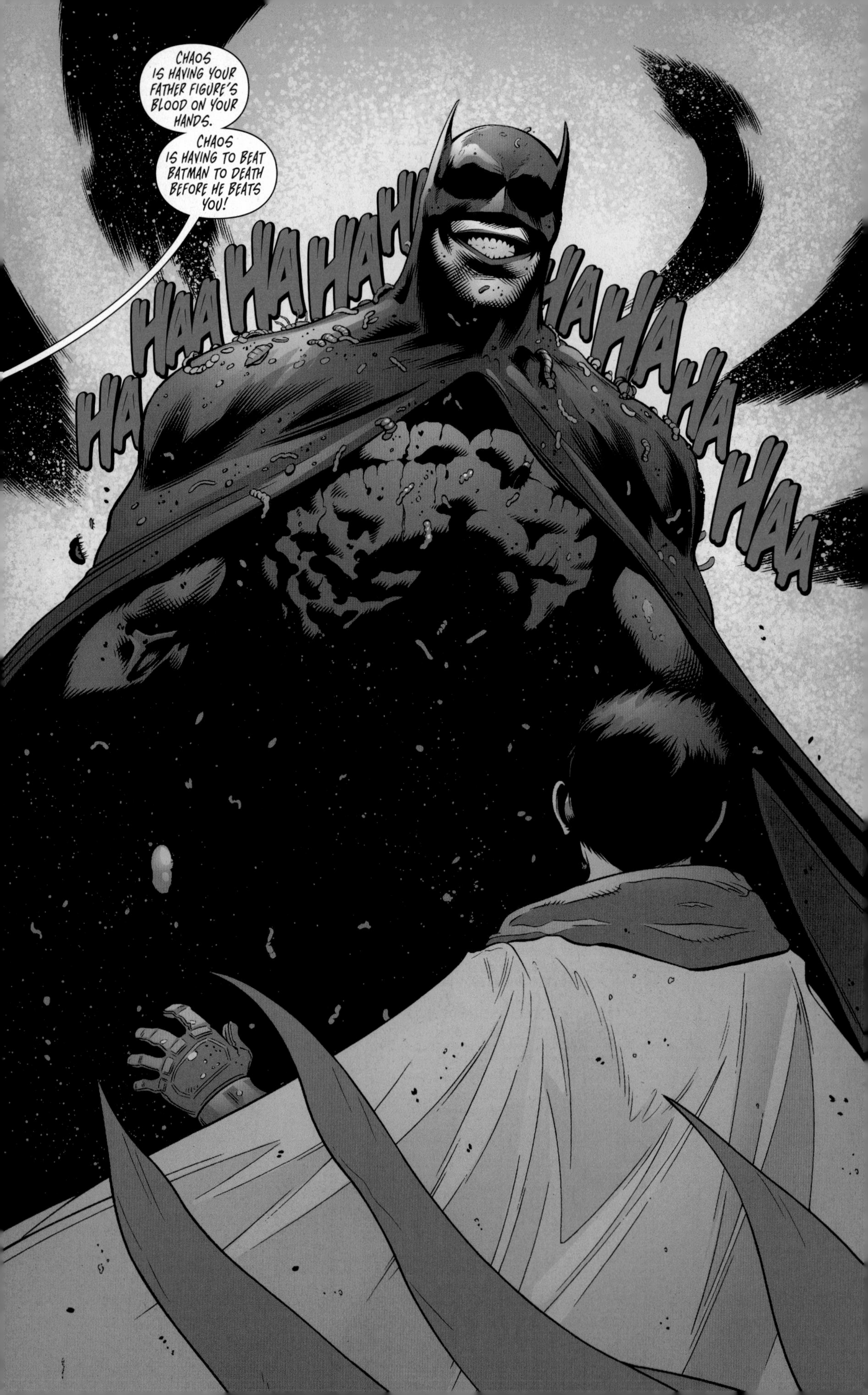
CHAOS IS HAVING YOUR FATHER FIGURE'S BLOOD ON YOUR HANDS.
CHAOS IS HAVING TO BEAT BATMAN TO DEATH BEFORE HE BEATS YOU!
HA HAA HAHAHAHAHAHA
HAHAHAHAHAHAHAA

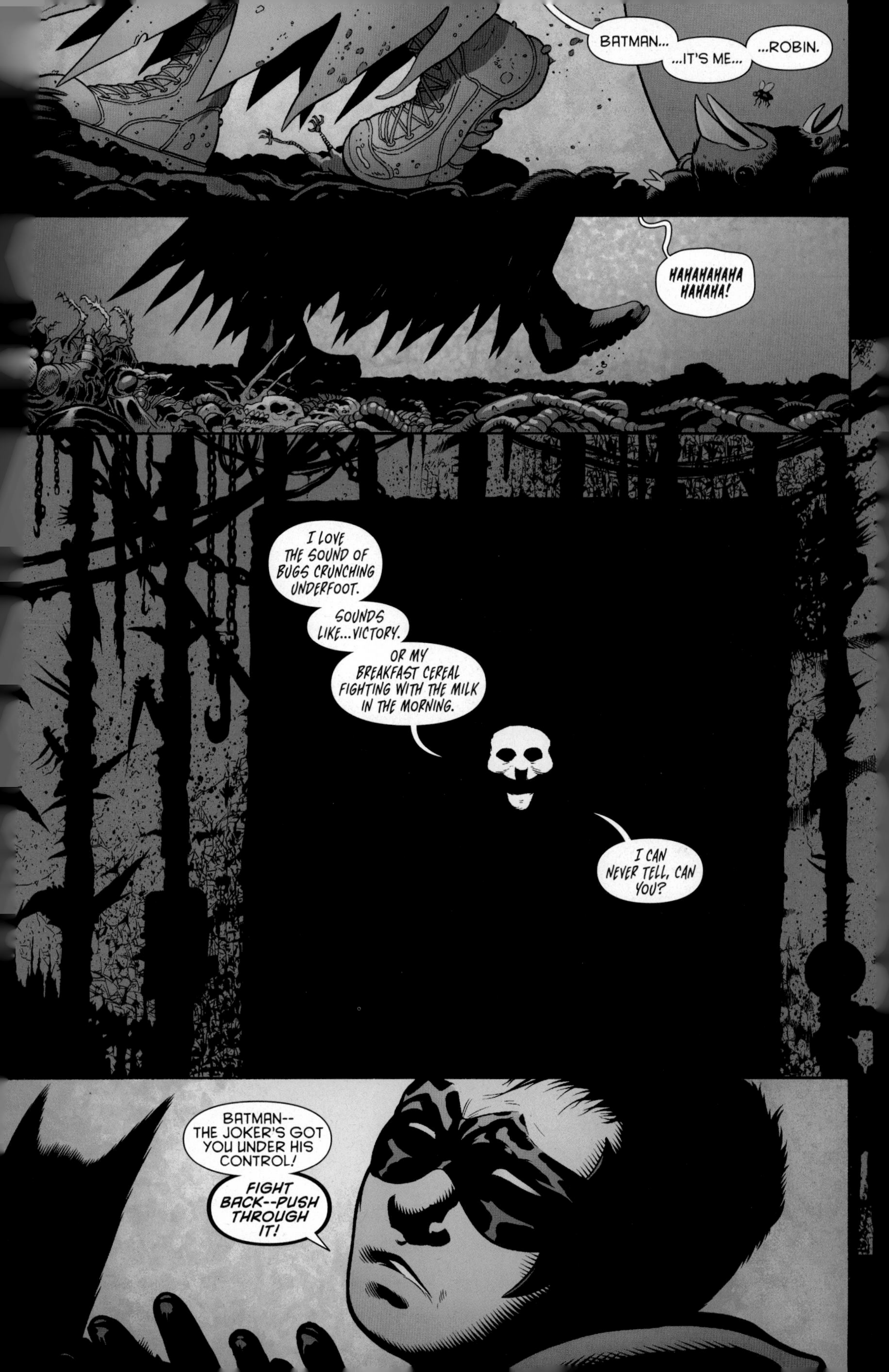
BATMAN...
...IT'S ME...
...ROBIN.
HAHAHAHAHA HAHAHA!
I LOVE THE SOUND OF BUGS CRUNCHING UNDERFOOT.
SOUNDS LIKE...VICTORY.
OR MY BREAKFAST CEREAL FIGHTING WITH THE MILK IN THE MORNING.
I CAN NEVER TELL, CAN YOU?
BATMAN-- THE JOKER'S GOT YOU UNDER HIS CONTROL!
FIGHT BACK--PUSH THROUGH IT!

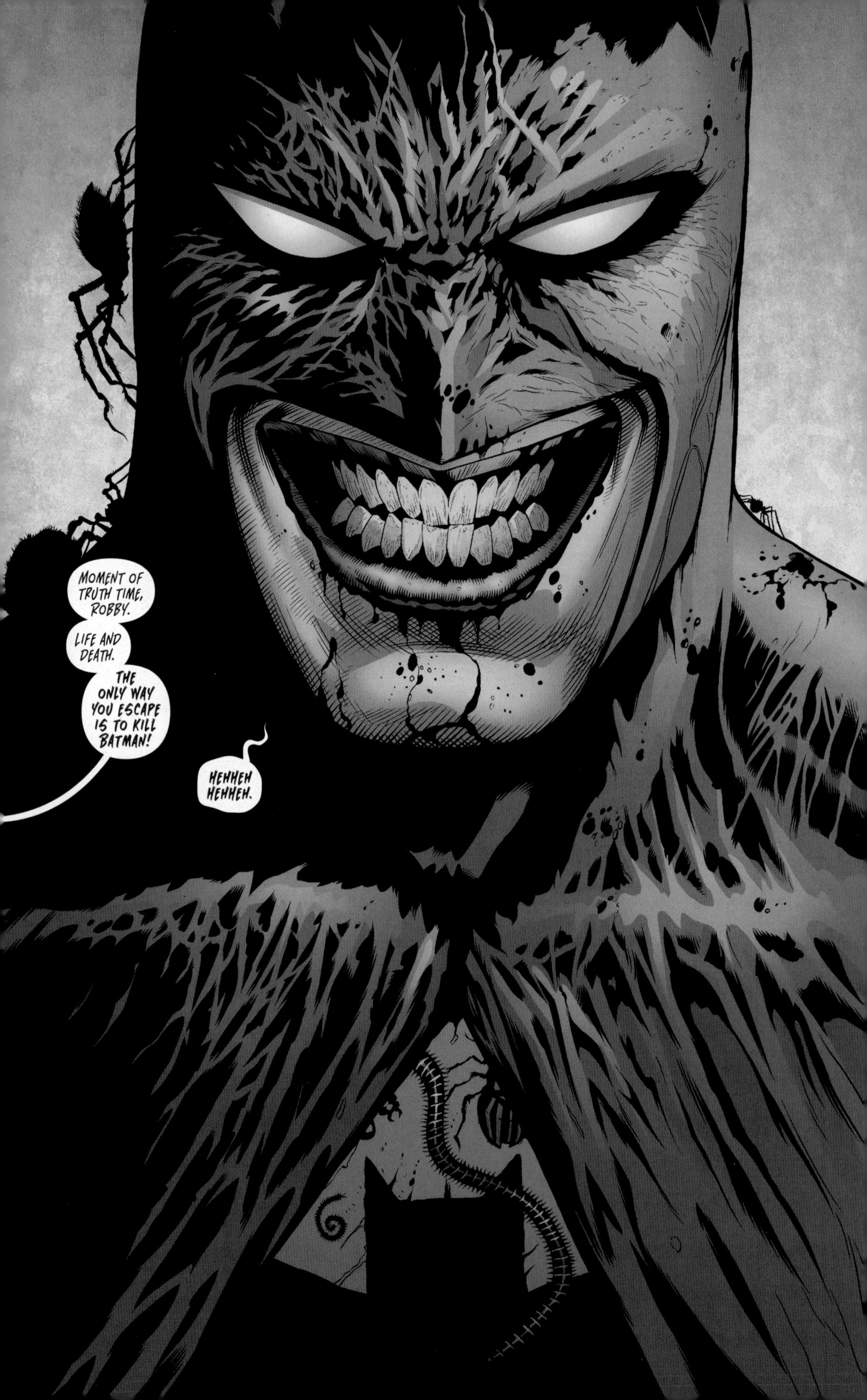
MOMENT OF TRUTH TIME, ROBBY.
LIFE AND DEATH.
THE ONLY WAY YOU ESCAPE IS TO KILL BATMAN!
HEHHEH HEHHEH.

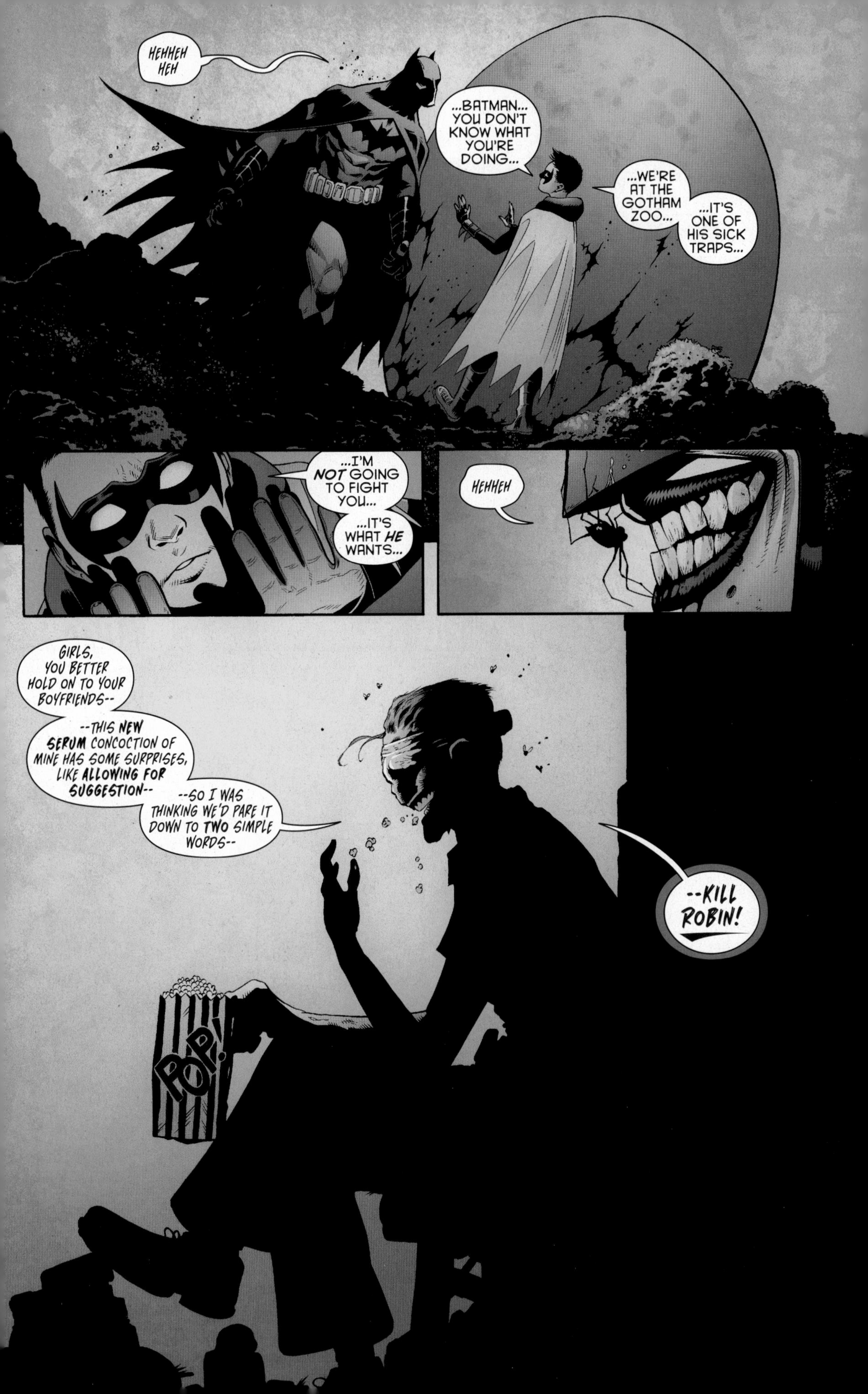
HEHHEH HEH
...BATMAN... YOU DON'T KNOW WHAT YOU'RE DOING...
...WE'RE AT THE GOTHAM ZOO...
...IT'S ONE OF HIS SICK TRAPS...
...I'M NOT GOING TO FIGHT YOU...
...IT'S WHAT HE WANTS...
HEHHEH
GIRLS, YOU BETTER HOLD ON TO YOUR BOYFRIENDS--
--THIS NEW SERUM CONCOCTION OF MINE HAS SOME SURPRISES, LIKE ALLOWING FOR SUGGESTION--
--SO I WAS THINKING WE'D PARE IT DOWN TO TWO SIMPLE WORDS--
--KILL ROBIN!
POP!

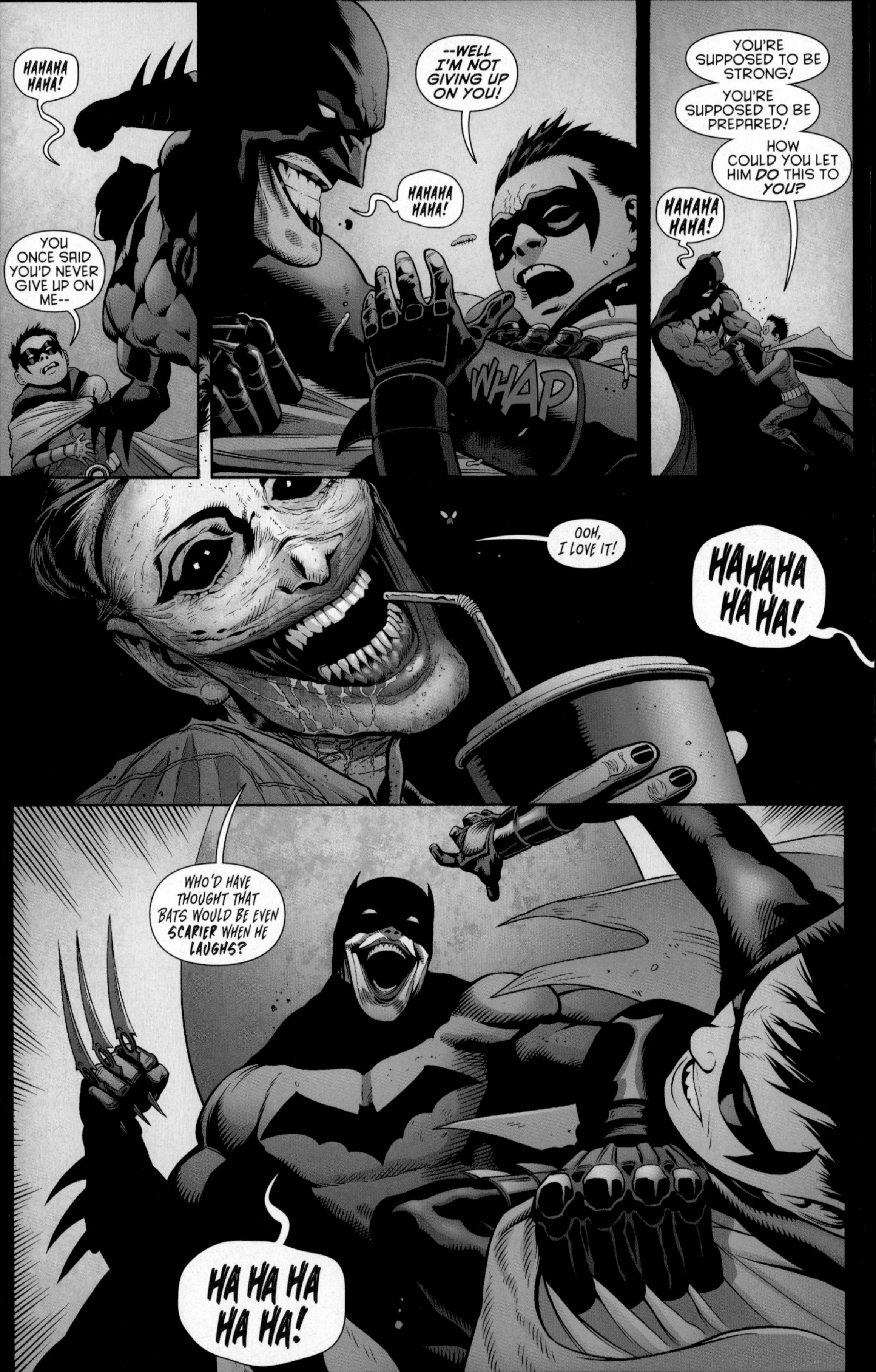
HAHAHA HAHA!
YOU ONCE SAID YOU'D NEVER GIVE UP ON ME--
--WELL I'M NOT GIVING UP ON YOU!
HAHAHA HAHA!
WHAP
YOU'RE SUPPOSED TO BE STRONG!
YOU'RE SUPPOSED TO BE PREPARED!
HOW COULD YOU LET HIM DO THIS TO YOU?
HAHAHA HAHA!
OOH, I LOVE IT!
HAHAHA HA HA!
WHO'D HAVE THOUGHT THAT BATS WOULD BE EVEN SCARIER WHEN HE LAUGHS?
HA HA HA HA HA!

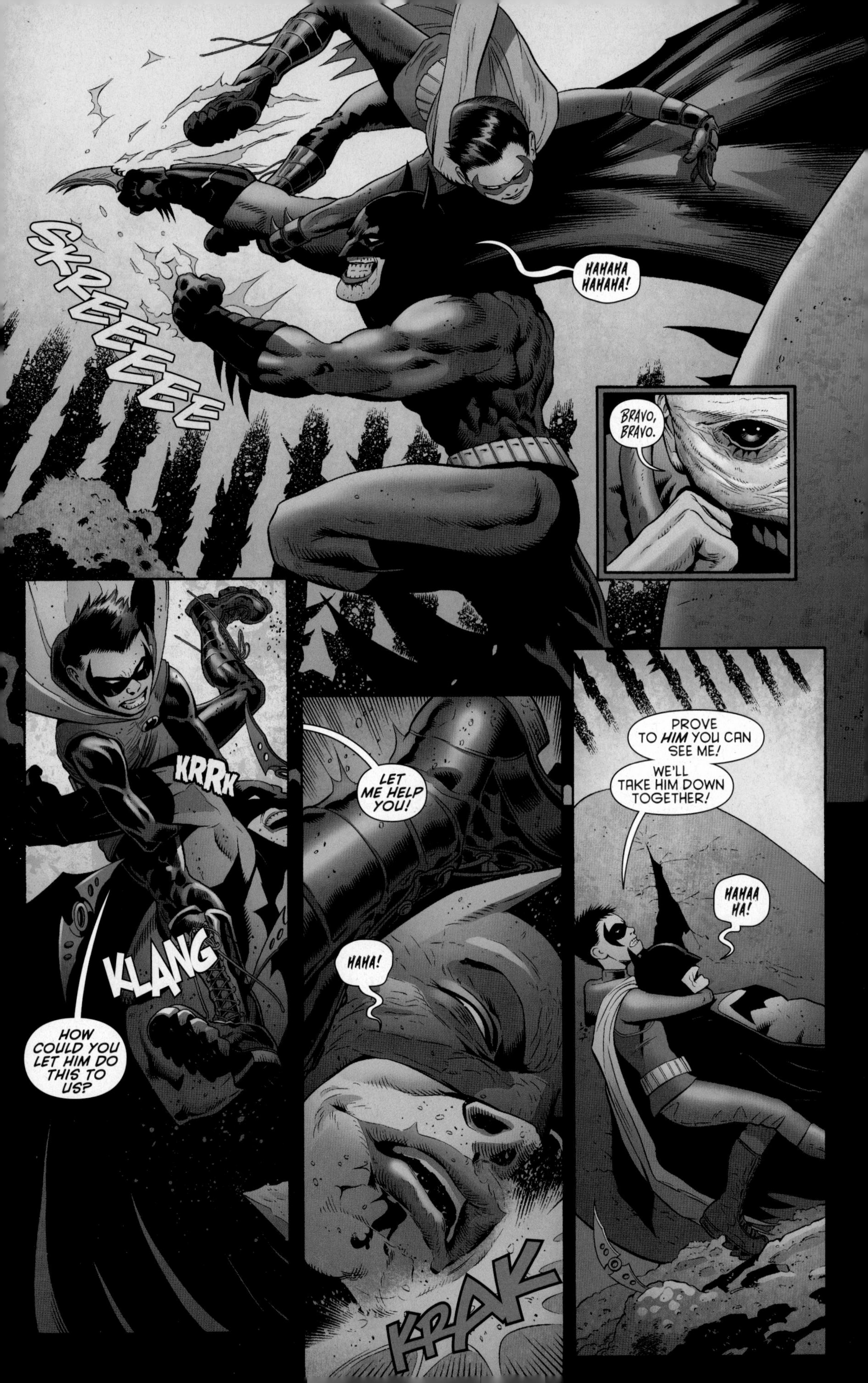
SKREEEEEE
HAHAHA HAHAHA!
BRAVO, BRAVO.
KRRRK
KLANG
HOW COULD YOU LET HIM DO THIS TO US?
LET ME HELP YOU!
HAHA!
KRAK
PROVE TO HIM YOU CAN SEE ME!
WE'LL TAKE HIM DOWN TOGETHER!
HAHAA HA!

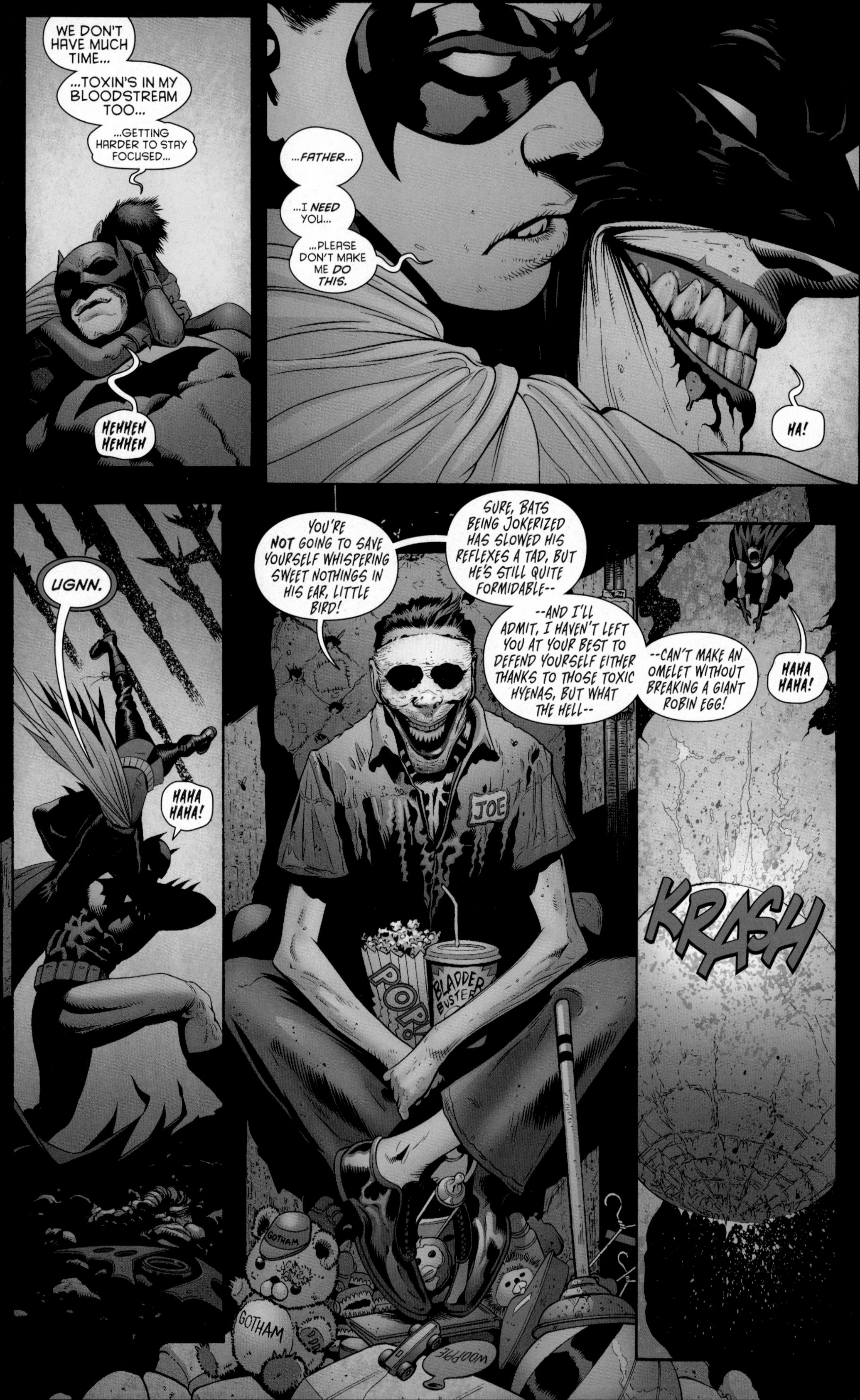

WE DON'T HAVE MUCH TIME...
...TOXIN'S IN MY BLOODSTREAM TOO...
...GETTING HARDER TO STAY FOCUSED...
HEHHEH HEHHEH
...FATHER...
...I NEED YOU...
...PLEASE DON'T MAKE ME DO THIS.
HA!
UGNN.
HAHA HAHA!
YOU'RE NOT GOING TO SAVE YOURSELF WHISPERING SWEET NOTHINGS IN HIS EAR, LITTLE BIRD!
SURE, BATS BEING JOKERIZED HAS SLOWED HIS REFLEXES A TAD, BUT HE'S STILL QUITE FORMIDABLE--
--AND I'LL ADMIT, I HAVEN'T LEFT YOU AT YOUR BEST TO DEFEND YOURSELF EITHER THANKS TO THOSE TOXIC HYENAS, BUT WHAT THE HELL--
--CAN'T MAKE AN OMELET WITHOUT BREAKING A GIANT ROBIN EGG!
JOE
POP
BLADDER BUSTER
GOTHAM
GOTHAM
WOOPPEE
HAHA HAHA!
KRASH

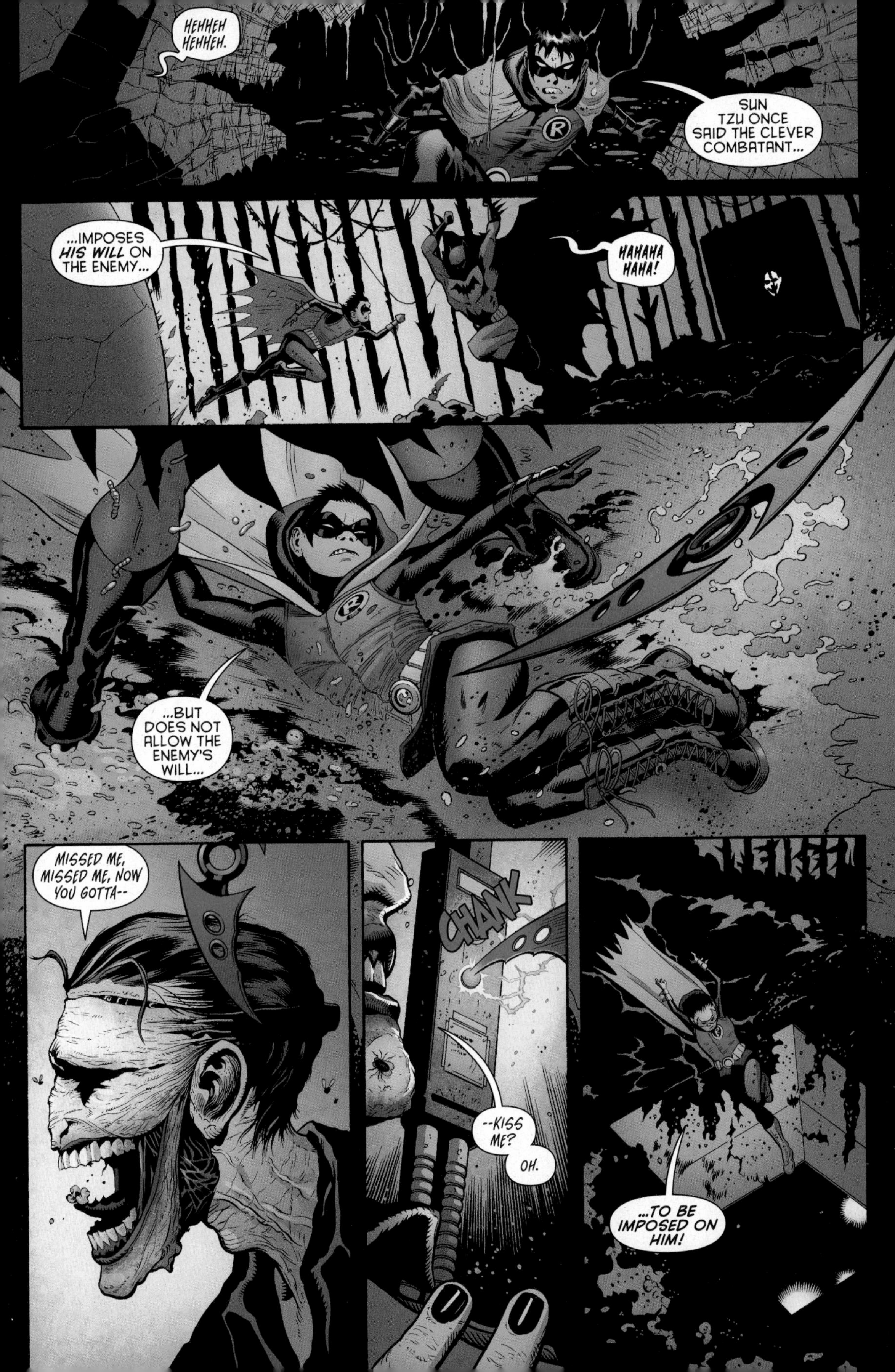
HEHHEH HEHHEH.
SUN TZU ONCE SAID THE CLEVER COMBATANT...
...IMPOSES HIS WILL ON THE ENEMY...
HAHAHA HAHA!
...BUT DOES NOT ALLOW THE ENEMY'S WILL...
MISSED ME, MISSED ME, NOW YOU GOTTA--
CHANK
--KISS ME?
OH.
...TO BE IMPOSED ON HIM!

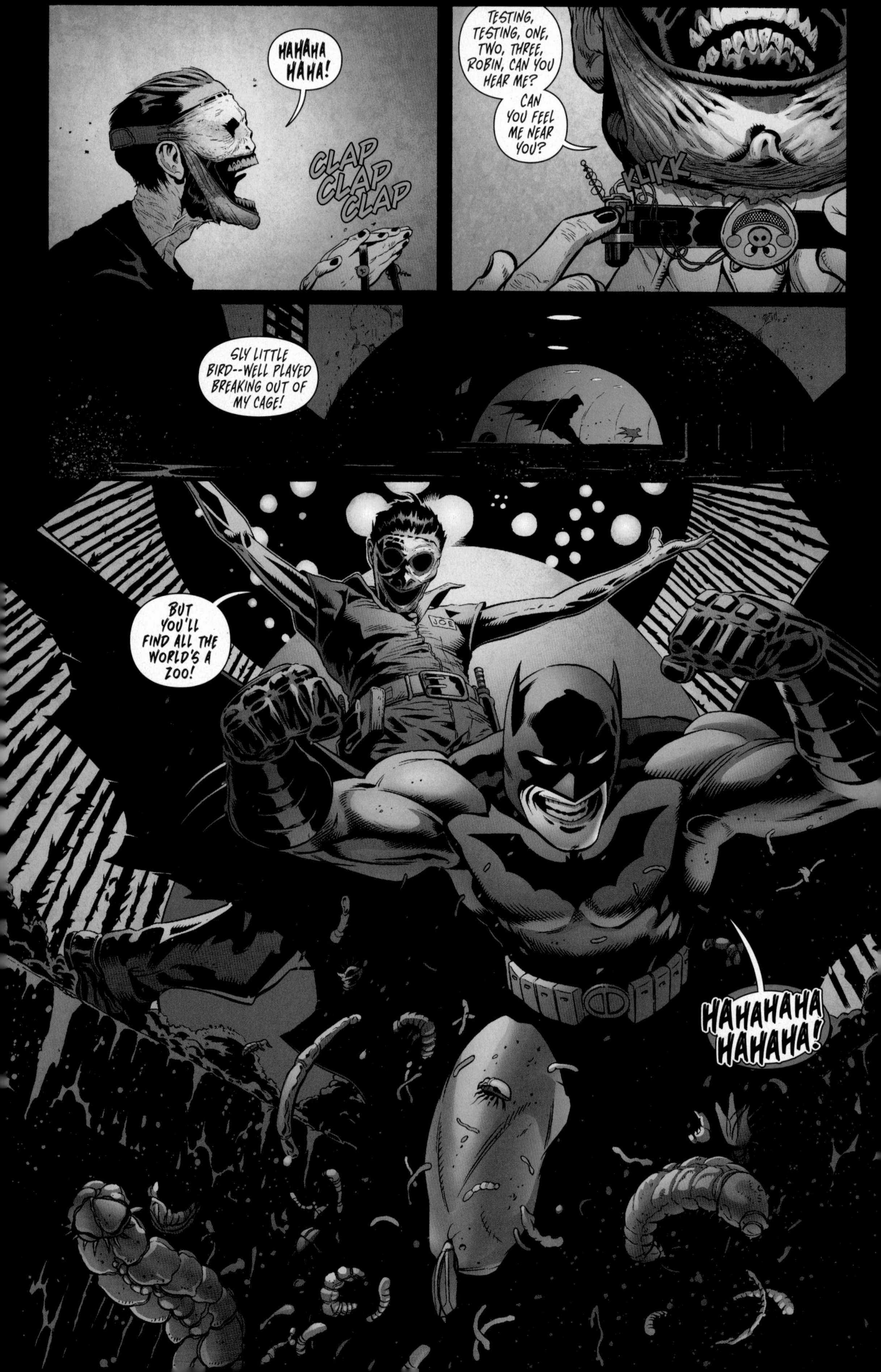
HAHAHA HAHA!
CLAP CLAP CLAP
TESTING, TESTING, ONE, TWO, THREE, ROBIN, CAN YOU HEAR ME?
CAN YOU FEEL ME NEAR YOU?
KLIKK
SLY LITTLE BIRD--WELL PLAYED BREAKING OUT OF MY CAGE!
BUT YOU'LL FIND ALL THE WORLD'S A ZOO!
JOE
HAHAHAHA HAHAHA!

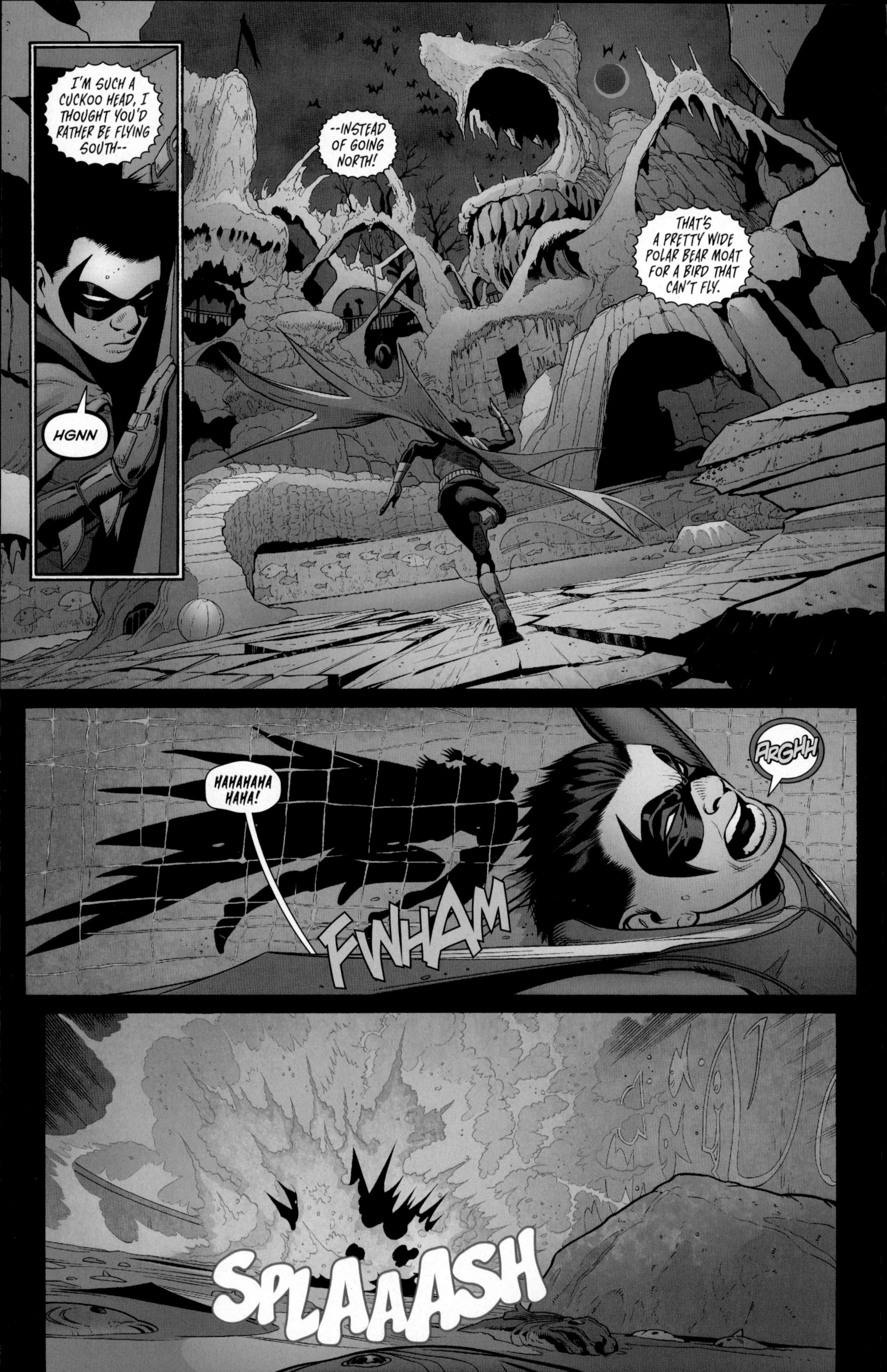
I'M SUCH A CUCKOO HEAD, I THOUGHT YOU'D RATHER BE FLYING SOUTH--
HGNN
--INSTEAD OF GOING NORTH!
THAT'S A PRETTY WIDE POLAR BEAR MOAT FOR A BIRD THAT CAN'T FLY.
HAHAHAHA HAHA!
ARGHH
FWHAM
SPLAAASH

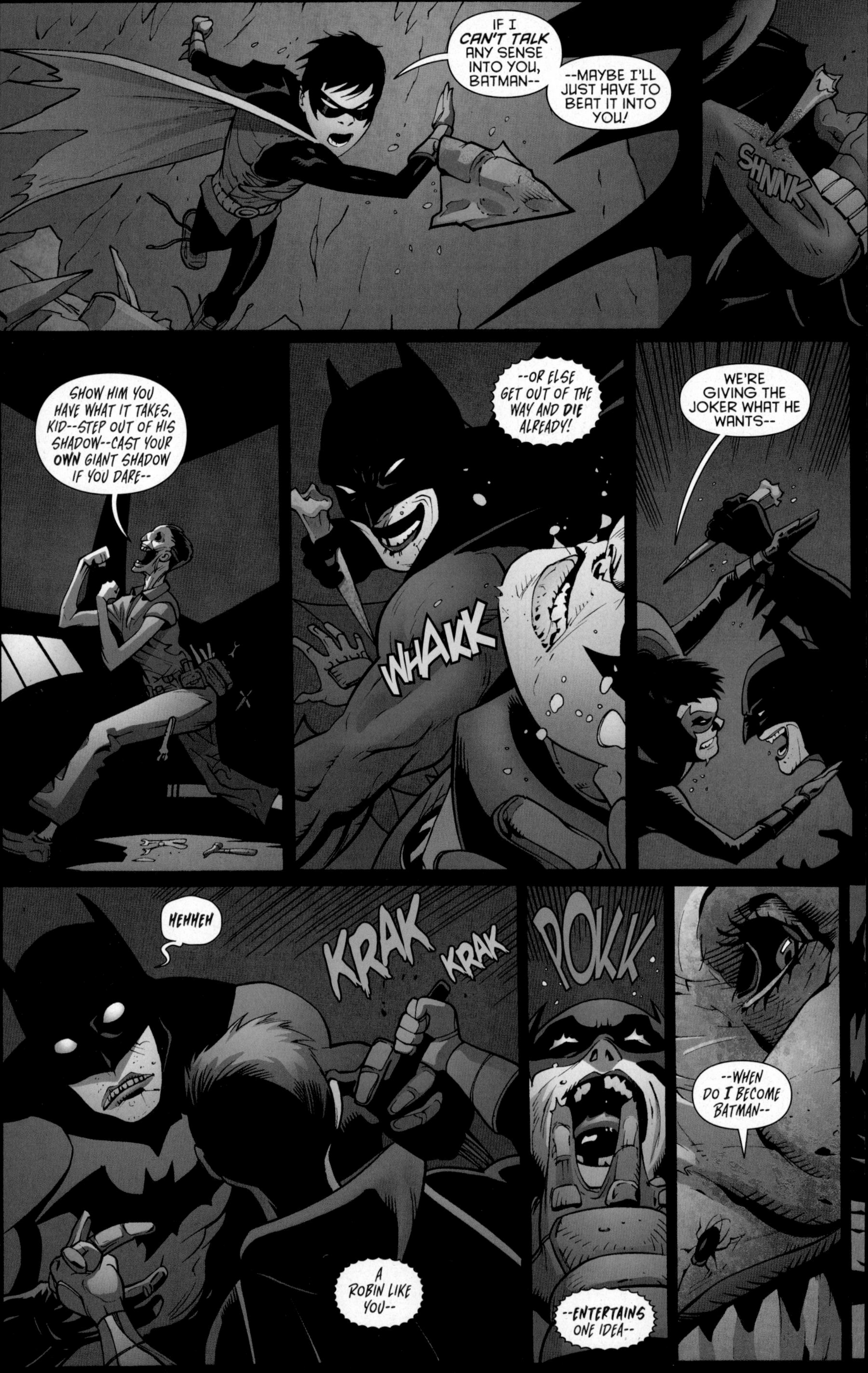
IF I CAN'T TALK ANY SENSE INTO YOU, BATMAN--
--MAYBE I'LL JUST HAVE TO BEAT IT INTO YOU!
SHNNK
SHOW HIM YOU HAVE WHAT IT TAKES, KID--STEP OUT OF HIS SHADOW--CAST YOUR OWN GIANT SHADOW IF YOU DARE--
--OR ELSE GET OUT OF THE WAY AND DIE ALREADY!
WHAKK
WE'RE GIVING THE JOKER WHAT HE WANTS--
HEHHEH
KRAK
KRAK
A ROBIN LIKE YOU--
POKK
--ENTERTAINS ONE IDEA--
--WHEN DO I BECOME BATMAN--

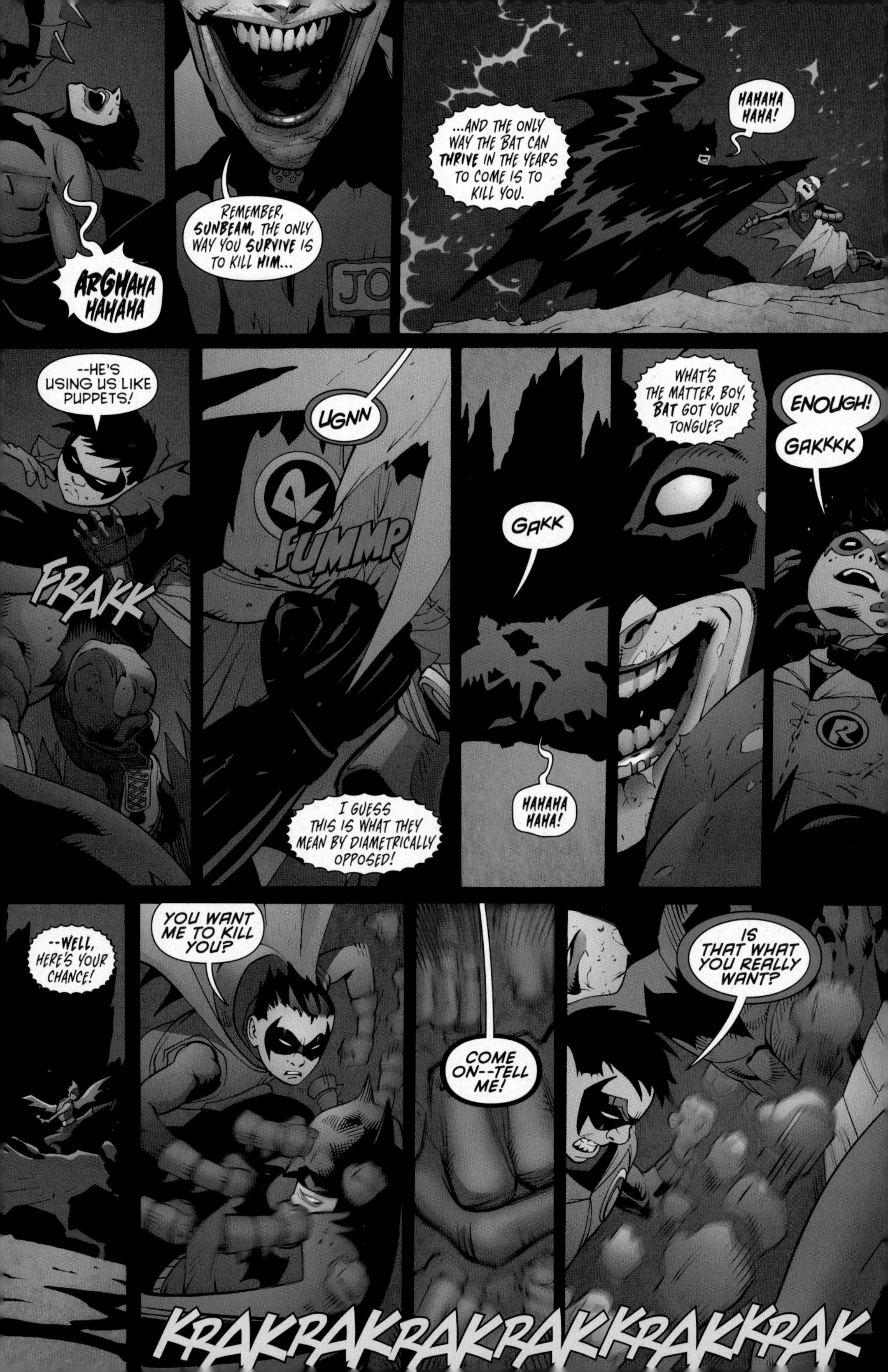
ARGHAHA HAHAHA
REMEMBER, SUNBEAM, THE ONLY WAY YOU SURVIVE IS TO KILL HIM...
...AND THE ONLY WAY THE BAT CAN THRIVE IN THE YEARS TO COME IS TO KILL YOU.
HAHAHA HAHA!
--HE'S USING US LIKE PUPPETS!
FRAKK
UGNN
FUMMP
I GUESS THIS IS WHAT THEY MEAN BY DIAMETRICALLY OPPOSED!
GAKK
HAHAHA HAHA!
WHAT'S THE MATTER, BOY, BAT GOT YOUR TONGUE?
ENOUGH!
GAKKKK
--WELL, HERE'S YOUR CHANCE!
YOU WANT ME TO KILL YOU?
COME ON--TELL ME!
IS THAT WHAT YOU REALLY WANT?
KRAKRAKRAKRAKRAKKRAKKRAK

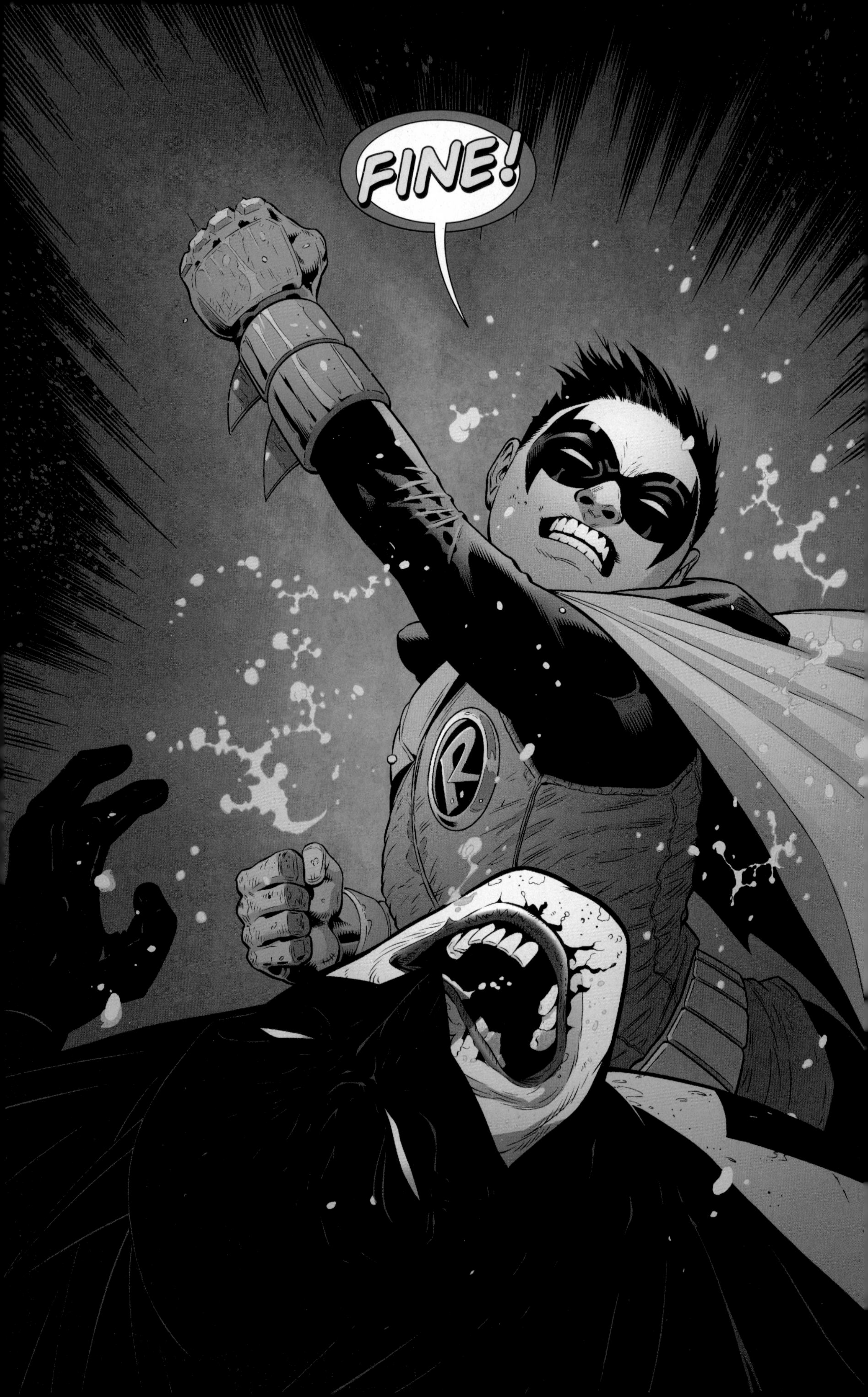
FINE!

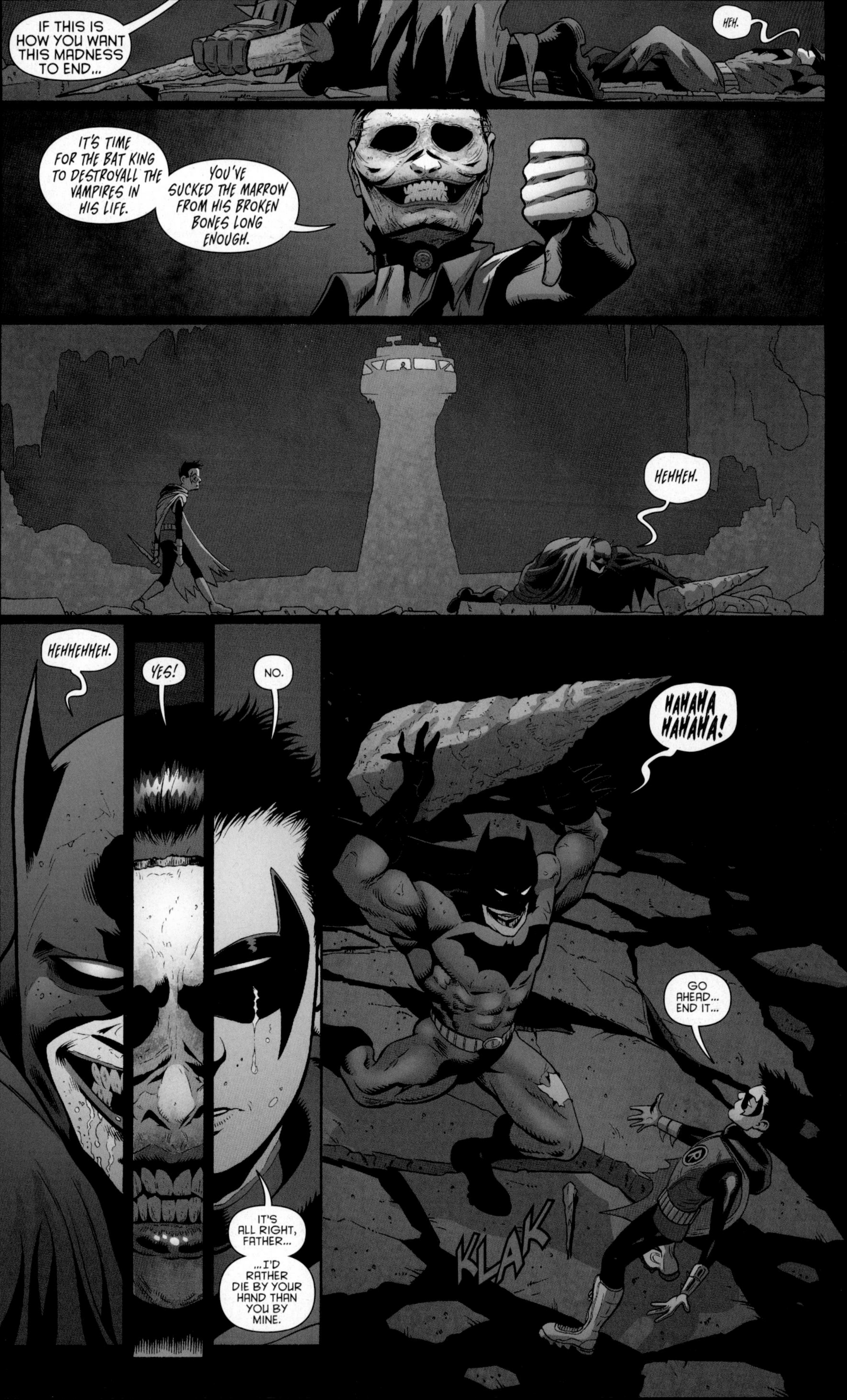
IF THIS IS HOW YOU WANT THIS MADNESS TO END...
HEH.
IT'S TIME FOR THE BAT KING TO DESTROY ALL THE VAMPIRES IN HIS LIFE.
YOU'VE SUCKED THE MARROW FROM HIS BROKEN BONES LONG ENOUGH.
HEHHEH.
HEHHEHHEH.
YES!
NO.
IT'S ALL RIGHT, FATHER...
...I'D RATHER DIE BY YOUR HAND THAN YOU BY MINE.
HAHAHA HAHAHA!
GO AHEAD... END IT...
KLAK

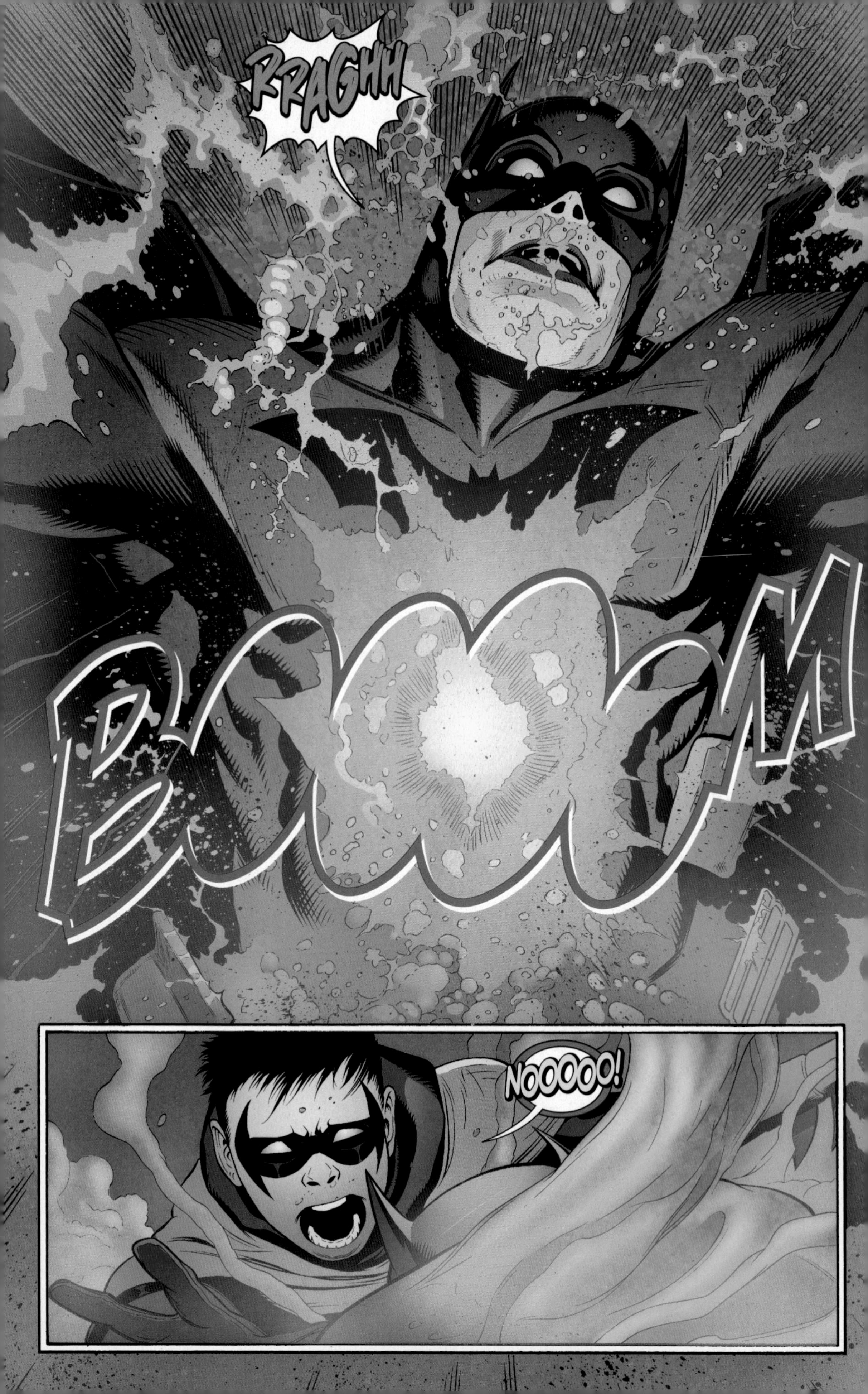
RRAGHH
BOOOM
NOOOOO!

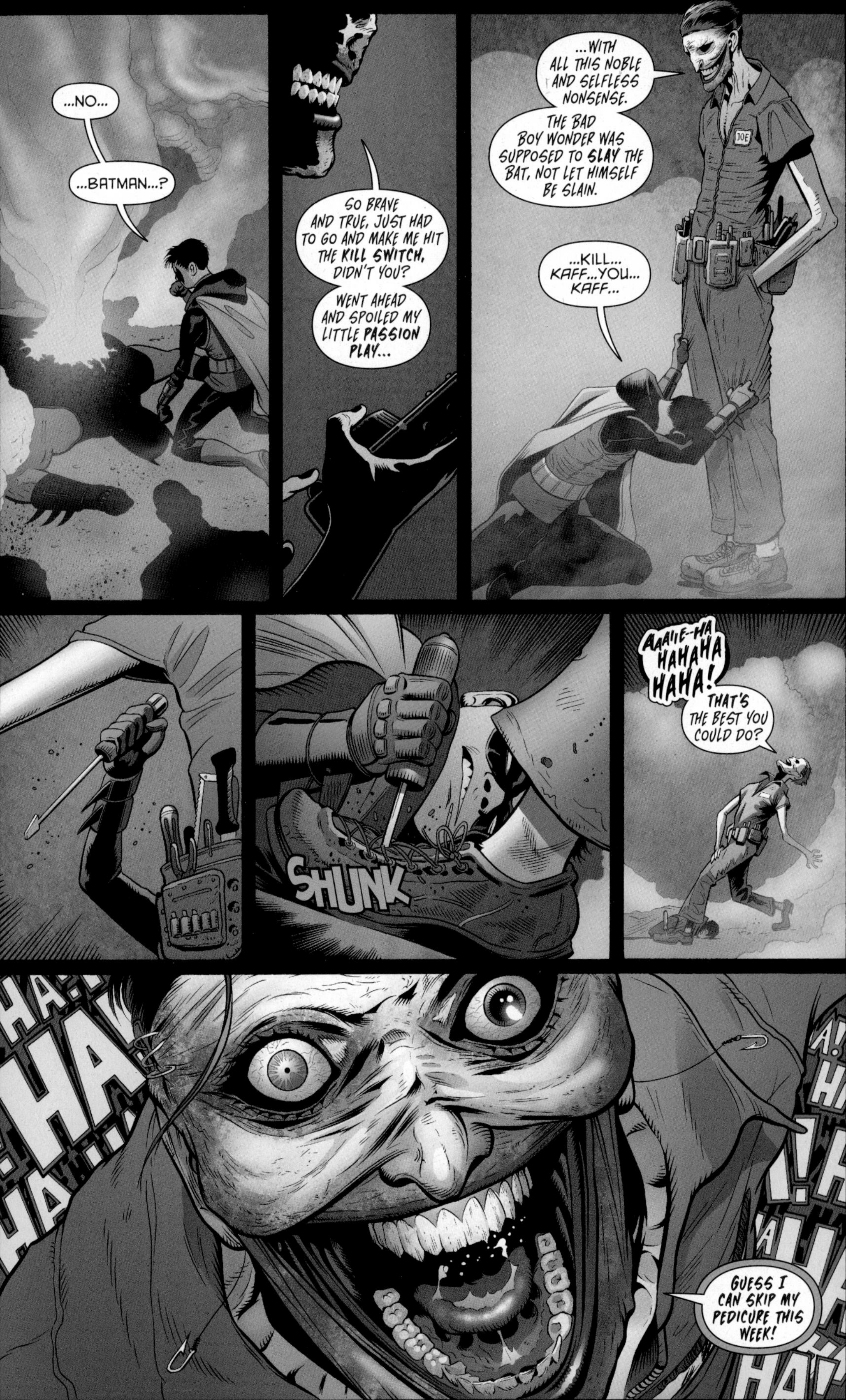
...NO...
...BATMAN...?
SO BRAVE AND TRUE, JUST HAD TO GO AND MAKE ME HIT THE KILL SWITCH, DIDN'T YOU?
WENT AHEAD AND SPOILED MY LITTLE PASSION PLAY...
...WITH ALL THIS NOBLE AND SELFLESS NONSENSE.
THE BAD BOY WONDER WAS SUPPOSED TO SLAY THE BAT, NOT LET HIMSELF BE SLAIN.
JOE
...KILL... KAFF...YOU... KAFF...
SHUNK
AAAIIE-HA HAHAHA HAHA!
THAT'S THE BEST YOU COULD DO?
GUESS I CAN SKIP MY PEDICURE THIS WEEK!

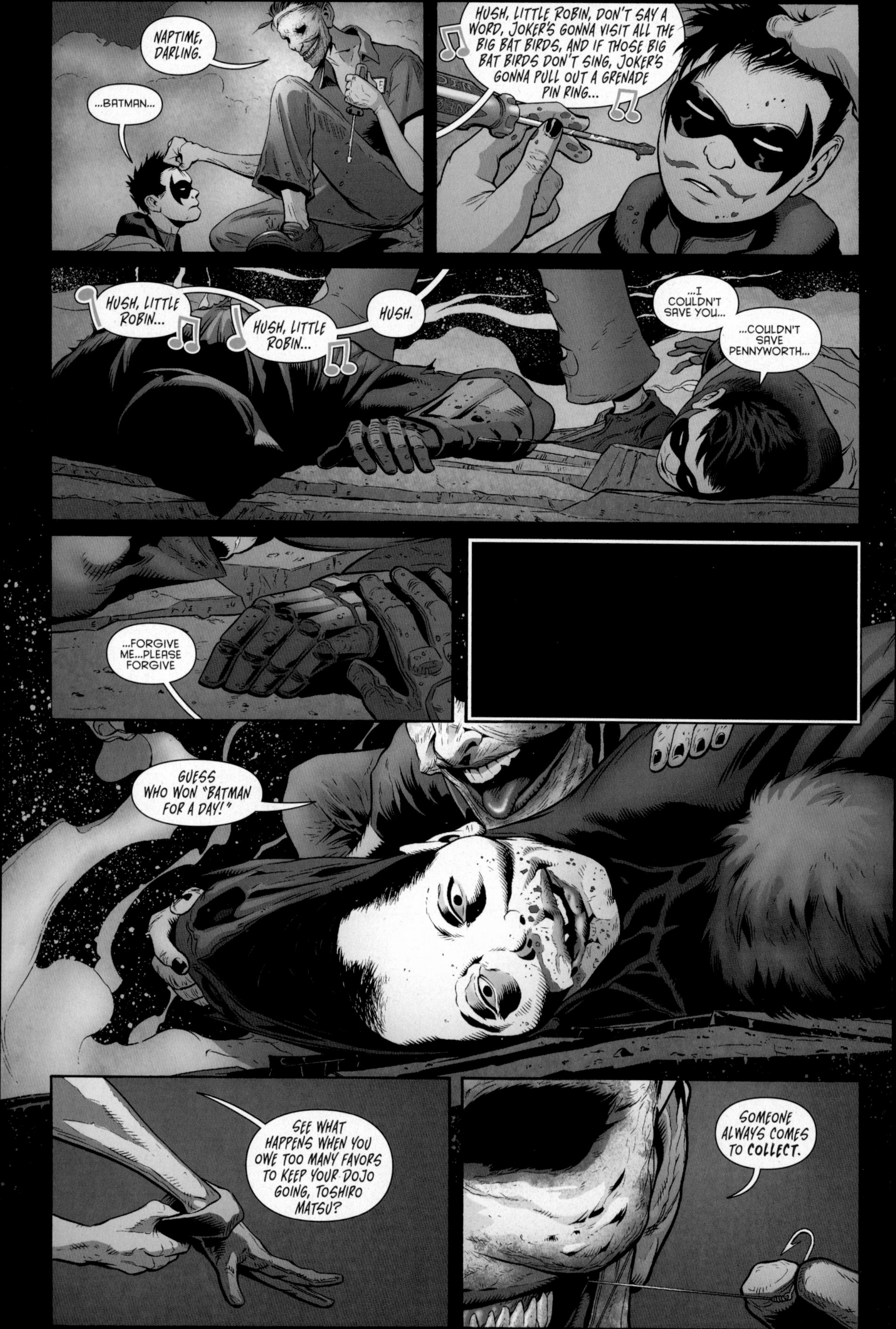
NAPTIME, DARLING.
...BATMAN...
HUSH, LITTLE ROBIN, DON'T SAY A WORD, JOKER'S GONNA VISIT ALL THE BIG BAT BIRDS, AND IF THOSE BIG BAT BIRDS DON'T SING, JOKER'S GONNA PULL OUT A GRENADE PIN RING...
HUSH, LITTLE ROBIN...
HUSH, LITTLE ROBIN...
HUSH.
...I COULDN'T SAVE YOU...
...COULDN'T SAVE PENNYWORTH...
...FORGIVE ME...PLEASE FORGIVE
GUESS WHO WON "BATMAN FOR A DAY!"
SEE WHAT HAPPENS WHEN YOU OWE TOO MANY FAVORS TO KEEP YOUR DOJO GOING, TOSHIRO MATSU?
SOMEONE ALWAYS COMES TO COLLECT.

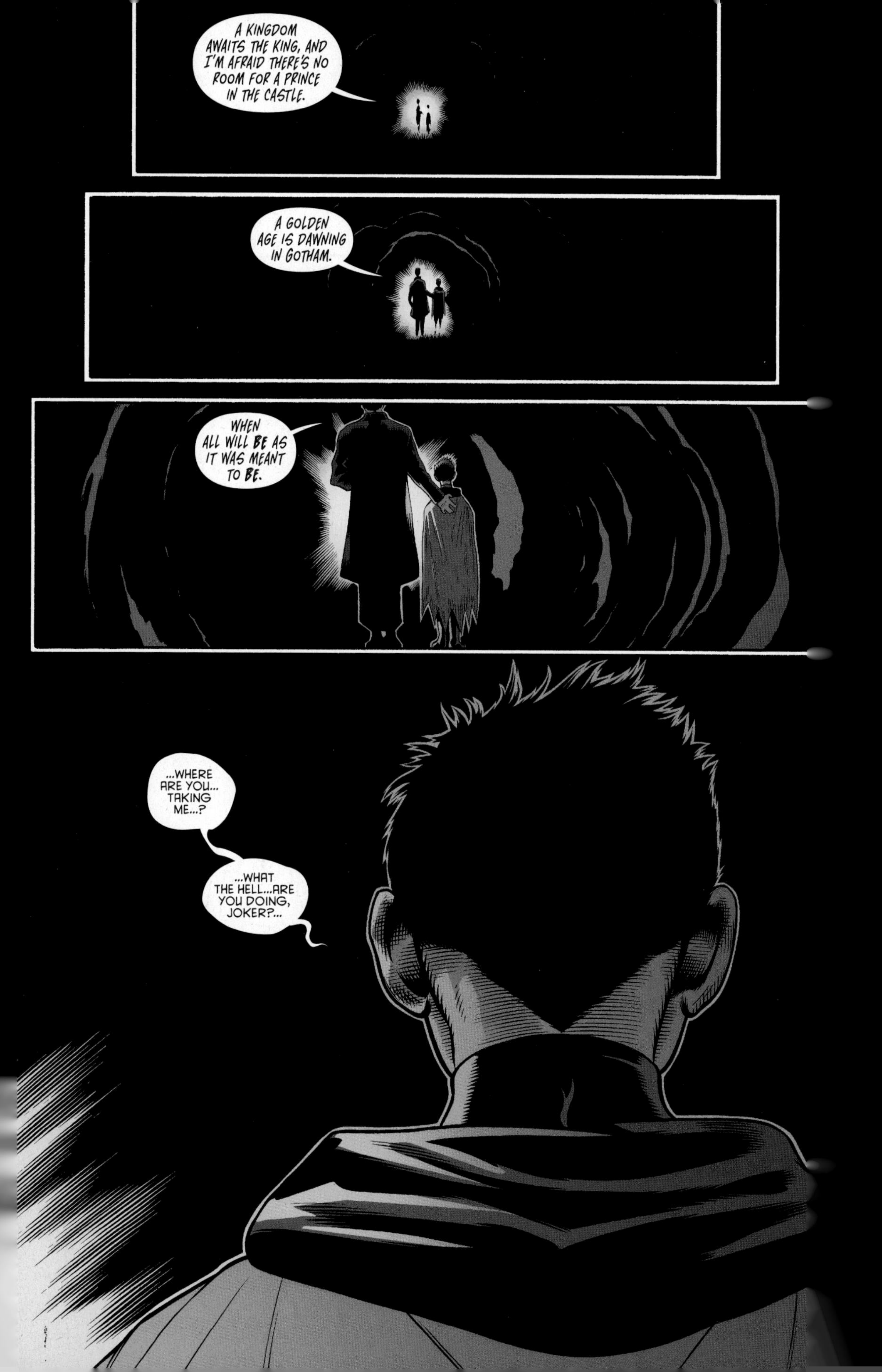
A KINGDOM AWAITS THE KING, AND I'M AFRAID THERE'S NO ROOM FOR A PRINCE IN THE CASTLE.
A GOLDEN AGE IS DAWNING IN GOTHAM.
WHEN ALL WILL BE AS IT WAS MEANT TO BE.
...WHERE ARE YOU... TAKING ME...?
...WHAT THE HELL...ARE YOU DOING, JOKER?...

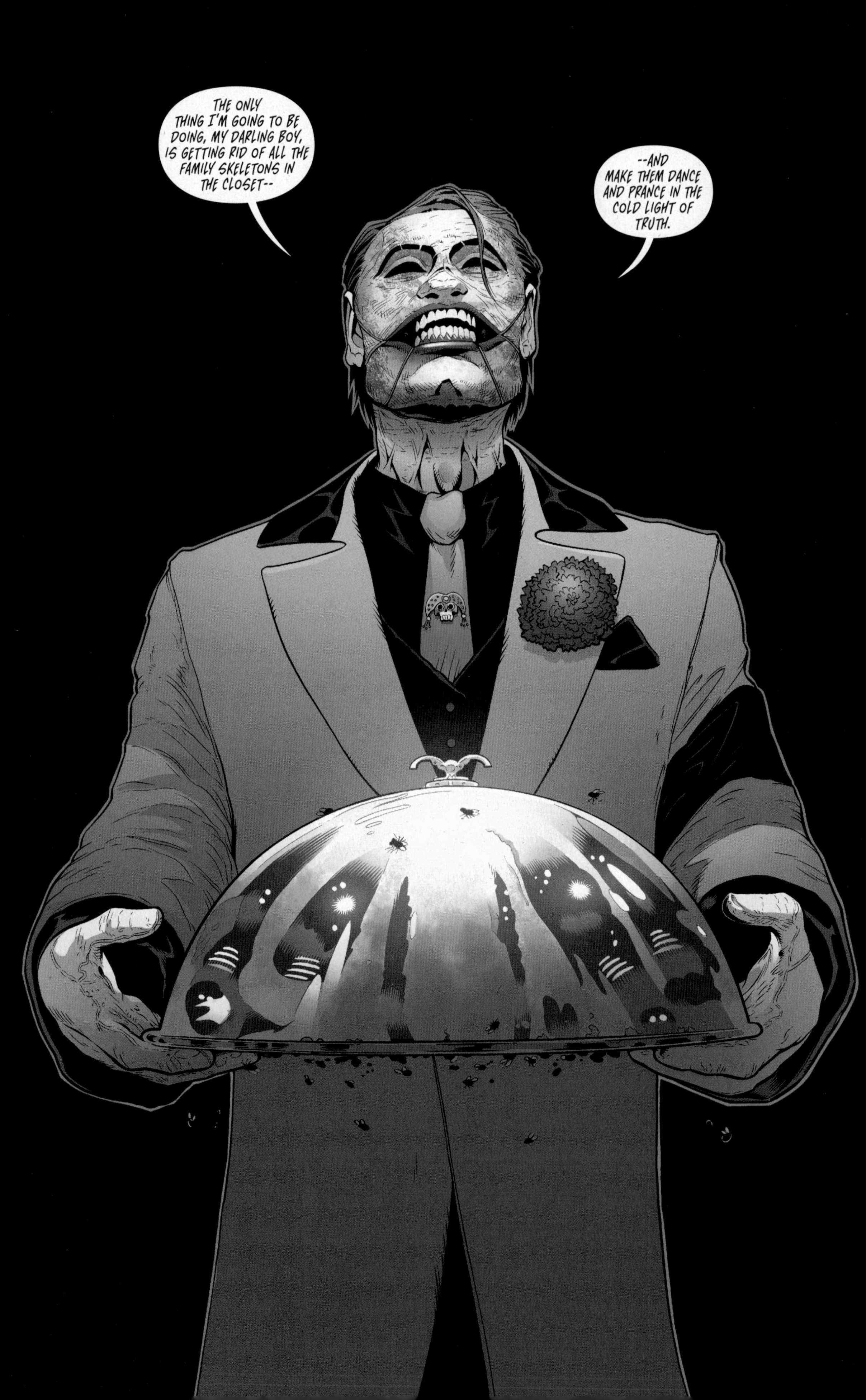
THE ONLY THING I'M GOING TO BE DOING, MY DARLING BOY, IS GETTING RID OF ALL THE FAMILY SKELETONS IN THE CLOSET--
--AND MAKE THEM DANCE AND PRANCE IN THE COLD LIGHT OF TRUTH.

CONCLUSION

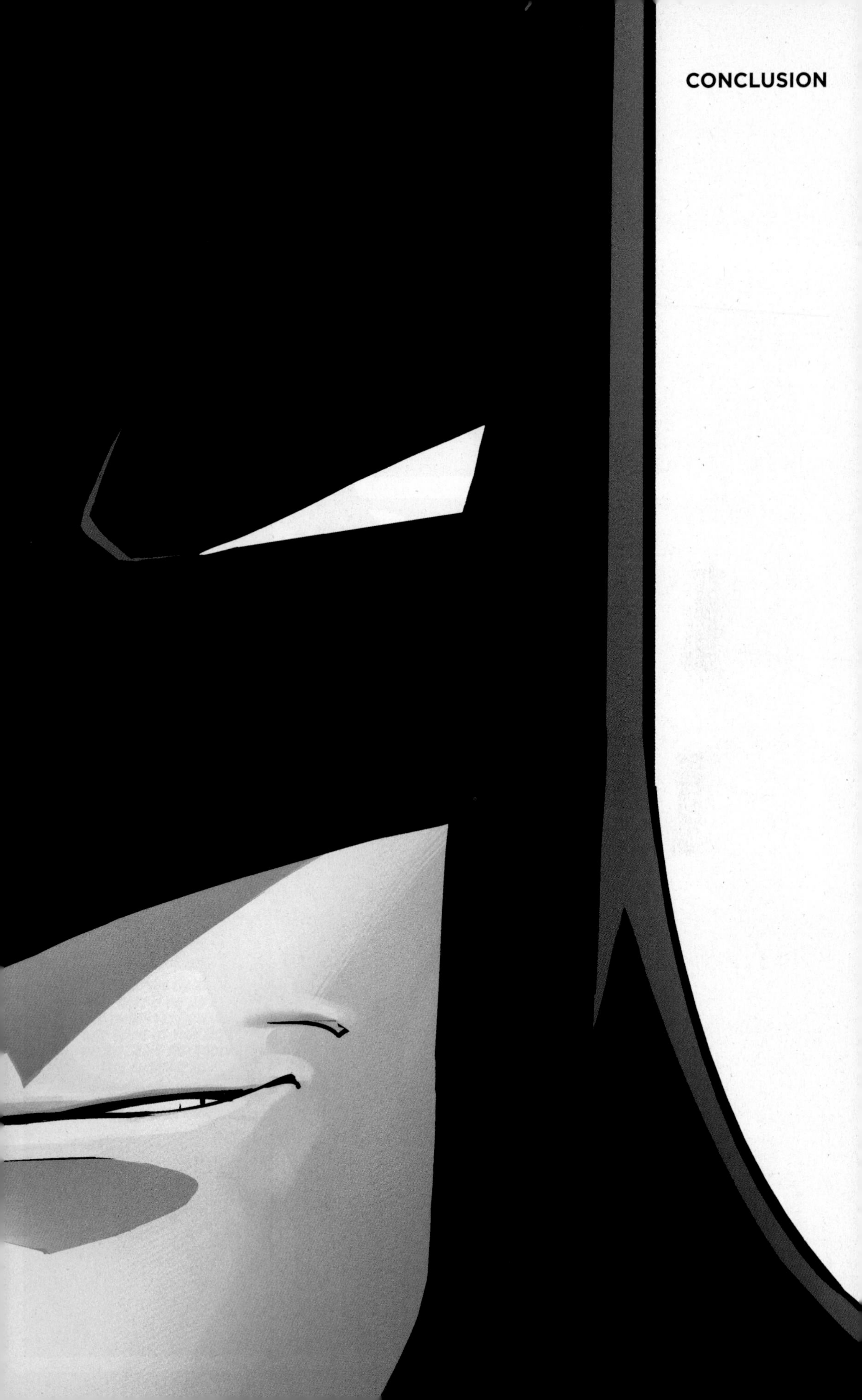

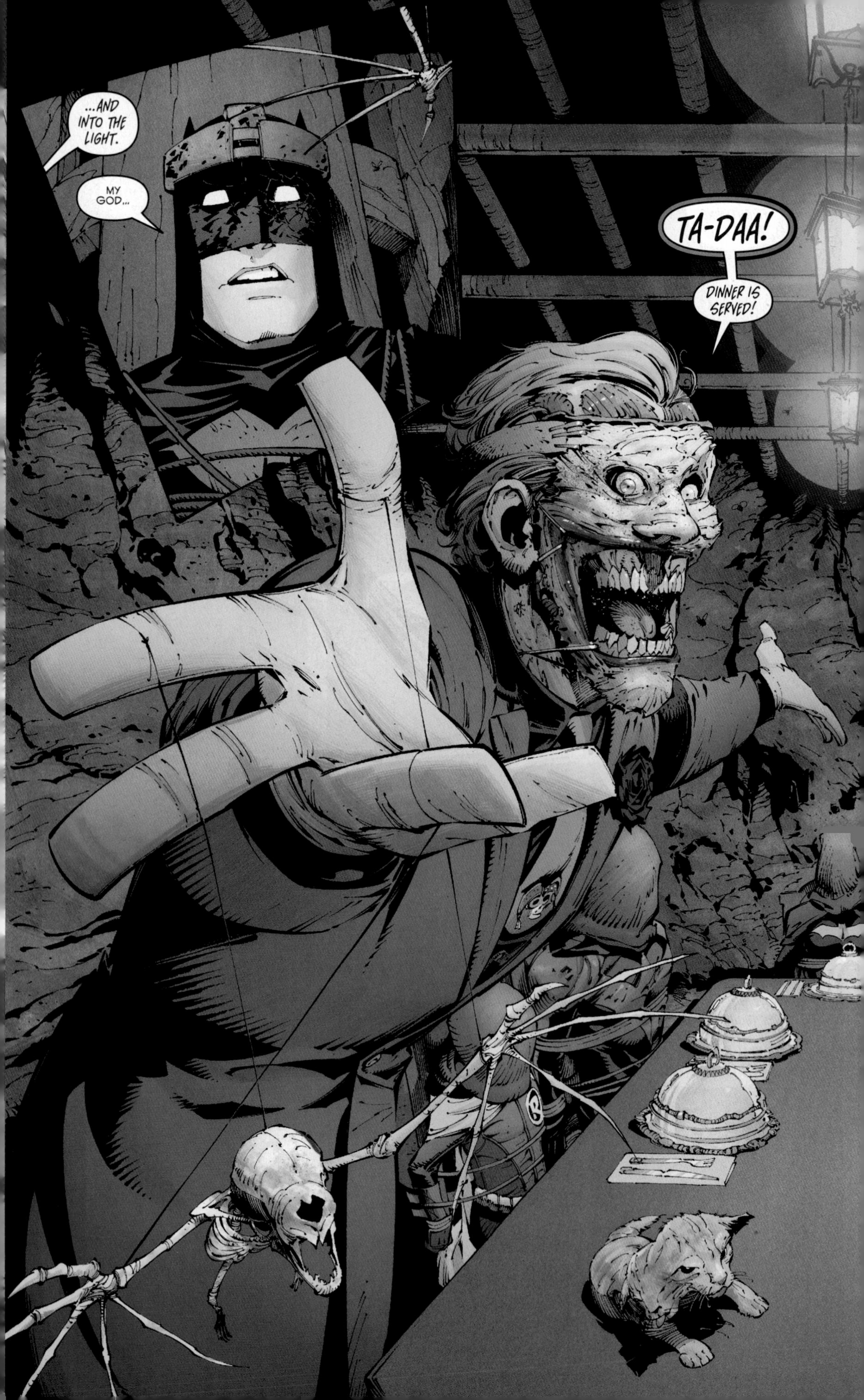
...AND INTO THE LIGHT.
MY GOD...
TA-DAA!
DINNER IS SERVED!

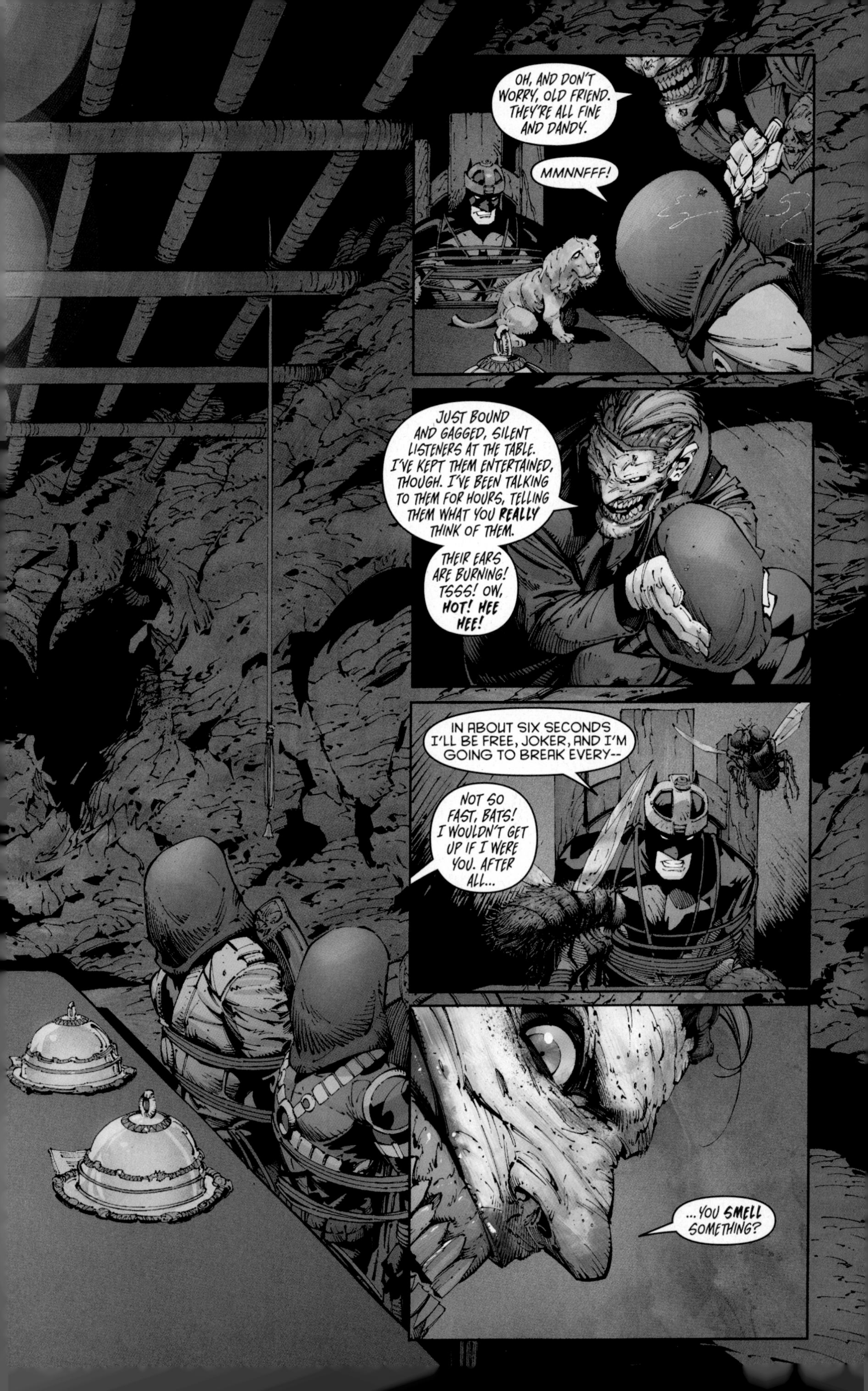
OH, AND DON'T WORRY, OLD FRIEND. THEY'RE ALL FINE AND DANDY.
MMNNFFF!
JUST BOUND AND GAGGED, SILENT LISTENERS AT THE TABLE. I'VE KEPT THEM ENTERTAINED, THOUGH. I'VE BEEN TALKING TO THEM FOR HOURS, TELLING THEM WHAT YOU REALLY THINK OF THEM.
THEIR EARS ARE BURNING! TSSS! OW, HOT! HEE HEE!
IN ABOUT SIX SECONDS I'LL BE FREE, JOKER, AND I'M GOING TO BREAK EVERY--
NOT SO FAST, BATS! I WOULDN'T GET UP IF I WERE YOU. AFTER ALL...
...YOU SMELL SOMETHING?

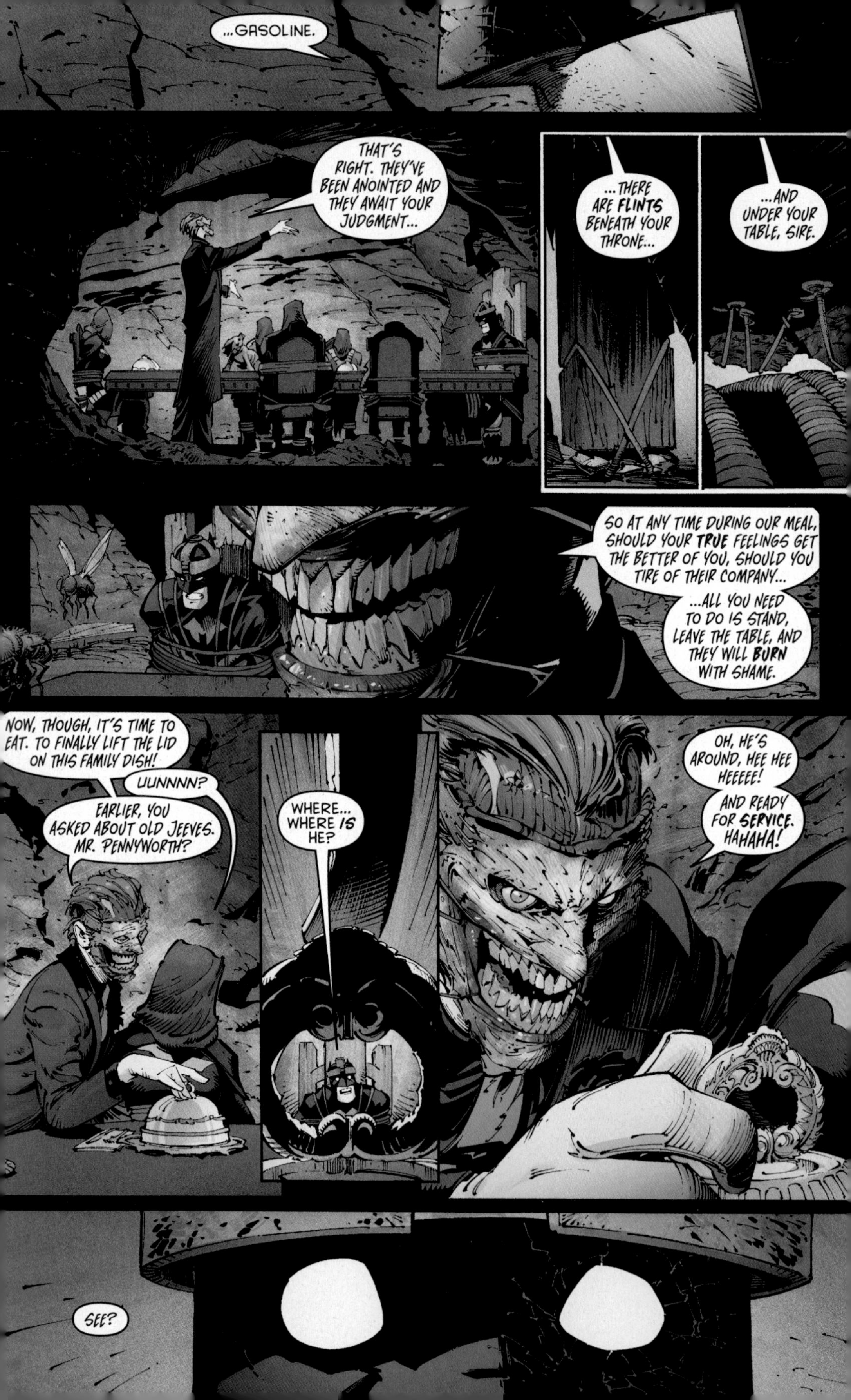

...GASOLINE.
THAT'S RIGHT. THEY'VE BEEN ANOINTED AND THEY AWAIT YOUR JUDGMENT...
...THERE ARE FLINTS BENEATH YOUR THRONE...
...AND UNDER YOUR TABLE, SIRE.
SO AT ANY TIME DURING OUR MEAL, SHOULD YOUR TRUE FEELINGS GET THE BETTER OF YOU, SHOULD YOU TIRE OF THEIR COMPANY...
...ALL YOU NEED TO DO IS STAND, LEAVE THE TABLE, AND THEY WILL BURN WITH SHAME.
NOW, THOUGH, IT'S TIME TO EAT. TO FINALLY LIFT THE LID ON THIS FAMILY DISH!
UUNNNN?
EARLIER, YOU ASKED ABOUT OLD JEEVES. MR. PENNYWORTH?
WHERE... WHERE IS HE?
OH, HE'S AROUND, HEE HEE HEEEEE!
AND READY FOR SERVICE. HAHAHA!
SEE?

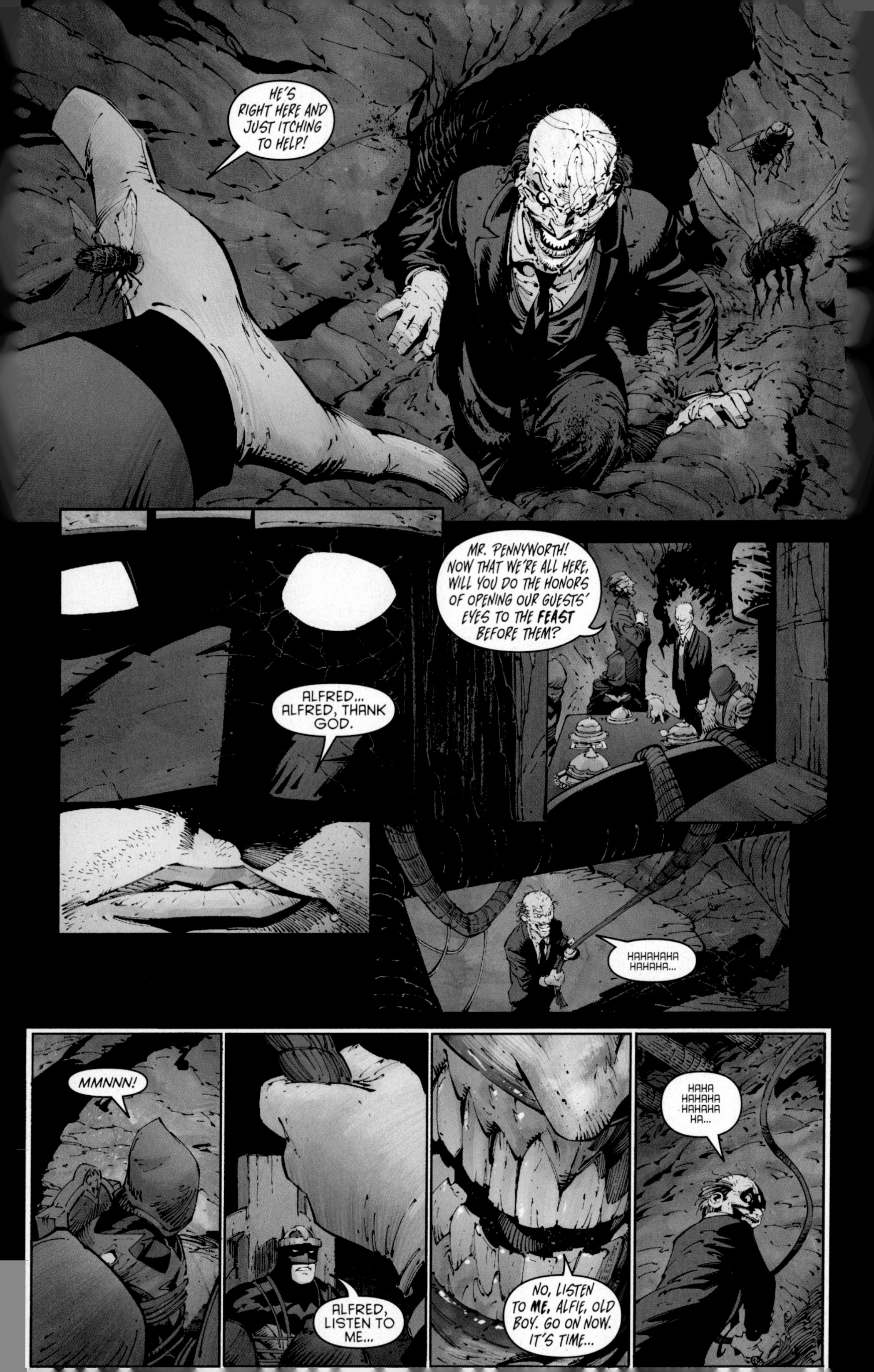
HE'S RIGHT HERE AND JUST ITCHING TO HELP!
MR. PENNYWORTH! NOW THAT WE'RE ALL HERE, WILL YOU DO THE HONORS OF OPENING OUR GUESTS' EYES TO THE FEAST BEFORE THEM?
ALFRED... ALFRED, THANK GOD.
HAHAHAHA HAHAHA...
MMNNN!
ALFRED, LISTEN TO ME...
NO, LISTEN TO ME, ALFIE, OLD BOY. GO ON NOW. IT'S TIME...
HAHA HAHAHA HAHAHA HA...

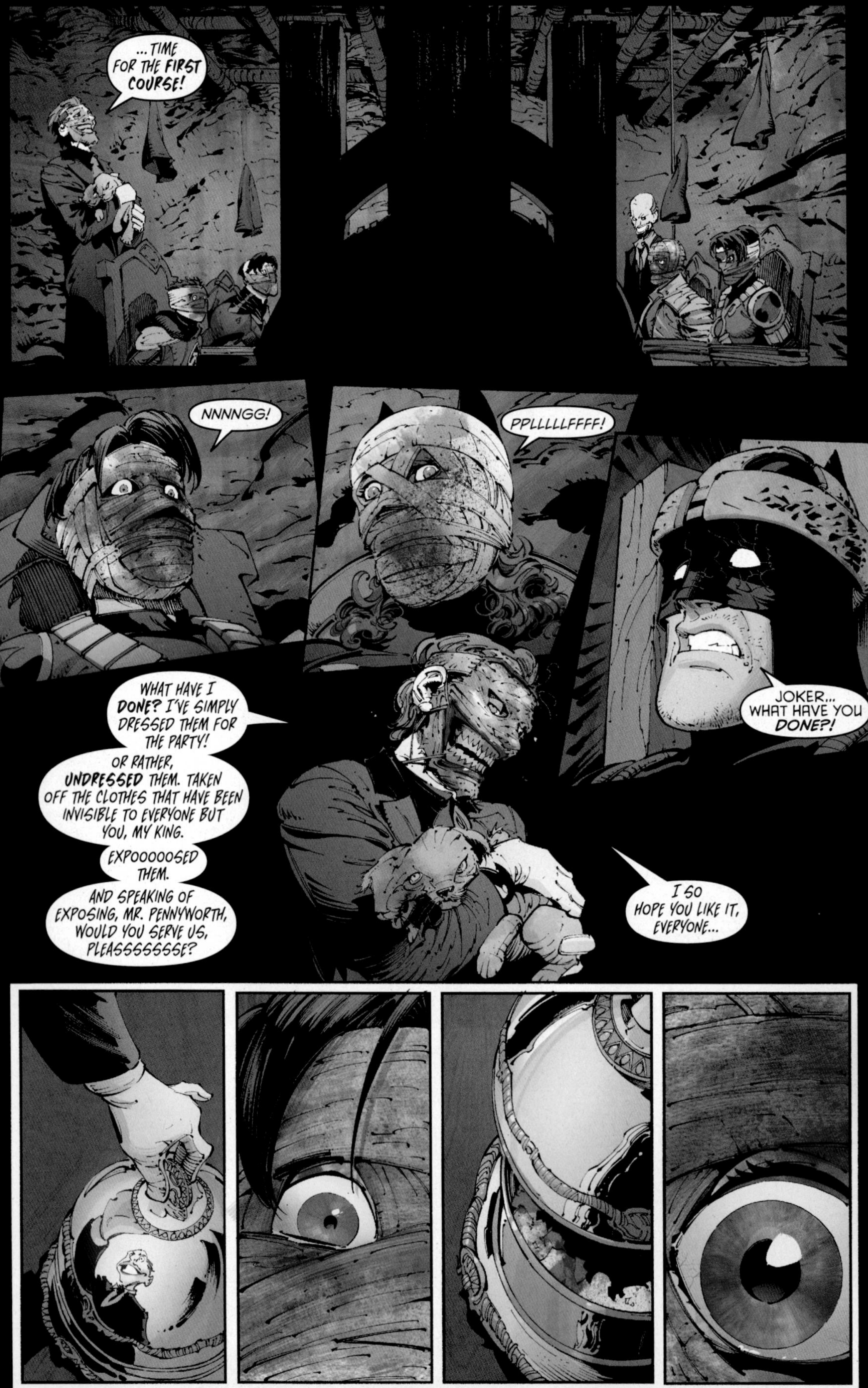
...TIME FOR THE FIRST COURSE!
NNNNGG!
PPLLLLLLFFFF!
JOKER... WHAT HAVE YOU DONE?!
WHAT HAVE I DONE? I'VE SIMPLY DRESSED THEM FOR THE PARTY!
OR RATHER, UNDRESSED THEM. TAKEN OFF THE CLOTHES THAT HAVE BEEN INVISIBLE TO EVERYONE BUT YOU, MY KING.
EXPOOOOOSED THEM.
AND SPEAKING OF EXPOSING, MR. PENNYWORTH, WOULD YOU SERVE US, PLEASSSSSSSE?
I SO HOPE YOU LIKE IT, EVERYONE...

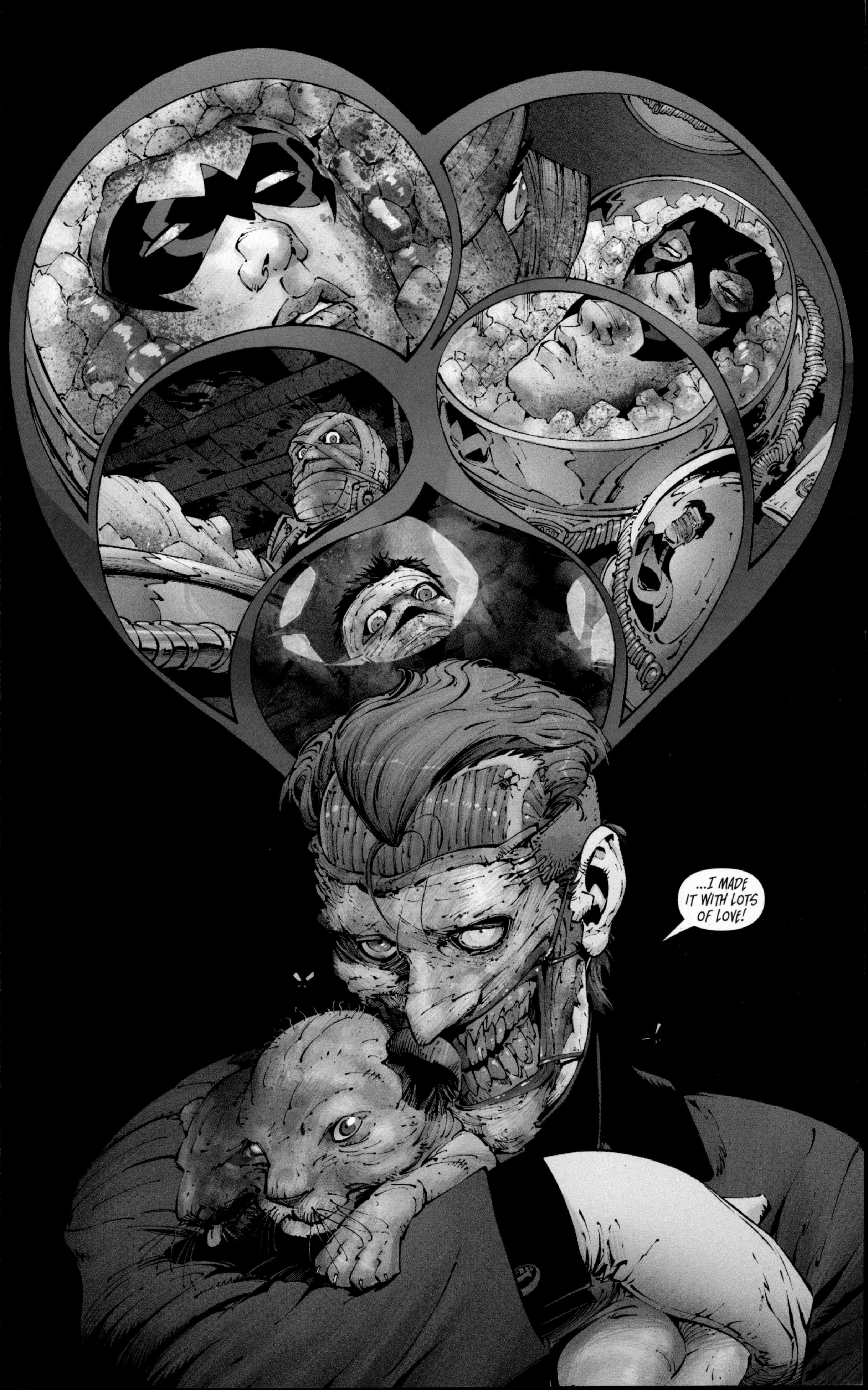
...I MADE IT WITH LOTS OF LOVE!

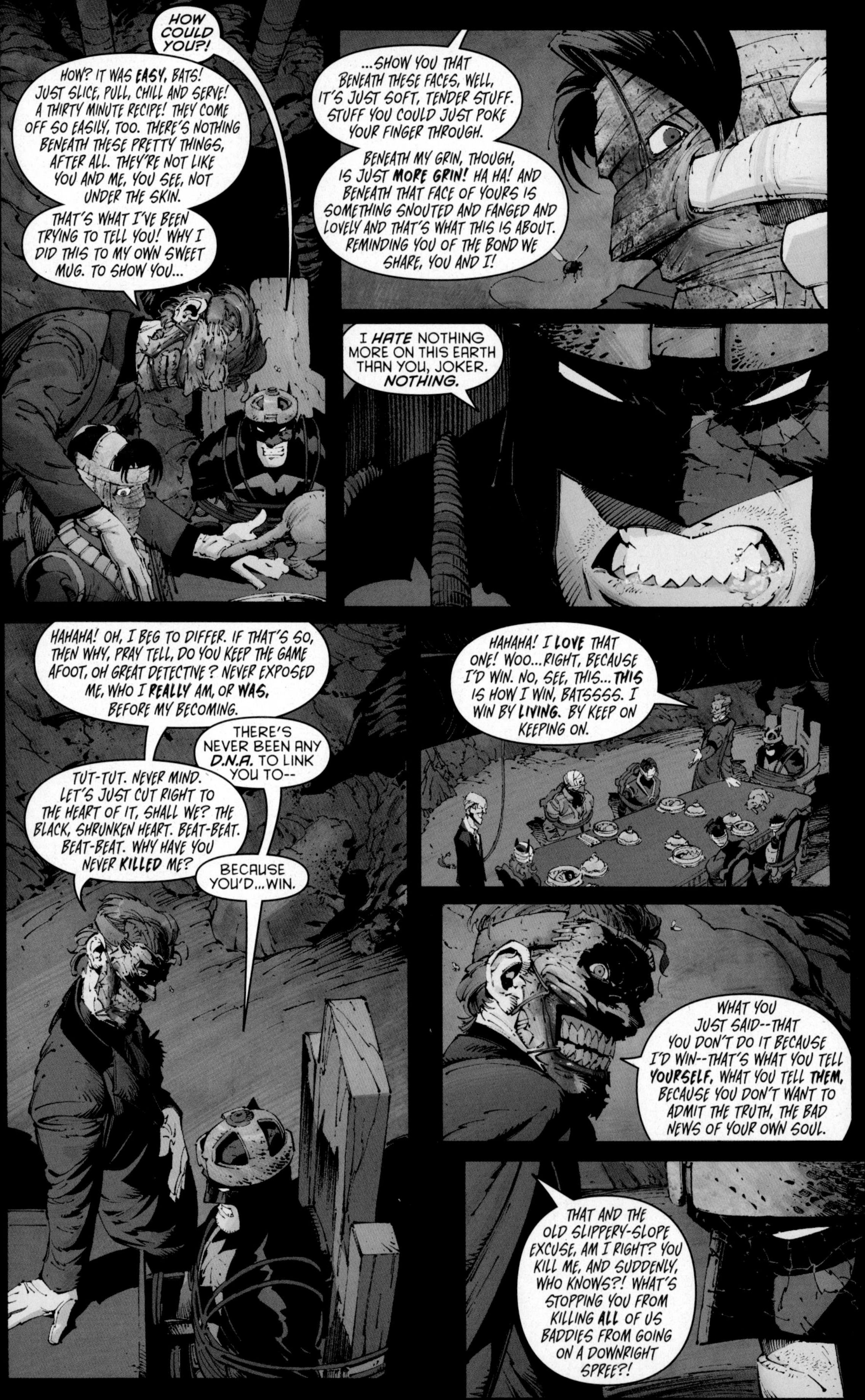
HOW COULD YOU?!
HOW? IT WAS EASY, BATS! JUST SLICE, PULL, CHILL AND SERVE! A THIRTY MINUTE RECIPE! THEY COME OFF SO EASILY, TOO. THERE'S NOTHING BENEATH THESE PRETTY THINGS, AFTER ALL. THEY'RE NOT LIKE YOU AND ME, YOU SEE, NOT UNDER THE SKIN.
THAT'S WHAT I'VE BEEN TRYING TO TELL YOU! WHY I DID THIS TO MY OWN SWEET MUG. TO SHOW YOU...
...SHOW YOU THAT BENEATH THESE FACES, WELL, IT'S JUST SOFT, TENDER STUFF. STUFF YOU COULD JUST POKE YOUR FINGER THROUGH.
BENEATH MY GRIN, THOUGH, IS JUST MORE GRIN! HA HA! AND BENEATH THAT FACE OF YOURS IS SOMETHING SNOUTED AND FANGED AND LOVELY AND THAT'S WHAT THIS IS ABOUT. REMINDING YOU OF THE BOND WE SHARE, YOU AND I!
I HATE NOTHING MORE ON THIS EARTH THAN YOU, JOKER. NOTHING.
HAHAHA! OH, I BEG TO DIFFER. IF THAT'S SO, THEN WHY, PRAY TELL, DO YOU KEEP THE GAME AFOOT, OH GREAT DETECTIVE? NEVER EXPOSED ME, WHO I REALLY AM, OR WAS, BEFORE MY BECOMING.
THERE'S NEVER BEEN ANY D.N.A. TO LINK YOU TO--
TUT-TUT. NEVER MIND. LET'S JUST CUT RIGHT TO THE HEART OF IT, SHALL WE? THE BLACK, SHRUNKEN HEART. BEAT-BEAT. BEAT-BEAT. WHY HAVE YOU NEVER KILLED ME?
BECAUSE YOU'D...WIN.
HAHAHA! I LOVE THAT ONE! WOO...RIGHT, BECAUSE I'D WIN. NO, SEE, THIS... THIS IS HOW I WIN, BATSSSS. I WIN BY LIVING. BY KEEP ON KEEPING ON.
WHAT YOU JUST SAID--THAT YOU DON'T DO IT BECAUSE I'D WIN--THAT'S WHAT YOU TELL YOURSELF, WHAT YOU TELL THEM, BECAUSE YOU DON'T WANT TO ADMIT THE TRUTH, THE BAD NEWS OF YOUR OWN SOUL.
THAT AND THE OLD SLIPPERY-SLOPE EXCUSE, AM I RIGHT? YOU KILL ME, AND SUDDENLY, WHO KNOWS?! WHAT'S STOPPING YOU FROM KILLING ALL OF US BADDIES FROM GOING ON A DOWNRIGHT SPREE?!

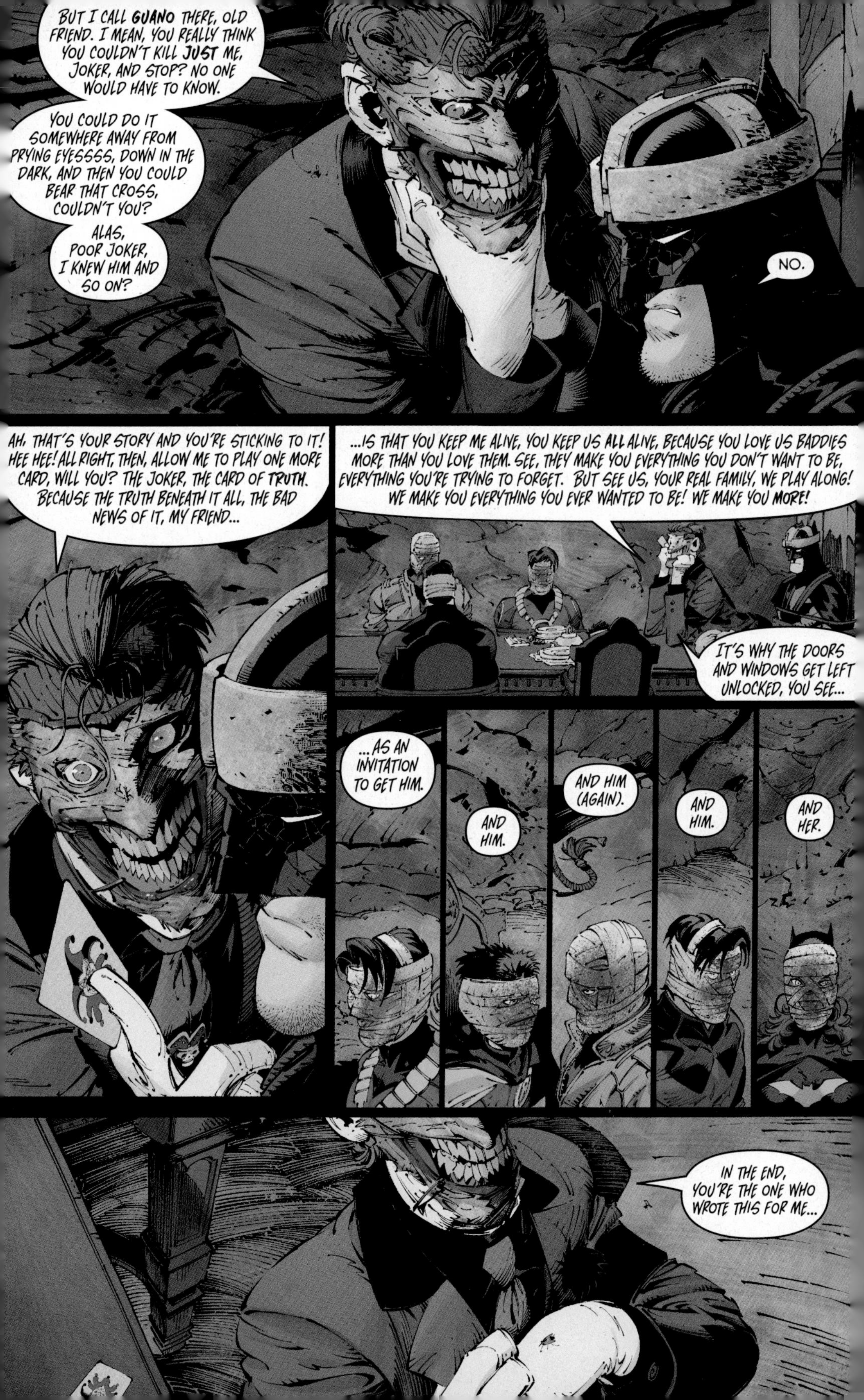
BUT I CALL GUANO THERE, OLD FRIEND. I MEAN, YOU REALLY THINK YOU COULDN'T KILL JUST ME, JOKER, AND STOP? NO ONE WOULD HAVE TO KNOW.
YOU COULD DO IT SOMEWHERE AWAY FROM PRYING EYESSSS, DOWN IN THE DARK, AND THEN YOU COULD BEAR THAT CROSS, COULDN'T YOU?
ALAS, POOR JOKER, I KNEW HIM AND SO ON?
NO.
AH, THAT'S YOUR STORY AND YOU'RE STICKING TO IT! HEE HEE! ALL RIGHT, THEN, ALLOW ME TO PLAY ONE MORE CARD, WILL YOU? THE JOKER, THE CARD OF TRUTH. BECAUSE THE TRUTH BENEATH IT ALL, THE BAD NEWS OF IT, MY FRIEND...
...IS THAT YOU KEEP ME ALIVE, YOU KEEP US ALL ALIVE, BECAUSE YOU LOVE US BADDIES MORE THAN YOU LOVE THEM. SEE, THEY MAKE YOU EVERYTHING YOU DON'T WANT TO BE, EVERYTHING YOU'RE TRYING TO FORGET. BUT SEE US, YOUR REAL FAMILY, WE PLAY ALONG! WE MAKE YOU EVERYTHING YOU EVER WANTED TO BE! WE MAKE YOU MORE!
IT'S WHY THE DOORS AND WINDOWS GET LEFT UNLOCKED, YOU SEE...
...AS AN INVITATION TO GET HIM.
AND HIM.
AND HIM (AGAIN).
AND HIM.
AND HER.
IN THE END, YOU'RE THE ONE WHO WROTE THIS FOR ME...

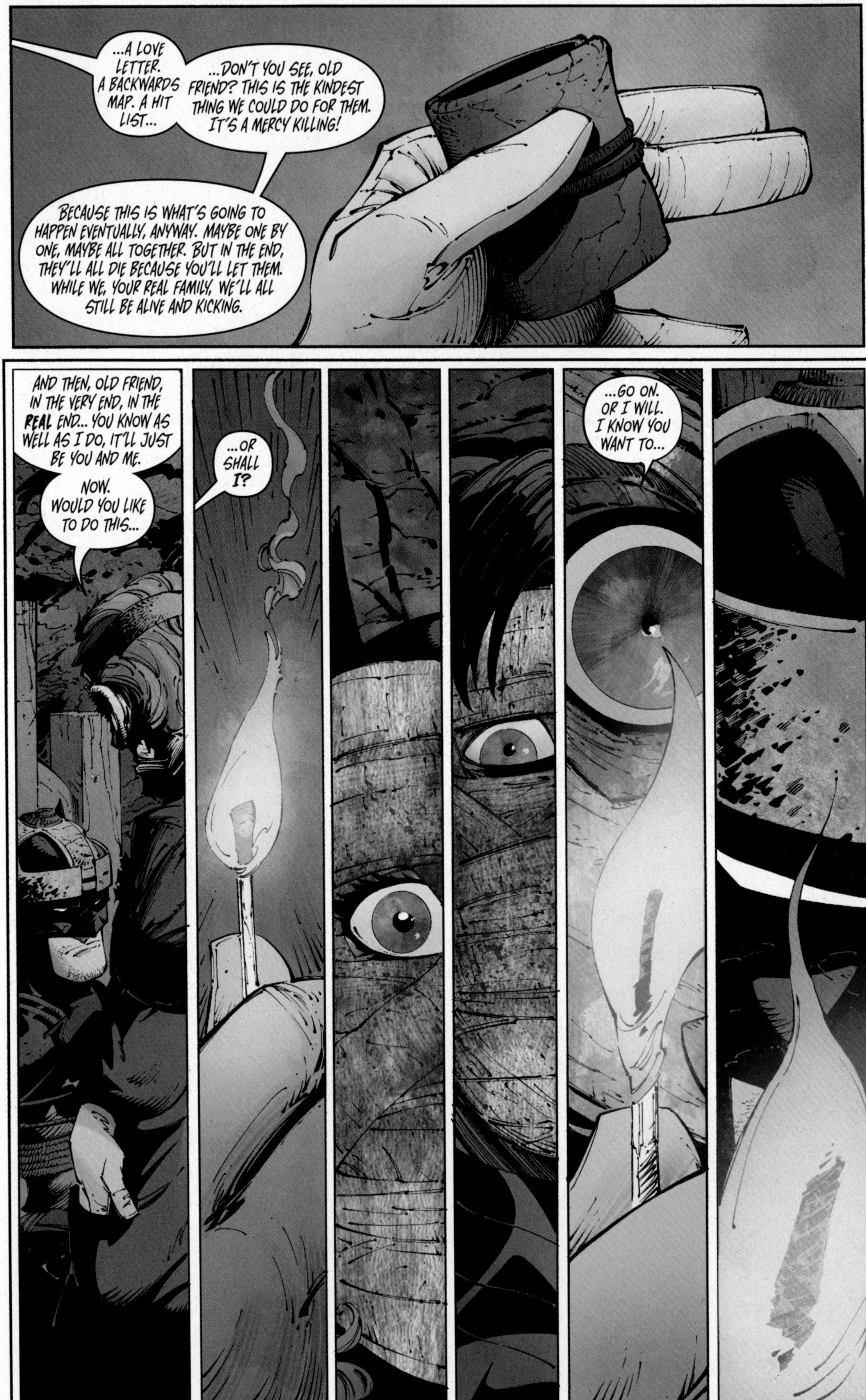
...A LOVE LETTER. A BACKWARDS MAP. A HIT LIST...
...DON'T YOU SEE, OLD FRIEND? THIS IS THE KINDEST THING WE COULD DO FOR THEM. IT'S A MERCY KILLING!
BECAUSE THIS IS WHAT'S GOING TO HAPPEN EVENTUALLY, ANYWAY. MAYBE ONE BY ONE, MAYBE ALL TOGETHER. BUT IN THE END, THEY'LL ALL DIE BECAUSE YOU'LL LET THEM. WHILE WE, YOUR REAL FAMILY, WE'LL ALL STILL BE ALIVE AND KICKING.
AND THEN, OLD FRIEND, IN THE VERY END, IN THE **REAL** END... YOU KNOW AS WELL AS I DO, IT'LL JUST BE YOU AND ME.
NOW. WOULD YOU LIKE TO DO THIS...
...OR SHALL **I**?
...GO ON. OR I WILL. I KNOW YOU WANT TO...

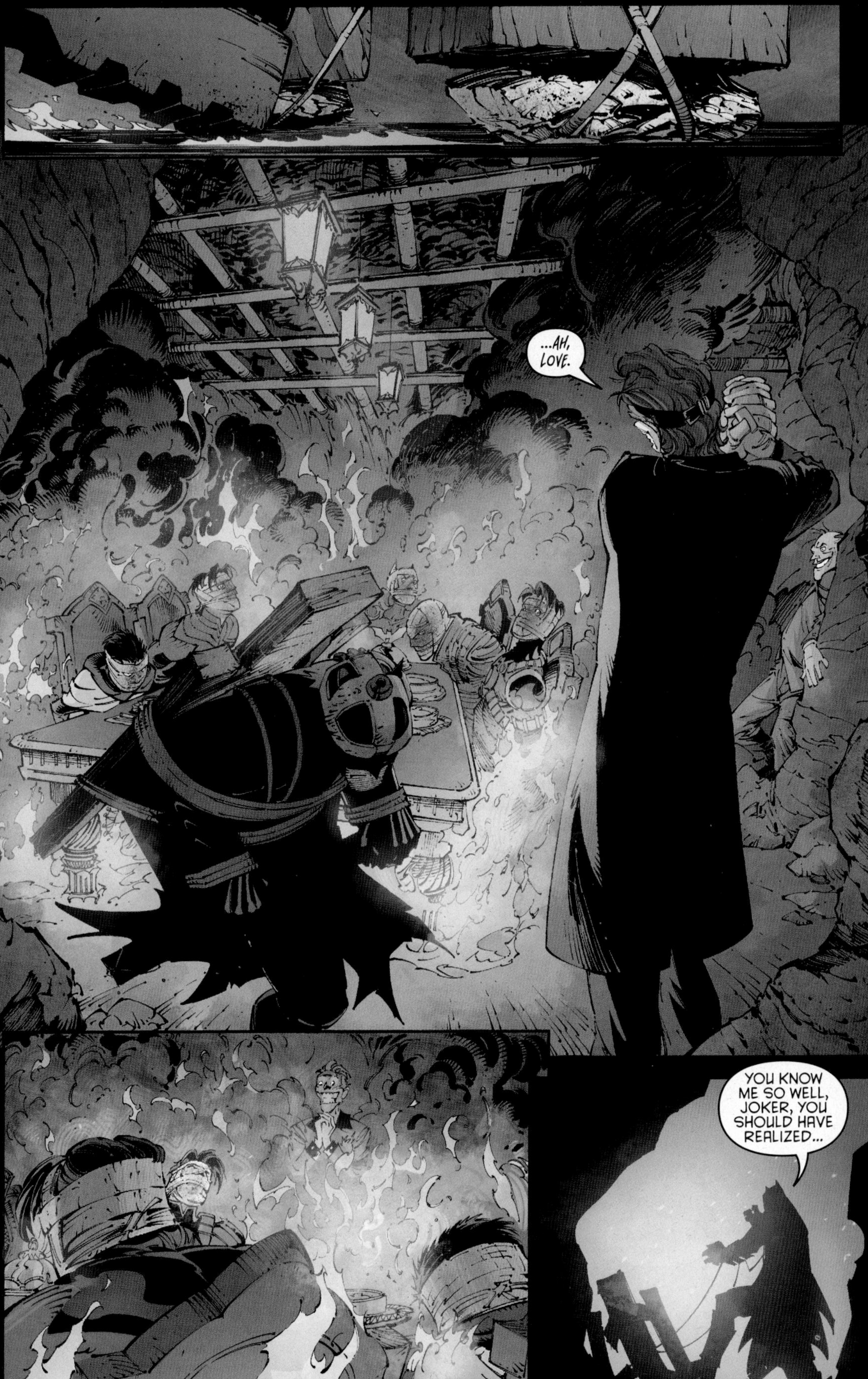
...AH, LOVE.
YOU KNOW ME SO WELL, JOKER, YOU SHOULD HAVE REALIZED...

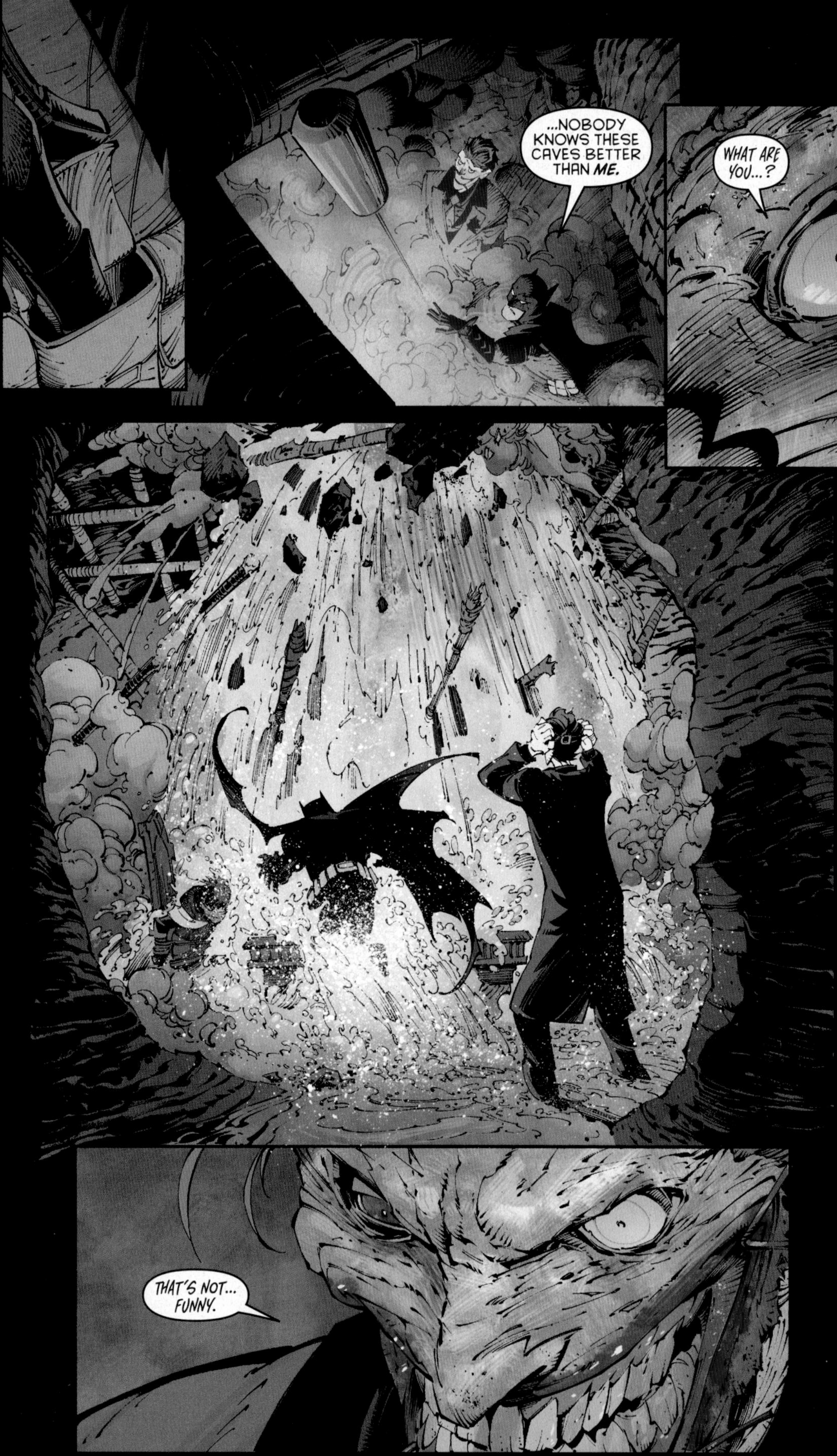
...NOBODY KNOWS THESE CAVES BETTER THAN ME.
WHAT ARE YOU...?
THAT'S NOT... FUNNY.

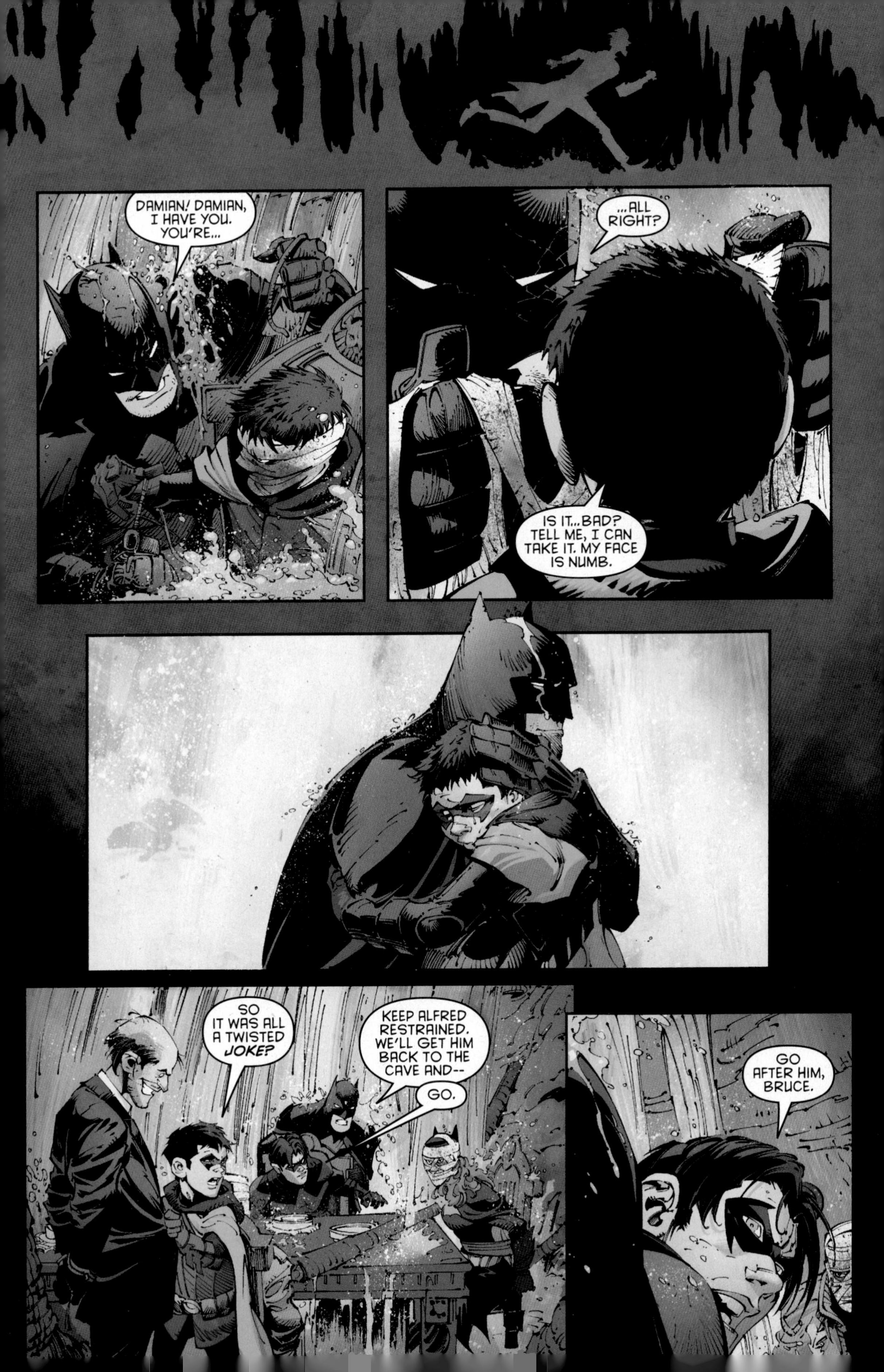
DAMIAN! DAMIAN, I HAVE YOU. YOU'RE...
...ALL RIGHT?
IS IT...BAD? TELL ME, I CAN TAKE IT. MY FACE IS NUMB.
SO IT WAS ALL A TWISTED JOKE?
KEEP ALFRED RESTRAINED. WE'LL GET HIM BACK TO THE CAVE AND--
GO.
GO AFTER HIM, BRUCE.

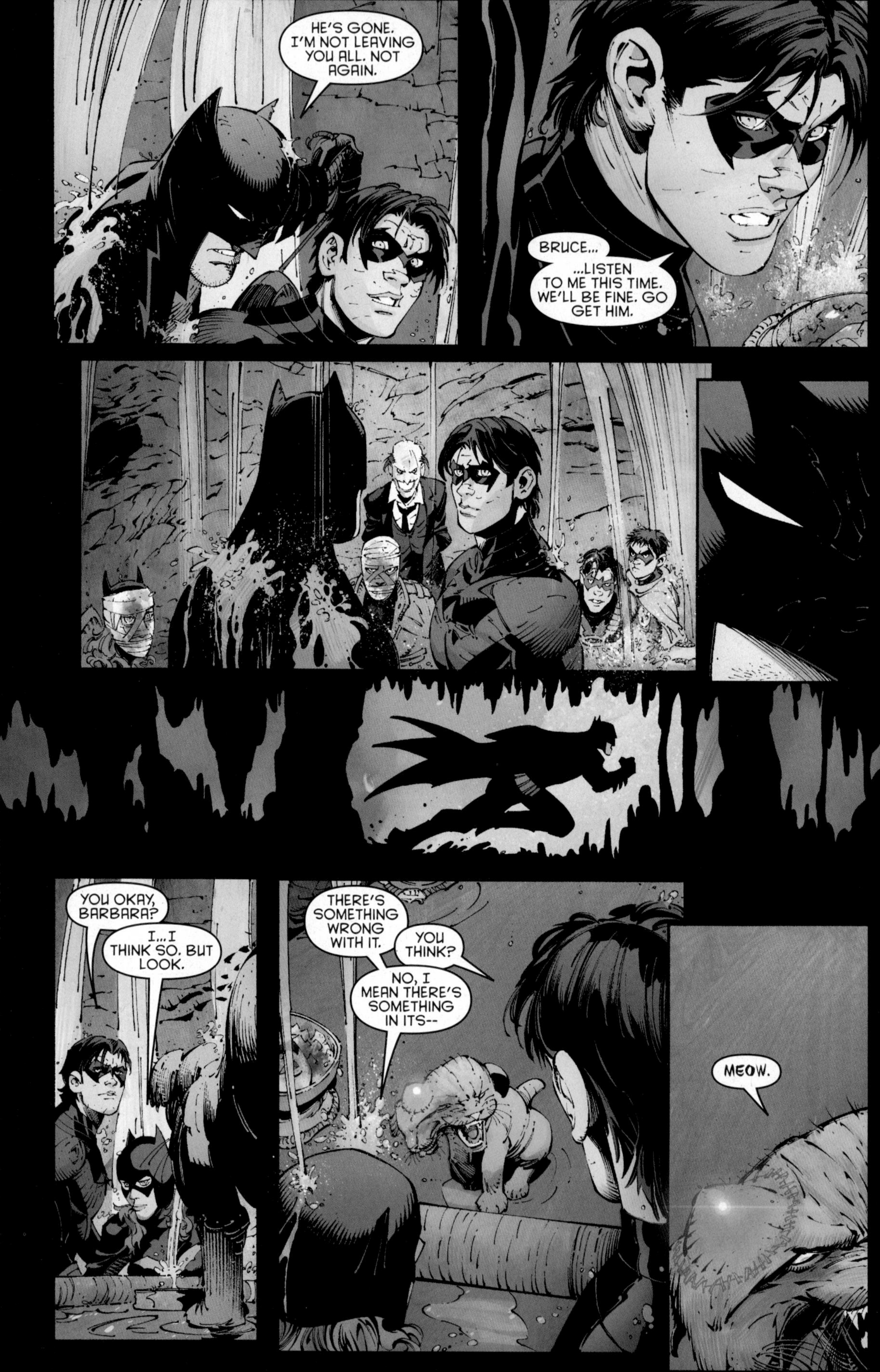
HE'S GONE. I'M NOT LEAVING YOU ALL. NOT AGAIN.
BRUCE...
...LISTEN TO ME THIS TIME. WE'LL BE FINE. GO GET HIM.
YOU OKAY, BARBARA?
I...I THINK SO. BUT LOOK.
THERE'S SOMETHING WRONG WITH IT.
YOU THINK?
NO, I MEAN THERE'S SOMETHING IN ITS--
MEOW.

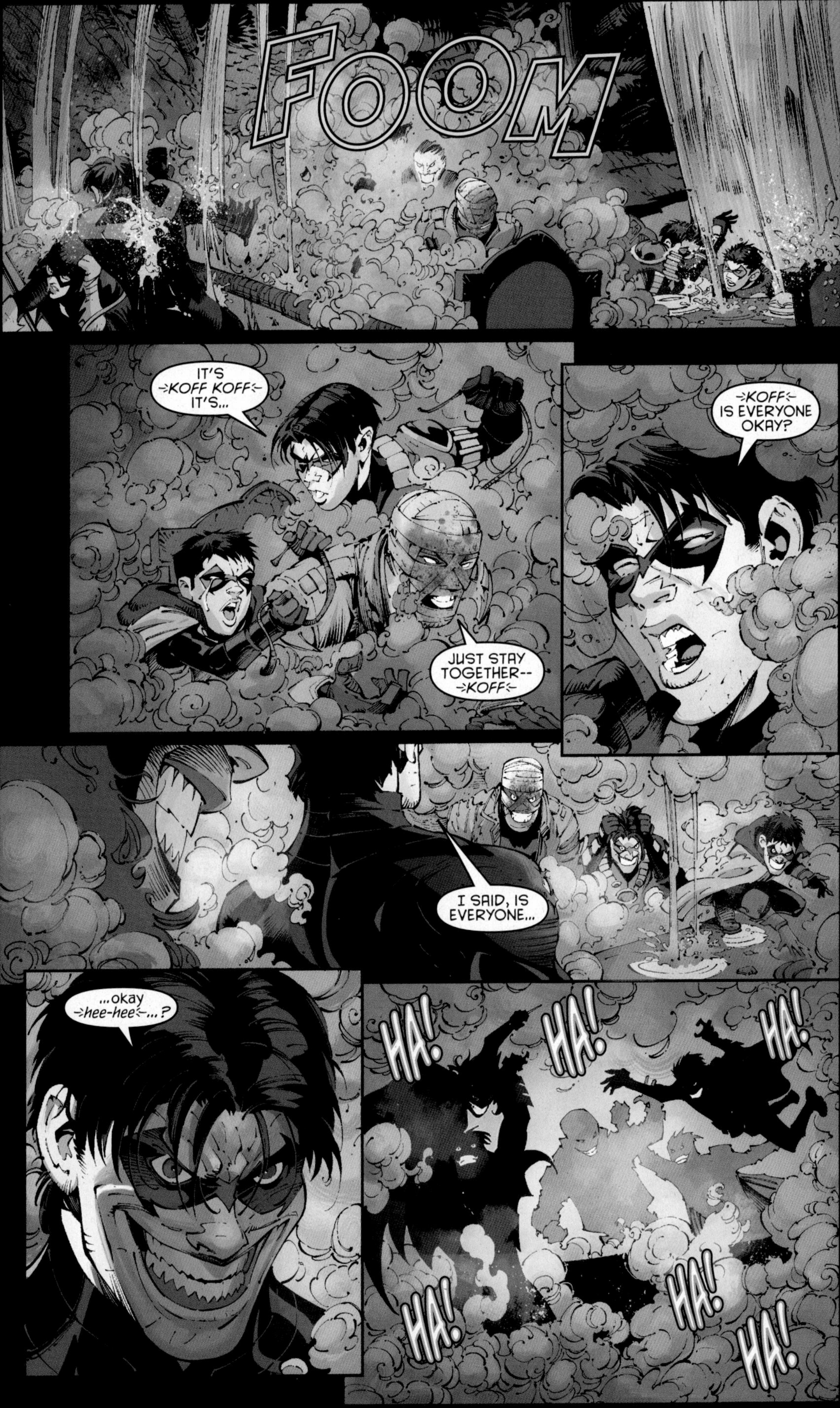
FOOM
IT'S -KOFF KOFF- IT'S...
JUST STAY TOGETHER-- -KOFF-
-KOFF- IS EVERYONE OKAY?
I SAID, IS EVERYONE...
...okay -hee-hee-...?
HA! HA! HA!
HA! HA! HA!

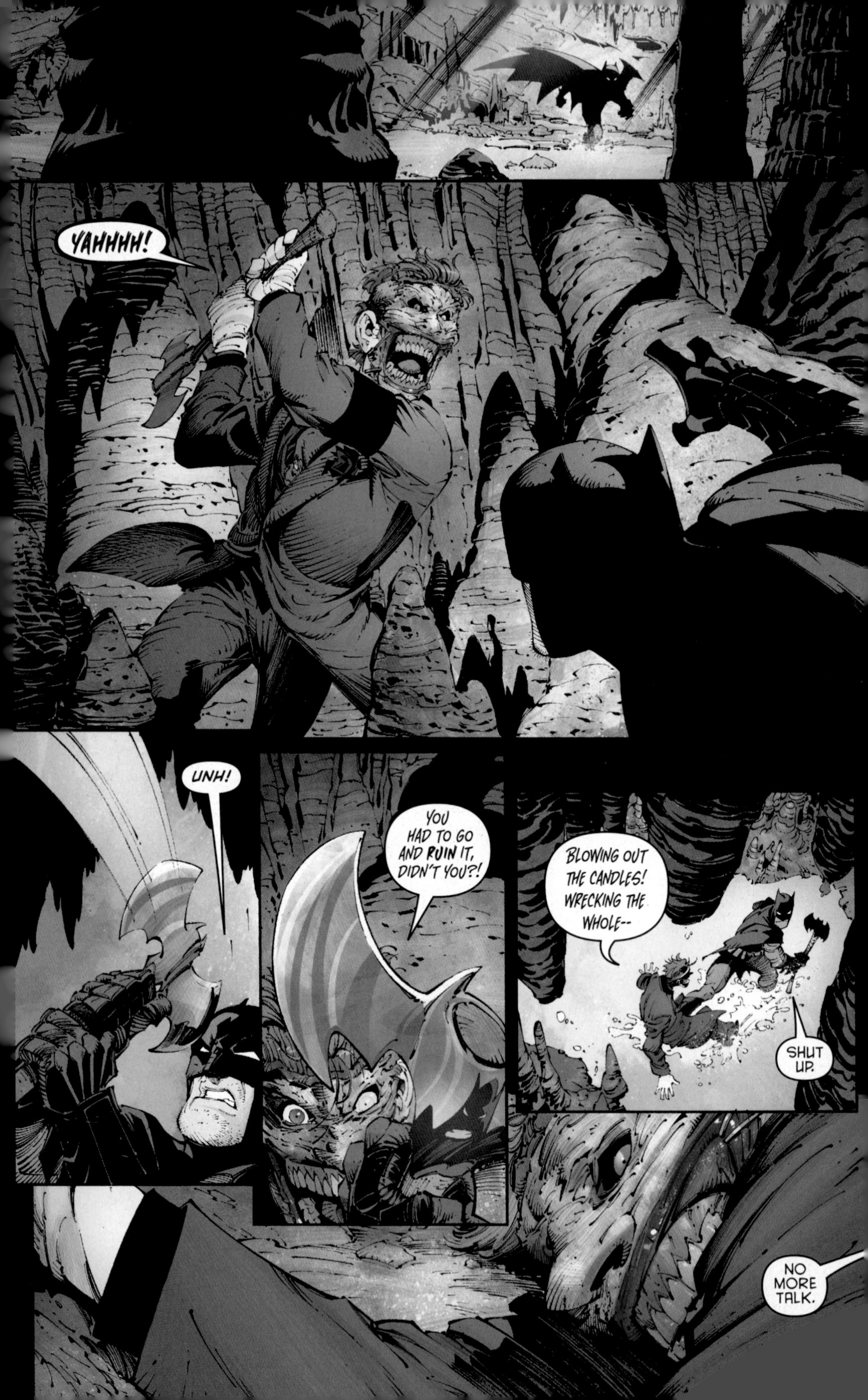
YAHHHH!
UNH!
YOU HAD TO GO AND RUIN IT, DIDN'T YOU?!
BLOWING OUT THE CANDLES! WRECKING THE WHOLE--
SHUT UP.
NO MORE TALK.

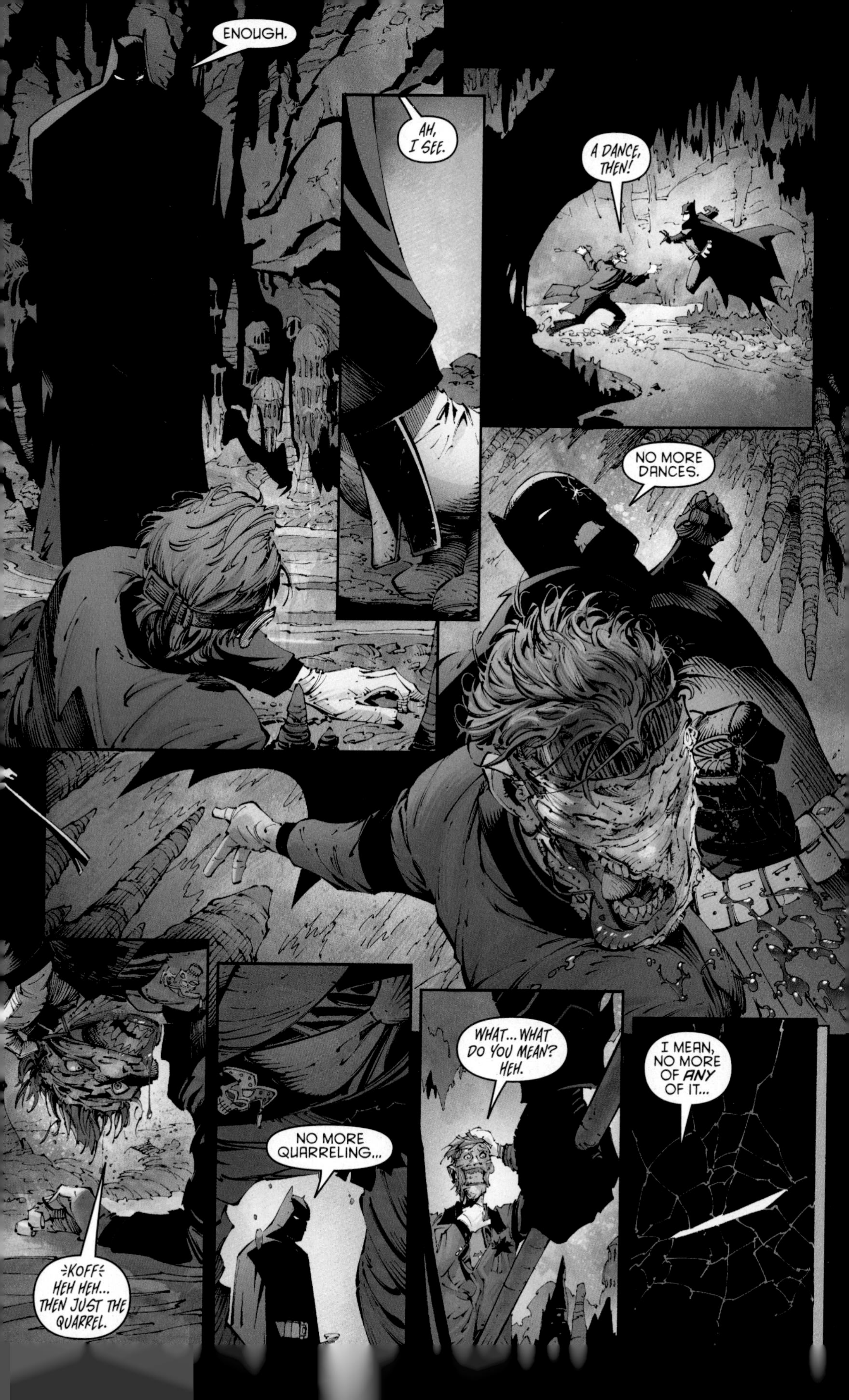
ENOUGH.
AH, I SEE.
A DANCE, THEN!
NO MORE DANCES.
KOFF HEH HEH... THEN JUST THE QUARREL.
NO MORE QUARRELING...
WHAT... WHAT DO YOU MEAN? HEH.
I MEAN, NO MORE OF ANY OF IT...

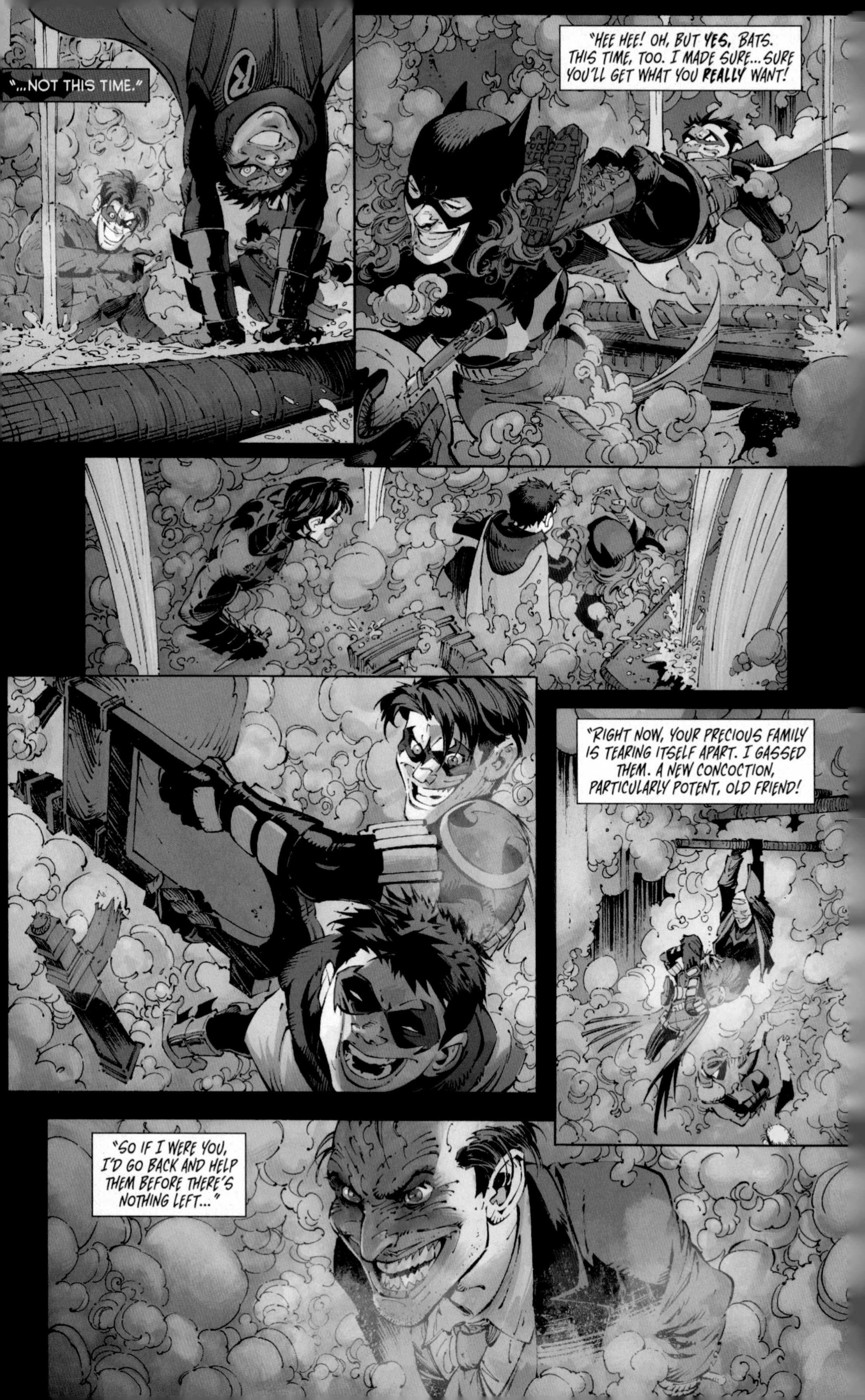
"...NOT THIS TIME."
"HEE HEE! OH, BUT YES, BATS. THIS TIME, TOO. I MADE SURE... SURE YOU'LL GET WHAT YOU REALLY WANT!
"RIGHT NOW, YOUR PRECIOUS FAMILY IS TEARING ITSELF APART. I GASSED THEM. A NEW CONCOCTION, PARTICULARLY POTENT, OLD FRIEND!
"SO IF I WERE YOU, I'D GO BACK AND HELP THEM BEFORE THERE'S NOTHING LEFT..."

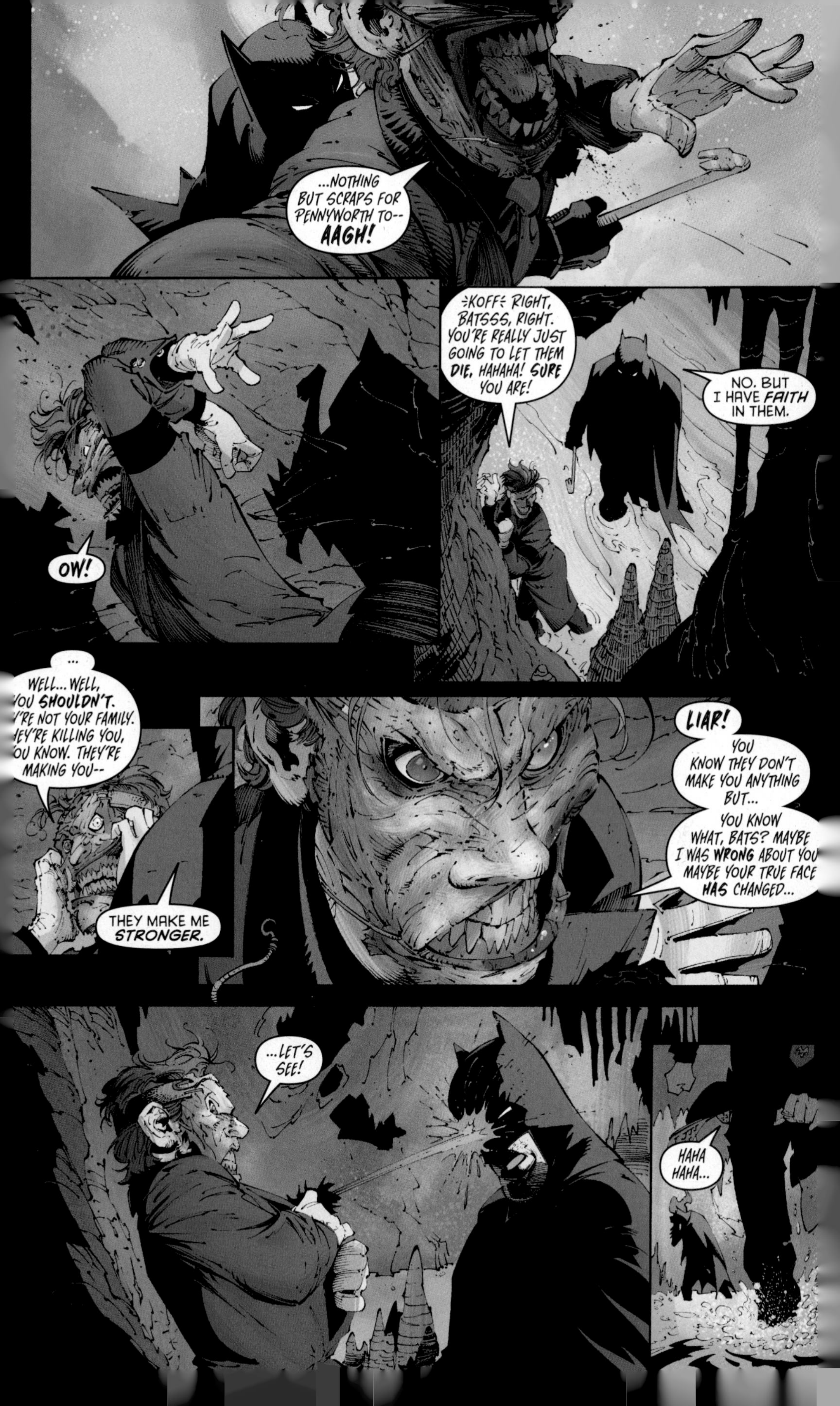
...NOTHING BUT SCRAPS FOR PENNYWORTH TO-- AAGH!
OW!
≷KOFF≶ RIGHT, BATSSS, RIGHT. YOU'RE REALLY JUST GOING TO LET THEM DIE, HAHAHA! SURE YOU ARE!
NO. BUT I HAVE FAITH IN THEM.
...
WELL...WELL, YOU SHOULDN'T. 'RE NOT YOUR FAMILY. HEY'RE KILLING YOU, OU KNOW. THEY'RE MAKING YOU--
THEY MAKE ME STRONGER.
LIAR!
YOU KNOW THEY DON'T MAKE YOU ANYTHING BUT...
YOU KNOW WHAT, BATS? MAYBE I WAS WRONG ABOUT YOU MAYBE YOUR TRUE FACE HAS CHANGED...
...LET'S SEE!
HAHA HAHA...

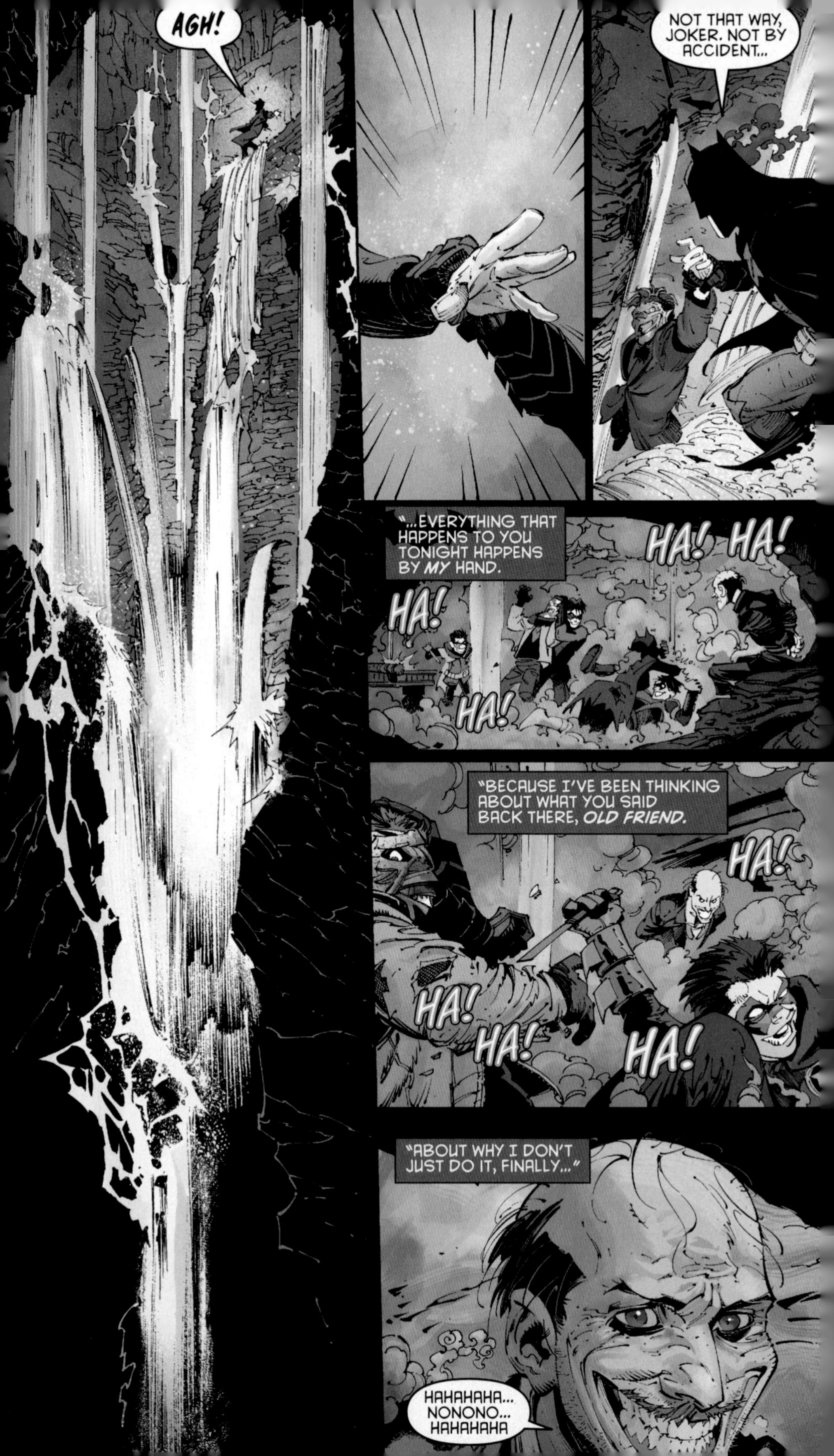

AGH!
NOT THAT WAY, JOKER. NOT BY ACCIDENT...
"...EVERYTHING THAT HAPPENS TO YOU TONIGHT HAPPENS BY *MY* HAND.
HA! HA!
HA!
HA!
"BECAUSE I'VE BEEN THINKING ABOUT WHAT YOU SAID BACK THERE, *OLD FRIEND.*
HA!
HA!
HA!
HA!
"ABOUT WHY I DON'T JUST DO IT, FINALLY..."
HAHAHAHA... NONONO... HAHAHAHA

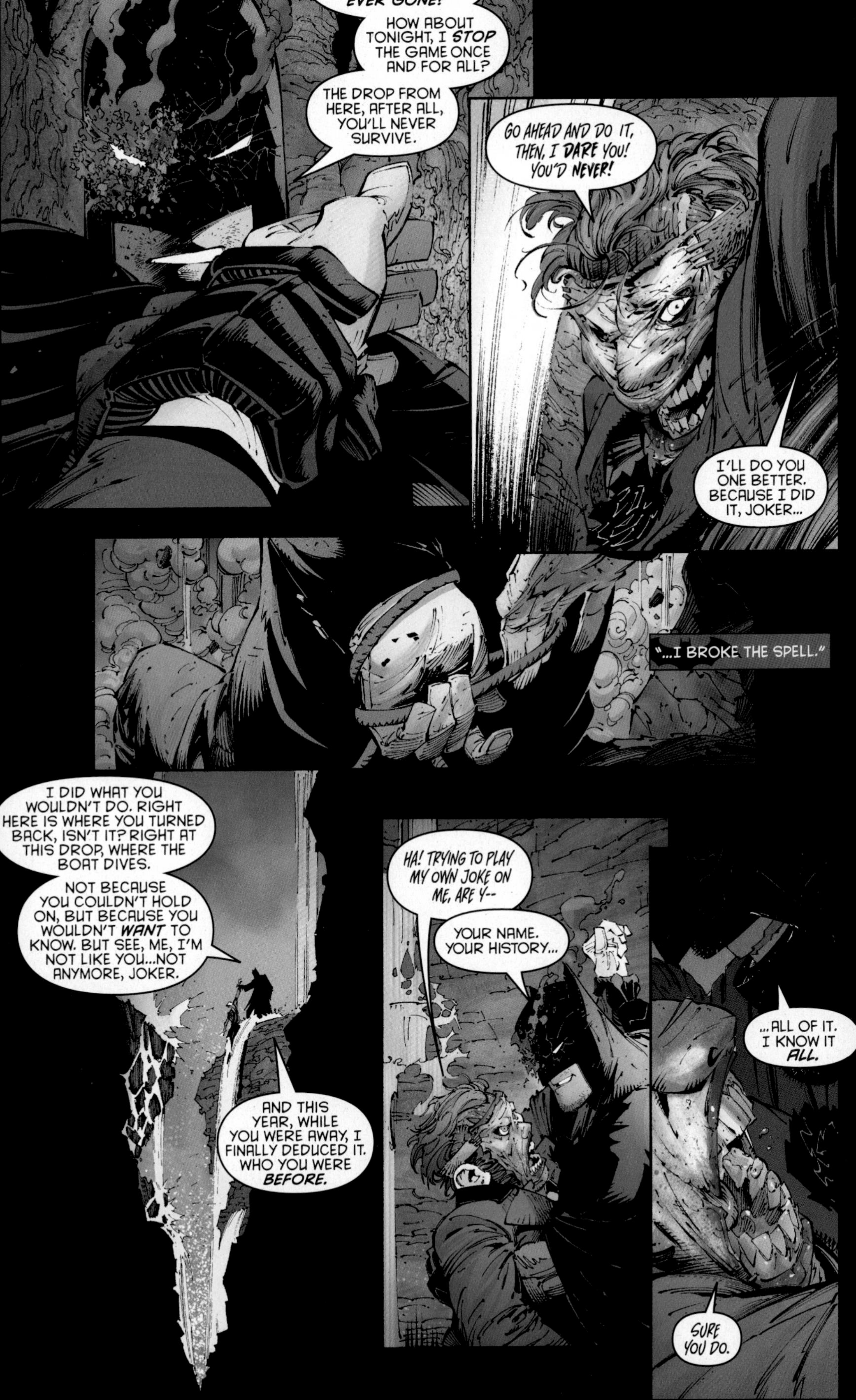
EVER GONE!
HOW ABOUT TONIGHT, I STOP THE GAME ONCE AND FOR ALL?
THE DROP FROM HERE, AFTER ALL, YOU'LL NEVER SURVIVE.
GO AHEAD AND DO IT, THEN, I DARE YOU! YOU'D NEVER!
I'LL DO YOU ONE BETTER. BECAUSE I DID IT, JOKER...
"...I BROKE THE SPELL."
I DID WHAT YOU WOULDN'T DO. RIGHT HERE IS WHERE YOU TURNED BACK, ISN'T IT? RIGHT AT THIS DROP, WHERE THE BOAT DIVES.
NOT BECAUSE YOU COULDN'T HOLD ON, BUT BECAUSE YOU WOULDN'T WANT TO KNOW. BUT SEE, ME, I'M NOT LIKE YOU...NOT ANYMORE, JOKER.
AND THIS YEAR, WHILE YOU WERE AWAY, I FINALLY DEDUCED IT. WHO YOU WERE BEFORE.
HA! TRYING TO PLAY MY OWN JOKE ON ME, ARE Y--
YOUR NAME. YOUR HISTORY...
...ALL OF IT. I KNOW IT ALL.
SURE YOU DO.

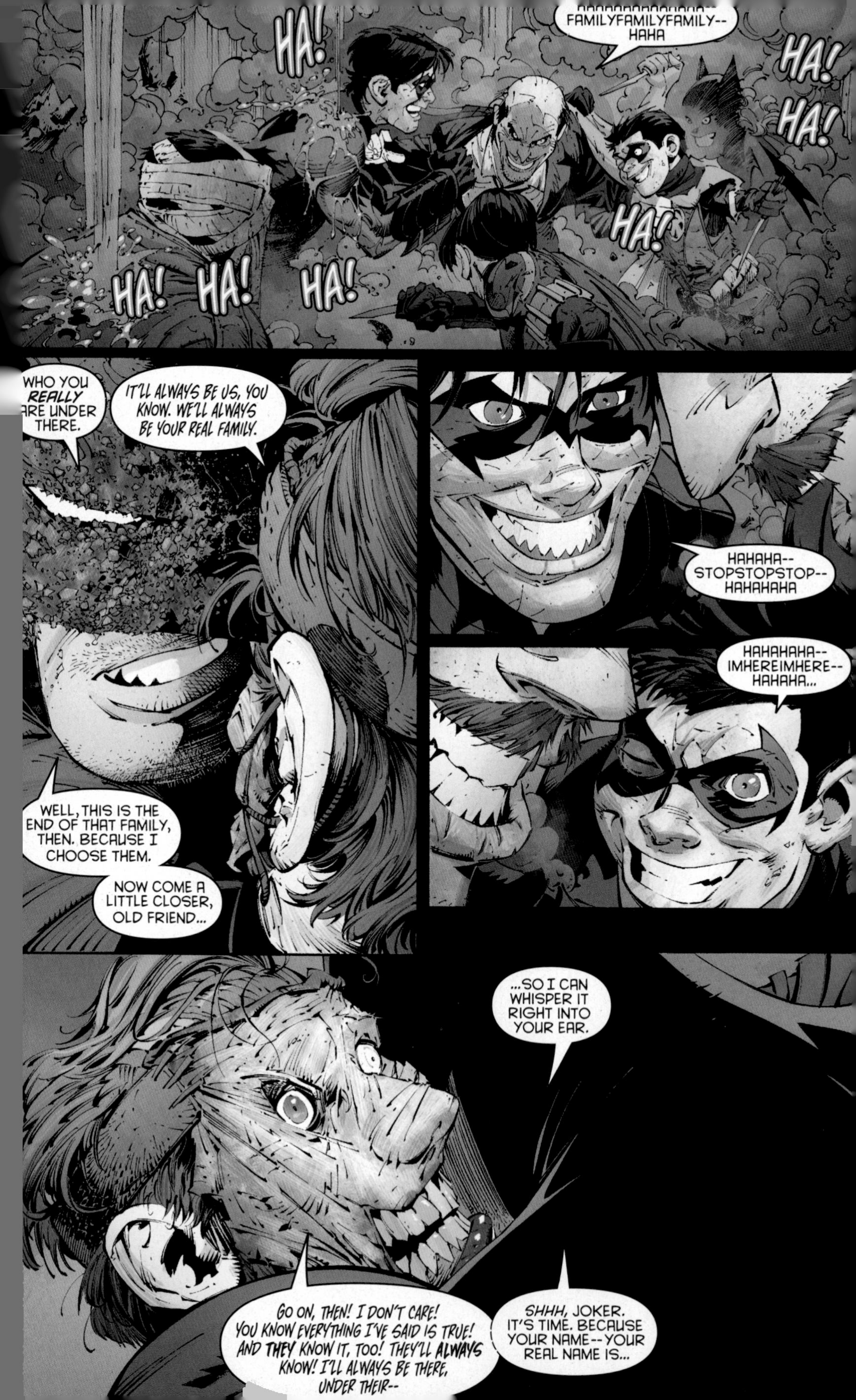
HAHAHAHAHAHAHA--
FAMILYFAMILYFAMILY--
HAHA
HA!
HA!
HA!
HA!
HA!
HA!
HA!
WHO YOU REALLY ARE UNDER THERE.
IT'LL ALWAYS BE US, YOU KNOW. WE'LL ALWAYS BE YOUR REAL FAMILY.
HAHAHA--
STOPSTOPSTOP--
HAHAHAHA
HAHAHAHA--
IMHEREIMHERE--
HAHAHA...
WELL, THIS IS THE END OF THAT FAMILY, THEN. BECAUSE I CHOOSE THEM.
NOW COME A LITTLE CLOSER, OLD FRIEND...
...SO I CAN WHISPER IT RIGHT INTO YOUR EAR.
GO ON, THEN! I DON'T CARE! YOU KNOW EVERYTHING I'VE SAID IS TRUE! AND THEY KNOW IT, TOO! THEY'LL ALWAYS KNOW! I'LL ALWAYS BE THERE, UNDER THEIR--
SHHH, JOKER. IT'S TIME. BECAUSE YOUR NAME--YOUR REAL NAME IS...

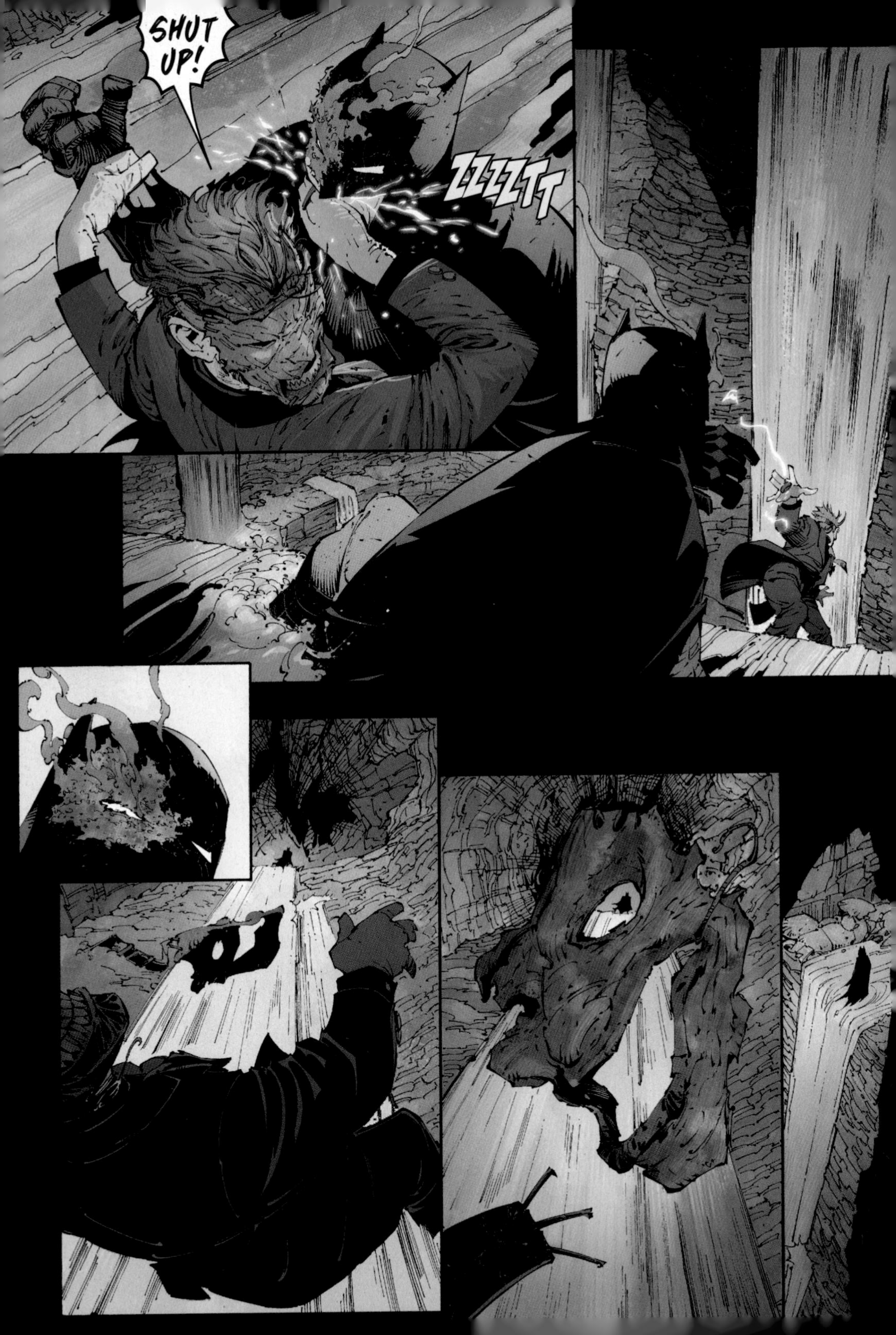
SHUT UP!
ZZZZTT

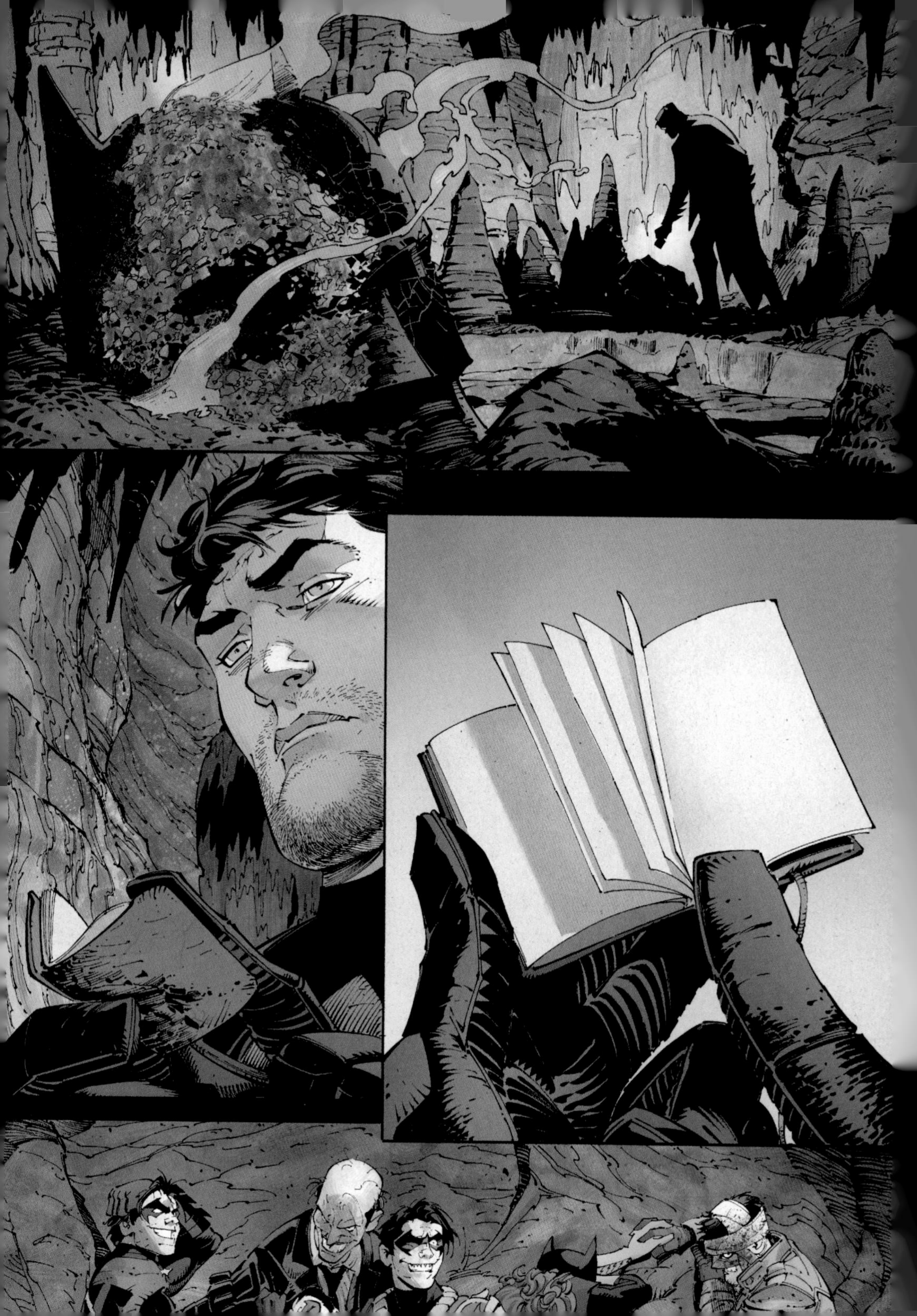

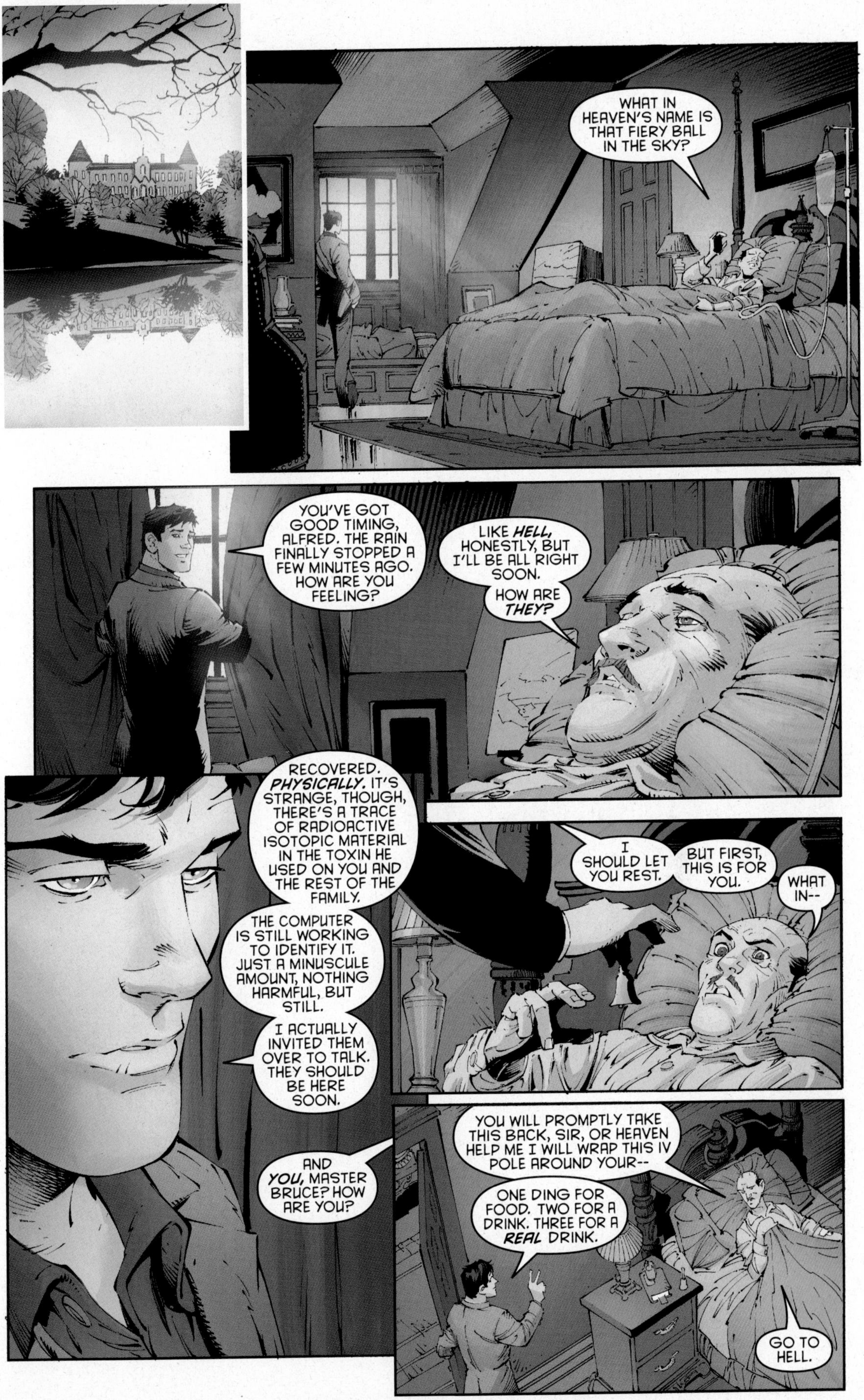

WHAT IN HEAVEN'S NAME IS THAT FIERY BALL IN THE SKY?
YOU'VE GOT GOOD TIMING, ALFRED. THE RAIN FINALLY STOPPED A FEW MINUTES AGO. HOW ARE YOU FEELING?
LIKE HELL, HONESTLY, BUT I'LL BE ALL RIGHT SOON.
HOW ARE THEY?
RECOVERED. PHYSICALLY. IT'S STRANGE, THOUGH, THERE'S A TRACE OF RADIOACTIVE ISOTOPIC MATERIAL IN THE TOXIN HE USED ON YOU AND THE REST OF THE FAMILY.
THE COMPUTER IS STILL WORKING TO IDENTIFY IT. JUST A MINUSCULE AMOUNT, NOTHING HARMFUL, BUT STILL.
I ACTUALLY INVITED THEM OVER TO TALK. THEY SHOULD BE HERE SOON.
AND YOU, MASTER BRUCE? HOW ARE YOU?
I SHOULD LET YOU REST.
BUT FIRST, THIS IS FOR YOU.
WHAT IN--
YOU WILL PROMPTLY TAKE THIS BACK, SIR, OR HEAVEN HELP ME I WILL WRAP THIS IV POLE AROUND YOUR--
ONE DING FOR FOOD. TWO FOR A DRINK. THREE FOR A REAL DRINK.
GO TO HELL.

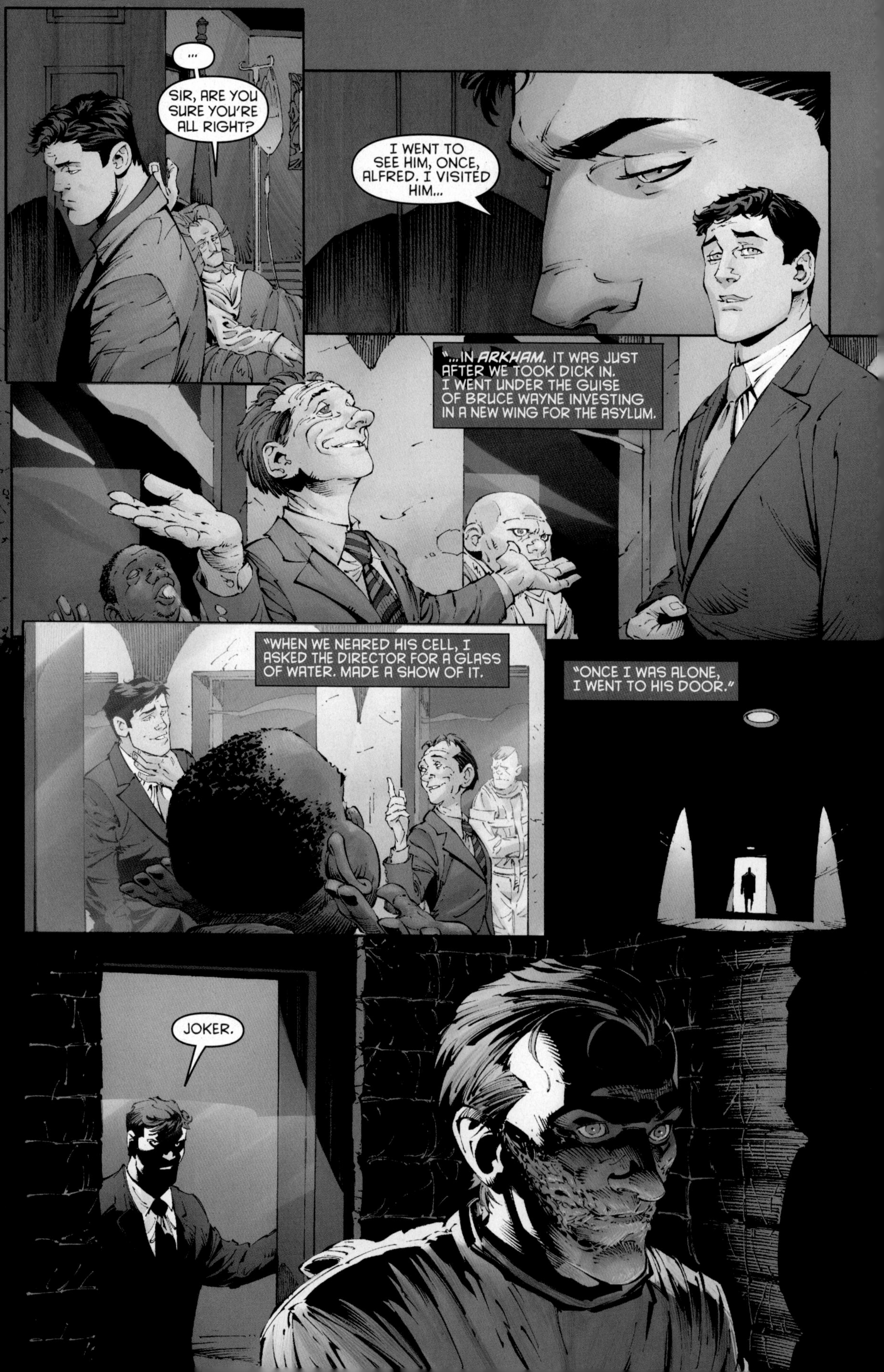
...
SIR, ARE YOU SURE YOU'RE ALL RIGHT?
I WENT TO SEE HIM, ONCE, ALFRED. I VISITED HIM...
"...IN ARKHAM. IT WAS JUST AFTER WE TOOK DICK IN. I WENT UNDER THE GUISE OF BRUCE WAYNE INVESTING IN A NEW WING FOR THE ASYLUM.
"WHEN WE NEARED HIS CELL, I ASKED THE DIRECTOR FOR A GLASS OF WATER. MADE A SHOW OF IT.
"ONCE I WAS ALONE, I WENT TO HIS DOOR."
JOKER.

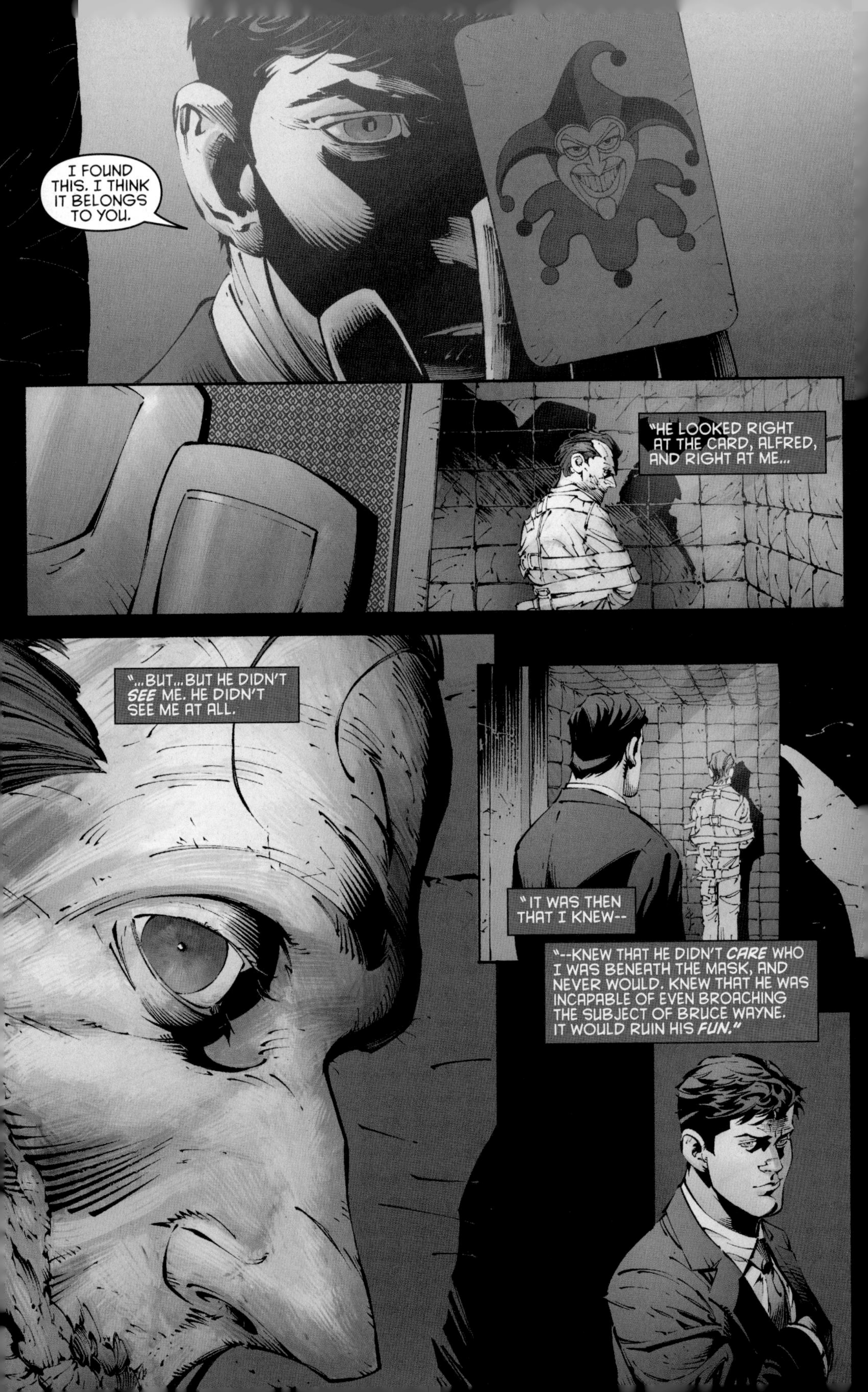
I FOUND THIS. I THINK IT BELONGS TO YOU.
"HE LOOKED RIGHT AT THE CARD, ALFRED, AND RIGHT AT ME...
"...BUT...BUT HE DIDN'T *SEE* ME. HE DIDN'T SEE ME AT ALL.
"IT WAS THEN THAT I KNEW--
"--KNEW THAT HE DIDN'T *CARE* WHO I WAS BENEATH THE MASK, AND NEVER WOULD. KNEW THAT HE WAS INCAPABLE OF EVEN BROACHING THE SUBJECT OF BRUCE WAYNE. IT WOULD RUIN HIS *FUN*."

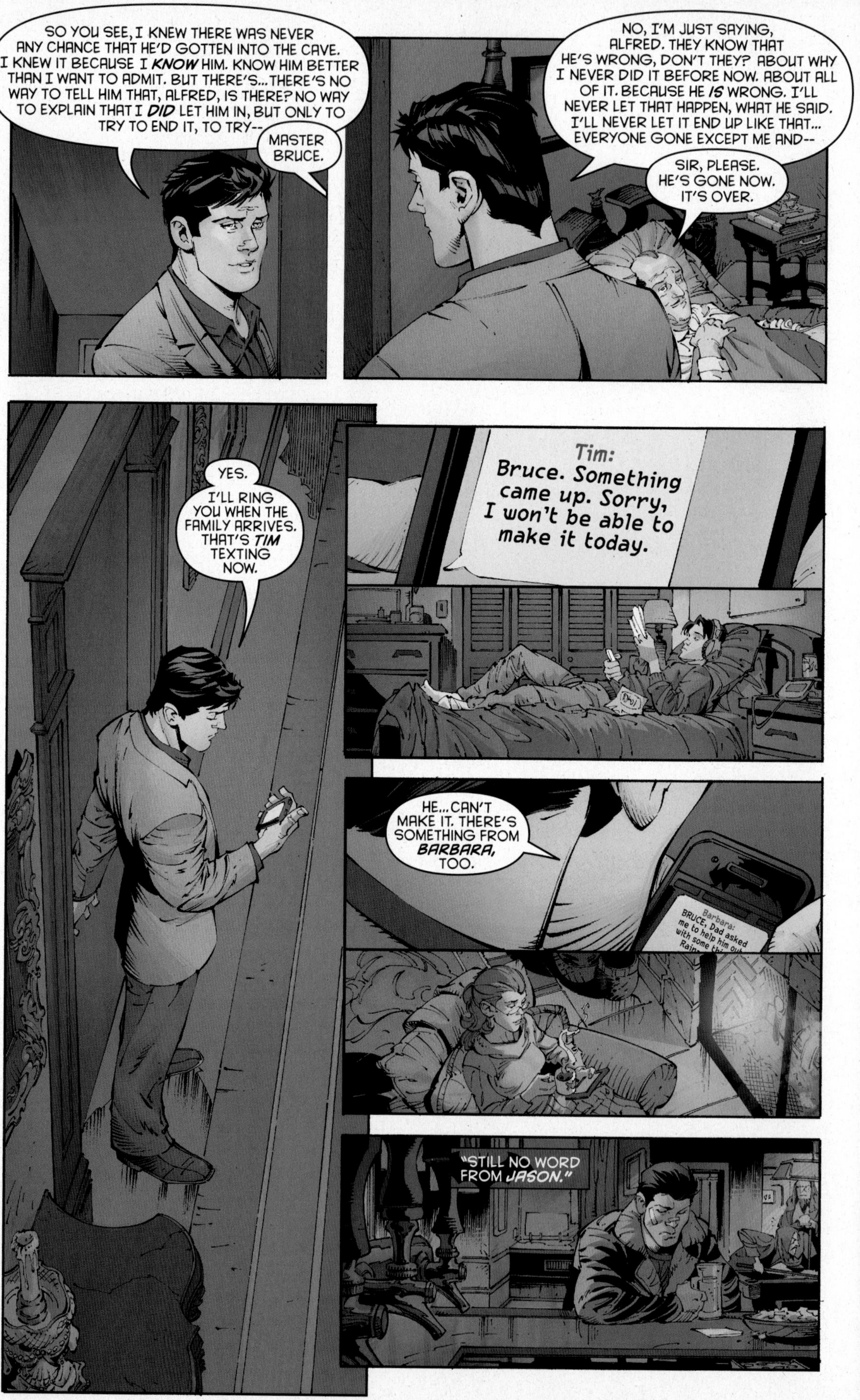
SO YOU SEE, I KNEW THERE WAS NEVER ANY CHANCE THAT HE'D GOTTEN INTO THE CAVE. I KNEW IT BECAUSE I *KNOW* HIM. KNOW HIM BETTER THAN I WANT TO ADMIT. BUT THERE'S...THERE'S NO WAY TO TELL HIM THAT, ALFRED, IS THERE? NO WAY TO EXPLAIN THAT I *DID* LET HIM IN, BUT ONLY TO TRY TO END IT, TO TRY--
MASTER BRUCE.
NO, I'M JUST SAYING, ALFRED. THEY KNOW THAT HE'S WRONG, DON'T THEY? ABOUT WHY I NEVER DID IT BEFORE NOW. ABOUT ALL OF IT. BECAUSE HE *IS* WRONG. I'LL NEVER LET THAT HAPPEN, WHAT HE SAID. I'LL NEVER LET IT END UP LIKE THAT... EVERYONE GONE EXCEPT ME AND--
SIR, PLEASE. HE'S GONE NOW. IT'S OVER.
YES.
I'LL RING YOU WHEN THE FAMILY ARRIVES. THAT'S *TIM* TEXTING NOW.
Tim:
Bruce. Something came up. Sorry, I won't be able to make it today.
HE...CAN'T MAKE IT. THERE'S SOMETHING FROM *BARBARA,* TOO.
Barbara:
BRUCE, Dad asked
me to help him out
"STILL NO WORD FROM *JASON.*"

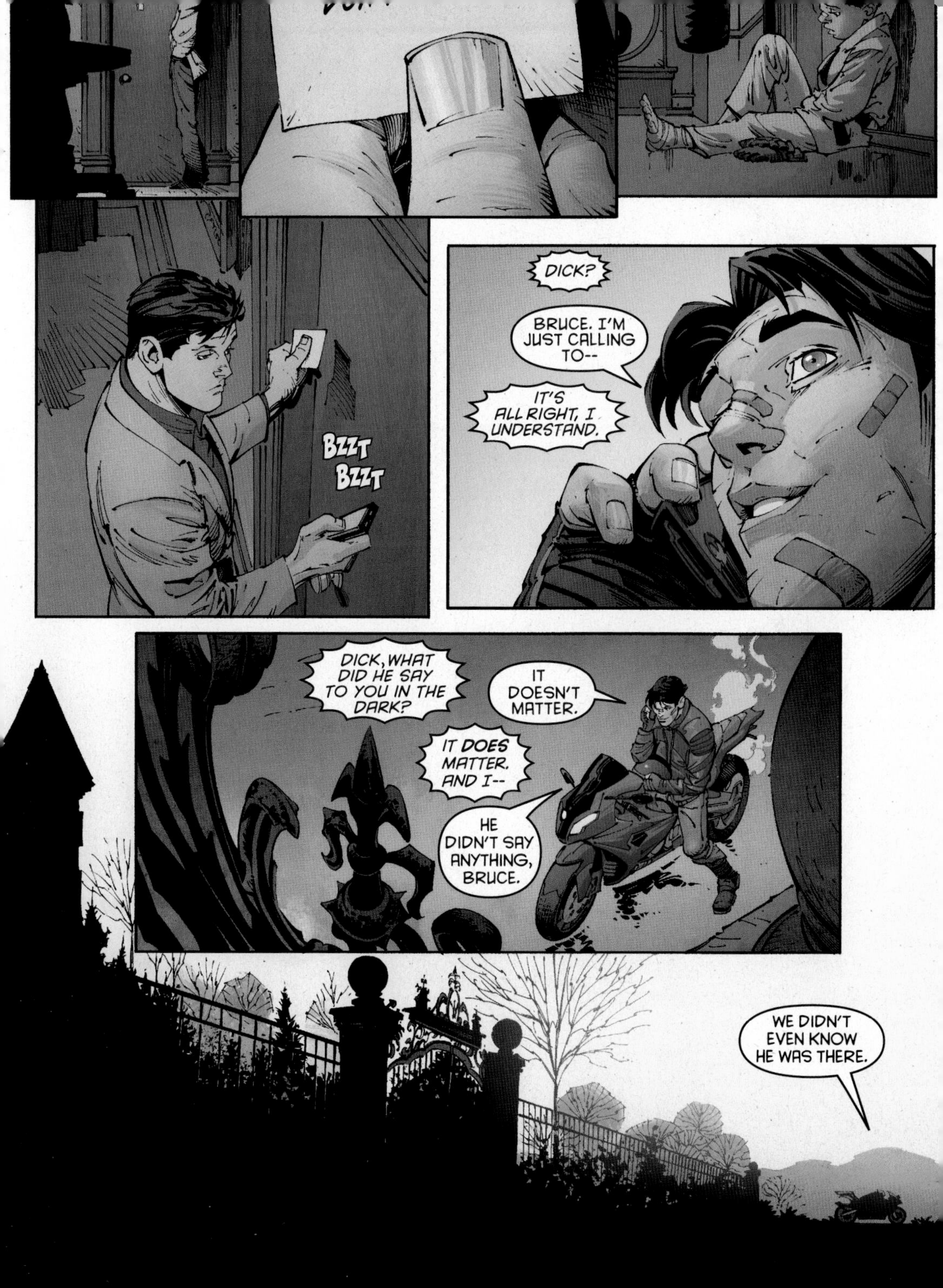
BZZT
BZZT
DICK?
BRUCE. I'M JUST CALLING TO--
IT'S ALL RIGHT, I UNDERSTAND.
DICK, WHAT DID HE SAY TO YOU IN THE DARK?
IT DOESN'T MATTER.
IT DOES MATTER. AND I--
HE DIDN'T SAY ANYTHING, BRUCE.
WE DIDN'T EVEN KNOW HE WAS THERE.

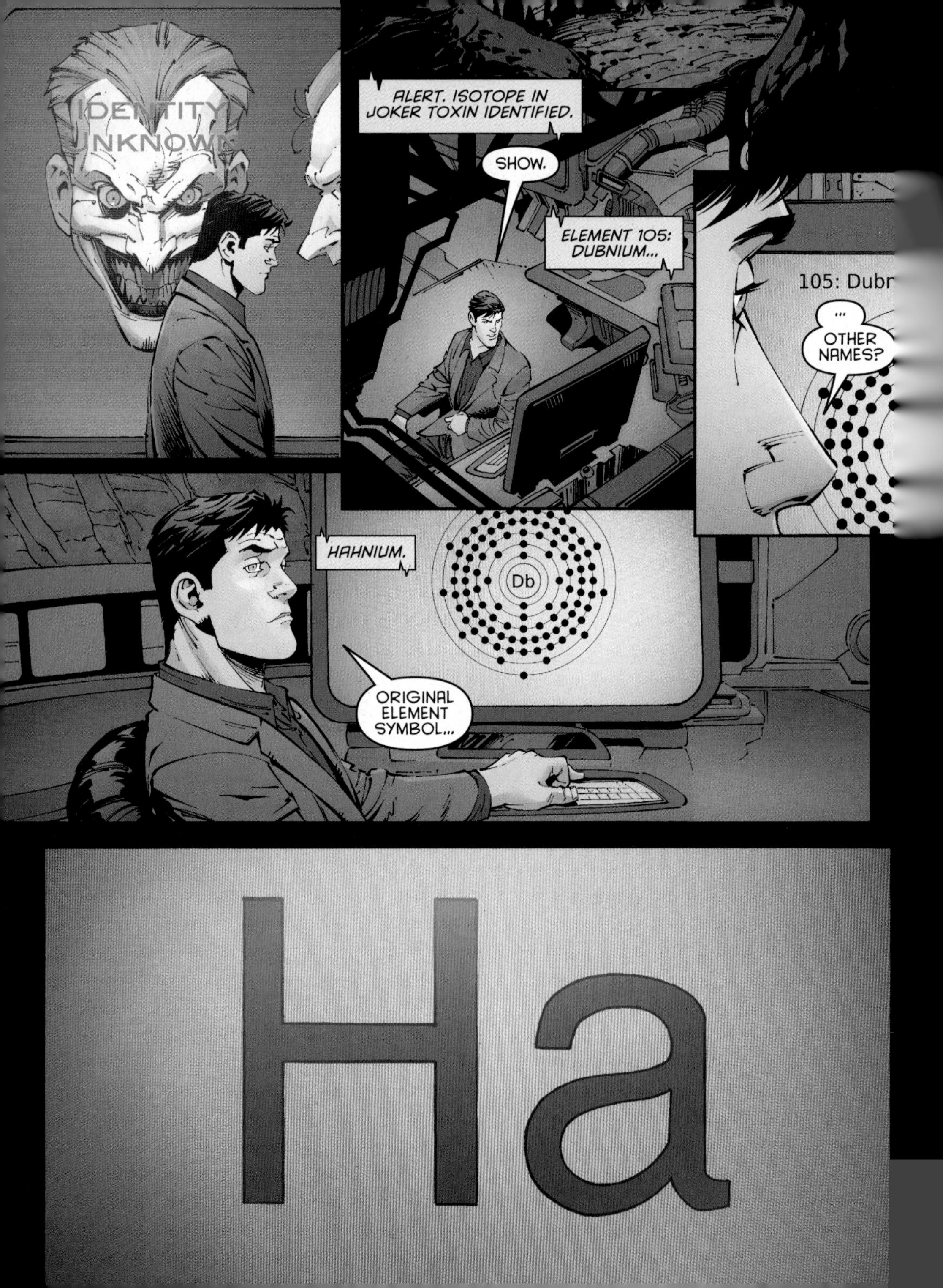
IDENTITY UNKNOWN
ALERT. ISOTOPE IN JOKER TOXIN IDENTIFIED.
SHOW.
ELEMENT 105: DUBNIUM...
105: Dubn
... OTHER NAMES?
HAHNIUM.
Db
ORIGINAL ELEMENT SYMBOL...
Ha

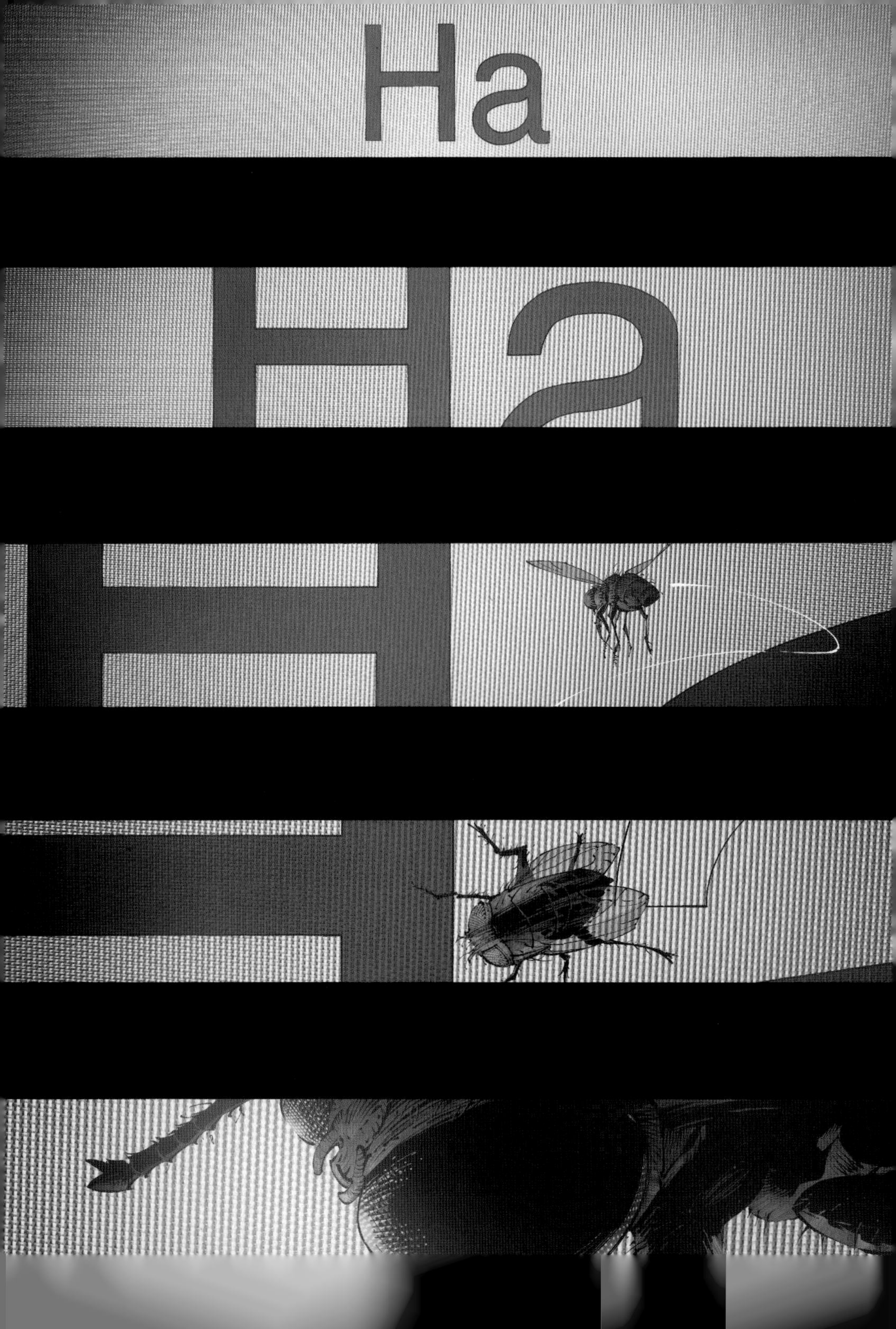
Ha

EPILOGUE

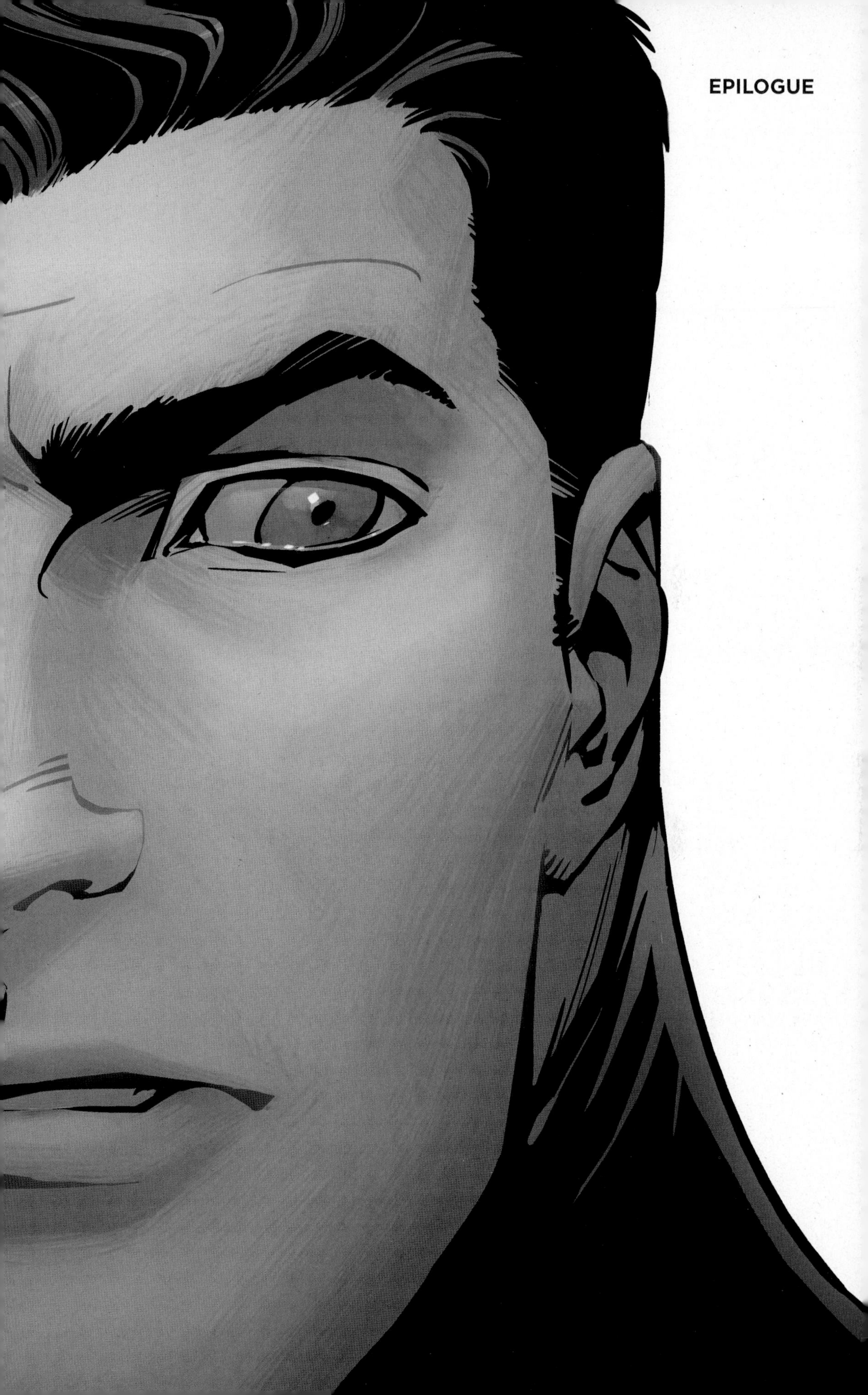

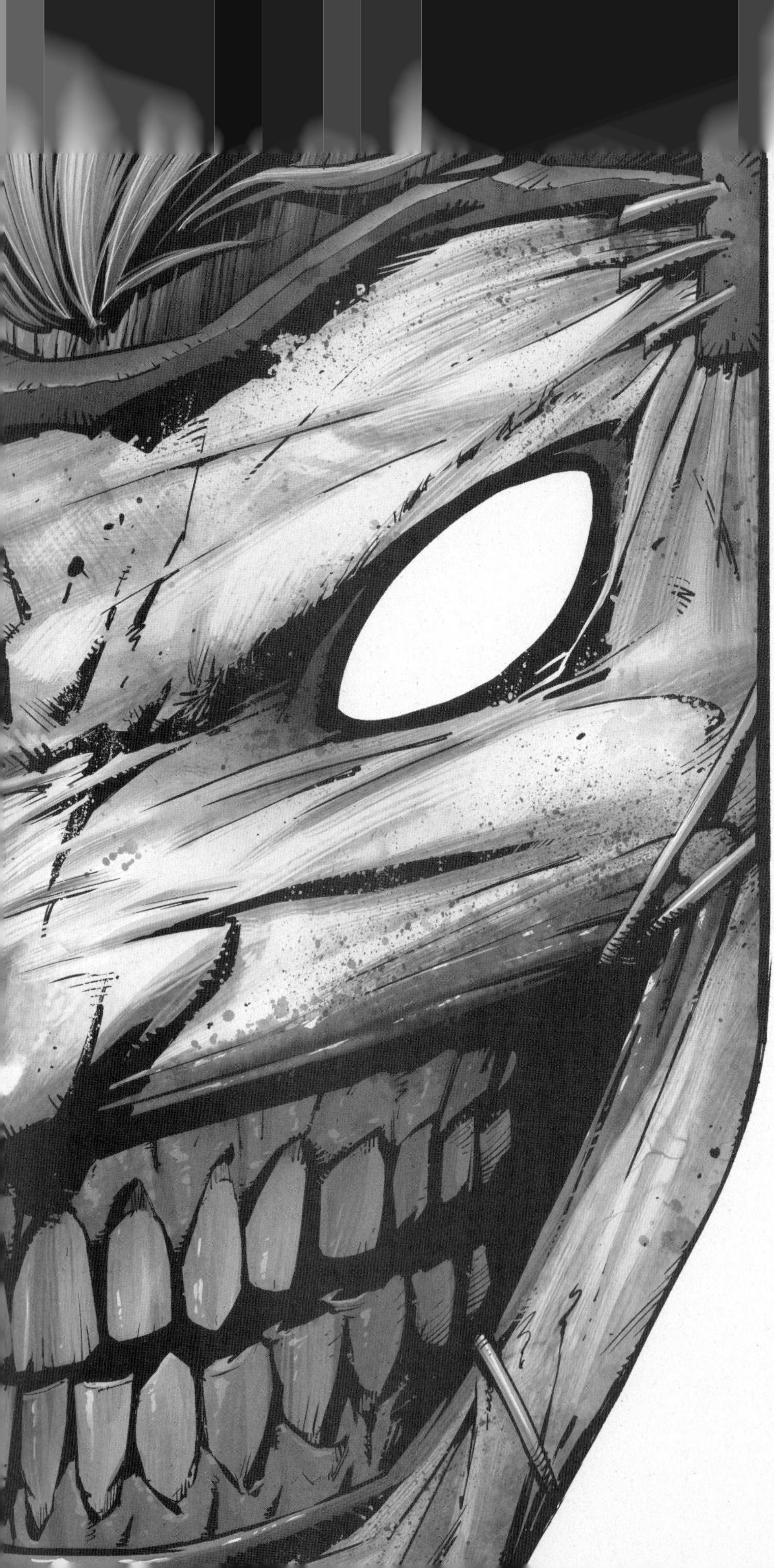

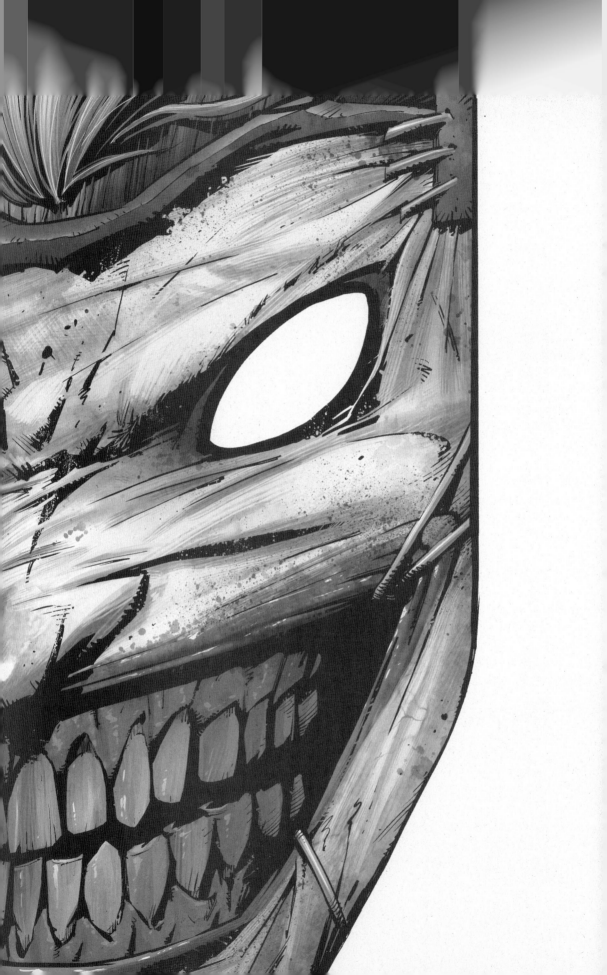

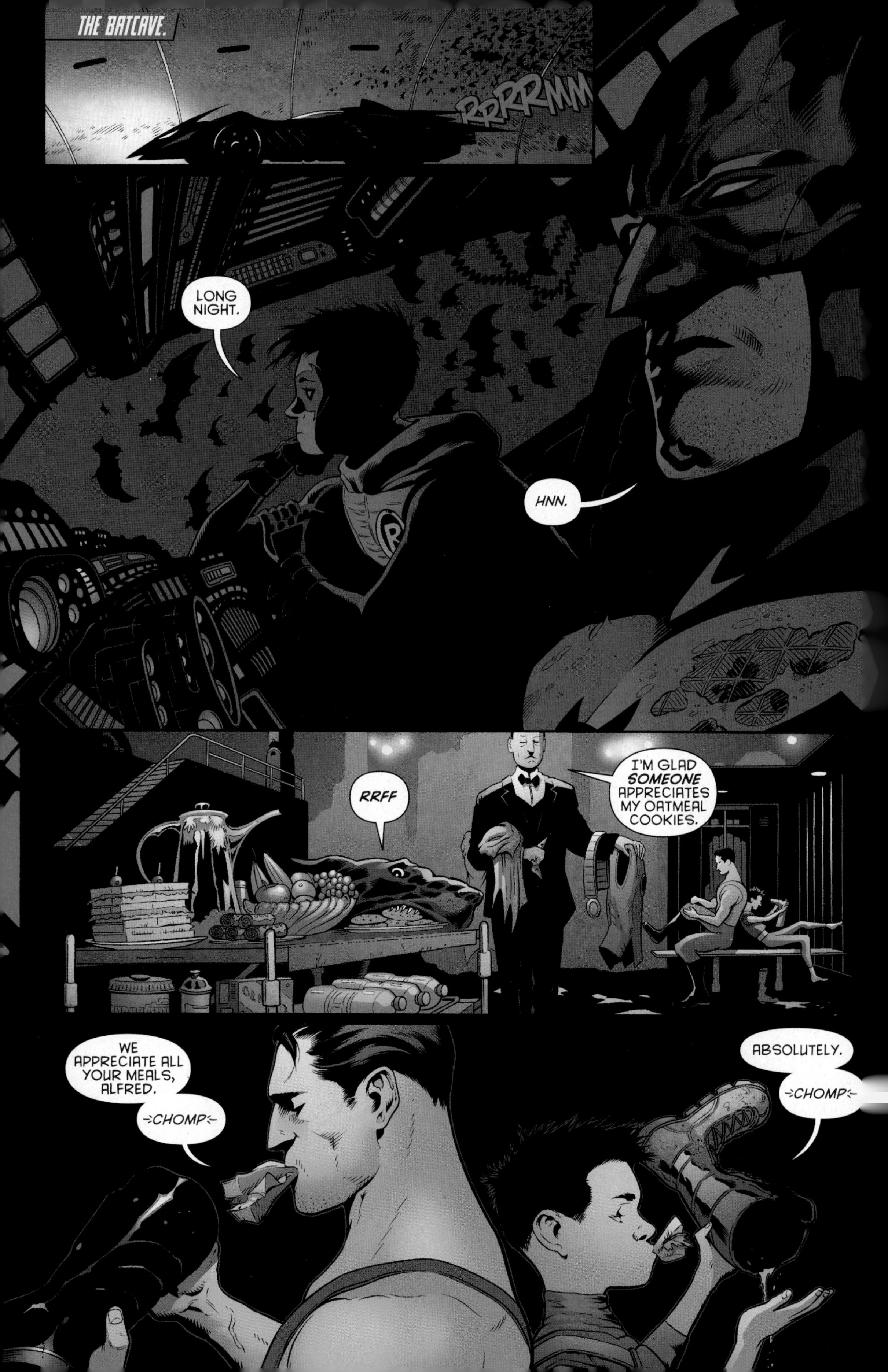
THE BATCAVE.
RRRRMM
LONG NIGHT.
HNN.
RRFF
I'M GLAD SOMEONE APPRECIATES MY OATMEAL COOKIES.
WE APPRECIATE ALL YOUR MEALS, ALFRED.
CHOMP
ABSOLUTELY.
CHOMP

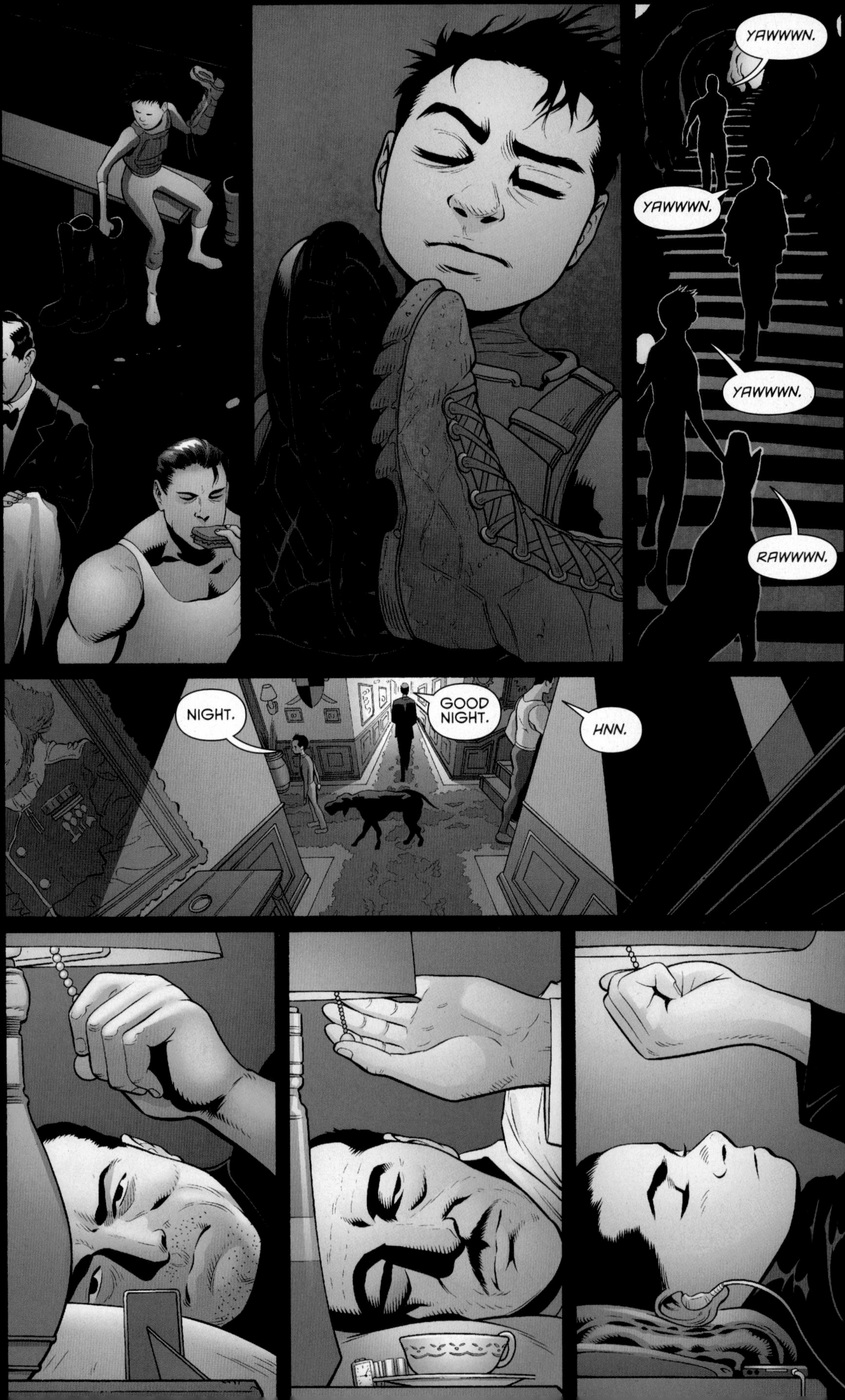
YAWWWN.
YAWWWN.
YAWWWN.
RAWWWN.
NIGHT.
GOOD NIGHT.
HNN.

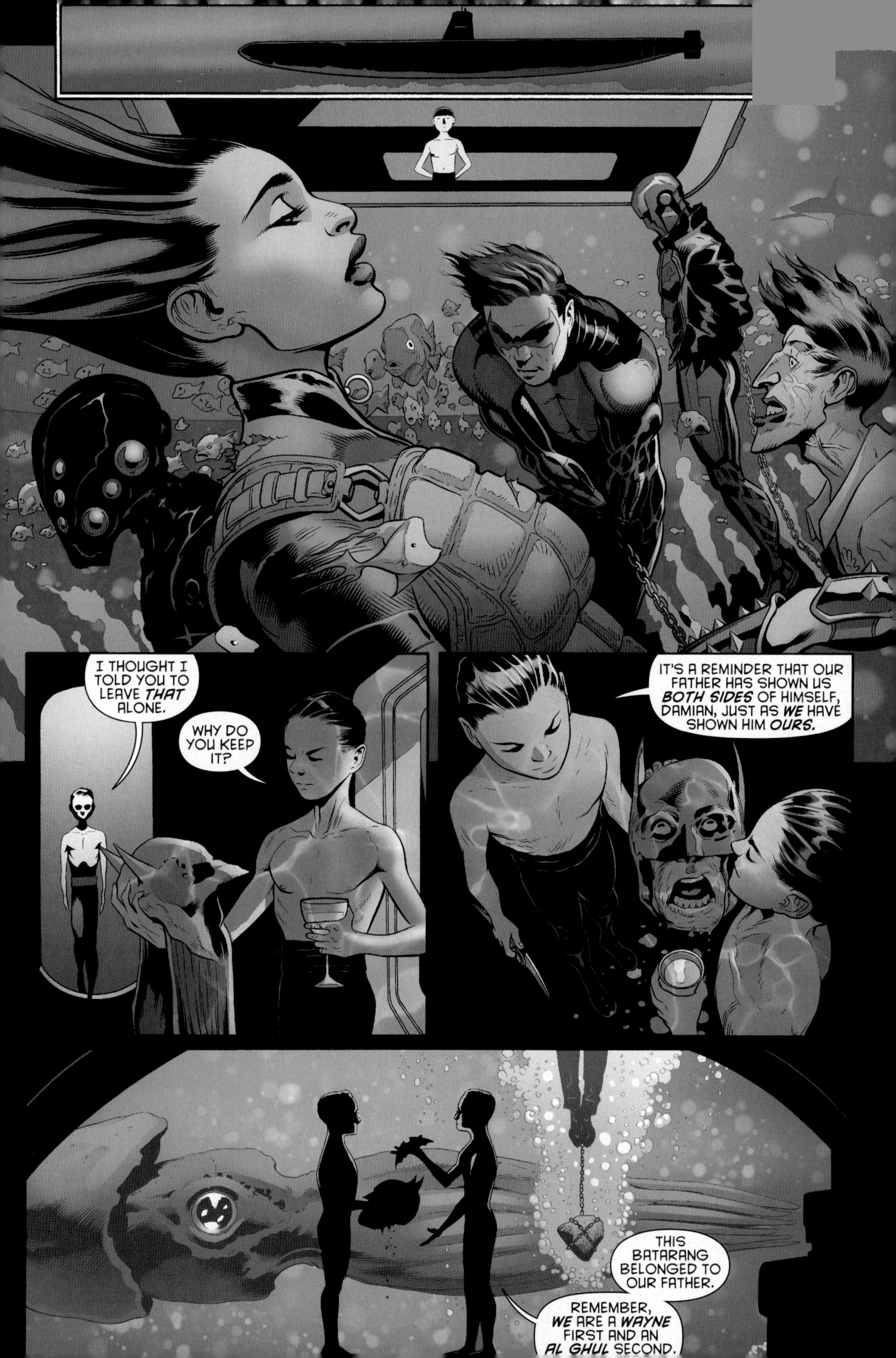

I THOUGHT I TOLD YOU TO LEAVE *THAT* ALONE.
WHY DO YOU KEEP IT?
IT'S A REMINDER THAT OUR FATHER HAS SHOWN US ***BOTH SIDES*** OF HIMSELF, DAMIAN, JUST AS ***WE*** HAVE SHOWN HIM ***OURS.***
THIS BATARANG BELONGED TO OUR FATHER.
REMEMBER, ***WE*** ARE A ***WAYNE*** FIRST AND AN ***AL GHUL*** SECOND.

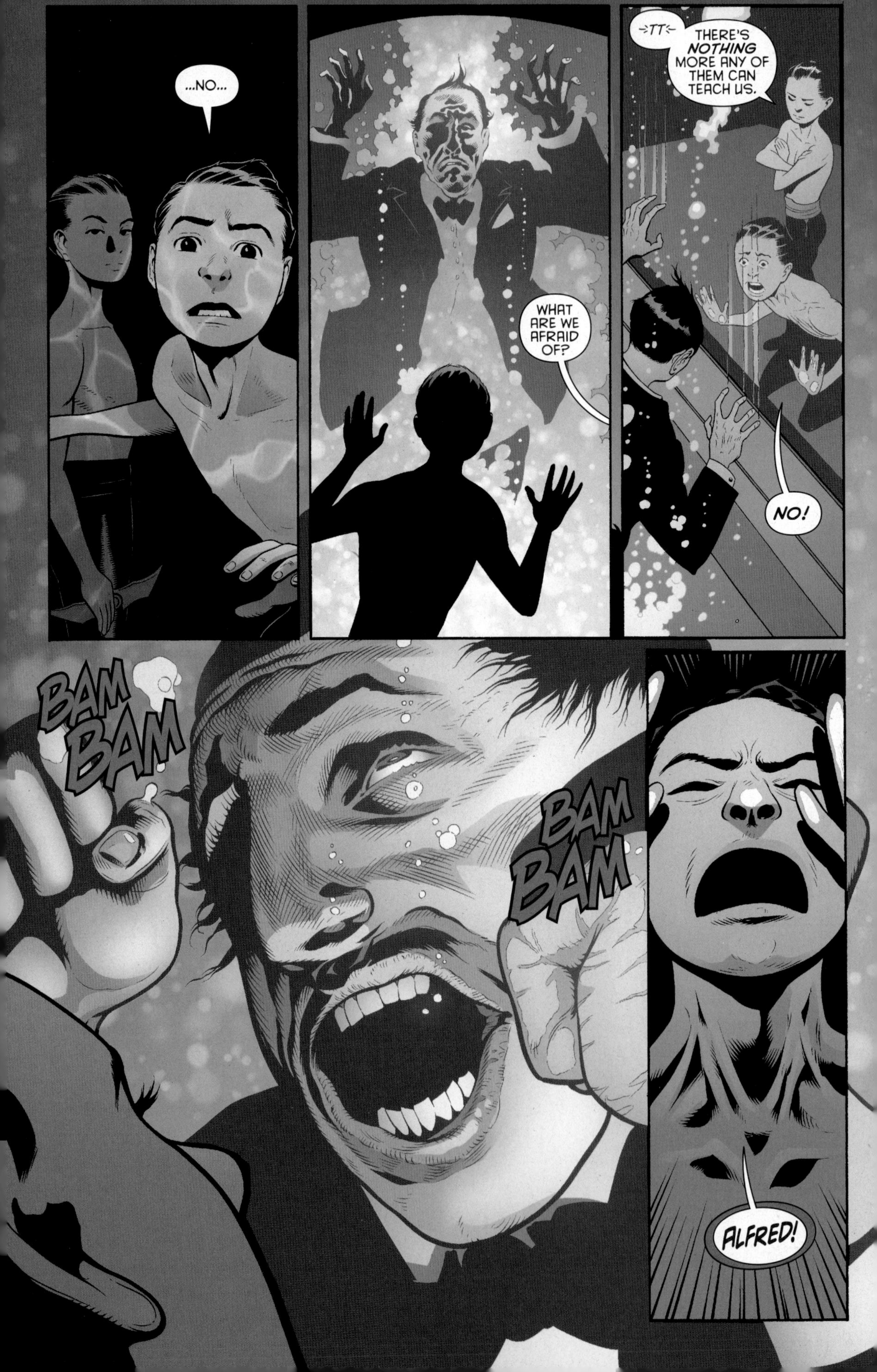
...NO...
WHAT ARE WE AFRAID OF?
TT
THERE'S NOTHING MORE ANY OF THEM CAN TEACH US.
NO!
BAM BAM
BAM BAM
ALFRED!

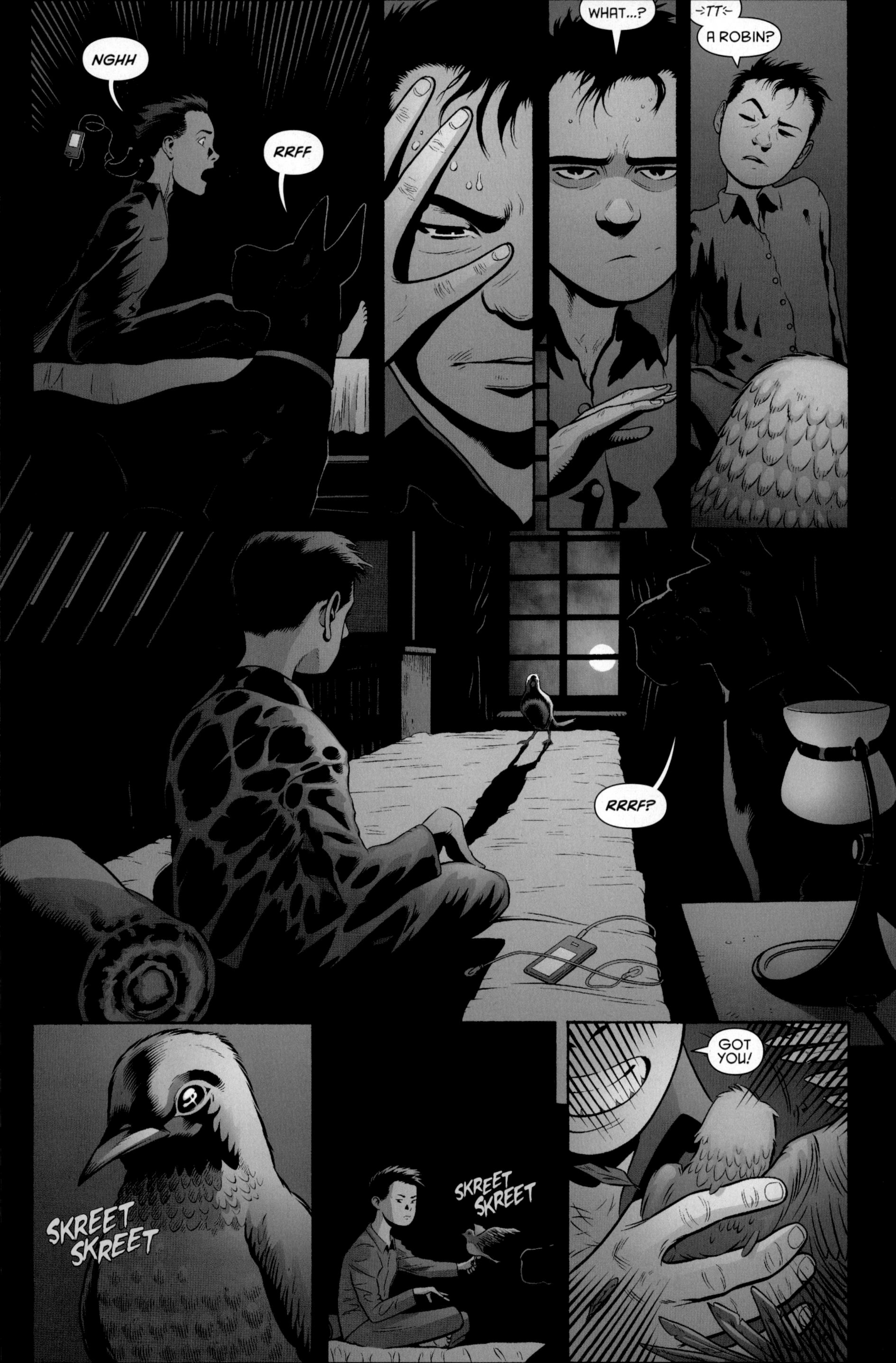
NGHH
RRFF
WHAT...?
TT
A ROBIN?
RRRF?
SKREET SKREET
SKREET SKREET
GOT YOU!

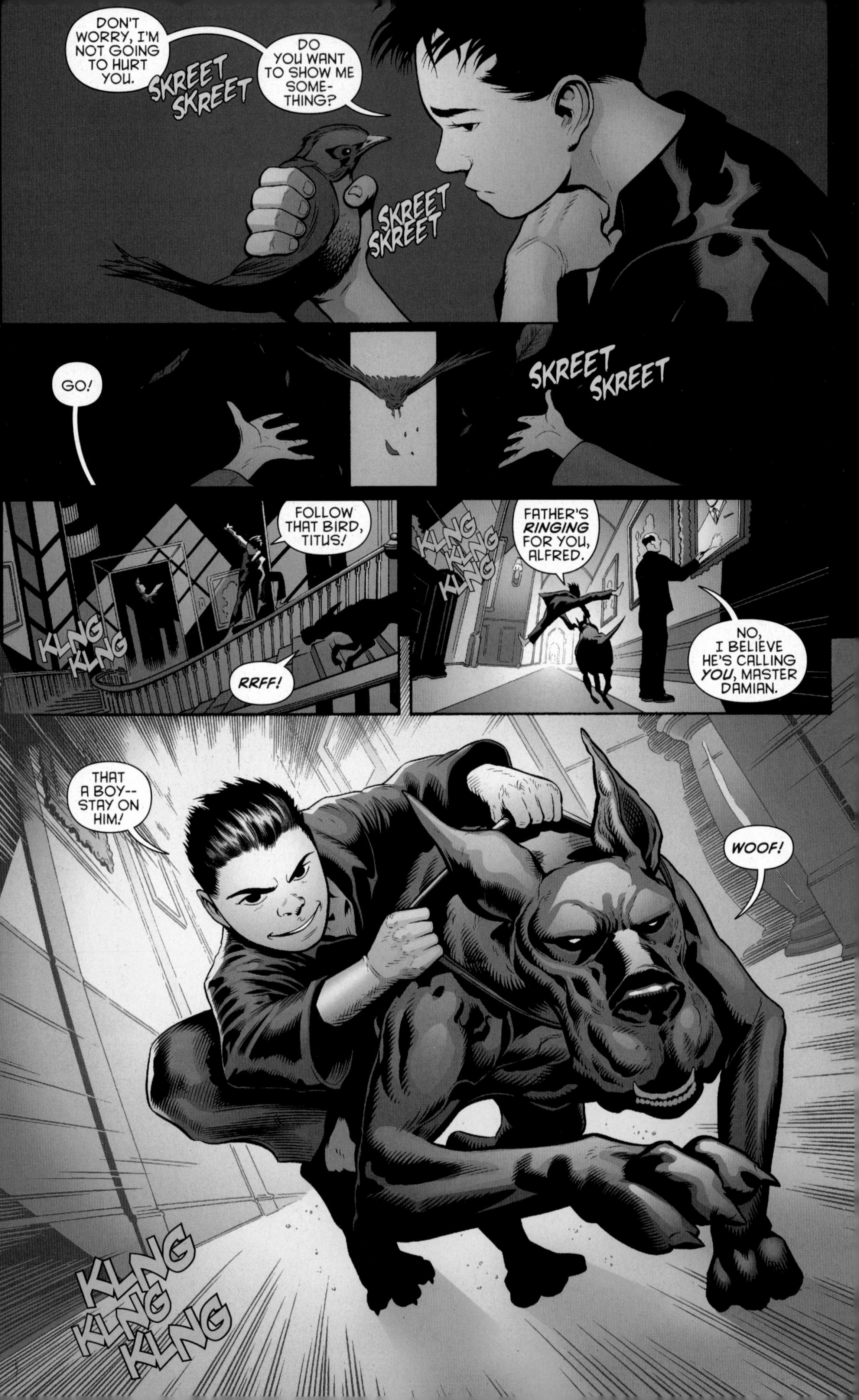
DON'T WORRY, I'M NOT GOING TO HURT YOU.
SKREET SKREET
DO YOU WANT TO SHOW ME SOME-THING?
SKREET SKREET
GO!
SKREET SKREET
FOLLOW THAT BIRD, TITUS!
KLNG KLNG
RRFF!
KLNG KLNG KLNG KLNG
FATHER'S *RINGING* FOR YOU, ALFRED.
NO, I BELIEVE HE'S CALLING *YOU*, MASTER DAMIAN.
THAT A BOY--STAY ON HIM!
WOOF!
KLNG KLNG KLNG

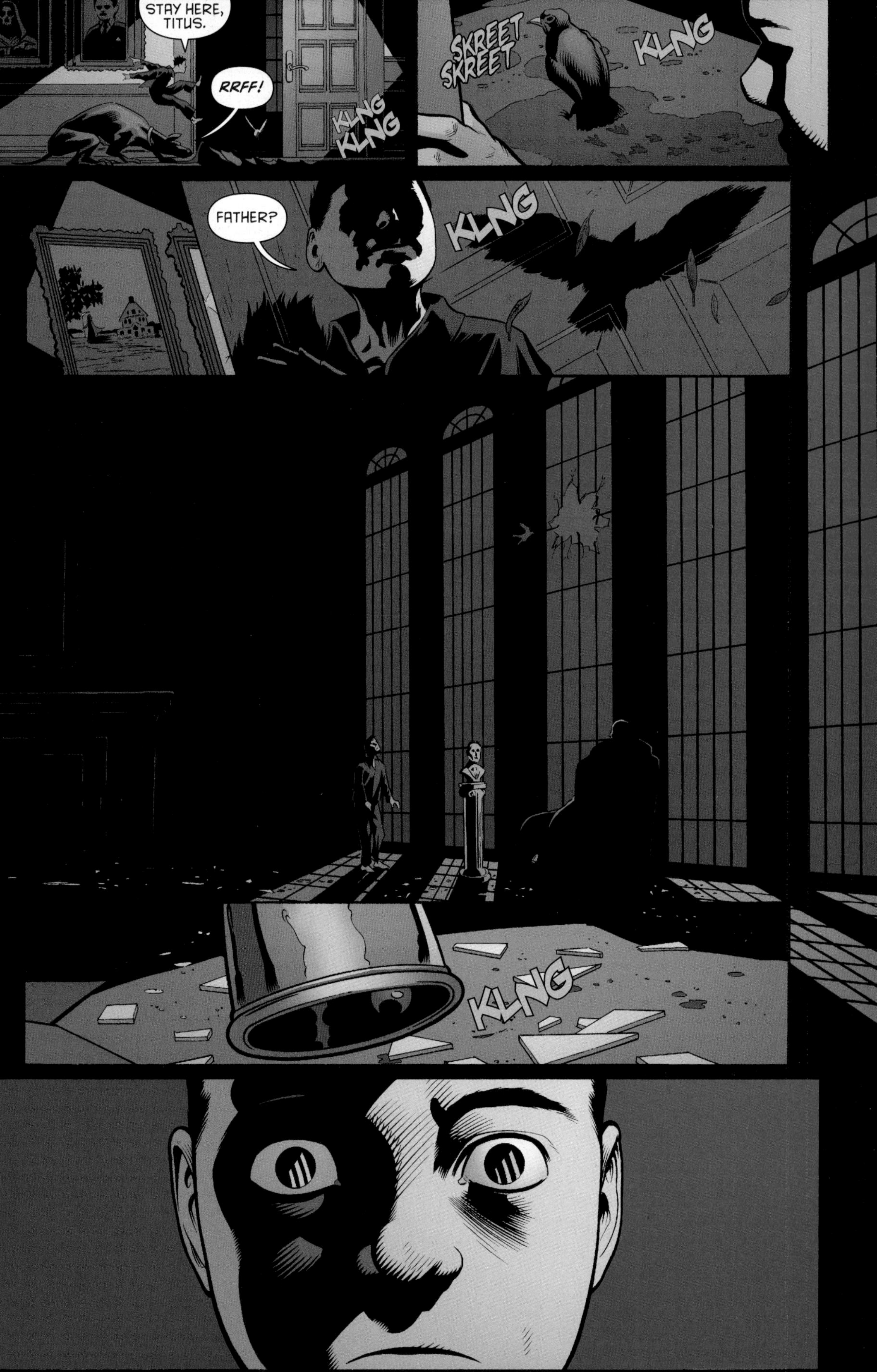
STAY HERE, TITUS.
RRFF!
KLNG KLNG
SKREET SKREET
KLNG
FATHER?
KLNG
KLNG

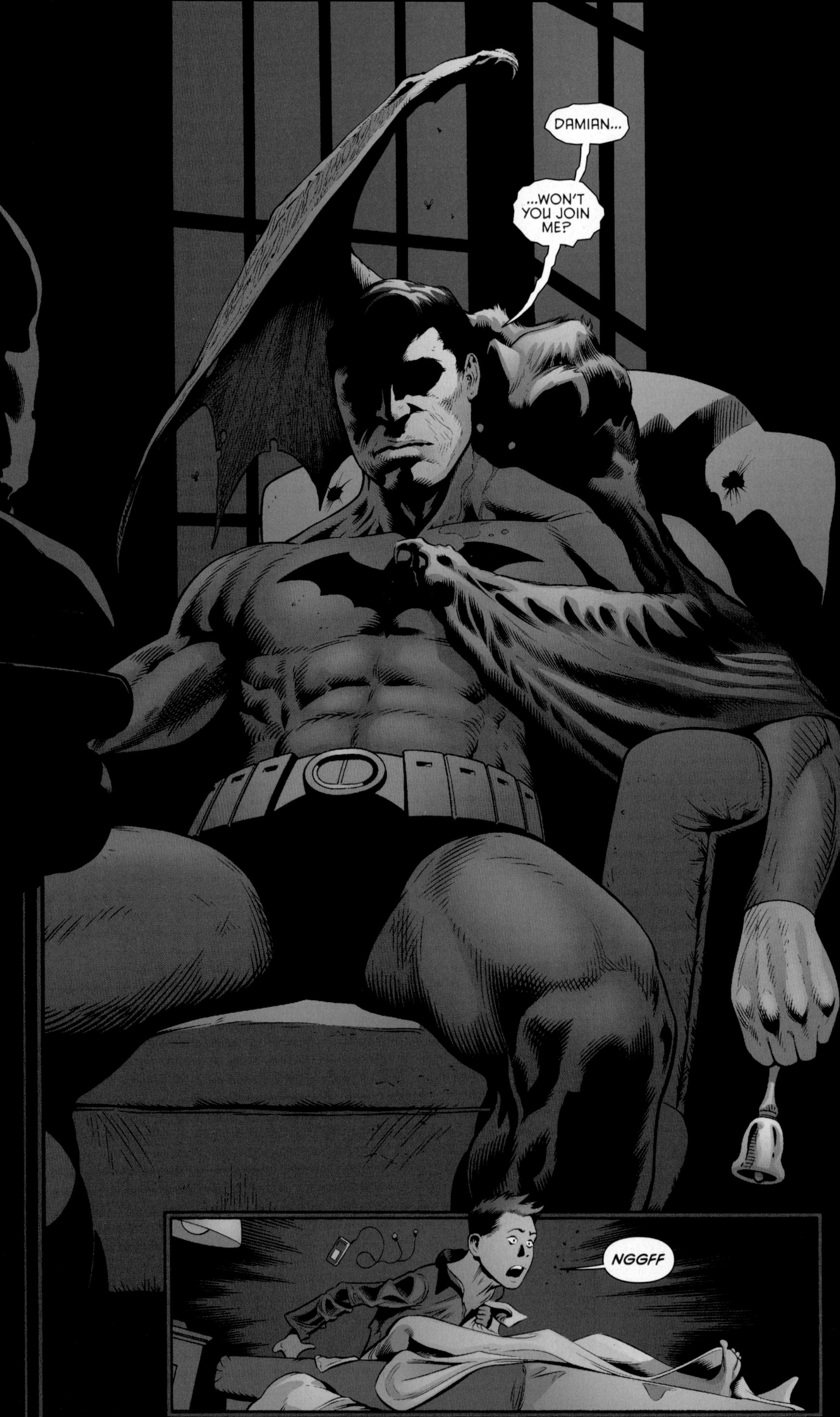
DAMIAN...
...WON'T YOU JOIN ME?
NGGFF

WHAT DO YOU THINK, ALFRED?

QUITE BEAUTIFUL, MASTER THOMAS. WOULD YOU LIKE ME TO WRAP IT?

ARE YOU QUESTIONING MY WRAPPING SKILLS?

ACTUALLY, THERE'S NO QUESTION THAT FOR SUCH A TALENTED SURGEON, YOU HAVE NO GIFT-WRAPPING ABILITY WHATSOEVER.

THEN SAVE ME FROM MYSELF, MISTER PENNYWORTH.

SAVE YOU, I SHALL, SIR.

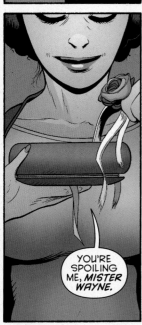

YOU'RE SPOILING ME, MISTER WAYNE.

I BELIEVE THAT'S MY SACRED DUTY FOR THE NEXT FIFTY YEARS OR SO, MRS. WAYNE.

WE LEAVING YET, DAD?

AND I THINK WE NEED A LITTLE HELPER TO PUT THESE ON.

...TOUGH TO FIT INTO THE LOOP...

GOOD JOB, BRUCE. YOUR HANDS ARE STEADIER THAN MINE.

NOTHING LIKE A NIGHT ON THE TOWN WITH MY HANDSOME BOYS.

MMM?

KRAK KRAK

KRAK KRAK KRAK KRAK

MASTER BRUCE... DAMIAN, DO YOU NEED SOME ASSISTANCE?

KRAK KRAK KRAK

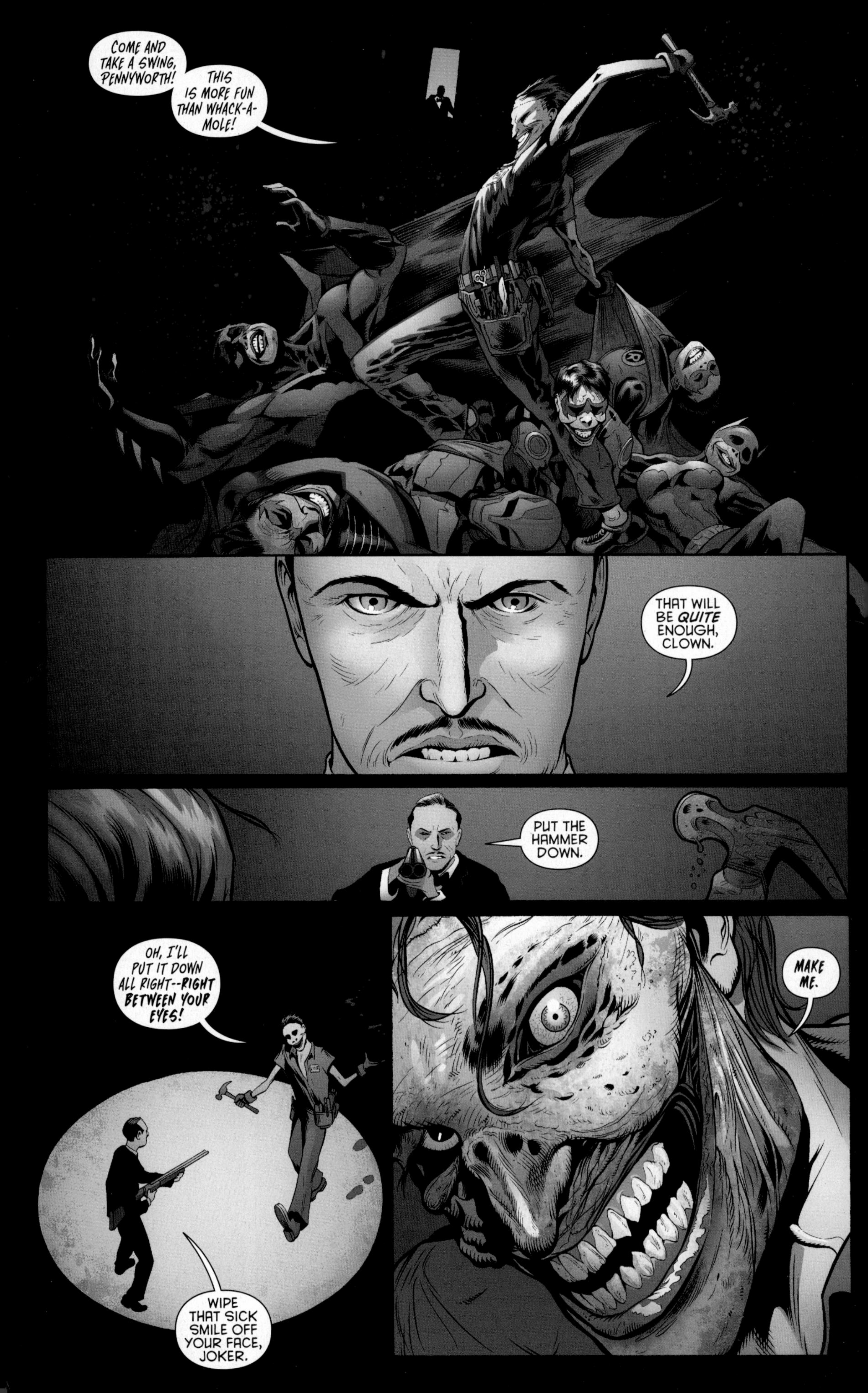
COME AND TAKE A SWING, PENNYWORTH!
THIS IS MORE FUN THAN WHACK-A-MOLE!
THAT WILL BE *QUITE* ENOUGH, CLOWN.
PUT THE HAMMER DOWN.
OH, I'LL PUT IT DOWN ALL RIGHT--**RIGHT BETWEEN YOUR EYES!**
WIPE THAT SICK SMILE OFF YOUR FACE, JOKER.
MAKE ME.

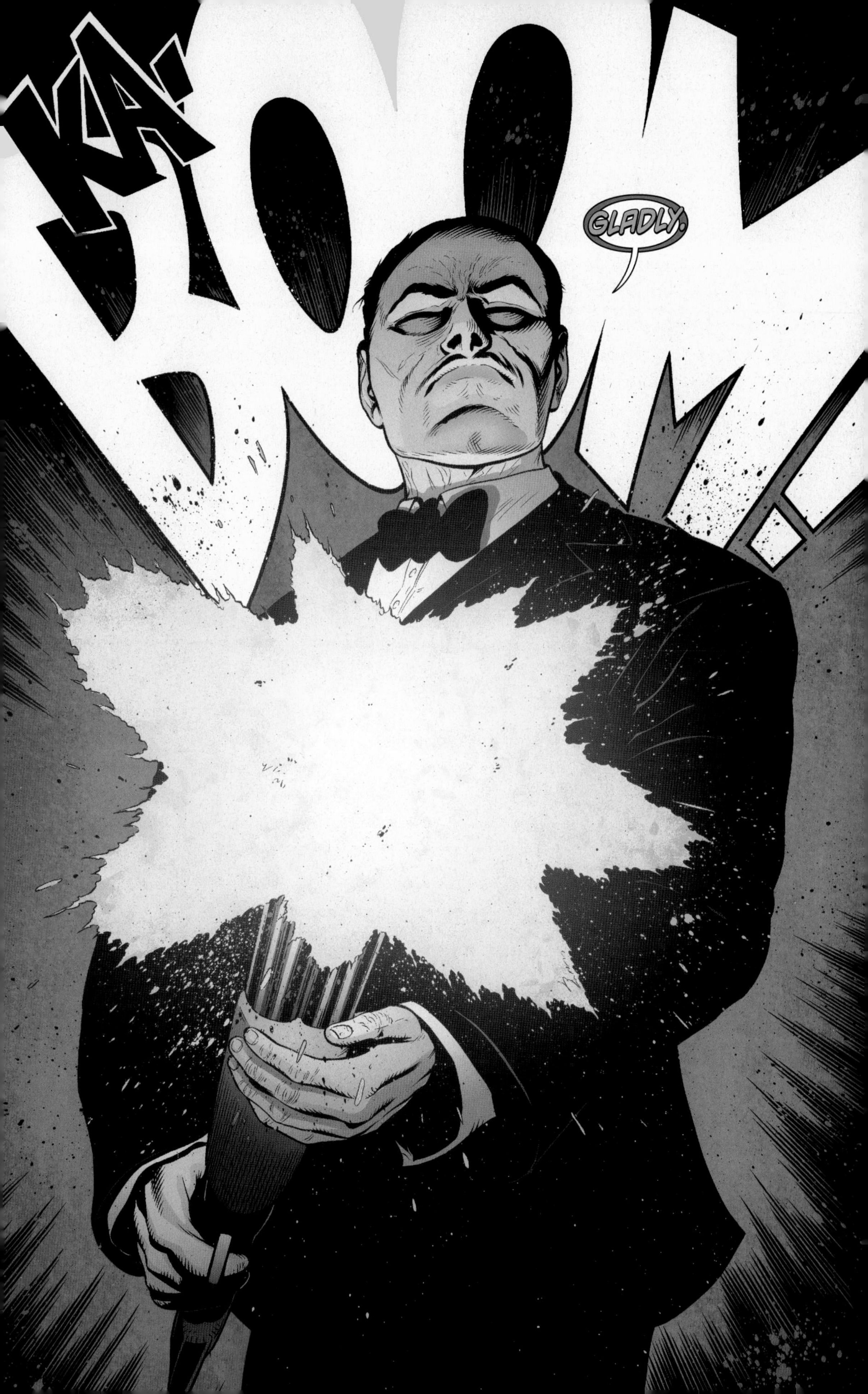
KA-BOOM!
GLADLY.

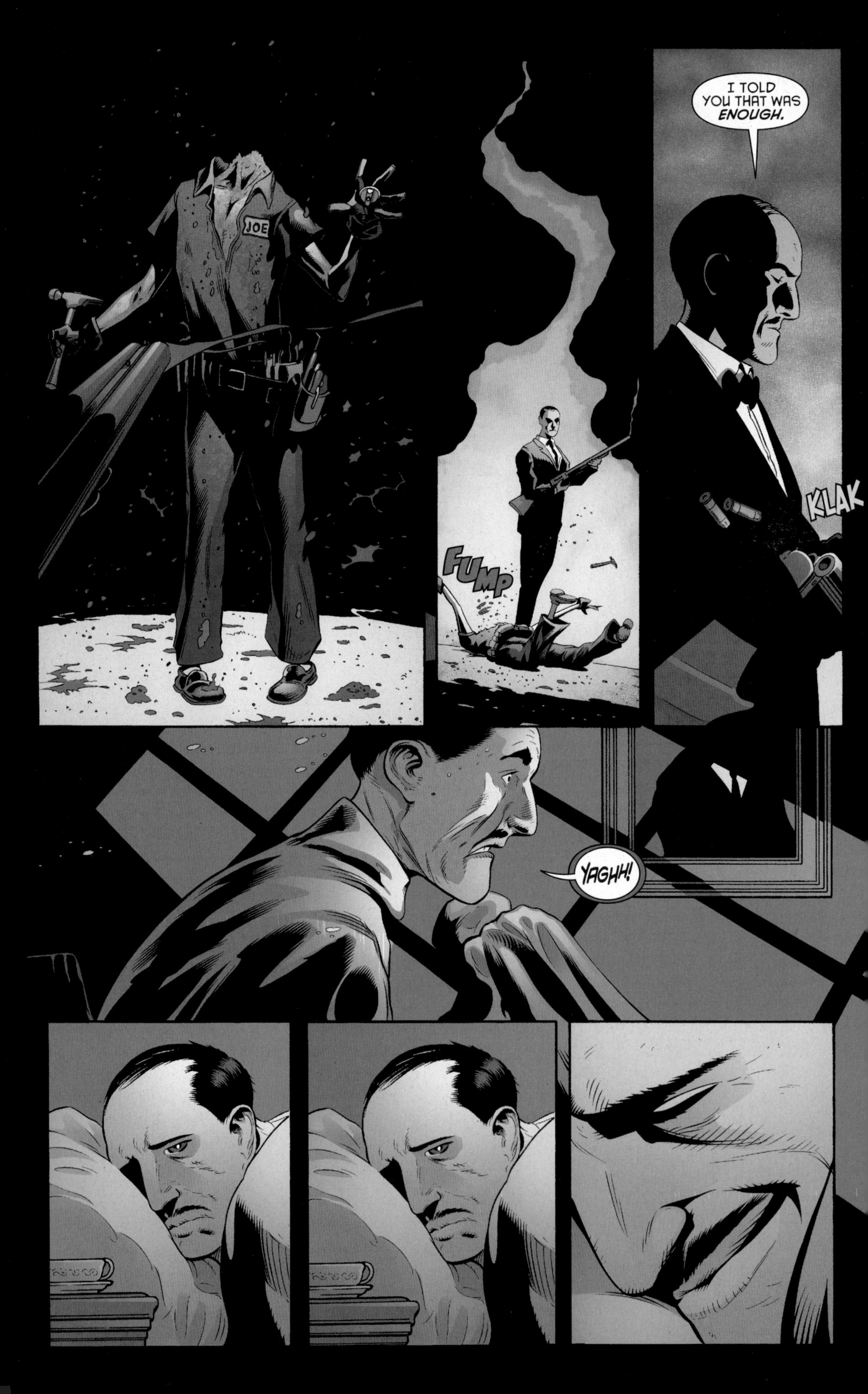
JOE
I TOLD YOU THAT WAS ENOUGH.
FUMP
KLAK
YAGHH!

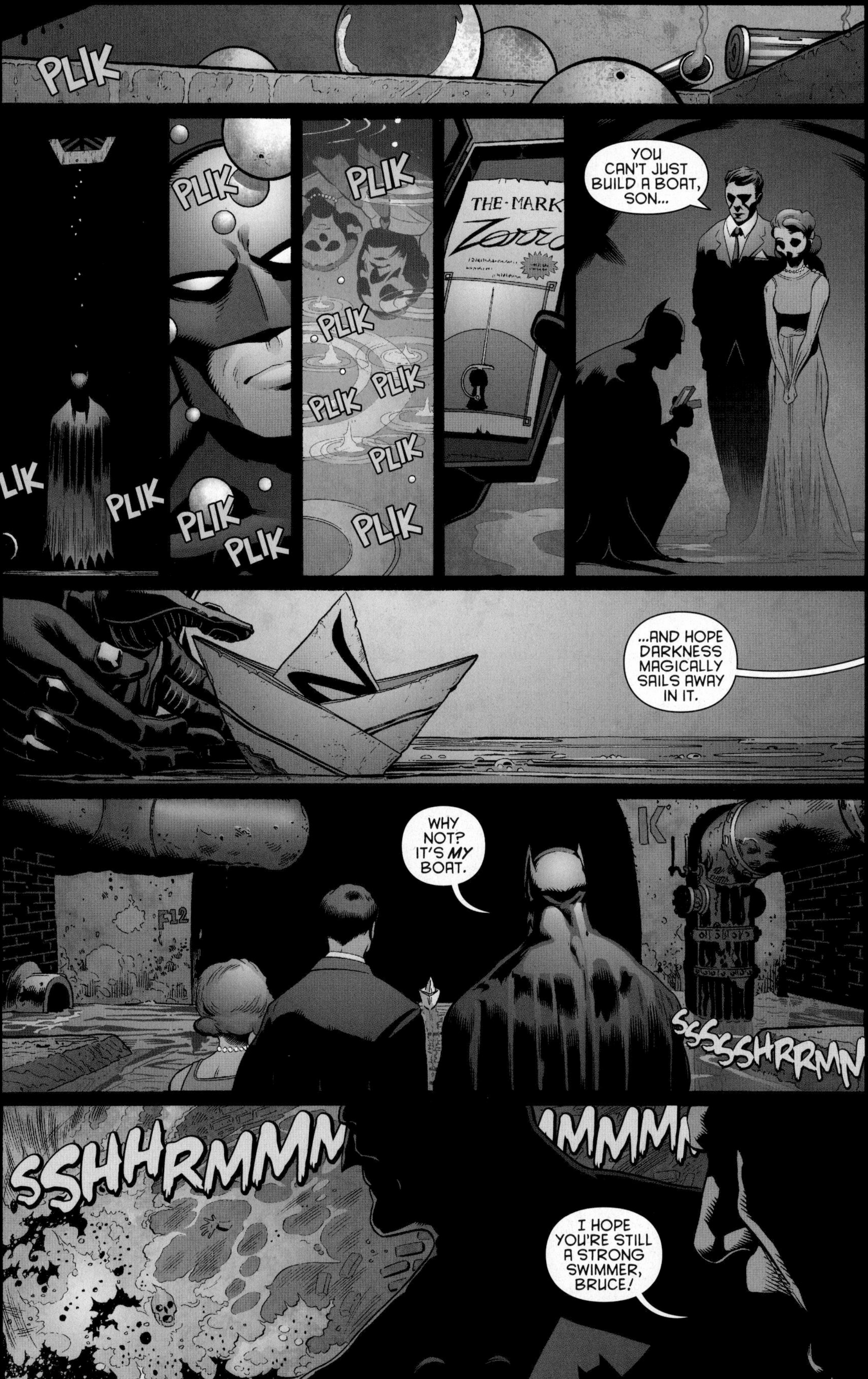
PLIK
PLIK
PLIK
PLIK
PLIK
PLIK
PLIK
PLIK
PLIK
PLIK
PLIK
PLIK
THE-MARK
Zorro
YOU CAN'T JUST BUILD A BOAT, SON...
...AND HOPE DARKNESS MAGICALLY SAILS AWAY IN IT.
WHY NOT? IT'S *MY* BOAT.
F12
SSSSSSHRRMN
SSHHRMMMN
MMMMN
I HOPE YOU'RE STILL A STRONG SWIMMER, BRUCE!

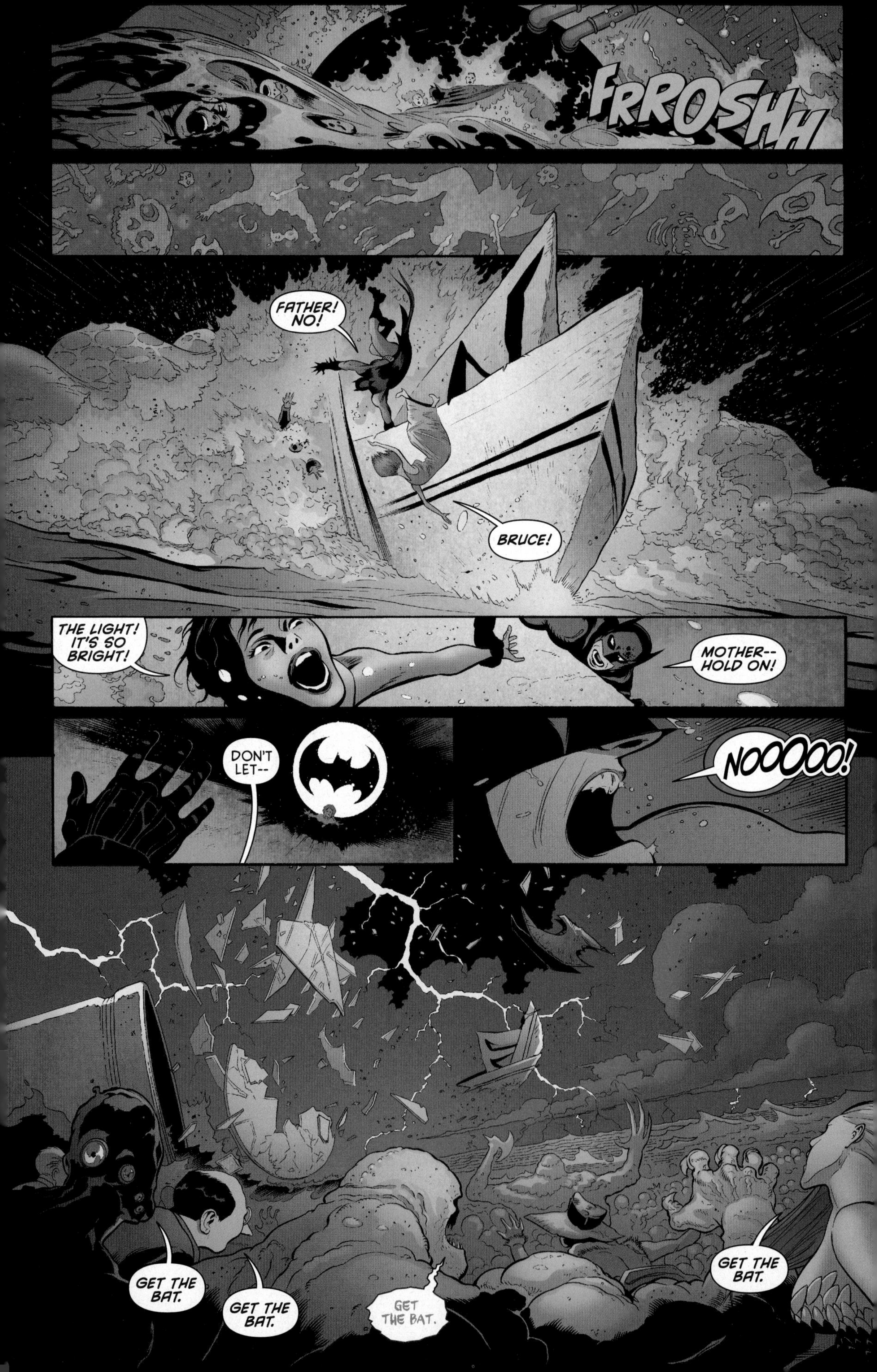
FRROSHH
FATHER! NO!
BRUCE!
THE LIGHT! IT'S SO BRIGHT!
MOTHER-- HOLD ON!
DON'T LET--
NOOOOO!
GET THE BAT.
GET THE BAT.
GET THE BAT.
GET THE BAT.

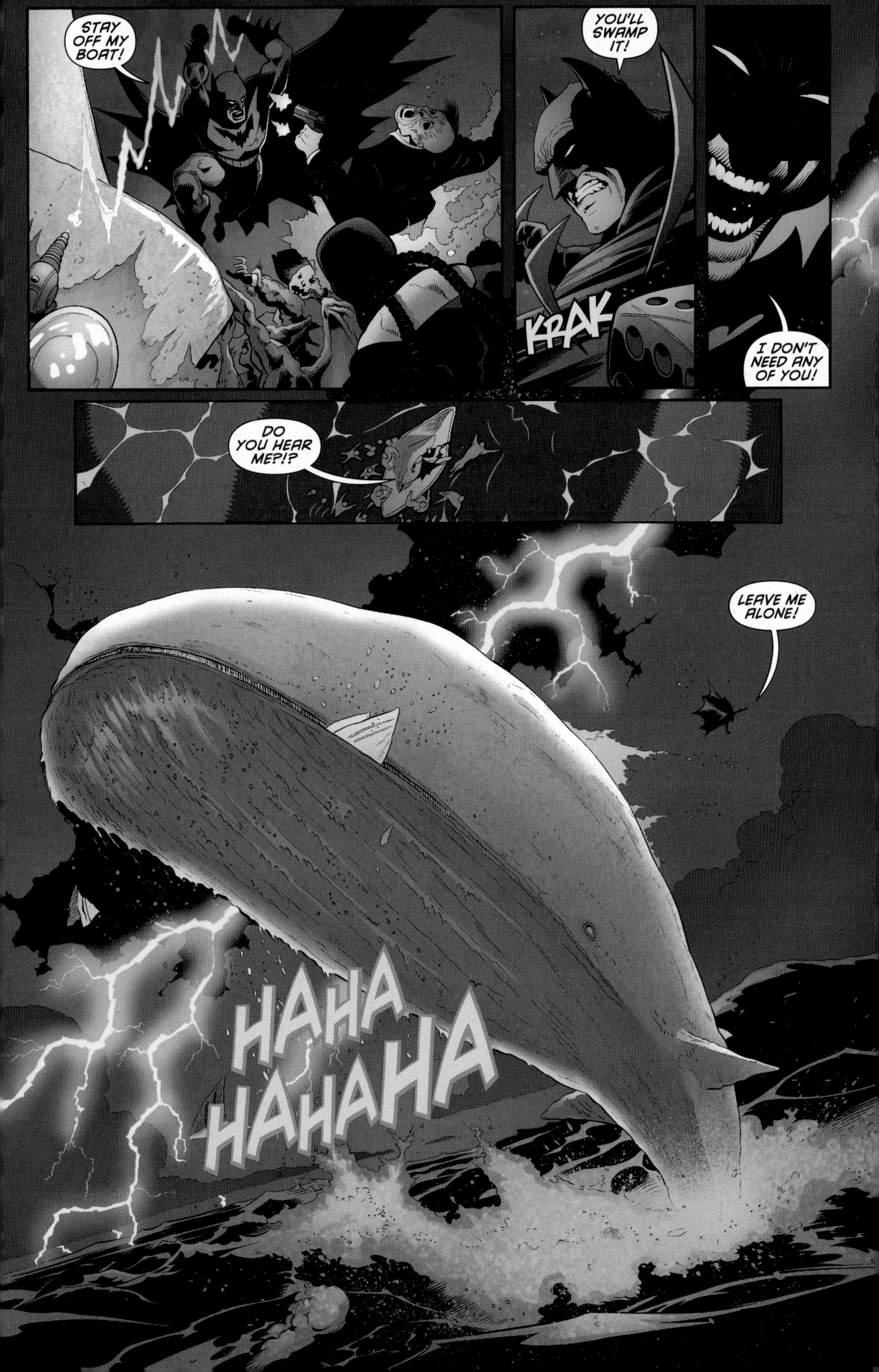
STAY OFF MY BOAT!
YOU'LL SWAMP IT!
KRAK
I DON'T NEED ANY OF YOU!
DO YOU HEAR ME?!?
LEAVE ME ALONE!
HAHA HAHAHA

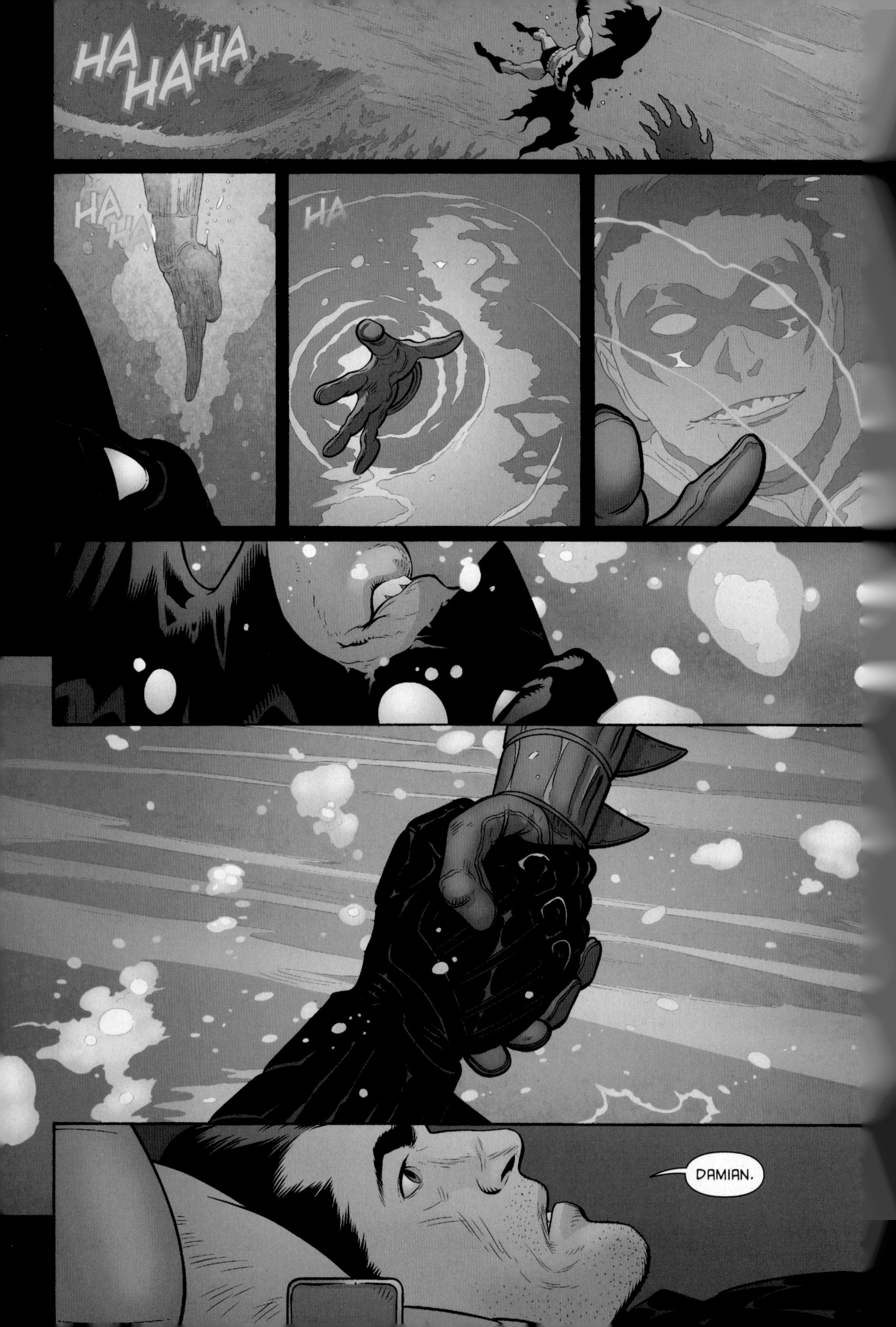
HA HA HA HA
HA HA
HA
DAMIAN.

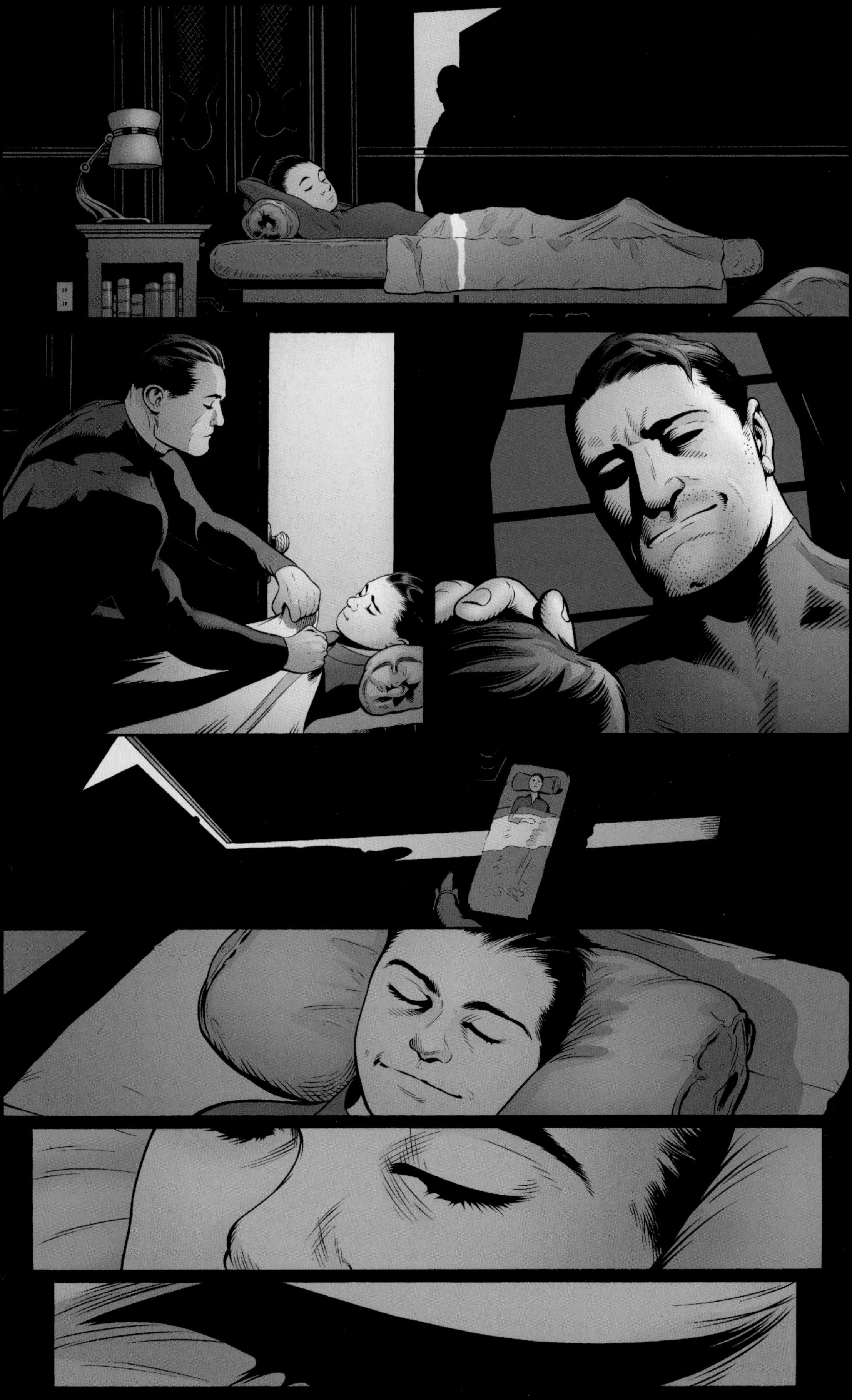

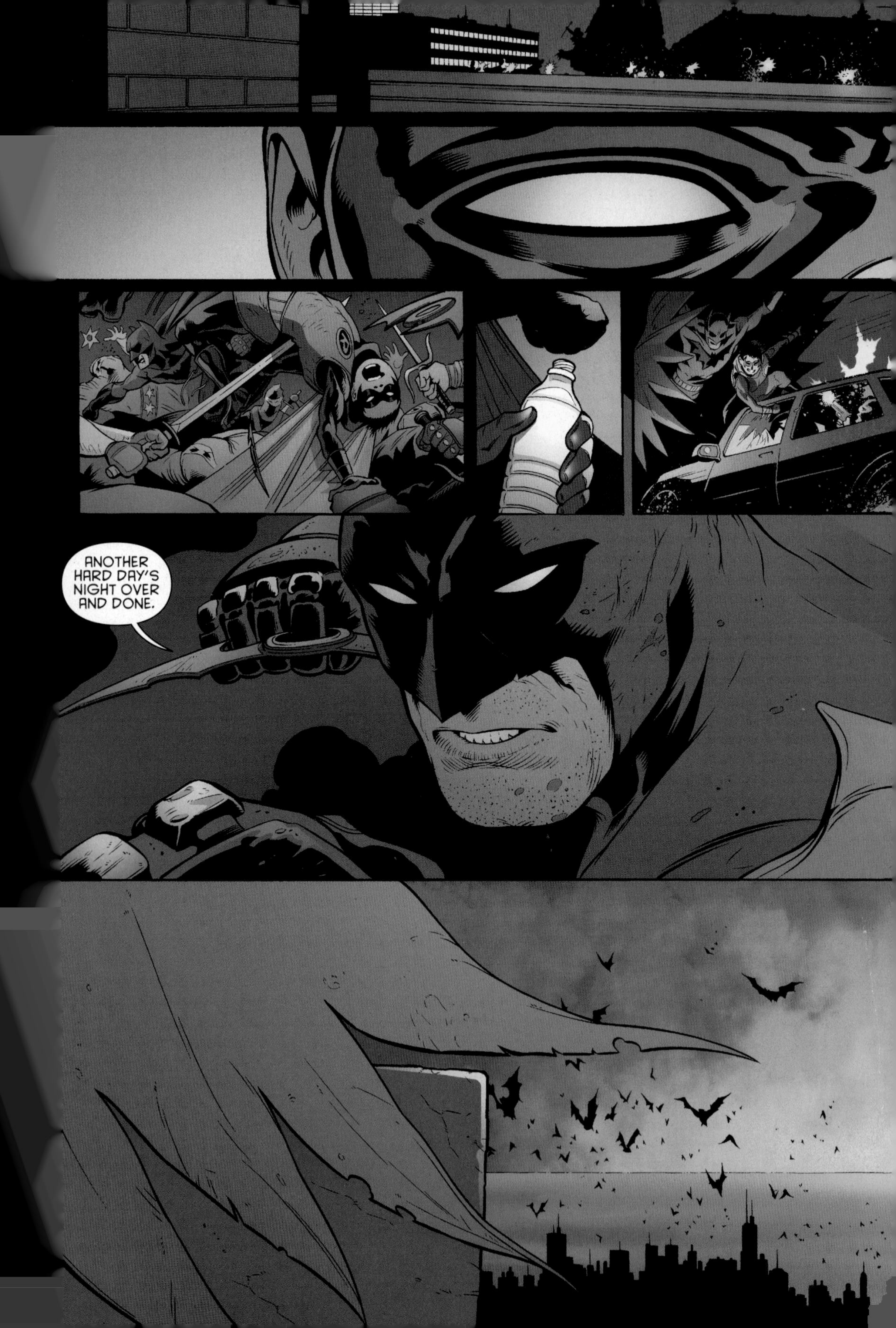
ANOTHER HARD DAY'S NIGHT OVER AND DONE.

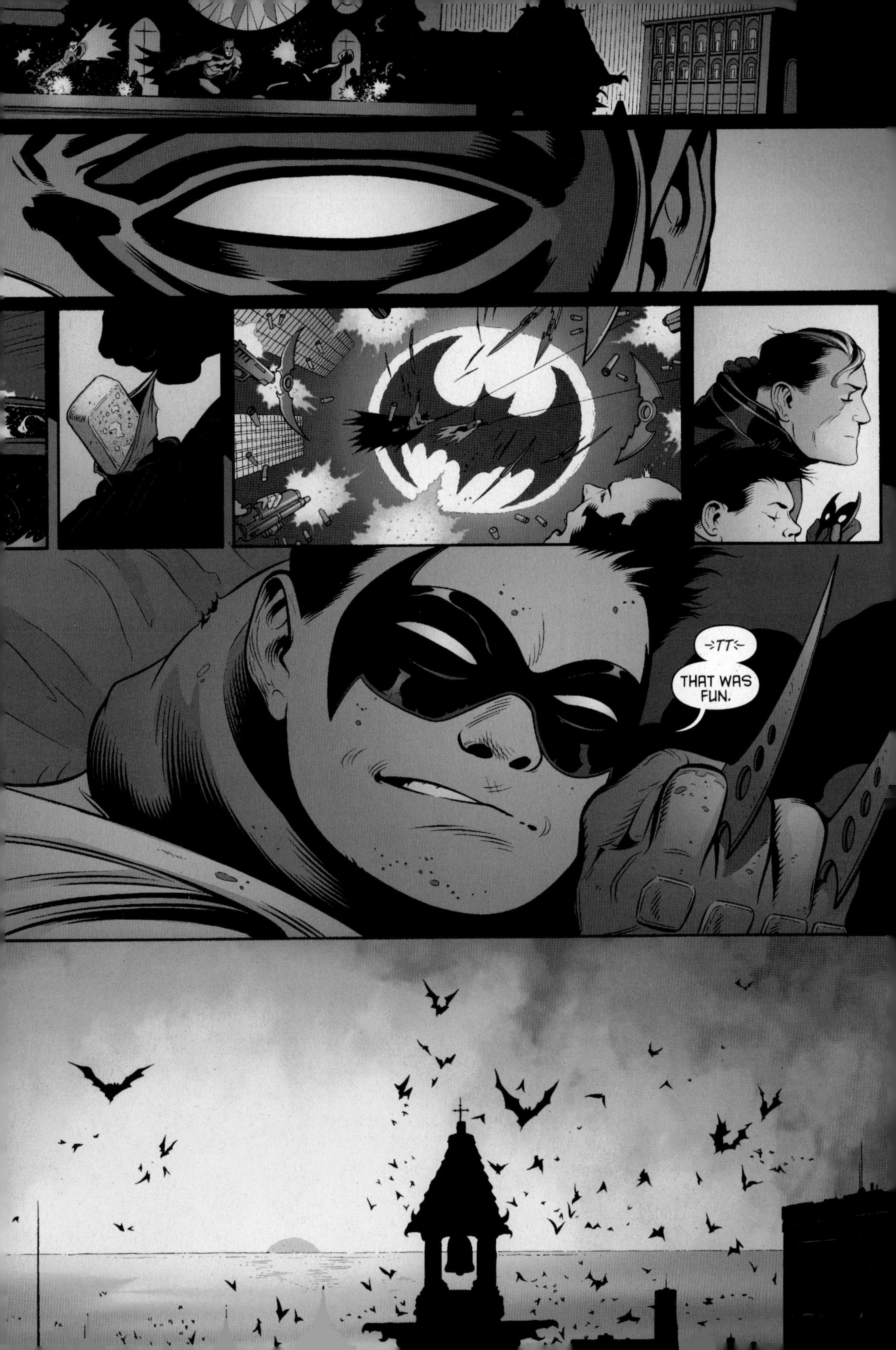
-TT-
THAT WAS FUN.

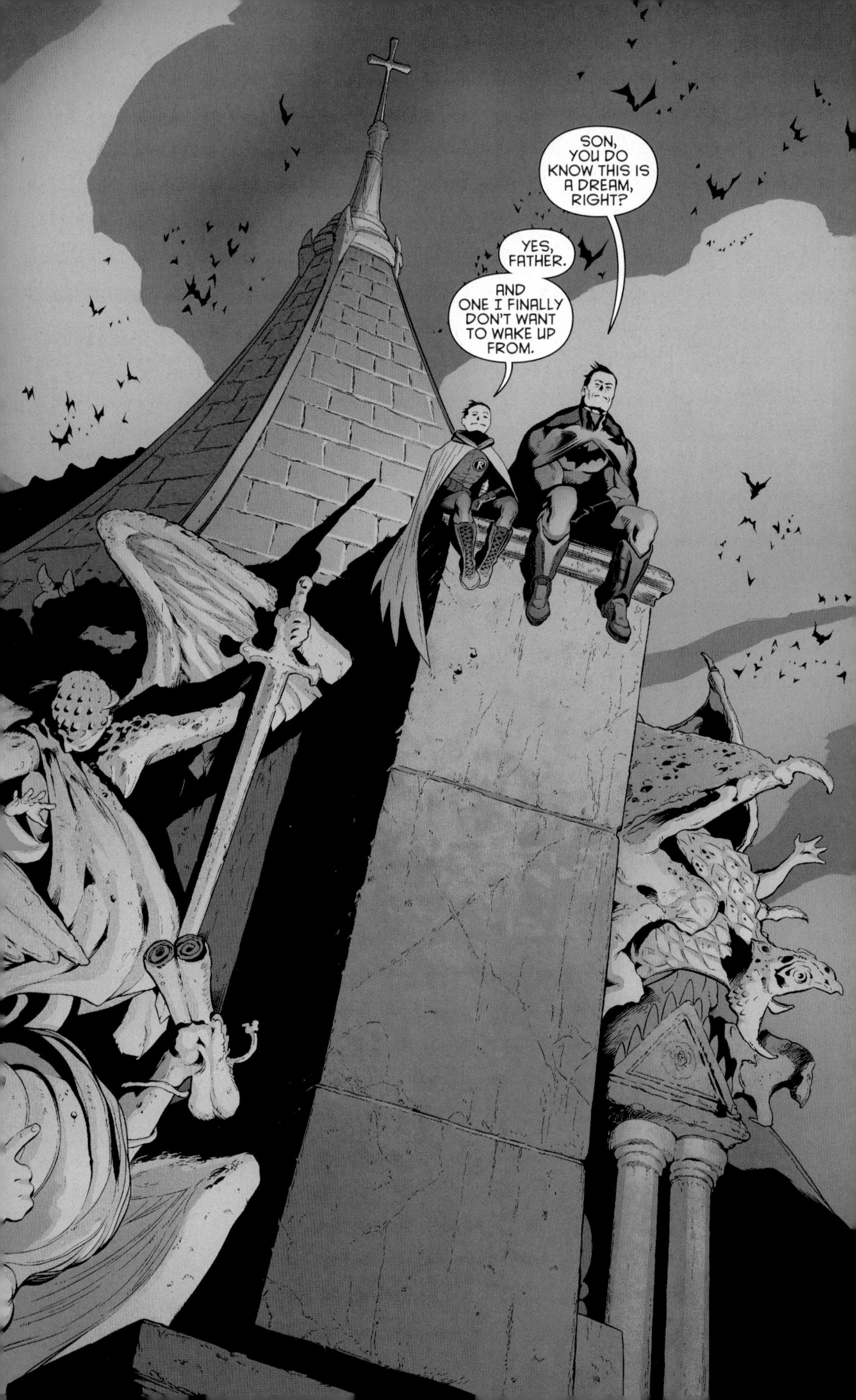
SON, YOU DO KNOW THIS IS A DREAM, RIGHT?
YES, FATHER.
AND ONE I FINALLY DON'T WANT TO WAKE UP FROM.

DETECTIVE COMICS #15 unused cover by **JASON FABOK & JEROMY COX**

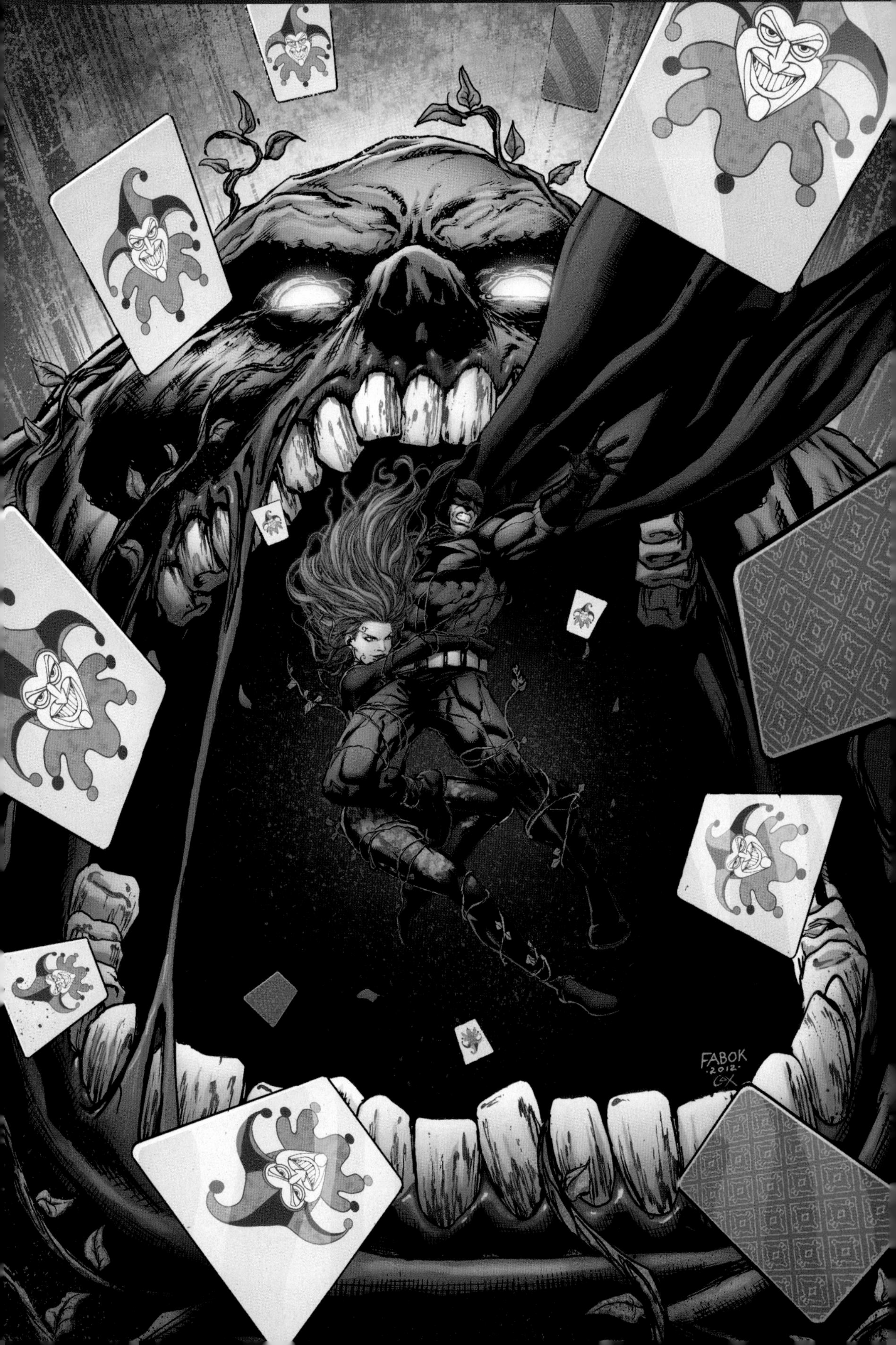
FABOK
·2012·
COX

DETECTIVE COMICS #16 cover by **JASON FABOK** & **JEROMY COX**

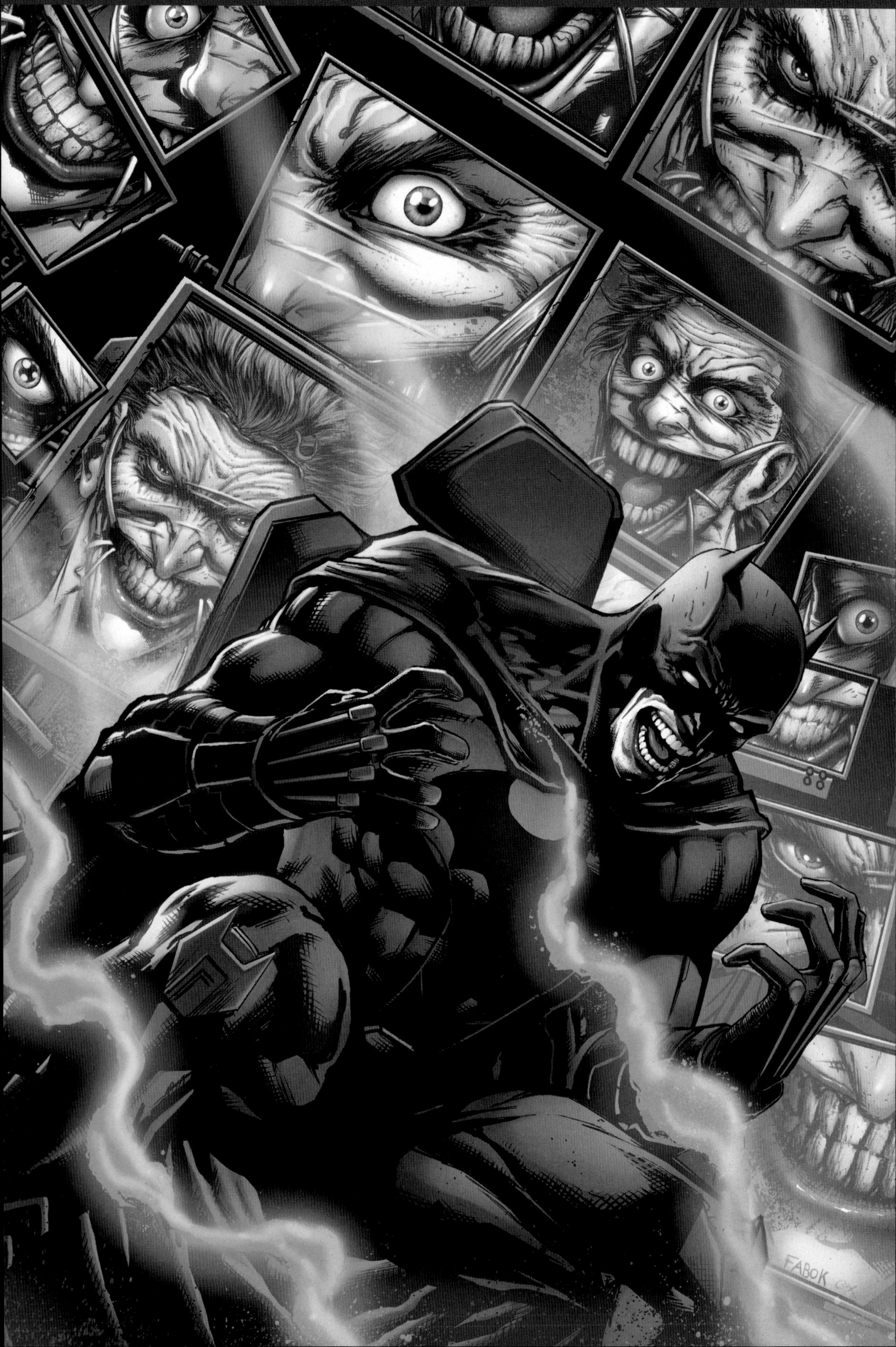
FABOK COX

DETECTIVE COMICS #17 cover by **JASON FABOK** & **JEROMY COX**

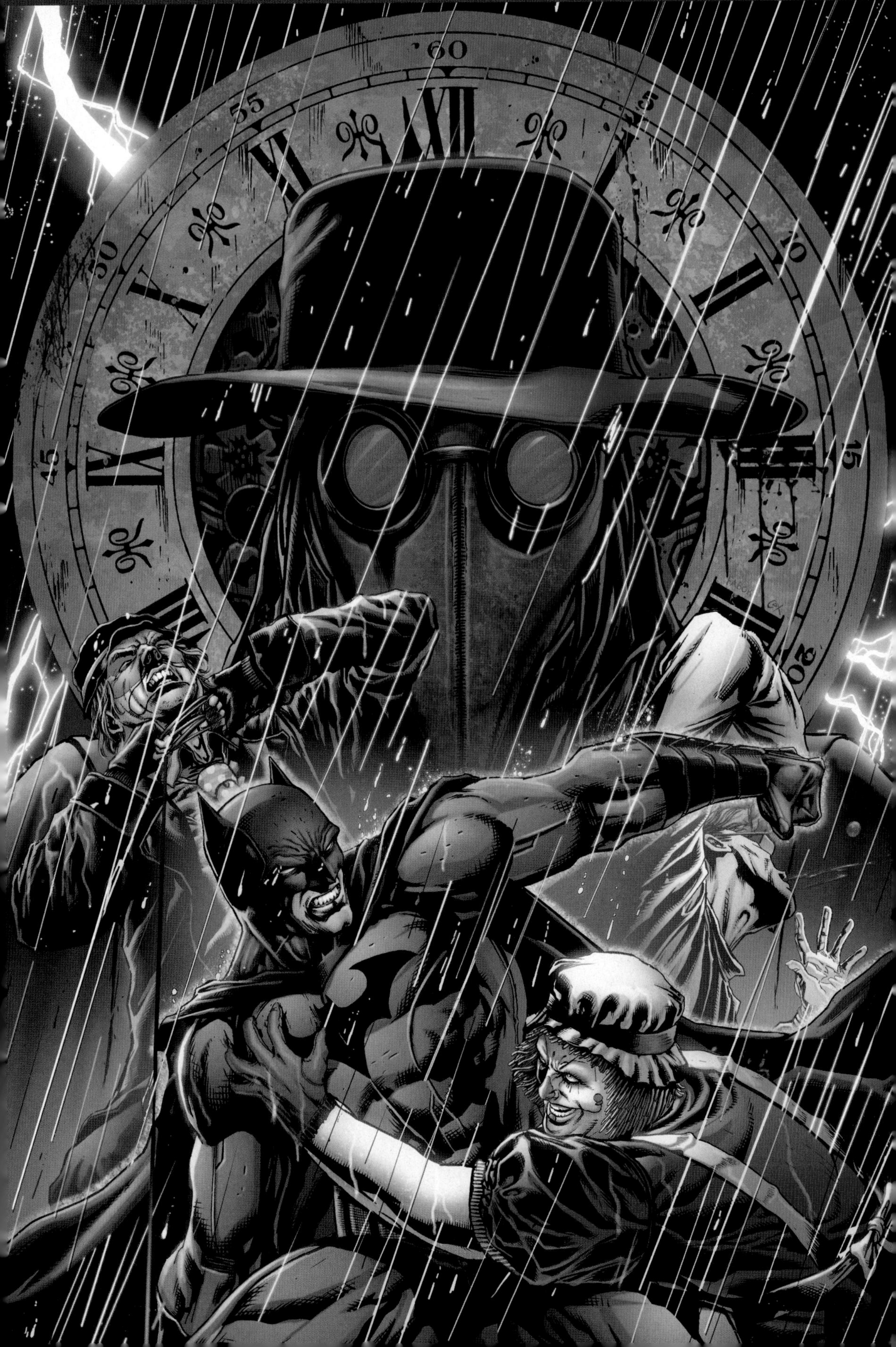

CATWOMAN #13 variant cover by **ANDY CLARKE**

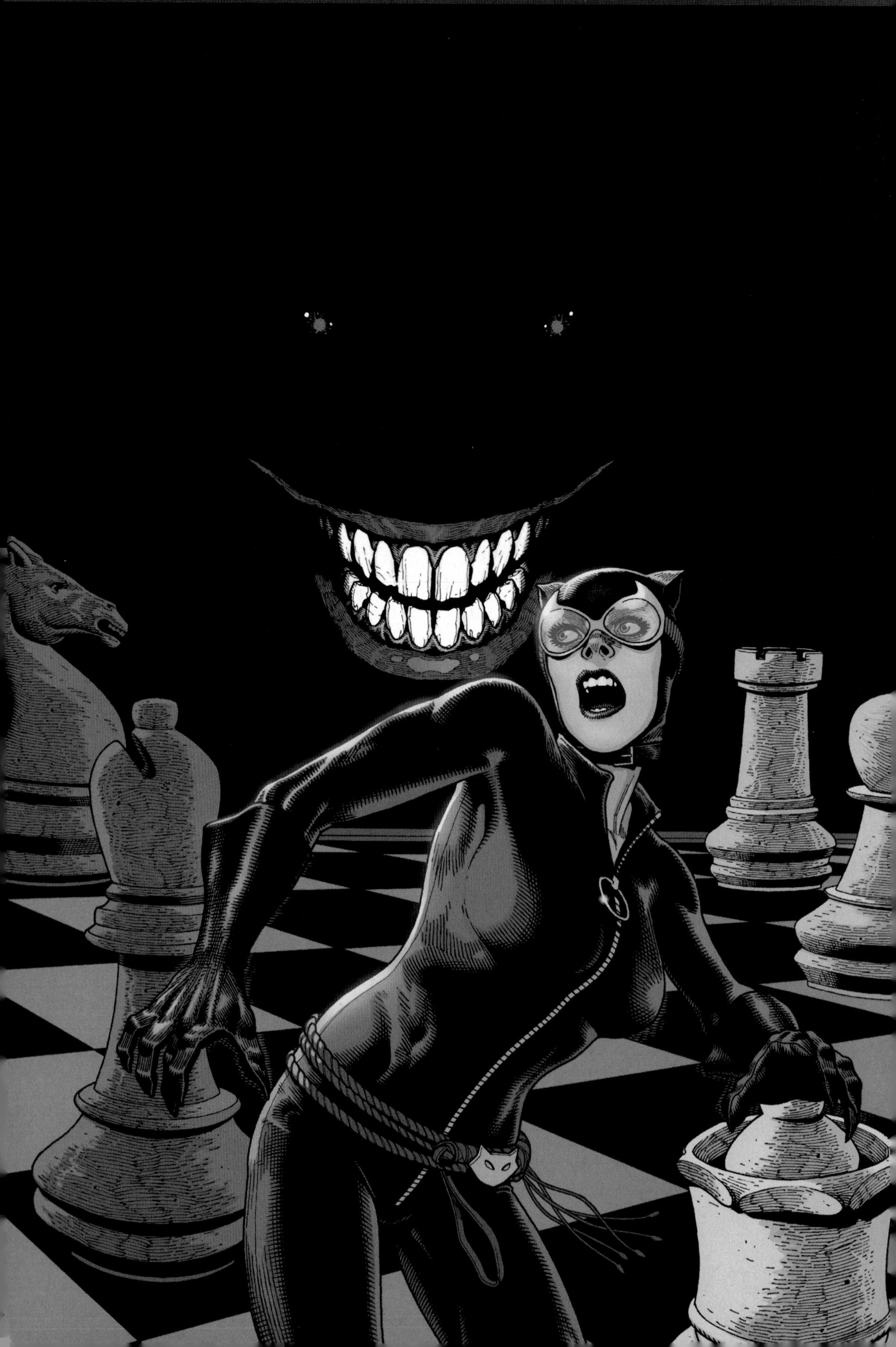

CATWOMAN #14 cover by TREVOR McCARTHY

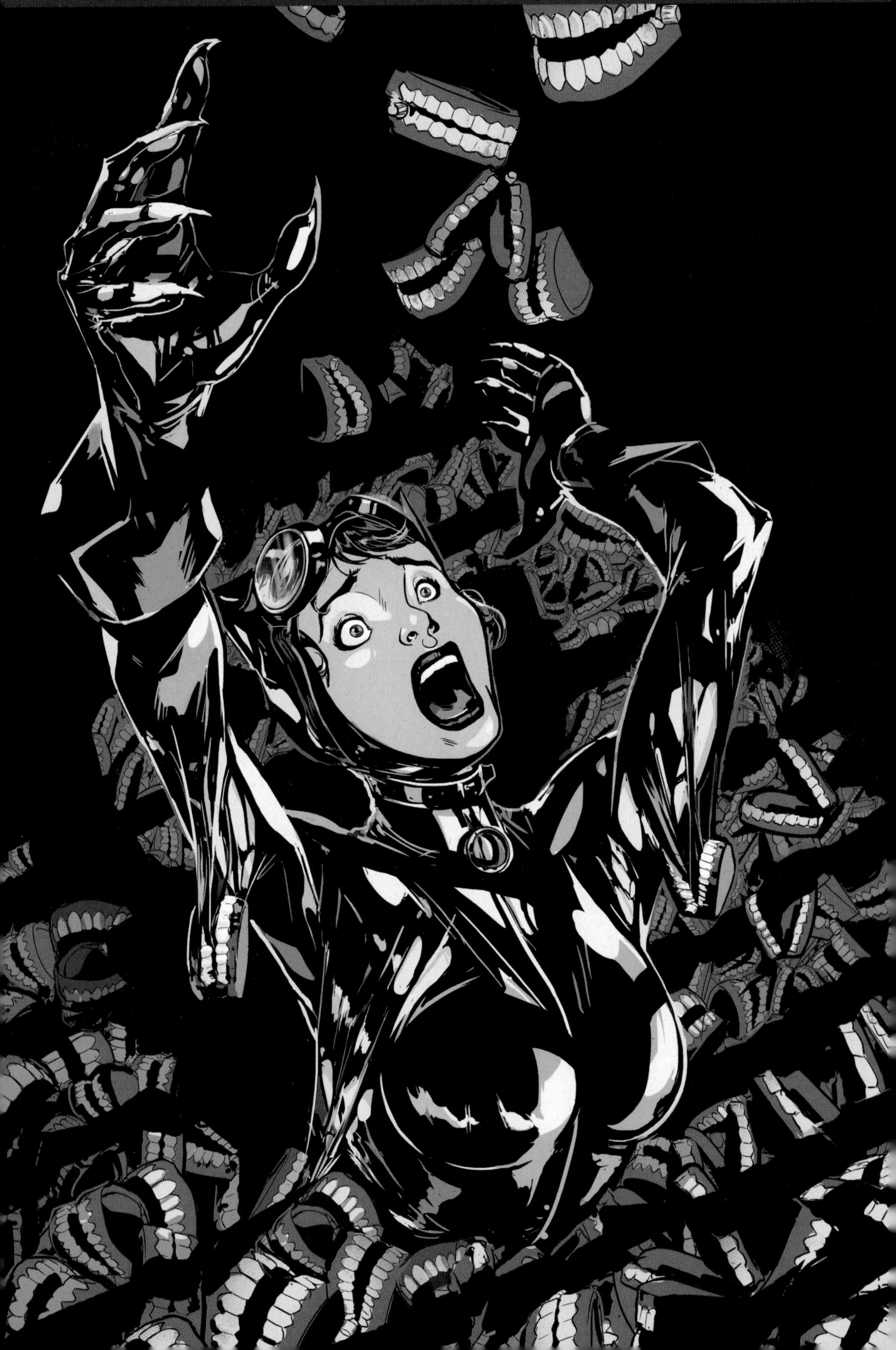

SUICIDE SQUAD #14 variant cover by **KEN LASHLEY & MATT YACKEY**

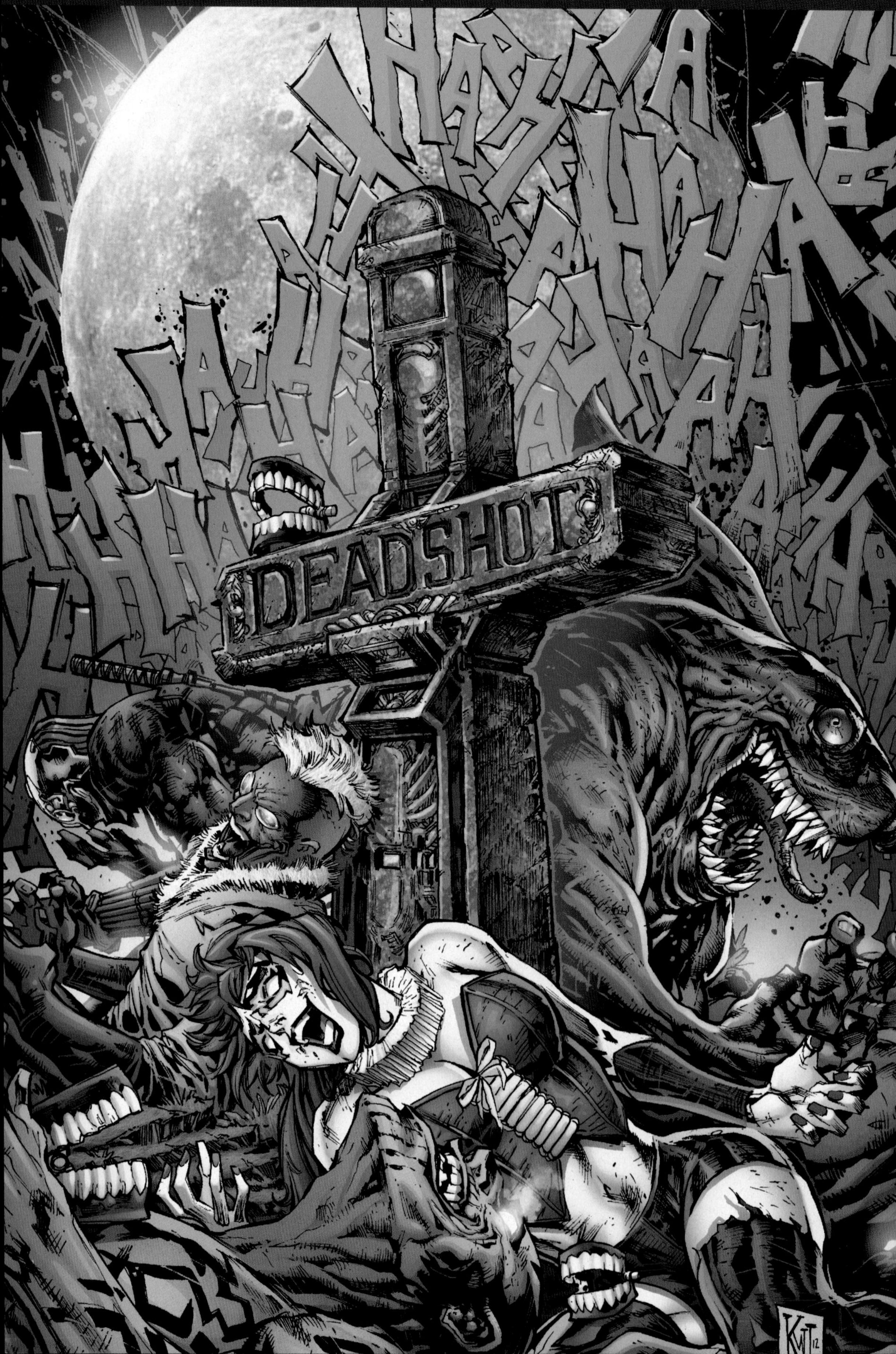
DEADSHOT

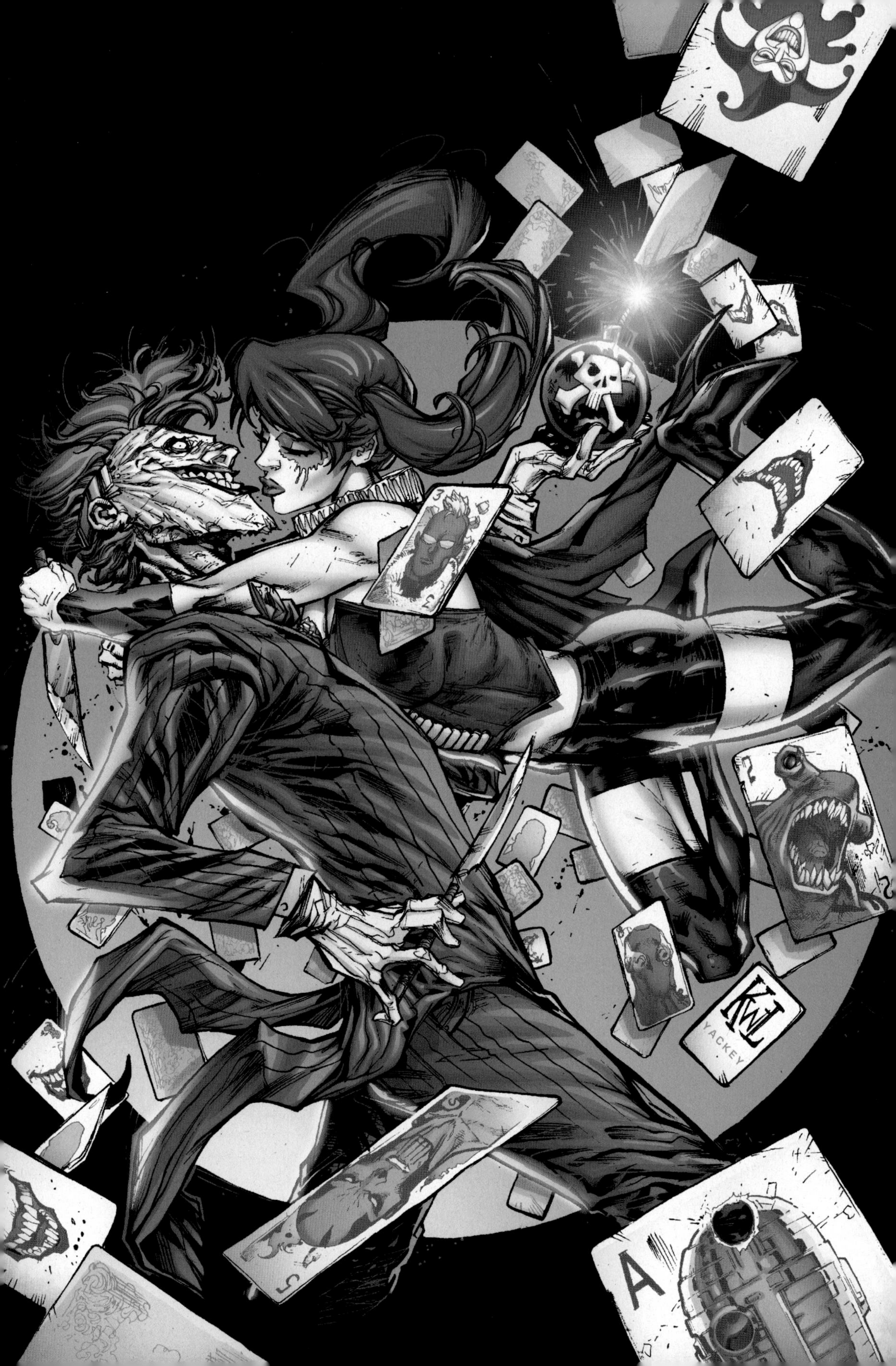
YACKEY

BATGIRL #14 cover by **ED BENES & ULISES ARREOLA**

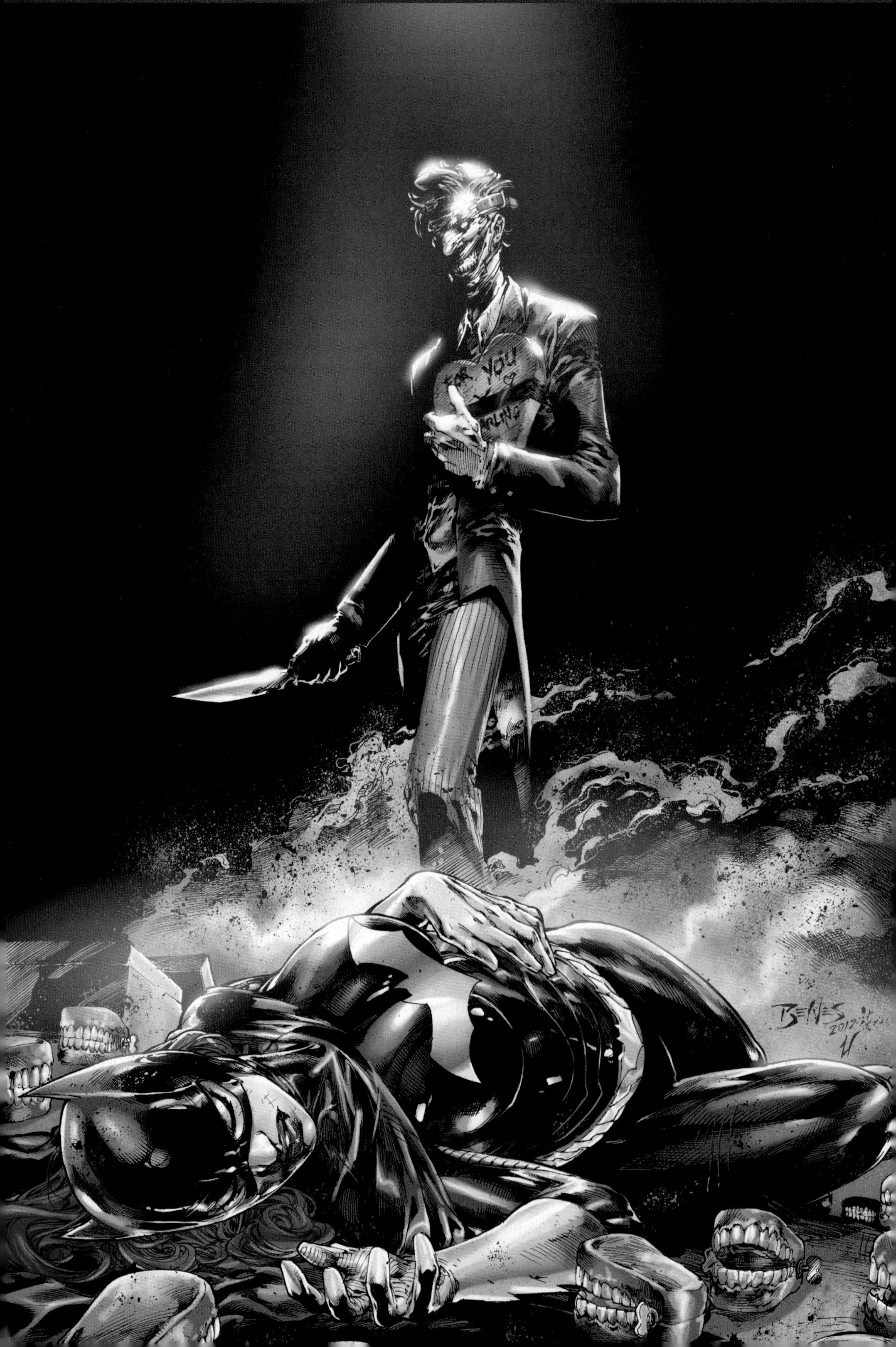

BATGIRL #15 cover by **ED BENES & ULISES ARREOLA**

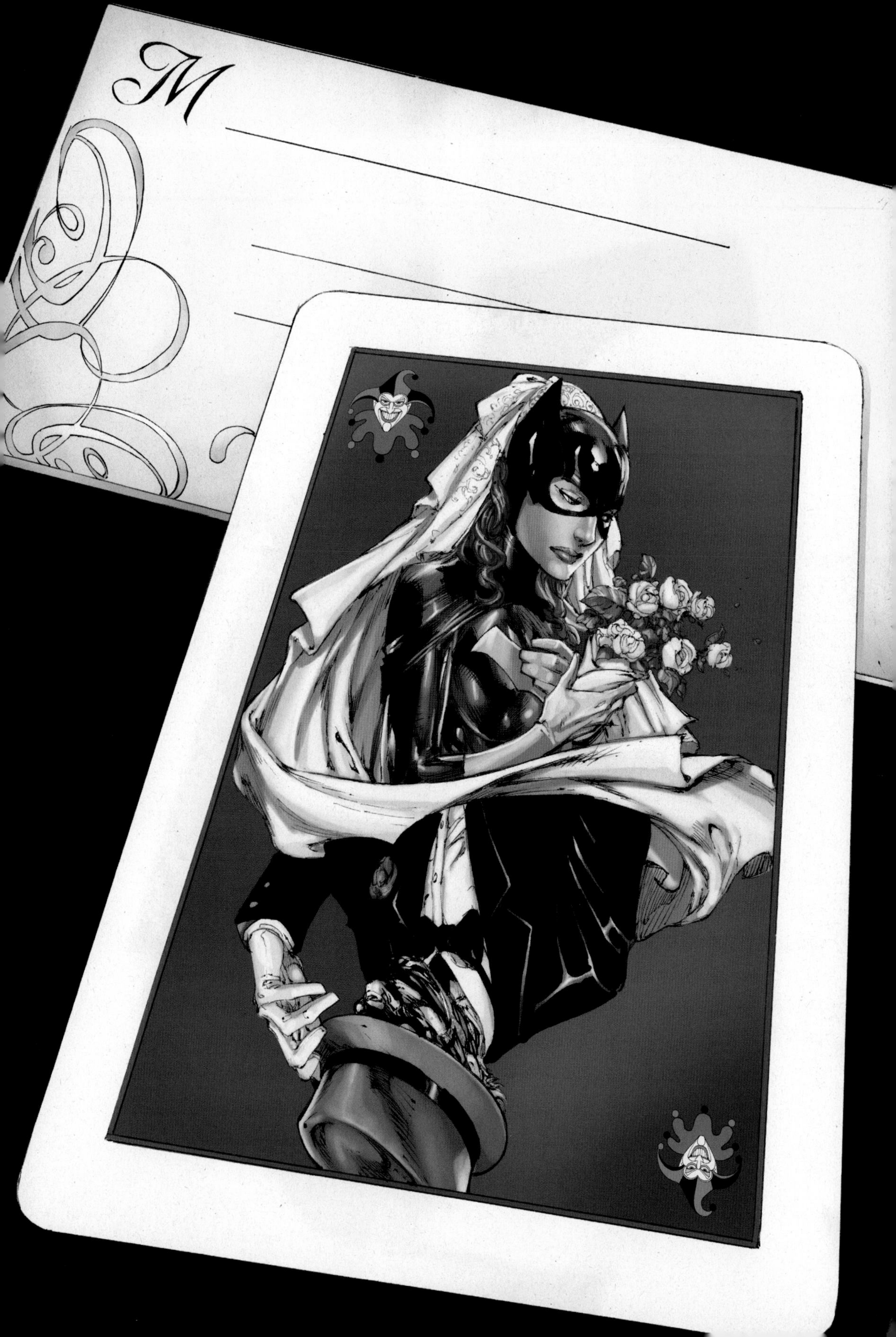

BATGIRL #16 cover by **ED BENES & ULISES ARREOLA**

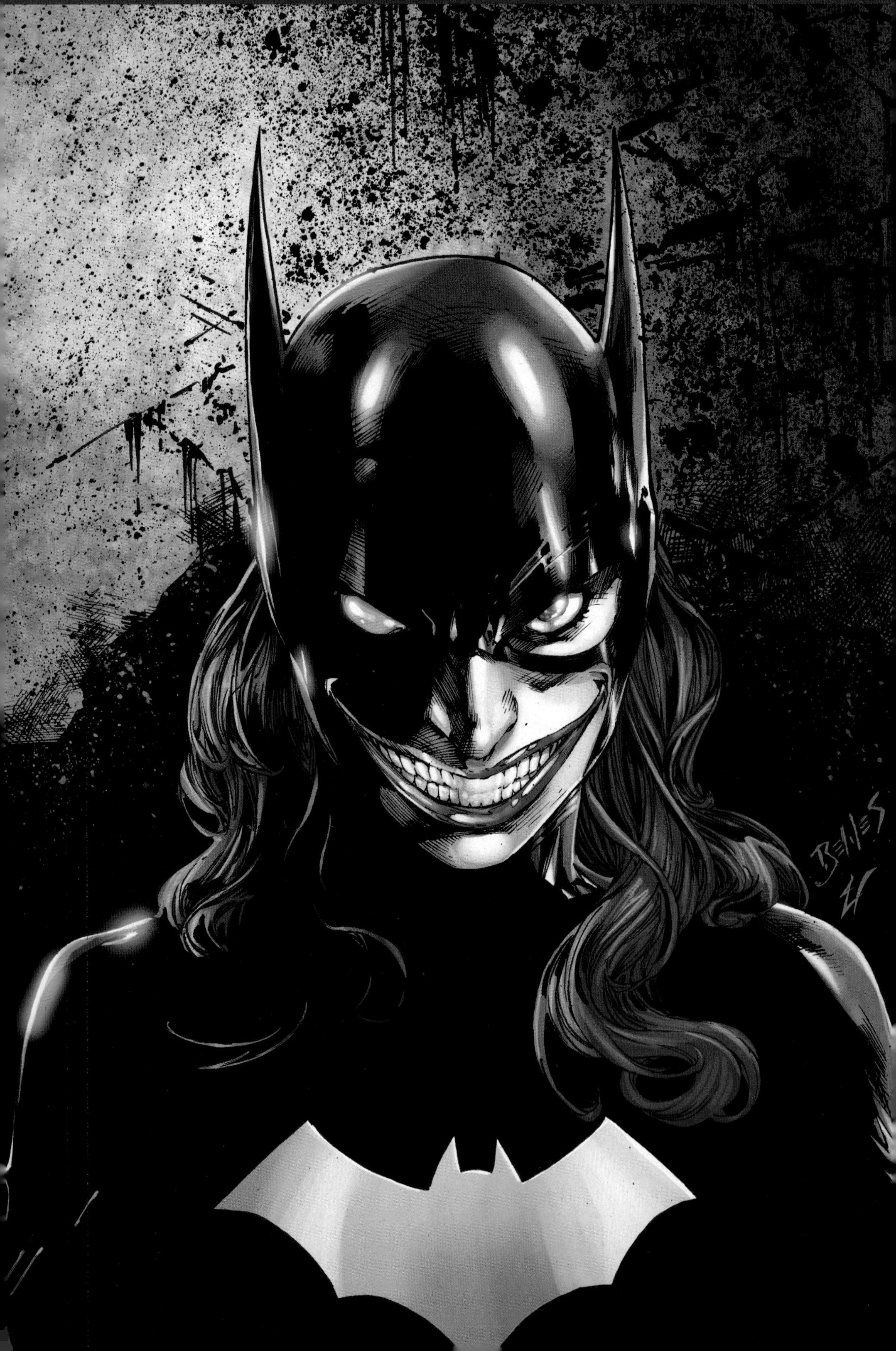

RED HOOD #15 unused cover by **BRETT BOOTH, NORM RAPMUND & ROD REIS**

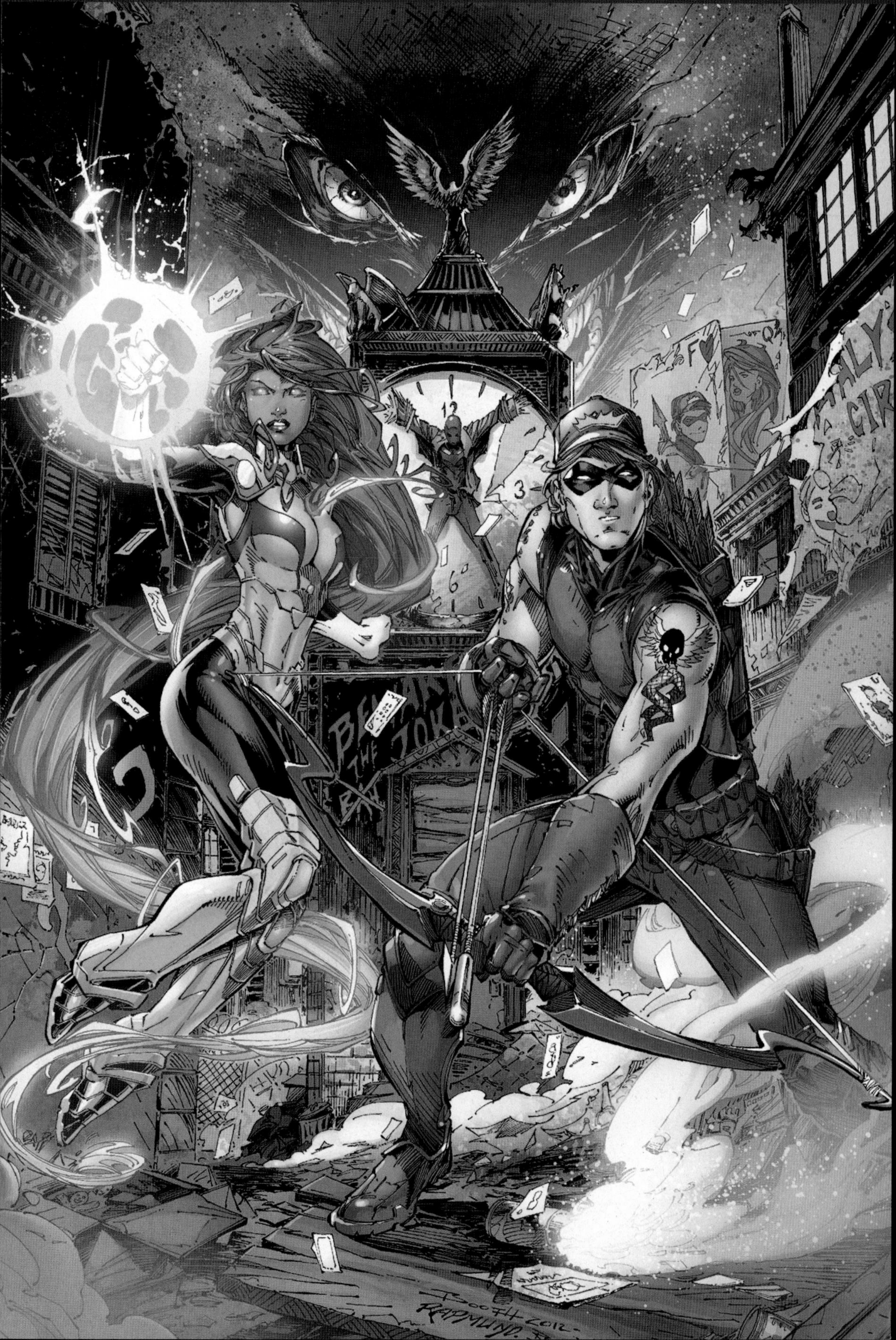

RED HOOD #16 cover by **TYLER KIRKHAM, BATT & ALEX SINCLAIR**

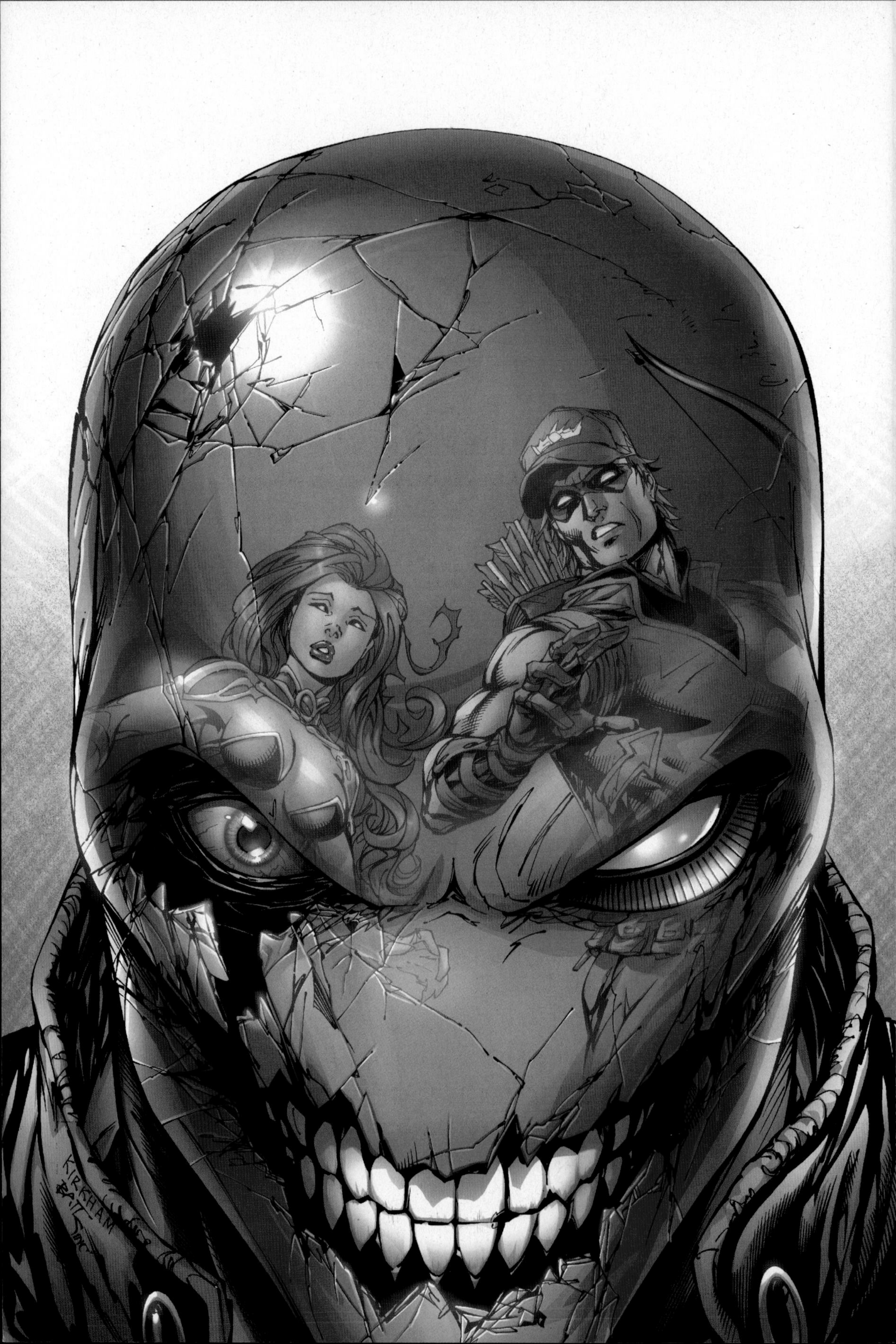

TEEN TITANS #15 unused cover by BRETT BOOTH, MARK IRWIN & ANDREW DALHOUSE

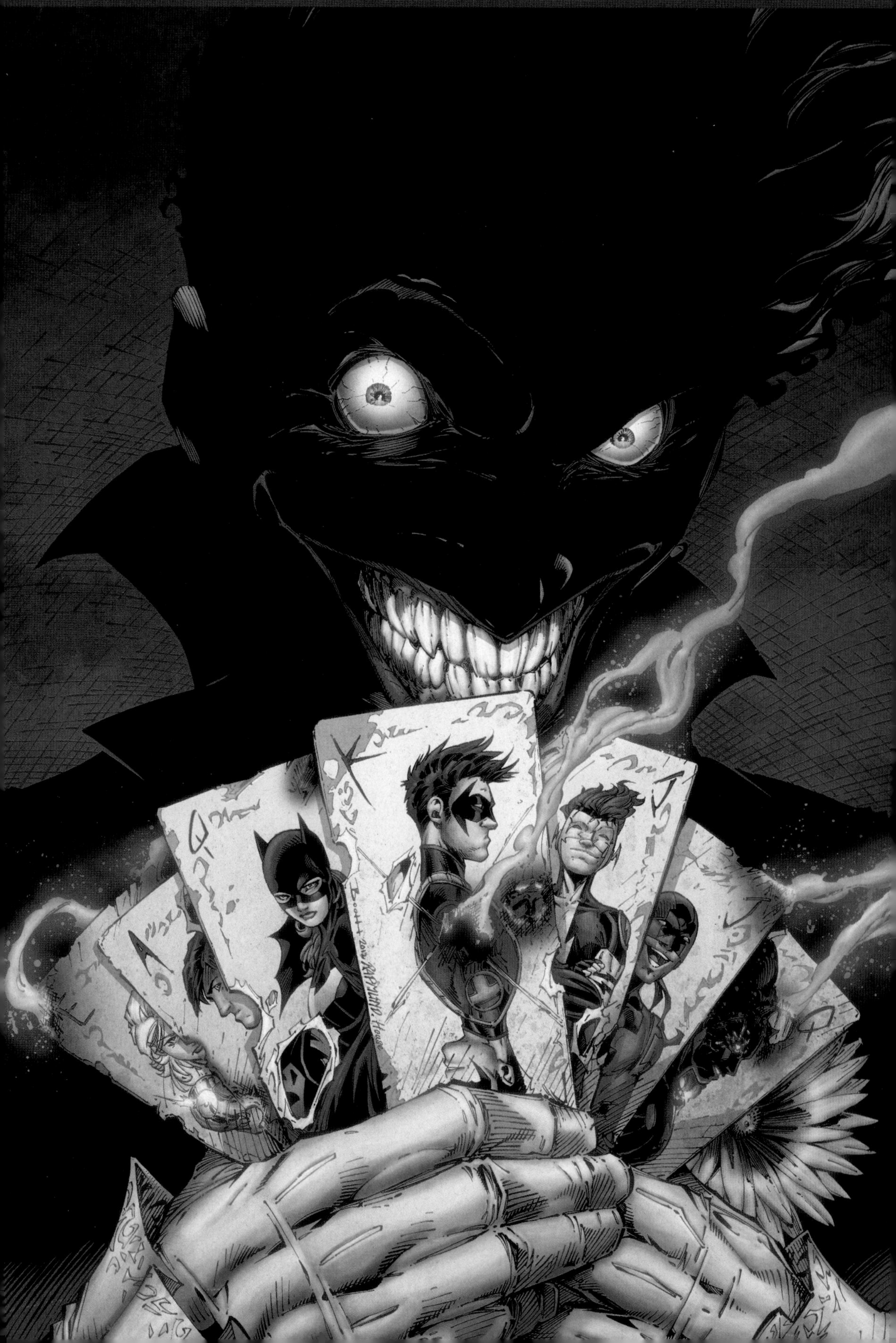

TEEN TITANS #16 cover by **BRETT BOOTH, NORM RAPMUND & ANDREW DALHOUSE**

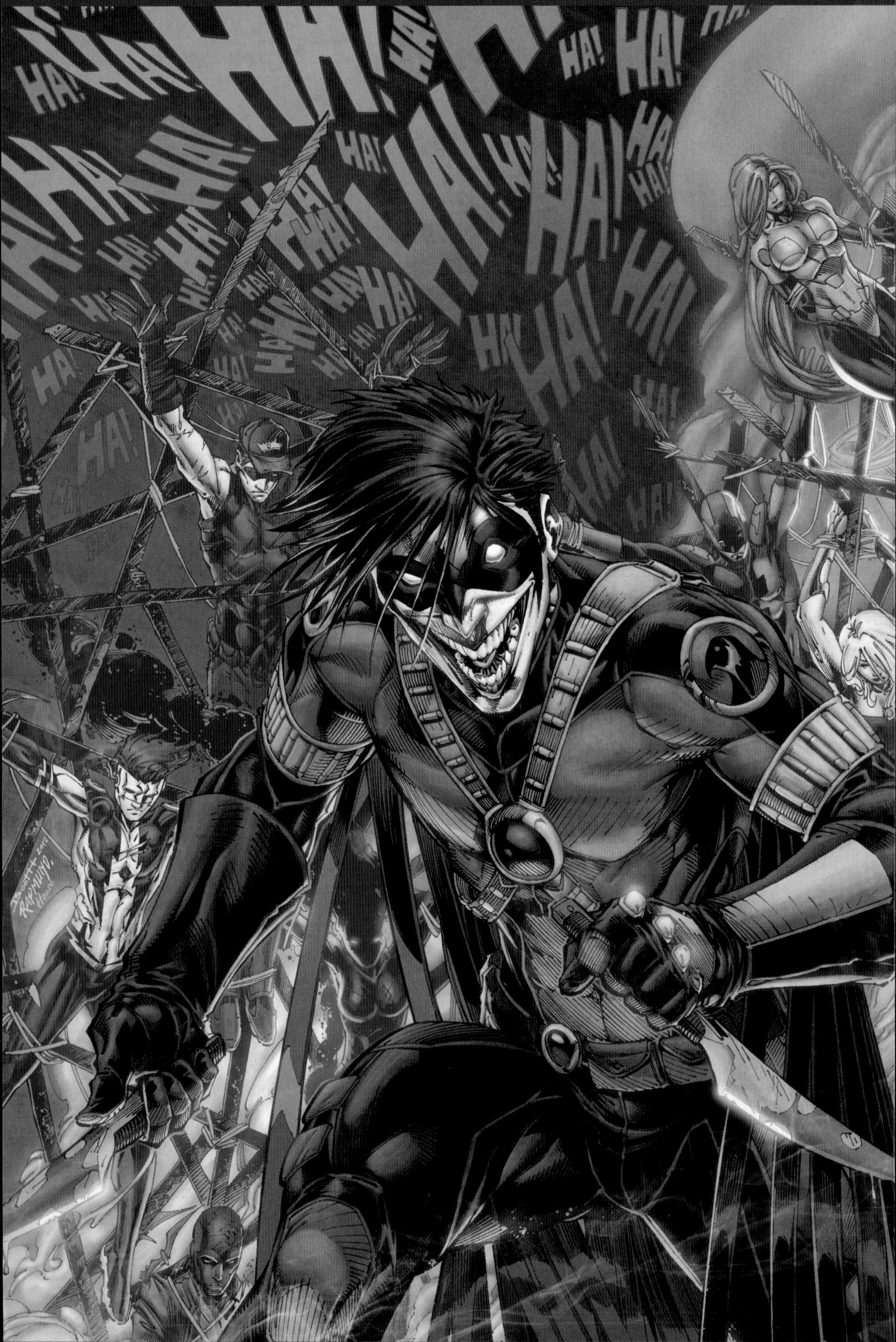

HA! HA! HA! HA! HA!
HA! HA! HA! HA! HA!
HA! HA! HA! HA! HA!
HA! HA! HA! HA! HA!
HA! HA! HA! HA! HA!

TEEN TITANS #15 cover by GREG CAPULLO & FCO PLASCENCIA

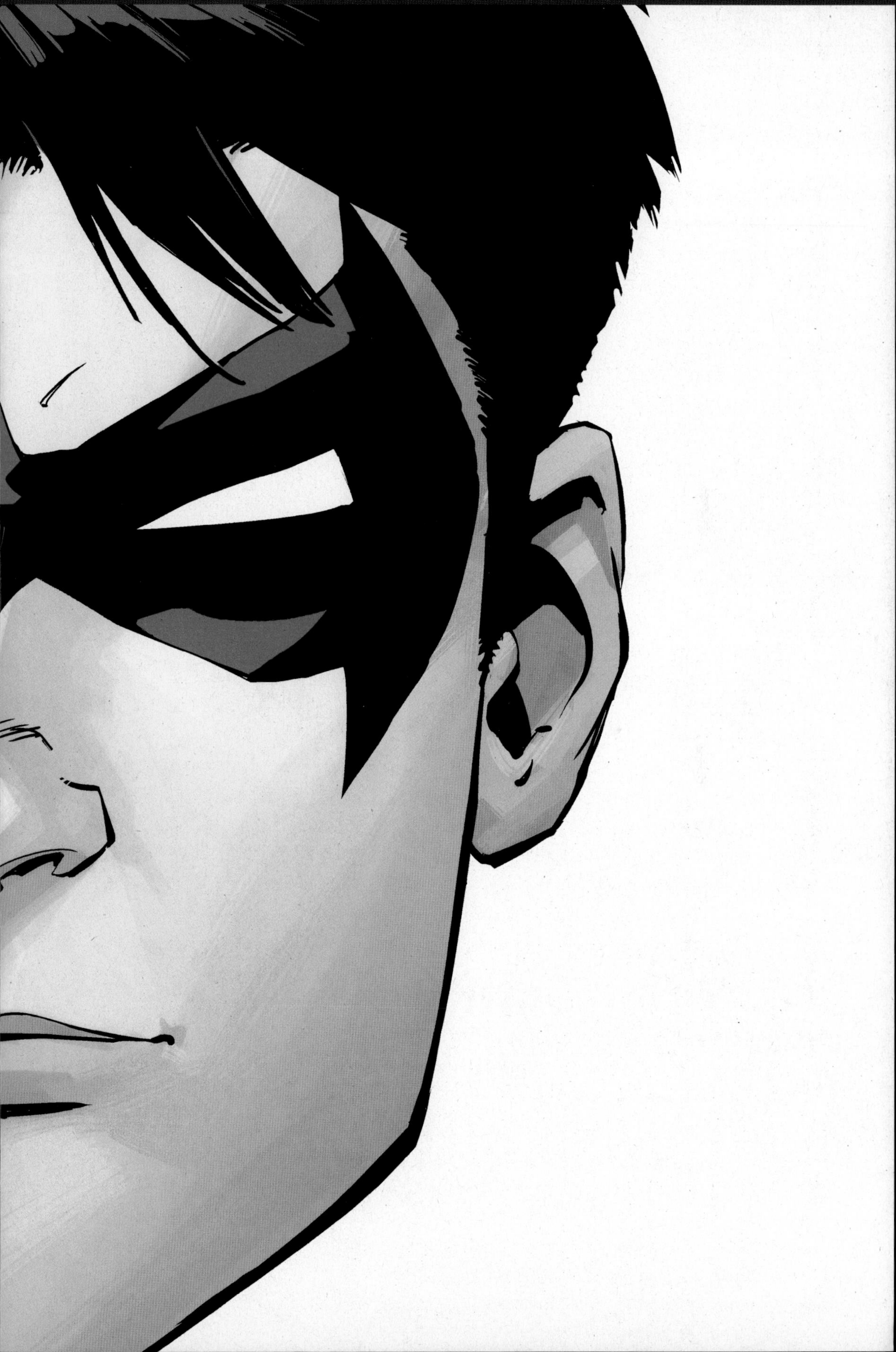

NIGHTWING #15 unused cover by **EDDY BARROWS, EBER FERREIRA & ROD REIS**

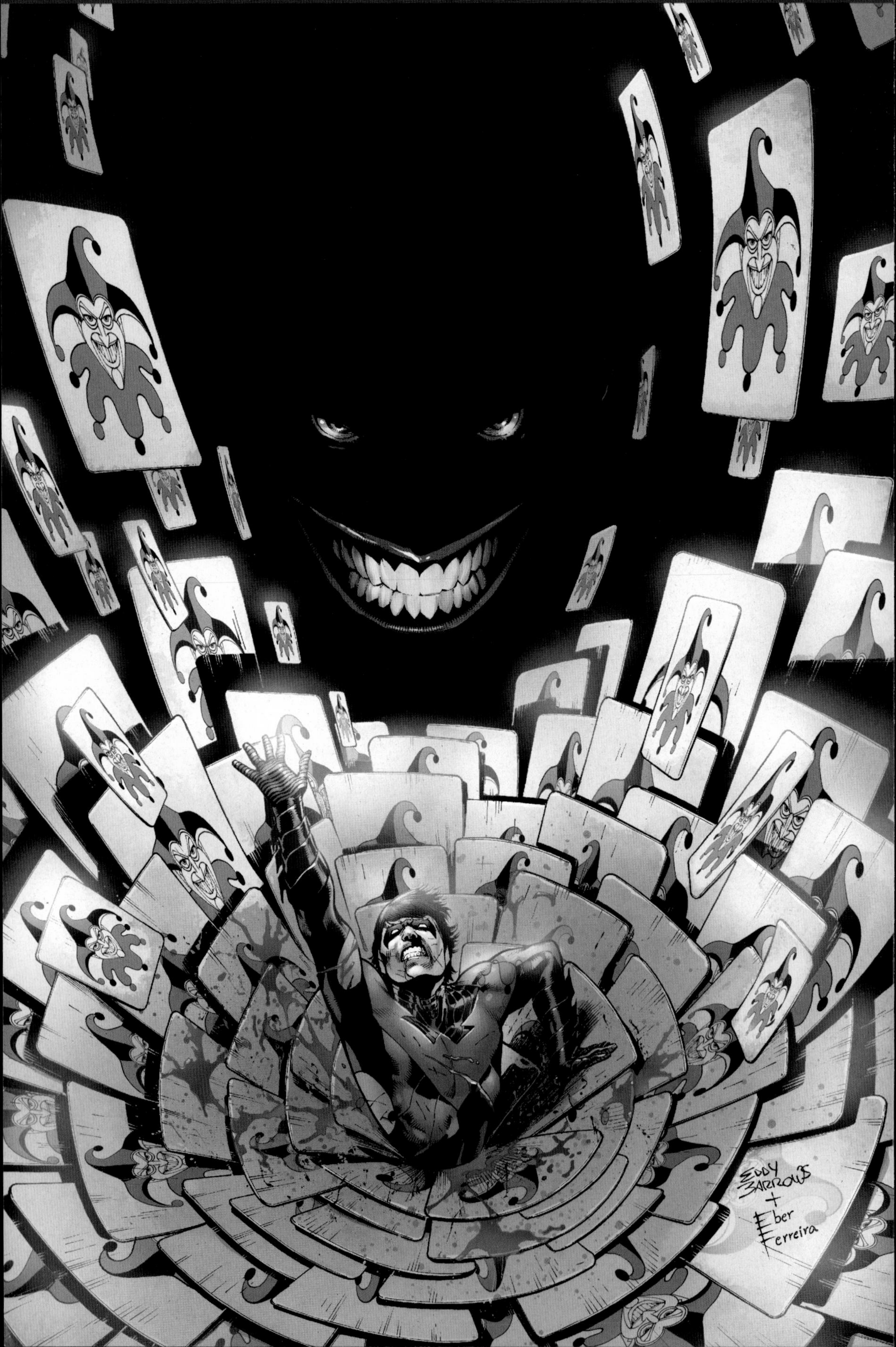
EDDY BARROWS
+
Eber Ferreira

NIGHTWING #16 cover by **EDDY BARROWS, EBER FERREIRA & ROD REIS**

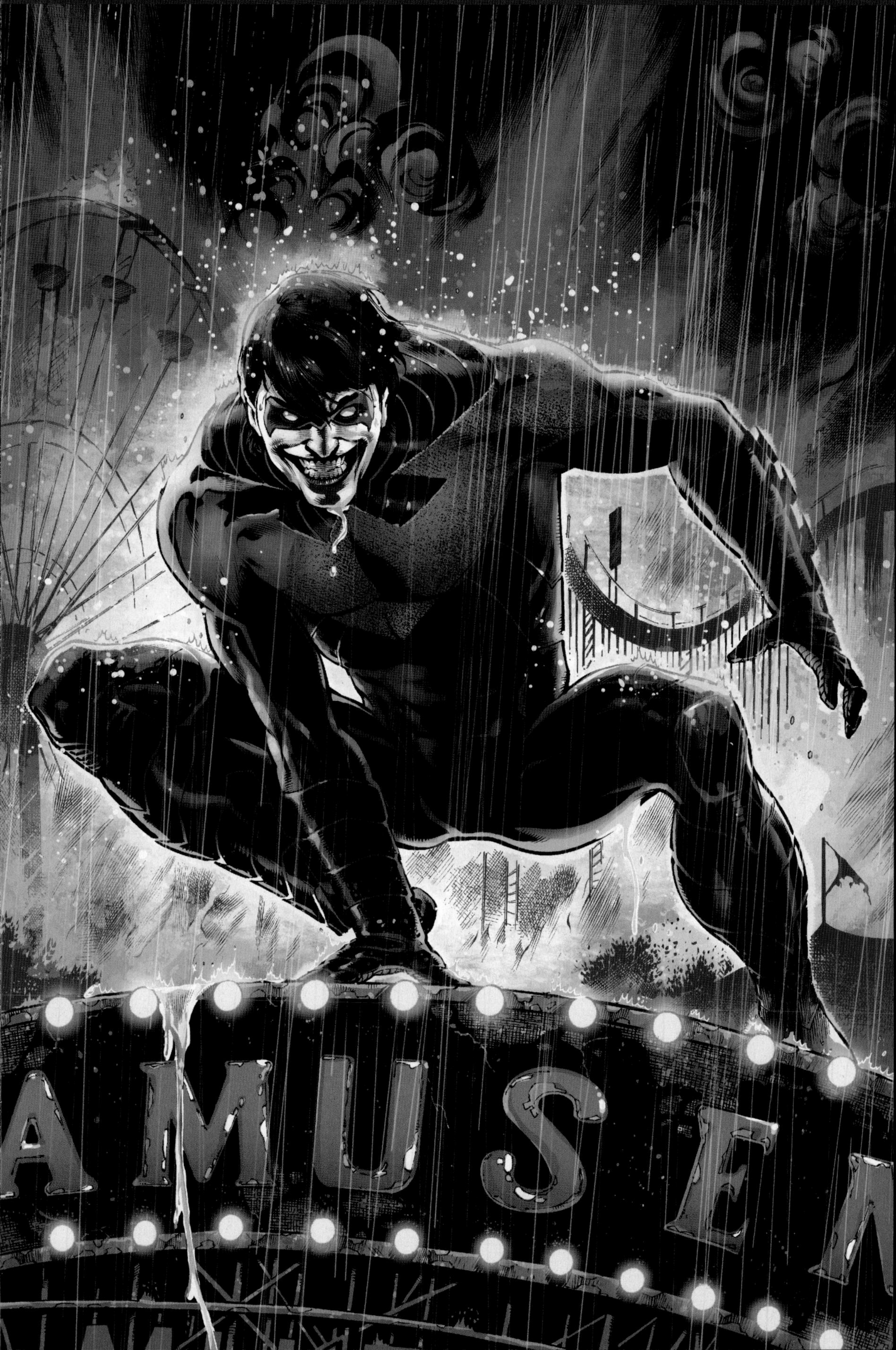
AMUSE

BATMAN AND ROBIN #15 unused cover by **PATRICK GLEASON, MICK GRAY & JOHN KALISZ**

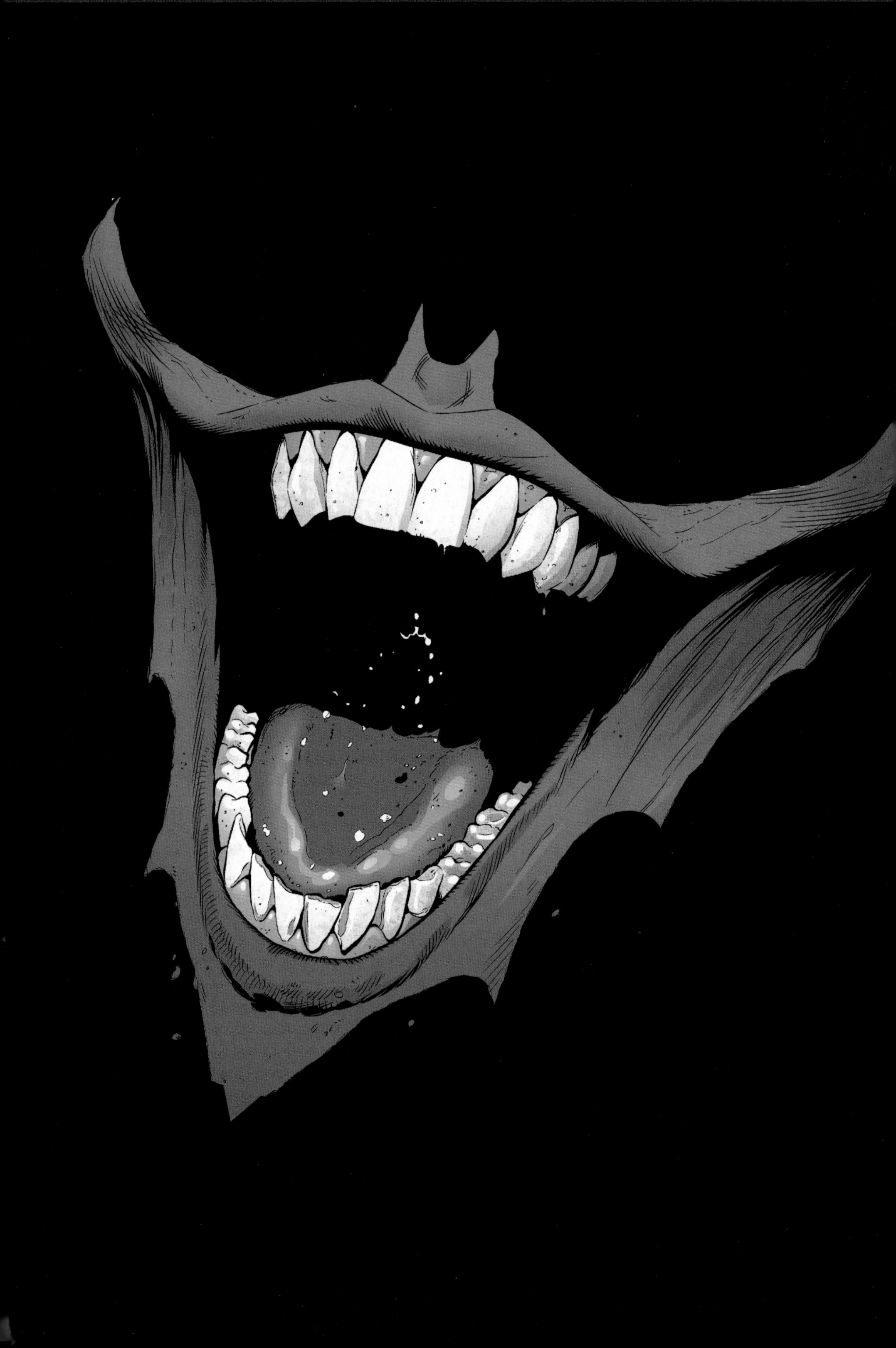

BATMAN AND ROBIN #16 cover by **PATRICK GLEASON, MICK GRAY** & **JOHN KALISZ**

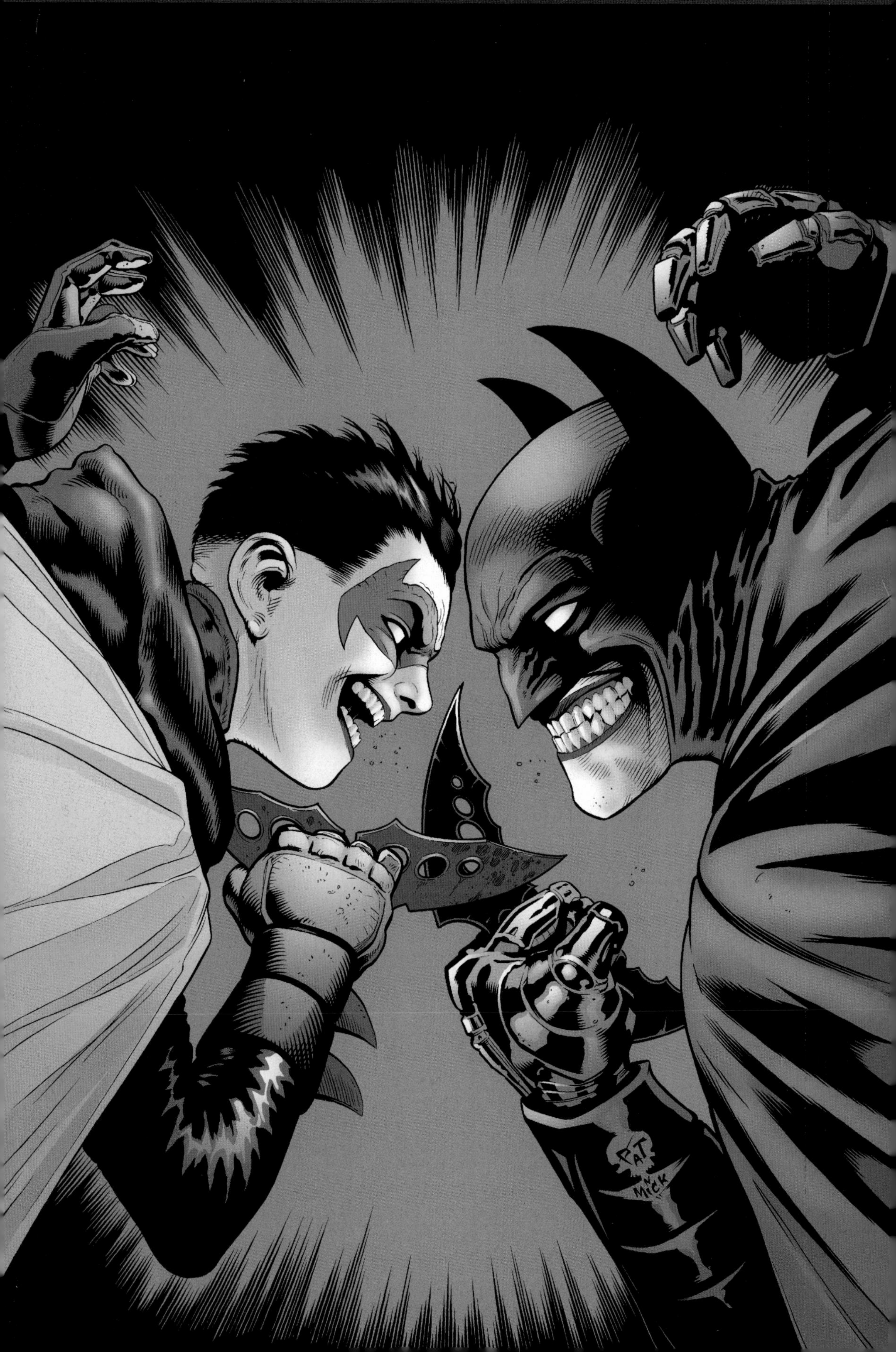
PAT N MICK

BATMAN AND ROBIN #17 cover by **PATRICK GLEASON, MICK GRAY & JOHN KALISZ**

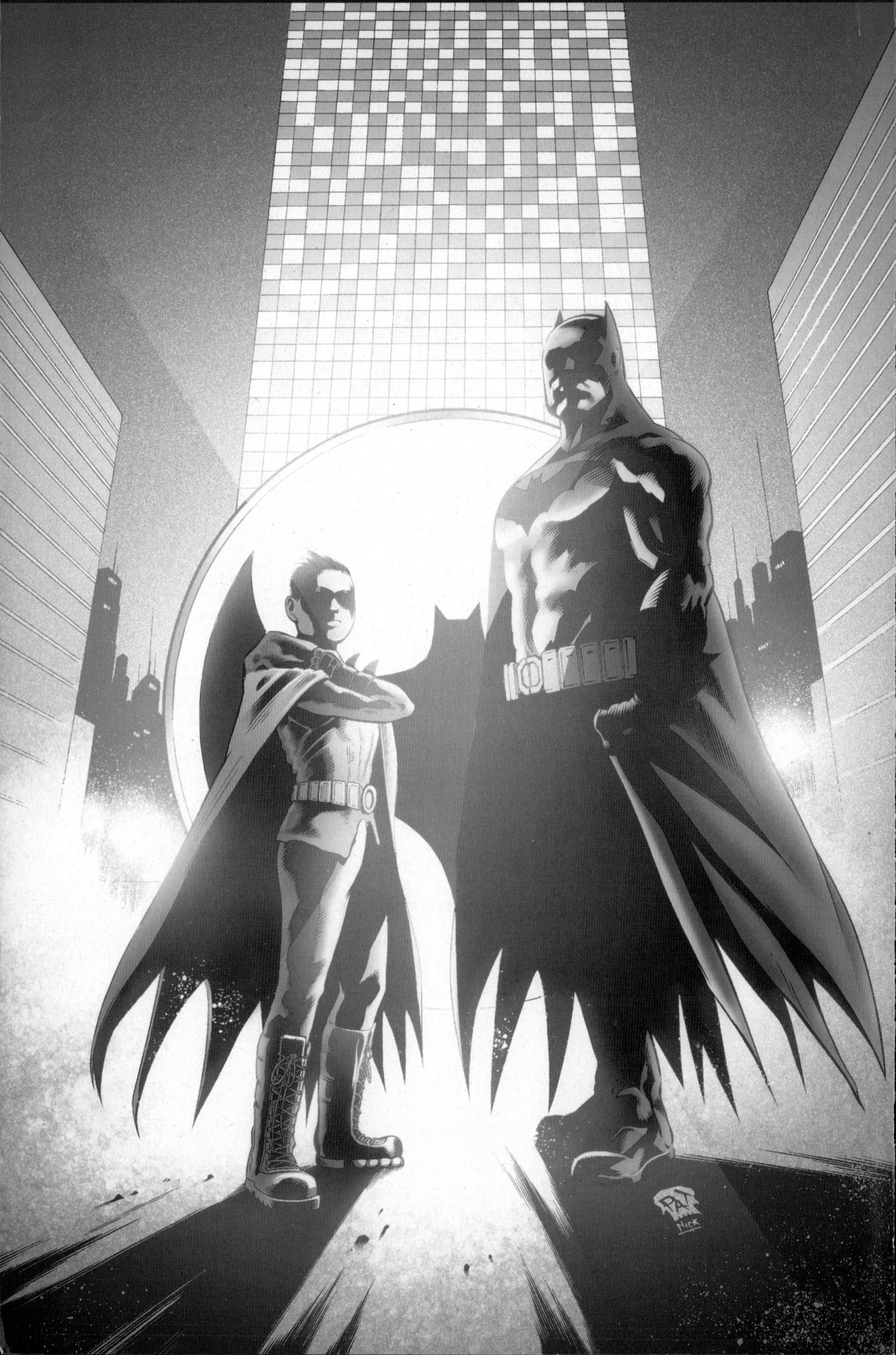

"A stunning debut. This is definitely in the top rank of the revamp."
—THE ONION / AV CLUB

"Snyder and Capullo reach new heights of collaboration here, with Capullo making inspired storytelling choices that add additional layers to Snyder's narration and dialog."
—VANITY FAIR

START AT THE BEGINNING!

BATMAN VOLUME 1: THE COURT OF OWLS

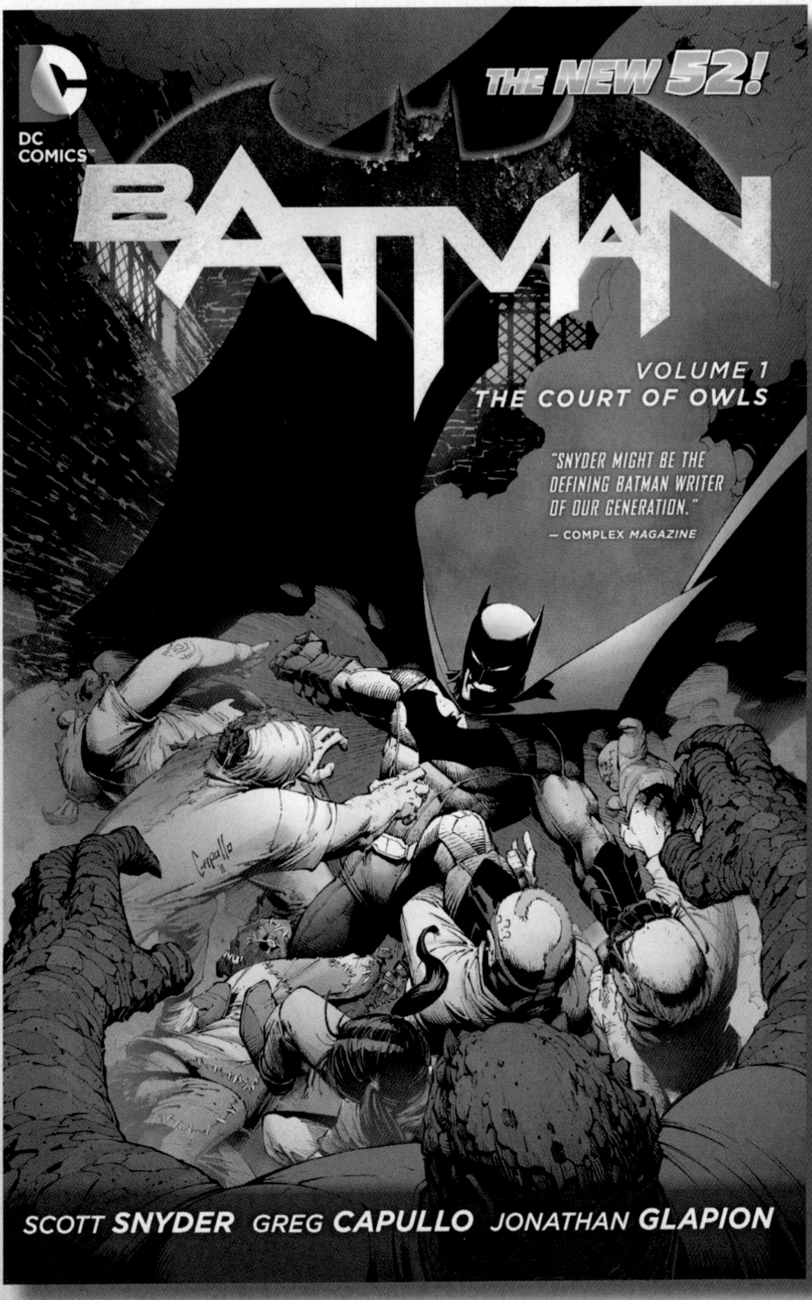
DC COMICS
THE NEW 52!
BATMAN
VOLUME 1
THE COURT OF OWLS
"SNYDER MIGHT BE THE DEFINING BATMAN WRITER OF OUR GENERATION."
— COMPLEX MAGAZINE
SCOTT SNYDER GREG CAPULLO JONATHAN GLAPION

BATMAN & ROBIN
VOLUME 1:
BORN TO KILL

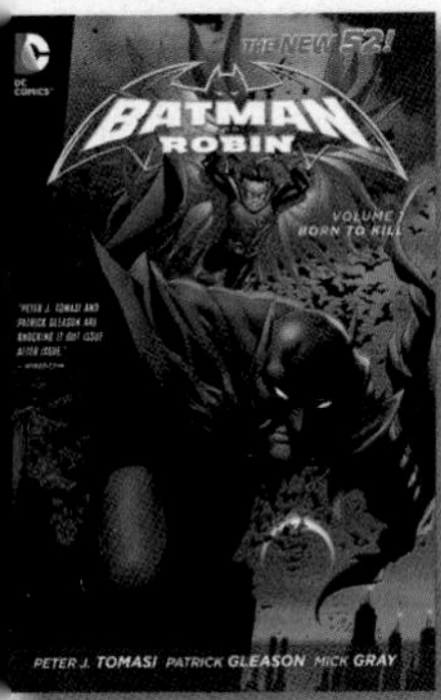
THE NEW 52!
BATMAN AND ROBIN
VOLUME 1 BORN TO KILL
PETER J. TOMASI PATRICK GLEASON MICK GRAY

BATMAN: DETECTIVE
COMICS VOLUME 1:
FACES OF DEATH

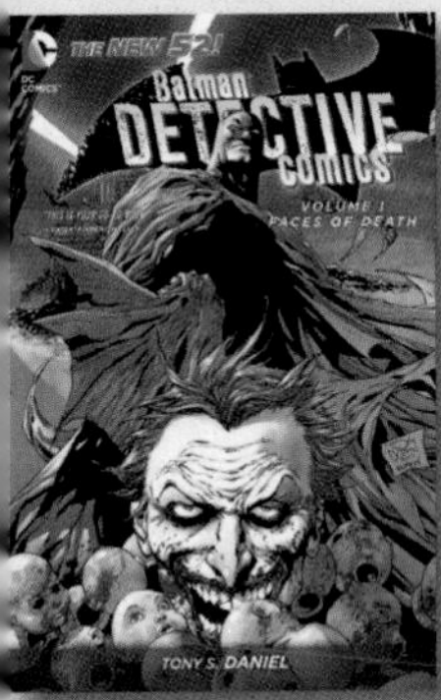
THE NEW 52!
Batman DETECTIVE Comics
VOLUME 1 FACES OF DEATH
TONY S. DANIEL

BATMAN: THE DARK
KNIGHT VOLUME 1:
KNIGHT TERRORS

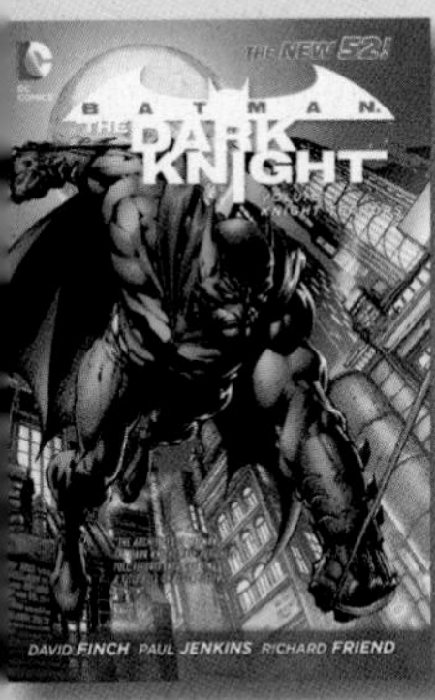
THE NEW 52!
BATMAN THE DARK KNIGHT
DAVID FINCH PAUL JENKINS RICHARD FRIEND

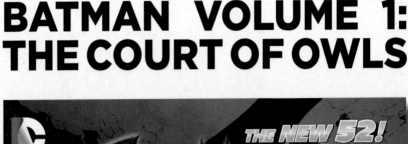

"Simone and artist Ardian Syaf not only do
justice to Babs' legacy, but build in a new
complexity that is the starting point for a
future full of new storytelling possibilities
A hell of a ride."—IGN

START AT THE BEGINNING!

BATGIRL
VOLUME 1: THE DARKEST REFLECTION

**BATGIRL VOL. 2:
KNIGHTFALL
DESCENDS**

**BATGIRL VOL. 3:
DEATH OF THE FAMILY**

**BATWOMAN VOL. 1:
HYDROLOGY**

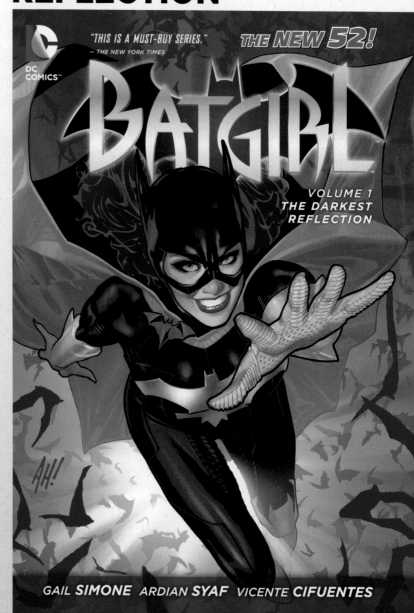

"THIS IS A MUST-BUY SERIES."
— THE NEW YORK TIMES

THE NEW 52!

VOLUME 1
THE DARKEST
REFLECTION

GAIL **SIMONE**   ARDIAN **SYAF**   VICENTE **CIFUENTES**